This is a detailed and comprehensive survey of music in the late Middle Ages and early Renaissance. By limiting its scope to the 120 years which witnessed perhaps the most dramatic expansion of our musical heritage, the book responds, in the 1990s, to the tremendous increase in specialized research and public awareness of that period.

Three of the four main Parts (I, II, IV) describe the development of polyphony and its cultural contexts in many European countries, from the successors of Machaut (*d.*1377) to the achievements of Josquin des Prez and his contemporaries working in Renaissance Italy around 1500. Part III, by contrast, illustrates the musical life of the institutions, and musical practices outside the realm of composed polyphony that were traditional and common all over Europe.

The book proposes fresh views in each chapter, discussing dozens of musical examples, adducing well-known and hitherto unknown documents, and referring to and evaluating the most recent scholarship in the field. The issues discussed include the impact of the Great Schism on music, a re-evaluation of English influence in Europe, the 'invention' of the musical 'masterwork' in the 1450s and the 'encounter of music and Renaissance' in late fifteenth-century Italy and Spain.

THE RISE OF
EUROPEAN MUSIC,
1380-1500

THE RISE OF
EUROPEAN MUSIC,
1380–1500

REINHARD STROHM

CAMBRIDGE
UNIVERSITY PRESS

Published by the Press Syndicate of the University of Cambridge
The Pitt Building, Trumpington Street, Cambridge CB2 1RP
40 West 20th Street, New York, NY 10011-4211, USA
10 Stamford Road, Oakleigh, Victoria 3166, Australia

First published 1993

Printed in Great Britain at the University Press, Cambridge

A catalogue record for this book is available from the British Library

Library of Congress cataloguing in publication data

Strohm, Reinhard.
The rise of European music, 1380-1500 / Reinhard Strohm.
p. cm.

ISBN 0 521 41745 7

1. Music – Europe – 500-1400 – History and criticism.
2. Music – Europe – 15th century – History and criticism. I. Title.
ML240.2.S87 1993
780′. 9′02 – dc20   92-2736   CIP   MN

ISBN 0 521 41745 7

ME

CONTENTS

ILLUSTRATIONS

TABLES

PREFACE

This book, written over the years 1983-9, was originally commissioned by Malcolm Gerratt for J. M. Dent & Sons Ltd. At the very end of 1987, Dent became part of Weidenfeld & Nicolson, though the concept of the book was not changed by either the publisher or the author. In early 1991, some weeks after Malcolm Gerratt had been compelled by circumstances to leave Dent, the publishers wrote to me to say that they felt the book would now be too academic for their list and that they wanted to arrange for a different publisher to take it on. Fortunately this did not prove difficult and I signed a new contract with Cambridge University Press in June 1991. By the end of 1990, Mr Gerratt had been able to supervise the main revisions. I owe him my warmest thanks for his continuous encouragement, expert advice and editorial care, without which the project might have faltered altogether. For the more detailed editing up to that point, I am indebted to the efforts and the competence of Ingrid Grimes. After the change to Cambridge University Press, the remaining half of the editing was carried out, with unusual musicological expertise and editing skill, by Ann Lewis.

It is my hope that those colleagues in the field of music history who took on the responsibility of advising me on matters of content will find that their labours were not lost. The greatest contribution by far was made by David Fallows, who commented on the whole typescript. His corrections and suggestions, plus the ensuing correspondence between us about controversial questions, would fill a potentially exciting volume by themselves. It goes without saying that the input from a leading authority such as David Fallows has substantially raised not only the value of the book, but also my own awareness of fifteenth-century problems.

Similarly, both the book and I gained very much from the prudent and patient advice given by Margaret Bent, Leeman L. Perkins, Jessie Ann Owens and Ursula Günther, all of whom read individual chapters and communicated their reactions to me.

The collaboration with such excellent scholars who are committed to serving not so much individual interests as the instruction of all is the very context from which my own studies have grown. Apart from those named elsewhere, I am particularly grateful to Brian Trowell and Pierluigi Petrobelli, scholars whose practice taught me more than many musicological books, and to all the

xiii

other colleagues and friends who made important suggestions, or presented me with their own published or unpublished findings and writings: Thomas Walker, Kurt von Fischer, Giulio Cattin, Walter Salmen, Karlheinz Schlager, Alejandro E. Planchart, Wulf Arlt, Nino Pirrotta, Martin Staehelin, Claude V. Palisca, Craig Wright, Howard M. Brown, Ernst Apfel, Allan W. Atlas, Lewis Lockwood, Maricarmen Gómez, Jaap van Benthem, Jaromír Černý, Mirosław Perz, F. Alberto Gallo, Kristine Forney, Christoph Petzsch, Keith Polk, Andrew Wathey, Anna Maria Busse Berger, Paula Higgins, M. Jennifer Bloxam, Barbara H. Haggh, Walter Kreyszig, Virginia Newes and Rob C. Wegman.

The historians Peter Burke and Hannes Obermair must be mentioned specially, as they generously entrusted me with unpublished material without having reason to know me at all.

The typescript of the main text and footnotes was completed in July 1989. Literature appearing after that date was not normally considered, except when this became necessary in the course of an actual textual revision, or when I had been allowed to use typescript contributions the publication of which was then delayed. I have yielded to the temptation of adding references to a few particularly interesting publications appearing as late as mid-1990, although their contents were not necessarily taken into account. Several of the contributions that appeared too late for being properly discussed here were written by Rob C. Wegman.

Research for this book has been supported, in the summer of 1987, by a travel grant from the American Council of Learned Societies and a complementary grant from the Whitney Griswold Fund of Yale University.

Most of the work was carried out on the basis of literature held in the Yale University Library, New Haven, and the British Library, London. Further items, including manuscripts and archival documents, were consulted in the Bayerische Staatsbibliothek, Munich; the Stadtarchiv, Vienna; the Tiroler Landesarchiv, Innsbruck; the Archivio Comunale, Bolzano; the Österreichische Nationalbibliothek, Vienna; the Archivio di Stato, Trent; the Bibliothèque Royale Albert Ièr, Brussels; the Rijksarchief, Ghent; and the research libraries and archives of Bruges. To all the librarians and archivists of these institutions I wish to express my heartfelt thanks.

The Music Librarian of the University of London, musicologist and friend Anthea Baird, gave me the characteristically charming and congenial support known to all scholars who have worked with her.

Janet M. Smith shared with me most of the anxieties and frustrations of writing this book during our years in America; I hope she will find the result worthwhile.

I was able to benefit much from my students and doctoral advisees at Yale University, particularly Ruth Hall, who worked on the bibliography and provided a useful critique of my prose, and Leslie Kearney who helped with the thinking.

After two of my students, I should also mention two of my teachers: the music historians Thrasyboulos Georgiades and Carl Dahlhaus. In the present context, let me remember them not so much for the light they gave to musicology in general as for the profound understanding they had, and communicated to me, of the music of the fifteenth century.

INTRODUCTION

I

Among the breathtaking developments of European civilization in the fifteenth century – which can be described as the 'Waning of the Middle Ages' and as the 'Renaissance' at the same time – there was also the rise, or the emancipation, of music to a major human resource and a universal language.

Our age is reluctant to acknowledge 'progress' in history, even where that word is used without implying a value judgement. We have adopted a relativist approach to history, partly because we accept that many 'progresses' of humankind have ended in chaos. But European music, it seems, is not among these stories of failure: after centuries of growth, it continues to be a restoring and healing element in society. Its influence on our lives and thinking may even have increased. Let us hope that the music of today's world will retain its ability to teach people how to respect each other.

Although it is widely believed today that the idea of historical progress was a product of the Enlightenment, a number of medieval and Renaissance writers acknowledged progress at least in certain areas of human endeavour (and not only for theological reasons). Music was judged by them as capable of continuous development and, indeed, ever greater aesthetic perfection. This humanistic view was held, for example, by the fourteenth-century writer Johannes Boen, who argued that music would probably soon develop to unheard-of refinement, as it had already made such great progress since its inventor Pythagoras (see p. 38). The fifteenth-century music theorist Johannes Tinctoris judged that only the composers of his own lifetime had produced music worth hearing (see p. 127).

Now, post-Enlightenment historicism has taught us not to discriminate against the old in favour of the new. The opposite view to that of Tinctoris was held, for example, by the influential nineteenth-century music historian François-Joseph Fétis, who disliked the musical avant-garde of his time and pioneered the appreciation of music of the past as an aesthetic experience in its own right.[1] It is not even a paradox that these two men, born only about 30 miles apart in what is now southern Belgium, devoted themselves to the appraisal of exactly the same repertory: the polyphonic music created in

---

[1] For example in his *Esquisse de l'harmonie considérée comme art et comme science systématique* (Paris, 1840).

England, France and the Low Countries in the fifteenth century. Tinctoris, the Renaissance humanist, approved of this music because its novelty demonstrated to him the continuing progress towards an *ars perfecta*. Fétis, the Romantic historicist, approved of it because it was an ancient tradition of his beloved homeland: two reasons so contrary to each other as to convince anyone of the fallibility of historical hindsight. Perhaps both judgements were wrong, and we might accuse Tinctoris of a chronological, Fétis of a geographical bias. But why, then, do they in effect agree?

The present writer considers that these two value judgements, although made for seemingly opposite reasons, were both right. From the point of view of human attitudes towards the world, there is no fundamental contradiction between the cultivation of ancient roots, and the urge for novelty, freshness, emancipation. Whereas undoubtedly many people in the fifteenth century enjoyed musical traditions simply as they were – and this will be further elaborated in Part III of this book – some must have believed in the progressive potentials of the art, too. It was this belief which then unfolded into history, creating new traditions. We are speaking not so much of real change or measurable progress as of people who, by dedicating themselves to perfecting their art, created lasting values. To explain why and how such values were created in fifteenth-century music is the main purpose of the present study.

The period from 1380 to 1500 in Europe was transitional like any period in history: it was not in any way self-contained. Nevertheless, certain changes happened to music then which have since become stable traditions. One of them was the phenomenon that composers became accustomed to apply the best of their art to musical works for the enjoyment of *listeners*. Another was the fact that composed polyphony ('harmonic' or 'part-music'), aspired to being understood by every *individual* in Europe like his or her own language. As a result of both, Europe imparted a significance to the role of the *composer* such as no other musical culture has ever done.

Today, the European language of music has developed into a world language, and the European attitude towards music has become a model all over the world. We go further today by accepting that music of whatever kind and ancestry is universal, and that every human being has a right to music, for personal recreation or any other purpose. Such beliefs, however, are rooted in the opinions of fifteenth-century European musicians – humanists and others. Similarly, the structural (harmonic, contrapuntal) principles of fifteenth-century music are still implied in ours, although they are now valid on a more universal plane. They are connected with the idea that music can convey meaning and emotion not only by reference to its generic form, text, performance circumstance – but directly, as it were, by its *individually composed structures*. This is possible – i.e. these structures are 'eloquent' – because they have absorbed multiple conventions and intentions of people, imitations of art and nature, symbols of eternity. This makes them potential resources which individual listeners across the countries and centuries can unlock. The concept of universality and the ability to re-create the individual mind are complementary features of European music which it will take a long time to eradicate. For these lasting values, we acknowledge a debt to individual composers: masters such as Guillaume Dufay and Josquin des Prez created them at a time when medieval and Renaissance cultures overlapped.

It would be foolish, of course, to deny the dignity or occasional artistic complexity of earlier music heard in Europe. Neither can it be doubted that certain musical repertories enjoyed wide, 'international' circulation in the Middle Ages. The European nations did not yet exist as political entities (the rise of European music accompanies their making), and this could mean that, under specific circumstances, political–cultural barriers could be quite easily crossed. But we should not really believe that medieval music, for example 'Gregorian chant', was a universal language. The organization of the Church and its practices, the ritual language (Latin) and to some extent the individual texts of the liturgy were common to Catholic Europe. The chant melodies, however, were subject to many local dialects and fiercely defended traditions of performance. The most effective struggles for the supra-regional unification of plainsong – those led by some mendicant orders and also limited to them – were also the forerunners of the more general trend towards universality which characterized fifteenth-century polyphony.

Furthermore, precisely the most generally shared features and circumstances of medieval music tended to be pre-artistic in nature. What was common to musicians of many regions was not so much the art in the sense of musical works, as the art in the sense of know-how, of practice. It is possible to speculate that the musical folklore of many European countries had, in the Middle Ages, common characteristics (some of which were shared, besides, with Arab and Eastern peoples): but on the high level of the individual art-work, musical style was particular and special, even idiosyncratic. What happened at the very end of the Middle Ages was the creation of individualized music (dignified less through the support of its high-ranking patrons than through its own artistic expertise and endeavour) that had *absorbed* the common and simple traditions and thus became itself a common language.

This language was that of polyphony, music performed in different lines (and usually by different people) simultaneously. Polyphonic music, which had existed in Europe since the Dark Ages, but either as a general, simple know-how or – occasionally – as an artistic speciality, has become *the* musical art-form of later centuries in Europe. We identify this art-form with a quest for communication and relationships: it is a symbol of togetherness and harmony – or of diversity and counterpoint, according to how we accentuate it. Neither this symbolic function of polyphony nor its predominance in the repertory was given to it by Nature. Rather, polyphony attained this status in the fifteenth century, when the greater complexity it offered over monophonic ('one-line') music appeared novel and 'progressive' to its listeners, stimulating more and more gifted minds to cultivate it.

Late medieval Europe witnessed an unprecedented expansion of the means of artistic creation and the access to art, triggered by an overall improvement (despite setbacks) of material conditions. For example, the use of musical instruments in art-music increased rapidly. This was partly because far more people could now afford them. The archives continuously document the introduction of new forms and uses of music, the ever greater expenditures on music, and its greater availability to lower social classes. Art-music began to travel more quickly and to be codified on paper. The fact that there are documents which tell us much about fifteenth-century music that we will never know about earlier repertories, points to an expanded public cultivation and consumption of music. The fact that there are perhaps ten times as many written compositions extant from that century as from the preceding one, suggests a considerable increase in the production of artistically complex (and therefore, written) music. Both facts together imply that relatively more social groups had now access to it than ever before. By the end of the fifteenth century, the ordinary people of several European towns could listen to free concerts with music by Josquin or Obrecht in the local parish church or indeed *in the streets*. The region where such a practice had already been common for generations – the Low Countries – was not surprisingly the one which was now producing the leading performers and composers of polyphony.

The development of fifteenth-century music is like a breaking of barriers everywhere, a flooding with ideas, an irrigation of deserts. Admittedly, this flood must also have submerged musical traditions or unwritten practices of which we now know nothing. But many local or 'common' practices that had never been written down were now absorbed into written art-music and thus at least documented; others were reported in writing by archivists, poets and musical theorists, or in design and colour by painters and architects. To the fifteenth century, we owe the invention of printing and music printing – although the latter became a typical mode of transmission only in the next century. Conversely, it is to fifteenth-century documents that we owe much of our understanding of medieval musical traditions: fifteenth-century people transmitted them because they cherished them. Because of this pivotal character of the period, we have to examine not only the leading innovations in art-music but also at some length what are called here the 'common traditions' of music: those common to upper and lower social classes, and shared by many countries and centuries of the European Middle Ages.

At the same time, this book describes the development of late medieval music as a step which music made towards ourselves. What was left behind deserves our respect, our careful evaluation, and perhaps our nostalgia. But only the comparison of tradition with what was newly created can help us recognize ourselves. Consider just one example: to discuss aspects of mode and tonality only in medieval, traditional terms, would mean to pass over the moment as insignificant when composers first conceived the idea of expressing sadness with the minor mode. Do we really want to miss this event in our history of music? It is hindsight that illuminates the past, although it is fallible and may throw a distorting light on the objects. But without any light, would we be able to guess that our perspective had to be adjusted? This problem is related to the question to what sort of historical reality the Renaissance concept actually corresponds. A medieval mind would presumably have explained what happened around 1400 entirely in medieval terms. It is the people born two and three generations later who reacted to the feeling that a change had taken place by identifying themselves with a new age, and it is us who try to explain those things that do not fit our view of the Middle Ages by constructing a new historical 'period'. Perhaps, the Renaissance exists in so far as we need it to rationalize our image of earlier periods.

Today, we are aware of music through performances, recordings, the media, books, conversation, education. Knowledge, taste and fancy make us choose and reject types of music. Musical sounds are part of our culture, and they decorate – or deface, as the case may be – our homes. This situation is not given by Nature, but has developed historically in the context of the privatization and individualization of the arts in late medieval Europe. Johannes Tinctoris may have rejected the music of earlier centuries (although his statement is highly rhetorical), but the fact that he had access to it, and exerted his critical judgement on it, already connects him with the humanistic, enlightened and historicist culture of our century. This century's cultivation of 'Early Music' is nothing but a further step towards the appropriation of all music by all people, as critical individuals.

II

An introduction should presumably tell the reader what to expect from the book and what not. This is difficult in the present case, because it is uncertain what anyone should expect from a single-author book on the history of European music in the fifteenth century. Charles van den Borren's *Etudes sur le quinzième siècle musical* (Antwerp, 1941) stands alone in making this century its sole subject, but it does not cover the areas which its eminent author had not studied first-hand. Even greater excellence but also greater selectivity is found in Manfred Bukofzer's *Studies in Medieval and Renaissance Music* (New York: Norton, 1950): a bundle of scholarly essays mainly on fifteenth-century topics, each of which has profoundly influenced later researchers. Bukofzer had developed his approach as a critical response to the German leader in the field, Heinrich Besseler. From Besseler's survey-volume *Musik des Mittelalters und der Renaissance* (Potsdam: Athenaion, 1931), Bukofzer borrowed really only the view, expressed in the title, that the Middle Ages and the Renaissance should not be separated too sharply.

Most other authors have preferred to tie the fifteenth century together with the sixteenth, usually presenting these 200 years as the 'Renaissance' period of music. One great scholar avoided the label: André Pirro in his *Histoire de la musique de la fin du XIVe siècle à la fin du XVIe* (Paris: Renouard, 1940). Pirro worked without grand patterns and periodizations. He was the only one who could envision musical thought and musical life in a true synthesis, arising from the endless diversity and detail found by him in archival documents, contemporary literature, works of art and musical scores. By contrast, the tremendous achievement of Gustave Reese's *Music in the Renaissance* (New York: Norton, 1954) lies in its control of modern scholarship: the book covers that generation's knowledge of fifteenth- and sixteenth-century music to a degree which it will be impossible to reach in the future due to the further rapid expansion of scholarship. Historiographically, the view presented by Reese is that of an expanding musical 'language' which originated in central areas (France, Netherlands and Italy) but then reached the other parts of Europe by way of 'diffusion'. Since this diffusion took place mainly in the sixteenth century, the two centuries logically belong together under the criterion of musical 'language', i.e. style. It must be acknowledged straightaway that it was Gustave Reese's book which, by taking the concept of 'diffusion' seriously, put an end to the reign of music histories that had focused on only three European countries.

In the present book, I accept Reese's geographical model of centrality and diffusion as one possible way of looking at the subject. The model has been used in altered forms, and for more than one historical development. Also, the meaning of the essential term may have changed a little since Gustave Reese. In the 1990s, we can more easily acknowledge that 'diffusion', from the point of view of the 'peripheries', also means their participation in, and contribution to, a common history. Reese's rigid periodization of music history on the sole basis of polyphonic musical style has been rejected. The growth of certain polyphonic styles is presented with an awareness of their relative weight in a cultural framework. For example, the observation that traditional, unwritten practices of minstrels and choristers began to surface in learned compositions of the Dufay period (in these matters we have learned much from Besseler and Bukofzer), is also used as a judgement on the role of music in society.

The 'Renaissance' is interpreted in this book as a consciously created socio-cultural environment, not a style characteristic of music. To describe this environment to its full chronological extent was not really my task, and the music heard in sixteenth-century Renaissance environments differed, for my ear, sufficiently from that of the preceding century to require a fresh chronicler. Besides, the Renaissance environment was not universal in Europe around 1500, and many medieval ways of life were indeed just disappearing then. Thus, consideration of both musical art and musical life made it feasible to unhook the fifteenth century from the following one, and to free it from the precursor's role it has to play in most books on 'Renaissance music'. It is admitted, of course, that the rise and expansion of the dominating polyphonic language was still far from settled around 1500. Many histories of music devote a chapter to 'Josquin and his contemporaries' in the decades 1480–1520. It can perhaps be accepted that this book does not descend to all the epigones, but closes on a high note provided by Josquin des Prez himself.

While the narrative thus fails to reach the new departure of the German Reformation (1517), its starting point (*c.*1380) is defined in terms of ecclesiastical history. This inconsistency can be defended: not only do successive historical periods rarely begin by virtue of the same criterion,[2] it is also possible to view the Great Schism as more momentous for music history than even the Lutheran reform. In any case, music was in 1520 more emancipated from the life of the Church than in 1380, and the specifically musical roots of Protestantism – congregational singing, for example – lie in the fifteenth century (see p. 271). In the first chapters of this book, the social and spiritual disruptions of the Schism, which harboured the beginning of religious reform, allow us to sketch a context and contrast for stylistic departures in music around 1400. They are also presented as the historical trigger for the long-lasting leadership of Netherlands musicians south of the Alps – probably the phenomenon that best characterizes the situation of music in Renaissance Italy.

How should one divide the history of music in Europe between 1380 and 1500? The reader will find that my basically chronological outline is interrupted (in Part III) by a non-chronological discussion of practices of musical life, under the heading of the 'common traditions'. These traditional practices, which developed at a different pace from that of polyphonic styles, are considered first in terms of institutional history, i.e. as musical services to organized communities, ecclesiastical and secular. Then, the musical genres of monophonic chant and vernacular song, simple polyphony and instrumental music are outlined. These were not the only types of music serving communities, but the implication is that instrumental playing and composing, for example, was in the fifteenth century still a 'non-authorial' art, less subject to individualization than vocal polyphony. This statement may be a simplification, but it has suggested itself in the absence of better documentary and analytical control of such music. In any case, the reader may find in this Part the seeds for further research on subjects such as musical education, the relationships between music and theatre or music and liturgy, instrumental versus vocal music (a difference of practices at first, later also of repertories), or written versus unwritten music (always a difference of practices, not of repertories).

In the other Parts of the book, the chronological frame is overlaid, to varying degrees, with a geographical organization. Before explaining the interplay between the two principles, I must confess that the self-imposed task of a wide geographical spread was also the one I felt least adequately prepared for. The references to regions such as Scotland and Scandinavia are token acknowledgments; the music of the east-central European countries is not sufficiently described, although its growing attachment to the rest of Europe is emphasized.

---

[2] The relationships between 'periods' of history are so inconsistent because each of them has been carved from different primary material by different generations of scholars with different criteria in mind.

The music of eastern Europe, belonging to the Orthodox sphere and then partly under Ottoman rule, has not been considered part of this history. The musical history of the Iberian peninsula is not given its due; composers and works in France after *c.*1480 are not discussed. Better coverage was not possible under the constraints of my authorship, and I had to give higher priority to balance than to coverage.

In each of Parts I, II and IV, the book indulges in a different historiographic model combining chronology and geography. In Part I, it is claimed that French polyphony after Machaut (*d.*1377) – the Ars nova transformed into the Ars subtilior – carried forward its traditionally central role, radiating its influence to the neighbouring countries, which is a model of expansion, but also – as pointed out above – of participation. These countries, however, began to form a chain whose artistic coherence was increasingly strengthened by the effects of the Schism. Their music emancipated itself from a 'peripheral' status to that of 'lateral' (i.e. equal-ranking) traditions. Thus, the momentum of the musical development itself radiated from inside to outside.

Part I, ending with the re-unification of the Roman Catholic Church in 1417, overlaps chronologically with Part II, beginning around 1400 in Burgundy and England. The doubly-covered years are seen as a period of competition between the old and the new. The reasons and the modalities of this stylistic transformation are still incompletely understood, but much of the impetus seems to have been generated by the absorption of 'humble' traditions into art-music, especially in the courtly French chanson. From here onwards, Part II takes two itineraries that actually cross each other geographically. It is suggested that these large streams flowing from north to south and from west to east constituted the main channels of artistic expansion. We can observe this expansion whether we follow the path of composers – Dufay's in the 1420s, for example – or the actual transmission of musical works through manuscripts and travelling performers – from England to the Council of Basle in the 1430s, for example. The difference from the previous (radiating) model is that England has now turned into a second fountainhead of stylistic developments, so that central and southern Europe already receive a mixture of Franco-Netherlands and English experiences.[3] Despite the waterways-metaphor, this diffusion is not to be considered a necessity of Nature. What impelled it from within, was not the expansive power of a single aesthetic principle such as tonal harmony, but rather – and I admit that my historiography is here out on a limb – the sheer excellence and reputation of individual works and composers.

Not even a Dunstable motet or a Dufay hymn, however, could travel by its own steam. What motivated their dissemination from without were fundamental socio-economic changes in continental Europe that made it equally possible for the princes of northern Italy, the merchants of Antwerp, or the university scho-

---

[3] The pattern strangely resembles that of the diffusion of Christianity from Rome and Gaul via the British Isles to central Europe in the sixth to eighth centuries.

lars of Kraków, to develop a desire for the most modern and sophisticated European music, whether they enjoyed it in church, in taverns, in public feasts, or in a solitary chamber. The strongest barrier against such hedonism had been the Church's objection to artistic polyphony; the strongest force now to break the barrier was the privatized devotion of the wealthy classes of secular society. Art-music was still a privileged pastime, but it already began to exert its individual appeal through mass production, long-distance transmission and pan-European, standardized forms.

The model which Part IV imposes on post-1450 Europe appears to be self-contradictory. On the one hand, the discourse is articulated geographically in four large areas (only one of which, Britain, corresponds to a modern nationality); on the other hand, what is described is supposed to be a further integration of European musical repertories and aesthetics. But diversity and participation were not mutually exclusive. First of all, diversity and even 'nationality' became trademarks in the European exchange. Thus, the Fleming Johannes Wreede, who had migrated to Castile, composed with his 'Pange lingua' a model piece in the Spanish style; but it is doubtful whether the style had actually existed before him. The Italian frottola and the German *Tenorlied* have in common not only an ostentation of national traditions of poetry, but also their harmonic and contrapuntal language, which in turn is derived from the polyphonic chanson style as shaped by mid-century English and French composers. Secondly, the diverse regions, centres and individuals realized their cultural ambitions through increasing participation in the mainstream repertories arriving from the Netherlands. In a cultural climate of intellectual emancipation and patronage in courts and towns, participation was soon followed by creative contributions that imitated the models. But how could the emulators develop originality, whether national or individual?

The key to the dialectic lies, I believe, in certain events taking place in the 1450s – a synthesis of experiences, a sudden upturn of compositional ambitions, a musical gesture which made all Europe listen and understand. The idea of the original masterwork in music, the *opus perfectum et absolutum*, grew in itself from acts of emulation. Unless you measured yourself against the best of your predecessors, against all the structural invention and all the communicative intention that music had ever been able to carry, your composition was imperfect. This compelling rule, to which Ockeghem, Busnois and the late Dufay subjected themselves, engendered its own imitators almost automatically. It was like a formula to spread a certain aesthetic, artificially and often superficially. No wonder that the emulators overplayed their results, trying to outclass their teachers not only in standard forms but in ever more extravagant creations. But the artist who really mastered the rule would necessarily have to supersede even Dufay, Busnois and Ockeghem. In order to do that, Josquin would also have to sum up the Middle Ages.

Josquin achieved this in the Italian Renaissance environment because ambition and the quest for perfection was most welcomed here, in music as well as in the other arts. Musical emulation was neither invented in Italy nor a characteristically Italian idea. It was a humanistic and pedagogical idea, well known to the Middle Ages. But in Italian Renaissance institutions, northern composers could turn the old idea into a working practice. Here, the practice had been appreciated since the time of Landini; here it appeared comparable and compatible with the humanistic imitation of ancient models; here it could be oiled by noble patronage.

The musical cultures of Italy and Spain form the closing element in our progress through post-1450 Europe. These cultures could absorb most of the impulses which traditionally travelled from north to south; they had the most favourable material conditions, and perhaps also the most articulate musical folklores (which would have generated good musical ears and formed reservoirs that could influence new art-music). The role of central Europe appears more as that of a mediator between the west and the south; the Netherlanders and their music travelled through, heading for greater achievements under even more auspicious conditions. What the Germans, Poles or Bohemians could add to their experience, was often taken across the Alps as well (by Isaac, for example). But having said all this, any of the European pathways were now used by music and musicians in both directions.

The 'chain' once formed by the lateral traditions had renewed itself with the inclusion of France and Iberia. The most characteristic contrapuntal technique which the late fifteenth century created is 'pervasive imitation', a texture in which the voices relate to each other like potential equals. The technique makes the musical voices do what the developing European nations did with each other's music. The European musical language was created by peoples imitating and respecting each other.

One possible exception to this happened with regard to Britain. It is likely, although by no means proven yet, that continental music was not emulated in parts of England for a short while in the later fifteenth century. The English musical institutions must have been so busy with their own overflowing creativity that the more provincial ones lost sight of Europe – probably because there happened to be fog in the Channel. We know that the English made up for any sin of proud self-sufficiency in the two centuries after Purcell. What a splendid thing it is to live in a country that belongs to Europe, is open to the world, but occasionally even forgets that there is life beyond the straits of Dover.

PART I

THE AGE OF THE GREAT SCHISM
(1378-1417)

INTRODUCTION

The forty years of the Great Schism were not a unified period of cultural history, nor even of political history. Nevertheless, the particular dynamic of a conflict dividing the whole Christian world seemed to be at work in all the historical processes, almost as a unifying element on a higher plane. Thus, *unity within conflict* is the underlying theme of Part I of this book, though by no means all the (musical) conflicts originating in this period can be fully explored in this Part.

Since the papacy had been the most powerful institution of the Middle Ages, influencing everybody's life, the election of two competing popes in 1378 signified more than a crisis of ecclesiastical administration. The fact that Christian Europe suddenly found itself split into two mutually exclusive areas of obedience (see Map 1) triggered numerous smaller realignments in its organization, down to the level of the individual.

The Schism also accompanied or exacerbated other fundamental changes of European life. As a political conflict, it helped promote the assertion of national states and their cultures apart from the central powers of pope and emperor. On the lower levels of intellectual and religious life, the Schism nourished spiritual tensions and social discontent which, in turn, were preconditions of humanist and Protestant renewal.

This was also the time of the Black Death: the plague had reached Europe in 1347, and it continued to return for generations, depopulating and dehumanizing the countryside and, to an even greater extent, the cities. At the same time, Europe experienced the growth of a capitalist economy, based on a network of long-distance trade, which had been developed by the merchant classes of Italy and Flanders. The Schism, the plague, and the new forms of economy lacerated the texture of medieval society, opening wide gaps for individual enterprise, new thinking and heresy, for personal success and collective participation in power.

The significance of the Schism for cultural history, and for music in particular, may be examined from three different angles. First, the Schism was above all a political conflict within the highest ranks of the Church, and between the secular powers which supported either side.[1] To the extent that music was susceptible to political interpretation, and exploitable for political ends, it could be

---

[1] Walter Ullmann, *The Origins of the Great Schism. A Study in Fourteenth-Century Ecclesiastical History* (London: Burns, Oates and Washbourne Ltd., 1948 / R Archon Books, 1967); Noël Valois, *La France et le Grand Schisme d'Occident*, 4 vols. (Paris, 1896–1902).

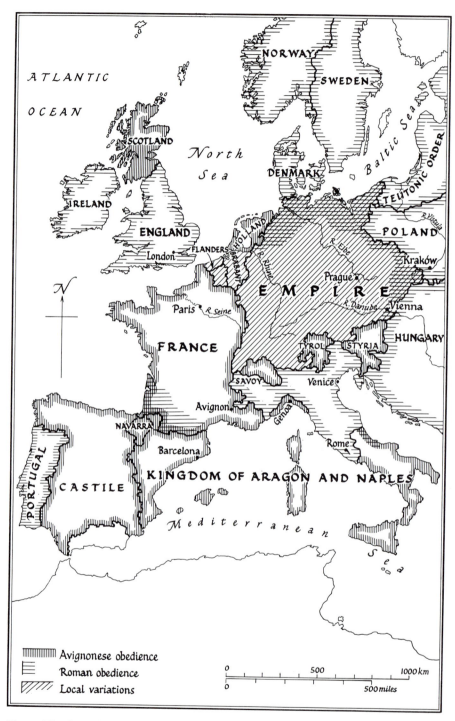

Map 1. The Great Schism in 1378

drawn into the debate just like literature and the other arts. The extent to which this happened may still have been limited, but it was greater than in earlier periods of history. Second, the Schism raised a spiritual problem for the Christian community at large. The struggle of the ecclesiastical authorities for popular support, the criticism voiced by theologians and other intellectuals, the general uncertainty of devotion and the yearning for peace must all have affected the contents and forms of religious art, including music. Third, the division of Europe in two – later three – competing 'obediences' directly affected the systems of patronage and the careers of musicians, especially if they were seeking ecclesiastical appointments or benefices away from home (for example, at the papal court). It is mainly on this level of cultural history that the period of the Schism and of the Church Councils (1378–1449) had a lasting effect on European music history.

The Schism originated as a political conflict within the Sacred College of cardinals – an oligarchic group of prelates who, as electors of the pope, controlled the wealth of the papacy as supplied by taxes, rents and other income from all over Europe. Many cardinals were members of French or Italian ruling houses from which they received political support and whose interests they served. The crucial events of 1378 happened at the end of a period during which three successive popes of Avignon (Innocent VI, *r.* 1352–62; Urban V, *r.* 1362–70; and Gregory XI, *r.* 1370–78) had tried to establish a secular *dominium* for themselves in Italy with military campaigns, aiming at a return to the Roman See. Gregory XI actually entered the Eternal City, intending to remain there, in January 1376. When he died on 27 March 1378, the election of his successor was bound to prejudice the question whether Italian or French prelates would retain their control of papal wealth and power. On 8 April the Sacred College, apparently under pressure from the Roman aristocracy and populace, elected the Archbishop of Bari, Bartolomeo Prignano. But this intractable Neapolitan immediately emerged as a despot for whom the task of reforming the Church was identical to curtailing the income and influence of the cardinals. A French-led majority of the cardinals revolted. Reconvening the conclave in the little town of Fondi, they elected one of their own circle, Count Robert of Geneva, as Pope Clement VII. On Clement's return to Avignon in 1381, two competing administrations had been set up which now perpetuated themselves. When Prignano (Urban VI) died in 1389, the Roman group elected Boniface IX instead of recognizing Clement VII. After the latter's death in 1394, the Avignon group was inconsiderate enough to give him a successor out of their own ranks, in the person of Pedro de Luna, Cardinal of Aragon. During his papacy as Benedict XIII, successive elections in Italy continued the Roman line with Innocent VII (*r.* 1404–6) and Gregory XII (*r.* 1406–17). The Council of Pisa in 1409, arranged after much pressure from secular powers and reformist groups within the Church, succeeded only in adding a third pope (Alexander V) to the other two who refused to abdicate. The Schism was brought to an end when the Council of Constance (1414–18) deposed both Alexander's successor, John XXIII, and Benedict XIII, whereupon Gregory XII abdicated. The newly elected Pope Martin V (Oddo Colonna, a Roman aristocrat) owed his uncontested supremacy to an alliance of the Church reformers with the leader of the Empire (King of the Romans), Sigismund of Luxembourg.

Political uses of music had already been prominent in the Parisian *Roman de Fauvel* (completed 1316), a literary and musical diatribe against the Order of the Templars. The *Roman* contains the earliest 'isorhythmic' motets, several of them by Philippe de Vitry. This new genre was to remain a vehicle for political ideas for over a century. Vitry continued to compose such motets, one of which was for Pope Clement VI (1342 or 1350).[2] This work and many other motets of the period embodied the political and moral views of high-ranking clerics like Vitry himself, and contributed to widely discussed subjects such as the reform of the Church. Sometime between 1371 and 1376, the anonymous motet 'Pictagore / O terra sancta' was addressed to Gregory XI, exhorting him to transfer the Holy See to Rome.[3] (The same appeal was made in those years by the saint and visionary Catherine of Siena.) Among polyphonic works for the first schismatic pope, Clement VII, there is the Latin ballade 'Inclite flos orti Gebennensis' ('Renowned flower of the Genevan garden'), composed by his chaplain Matheus de Sancto Johanne.[4] There are also two French ballades that advertise the courtly distinction and power of this secular-minded pontiff: 'Courtois et sages' by Magister Egidius,[5] and 'Par les bons Gédéon et Sanson' by the influential musician Philipoctus de Caserta.[6] Philipoctus celebrates the 'souverain pape qui s'apelle Clément', and wishes that the people of God be delivered from the dire effects of the Schism. He must have written this ballade soon after Clement's election, and thus while the pope was still in Italy. Neither Philipoctus nor Magister Egidius are known to have belonged to the papal chapel in Avignon. (See also pp. 54 f.)

Musical works like these were not necessarily propagandist in the sense of reaching wide audiences. They were probably performed by the pope's *capellani* at small after-dinner parties (*potus in aula*) following the papal Vespers service, for the pope's innermost circle of officials and guests.[7] Celebratory ballades for secular princes originated under very similar conditions and, like the papal works, circulated in precious manuscript copies among the most sophisticated secular courts.

A motet in honour of the Roman Pope Urban VI has recently been identified.[8] It was perhaps performed for an even smaller audience. Its text, 'Alme

---

[2] 'Petre clemens / Lugentium': edited in Vitry, *Works*, 97.

[3] Tomasello, *Music and Ritual*, 26–9.

[4] Ursula Günther ed., *Zehn datierbare Kompositionen der Ars Nova* (Hamburg: Musikwissenschaftliches Institut der Universität, 1959), no. 9; Apel ed., *FSC*, vol. 3 (1972), no. 296. Discussed in Günther, 'Datierbare Balladen', 16 (1962), 156–61. See also Tomasello, *Music and Ritual*, 41.

[5] Günther, 'Datierbare Balladen', 16 (1962), 154–6; Apel ed., *FSC*, vol. 1 (1970), no. 21.

[6] Günther, 'Datierbare Balladen', 16 (1962), 161–6; Apel ed., *FSC*, vol. 1 (1970), no. 82.

[7] Tomasello, *Music and Ritual*, 120 f.

[8] Lefferts, *Motet*, 184.

pater, pastor vere', refers to Urban's quarrels with the court of Naples in 1385, which forced him to flee with only a few remaining supporters across the peninsula. He brought several cardinals with him as prisoners, because they had plotted against him. In his besieged castle of Nocernia near Naples, the pope may have listened to this motet, while – as is alleged – the cries of his tortured prisoners were audible in all the rooms. The music of this work is found in an English source, and the poem may well have been written by the one cardinal who had not yet fallen into disgrace, the Englishman Adam Easton.

The spiritual anxieties and the quest for a solution to the Schism were probably more on the minds of other social classes. In cathedrals and other local churches, the celebrant would include the wish for Christian unity and peace in his prayers at the altar. It was not incongruous, then, when such sentiments were also included into the text of the Mass. Specially written tropes (musical-textual additions), often for the Gloria in excelsis, more and more frequently addressed the Schism, as for example in Johannes Ciconia's setting, 'Suscipe, Trinitas, hoc pacis jubilum; horrendi scismatis remove nubilum' ('Accept, Holy Trinity, this peaceful rejoicing; remove the cloud of the horrible Schism').[9]

The peace celebration mentioned in this Gloria was possibly that after the election of John XXIII in 1410, whose support exceeded that of the other schismatic popes. His main legal adviser, Cardinal Francesco Zabarella of Padua (1360-1417), was not only a patron of the composer Ciconia but, more importantly, one of the leading spirits of the 'conciliar movement'. This pressure-group, which included most prominent theologians, hoped to end the Schism either by persuading one of the competing popes to abdicate (*via cessionis*), or by convening an ecumenical council to regulate the question (*via concilii*). Zabarella himself prepared the Council of Constance in negotiations between John XXIII and King Sigismund. It is perhaps no coincidence that also other leading 'conciliarists' and friends of Zabarella were patrons or supporters of music. The famous theologian and poet Jean Charlier de Gerson (1363-1429) wrote much about music, and reformed the choir schools of Notre Dame, Paris (1408) and St Donatian's, Bruges (1396).[10] Together with Zabarella and Gerson, Cardinal Pierre d'Ailly (1352-1420) is considered one of the most influential figures of the Council of Constance. An eminent scholar, whose writings still proved useful to Christopher Columbus, he was Bishop of Cambrai when Guillaume Dufay was a choirboy there (1409-11). The suggestion that d'Ailly himself took the young musician with him to the Council does not seem too far-fetched.[11]

An international group of 'conciliarists' at the University of Paris also included the German professors Heinrich von Langenstein (1325-97) and Konrad von Gelnhausen, whose writings about the Schism ('Epistola pacis', Lan-

---

[9] Ciconia, *Works*, no. 7.
[10] Strohm, *Bruges*, 20; Joyce L. Irwin, 'The mystical music of Jean Gerson', *EMH* 1 (1981), 187-201.
[11] Fallows, *Dufay*, 16 f.

genstein, 1378; 'Epistola concordie', Gelnhausen, 1380; 'Epistola concilii pacis', Langenstein, 1381) express the general yearning for peace and reconciliation. An echo of such feelings also sounds in two Gloria settings of the time,[12] where the cry 'pax' is pronounced by the three voices one after the other – a symbol of the divided Christendom?

Example 1*a* Antonius Zacharias de Teramo, Gloria 'Anglicana'

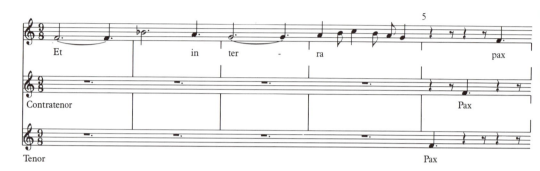

Example 1*b* Johannes Ciconia, Gloria

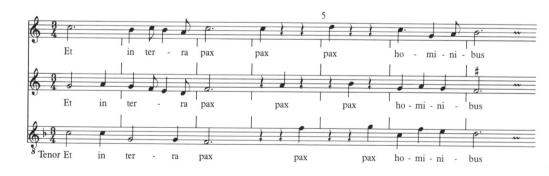

12 Zacharias: von Fischer–Gallo eds, *Italian Sacred and Ceremonial Music*, no. 9; Reaney ed., *EFM*, vol. 6 (1977), no. 20. Ciconia: *Works*, no. 1.

Ceremony and ritual gained in significance for the faithful when expressing contemporary concerns. The popes and the higher clergy had at least to pretend that they had an open ear for ecclesiastical abuses. In areas of contested allegiance, such as the Low Countries, Germany and (from 1395) France, local prelates were under pressure to demonstrate the reformist zeal of 'their' pope. Criticism of the Church was frequently expressed in poetic and musical forms, for example in motets. One such work which denounces simony – the practice of selling ecclesiastical positions to the highest bidder – is 'Degentis vita', a work possibly composed in northern France around 1380 (see pp. 42 f). Another, addressing similar issues, is 'In precio precium / Si nichil attuleris' by Hubertus de Salinis, possibly written in Florence around 1410.[13] Critical and satirical works were heard within the papal circle itself. The papal chaplain Matheus de Sancto Johanne wrote a motet for performance immediately after Mass, 'Are post libamina', in which poignant criticism is expressed of papal and other musicians, albeit not of the authorities themselves.[14]

The popes of Rome and Avignon also competed by enriching the liturgy with new devotions of wide, popular appeal. In 1385, Clement VII seems to have officially adopted the Feast of the Presentation of Our Lady (21 November), which had been celebrated at Avignon as early as 1372. Its programme was created by the chancellor of the King of Cyprus, Philippe de Mezières, who had encountered this ceremony in the Eastern Church.[15] Philippe composed a kind of miracle-play which included the use of instruments, and at least one song in the vernacular: a 'rondellus-like song of the Blessed Virgin' (*canticum ad modum rondelli de Beatissima virgine*), intended to 'excite the people to devotion'. On the Roman side, Urban VI agreed to the introduction of another popular Marian devotion, that of the Visitation of Our Lady (2 July). An original rhymed text for this Office was the work of Urban's Cardinal Adam Easton.[16] Its poetic style (for example in the free treatment of the iambic scansion) resembles the motet text 'Alme pater' mentioned above. Easton wrote his Office over the melodies for the Office of St Francis by Julian of Speyer; but at least one new musical setting of a Visitation Office was composed at the time. Its author was a canon of Liège, Henri Dézier de Latinnes, cantor of the Roman popes Urban VI and Boniface IX.[17]

---

[13] Reaney ed., *EFM*, vol. 7 (1983), no. 8. The text is an Ars antiqua conductus in two stanzas; Hubertus set the two stanzas to be sung simultaneously. The first is also found in the *Roman de Fauvel* (F-Pn fr. 146; see Emilie Dahnk, *L'hérésie de Fauvel* (Leipzig, 1935), 34 f), but the complete text is otherwise only found in the famous manuscript of Ars antiqua polyphony, *I-Fl plut. 29.1* (codex *F*), fol. 227. This manuscript belonged to the Medici family by 1456 at the latest: see Rebecca A. Baltzer, 'Notre Dame manuscripts and their owners: lost and found', *JMus* 5 (1987), 380.

[14] Hughes–Bent eds, *OH* no. 146; see Bent, 'Progeny', 5–20 for this and the related motet 'Post missarum solemnia'. See also p. 83 below.

[15] Tomasello, *Music and Ritual*, 34 f.

[16] *AH*, vol. 24, 89–94.

[17] O.-J. Thimister, *Nécrologe du clergé du diocèse de Liège 1801 à 1894* (Liège, 1894), 127 f. See also p. 323 below.

Around the turn of the century, both popes institutionalized the widespread devotion to Mary's mother, St Anne. The subject belongs, like those of the Presentation and the Visitation, in the sphere of Mary's 'family life'. The stories told in these liturgies are almost assemblies of 'genre' pieces, just as in Marian poems and altar paintings created for churches everywhere in Europe. They all have in common a deliberate appeal to women and to middle-class congregations.

It is difficult to assess what the situation of the Church may have meant for music on the lower levels of society. There are signs to indicate that the various unofficial or heretic devotions which had existed throughout the Middle Ages, gathered particular strength in this period. Movements like those of the *devotio moderna* in the Netherlands, the radical mendicant orders and *laudesi* in Italy, or the Bohemian heretics around Hieronymus of Prague and Johannes Hus actively developed unofficial sacred music, including hymns and processional songs in the vernacular (see also p. 327). These trends represented not so much an alienation from religious bonds as an answer to the disarray of a secularized Church authority.

Just a glimpse of a popular musical reaction to the Schism is provided by an order of the Parisian police of 1395:

> Défense est faite a tous menestriers de bouche et recordeurs de ditz que ils ne facent, dyent ne chantent, en place ni ailleurs, aucuns ditz rhymés en chansons qui facent mention du pape, du roi et des seigneurs de France en regard de ce qui touche le fait de l'union de l'Église.[18]

> [It is forbidden to all singing minstrels and song-makers to compose, say or sing, whether here or elsewhere, any musical ditties that make mention of the pope, the king, or the lords of France, with reference to the fact of the unity of the Church.]

Apparently, it had become a popular form of entertainment to 'make, say or sing rhymed chansons' in derision of the pope (or the King of France, who supported him) in the streets. There was enough popular unrest in France at the time, but the fear that singing minstrels ('menestriers de bouche') and poets ('recordeurs de ditz') might instigate it, is remarkable. It seems that music did become a vehicle for those political tendencies which, in 1395, forced the King of France to 'subtract' the allegiance of Royal France from the Avignon pope.

The changes which most significantly affected music in this period took place on the level of the material conditions of the musicians themselves. We may distinguish two related effects. The first, general effect was a sharp increase of supra-regional communications between musicians (caused by the almost frenetic diplomatic activity and the frequent travels of their patrons), which reached a climax in the enormous conciliar gatherings. Many hundreds of musicians attended the Council of Constance, for example. The second, more specific effect arose from the realignment of ecclesiastical spheres of influence. Both effects concerned the musical members of the Church itself – the lower

---

[18] Cited after Boutet-Strubel, *Littérature*, 168. See also François Lesure, 'Quelques chansons diffamatoires et séditieuses en France du XVe au XVIIIe siècle', *AnM* 37 (1982), 9–14; Cazeaux, *French Music*, 69.

clergy and the chaplains who made a living through music – as well as the many secular musicians in the service of popes and prelates.

To give a few examples: the harper and composer Jacob de Senleches was, between 1382 and 1383, a chamber valet of Cardinal Pedro de Luna, a Church diplomat who journeyed as far as Scotland.[19] We do not know what happened to Senleches when his master became pope in 1394. (See also pp. 55 f.) In the 1380s and 90s Jean de Noyers dit Tapissier was a 'valet de chambre' of Duke Philip the Bold of Burgundy, and accompanied the duke on military and diplomatic journeys, for example to Avignon and Milan in 1391.[20] Tapissier is one of those composers who wrote a work calling for an end of the Schism: the motet 'Eya dulcis atque vernans rosa' supports the cause of the French dynasty in the conflict.[21] Musicians like him were courtiers and cultural agents of their princes, not simple musical entertainers. Their function was also one of 're-presentation'. When between 1402 and 1407 Pope Benedict XIII had lost most of his supporters and was practically a fugitive in Italy, he nevertheless took his whole chapel with him, and even replenished its personnel.[22] For him, as for the Renaissance princes, cultural display in the form of a functioning sacred ritual was almost a symbol of legitimacy. For similar reasons, princes would take at least heralds and trumpeters with them on long-distance trips. A well-documented case is the expedition to eastern Europe and the Holy Land undertaken by Henry of Derby, later King Henry IV, in 1392–3.[23] Princes also recruited musicians from further afield, or 'poached' them from a competitor, to demonstrate their cultural superiority.

At the papal courts, such tendencies went hand in hand with the growth of the papal administration itself, and with the tightening of the grip on ecclesiastical benefices around Europe, as exerted by the *curia*.[24] Any papal administrator, whether a chaplain, *scriptor* or even cook, could be hired from abroad, and be rewarded with a church benefice in his homeland. When he died or was deprived of his position for spiritual or disciplinary offences, the benefice would usually revert to the pope, who gave it to a successor of his own choosing. During the Schism, when virtually all the servants of one pope were considered heretics by the other, a benefice reverted to the *curia* if its holder defected to the rival pontiff. Conversely, it could be offered as reward to a counter-defector. In this way, many clerics furthered their careers by deserting one pope for another. The Italian composer Antonius Zacharias de Teramo owed his curial office of *scriptor* of papal letters to the defection of his predecessor (in 1391).[25] The growing papal administration, including its chapel, drew

---

[19] Günther, 'Zur Biographie', 195; Gómez, *La música*, vol. 1, 40 f; Tomasello, *Music and Ritual*, 42 f. See also p. 308 below.

[20] See n. 89 below.

[21] Reaney ed., *EFM*, vol. 1 (1955), no. 3.

[22] Günther, 'Zur Biographie'; Tomasello, *Music and Ritual*, 69–72.

[23] Toulmin Smith, *Expeditions*.

[24] Starr, *Papal Court*, 15–62 ('Ars et praxis beneficiorum').

[25] Ziino, 'Magister Antonius', 311 f.

to the *curia* many gifted clerics who in earlier periods would have exerted their skills at home. This effect was particularly strong in the Low Countries, an area of contested allegiance during the Schism.

Already before 1378, the Avignonese popes and their cardinals had become accustomed to supplying themselves with musicians from the Low Countries. Statistics show that the dioceses from which most of the papal musicians came were those of Liège, Cambrai, Tournai and Thérouanne, followed at some distance by those of Arras, Amiens, Rouen, Noyon, Laon and Rheims.[26] The music of Avignon was thus dominated by influences from the southern Netherlands and northern France. But what happened after 1378 was the *diversion* of these influences from Avignon to Rome – and therefore the beginning of the epochal migration of Netherlands musicians to Italy.

This development had already started with the musicians accompanying the papal envoys who campaigned in Italy before 1378. Cardinal Gil Albornoz,[27] for example, employed the 'tenor' Johannes de Burgo (Bourges?), the *magister capelle* Bernardus de Luschis, and a priest from Liège, Thierry dictus Bona, who died in 1379 as *magister capelle* of a Roman cardinal. When Pope Gregory XI entered Rome in 1376, his *magister capelle* was Johannes Volcardi from Oerderen near Antwerp. Volcardi remained in Italy after 1378 as *magister capelle* of Urban VI, receiving large benefices in Antwerp and other places near his home, but losing the deanery of Antwerp itself when that city went over to Avignonese obedience in 1381. In recompense, Volcardi received other benefices in western Flanders, which was still under Roman control. A whole series of musicians in Roman service came from the diocese of Liège, where the popes controlled many benefices. In the church of St Servatius at Maastricht, for example, the canons were almost without exception curial administrators.[28]

Musicians from Liège and its diocese were, in fact, the most influential group of northerners in Italy for a long time to come. Composers such as Johannes Ciconia, Hubertus de Salinis, Johannes Franchois de Gembloux, Hugo and Arnold de Lantins and several others represented a nucleus of technical skill and stylistic innovation in the late fourteenth and earlier fifteenth centuries. In due course, we shall compare their achievements with those of their colleagues from other regions, and within a European musical context which stretches from England through the Low Countries and Germany to Renaissance Italy.

---

[26] Günther, 'Zur Biographie'; Tomasello, *Music and Ritual*, 210 (fig. 28).

[27] On Albornoz, see Suzanne Clercx-Lejeune, *Johannes Ciconia. Un musicien liégeois et son temps (vers 1335–1411)*(Brussels, 1960), vol. 1, 22 f. For the revision of Ciconia's biography, see p. 96 below.

[28] Further on these Roman chaplains, see Ziino, 'Magister Antonius'; Strohm, 'Magister Egardus'.

THE CENTRAL TRADITION

Trends in sacred music

The papal court of Avignon was a major centre for the cultivation of sacred polyphony, before and after 1378. The popes, who hired their chaplains from all parts of France and the Low Countries, providing them with privileged benefices, could avail themselves of the strongest traditions of polyphony which this age had to offer. They also cared for the musical education of their younger clerics: Urban V (1362–70) sent seven boys and a magister, who had to be 'most expert in the science of music', to the University of Toulouse, where the boys were expected to sing at High Mass, while also being educated in other subjects.[29] In the liturgy of the papal chapel itself, however, artistic polyphony was not necessarily indispensable. According to Andrew Tomasello, the ceremonies of the highest solemnity – the Pontifical Mass, and First Vespers on Solemn Feasts – lacked polyphonic music. For most weeks of the year the chaplains discanted regularly only in the less solemn Masses 'in the presence of the Pope' (*coram Papa*) and at Second Vespers, where it seems that they performed sections of the Ordinary of the Mass, Office hymns and perhaps other chant-based genres.[30]

The musical sources suggest that the papal repertory of Avignon was more or less of the same kind as the liturgical music of other leading institutions within the area, for example the royal chapels of France or Aragon. The surviving works belong mainly to the genres just mentioned (Mass Ordinary, Office hymns, a few other items for Vespers). The pieces are more suited to ordinary feast-days and Sundays than to special or solemn occasions (quite unlike the pioneering polyphony of Notre Dame of Paris in the preceding centuries). They are simpler in artistic approach than the new genres of the isorhythmic motet and the secular chanson.

There is, nevertheless, a fair amount of stylistic differentiation and individualization. In terms of compositional technique, three main styles have been identified:

'motet style' with a texted upper voice (duplum), often also a triplum above it, and a slower-moving, textless tenor, plus sometimes a textless contratenor;

[29] Haberl, *Bausteine*, III, 23 f; Tomasello, *Music and Ritual*, 22.
[30] Tomasello, *Music and Ritual*, 116 f.

'discant' or 'chanson' style with one texted upper voice and two slower-moving textless, lower voices;

'simultaneous style', where all the three or four voices may be texted and where the rhythmic differentiation between them is slight.[31]

There are many other variants, and sometimes the sources do not agree about the number of voices involved, or the absence or presence of text in them. Sometimes the different requirements of liturgical genres make themselves felt; when, for example, a Kyrie or Agnus Dei setting in 'simultaneous style' proceeds in long, florid melismas in all three voices just as in a passage of a secular chanson. The genres that have much text, such as the Gloria and Credo, are often set very homorhythmically in all voices so that they resemble the 'simultaneous style', even when text is absent from the lower voices in the manuscripts, which would normally suggest 'motet' or 'discant' styles. Other liturgical genres of this repertory such as hymns are mostly in 'simultaneous style', probably alternating between chant verses and polyphonic verses. Similar to the hymns are a few 'Benedicamus domino' settings which can be sung at the end of Vespers or Mass. The uses of chant are differentiated and sophisticated in all the genres found. Many Mass settings have no relation to chant melodies; but in others, the respective plainsong may be used in the tenor or, ornamented, in the top voice. All sections of the Mass can receive *tropes*: added texts which may refer to a specific festivity or dogma. Only a few of these texts occur also in contemporary plainsong books, for example the Marian trope 'Spiritus et alme' for the Gloria. Otherwise, the repertory exhibits a number of rare trope texts, some of which may have originated with the polyphonic settings themselves.

The habit of combining all five sections of the Mass Ordinary into a musical cycle began in this period. The earliest example is the 'Mass of Tournai', copied around the middle of the century.[32] Together with the well-known 'Messe de Nostre Dame' by Guillaume de Machaut and other anonymous cycles, the 'Mass of Tournai' seems a fair beginning to a musico-liturgical tradition which still continues today. It appears, however, that there was no great interest among French musicians to develop this novelty. The papal chaplains themselves do not seem to have taken it up.

Much of the sacred polyphony under discussion here (and not only the Mass cycles) originated in establishments other than the papal chapel. Only one surviving manuscript (*F-APT 16bis*) may be said to reflect the music of Avignon: one of the *magistri capelle* of the pope, Richardus de Bozonvilla, had a hand in its compilation. The manuscript was completed shortly after 1400 in the Cathedral of Apt, 50 miles east of Avignon.[33] This does not mean that all the music in that manuscript was necessarily composed by papal musicians. Among

---

[31] Stäblein-Harder ed., *Mass Music*; Hoppin, *Medieval Music*, 378–84.
[32] Charles van den Borren ed., *Missa Tornacensis*, CMM 13 (Rome: AIM, 1957).
[33] Tomasello, *Music and Ritual*, 123–50.

the fourteen names in the Apt MS that seem to be composer ascriptions, only one - Pellisson - has been identified with a musician in the pope's service: under his real name, Johannes de Bosco (1391-6).[34] If this identification is correct, we have a total of four works by this composer - all Mass sections - only two of which appear in the Apt MS. He may well also have composed for other employers, including perhaps Duke Louis II of Anjou (*c.*1390-93). With other identifiable composers in the Apt MS, the picture is similar. Among them are famous personalities such as Jean de Noyers dit Tapissier (*fl.*1370-1410) and Magister Baude Cordier (see pp. 64 f). Steve de Sort (Sortes) was a cantor and organist of King Martin I of Aragon from at least 1398 to 1405.[35] No liturgical music and no works in the Apt MS exist today by other known composers who were papal chaplains, for example Matheus de Sancto Johanne (see above) or Johannes Symonis dit Hasprois (chaplain from 1393 to *c.*1403).

All this may simply be explained by the loss of sources deriving directly from the chapel at Avignon. But there is a certain logic even in the source transmission as we have it: liturgical polyphony, mainly for Mass, was a genre which by definition could be used in many establishments, even in different countries. The composers and singers of this repertory, many of whom spent only part of their careers at Avignon, may have had a personal interest in taking their works with them when they changed service. Conversely, the music of the papal court as a whole rivalled that of the secular princes also with the highly individualized, artificial genres of the isorhythmic motet and the courtly ballade.

Some of the Latin-texted music in the even more famous manuscripts at Ivrea (*I-IV 115*) and Chantilly (*F-CH 564*) may also have originated at the papal court. The former source, which contains Mass sections and motets (apart from secular music), was either compiled around 1370 at the court of Count Gaston Fébus, or - on the basis of central French exemplars - at the Cathedral of Ivrea (Piedmont).[36] The Chantilly Codex (*c.*1400) draws its material from several centres in any case.[37]

The internationalism or, at least, inter-regionalism of the papal establishment may be illustrated by three compositions in the Apt MS which were so widely popular at the time that they survive even today in five or six sources, each from different countries.[38] The anonymous Gloria 'Qui sonitu melodie', for

[34] *Ibid.*, 235 f.

[35] Gómez, *La música*, 94-8.

[36] See, respectively: Günther, 'Problems of dating'; Karl-Josef Kügle, *The MS* Ivrea 115: *Studies in the Composition and Transmission of Ars Nova Polyphony*, Ph.D., New York U., 1986. An inventory of the manuscript is to be found in *RISM B IV. 2*, 282-304.

[37] Günther, 'Unusual phenomena', 102-7. An inventory of the manuscript is to be found in *RISM B IV. 2*, 128-60.

[38] All edited in Stäblein-Harder ed., *Mass Music*. See also Amédée Gastoué ed., *Le manuscrit de musique du trésor d'Apt* (Paris: Droz, 1936). For the Spanish sources of this and other sacred music, see Gómez, 'Musique et musiciens'; *idem*, 'El manuscrito M 971' (with facsimile edn of the manuscript containing the 'Mass of Barcelona' and the motets 'Degentis vita' and 'Apollinis eclipsatur').

three voices, may have originated in southern France; its earliest source is the Ivrea Codex. By 1420 the piece had also been distributed in Italy, Austria and Germany. It is in simple chanson style, with a lively and fluent melody in the top voice (in *prolatio major*, 6/8 in transcription) and a rhythmically simple duet of tenor and contratenor a fifth below. The trope text is a beautiful piece of poetry, in stanzas of octosyllables each concluded with a quadrisyllable. It celebrates the life of Christ, and ends with a reference to the Assumption of Mary into Heaven. The work was probably composed for the feast of the Assumption (15 August) – a feast endowed with much music in churches at this time, and invariably illustrated by angels' concerts in paintings of the subject.

The Credo by 'Sortes', presumably the Aragonese composer Steve de Sort, is preserved in manuscripts from France, Aragon, Italy and the Low Countries; it is labelled 'de rege' ('of the king') in the Ivrea Codex. The title may refer to a feast of Our Lord; or the work could have been intended for a royal ceremony. Stylistically, this Credo resembles the Gloria 'Qui sonitu', although the declamation is even simpler and mostly syllabic. An exception is the melismatic 'Amen', which has a striking sequential pattern of five beats in the top voice.

The Credo labelled 'Bonbarde' in the Apt MS may now be discussed in more detail.[39] The description seeks to clarify how the work comprises a successfully contrived system of *relationships*: between pitches, note-values or phrases, between music and words, between polyphonic voices. In this way, procedures may become apparent that were, in my opinion, relevant for all music of this era.

Example *2a* Perrinet de la Bombarda? Credo 'Bonbarde'

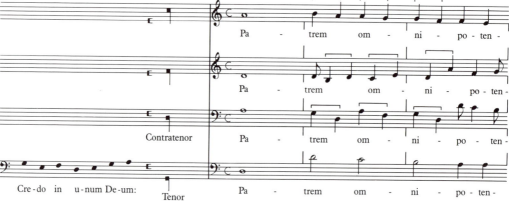

---

[39] Stäblein-Harder ed., *Mass Music*, no. 55. The deviations of the example from this edition are based on variant manuscript readings.

Example *2a* (*cont.*)

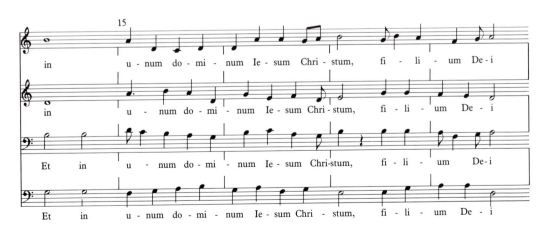

Example 2*a* (*cont.*)

Example *2a* (*cont.*)

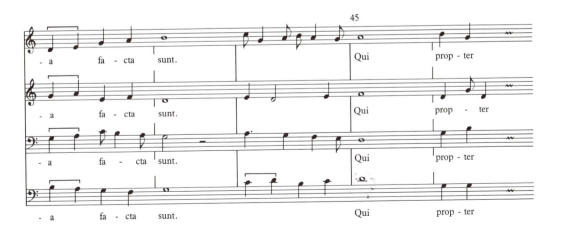

This is a four-voice composition in 'simultaneous style', and one of the long-gest pieces in the repertory (182 bars in the edition). In the Apt MS, it requires three full openings. The Credo is articulated in five large sections (bars 1–35, 36–61, 62–80, 81–109 and 110–45), followed by a separate 'Amen'. The first five sections are analogous to each other in their internal organization, remotely like variations of a given pattern. They coincide to some extent with the major subdivisions of the text. The end of section five ('Et vitam venturi seculi') is differentiated by longer note-values and a more melismatic declamation, lead-ing to the wholly melismatic 'Amen'. Otherwise, the text is declaimed syllabi-cally, mostly in semibreves (crotchets in transcription), and underlies all four voices. Its performance would take approximately as much time as the singing of the Credo in plainsong. Other Credos of the period, by comparison, go even faster, as the syllables are set in shorter note-values: the sense of the words is often obscured. The composer of this Credo observes liturgical dignity, gives each phrase time to breathe, and separates syntactic units by cadences and longer notes.

The tenor will be considered first, as it determines the other voices. Its melody is not one of the known Credo plainsongs, although it resembles some of them,[40] for example by its restriction to the octave range *d–d'* (exceeded only rarely with steps to *e'*) and its use of melodic shapes which are typical for the first mode. The intonation on the words 'Credo in unum Deum' is, as usual, not found in the manuscripts. As with the phrase 'Gloria in excelsis Deo', these initial words were never set by late medieval composers, but intoned by the celebrant.[41]

In the first two phrases of the tenor ('Patrem . . . terre'), the divisions of the text are emphasized by longer note-values. Also the melodic contours embody the sense of the words. The word 'Patrem' at once establishes the melodic frame *d–d'*. Then the melody descends by step to *a*, and falls back a fifth to *d*, with the word 'omnipotentem'. 'Factorem celi et terre' elaborates on 'omnipoten-tem'. Its line circles from *g* via *b* back to *d*, all in stepwise motion and complet-ing the stepwise descent of the first line. In the next phrase, the upper fourth of the melodic frame is traversed twice in stepwise motion, precisely once for each of the two rhyming words 'visibilium' and 'omnium'. Another circling line then completes the descent to *d*, corresponding to the line 'factorem celi et terre'. At the first full stop of the text, the octave-frame is not only filled with all the diatonic pitches, but also 'interpreted' by the internal subdivisions *d'–a–d* and *d'–b–d*. The next phrase, which introduces God the Son, has three, not two sub-phrases, divided by weaker caesuras. The separating notes *e* and *d* are only minims, and they are not left by leap as in the previous subdivisions.

---

[40] It is related to Credo IV of the present Vatican editions (see *LU*), which was often sung polyphoni-cally around 1400. Another related melody, set in two-part counterpoint, is in the Italian gradual *I-PIca* s.n., fol. 86v. See also p. 338 below.

[41] This is specifically prescribed in the Ceremonial of the Council of Constance, for example (see also p. 114).

After the full stop of bar 20, however, a full bar's rest constitutes the strongest division so far.

With 'et ex patre . . . secula', the melodic style changes somewhat. Pairs of repeated pitches are introduced, and even a pair of declamatory quavers on 'omnia'. Appended to this phrase is a melismatic excursion on the vowel 'a'; it is circular in shape and lasts as long as a texted sub-phrase of its own.

As a sharp contrast, 'Deum de Deo' brings a pattern not derived from the words. It implies triple metre, and is reminiscent of the 'modal' rhythmic patterns of the thirteenth century. The pattern is repeated eight times, fragmenting the text into small splinters of mostly one word only. Melodically, there is a repetition pattern A B A' B' / A'' C A'' B', which also involves strict transpositions of A and B. The symmetrical grouping into $(2 + 2) + (2 + 2)$ units may reflect the parallels within the text, or even its meaning: the similarity of the Son to the Father.

The phrase starting with 'Genitum' reverts to the earlier syllabic declamation, again spanning the octave *d–d'*, which is stated at the beginning as a falling interval. The contour of 'Per quem . . .' boldly traverses two overlapping fourths by leap (*d'–a*, *c'–g*), and then the tritone interval *b–f* by step. This is the first phrase to end on a non-final pitch (*g*), reconnected to *d'* by a melismatic bridge (bar 44).

The contratenor has the same range as the tenor (*d–e'*) and tends to move within the fifth above the tenor when that voice is in the lower register, but the fifth below when the tenor is in the upper. The middle-range notes of the tenor, *g* and *a*, are often doubled by the contratenor in unison. The two upper voices, one storey higher, also share a range (*b–c''*), crossing each other often, and almost consistently exchanging places from one cadence to the next. When the lower voice-pair has the fifth *d–a*, the upper pair usually repeats that fifth an octave higher. This sonority of only perfect consonances (1–5–8–12) occurs throughout the work at major cadences on *d*, including the last chord. The imperfect consonance of the third is also often avoided in cadential chords on *a*; but it is usually present where the tenor comes to a halt on *g* or *e*. No cadences are formed on *f*, *b* and *c'*: this differentiated use of final chords corresponds to the structure of the first mode.

The three voices other than the tenor create many dissonances, more often with each other than with the tenor. Most dissonances are caused, of course, by small, ornamental note-values and by the syncopations which pervade the whole composition. In bars 1–20, the two upper voices alternate in creating syncopation. For long stretches, one voice is 'disaligned' with the other at the distance of a quaver. In bars 2–3, for example, the second voice seems 'delayed' by one quaver, and the counterpoint could be normalized by omitting one quaver at the beginning. This would produce 'note-against-note' counterpoint for the upper voices, and all the dissonances between them would disappear. The syncopation appears as a written-out rubato effect which is not essential to the composition. Rhythmic normalization would not remove *all* the dissonances, however. At the end of bar 2, the interval of a ninth, *f-g'*, between contratenor and top voice cannot easily be eliminated. In bar 5, rhythmic normalization of the second voice would make it consonant with the tenor but create problems with the top voice and contratenor.

The contratenor accords particularly well with the tenor, but not at all with the upper voices. Apart from dissonances, it often has 'forbidden' parallels with them. In bars 6–7, it doubles the second voice, in bars 9–10 the first. Where there are full triads, the contratenor invariably doubles a chord component also present in one of the other three voices. None of the other voices is as 'superfluous' as that. The disregard of the upper voices for the contratenor is so strong that they even avoid the fourth against the tenor where the contratenor has a third or fifth underneath the tenor (bars 2, 5 and 8), so that the sonority would still be consonant if the contratenor were omitted. This must mean that the upper voices were composed against the tenor – and also with regard to each other – but that the contratenor was composed against the tenor on its own, not considering the upper voices (see Fig. 1).

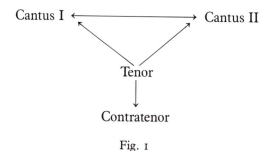

Fig. 1

A striking series of parallels occurs in bar 62:

Example 2*b*

Example 2*b* (*cont.*)

The poor voice-leading here is perhaps alleviated by the exceptionally rapid declamation. But in bar 66, the contratenor has gratuitous quavers which simply ornament the pitches of the top voice, like a 'heterophonic variant' of the top line rather than a counterpoint against it. Instead of the parallel octaves of bar 62, top voice and contratenor have parallel sevenths in bar 69. A similar passage in bar 38, with accented sevenths, may reveal that these are all ornamentations of the same progression in octaves (*c'–b–a–g*). It is always the contratenor which disobeys contrapuntal rules, but which thickens and enlivens the texture.

Let us return for a moment to the passage with rhythmic patterning in bars 28–35. This is similar to a frequent device of the time, the *hoquetus*. Here, the voices complement each other rhythmically in a lively, repetitive pattern which includes many rests. In our passage, precise complementation of rhythm takes place between the tenor and the upper voices. The rhythmic figure repeated in all of them at the distance of one crotchet is exactly three crotchets long. What role is left for the fourth voice, the contratenor? It has a rhythmic figure of its own, which is only half as long as the other figure (simply quaver–crotchet), and has no rests. This produces a kind of thickening substructure to the *hoquetus* itself: the contratenor has an individual task with regard to rhythm and texture. The upper voices, on the other hand, differ from the tenor in *melodic* terms: the tenor is melodically patterned, the upper voices are free.

Similar *hoquetus* passages recur in the Credo at the ends of the five major sections, and thus articulate the large-scale organization of the piece. As here, they are all cleverly worked out to the smallest detail. Melody, rhythm, counterpoint and texture are all employed as independent parameters to organize and differentiate the whole. And yet, the total effect of the piece is remarkably homogeneous, with innumerable quasi-repetitions. Also because of the prevailing thick textures, the aural impression of the piece could be compared to that of a piece for organ or wind ensemble, with tutti registration throughout. Hanna Stäblein-Harder remarks on the Credo: 'The three upper voices . . . are considerably influenced in their structure by the T[enor], which constantly appears to vary certain melodic turns. The voice appears to resemble the improvisations of a skilful instrumentalist.'[42]

Actually, the 'improvisational' character seems to apply even more to the added voices: the contratenor with its heterophonic ornaments, the upper voices with their rubato-syncopations. But we do not need to assume *instrumental* performance, since vocal improvisation and diminution (for example, over a given chant) were not unheard-of in medieval times. Following unwritten rules and assigning each voice a specific range and task, singers would produce a series of similar but not identical patterns, especially before cadences. A basic 'note-against-note' declamation would keep the text audible, making it proceed at the pace of the plainsong itself.

It appears that such practices were known even in papal circles, where their unpretentiousness might have assumed the value of austerity or liturgical dignity. In his notorious Bull 'Docta sanctorum patrum' of 1324/5, the austere and somewhat eccentric Dominican Pope John XXII thundered against the modern church music of his time: against the introduction of small note-values and newly invented note-shapes such as semibreves and minims; against *hoqueti* which lacerated the text and the plainsong; against added 'discantus' voices and secular motet texts. He deplored that the chants of the Antiphonal and Gradual were despised and misunderstood, their declamation confused, their modal character ignored, their performance rushed.[43] Most scholars believe that the Bull had little or no effect on musical practice; but there are some partial repercussions of its precepts during this century. The Carmelite order, at least,

[42] Stäblein-Harder ed., *Mass Music*, Critical Text, 66.
[43] Helmut Hucke, 'Das Dekret "Docta Sanctorum Patrum" Papst Johannes' XXII', *MD* 38 (1984), 119–31.

introduced a few similar-sounding statements into its general statutes. Traces of this aesthetic may be discerned in the music of Avignon itself. The Credo 'Bonbarde', for example, does respect the pace and audibility as well as the linguistic structure of the sacred text. Even the melismatic interludes and *hoqueti* rather enhance its understanding. The composition may also be related to one of the positive suggestions of the Bull. It says that polyphony at Mass is not altogether forbidden but should be limited to major feast-days, when the plainsong might be embellished by perfect consonances such as the octave, fifth and fourth. In the Credo 'Bonbarde', the sonority 1–5–8–12 is always re-established on the final *d*. In the Apt MS, the voices are actually labelled according to this distribution, namely 'v^a' (fifth), 'viii^a' (eighth) and 'xii^a' (twelfth) above the tenor. The voice-names 'contratenor', 'motetus' and 'triplum' are avoided. The same strange labels occur also in the next piece of the manuscript, a Credo by Jacobus Murrin, and in an anonymous hymn for St Anne ('Orbis exultans') in the closely related source *F-APT 9*.[44] It appears that these pieces advertised their compatibility with the old-fashioned practices of harmonizing a plainchant as permitted by the Bull of 1324/5.

Strangely enough, a link with instrumental music nevertheless exists. Stäblein-Harder has suggested that the composer of this Credo, whose name is given in other manuscripts as 'Perneth' or 'Prunet', was a tenor-shawm player – thus offering an explanation for the heading 'Bonbarde' in the Apt MS. A fitting candidate for this name has now been found. He is 'Perrinet (Perrequì) de la bombarda', a minstrel who was requested to join the court of Aragon in a letter by King John I of 6 June 1393. Perrinet was promised the high salary of 100fl.; a companion whom he was expected to bring with him, was offered 50fl.[45] We do not know from where the two musicians came or whether they actually arrived at the Aragonese court. But the possibility remains that the Credo was composed for the papal chapel, an institution well above Perrinet's own social standing. On the other hand, the chaplains could hardly get hold of a Mass setting better suited to both the dignity and the secular splendour of their establishment. In any case, this Credo with its monumental simplicity and improvisatory needlework influenced the standards of fifteenth-century Mass music. It was copied by the next generation of musicians in sources from Italy, Germany and Spain.[46]

Aesthetic ambitions of the Ars subtilior

An important sector of what is presented here as the 'central tradition'[47] of late fourteenth-century music has also been described as the 'mannerist style' (by

---

[44] Tomasello, *Music and Ritual*, 146.

[45] Gómez, *La música*, doc. 132; *idem*, 'El manuscrito M 971', 7 f.

[46] Gómez, 'Musique et musiciens', 85.

[47] I derive this term from the model 'centre/periphery', despite its possible implications of a value judgement which I do not share. I have replaced 'periphery' by 'lateral traditions', however: see pp. 62 f.

Willi Apel)[48] or as the 'Ars subtilior' (by Ursula Günther).[49] The latter name, in particular, expresses very well the aspirations of composers working around 1380–1410 in the areas of Avignonese obedience, i.e. southern France, Spain (the kingdoms of Aragon, Navarre and Castile) and some affiliated territories such as Savoy, Lombardy and Cyprus. The quest for a subtler manner of composing characterizes in particular the secular polyphony of this group, including in some sense their isorhythmic motets (see below). But as we have seen, the sacred music of the same area shows trends towards simplicity as well. In pieces such as Perrinet's Credo, they appear together with more complex procedures; elsewhere they appear undiluted, for example in some very simple Kyries and hymn settings of the Apt MS.

The musical style known as the Ars subtilior was only one tendency within a rich tradition of music-making that took place within a context of patronage and of dynastic display which allowed musicians considerable freedom of activity. The most enterprising of them were continuously crossing the borders between the sacred and secular, vocal and instrumental, clerical and princely spheres. Musically, they all depended on the great models of the French Ars nova: this makes them representatives of the 'central tradition'. But the practitioners of the Ars subtilior sought to expand the tradition's limits by further refinement, exaggeration and amalgamation. By contrast, the 'lateral traditions' of music, which we will discuss later, resulted from interactions between the Ars nova and regional traditions already present in countries further to the west, north and east. Broadly speaking, these interactions were learning processes. For the musicians of the central tradition, however, who were firmly grounded in the Ars nova of Vitry and Machaut, the question was more a matter of how to go beyond maturity.

The cultural climate of the central tradition may be characterized, for example, by the careers of some of its composers. The harper Jacob de Senleches first served the court of Castile and later Cardinal Pedro de Luna of Aragon. Johannes Symonis dit Hasprois was a cleric from Cambrai who worked at the French royal court (in 1380), at the court of Portugal, and for the popes Clement VII and Benedict XIII. (His surviving music consists of secular chansons only!) Aragonese rulers requested musicians and compositions from Avignon. In 1379 Duke John of Gerona asked his ambassador in Avignon to send six 'bons xantres' to serve in his chapel (specifying that they should not be married): 'And, we wish that they bring with them the complete music of the Mass, and a book where there are many motets, rondeaux, ballades, and virelais. But make sure that none of them has previously served the Duke of Anjou.'[50] Duke

---

[48] Apel ed., *FSM*, 10–13.

[49] Ursula Günther, 'Das Ende der Ars nova', *Mf* 16 (1963), 105–20.

[50] Gómez, *La música*, doc. 223. Here and in other quotations from the document, a substitution of 'en' for 'e' has led to the misunderstanding that the Mass and the other music were requested in the same book. For the correction, see Giampaolo Mele, 'Una precisazione su un documento di Giovanni Duca di Gerona e primogenito d'Aragona, riguardante la sua cappella musicale', *AnM* 38 (1983), 255–60.

John also expressed curiosity as to whether the singers played instruments including bagpipes, 'as we have them in many varieties'. Ten years later, the same prince – now King John I of Aragon – sent another request: 'We wish that you have a book made for us where there are notated between 15 and 20 motets, . . . and where there are ballades, rondeaux and virelais of prime quality [que sien la flor], and have it prepared by the singers of the pope, because they know the best quality of that' ('la flor d'aço').[51]

The papal chaplains, it would seem, could run a business on the side by duplicating their music for other courts. Or they could join other masters personally, on the strength of their instrumental as well as vocal skills. John I was obviously familiar with French manuscripts which contained a mixture of motets and secular polyphonic songs (French was the *only* vernacular language used for polyphony in the central tradition). Such manuscripts could have been similar to the Chantilly Codex, which contains precisely 100 chansons (as do some literary anthologies of this period), plus 13 motets. They could also have been similar to the Ivrea Codex which contains all the genres mentioned, including polyphonic Mass settings. As already mentioned (p. 25), Ursula Günther connected this manuscript with the flamboyant court of King John's relative, Count Gaston Fébus of Foix and Béarn (1343–91). In his small county along the Pyrenees, the arts of music, poetry and hunting blossomed like nowhere else. To all these arts, precious illuminated codices were dedicated. Musicians praised the patronage of the ruler with at least eight dedicatory compositions; a ninth piece may be the troped Kyrie 'Sol justicie' which seems to address the prince himself, in place of God, with the epithet 'Sun of justice'. Similar celebratory works, often of a cryptic and heraldic nature and likely to be performed at feasts such as courtly weddings or anniversaries, are also known from the courts of Anjou, Berry, Burgundy, Milan and Savoy. Next to poetry itself (the *seconde rhétorique*), music was a kind of third rhetorical art,[52] exercised in acts of homage and as an ornament of politics and leisure. Perhaps the most amazing document of this musical culture is the Cyprus Codex (*I-Tn J.II. 9*), compiled for the French Lusignan dynasty of Cyprus about 1415.[53] It is the largest of the surviving collections, with 229 pieces, encompassing all genres. None of them is found in the other sources, but many are strict imitations of the dominating styles, or even of specific models. This Cypriot repertoire seems to have been created *on the spot* for a court wishing to emulate those of the French cousins and rivals.

If the stylistic detail of much of this music is 'subtler' than that of the Ars nova, the cultural attitude of the patrons is perhaps somewhat less so. The underlying condition for this musical activity was great feudal wealth, and a

---

51 Gómez, *La música*, doc. 243. Further on the singers of John I, see Giampaolo Mele, 'I cantori di Giovanni I Il Cacciatore Re d'Aragona (anni 1379-96)', *AnM* 41 (1986), 63-104.
52 On their connection, see especially Gallo, *Music of the Middle Ages II*, 45-8.
53 Richard H. Hoppin ed., *The Cypriot-French Repertory of the Manuscript Torino, Biblioteca nazionale, J.II.9*, CMM 21/1-4 (Rome: AIM, 1960-63).

taste for only the very best ('la flor'). But the patrons left it to the paid specialists to determine what the 'very best' actually was.

The compositional styles of the Ars subtilior, suitably characterized by a comparative term, had grown from a strong and self-conscious heritage of craftsmanship within the musical discipline itself. 'Subtilitas' was a general ideal of the time: for example, the venerable theologian Duns Scotus (*d.* 1308) had been honoured with the sobriquet 'Doctor subtilis'. The transfer of the term to music introduced a most remarkable historical dynamic.[54] We find this in the *Musica* of Johannes Boen, a treatise written *c.*1355.[55] Boen was a Dutch priest who spent much time at the University of Paris. When speaking of the terms for the signs b flat and b natural, Boen says that the expressions 'round b' and 'square b' are used by uneducated people, as they refer to external shapes only. Others, *more subtly*, speak of 'soft b' and 'hard b', which is how these notes sound to the ears.[56] He thus praises the subtlety of mind and ear of those who can appreciate the metaphoric expressions 'soft' and 'hard' as convincing descriptions of the aural effect. In another passage, Boen contrasts the uneducated singers of his own nation (the 'Alemani') at the University of Paris with others (probably French singers) who can sing a hymn melody 'subtiliter'.[57] But in his most remarkable statement, he identifies 'subtilitas' with a *historical development of style*:

> According to the diversity of time and region, many new and unheard-of things will arise, as for example the performance of the comma and of three minor semitones [i.e. small divisions of the whole tone] and many similar things which, although they have not yet been heard, perhaps with the passing of time will become audible through the use of new instruments and vocal skills: just as, before Pythagoras, there was no such subtlety of singing as is used in our times, nor do we use such fractions of melody ['fracturam in cantu'] as do the English, the French and the Italians.[58]

This extraordinary passage leaves no doubt that Boen expects a refinement or 'greater subtlety' of tuning and rhythm as a result of the passing of historical time – on the evidence that some nations are already ahead of others in this development. He thus predicts the 'Ars subtilior' and, perhaps, later developments as well.

---

[54] See also Nino Pirrotta, '"Dulcedo" e "subtilitas" nella pratica polifonica franco-italiana al principio del '400', *RBM* 2 (1948), 125–32; repr. in *idem*, *Musica tra Medioevo e Rinascimento* (Turin: Einaudi, 1984), 130–41.

[55] Wolf Frobenius, *Johannes Boens Musica und seine Konsonanzenlehre* (Stuttgart: Musikwissenschaftliche Verlagsgesellschaft, 1971). Pirrotta's conceptual pair *dulcedo* and *subtilitas* is found in the treatise in the *Prohemium*, 32, line 2.

[56] Frobenius, *Johannes Boens Musica*, 51 f, line 7.

[57] *Ibid.*, 33, line 12.

[58] *Ibid.*, 45, lines 25–6.

The pride of the isorhythmic motet

Other significant references to the term appear in the *Tractatus figurarum* whose probable author is the composer Philipoctus de Caserta (*fl.*1370–90).[59] Speaking of the development of motet composition – again a surprisingly historical framework to the argument – he distinguishes the early style of the motet 'Tribum quem / Quoniam secta' (probably by Vitry) from the later, subtler style ('subtiliorem modum') introduced by the same masters, and exemplified by 'Apta caro / Flos virginum'. Then a new generation of composers invented even 'greater subtleties' ('maiores subtilitates'), 'to perfect what had been left unfinished by their predecessors'.[60]

The fourteenth-century method of composing motets is well known.[61] The principle of isorhythm (a term coined by Friedrich Ludwig) was derived from the patterned structure of thirteenth-century motet tenors, where repetitive rhythms (a continued alternation of long and short, for example) were applied to chant melodies, and the whole line then segmented by inserted rests into shorter or longer sections (the so-called *ordines*). In fourteenth-century motets, each of these sections had exactly the same internal rhythm and was known as a *talea* (literally a 'cut'). The melodic contour of the chant, which progressed independently of the rhythmic segmentation, was called a *color* (i.e. an ornament). The melody could also be repeated, and this often happened in a simple arithmetical ratio to the rhythmic repeats, for example when 6 *taleae* = 2 *colores*. Each of these two *colores* could be called one complete tenor 'period'; they are identical in this case. The earliest isorhythmic motets are found in the *Roman de Fauvel* (completed 1316), and up to six of them may be by Philippe de Vitry. Guillaume de Machaut's 23 motets are the most important contribution to the genre after Vitry, from whose works they are distinguished by much greater use of French texts and other characteristics. By 1351 at the latest, the form was practised in England, too, as attested by the author of the treatise *Quattuor principalia* (see p. 81). In terms of performance, the isorhythmic motet remained a vocal genre with more than one text and a certain hierarchy of the voices. Usually, the one or two texted upper voices (motetus or duplum, and triplum) were constructed over a ready-made tenor or tenor–contratenor scaffolding, and they related to this pre-established scaffolding like an elaboration to a fundamental thesis.

What were, then, the 'greater subtleties' with which some composers after Vitry 'perfected what had been left unfinished by their predecessors'? (We should note in this expression the emphasis on a coherent tradition: the later

---

[59] Coussemaker ed., *CS*, vol. 3, 118–28. Wulf Arlt, 'Der *Tractatus figurarum* – ein Beitrag zur Musiklehre der "Ars subtilior"', *Schweizer Beiträge zur Musikwissenschaft* 1 (1972), 35–53, rejects contemporary attributions of the treatise to Egidius de Murino and Philipoctus de Caserta; but see p. 59 below.

[60] Coussemaker ed., *CS*, vol. 3, 118 f.

[61] For basic information, see Gilbert Reaney, 'Ars nova in France', in *NOHM III*, ch. I, 6 ff; Ernest H. Sanders, 'Motet, #I, 3' in *The New Grove*; Gallo, *Music of the Middle Ages II*, ch. II.9.

composers only unfolded what was already implied in the earlier forms of the genre.) In an effort to define style criteria by which to recognize these later works, Daniel Leech-Wilkinson[62] stressed the significance of stricter rhythmic repetitions also in the upper voices (pan-isorhythm), and of *proportional diminutions* of the tenor periods themselves: as, for example, when in a structure of 6 *taleae* = 2 *colores* the second period or *color* (comprising *taleae* 4–6) is sounded in halved note-values. Such pieces, some of which have far more complicated structures, are found in the Ivrea Codex of *c*.1370, but some appear no earlier than in the Chantilly Codex of *c*.1400, for example 'Inter densas / Imbribus' and 'Sub Arturo / Fons citharizantium'. The former work was written in honour of Count Gaston Fébus; the latter was probably composed by an Englishman (see p. 82).[63]

'Porcio nature / Ida capillorum', a motet found in the Ivrea Codex, can serve as an example for the proportional layout of the tenor which goes beyond the procedures of Vitry. In this work, the tenor periods relate in the ratio 6:4: 3:2 in length, but only one period is actually written out. By applying four different mensurations to this basic series of note-shapes, the composer not only changes the total length of the period, but also its internal rhythm. In the perfect (triple) mode or tempus, the second of two breves or semibreves is doubled in value according to the rule of *alteratio*, whereas in the imperfect (duple) mode or tempus it has to be read at face value. A verbal rubric ('canon') explains the procedure.

Example 3 Magister Henricus, 'Porcio nature / Ida capillorum'

[62] Daniel Leech-Wilkinson, 'Related motets from fourteenth-century France', *PRMA* 109 (1982–3), 1–22; see also Ursula Günther, 'The fourteenth-century motet and its development', *MD* 12 (1958), 27–58.

[63] Most of the surviving French motets of the post-Machaut generation are edited in Harrison ed., *Motets of French Provenance*, and Günther ed., *Motets of Chantilly*.

Example 3 *(cont.)*

half values (imperfect tempus)

The intended duration of the note is not self-evident from its visual shape, but changes according to the context, as defined by the mensural code applied in each case. The principle that the meaning of a sign depends on its context is, of course, fundamental to Western musical notation (as to other linguistic codes). The opposite principle of 'orthochronic notation' (where each sign corresponds to one duration only) has always been confined to special purposes. In this composition, and many related ones from the late fourteenth and fifteenth centuries, an intellectual game arises from the separation of sign and meaning, by making it explicit. What appears to be a single series of signs, has to be read in four different ways to produce the structure of the whole work. This requires a verbal 'canon' to explain the code, demonstrating that the signs in themselves are ambiguous. The idea gained enormous significance not only for the later history of the isorhythmic motet, but even more so for that of the Franco-Netherlands cantus firmus Mass. The Ars subtilior composers also operated with similar verbal 'canons' in secular music (see the discussion below of 'Medée fu').

Another Ars subtilior motet, 'Inter densas / Imbribus', goes so far as repeating a series of only six tenor notes in eight different mensurations. The upper voices remain uninfluenced by this layout. Conversely, the motet 'Multipliciter amando / Favore' has a very simple tenor layout (3 *taleae* = 2 *colores*), whereas the upper voices challenge the performer with syncopations, *hoqueti* and passages in coloured notation. In many cases, the game of changing mensurations and proportions gains musical significance. In 'Rex Karole / Leticie pacis', the change from perfect to imperfect mensuration within each of the five *taleae* coincides with a drastic change of rhythmic and melodic style in the upper voices, which produces an audible contrast of textures (see also p. 67).

The intellectual and musical enterprise of the Ars subtilior composers can also be recognized in various transfers of techniques from the motet to other genres, and in attempts at a fusion of genres. Isorhythm itself found its way from motet to Mass composition. This was a rather bold step because the Mass text is largely irregular, like prose, whereas motets require newly written, patterned poetry which is more amenable to their strict formal schemes. In contrast to the simple rhythmic patterns in Machaut's Mass (Kyrie, Sanctus and Agnus), genuinely isorhythmic Glorias occur in the Ivrea Codex (nos. 44 and 61).[64] These settings segment their text systematically, as if it were metrical

---

[64] Stäblein-Harder ed., *Mass Music*.

poetry; the same was possible with the frequently used Mass tropes, many of which were poetry anyway. Hybrids between Mass and motet also include the troped settings of the words 'Deo gratias' or 'Ite missa est' for the end of Mass.

The introduction into the Mass of chanson textures ('discant style') may also be interpreted as a conscious transfer of genre characteristics. In addition to generally songlike textures, Mass composition inherited the device of strict canon from the secular genres of *chace* and *caccia*.[65] Since the technique (usually called *fuga*) was also a symbol for hunting, its use in the church service created a two-layered metaphor, as it were. (Johannes Boen would have called this a 'subtlety'.)

The *poetry* of the Ars subtilior was in itself like a great collective exercise in subtlety and genre-transfer. Many motet and ballade texts try to astonish the listener by combining heterogeneous images, or by mixing classical-mythological with medieval–biblical language. There are also political, devotional, military and erotic vocabularies. The title 'Baralipton' for a Gloria in the Apt MS even seems to refer to a term of logics. The poems also mix classical and medieval metres and, of course, Latin and French.

These are perhaps the signs of an eclectic or even epigonal culture. But they are also artistic strategies full of vitality and purpose. The author wants to make his work as individual and inimitable as possible. Many motet writers record their names in the texts themselves. In 'Porcio nature / Ida capillorum', for example, Magister Henricus mentions himself in the triplum text as the author of both the music ('cantamen') and the poem ('dictionale gregamen'). B. de Cluny recommends himself to the audience in 'Apollinis / Zodiacum'. In 'Alma polis / Axe poli', the composer is identified as Egidius de Aurelia (Gilles of Orléans?), the poet ('carmineus') as J. de Porta. These two works, as well as 'Sub Arturo / Fons citharizantium' and 'Musicalis scientia / Scientie laudabili', name not only the author, but whole groups of musicians with whom he is associated. 'Musicians' motets' like these, which underscore the author's own standing within a great tradition, are joined by other motets and ballades whose subject matter is musical theory and practice in general.

Even greater self-consciousness is found in the widely known motet 'Degentis vita / Cum vix'.[66] Its tenor is labelled 'Vera pudicitia' ('True modesty') – but this apparent reference to a non-existing plainsong is pure ostentation. The text of the top voice expresses bitter criticism of a decadent Church, of its practice of simony and nepotism, and of the decline of learning. The author recommends himself to Christ and the Virgin as a poor, unlucky intellectual ('scientificus'), whose claim to a benefice has been severely disappointed. The language of this 'modest' man is anything but conventional, as the following excerpts show:

---

[65] Newes, 'Imitation'; *idem*, 'Chace, caccia, fuga: the convergence of French and Italian traditions', in Günther ed., *1380–1430: An International Style?*, 27–57.

[66] Harrison ed., *Motets of French Provenance*, no. 23; Günther ed., *Motets of Chantilly*, no. 2 (with divergent interpretations of the text). I translate 'degentis' as if it were 'egentis', assuming poetic license; 'the life of the living' makes too little sense.

[Degentis vita, quid prodest arte polita? . . .]
The life of the poor, what is it worth even if polished by art?
Nothing, but even the garnished hand is unfit for reward.
The prebend is not given for sweet manners or love of art . . .

[Cum vix artidici promoti sint ad habere . . .]
When hardly the rhetoricians are promoted to wealth,
The astronomers and logicians, what can I, Petrus, do?
Have mercy, even on the modest man, albeit learned,
Have mercy . . .

[Leno, scurra, malis et adulans, qui joculatur . . .]
The pimp, the *beau*, the one who flatters the wicked,
The entertainer, the hanger-on, the nondescript are quickly satisfied.
Having nothing in common with these, but more with the poor,
I pray thee, Flower of Flowers, share with me the heavenly realms . . .

The sentiment expressed here – the true artist sees himself at the bottom of the social ladder – is an age-old complaint. Our author does not neglect to display his linguistic virtuosity, his religious devotion, and above all – his own name (Petrus). As a learned motet, the work was surely intended to be distributed and to convey its criticism to like-minded clerics. Under the cloak of humility, it is a lesson in intellectual self-esteem, and must have been recognized as such by the many other musicians who copied it.

Writing and performing secular music

The musical characteristics of the 'mannerist style', or the 'Ars subtilior', were first identified in secular songs of this period.[67] We continue to think of this style as a secular, soloistic art, as accompanied song. Its surface phenomena are irregularities of rhythm, including syncopation, shifts of accent and grouping, richly ornamented melodic lines and ornamental dissonances. The isorhythmic motet, by contrast, is appreciated for its large-scale structure, its contrapuntal and arithmetic groundplans. Probably, we should not distinguish so sharply between the genres. Research suggests that large-scale planning, for example of modal and arithmetic structures, is not absent from the secular chanson altogether.[68]

The top line of a three-part chanson, usually the only texted line, is responsible for the poetry as regards its contents and metrical form. In many songs

---

[67] See, respectively, Apel ed., *FSM*, 10–13; Günther, 'Das Ende der Ars nova' (n. 49 above); *idem*, 'Datierbare Balladen'.

[68] Examples of such analysis are found in Jehoash Hirshberg, *The Music of the Late Fourteenth Century: A Study in Musical Style*, Ph.D., U. of Pennsylvania, 1971; Laurie Koehler, 'Subtilitas in musica: a reexamination of Johannes Olivier's "Si con cy gist"', *MD* 36 (1982), 95–118; Howard M. Brown, 'A ballade for Mathieu de Foix: style and structure in a composition by Trebor', in Günther ed., *1380–1430: An International Style?*, 75–107.

there is an apparent contrast between the lyrical spontaneity of the top line and the simpler rhythms of tenor and contratenor. This has led to the view that the lower voices are to be played on instruments, and that they function as a harmonic accompaniment. But it has never been demonstrated that tenor and contratenor could not also have been sung. It seems established that composers planned the top line (cantus) and the tenor first, as a fundamental duet, and then added the contratenor, and perhaps a triplum as the fourth voice in the highest register. While there is little doubt as to the secondary function of the contratenor and triplum (the sources attest that either of them could be omitted), the tenor is an essential voice. I would not go so far as to call these pieces 'vocal duets with additional *ad libitum* voices', however. Rather, the essential duet of cantus and tenor may often have been composed by a singer who accompanied himself on an instrument, for example the harp. The seemingly improvisatory style of many cantus parts could have been achieved by subsequent elaborations – for instance, by singing new vocal versions against the tenor, played on the harp.[69]

There are devices in the rhythmic–melodic style of the chansons which can be interpreted as 'secondary improvisation': that is, as elaborations of a given contrapuntal skeleton. One of them may be the so-called 'displacement syncopation', explained by Apel as a kind of written-out rubato.[70] This is the delayed or anticipated performance of one line against another given line, or against a pre-established rhythmic pattern. We have encountered the device in Perrinet's Credo, where it can usually be 'normalized' to a simpler contrapuntal framework. In this way, analysis effectively reconstructs a more original state of the composition.

Example 4*a*

Nevertheless, the complex rhythmic notation of many Ars subtilior songs, which reproduces the smallest nuances of the texted line, is not ordinarily the result of written-out embellishments that were extemporized in performances. The rhythmic complications are really part of the compositions themselves. For example, they often affect the counterpoint with the other voices, as is attested by the author of the *Tractatus figurarum* (see p. 59). His main goal is to describe notational tools that can cope with the ever more complex and

---

[69] Page, 'Performance', adduces evidence that a fifteenth-century song could be composed with the aid of the harp.

[70] Apel ed., *FSM*, 11.

individualistic rhythms of his time. He says in one place that 'it would be a great inconvenience if that which is orally performed could not be written' ('satis inconveniens videretur illud scribere non posse quod ore profertur').[71] He does not concentrate, however, on the writing down of improvised ornaments, but of proportional ratios between different voices of a chanson. He teaches how to notate '3 against 2', '4 against 3', and so forth up to '9 against 8' between cantus and tenor. Such devices must occasionally have been planned by a virtuoso performer without being written down, but even then they would have been premeditated, not improvised. They imply precise arithmetic control of vertical sonorities.

The parameters that were not completely fixed in the notation were neither contrapuntal nor melodic–rhythmic categories, but tuning and *musica ficta*. Nobody, in fact, seems to have complained about the inconvenience of not being able to write down *musica ficta* which was heard in performance.

The premeditation of complex rhythms[72] was perhaps easier in a notational system which did not count every single note against a recurrent 'beat'. Rather, it grouped units of two, three or four equal values together (seldom more), which could then be equated with another rhythmic group in another voice, or within the same voice. For example, 'displacement syncopation' as in Example 4*a* looks puzzling only in modern notation, where the ties have to visualize the 'beat'. In the original notation, we have only to read four equal note-values (perfect semibreves), made up of three smaller note-values (minims) each. In Example 4*b*, it would be downright unmusical to sing the syncopated notes, which are unequal in length, against a recurrent 'beat':

Example 4*b*

We have rather to commit to memory the isolated quaver at the beginning, until it can be completed by the two quavers after the syncopation. The original notation facilitates such interruptions of a rhythmic unit by giving the inserted syncopation a different colour (if its internal grouping differs from that of the other units, as here: 4 + 2), or by setting it apart between dots (*punctus syncopationis* or *transportationis*). Such visual aids were also needed for the more complex 'split syncopation', where the syncopated unit is itself interrupted:

Example 4*c*

[71] Coussemaker ed., *CS*, vol. 3, 119.

[72] Useful surveys of fourteenth-century French notation are Hoppin, *Medieval Music*, 477–84; Apel, *Notation*, 403–35. On proportions, see Anna Maria Busse Berger, 'The origin and early history of proportion signs', *JAMS* 41 (1988), 403–33.

These examples would typically be sung against a tenor in a simpler rhythm: for example, of four dotted crotchets. The singer would know in advance that a total of twelve quavers was at his disposal for the whole passage. He would think in terms of larger units which he then filled with asymmetrical detail.

Such a 'hierarchical' procedure was quite comparable to the compositional structure of isorhythmic motets. It involved, whether in composition or in performance, first a 'mapping out' of stretches of time and then a 'filling them in'. In motets, this kind of thinking separated the two parameters of 'rhythm' (*talea*) and 'pitch' (*color*), which were taken care of one at a time. The procedure was also analogous to that of a painter who first drew the lines and then coloured the spaces; it was analogous to that of the orator who first organized his material (*dispositio*) and then worked it out (*elocutio*). The actual delivery of the speech followed (*actio, pronuntiatio*), which could well be compared to a musical performance. In music, where the art of *pronuntiatio* may still involve relevant decisions, for example about *musica ficta*, *elocutio* has already taken care of the rhythm. It may also have produced the added and less essential voices: contratenor and/or triplum. These voices are neither left entirely to improvisation nor are they intrinsically irrelevant (like *ad libitum* parts in Baroque music, for example). Rather, they represent an unfolding of the composer's art. We may compare them to the 'heightening' of book illuminations with white and gold: an unnecessary but beautiful addition.

The ballade of the faithful Medea

In the discussion of Perrinet's Credo, we concluded that the contratenor, while improvisational in surface style, alters and enhances the texture. Its status is therefore compositional (*elocutio*). We shall now consider a secular piece from the Ars subtilior where the contratenor, albeit an added voice, is even more closely wrought into the composition. The anonymous three-voice ballade 'Medée fu en amer véritable' is, in addition, an example of the famous rhythmic complexities of the style.[73] The piece is found in three manuscript sources, dating from *c*.1400 until *c*.1430, but it was surely composed around 1370–80. It has been considered to be one of the earliest works with proportional changes of metre within the texted line, the cantus. Whereas the tenor is in ℭ mensuration throughout (6/8), the cantus and contratenor also use ○ (3/4) and the proportional signs '2', '3' and '4', plus isolated coloured notes. As a verbal 'canon' in the manuscripts explains, under the sign '3' three minims have to be sung against two in the tenor; under '2', four against three (!), and under '4', four against two. The first of these proportions (*sesquialtera*) appears in the transcription as quaver triplets, the second (*sesquitertia*) as quaver duplets, and the last (*dupla*) as regular semiquavers in the cantus (bars 6–7, 28–33, and 23):

[73] Previous editions are Greene ed., *Manuscript Chantilly*, PMFC, 18, no. 26; Apel ed., *FSC*, vol. 2 (1971), no. 165; Reaney ed., *EFM*, vol.4 (1969), p. 51; Hoppin ed., *Anthology*, no. 68. Our example attempts some improvements over all these editions. See also Hoppin, *Medieval Music*, 483 f.

Example 5 'Medée fu', Chantilly Codex

Example 5 (*cont.*)

Example 5 (*cont.*)

The appearance in modern notation is deceptive. What we notate as triplets, duplets and semiquavers all look like ordinary minims in the original. But their values are reduced in the ratios 3 : 2, 4 : 3 and 2 : 1, as directed by the added figures.[74] The simplest of these reductions, 2 : 1, is expressed in our notation by a sign completely different from the other two: not a superscript figure but a flag attached to the stem of every note, of which it halves the value. This

---

[74] A facsimile of the piece is in Gallo ed., *Codice Panciatichi*, fols. 2v and 107v.

device may actually have been unknown to our composer. His smallest note-value is the minim (transcribed here as quaver); when he wants it to lose half its value, he has to prescribe a proportion, just as in the other cases where he wants it to lose a third or quarter of its value. Probably soon after this piece was composed, the colouring of notes to signify duple proportion (half value) came into use: same shape but different colour. But coloration was also used to express other proportions; and in order to avoid confusion, modifications of the note-shape were introduced to express the smallest values, for example flags and double-stems: same colour but different shape.[75]

Modifications of note-shape (various kinds of flags and stems) were widely used in Italy, and spread to French music around 1380 – whereas coloration was a French practice which reached Italian music about the same time. The *Tractatus figurarum*, dating from the 1380s, teaches both devices for values smaller than the minim. In 'Medée fu', there are no flags, and coloration is used only for semibreves with the meaning of *sesquialtera*: that is, they lose a third of their value and become imperfect rather than perfect. (We express this by simply leaving out the dot.) This coloration happens, for example, in bars 25–6 in the cantus, and is indicated in the transcription by broken brackets. The three semibreves (crotchets) form a syncopated unit together; although they are interrupted by other notes, they can easily be perceived as a unit in the original notation since they are coloured.

In the music of 'Medée fu', the smaller note-values come in groups which ornament simpler progressions, and are an elaboration of the structure. A different status applies to the changes of metre in the cantus and contratenor. These produce conflicting mensurations between the voice-pairs cantus/contratenor, contratenor/tenor and tenor/cantus, which seem to interlock with the total layout of the piece:

	cantus	*contratenor*	*tenor*	*symbol*
bars 1–11	6/8	6/8	6/8	A
bars 12–19	3/4	6/8	6/8	B
bars 20–28	6/8	3/4	6/8	C
bars 29–38	6/8	6/8	6/8	A
bars 39–48	6/8	3/4	6/8	C
bars 49–61	3/4	6/8	6/8	B

The succession of symbols A B C A C B clearly suggests a kind of symmetry. Each symbol or 'mensuration type' appears twice. Type 'A', without mensural conflict between the voices, appears for a total of 21 bars, 'B' for either 19 or 21 bars depending on whether one counts the repeat-bars 18 and 19; 'C' appears for 19 bars. Type 'A' opens both groups of three; type 'B' closes the two major

---

[75] The relationship 'same shape / different colour' survives in the relationship between our minim and crotchet; 'same colour / different shape' survives in the relationship between our crotchet and quaver.

sections of the piece, since the double-bar is at bar 19. The mensuration is thus used as a structural tool, comparable to the 'mapping out' of *taleae* in a motet. Note that cantus and contratenor never go together in mensural conflict against the tenor: this voice-pair is less closely related than the other two pairs.

It must be added that these mensural conflicts have little significance for local rhythm. The juxtaposition of 3×2 and 2×3 does not lead to particularly complex groupings here. It rather serves the layout (*dispositio*) of the material as a whole.

The total layout of the piece is, of course, also determined by the text. The poem is a ballade in three stanzas of eight lines each, with ten syllables each except for line 5 which has seven. As in all ballades with this number of lines, the stanza divides in two halves with the rhyme-scheme a b a b / c c d d – where *a* and *c* are feminine rhymes, alternating in the first half, paired in the second. The rhyme-syllables are identical in all three stanzas (not only the rhyme-scheme, as was more usual), and the refrain-line 8 is identical as a whole. The musical setting is identical in all three stanzas, of course, but the refrain-line stands out by repeating not only music but also words. Within each stanza, lines 1–2 and 3–4 are also given the same music, only differentiated into *ouvert* and *clos* cadences (first and second endings). We have therefore *six* musical phrases (as against eight lines of text), of which in the total performance the first two phrases will receive six different texts, phrases 3–5 three different texts, and phrase 6 only one text.

Thus, in a ballade of this type the textual and musical repetitions plus their combination yield the significant ratios $2:3:1$ (musical phrases), $4:3:1$ (textual lines) and $6:3:1$ (their combination). These ratios incorporate the perfect concordances of the twelfth ($3:1$), octave ($2:1$), fifth ($3:2$) and fourth ($4:3$). In our piece, these ratios are structurally employed in the rhythmic proportions of the cantus line and in the layout of the mensural conflicts, as explained above.

An interpretation of the content of the poem,[76] together with the word-setting, could take as its point of departure the *refrain*: a punch-line which surprises by rhyming with the preceding line in identical sounds ('amy' = 'a my'). This well-known literary device becomes, in our context, a game about identity and ambiguity. With the very last syllable of the text, the poet substitutes himself for the 'amy', the ancient lover Jason, and completes the comparison of his lady with the famous anti-heroine, Medea. Poems which quote ancient heroes and lovers to compare them with contemporary people were extremely fashionable at the time. Usually the intention was that of a rhetorical hyperbole (exaggeration): the patron is said to be more glorious even than Alex-

---

[76] For the literary context see Boutet-Strubel, *Littérature*, 145–209; Daniel Poirion, *Le poète et le prince. L'évolution du lyrisme courtois de Guillaume de Machaut à Charles d'Orléans* (Grenoble: Faculté des lettres et sciences humaines, 1965); Nigel Wilkins, *One Hundred Ballades, Rondeaux and Virelais from the Late Middle Ages* (Cambridge University Press, 1969) (commenting on forms and on individual poets).

ander or Julius Caesar, the lady more beautiful than Helen, the lover more wretched than Lancelot or Tristan. In this ballade, however, the comparison works against the lady: she is less faithful even than Medea, Helen and Bryseida – none of whom is particularly famous for her virtue. The poem begins as if it were a song in praise of a rather unlikely figure – until the refrain brings home the verdict upon the poet's own mistress. The effect is linguistically enhanced by the strong, accented endings of the important phrases, with verb-forms in *passé simple*: 'fu', 'enama', 'laissa' etc. The musical setting reflects this in the strikingly syllabic declamation at the *ouvert* and *clos* cadences. The pair of identical rhymes at the end falls on cadential chords which are analogous to the *ouvert* and *clos*, but the chord on 'amy' (bar 42) is unexpected, irregular and unstable. The major sixth b–$g^{\sharp}{}'$, with the supporting e in the contratenor, does not find a proper resolution in bar 43 (the lower a is missing), nor in bars 47–8 (the contratenor subverts the sonority), but only in transposed form at the end, where the contratenor has regained its normal position in the middle (bars 60–61).

The melodic–rhythmic elaboration of all three voices is remarkably consistent, in spite of the apparent spontaneity of the lines. To give a few examples: a sequential pattern of falling thirds in the cantus, which fills a descent from a' to d', recurs three times (bars 2–4, 29–32 and 55–60). It ornaments the words 'Medée', 'chaière' and 'a my'. A cadential formula of two descending note-pairs (scale-degrees '3 2 2 1') appears in bars 6, 23, 28, and 36, and in bar 60 in the contratenor; it is singled out by almost immediate repetition in bars 44 and 46. Even more essential to the vocabulary is the formula '3 2 3 1'. It is 'smuggled in' for the first time in the cantus, bar 7, and then recurs in various rhythms in bars 9, 10, 15, 37, 38, 40 and 50; contratenor bars 35, 40–41, 57, 59 and, with expanded contour, in bar 13. The tenor has only the expanded contour, laid out over bars 2–4 and 9–11. The 'primary form' of this motive may be that of bars 15 and 50, in triple metre. (This is the form most often found in other pieces of the time.) The motive is part of the substance of the song as a melodic idea, and the rhythms are different elaborations of it: the reverse relationship between melody and rhythm than that obtaining between *talea* and *color*.

Cantus and tenor form a structurally complete duet which is further articulated by the contratenor. One can clearly recognize the merely ornamental dissonances between cantus and tenor, for example the accented ones in bars 2, 55 etc., or the neighbour-notes and passing dissonances which inevitably arise from the melodic formulas '3 2 2 1' and '3 2 3 1'. The sequential pattern of falling thirds (bars 2–4 etc.) is dissonant only by virtue of the rubato-like delays. But the contratenor adds a great amount of dissonance and also harmonic 'interpretation' of its own. It 'undermines' the regular cadences of cantus and tenor in bars 8–9, 24, 29 and elsewhere; it acts as a false tenor in bars 41–2. Its dissonances, apart from the ornamental ones which may clash with both cantus and tenor (for example the g in bar 2), are of two kinds. In passages like bars 3–4, the contratenor is consonant with the tenor against the cantus; in passages like bar 40 it is consonant with the cantus alone. The former cases are more frequent, but the latter cases show that the contratenor takes into account both the structural voices. Sometimes, it seems to soften dissonances between them, such as in bar 15 (*d*) and bar 22 (*f*). It achieves the greatest freedom where the other voices are most consonant (bars 8, 12–14 and 57–60).

The contratenor's rhythmic complications, especially the passages in proportion and the syncopations (as in bars 2, 6, 10 and 43–4), are derived from the vocabulary of the cantus. The tenor has no such rhythms. We noted, however, that the contratenor is in mensural conflict with the cantus except where all three voices agree in mensuration. The contratenor of this work has a different status from that of the Credo 'Bonbarde'. It does not obey the tenor alone, but is an interloper between the structural voices, constantly changing allegiance.

'Medée fu en amer véritable' is a masterwork which has come down to us only anonymously. An attribution to Johannes Symonis dit Hasprois has been proposed, but on insufficient grounds.[77] Anonymous works are frequent in the Ars subtilior tradition, particularly among those pieces which continued to be copied in the fifteenth century, as in our case. We must be cautious in a search for significant stylistic trends in this repertory, or for 'leading' composers. Few individuals are credited with more than six works in all the sources taken together. With all due reserve, a rough chronological grouping may nevertheless be suggested.[78]

Composers and patrons

A first group of composers still seems to reflect the influence of Guillaume de Machaut (*d.*1377), while going beyond his procedures in individual ways. Magister Grimace and Pierre des Molins have been considered Machaut's contemporaries; their surviving songs lack the complexity of the Ars subtilior. A certain F. Andrieu set a bi-textual ballade by the poet Eustache Deschamps lamenting the death of Machaut ('Armes amours / O flour des flours'); he may be the same man as a Magister Franciscus who wrote a ballade for Count Gaston Fébus, 'Phiton, Phiton, beste tres venimeuse', which actually quotes from a late song by Machaut, 'Phiton le merveilleus serpent'. Another ballade by Franciscus, the widely distributed 'De Narchisus', was certainly composed before 1376.[79] Jehan Vaillant had a music school in Paris around 1380, where he also

---

[77] Reaney ed., *EFM*, vol. 4 (1969), p. xiii, claims that the proportion canon of 'Medée fu' is 'practically identical' with that of Hasprois' ballade 'Ma doulce amour', proposing an attribution to that composer. In fact, the proportion canon is not the same, but is identical to that of Johannes Cuvelier's ballade 'L'orques Arthus'. This may, or may not, reflect on the authorship of the anonymous piece.

[78] The pieces mentioned in the following survey are all transcribed (not necessarily reliably) in Apel ed., *FSC*, vols. 1–3.

[79] Its copy in the Trémoille MS (*F-Pn n. a. f. 23190*) contains that date. Copies of 'De Narchisus', 'Phiton, Phiton' and of the double-texted ballade 'Se Zephirus / Se Jupiter' by Grimace, have recently been found in a Hungarian fragment: see Brewer, *Ars nova*, app. XX.

served King Charles V (1364–80). He was interested in poetic genres other than the ballade; his most celebrated work is 'Par maintes fois', a virelai (see p. 86) for springtime with imitation of various bird-calls. Such onomatopoetic songs, mostly of a pastoral nature, have been labelled 'realistic virelais' (Willi Apel) or 'mimetic songs' (Margaret Hasselman). Specimens had existed well before 1370, but Machaut did not cultivate the genre. There are non-pastoral items, too: Grimace's virelai 'A l'arme, a l'arme' introduces military imagery by imitating trumpet fanfares.

Vaillant's enterprising outlook also produced an isorhythmic rondeau ('Pour ce que je ne say'), and a double-texted rondeau ('Dame doucement / Douz amis'), where the lovers have a dialogue in canon at one point. This piece was composed as early as 1369.[80] Vaillant must have known the slightly younger composer Solage, since both men were connected with the court of Duke Jean de Berry from about 1380. Two of Solage's ten surviving works seem to have been written for the wedding of the duke's son with Catherine de France in 1386, and another praises Duke Jean himself. Solage left four songs in four parts, which are said to be close in style to Machaut – but their simple chordal textures have a flavour quite of their own. One is the witty ballade 'Plusieurs gens voy', ostensibly written about the composer's jacket, and alluding to extravagant dress fashions in Paris. In reality, the piece makes a pun on a woman's name, 'Jacquete'. Fashions in Paris are indeed satirized in Solage's excessively chromatic rondeau 'Fumeux fume', and in the ballade 'Puisque je sui fumeux' by Johannes Symonis dit Hasprois. Around 1370, there existed the extravagant Parisian club of the 'fumeux' (the 'whimsical'), led by the poet Eustache Deschamps,[81] and seemingly alluded to in the songs of Solage and Hasprois.

Like Vaillant and Solage, Symonis moved away from Paris after 1380; he went to Portugal and to Avignon, as mentioned above. A similarly colourful career seems to have been that of Johannes (or Jacquemart) Cuvelier. He wrote a chronicle on the life of the Royal High Constable Bertrand du Guesclin, and we also know that he wrote the poems of his ballades himself. One of them, 'Se Galaas', is dedicated to Gaston Fébus. It is his simplest work with regard to rhythmic style and may be early. A certain Guido, whose ballade 'Or voit tout' and rondeau 'Dieux gart qui bien le chantera' and 'Robin muse / Je ne say' all have music and its stylistic progress as their subjects, has been identified with the papal chaplain Guido de Lange, who is documented between 1362 and 1374. But the present view of Guido is that he initiated certain idioms of the Ars subtilior no earlier than *c.*1375–80. We do know of song composers who were papal chaplains at Avignon. There are at least Johannes Symonis, Johannes Haucourt (de Alta Curia) and Matheus de Sancto Johanne. The author of the ballade 'Courtois et sages' for Pope Clement VII, Magister Egidius, was not a

---

[80] Ursula Günther, 'Vaillant, Jehan' in *The New Grove*.
[81] Pirro, *La musique à Paris*, 23 f.

papal chaplain. He is also the composer of the wedding ballade for Jean de Berry of 1389, 'Roses et lys'.[82]

A piece apparently written for the same occasion and in the same, highly complex style is 'Passerose de beauté' by Johan Robert. He is also called 'Triboll' and 'Trebor' in the sources, and he himself used the anagrams 'Trebol' and 'Borlet' for his name.[83] He is documented at the court of Navarre in the 1390s. Unlike Symonis, Solage, Cuvelier and Egidius, whose style seems to have developed between *c*.1370 and *c*.1390, Robert belongs to a younger group of musicians by whom we have exclusively works of the most advanced individualism and subtlety, and whose main sphere of activity seems to have been in the south. Apart from Robert, this central and most characteristic group of Ars subtilior composers includes a certain Rodericus (who used the anagram 'S. Uciredor'), as well as Jacob de Senleches and the Italian Philipoctus de Caserta.[84] It is their technical mastery (or some of its individual features) which was then taken up but later abandoned by a third, youngest group of composers whose careers led them outside the central tradition: Baude Cordier (= Baude Fresnel?, *d*.1397/8) and Jean de Noyers dit Tapissier (*d*.1410 or earlier), who both served the Burgundian court; Anthonellus Marot de Caserta and Matheus de Perusio (*d*.1418 or earlier), who worked in northern Italy; Hubertus de Salinis and Johannes Ciconia, both from the diocese of Liège, who contributed one work each to the Ars subtilior, but after *c*.1400 pioneered a different, Italianate style.

The central group is best exemplified in Jacob (Jacomì) de Senleches. Coming probably from Senlecques near Calais, he served the Castilian court as 'juglar de arpa' until 1382, then visited the court of Navarre and entered the household of Cardinal Pedro de Luna, who became Pope Benedict XIII in 1394. Of Jacob's six surviving works (three ballades, three virelais), all but one are highly personal and even autobiographical in their texts. Perhaps the earliest song is the ballade 'Fuions de ci', where the musician laments the death of his patroness, Queen Eleanor of Castile (1382). In the transposed fifth mode ('Bb major') and in a low range, the interlocking voices produce a remarkably full, chordal texture. The refrain-line ('. . . since we have lost Alionor') forms full triads on Bb, *c*, *d*, *eb*, *f*, *g* and, in passing, even *a* (bar 50), see Ex. 6. This line also contains (from bar 47) three sequential patterns of interlocking thirds (as found in 'Medée fu', but less regular in rhythm). Such melodic patterns, often cut short at the end by one or two energetic quavers and a move in

---

[82] Günther, 'Datierbare Balladen', 16 (1962), 151-4.

[83] On his life and works, see Gómez, *La música*, 99-101; *idem*, 'La musique à la Maison Royale de Navarre à la fin du Moyen-Age et le chantre Johan Robert', in Günther ed., *1380-1430: An International Style?*, 109-51.

[84] The spelling 'Philipoctus' is only a Latinization; 'ct' is pronounced like 'tt'. On him, see Gilbert Reaney, 'Philippus de Caserta' in *The New Grove*; Nigel Wilkins, 'Some notes on Philipoctus de Caserta (c.1360?-c.1435)', *Nottingham Medieval Studies* 8 (1964), 82-99 (with edn of the chanson texts and the treatise *Regule contrapuncti*; biographically unreliable). For revisions, see below.

the opposite direction, appear in several of Jacob's songs – to particular effect in the virelai 'En ce gracieux temps joli', which describes a competition between nightingale and cuckoo. The beautifully patterned, descending phrases of the nightingale's 'oci, oci' contrast with the simplistic 'cocu', which consists, of course, of one descending third only. The motive is heard in witty imitation between the cantus and the triplum. This satirical song is only ostensibly a 'realistic virelai': in reality, the composer is attacking his musical rivals 'who know only one little chanson' – that is, the 'cocu'. His own style, however, is that of the nightingale: the piece contains a stylistic self-characterization.

Example 6 Jacob de Senleches, 'Fuions de ci'

Also in two other songs, Jacob attacks his rivals or mediocre imitators. In 'Je me merveil / J'ay plusieurs fois', he explicitly accuses them of forgery and plagiarism; at that point, he makes the two texted voices share the same text and proceed in strict canon. In 'Tel me voit', he complains that they do not want to let him sing, out of jealousy. Jacob's ballade 'En attendant esperance' belongs to a network of poetic and musical quotations which reaches back to Machaut. It quotes, in its refrain-line, the music and text of the widely known rondeau 'Esperance qui en mon cuer s'en bat' - on the keyword 'esperance', of course.[85]

If we draw biographical conclusions from Jacob's song texts (and we have to, because the documents are so scarce), then the only love in his life might have been – his harp. She (and not his wife, as has been suggested), is the 'povre compaigne', whom he tells in 'Fuions de ci' to flee with him from the now inhospitable Castilian court. To the instrument, his travelling partner and Muse, Jacob dedicated his most surprising composition, the canonic virelai 'La harpe de melodie'. The work must be interpreted in the light of its notation as found in one of the sources (*US-Cn 54*, see below): the image of a harp whose strings serve as staves for the music.[86] Each line is represented by a string, whereas the spaces are not used; the piece is almost fully diatonic, as was the tuning of the harp.[87] Because he wished to notate the work in this guise, it was necessary for Jacob to use a complicated notation with three colours, which call for double augmentation and other proportional changes. An accompanying verbal 'canon' – in the poetic form of a rondeau – explains the performance of the virelai. The singer is directed to imitate ('chasser') his own line in strict canon on the harp. Even if the tenor was performed by a helper (perhaps a second harper), the singing and playing of both canonic voices at the same time required some virtuosity. The composer must have developed such skills in many 'dialogue' performances alone with his instrument. The text of the virelai itself recommends the harp's melodiousness and visual beauty to the audience. Harmony, it says, can here be sung, heard and seen. During a performance at court, the actual harp picture may have been submitted to a patron in the audience. The composer himself must have designed the prototype of the picture, of which the surviving specimen is a faithful copy. It now forms part of a

---

[85] An excellent account of the phenomenon of 'intertextuality' in the Ars subtilior is Ursula Günther, 'Zitate in französischen Liedsätzen der ars nova und ars subtilior', *MD* 26 (1972), 53–68. (Jacob's quotation of 'Esperance' is not mentioned there.)

[86] Reproduced as colour jacket cover of Hoppin ed., *Anthology*. Editions of music and text are in Hoppin ed., *Anthology*, no. 69; Apel ed., *FSC*, vol. 1 (1970), no. 92; Greene ed., *Manuscript Chantilly*, no. 67; Nors S. Josephson, 'Die Konkordanzen zu "En nul estat" und "La harpe de melodie"', *Mf* 25 (1972), 292–300. An evaluation of the piece as well as its social and aesthetic implications is Reinhard Strohm, '"La harpe de melodie" oder Das Kunstwerk als Akt der Zueignung', in H. Danuser *et al.* eds, *Das musikalische Kunstwerk: Festschrift Carl Dahlhaus zum 60. Geburtstag* (Laaber: Laaber Verlag), 305–16.

[87] On the instrument and its uses, see Howard M. Brown, 'The Trecento harp', in Boorman ed., *Studies*, 35–73.

volume of manuscript treatises on music, compiled *c.*1391 in Pavia by a certain 'Frater G. de Anglia'.[88] He was perhaps a member of Pavia University, founded by Gian Galeazzo Visconti of Lombardy, who had his main residence in that city. It is possible that 'La harpe de melodie' was actually composed in Lombardy.

Two other works of similar pictorial design are known from this period, both by Magister Baude Cordier. They open the famous Chantilly Codex, which also contains 'La harpe de melodie' (although, significantly, not in pictorial form). In Cordier's circle-shaped canonic rondeau 'Tout par compas sui composés', the song speaks to the performer in the first person, advising him how to perform itself – as does Jacob's virelai in the accompanying rondeau. In the heart-shaped rondeau 'Belle, bonne, sage', Cordier gives his own heart to his lady as a New Year's gift (*estrenne*) – pictorially and musically. These two pieces may well have originated as reactions to Jacob's harp piece.

If a direct link between the pictorial songs by Senleches and Cordier is accepted, this would strengthen the suggestion of Craig Wright that Baude Cordier was identical with the Burgundian 'valet de chambre' and harper Baude Fresnel (*d.*1397/8) who was, in fact, a member of the retinue of Duke Philip the Bold when he visited Milan in 1391.[89]

The elegant courtly life under Gian Galeazzo Visconti (1385–1402) has not been investigated in detail. Eustache Deschamps speaks of the singing and dancing, as well as of other worldly pleasures at this court, in his ballade of *c.*1391, 'Il fait très beau démourer en douz chastel de Pavie', written on the occasion of a visit by the French princes to Lombardy.[90] The Viscontis were closely linked to the French royal family. Gian Galeazzo had married Isabelle, a daughter of King Charles V, in 1360, thus inheriting the title of Comte de Vertus (a small county in the Champagne which was her dowry). In 1389 his daughter Valentina married the younger brother of Charles VI, Duke Louis of Orléans. The musical interests of these two ladies are well known; Valentina owned several harps and knew how to play them. She was the mother of the famous poet and music-lover Charles d'Orléans, born in 1394.[91]

Gian Galeazzo and his predecessor Bernabò Visconti (*d.*1385) were musical

---

[88] *US-Cn 54.* See Kurt von Fischer, 'Eine wiederaufgefundene Theoretikerhandschrift des späten 14. Jahrhunderts', *Schweizer Beiträge zur Musikwissenschaft* 1 (1972), 23–33.

[89] Craig Wright, 'Tapissier and Cordier: new documents and conjectures', *MQ* 59 (1973), 177–89; *idem, Burgundy*, 123–34. The identification has been challenged, most recently in Günther, 'Unusual phenomena', 89 ff, on the assumption that the pictorial pieces in *F-CH 564* are autographs – whereas the manuscript must date from *c.*1400 or later and Fresnel was already dead by 1398. There is no real evidence for the pieces being autographs: if this assumption is discarded, the identification remains acceptable. Implications for Cordier's historical status as a composer will be discussed below (p. 141).

[90] Eustache Deschamps, *Oeuvres inédites*, ed. P. Tarbé (Paris, 1849), vol. 1, 116 f; *idem, Oeuvres complètes*, ed. Auguste de Queux and Gaston Raynaud, vol. 5 (Paris, 1887), 314–16.

[91] Pirro, *La musique à Paris*, 11 f; Généviève Thibault, 'Emblèmes et devises des Visconti dans les oeuvres musicales du Trecento', *L'Ars Nova* 3 (1970), 131–60, especially 152 ff.

patrons themselves.[92] Philipoctus de Caserta composed his ballade 'En attendant souffrir m'estuet' in honour of Bernabò's motto, 'Souffrir m'estuet'. The courtly circle is referred to in this text under the metaphor of the 'fontayne', an image which is otherwise known as the name of musical–rhetorical societies, for example in Ghent. The canon 'Le ray au soleil' by Johannes Ciconia is a celebration of the Visconti arms, as are the madrigals 'Alba tortorella' and – conceivably – 'La fiera testa' by Bartolino da Padova. It seems that Philipoctus actually lived at this court. Besides 'En attendant souffrir' and 'Par les bons Gédéon' of 1378 (see p. 16), he left another topical work, the ballade 'Par le grant sens d'Adriane la sage'. This celebrates the military expedition of Louis I of Anjou against Charles of Durazzo, ruler of Naples (r. 1382–4). Duke Louis, of course, was the brother of Isabelle de France and thus Gian Galeazzo's brother-in-law. He spent some time at his court in 1382, receiving financial aid for the preparation of his campaign (despite the fact that Lombardy officially belonged to the Roman obedience).[93] This visit may well have provided the occasion for Philipoctus's ballade 'Par le grant sens'.

The *Tractatus figurarum* (see p. 39) is contained in the Pavia MS of 1391 mentioned above, where it appears next to 'La harpe de melodie'. This treatise is probably by Philipoctus: the attribution of the Pavia copy to 'Magister Philippus Andree' is contradicted only by later sources of inferior value.[94]

The music of Philipoctus deserves much further study. All of his surviving six chansons use long-range syncopations and proportional passages, expressed by coloration or special note-shapes as taught in the *Tractatus figurarum*. But there is something like a stylistic division in two groups. The ballades in minor prolation (2/4 in transcription), 'Par les bons Gédéon' and the very similar 'Il est nulz homs', as well as 'Par le grant sens' (in major and minor prolation), have more angular melodies, especially in the active, leaping contratenors. The other three ballades, 'En attendant souffrir', 'De ma doulour' and 'En remirant', are in major prolation (6/8 and 9/8). Their melodic smoothness is reminiscent of French masters such as Cuvelier and Magister Egidius; two of the texts contain quotations from Machaut. These three songs are all in the first mode, transposed flatwards, whereas none of the other three pieces has a flat key signature. The sole surviving sacred work by Philipoctus, a Credo found only in an Italian source,[95] is a simpler variant of the style of the minor prolation group. Possibly this group represents a slightly earlier (perhaps more Italianate) style, whereas the second group conforms more closely to the central tradition.

'En attendant souffrir' has been copied in the Chantilly Codex with a wrong attribution to a certain 'Jo. Galiot', of whom nothing is known. This name also appears in Chantilly with the ballades 'En attendant d'amer la douce vie' and

---

[92] See also Strohm, 'Filipotto da Caserta', and p. 92 below on the Pavia connections of the inventor of the harpsichord.

[93] Valois, *La France* (see n. 1 above), vol. 2, 32 ff.

[94] Strohm, 'Filipotto da Caserta', refuting Arlt, 'Der *Tractatus figurarum*' (n. 59).

[95] von Fischer-Gallo eds, *Italian Sacred Music*, no. 14.

'Le sault perilleux' (not extant in other sources) as well as – again erroneously – with Jacob's 'En attendant esperance'. Clearly, the three works beginning 'En attendant' stem from the same circle of composers. In each case, the common words of the beginning are followed by a quotation: '. . . d'amer la douce vie' quotes Machaut ('En amer a douce vie', a rondeau from his *Remède de Fortune*); '. . . souffrir m'estuet' the motto of Bernabò Visconti; and '. . . esperance' the rondeau mentioned above. An explanation of these relationships could be that not only Philipoctus, but also Jacob de Senleches and Jo. Galiot had dealings with the Viscontis. In fact Galiot's ballade 'Le sault perilleux' speaks of the same 'fontayne', and in the same terms, as does 'En attendant souffrir'. This piece occupies the most richly illuminated page of the Chantilly Codex (fol. 37r), the heraldic symbols of which have not been deciphered.[96] Could it be that the 'Galiot' misattributions have something to do with the origins of the Codex, or even that 'Jean Galiot' represents a mishearing of 'Jean-Galéas' Visconti?

The network of quotations extends further than this. Johannes Ciconia's ballade 'Sus un fontayne' – his only contribution to the Ars subtilior style – pays homage to Philipoctus by quoting, in text and music, his three ballades 'En attendant souffrir', 'De ma doulour' and 'En remirant'.[97] The text speaks of the composer's desire to see that 'noble flower who sang so sweetly under the fountain'. The conclusion is inescapable that Philipoctus was Ciconia's teacher or mentor and that the two men met under the patronage of the Visconti 'fountain'.

The extent to which the French gothic styles survived in the northernmost territory of Italy around 1390–1400, is magnificently demonstrated by the gothic cathedral of Milan, built in that period under Gian Galeazzo. Around the time of the duke's death in 1402, the latest prominent composer of the Ars subtilior, Matteo da Perugia,[98] was appointed *biscantor* at Milan Cathedral. Whether or not this musician had previously served the duke, he became a member of the household of the Archbishop of Milan, Pietro Filargo, at Pavia between 1405 and 1408.

Matteo's 24 secular and 6 sacred compositions survive almost exclusively in a manuscript which may have been intended as a gift for Cardinal Filargo when he became Pope Alexander V in 1409. This codex (*I-MOe α. M. 5.24*; *ModA*) was enlarged, probably after the pope's death in May 1410, with more works mainly by Matteo, who had re-entered the cathedral service at Milan.[99] He seems to have been responsible for its compilation from the beginning. The

---

[96] The page has often been reprinted, as it shows singing chaplains. 'Le sault perilleux' was known in Vaillant's music school in Paris. Günther, 'Unusual phenomena', 96 f.

[97] This was first recognized by Ursula Günther; see Günther, 'Zitate' (n. 85), 64 ff.

[98] Often cited as Matheus de Perusio. On his life and works (with edn), see Fabio Fano, *La Cappella musicale del Duomo di Milano*, 1: *Le origini e il primo maestro di cappella: Matteo da Perugia* (Milan: Ricordi, 1956). His sacred works are also in von Fischer–Gallo eds, *Italian Sacred and Ceremonial Music*. His French-texted works are completely edited in Apel ed., *FSC*, vol. 1 (1970); and in Greene ed., *French Secular Music*.

[99] Ursula Günther, 'Das Manuskript Modena, Biblioteca Estense, α.M.5.24 (*olim lat.568 = Mod*)', *MD* 24 (1970), 17–67. For arguments against a connection between the manuscript and the papal court of John XXIII in Bologna, see Strohm, 'Magister Egardus'.

older section includes many works by Jacob de Senleches, Philipoctus, Hasprois, Magister Egidius and other representatives of the Ars subtilior. To some extent Matteo's own music rivals these idioms, though it also introduces more modern mannerisms such as running semiquaver melismas, triadic contours, syllabic declamation or homorhythmic progressions in all the voices. Matteo set only one Italian text but wrote some two-voice rondeaux in a style close to that of the Italian ballata. His sacred music, likewise, combines traditional French devices (such as isorhythm) with others found more often in Italian music, for example duets for two equal upper voices. He was not really an innovator, but rather an eclectic whose speciality seems to have been complicated contratenors. He added several such voice parts to works by other composers – perhaps for his own use as a singer.

For Anthonello da Caserta (Anthonellus Marot), the Ars subtilior styles were similarly a matter of eclectic choice; he also composed Italian-texted songs in a radically different manner. His eight works to French texts are all contained in the older part of *ModA*, which suggests that he collaborated with Matteo da Perugia at some stage.[100] Matteo, in his turn, wrote a contratenor for one of Anthonello's ballatas. Anthonello is also referred to as 'Abbas de Caserta', which poses the question as to whether he also resided in that town near Naples at any time. Probably, Caserta was his home and he went north to join the Visconti court of Lombardy (as did Philipoctus de Caserta), where stylistic complexity, as found in his French songs, was appreciated. His ballata 'Del glorioso titolo d'esto duce' could refer to the elevation of Marquis Gian Galeazzo Visconti to the rank of Duke of Milan in 1395.[101] According to an older theory, the piece was composed for the French Anjou dynasty in Naples around 1410.[102] This court may have been, like the Lusignan court of Cyprus, one of the last strongholds of French feudal culture in the Mediterranean.

[100] The French songs are in Apel ed., *FSC*, vol. 1 (1970), the Italian songs in PMFC, vol. 9.

[101] John Nádas, 'The Lucca Codex and MS San Lorenzo 2211: native and foreign songs in early Quattrocento Florence', unpublished paper, AMS Annual Meeting, Austin, 1989. The contents of this paper are not fully incorporated here. That Anthonello worked in Lombardy had been surmised in Strohm, 'Filipotto da Caserta'.

[102] Ursula Günther, 'Anthonello de Caserta' in *The New Grove*.

2

THE LATERAL TRADITIONS

This book proposes a distinction between the 'central tradition' and the 'lateral traditions' in the music of the late fourteenth and early fifteenth centuries. The central tradition, described above, was the true heir of the Ars nova, and it concentrated on developing this heritage until its exhaustion around 1410. The lateral traditions in the countries surrounding France had emerged as a result of individual interaction between the Ars nova and regional practices. It was a process of assimilation that was achieved more swiftly and decisively in some places than others. Germany, for example, remained relatively uninfluenced by the Ars nova until the end of the fourteenth century, and Poland perhaps until even later. In Bohemia, on the other hand, the Luxembourg dynasty (with Emperor Charles IV, 1347–78, and his successor Wenceslas, 1378–1419) and the University of Prague may already have imported French music and music theory during the lifetime of Machaut, who had served Charles's father, King John. The most independent of the lateral traditions in the fourteenth century were found in England and Italy, the least independent in the Netherlands (for reasons which will immediately become apparent). During the period of the Great Schism, all these lateral traditions began to interact with each other, by-passing the centre, as it were. This process, in which the Ars subtilior became increasingly isolated, led to the new European context of early fifteenth-century music mentioned earlier. The most tangible expression of this new coherence within European music was the huge international meeting of the Council of Constance (1414–18).

This study is mainly concerned with composed polyphonic music. However, monophonic and instrumental music, together with primitive types of polyphony (see Part III, Chapter 2) – music which was usually transmitted orally – existed within the same socio-cultural conditions and was subject to similar trends. The music of the minstrels must have travelled on the same European routes as did polyphony. Surviving evidence about the distribution of primitive polyphony suggests the possibility of an even closer contact between the lateral traditions than is found in other music. Examples of Iberian music which stand apart from the central tradition, the pilgrimage songs in the 'Llibre Vermell' of Montserrat (*c.*1400),[103] are strangely analogous in general approach and func-

---

[103] Higinio Anglès, 'El "Llibre Vermell" de Montserrat y los cantos y la danza sacra de los peregrinos durante el siglo XIV', *AnM* 10 (1955), 45–78; Maria Carmen Gómez Muntané, *La música medieval* (Barcelona: Dopesa, 1980), 103–8.

tion to the song collection in the Anglo-Irish 'Red Book of Ossory' (mid-fourteenth century), where popular melodies are suggested to be sung with the sacred poems.[104] Some cathedral sources of liturgical polyphony from Spain and Mallorca reflect practices also found in Italy, Austria and Bohemia (see p. 338).

To some extent, our picture conforms with the development in the fine arts and literature. In this period, the 'international style' or 'international Gothic' spread over areas such as northern Italy, Austria, Bohemia, England and the Low Countries, gradually diminishing the dominance of France.[105] While Jehan Froissart (1337-1410) and Eustache Deschamps (1346-1406), the exponents of French literature in the generation after Machaut, remained essentially faithful to native traditions and Valois patronage, Geoffrey Chaucer (*c*.1342-1400) widened his outlook to absorb the influence of Dante, Petrarch and Boccaccio.

Paris and the Low Countries

It seems that during the lifetime of Machaut, the art-music of the Low Countries was not essentially distinct from the French Ars nova. By 1380 Netherlands musicians populated the University of Paris, the papal chapel of Avignon, the royal chapel and the households of the dukes of Anjou, Berry and Burgundy – the three uncles of King Charles VI (1380-1422) who were the true political managers of the country. Paris was the focus of their cultural and political ambitions, and a melting-pot of artistic trends coming from many provinces and countries.[106] But the relatively weak central power of Charles VI encouraged a growing centrifugal tendency in the arts. Duke Jean de Berry, this great patron of the arts and music, spent his later years predominantly in Bourges (see also p. 144). On the other hand, under the impact of the Burgundian rise to power, much of northern France – and even Paris itself – was drawn into the context of the lateral tradition of the north.

Let us compare the situation of music in Paris around 1370-80 with that of 1400-10. The great musical institutions of the capital flourished throughout this period,[107] but their personnel and artistic orientation gravitated more and more towards Burgundy. Around 1380, some important composers of the Ars subtilior – Vaillant, Solage, Cuvelier, Hasprois – were active in Paris, as were organists and minstrels of the Valois princes. Many of these musicians had or established further contacts with the southern courts of Foix, Avignon, Aragon, Navarre and even Portugal.[108] The itinerant chapel of the king was heard at the court of Gaston Fébus of Foix, for example. By 1400 the leading composers of Paris were mostly employed by Duke Philip of Burgundy (1369-1404),

---

104 Wilkins, *Chaucer*, 95-7; Bukofzer, 'Popular and secular music', 118 f.
105 Discussions of its relevance for music are found in Günther ed., *1380-1430: An International Style?*
106 Pirro, *La musique à Paris.*
107 For the Cathedral of Notre Dame, see Wright, *Music and Ceremony.*
108 Günther, 'Zur Biographie'.

who from 1384 had established his power-base in Flanders. His musicians such as Magister Baude Cordier, Jean de Noyers dit Tapissier and Jean Carmen, or his organist Jean de Visée, shuttled between Paris and the northern cities of Lille, Bruges and Ghent.[109] A particularly talented younger composer, Nicholas Grenon, started his career in 1399 as a clerk at Notre Dame in Paris, but then chose to move northwards, not southwards: he taught at the cathedral school of Laon in 1403, and of Cambrai from 1408.[110] The Parisian music school founded by Johannes Vaillant around 1380 has been mentioned; at the turn of the century it was Tapissier (*d.*1410 or earlier) who taught music privately in Paris while in the service of the Duke of Burgundy, whose choirboys he also educated. Another composer who studied with him was Thomas Fabri. He seems to have received earlier training in Bruges, returning there as succentor between 1412 and 1415.[111]

The Paris-based poetical and musical society called the 'Fumeux' and directed by Eustache Deschamps (*c.*1370) has already been mentioned (see p. 54). In 1401 another society was founded in the Parisian residence of Duke Philip (the Hôtel d'Artois), whose leading members were largely connected with his household: the 'Cour d'amour'.[112] The organization and elaborate ceremonials of this society were analogous to those of other aristocratic or bourgeois guilds and fraternities in France. (They included, for example, a weekly Mass service with organ and discant, plus an anniversary service on St Valentine's Day.) But its explicitly stated literary goals were in opposition to older chivalric ideals and their embodiment in the ever-famous 'Roman de la Rose'. They gave priority to the praise and the defence of the ladies, eschewing most of the misogynistic tone still predominant in Froissart and his generation. A song like 'Medée fu' might not have been appreciated in this circle. Its poetics were more akin to the writings of Christine de Pisan (*c.*1363–*c.*1431), an author much appreciated at the Burgundian court. Among the 24 'ministres' of the 'Cour amoureuse', there were at least three musicians in Burgundian employ: Jean Carité, Jean de Villeroye dit Briquet, and a theologian of the university, Johannes de Mullechner of Austria, who was renowned as a vielle-player but also served Duke Philip as a diplomat.

As Craig Wright has shown, two motets on the Schism by Jean Carmen and Jean Tapissier must both have been composed for the Burgundian court, since they are musically interrelated.[113] Tapissier and Cordier, in turn, collaborated not only as ducal employees but also in the composition of a 'Mass pair', Cordier writing the Gloria, Tapissier the Credo. These works, as well as a Sanctus by Tapissier, are found in the Apt MS (see p. 25). Wright explains that this

---

[109] Wright, *Burgundy*, 165 ff and *passim*.
[110] On his later career in the chapels of Berry, Burgundy and the pope, see p. 149.
[111] Strohm, *Bruges*, 108–13.
[112] Pirro, *La musique à Paris*, 23–5; Wright, *Burgundy*, 134–7.
[113] Wright, *Burgundy*, 131 and n. 54.

survival of their music is not a result of their personal connections with Avignon, but rather because they travelled there with the duke, in 1391 and in 1395.[114] And the duke's mission was to persuade Pope Benedict XIII to abdicate, not to strengthen his position.

Tapissier is mentioned, together with Jean Carmen and Jean Cesaris (a composer connected with the dukes of Berry and Anjou), as a leading composer of Paris in the often-quoted lines by Martin le Franc ('Le champion des dames', *c*.1440):

> Tapissier, Carmen, Cesaris
> N'a pas longtemps si bien chanterrent
> Qu'ils esbahirent tout Paris
> Et tous ceulx qui les frequenterrent;
> Mais oncques jour ne deschanterrent
> en melodie de tel chois,
> Ce m'ont dit qui les hanterrent,
> Que G. du Fay et Binchois.[115]

[Tapissier, Carmen, Cesaris – / not long ago they sang so well, / that they astonished all Paris, / and all those who frequented them; / But never did they sing discant / with such exquisite melody / (people who heard them told me so), / as G. du Fay and Binchois.]

This statement is made from hearsay, of course (in the true sense of the word); one also wonders whether 'Cesaris' may have been selected for the rhyme's sake. But the information is believable. It makes a connection with the leading composers around 1440: Dufay and Binchois excelled the masters not of the Ars subtilior, but of the Franco-Burgundian tradition.

Musical life in northern France and in the Netherlands unfolded not only at court, but also in the great cities and cathedrals. This is a further distinction from the more exclusively princely and feudal culture of the central tradition. The southernmost city of the Low Countries was the imperial town of Cambrai, a kind of musical gateway to the north. The town itself was French-speaking, but it had a large diocese encompassing parts of Hainaut and all of Brabant to the mouth of the river Escaut. The mainly Flemish-speaking population tended to support the Roman popes after 1378. In 1385 Cambrai became the scene of a magnificent double wedding of the son and daughter of Philip the Bold of Burgundy to the daughter and son of Count Albert of Holland, Zeeland and Hainaut. The ceremonies included much music, sacred and secular, in the presence of the French and Dutch princes and guests.[116] It is possible that some of this music actually survives in a collection of fragments found at Cambrai (*F*-

---

[114] *Ibid.*, 127 f. On the identification of Cordier with the ducal harper Fresnel, see n. 89 above.
[115] After Reese, *Renaissance*, 12 f.
[116] Pirro, *La musique à Paris*, 11.

CA 1328) which come from sacred and secular codices of the area.[117] Although we are dealing with diverse fragments only, it seems that even the most recent pieces found here eschew the most advanced Ars subtilior idioms. This music is simpler and more old-fashioned in some ways, but innovative in others. There is, for example, a 'mimetic' motet in Flemish, a canonic Credo-motet which at the same time paraphrases the Credo chant itself, and a 'realistic' ballade where the partners share the same line in a love-dialogue: 'J'aym.' 'Qui?' 'Vous.' 'Moy?'. The composer's name, Paullet, is transmitted in a concordant copy in the Italian codex *GB-Ob 213* dating from as late as *c*.1430.

Liturgical polyphony at Cambrai Cathedral is exemplified by the hymnal *F-CA 29*, the compilation of which began under the chaplain Johannes de Fontanis in 1381 but which remained in constant use until the early sixteenth century, well after Dufay's time. Practically every intervening generation added new hymns, thirteen of which are polyphonic (and one in fauxbourdon, see p. 180). There is no doubt that polyphonic singing was practised in the Cambrai choir school well before Dufay became a choirboy in 1409. (On that period, see p. 152.)

Only in recent years has there been a fresh awareness of the Dutch/Flemish contribution to fourteenth-century polyphony, stimulated by the discovery of manuscript fragments in many libraries of the area, and by rapidly growing archival evidence. The most impressive body of documents is contained in Craig Wright's study of music at the Burgundian court. This itinerant institution inherited its traditions – and musicians – mainly from royal France, but to some extent also from the court of the last independent Count of Flanders, Louis de Male (*d*.1384). The court chapel, the ducal and civic minstrels and the local clergy in the major Flemish cities regularly co-operated in the context of religious and secular festivals and pageants. Similarly favourable conditions for public music-making seem to have existed in the duchy of Brabant with Antwerp, Brussels and Malines, in the prince-bishoprics of Utrecht and Liège, and in the counties of Holland, Zeeland and Hainaut, whose court was located in The Hague and intermittently in Le Quesnoy (Hainaut).[118] The Burgundian dynasty, which also owned the Artois (with Arras), later acquired for itself the three counties just mentioned plus Brabant. Apart from the courts, the strongest native tradition of music was concentrated in the cathedrals and collegiate churches. The clergy had much access to music and music theory from royal France, largely through the University of Paris, and also found ready financial support for sacred music from wealthy citizens in the respective towns. The Onze-Lieve-Vrouwe-Broederschap (Fraternity of Our Lady) in 'sHertogen-

---

[117] Irmgard Lerch, *Fragmente aus Cambrai. Ein Beitrag zur Rekonstruktion einer Handschrift mit spätmittelalterlicher Polyphonie*, 2 vols. (Kassel etc.: Bärenreiter, 1987); David Fallows, 'L'origine du MS 1328 de Cambrai', *RdM* 62 (1972), 275–80.

[118] On the court of Holland, see especially F. P. van Ostroom, *Het word van eer* (Amsterdam, 1987); and Janse, 'Muziekleven'.

bosch is only one of the many associations of laymen which patronized sacred music. Their first codex containing polyphony (*liber motetorum*) is documented already in 1336.[119] Fragments of several other such 'motet books' have survived; they show that this type of codex contained by no means only motets – most notably by Vitry and his immediate successors – but also sections of the Mass Ordinary and often also secular songs in French or Dutch/Flemish.[120] St Donatian's in Bruges had one such manuscript before 1377, St James's in Ghent (a parish church!) by 1387.

The widespread interest in the motets and treatises of Vitry may go back to his own lifetime, and to the personal contacts he demonstrably had with clerics resident in the area. Among more recent motets, apparently preferred items include critical and satirical works such as 'Degentis vita' (see pp. 42 f), and 'musicians' motets'. In 'Musicalis scientia / Scientie laudabili' and 'Apollinis eclipsatur / Zodiacum', the musicians mentioned in the texts largely hail from northern towns such as Douai, Bruges, Thérouanne, Arras, Valenciennes and Tirlemont.[121] The motets of Machaut, and his Mass, were perhaps less well known in the area, although at least one manuscript of his oeuvre was at some time located in Flanders.[122]

A typically Netherlands advance beyond the Vitryan tradition can be seen in the motet 'Rex Karole / Leticie, pacis', which was probably composed for the magnificent diplomatic congress of Bruges in 1375-6.[123] The negotiations between England and France, supervised by the Duke of Burgundy and attended by princes and musicians from many other regions,[124] led only to a one-year truce, but the motet nevertheless celebrates Charles V as a peacemaker. In a late source, the composer's name is given as 'Philippus Royllaert'. The motet marks the point of stylistic development where the central and the lateral traditions begin to diverge. The musician who copied it in the Chantilly Codex may have been mildly interested in its structural scheme (five *taleae* distributed over two *colores*; change of mensuration within the *talea*), and perhaps in its French royal connection. The musicians in England, in Italy, in 'sHertogenbosch and in Strasbourg where it was also copied, may have appreciated its recurrent contrasts of texture, its simple 3/4 metre and its canonic beginning. The latter three characteristics appear again in motets by Ciconia, composed in Italy a generation later.

The three-voice motet 'Comes Flandrie / Rector creatorum', which celebrates

---

[119] Smijers, *Broederschap*, 5 ('magistro Waltero scriptori 12 gr. de motetis').

[120] Further on *libri motetorum* and their contents, see Strohm, *Bruges*, 103 ff.

[121] A full list of musicians' names mentioned in the motets is in Harrison ed., *Motets of French Provenance*, 205.

[122] *F-Pn fr.1584* (MachA) belonged to the Bruges family de Gruuthuse in the fifteenth century. In addition, *F-Pn fr.9221* (MachE) was produced for, or bought by, Duke Jean de Berry *c.*1400, probably in Flanders.

[123] Günther ed., *Motets of Chantilly*, no. 5.

[124] Wright, *Burgundy*, docs. 9-22.

a victory of the Count of Flanders in 1381 or 1382, is more remote from the central tradition.[125] Although it is a 'musicians' motet', mentioning Boethius and elements of music theory, it is not isorhythmic. It mimics the sound of chime-bells and thus recalls the 'mimetic' songs of the time, which were popular in the Netherlands. Besides circulating French examples of the genre (Vaillant's 'Par maintes fois' and the anonymous 'Orsus, vous dormes trop'), Flemish-speaking musicians composed new pieces, for example '(Go)eden kaccharinc' (a street-cry motet) and '(Ic beghi)nne mijn liedekijn' in a fragment which is perhaps from Bruges (*NL-Uu 37 I*).[126]

Mass Ordinary settings are frequent in the *libri motetorum* of the area, although few of them survive complete. Some settings were obviously imported from Avignon or other southern centres, but more were composed locally. The earliest-known Mass cycle, the 'Mass of Tournai',[127] may be a combination of sections of different origin, assembled for use at Tournai Cathedral. A special confraternity 'de la messe de Nostre Dame' existed at Tournai in 1350. An endowment made by the bishop in 1349 requested regular performances of a Lady Mass at a special altar in the transept of the cathedral.[128]

The practice of endowed or 'votive' Lady Masses is amply documented in the Low Countries and also in England. They were often called *Missa de Salve* because of the introit 'Salve sancta parens' which begins the service. Special Lady Chapels were dedicated to the purpose, and some of these are still the showpieces of English cathedrals (see Plate 1). Flemish sources tell us that usually the succentor, the organist and the choirboys participated in the polyphony, the latter contributing at least the Marian trope of the Gloria, 'Spiritus et alme'.

In the surviving Glorias and Credos in particular, motet-like tenor construction and unification of the two movements sometimes foreshadow the later tenor Mass. One Gloria exists which uses a non-Mass chant in the tenor – a device not known from French music before the 1420s. The piece, apparently from Ghent (*B-Gr 133*), dates from about 1390.[129] It is not isorhythmic but resembles the so-called 'isomelic' technique of the fifteenth century: the antiphon 'Gloria in excelsis Deo' for Lauds on Christmas Day is sounded twice in the tenor with exact repetition of pitches but different rhythms. The choice of this particularly 'appropriate' antiphon suggests that a non-Mass cantus firmus was still a novelty, and that perhaps an exception was made for Christmas. The Low Countries also

---

[125] Strohm, *Bruges*, 103 f and ex. 1.

[126] Edward Stam, 'Het Utrechts fragment van een Zeeuws-Vlaamse marktroepen-motetus', *TVNM* 21 (1968), 25–37 (with facs and transcription); Strohm, *Bruges*, 105 f.

[127] After the edns of Leo Schrade in PMFC 1 (1956) and Charles van den Borren in CMM 13 (1957), there is now a richly commented facs edn and transcription: Jean Dumoulin, Michel Huglo, Philippe Mercier and Jacques Pycke eds, *La Messe de Tournai* (Tournai: Archives du Chapitre Cathédral, and Louvain-la-Neuve: Université Catholique, 1988).

[128] Strohm, *Bruges*, rev. edn, 102 and added fn. p. 259. The editorial commentary by Michel Huglo (see n. 127) draws the same conclusions about the origin of the Mass.

[129] Strohm, 'Ars nova fragments', Gloria no. 2 (with facs).

1 St Alban's Cathedral, the Lady Chapel

produced some 'Deo gratias' motets for the end of Mass, as in the Tournai cycle (see p. 83).

In the surviving fragments of courtly chansonniers from this region and period, typical Ars subtilior pieces are not excluded but are in a minority. They occur most often in the fragmentary Utrecht chansonnier (*NL-Uu 37 II*), a manuscript which possibly originated at the French-speaking court of Brabant around 1400. Only one piece has a Flemish text here. The larger Leiden fragment (*NL-Lu 2720*), on the other hand, abounds with simpler, naturalistic or 'mimetic' songs in both languages.[130] Several are of an ebullient, convivial nature, and have declamatory text underlying all voices. In two of the most exuberant songs ('Faites chi verser de che bon vin cler' and 'Cheulz qui volent retourner en lanois'), localities near Cambrai are mentioned (the Laonnais region,

---

[130] Biezen–Gumbert eds, *Two Chansonniers*; Helene Wagenaar-Nolthenius, 'De Leidse fragmenten. Nederlandse polifonie uit het einde der 14e eeuw', in Robijns ed., *Renaissance-Muziek*, 303–15.

and the village of Haspre); they may well have originated among students and clerics of Cambrai. In some other pieces, for example the Latin-texted praise of music, 'Letificans tristantes', the counterpoint recalls the style of the English cantilena (see p. 76). Two composers are named: Martinus Fabri and Hugo Boy Monachus. Both were singers of Count Albert of Holland at The Hague in 1395.[131] Hugo Boy, the monk, seems to have been at home in Dordrecht. For some kind of wrongdoing, he was once sentenced to go on a pilgrimage to Rome; his song is a prayer to Lady Venus ('Genade Venus, vrouwe tzart').

Two songs in this chansonnier seem particularly significant. 'Hu, hula hu! Se ma canchon' is evidently a mock-song on a (clerical?) colleague.[132] The tenor has its own text, a goliardic ditty which is once repeated identically, while the words and music of the upper voice continue differently. The tune in the tenor, albeit not a folksong, has the characteristics of a pre-existing song:

Example 7 'Hu, hula hu! / Au debot', Leiden fragments

Fabri's courtly ballade 'N'ay je cause'[133] looks at first glance quite similar to some specimens of the Ars subtilior, particularly of the older and simpler types. Also the poem belongs to that stylistic group. Some musical aspects, however, contradict this. The editors were surely correct in placing the text not only under the cantus but also under the tenor, which is the simplest and most singable line. It even gives the impression of a pre-existing tune (see Ex. 8). Most of the tenor line in the first half of the ballade is rhythmically grouped in 3/4 bars, although the metre is 6/8. The tenor line divides into five phrases of four bars each, which seem to echo each other, melodically and rhythmically.

---

[131] Janse, 'Muziekleven', 143 and 154.
[132] Biezen–Gumbert eds, *Two Chansonniers*, no. L 10.
[133] *Ibid.*, no. L 6.

Example 8 Martinus Fabri, 'N'ay je cause'

Example 8 (*cont.*)

The repetition scheme is 'A A¹ B C A²'. Such regularity and repetitiveness of phrases does not call to mind the Ars subtilior, but rather, earlier fourteenth-century song, on the one hand, and the later 'Burgundian' chanson, on the other. Only two phrases are needed for the text declamation, the others are vocalized – which is remarkable, since phrases one and two relate to each other like antecedent and consequent, involving a quasi-transposition. This device is surely more typical of chansons around the time of Binchois. In the texted phrases the decasyllabic verses are accommodated with the help of upbeats and of pitch-repeating quavers (bars 7 and 15) which do not produce good word-setting. There is a suspicion, then, that the tenor line originally fitted *octosyllabic* verses (and perhaps more than two): quite possibly a Germanic four-stress type of verse.

The cantus goes at first with the tenor rhythm but then introduces 'delayed syncopation', smaller note-values and genuine 6/8 groupings. The contratenor even has 'split syncopation' as early as bars 1–3, and wide leaps; it obscures the regularity of the tenor even more than does the cantus.

The second half of the song is very different from the first. Their only tangible link is the repetition of the *first* tenor phrase at the very end, a very unusual choice for a musical refrain in a ballade. (There is also a fleeting similarity between bars 3–4 and 49–50.) Besides, the cantus and contratenor differ when the first phrase comes back at the end – which again speaks for an independent origin of the tenor. Apart from the refrain, the second half is in 6/8 throughout. Cantus and tenor regularly alternate in a 'question and answer' fashion; in bars 51–2 they even mimic each other in strict imitation. After each of these three little dialogues, they sing together. This interesting textural articulation is enhanced by a strange but logical distribution of phrase-lengths (counting units of ♩.):

```
Cantus: -- 3 4 -- 3 8 -- 3 12
Tenor:   2 -- 4 2 -- 8 2 -- 12
```

The total number of units (39) just fails to equal that of the first half (40). The strange incongruence of the two halves may suggest that the composer worked with given material which covered only the first half. He then expanded it into a full ballade form and added a cantus and contratenor. The tenor tune of the first half may have been a Dutch monophonic song, of five octosyllabic verses. In transforming the song, Fabri did his best to disguise its humble origin. Some of the complications he added were borrowed from the courtly style of the central tradition, but others (the textural contrasts and imitations) were progressive, or better 'lateral', characteristics.

The musicians from the Low Countries, whom we encounter in these fragments, were working at the extreme margins of the central tradition. But their local idiosyncrasies and, after all, their innovations, combined into a vocabulary later found in Binchois, Dufay and their contemporaries. There could even be biographic connections. The chansonnier *NL-Lu 2720* was probably used at the court of Holland, Zeeland and Hainaut, where Binchois' father, Jean de Binche, served as councillor. Perhaps the use of the manuscript extended into the time of Countess Jacqueline (r. 1417–29), who may have been personally acquainted with Binchois.[134] As regards the convivial songs from the Cambrai region, they may have been sung around Cambrai Cathedral while Dufay was a choirboy there.

The recently discovered Groningen fragment of polyphonic keyboard music from this period[135] recalls the fact that the organ is sometimes quoted in the context of polyphonic performances in archival records. These documents typically identify the organist as a regular participant in paid discant Masses.[136] The following all contain unambiguous references to polyphonic playing on the organ: the description of a ceremony in Bruges, 1384, where the organist played a 'motet';[137] a painting of the same decade of Brabantine origin in the Royal Art Gallery in Brussels, showing the 'Coronation of the Virgin' with a musician angel who applies both hands to the keyboard, van Eyck's 'Adoration of the Lamb' (of the 1420s), where the angel at the organ plays a chord of three notes, while others in the opposite panel are singing. Besides the pipe organ, particularly if of a small size, stringed keyboard instruments were in great demand and may occasionally have been used for polyphony. A predilection for the exchiquier (chekker, *Schachpret*) was shared by Machaut, King John of France (r. 1350–64) and Jean Charlier de Gerson. In one of its guises it was probably a kind of clavichord, very suitable for domestic and secular music-making.[138] This may have been the intended instrument for the Groningen fragment which contains two French songs in keyboard arrangements. They are 'Esperance qui en mon coeur s'en bat', the rondeau also quoted by Senleches, and the widely known virelai 'Mais qu'il vous viengne' – here appearing with the initial words 'Empris domoyrs' (i.e. 'd'amours'). The notation is the one known as 'Italian keyboard tablature', which uses only mensural notes, arranged in score. (The English and German keyboard tablatures of the period also use figures.) The implications of this Italian connection, and the style of the arrangements, will be discussed later on.

'Esperance' is also found in the Ghent fragment *B-Gr 133* mentioned above, which makes it likely that the piece was well known at the Burgundian court. Other French chansons which were appreciated in Burgundian Flanders are

---

[134] Parris, *Binchois*, 8–28 (but see Fallows, 'Binchois' in *The New Grove*, 712). Some notices about Jacqueline's expenses on music are in Frans de Potter, *Geschiedenis van Jacoba van Beieren (1401-36)* (Brussels: Académie Royale de Belgique, 1881), 81–3.

[135] Maria van Daalen and Frank Ll. Harrison, 'Two keyboard intabulations of the late fourteenth century on a manuscript leaf now in the Netherlands', *TVNM* 34 (1984), 97–108 (with facs and transcriptions).

[136] Strohm, *Bruges*, 15, 26 f, 32, 40, 46–9, 53, 57, 64, 70 f. Generally on organ music of the time, see Yvonne Rokseth, *La musique d'orgue*, 1–29; *idem*, 'Instrumental music', 412–25.

[137] Strohm, *Bruges*, 18.

[138] The name did perhaps not refer to one type of instrument, but to a standard (chessboard) decoration: see Christopher Page, 'The myth of the chekker', *Early Music* 7 (1979), 482–9.

assembled in a chansonnier fragment also found in Ghent, of *c*.1390–1400 (*B-Gr 3360*). These pieces are all in the older and simpler Ars nova styles, eschewing the complications of the Ars subtilior.[139] Apparently, their very conservatism made them widely acceptable outside France. Most of them were copied again in Italian, English and German manuscripts of *c*.1400–1420. How did they reach all these countries?

Apart from the effects of the Schism, it was surely the Flemish–Burgundian culture which chained the lateral traditions of music together. The wealthy trading centres of the region were excellently connected with the Italian and German cities, and with Britain. Merchants, clerics and intellectuals from all those countries actually lived in Flanders. The reputation and the diplomatic activities of the Burgundian court fostered even more exchanges of music, musicians and other artists than in Avignon. Around 1400, foreign bankers and diplomats in Bruges and Ghent were also patrons of local music. The Bruges confraternity of the 'Dry Tree', which consisted mainly of Florentine merchants, had already instituted its weekly Lady Mass in discant by 1396.[140] Dino Raponacute;di, a banker from Lucca who was the most important financier of the Burgundian court, endowed his own personal discant Mass in Bruges by 1414.[141] Such patronage extended to the hiring of minstrels, the trade in musical instruments, and the provision of music for ballrooms and banquets.

A considerable amount of French-texted secular music collected in Italy around 1390–1420 was derived from Netherlands sources. Good examples are the first part of the Reina Codex (*F-Pn n. a. f. 6771*), copied about 1400 in the Veneto region, which contains many songs also found in the Low Countries and one even with Flemish words; and the codex *F-Pn 568* (*Pit*), compiled *c*.1407 in Lucca for a Florentine merchant family.[142] Not only clerics, but also secular musicians, and their instruments, had by that time reached Italy from the Low Countries (see also p. 90). In the area of sacred music and the motet, Italian reliance on the northerners is by no means confined to such remarkable oeuvres as that of Johannes Ciconia. Two of his northern colleagues in Italy, Johannes Ecghaerd ('Magister Egardus') from Bruges and Hubertus de Salinis from the diocese of Liège, have left their music in both Italian and Netherlands sources (see pp. 99 f).

England

The musical situation of England in our period can be – and has been – described in many different guises.[143] The traditions leading up to the famous Old

---

[139] Strohm, 'Ars nova fragments'.
[140] Strohm, *Bruges*, 70 f.
[141] Strohm, *Bruges*, 15. Raponacute;di died in 1414, but the endowment came into effect in 1417.
[142] On both manuscripts see also pp. 89 f below.
[143] Harrison, *Britain*; idem, 'English church music'; Bukofzer, 'Popular and secular music'; Sanders, 'England'; Hoppin, *Medieval Music*, 502–24 ('An English epilogue'); Wilkins, *Chaucer*, 74–110.

Hall MS (*OH, GB-Lbl add.57950*) of *c*.1415–20 have been characterized as an epilogue to the Middle Ages, as a transition, or even as the beginning of a new era. Lack of securely datable sources before the Old Hall MS makes it difficult to decide not only how English music developed during the period of the Schism, but also which genres and styles should be considered. The numerous sources of sacred polyphony survive mostly only as fragments, and are in many ways inconclusive.[144] We know very little about music in the secular sphere, and the most instructive accounts of this have to be sought in the works of Chaucer. The most authoritative writer on British medieval music, Frank Ll. Harrison, excludes the subjects of minstrels and popular music from his discussion.

It seems likely that the population at large must have known art-music mainly through their churches – to an extent quite uncommon in Europe. Unlike the Continent, England had a very musical *monastic* clergy then. The musical productivity of the Benedictine cathedrals (Canterbury, York, Norwich, Worcester etc.) equalled or exceeded that of the 'secular' cathedrals (Salisbury, Lincoln, Exeter, London St Paul's etc.); the great abbeys, such as St Alban's, Waltham, Westminster, Fountains and Bury St Edmunds, were also active musical centres. Increasingly important was the contribution of colleges and collegiate churches. The small élite of educated clerics serving these institutions was less secluded from the common people than were, by comparison, the continental sacred and secular courts – or else its tastes in music were less esoteric.

There is, for example, the sizeable repertory of the *cantilena*,[145] a type of composition in three texted parts which may be a relative of the conductus of the Ars antiqua. The texts are sacred and in Latin, but non-liturgical, many are in honour of the Virgin and the Saints. Most of this music was probably composed by clerics and monks, but the official documents of worship – the liturgical books – do not include any of it. The purposes of the cantilena were 'votive, devotional, processional and recreational',[146] and their performance may have involved people of varied education. The genre waned in the later fourteenth century; surviving specimens from this period sometimes show admixtures from the motet or from instrumental music.

A liturgical counterpart to the cantilenae is to be found in the three-voice settings of the Mass Ordinary, and of antiphons, sequences and tropes. This is the most extended repertory. In a majority of cases, the polyphony was written against the appropriate plainsong and was thus performed in the church service. The style of these works is known as *English discant*, a method of extem-

---

[144] For sources, see: Frank Ll. Harrison and Roger Wibberley eds, *Manuscripts of Fourteenth-Century English Polyphony: A Selection of Facsimiles* (London: The British Academy, 1981) (EECM, vol. 26); William Summers ed., *English Fourteenth-Century Polyphony: Facsimile Edition of Sources Notated in Score* (Tutzing: Schneider, 1983). On provenances, see also Bent, 'Transmission'; Lefferts, *Motet*, 24 f and app. 2.

[145] Sanders, 'Cantilena and discant'. Editions in: Sanders–Harrison–Lefferts eds, *English Music II* (*PMFC*, vol. 17).

[146] *PMFC*, vol. 17, x.

porizing or composing an added voice (discantus) to a given plainsong with little or no disparity of rhythm.[147]

The homorhythmic style, which is analogous to the continental 'simultaneous style', is the most significant feature of the liturgical settings and the cantilenae, and corresponds to their notation in 'score'. This was not a score in the modern sense, nor like the keyboard scores of the period; the voices were written above each other line by line, and the text was only written beneath the bottom voice. The vertical alignment of the notes was only approximate, and could be obscured by the use of ligatures. The simultaneity of the notes was controlled not by a metrical system such as barlines, but by the underlaid syllables which were pronounced in all the voices simultaneously. Smaller note-values often embellished individual passages of a single voice, so that the result was not actually 'note-against-note' counterpoint, but 'syllable-against-syllable' performance. The score notation, although approximate, was indeed an aid in performance (and thus suggests that the manuscripts were actually used in performance, which would not have been a matter of course). Moreover, the chant settings demonstrate that the conventional pronunciation of the chant, including its ligatures and syllable distribution, governed the total rhythm. The plainsong is the 'soul' of these pieces; in contrast to its objectivizations in the isorhythmic motet and later in the cantus firmus Mass, here it still lives its own life as a song.

Composing such pieces meant writing down a manner of performing the chant, and this is why the theorists of English discant made no clear distinction between composition and execution. Their rules tell the singer of the discantus which intervals to take when the chant makes a certain step.[148] This makes sense only when the performer of the discantus knows the progressions of the chant beforehand *and* can calculate their rhythmic pace. This would not be possible with a rhythmically distorted motet tenor! Very frequently, the chant-carrying voice of the written compositions has equal note-values throughout, which is how the plainsong was most often performed. When this voice is written with some inserted rests, longer note-values or short strokes of division without precise rhythmic meaning – that, too, was a usual manner of articulating plainsong. Sometimes, simple 'external' rhythms, such as strict alternation of long and short notes, were imposed on all the voices. These would have been just as calculable as 'monorhythm'. More complicated rhythms in the added voices, such as 6/8 with many ornamental notes, must be ascribed to the influence of the motet. In Example 9, an English discant setting of the earlier fourteenth century,[149] the plainsong in the middle voice (an antiphon) is treated 'monorhyth-

---

[147] Sanders, 'Cantilena and discant'; *idem*, *Medieval English Polyphony*, 287–318; Harrison, 'English church music', 95–8.

[148] Apfel, *Studien*, vol. 1, 57–85; *idem*, *Diskant und Kontrapunkt in der Musiktheorie des 12. bis 15. Jahrhunderts* (Wilhelmshaven: Heinrichshofen, 1982), parts I and II; Sanders, *Medieval English Polyphony*, 313–18.

[149] PMFC, vol. 17, no. 7. Facsimiles of the manuscript (*GB-Cu Kk.1.6*) in Harrison, *Britain*, pl. 22; Harrison-Wibberley eds, *Manuscripts* (n. 144), pl. 102; Summers ed., *English Fourteenth-Century Polyphony* (n. 144), pl. 29.

mically' with few exceptions. Most of the chant ligatures (except on 'vir-') are spread out, giving each note of the chant melisma the same length as the notes which carry a syllable of their own:

Example 9 'Paradisi porta', *GB-Cu 6*

Our example also demonstrates essential characteristics of English harmony. The plainsong is in the middle voice, as was usual in England but very rare on the Continent. The voices occupy overlapping but distinct ranges, adding up to a total range of 14 notes. The texture is suitable for a group of adult singers with modest individual ranges. The upper voices never cross, the lower pair only once (at 'iterum'). All crotchets (originally breves) are consonant with the chant

– except that the top voice often has a fourth above the chant when this is supported by the bottom voice with a third or fifth below. The first-mode plainsong is transposed up a fifth, but the piece is harmonized in D (not A), as the major cadences show. Most of the final chords of phrases lack the third, but full triads are frequent in the middle of phrases.

The inhabitants of the British Isles (not just the English) had an age-old predilection for thirds and sixths, which particularly characterizes the harmony of the cantilenae. In that genre, parallel progressions in 6-3 sonorities (or 10-5 or 10-6) are justly considered typical for the insular style. In the chant-based genres, however, theorists and composers alike restrict the use of parallels in favour of contrary motion. In our piece, some parallel fifths and octaves do occur, but 6-3 parallels are absent. Rather, the chord-type is carefully varied with each chant note. A peculiarity typical of English discant is often to be found at cadences where the chant repeats its pitch, so that the bottom voice, which reaches the final note by step, produces a 6-4 chord. In Example 9, this sonority is carefully treated as a passing embellishment, or as a kind of suspension.

Theory and practice of English discant do not go entirely hand in hand, since the former teaches only two-part counterpoint, whether written or extemporized. In the treatise *Quatuor principalia* by Pseudo-Tunstede (1351), the author observes that it is impossible to sing discant above a chant while another voice is discanting below, unless the singer observes the rules about good consonance with the lowest notes at the same time.[150] This more difficult type of music – which Ernst Apfel described as 'multiple two-part counterpoint' – is precisely what the written English discant repertory represents.[151] Here, the composer could take account of both the plainsong and the bottom voice when writing the top voice. If the lower voices crossed, he had to take account of whichever was the lowest note at the time.

As with many stylistic principles of English music, their antithesis can also be found, sometimes within the same genre. If the English discant technique separated voice-ranges, giving the chant a fixed place in the middle, it also produced the 'migrant' cantus firmus.[152] Here, some notes of the chant were passed from the middle voice to one of the outer voices when going very high or low (see Ex. 31). The purpose of this device, which became a sophisticated technique in the fifteenth century, was originally to avoid voice-crossings that made it difficult to keep track of the lowest notes. By contrast, continental musicians allowed many crossings between tenor and contratenor, as the cantus

---

[150] Coussemaker ed., *CS*, vol. 3, 354-64; vol. 4, 278-98, ch. 40. A German translation, with further literature, is in Ernst Apfel, *Die Lehre vom Organum, Diskant, Kontrapunkt und von der Komposition bis um 1480*, 2nd edn (Saarbrücken: Author, 1989), 190-211 and n. 74.

[151] Ernst Apfel, *Geschichte der Kompositionslehre von den Anfängen bis gegen 1700*, 5 vols. (Saarbrücken: Author, 1985), vol. 1, 118-63; Klaus-Jürgen Sachs, *Der Contrapunctus im 14. und 15. Jahrhundert* (Wiesbaden: Steiner, 1974), 123 ff.

[152] Bukofzer, *Studies*, 46-8; Sanders, *Medieval English Polyphony*, 304-10.

was composed exclusively against the tenor (except in four-part motets). The *Pseudo-Chilston* treatise of the early fifteenth century seems to recognize such a continental alternative when distinguishing between the English 'counter' and the 'countirtenor'. The former is always a bottom voice and always essential to the harmony; the latter may cross into the middle, becoming a 'mene', but is essential only where it stays below the tenor.[153] That is not the same as the continental contratenor which is always inessential, even where it is the lowest voice (except in four-part motets). The English 'countirtenor' and the migrant cantus firmus are inversely related: the former technique leaves all the chant notes in the tenor but makes it exchange the lowest position with the 'countirtenor', the latter distributes chant pitches between the lower voices, but helps keep all the lowest notes within a single voice.[154]

By the early fifteenth century, two other practices had also surfaced: the 'sight' techniques, which include (but are not restricted to) *faburden*, and the 'squares' (see p. 210). Both are aids for dealing with a cantus firmus and thus related to English discant rules. The 'sight' techniques allow for extemporized additions of voices to a given plainsong, and the 'squares' were written-out 'countirtenors' for given chants used in other contexts.

Most of the techniques have in common the fact that they could be used in a polyphonic performance to accommodate singers of the plainsong who *did not sing from the book* but by heart, or who sang from the actual plainsong book, or who sang from a polyphonic manuscript but were spared the mensural complexities in their 'monorhythmic' part. I suggest that English liturgical polyphony sometimes involved choral performance of the chant-carrying voice, *in addition* to the notated polyphony. The notated tenor or 'mene' only doubled the chant – as far as it contained it at all. The same practice would have applied when the organ participated: the organist played the chant, and the singers of the written polyphony (who could stand far away from the organ) accompanied him.[155]

Popular, secular and instrumental music in England has not been thoroughly

---

[153] Andrew Hughes, 'Chilston' in *The New Grove*; Ernest H. Sanders, 'Discant #II: English' in *The New Grove*.

[154] On counterpoint in four-part motets, see also p. 236 below. A conflation of the lowest notes of four-part pieces within one voice was used also on the Continent, perhaps for composition drafts or rehearsal: such a voice was called *solus tenor*. Margaret Bent, 'Some factors in the control of consonance and sonority: successive composition and the solus tenor', in Perkins, 'Euphony in the Fifteenth Century', 625–33; Davis Shelley, 'The solus tenor in the 14th and 15th centuries', *AcM* 39 (1967), 44–64, and 40 (1968), 176–8.

[155] Many writers still reject the idea of organ participation in polyphony before *c*.1500, but see Harrison, *Britain*, 207–15, and for the fifteenth century, p. 278 below. Chant-carrying voices in 'monorhythm' were eminently suitable for performance on a large organ, even when the singers stood at some distance from it. In certain English pieces, some chant-notes are missing but would be consonant if inserted (for example in the 'Sancta Maria virgo', PMFC, vol. 17, no. 8): this could mean that the chant was performed by the general choir or the organ, or both, *in addition* to the written polyphony. Further on English fourteenth-century performance practice, see Roger Bowers, 'The performing ensemble for English church polyphony, c.1320–c.1390', in Boorman ed., *Studies*, 161–92 (with a cautiously positive remark concerning the organ on p. 172 f).

investigated.[156] Apart from the cantilena, some of the older genres which sometimes had English words were still in use in the late fourteenth century – for example the rondellus and related forms of canon and voice-exchange. The cantilena 'Angelus ad virginem', known in more than one version, received a vernacular translation.[157] It has been argued that the polyphonic *carol*, whose sources date from the fifteenth century, emerged from earlier liturgical uses.[158] Even then, its typical social contexts would have been processions, Christmas festivities (lullabies, Marian songs) and the sacred theatre, where educated musicians addressed less educated audiences.

For the courtly and collegiate circles, another possibility may have been available: imported secular polyphony either with the original lyrics or with English contrafactum texts. Nigel Wilkins has endeavoured to identify actual French chansons which he thinks might have been sung in England.[159] Such practices could have originated during the English campaigns in France, or while the French King John was a prisoner in England (1357–60), as he was at first allowed to keep his own musicians with him. Travels by nobles, intellectuals and merchants to the Continent would have supplied new material. French songs are indeed found in two English manuscripts from the beginning of the fifteenth century: *GB–Cu add.5943*[160] and *US–Wc 14*.[161] English contrafacta of French chansons have not yet been found.

Non-liturgical polyphony focused, however, on the genre of the *motet*.[162] The magnificent insular motet tradition goes back well into the thirteenth century. By the mid-fourteenth century, English composers were acquainted with the style and notation of the Ars nova motet. But the insular approach was remarkably independent: in notational usages (of which there were many),[163] in rhythm (with a striking preference for 9/8 groupings), and in the clear and simple periodic schemes of the tenor, which never equalled the arithmetic extravagances of the Ars subtilior motets. It may be that the motet in England was socially more broadly based than in France. Although it was cultivated mostly in university and monastic circles, its often songlike structures may have appealed to wider audiences. Most of the known works are sacred or devotional in character. Latin texts predominate by far, and the use of French or English is mainly found within early pieces which presumably quote popular tunes such as the tenors 'Dou way Robin', 'Marionette douche' and 'Hey lure lure'. An English preference for non-Gregorian tenors or 'grounds' has been noted, and further tenors (or other lines) of vernacular origin may still be hidden in the existing composi-

---

[156] Surveys are Bukofzer, 'Popular and secular music'; Wilkins, *Chaucer*, 92–124.

[157] Wilkins, *Chaucer*, 94.

[158] Harrison, 'Benedicamus'.

[159] Wilkins, *Chaucer*, 106–10; *idem*, *Chaucer Songs* (Woodbridge: Brewer, 1980).

[160] Wilkins, *Chaucer*, 107–10 and n. 257.

[161] Lefferts, *Motet*, 308–10. The manuscript contains, besides the motet 'Rex Karole', the convivial French–Latin song 'Deus compaignouns de Cleremunde', probably of northern French origin.

[162] Lefferts, *Motet*.

[163] Margaret Bent, 'A preliminary assessment of the independence of the English Trecento notations', *L'Ars Nova* 4 (1975), 65–82.

tions. Motet poets and composers were especially influenced by Latin monody, for example the sequence (with musical repetitions of paired verses). The lai (a monophonic, stanzaic song) and the instrumental *estampie* (*stantipes, ductia*) may also have offered formal models. Peter M. Lefferts emphasizes the sequence style in a triplum from a fragmentary motet in a Bury St Edmunds manuscript ('Eya templum Salomonis').[164]

This beautiful piece of poetry was intended for the feast of dedication of a church. Other motet texts celebrate Christmas, Marian feasts and, in particular, local or national patron saints. This points to a function of the motets which was distinct from their continental uses, at least of the central tradition: the performance during church festivities and processions in the presence of the congregation.

While the English discant repertory does not seem to have undergone major stylistic or functional changes before *c.*1400, there are changes in the use and status of the motet by 1370 at the latest. It may be in the context of the Anglo-French war that Johannes Alanus composed the exceptional work 'Sub Arturo / Fons citharizancium'. Its text praises the members of an English royal chapel under the guise of the King Arthur legends.[165] Its arithmetic layout, with proportional reductions of the tenor in the ratios 9 : 6 : 4, recalls the latest developments in the French motet around 1370. Brian Trowell has suggested that the composer was John Aleyn, a 'King's clerk' and later canon of Windsor (*d.*1372), and that he wrote the work for a meeting of the Order of the Garter.[166] In that case, would he not have adopted a more indigenous style? It is perhaps more likely that this 'musicians' motet', which amounts to political propaganda, was written during an English campaign in southern France, and in a style familiar to musicians of the Avignonese orbit.[167] 'Sub Arturo / Fons' is symptomatic of events to come, not only because it is so close to the French tradition, but also because it is royal and secular. The war probably generated new interest among royal chaplains and other musicians for the continental motet. From the 1380s onwards, six English sources contain such works. They include motets by Vitry, and such well-known unattributed works as 'Apta caro', 'Rex Karole', 'Degentis vita' and 'Inter amenitatis / O Livor'. The 'musicians' motet' 'Musicorum collegio / In templo dei'[168] must have been composed in northern France,

---

[164] Lefferts, *Motet*, 178 f (fig. 48).

[165] Harrison ed., *Motets of French Provenance* (sic), no. 31; Günther ed., *Motets of Chantilly*, no. 12; Margaret Bent ed., *Two Fourteenth-Century Motets in Praise of Music* (Newton Abbot: Antico Edition, 1977) (together with 'Apollinis / Zodiacum'). 'J. Alanus' cites himself as the composer in the text. This may be the only attributed English composition surviving in a fourteenth-century copy.

[166] Brian Trowell, 'A fourteenth-century ceremonial motet and its composer', *AcM* 29 (1957), 65–75. Trowell's dating of 1358 has been challenged by Bent, 'Transmission', 70 ff.

[167] Günther ed., *Motets of Chantilly*, commentary on no. 12. An English source of the work has recently come to light (*GB-YOX*): see Lefferts, *Motet*, 300–302. The work could nevertheless have been imported from France (albeit written by an Englishman), since *GB-YOX* also contains 'Degentis vita' (see pp. 42 f above).

[168] Harrison ed., *Motets of English Provenance*, no. 35.

as it praises the singers of a 'curia Gallicorum' who perform a weekly Marian office. Some of them, to judge by their names, appear to be Netherlanders; one is called 'J. Anglicus'. The proportional structure of the work is related to 'Sub Arturo', but even more resembles 'Porcio nature / Ida capillorum', a motet in honour of St Ida of Boulogne (see pp. 40 f and Ex. 3).

The latest species of motets, the 'Deo gratias' substitute, is found in sources up to and including the Old Hall MS which contains a pair of such works: 'Are post libamina / Nunc surgunt', attributed to 'Mayshuet', and the anonymous 'Post missarum solemnia / Post misse modulamina', which paraphrases a text already found with different music in the Ivrea Codex.[169] The triplum text of 'Are post' states that its author composed it first to French words, but then 'reformed it in Latin so that it now pleases the English'. In its original form with a French triplum (possibly a love-song) and a Latin duplum (expressing a moral admonition), the work would closely resemble the 'Deo gratias' motet at the end of the Mass of Tournai, 'Se grasse n'est / Cum venerint miseri degentes / Ite missa est'. Mayshuet is probably identical with the papal chaplain Matheus de Sancto Johanne, who came from the monastery of Saint-Jean in the diocese of Thérouanne, and had a benefice in the neighbouring diocese of Tournai.[170] 'Deo gratias' motets of probably English origin are 'Humane lingue organis / Supplicum voces / Deo gratias'[171] in the Fountains fragments (see below), and two fragmentary works in other English sources.[172] The genre of the 'Deo gratias' motet is also documented in the lateral traditions.[173]

The Fountains fragments,[174] from a codex written in 'white' (hollow) notation around 1400 (and thus at least a generation before this kind of notation became common), exhibit further continental connections. There is a Gloria also found in the Old Hall MS, and there attributed to an otherwise unknown 'Rowlard'. He could be Philippus Royllart, the composer of 'Rex Karole'. The piece is in a relatively simple chanson style and might be considered up-to-date for a northern French environment in the 1380s. There is also the motet 'Alme pater', arguably composed by an Englishman for Pope Urban VI in Italy (see pp. 16 f).[175]

The earliest-known keyboard tablature also belongs in the context of the lateral traditions. Craig Wright associates the Robertsbridge fragment (*GB-Lbl add.28850*) with the prisonership of King John of France in England, 1357-60.

---

[169] Hughes-Bent eds, *OH*, nos. 146 and 147. See Harrison, *Britain*, 226 ff; Bent, 'Progeny', 5-20; and p. 205.

[170] Tomasello, *Music and Ritual*, 252 f.

[171] Harrison ed., *Motets of English Provenance*, no. 36. See also Lefferts, *Motet*, 265.

[172] One is from a four-part motet 'O cipressus' ending with 'danda dei gratias' (communication from Margaret Bent) in the Maidstone fragment from Canterbury (see Bent-Bent, 'Dufay, Dunstable, Plummer', 397). The other is a Credo ending 'Deo gratias' (!), in *US-NYpm 978*.

[173] Strohm, *Bruges*, 29, 46, 104 f and 132. Marchetto da Padova composed such a work (see p. 96). For the 'Deo gratias' at the Council of Constance, see p. 114.

[174] *GB-Lbl add.40011 B*; *LoF* (the 'younger' Fountains fragments). See Bukofzer, *Studies*, 86-112; Lefferts, *Motet*, 265 f; *CC*, vol. 2, 77 f.

[175] Edited in Edward Kershaw ed., *The Fountains Fragments* (Newton Abbot: Antico Edition, 1988), nos. 2 and 18. Facs edn: Margaret Bent ed., *The Fountains Fragments* (London: Boethius Press, 1986).

The king liked instrumental music and was given an exchiquier for his private entertainment by Edward III.[176] Among the French musicians, who accompanied him to England and who could have disseminated pieces like those found in the Robertsbridge source, were Gace de la Buigne, King John's *magister capelle*,[177] and the chamber valet Perotus de Molyno (whom Wright identifies with the composer Pierre des Molins). By a strange coincidence, Pierre's two surviving compositions circulated widely within the lateral traditions and are found in instrumental arrangements in Germany and Italy.[178] In the Robertsbridge tablature, we find arrangements of two motets from the *Roman de Fauvel* and another Latin-texted piece, as well as two *estampies* and an untitled ballade arrangement. Both the chamber organ and the exchiquier would be suitable for performance. The keyboard notation is comparable to that of the earliest German organ tablatures from *c.*1425, but unlike the 'Italian' type of tablature in the Dutch Groningen fragment (see above). Nevertheless, the practice of arrangements as such connects all these four countries.

Much of the music collected in the royal Old Hall MS can be seen as the beginning of a new age. The earlier and main layer of the codex seems to have been copied *c.*1415–20 for the chapel of Duke Thomas of Clarence (*d.*1421), the younger brother of Henry V.[179] This was at a time when the English were attending the Council of Constance in large numbers, and when chapel musicians followed the Agincourt campaign of Henry V. This may have affected the style and outlook of the court composers, foremost among whom was Duke Thomas's chaplain, Lionel Power. It can be argued that even the traditional English discant settings collected in the earlier layer of the Old Hall MS partly absorb the influence of continental chanson style (see pp. 202 f). The pieces in isorhythmic and canonic techniques were, in relation to the English tradition, the work of an avant garde. And some of the music in simpler, chanson-related styles even belongs in the context of English–Continental interactions *after* the period of the Schism.

Italy

The secular music of fourteenth-century Italy has long received scholarly attention. The uniqueness of its mensural notation attracted musicologists such as Hugo Riemann and Johannes Wolf, and its poetry was studied by the nineteenth-century Italian poet and historian Giosué Carducci. Today there exist many recordings of the music, and more than one comprehensive edition of the

---

[176] Wright, *Burgundy*, 16 f and n. 29. On the manuscript, see Rokseth, 'Instrumental music', 419–22. Among the various edns, note PMFC, vol. 17, nos. 58–61, followed by some instrumental pieces from other English sources.

[177] Génévieve Hasenohr, 'Gace de la Bigne, maître chapelain de trois rois de France', in *Etudes de langue et de littérature du moyen age. Offertes à Félix Lecoy* (Paris: Champion, 1973), 181–9.

[178] Strohm, 'Ars nova fragments', 116 and n. 23; see also p. 93 below.

[179] Bowers, 'Some observations'; Bent, 'Progeny', 26 f.

secular polyphony.[180] Its foremost editor and researcher, Nino Pirrotta, has always stressed the significance of the lyrics for which this music was composed, and has suggested that the large and sometimes splendid manuscripts which contain it were intended as collections of poetry in the first place. A similar view might be held with regard to the manuscripts of Machaut's 'complete' works; but the Italian production, albeit dominated by Francesco Landini (*d.*1397), was a much more collective effort. Also, these musical lyrics intersect more with other aspects of Italian culture of the period, including sacred polyphony and a strong undercurrent of monophonic song and unwritten musical practices, which have been untapped in the writings of Pirrotta. The intersections with the works of the Italian classics, Dante Alighieri (1265-1321), Francesco Petrarca (1304-74) and Giovanni Boccaccio (1313-75), are few but significant.[181] Boccaccio mentions in his *Decamerone* (1348-53) many musical performances (all of them monophonic, it seems) within the Florentine circle whose pastimes he describes. He mentions actual songs which were performed, including his own, and the instruments which were used. This is one of the features which Chaucer imitated in the *Canterbury Tales*.

The Florentine Franco Sacchetti (*c.*1332-1400) was the most prolific author of musical lyrics. His *Libro delle rime*[182] contains many poems, arranged in chronological order, which illustrate contemporary life and ideas in a fashion comparable to the work of Eustache Deschamps. Sacchetti names the authors of 34 polyphonic settings of his poems, including himself, Landini, and other known musicians such as Jacopo da Bologna, Gherardello, Giovanni da Cascia, Nicolò da Perugia and Lorenzo da Firenze. Other contemporary and later writers also pay respect to musicians, for example Giovanni Gherardi da Prato in his *Paradiso degli Alberti* (*c.*1420) and Filippo Villani in his chronicle of Florence. In both these narrations, Landini is very honourably mentioned. The awareness of music and poetry as contributors to civilization in general, and the focus on the outstanding artist, are surely traits which typify the Italian Renaissance. This would support the view of Hugo Riemann who described this music as part of a *Florentinische Frührenaissance*. More recent scholars have, more wisely perhaps, separated Italian fourteenth-century music from the Renaissance. Kurt von Fischer uses the neutral term 'Trecento music',[183] and Nino Pirrotta adopts 'Ars nova' for it, emphasizing not so much its French

[180] Nino Pirrotta ed., *The Music of Fourteenth-Century Italy*, CMM 8/1-5 (Rome: AIM, 1954-64); Thomas W. Marrocco ed., *Italian Secular Music* (PMFC, vols. 2, 7, 8, 9, 10 and 11; 1956-78).

[181] Nino Pirrotta, 'Dante "musicus": gothicism, scholasticism and music', *Speculum* 43 (1968), 245-57; also in *idem*, *Music and Culture*, 13-25; *idem*, 'Ars nova and Stil novo', *Music and Culture*, 26-38; Pierluigi Petrobelli, '"Un leggiadretto velo" e altre cose petrarchesche', *RIM* 10 (1975), 34-45.

[182] Franco Sacchetti, *Il libro delle rime*, ed. Alberto Chiari (Bari: Laterza, 1936); *idem*, *Le rime*, ed. Franca Brambilla Ageno (Florence: Olschki, 1989). See also Gallo, *Music of the Middle Ages II*, ch. III.16; *idem*, 'The musical and literary tradition of fourteenth-century poetry set to music', in Günther-Finscher eds, *Musik und Text*, 55-76.

[183] For example in his fundamental *Studien*. In a recent study, however, he develops sympathies with Riemann's view: Kurt von Fischer, 'Sprache und Musik im italienischen Trecento: Zur Frage einer Frührenaissance', in Günther-Finscher eds, *Musik und Text*, 37-54.

connections as its peculiar freshness. For the decades around 1400 that we shall discuss, the issues of 'national' independence and of innovation appear indeed to be related.

It is likely that early Italian polyphonists such as Magister Piero, Jacopo da Bologna and Giovanni da Cascia developed forms and styles from popular and unwritten models. This is the more remarkable as they served (around 1350) a select, aristocratic society at the courts of Verona and Milan. The genres which they cultivated were the madrigal, a uniquely Italian form, and the *caccia*, which is analogous to (but distinct from) the French *chace* and other forms of strict canon known in several countries. The madrigal received its name probably from 'carmen matricalis', that is, a poem in the mother tongue. This distinguished it from the learned Latin poetry of the Church and the universities, and made it more accessible to the secular nobility, whose heraldic, pastoral and amorous interests it reflected. The *caccia*, with its naturalistic or even 'impressionistic' portrayals of hunting or similar social activities, similarly celebrated the life of an élite.

Truly popular, however, was the ballata, which in the mid-fourteenth century was often set monophonically (but mensurally). The genre belongs to a wide European network of dance-songs such as the French and English carol(e) and the Spanish cantiga. Formally similar is the Italian sacred *lauda*, which at least in the thirteenth century must have been used for religious dances and remained an ingredient of processions and pilgrimages. The ballata is also formally close to the French virelai, at least in its repetition scheme of *ripresa* (refrain), *mutazione* (*ouvert/clos*) and *volta* (tierce):

Text	a	b b′	c	a
Music	A	B B	A	A
	ripresa	*mutazione*	*volta*	*ripresa*

(This scheme represents a single stanza; the *ripresa* may not be repeated after each stanza, if there is more than one.)

In the later fourteenth century, the ballata had become a poetic art form with different sub-genres, which writers of the time classified according to the number of lines they contained. This distinguished it from the virelai which was freer in its rhyme-scheme. This later, literary ballata rarely indulges in the naturalistic imagery of the French 'mimetic' virelais; it was the *caccia* that performed this function. Where such ballata texts occur, their sense is more often figurative or satirical, as it was in some madrigals and *caccie* as well.

The achievement of Florentine bourgeois poets and composers around Francesco Landini is that they widened the stylistic and expressive range of the ballata. Nicolò da Perugia, Andrea de' Servi (*d.*1415) and Paolo da Firenze (*d.*1419), among others, made it a musically complex genre in which they covered every imaginable secular topic. The texts and the music of Landini's 141 ballate, in particular, range from the erotic, the pastoral, the descriptive to the contemplative, the moral and the political. He wrote at least some of the poems himself. A (non-musical) sonnet by him was entered into Sacchetti's poetry collection, and he is the author of a long Latin poem which apparently honours the philosophy of William of Ockham. Landini's ballata 'Contemplar le gran cose c'è onesto' ('To contemplate the great things, that is worthy') expresses clearly and in simple form the basic tenets of Ockham's theology: the distinction between intellect and faith which frees both these human capabilities to pursue their own goals.[184] It has been argued that these 'Ockhamist' texts show Landini to be a sympathizer of pro-Franciscan and even pro-French circles in Florence, as opposed to Italian nationalist and anti-Avignon trends nourished by Petrarch's political ideas. In fact, Landini wrote a madrigal in praise of Philippe de Vitry: 'Si dolce non sonò con lir' Orfeo' ('Not even Orpheus with the lyre sang so sweetly').[185] This 'song about music' quotes mythical musicians, and alludes to the French composer as a 'singing cock' ('gallo'). The isorhythm of the concluding section of the madrigal, the ritornello, is a musical reference to Vitry.

The veiled allusions and the ambiguous language give the piece a greater subtlety than, for example, Jacopo da Bologna's madrigal and *caccia* over the text 'Oselletto selvaggio per stagione' ('Little bird of the woods, in the spring season'). This poem directs the bird metaphor against uneducated but ambitious singers who all want to be masters like Philippe and Marchetto. (The imagery recurs with the same polemical intent in Senleches's virelai 'En ce gracieux': see p. 56.) Landini's madrigal already points to the *subtilitas* and disembodied imagery of Ciconia's homage to Philipoctus, 'Sus un fontayne'.

Francophile tendencies in Florence have been contrasted, perhaps too sharply, with a more traditionalist and nationalist approach of north Italian musicians such as Bartolino da Padova (see below). Compositional and notational traits that can pass as 'French-influenced' include coloured notation and proportions, the musical differentiation of *ouvert/clos* (*verto/chiuso*) in the ballata, the omission of text from the tenor, and the replacement of the traditional second upper voice in three-part writing with a contratenor. The peculiar Italian notational system, as first described in Marchetto da Padova's *Pomerium* (1326), divided the breve in 4, 6, 8, 9 or 12 smaller values, setting breve-units apart between dots. It differentiated the smaller values by stems and flags, and had its own rules for what the French were calling 'alteration' and 'imperfection'. Many of these native features tend to disappear in the late copies of the music which we have, and yield to procedures more compatible with the French system of the *quatre prolations* as designed by Vitry and Jehan des Murs.[186]

Nationalist or restorative tendencies have been said to prevail in the writings

---

[184] Michael F. Long, 'Landini and the Florentine cultural élite', *EMH* 4 (1984), 83–99.

[185] Kurt von Fischer, 'Philippe de Vitry in Italy and an homage of Landini to Philippe', *L'Ars Nova* 4 (1975), 225–35.

[186] This process has first been outlined in von Fischer, *Studien*. See also Apel, *Notation*, 368–402; Michael F. Long, *Musical Tastes in 14th-Century Italy: Notational Styles, Scholarly Traditions, and Historical Circumstances*, Ph.D., Princeton U., 1981, chaps. II–V.

of the leading Italian theorist after 1400, Prosdocimus de Beldemandis of Padua (*d*.1428).[187] But his treatise which explicitly teaches Italian notational tradition (*Tractatus pratice cantus mensurabilis ad modum Ytalicorum*, 1412) is only one of his varied works. In the same city, Johannes Ciconia wrote treatises which transmitted his broad, Franco-Italian learning to his colleagues and pupils.[188] A common goal of the two men may have been to keep the divergent traditions alive, distinguishing between them simply for the sake of didactic clarity.

A more problematic oeuvre is that of Bartolino da Padova (*fl.* 1380–1400), whose heraldic madrigals for courtly employers have been seen as a restoration of the older genre and style. But there is some doubt about their actual dates, and indeed about their political orientation, which might have influenced the style. His madrigal 'La douce chiere' is an ambiguous work in more than one sense:[189]

Example 10 Bartolino da Padova, 'La douce chiere'

[187] For biography, edns and literature, see F. Alberto Gallo, 'Prosdocimus de Beldemandis' in *The New Grove*.

[188] Suzanne Clercx, 'Johannes Ciconia théoricien', *AnnM* 3 (1955), 39–75.

[189] Marrocco ed., *Italian Secular Music* (PMFC, vol. 9), no. 11; Nigel Wilkins ed., Bartolino da Padova, *Three Madrigals* (Newton Abbot: Antico Edition, 1976).

Example 10 (*cont.*)

d'un   fier   a - ni - mal

Typically Italian are the cadence of cantus and tenor in the unison (bar 12; the piece also ends in that way) and the rapidly alternating divisions of the breve into six or eight minims. The declamation of the French words is not idiomatic; the treatment of the inessential contratenor, on the other hand, is typically French. The text refers to armorial devices, perhaps of the Visconti (which could explain the French features) or perhaps of the Carrara dynasty of Padua. Bartolino also composed a more unambiguously Italianate madrigal praising the Carraras ('Imperiale sedendo', probably 1401). His madrigal 'La fiera testa' clearly describes the Visconti arms – but we do not know whether in support or defiance of that dynasty.[190] These works by Bartolino were widely copied; they are not individual oddities but mirror the political and cultural contrasts of his country.

The divergent efforts either to separate or to integrate Italian and French procedures, which reflected the uneasy 'fraternity' between the two countries, reached a climax around 1400 or shortly after. To start with the simplest generalization: French language and French song were used and performed in many centres.[191] Of course, those who wished to enrich the indigenous repertory with French music, also studied and used its musical notation. Many manuscript collections contain the imported material. Whereas the Florentine Panciatichi Codex (*I-Fn 26*) is essentially an anthology of native songs (mainly by Landini), to which some Ars subtilior pieces were added later,[192] the Tuscan collection *F-Pn 568* (*Pit*) mixes native and French songs almost indiscriminately.[193] The

[190] On these historical and stylistic questions, see Pierluigi Petrobelli, 'Some dates for Bartolino da Padova', in Powers ed., *Studies in Music History*, 85-111.

[191] For some details, see Fallows, 'French as a courtly language', 429-32.

[192] Gallo ed., *Codice Panciatichi*; John Nádas, 'The structure of MS Panciatichi 26 and the transmission of Trecento polyphony', *JAMS* 34 (1981), 393-415.

[193] Gilbert Reaney, 'The manuscript Paris, Bibliothèque Nationale, fonds italien 568 (*Pit*)', *MD* 14 (1960), 33-63; Ursula Günther, 'Zur Datierung des Madrigals "Godi, Firenze" und der Handschrift Paris, B.N. fonds it. 568 (*Pit*)', *AMw* 24 (1967), 99-119.

Reina Codex (*F-Pn n. a. f. 6771*) from Venice or Padua, *c.*1400, represents in one book two collections clearly distinguished by language.[194]

The famous Squarcialupi Codex (*I-Fl 87; Sq*), compiled by the versatile composer and theorist Don Paolo da Firenze *c.*1415-19, is intended as a monument to the great Italian song composers and poets. Paolo arranged the music chronologically according to the time of the composers' deaths, leaving empty space for works by living composers.[195] At least one other large manuscript was produced in Florence around that time with a similarly 'antiquarian' intent: the collection San Lorenzo 2211 (*I-Fl 2211*).[196] In contrast to this approach, the Florentine collection *GB-Lbl add.29987* (*Lo*) liberally accepts foreign and even instrumental music.[197] Florentine society did not only employ foreign musicians in church: a certain Giovanni di Daniele di Fiandra (i.e. of Flanders) is cited in 1402 as the teacher of two boys who used to sing for the *signoria* (the city magistrate), probably at banquets.[198] One wonders which pieces or languages they used.

The pastimes of Italian secular society – noble and high-bourgeois – are amusingly illustrated in Simone Prodenzani's epic *Il Saporetto* (*c.*1425).[199] It features the musical performances of a fictitious character, Solazzo, who with his friends sings or plays ballate and other pieces, most of which are cited with the names of their composers: from Jacopo da Bologna and Bartolino da Padova to Antonius Zacharias and Johannes Ciconia. He sings popular songs from different Italian regions and plays Spanish and German tunes on the 'Flemish organs' ('organi framegni'), dance-tunes on bagpipe and lute, madrigals on the harp, and liturgical pieces as well as polyphonic chansons ('La harpe de melodie', for example) on the organ.

Solazzo's repertory is largely identifiable in north Italian collections of *c.*1400-1420, and his keyboard playing neatly fits the evidence of the north Italian Faenza MS (*I-FZc 117*).[200] This is the earliest surviving large codex of polyphony in tablature, compiled perhaps *c.*1410-20, and an extraordinary monu-

---

[194] Kurt von Fischer, 'The manuscript Paris, Bibl. Nat., Nouv. Acq. Frç. 6771 (Codex *Reina* = *PR*)', *MD* 11 (1957), 38-78; Nigel Wilkins, 'The codex Reina: a revised description', *MD* 17 (1963), 57-73; Kurt von Fischer, 'Reply to N. Wilkins' article', *MD* 17 (1963), 75-7.

[195] I.e. by himself and by the Florentine organist Giovanni Manzuoli. See Kurt von Fischer, 'Paolo da Firenze und der Squarcialupi-Codex', *Quadrivium* 9 (1969), 5-24. On Paolo's biography, see Ursula Günther, John Nádas and John A. Stinson, 'Magister Dominus Paulus Abbas de Florentia: new documentary evidence', in Günther ed., *1380-1430: An International Style?*, 203-46.

[196] Much of the music has been erased. See Frank D'Accone, 'Una nuova fonte dell'Ars Nova Italiana: Il codice di San Lorenzo 2211', *Studi Musicali* 13 (1984), 3-31.

[197] Facs edn: Gilbert Reaney ed., *The Manuscript London, B.M. add.29987*, MSD 13 (Rome: AIM, 1965); Gilbert Reaney, 'The manuscript London, B.M.Add.29987', *MD* 12 (1958), 67-91. Generally on Florentine manuscripts, see John Nádas, 'Song collections in late medieval Florence', in Strohm (chairman), *Costituzione e conservazione*, 126-37.

[198] Gino Corti, 'Un musicista fiammingo a Firenze agli inizi del Quattrocento', *L'Ars Nova* 4 (1975), 177-81.

[199] Santorre Debenedetti ed., *Il 'Solazzo' e il 'Saporetto' con altre rime di Simone Prudenzani d'Orvieto* (Turin, 1913).

[200] First described by Dragan Plamenac. See Dragan Plamenac ed., *Keyboard Music of the Late Middle Ages in Codex Faenza 117*, CMM 57 (Rome: AIM, 1972). Facs edn: Armen Carapetyan ed., *The Codex Faenza, Biblioteca Comunale, 117 (Fa)*, MSD 10 (Rome: AIM, 1961).

ment to musical techniques as well as musical life. As for the latter, the 48 pieces (of which ten can be identified as involving sacred plainsongs) seem to have belonged to the repertory of keyboard players who used to arrange all kinds of music for their purposes. Sixteen pieces have titles identifying them as French songs, and fourteen have Italian titles. Most of the originals are known from collections of the time, for example the older part of the Reina Codex; the selection is typical for the 'lateral traditions'. Two pieces are probably *estampies*: (no. 21, labelled 'Tumpes' (i.e. perhaps 'Stampes') and no. 23). There are also some arrangements of possibly monophonic dance tunes – among them the titles 'Sangilio' (no. 22) and 'Belfiore dança' (no. 36) which have been interpreted as pointing to Ferrarese provenance. 'Belfiore' was, in fact, the name of a famous palace owned by the Este family.[201] The codex was found in the Carmelite friary of Ferrara, where it can be traced back to the fifteenth century (on its use by Carmelite musicians of John Hothby's circle, see p. 298). It may, therefore, be suggested that the compiler and first owner was a Carmelite friar of Ferrara, who played polyphonic keyboard music in church as well as for entertainment, for example in aristocratic houses. Also one of Solazzo's musical friends in the *Saporetto* was a friar, 'frate Agustino'; and one of the composers whose *canzoni* were performed and praised by the author was called 'frate Biasgo' (i.e. Blasius). A certain Blasius de Este was master of the choirboys at Padua Cathedral in 1421; he probably came from the town of Este in the neighbourhood.[202]

Three more Italian specimens of tablature exist from the same period. Two pieces, one of which is an arrangement of Landini's famous ballata 'Questa fanciulla, Amor', are found in the older part of the Reina Codex (*c.*1400); there is a fragment, probably of Paduan origin (*I-Pas 553*; *c.*1400), with the plainsong elaboration of a Gloria, and there is a somewhat later Kyrie, also over a plainsong, from Umbria (*I-Ac 187*).[203]

The notation and technique of the Faenza arrangements have often been discussed.[204] Because of the layout in score and the essential analogies with the other early keyboard scores (including the Robertsbridge and Groningen fragments: see pp. 83 f), there is hardly any doubt that the function of the Italian manuscripts was to serve keyboard players. The Italian and Groningen sources have in common with each other, and with later Italian keyboard tablatures, the use of mensural notation in score for both hands. Some individual transcrip-

---

[201] Adriano Cavicchi, 'Sacro e profano. Documenti e note su Bartolomeo da Bologna e gli organisti della cattedrale di Ferrara nel primo Quattrocento', *RIM* 10 (1975), 46–71.

[202] See also Allan W. Atlas, 'On the identity of some musicians at the Brescian Court of Pandolfo III Malatesta', *CMc* 36 (1983), 11 n. 6.

[203] See, respectively, Rokseth, 'Instrumental music', 423; Cattin, 'Ricerche S. Giustina', 32 f and pl. VI; Agostino Ziino, 'Un antico "kyrie" a due voci per strumento a tastiera', *NRMI* 15 (1981), 628–31. *I-Ac 187* and *I-Pas 553* are transcribed in PMFC, vol. 13, nos. A 1 and A 2.

[204] See, in particular, Michael Kugler, *Die Tastenmusik im Codex Faenza* (Tutzing: Schneider, 1972). For the musical style of the arrangements, see also p. 122 below; for questions of notation and later sources, see pp. 368–70 below.

tions may have originated for performance on lutes and harps.[205] This might be the case with those pieces where overlapping ranges cause awkward crossings of the hands. The problem can be solved on the keyboard, however, by octave displacements, particularly in the left hand.[206]

It seems as if these Italian sources were related not only to the organ (used as a polyphonic instrument), or the exchiquier or clavichord (called 'menacordo' by Prodenzani), but to an often-forgotten historical event for which there is documentary evidence: the invention of the harpsichord (It: *clavicembalo*). In 1397 the Paduan lawyer Giovanni Lambertacci wrote to his son-in-law, then at university in Pavia, that his friend Hermannus Poll, from Vienna, a medical doctor most expert in various musical instruments, had invented an instrument which he called *clavicembalum*.[207] The extraordinary biography of this Viennese doctor has since come to light.[208] He completed his wide-ranging studies in Pavia in the 1390s – the place and time of Gian Galeazzo Visconti's musical patronage – and in 1400 became the physician of the new German king, Ruprecht of the Palatinate. Within a year, he fell victim to an allegation of having attempted to poison the king on the instigation of Gian Galeazzo. At this time, not only the political tensions, but also the cultural connections, between the Carrara dynasty of Padua and the Visconti of Lombardy focused precisely on the alliance with or against the German king, who was preparing to campaign in northern Italy. It is tempting to think that Padua and Pavia, the two university cities where Poll had contacts, were also at the forefront of the development of polyphonic instrumental music. (See also pp. 58 f on Jacob de Senleches.) Whether or not Hermann Poll was really a paid agent of the Visconti and a murderer, he was executed in Nuremberg in 1401, leaving behind the memory of 'an outstanding physician, handsome, well-mannered, 31-year-

---

[205] Robert Huestis, *Transcriptions from the Faenza Codex* (Westwood: Author, 1971); Timothy J. McGee, 'Instruments and the Faenza Codex', *Early Music* 14 (1986), 480–90. McGee goes too far in proposing that most early keyboard tablatures should be 'reclassified as for lute, harp and/or keyboard' (p. 488). The score notation is impractical for more than one player, and there is overwhelming pictorial evidence against the use of written music by harpists or lutenists at that time. McGee denies the existence of double-stops in Faenza, concluding from their *absence* that 'none of the manuscript's contents were for keyboard' (p. 484). As a matter of fact, there are double-stops in six pieces (nos. 3, 9, 17, 23, 26 and 41). They are also present in *I-Pas 553* – a source close in place and time which McGee does not mention. On the other hand, he suggests that the German arrangement 'tenor bonus III. Petri' (see p. 373) is for lute duet: its top line has 33 double-stops and one quadruple-stop.

[206] Contemporary instruments had ranges of approximately three octaves, making it possible to play the lower voice an octave lower, i.e. 'at pitch', since they were 4' instruments. Alfons Huber, 'Baugrößen von Saitenklavieren im 15. Jahrhundert', in *Musik und Tanz zur Zeit Kaiser Maximilians I.*, ed. by W. Salmen (Innsbruck: Helbling, 1992), 153–175; Edward M. Ripin–Howard Schott, 'Harpsichord, #I' in *The New Grove*.

[207] André Pirro, 'Pour l'histoire de la musique', *AcM* 3 (1931), 51.

[208] Standley Howell, 'Medical astrologers and the invention of stringed keyboard instruments', *Journal of Musicological Research* 10 (1990), 3–17; Reinhard Strohm, 'Die private Kunst und das öffentliche Schicksal von Hermann Poll, dem Erfinder des Cembalos', in *Musica Privata. Die Rolle der Musik im privaten Leben. Festschrift für Walter Salmen zum 65. Geburtstag* (Innsbruck: Helbling, 1991), 53–66.

old master of arts, very literate and a doctor of medicine, an excellent musician on the organ and other musical instruments'.[209]

By 1420 the effects of the Schism and the buoyant commerce with the north had drawn many foreign musicians, and their vocal or instrumental skills, to Italy. This wave of immigration and importation had finally submerged the last branches of the Ars subtilior which had flourished in Lombardy and perhaps elsewhere. It seems that this process had begun not at the secular courts, but in the cathedrals and in the papal chapel in Rome – with sacred music.[210]

Liturgical polyphony of a simple kind had existed in the fourteenth century all over the peninsula. The path to elaborate church polyphony was sought around 1370 by some Florentine composers who imitated the style of the native madrigal but also adopted elements of the primitive traditions.[211] The Roman popes from 1378, however, preferred Franco-Netherlands polyphony. It was performed in the papal chapel by foreign chaplains, together with native singers from the papal territories in central Italy. This must be the reason why several manuscript fragments of mostly foreign sacred music are now found in central Italian places such as Cortona, Perugia, Foligno, Todi, Atri, Rome itself, and Grottaferrata: local cathedrals absorbed music which had reached the peninsula through papal chaplains.[212] The most important source, the choirbook fragment of Grottaferrata (*I-GR 197*), contains the Gloria 'Qui sonitu melodie' and the Credo 'Bonbarde', for example.[213] *I-FOL* has an English and two French settings of the Gloria,[214] *I-Rvat 1419* a 'Kyrie rondello' in the form of a French rondeau, as well as the Kyrie 'Summe clementissime' by Johannes Graneti, a work also known from French and Spanish manuscripts.[215] These sources also include French chansons – by Vaillant, Trebor, Pierre des Molins and Philipoctus – which may have been performed by the same chaplains. A smaller but comparable group of pieces survives in Cividale (Friuli), where Pope Gregory XII held a Council in 1409.[216] The composer Antonio da Cividale (Antonius de Civitate Austrie), probably a papal chaplain then, is represented in the Cividale fragments with a two-voice Gloria in a primitive style, quite unlike his other (and probably later) works.[217] We also find the Credo 'de rege'

[209] Jacob Grob, 'Bruchstücke der Luxemburger Kaiserchronik des Deutschen Hauses in Luxemburg', *Publications de la section historique de l'Institut Grand-Ducal de Luxembourg*, vol. 52 (1903), 398.

[210] Von Fischer–Gallo eds, *Italian Sacred Music* (PMFC, vol. 12); idem, *Italian Sacred and Ceremonial Music* (PMFC, vol. 13), and the review of PMFC vol. 12 by Margaret Bent in *JAMS* 32 (1979), 561–77. For discussion, see Bill J. Layton, *Italian Music for the Ordinary of the Mass, 1300-1450*, Ph.D., Harvard U., 1960; Kurt von Fischer, 'The sacred polyphony of the Italian Trecento', *PRMA* 100 (1973-4), 143-57.

[211] Kurt von Fischer, 'Il ciclo dell'Ordinarium Missae del MS F-Pn 568 (*Pit*)', *L'Ars Nova* 5 (1985), 123-37.

[212] For source list and bibliography, see PMFC, vol. 13, 260 f and 290 ff.

[213] Ursula Günther, 'Quelques remarques sur des feuillets récemment découverts à Grottaferrata', *L'Ars Nova* 3 (1970), 315-97.

[214] Janet Palumbo, 'The Foligno fragment: a reassessment of three polyphonic Glorias, ca. 1400', *JAMS* 40 (1987), 169-209.

[215] See the comments on the edns in PMFC, vol. 12, no. 1, and vol. 13, no. 1.

[216] Inventory in *RISM B IV*, vol. 4, 746-54.

[217] Edited in Reaney ed., *EFM*, vol. 5 (1975).

by Sortes, and a rather Italianate Credo by Philipoctus de Caserta.[218] An intriguing Gloria fragment by Rentius de Ponte Curvo, a priest of Cividale, 1407–8, is composed over a non-Mass chant, the responsory 'Descendit angelus'.[219] Is this a relation of the 'Christmas Gloria' from Ghent (see p. 68)?

Many music fragments of Paduan origin attest to a vivid polyphonic practice around 1390–1420 in that cathedral, and in the local abbey of Santa Giustina.[220] Ciconia is documented as having been at the cathedral from 1401 until his death in 1412. The other known musicians include the composer Gratiosus de Padua[221] and the copyist Rolandus de Casale, a monk of Santa Giustina, who compiled several music books, partly of large size, repeatedly adding his signature. Some of the codices must have been commissioned from outside, because the Benedictine reform which began in 1407 severely restricted vocal polyphony in the abbey. The resemblance of the surviving Paduan manuscripts to Netherlands *libri motetorum* is striking. Although fragmentary, it is clear that the backbone of their contents was the Mass Ordinary, with interspersed motets and chansons in both French and Italian, possibly intended for the instruction of the choirboys and for clerical entertainment. The many foreign works include the Credo 'Bonbarde' (labelled 'Perneth'), Senleches's virelai 'En ce gracieux', and a Sanctus–Agnus pair headed 'Sant Omer' which recalls the modal rhythms in the older sections of the 'Mass of Tournai'[222] (see Ex. 11). This was surely not a local composition: its title must refer to the town in the Artois from where it came. In the same fragment, however, a Sanctus 'Barbitonsoris' exhibiting the same archaic rhythms could be a local imitation. A Sanctus 'Mediolano', on the other hand, seems a companion-piece to the Credo 'Bonbarde' with its syncopations and thick, four-voice texture. It is of little consequence whether the title

Example 11 Sanctus 'Sant Omer', Padua fragments

[218] PMFC, vol. 12, no. 14.
[219] PMFC, vol. 13, no. A 3.
[220] Cattin, 'Ricerche S. Giustina'; Inventory: *RISM B IV*, vol. 4, 668–71 and 989–1002.
[221] On him, see Anne Hallmark, 'Gratiosus, Ciconia and other musicians at Padua Cathedral: some footnotes to present knowledge', *L'Ars Nova* 6 (1992), 69–84.
[222] From *I-Pu 1475*, no. 1.

Example 11 (*cont.*)

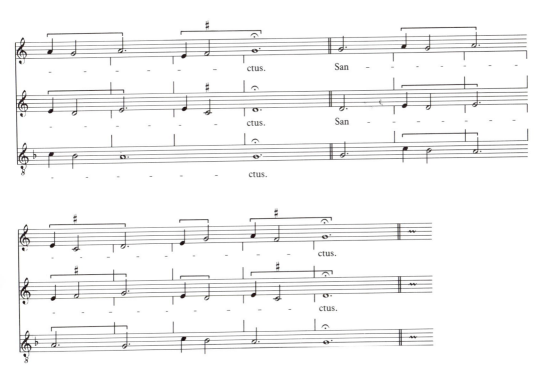

refers to the place of composition (Milan) or a composer 'X. de Mediolano'.[223] We cannot precisely delineate a local Paduan repertory in these fragments, nor should we: the ecclesiastical network must have provided contacts with many other cathedrals, and with the papal chapel.[224]

An influential composer who seems to have moved within this network was the Fleming Magister Egardus.[225] As mentioned above, his full name was Johannes Ecghaerd, and he was succentor in Bruges in 1370–1, but left for Italy around 1390. He may perhaps be identified with a papal *scriptor* 'Eckardus' of 1394. Of his three surviving works, the most unusual is a Latin canon in which he probably addresses his former student at Bruges, Thomas Fabri. In a strictly isorhythmic Gloria, Egardus uses French mensurations and rhythmic detail often found in Avignonese Mass settings; but the upper voices share the text in alternating phrases, a textural device which has been regarded as typically Italian. Egardus may have composed the piece in the north, as it was also copied in a Flemish manuscript of the time (*NL-Uu 37 I*). Another three-voice

223 The pieces 'Barbitonsoris' and 'Mediolano' are in *PMFC*, vol. 12, nos. 19 and 18.
224 Ann Hallmark, 'Some evidence for French influence in northern Italy, c.1400', in Boorman ed., *Studies*, 193–226.
225 Strohm, 'Magister Egardus'.

Gloria, freely composed, has a chanson-like distribution of voices (tenor and contratenor share the same range), but gives text to all three of them, as was usual in Italy. Here, the textural interest is produced by the non-simultaneous word-underlay in all the voices. The voices seem to speak to each other in perfectly natural declamation – a novelty for the contratenor – although not in actual imitation.[226] The work evidently influenced one of the best-known Mass settings by Ciconia, his Gloria–Credo pair, nos. 1–2,[227] where the gentle dialogue of Egardus's voices is enhanced to almost dramatic scenes.

If Ciconia imitated a work by a Netherlander active in Italy, questions not only of style but also of biography arise.[228] According to the present state of knowledge, Ciconia cannot have been born much before 1370. If he arrived in Italy about 1390 or later, he must have collected considerable musical experience in the north, quite possibly as a choirboy at Liège Cathedral. As a cleric of the staunchly 'Urbanist' (i.e. pro-Roman) diocese of Liège, he would not have dreamed of going first to Avignon. But Milan is possible, where he seems to have dedicated his piece of apprenticeship in the Ars subtilior idiom, 'Sus un fontayne', to Philipoctus de Caserta. In 1401 he surfaced in Padua as the holder of a modest clerical benefice bestowed by the powerful patron Francesco Zabarella, archpriest of the cathedral, in whose honour Ciconia wrote two of his splendid ceremonial motets, 'Doctorum principem / Melodia' and 'Ut te per omnes celitum / Ingens alumnus'. Others praise Paduan and Venetian dignitaries, and the two cities themselves. (The 'Most Serene Republic' had conquered Padua from the Carrara family in 1405 and thus became Ciconia's overlord.) Ciconia's ascribed motets, like his Italian songs (see below), must all have been written in the last decade of his life, which ended in 1412.

With his motets, Ciconia has been said to be indebted exclusively to Italian tradition.[229] This tradition is not documented by many works but is certainly distinct. Its founder is Marchetto da Padova, not only with his treatise *Pomerium* which is in essence an *ars mottetorum*, but also with the motet 'Ave regina celorum / Mater innocentie / Ite missa est'.[230] The text includes his name as an acrostic. This work is a 'Deo gratias' substitute. Its liturgical tenor is in the middle voice, as in English discant and in the 'Deo gratias' motet concluding the 'Mass of Tournai'. Later Italian motet composers are mostly anonymous, although Landini may be among them. Isorhythm, where at all found in these

---

[226] PMFC, vol. 12, no. 7.

[227] Ciconia, *Works*, nos. 1–2.

[228] The most detailed biographical account has been offered by Suzanne Clercx-Lejeune, *Johannes Ciconia. Un musicien liégeois et son temps (vers 1335–1411)*, 2 vols. (Brussels, 1960). The presumed birthdate of *c*.1335 and its implications have been challenged by David Fallows, 'Ciconia padre e figlio', *RIM* 11 (1976), 171–7. A summary of the biography as accepted here is given by Margaret Bent and Anne Hallmark in Ciconia, *Works*, introduction.

[229] Ciconia, *Works*, introduction, p. xii. See also Margaret Bent, 'The fourteenth-century Italian motet', *L'Ars Nova* 6 (1992), 85–125 . Works by other composers are in PMFC, vols. 12 and 13.

[230] F. Alberto Gallo, 'Marchetus in Padua und die "francovenetische" Musik des frühen Trecento', *AMw* 31 (1974), 42–56.

works, remains simple; sometimes the tenor is restated identically in more than one section. A soloistic *introitus* for an upper voice is occasionally prefixed. The two upper voices tend to be equal in range and function, as is also the case in much secular music of the Italian Trecento. It must be said, however, that these traits are also found in motets from France and the Low Countries which were copied in Italy at the time. They include such well-travelled works as 'Impudenter circuivi' (probably by Vitry), 'Rex Karole', 'Almifonis melos', 'Apollinis eclipsatur', 'Apta caro' and others, which cannot be discarded as possible models for Ciconia.

Only four of Ciconia's eight extant motets[231] have an isorhythmic layout in tenor and contratenor; *talea* and *color* always coincide. This amounts to simple restatements of the lower voices, above which the upper voices also repeat their rhythms, except in 'Doctorum principem'. This work presents the tenor / contratenor in three different mensurations, producing drastic changes in the four-part texture; more textural articulation results from duet passages and rhythmic patterning of long stretches of music. Internal repetitions of such textures even cut across the three basic sections, and the melodic contours of the upper voices recur in each section in analogous places. That Ciconia can use melody and texture as structural elements is due to his rich invention. We have only to look at the opening passages of Example 12 to confirm this. Besides the various rhythmic and textural patterns displayed here, there is also a broadly planned harmonic feeling. The opening is like a grand portal over the F chord, performed as a melisma on the vowel 'O'. The long stop with a pre-cadential sonority in bars 6-7 is unexpectedly resolved by the top voice alone in bar 8. Bars 15-17 prolong a G chord (oscillating with F) with just the rhythms used

Example 12 Johannes Ciconia, 'Doctorum principem / Melodia suavissima'

[231] Ciconia, *Works*, nos. 12-19. Two other works, nos. 20-21, are probably by Ciconia.

97

Example 12 (*cont.*)

Example 12 (*cont.*)

de - tur o - pe - ra

earlier for F. Also the text and its meaning are involved: bar 18, 'ergo' ('there-fore') is clearly a resolution and a new beginning. The relationship of the voices in the whole work is that of a tenor foundation to which the upper voice-pair is added. Also the contratenor must have been designed from the start, as is demonstrated by its mirror-like reflection of the tenor in the opening bars. For sections two and three, pitch and rhythm of the tenor / contratenor foundation were predetermined in any case.

In a strictly technical sense, then, Ciconia did not compose this work from the upper voice-pair down to the accompanying tenor, as has been claimed to be the technique of his motets. Nevertheless, the melodic–rhythmic behaviour of the upper voices, and the sound of the whole texture, do recall older Italian music where the upper voice-pair was primary. The sources of Ciconia's style emanate both from Italy and the northern tradition. Openings in echo imitation between the upper voices, for example, are not only typically Italian but also found in 'Rex Karole' and in motets by Hubertus de Salinis.[232] Text-sharing between the upper voices characterizes not only Ciconia's motets 'O felix tem-plum' and 'O Padua sidus', but also the isorhythmic Gloria by Magister Egardus (see above), where the rhythmic–melodic detail, furthermore, strikingly resem-bles passages of 'Doctorum principem'. The practice of two equal top parts in the same range can be traced in northern performance practices well before 1400. Archival documents tell us that choirboys were often required to sing passages of the Mass on their own, especially the Gloria trope 'Spiritus et alme'. A Gloria in the Flemish source *NL-Uu 37 I* has high duet passages for precisely those sections, although it is otherwise in the conventional three parts with a low contratenor.[233] The practice of dividing the cantus part in two for special

[232] Published in Reaney ed., *EFM*, vol. 7 (1983).
[233] Metha-Machteld van Delft, 'Een Gloria-Fragment in de Universiteitsbibliotheek te Utrecht', *TVNM* 19 (1960), 84–5; Strohm, *Bruges*, 52 and 105.

sections is widespread in Italian Mass music after 1400 until Dufay's genera-tion.[234] It is almost the norm in the settings by Hubertus de Salinis, who was a contemporary of Ciconia from the diocese of Liège. Like Ciconia, he left a single *essay* in the Ars subtilior style, the ballade 'En la saison' written before 1398 for the du Guesclin family. His Latin-texted works all survive in Italian sources, and it can be surmised that he was active in Florence around 1410.[235] His Gloria 'Jubilatio' praises the end of the Schism, but may refer to the election of Pope Alexander V at Pisa in 1409 rather than to 1417. It is also contained in the Flemish source quoted above, *NL-Uu 37 I*.[236]

We must now turn to the most important Italian composer of this time, whose music epitomizes the questions of Italian independence and innovation. Antonius dictus Zacharias, from Teramo in the Abruzzi region, has received a proper biography only recently, with the effect that we can now credit him with all the works variously ascribed to 'Magister Zacharias', 'Antonius Zachara' or even 'Magister A. dictus Z.'.[237] He was *cantor*, and became *scriptor*, at the Roman *curia* in 1391. This is remarkable as he was a married man and also a crippled dwarf (which is what the sobriquet 'Zacharias' may refer to). Around 1407-9, he defected from the Roman pope and is later documented in the chapel of Pope John XXIII at Bologna; he may have died in this service, perhaps during the Council of Constance. His sacred music and Italian songs were widely copied at home and abroad.[238] It is not clear why he seems not to have left any motets. As with Ciconia and Salinis, we have by him a single 'Ars subtilior *essay*': the extravagant Latin song 'Sumite karissimi'. Its text contains a cryptic 'recommendation' (spelled as a rebus) to friends or colleagues, perhaps of the papal chapel. In this employment, Antonius was surrounded by Netherlanders, who may have included 'Eckardus' (Magister Egardus?) in 1394.

In his music for the Mass,[239] Antonius was one of the first composers to use 'parody' techniques (in the strict sense), borrowing musical material for three settings from his own ballatas 'Rosetta che non cambi mai colore', 'Deus Deo-rum, Pluto' and 'Un fior gentil m'apparse'. These settings appear to be late works. Much earlier (c.1400?) is the Mass pair Gloria 'Micinella' – Credo 'Cur-sor', the titles of which may indicate, respectively, the brevity and the swiftness of the pieces. They go together in mode, range, tenor layout and in much of the rhythmic–melodic detail; they are for four voices, and 'isorhythmic' in the sim-

---

[234] See, for example, Margaret Bent, 'New sacred polyphonic fragments of the early Quattrocento', *Studi Musicali* 9 (1980), 137-56; von Fischer, 'Bemerkungen', 167 f.

[235] See p. 55 and n. 13 above: the connection with Florence is suggested by the fact that the Ars antiqua codex *F*, from which Salinis may have taken a text, belonged to the Medicis by 1456 at the latest, and corroborated by the presence of two motets by him in the manuscript *San Lorenzo 2211*.

[236] Published in Reaney ed., *EFM*, vol. 7 (1983), no. 1. The concordance in *NL-Uu 37 I* (no. 13) has not hitherto been noticed.

[237] Nádas, 'Further notes on Magister Antonius'.

[238] Edited (under variant names) in Reaney ed., *EFM*, vol. 6 (1977). The sacred works also in PMFC, vol. 13, the secular songs in PMFC, vol. 10.

[239] See von Fischer, 'Bemerkungen'.

ple manner of restating the lower voices identically several times. There is great textural interest and rhythmic energy in the interplay of the voices; the counterpoint and the modal contours of the tenor recall the Credo 'Bonbarde', which Antonius may well have known. In turn, his Mass pair has an unmistakable follower in Ciconia's Mass pair nos. 3-4 where, as in Ciconia's reaction to Egardus (see p. 96), all the effects are enhanced and clarified. Antonius is particularly fond of soloistic or duet openings and has text-sharing upper voice-pairs. As mentioned earlier, such devices are common to the Italian and northern lateral traditions: besides the works mentioned above, a Gloria from Ghent can be cited, where the three voices enter non-imitatively one after the other.[240] Flemish colleagues in the papal chapel may also have been mediators for a suggested English influence on Antonius. His Gloria 'Anglicana' (see Ex. 1a) was probably so named because it uses the 9/8 metre then common in England, although this does not prove that he knew English music personally. The fact that his Gloria 'Gloria, laus, honor' was even copied in the Old Hall MS is equally inconclusive: his music could have travelled abroad without him, perhaps via the Council of Constance (see also p. 118).

The Italian songs of Antonius Zacharias fully reveal a spirited, eccentric personality, who enjoys cryptic games with words and numbers, *hoqueti* and canonic artifices – but whose melody and declamation always come out as pure and simple. The tri-textual ballata 'Je suy navrés' is a mock-song on the beauties and the academic ambitions of Florence. It starts with a comical French dialogue between two lovers of the city, while the contratenor contributes incomprehensible local slang:

Example 13 Antonius Zacharias de Teramo, 'Je suy navrés'

---

[240] Strohm, 'Ars nova fragments', plates 2-3 (of *B-Gr 133*).

Example 13 (*cont.*)

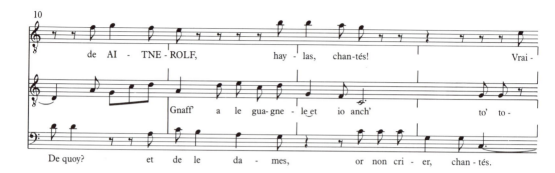

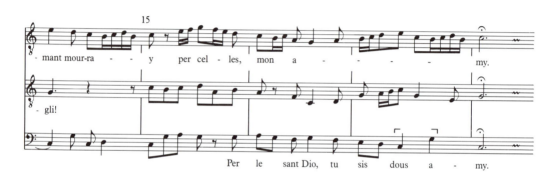

This piece is not only a joke: it is also an exercise in gently rolling melismas and almost purely consonant part-writing. The tenor has a remarkably 'bass-like' contour; the '2–1' and '5–1' cadential descents are treated almost as if they were equivalent (compare bars 14 and 17).

In the ballata 'Un fior gentil', Antonius spells the name 'CHARAMILLA' with numbers and cryptic crossword-clues ('aspiratio' = CH; 'prima' = letter 'A'; 'bina ne va per rima' = RAMI; 'due cinquanta' = LL). A girl named 'Ciaramella' is also the dedicatee of one of his most folkloristic songs.[241]

Unlike Antonius Zacharias, Johannes Ciconia seems to have spent great compositional efforts on the old-fashioned genre of the madrigal. There is some doubt as to how these pieces should best be interpreted: as part of the nationalist revival mentioned above (which is suggested by the partly aristocratic–heraldic texts), or as purely stylistic exercises, blending various musical traditions. Ciconia the 'Italian' can be pinpointed much more easily in his ballate, especially 'O rosa bella' and 'Lizadra donna', which self-consciously allude to folk traditions but are worlds away from the 'Ciaramella' idiom of Antonius.

---

[241] Transcribed and discussed in Pirrotta, 'Zacharus Musicus'.

A popularizing element in Italian song had been gaining momentum since the 1390s. Linguistic and musical traits of pseudo-folkloristic, extemporized song can be traced in some ballatas of the Reina Codex; their context was a noted fashion in north Italian circles for the so-called *siciliane*.[242] The popular lyrical genres of the *strambotto* and the *barzelletta* are already present here, although cast into the external form of the ballata. A manuscript of about 1410, the Mancini or Lucca Codex (*I-Las 184*; *Man*) and related fragments, contain many songs in this manner.[243] The music comes from various places and largely coincides with Solazzo's repertory in *Il Saporetto* (see above). In the poetry, the octosyllabic line of the barzelletta makes its first musical appearance ('Deh, tristo mi topinello'). Also, popular-sounding irregularities of scansion, such as surplus syllables, are introduced – and are to stay with Italian musical lyrics for generations. Most of the songs are small in scope, some diminutive; two-part writing is the norm. As regards the poetry, there is a large group of simple, poignant love-songs which often use the same sentimental vocabulary. An example is 'Mercè te chiamo, o dolce anima mia', which has an imitative, declamatory opening leading to mainly homophonic textures. Ciconia's 'Mercè, o morte' is an even more romantic song with its sighing word-gestures which are repeated as in an opera aria.[244]

The circle of poets and composers involved in this new fashion seems to have been large. Its foremost literary figure was the Venetian aristocrat Leonardo Giustinian (*c*.1390–1446), who was so successful with his semi-improvised, popularizing love-songs that a whole genre emerging from them has received his name: 'giustiniane' or 'veneziane'. He may be the author of the ballata 'O rosa bella' which surely exemplifies his poetic style.

The three-voice setting by Ciconia[245] is an outstanding, even incredible achievement for a composer (and not even a native Italian) of this generation:

Example 14*a* Johannes Ciconia, 'O rosa bella'

[242] Nino Pirrotta, 'New glimpses of an unwritten tradition', in *idem*, *Music and Culture*, 51–71; F. Alberto Gallo, 'Due "Siciliane" del Trecento', *AnnM* 7 (1964–77), 43–50.

[243] An up-to-date facs edn and inventory (including newly discovered leaves) is John Nádas and Agostino Ziino eds, *The Lucca Codex (Codice Mancini)* (Lucca: Libreria Musicale Italiana Editrice, 1990).

[244] Ciconia, *Works*, no. 39. The authenticity of the piece has meanwhile been established by the discovery of an attribution in *I-Las 184*.

[245] Ciconia, *Works*, no. 34.

Example 14*a* (*cont.*)

la,   o   dol - ce a - ni - ma   mi - a,   o   dol - ce a - ni - ma   mi - a,   o

dol - ce a - ni - ma   mi   -   -   a,

Only lack of space prevents us from discussing the complete piece. At 70 bars' length, it is unusually extended for the simplistic genre from which it grew and for the limited number of words it represents. It has a wider than usual range of 12 notes (f–c'') in the cantus. Such expansion serves, above all, the melody. Hardly anywhere in Italian song before Dufay's 'Vergene bella' (see p. 156) have there been such long, articulated lines, with motives that seem to renew themselves with each word-related gesture. The impulse of the first three words, 'O rosa bella', carries the melody forward over a whole long phrase. The first vowel, an astounded 'O', appears to generate a kind of dance-prelude which then settles on the first actual word, 'rosa'. Then the rose begins to grow, as it were, rhythmically and melodically, until the charming word 'bella' takes over. This word dances back over the whole octave g'–g, like a stream of water over a Roman fountain.

In the second phrase, the passionate repetitions become more incessant: the exclamations 'o' pull the line upwards. Subtle motivic relationships between the gestures have already surfaced (compare, for example, bars 1–2 with bars 7–8): sequential and imitative patterns exist within the single line. From bar 19, however, these patterns expand into a real dialogue of cantus and tenor, and the repeated exclamations of the lover become dramatically impatient:

Example 14*b*

Non mi las - sar   mo - ri - re,   non mi las - sar   mo - ri - re

Tenor   Non mi las - sar   mo - ri - re,   non mi las - sar   mo -

non mi las - sar   mo - ri - re,

- ri   -   -   re,

In bar 23, the peaking *b* in the cantus, the sudden break of the melodic contour and the accented dissonance on 'las-' make it appear as if every syllable were crying out by itself. Such dramatic presentation of the words surpasses, in my opinion, most of the merely competent word-setting in fifteenth-century Italian song, and instead looks forward to the Renaissance madrigal.

3

THE COUNCIL OF CONSTANCE

A new publicity of music

The Council of Constance, which lasted from November 1414 to May 1418, was a significant event in the history of music in several respects. The main tasks which the Council fathers had set themselves – above all, the removal of the Schism, the reform of the Church and the defence of its dogma against Wyclifite and Bohemian heresy – did not directly impinge on music and liturgy (although a liturgically relevant, if marginal, point on the agenda was a calendar reform). Indirectly, however, the decisions taken in Constance did influence the course of music history. The unification of the Western Church under Pope Martin V (elected 11 November 1417) helped to turn the Roman papacy into the most conspicuous centre of sacred music for the next two centuries, and thus to associate music with the Italian Renaissance. On the other hand, the legally indefensible execution of the Czech 'heretics' Johannes Hus and Hieronymus of Prague, and the failure to produce any genuine ecclesiastical reform, fuelled religious dissent in Bohemia and elsewhere, and with it the rise of non-conformist, popular and even nationalist tendencies in religious music. The ceremonial life of the Council itself, which had to integrate so many divergent local customs, at least strengthened the idea of a Roman-based reform of the ritual, which was to culminate in the Council of Trent in the next century.[246]

More important, perhaps, the Council brought together music and musicians from almost anywhere in Europe. These people could now meet and learn from each other directly – exchange material, perform together, switch employers and plan new careers. Written and unwritten music of many kinds found new areas of distribution. Last but not least, the ceremonial and musical activities of some of Europe's greatest institutions descended on a small town in southern Germany with only 6000 to 8000 inhabitants, making it a 'mirror of the (musical) world'. This was to be a challenge not only to subsequent Church Councils, but even more to the cultural pride of European cities. Music gained a kind of public exposure here which was more typical of the ages to come. The common people of Constance could hear the pope's private chapel sing in public; chants like the *Te Deum laudamus* were sung in the streets by crowds of thousands –

---

[246] Generally on the Council, see Franzen–Müller eds, *Das Konzil von Konstanz*.

scenes which resemble the style of modern mass culture. Among the perhaps 50,000 to 70,000 guests who attended the Council over these years there were many hundreds of professional musicians (the highest figure given is 1700) – not including the musicians of clerical or aristocratic status.

Music for public and representative purposes features prominently in the existing reports about the Council. It may be more than a coincidence that the first mention of King Sigismund – the Council's secular overlord – in the minutes of the city magistrate refers to New Year's gifts presented to his heralds and trumpeters (January 1415).[247] After the Council, the city obtained the privilege of having its own civic trumpeters, which reflects not so much a raised status of the city as its higher concern for musical self-presentation.

In this sense at least, it also marked the climax of a medieval tradition: the use of music in order to display authority.[248] The main chronicler of the events, Ulrich Richental,[249] speaks for many when he emphasizes the splendour of the processions and stately receptions, which were regularly accompanied by wind bands of trumpeters ('prusuner') and shawmists ('pfifer'), their instruments emblazoned with the coats of arms of their employers. During the greater processions and cavalcades through the town, several different wind bands would at times perform simultaneously ('in widerstrit'). When, for example, the king received the 'golden rose' from Pope John XXIII, he rode through the streets with all the princes and nobles, and with 23 trumpeters and 40 pipers who had been recruited from different princely bands. The king's authority was in danger when Pope John secretly fled the town on 20 March 1415, to avoid being deposed. The next morning, Sigismund himself rode through the town with trumpeters who preceded his personal announcements with fanfares. To make everybody fall silent and listen to him, the king commanded the trumpeters to 'play in a stately manner' ('stäteglichen uff prusunen').[250] The royal and princely wind bands and, of course, the many freelance musicians, could apparently be chartered privately. The particularly splendid festival of the Florentine money-changers (St John's Day, 24 June 1415) was advertised throughout the town by five 'prusuners' and three 'pfifer'.

This and other public performances have been portrayed in the illustrations of Richental's chronicle, which exists in several copies. Although the drawings (and the chronicle itself) originated years after the events, many details are trustworthy, for example the recurrent combinations of natural trumpets, straight or S-shaped slide-trumpets, and shawms of various sizes.[251] On one

---

[247] Schuler, 'Konstanz', 163 f.

[248] Žak, *Musik als 'Ehr' und 'Zier'*, 149–51.

[249] Richental's chronicle, written perhaps in the 1430s, survives in several manuscript versions. A facs edn of the manuscript now in the Rosgarten-Museum, Constance (see also pl. 2), with edn and commentary, is Richental, *Chronik*. Little is known about the author except that he was a local man of social standing.

[250] Richental, *Chronik*, 63.

[251] See the facs edn (n.249), fols. 39, 66v, 75; Bowles, *Pratique musicale*, pl. 25; Žak, *Musik als 'Ehr' und 'Zier'*, pl. 8.

occasion Richental documents polyphonic playing. The large English delegation under Richard Beauchamp, Earl of Warwick, arrived in January 1415 with three trombonists ('prusuner') and four shawmists; the trombonists 'played in three parts, one above the other, as one usually sings'.[252] Beauchamp's minstrels are mentioned again when they announced the English Feast of St Thomas of Canterbury throughout the town, on the Eve (28 December 1416). There were four of them this time, and they carried the royal English arms on their instruments. They played again after Mass on St Thomas's Day (29 December), outside the church, though they may not have appeared in the actual services (as has been claimed), which were adorned with loud bell-ringing, candlelight and organ-playing. The Vespers service furthermore ('darüber') included three-part vocal polyphony.[253] The singers in question may have been those of the retinue of the bishops of Norwich and Lichfield, who had arrived in September 1416, having already made a big impression during a performance in Cologne, on the way. Chapel musicians from Canterbury, Salisbury or, indeed, the royal establishments may have been present individually at Constance.

The nationality of Beauchamp's trombonists is uncertain. Although their polyphony struck Richental as something new, polyphonic playing may have been known to other wind bands – or have become known to them through the English example.

There are many vocal compositions of the early fifteenth century which seem to imply the use of brass instruments. Most of these pieces, however, contain only imitations of 'trumpet' styles (see also below). A few surviving pieces might have been genuine instrumental compositions, not intended to carry a text. One of these is likely to have been performed during the council: the textless 'Tuba gallicalis' (see Ex. 15) of the Strasbourg Codex (*F-Sm 222*; *Str*).[254]

The only extant (recent) copy of this piece leaves room for doubt concerning some notes, but many of the dissonances between the contratenor and the outer voices must be authentic. The contratenor is clearly designed for a natural brass instrument, which uses only the partial tones 4, 6, 7, 8, 10 and perhaps 9.[255] The *tuba* – as we may call this individual voice – has many unavoidable clashes with the free melodic top line, particularly when playing the pitches c and c'.

---

[252] 'prusonettend überainander mit dry stimmen als man gewonlich singet': Schuler, 'Konstanz', 165.

[253] 'darüber tenor, discant und medium ze vesper zit': Schuler, 'Konstanz', 159. This particular passage about polyphony is missing in another version of the chronicle. It must nevertheless be authentic; the peculiar combination of voice-labels, including the English and central European *medium* instead of contratenor, is also known from musical sources of this time and region.

[254] For an inventory of the manuscript and literature, see *RISM B IV*, vol. 3, 550–92. The manuscript was burnt in 1870, but a partial copy and complete thematic index by E. de Coussemaker exists, see (Edmond de Coussemaker), *Le manuscrit musical M 222 C 22 de la Bibliothèque de Strasbourg*, ed. A. Vander Linden (Brussels: Office International de Librairie, n.d.). On the instrumental pieces discussed here, see Charles van den Borren, 'La musique pittoresque dans le manuscrit 222 C 22 de la Bibliothèque de Strasbourg', in *Bericht über den musikwissenschaftlichen Kongreß in Basel 1924* (Leipzig 1925), 88–105 (with unreliable transcriptions on p. 96 ff); Ramalingam, 'Trumpetum' (with correct transcriptions).

[255] The only d', in bar 8, may be an error for c'.

Example 15 'Tuba gallicalis', *F-Sm 222*

Example 15 (*cont.*)

This happens even in pre-cadential ('dominant') sonorities and produces a bourdon-like sound.

Considering the individual voice-pairs, the *tuba* appears to be written against the tenor alone, with which it forms many perfect consonances – including the fourth, however! The precadential 6-4 chords are as striking as they are inescapable. The frequent triadic pitch-exchanges within the C sonority (bars 1–7, 12–14) and some archaic progressions such as fifth–octave (bars 8–9, 27), may belong to older practices of extemporized polyphony. The repetitive 6/8 rhythms also point to fourteenth-century styles. The tenor does not much resemble contemporary vocal lines either, as it uses only the diatonic pitches from *c* to *c'*, with much emphasis on the triad. This part could be designed for the slide trumpet or trombone, which was not necessarily chromatic or in any way as flexible as the modern trombone.[256] The top part, however, could be performed on a tenor shawm – the third partner of such ensembles, shown in several illustrations of the chronicle. Its line is carefully composed against the tenor alone, with mostly correct progressions on the structurally important notes. The few exceptions include the fourth in bar 14 (which is problematic in the source) and the ornamented parallel octaves in bar 27. Such parallels (albeit with the contratenor) were tolerated in a work like the Credo 'Bonbarde' (see Ex. 2). The present example is even more likely than the Credo 'Bonbarde' to have been composed by an instrumentalist for his own purposes, perhaps for himself and an accompanying trombonist. When the two had to perform with a natural brass player as well – for the sake of greater festive noise – this person would have devised his extemporized part against the tenor alone which he had to learn by heart, of course. The final participants in a performance might include not only these three, but an unlimited number of minstrels.

All these observations, together with the title 'Gallic trumpet-piece', make it unlikely that the piece matches the musical style of the English trombone

---

[256] For the most recent information about the trombone at this time, see Keith Polk, 'Instrumental music', 167–74; and the contributions by Keith Polk, Herbert W. Myers and Ross W. Duffin in *Early Music* 17 (1989), 383–402.

soloists. They produced a sound which reminded Richental of polyphonic *sing-ing*, perhaps because of the greater flexibility of their slide-instruments which they used for all three parts. We must draw the important conclusion that polyphonic playing by wind bands had by 1415 already developed different stylistic branches. This is also suggested by another *tuba* composition: the 'Tuba Heinrici de Libero Castro' in the Strasbourg Codex immediately preceding 'Tuba gallicalis'. This piece has a texted top voice, 'Virgo dulcis atque pia', which is playable on a natural trumpet using the partial tones 6–12 with adjustment for 7(*a*). The tenor, and the contratenor 'tube', however, would require slide trumpets, although their parts are even more fanfare-like. This piece stands thus on the borderline of a type of vocal music where the triadic formulas have become a pictorial device and are not necessarily intended for brass instruments. Whether or not the composer, Heinrich of Freiburg, intended 'Virgo dulcis' to be sung, it is likely that he was inspired by polyphonic wind band performances such as could be heard at Constance.[257]

Sacred ceremonies

Sacred music was, of course, the mainstay of the conciliar ceremonies. It must have been performed in many places: the cathedral, the collegiate churches of St Stephen and St John, the parish churches and also the monasteries, where the larger delegations were housed. Richental reports on a Greek Mass in the private lodgings of the Patriarch of Kiev, and he mentions the Hebrew chants of the Jewish community, when they met the pope and the king in the streets to obtain a renewal of their privileges. According to Schuler, the musical chapels present in Constance included those of the pope, the king and the latter's deputy, the Count Palatinate of Heidelberg.[258] Pope John XXIII arrived with his chapel and other retinue (about 600 people) at the end of October 1414.

A chapel list of 3 November gives the names of seven *cantores* or *tenoriste*. Most of these musicians stayed on, when John XXIII was deposed by the Council in May 1415, and again most of them were reappointed after the election of Martin V in November 1417.[259] This continuity is significant: it must have extended to the musical repertory which the chapel singers had brought with them from Italy.

Almost all the singers themselves, however, hailed from northern France and the Low Countries. The only singer in the chapel of King Sigismund who is known by name, Simon Ranarii, was probably a Netherlander, too: he is

---

[257] Further considerations about the pieces and their style are offered by Ramalingam, '*Trumpetum*', who establishes that the Bohemian theorist Paulus Paulirinus (see p. 292 below) speaks in fact of a 'tuba gallicana' as the instrumental model for a harsh-sounding contratenor part ('vox sonora aliquantulum rauca') in a vocal piece called 'trumpetum'.

[258] Schuler, 'Konstanz', 158.

[259] Schuler, 'Konstanz', 155 f. See also *idem*, 'Kapelle Papst Martins V'.

documented as succentor in Bruges between 1422 and 1426.[260] It is strange that none of the composers who had been connected with the popes before 1415 can actually be located at the Council. Antonius Zacharias of Teramo served John XXIII until 1413, but then all documentation about him ceases.[261] Matteo da Perugia, somehow connected with Alexander V around 1409/10 (see p. 60), died in Milan in or before January, 1418. None of his works seems ever to have crossed the Alps. Antonius Zacharias had been a member of the chapel of Pope Gregory XII until at least 1407;[262] this pope did not attend the Council but sent a large delegation under Carlo Malatesta of Rimini to negotiate his abdication (which was announced in June 1415). Carlo's retinue included musicians,[263] though it would be a mere guess to say that singers of Pope Gregory XII visited Constance with the Malatesta delegation. Nicolaus Simonis de Leodio, an earlier servant of this pope, was then definitely employed in Italy (see p. 117). We can rule out the presence of a chapel serving Pope Benedict XIII because he did not send a delegation. On the other hand, musicians such as Antonius Zacharias, Hubertus de Salinis or Nicolaus Zacharie of Brindisi (see below), could have come to Constance from any chapel, even in a non-musical capacity, and have had their compositions performed. Musicians from France and the Low Countries were surely also present. It is possible that the young Guillaume Dufay attended the Council, either with delegates from his cathedral (Cambrai) or in some personal connection with Cardinal Pierre d'Ailly.[264] He may have been one of those musicians who changed career at Constance, making his way to Italy with the Malatesta retinue.

How was sacred music performed at Constance? Many of the outdoors ceremonies – the processions, or the public blessings given by the pope from the balcony of the episcopal palace – were accompanied by the papal singers with chants and possibly ceremonial motets. In liturgical services such as Mass and Vespers, which are frequently depicted in Richental's chronicle, the chapel seems to have been divided in two groups of three or four singers each (the usual number of papal *cantores* at this time was in fact seven). Each group has its own choirbook and is directed by its own leader who seems to be making signs with the fingers of his left hand. Comparison with other contemporary illustrations suggests that the leader is not pointing out the notes in the book but that the signs are rhythmic ones – which must mean that mensural music is being performed.[265]

The picture reproduced in Plate 2 belongs to the coronation ritual of Martin

---

[260] Schuler, 'Konstanz', 158; Strohm, *Bruges*, 187.
[261] Nádas, 'Further notes on Magister Antonius', 179. The papal chaplain Johannes de Semeriaco (see Nádas, p. 180, and Schuler, 'Kapelle Papst Martins V', 38 f) might have been the composer 'Cameraco' or 'Cameracy' represented in *F-Sm 222* with a chanson (no. 126) and a Credo (no. 194).
[262] Ziino, 'Magister Antonius', 327.
[263] Atlas, 'Pandolfo III Malatesta', 70.
[264] Fallows, *Dufay*, 16 f; Schuler, 'Konstanz', 159.
[265] See, for example, Tomasello, *Music and Ritual*, pl. 4.

2 The papal chapel at the Council of Constance. Ulrich Richental, *Chronik*, fol. 103r.

V on 21 November 1417.[266] It actually took place outdoors; an immense crowd was watching it, which may be the reason why Richental says he could not hear the singers very well. Alternatively, their 'soft singing' may have been due to the fact that it was polyphonic, and that upper lines were produced in falsetto. (Choirboys are never shown in the drawings of the chronicle, and were apparently not used for polyphony in the papal chapel then.) The enormous candles, held by vergers standing behind the singers, and the division into two groups, are also found in other illustrations when Mass services are shown.

266 From the manuscript Constance, Rosgarten-Museum, fol. 103r.

An organ is never visible; polyphony seems to have been purely vocal, and the church organ would have been used only for certain plainsong items (Kyrie, sequences, hymns, *Magnificat*, *Te Deum*) in alternation with the full choir, as was customary. The two groups in our picture are surely not performing psalms antiphonally: any cleric would do this by heart, and the psalms belong to the Divine Office which was celebrated, of course, by the local clergy according to their round of duties.[267] It seems to follow that the division of the singers serves a purely musical purpose, most probably that of alternating contrasting sections in Mass music or motets.

It is precisely from this period that we have numerous Mass settings scored in an *alternatim* fashion – for example by contrasting, verse by verse, a soloistic duet of high voices with a fuller three-voice ensemble.[268] It so happens that the Gloria 'Jubilatio' by Hubertus de Salinis (see p. 100), which is written in this manner, celebrates the end of the Schism. Although it was probably composed in 1409 for the election of Pope Alexander V, it may well have been repeated at Constance.

There are other extant works which could have been heard in conciliar ceremonies. One is a 'Deo gratias' motet which was probably sung after Mass.[269] Its (originally) three voices sing three different but related texts, exhorting the high clergy, the secular lords, and finally all the faithful to give thanks to God:

> (Triplum:) Deo gratias papales presules et cardinales . . .
> (Motetus:) Deo gratias solvant principum et regum nobilitas . . .
> (Tenor:) Deo gratias fidelis quisque solvat qui in celis . . .[270]

We know from the ceremonial books of the Councils of Constance and Basle[271] that the singers had to answer the celebrant's words 'Ite missa est' or 'Benedicamus domino' with 'Deo gratias'. The same regulations tell us, furthermore, that in pontifical Masses in the pope's presence (*coram Papa*), the celebrant had to intone the Kyrie, Gloria and Credo but then say the remainder of the words privately (*submissa voce*), whilst the *cantores* completed these items musically. The Sanctus and Agnus Dei were not intoned by the celebrant, but he had to speak them, too. Finally, we must note that the church bells and – at least on particularly joyous occasions – trumpeters were heard during Mass.[272] There is no proof that they ever took part in polyphonic performances in church, however.

---

[267] On the local traditions and antiphonal singing, see Schuler, 'Konstanz', 151–4 and 157 f, respectively. The liturgy of the conciliar sessions included the solemn singing of the hymn 'Veni creator spiritus' in alternation between the conciliar delegates and the *cantores*; see Koep, 'Liturgie', 251.

[268] See also pp. 248 f below on *alternatim* techniques.

[269] The 'Deo gratias' played a role not only in conciliar Masses, but also in the liturgy of the actual sessions: Koep, 'Liturgie', 247 and 251.

[270] For this work, see Ward, 'A central European repertory', 332 f, and Strohm, *Bruges*, rev. edn, 105 n. 11 and 262 (identifying the original third voice in a manuscript from Gdańsk).

[271] Koep, 'Liturgie'; Schimmelpfennig, 'Zum Zeremoniell'.

[272] Schuler, 'Konstanz', 165.

Mass settings from this time with designations such as *tuba* or *trompetta* document a general popularity of the 'trumpet style' in vocal execution (see above).[273]

A 'conciliar repertory'

Since no manuscripts of sacred music survive which can have originated at the Council itself, a search for 'conciliar music' must turn to geographically and chronologically related sources. It seems right to seek some of this music in the older layer of the Strasbourg Codex, begun about 1420. An eye-witness and chronicler of the Council, Reinbold Slecht, was in fact cantor at a collegiate church of Strasbourg.[274] Similar connections can be suggested for the fragmentary choirbook of St Stephen's, Vienna (*D-Nst 9/9a* and *A-M 749*), since the interest of Viennese prelates and university clerics in the Council was intense. Several Polish manuscripts of about 1440 still seem to absorb music heard at Constance, although the most important of them – *PL-Wn 8054* (*Kras*) and *PL-Wn 378* – also contain more recent material (see p. 260). The initiative of transmitting this repertory might be ascribed to Polish musicians visiting the Council – or even musicians formerly employed in Italy who changed patrons there.[275] Finally, there are many smaller fragments and musical treatises, originating along the eastern border of the Holy Roman Empire (found at Gdańsk, Poznań, Wrocław, Kraków, Kremsmünster and Vienna), which reflect an interest in Ars nova music until after 1430: possibly an interest aroused by the events of Constance.[276] Taken together, these sources indeed suggest that central Europe was joining the *lateral traditions* of western Europe and Italy a generation late, as it were. Artistic polyphony was now being transmitted to places where it had scarcely been known before, or received enormous encouragement in centres where it must have been exceptional – such as Strasbourg and Constance itself.[277]

The western and Italian sacred music found in the sources we have associated with the Council, falls in two repertorial groups. Both seem to have been imported from the south. The older group comprises the best-known Ars nova motets such as 'Apollinis eclipsatur', 'Ida capillorum', 'Degentis vita', 'Rex Karole', and a number of works by Vitry; there are also Mass settings from the central tradition, including the Credo 'Bonbarde' and the Gloria 'Qui sonitu

---

[273] Ramalingam, '*Trumpetum*', 155 f, has a list of sacred works and chansons with 'actual trumpet parts' by Grossin, Loqueville, Arnold de Lantins, Franchois and Fontaine, which I consider, without exception, as vocal imitations of the style. The famous if crude 'Gloria ad modum tube' by Dufay (*Opera omnia*, vol. 4, no. 22), with canonic upper voices, looks to me like a youthful *tour de force* in these modern fashions – perhaps written at Constance.

[274] Vogeleis, *Quellen und Bausteine*, 97; Schuler, 'Konstanz', 157 and n. 52.

[275] An opinion expressed in Pirrotta, 'Zacharus Musicus', 159; and in von Fischer, 'Bemerkungen', 166 f.

[276] See Strohm, 'Native and foreign polyphony', 209 ff, and p. 260 below. An apparently earlier phase of influence is investigated in Brewer, *Ars Nova*.

[277] Documents on the musical history of Strasbourg are collected in Vogeleis, *Quellen und Bausteine*.

melodie'. Almost all of these works had been known in Italy by about 1400. Sometimes, amusing anomalies occurred once this music found its way into central European sources. 'Degentis vita', for example, received a new contratenor[278] (in *D-Nst 9/9a*) which destroys the isorhythmic scheme and creates many dissonances. The composer of this voice erroneously believed that not only the rhythm but also the melody had to be repeated literally in the second half of the piece! It cannot be ruled out that this misunderstanding originated in Italy, where such simpler types of 'isorhythm' were frequent. 'Apollinis eclipsatur', the famous 'musicians' motet', underwent changes of this kind, too. In a late Viennese source (*A-Wn 5094*, see p. 260), it survives as a textless 'rondellus', apparently arranged for the keyboard, and comprising only the motetus and contratenor(!). The original version of the motet, however, was also known in central Europe. It was often quoted in treatises as a didactic example, and copied correctly in *F-Sm 222*. Other 'motets about music' were apparently written in imitation of it, for example 'Sonorum varietas' by a certain 'Heinricus', and the anonymous motet 'Musicorum inter collegia' (*F-Sm 222* no. 166), which is also labelled 'Rex rondellorum'. The beginning of this piece quotes 'Apollinis eclipsatur'. The famous plainsong tenor of the French work, 'In omnem terram exivit sonus eorum', which also appears in the English motet 'Sub Arturo plebs', appealed to self-conscious musicians in Germany as well. These psalm words are written, as a kind of motto, at the beginning of the Constance manuscript of Richental's chronicle. We may adopt the quotation 'Their sound went out in all the lands' as a musical emblem of the Council itself.

A more recent body of music which entered central Europe by way of the Council, was not only transmitted through Italy, but itself of Italian origin. This group comprises mainly Mass settings by Ciconia, Antonius Zacharias, Magister Egardus, Antonius de Civitate and probably Hubertus de Salinis (see above). Surprisingly, the 'parody' Mass settings by Antonius Zacharias and Bartolomeo da Bologna are absent, as are all the ceremonial motets by Ciconia! These splendid works, for example 'Doctorum principem' for Francesco Zabarella, would have found an ideal setting at Constance, where the cardinal concluded his career (*d.*1417). Other Italian motets could have been given new texts if their celebratory words had been an obstacle – but they are missing from our sources as well.[279]

This is even stranger as the genre of the ceremonial motet was by no means absent from the conciliar repertory. One work, the motet 'Argi vices Polyphemus / Tum Philemon' explicitly honours Pope John XXIII.[280] Whether com-

---

[278] Printed in Harrison ed., *Motets of French Provenance*, no. 23; Günther ed., *Motets of Chantilly*, no. 2. On the work, see also pp. 42 f above.

[279] One or more central European sources with such works could, of course, be lost; but the omission of Italian motets from the extant sources remains a fact. Is this the reason why we do not have a single motet by Antonius Zacharias?

[280] Edited in PMFC, vol. 13, no. 49. See also de Van, 'A recently discovered source', 12–14; Newes, 'Imitation', 51.

posed already for the pope's coronation in 1410 or later, the work was almost certainly performed in Constance, at least in the private lodgings of John XXIII in the monastery of Kreuzlingen, where Duke Frederick of Austria, Count of Tyrol, the greatest supporter of the pope, also lodged. On 20 March 1415 the duke helped Pope John XXIII to flee from Constance to pre-empt his deposition, and thus incurred the wrath of King Sigismund to the point of forfeiting his territories. The deposition took place nevertheless; but the celebrative motet surfaces again in a copy made in the late 1430s in the Aosta Codex (*I-Ao*) – quite probably for Frederick of Tyrol himself (see p. 254).

The text cites, besides Pope John XXIII, the poet ('Guilhermus') and the composer ('Nicolaus'). The latter has variously been identified with the singer Nicolaus Simonis from Liège, who served Pope Gregory XII in 1409, or with Nicolaus Zacharie from Brindisi, a composer first documented in 1420 in the chapel of Martin V, or even with Nicholas Grenon. The question is important because the motet seems so close to what may be perceived as a specifically Italian tradition. It is strictly isorhythmic although it has only simple repetitions of tenor periods; its introductory canon apparently impressed the young Dufay (see p. 161), and the upper two voices form a duet in the same range, just as in much Italian music.

Although the French composer Grenon had hitherto unexplained contacts with Italy just around this time (see p. 149), he was master of the choirboys of the chapels of Berry and Burgundy between 1409 and 1419, and thus hardly able to travel to other countries. Also Nicolaus Simonis 'Françeis' from Liège seems to be documented at Italian cathedrals (Treviso and Cividale) continuously between 1411 and 1419.[281] A musician in the service of Pandolfo III Malatesta at Brescia, a certain 'Nicholaus de Burgundia lod(on)ensis' or 'de Liessa', has also been put forward.[282] Neither man is otherwise known to have been a composer, and both were closely dependent on the party of Pope Gregory XII, which would make them unlikely composers of a motet praising John XXIII. Barring the speculation that Grenon wrote the work in France (sometime between 1410 and 1415), and it was sent to the pope, we should restore it to Nicolaus Zacharie of Brindisi. This composer's works help, in their own way, to bridge the gap between Ciconia and the early Dufay.

The fact remains that the 'Italian idiom' of the motet is also a northern idiom (see also p. 97): texture and form of 'Argi vices' are as close to Grenon's motet 'Ad honorem sanctae Trinitatis / Celorum regnum' as they are to 'Letetur plebs' by Nicolaus Zacharie. 'Argi vices' fits Constance very well with its internation-

---

[281] Pierluigi Petrobelli, 'La musica nelle cattedrali e nelle città', *Storia della cultura veneta. Il Trecento* (Venice: Neri Pozza, 1977), 467 f. In the documents, Nicolaus Simonis is called 'Françens', probably to be read as 'Françeis'.

[282] Atlas, 'Pandolfo III Malatesta', 68 f, proposes to identify this man at Brescia with Nicolaus Simonis at Cividale, although the times of their tenures coincide. Nicholaus de Liessa surely comes from Liesse near Laon, as the identification 'lodonensis' (= laudunensis) confirms; 'from Liège' would be 'leodiensis'.

ality – although it seems more old-fashioned than, and indeed strikingly inferior to, the other two works.[283]

It may be that the sacred music heard at Constance fell short of the latest stylistic developments. This concerns, for example, the advances of English music. Whilst English musicians seem to have picked up continental music at Constance, probably including the Gloria 'Gloria, laus honor' by Antonius Zacharias, it is doubtful how much of their most recent music was heard there.

As mentioned, Antonius Zacharias's Gloria 'Anglicana' (see p. 101 and Ex. 1*a*), probably a late work, was not necessarily written in conscious imitation of English music. A case could be made, however, for an anonymous 'Salve regina' from *F-Sm 222* (no. 93), which is also found in a Durham processional.[284] The piece is a strict three-voice canon, a *rota* in fact, and thus belongs to an established insular genre. On the other hand, canons with sacred and secular texts abound in the Strasbourg source. The fashion was at its height on either side of the Channel; and in that context, the English 'Salve regina' stands out as fairly archaic in style. There is a remote possibility that some modern English works of Dunstable's generation which were copied in the Italian Codex *I-Bc Q 15* not long after 1420 (see p. 136), passed through Constance to Italy. This is most unlikely, however, as none of them shows up in a central European source before *c*.1435. Finally, the 'Magister Alanus' by whom there are four songs in *F-Sm 222*, has tentatively been identified with either Johannes Alanus, the English composer of 'Sub Arturo plebs' (see p. 82), or a certain 'Aleyn' found in the Old Hall MS or both.[285] As a matter of fact, the pieces belong to a composer who imitated the French central tradition and was active before *c*.1400. Even if 'Magister Alanus' was an Englishman, he did not represent English music as heard at the Council.[286]

The other riddle of this repertory is its apparent lack of music by the Franco-Burgundians working after about 1400. As with 'Magister Alanus' and 'Nicolaus', we could liberally interpret some composers' names given in *F-Sm 222*. A Gloria by 'Richart' (no. 148) could then be credited to Richard Loqueville of Cambrai or even to the Burgundian chaplain Richard de Bellengues, dit Cardot; another by 'Lampens' could go to either Hugo or Arnold de Lantins, active in Italy from 1420 onwards. But exactly as in the cases of 'Argi vices' and the Alanus songs, each composition put forward turns out to have the features of an older generation. The sound which went from Constance to so many lands was the sound of the Ars nova.

---

[283] Edn in Borren ed., *Polyphonia Sacra*, no. 31 and no. 48, respectively.

[284] Nick Sandon, 'Mary, meditations, monks and music', *Early Music* 10 (1982), 43–55. The manuscript context of the Durham source is unambiguously English.

[285] David Fallows, 'Alanus, Johannes' in *The New Grove*.

[286] Two songs are German, and one of them, 'Min frow, min frow', is an imitation of Magister Grimace's virelai 'A l'arme, a l'arme' with its fanfare-like cries. The virelai 'S'en vous pour moy', whose original French text is underlaid to the copy in the older part of the Reina Codex, is an unsuspicious Ars nova piece. The pieces seem to have been entered into *F-Sm 222* as a second layer, perhaps in the mid-1420s; it is possible that they have nothing to do with the Council.

Secular song and its transformations

Perhaps, this soundscape changes somewhat when we add secular song to it. The chroniclers, as can be expected, say nothing about such lowly musical practices. The streets, the taverns and the private houses must have been full of singing and playing, however. Among the minstrels mentioned by Richental, there were fiddlers, lutenists and other performers of 'soft music' (*basse musique*), suitable for private entertainment. Many clerics, too, must have enjoyed singing for their own entertainment – in the inns after nightfall, for example – and many would have owned instruments. If the secular princes did not have a chapel, they at least had individual singers, harpists or keyboard players in their households. The most prominent representatives of all these musicians at Constance were Antonio Tallander alias Mossèn Borra and Oswald von Wolkenstein: the first a famous Aragonese minstrel, the other a Tyrolean knight and Minnesinger.[287] Both men served the same patron, King Sigismund. We know nothing about Tallander's music, but Oswald's is carefully collected in two major manuscripts dedicated to his musico-poetic *opera omnia*, totalling over 130 songs.[288]

In their own way, these songs document the reception of foreign polyphony in Germany at the time of the Council. The fact is that many of Oswald's 39 polyphonic lieder are arrangements of foreign compositions, and that the majority of them can be dated, on the basis of their texts, within the years 1415–17.[289] Oswald was a councillor to the king in those years, staying with him in Constance in 1415 and 1417, and also during the long diplomatic travel which Sigismund undertook to southern France, Navarre, Paris and England in 1416, to rally support for his proposed solution to the Schism. This adds a taste of internationality to Oswald's production at the time, especially because the expedition met the chapels and minstrels of Paris, of the Burgundian court and of King Henry V.[290] Even so, these encounters were qualitatively not very different from what could be experienced in Constance.

It seems that Oswald wrote the polyphonic songs listed in Table 1 during or immediately after the Council (the numbers follow Pelnar's edition).

[287] Schuler, 'Konstanz', 164 and 167.

[288] Facs edns: MS 'A' (*A-Wn 2777*): *Oswald von Wolkenstein. Handschrift A*, ed. Francesco Delbono (Graz, 1977); MS 'B' (*A-Iu, n.s.*): *Die Innsbrucker Wolkenstein-Handschrift B*, ed. H. Moser and U. Müller (Göppingen: Kümmerle, 1972). Complete edns: Oswald von Wolkenstein, *Geistliche und weltliche Lieder, ein- und mehrstimmig*, ed. Josef Schatz and Oswald Koller, *DTOe IX/1*, vol. 18 (1902); Oswald von Wolkenstein, *Die Lieder*, ed. Karl Kurt Klein *et al.*, 2nd edn (Tübingen, 1975); Oswald von Wolkenstein: *Die Lieder*, ed. Klaus J. Schönmetzler (Munich: Vollmer, 1979).

[289] Complete edn of the polyphonic songs: Pelnar, *Die mehrstimmigen Lieder Oswalds*. For the dates given in the table below, see Norbert Mayr, 'Oswald von Wolkensteins Liederhandschrift A in neuer Sicht', in Hans-Dieter Mück and Ulrich Müller eds, *Gesammelte Vorträge der 600-Jahrfeier Oswalds von Wolkenstein, Seis am Schlern 1977* (Göppingen: Kümmerle, 1978), 351–71.

[290] Schuler, 'Konstanz', 167; Pirro, *La musique à Paris*, 30; Wright, *Burgundy*, doc. 166 (of 17 November 1416); Higinio Anglès, *Historia de la música medieval en Navarra* (Pamplona: Diputación Foral de Navarra, 1970), 329 f, and p. 197 below.

Table 1 *Arrangements of foreign songs by Oswald von Wolkenstein*

No. Foreign model	German source	Oswald's text	Date
46 Je voy mon cuer	F-Sm, CS-Pu	Du außerweltes schöns	16/17
47 N'ay je cause	–	Frolichen so wel	16/17
48 Jour a jour	F-Sm, Em	Stand auf Maredel	after 18?
50 Par maintes fois	F-Sm, Em	Der mai mit lieber zal	before 15?
52 Fuiés de moy	A-M, F-Sm, CS-Pu	Wolauff, gesell	15/16
53 En tes douz flans	F-Sm	Frolich, zärtlich	16–18
54 Qui contre	F-Sm, A-Wn	Froleich geschray	22(?)
56 ('*piroletum*')			
Musica frawein	D-WI, D-TRs	Tröstlicher hort	17
65 Questa fanciulla	F-Sm, Em	Mein herz das ist versert	16/17
72 Talent m'est pris	F-Sm	Die minne füget niemand	15
88 A son plaisir	F-Sm, Em	Vierhundert jar	16/17

The foreign songs on which these arrangements are based, were probably available to Oswald at Constance; this is the more likely as they were also copied in central European sources that are indirectly related to the Council (on these sources, see also below).

In order fully to understand these contrafacta, we must consider how fluid the shape of even a polyphonic song could be at the time. Some musicians may have performed simply one voice of it, or have added or substituted voices (especially the contratenor). Others may have arranged the song for instruments such as harp, lute, gittern, chamber organ, clavichord, exchiquier, harpsichord, even winds.[291] There were straightforward contrafacta (i.e. substitutions of another text – often a sacred one); but there were also rewritings of the music, and transfers of the text from one voice to another. Oswald's songs in this category are all arrangements with musical changes, and often with a transfer of the text from the superius to the tenor. Oswald tends to omit original contratenors, and never adds a completely new voice such as a triplum or contratenor.[292] His method of reworking must have relied much more on the ear than on written notation, and may have involved a supporting instrument such as the harp. He would have learnt the foreign songs by heart (perhaps not with all their voices), and then shaped his new poems for them. The final, polyphonic versions of his arrangements as they were later codified in his song manuscripts, were almost certainly put together with the help of literate musicians who had access to some of the foreign originals.

As can be seen from Table 1, the repertory adapted here belongs to the lateral traditions, and also includes some older songs which had become part of these traditions. These include Vaillant's virelai 'Par maintes fois', and the old *chace* 'Talent m'est pris', two onomatopoetic songs; 'Fuiés de moy' which presumably predates 1376; and 'Jour a jour' which certainly predates 1384.[293]

[291] See also Strohm, 'Native and foreign polyphony', 212 f and 217.

[292] The contratenors in Oswald's versions of 'Je voy mon cuer' (no. 46) and 'Qui contre fortune' (no. 54) have not yet been found in French sources, but were surely also composed in the west.

[293] On these and other old songs which became the staple fare of the lateral traditions, see Strohm, 'Ars nova fragments'.

'Questa fanciulla, amor' is, of course, by Francesco Landini, and 'N'ay je cause' by Martinus Fabri, who worked in Holland (see pp. 70 f). I believe that Oswald's models give a representative sample of the secular songs that could be heard during the Council in various versions and social contexts.

Most of the French songs were well known in Italy by 1415, as is attested by their sources (including the arrangements in *I-FZ*) and by citations in *Il Saporetto* (see pp. 90 f). They reached Oswald apparently in vocal versions, but sometimes without the original texts. In fact, their German copies (in *F-Sm, CS-Pu, Em, A-Wn 5094* etc.) usually give them sacred contrafactum texts or have only garbled French incipits. An example is 'Addo plasier' in the Strasbourg MS for 'A son plaisir' by Pierre Fontaine; next to that garbled incipit, there appears the title of Oswald's arrangement (!), 'Vierhundert jar'. This suggests that the Strasbourg scribe knew Oswald's version, too, perhaps through contacts with Constance. This would make Oswald's arrangement the earliest testimony of Fontaine's seminal compositions (on him, see p. 148), and also place some music of the most advanced style within the conciliar orbit.[294]

Oswald's arrangements are invariably closer in notational detail to the German sources than to the foreign ones. This partly reflects the procedure of his scribes who compiled his songs from *c.*1422, but also shows that he was by no means alone in performing and arranging foreign songs. Other Germans may even have preceded him.[295] The MS *CS-Pu XI E 9*, a song collection copied in Strasbourg *c.*1415–20,[296] and the oldest repertory in *Em* (*D-Mbs lat. 14274*), a source copied around 1440 in Vienna,[297] surely have independent links with the foreign material brought to Germany in this period. At least one other large collection must have existed about 1420 in Vienna, at the collegiate school of St Stephen's or at the abbey of St Dorothy.[298] *CS-Pu XI E 9* and *F-Sm 222*, the Strasbourg sources, are especially rich in music from the Low Countries, with French and Flemish texts. *F-Sm 222*, furthermore, has many German polyphonic songs, probably comprising arrangements or contrafacta, together with original compositions. If we add to this the lieder of the Monk of Salzburg and of Heinrich Laufenberg (see p. 341), we have a very large corpus of German song around 1400, both monophonic and polyphonic, sacred and secular, which surrounded and stimulated Oswald's own produc-

---

[294] At least, both the original and the arrangement were known in south-west Germany by the early 1420s when 'Addo plasier' was copied. Welker, 'New light on Oswald', 200, and Fallows, 'Two equal voices', 229 and 240, identify three other songs by Grenon ('La plus jolie et la plus belle') and anonymi which Oswald arranged considerably later, probably around 1430. On 'La plus jolie', see also p. 149 below.

[295] The original of 'Tröstlicher hort' (no. 56) must have been a lost Ars nova virelai ('piroletum'), which was known in central Europe before 1415, and quoted in treatises already under two different titles ('Musica frawein' and 'Tonat agmen celestis curie'), before Oswald took it up. Brunner–Ganser–Hartmann, 'Windsheimer Fragment', 200, with facs of *D-WI*. The authors attempt to prove German origin for this composition, underestimating the stylistic variety within the Franco-Netherlands tradition.

[296] *RISM B IV*, vol. 3, 255–62; Friedrich Kammerer, *Die Musikstücke des Prager Kodex XI e 9* (Augsburg and Brno, 1931); Strohm, 'Ars nova fragments', 121.

[297] On this source, see p. 259 below.

[298] Strohm, 'Native and foreign polyphony', 210.

tion. It remains to be investigated whether he actually met foreign chanson composers at Constance or on his travels, and whether Nicholas Grenon or Pierre Fontaine were among them.[299]

To exemplify the work of arrangers other than Oswald, there is hardly a better case than that of 'En discort sunt Desir et Esperance': a ballade from the lateral tradition, first found in *NL-Uu 37 II* (see p. 69). This Ars nova song found an enthusiastic reception in central Europe, where it usually appears, in practical and theoretical sources, with the sacred text 'Virginem mire pulchritudinis'.[300] Two keyboard arrangements also exist: in the Faenza Codex and in the later Buxheim Organ Book. In Example 16, I have selected for comparison the original cantus and tenor, the cantus of the sacred contrafactum according to the Polish source *Kras (PL-Wn 8054)*[301] and the embellished cantus from Faenza.[302] The tenor is identical in all three versions; the Faenza MS – as usual – omits the contratenor, and transposes the piece up a fifth.

What is shown are only the first two lines of the ballade, without the concluding melismas of the second. The French words are spread over a variety of longer and shorter musical phrases, which serve to highlight the syntactic ingredients of the text (the symbolic figures 'Desir' and 'Esperance' from the *Roman de la Rose* receive prominent treatment). Simple melodic–rhythmic

Example 16 'En discort' (three versions)

---

[299] The minor Flemish composer Thomas Fabri (see also p. 145) was perhaps at Constance: a manuscript with three songs by him, now surviving in Austria (*A-HEI*), could well have been produced in the international atmosphere of the Council. Strohm, *Bruges*, 109 ff; *idem*, 'Native and foreign polyphony', 211 f.

[300] Ward, 'A central European repertory', 329 f.

[301] *Kras*, no. 14; see Perz ed., *Sources of Polyphony*, vols. 13, 59; and 14, no. 14. The contrafactum is compared with others in eastern sources in Mirosław Perz, 'Zur Textunterlegungspraxis in der Mehrstimmigkeit des 14. und 15. Jahrhunderts und über einige in Polen neu- und wiedergefundene Quellen dieser Zeit', in Günther–Finscher eds, *Musik und Text*, 327–49.

[302] Of the various edns of the Faenza version, see the synopses of the original and keyboard arrangement in Apel ed., *FSC*, vol. 2 (1971) no. 3, and Plamenac ed., *Keyboard Music . . .* (n. 200 above), no. 3.

Example 16 (*cont.*)

formulas keep returning, for example the syncopated descent of bar 2 and the '3-2-3-1' motive of bars 5-6. The two arrangements are, of course, divergent in purpose and style, but they have one principle in common: *horror vacui*. Whereas the contrafactum splits all the longer values into repeated pitches, to accommodate a text about five times as long as the original, the keyboard version adds so many ornamental runs and flourishes that the primary notes can hardly be recognized. Both adaptations occasionally agree in filling the 'gaps' with repeated notes (bars 4 and 8); because of the added rhythmic activity, the concise '3-2-3-1' motive loses profile. The keyboard arranger makes an effort to distinguish the cadential bars 3 and 7 by special embellishments, and also rhythmically equates bars 3 and 5, as does the original. The vocal arranger rattles on across most structural points. On the other hand, the keyboard arranger seems to lose interest in the embellishing efforts after bar 10 (the previous style is taken up only later in the piece), whereas the vocal arranger discovers at last in bar 14-15 that there can be linguistic equivalents to the musical repeats of the chanson: 'cythara', 'prosodia'. Much as these arrangements all need to be judged in the context of their respective cultural environments, they have in common a certain mindless 'music-making', which replaces the distinct gestures of the original.

This may be seen to be the same spirit which, in the last stages of the Ars nova and Ars subtilior, tended to ornament and embellish rather than express, and which was in permanent search of detail, ever smaller note-values, verbosity, and repetition. Whether in the central or in the lateral traditions, elaboration (*elocutio*) got the better of invention. And yet, the same traditions which were coming to an end here, also harboured new creative forces: a paradox that still awaits a full interpretation.

PART II

THE AGE OF DUFAY AND DUNSTABLE

INTRODUCTION

The names of great composers are legitimately employed to characterize an age which itself acknowledged their leadership. Johannes Tinctoris, in his *Liber de arte contrapuncti* of 1477, praised the great progress which the musical art had made in the previous forty years among contemporary composers whose teachers (*praeceptores*) had been Dunstable, Dufay and Binchois.[1] In another context, he spoke of the music of his time as a 'new art', of which the 'fount and origin' (*novae artis fons et origo*) was held to be among the English composers, whose chief (*caput*) was Dunstable.[2] Again, the names of Dufay and Binchois are joined to that of Dunstable. Tinctoris's quest for leaders and origins may be regarded as typical of a Renaissance scholar and a reflection of his own environment rather than of the historical facts. Nevertheless in his epic *Le champion des dames* (*c*.1440), Martin le Franc had already praised the new style of Dufay and Binchois as superior to that of Tapissier, Carmen and Cesaris at the beginning of the century (see p. 65). He goes on to explain the reasons for Dufay's and Binchois' success:

> Car ilz ont nouvelle pratique
> De faire frisque concordance
> En haulte et basse musique,
> En fainte, en pause et en muance;
> Et ont prins de la contenance
> Angloise, et ensuy Dompstable;
> Pour quoy merveilleuse plaisance
> Rend leur chant joieux et notable.

[For they have a new practice of making pleasant consonance in *haute* and *basse musique*, pause and mutation. They have taken up the English countenance and followed Dunstable, whereby marvellous pleasure makes their song joyful and significant.]

There is hardly any word in these lines which does not require – and has not attracted – musicological comment.[3] We may concentrate on two aspects.

---

[1] Tinctoris, *Opera theoretica*, vol. II, 12. For an English translation of the preface of this work, see Strunk, *Source Readings*, 7–9.

[2] The preface of his *Proportionale musices* of the early 1470s; see Tinctoris, *Opera theoretica*, vol. IIa, 10. Translation in Strunk, *Source Readings*, 5.

[3] According to Fallows, 'Contenance angloise', le Franc did not speak of a sudden or tangible English influence, nor did he refer it clearly to one of the musical terms mentioned in the first half of the stanza.

Martin le Franc, a poet who cannot necessarily be credited with musical know-how, endeavours in the first four lines to use technical terms relating to polyphonic composition as well as performance practice. The latter is represented by the following terms: '*haute musique*' (music for wind bands); '*basse musique*' (music for soft instruments and voices); '*fainte*' (probably *musica ficta*); '*pause*' (probably not simply 'rests' but also long-held notes with improvised embellishments, see p. 167) and '*muance*' (mutation, i.e. the change of the solmization hexachord when the line steps outside it). All these traditional elements, however, are used according to a 'novel practice' which makes 'pleasant concordance' – implying polyphonic composition. Since the poet translates several established Latin terms into their French equivalents (*concordantia* is one of them), we may also retranslate the inconspicuous word 'faire' into its Latin equivalent, 'facere': that is, 'componere'.[4]

The other point of interest is, of course, the much-discussed citation of Dunstable and the '*contenance angloise*'. It is possible that this term refers to performance practice, too, although connected with a famous composer. The term is otherwise unknown in music and may have been coined ad hoc. It could therefore be argued that the poet meant English performing and composing techniques for which he did not know a better term: 'English discant' or 'faburden'. These are harmonic techniques, characterized by the avoidance of dissonance ('euphony') and many imperfect consonances. Although they did to some extent influence continental composers in this period, they are absent from the works of Dunstable, to whom the poet's praise is mainly addressed. '*Contenance*' must rather refer to the melodic, harmonic and rhythmic style of written works. The word means something like 'deportment', 'gesture' or 'attitude', as in the postures and movements of a dancer or actor. When applied to a written composition, it may fit as a metaphor describing melodic–rhythmic shapes. Heinrich Besseler was perhaps close to this understanding of the term when he coined the formula *neuer Stromrhythmus* ('new flowing rhythm') for Dufay's music around 1430.[5]

Euphony and imperfect consonances in the performance of plainsong-based genres, flowing rhythm, and also sensuous melodic shapes, were shared achievements of England and the Continent. These achievements were also the result of a longer evolution, on either side of the Channel. By about 1440 the specifically English performing techniques of English discant and faburden had long been submerged in written styles, or even been abandoned by the leading English composers. Le Franc cannot have thought that a Dunstable was needed to communicate these techniques to Dufay. In the lines containing the term

---

[4] 'Facere' denoted the creation of a work in general, and especially of art. *Res facta* (a term used by Tinctoris) is 'the composed musical work'. *Choses faictes* are composed pieces: see Blackburn, 'Compositional process', 262 ff. Lionel Power wrote his treatise 'upon the gamme' (see Sanford B. Meech, 'Three musical treatises in English from a fifteenth century manuscript', *Speculum* 10 (1935), 235–69) 'for hem that wil be syngers, or makers, or techers'.

[5] Besseler, *Bourdon*.

contenance angloise and the name of Dunstable, he expresses respect for musical works, not for faburden or English discant. As regards the 'novel practice' of euphony, pauses and mutations, *haute* and *basse musique*, he does not say that these techniques were English. He is simply rounding out his picture, emphasizing the comprehensiveness of the change he saw in musical style.

In the following chapters the 'novel practice' of Dufay's and Dunstable's time is discussed as one of the achievements of *written* composition. The performance techniques and styles which le Franc also mentions were absorbed within this novel practice. No aspect of this process of absorption was limited to England. The continental and insular developments will be treated separately at first – not because there was no interaction but because a synthesis only becomes apparent just before the 1430s. From that time onwards, the evidence allows us to speak – whether under the aegis of the *contenance angloise* or not – of a musical age of Dufay *and* Dunstable.

Our period encompasses the active careers of John Dunstable (*d*.1453), Lionel Power (*d*.1445), Gilles de Bins dit Binchois (*c*.1400–60), Hugo de Lantins (*fl.* 1420–30), Arnold de Lantins (*d*.1432), and of many contemporaries of similar stature. Dufay, born perhaps in 1397,[6] lived until 1474, but his style and career took decidedly new turns in the early 1450s. At the beginning of the century, the formation of a new style ('novel practice') had overlapped with a continued cultivation of Ars nova idioms. This is exemplified by the music heard at the Council of Constance (1414–18), and by the older works in the Old Hall MS, copied in approximately the same years. This overlap characteristically occurred within the lateral traditions, where the new was born out of the old, while the central tradition did not accept the new elements and died out.

The Council of Constance initiated a slow process of Catholic centralization under Rome. But Pope Martin V (*r*. 1417–31), and even more his successor Eugene IV (*r*. 1431–47), faced resistance within the Church as well as from national and fringe movements. At the Council of Basle (1431–49), the die-hard conciliarists were dominant, and even created an antipope, Felix V (1439–49). The rising European powers of Aragon, Habsburg and France settled their conflicts with Rome only in the 1440s, having gained significant control over the affairs of the Church in their own territories. The Hussite campaigns in Bohemia and much beyond its borders – a direct result of Constance – lasted throughout the early 1430s; the religious dissent in Bohemia survived into the following century.

The decades of France's domination by England (1415–35) were the time when the Burgundian rather than the French royal branch of the Valois dynasty was most conspicuous in Europe. The court of Duke Philip the Good (1419–67) was like a spider in the web of international relations; its eclectic and flamboyant culture typified the feudal aspirations of the age.[7]

[6] Planchart, 'Guillaume Du Fay's benefices', 122–4.

[7] Vaughan, *Philip the Good; idem, Valois Burgundy* (London, 1975); Otto Cartellieri, *The Court of Burgundy* (London, 1929); Marix, *Histoire*; Dahnk, 'Musikausübung'. See also pp. 462–3 below.

The kingdom of France slowly found its way back from the humiliation at Agincourt (1415) to the position of a powerful, modern state in the later reign of Charles VII (*r.* 1422–61). This recovery, punctuated by the exploits of Jeanne d'Arc (burnt at the stake in 1431) and by the peace of Arras with Burgundy and England (1435), also helped the recovery of French cultural life.

If the period of the Great Schism (1378–1417) had been the time when regional practices outgrew provincialism and came in contact with each other, the following decades developed new coherence all across Europe. To borrow the metaphors with which Manfred Bukofzer contrasted Handel with Bach,[8] the age before 1417 saw a 'co-ordination' of regional styles, the later age a 'fusion'. This synthesis was achieved on the level of written art-music, and in the works of composers strong enough to absorb and transform traditions. Not only Dufay and Binchois, but also Dunstable and Lionel Power drew on the double heritage of a central (French) tradition and of their respective 'vernacular' idioms. All of them absorbed simpler or unwritten musical practices. Where the best music of their period excels in simplicity, clarity and balance, it pays tribute to the *undercurrents* of fourteenth-century music: but it also ennobles them. In France and in the Low Countries, simple, genre-bound styles had survived underneath the greater subtleties of the leading composers: the pastoral, convivial or popularizing rondeau, the 'realistic virelai', the modest liturgical chant settings performed in local cathedrals as well as in the papal chapel of Avignon. In England before the time of the Old Hall MS, polyphonic music was usually transmitted anonymously: it served communities, not career ambitions. In Italy, artistic renewal around 1400 chose the popularizing path with simple, heartfelt love-songs and *giustiniane*. An artist of Ciconia's stature could transform these trends into music of epochal significance.

Instrumental music, and the realistic imitation of the sounds of nature in music, had been beloved children of the Ars nova – but they had been children. Nobody had put his name to keyboard arrangements of songs, or to organ versets. No Ars nova composer had indulged in 'tuba' or 'trompetta' music – but Dufay did. Other humble idioms, for example fauxbourdon and faburden, had grown up by his time. Besseler has claimed that Dufay 'created the fauxbourdon piece' in his 'Missa Sancti Jacobi'.[9] Pieces with unwritten fauxbourdon technique must, however, have been performed in many churches by then. What Dufay probably did create was the idea that fauxbourdon was not too lowly a practice to enter a written Mass composition by Dufay.

This new 'social order' of musical idioms and genres began to emerge, in my opinion, around 1400 in the Franco-Netherlands area. Statistics derived from the surviving manuscripts show that the small-scale rondeau became more frequent at the expense of the large-scale ballade. The statistics are misleading in so far as they suggest a change within the same thread of historical develop-

---

[8] Manfred Bukofzer, *Music in the Baroque Era from Monteverdi to Bach* (New York: Norton, 1947), chaps. 7 and 8.
[9] Besseler, *Bourdon*, 17–19.

ment. In reality, the aesthetic of the simpler rondeau had been well established at the Burgundian court of Philip the Bold (*d.*1404), while southern French circles were still developing the most complex forms. In Burgundian Flanders, in Paris and at the courts of Berry and Anjou, the simple charm of the rondeau fascinated high society, and the *cour d'amour* cultivated a more emotional or 'feminine' aesthetic of courtly love. The dedicatory genres of the New Year and May song flourished: as they were based on the custom of giving one's sweetheart a New Year's gift (*estrenne*), or flowers in May, these courtly chansons actually ennobled folklore.

The rising middle classes of northern France and the Low Countries, particularly the merchants with their spending power, demanded a bigger share of the art, especially in sacred music. They were interested in the devotional aspects of the liturgy. Composers began to respond to this new type of patronage by writing their finest music to devotional texts, or by contributing simple, functional plainsong settings such as hymns, antiphons for Compline (a service which burghers could attend after work), or votive Masses for Our Lady. The ceremonial motet survived into the 1440s, albeit in the simpler forms developed in Italy and England. Non-isorhythmic motets in song styles or sometimes over well-known cantus firmi began to occupy an increasingly important place in musical production.

A sizeable amount of actual folklore entered art music in this period, certainly more than we can identify today. The peculiarities of the popular *siciliane* were taken up in Italian art-song around 1400, and Dufay rather often elaborates dance-tunes or folksongs. This he does do not with the attitude of the folklorist or antiquarian, but as an universalist who wants to assimilate all music.

We are dealing here not with negative but with positive processes of innovation. The complexities of the Ars subtilior disappear, because the musicians divert their best efforts to *something else*. By the same token, they raise humbler genres and techniques to higher complexity. Behind the unassuming mask of simple rhythms, small-scale forms, naive poetic vocabulary, there is often a sophisticated balance of motivic and tonal design, and a great control of dissonance. Free, declamatory imitation widely replaces strict canonic technique. In the hands of a good composer, free imitation is of greater artistic interest than strict canon, as is attested by much Renaissance music. While canon tends to obscure the words, imitation often enhances them, both in their expressive and their formal qualities.

In the next chapter, an attempt will be made to describe the genesis of the new style of fifteenth-century music in more detail. One rather fundamental stylistic element which distinguishes the new style from the old, may be discussed already here: the development of rhythm and its notation.

These categories have often been considered essential for the genesis of fifteenth-century music. Most attention has been paid to changes in the use of mensurations. No particular development can be observed in the use of C (*tempus imperfectum cum prolatione minori*; often transcribed as 2/4), which was infrequent anyway. There was a shift, however, among the triple metres from the predominance of ₵ (*tempus imperfectum cum prolatione maiori*; 6/8) to that of ○ (*tempus perfectum cum prolatione minori*; 3/4). Besseler spoke of an actual '*Notationsumschwung*' (a U-turn in notational habits) towards 1430, giving Dufay most of the credit for it.[10] In his view, the broader triple pace of 3/4 (○) as opposed to the narrower gait of 6/8 (₵) constitutes a 'new flowing rhythm' around 1430.

A newly introduced mensuration, ф (6/4 or 3/2), also demonstrates this tendency. Its first known occurrence is in the heart-shaped rondeau 'Belle, bonne, sage' by Baude Cordier (see p. 58); by the early 1420s, the mensuration was well known. It seems to have had the function of presenting the rhythmic groupings of ₵ in doubled note-values. If these values are then performed at twice their usual speed – as might be suggested by the slash through the circle – the rhythmic effect is offset, making the new metre seemingly unsuitable for a new rhythmic conception.

In reality, however, the visual effect of the longer note-values of both ф and ○ must have been significant for performers at the time. The adoption of these longer values was primarily a reaction to a general slowing down of performance tempos, which can be observed throughout the later Middle Ages (and beyond). Instead of introducing ever smaller note-values for ornaments, as had happened in the Ars subtilior, many musicians now decided in favour of longer note-values performed at faster speeds, which seemed more convenient for the writing and reading of music. (Again, similar 'compensatory' changes of notation can be observed in later ages.) It is by no means certain that ф was always performed at double speed:[11] the new notation also conveyed a different musical feeling that can best be shown when comparing the traditional metres ₵ (6/8) and ○ (3/4).

These two metres had already been part of the four admitted by Philippe de Vitry and Jehan des Murs in the early fourteenth century (the *quatre prolations*). They were used alongside each other throughout that century, their durational relation being that of minim equivalence (quaver in transcription). Their rhythmic 'vocabularies' related in about the same way as in our 6/8 and 3/4 metres. While the 6/8 type was preferred for the great Ars subtilior ballade and also for much sacred music, the 3/4 type became more characteristic of simpler music, particularly of the rondeau as cultivated at the Burgundian court towards

---

[10] Besseler, *Bourdon*, 109 ff. These and other perceived changes in notational practice have been used for the dating of Dufay's works: Charles Hamm, *A Chronology of the Works of Guillaume Dufay, Based on a Study of Mensural Practice* (Princeton University Press, 1964).

[11] For its beginnings, see Ursula Günther, 'Der Gebrauch des tempus perfectum diminutum in der Handschrift *Chantilly 1047*', *AMw* 17 (1960), 277–97. Planchart, 'Relative speed', argues in favour of a 3 : 2 relationship between the durations under ○ and ф; but Anna Maria Busse Berger, 'The myth of the *diminutio per tertiam partem*', *JM* 8 (1990), 398–426, shows that diminution by half is consistently supported by theorists. Eunice Schroeder, 'The stroke comes full circle: ф and ₵ in writings on music, c.1450–1540', *MD* 36 (1982), 119–66, found that mid-fifteenth-century writers interpreted the stroke as a sign of diminution by half.

1400. But then a strange thing happened. The 6/8 pieces showed the expected tendency to acquire more and more small, ornamental values (semiminims: i.e. semiquavers), and thus reflected the general slowing down of performance tempos. In small-scale pieces in 6/8 without virtuoso ornamentation, such as Baude Cordier's 'Se cuer d'amant' (see Ex. 19), the main motivic events happened on the minim (quaver) level. Pieces written in ◯, however, retained a faster pace and were reluctant to pick up small note-values, retaining their breves (minims) and semibreves (crotchets) instead. The result was that much music in ◯ metre composed between *c.*1400 and *c.*1430, and especially the small-scale chansons of Franco-Netherlands composers, still conformed to the leisurely triple groupings in breves and semibreves (♩ ♩ ♩ ♩) already used by Machaut, whereas the chansons in ₵ written at the same time seem to reproduce similar groupings in halved values (♪ ♩ ♩ ♪). Compare, for example, two chansons by Binchois and Dufay – both of the 1420s, and copied just a few pages away from each other in the same manuscript:[12]

Example 17*a* Binchois, 'Joyeux penser' (contratenor omitted)

Example 17*b* Guillaume Dufay, 'Je ne puis plus / Unde veniet' (contratenor omitted)

[12] *GB-Ob 213* (see below). 'Je ne puis plus / Unde veniet' is edited in Dufay, *Opera omnia*, vol. 6, no. 29; 'Joyeux penser' is in Binchois, *Chansons*, no. 21.

Example 17b (*cont.*)

According to the theoretical tradition of the *quatre prolations*, Dufay's quavers should have the same duration as those of Binchois (minim equivalence). For the first phrase of the song, this would be musically absurd. Dufay's piece must surely be performed faster, because it has more or less the same rhythmic groupings and declamatory pace here as Binchois' piece, but in doubled note-values. It is unlikely that it should go twice as fast, however, because in the last phrase, Dufay introduces many quavers, whereas Binchois does not have a corresponding number of semiquavers – with the result that the note-values look roughly the same in both pieces. We must conclude that Dufay's chanson is to be performed at *less than twice* the tempo of that of Binchois. The appropriate pulse might be 'crotchet = 120' in the former piece, but 'quaver = 150' in the latter.

The performance tempos in the two mensurations can thus not be compared any longer by a strict, proportional equivalence (as in Vitry's time). Now, performance traditions have gradually transformed the relationship and eroded the mathematical ratio. The ○ metre, 3/4, has retained the relatively swifter pace and the longer note-values of the earlier times, whereas the ₵ metre, 6/8, has duly slowed down to the point of losing most of its long values.

The slowing-down effect had one important limitation. Values smaller than a quaver were traditionally thought unfit to carry individual syllables, regardless of the mensuration. Few composers dared break this barrier; most of them used the smaller values for ornamental melismas only. In any mensuration, semi-quavers and even smaller values usually came in groups or pairs, not singly. In effect, the 6/8 metre could not activate the shortest values to the same extent as 3/4 could activate the longest. The 3/4 mensuration ended up as being more flexible, giving access to an additional level of note-values.

Dufay's chanson 'Je ne puis plus ce que j'ay peu / Unde veniet auxilium mihi?' was quite possibly conceived as a demonstration (among other things) of the flexibility of the 3/4 metre. While the tenor of this piece speeds up in proportional diminutions as in an isorhythmic motet, the cantus stays in the same metre. It simply hurries along with the tenor in more and more quavers, covering the full range of note-values across three diminutions of the tenor. This demonstration of the flexibility of ○ also seems symbolic with regard to the text. The tenor represents an old man and his increasingly anxious cries for help. He 'can no longer do what he used to'; that is, he is old-fashioned and inflexible, needing a proportional 'operation' to achieve a different speed. The cantus, on the other hand, represents the 3/4 mensuration which has retained its youthful muscles and can accelerate as desired.

I

NORTH AND SOUTH

The genesis of the new style on the Continent

Before anything can be said about stylistic developments, it is useful to examine our underlying chronological and geographical assumptions, which largely depend on the availability of manuscript sources.[13] A huge number of them survives, but they rarely disclose dates or places of composition for individual works. The main problem is their unbalanced geographical distribution. Before *c.*1430 the largest sources are mostly of Italian origin; nevertheless, they contain more music by northern composers than by Italians. On the other hand, we have none of the large choirbooks which northern cathedrals and court chapels must have owned at that time, and we have virtually no chansonniers of French origin for the first quarter of the century. If we had those sources, our picture would probably be even more slanted in favour of this area. Perhaps we would then also have more music of English origin.

The largest Italian collection is *I-Bc Q 15 (BL)*. The codex was begun in the Veneto about 1420, and completed probably in Vicenza about 1436; its over 300 works include Mass settings (in pairs and cycles), sacred and secular motets, antiphons, hymns, sequences, *Magnificat* settings and French chansons. Several pieces in the earliest layer are by English composers.[14]

The largest secular collection is *GB-Ob 213 (O; Ox)*, with 259 secular songs in French and Italian, plus 66 sacred pieces (none of them English).[15] This manuscript was compiled close to 1430 in the Veneto, and completed soon after 1436. It is the earliest continental manuscript surviving complete that is written entirely in 'white' (i.e. hollow) notation. It is a significant source also in that it

---

[13] Information on the manuscripts mentioned in the following chapter is also available in the *Census Catalogue (CC)*, and for some manuscripts in *RISM B IV*.

[14] The only published inventory is Guillaume de Van, 'Inventory of manuscript Bologna, Liceo Musicale, Q 15 (*olim* 37)', *MD* 2 (1948), 231–57. A forthcoming study by Margaret Bent will greatly revise and update this information. See, for the moment, Bent, 'A contemporary perception'.

[15] Inventory: Gilbert Reaney, 'The manuscript Oxford, Bodleian Library, Canonici Misc. 213', *MD* 9 (1955), 73–104. Detailed studies: Schoop, *Entstehung und Verwendung*; Graeme M. Boone, *Dufay's Early Chansons: Chronology and Style in the Manuscript Oxford, Bodleian Library, Canonici misc. 213*, Ph.D., Harvard U., 1987. Higgins, 'Music and musicians', proposes that some of the material in fasc. 5–8 came from the court of Jean de Berry at Bourges, since several composers represented here were active at the Sainte-Chapelle (G. Legrant, Grenon, Fontaine, Cesaris, Charité and Paullet). See also pp. 144 f below.

mentions dates and places above several works. Some of these seem to be dates of composition, others perhaps not (the dates range from 1423 to 1436). The oldest music, partly of the fourteenth century, is concentrated in the fascicles 5-8, which were written first. The compiler of this collection also had access to a small manuscript of Franco-Netherlands origin, *F-Pn n. a. f. 4379*, part II (*PC II*), and he copied tenors from songs in his possession into the manuscript *F-Pn 4379*, part III (*PC III*). A similar little chansonnier of French origin was attached in the 1420s to the older Reina Codex (*F-Pn n. a. f. 6771*, part III; *PR III*), probably by a collector in the Veneto. Loosely related to this group of sources is the chansonnier *F-Pn n. a. f. 4917 (Pz)*, with 34 French and Italian songs. A slightly later north Italian manuscript, *I-Bu 2216 (BU)*, has 85 works of various genres: many of them are Italian, four English.[16]

All these manuscripts demonstrate how much a circumscribed group of north Italian musicians appreciated northern music. Of course, such enthusiasm can characterize this whole period only by default of other information. Among the very few Franco-Netherlands sources of this time, there are the fragments *F-Dm 2837*[17] (c.1420-25), *F-Pn n. a. f. 10660*,[18] and *E-MO 823* (c.1420-30).[19] The complete Burgundian chansonnier *E-E V. III. 24 (EscA)* and the closely related 'Binchois fragment' (*D-Mbs 3192*) may be as late as c.1440, although they contain earlier material.[20] Apparently dating from the 1440s is a pair of folio-size choirbooks from Cambrai Cathedral *F-CA 6* and *F-CA 11*. Sharing between them the majority of their respectively 16 and 19 pieces, the volumes may have been used simultaneously by two groups of singers in the cathedral choir.

Central and eastern European sources of the 1430s and 1440s are more numerous. The Council of Basle (1431-49) and related political events led to the compilation of such choirbooks as the Aosta MS (*I-AO; Ao*) and the Trent Codices 87 and 92 (*I-TRmn 87, 92; Tr 87, 92*) around 1435-43. All these codices are, unlike the coeval French sources, written in 'white' notation. The 'St Emmeram Codex' (*D-Mbs lat.14274; Em*), a big Viennese anthology, was compiled by a university scholar in the same years. Apart from related fragments, the numerous pieces added to the Strasbourg Codex (*F-Sm 222*) over the years c.1425-45

[16] Inventory: Heinrich Besseler, 'The manuscript Bologna, Biblioteca Universitaria 2216', *MD* 6 (1952), 39-65. Facs edn and study: F. A. Gallo ed., *Il codice musicale 2216 della Biblioteca Universitaria di Bologna*, 2 vols. (Bologna: Forni, 1970). A new study of the manuscript by Janet Palumbo is forthcoming (Ph.D., Princeton U.).

[17] Craig Wright, 'A fragmentary manuscript of early 15th-century music in Dijon', *JAMS* 27 (1974), 306-15.

[18] See, most recently, Fallows, 'Two equal voices', 234 f.

[19] Maria Carmen Gómez, 'El manuscrito 823 de Montserrat (Biblioteca del Monasterio)', *MD* 36 (1982), 39-93. Fallows, 'Two equal voices', 234 n. 5, concludes from an Italian watermark that the manuscript may be Italian, but Italian paper was used in all Europe at that time. Fallows also seems to consider the Reina Codex part III as being Italian, whereas I believe it is French.

[20] Walter Kemp, 'The MS Escorial V.III.24', *MD* 30 (1976), 97-129; Slavin, *Binchois' Songs*. I am referring to *EscA* as 'Burgundian' here because it can be argued that it was used at the ducal court; sources which may have originated in the ducal territories but cannot be linked to the court (for example, *Dijon 2837*) are classified here as 'Franco-Netherlands'.

are worth mentioning. The Polish source *Kras*, of *c*.1440, has some music written in a contemporary idiom, and the same is true of other Polish and Silesian
fragments from these decades.

The bulk of English sacred music of the early fifteenth century reached central Europe as late as in the Aosta, Trent and St Emmeram codices – a sure
sign that the Council of Basle was far more instrumental in its distribution
than Constance had been. A choirbook of *c*.1448 from the Este court in Ferrara, *I-MOe α.X. I. II* (*ModB*), contains, besides liturgical music and motets
by Dufay and Binchois, a surprising number of English works – a phenomenon
which will be discussed below (p. 265).

The compositions found in the great collections of the early fifteenth century
are not only of diverse national origins (which in itself is something of a
novelty) but also of different ages. The musicians who copied these sources
were interested in the music of at least three generations. One wonders how
the older pieces were *performed* or, in some cases, whether they were performed
at all. For example, two ballades copied in *GB-Ob 213* around 1430 must have
existed by 1390: 'Medée fu' (see Ex. 5) and 'J'aym. Qui?' by Paullet (see Ex. 18).
Whereas the former work may have presented some difficulty to modern singers
with its outdated rhythmic proportions, the simple 'J'aym. Qui?' is hardly
distinguishable from more recent chansons. Its rhythmic vocabulary, especially
the witty parlando-imitation, is very similar to that of Dufay's celebrated bal-

Example 18 Mahieu Paullet, 'J'aym. Qui? Vous. Moy?'

Example 18 (*cont.*)

lade of the early 1430s, 'Se la face ay pale'. The style of 'Medée fu', on the other hand, was not imitated by any composer after *c.*1420. This Ars subtilior ballade was simply an old, famous work which musicians chose to retain in their manuscripts – whereas the little ballade by Paullet plays a role in the genesis of the new style.

It is legitimate to search for origins in the history of musical style, whether or not it can be shown that composers were consciously striving for innovation. We cannot help attributing significance to the chronological priority of ideas, whether or not we relate it to some kind of superiority. But chronological priority is not always easily demonstrated. Many works of our period have no author's name attached and no other external clue as to their date; some are attributed to authors for whom we have no biographies.

The development of Italian music around 1400–25, for example, is difficult to trace, since we have reliable dates for some composers, and not for others. The most famous names are those of Johannes Ciconia (*d.*1412), Antonius Zacharias (*d.*1415) and Hubertus de Salinis (*fl.* ?1395–1417; see p. 100). Did they precede, and influence, all the other composers working in Italy before the appearance of Dufay in 1420? Or were some of the apparently lesser men important originators, too? The group in question includes the following composers:

Antonio da Cividale (*fl.* 1400–30?);
Bartolomeo da Bologna (a Benedictine prior and organist at Ferrara Cathedral, *fl.* 1407–*c.* 1430);
Cristoforo de Monte (of Feltre, *fl.* 1410–30?);[21]

[21] He obtained the doctorate at Padua University on 26 October 1410, in the presence and perhaps under the guidance of the later famous humanist Vittorino da Feltre, his fellow countryman. Two months later, a Simone de Lellis de Teramo obtained the degree, in the presence of 'presbiter' (!) and doctor Anthonius de Teramo, magister Anthonius de Luca, and – Pandolfo Malatesta! G. Brotto and G. Zonta, *Acta Graduum Academicorum Gymnasii Patavini* (Padua, 1922), nos. 132/3 and 136, respectively.

Prepositus Brixiensis (singer at Padua Cathedral 1421–5, perhaps identical with an earlier *prepositus* Melchior from Brescia);[22]
Nicolaus Zacharie of Brindisi (*fl.* 1415–30?);
Antonius Romanus (*cantor* at St Mark's, Venice, in 1420 and 1425);
Petrus Rubeus (of Parma, composer and theorist, 1378–1438);
Bartholomeus Brolo from Venice (*fl.* 1420–40?).[23]

Unless the scarce survival of their works misleads us, these composers seem to be followers, not leaders, in a stylistic development initiated by Zacharias, Salinis and Ciconia. There is little proof as yet. Bartolomeo da Bologna, for example, wrote 'parody' Mass sections over two of his own ballatas (a Gloria 'Vince con lena' and a Credo 'Morir desio'), as did Zacharias: we do not know who got the idea from whom. Several of these Italian composers also wrote French chansons: without exception, these pieces are more old-fashioned than the chansons written by Hugo and Arnold de Lantins in Italy in the 1420s. In Latin-texted music and in the Italian ballata, however, it is possible that the influence of Antonio da Cividale and Bartolomeo da Bologna rivalled that of Zacharias and Ciconia on the Dufay generation.

The fact that music by northern composers was so amply copied in Italian manuscripts of this time, may already give some clue as to the centres of stylistic leadership. But the chronological position of the northerners represented in Italian manuscripts is not always certain, and not all of their works can pass as innovative. This is the case, for example, with two ballades by Johannes Symonis dit Hasprois, which appear in the Chantilly Codex around the turn of the century, and still in *GB-Ob 213* thirty years later ('Puisque je suis fumeux' and 'Ma doulce amour'). The author is documented as early as 1378, and the chansons in question are true examples of the Ars subtilior, copied in *GB-Ob 213* out of a desire to preserve them for posterity. The same source contains two excellent chansons by a certain 'Haucourt' or 'Acourt', in a style that seems typical of 1430. (Hacourt is a village near Liège.) It is most unlikely that their author was Johannes de Altacuria, a papal chaplain until *c.*1403: the only surviving work by Johannes (in *F-CH 564*) is totally different in style. Thus, both Hasprois and Altacuria have to be distinguished from the generation mainly represented in *GB-Ob 213*.[24] Another questionable identification is that of 'Bosquet', the composer of two Mass sections found in *I-Bc Q 15*, *F-Sm 222* and elsewhere, with the Avignonese chaplain Johannes de Bosco alias Pellisson (see p. 25), by whom we have two much more old-fashioned Mass sections in the Apt MS.[25]

---

[22] Atlas, 'Pandolfo III Malatesta', 71 f.

[23] For editions, see Reaney ed., *EFM*, vols. 5 (1975) and 6 (1977); Stevens ed., *Venetian Ceremonial Motets*; Antonius Romanus, *Opera*, ed. F. A. Gallo (Bologna, 1969).

[24] See, respectively, Ursula Günther, 'Hasprois, Johannes Symonis' and 'Haucourt, Johannes' in *The New Grove*. I cannot accept the attributions to Hasprois proposed by Reaney and Günther (see also p. 53 above), and am certain that Altacuria is not the author of Haucourt's pieces.

[25] Reaney ed., *EFM*, vol. 2 (1959). See also p. 145 below on Johannes de Bosco at the Sainte-Chapelle of Bourges in 1405 and 1406.

Several important works in *I-Bc Q 15* and elsewhere by 'Johannes François de Gemblaco' (see also p. 173) have been connected with a chaplain of Duke Philip the Bold (*d.*1404) who carried that name: he was first heard of in 1378, last in 1415. The works in *I-Bc Q 15* must belong to a younger man (more often spelled Johannes Franchois), who seems to have come from Liège to Italy around 1420.[26] Bertrand Feragut from Avignon, active in Italy from 1415 until the 1440s,[27] composed a motet in praise of Vicenza and its Venetian bishop Francesco Malipiero in 1433 ('Excelsa civitas Vincentia'). In the copy in *I-Bc Q 15*, Malipiero's name has been erased and replaced by that of an earlier bishop, Pietro Emiliano, making it appear as if the work had been composed for his accession in 1409. A later scribe restored the original name, adding to the confusion.[28] This work with its pure chanson format would be revolutionary in the motet genre in 1409; in reality, it is indebted to models of Dufay and Arnold de Lantins of the 1420s (see p. 162). Feragut's only extant chanson, 'D'yre et de dueil', is probably an early work, showing the influence of Matteo da Perugia, whose successor at Milan Cathedral the French composer became in 1425. It seems impossible that this piece should postdate the motet. Finally, it has now been established that the composer Benoit ('Benotto di Giovanni'), active in Ferrara and Florence in the 1440s, was identical with the papal singer Benedictus Sirede,[29] and had no connection with Guillaume Benoit, a master of choirboys at Notre Dame, Paris, in 1405, or Guillaume Benoit, a singer in the service of William de la Pole, Earl of Suffolk, in 1424.

By contrast, we can observe the breaking of new ground in the compositions of Magister Baude Cordier, since he must indeed be identifiable as Philip the Bold's harper Baude Fresnel, who died in 1397 or 1398.[30] At least one work by Cordier – an elegant chanson-style Gloria in the Apt MS – was copied before 1400, and forms a pair with Tapissier's Credo (see p. 64). Cordier's two superb, innovative chansons 'Tout par compas' and 'Belle, bonne, sage' (see p. 58), would in their pictorial copies in the Chantilly Codex have to be dated around 1410 at the very latest, even if the identity Fresnel / Cordier were denied. Cordier, like Ciconia and Salinis, also produced an 'Ars subtilior essay': the rondeau 'Amans, amés sécrètement'. But with its tiny dimensions, it is almost a spoof: it has only two lines of text, and precisely 100 minims before the final, but uses no fewer than ten different mensuration signs! Apart from the deliberately complex rhythms, there is more 'secrecy' to the piece than meets the eye. At mid-point on the word 'sécrètement', the modal unity is interrupted by a striking C♯ sonority.

For the most modern-sounding chansons by Cordier, the small-scale rondeau 'Se cuer d'amant' (Ex. 19) is typical:

---

[26] José Quitin, 'A propos de Jean-François de Gembloux et de Johannes de Limburgia', *RBM* 21 (1967), 118–24. Wright, *Burgundy*, 62–5, defends the identity of the two men.

[27] Atlas, 'Pandolfo III Malatesta', 63–8.

[28] This state of things in the manuscript has only recently been uncovered: see Bent, 'A contemporary perception', 187 f.

[29] Starr, *Papal Court*, 106–13.

[30] Wright, *Burgundy*, 123–34; see p. 58 above. Cordier's works are edited in *EFM*, vol. 1 (1955).

Example 19 Baude Cordier, 'Se cuer d'amant'

The piece is remarkable for its concentration and economy of means. The voices advance in a cautious pace, with crotchet and quaver steps, often in disalignment with each other. This 'shredded texture' (Willi Apel) emphasizes the quavers. The basic rhythmic unit is not the dotted minim but the dotted crotchet; 39 such units appear before the final. Sometimes two or three units are combined into larger gestures, for example by hemiolas. Dissonances are restricted to the length of a quaver, rarely 'accented', and often treated as regular suspensions. The contratenor is of the 'combinatory' kind so often observed in later music. In the cadences of bars 4–5, 10–11 and 14, it acts as cantus, pushing the real cantus into the triplum position. In bars 7–8, 10 and 17, it cadences in its home position in the middle. In bars 5 (end), 6 (beginning) and 15, however, it is the bass of a 'V–I' or 'double-octave' cadence. The octave-leap formula (a possibility in bar 15, for example) is absent from the whole piece, which suggests that it was written before c.1400. On the other hand, one might seek the beginning of more modern harmonic approaches in a formation such as bar 14, where the cantus (in triplum position) descends from *c″* to *b′*, forming a diminished fifth over the leading note *f♯′*, instead of taking the more traditional step *c♯″–d″*.

The work has a clear overall shape with straightforward declamation of the four texted lines, plus connecting melismas. But there are also strategic recurrences of structural motives. Among them is the triad over *g′* (cantus: bars 1, 8 and 11) with its expansion to an octave in the lower voices (bars 5 and 11–12). The fifth over *g′* also appears in stepwise descent (bars 5 and 14–15), and in longer values in the tenor (bars 9–11), where it connects the two halves of the rondeau. Closely related is the particular descending gesture of the words 'cuer d'amant', on *d′*. It is echoed at once in the tenor a fifth lower, setting the scene for bar 5 which consists of three structural motives: the stepwise descent of the fifth on the words 'soy humilier', the octave descent in the contratenor, and the canonic imitation of 'cuer d'amant' in the tenor. The whole phrase describes, of course, the word 'humilier'. The 'cuer d'amant' motive returns somewhat hastily in bar 13: like a quick reminder to the lady of her lover's humble service, before he dares ask for reward in the very last line.

At that point, two descending fifths combine to form the expansive gesture of a seventh: its component *c″–f′* comes from bar 6, and the component *a′–d′* ('cuer d'amant') has been heard in bar 12, in the same rhythm. The descending seventh also answers that in bar 2 from *d″* to *e′*, which had not reached a full close yet. Upward-leaping sevenths had been heard in bars 4 and 14, at the junctures of text phrases. Thus, the final phrase is the first complete and conclusive gesture, secretly prepared, of this timid lover. His initial hesitations had also been expressed by the cautious rhythmic pace and the modal ambiguities of bars 5–15.

Many strategies of this setting were to stay with the 'Burgundian' chanson for decades. Typical of songs around 1400–20 is the introductory melisma (which may or may not have to be sung on the anticipated first syllable). A further development, however, was to be a distinction of texted and melismatic phrases throughout a piece, and their formal and sometimes motivic correspondence, like question and answer. This arrangement can be found, for example, in the perfect little two-part rondeau 'Ma seul amour' by Jean de Villeroye dit Briquet, a *ministre* of the *cour d'amour* in 1416. Briquet had already served the Burgundian court since 1388, but as a diplomat rather than a musician, which may be the reason why we only have this one piece by him.[31] This may speak for a high general level of musical expertise among the Burgundian courtiers.

Baude Cordier can well be compared with the 'Parisian triumvirate' Tapissier, Carmen and Cesaris. These composers are all documented as active musicians before 1410, in central and northern France; their works, especially the motets, constitute a break with the Ars subtilior.[32] 'Pontifici decori' by Jean Carmen, for example, is only approximately isorhythmic, has two canonic upper voices sharing the same text, and a flowing tenor–contratenor duet without rests, that provides full harmonies throughout (although the contratenor is often awkwardly dissonant). 'A virtutis ignicio / Ergo beata nascio' by Johannes Cesaris comes close to Ciconia: rolling coloraturas embellish full, static harmonies; sharply delineated areas of motivic interplay and *hoqueti* add textural contrast. Motets by Billart (probably a Parisian) and Nicholas Grenon show similar approaches, although their dates of composition are not precisely known.[33] (None of these motets yet adopts the three-voice chanson format, however.)

The secular music by Johannes Cesaris is remarkable in several respects.[34] 'Bonté lialté' features surprising chromaticism, 'A l'aventure va Gauvain' (a satirical song) witty parlando-style imitations. The rondeau 'Pour la doulour / Qui dolente n'aura' consists, in the form transmitted in *GB-Ob 213*, of only two high, texted voices: cantus and tenor. A low contratenor may have existed but is not indispensable. The voices constantly cross, and reach octave, unison or fifth on the finals *g*, *e*, *d*, and *c*. The pitch *eb* is used as a flattened third above *c*, and as a flattened supertonic above *d*. 'Se vous saviés' has regular octave-leaps of the contratenor at cadences, which were to become typical of the fifteenth-century chanson.

Between 1406 and 1409 Cesaris belonged to a group of innovative musicians then employed by the culturally ambitious Duke Jean de Berry. The duke's patronage of the visual arts and his splendid library have been exhaustively studied. Evidence has been found only recently[35] of the musicians whom he assembled in his palace and Sainte-Chapelle of Bourges (consecrated in 1405). They included the organists Guillaume le Bourgoing and Jehan Foliot, as well as Cesaris himself; that these organists performed polyphony together with chapel singers is strongly suggested by the fact that, in 1408, Foliot sold to the

---

[31] *EFM*, vol. 2 (1959). On the composer, see Wright, *Burgundy*, 134–7.
[32] The works of all three are in *EFM*, vol. 1 (1955).
[33] *EFM*, vol. 7 (1983) (Grenon); Borren ed., *Polyphonia Sacra*, no. 24 (Billart), nos. 30 and 31 (Grenon).
[34] See also Dannemann, *Musiktradition*, 46 f, 52.
[35] Higgins, 'Music and musicians'.

chapter of the Sainte-Chapelle a 'book of motets and Patrems which was delivered to Cesaris for the choirboys'.[36] Furthermore, clerks of the chapel from 1405 included Pierre Fontaine (who had earlier served the Burgundian court, where he was to return around 1415), Guillaume Legrant, Mahieu Paullet and Johannes de Bosco. The last-named was perhaps the Johannes de Bosco alias Pellisson who had already served Pope Clement VII; whether he is also identical with the composer Bosquet is not yet established (see p. 140). Paullet is known to us as the composer of 'J'aym. Qui?' (Ex. 18), and was surely active already before 1400, perhaps at Cambrai. From 1409 to 1412 Nicholas Grenon was Cesaris's successor as master of the choirboys.

Grenon, Fontaine and Legrant, with their connections to other centres such as Paris and the Burgundian court, are typical of this generation around 1400–10. In their careers, northern cathedral traditions (especially of musical education) begin to merge with the patronage of the courts. Some of these composers also went abroad. A few minor representatives of this group may be mentioned first.

Thomas Fabri, apparently taught by Johannes Ecghaert (Magister Egardus) in Bruges and by Tapissier in Paris, was succentor in Bruges between 1412 and 1415. He must have travelled to the south, perhaps to the Council of Constance, where a chansonnier containing his three secular songs was presumably compiled. His most modern-sounding piece is the Flemish May-song 'Die mey so lieflich wol ghebloit', which resembles Baude Cordier's rondeau 'Belle, bonne, sage' with its leisurely 3/4 pace and opening imitation.[37] His Gloria, in 'simultaneous style', forms a pair with a Credo by Tapissier, and is in fact headed (in *I-Bc Q 15*) 'Tomas Fabri scolaris Tapisier'[38] (this notwithstanding the fact that a Gloria by Cordier in *I-Bc Q 15* also goes together with the same Credo: see p. 64.) Here is evidence of the new practice of composers collaborating on Mass pairs in friendly competition. The settings themselves may all predate 1400.

Gilet Velut seems to have been a *petit vicaire* at Cambrai Cathedral in 1409, and in 1411 arrived in Cyprus with Charlotte de Bourbon.[39] His isorhythmic motet 'Benedicta viscera / Ave mater' has an ambitious proportional layout, but flowing cantus lines and much textural variation as has Ciconia. Velut wrote a Gloria and a Credo which do not form a pair, although are placed together in *I-Bc Q 15*. The Credo is more reminiscent of the style of Cordier's Gloria (see above), whereas the Gloria, in chanson style, recalls Tapissier's Sanctus in the Apt MS. One wonders whether Velut's rondeau 'Je voel servir' (Ex. 20) was known around 1410 at Cambrai, because of its stylistic similarity to the early Dufay. Noteworthy are its 'V–I' cadences with a falling fifth in the tenor or contratenor:

---

[36] Higgins, 'Music and musicians', 691.
[37] His three complete secular works are in Strohm, *Bruges*, mus. exx. 2–4.
[38] Edited in *EFM*, vol. 1 (1955).
[39] His extant works are in *EFM*, vol. 2 (1959).

Example 20 Gilet Velut, 'Je voel servir'

Similar cadences are also frequent in the music of Cesaris, together with the octave-leap formula. This suggests that both types became widely used at about the same time. The 'V–I' cadence, occasionally found even in Machaut, did not represent a later, harmonically advanced stage of composition, nor did it require an extended range of the contratenor, as claimed by Heinrich Besseler. He interpreted such formulas as bars 17–19 in Example 20 ('double-octave cadence') as innovations of Dufay.[40]

Franchois Lebertoul also sang in the Cambrai choir in 1409 and 1410. His five extant compositions,[41] although not distinguished, would have been modern for that time. 'O mortalis homo' is a very strange piece: a sacred ballade with three different Latin texts (reminiscent of a cantio) in the three voices. Perhaps it is a contrafactum of a true ballade. It is an isolated composition, and we have no clue as to when it was composed. Similar dating problems beriddle the only surviving piece by Jacques Charité (also called Jean Carité), the triple-texted rondeau 'Jusques à tant'.[42] With its 'V–I' cadences, descending chains of 6–3 sonorities, corresponding phrases and singable lines for all three

[40] Besseler, *Bourdon*, 38: 'Diese von Dufay geschaffene Schlußform'.
[41] *EFM*, vol. 2 (1959).
[42] *EFM*, vol. 2 (1959); Stainer ed., *Early Bodleian Music*.

voices, it embodies the chanson style of the 1420s. Charité was a chaplain of Jean de Berry at Bourges from 1401 to 1416, and a canon of Bourges in 1422; he is also documented at the Burgundian court and in Bruges, 1406–11, and was a member of the Parisian *cour d'amour*.[43]

Similar pieces have also been written by Jacques Vide.[44] He was perhaps a choirboy at Notre Dame, Paris, in 1405, but by 1410–11 already held a canonry at Bruges. He may have been in Italy around that time; he spent the last documented years of his life (1423–33) at the court of Burgundy. His songs 'Las, j'ay perdu' and 'Et c'est assés' reflect the same trend towards the small-scale and a greater economy of means, as do 'Se cuer d'amant' and 'Ma seul amour'. They survive with two voices only (like 'Ma seul amour'); but Italian scribes, for example that of *GB-Ob 213*, had a tendency to omit contratenors and also to add text to the tenor. In 'Et c'est assés', the two voices often cadence at the unison or fifth, so that a lower contratenor seems desirable. It would tend to supply 'V–I' cadences. In Vide's three-voice songs, the contratenors are more conventional.

Vide's chansons reveal a great melodic gift; one of their special traits is the declamatory opening with three or even four repeated pitches, later favoured by Binchois. A fine study by Wulf Arlt reveals subtle text-setting procedures in Vide's 'Las, j'ay perdu' and 'Il m'est si grief'.[45] The latter song comes up with two different contratenors in the manuscripts. One has the high range g–g', is texted like a triplum, is at times incompatible with the cantus (bars 10–11) and obscures the phrasing. The lower and rhythmically more active contratenor (in *EscA*) must be more recent. It does not fit very well either (bar 14), but introduces fanfare-like leaps within the octave c–c'. Probably neither contratenor is by Vide. His 'Amans doubles, or doublés' has also been tampered with in the manuscripts. It is in the usual three-voice format, but a texted triplum has been added which does not accord with the contratenor; the cantus and tenor, too, seem to have been modified in the process. The last line starts with an imitated triadic motive in the three original voices: the added triplum repeats that motive as well, but in a clumsy fashion, creating unnecessary dissonances.

A great amount of revising and reworking of chansons took place in this period, often done by lesser musicians on the basis of experiments in actual performance. The addition of a high voice (triplum) was rarer than in the fourteenth century, but contratenors were added or substituted more often.[46] Scholars have sometimes endeavoured to see more modern harmonic practices in these new voices. Besseler, for example, considers the substitution of a low–range contratenor as the foreshadowing of tonal harmony. According to him, Dufay's

---

[43] Wright, *Burgundy*, 81 f n. 209, and 135 f; Strohm, *Bruges*, 20; and, most recently, Higgins, 'Music and musicians', where it is shown that the diverse documents refer to the same man.

[44] Seven of his eight extant chansons are in Marix ed., *Musiciens*, nos. 11–17.

[45] Wulf Arlt, 'Der Beitrag der Chanson zu einer Problemgeschichte des Komponierens. "Las! j'ay perdu . . ." und "Il m'est si grief" von Jacobus Vide', in Beihefte zum *AMw*, 23 (1984), 57–75.

[46] A good discussion of this practice is Korth, *Kantilenensatz*.

contratenors whose range requires six-line staves ('*Sechslinien-Kontratenor*') combine the traditional role of the contratenor with that of a harmonic foundation ('*Harmonieträger*').[47] He connects these bourdon-like voices with the use of a trombone or slide trumpet. Although this last argument finds support in contratenors labelled 'trompette' and in fanfare-like idioms, it is not therefore established that these contratenors were heard as the harmonic foundation. Indeed, they often hit the bottom note without providing the 'root' of the chord.

As mentioned above (p. 61), Matteo da Perugia specialized in rewriting the contratenors of other composers. His contratenors have wide ranges, but none is fanfare-like or particularly 'harmonic'. They rather reflect the skills of a specific singer, perhaps Matteo himself.

Among the pieces affected by such manipulations, the name of Pierre Fontaine occurs strikingly often. Some of his songs have low and wide-ranging contratenors; they include the substitute 'contratenor trompette' for his rondeau 'J'ayme bien celui', which Besseler ascribed to Dufay.[48] This voice has the magnificent range *D–d'* and several 'V–I' cadences (but not at the mid-point fermata). Three other songs by Fontaine received contratenors by three different colleagues: 'Pour vous tenir' (contratenor by Matteo da Perugia, datable before 1418, when Matteo died); 'A son plaisir' (contratenor by Guillaume Legrant); and 'Sans faire de vous departie' (contratenor by Francus de Insula). 'Pour vous tenir' received, furthermore, a triplum which – like that of Vide's 'Amans doubles' – creates unnecessary dissonances at the imitative beginning of the last line and elsewhere.[49]

Fontaine seems to have been a popular, perhaps slightly eccentric figure among his colleagues. After his employment between 1405 and 1407 at Bourges (see above), his career is documented from *c.*1415 to 1447: he spent much of his time at the Burgundian court, and between 1420 and 1427 sang in the papal chapel. Dufay's convivial song 'Ce moys de may' quotes a 'Perrinet', possibly Fontaine, and he is addressed in a witty rondeau in the style of Binchois, 'Fontaine a vous dire le voir'. His leisurely 'Mon cuer pleure' was used for a lost Mass cycle by the Burgundian chaplain Guillaume Le Rouge (Ruby). There is a certain experimentalism about his songs, three of which are in B♭.

His own version of 'Pour vous tenir' has a low-range contratenor. Harmonically, the piece makes perfect sense, although it is a little eccentric in its harmonic inertia, and sometimes lacks either supertonic or leading note in a cadence. The important thing is that Matteo's substitute contratenor is much more *conventional* than Fontaine's. The same is probably true for 'J'ayme bien celui', where the more conventional contratenor is anonymous, and 'A son plaisir' and 'Sans faire de vous départie', where only the conventional contratenors by Legrant and Francus de Insula, respectively, survive. The tenor of 'Sans

---

[47] Besseler, *Bourdon*, 81 ff.
[48] Dufay, *Opera omnia*, vol. 6, no. 86 (see also Ex. 48*a*). Besseler, *Bourdon*, 49.
[49] This version is printed in Marix, *Musiciens*, no. 8. The version with Matteo's contratenor is in Korth, *Kantilenensatz*, 99.

faire' also became a *basse danse* melody: further evidence that others liked to tamper with Fontaine's tunes.[50] I suggest that his original contratenors were mostly written in a 'trompetta' style that may have been his speciality as a singer or player.

Matteo da Perugia also wrote a contratenor for the ballade 'Je ne requier' by Nicholas Grenon (which again places this song before 1418).[51] This composer's career is now fully documented. His spheres of activity were the cathedrals of Paris, Laon and Cambrai until 1409, then the ducal chapel at Bourges, from 1412 the Burgundian court, the papal chapel (in the 1420s), and then once again Cambrai Cathedral, where he died in 1456. In most of these positions he taught choirboys. His links with Italy, also attested by Matteo's reworking, seem to predate 1418. In fact, all his three motets are close in style to Italian music around 1410-15, especially 'Nova vobis gaudia' (a Christmas song), with the joyful parlando-rhythms of the upper voices (presumably written for choirboys). Another early work is the rondeau 'Se je vous ay', where the three voices tend to exchange registers and functions, taking over each other's motives. The tenor of this rondeau has text in the Italian manner which seems appropriate, since it is at the top of the texture no fewer than six times. Registral experiments like these also occur in 'Je suy defait' and in the broadly flowing virelai 'La plus belle et doulce figure'. A similar text is sung in the rondeau 'La plus jolie et la plus belle' by three voices in a more or less homorhythmic fashion; there are several registral exchanges between them.[52]

It is interesting that Oswald von Wolkenstein made an arrangement (for two voices) of this early song by Grenon, which he apparently picked up in Piacenza (Lombardy) in 1432. Well before that time, he had arranged Fontaine's 'A son plaisir' (see p. 121). Could the Grenon song, present in Italian sources from before 1430, also have been around in Italian or German circles as early as *c.*1416?[53]

Grenon is neither the first nor the only composer to use a popular-sounding, homophonic style. It may be traced back to sacred music in 'simultaneous style' (including conductus and cantilena), and is found in the rondeau 'Va t'en, mon cuer' by Gacian Reyneau of Tours, who from 1398 worked at the court of Aragon.[54] 'Va t'ent, souspier' by Etienne Grossin (see p. 177) resembles that style, too. There are several anonymous songs of this kind, and the virtually anonymous Francus de Insula also wrote one: the very simple, pastoral ballade 'L'autre jour jouer m'aloye'. 'Ce rondelet je vous envoye', by Johannes Reson, which survives in two equal voices only, has a literal voice-exchange between

[50] Crane, *Materials*, no. 89.
[51] Edited with Grenon's other extant works in *EFM*, vol. 7 (1983).
[52] On most of these works, see Dannemann, *Musiktradition*, 62 ff and 71 ff.
[53] Oswald, *Lieder*, no. 88 ('Vierhundert jar') and no. 103 ('Wer die ougen'); Pelnar, *Die mehrstimmigen Lieder Oswalds*, nos. 33.88 and 32.103. The identification is due to Welker, 'New light on Oswald', where it is argued that they show Oswald up to date with the modern 'Burgundian' polyphony.
[54] Higini Anglès, 'Gacian Reyneau am Königshof zu Barcelona in der Zeit von 139 . . . bis 1429', in *Studien zur Musikgeschichte*, 64-70.

cantus and tenor in the first two lines.[55] There are other songs for two equal voices, whether with one or two texts; they seem to be a speciality of the early fifteenth century.[56] Such fashionable simplicity may consciously refer to the old techniques of voice-exchange and rondellus as well as the then scarcely documented English (and continental?) practice of gymel.

Most of the examples quoted so far have merry, pastoral texts, and their music has affinities with dance. A similar popularizing tradition is found in three interrelated virelais by Guillaume Legrant. This composer, whose real name was Le Macherier, may have been one of the younger clerks of the Bourges chapel in 1405, since he was still alive (at Rouen) in 1449. Between 1418 and 1421 he sang in the papal chapel.[57] The three virelais seem to tell a little story. The first, 'Ma chière mestresse', comes from the mouth of a young lover who pleads to his girlfriend; the second text is sung by the girl, who accepts him as a suitor ('Pour l'amour de mon bel amy'); and the third, 'Or avant, gentilz fillettes', has texts in all three voices and is probably intended to be sung collectively by a girls' chorus. The girls invite each other to make garlands of flowers, and complain about the cold month of March which has killed the violets, but praise April when they can all go out to the woods, pick flowers and sing 'balades, rondeaux, et de belles chansonettes'. The three songs might fit into a pastoral play of the 'Robin and Marion' type. Musically, the songs are simple and homophonic, with many voice-crossings and full triads, and in duple metre. Each is prefixed with a textless prelude of only a few chords, as if a lute or gittern were setting the pitch:

Example 21*a* Guillaume Legrant, 'Ma chiere mestresse'

The chromaticism of this phrase recurs in all three songs, involving all the accidentals from G♯ to E♭. It may or may not be another popularizing element. It is employed for illustrative effect at least in 'Or avant', where at the mention of 'death' and the 'cold knives of March' the voices suddenly slow down to a triple metre and sombre, chromatic harmonies. In the other sections of this song, hopping quavers with some imitation between them seem to depict the merry company. This 'theatrical' music may well have belonged to a courtly parody of old-fashioned pastoral theatre.

---

[55] Both printed in *EFM*, vol. 2 (1959).
[56] Fallows, 'Two equal voices'.
[57] His works are in *EFM*, vol. 2 (1959).

Example 21*b* Guillaume Legrant, 'Or avant gentilz fillettes'

Car ce Mars de ses mar - teaux a tu - é les vi - o - let - tes:

Contratenor Car ce Mars de ses mar - teaux a tu - é les vi - o - let - tes:

Tenor Car ce Mars de ses mar - teaux a tu - é les vi - o - let - tes:

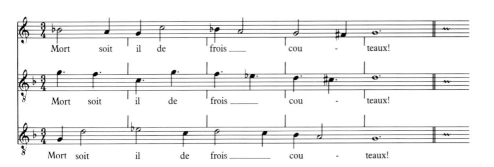

Mort soit il de frois ____ cou - teaux!

Mort soit il de frois ____ cou - teaux!

Mort soit il de frois ____ cou - teaux!

From dance and theatre, it is not far to the taverns: the convivial or drinking songs were certainly a part of the popularizing tradition. Dufay wrote several of them, full of gaiety but also artifice. He may have learned this sort of music as a choirboy at Cambrai. As mentioned above (p. 69), two convivial songs in the Leiden MS (*NL-Lu 2720*) refer directly to places near Cambrai: 'Cheulz qui volent retourner en lanois' and 'Ho! ho! ho! Faites chi verser De che bon vin cler!' These pieces are musically related to the homophonic, dance-like songs described above, and seem to rely on primitive or unwritten types of partsong.

The 'difficulty' with Dufay is, however, that hardly any of his songs resembles any specific model, although simple and traditional techniques pervade and enrich much of his music. His famous rondeau of 1426, 'Adieu ces bons vins de Lannoys',[58] is a case in point. It is believed that he composed it at the end of a stay in northern France (*c.*1424–6) before returning to Italy. The song resembles 'Cheux qui volent retourner en lanois' not only with its textual allusions and abundant use of the rhyme '-ois', but also in subtle musical ways such as the manner in which one line after the other emerges from the texture to circle downwards. A similar idea of voice-exchange is treated more systematically in Dufay's rondeau 'Resvelons nous, resvelons, amoureux'. Here, tenor and contratenor dance around each other in strict canon with the ostinato tune (*pes*) 'Alons ent

---

[58] *Opera omnia*, vol. 6, no. 27. See also Fallows, *Dufay*, 86 ff.

bien tos au may'. This is a musical and quasi-theatrical depiction of one of the pastimes which 'Cheulz qui volent' enumerates: 'karoler et danser, tumer et trikebaler, tout ensy que font hansprois'. These activities take place 'au bois', of course, and what can happen there among the merry company is described in 'Faites chi verser' in more explicit terms. It may seem improper to draw the noble 'Adieu ces bons vins' into this picture. But the rondeau is, after all, a drinking song, in which the author greets not only his own sweetheart but also his wines, his drinking companions, and even local 'dames' and 'borgois'. With his new art, Dufay ennobles the musical folklore of his native past, but at the same time distances himself from its lowly aesthetics. In this sense, too, 'Adieu ces bons vins' is a farewell.

Dufay's musical background was, of course, the cathedral: the performance of liturgical music must have played an important role in the formation of his style.[59] Of several composers who passed through Cambrai during his early years, only Richard Loqueville left significant liturgical compositions, and these influenced Dufay. Loqueville was master of the Cambrai choirboys from 1413 until his death in 1418, although he was a layman and had previously served the Duke of Bar as a chaplain and harper.[60] His extant secular music, and an isorhythmic motet ('O flos in divo / Sacris pignoribus'), seem of little significance. There is, however, a Gloria in three-voice chanson format (no. 7), and another Gloria (no. 6) written in the alternating manner which the Italians called 'a versi': duet sections of two high, soloistic voices alternating with full sections in chanson texture. This kind of soli–tutti alternation, often indicated by the voice-labels 'unus' and 'chorus', is also found in works by Ciconia, Zacharias, Salinis and Guillaume Legrant, and seems to have been used in the papal chapel at Constance (see p. 114).

Dufay and Binchois took it up as well, and it is therefore important that Loqueville's Gloria documents the practice before 1418 in a northern cathedral. Loqueville's solo sections are provided, in a later manuscript (*A-ZW*), with a 'contratenor trompette'. Whether composed by him or not, it is possible that the addition of a part in trumpet style was also a northern practice. Loqueville's Gloria–Credo pair (no. 8) comes up with another fashionable technique, called 'cursiva' by the Italians.[61] Verse by verse, only one upper voice sings the text, while the other vocalizes. This text-sharing is also found in a Gloria by Magister Egardus (see pp. 95 f) and in the Old Hall MS; Ciconia and the Italians adopted it, and so did Dufay and Binchois.

Loqueville's four-part Sanctus 'Vineux' displays yet another technique that was important for Dufay. It is a cantus firmus composition with a Sanctus plainsong in the tenor. This particular melody is also found in monophonic

---

[59] On Cambrai in those years, see Pirro, *Histoire*, 54-7; Fallows, *Dufay*, 7-17.

[60] David Fallows, review of Wright, *Burgundy*, in *JAMS* 34 (1981), 551 f. Loqueville's works are in *EFM*, vol. 3 (1966).

[61] The terms 'a versi', 'cursiva' and 'virilas' ('men's voices only') occur in the manuscript *GB-Ob 213* and are explained in Schoop, *Entstehung und Verwendung*, 49 f.

sources, but with a mensural rhythm(!); it belongs to a group of rhythmicized Mass plainsongs which apparently circulated in the Franco-Netherlands area. Some are copied in the Cambrai choirbooks *F-CA 6* and *11* (see also p. 325). The 'Vineux' melody received its name from a locality, the wine-producing region around Nouvion-le-Vineux in the Laonnais, where Dufay held a benefice in the late 1420s.[62] Thus it is no surprise that he used this plainsong himself as cantus firmus of a Sanctus–Agnus pair, perhaps *c*.1425 on his return from Italy. He also adopts the same Sanctus trope as Loqueville: the Easter trope 'Qui januas mortis confregisti' ('You, who shattered the gates of Death'),[63] which may or may not be originally connected with the melody. Dufay's setting does not quote Loqueville's musically, but may have been intended for a similar liturgical use.

Besseler published Dufay's 'Vineux' pair together with one of his Kyries, and suggested a cyclic relationship.[64] The tenor of the Kyrie is indeed similar in mode and range to the 'Vineux' melody; Dufay either modelled it after the 'Vineux' plainsong, or found a fitting plainsong Kyrie somewhere else.[65] David Fallows added another facet by connecting this presumed cycle with Dufay's oddly named Gloria 'de Quaremiaux'.[66] He dates this composition around 1425 because of its similarities with 'Adieu ces bons vins'. The Gloria has a pre-existing tune in the tenor, which is repeated like an ostinato, but in different mensurations. Its simple phrase-structure and songlike independence have been emphasized by Besseler, who called it a 'French folksong', and in a detailed study by Bockholdt.[67]

The 'de Quaremiaux' melody could have been a dance-song for Shrove Tuesday (*quadragesimalis*). The question remains open as to whether Dufay can have intended his Mass cycle for both Shrove Tuesday and Easter (the 'Vineux' trope), and whether he planned to combine secular and sacred cantus firmi in the same work.

Dufay and his colleagues in Italy (1420–c.1436)

The miracle of the early Dufay arises, to a large extent, from his ability to absorb and transform divergent stylistic ideas, surpassing them all. Most of his continental colleagues differ from him in their more anxious cultivation of only

[62] David Fallows, 'Dufay and Nouvion-le-Vineux: some details and a thought', *AcM* 48 (1976), 44–50; Fallows, *Dufay*, 173–5 and pl. 14.
[63] The plainsong suits both the Sanctus and the Agnus Dei, as was often the case. On the uses of related tropes by Arnold de Lantins and Clibano, see p. 177.
[64] *Opera omnia*, vol. 4, no. 2; Bockholdt, *Messenkompositionen*, vol. 2, 30–34.
[65] The Kyrie tenor is not a plainsong recorded in Landwehr-Melnicki, *Kyrie*. It is unlikely that it formed a chant cycle together with 'Vineux' – although such cycles did exist: see p. 325.
[66] *Opera omnia*, vol. 4, no. 23; Fallows, *Dufay*, 88; this suggestion already in Bockholdt, *Messenkompositionen*, vol. 1, 79 f.
[67] Bockholdt, *Messenkompositionen*, vol. 1, 18–47.

a few musical trends. This can best be observed where their respective careers actually crossed.

From *c*.1420 to *c*.1423 Dufay worked for the Malatesta dynasty in Rimini and Pesaro (see Map 2). It had long been known that other notable composers such as Antonio da Cividale, Antonius Romanus, Hugo and Arnold de Lantins were active at the same time in this area, mainly in Venice. Alejandro Planchart recently discovered a document that places the Lantins couple (we do not know whether they were brothers) in the service of Malatesta di Pandolfo, head of the Pesaro branch of the dynasty, in 1423.[68] In 1420 a marriage was arranged between Malatesta's daughter Cleofé and Theodore II Palaiologos, Despot of the Morea (Peloponnese). For this occasion, Dufay composed his isorhythmic motet 'Vasilissa ergo gaude', and Hugo de Lantins his ballata 'Tra quante regione il sol si móbele'. Dufay also wrote the ballade 'Resvelliés vous' for the wedding of Cleofé's brother Carlo Malatesta to Vittoria Colonna in 1423, and presumably in 1426 the Italian-texted motet 'Apostolo glorioso / Cum tua doctrina' for the church of St Andrew in Patras (Peloponnese), where another brother, Pandolfo, was bishop.[69]

Carlo Malatesta of Rimini, perhaps Dufay's actual employer and described as 'one of the most lettered men . . . of our time',[70] would seem a feasible patron for Dufay's greatest work set to Italian words, Petrarch's canzone 'Vergene bella, che di sol vestita'.[71] Dufay set the first stanza only, moulding the irregular rhyme-scheme into a tripartite form somewhat reminiscent of the great courtly ballade with a single refrain line as the third section (as in 'Medée fu'). The decreasing length of the three sections, corresponding to 6 + 6 + 1 verses of text, is counterbalanced by Dufay's mensurations ($\phi \bigcirc \phi$) in such a way that a total length of precisely 600 regular minims results.[72] Similar, if more complicated, arithmetic structures have been detected in the wedding chanson of 1423, 'Resvelliés vous',[73] a ballade of exactly the same, old-fashioned structure – with a single refrain line – as 'Vergene bella' and with a comparable distribution of text verses: 4 + 4 + 1. This grand, celebrative work pulls out all the stops of virtuosity, from imitations and motivic recurrences to chains of fermata

---

[68] Planchart, 'Guillaume Du Fay's benefices', 124. Other biographical matter is discussed in Fallows, *Dufay*, ch. 3.

[69] For the Dufay works, see *Opera omnia*, vols. 1 (motets) and 6 (chansons). The complete secular works by Hugo and Arnold de Lantins (as well as Jean Franchois) are in van den Borren ed., *Pièces polyphoniques*.

[70] Fallows, *Dufay*, 251.

[71] *Opera omnia*, vol. 6, no. 5. My suggestion of a date near 1423 is new and will be further supported below. Fallows, *Dufay*, 129, calls it a 'relatively early work'.

[72] This assumes a tempo relationship of 3 : 2 (perhaps MM 120 : 80) between the values under ϕ and $\bigcirc$, which in this piece is musically convincing (but see n. 11 above). The final longs of the three sections must (as usual) not be counted, being 'unmeasured' – but the crotchet rest (semibreve rest in the original) after the second final is measured and must be counted. Then, the first and third sections total an equivalent of 400 regular minims, the second has 200.

[73] Allan W. Atlas, 'Gematria, marriage number, and golden sections in Dufay's "Resvellies vous"', *AcM* 59 (1987), 111–26.

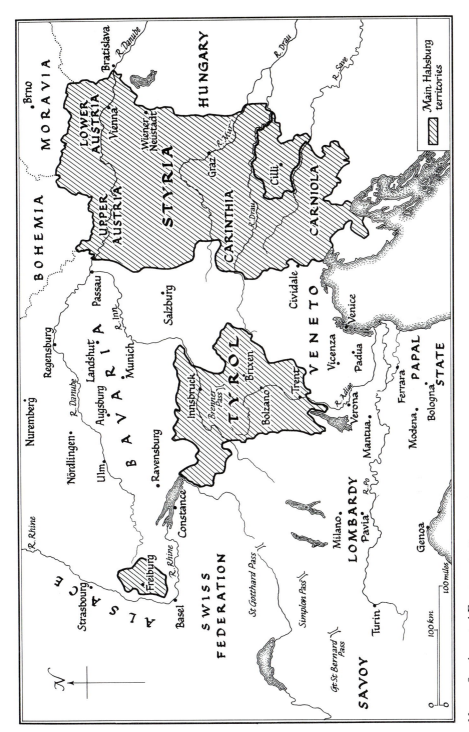

Map 2. South central Europe c.1450

chords and rolling coloraturas. It is unpredictable, even dramatic. 'Vergene bella', as a sacred composition, is more restrained with its even and flowing pace, but rich in word-related gestures. It has affinities with the genre of the Italian *lauda*, which attracted several northern composers in the 1420s (see also below). Dufay's imitative opening is in fact echoed (perhaps consciously) in two genuine *laude*, found in a Venetian monastic manuscript of the 1440s:[74]

Example 22a Guillaume Dufay, 'Vergene bella'

Example 22b anonymous lauda, *I-Vnm It. IX, 145*, fol. 39v

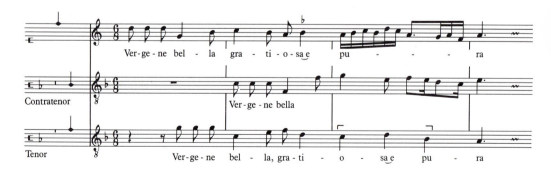

[74] *I-Vnm It. IX, 145.* Published in Giulio Cattin ed., *Laudi quattrocentesche del Cod. Veneto Marc. It. IX 145* (Bologna, 1958), nos. 1 and 8.

Example 22c anonymous lauda, *I-Vnm It. IX, 145*, fol. 31r

Fallows lists other connections between Dufay and Hugo de Lantins that date from the early 1420s: these include a Mass pair of which Hugo wrote the Gloria, Dufay the Credo.[75] Furthermore, Dufay's drinking song 'Hé, compaignons, resvelons nous' is addressed to a merry company of named friends which Planchart has been able to identify with musicians active at the Malatesta court of Pesaro, including the two Lantins.[76] I believe that the same environment also generated some Italian love-songs by Hugo and Dufay, in the tradition of the Venetian *giustiniane*. This style is clearly present in Hugo's 'Io sum tuo servo, o dolce anima bella', 'Mirar non posso ni conçerner, donna', 'Per amor de costey che vol ch'io cante' and arguably so in Dufay's 'L'alta bellezza tua, virtute, valore' and 'La dolce vista del tuo viso pio'. All are ballatas with certain formal irregularities identifiable as north Italian regionalisms (for example surplus syllables), and they sometimes use the word repetitions and brief echo imitations cultivated in Ciconia's circle (see pp. 103 f). The robust declamatory gestures of Ciconia's 'O rosa bella', for example, are found again in Hugo's ballata 'Io sum tuo servo'. This text involves Venetian dialectal elements, and the interruption of the word 'servo' comes straight from the mannerisms of the *giustiniane*:

Example 23 Hugo de Lantins, 'Io sum tuo servo'

---

[75] *Opera omnia*, vol. 4, no. 3; discussed in Fallows, *Dufay*, 175–7.
[76] Planchart, 'Guillaume Du Fay's benefices', 124 f.

Example 23 (*cont.*)

[I am your servant, my beautiful sweetheart: through your fault you have taken my speech away.]

The rich sonorities of this piece, however, and the logic of his balanced phrases are Hugo's own contribution. Their background is the northern chanson. Hugo weaves his voices more densely together than does Ciconia, so that only the frequent registral exchanges prevent parallel triads. He loves imitation, both melismatic and declamatory (as in the example). Beautiful patterns of imitative sequences can be found in his 'Tra quante regione',[77] and the last phrase of Dufay's 'Vergene bella' seems to be indebted to this model.

[77] Borren ed., *Pièces polyphoniques*, no. 32, bars 52–65.

In Hugo's twelve extant French chansons, dense textures and a great equality or interchangeability of the voices are just as characteristic. They recall, if anything, Grenon or Vide. The composer also experiments in juxtaposing unrelated triads, and creating *musica ficta* riddles (as in his ostensibly sombre rondeau 'Plaindre m'estuet'), which connects him with Cesaris and Guillaume Legrant. Almost all his songs, and several by these other northern composers, were copied in the Italian sources with text in both cantus and tenor, or even in all three voices. On the one hand, this is an Italian characteristic that dates back to the Trecento madrigal; on the other, it is equally appropriate to the imitations and voice-exchanges of this new chanson style.

The respective merits of Hugo and Arnold de Lantins will perhaps exercise future musicology in a similar way that art historians have had to discuss the respective contributions of Hubert and Jan van Eyck. Attribution problems are small: only two songs are disputed between the two composers. But among the other fourteen by Arnold, several are in the characterful, sombre mood of Hugo. Was Arnold the younger of the two men and did he imitate Hugo, or was it the other way round? Arnold's counterpoint is at times less polished, and he more often enjoys drastic gestures, parlando declamation and bouncing rhythms, for example in 'Puis que je voy', 'Or voy je bien' and the possibly autobiographical 'Puisque je suy cyprianés' (the only chanson by either composer in duple metre). Arnold's more versatile approach, and his larger output of Latin-texted music, may reflect a longer stay in the changing Italian environment. Hugo composed a setting of the *laudes regiae* 'Christus vincit' – an acclamation for political rulers – for Doge Foscari of Venice in 1423;[78] but he cannot be traced anywhere beyond the early 1420s. Arnold composed two songs in Venice in March 1428; in 1431–2, he sang in the papal chapel with Dufay. He died in June 1432, leaving a rectorship in the diocese of Liège.[79]

The interaction between north and south, which is exemplified in Dufay's career of the 1420s and 30s, had been a familiar matter for musicians from the Liégeois since 1378. The northerners who populated the papal chapel and the Italian courts and cities could compose 'Burgundian' chansons in Italy, and Italianate music for their home cathedrals. Many of them kept in touch with their native institutions, expecting to return there sooner or later. There are many extant 'New Year's' songs by Dufay and the two Lantins that were probably sent home as seasonal gifts: this particular genre (see p. 131) has never been cultivated by Italian patrons. Conversely, the northerners were attracted to the Italian sacred *lauda*, and contributed some Latin-texted settings to the genre.[80] Whereas the Italian *lauda* is formally congruent with the ballata, the

---

[78] F. Alberto Gallo, 'Musiche veneziane nel ms.2216 della Biblioteca Universitaria di Bologna', *Quadrivium* 6 (1964), 107–16; see also Ernst H. Kantorowicz, *Laudes regiae* (Berkeley and Los Angeles, 1946).

[79] According to documents discovered by Alejandro E. Planchart. See Planchart, 'Guillaume Du Fay's benefices', 125.

[80] A thorough discussion and edition is Diederichs, *Lauda*.

Latin *lauda* resembles other strophic genres such as hymns. Musical hallmarks of the polyphonic settings include homorhythmic declamation and symmetrical, clearly separated phrases, often dictated by a pre-existing (or at least song-like) tune in the tenor. Most pieces are in a straightforward triple metre (O). Johannes de Lymburgia wrote at least five *laude* and many other similar pieces, which are usually referred to as motets. This represents a sizeable part of his 46 extant works, all found in *I-Bc Q 15*. The codex is therefore thought to be connected with the composer himself. Johannes can be traced at Liège in the 1420s, and he became instructor of young clerics in *cantus figuratus* at the cathedral of Vicenza in 1431.[81] His *laude* and devotional motets would have been appropriate for festive but informal singing in side-chapels and the cathedral refectory. 'Salve, virgo regia' could serve as an example for this simple, incisive music.[82] The form and distribution of rhymes is exactly as in a ballata (aa / bb / ba), except that the last pair of lines – the *volta*, 'b a' – has new music instead of being sung on the music of the first pair (the *ripresa*). The three-part setting is largely homorhythmic, and all the three voices carry text.

Similar in form, but using the same music for the second and third sections (*stanza* and *volta*), is the *lauda* 'In tua memoria' by Arnold de Lantins.[83] Its tenor is a beautiful first-mode melody and could have existed as a monophonic tune. There are also *lauda*-like compositions by Johannes Brassart, Johannes de Sarto and H. Battre: all Liégeois composers of whom the last two do not seem to have been to Italy. It seems that there existed a parallel northern tradition of such devotional songs.

The Latin *lauda* occupies one end of a continuous spectrum of forms and styles of which the isorhythmic motet occupies the other. Latin-texted, non-liturgical compositions of this period cannot always be strictly classified because Dufay and his colleagues deliberately overstepped genre divisions. Their settings of antiphons and hymns often resemble free devotional songs; Dufay's heroically simple 'Ave regina celorum (I)' could pass as a Latin *lauda* were it not for its liturgical text.[84] In turn, a non-isorhythmic motet such as Dufay's 'Flos florum' borders on song and antiphon setting. Whereas ceremonial and occasional texts, using specially composed poems, are hallmarks of the motet, even some isorhythmic motets have traditional texts and may have served more recurrent, devotional uses.

At least nine works by Dufay of the 1420s currently pass as *motets*, on account of their relative length and complexity. Five of them are isorhythmic.[85]

---

[81] Gallo–Mantese, *Ricerche*; José Quitin, 'A propos de Jean-François de Gembloux et de Johannes de Limburgia', *RBM* 21 (1967), 118–24; Jerry H. Etheridge, *The Works of Johannes de Lymburgia*, Ph.D., U. of Indiana, 1972. Margaret Bent reminds me that the identity of the Lymburgia at Liège with the one at Vicenza might be doubted.

[82] Diederichs, *Lauda*, 344 f.

[83] Diederichs, *Lauda*, 350–52; Borren ed., *Polyphonia Sacra*, no. 42.

[84] *Opera omnia*, vol. 5, no. 49.

[85] Note the distinction 'isorhythmic motets' / 'cantilena motets' in Fallows, *Dufay*, chaps. 9 and 10, and 234 f. The former are nos. 6–11 in *Opera omnia*, vol. 1, the latter are nos. 1–4.

A similar proportion of isorhythmic and non-isorhythmic works is to be found in Ciconia's oeuvre, which could have served in its entirety as a model to the young Dufay.

Fallows suggested a direct link between Dufay's earliest motet, 'Vasilissa ergo gaude', and Ciconia's 'Ut te per omnes / Ingens alumnus'.[86] The isorhythmic scheme, however, is simple enough to have been chosen independently by Dufay. Other features of 'Vasilissa' belong to the motet tradition in general. The canonic *introitus*, for example, was a frequent feature, occurring in 'Rex Karole' (p. 97) as well as in Grenon's 'Ad honorem / Celorum regnum' and in 'Argi vices Polyphemus' by Nicolaus (Zacharie?).[87] Antonio da Cividale, too, wrote an introductory canon with a supporting lower voice in 'Strenua quem duxit / Gaudeat' in *c*.1412.[88]

'Vasilissa' seems most closely related to 'Argi vices', where the distance of the canonic entries is shorter, but the canon itself similarly long and complex. Dufay's work, in turn, has been imitated in the anonymous motet 'Clarus ortus / Gloriosa mater', written for a member of the Colonna family in 1430 or shortly thereafter. Hugo de Lantins' St Nicholas motet, 'Celsa sublimatur / Sabine presul', also has a short introductory canon, though it is a more modest work. The text-sharing of the upper voices in 'Vasilissa' can likewise be found in older compositions, including Grenon's 'Nova vobis gaudia refero' and Carmen's 'Pontifici decori speculi'.[89]

Dufay's non-isorhythmic 'Inclita stella maris' has an ingenious mensuration canon for the two upper voices, which it explicitly assigns to 'pueri'.[90] Many motets collected in *I-Bc Q 15* (a cathedral book) could indeed have served the needs of choir schools. Their texts address the Virgin or popular saints such as St Sebastian, St Andrew, St George, St Katherine, St Barbara and, above all, St Nicholas, the patron of choirboys. He was widely celebrated with music on the clerical feasts of the Christmas period (see also p. 514). Recurrent festivities of the liturgical year may indeed have given rise to Dufay's motets nos. 1–4 (non-isorhythmic) as well as nos. 8 and 9 (isorhythmic).

In the former group, 'Flos florum' (from the early 1420s) seems to have been a stylistic trendsetter. Perhaps the most intriguing feature of this beautiful work is its chanson format for three voices with only one text. As in the French chanson, the cantus and tenor form a contrapuntally correct duet at approximately a fifth's distance, and the contratenor is an inessential addition within the tenor's range. If we look at the piece as a motet, this is remarkable: it is easier to understand 'Flos florum' as a song with a sacred text. Probably, the transfer of chanson format to the motet genre had come through sacred contrafacta or Latin-texted imitations of song forms (such as Lebertoul's ballade

---

[86] *Dufay*, 108.
[87] Newes, 'Imitation', 49–52, and p. 117 above.
[88] *EFM*, vol. 5 (1975); Borren ed., *Polyphonia Sacra*, no. 29.
[89] Grenon's 'Nova vobis' is in *EFM*, vol. 7 (1983), the other motets in Borren ed., *Polyphonia Sacra*.
[90] See also Fallows, *Dufay*, 131 f.

'O mortalis homo'), and through *lauda* and antiphon settings (such as the remarkably chanson-like 'Salve regina' by Hubertus de Salinis). There is an important analogy here with the English development of the antiphon in chanson format, which took place in those same years (see pp. 211 f) – although at first there was not much of a stylistic resemblance between the English and Continental settings.

The textural, motivic and contrapuntal ideas of 'Flos florum' were further developed by Dufay in 'O beate Sebastiane' and 'Ave virgo'. Arnold de Lantins, Johannes de Lymburgia and Bertrand Feragut also contributed to the new species of 'motets in chanson format'. Some texts are partly liturgical (as in Arnold's 'Tota pulchra es' and 'O pulcherrima', and Feragut's 'Ave Maria'), others are occasional or celebrative (Feragut's 'Francorum nobilitati' and 'Excelsa civitas Vincentia'),[91] while the remainder are devotional poems (Dufay's 'Flos florum' and 'Ave virgo'). None is isorhythmic, and there is no use of plainsong.

'Flos florum', with its bright tonal colours, transparent texture and coloraturas in the cantus, might have been a direct model for 'O pulcherrima mulierum' and 'Excelsa civitas'. Feragut composed the latter for Vicenza, probably in 1433 (see p. 141). Where Dufay gives florid ornaments to his phrase concerning flowers ('florum'), Feragut has long runs of quavers at 'decorata decore'. What he lacks is the freshness with which Dufay reacts to each new textual impulse (for example with low registers and flattened thirds at 'spes venie'). Arnold's 'O pulcherrima' is melodically very similar to both the other pieces, but is differentiated by a slightly stiffer, declamatory approach, and an absence of word-painting. All three compositions end with a string of fermata-held chords for the last line of text, a device which was then frequently used for textual emphasis (see p. 167). As might be expected, Dufay's harmony is by far the most adventurous in that passage, since it introduces E♭ and A♭ into the F major context. I would suggest that Arnold's and Dufay's works are contemporary, or even that Arnold's is earlier, and influenced Dufay.

The excellent discussion of Dufay's isorhythmic motets by David Fallows needs little elaboration here.[92] According to him, 'Rite majorem / Artibus summis' is an important step forward with its isomelic design in the upper voices (prefigured in Ciconia but not found in Dufay's earlier works) and the concern for large-scale tonal contour across all four sections.[93] Both features recur, more explicitly, in 'Nuper rosarum flores' of 1436. 'Rite majorem' was written on behalf of Dufay's patron Robert Auclou, curate of St-Jacques-de-la-Boucherie in Paris: the text spells the acrostic 'Robertus Aclou curatus Sancti Jacobi'. Auclou had become secretary to Cardinal Louis Aleman, papal governor of Bologna, around 1425–6; Dufay was in Bologna under the protection of Aleman and Auclou by April 1427. The text of his motet is couched in the form of

---

[91] All these are edited in Borren ed., *Polyphonia Sacra*.
[92] Fallows, *Dufay*, ch. 9.
[93] Fallows, *Dufay*, 109 f. See also Samuel E. Brown, Jr., *The Motets of Ciconia, Dunstable, and Dufay*, Ph.D., Indiana U., 1962, 38–50, 181–8, 280–93.

a prayer for Robertus to his patron, St James the Greater, and entirely written in Sapphic hendecasyllables. This is new in Dufay's oeuvre. Classical metres – but only hexameters or elegiac distichs, the most common ones – are used in four later motets dating from 1431 onwards. An Italian humanist environment may be posited for the performance of 'Rite majorem', which strengthens the date of 1427 and the connection with the 'Missa Sancti Jacobi' as proposed by Alejandro Planchart.[94]

A civic uprising in Bologna in 1428 forced Cardinal Aleman to flee the city for Rome. He surely took Auclou and Dufay with him. By the end of the year, the composer had entered the papal chapel, where he was to stay until 1433. Between the election of Pope Martin V in 1417 and his death in 1431, the chapel flourished, usually numbering nine to eleven *cantores* plus other personnel.[95] Many singers were from Cambrai or other cathedrals in the Low Countries. Some were composers: Guillaume Legrant, who was a chapel member between 1419 and 1421; Pierre Fontaine, 1420–22; Richard de Bellengues dit Cardot, 1422–5; Philippe Foliot, 1424–5; Nicholas Grenon, 1425–7. The last-named trained the choirboys (as often in his career); they seem to have left with him when he went back to Cambrai. Among the initial four (then six) boys was Bartholomeus Poignare, who entered in 1425 at the age of seventeen, but stayed until 1433 when he returned to his native Douai. He is also known as a composer. Another attempt to use choirboys in the chapel was made in 1438; it is not known why this was also short-lived. Like Dufay, the composer Gautier Libert entered in 1428. Under Pope Eugene IV (elected March 1431), the composers Johannes Brassart from Liège, Arnold de Lantins (replacing Brassart), Guillermus Malbecque and Georgius Martini served alongside Dufay.[96] Martini had previously been cantor at Treviso Cathedral, but in 1432 returned to his native Bruges.[97] It is likely that more of Dufay's northern colleagues in the papal chapel also held appointments, at least intermittently, in some Italian cathedrals.

It has been suggested that Dufay composed little during these years at the papal court. About 1432, his status advanced to a secondary position next to the *magister capelle*, Egidius Flannel dit l'Enfant; perhaps he pursued his law studies (possibly begun at Bologna) at the curial university. He did compose three of his most significant motets, however: 'Ecclesie militantis / Sanctorum arbitrio' for the inauguration of Pope Eugenius IV in 1431; 'Balsamus et munda cera' for a papal ceremony on 7 April 1431; and 'Supremum est mortalibus bonum' for the peace between the pope and King Sigismund, and his coronation as Holy Roman Emperor in May 1433. The text of 'Ecclesie militantis' exalts the strength of a peaceful Roman Church, and has been interpreted as a

---

[94] Planchart, 'Guillaume Dufay's Masses', 26–33. See also p. 178 below.
[95] Manfred Schuler, 'Zur Geschichte der Kapelle Papst Martins V', *AMw* 25 (1968), 30–45; Haberl, *Bausteine*, I, 56–66, and III, 31–3.
[96] Manfred Schuler, 'Zur Geschichte der Kapelle Papst Eugens IV', *AcM* 40 (1968), 220–27.
[97] Strohm, *Bruges*, 24 and 117.

political manifesto for the new pope, the Venetian Gabriele Condulmer. The political intent is further specified by the words of the contratenor:

> Bella canunt gentes: querimur, pater optime, tempus;
> Expediet multos, si cupis, una dies.
> Nummus et hora fluunt, magnumque iter orbis agendum,
> Nec suus in toto noscitur orbe deus.

[The gentiles are calling for war: we lament the times, best of fathers; / a single day, if you so wish, will send out many men. / Money and time are flowing away, and a great march through the world has to be completed; / and yet, God is not known to the whole world.]

This can only be a call upon the Holy Father to expedite troops against the Ottoman Empire, which was threatening Constantinople and the Venetian possessions in the eastern Mediterranean. Eugenius IV had too much strife within his own orbit to be able to react to this call: Pius II was to be the only pope to prepare a campaign, when it was too late, between 1459 and 1464.[98]

'Ecclesie militantis' is Dufay's most ambitious isorhythmic work, combining musical splendour with learnedness. Its five voices form three distinct layers of music and words. The triplum and motetus, written within the same range, perform the two sections of the main text; two tenors interlock with very few chant notes for the words 'Ecce nomen domini' and 'Gabriel' (referring to the pope's secular name); the single contratenor three times recites the motto 'Bella canunt' (quoted above) which is written in elegiac distichs and in almost perfect Horatian Latin. The motet has six sections, each with a different rhythmic interplay between the different mensurations in its three layers. Isomelic design is used for the triplum and motetus, ostinato for the contratenor, and proportional diminution for the tenors.

With this overpowering musical rhetoric, we could compare the 'minimalist' attitude of another isorhythmic motet probably composed for Pope Eugenius, 'Magne decus potencie / Genus regale Esperie' by Johannes Brassart. It has the usual four voices, is isorhythmic in the tenor only, with one diminution, and has an unbroken flow of conventional triple rhythms in the upper duet. In a sense, Brassart's much simpler approach was more typical of *c.* 1431. This trend may then have prevailed in the chapel of King Sigismund, whose chaplain and *rector capelle* Brassart became in 1434.[99]

---

[98] A different view is offered in David Crawford, 'Guillaume Dufay, hellenism, and humanism', in *Music from the Middle Ages through the Twentieth Century. Essays in Honor of Gwynn McPeek*, ed. C. P. Comberiati and M. Steel (New York etc.: Gordon and Breach, *c.*1989), 81–93. Here, the 'militancy' of the motet is not interpreted as relating to the Turks in 1431 but rather to the Greeks in 1438. Crawford notes that only seven days elapsed between the pope's election and coronation; the motet will, in fact, have been performed when it was ready some time later.

[99] Mixter, *Johannes Brassart* I, 49–50. The motet is in Brassart, *Opera omnia*, vol. 2, and Brassart, *Sechs Motetten*. The text of the motet strongly suggests that it was composed for a pope, as noted already in August Wilhelm Ambros, *Geschichte der Musik*, 1st edn (1868), vol. 3, 495. Under the circumstances of Brassart's career, this can only have been Pope Eugenius.

Dufay's motet 'Supremum est mortalibus bonum' seems to make concessions to this trend. Its simple isorhythmic design is confined to the tenor (ostensibly a plainsong: 'Isti sunt duo olive'). There are never more than three voices singing: the introduction, the final 'Amen' and other passages are high duets with a supporting lower voice, some of them actual fauxbourdon trios. The other passages have triplum, motetus and tenor; as Fallows noted, there are many parallel 6–3 sonorities in these passages, too.[100] Isomelic design connects the upper lines of the third and sixth *taleae*:

Example 24*a* Guillaume Dufay, 'Supremum est mortalibus bonum'

100 Fallows, *Dufay*, 116 f.

Example 24a (*cont.*)

[Joyfully open lie gentle hills; in peace the wealthy man is making his way; in safety the ploughman inhabits the fields . . . And those, o peace, who gave you to us – may they possess the realm forever: Eugenius and King Sigismundus.]

Note the hidden imitation at the fifth between 'Pace dives' (bars 45–6) and 'Tutus arva' (bar 49): the second time, the motive results from the interplay of the voices. This turning motive, g'–e'–f'–g', and its retrograde, the under-third cadential formula g'–$f\sharp'$–e'–g', pervade much of the work. The altered pitch eb' at 'Pace dives' is taken up differently on the words 'Tutus arva', reflecting the opposition and analogy between the two text verses. A similar balance exists between *taleae* three and six as a whole, with related melodies (bars 41–3, 48–52 and 86–90, 93–7), and with related but not identical harmonies over a ciacona-like tenor c'–bb–c'–g (bars 48–52 and 93–7). Three times (bars 52, 56 and 97), the last g is brightened up by its major tenth above.[101]

Both passages are followed by melismatic duets. The second (bars 97–101) spins out the words 'regnum sine fine' in a patterned manner reminiscent of Hugo's 'Tra quante regione' at the words 'Tu fosti albergo d'Elena regina'.[102] The sequential patterns probably symbolize eternity. As in Hugo's piece, where long-held chords follow, announcing the patronal name ('Madonna Cleofé'), Dufay goes on to announce the names of pope and king in a famous passage in fermata chords:

Example 24*b*

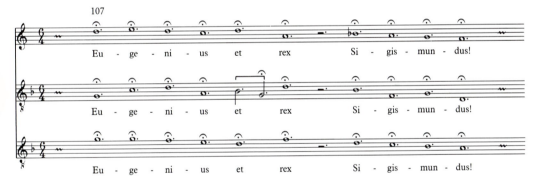

Fermata-held progressions like these, which we have encountered in other works of the time (p. 162), were probably performed with embellishments on each chord – a device called *noëma* or *cantus coronatus*.[103] It was often used in Mass settings for the names of Christ and Mary. This is as if the name were appearing in capital letters in a painting or on a grand portico. The term *cantus*

101 The passages are disfigured by some misprints in *Opera omnia*, vol. I, no. 14.
102 Borren ed., *Pièces polyphoniques*, no. 32.
103 Charles W. Warren, 'Punctus organi and cantus coronatus in the music of Dufay', in Atlas ed., *Dufay Quincentenary Conference*, 128–43.

coronatus, derived from the term for the fermata sign, corona, also assumes an obviously symbolic connotation here.

Dufay's text is one of the most touching Latin poems set to music in this century. Its rhymed, unsophisticated verse (medieval decasyllables) and leisurely string of thought praise peace and its effects. Some verses seem to open windows on to a wide and beautiful Italian landscape. Dufay reacts not only structurally (as seen in bars 45–9) but also pictorially to the words. At the mention of a maiden's golden locks ('virginem ornare auro comam crinesque nodare'), the first ornamental note-values crease the melodic flow (bars 31–2 and 36). At 'gentle hills' ('collesque suaves', bar 44), the top line takes a little excursion upwards, gently arched in quaver patterns. At 'diu expectata' ('long-awaited', bars 59–63), the cadence is deferred by denser dissonances. When peace is apostrophized as 'eterna, firma' (bars 71–5), the longest note-values of the motet appear in the top voices.

Dufay's praise of peace was to be belied by factional strife in Rome soon after. The pope had to flee the city, and many chapel members left him. Dufay went to the court of Savoy in 1434, but rejoined the chapel in Florence in spring 1435. He stayed there for another two years, composing his three 'Florentine' motets 'Mirandas parit', 'Salve flos Tuscae gentis / Vos nunc' and 'Nuper rosarum flores'. The first is a eulogy to Florentine girls, and one in particular – apparently referred to as 'Helen' – who must have been a local noblewoman. 'Salve flos' praises both the city and, again, its women. It seems somehow autobiographical, although the mention of the composer's own name in the text is a tradition of the genre and does not prove this point. The many classical allusions in both these motet texts have been noted; but the hexameters are awkward enough to have been written by a newcomer to humanist fashions such as Dufay himself. Conversely, the metre and imagery of 'Supremum est' would have been within the scope of his cathedral training.[104]

'Nuper rosarum flores' was written for the pompous and widely noted consecration of Florence Cathedral on 25 March 1436, the feast of the Annunciation. The gothic church of Santa Reparata was re-dedicated to 'Santa Maria del Fiore', after the completion of Filippo Brunelleschi's magnificent new dome. The architect had trained himself for this task by studying the dome of the classical Roman Pantheon. The performances of the papal singers (and instrumentalists, but not necessarily within the same works) in the presence of Eugenius IV have been described in exaggerated terms by the humanist Giannozzo Manetti.[105] Two modern writers have sought analogies between the isorhythmic design of Dufay's motet and the architectural dimensions of the cathedral itself.[106] Such an idea was apparently not unknown in the Middle Ages. But

---

[104] Humanist leanings in motet texts and their settings are emphasized in Willem Elders, 'Humanism and early Renaissance music: a study of the ceremonial music by Ciconia and Dufay', *TVNM* 27 (1977), 65–101; *idem*, 'Guillaume Dufay as musical orator', *TVNM* 31 (1981), 1–15.

[105] Žak, 'Quellenwert'.

[106] Rolf Dammann, 'Die Florentiner Domweihmotette Dufays', in Wolfgang Braunfels, *Der Dom von Florenz* (Olten etc.: Urs-Graf Verlag, 1964), 73–85; Charles W. Warren, 'Brunelleschi's dome and Dufay's motet', *MQ* 59 (1973), 92–105.

there are serious problems with this theory here: for example, the fact that the proportions of the building as a whole, approximately comparable to those of the motet, had existed long before 1436 and were thus the one thing that did not require a celebration.

The verses of 'Nuper rosarum flores' mention the event of the consecration and implore the Virgin to intercede for the Florentine people. They also draw two liturgical allusions into the context. One is to the feast of the dedication of a church, represented by its introit 'Terribilis est locus iste', which is partially recited by the two canonic tenors. The other allusion is to the foundation legend of the Roman Basilica of Santa Maria Maggiore, the mother church of all Marian foundations and thus also of 'Santa Maria del Fiore'. Snow had fallen on the Esquiline hill in the midst of summer – on 5 August – to signal the wish of the Virgin for a church to be built for her in that place. The text of 'Nuper rosarum flores, hieme licet horrida . . .' creates an inverted foundation legend for the Florentine church: in the midst of winter, Pope Eugenius IV presents the City of Florence with a rose – the famous 'Golden Rose' which the popes traditionally presented to allied secular powers. That the motet text speaks of this ceremony as a somewhat miraculous event ('roses in the snow') and connects it with the dedication of the cathedral, must be because this re-foundation was understood as a sequel to the foundation of Santa Maria Maggiore. It is likely that Eugenius IV intended the Florentine church to be his papal basilica for years to come. In Dufay's motet, the two tenors which follow each other in strict canon at the fifth seem to symbolize the relationship between mother church and daughter church; similarly, the text derives from a past event ('Nuper') a present one ('Hodie').

The concept of duality – past and present, mother and daughter etc. – is built into the harmonic structure of the motet. Modal duality arises from the two tenors within the same (second) mode but a fifth apart, on d' and g. Both these finals have either the major or the minor third above them, so that four cross-related sonorities result:

D major – g minor
d minor – G major.

The first pair forms a *harmonic* relationship, relying on the accidental $f\sharp$, the second a *modal* relationship between the pentachords of the Dorian mode (d–a) and the Mixolydian (g–d'). In the manuscript, B flats at the clefs of the lower three voices rival with B naturals of the triplum, which are sometimes revoked by specially written flats. This device, somewhat improperly called 'conflicting signatures', is known from English as well as continental music of the time.[107] It is remarkable, however, that Dufay writes so many accidental sharps and

---

[107] For an introduction on the relationship of accidentals and modes, see Margaret Bent, 'Musica ficta' in *The New Grove*; Berger, *Musica ficta*, ch. 3; Brown ed., *Florentine Chansonnier*, ch. XIV. A modal analysis of 'Nuper rosarum' is Patricia Carpenter, 'Tonal coherence in a motet of Dufay', *JMT* 17 (1973), 2–65.

flats explicitly – apparently because he does not wish to leave his harmonic relationships to the whim of performers. His tenors produce not only *g* and *d'*, but also *f*, *a*, *b*♭ and *c'* as the lowest pitches. The harmony thus comprises all the triads of the harmonic series, D–G–C–F–B♭, and also all the finals of the hexachordal scale, *f–g–a–b*♭–*c'–d'*.

The universality of the work is also one of stylistic resources and techniques of detail. Unlike 'Ecclesie militantis', however, the gentle flow of 'Supremum est' prevails. The emphasis is on long duets of the top voices with much sequential patterning and imitation, on broad triple rhythms and pentatonic gestures, on 'divisi' notes in the upper voices producing chordal fullness. Isomelic recurrences are clearly audible. The isorhythmic scheme (the proportional diminution of the tenors is 6 : 4 : 2 : 3) does not produce much textural contrast: Dufay's formal clarity no longer depends on the isorhythmic scheme. This may be seen as a final step away from Ciconia, and a step possibly made with English music in mind.

The genre in which England was going to make its most characteristic contribution to European music was the cyclic tenor Mass. It is therefore useful to assess what continental composers achieved in *Mass Ordinary settings* before the English impact was felt.

In the early to mid-1420s, Dufay and his colleagues in Italy revived the concept of the Mass Ordinary cycle, consisting of the five invariable musical items of the Mass service: Kyrie, Gloria, Credo, Sanctus and Agnus Dei.[108] Several such cycles had been composed in fourteenth-century France (one by Machaut). No specimens are found in sources between *c.*1380 and *c.*1420 – although surviving Mass pairs or single items from this period may have belonged to cycles. By about 1430, however, the cyclic arrangement of musically related Mass sections was a common practice, at least in northern Italy.[109] Dufay had by then composed two complete cycles, the so-called 'Missa sine nomine' (*c.*1423–6) and the 'Missa Sancti Jacobi' (*c.*1427); similar works survive (not always complete) by Arnold de Lantins, Johannes Reson, Johannes de Lymburgia, Reginald Liebert and Etienne Grossin. In his 'Missa sine nomine', Dufay uses motivic material also found in his ballade 'Resvelliés vous' of 1423,[110] in a manner reminiscent of the 'parody' Mass settings by Antonius Zacharias and Bartolomeo da Bologna. It is not clear, however, whether Dufay derived the Credo from the chanson or vice versa. It seems, in any case, that he composed his Gloria and Credo first, as independent pieces, and then completed a full cycle with Kyrie, Sanctus and Agnus; the latter three sections are musically more similar to each other than they are to the former two. This type of 'layered' cycle was

---

[108] On Dufay's works in the genre, see Fallows, *Dufay*, ch. 14 ('The early Mass music'); Bockholdt, *Messenkompositionen* (with edition in original note-symbols). Although Bockholdt's edition is better, I am following here the numeration of Dufay, *Opera omnia*, vol. 4, as does Fallows.

[109] Important analyses of composing and copying practices are: Charles Hamm, 'The Reson Mass', *JAMS* 18 (1965), 5–21; Gossett, 'Techniques of unification'; Bent, 'A contemporary perception'.

[110] Fallows, *Dufay*, 165–8. On the ballade, see p. 154 above.

frequent. Musicians would take an already existing Mass pair (Gloria–Credo or Sanctus–Agnus) or even some unrelated sections, and complete them by adding the missing sections, irrespective of whether the pre-existing ones were their own work. In addition, copyists of polyphonic manuscripts took the liberty of placing Mass sections together in cycles whether or not this had been the intention of the composers, according to their musical judgement. Criteria for such co-ordination would include similarity of clefs, modes, ranges, common melodic openings ('mottos') or formal analogies between the sections. On the other hand, some cycles intended as such by composers (such as the one by Reson) were redistributed in the manuscripts. The Gloria and Credo, for example, could be placed as an independent pair far away from the other sections. It is likely that this is why many components of originally full cycles are lost today. The suggestion that Dufay composed a full cycle incorporating the 'Vineux' melody (see p. 153) rests upon this premiss.

What were the reasons for these practices of composing and performing? First of all, there must have been a need at some institutions for Mass cycles exceeding the supply of composed cycles, since copyists had to make up 'pastiches' of heterogeneous origin. Other institutions, however, had no such need, since in their manuscripts the sections of existing cycles were treated independently. This strongly suggests that decisions about cycles had to do with particular conditions – liturgical or organizational – in individual establishments. Secondly, the criteria used by composers to make the five Mass sections 'go together', or by copyists and performers to co-ordinate them, were the same as had been applied to the writing of conventional Mass pairs. The progress from pair to cycle did not generate any new aesthetic of musical 'unification', and did not depend on a single unifying factor such as a borrowed cantus firmus common to all the sections (the English type, see p. 228). The most 'unified' work from this sphere is an anonymous Gloria–Credo pair in the codex *I-Bc Q 15*, where one section is an exact 'parody' or paraphrase of the other.[111] This sort of unity, or rather, 'uniformity', was actually an obstacle to cyclic unification, because five sections as uniform as these two would not have constituted a viable work.

It seems, then, that the cyclic Mass was fostered by pragmatic, rather than aesthetic, considerations. In the Mass services throughout the year, the Gloria is not sung in Lent and the Credo only on Sundays and feast-days, so that Kyrie, Sanctus and Agnus were sung more often, a fact that apparently conflicts with their smaller number in polyphonic sources. The reason is that polyphonic settings would be admitted in many churches only on festal occasions anyway: a Gloria–Credo pair might be sung on a feast-day when the other sections were left to plainsong. This accounts for many Mass pairs of festal character still being written in the 1420s and 30s; for example, with special

---

[111] Gossett, 'Techniques of unification', 222–31. For a discussion of the over-used concept of 'unification', see Strohm, 'Einheit und Funktion'.

tropes, or in four voices rather than three. Dufay's Gloria–Credo pairs nos. 4 and 5, and Sanctus–Agnus pairs nos. 6 and 7, belong to this group.[112]

The genre of the full cycle, however, must have corresponded to a practice slightly outside the regular liturgy. Patrons, congregations and performers would the more appreciate the 'cyclic idea', the more also the Mass service, which they were attending, was distinct. There is enough evidence from the days of the 'Mass of Tournai' (see pp. 68 f) to show what kind of distinction this can have been: that of a specially funded *votive Mass* for a patron saint or Our Lady, performed annually, weekly or daily outside the high choir, often in a Lady Chapel. As far as the destination of the early cycles can be established at all, a surprising number of them are Lady Masses. The cyclic form was essentially connected with their recurrent use, since – by the prominence of the heavenly or the financial support of the earthly patron – they were sheltered from the vicissitudes of the calendar. Recurrent use made it advisable to group the five sections together in a manuscript (even if they were not composed together), so that the performers did not have to put bits and pieces together every Saturday, for example. It also led to 'unification' by such considerations as common clefs, modes and voice-number, because the same small group of performers would regularly be charged with this supernumerary service. A common musical 'tag' such as a recurring motto would serve them, and the audience, to identify each section as belonging to their special Mass service. If the cycle was copied into a larger, miscellaneous manuscript, it would preferably be placed at the beginning (as in *I-Bc Q 15*), or in some other distinctive place, for example as a separate fascicle. Such 'fascicle manuscripts'[113] could also be handled on their own, for example in a side-chapel where the special service might take place. Other institutions without the funds for such votive Masses could nevertheless use the individual sections independently in the regular service. This practice, and the scarce survival of smaller 'fascicle manuscripts', have probably deprived us of many components of once-complete Mass cycles, and of entire cycles.

As stated above, unifying devices are discernible in Mass pairs, too. It is worthwhile examining for a moment what kinds of devices there were, and what interests they served. In Bartolomeo da Bologna's Gloria and Credo on his ballatas 'Vince con lena' and 'Morir desio', respectively,[114] the recognition of the secular 'parody models', and thus of the 'pair', was perhaps not intended for uninitiated ears. Dufay's Gloria–Credo pair no. 4 is famous for its quotations from two apparent folksongs in the 'Amen' sections. Although they are audible 'tags', the songs are disguised by having alternative words in Latin: pious tropes for Easter. Only the performers could *read* the original words in their manuscript: 'Tu m'as monté sur la pance et rien n'ay fait' and 'La villanella

[112] Dufay, *Opera omnia*, vol. 4.
[113] Their importance in the transmission of polyphony of the time has been emphasized in Hamm, 'Manuscript structure'.
[114] Edited in *EFM*, vol. 5 (1975), and Borren ed., *Polyphonia Sacra*, nos. 6 and 7.

non è bella se non la dominica', respectively. Each voice, in turn, gets a chance to sing the tunes: clearly Dufay wanted to amuse his Franco-Italian colleagues who sang, not the audience.[115] Johannes Franchois seems to have made use of a similar tune. In the version of his Credo in *I-Bc Q 15*, the 'Amen' contains a little dance melody (bars 13–15):

Example 25 Johannes Franchois, Credo

---

[115] See also Besseler, *Bourdon*, 182–5; Pirro, *Histoire*, 73 f. Peter Gülke, 'Das Volkslied in der burgundischen Polyphonie des 15. Jahrhunderts', in *Festschrift Heinrich Besseler zum 60. Geburtstag* (Leipzig, 1961), 179–202.

Example 25 (*cont.*)

A simpler 'Amen' exists for this Credo without this tune (has it been ex-purgated?), but the version of *I-Bc Q 15* is probably authentic. The various types of imitation and the strict motivic patterning found here (see tenor, bars 9-12; cantus and tenor, bars 18-20) occur elsewhere in Franchois' music. The beginning of this 'Amen' sounds almost like Baroque fugal writing.[116]

This pair as a whole uses imitation as a unifying device; the same *soggetti* even recur in both sections. Franchois probably owes his flair for imitation and sequential patterning to the Liège tradition, as exemplified by Ciconia, Salinis and Hugo de Lantins. Sequential patterning is also found frequently in the cycle by Johannes Reson. We may have to look in the diocese of Liège for Reson's origins (but in some north Italian cathedral for his place of activity).

'Intertextual' relationships are frequent in Mass pairs. When Hugo de Lantins and Dufay produced a pair together (see p. 157), the insiderish effect on the performers would have been lost had the two sections not actually been sung in the same service. A Gloria–Credo pair by Guillaume Legrant, dated 1423 in *GB-Ob 213*,[117] cultivates a striking chromaticism as do his three virelais (see p. 150). These non-harmonic alterations (a unifying device?) seem to have influenced Dufay's Gloria–Credo pair no. 5, even to the point of borrowing a special effect: the unusual pitch *ab* is reserved until the end of the Gloria, whereas the Credo brings it in at once and repeats it towards the end in a passage corresponding to that in the Gloria (see Ex. 26).

Alterations like these do not arise from the regular application of *musica ficta* rules, nor do they affect a leading note or penultimate chord. Besseler called them '*Terzfreiheit*' (free use of major or minor third). Although a frequent mannerism in sacred and secular works of the time, it is also used as an expressive device. In Dufay's cheerful rondeau, 'J'attendray tant', for example, the only *eb* in the 'C major' context occurs on the word 'desplayra'.[118]

[116] Borren ed., *Polyphonia Sacra*, nos. 13 and 14; the authentic 'Amen' is no. 14bis.
[117] *Polyphonia Sacra*, nos. 18 and 19. The date might, in this case, be close to the time of composition.
[118] Further on the classification of accidentals, see Margaret Bent, 'Musica recta and musica ficta', *MD* 26 (1972), 73-100; Hughes, *Manuscript Accidentals*; Berger, *Musica ficta* (especially ch. 8).

Example 26 Guillaume Dufay, Gloria–Credo pair no. 5

There are three surviving Gloria–Credo pairs by Arnold de Lantins.[119] The most interesting (*Q 15*, nos. 90–91) is written in low clefs and with two flats for tenor and contratenor, a sound familiar from English music.[120] If, as must be assumed, the low range of the pair is a unifying device, then it was probably not transposed upward in performance (unless one assumes, again, that the device was intended more for the eyes of the performers than the ears of the listeners).

Arnold de Lantins surely provided music for votive services. To a Marian Gloria–Credo pair by Ciconia, he added the sections Kyrie, Sanctus and Agnus, plus the introit 'Salve sancta parens', to achieve a complete Lady Mass. In these sections he used the appropriate Marian plainsongs as tenors. This is a 'Missa de Salve' as practised in Netherlands churches on the basis of endowments (see p. 68).

Arnold also left a Mass cycle entirely of his own, the 'Missa Verbum incarnatum'. It should rather be called 'Missa O pulcherrima mulierum', because it is based on Arnold's own setting of that Marian antiphon.[121] Both antiphon and Mass sections share a common initial motto (it resembles the beginning of Dufay's 'Flos florum'); the Credo continues similarly as in 'O pulcherrima'. Further reminiscences appear at the beginning of all six middle sections, and in the fermata chords at the ends. It is a unity expressed in a common melodic–rhythmic vocabulary, a constant recurrence of the same formulas, especially striking in the section 'Dilectus meus' (bars 26 ff) of the antiphon and in the 'Et incarnatus' of the Mass, where literal quotations are easy to find.

The mensuration schemes of the antiphon and the Mass sections together form a coherent sequence:

Antiphon	₵	○	₵	
Kyrie	₵	○	₵	C
Gloria	₵	○	₵	
Credo	₵	○	₵	C
Sanctus	₵̸	○	₵̸	
Agnus	₵̸	○		C

Without the antiphon, the series would not be symmetrical (2 + 2 + 2; corresponding items 1–3–5 and 2–4–6; since the Sanctus–Agnus pair is more independent, the Gloria would not have a match if the antiphon were missing).

The cycle has been labelled 'composite', because the Sanctus and Agnus are set apart by their ₵̸ mensuration. The two mensurations are equivalent at least aurally (see p. 132); the fact that the composer chose a different notation in

---

[119] His Mass music is discussed and edited in Jean Widaman, *The Mass Ordinary Settings of Arnold de Lantins: A Case Study in the Transmission of Early Fifteenth-Century Music*, Ph.D., Brandeis U., 1987.

[120] Similar ranges and clefs are found in a Gloria by Binchois (*Polyphonia Sacra*, no. 8) and two by Hugo de Lantins (*Polyphonia Sacra*, nos. 15 and 17).

[121] Borren ed., *Polyphonia Sacra*, nos. 1–5 (Mass), and no. 43 (antiphon).

the more melismatic sections of the cycle does not prove that he wrote them at a later time. The decision would hardly have been taken because he did not know of this alternative notation before. Rather, he wanted some degree of variety to counteract total 'unification'.

The title of the work, given by the editor, derives from its Kyrie trope 'Verbum incarnatum'. The Sanctus has the trope 'Qui hominem limo condidisti'. Both texts could be related to the same poem or group of poems which also included the stanzas 'Qui januas mortis confregisti' and 'Qui vertice Thabor affuisti', connected with the 'Vineux' melody (see p. 153). All these texts refer to the life of Christ, which would seem to conflict with the possibly Marian destination of Arnold's cycle, on account of its connection with the antiphon. The work may have been a votive Mass for the Advent season, when the Virgin and her son are praised together.[122]

Arnold's Gloria has a canonic introduction, underpinned by a contratenor part which is labelled '*tuba sub fuga*'. This festive device is reminiscent of the 'trompetta' voices in Mass sections by Loqueville and Dufay (see p. 115). Etienne Grossin wrote a cyclic 'trompetta' Mass, where duos with a trombone-like lower voice alternate with sections in chanson format, labelled 'chorus'.[123] There is no Agnus; in the Sanctus, the 'Pleni' and 'Osanna' verses are monophonic, consisting of chant-like but mensural tenor melodies. The work probably existed before 1430, and may have been intended for a festive occasion when a specialized 'trompetta'-style singer was available. It would thus not have been a votive Mass. Grossin was a chaplain of the church of St Merry in Paris from 1417, and a clerk of Notre Dame in 1421; musical sources refer to him as 'Grossim de Parisiis'.[124] Of his surviving works, some are stylistically very close to Loqueville (*d.*1418). An isolated Gloria (no. 16) has a 'trompetta' contratenor like the Mass. There is also a Kyrie which uses fauxbourdon in alternating sections; we cannot rule out the possibility that it was composed before, or independently of, Dufay's earliest fauxbourdon piece of *c.*1427 (see p. 179). Grossin's Kyrie is found in the Polish *Kras* MS, where there are also fragments of an apparent Mass cycle: one Gloria known to be by him, and anonymous settings of a Kyrie (? textless) and a Credo to go with it.[125] Their tenors are not identical but modally similar, in the manner of Dufay's 'Vineux' group. The tenor of the Gloria is stated three times identically (and may therefore be a pre-existing melody) but under different mensurations, much in the manner of Dufay's Gloria 'de Quaremiaux'. This was perhaps a cycle of which the Sanctus and Agnus were performed in mensural plainsong.

There is growing archival evidence that polyphony at Mass was a regular practice in many wealthier establishments. In princely chapels, for example, the sovereign could command as many polyphonic performances of the Mass as

[122] Further on the Mass, see Strohm, 'Einheit und Funktion', 149–55.
[123] Reaney ed., *EFM*, vol. 3 (1966).
[124] See also Wright, *Music and Ceremony*, ch. 8.
[125] Perz ed., *Sources of Polyphony*, vols. 13 and 14, nos. 7, 8 and 12.

he wanted, because he funded them. Duke Philip the Good of Burgundy maintained not only his itinerant *chapelle domestique*, which regularly sang polyphony at Mass; he also endowed daily Lady Masses in 'discant' with choirboys at St Peter's, Lille, and in the Sainte-Chapelle, Dijon, in 1425.[126] Other rulers probably acted analogously. In such cases, there can be no question of the chaplains' having to assemble new combinations of Kyrie, Gloria etc. every day: it can be assumed that fixed cycles were used.

In 1405 the statutes of the Sainte-Chapelle of Bourges, the newly founded establishment of Duke Jean de Berry, requested even more magnificent musical services:

> Jubemus quod in omni missa cujuscumque solemnitatis sit . . . semper officium, responsorium, alleluja, offertorium et postcommunio discantabuntur, et similiter Kyrie eleison, Gloria in excelsis, Prosa, Sanctus, Agnus, nisi organisentur.
>
> [We decree that in every Mass of whatever solemnity . . . always the introit, gradual, alleluja, offertory and postcommunion be sung in discant, and likewise the Kyrie, Gloria, sequence, Sanctus and Agnus, unless they are played on the organ.][127]

In the case of the Mass Ordinary, this is almost a recipe for the introduction of fixed cycles. We do not know, of course, how much of the statute was carried out in reality. The amount of polyphony required for the Mass Proper (introit etc.) would be impressive, because in that genre each Sunday or feast had its own texts! Very little polyphony for the Mass Proper from that time and region exists today. Perhaps the 'discant' used for the Proper items consisted of some unwritten singing practice, such as fauxbourdon.

Nevertheless, the document may provide a background for two surviving 'plenary cycles' – so named because they contain the Mass Ordinary *and* Mass Proper items: Reginald Liebert's Marian cycle and Dufay's 'Missa Sancti Jacobi'.[128] More plenary cycles were assembled from heterogeneous material in the Codex *Tr* 92 (see p. 253), which seems to indicate that the practice was well known outside France.

Liebert's cycle may be a votive Mass for Our Lady, written for an unknown institution. Dufay's work originated in Bologna about 1427, apparently in connection with the motet 'Rite majorem' for Auclou (see above). Alejandro Planchart has shown that the texts of the Proper items belonged to the liturgy of the Bolognese Franciscan house S Giacomo Maggiore.[129] This large establishment, well connected with the university, may have ordered the work for recurrent celebrations of its patron, St James the Greater. Dufay responded with a com-

---

[126] Marix, *Histoire*, 162 f.

[127] Higgins, 'Music and musicians', 691. The extract had been published by earlier writers, for example Peter Wagner, *Geschichte der Messe* (Leipzig, 1913), vol. 1, 80 f (where it is dated 1407). An interesting liturgical peculiarity is the mention of the sequence, an item of the Mass Proper, among the Ordinary items instead of the Credo. See also pp. 435 f.

[128] The Liebert cycle is printed in *DTOe XXVII/1*, vol. 53; the Dufay in *Opera omnia*, vol. 2 no. 2.

[129] Planchart, 'Guillaume Dufay's Masses', 26–33. See also Fallows, *Dufay*, 168–73.

position so rich in polyphonic techniques that it could be regarded as a summa
(or musical universe) of Mass composition of his day.

The cycle is made up of several layers, distinguished by technique but probably *not* by chronology of composing. There is a 'trio' of Kyrie, Gloria and Credo
in chanson format, with intervening duos; a Sanctus–Agnus pair for four
voices, with the appropriate plainsong paraphrased in the tenor, plus intervening duos; the introit 'Michi autem', the alleluia 'Hispanorum clarens stella' and
the offertory 'In omnem terram' also for four voices with their chants in the
tenor. The repetition of the introit antiphon (that is, the second part of the
introit) and the post-communion 'Vos qui secuti estis' are linked with the Kyrie
by having their chants ornamented in the cantus; but 'Vos qui secuti estis'
stands out by using fauxbourdon. Various motivic recurrences, and a general
plan of mensurations, embrace the whole cycle.

The two main techniques of plainsong treatment are the 'discant paraphrase'
(with an ornamented version of the chant in the top voice), and what could be
called the 'antiphon type' (with the plainsong as a non-isorhythmic tenor). Both
techniques had been cultivated in France and England before, whereas the
Italians did not normally use plainsongs for Mass settings before that time.
Dufay and other Franco-Netherlands composers, such as Loqueville, Arnold de
Lantins and Grossin, prepared the extensive use of non-isorhythmic plainsong
tenors in the Mass observed in central European sources after 1430.

The post-communion uses fauxbourdon in its earliest written and datable
specimen:

Example 27 Guillaume Dufay, 'Missa Sancti Jacobi': post-communion

Example 27 (*cont.*)

According to Dufay's direction here, a non-written contratenor (or second cantus) has to be sung in strict parallel fourths below the cantus. The cantus, which paraphrases the plainsong, forms a contrapuntally complete duet with the tenor, as in a chanson; where these voices proceed in parallels, full 6–3 parallels are formed with the middle voice. But just as often, the outer voices proceed in contrary motion, and are rhythmically independent from each other. At the beginning of most phrases, the tenor 'leads in' with a free, soloistic gesture, so that the characteristic sixth is established almost casually in the process.

It has often been remarked that this is quite unlike the English faburden practice, where the plainsong is scarcely or not at all rhythmicized, in the middle voice, and is accompanied by the outer voices in syllable-against-syllable style.[130] In the present piece, and in virtually all subsequent fauxbourdon settings on the Continent, the plainsong is first transformed into a chanson-like upper voice, to which first a freely composed tenor and then a strictly parallel contratenor are added. Unlike faburden, this technique cannot be extemporized from the plainsong book. An epochal transformation of an unwritten practice into a compositional style has taken place.

A more primitive stage of such an unwritten practice on the Continent seems to survive in a piece of the Cambrai hymnal *F-CA 29*. Here, the hymn 'Cultor dei memento' (fol. 159v) carries the rubric '*a faulz bourdon*'.[131] The single notated melody of the hymn is identical with the plainsong in most stanzas, but in the second stanza ('Fac cum sonante sono') it is notated a third higher in the middle of phrases. If this stanza is performed with an extemporized contratenor strictly a fifth above the plainsong, and with a cantus strictly an octave above it (by choirboys who would sing in that register anyway), then the result is identical to English faburden (see p. 209).

Although the hymn was copied into this old hymnal in the mid-fifteenth century – conceivably under Dufay's own supervision – it may reflect an older

---

[130] Despite important differences of opinion about the development, this diagnosis is essentially shared between Besseler, *Bourdon*, 96 ff, and Trowell, 'Faburden – new sources'.

[131] Wright, 'Performance practices', 315–21 (with transcription); Brian Trowell, 'Faburden' in *The New Grove*.

practice at Cambrai. The plainsong of 'Cultor dei' is measured in a simple triple metre; several other hymns in the book copied in 1381 are measured in this way and may also have been performed with improvised faburdens. Dufay, if he had anything to do with the hymnal, would seem to have endorsed an older practice with which he grew up at Cambrai. Had the technique been new to his colleagues around 1450, the *'faulz bourdon'* rubric would have confused them no end, being so different from the newer written fauxbourdon pieces used by the same choir. This hymn could be the tip of an iceberg: an isolated survivor of a *continental* faburden technique which in the 'Missa Sancti Jacobi' appears already stylized and transformed. Nevertheless, Dufay's motive for turning to the primitive technique in this Mass may well have been to meet the challenge of English sacred music, which by 1427 had arrived on the Continent.

The chanson and Binchois

The development of French polyphonic song in the 1420s and early 1430s is difficult to trace. We usually refer to this body of music as the 'Burgundian chanson', mainly in view of the contribution of Binchois – but a significant number of his 60-odd surviving songs must have been written before he actually entered the Burgundian household around 1429.[132] As we have seen, Dufay and the two Lantins made important contributions to the genre while in Italy; the same can be surmised about Pierre Fontaine, Nicholas Grenon, Gautier Libert and others who served in the papal chapel in the 1420s. That French polyphonic song had been accepted at Italian courts (including the papal *curia*) as a sort of international coinage is confirmed by the French songs composed at this time by Italians such as Antonio da Cividale, Bartolomeus Brolo, Prepositus Brixiensis, Do. Vala and several others, and collected in sources such as *I-Bu 2216* and *GB-Ob 213*.[133] Nor is it contradicted by the probability that Dufay's song 'Craindre vous vueil' originated as the Italian song 'Quel fronte signorille in paradiso' which he set while in Rome (*GB-Ob 213* specifies 'Rome composuit' above the latter version).[134] The French text contains the acrostics 'Cateline' and 'Dufai': this version, with a woman's name as the dedicatee, may have been a dedicatory piece in the manner of 'New Year' and 'May' songs which northerners apparently sent home from Italy (see p. 159).

Because of the frequent journeys undertaken by these composers, and the scarce documentation for dates and origins of chansons, neither an 'Italian' nor a 'Burgundian' group can stylistically be identified. Northern cathedrals (Cambrai, Liège, etc.) were certainly centres of song composition. There are many anonymous pieces, and many composers' names simply tell us nothing. For

---

[132] The songs are edited in Binchois, *Chansons*. For proposed additions, see Walter Kemp, 'The MS Escorial V.III.24', *MD* 30 (1976), 97–129.

[133] Fallows, 'French as a courtly language'.

[134] Bent, 'Songs of Dufay', 454–9, supports the priority of the French text.

example, we know nothing about Reginald Liebert, nor whether he was connected with either Gautier Libert, or with Clement Liebert (Hébert?) who was a Burgundian chaplain in 1441.[135] Haucourt (of *GB-Ob 213*) could be linked to Hacourt near Liège, and Johannes Franchois hailed from Gembloux in the same diocese. Adam (also *GB-Ob 213*) was perhaps Adamo Grand, Master of the Choirboys of Savoy in 1433 and later,[136] or Adam Hustini de Ora from Cambrai, who sang in the Habsburg chapel in 1442/3. Jacobus Coutreman was an organist and succentor in Bruges, 1417–32.[137]

The towering position of both Dufay and Binchois in this field led some of their contemporaries to regard them erroneously as kindred spirits.[138] However, Binchois' mannerist approach cannot really be equated with the greater universality of Dufay's talents. While the former earned his enormous reputation in the one genre in which he excelled as a composer, performer, and possibly even poet, Dufay's creativity unfolded along many more musical lines. His surviving chanson oeuvre[139] is larger than that of Binchois or anyone else, and more diversified than that of any composer since Machaut. Many of its experiments are atypical of the mainstream of the genre. Unless manuscript losses cruelly mislead us, Dufay had ideas which even Binchois simply never tried.

There are, for example, bold departures from the standard three-voice format, and a striking number of cantus firmus compositions. Next to the convivial song 'Resvelons nous' (no. 28), which has an ostinato canon in the lower voices, the edition has the rondeau 'Je ne puis plus' (no. 29) based on the cantus firmus 'Unde veniet auxilium mihi' (see p. 133). In other pieces there is no genuine tenor at all, or its function is artfully disguised and given to a voice labelled differently: 'Je me complains piteusement' of 1425 (no. 14) with the voice-names 'primus', 'secundus' and 'tertius'; 'Par droit je puis' (no. 43) with two canonic upper voices and a duet of contratenors, one of which can be omitted – but no tenor. 'Hé, compaignons, resvelons nous' (no. 49) is in the same format. The voices frequently exchange functions, particularly the lower pair; the voice-exchange technique correlates with ostinato-like harmonies, so the piece sounds almost like 'variations over a V-I ground'. With its bouncing rhythms in the manner of a rustic dance, this rondeau is sharply distinguished, despite a similar technique, from the supple four-voice rondeau 'Ma belle dame souveraine' (no. 44). This enchanting song has its tenor, cantus and triplum in the same range, with many voice-crossings disguising the cantus–tenor duet. Another song for four voices, 'Mon cuer me fait' (no. 54), shows the traditional hierarchic order of cantus–tenor duet with added contratenor and triplum.

---

[135] Marix, *Histoire*, 199.

[136] Fallows, *Dufay*, 40.

[137] Strohm, *Bruges*, 21.

[138] They were named together at least by Martin le Franc (see p. 65; also a portrait of both of them is in the manuscript) and Tinctoris (p. 127).

[139] Edited in Dufay, *Opera omnia*, vol. 6. Henceforth, numbers in the text refer to this edition. A revised edition by David Fallows is announced. A recent study of chronology and style is Boone, *Dufay's Early Songs* (n. 15 above).

'Pour l'amour de ma doulce amye' (no. 48), however, may be compared to the four-voice chansons of Vide and Fontaine: the contratenor and triplum are alternatives and should not be sounded together. In his genuine four-part songs, Dufay tends to eliminate archaic progressions such as parallel octaves, which in the 1420s were still acceptable to him in Mass and motet styles.

'Pour l'amour', 'Mon cuer me fait' and 'Hé, compaignons' are conceived in ϕ mensuration, perhaps in order to admit more dissonances on semibreves. These are all early pieces, as is the three-part rondeau 'Belle, vueillés vostre mercy donner' (no. 47), the only other early song with genuine ϕ mensuration. Two other early songs, 'Belle, vueillés moy retenir' (no. 30) and 'Ma belle dame, je vous pri' (no. 31), have the unusual sign $\odot$ (9/8) in the cantus. The lower voices of no. 30 are in ordinary $\bigcirc$ (3/4) metre, their imperfect semibreves (crotchets in transcription) being equivalent to the perfect semibreves (dotted crotchets) of the cantus. The latter voice is, therefore, not in a real 9/8 metre, but in a 3 : 2 proportion to the tenor – which should be expressed as triplets in 3/4. Such proportions (whether expressed by proportional signs, coloration or flagged stems) are, of course, frequent in French and Italian songs of the time. The distinction of 'Belle, vueillés moy retenir' is that its cantus is written in this proportion throughout. 'Ma belle dame', on the other hand, is in a genuine $\odot$ metre (9/8) in all the voices. Its semibreve (crotchet) pulse should be 1½ times as slow as that of 'Belle, vueillés'. The two songs both have 'conflicting signatures': two flats in the lower voices against nothing in the cantus. In 'Belle, vueillés', this device could be regarded as an analogy to the metrical conflict of 3 against 2 notes per beat. But it is 'Ma belle dame' – perhaps a later essay in the same idea of voice conflicts – which exploits the resulting cross-relations for harmonic effect. (See also p. 174 on *Terzfreiheit*.)

Dufay uses duple metre in only three songs from this period, and all are special: 'Entre vous, gentils amoureux' and 'Bien veignes vous' have a strict canon between cantus and tenor; the latter and 'Belle, que vous ay' have three different mensuration signs in the three voices. In 'Bien veignes vous', this results in a mensuration canon.

His fondness for canons – not merely 'canonic writing' – is exemplified by a number of pieces based entirely on a particular canon technique. This 'scholarly respect for age-old traditions'[140] distinguishes Dufay as much from Binchois and others as does his frequent use of pre-existing melodies. Dufay's free imitation is quite different. He makes plentiful and varied use of it but rarely ever makes it the basis of a composition. He favours the simple types of imitation: at the unison, and with subjects in stepwise motion, producing parallel thirds. The device is often only an opening gambit. Many imitations are simply triadic fillings of a chord, and cease when the harmony changes. Examples of this lighthearted approach are found in 'Ce jour de l'an' and 'Ce moys de may', where all the voices 'sing and dance together' pictorially.

---

[140] Fallows, *Dufay*, 133.

Dufay's tendency to set himself specific compositional tasks, the solution of which is then artfully disguised, is very different from the attitude of Binchois. This master of melody and courtly performer apparently does not explore the depths of the art. It is useless to search for directly comparable songs in the oeuvres of the two. Many idioms are the same, but not a single piece puts them all together in the same way. Some simpler songs by Dufay are vaguely reminiscent of the general style of Binchois: 'Je ne requier', 'Se madame je puis veir' and 'Estrines moy', for example. Each of them is special in some other sense. It is notable that Dufay's songs which most closely approximate to the general style of Binchois tend to be in O metre, whereas his ¢ pieces are far more individualized. Often the former pieces are 'dedicatory' songs for the New Year and May. Did Dufay deliberately adopt more conventional idioms in this genre?

We must now turn to Binchois himself. Despite the great number of his songs, a style chronology can be constructed only with difficulty.[141] Manuscript dates are of little help. Rhythm and mensuration, and the role of the contratenor, would suggest that there is an earliest group of approximately six to ten songs which all use ¢ in a similar way and which all have 'combinatory' contratenors with regular octave-leaps but also many middle-position cadences and the occasional 'bass-like' gesture (for discussion of these devices, see p. 146). Modes and ranges tend to focus on F, D and C, with the lowest note usually a fourth below these finals. The polyphonic texture is always of a similar density, cantus and tenor overlapping by a fifth, and tenor and contratenor by an octave. Rehm constructs an earliest group of six songs, all rondeaux: 'Tristre plaisir' (on a poem by Alain Chartier), 'Adieu m'amour', 'Amours et qu'as tu', 'Je me recommande', 'En regardant' and 'Nous vous verens'.[142] I see no reason not to add the rondeaux 'Amoureux suy' (the only one in the group with opening imitation), 'Joyeux penser' and 'Mes yeux ont fait', as well as the ballades 'Amours, merchi' and 'Je loe amours'.

Most distinctive in these songs is the careful balance between the cantus phrases, whether declamatory or melismatic. Binchois exploited this 'Burgundian' tradition to the full, even to the point of making all phrases almost the same length ('Je me recommande'). More often, he varies the length somewhat, in a judicious manner. The melismatic phrases, separated from the preceding texted phrases by a minim rest, often correspond to them with rhythmic–melodic material. No doubt they were sung. There are also shorter melismatic extensions at the end of texted phrases which emphasize the rhyme-syllables. The shortest piece with only 12 bars before the final, 'Nous vous verens', has no separate melismas but extends the first and last lines with two-bar melismas. Usually the melismatic phrases are distributed more or less evenly between the

---

[141] The following paragraphs refer to the edition by Wolfgang Rehm: Binchois, *Chansons* and its preface. See also Slavin, *Binchois' Songs*.
[142] Binchois, *Chansons*, 13*.

two halves of a piece; there may be between one and four of them in each half, plus some extended rhyme-syllables.[143]

'Adieu m'amour' is an example of a typical Binchois rondeau, and of the genre itself:[144]

Example 28 Binchois, 'Adieu m'amour'

---

[143] 'Tristre plaisir' is the only early rondeau which *begins* with a melisma; it also inserts more melismas in the middle of phrases. The poetry is special here, featuring opposed images in the rhetorical tradition of the *oxymoron* (such as in 'bitter-sweet').

[144] Binchois, *Chansons*, no. 3.

Example 28 (*cont.*)

A - dieu mon con - fort et li - es - - - se.

J'ay grant desir de prendre adresse,
Pour quoy, vous puisse reveir.
Adieu m'amour etc.

Souvengne vous belle dé esse
De moy qui suy vo' sans faiuir,
En volonté de revenir
Pensant a vo' belle jounesse.
Adieu m'amour etc.

This is a rondeau with a four-line refrain. The metrical balance of the four texted lines and melismas is shown in the following diagram (mel = separate melismatic phrase; ext = rhyme-syllable extension):

Text line		1	mel	2	mel	/	3	ext	4	ext	
Length in ♩.		5	5	5	5	/	5	5	4	2	+ final (4)

The symmetry may appear striking. It has come about because the composer has scrutinized his text, which has four octosyllabic verses (32 syllables), all of which begin with the same word, 'adieu'. This repetitiveness also corresponds to the stubbornly repeated cadential formulas. On the other hand, the musical motive of the opening word 'adieu' is itself subtly differentiated each time.

There is identical musical material in bars 7–8 and 18–19, though it appears in non-corresponding positions: it is the cadence of the second line in bars 9–10 which would have to correspond to the final cadence. And in a sense, it does: bars 17–19 sum up, in reverse order, the two cadential motives of bar 7 and bar 9.

The melodic contours of the phrases are strategically designed. The cantus of bars 1–5 has the essential outline $f'-c'-a'-f'$, with the tenor first falling in parallels and then rising, $f-c-f$. In bars 6–10, the same contours are repeated higher in the same triad, $a'-f'-c''-a'$ in the cantus and $d'-f-a$ in the tenor. In bars 11–15 the cantus descends to d' and c', and the tenor similarly from c' to c – which probably illustrates the word 'servir'. The cantus of bars 15–20, however, spans a great arch through the octave $c'-c''$ (a reversal of the previous tenor contour) and falls back to f', while the tenor is stabilized within the fifth $f-c'-f$. A bold, rising gesture like that of the cantus in bars 15–17 is often found in last lines of Binchois, but it is particularly appropriate here, to the joyful words 'confort et liesse'.

The counterpoint of the piece is not very polished. For the sake of linear logic, some accented or declamatory dissonances occur between cantus and tenor (bars 11 and 12); in bars 2, 9, 17 and 18 these result from the tenor's 'anticipated' step within a hemiola. The purpose of the hemiolas is a drive to the cadence; it is fitting that the final line has the cadential drive twice over. The contratenor either moves essentially in parallel fourths with the cantus, or supplies alternating fifths and octaves (sometimes thirds) under the tenor when that voice is high. The leaping gestures in bars 6–7 and 17–18 are 'bass-like', but none of them reaches the actual cadence. One has the impression that the many repeated pitches, some of which cause unnecessary dissonances (bars 3, 6 and 9), are there to remind the listeners of the contratenor's presence. This characteristic contratenor style, adopted by earlier composers, would lend itself quite well to performance on a plucked instrument.

The performance of the complete rondeau would involve distributing the text in the following manner (the numbers denote the text lines, '+' and '–' the feminine and masculine rhyme-syllables, respectively):

Music:	A	B	C	D
refrain:	1 +	2 –	3 –	4 +
half-stanza:	5 +	6 –		
half-refrain:	1 +	2 –		
stanza:	7 +	8 –	9 –	10 +
refrain:	1 +	2 –	3 –	4 +

The total of 16 lines (4 × 4) is irregularly provided with music in so far as the second unit of four (half-stanza and half-refrain) goes through the same music twice. Without this unit, the song would be in the simplest A B A form. It is characteristic of the rondeau, however, that the progress of the poetic text is 'set back' after line 6 by starting with 1 again, whereas the music has already started to repeat after line 4. All the musical material is presented at the outset, whereas the poem unfolds in two more steps.

It has often been asked whether the composers reckoned, in their setting of the refrain, with the further enrichment of poetic meaning through the additional text lines. In our case (and in many others), judicious placement of words and rhythms in the refrain avoids at least wrong declamation of the new words. The poet could provide for that, but to do more would have been somewhat counterproductive, as the new text should rather create new tension between words and music. The overall form, with its many repeats of the first half of the refrain (its music appears five times, its text three times) and its fewer repeats of the second half (music three times, text twice), ensures that tensions arising from the progression of the poetic text are soon resolved.[145]

Besides the rondeau species described here (the 'rondeau quatrain'), the other main species was the 'rondeau cinquain', with five refrain lines of which three make up the first section. The standard rhyme-scheme 'ab / ba' is extended to 'aab / ba'. Rhymes 'a' and 'b' are still usually differentiated by feminine and

---

[145] Such questions are further investigated in Howard Garey, 'The fifteenth-century rondeau as aleatory polytext', in Winn ed., *Musique naturelle*, 193–236.

masculine endings. In the rondeau cinquain, a total of 21 text lines is sung: 5 + 3 + 3 + 5 + 5.

Verse metres in the rondeau are almost exclusively octosyllabic or decasyllabic (the special form of the 'rondeau layé' inserts two or more shorter lines), so that the total number of syllables pronounced in a rondeau refrain can be 32 (8 × 4), 40 (8 × 5 or 10 × 4) or 50 (10 × 5). The composers were well aware of these significant numbers.

Together with the ballade and the virelai, the rondeau belongs to the so-called *formes fixes* of fourteenth- and fifteenth-century French poetry. All of them were occasionally transferred to other languages (English, Dutch, German); only the virelai had a native analogy in the Italian ballata and *lauda*, and in the Spanish villancico. The musical genre of a *forme fixe* could usually be determined even if the piece in question had no text: the ballade had an *ouvert/clos* (first and second ending) at the end of the first half, the virelai at the end of the second half, and the rondeau had none.

Binchois' manner of composing secular songs seems fully established from the outset; later developments happen almost casually. He adopts the 3/4 metre (O) before *c.*1430, but keeps composing in 6/8 (C) until at least that time. The rondeau 'Jamais tant' exists in both metres in two different sources. What is probably the earlier version, in 6/8 (in the earlier source *PR III*), seems to have been transcribed into doubled note-values in 3/4 in *GB-Ob 213*, with interesting smaller modifications. Binchois occasionally writes low and wide, 'bass-like' contratenors, or uses less conventional harmonies. Most of these features reflect the expression of the individual texts rather than a stylistic development. For example, the rondeau 'Ay, douloureux' owes its low ranges, imitative gestures and modal conflict (between the C Dorian of the lower voices and the G Dorian/Mixolydian of the cantus) to the very plaintive words. The only consistent development seems to be the increase of melismas in the first lines of the songs. The style of a group of seven songs found only in sources post-dating 1445 confirms these as late (see p. 442).

Two of the most famous Binchois songs must be discussed here also for the impression they made on his contemporaries: 'De plus en plus' and 'Dueil angoisseus'. The rondeau 'De plus en plus se renouvelle' (see Ex. 29) features not only a charming tune and an ingenious arithmetic construction; it may also have symbolic–biographical connotations.[146]

Note that the strikingly 'tonal' implications of cantus and tenor in the first line are counteracted by the contratenor, which arpeggiates the G triad in the *first* half of bar 1 and the C triad afterwards, whereas we would hear the harmony the other way round, as 'I-V'. The contratenor similarly outlines an arpeggio after the cadence in bar 4, and from bar 8 leads on to the striking texture of bars 9–11, where the cantus is at the bottom, perhaps to express the humility of the lover. In this instance, the words of the subsequent units seem

---

[146] Binchois, *Chansons*, no. 12.

Example 29 Binchois, 'De plus en plus'

to justify the music more clearly: line 8 is 'que je vueil de tout obéir', and line 11 'que je voudroie bien morir'. The active contratenor of this piece adds new rhythmic interest at cadence-points (a device which became more standard in the mid-fifteenth century) and even adds 'expressive' ideas of its own (bars 6 and 11). This suggests a somewhat later date for the piece than the previous one, despite the 6/8 notation.

'Adieu', 'renouvelle' and 'souvenir' are key-words in poems set by Binchois in the 1420s: see, for example, the texts of 'Mon cuer chante joyeusement' and

'Amours et souvenir de celle'. The aesthetic of 'love from afar', of 'remembrance' and 'renewal', is removed from the 'Burgundian' seasonal, convivial or pastoral songs. The text of Dufay's 'Adieu ces bons vins' strikes us as almost a parody of Binchois' 'Adieu' chansons. Can we identify the circles where the sentimentality of Binchois' poems was appreciated, and perhaps draw conclusions as to his early career?

As mentioned (p. 74), he probably grew up in some connection with the court of Hainaut and its last countess, Jacqueline (r. 1417–29). If any of the songs in the Leiden MS attracted his interest, then these were unlikely to have been the Dutch and convivial songs, but rather such pieces as the strikingly melancholic May song 'Renouveler me feist' or the sentimental 'Adieu vous di'.[147] From 1424 at the latest, Binchois was in contact with English princes during their occupation of northern France. This contact was perhaps brought about by Countess Jacqueline, who had fled to London where, in 1423, she married Duke Humphrey of Gloucester – as a support against her political rival, Burgundy. In 1424 Binchois was in Paris, where he wrote a chanson, 'Ainsy qu'a la fois me souvient' (now lost), to please William de la Pole, Earl of Suffolk. This great lover of French poetry and music, and close friend of the poet Charles d'Orléans (a prisoner of the English from 1415 to 1440), may have given Binchois access to the poetry of the Duke of Orléans and others (Garenciennes, Chartier) as well as his own. An anonymous setting of Suffolk's poem 'Je vous salue' is possibly by Binchois, and the composer's rondeau 'Mon cuer chante', on a text by Charles d'Orléans, may have been written for Suffolk as well.[148] This latter poem also resembles 'De plus en plus'.

It is interesting that 'De plus en plus' has been quoted in the motet 'Anima mea liquefacta est' by Lionel Power.[149] The song was surely later known in the Parisian circle of Ockeghem who composed a Mass over it (see p. 474). The Anglo-French contacts in Paris in the 1420s go much further than this (see also p. 239). It was probably around this time that John Dunstable served Duke John of Bedford, the English regent in France.[150] John of Bedford and Humphrey of Gloucester were, of course, brothers of King Henry V. Their uncle Henry Beaufort, Cardinal of Winchester (his motto was 'Me souvent souvant'), repeatedly visited the Continent at that time, and has been mentioned in connection with Lionel Power.[151]

It is unlikely that Binchois was ever an ordinary 'soldier', as could be deduced from two lines in Ockeghem's *complainte* on his death (1460), 'Mort, tu as navré de ton dart':[152]

---

[147] Biezen-Gumbert eds, *Two Chansonniers*, L 8 and L 13.

[148] David Fallows, review of Julia Boffey, *Manuscripts of English Courtly Love Lyrics* in *JRMA* 112 (1987), 132–8. On the poets of Binchois' era, see also Lowinsky, '*TYMOTHEOS*', 96 ff.

[149] Shai Burstyn, 'Power's *Anima mea*'.

[150] See n. 234 below, and Pirro, *Histoire*, 95 f.

[151] Bowers, 'Some observations', 110. I erroneously extended this into an actual employment of Power with Beaufort in Strohm, *Bruges*, 120.

[152] Marix, *Histoire*, 176. On this piece, see also pp. 413 f.

En sa jeunesse fut soudart
De honnorable mondanité,
Peu a esleu la milleur part
Servant Dieu en humilité.

[In his youth he was a warrior / of honourable worldliness; / but then he chose the better part, / of serving God in humility.]

The 'honourable worldliness' seems to refer to the service of a secular prince, however, perhaps as a squire. Given the high social standing of his father as a court councillor, Gilles may have belonged to the gentry. His services to his patrons – whether Suffolk, Countess Jacqueline or even Gloucester – must have been mainly musical, as those of a chamber valet and harper. He may have been a poet as well, and certainly sang his own compositions, perhaps accompanying himself on the harp. He is portrayed with a harp (the chivalric instrument) in a famous miniature of le Franc's *Le champion des dames* which also shows Dufay with a small organ.[153] By about 1429, when his native Hainaut had become Burgundian territory, Binchois had entered the household of Duke Philip the Good. At the beginning of 1430 he received a canonry *de privilegio* in Bruges because he was a member of the ducal chapel.[154]

Nevertheless, his contacts with English patrons could have lingered on. Suffolk left the Continent in 1431. It is in this context that I would like to place an alleged portrait of the composer: the famous painting by Jan van Eyck, now in the National Gallery, London (see Plate 3). The painting is dated 10 October 1432, and carries the inscriptions 'Tymotheos' (in Greek letters) and 'LEAL SOVVENIR'.[155] Erwin Panofsky first suggested that this unknown man may be Binchois, as the name of Timotheos refers to a legendary musician: the celebrated kithara player of Alexander the Great.[156] The sitter does not hold a musical attribute such as a stringed instrument, but the scroll of paper in his hand may refer to poetry which he wrote or set. Binchois was a Burgundian chaplain in 1432: it has been thought that the painting was executed for Duke Philip, who would have been flattered by the indirect allusion to him as Alexander the Great. This is contradicted by the motto 'LEAL SOVVENIR'. Duke Philip would not need a 'souvenir' portrait of the young man who had joined his chapel recently and who was with him all the time. Both the motto and the allusion to Alexander would more aptly refer to William de la Pole, a famous leader of English troops and a *former* employer of Binchois, who had now returned to England. If a 'souvenir' portrait of his former harper was to be commissioned for him (or by him), the choice of Jan van Eyck, the greatest portrait painter of the age, was most appropriate. Van Eyck worked

---

153 Fallows, *Dufay*, pl. 7.
154 Strohm, *Bruges*, 24.
155 Martin Davies, *Early Netherlandish School*, 3rd, rev. edn (London, 1968), 54 f.
156 Accepted and expanded in Lowinsky, *'TYMOTHEOS'*; see also David Fallows, 'Binchois, Gilles de Bins dit' in *The New Grove*, 710.

3 Jan van Eyck, Portrait of a Young Man, 1432 (Binchois?)

in Bruges; we can now determine that Binchois actually stayed in that town around the time the portrait was completed (10 October 1432).[157]

The most important clue, however, is hidden in the motto itself – as happens also elsewhere in Van Eyck's oeuvre. 'Souvenir' is a key-word in the kind of

---

[157] Bruges, Bisschoppelijk Archief, Reeks G.65 (*Tabulae dietarum*), 1432-3: Binchois was present in the choir of St Donatian's on four days in September and five in October, four in November and twelve in December, which very probably means that he was in the town continuously for these months.

poetry Binchois used to set, also for Suffolk. 'LEAL SOVVENIR' is an anagram of 'NOVVELLES AIRE', (i.e. 'novel tunes'),[158] and a quasi-anagram of
'SE RENOVVELLE'. The motto in the painting appears carved into marble,
the symbol of lasting remembrance, especially of a poet or artist. It expresses
the wish that the patron may 'renew' his 'true recollection' of the 'novel tunes'
ever more, 'de plus en plus'.

The famous ballade by the English composer Walter Frye, 'So ys emprentid
in my remembrance' (see p. 392), uses the same imagery in its first line. This
song was written later, but a connection between Frye and the Earl of Suffolk
(*d.*1450) can by no means be excluded.

The traditional genre of the ballade was indeed still favoured by Anglo-French
circles in this period. The ballade 'Je languis en piteux martire' in Dufay's
Opera omnia has recently been claimed for none other than John Dunstable.[159]
In that case, the composer would have written it while in France with the
Duke of Bedford. The seven ballades by Binchois are musically rather different. All are important works, but historically most significant is 'Dueil angoisseux', on a text by Christine de Pisan. She is said to have written it on the death
of her husband; this may have been known to Binchois or his patrons when
he set it to music. A fitting occasion for its performance would have been the
funeral of Bedford's wife, Anne of Burgundy, who died prematurely in Paris in
1432; since the Burgundian court was then assembled in Bruges for the Festival
of the Order of the Golden Fleece (30 November 1432), her obsequies were
incorporated within the feast itself.[160]

'Dueil angoisseux' survives in seven music manuscripts, and in several versions, distinguished by different contratenors. The earliest has a cantus–tenor
duet, and an active contratenor (range *f–g'*), which is in the middle of the texture and has a single octave-leap cadence (bars 39–40).[161] A second version
has two contratenor parts (ranges *f–f'* and *Bb–e'*), intended to be performed
together (edition: no. 50a). This four-part version adds 'V–I' cadences in the
bass and is rich in full triads, often with the major third at the top of the texture. In another, three-part version, the contratenor, replacing the two voices
just mentioned, is labelled 'solus contratenor' (edition: no. 50). It has the lower
range *Bb–f'* and draws on the motives of all the previous contratenors. It could
be the work of a skilful arranger other than Binchois himself. The three versions did not necessarily originate at different times, except that the 'solus contratenor' presupposes the existence of the other three contratenors. Example 30
is the beginning of the original version.

---

[158] *Aire* (*ayre, aere*), the ancestor of *aria*, is an old French word denoting 'manner' or 'guise'; it was used
in fourteenth- and fifteenth-century Italy to indicate a melodic manner or a type of musical
measure.

[159] Bent, 'Songs of Dufay', 458 f; see also p. 239 below.

[160] Strohm, *Bruges*, 96; evidence for the presence of Binchois in Bruges then is, again, the *Tabula
dietarum* for 1432–3 (see n. 157 above).

[161] This version is not among those published in Binchois, *Chansons*, no. 50/50a. It uses the *contratenor
primus* as printed separately on p. 73.

Example 30 Binchois, 'Dueil angoisseux'

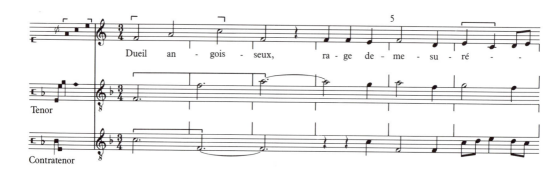

Dueil an - gois - seux, ra - ge de - me - su - ré - -

Tenor

Contratenor

- - - e,

Apart from the funeral of Anne of Burgundy, other occasions for the composition and performance of 'Dueil angoisseux' could be suggested, for example Christine de Pisan's own death (1431?). The song may have been used on more than one occasion, which would have caused its various incarnations. With this ballade Binchois established the genre of the musico–poetic *complainte* (lament) as a tradition of outstanding polyphonic masterpieces, which continued well into the Baroque period (see pp. 413 f).

Perhaps most remarkable about this song are the opening gestures (which employ a very broad triple grouping in coloured breves), and the harmonic inertia of the lower voices. They may have induced the scribe of the chansonnier *EscA* to attach the mensural sign ϕ : unprecedented in Binchois' secular oeuvre but possibly authorized by the composer in this case.[162] A few other songs by Binchois share this expansive metre and quiet pace (the rondeaux 'Adieu, adieu mon joyeulx souvenir', 'Adieu, jusques je vous revoye', 'Adieu, ma doulce', 'Adieu mes tres belles amours', 'Amours et souvenir', 'Ay douloureux', 'Plains de plours'), but none has this specific mensural sign nor the grand gestures of 'Dueil angoisseux'. In no other song does Binchois use the cadential formula in triplets (bars 20 and 52) so characteristic of English sacred music that it has actually been called an 'English figure'.

---

162 Rehm ed., *Manuscript EscA*, fols. 37–8.

The triadic opening of 'Dueil angoisseux', which incorporates perhaps the most beautiful tenor gesture in Binchois' songs, is also typical of English sacred music. Such motives resounded in the memories of other musicians, too: Dufay's ballade 'C'est bien raison' (of 1433 or later) starts with this F major triad, though it is a buoyant, festive song in the Italian manner. The idea is also used in several mid-century pieces found in the Trent Codices, such as the Mass cycle composed over 'Dueil angoisseux' by John Bedyngham, which makes great play of it.[163] Binchois himself never repeated it.

Of the other six ballades by Binchois, every single one deserves the greatest attention. We can only cite, by way of example, the passage in 'Adieu mon amoureuse joye' (bars 18–21) where the wordless cantus line expires at the bottom of the texture, and the gap to the next phrase is filled by the other two voices with an exact repeat of the same descent, like a sympathetic echo; or the particular motivic consistency of 'Ma dame que j'ayme', a piece built on the motive *a'–g'–e'*, which also has a surprising sequential pattern in bars 16–18. 'J'ay tant de deul' opens with a textless phrase in F major, after which the words outline an E minor triad; by bar 9, the 'home key' of G Dorian has been reached. In bars 25–28, the lamenting words 'N'ay je cause de les clore souvent'[164] include the painful cross-relation *e''–eb'* between cantus and tenor. But the cantus of these bars fits precisely the tenor melody of Martinus Fabri's joyful 'N'ay je cause' of the Leiden MS.[165]

In contrast to Dufay's many secular compositions over pre-existing material, Binchois wrote only one: 'Files a marier', the tenor of which is the popular song 'Se tu t'en marias'.[166] The text of the two upper voices was also sung to a *basse danse* melody. The whole song was probably written for entertainment at a ballroom dance, warning young girls against a precipitate marriage. The parlando declamation closely reminds of 'La belle se siet' ascribed to Dufay, a polyphonic ballade over a 'folksong' (but in contrasting mood).

We have only two motets by Binchois, both of which can be dated before 1432 and are written for ceremonial use at the Burgundian court.[167] 'Nove cantum melodie / Tanti gaude' celebrates the christening of Duke Philip's first son, Anthoine, in Brussels on 18 January 1431.[168] The text mentions no fewer than 17 members of the ducal chapel by name, supplying a 'chapel roster' for this time which is otherwise lost. The chaplains and *clercs* cited include the composers Binchois, Pierre Fontaine, Symon le Breton, Jean Carbonnier,

---

[163] On this work, see pp. 404 f.

[164] 'Should I not close my eyes often, letting this (painful) remembrance go away, when through my eyes I suffer such torment?'

[165] See Ex. 8, bars 4–8.

[166] Binchois, *Chansons*, no. 55; see Martin Picker, 'The cantus firmus in Binchois' *Files a marier*', *JAMS* 18 (1965), 236 f. The tune may be an original dance-song. There is an anonymous Mass cycle built on it: see p. 423.

[167] A third work, 'Veneremur virginem', is really a setting of a sequence text, although it may have an as yet unidentified, borrowed tenor. Edited in Parris, *Binchois*, no. 60.

[168] Marix, *Histoire*, 28 f and 168 (with misprint implying 1430). The fragmentary music is edited in Marix ed., *Musiciens*, 212.

(Richard de) Bellengue, Philippe Foliot and Guillaume Ruby. The work is inspired by the 'musicians' motets' of the fourteenth century, and perhaps by 'Sub Arturo / Fons' (see p. 82) in particular. It is not completely preserved, but the tenor is clearly isorhythmic, and includes two proportional diminutions of a *talea* of five notes and a *color* of ten. The melody is a plainsong 'Christe eleison'.[169] The cantus and two high contratenors sing three successive stanzas of text simultaneously: a distribution also observed in Dufay motets.[170] The text celebrates not only the chapel itself and the newborn child, but also his patron saint, Anthony of Padua.

The motet 'Domitor Hectoris, Paride domitus' is a curious work which I have identified elsewhere as a funeral or memorial motet for Duke John the Fearless, who was murdered in 1419.[171] It is impossible that Binchois composed it so early; a plausible date might be the tenth anniversary of the funeral, 14 September 1429. This may well have been about the time of Binchois' entry into the Burgundian chapel. The musical style of 'Domitor Hectoris' (see Ex. 40), as well as the various idioms found in Binchois' liturgical music, cannot be fully appreciated without considering English sacred polyphony, discussion of which is now overdue.

[169] Parris, *Binchois*, 98 (no. 42) identifies it with *Liber Usualis*, 83. Binchois' Kyrie no. 33 seems to be based on the same melody.
[170] Fallows, *Dufay*, 111 f.
[171] Strohm, *Bruges*, 95. The motet is published in de Van, 'A recently discovered source'.

2

WEST AND EAST

Anglo-continental relations and the Old Hall Manuscript

The musical relationship between England and the European continent – two partners of slightly unequal size – was of a special kind in the fifteenth century, a kind never to recur in history. It was exemplified by a massive adoption of England's music by continental musicians, and an admiration for her composers the like of which neither William Byrd nor Henry Purcell were to enjoy. Continental colleagues were aware of typically English musical techniques – discant, faburden – but even more, of the achievements of English composers such as Dunstable and Lionel Power, in whose works Martin le Franc seems to praise a certain *contenance angloise* (see pp. 127 f).

English fourteenth-century music, for all its worth, had not yet found such heralds and ambassadors: a corollary of its collective, functional orientation perhaps. What was shared with and sometimes communicated to other countries, did not go much beyond aspects of usage and professional know-how, transmittable also in unwritten form and by minstrels. The Constance Council chronicler Richental admired the manner of playing of the English trombonists, not the piece they performed.[172] When King Sigismund visited England in 1416, he must have been impressed by the 'heavenly' singing and 'ample' size of the chapel of Henry V, to borrow the words of a contemporary panegyrist.[173] Another poem purports to reproduce King Sigismund's own impression of England in the form of his farewell:

> Farwel, with glorious victory,
> Blessid Inglond, ful of melody.
> Thou may be cleped [called] of Angel nature;
> Thou servist God so with bysy cure.
> We leave with the[e] this praising,
> Whech we schul evir sey and sing.[174]

---

[172] See p. 108 above.

[173] 'Psallit plena deo cantoribus ampla capella: Carmine sidereo laudabilis est ea cella'. See Harrison, *Britain*, 22.

[174] From the *Discessus Sigismundi* (1416), as recorded in John Capgrave, *The Chronicle of England*, ed. F. C. Hingeston (London, 1858), 313-15; quoted here after William C. McDonald, 'The "Discessus Sigismundi": an unknown political poem from the time of the Council of Constance (1416)', *Jahrbuch der Oswald von Wolkenstein Gesellschaft* 4 (1986-7), 249-56.

This, too, was an acknowledgement not of English musical works, but of the status and resources of the chapel (which by *c.*1420 had 6 choristers and 32 gentlemen), and of its liturgical practice, as well as of the fine art of singing generally found on English soil.[175]

However, these resources and this network of musical practice, developed in the fourteenth century, now became the foundations of high individual achievement.[176] The time had come when not only monastic and collegiate centres, but also royal and princely patrons, were drawing musical talents together; when the Great Schism and the Anglo-French War were leading British musicians abroad, and feeding back new experiences to those at home. Composers, in particular, felt the need to compete with their continental colleagues, and with each other, as individuals. This attitude had first surfaced in the royal chapel motet 'Sub Arturo / Fons' (see p. 82), a work that documents the new desire of musicians to make their names known.

For the first time, appreciation of individual achievement characterizes an entire musical codex: the Old Hall MS, which dates from the decade around 1420.[177] The deliberately individualistic style of many of its works, and the simple fact that it transmits as many composer attributions as any continental source of the period, are unprecedented in England.

Of the 147 compositions in the manuscript, about two-thirds are attributed to 24 composers. As far as we can tell from biographical data, these composers are not a homogeneous group; they must have worked in various parts of England. A number of them, however, are linked to royal households under Henry IV (*r.* 1396–1413) and Henry V (*r.* 1413–22). One of the composers, indicated as 'Roy Henry' above two pieces (nos. 16 and 94), is today thought to have been Henry V. Of the few motet texts in the manuscript which seem to allude to contemporary people or events, all have been more or less convincingly connected with the reign of this monarch, none so with Henry IV.[178] There is also an interesting connection with foreign music, or with the presence of English musicians in France during the military campaigns of 1415–21 (see below). Special profile is given to one 'J. Cooke', probably the John Cook who is traceable as a member of the royal chapel in 1402 and between 1413 and 1419 (if the respective documents refer to the same man). The most amply represented composer (with 21 or more works) is Lionel Power, who was a chaplain of Thomas Duke of Clarence in 1419. From this fact it has been concluded that the whole manuscript was compiled for the chapel of Clarence, a

---

[175] See the beautiful pages on English music of this time in Pirro, *Histoire*, 95–9.

[176] Generally on this process, see Bowers, 'Obligation, agency and laissez-faire'.

[177] Edition: Hughes–Bent eds, *OH*. Studies: Hughes–Bent, 'Old Hall MS'; Margaret Bent, 'The Old Hall Manuscript', *Early Music* 2 (1974), 2–14; *idem*, 'Sources of the Old Hall music', *PRMA* 94 (1967–8), 19–35; Bukofzer, *Studies*, 34–85 (= ch. II); Harrison, *Britain*, 228–57; *CC*, vols. 2, 82 f, and 4, 427.

[178] Bukofzer, *Studies*, 73–80; Hughes–Bent, 'Old Hall MS', 106 f (a misinterpretation of the motet text 'Salvatoris mater' makes it appear to refer to Henry IV and to Henry V, his 'filius' or 'natus' – but this is the son of the Virgin).

younger brother of Henry V.[179] After the duke's death in battle in 1421, work on the codex seems to have been interrupted for a while, until it was continued by other hands -- probably for the chapel of Henry VI. Fragments exist of a related, slightly later codex which was compiled for this chapel in the 1420s (*H6*).[180] In the Old Hall MS itself, Cooke and Power continue to be present in the later additions, a fact that may or may not reflect their careers after 1419/21. Composers who appear in the additions for the first time include John Burell, Thomas (?) Damett and Nicholas Sturgeon.[181]

Considered as a whole, the music found in the Old Hall MS is certainly representative of the English courtly environment around 1420, though there are doubts as to how complete a picture it offers of English polyphony. For example, the codex contains only one verified work by John Dunstable: his motet 'Veni sancte spiritus / Veni creator'.[182] It has been added, anonymously, in the later layer. Was Dunstable here denied the recognition awaiting him abroad, or does the Old Hall MS contain other, unattributed works by him? Dunstable, whose music heralds English musical eminence, may have written other ambitious works before *c.*1420, which are not in the codex; for example, the isorhythmic motet 'Preco preheminencie / Inter natos mulierum'. It was probably performed at Canterbury on 21 August 1416, in a thanksgiving ceremony after the Duke of Bedford's victory at Harfleur; it is dedicated to St John the Baptist, the patron saint of John of Bedford and also of the composer.[183] 'Veni sancte spiritus / Veni creator' apparently reached the codex in the company of two works by John (?) Forest which may have been sung at the same Canterbury celebration: the motet 'Ascendit Christus / Alma redemptoris mater' and the antiphon 'Qualis est dilectus tuus'. The three works are grouped together in the codex as nos. 66–8. Forest's texts are both suitable for the Feast of the Assumption of the Virgin, into whose octave the Canterbury celebration fell; furthermore, a contemporary report confirms that one of the pieces sung there was 'Ascendit Christus', which is a rare antiphon text. The scribe of the Old Hall MS left the motet incomplete.[184]

There is a feeling of open-endedness not only to these attribution problems, but also to repertorial aspects of the collection and, in a sense, to some individual works. In 'Veni sancte spiritus / Veni creator', the tenor quotes as cantus firmus only the second and third lines of the Pentecost hymn 'Veni creator spiritus', starting abruptly with the underlaid words 'Mentes tuorum visita'.

---

[179] Bowers, 'Some observations', 109 f.

[180] Bent, 'Progeny', 26, 41–4.

[181] A survey of the available biographical information on the *OH* composers is in Hughes–Bent, 'Old Hall MS', 109–18; for more recent findings see the respective articles in *The New Grove*; Bowers, 'Some observations'; and Wathey, *Royal and Noble Households*.

[182] Published in Dunstable, *Complete Works*, no. 32.

[183] Bent, *Dunstaple*, 8. Sigismund, King of the Romans, was present at this feast.

[184] His attribution to Forest is contradicted, in the much later source *ModB* (see p. 264), by another to Dunstable. Similarly, 'Qualis est dilectus' is there attributed to 'Polumier' (i.e. 'Plummer') - but follows a copy of 'Veni sancte spiritus / Veni creator', correctly attributed to Dunstable.

In 'Ascendit Christus', the cantus firmus 'Alma redemptoris mater' breaks off in the tenor after the phrase 'virgo prius ac posterius' (see also p. 220). To use only a fragment of a plainsong as cantus firmus is a practice ultimately deriving from the organum and motet of the thirteenth-century Ars antiqua; it did not die out in English music until the sixteenth century. The motet 'Salvatoris mater' by Damett (*OH* no. 111) has a cantus firmus comprising the first half of a plainsong Benedictus, the second half being provided by Sturgeon's 'Salve mater domini' (*OH* no. 113); one syllable of the plainsong is omitted. Lionel Power composed a Gloria–Credo pair (*OH* nos. 24 and 84) over two modally related antiphons, both taken from the feast of St Thomas of Canterbury. In the same way, a sequel could have existed to 'Ascendit Christus', using the remainder of 'Alma redemptoris mater' as cantus firmus. Clearly, the Old Hall MS documents a tendency towards sophisticated pairs and sets, whether composed by a single author or in collaboration.

The contents of *OH* are mainly Mass compositions. They are arranged according to genre in Gloria, Credo, Sanctus and Agnus Dei settings; some antiphons copied between the Glorias and Credos (and therefore perhaps intended as sequence substitutes at Mass); and three small groups of motets inserted at the end of the earlier layer and on previously blank pages in the more recent layer. This arrangement is not entirely incomparable to those of the Apt MS or of *ModA*. There are, however, no Kyries. It was once assumed that Kyries were not set polyphonically at this time in England; but more recently, such settings have been discovered, and archival documents have been found referring to polyphonic Kyries at this time.[185] If Kyrie settings were available to the chapel of Thomas of Clarence, they may have been assembled in a different book. Precise reasons for this cannot yet be given; perhaps, they needed a different liturgical arrangement.

The extant Mass settings reflect the liturgy: they are often based on the appropriate Mass chants found, for example, in the Salisbury ('Sarum') graduals, and are grouped into ferial settings (for weekdays) and festal settings (for Sundays and feast-days). Several Mass pairs have been identified in the manuscript.[186] The techniques of relating the two sections vary, but sometimes involve isorhythmic structures; the Gloria–Credo pair by Lionel for St Thomas of Canterbury (nos. 24 and 84) comprises related, *borrowed* tenors. There are only Gloria–Credo or Sanctus–Agnus pairs, no other kinds of pairs, nor 'trios'. All this corresponds closely to continental practice around 1400–20. A full Mass cycle was subsequently added to the later manuscript *H6*, but most of its music is lost.

How does the music of the Old Hall MS, which served such a prominent musical centre, relate to general stylistic developments in and outside England?

---

[185] See the Kyries in Dunstable, *Complete Works*, or those discussed in Bent-Bent, 'Dufay, Dunstable, Plummer'. Wathey, 'Lost books', documents lost copies of Kyrie settings.

[186] The evidence is summarized in Andrew Hughes, 'Mass pairs in the Old Hall and other English manuscripts', *RBM* 19 (1965), 15–27. Some pairs link *OH* with the Fountains fragment (*GB-Lbl add.40011 B*; *LoF*), on which see also p. 83 above.

The oldest stylistic group in the manuscript is formed by Mass settings and some antiphons in the English discant technique, notated in score. We have seen (p. 77) that this style was established in fourteenth-century England as a manner of extemporizing above or below a plainsong, usually one voice at a time. Most surviving specimens are in three parts, however, which is presumably why they had to be written down and are therefore preserved. The settings in the Old Hall MS are in three parts and all go beyond the simplicity one would expect from extemporization. Pieces in 'syllable-against-syllable' style are present, but more often the voices are rhythmically differentiated. The plainsongs appear less frequently in the middle voice than was customary earlier. Besides the conventional transposition to the fifth above, other transposition intervals occur, and sometimes there are even different transpositions within the same piece. 'Migrant' cantus firmi are frequent.

Migration of the plainsong from the middle voice (mene) to the treble or counter had originally been an expedient to avoid voice-crossings, so that the composer, when setting the treble, could more easily keep track of the lowest notes, all assembled in the counter.

Example 31 Sanctus, *OH* no. 100

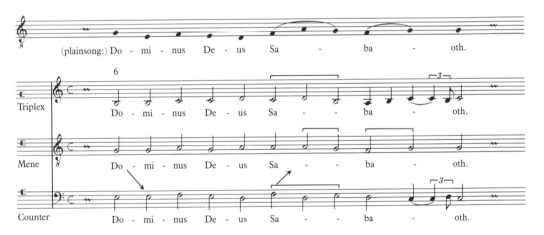

About 40 Old Hall settings observe this relatively genuine, 'layered' format of English discant. A more forward-looking group of about twenty settings also resembles English discant except that it introduces more frequent crossings between the lower (and upper) voices. Whereas in genuine English discant, at voice-crossings the mene would switch contrapuntal roles with the counter and be able to support fourths between the upper voices, here the counterpoint almost invariably *ignores* the crossings: fourths which would need support from the lowest voice are avoided. A typical result of this is the increase of full 5–3 sonorities, and even of parallel triads, at the point of crossings. Other typical formations are 8–6 and 8–3.

Example 32 Credo (plainsong in treble), *OH* no. 57

This militates against the spirit of English discant, which allowed an un-limited number of fourths between the treble and the mene. The new technique is analogous, however, to continental procedures, particularly the so-called 'simultaneous' and 'discant' styles in Mass settings (see pp. 23 f). There, the con-tratenor never acts as a harmonic foundation even when at the bottom, because the cantus–tenor framework is self-sufficient. (The contratenor is also responsi-ble for 'bad progressions' such as parallel octaves. In Example 32, too, the treble and counter form a correct duet, and the 'forbidden' parallels are all caused by the mene.) In other words, in this group of Old Hall settings, the traditional English mene has become a continental contratenor without any harmonic responsibility, and the counter has become a continental tenor, which has assumed all that responsibility regardless of its position in the texture.[187]

Not surprisingly, this change is linked to other departures from tradition. Where the mene is no longer the primary voice, it also tends not to carry the plainsong, which is often in the treble (in slightly ornamented form), or omit-ted altogether. The treble behaves more like the cantus of a chanson; the tradi-tionally distinct ranges of the lower voices are more equal. Rhythmic diversity of the voices, though not entirely absent from the genuine discant settings, greatly increases. Composers cultivating this style include W. Typp (Credo no. 62), Cooke (Gloria no. 7), Oliver (Credo no. 59) and – notably – Roy Henry (Gloria no. 16, Sanctus no. 94). The last-named also skilfully avoids the parallel triads which typify other pieces in this group. His Sanctus is one of the most advanced examples of this style in the manuscript. The Gloria, furthermore, borders on the style of chanson and motet. These two pieces are copied at the beginning of their respective Mass section groups, not because they were added later, but probably to honour the royal composer (Henry V).[188] This implies that the codex was begun after his accession (1413), and that by this time, more innovative styles had already been adopted.

[187] Further on contrapuntal considerations, see Apfel, *Studien*, especially 90 ff.
[188] Margaret Bent, 'Roy Henry' in *The New Grove*.

The settings in score notation are followed, in each section group, by others in part notation (*cantus collateralis*). This layout, which was used on the Continent and also in English motets, generated a stylistic freedom quite unknown to English discant. Lionel, Cooke, Byttering, Oliver and others admit florid treble lines, intricate syncopations between the voices,[189] and far more ornamental dissonances (a good example is Oliver's Sanctus, no. 120). If the plainsong appears at all, it is in the treble, or occasionally in the tenor (as in Lionel's nos. 118 and 141). The ○ mensuration becomes more frequent, particularly with Lionel, or alternates with ₵ or C in the same piece. The lower voices often move in longer note-values than the treble, or contrast with it in modal character, for example by having one flat more at the clef. Textual underlay to contratenor and tenor lines becomes fragmentary or disappears. On the other hand, the texts of Gloria and Credo are sometimes 'telescoped' between the upper voices, so that different text segments are sung simultaneously by the two voices, perhaps in order to make the settings shorter. The texture allows alternating duets to occur between different pairs of voices: a particularly logical outcome of part notation.[190]

Example 33 Byttering, Gloria

---

[189] Andrew Hughes, 'Mensuration and proportion in early fifteenth-century English music', *AcM* 37 (1965), 48–61.

[190] On stylistic developments starting at this point, see Curtis, 'Stylistic layers'.

Example 33 (*cont.*)

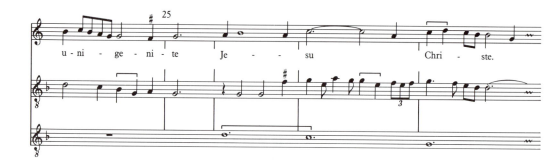

In a remarkable Gloria by Byttering (Ex. 33), the echo imitation with ascending, ornamented lines (bars 19–21) and the extended pre-cadential dissonances (bar 21) are strikingly individual traits. But there is here more than a hint of the style of Antonius Zacharias and Johannes Ciconia, for example in the declamatory imitations of bars 22 and 24.

This stylistic layer of the codex also comprises several isorhythmic motets. In Byttering's 'En Katherine solemnia' (no. 145), there is a continuous intertwining of the texted but melismatic lines of cantus and contratenor in many imperfect consonances: a style comparable to that of motets by Carmen or Salinis. Similarly, in Cooke's 'Alma proles' the cantabile writing for the upper voices anticipates later English motets, especially those of Dunstable. This motet has a text addressing St George, and praying for protection of the king in the war, which would seem to link this work with the campaigns of 1415. For the motet pair 'Salvatoris mater / O Georgi' by Damett and 'Salve mater / Salve templum' by Sturgeon (nos. 111 and 113), a date immediately after the Agincourt victory would make most sense. 'En Katherine solemnia / Virginalis concio', in turn, whose tenor 'Sponsus amat sponsam' refers to the mystical marriage of St Katherine, has been linked to the wedding of Henry V with Catherine de Valois (1420).[191] These tentative dates, however, now seem to conflict with the manuscript evidence: 'En Katherine' is in the original layer of the codex, whereas the motets by Cooke, Damett and Sturgeon are post-1421 additions. A solution is to reject the connection between Byttering's 'En Katherine' and the 1420 wedding: the piece honours a very popular saint, and could well have been composed around 1415 or earlier – with implications for Byttering's stylistic role.[192] The motets by Cooke, Damett and Sturgeon, however, may have entered the codex as later additions because their authors were absent at the

---

[191] Hughes-Bent, *Old Hall MS*, 106 f (with the correction given in n. 178 above), and Bent, 'Progeny', 26 ff.

[192] I agree here with Hughes; see Hughes-Bent, *Old Hall MS*, 105 f.

time of compilation: they may have followed the chapel of Henry V (not of Duke Thomas) to France between 1417 and 1421.

Byttering, Power and Pycard can also be credited with surprising and ambitious technical advances in Mass settings, especially in festal Glorias. Strict canon techniques (a personal mannerism of Pycard), an increase in the number of voices to four and even five, conflicting and syncopated rhythms, multicoloured notation to express proportional passages, and mensural independence of the voices: all these features are akin to the spirit of the French central tradition. It has now been suggested that Pycard was not an Englishman, but can be identified with a chaplain Jean Pycard, alias Vaux, who served John of Gaunt at Amiens in 1390.[193] It is tempting to conclude that his contributions to the Old Hall MS date from that period – which would make them innovative in comparison to the English works. Whatever the dates and places of origin of Pycard's works, there is at least one with a 'Sarum' plainsong as cantus firmus, the Gloria 'Johannes Jesu care'.[194] We have already mentioned (p. 83) Mayshuet / Matheus de Sancto Johanne and Rowland/Royllart, probably two other Franco-Flemish musicians who may have served English patrons and thus transmitted their works to English sources, including the Old Hall MS.

Unfortunately, most French sources of this period are lost for purposes of comparison. The Old Hall MS is, however, analogous in stylistic outlook to the Italian codex *ModA*, especially the most recent fascicles, which contain Mass settings by Matteo da Perugia and anonymous composers (*c.*1410–18; see pp. 60 f). This impression is reinforced when we compare the music with motet-style Mass settings not only of Lionel, Byttering and Pycard, but also of Queldryk, Pennard, Swynford, Typp and Tyes. Their procedures, and those of Matteo's circle, seem to be based on similar continental precedents (as found in the Ivrea Codex, for example) which are then variously and ingeniously developed. The use of borrowed tenors for Mass settings, or of strict canon of the lower voices, is no longer exceptional in either circle. There are direct analogies as well: the special form of isorhythm in Swynford's Credo no. 68, with its simple restatement of the complete tenor, but in mensural transformation, also occurs in two Glorias by Matteo in *ModA* (nos. 5 and 6).

The Old Hall MS contains pieces which could have changed hands at the Council of Constance: for example the Gloria 'Gloria, laus, honor' by Antonius Zacharias. A recently discovered document draws a musical connection between a certain Richard Queldryk and Lichfield Cathedral;[195] it so happens that the Bishop of Lichfield and his chaplains actually attended the Council (see p. 108).

The adoption of motet-like construction to the Mass Ordinary was an important step towards the later tenor Mass cycle. Unlike the 'simultaneous' and 'chanson' styles with contrapuntally inessential contratenor, in the four-voice motet the contratenor was designed as a structural voice complementing the

---

[193] Wathey, *Royal and Noble Households*, 180 n. 92.
[194] Bukofzer, *Studies*, 60 ff. On stylistic matters, see pp. 80–85.
[195] Wathey, 'Lost books', no. 39.

tenor. This was to be the structure in English cantus firmus cycles for four voices, and it initiated the genuine four-part counterpoint of the 'Renaissance' composers. A few works in the Old Hall MS already use the contratenor in this way even in 'chanson style' contexts: it occasionally acts as harmonic foundation in Cooke's Gloria no. 36, Lionel's Sanctus no. 117 and in an anonymous Gloria no. 34.[196] These cases reflect the influence of motet construction, rather than the continuation of English discant traditions, which these composers had by now abandoned.

Insular practices

A full picture of English polyphonic music in the first quarter of the century can only be gathered if we stray some distance from the Old Hall MS. We may begin by mentioning the *carol*, which in the fifteenth century was 'a well-defined form in English, Latin or macaronic verse consisting of a burden, always sung first, and a number of uniform verses or stanzas between which the burden was repeated'.[197] The general form, analogous to ballata, virelai, *lauda* and villancico, originally corresponded to the needs of collective singing, and performance was possibly shared between soloist and chorus. Full text in all the voices and score notation were also characteristic of the carol, and determine it as a purely vocal genre. This is, at least, the status which the pieces have in the earliest sources, such as the 'Trinity roll' (*GB-Ctc o.3.58*) which includes the 'Agincourt carol' ('Deo gratias, Anglia') and thus postdates 1415.[198] Only one other small source is as early as this (*GB-Lbl add.5666*); the bulk of the surviving material is found in later sources, mixed with liturgical music (*GB-Ob Selden B 26*; *GB-Lbl Egerton 3307*; *GB-Lbl add.5665*, the Ritson MS).[199]

It is clear from the distribution in these mostly provincial manuscripts that carol singing was then, as now, a national entertainment, cultivated mostly in clerical, monastic and collegiate circles, but also at court; schoolchildren must have been the main performers during the Christmas period. The practice as such may be compared to *Kindelwiegen* and *Ansingen* in German-speaking areas (see p. 295). According to some, the carol emerged out of Latin precedents, the paraliturgical cantilenas, hymns and substitutes for the 'Benedicamus domino' and 'Deo gratias'.[200] The connection with dance, as implied in

---

[196] These passages are identified and discussed in Apfel, *Studien*, vol. 1, 92–7, and Andrew Hughes, 'Some notes on the early fifteenth-century contratenor', *ML* 50 (1969), 382 f.

[197] Bukofzer, 'Popular and secular music', 121. This chapter (*NOHM III*, 107–33) and Bukofzer, *Studies*, 148–69, are fundamental for studies of the carol, as are Greene, *Carols*, and Stevens ed., *Mediaeval Carols*. See Harrison, *Britain*, 416–23. The term 'burden' for the refrain seems absent from fifteenth-century sources.

[198] See also *CC*, vol. 1, 130.

[199] *CC*, vol. 2, 44 f; vol. 2, 98 f; 89 f, and 43 f, respectively. The three last-named manuscripts are further discussed on p. 382 below. For the recently discovered fragments *GB-Ob Bodley 88**, see David Fallows in *EMH* 4 (1984), 313–29.

[200] Harrison, 'Benedicamus'.

the name, is indeed no longer obvious in the earliest, monophonically transmitted pieces, for example the cradle song 'Lullay, lullay . . . mi dere moder' (*GB-Cu add.5943*).[201]

The earliest and most essential group of carol composers were probably the teachers of choir schools and colleges. They instructed the schoolboys and choristers in various forms of singing, conducted them when performing for festivities, and may have sent them out in the streets to celebrate events such as the Agincourt victory.[202] For this social reason, most of the carol repertory in the fifteenth century is anonymous; the few named composers (Childe, Smert, Trouluffe) were provincial clergymen. But various stylistic similarities with Dunstable's music, for example,[203] attest to the musical standards of the carol authors. The two-part counterpoint of the carol is always remarkably consonant. Three-part writing is rare in the earlier sources, and restricted to refrain sections. These sections (often the repeat of the refrain only) resemble English discant in the earliest specimens, although plainsongs are never used. In the Selden and Egerton MSS, three-part chanson format with crossing lower voices appears, and perfect time (O) becomes more frequent than imperfect (C). The three-part pieces have fewer parallel 6–3 chords than might be expected, although individual instances of imperfect consonances and full triads are frequent as such; parallel perfect intervals are exceptions.[204] These characteristics distinguish the carol not only from faburden (see below), but also from the fourteenth-century cantilena whose social function was so similar. In contrast to these genres, and to all liturgical music, the carol is most often a setting of vernacular poetry: 'art song' not 'plainsong'. From about the mid-fifteenth century, a cross-fertilization between carol style and secular polyphonic song can be observed. For example, some carols of that period resemble the songs of Bedyngham and Frye (see pp. 302 f).

Despite some stylistic refinements, the fifteenth-century carol remained a *collective* genre of music, intended for devotion and entertainment among non-professional people, old and young. In some carols, the repeat of the burden is marked 'chorus', indicating the participation of unskilled singers: for instance all the schoolboys, rather than just the choristers.

The practices of *faburden* and fauxbourdon have been a matter of scholarly debate for generations. As I have tried to show above (p. 180), their origins cannot be understood without an investigation of unwritten performance practices in England *and* on the Continent. Neither term has yet been traced before the 1420s; the impressive list of surviving faburden pieces published by Brian Trowell contains no specimen that is demonstrably older.[205] Archival references

[201] Wilkins, *Chaucer*, 104 f (compared with a similar lullaby in *GB-Lbl add.5666*).

[202] The 'angeles syngyng' from London Bridge at the reception of Henry V in 1415 (see Bowles, 'Civic processions', 151, and Pirro, *Histoire*, 96) were surely schoolchildren.

[203] Some are described in Bent, *Dunstaple*, 22 ff.

[204] In Stevens ed., *Mediaeval Carols*, the editor enriches two-part settings with middle voices in parallel fashion, like faburden. The status of the added voices is entirely conjectural.

[205] Trowell, 'Faburden – new sources'.

which begin to appear around that time immediately confirm that faburden was important enough for the performance of the liturgy to be taught in choir schools. This may imply, as has been claimed by Ann B. Scott, that the technique existed much earlier under a different name such as '*cantus organicus*', or without a special name.[206]

Faburden – like fauxbourdon – was a liturgical practice, applied to genres like the Kyrie, *Magnificat*, *Te Deum*, hymn and processional psalm.[207] All except the last were typical 'organ genres'; faburden settings for the organ exist in great numbers from the late fifteenth century onwards. In 1430 the organist John Stele of Durham Cathedral was obliged to teach the monks and eight choirboys 'Pryktenote ffaburden deschaunte and counter'.[208] 'Pricked note' could refer, in a general sense, to notated music or, more specifically, to music written out in all its parts. 'Deschaunte' and 'counter' were the two kinds of extemporization against a plainsong, described together as English discant. Faburden resembled English discant in that it did not need to be written, or its only notated part was the plainsong, which would have been performed from the chant book. For the plainsong itself, the general choir or the organ (or both: see p. 80) were all that was needed. Supervision by a learned musician such as John Stele was required for the techniques of adding mensural voices.

The plainsong of both English discant and faburden was in the middle voice, often transposed up a fifth at sight. The task of the singer of the bottom voice (the 'counterer') was the most significant one: he had to perform exclusively consonant intervals (no fourths) against the chant. In this respect, English discant and faburden were the same; but the genres differed in the top line. The treble singer(s) of English discant had to consider both the plainsong and the counter, whereas the treble singer(s) of faburden considered only the plainsong, which they followed in parallel fourths throughout. Thus, faburden could be called a simplified version of three-part English discant (it may also have come into being that way); it was not too difficult a task for choristers or other novices to polyphony.

Apart from the special techniques of English discant and faburden, strict transposition of the plainsong to achieve parallel singing seems to have been practised in many institutions where written polyphony was deemed too challenging or modern. The singers used the 'sight' techniques, widely taught in treatises: they simply 'set their voices' at a different pitch from that of the notated plainsong, imagining a different clef. The 'mene sight' doubled the chant at the fifth above, the 'treble sight' at the octave, and the 'quatreble sight' at the twelfth: this resulted in perfect consonances throughout. The practice was centuries old and by no means confined to Britain; traces of it can even be found at the papal chapel of Avignon (see p. 35).

(see p. 80)
(see p. 35)

[206] Ann B. Scott, 'The beginnings of fauxbourdon: a new interpretation', *JAMS* 24 (1971), 345–63.
[207] All these genres are well represented in Trowell, 'Faburden – new sources'. For psalms, see also Denis Stevens, 'Processional psalms in faburden', *MD* 9 (1955), 105–10.
[208] The identification and dating of the document is by Roger Bowers. For this and other documents, see Brian Trowell, 'Faburden' in *The New Grove*.

Faburden, as a specific variant of the practice, is described in a single English treatise (by pseudo-Chilston, also known as 'Wylde's Anonymus', early fifteenth century),[209] where rules are given only for the singer of the bottom line, the faburdener. Brian Trowell interprets them thus: using a 'sight' technique the faburdener transposes the chant a fifth *down*, which yields the required perfect consonances at beginnings and ends of phrases, but he sings most notes in the middle of phrases a third *higher* – which in transposition yields the characteristic thirds below the chant. The chant is sung at pitch, and the treble a fourth above. This view provides an explanation of the term 'fa-burden': English 'burden' or French 'bourdon' is the lowest part, and the solmization syllable *fa* refers to the characteristic pitch B♭ (the lowest note of the hexachordal system that is called *fa*) which was obligatory for the faburdener since he transposed a fifth down, and plainsongs never have f♯.[210] The problem with this interpretation is that the transposition of the treble up a fourth is not taught as one of the usual 'sight' techniques. Ann B. Scott prefers the following explanation: the plainsong is performed by using the 'mene sight', that is, transposing it up a fifth, the treble by 'treble sight' up an octave, and the faburden part by alternating between plainsong notes sung at pitch (for the beginnings and ends of phrases) and others sung a third higher.[211] This view coincides more closely with the tradition of singing the chant in the 'mene', a fifth above notated pitch, and of singing the treble an octave above – which is what choirboys would do in any case, even without conscious transposition. It would also explain why rules are given only for the faburdener: his is really the only part where transposing skill is required, whereas the other singers apply generally known 'sight' techniques. The 'faulz bourdon' hymn in the Cambrai MS (*F-CA 29*, see p. 180) works very well in the manner described by Scott: the top voice is sung by choirboys an octave above the chant, and the chant itself is transposed up a fifth; in the stanza 'Fac cum sonante sono' the chant is written a third higher except at the beginnings and ends of phrases where it is at pitch, and this line would have to be performed as written. This manner of writing a faburden also occurs in English sources, and is there interpreted by Trowell as requiring downward transposition by a fifth.[212]

It has been suggested earlier (p. 80) that English discant could at times be performed by specialized singers *together with* the general choir and / or the organ, particularly in those pieces where the rhythm and phrasing of the plainsong is not altered in any way, or is 'monorhythmic'. Faburden seems to have been produced in this manner, too – although we cannot easily prove it, as most surviving pieces may have had to be written down precisely because their plainsong rhythm was modified. The organ seems the ideal instrument for the per-

[209] Andrew Hughes, 'Chilston' in *The New Grove*.
[210] Brian Trowell, 'Faburden and fauxbourdon', *MD* 13 (1959), 43–78. For the history of the terms, see also Dagmar Hoffmann-Axthelm, 'Bourdon' and 'Faburdon / fauxbourdon / falso bordone' in H. H. Eggebrecht ed., *Handwörterbuch der musikalischen Terminologie* (Wiesbaden: Steiner, 1972–)
[211] See n. 206 above.
[212] See, for example, the plate in Brian Trowell, 'Faburden' in *The New Grove*.

formance of plainsongs with faburdens in the liturgy; the transposition of the chant to the upper fifth is a mixture found on the medieval *Blockwerk* organ in any case. This sound must have been perfectly familiar to organists such as John Stele at Durham, who may have assembled the boys and the faburdeners (including choristers whose voice had broken) around his organ desk.

The greatest difference between unwritten faburden practices – which are difficult to reconstruct – and the written use of fauxbourdon *style* – with which the manuscripts abound – is the manipulation of the plainsong rhythm in the latter cases. Manipulation and stylization of plainsong melodies was a general, progressive trend; whereas the monorhythmic (possibly unwritten) performance was the earlier practice. Since the monorhythmic practice was typical of provincial England, and the stylized form more representative of the continental fauxbourdon pieces, the whole practice may have had older roots in England than on the Continent. We cannot be absolutely sure about this, as unwritten continental fauxbourdon practices may simply have disappeared without leaving any other trace than the hymn in *F-CA 29* (see above). Dufay's fauxbourdon in 'Vos qui secuti estis' (see p. 179) is much more advanced in this process of stylization. The process may, however, have begun with unwritten faburden practices known to Dufay in his early youth.

Dufay's particular form of fauxbourdon was imitated by many continental composers, but never picked up by the English. Their written compositions in faburden style never use the artifice of *not* writing out the faburden voice but prescribing it with a canon. They rarely have such strict parallel fourths between the top voices. Complete 6–3 parallels appear in their works rather haphazardly, and where they do, the cantus is simple and syllabic, not chanson-like as on the Continent. The closest we get to strict parallelism is in some liturgical pieces of the mid-century manuscript *GB-Lbl Egerton 3307* (see p. 383), and perhaps in Dunstable's *Magnificat*, which belongs to the same stylistic sphere.

Not even the simpler pieces in the Egerton MS, however, can be confused with the (mostly later) written specimens of actual faburden in England.[213] The majority of the latter occur in actual plainsong books; the faburden part is often the only one notated, and in so far as there is rhythmic notation at all, it is often intended for mensurally illiterate singers. Individual faburden parts are often written separately from their plainsongs; the purpose or result of this practice was that they were re-used in new, different pieces.

In this respect, faburden parts were akin to squares – vocal parts which fitted against certain plainsongs, but were notated on their own, so that they could become the starting-points for different settings.[214] Some of the most famous, often-used squares were copied in the Sarum gradual *GB-Lbl Lansdowne 462*, which also contains a faburden part. The reason for their copying may simply have been that they are in mensural rhythm. The earliest sources containing

---

[213] Listed in Trowell, 'Faburden – new sources'.
[214] Baillie, 'Squares'; Margaret Bent, 'Square' in *The New Grove*.

squares (or voice-parts later used as squares) seem to be the Fountains fragment (see p. 83) and the Old Hall MS. Some such voice-parts even found their way to the Continent (see p. 347). This is hardly surprising, since continental musicians were themselves wont to extract individual voices from polyphonic works and find other uses for them. Thus chanson tenors became dance-tunes, and melodies in German organ manuscripts were transmitted under headings such as 'tenor bonus' (see p. 373). The whole practice goes back at least to the fourteenth century, and in the fifteenth begins to merge with cantus firmus composition in general. Early Tudor composers such as Nicholas Ludford and William Mundy sometimes wrote Mass cycles over squares, rather than plainsong cantus firmi. Technically speaking, most of the English squares are counters (see p. 80): they are thus precisely analogous to the isolated faburdens.

From the Old Hall Manuscript to the Caput Mass

It is probably no coincidence that the works by Burell, Damett, Sturgeon and Forest which were added to the Old Hall MS shortly after *c*.1420 show few of the technical aspirations so remarkable in that source's earlier music. Simplicity was the trend of the time. Now, however, it was no longer the plainsong-bound simplicity of English discant or faburden: it was an aesthetic attitude freely chosen by composers themselves.

In English polyphony after 1420, three main lines of development may be observed. The first is represented by sacred music of various genres in the three-voice chanson format, which often used a melismatic idiom in all the voices. Plainsongs, if present at all, occur either as ornamented cantus lines, or sometimes as tenors in slower-moving but unsystematic rhythms. The second group comprises isorhythmic motets, with systematic manipulation of a plainsong in the tenor. This genre died out with the composers Dunstable, Benet and Forest, around 1440 or a little earlier. The third main development concerns the Mass cycle. Mass Ordinary settings had no contrapuntal or textural idiom of their own, but were modelled either on the isorhythmic motet or on chanson format (as in the Old Hall MS). The form of the cyclic Mass, however, required special solutions: one of these was the cantus firmus cycle. Works of this type were written from the 1420s onwards.

Chanson format as a contrapuntal and textural principle (see p. 161) is not identical with 'chanson style', let alone 'chanson form'. English sacred works which have this arrangement of the voices (cantus, tenor and contratenor) are, for all other purposes, *free* compositions, unfettered by the metrical restraints of vernacular or Latin poetry, or by the musical patterns of a manipulated cantus firmus. Their 'prose style' prefers a leisurely concatenation of phrases, irregularly articulated by means such as *reduced scoring* (i.e. interpolated duet passages), variations of the rhythmic pace, staggered entries, and elided cadences. All these characteristics, which were much less pronounced in the continental 'motets in chanson format' around the early Dufay (see p. 162), were to remain essential for the motet in the Renaissance. English composers of the early fifteenth century developed the free, non-isorhythmic motet: indeed, the classification of their antiphon settings as 'motets' anticipates a later terminology.[215]

The English composers of antiphons and Mass settings in chanson format attracted the attention of continental musicians from about 1420, and thus, became leaders in a European development. Only a few names occur time and again in continental manuscripts: Lionel Power, John Dunstable, John (?) Forest, John Benet and (after *c.*1440) John Bedyngham, John Plummer and Walter Frye. Many works remain anonymous, however, and many other names occur at least sporadically: Byttering, Gervays, Pyamour, Soursby, Neweland, Markham, Stone, Standley. The continental impact of these composers seems to have begun sometime after the compilation of the Old Hall MS; the original (English) sources of their works are mostly lost.[216]

Lionel Power's 'Salve regina',[217] one of the early works of this group (it is found in the earliest layer of *I-Bc Q 15*), exhibits not so much a 'typically English' harmonic style as an individual mastery of form and plainsong elaboration (see Ex. 34). As to the harmony of this piece, a preference for imperfect consonances and full triads, as well as occasional parallelisms, cannot be denied. As to the form and plainsong treatment, the piece may be said to have no systematic shape at all: it is fluent musical prose.

Our example comprises only the first, large section, which is based on plainsong. There follow three shorter sections with the words 'O clemens, o pia, o dulcis virgo Maria', each section preceded by a verse of the trope 'Virgo mater ecclesie', scored for duet. These sections also introduce different mensurations (¢ and C) and are not based on plainsong. Taken together, they are about as long as the entire first section, so that the work curiously divides into two halves with totally contrasting internal organization.

Bipartite structure in non-isorhythmic works is rather uncommon in the earlier fifteenth century. Perhaps, it arose here fortuitously. Lionel's first section paraphrases the whole of the plainsong 'Alma redemptoris mater' in the cantus. It could thus be argued that the work was originally intended as a setting of that antiphon, ending at the present mid-point. The composer could then have changed the words to 'Salve regina' and added the second half to accommodate the remainder of this new, longer text. A study of Lionel's plainsong treatment suggests, however, that the words 'Alma redemptoris' were never intended to be sung.

[215] Charles Hamm, 'The motets of Lionel Power', in Powers ed., *Studies in Music History*, 127-36; and Power, *Complete Works*, vol. 1 (The Motets): the nomenclature in those cases includes all the smaller liturgical settings.

[216] An investigation of the total output of these composers, and their continental sources, is Trowell, *Plantagenets*. See also *idem*, 'Some English contemporaries of Dunstable', *PRMA* 81 (1954-5), 77-92.

[217] Power, *Complete Works*, vol. 1, no. 10. On the composer's music, see Hamm, 'The motets' (n. 215); Margaret Bent, 'Power, Leonel' in *The New Grove*; on his life, see Bowers, 'Some observations'.

Example 34 Lionel Power, 'Salve regina'

Example 34 (*cont.*)

Example 34 (*cont.*)

Example 34 (*cont.*)

Example 34 (*cont.*)

The pitches of the chant are quoted one by one, with few added ornamental notes or skips; it is by rhythmic means alone that the composer arranges them into phrases. At first, the phrases of the 'Salve regina' text and those of the plainsong correspond rather well:

(Alma)   (redemptoris mater)
Salve regina   misericordie.

We could imagine the 'Alma redemptoris' text as being sung by the cantus. At the end of the third phrase (bar 20), however, the plainsong migrates to the contratenor; its notes for the words 'celi' and 'porta' coincide in cantus and contratenor at this point. Thus, the falling fifth of 'celi porta' is heard as a *simultaneous* interval; in the declamation at least one syllable of these words would have to be left out. Later in the piece, the 'Alma redemptoris' text would be declaimed in very uneven rhythms ('maris', bars 29–30), or its words would be split by rests ('cadenti', bars 33–7; 'mirante', bars 52–5). The chant migrates to the contratenor in bars 21–5 and bars 71–4; from bar 74 until bar 81 ('Ave'), it seems present in *both* these voices. Then it disappears – except for an allusion to it in bars 82–3, in transposition. The last phrase, 'peccatorum miserere', is not obviously present in the setting, but the cantus alludes to it a fourth higher.

This section ends on F; the whole work ends on C. Lionel has transposed the 'Alma redemptoris' melody from F to C (which was an English convention) – but he twists the end of this section back to F while abandoning the chant quotation. The presence of a migrant and transposed plainsong, the modal ambiguity of 'C versus F' and the 'conflicting key-signatures' in the different voices are as intentional as they are English characteristics of this period.[218]

The mensurations, too, are in conflict. The implied mensuration of the cantus is $\bigcirc$, but the lower voices have been notated in C. Their values have to be doubled by the performers to fit underneath the cantus. (It is immaterial whether one reads the lower voices in doubled or the cantus in halved values.) This conflict occurs quite frequently in works within the Old Hall MS (including some by Lionel), and was later to become a recognized English mannerism (see also p. 425). The precise ratio of 2 : 1 between the mensurations is, of course, certain because they are in force simultaneously. When performed in succession, other tempo relationships may have applied.[219]

The mensurations chosen here have some bearing on the counterpoint. There are irregular dissonances which last for one crotchet (semibreve in the original), for example in bars 4, 8 and 13; in bar 49 there is a 6–4 appoggiatura lasting a minim (breve). It may have seemed more acceptable to notate such eccentricities in halved values in the lower voices. The tempo is rather swift in any case, as Lionel very rarely resorts to quavers (minims) in the cantus. His implied cantus mensuration $\bigcirc$ still observes the quicker fourteenth-century pace. Musi-

---

[218] Further on conflicting signatures, see pp. 169 f.
[219] Anna Maria Busse Berger, 'The relationship of perfect and imperfect time in Italian theory of the Renaissance', *EMH* 5 (1985), 1–28.

cians active in northern Italy in the 1420s, who considered the cantus of this work to be in ϕ (this is how it was notated in *I-Bc Q 15*), would have used far more ornamental quavers in their own pieces with this time signature.

The interlocking rhythms, unpredictable smaller rests and registral exchanges in the 'Salve regina' combine to create an almost continuous triadic sonority, which at cadences gives way to bare fifths and octaves. The duet passages, too, have many imperfect consonances. But the great individual achievement of the piece lies not so much in the harmony as in the melodic shapes, phrasing and text setting. It is only with the words of the 'Salve regina' that these qualities become apparent, and this must therefore be the original text.

The music follows the words without any declamatory pressure. Individual words as well as entire phrases make specific gestures of their own, some of which (such as the falling fifth in bar 10) derive from the 'Alma redemptoris' chant. The attack of c'' – a chant note – in bar 26 is dramatized by the unexpected reappearance of the cantus in that high register. No less surprising is the continuation of the text beyond that point in the contratenor, to be joined in bar 31 by the tenor. This is not simply a copyist's idea: the musical texture itself resounds with the repeated cries of the 'exiled sons of Eve'. Another word-related – even rhetorical – gesture is the interruption, in a low register, at 'the valley of tears' in bar 42. The final invocation from bar 75 is the most remarkable. The great line of the word 'ostende' ('display') is like an outstretching of arms. That this is the only phrase of the cantus which begins on a *second* (weak) beat betrays an incredibly subtle planning of musical effects.

'Alma redemptoris mater' was one of the four Marian antiphons performed almost everywhere in Europe in special, recurrent services added to the regular liturgy at the instigation of pious foundations, for example. The other three were 'Ave regina celorum', 'Salve regina' and 'Regina celi letare'. In England, the practice of singing them polyphonically anticipated that of other countries, surely a reflection of the musically advanced state of the collegiate and choir schools.[220] Other antiphons for such 'votive' use received their first settings in England. Lionel and Dunstable set many of them: such non-festal, functional music had by this time attracted the interest of outstanding composers. The circumstances of performance were increasingly dictated by lay patronage (which yielded, for example, special emoluments to the performers of votive antiphons) and, consequently, the presence of lay audiences. Patronage could express itself in corporative forms, for example in the foundation of colleges which, according to their statutes, had regularly to perform certain antiphons in polyphony. On the Continent, similar practices arose at first in the Low Countries, where merchant citizens rivalled the patronage of princes. Nevertheless, this cultivation of art-music still differed essentially from later, more individualistic, types of patronage.

---

[220] On 'Salve regina' settings in England, see Harrison, *Britain*, 295–329 and *passim*; Bowers, *Choral Institutions*, 5082–4. Generally on votive services, see p. 274 below.

In antiphon settings it was apparently left to the discretion of the composers how and when their plainsongs were employed. This may to some extent distinguish the genre from Mass and Office compositions. Plainsong paraphrase in the cantus is very common in antiphons, though some pieces have the plainsong in the tenor. Lionel's five pieces with a plainsong in the middle voice are really English discant settings,[221] and must have been written earlier than his other twenty or so settings. Dunstable, by whom we have eighteen antiphon settings, very rarely uses plainsong at all. His 'Crux fidelis' has the chant in the middle voice, but is not an English discant piece. The plainsong is rhythmicized and sometimes stated literally, sometimes richly ornamented. In duet passages, it appears paraphrased in the treble.

A significant work with an actual cantus firmus is the antiphon-motet 'Ascendit Christus / Alma redemptoris mater' by Forest. If this really was performed in Canterbury as early as 1416, it would have been unusual for its time.[222] Its plainsong treatment, with a tenor that is rhythmically almost on a par with the other voices, has much in common with Mass settings of the so-called 'isomelic' type (see p. 424); but there is no evidence that such settings existed in England before 1420. The melody of 'Alma redemptoris' is ornamented very little initially; its transformation relies entirely on the freely chosen rhythms, which carve out phrases of considerable variety. The main divisions of the text are emphasized by inserted rests. The text would actually fit the tenor line, although the composer probably intended the tenor to sing 'Ascendit Christus', in common with both other voices. In all parts, repetitive rhythmic patterns and short imitations abound, especially in the duets.

It has been claimed that the cantus firmus ends with the antiphon's words 'virgo prius', leaving the theological statement 'virgo prius ac posterius' ('a virgin before and after') curiously incomplete.[223] In reality it seems that in the final duet of cantus and tenor, the cantus takes over the plainsong paraphrase a fourth higher, and concludes it up to the word 'posterius'. Only the last plainsong note of that word, g', is replaced by f with which the piece ends. The duets make striking use of recurring patterns, which gives the impression that the chant is hidden in both voices. This is by no means the same technique as found in a Credo 'Alma redemptoris mater' ascribed to 'Anglicanus', which similarly leaves the plainsong incomplete, and for which Forest has again been suggested as possible author.[224] Here, the cantus firmus is quoted once complete and a second time up to 'virgo prius' (there is thus no theological problem); the tenor treatment and melodic style are unlike Forest's. It is also improbable that he is the author of an anonymous 'Anima mea liquefacta est'

[221] *Complete Works* vol. 1, nos. 1–5.
[222] *OH* no. 68; see p. 199. As in some other cases, Bukofzer printed it in Dunstable, *Complete Works*, no. 61, without supporting its authenticity.
[223] Bukofzer, 'English church music', 204.
[224] Edited in *DTOe XXXI*, vol. 61, no. XLIX. Margaret Bent, 'Forest' in *The New Grove*, argues against the attribution; Bukofzer, 'English church music', 204.

without cantus firmus, the earliest source of which dates from *c*.1455.[225] Among the verified cantus firmus settings by Forest, there is the Credo over the responsory 'O mire pietatis homo' (for St Wulstan).[226] Its plainsong treatment is closer to that of 'Ascendit Christus' than that of the other Credo. Forest (or possibly Lionel) may be the composer of the motet 'O sanctissime presul / O Christi pietas', written for Bruges (see p. 241).

Antiphon settings or 'motets' without any use of plainsong were fairly common. In most of them, there is at least a modal or melodic compatibility with plainsong style; the slow-moving tenors of some Dunstable motets are reminiscent of chant, particularly when in the Lydian mode. More often, the composers exploit the intervallic freedom of the tenor for larger melodic gestures, for example fifths and octaves. Lionel and Dunstable almost never employ leaps of fifths and fourths in the tenor to support 'V–I' cadences, however, whereas this does happen in continental chanson style. Practices for setting text are varied; one principle seems to be that in passages of full scoring, text in the lower voices is optional, whereas the lower voice of a duet always has to sing words. Snatches of declamatory imitation, more common in Lionel than in Dunstable, may also require text in all the voices concerned. The same would apply to staggered but non-imitative entries of which there are more examples by Dunstable. In some antiphons by both composers, the intricate web of rhythms may briefly give way to homorhythmic declamation.[227] Forest's 'Qualis est dilectus tuus' (*OH* no. 67) has many declamatory passages where repeated pitches occur in both or all three voices. This piece also makes prominent use of thirds and full triads. Similar sweetness, and straightforward declamation, characterize the only surviving work by John Pyamour, 'Quam pulchra es'.[228] Pyamour was Master of the Choirboys of Henry V between 1416 and 1420 and served John of Bedford in 1427, perhaps simultaneously with Dunstable. This might explain the composition of Dunstable's own 'Quam pulchra es': his most famous work, but unusual for him in its use of homorhythmic declamation and compact triads almost throughout. Somewhat related, but more complex, is Forest's 'Tota pulchra es'.[229] These four works, and Lionel's motets nos. 24–6, all have texts from the *Song of Songs*, a fact which may in some way be related to their emphasis on chordal style.[230]

---

[225] *Tr* 90, no. 1046, with half-legible heading '. . . in agone composuit' ('. . . composed it on his deathbed'); ed. in *DTOe XL*, vol. 76, 86, and Noblitt ed., *Kodex Leopold*, no. 2. For the missing name, Feininger read 'Forest'; Bukofzer accepted this in 'Forest' in *MGG*.

[226] Edited in *DTOe XXXI*, vol. 61, no. XLVII.

[227] For example Dunstable no. 44 ('Quam pulchra es'), no. 45; no. 47, bars 13–15; Power nos. 24, 25 and 26.

[228] Marrocco–Sandon eds, *Medieval Music*, no. 96.

[229] *DTOe XL*, vol. 76, 80.

[230] Further on this group, see Shai Burstyn, 'Early fifteenth-century settings of Song of Songs antiphons', *AcM* 49 (1977), 200–27; *idem*, 'Dunstable and Forest: a chapter in the history of musical borrowing', *MR* 40 (1979), 245–56. On the special style of the antiphons in the Selden MS, see p. 382 below.

English composers of this generation also cultivated strictly liturgical genres, such as hymns, sequences, *Magnificat* settings and responsories, which were relative newcomers to artistic polyphony. By mid-century, we have sources supplying polyphony for diverse items of the Holy Week liturgy, including the Passion (see p. 383). Predictably, faburden style appears quite frequently in such pieces, particularly in the *Magnificat*, with its psalmodic character. Plainsongs are often used, but occasionally replaced by a square or faburden composed against the (absent) plainsong.[231] Nevertheless, this whole tradition of English sacred music is dominated by the new styles in chanson format, and retains remarkably few vestiges of English discant.[232]

Dunstable alone shares with Dufay the distinction that he wrote his most impressive works in the genre of the *isorhythmic motet* – at a time when appreciation for the genre was slackening.[233] It is unlikely that only these two composers repeatedly received commissions for motets, specified by the patron to be isorhythmic. Rather, they chose to write such works more often than others did, whether on commission or not. Dunstable recognized in the genre a particular challenge to his skills. A main characteristic of the isorhythmic motet is that it generates variety through repetition: this happens through the repetitions of both a rhythmic pattern (*talea*) and a melody (*color*) which may not coincide, so that the rhythm–pitch relationship is transformed. Arithmetical niceties of *talea–color* relationship, as cultivated in the fourteenth century, later gave way to simpler layouts. Another artifice was developed instead: strict transformation techniques. We may distinguish *proportional transformation* of the repeated statements, by which the notes retain their exact rhythmic relationships but are reduced or augmented in value (by proportions of integers, such as 1 : 2, 2 : 3 etc.), and *mensural transformation*, by which individual note symbols have to be read as different values under a new mensural sign (for example, when an imperfect semibreve becomes perfect without changing shape). Since a new mensuration does not affect all the note-shapes in the same way, the rhythmic relationships between the notes can be changed. Either type of transformation operates only with integers below 10; both techniques focus on the ratios 6 : 4 : 3 : 2, the series inherent in the mensural system itself.

Dunstable was a learned man, with a deep interest in mathematics and astronomy.[234] He was obviously fascinated by constructing works, complete in themselves, from a limited set of whole numbers. To the mathematician, it was a virtue to derive a maximum of conclusions from a minimum of assumptions. Brian Trowell has shown that Dunstable's motets are often based on simple arithmetic ratios such as the multiples of 2 and 3 below 10. He also extends

---

[231] As, for example, in a *Magnificat* on the faburden of the eighth tone, published in Marrocco–Sandon eds, *Medieval Music*, no. 94.

[232] For which see pp. 383 and 387 below.

[233] For an introduction, see Bent, *Dunstable*, 55–71.

[234] Bent, *Dunstable*, 2–6, collects the available biographical evidence. See, in addition, Wathey, 'Dunstable in France'.

his analyses to Mass settings and non-isorhythmic antiphons.[235] The 'building up' of mathematical structures over simplest ratios can involve multiplying factors chosen for symbolic or other reasons. (The actual number of chant-notes used, as well as their combined mensural length, might be such a factor.) Proportional transformation of the tenor statements would add to the complexity.

Another feature of the isorhythmic motet – albeit one shared with other genres – was textural variety. This arises from the contrast between a patterned cantus firmus melody, mostly in long notes and interrupted by rests, and a free-flowing duet of upper voices. Here, proportional diminution of the tenor's notes has the effect of making the tenor 'catch up' with the rhythmic activity of the other voices: an effect of convergence which can contribute to unifying a piece.

Of the eleven isorhythmic motets by Dunstable which survive complete, seven are in three parts and four in four. All except 'Specialis virgo' have two different texts in the upper voices, which in most cases are isorhythmic as well (or approximately so); when there is a fourth voice, it too is isorhythmic.

All tenors are plainsongs, often transposed and abbreviated; four of them do not start at the beginning of the chant. They are drawn from various liturgical genres – antiphons, sequences, hymns, responsories – but it is striking that they are predominantly *syllabic* plainsongs or passages thereof. Only 'Salve scema sanctitatis' (an early work, according to Trowell) has as its tenor the florid melisma of a responsory.

The content of the texts in upper voices and tenor usually correspond closely, converging on a liturgical theme which can be identified in most cases. The upper-voice texts are often derived from metrical poems, liturgical or paraliturgical. Unlike the texts set by Dufay, very few seem to have been written for the occasion for which Dunstable was composing. Many text pairs for the upper voices come from the same poetic source and allude to each other by assonance or alliteration (hallmarks of British medieval Latin poetry), as in 'Dies dignus decorari / Demon dolens dum domatur'. Classical metres such as hexameters are found, but the poetic style is always medieval, not classical as in humanistic poetry.

Apart from what has already been said, there is little hope of constructing a chronology based on the style of these works, nor can they be tied in with what little is known of the composer's biography. Since most of the texts are addressed to the Virgin or saints, their major feast-days must be deemed appropriate occasions for the composition. The only known exception seems to be 'Preco preheminencie' (see p. 199). 'Albanus roseo', for St Alban, may have originated in 1426 when John of Bedford visited that abbey. 'Dies dignus' is for another saint venerated at St Alban's: St Germanus.[236] The two works are similar in general layout and style, but not more conclusively than most motets.

---

[235] Brian Trowell, 'Proportion in the music of Dunstable', *PRMA* 105 (1978–9), 100–41.
[236] Dunstable, *Complete Works*, critical commentary on nos. 23 and 26.

Dunstable's melodic–rhythmic language, texture and harmony are indeed very consistent in all these works. Unlike Ciconia and others working before him on the Continent, he shuns drastic rhythmic contrasts. He favours a fairly even flow in the upper voices, using minims and few semiminims; the latter are largely avoided in the C metre, which suggests that it was performed faster than O, the other usual metre. No use is made of Ȼ and, apart from ornamental triplets, there are no proportional complications of the upper lines. (In this respect the music differs from that of Lionel.) Dunstable's harmony is very rich; full sonorities are achieved almost as a matter of course. Dissonances are controlled and rarely exceed the written value of a semibreve, preferably in 'unaccented' positions. In duet passages with small note-values, dissonance is equally restrained. These often intricate, fast-moving sections make for the greatest textural contrasts. Shorter duets (never trios) can also be interspersed within full sections. Phrases often overlap or are elided by voice entries, except at the end of *taleae*, where there may even be rests separating the sections. Many phrases begin with staggered entry of voices, but opening imitation is rare and sometimes limited to rhythmic imitation. Melodic contour favours expansive, long lines, which comprise declamatory as well as melismatic word-setting; there is a certain unpredictability as to the occurrence of any word. Scholars have yet to find pictorial or symbolic illustration of the words. As in other English works, the melody is often triadic or concentrates on the scale-degrees 3, 5 and 6 – a corollary of the prevailingly consonant style, since these scale degrees are all consonant with an unchanged pitch in the tenor. In passages with long held tenor notes there are in fact areas of melodic inertia in the upper voices. On the other hand, Dunstable likes to articulate his contours with small-scale changes of direction within larger, more static passages. Variety is an overriding principle, and – unlike Forest – he uses melodic or rhythmic patterning only rarely. Written accidentals hardly ever occur, but 'conflicting signatures' of the most common kind (one flat less in the top voice) are an inherent part of the language.

Dunstable's invention in resolving isorhythmic repetition into variety of detail can be shown by examining excerpts of 'Gaude, felix Anna':[237]

Example 35 John Dunstable, 'Gaude, felix Anna'

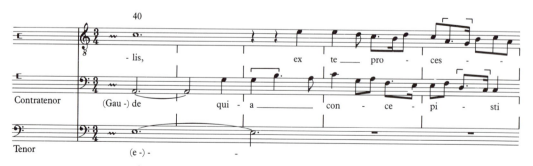

[237] Dunstable, *Complete Works*, no. 27.

Example 35 (*cont.*)

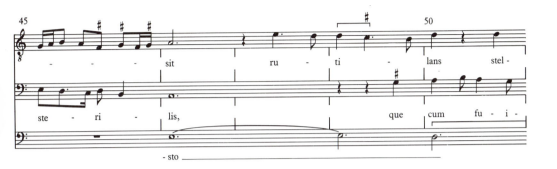

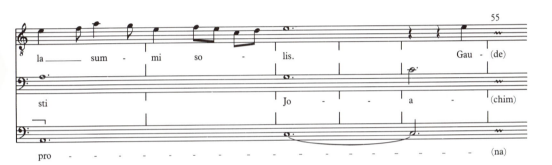

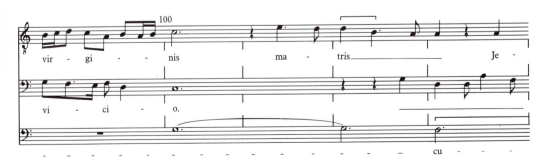

Example 35 (*cont.*)

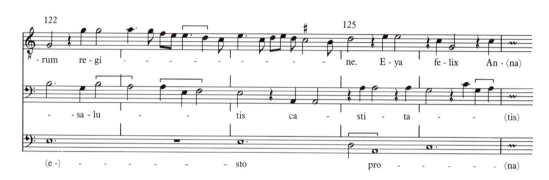

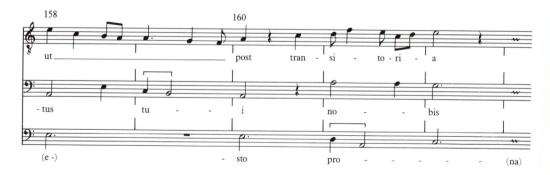

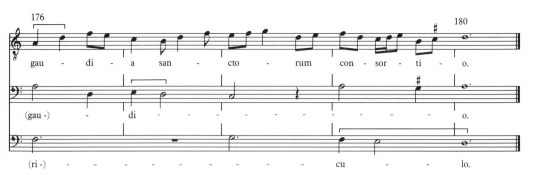

The six sections comprise the ends of the six tenor taleae. The upper voices here have one rare feature: *hoquetus*-like passages. (On *hoquetus*, see pp. 33 f.) These may have arisen from suggestions in the text: in bar 125, the cantus text begins its second half with the exclamation 'Eya', a word brought out by the note-repetition at the top of the texture. The other *hoquetus*-like motives, however, do not have such declamatory stringency.

When comparing the corresponding passages in the example, note that the first two, with the longest rests, open wide gaps for duets between the other voices (bars 45–7 and 97–9), with increased rhythmic activity. Because of the proportional diminution, the same tenor rests in the later sections are just sufficient for small interludes. The melodic contours of the cantus and contratenor in bars 122–5 and 131–5 reach far beyond the short duet passages, but both times the highest pitch of the cantus is reached where the tenor rests. Conversely, the cantus and contratenor are near their lowest points at the tenor rests in bars 159 and 177.

Harmonically, all six passages are different, but the first two are more analogous to the last two than to those in the middle. In bars 46 and 160, the tenor enters after its rest as the fifth degree of *A*, in bars 100 and 178 as the fifth degree of *c*, with the contratenor in 'root position'. These are unstable cadences, however, and are resolved when the tenor returns to 'root position' in bars 52, 107, 162 and 180. In contrast, in the middle sections the tenor enters in 'root position', taking over its pitch from the cadencing contratenor to form chords of E (bar 124) and G (bar 142). If we also consider the sonorities produced each time at the last tenor notes *before* the rests, we get a symmetrical set of progressions:

section 1 (bars 40–55): *(A) – (A) – c*
section 2 (bars 94–108): *f – (c) – d*
section 3 (bars 122–6): *e – e – c*
section 4 (bars 140–4): *f – g – d*
section 5 (bars 158–62): *(A) – (A) – c*
section 6 (bars 176–80): *f – (c) – d*

The harmonies correspond on a higher level (section pairs) like 'A B A', on the lower level (individual sections) like 'a b a b a b'. Yet another pattern can be perceived through melodic correspondences within the outer voices. Bars 44-5 and 98-9 are related by simple transposition in both voices. In bars 122-3 and 140-41, only the cantus line corresponds; in bars 159-60 and 177-8, only the contratenor line. Traces of melodic ('isomelic') correspondence can be found in other motets by Dunstable. The device of the 'motto-opening' in Mass cycles of this period is indeed related to the 'isomelic' repetitions in motet sections.

Dunstable's isorhythmic motets must have impressed not only the continental musicians who eagerly copied them (in the codex *ModB*, for example), but also his English colleagues. Few such works by other English composers survive – though, remarkably, there are three by John Benet.[238] The absence of the genre within Lionel's output is puzzling. There is also no evidence of any development beyond Dunstable's procedures.

In terms of the number of settings, and the artistic effort involved, the cyclic *cantus firmus Mass* (or *tenor Mass*, to distinguish it from settings with plainsongs in the cantus) was the most outstanding genre of sacred polyphony in the fifteenth and sixteenth centuries. It has therefore been considered a typical expression of the 'musical Renaissance', and its introduction has been likened to the adoption of the principle of central perspective in European painting.[239] This analogy seems to say that the musical material is focused 'horizontally' as well as 'vertically' on the single point of the tenor cantus firmus. The genre was obviously concerned with the problem of musical unity, or rather, diversity within unity.

Only lack of sources forbids us to state with certainty that the cantus firmus Mass originated in the hands of English composers *c*.1420-30. This may well have happened on French soil, however. A date as early as 1420 has been proposed for Dunstable's cycle 'Da gaudiorum premia'.[240] The cantus firmus is a Trinity responsory celebrating peaceful unions ('pacis foedera'), and the work may have been sung at the wedding of Henry V and Catherine de Valois on Trinity Sunday 1420, following the Treaty of Troyes. Dunstable was possibly in France at the time. No other extant cycle has features which point to such an early date; Lionel Power's Mass 'Alma redemptoris mater' may be equally early, but we lack any external factors for its dating. 'Da gaudiorum premia' was almost certainly performed in Paris for the coronation of Henry VI as King of France in 1431.[241] The Mass may have been composed for that ceremony,

---

[238] Brian Trowell, 'Benet, John' in *The New Grove*.

[239] See, for example, Bukofzer, *Studies*, 217-19.

[240] *Complete Works*, nos. 17-18 (Credo, Sanctus) and 69 and 72 (fragments of Kyrie and Gloria). For a discussion, see Bent, *Dunstaple*, 78 ff. The work had been classified as a Mass pair (Credo–Sanctus), until the two fragmentary sections were found. An Agnus Dei must have existed, too.

[241] Craig Wright, 'The coronation of Henry VI of England at Notre-Dame of Paris', in Honegger–Meyer eds, *La musique et le rite*, vol. 1, 433-8.

and its apparent suitability for the earlier event could be mere coincidence. Either way, it would be a celebratory, royal and political work.

The cantus firmus Mass is in a sense a combination of two distinct principles: that of composing the five sections of the Mass Ordinary as one work and for the same performance (as in the 'Mass of Tournai', and Machaut's cycle), and that of constructing Mass sections over 'borrowed' cantus firmi, in the manner of the isorhythmic motet. Before *c.*1420, both principles appear separately. Borrowed tenors for Mass sections are subsequently found on the Continent as well as in the Old Hall MS, where they occasionally constitute Mass pairs (see p. 200). But the usual procedure, especially in England, was for each Mass Ordinary item to be composed on its appropriate chant (a Kyrie on a Kyrie chant, Gloria on a Gloria chant etc.) if plainsong was used at all. Machaut's cycle has the appropriate chants in the Kyrie, Sanctus and 'Ite missa est' sections. Whole cycles using the appropriate chants in all the sections do not seem to exist. Continental cycles of the 1420s (by Dufay and Arnold de Lantins, among others: see p. 177) use plainsongs – including borrowed ones – in various ways, but never in a motet-like construction common to all the sections. This principle appears on the Continent only in the 1440s, when it is clearly an imitation of the English tenor Mass procedure.

It has been argued that the continental procedures, which included the use of recurring 'mottos' at the opening of each section, did not properly address the problem of unity. Furthermore, to have different plainsongs, each appropriate to its own text, made unification difficult. The tenor Mass thus solved the problem: if a borrowed tenor was used, each section could be constructed on it, because it was not appropriate to any one section.[242] This explanation is not quite convincing. Many fifteenth-century Mass cycles have no cantus firmus at all (the so-called 'Missae sine nomine') but are musically unified enough. If the appropriate chant prevented unity, it could be dropped; even in the fourteenth century composers used various 'parody' techniques, making Mass sections similar to each other, even when they had different tenors.[243] The introduction of the borrowed tenor therefore did not solve the supposed problem of musical unification.[244]

It may, however, have provided an answer to another question that was not purely musical. Why did the isorhythmic motets use borrowed tenors, and why did their peculiar construction become the model for the early tenor Masses? Borrowed tenors did not merely serve an aesthetic–formalistic goal: they seem to have had extra-musical significance with their liturgical (and possibly symbolic) connotations. The problem of balancing musical unity and variety faced the composer in any case; it was a general ideal. Dunstable's most unified Mass setting is actually a Gloria–Credo pair without cantus firmus: but a strongly

---

[242] Besseler, *Bourdon*, 135 f; Besseler, *Musik des Mittelalters*, 151; Bukofzer, 'English church music', 203.

[243] See, for example, Leo Schrade, 'A fourteenth-century parody mass', *AcM* 27 (1955), 13–39, and 28 (1956), 54 f.

[244] On this whole question, see also p. 171 above.

patterned mensural and textural layout recurs in both sections.[245] In 'Da gaudiorum premia', on the other hand, the point may have been less the use of a unifying cantus firmus as such, than the choice of that particular plainsong in connection with a Mass service.

Table 2 *The earliest cantus firmus Masses*

(in approximately chronological order)

no.	composer	title	voices	c.f. treatment	extant sections
1	Dunstable	Jesu Christe fili Dei vivi	3	strict	Gl, Cr
2	Dunstable	Da gaudiorum premia	3	strict	Ky-Sa
3	Power	Alma redemptoris mater	3	strict	Gl-Ag[246]
4	anon.	Salve sancta parens	3 (4)	strict	Gl-Ag[247]
5	Dunstable or Power	Rex seculorum	3	free	Ky-Ag[248]
6	anon.	Fuit homo missus a Deo	3	strict	Ky-Ag[247]
7	anon.	Quem malignus spiritus	3	almost strict	Ky-Ag[247]
8	Benet, Power or Dunstable	Missa sine nomine	3	no c.f. or free	Ky-Ag[249]
9	anon. (not Dufay)	Caput	4	strict	Ky-Ag[250]
10	anon.	Veterem hominem	4	strict	Ky-Ag[247]
11	Benet	Jacet granum	3	free	Gl, Sa[251]
12	anon.	Alma redemptoris	3	free	Ky, Gl[252] (pair only?)
13	anon.	Tu es Petrus	4	strict?	frg.[253]
14	anon.	Requiem aeternam	4	free	frg.[254]

In the early English tenor Masses (see Table 2), several types of cantus firmus treatment are found, only one of which is akin to the isorhythmic motet.[255] It is not exactly the same, however. In 'Da gaudiorum premia' (no. 2 in Table 2),

---

[245] *Complete Works*, nos. 11 and 12. See Bent, *Dunstaple*, 75 f.

[246] Lionel Power, *Mass 'Alma redemptoris mater'*, ed. Gareth Curtis (Newton Abbot: Antico Church Music, 1982); also in Feininger ed., *Documenta*, ser. 1A, no. 2 (1947).

[247] Bent ed., *Four Anonymous Masses*. The added fourth voice of the Mass 'Salve sancta parens' is probably inauthentic.

[248] Dunstable, *Complete Works*, nos. 19–22, 70.

[249] Dunstable, *Complete Works*, nos. 56–9, 71.

[250] There are four edns, none of them entirely correct: *DTOe XIX/1*, vol. 38, no. 1 (with complete facs of the copies in *Tr 89* and *Tr 88*); Feininger ed., *MPLSER* ser. I, tom. I, 2 (1951); Dufay, *Opera omnia*, vol. 2; Planchart ed., *Missae Caput*. On the transmission and English origin, see p. 240 below.

[251] Ed. in Trowell, *Plantagenets*.

[252] In *Tr 87*, nos. 133, 134. (A work in 'B♭' – *quinti toni irregularis*). No edn.

[253] Manfred Bukofzer, 'Caput redivivum: a new source for Dufay's Missa Caput', *JAMS* 4 (1951), 97–110 (with facs).

[254] Credo (the only complete section) ed. in Apfel, *Studien*, vol. 2, 142–5.

[255] It is described in Sparks, *Cantus firmus*, under the general heading 'structural cantus firmus'.

which belongs to this type, the full plainsong melody is stated complete once in each Mass section, with identical pitches and rhythms. Thus, there is no distinction of *talea* and *color*: the repetitions of rhythm and pitch always coincide. Variety is provided by a change of mensuration (from ○ to ℂ) midway through each section. The total tenor layout over the five sections is simply AB AB AB AB AB.

The other early cycles with strict tenor treatment do not go much beyond this simplicity. Lionel's Mass 'Alma redemptoris mater' (no. 3), possibly written in the 1420s, is identical in layout to 'Da gaudiorum'. Its plainsong breaks off in the middle, after the syllable 'po-' (of 'populo'), a peculiarity it shares with the anonymous 'Alma redemptoris' pair (no. 12).

The simplest tenor layout is sometimes varied by the addition of a third passage in ○ at the end of each section (scheme: A B C A B C . . .). This occurs in the anonymous cycles nos. 4, 6 and 7. In the four-part cycles, all apparently composed after *c.*1440 (nos. 9, 10 and 13), the cantus firmus is stated twice in each section, first in triple and then in duple metre. This 'double cursus' of the cantus firmus is more akin to true isorhythm, since pitches are repeated with varied rhythms. The new rhythm of the line in the second statements is, however, not in any way strictly derived from the old one, but newly composed. An important result of the 'double cursus' is that the tripartite items of the Mass Ordinary text – the Kyrie and Agnus Dei – are subjected to a strictly bipartite musical organization. This can also be observed in 'Da gaudiorum premia' (see above).

The most complex bipartite scheme is found in Dunstable's pair 'Jesu Christe fili Dei vivi'. Each section states the cantus firmus twice, and each statement also changes from triple to duple metre; the second statements are derived from the first by strict halving of the note-values (proportional diminution, 2 : 1). This could be expressed by the scheme A B a b A B a b. Although this scheme is not as complicated as those of Dunstable's isorhythmic motets, it comes closer to them than the other works on the list. I would suggest that 'Jesu Christe fili Dei vivi' is the earliest work, irrespective of whether it is a genuine pair or a fragment from a full cycle.

Sources that have not survived probably contained several more early Mass cycles. When there is only a pair or single section extant, we can rarely say whether they belonged to full cycles. In the case of Benet's 'Jacet granum' (no. 11), a cycle may have existed because the pairing Gloria–Sanctus would be unusual. However, there is another Sanctus by Benet on the same cantus firmus: if this were a fragment from another 'Jacet granum' cycle by the same composer, this would be truly remarkable. The plainsong is a responsory for St Thomas of Canterbury, to whom also Lionel's Gloria–Credo pair (*OH* nos. 24 and 84) is dedicated. Like the Lionel pair, a pair by Driffelde uses two related chants for the two sections: for the Sanctus the respond 'Regnum mundi' from a feast of Virgins and for the Agnus Dei its verse 'Eructavit cor meum'.

These works by Driffelde and Benet, and the Mass 'Rex seculorum' (no. 5) lack any strict patterning of the cantus firmus. There is at most a repeat of the tenor melody from section to section. The tenor rhythms are usually different, and there may be different melodic ornamentation in each section as well. In 'Rex seculorum', the mensural layout (the usual scheme O C O) and textural variations (intervening duets) recur in more or less analogous ways. But even corresponding passages of the plainsong occasionally fall under different mensurations in the different sections. It is not certain whether Dunstable or Lionel composed the Mass 'Rex seculorum', but in either case, one composer would have used both the strictest and the freest cantus firmus technique of the time.

John Benet seems to have cultivated the free approach, which also became the norm with younger composers such as Bedyngham, Plummer and Frye. Some Mass sections surviving in isolation without internal patterning of the tenor could, of course, have belonged to cycles of the strict type – if the other sections existed and indeed literally repeated the tenor. Forest's Credo 'O mire pietatis homo' and the anonymous Credo 'Alma redemptoris' (see p. 220) may be cases in point.

Attribution problems surround the 'Missa sine nomine' (no. 8), so named because it has either no borrowed tenor at all, or one that it so abundantly paraphrased (differently in each section) that it cannot be identified.[256] Continental copyists variously ascribed the cycle to Dunstable, Lionel and Benet. Benet is the most likely composer, since the other two were more famous and more prone to attract false attributions. In this work, the Gloria–Credo and Sanctus–Agnus pairs are more closely related internally than one is to the other. The long Kyrie, underlaid with the text 'Omnipotens pater', stands farther apart.[257]

Long texts such as 'Deus creator omnium', and 'Omnipotens pater', found for English Kyries in insular sources, are actually tropes (prosulae) originally underlying the melismatic Kyrie plainsongs for various feasts. The plainsongs themselves are often paraphrased in the cantus lines.[258] But the general form and the cantus firmi of these Kyries match those of the other Mass sections; in the 'Missa sine nomine', there is at least a common motto and an analogous mensural layout. It is not known whether the fact that these Kyries often survive separately has any liturgical or practical implication.

Texture and counterpoint in the early tenor Masses[259] can be divided more or less into two kinds. In the three-part works, the relationship between the voices resembles that of chanson format – even where the tenor is strictly repeated (another feature that distinguishes these works from true isorhythm). The contratenor can be written in the same clef as the tenor, but remains mostly in the middle, exploiting the upper half of its register. There are extended

[256] See also Curtis, 'Jean Pullois', where it is claimed that the work has a cantus firmus.
[257] Bukofzer discovered it, together with the Kyries of the Masses 'Da gaudiorum' and 'Rex seculorum', in a fragmentary English source. See Dunstable, Complete Works, commentaries on nos. 70–72.
[258] On the prosulae, and their rejection by continental scribes, see p. 240 below.
[259] For a detailed study, see Curtis, 'Stylistic layers'.

duets between cantus and contratenor during tenor rests or long-held notes. Duets with the tenor are rare, and usually do not constitute self-contained sections; only 'Rex seculorum' and the Gloria–Credo pair of the 'Missa sine nomine' use them in a systematic way. In three-voice passages, the behaviour of the contratenor may change according to that of the cantus firmus. At the beginning of the Credo 'Da gaudiorum premia', it is at first pushed into the highest register by the high plainsong pitches, but then (bar 14) dives below the tenor, so that its continuation is more like the contratenor of a chanson, even having an octave-leap cadence in bars 18–19:

Example 36 John Dunstable, Credo 'Da gaudiorum premia'

Example 36 (*cont.*)

The Mass 'Da gaudiorum premia' employs greater rhythmic complexity than all the other works, perhaps because it is one of the earliest. Although the tenor is predominantly simple, its beginning has a strange syncopation which enhances the motto effect. Only in 'Quem malignus spiritus' (no. 7) is there a similarly striking tenor entry (a maxima imperfected by a semibreve), which may have some symbolic connotation. In the other works, the tenor entries are almost disguised, and their rhythms avoid any artifice. The tenors of 'Jesu Christe fili Dei vivi' and 'Fuit homo' are virtually monorhythmic throughout.

The genuine four-part works are 'Caput', 'Veterem hominem' and 'Tu es Petrus'. Here, the texture and counterpoint of the four-part isorhythmic motet are fully adopted. A tenor–contratenor duet is composed first, the two voices sharing harmonic responsibility. The cantus is then written against whichever of these two voices is at the bottom, and the contratenor altus is fitted in last. This procedure is neither comparable to English discant, nor found in English music other than the isorhythmic motet. The composer of 'Caput' – certainly not Dufay, as has been believed – seems to emphasize its peculiarity when he makes his tenor *enter* in the fifth-degree position:

Example 37 'Missa Caput': Kyrie 'Deus creator omnium'

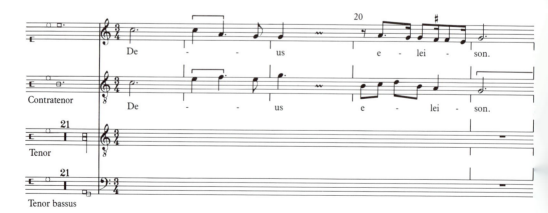

Example 37 (*cont.*)

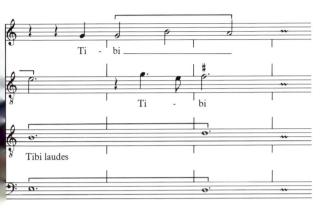

I do not know any other work of the period where the tenor enters in such a way, and with *b♮* at that. Of course, this pitch is the beginning of the cantus firmus; but the composer has selected his plainsong very deliberately. From the antiphon 'Venit ad Petrum', which belongs to the *Mandatum* ceremony for Maundy Thursday in the Salisbury liturgy, he took the final melisma sung to the word 'caput':[260]

Example 38 Antiphon 'Venit ad Petrum': the 'Caput' melisma

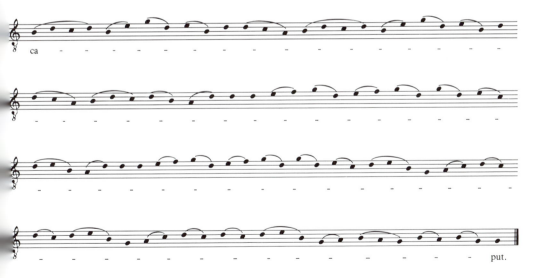

---

[260] This identification, and a lengthy analytical study of the work together with its namesakes by Ockeghem and Obrecht, is contained in Bukofzer's classic essay 'Caput: a liturgico-musical study', in Bukofzer, *Studies*, 217–310 (= ch. VII).

235

The composer's choice of this plainsong tenor is a bet against the odds. The seventh-mode range of the chant (*g–g'*) is the highest possible in the antiphon repertory, and this particular melisma emphasizes the upper fourth *d–g'* even more than the antiphon does elsewhere. The melodic contour, which involves many internal repeats, has almost no stepwise descents, normally so frequent in plainsong. Stepwise descents, however, would seem indispensable for a tenor cantus firmus, as they allow for proper cadences. With its beautiful ascending and descending thirds and falling fourths, the 'Caput' melody is most unsuitable for a polyphonic tenor. It rather sounds like an upper voice, sung at the top of the natural male voice. In fact, the high *g'* of the cantus firmus often appears in this Mass at the top of the whole texture, in cantus position.

This tenor could have been chosen only with the intention of supporting it with a lower contratenor of equal harmonic responsibility (to supply the missing root positions) and of the greatest textural importance (to fill the octave *d–d'*, since the tenor is so often above it). Accordingly, this voice is called 'tenor secundus' in the better sources – as in four-part isorhythmic motets by Dunstable. In this and other (later) four-part Masses, the label 'tenor bassus' is also found. Nevertheless, such low voices often carry the Mass text in English sources, whereas the tenor can only vocalize, or pronounce the plainsong text (which is the single syllable 'Ca-' in this case).[261] The upper voice-pair is differentiated in range and function, as would be the motetus and triplum in a four-voice motet: but the second voice often crosses beneath the tenor, usually by leap. It behaves more like a chanson contratenor than like a motetus. What we are describing is, in fact, the typical four-voice texture of Mass and motet as it was to remain well into the sixteenth century – where the only inessential voice is not the lower but the higher contratenor.

The texture of 'Caput' still differs from later works in its emphasis on unaccompanied duets of the upper voices. These duets often occupy self-contained sections (labelled 'duo' in English sources, without rests being written in for the *tacet* parts) and help to articulate the total form. There are, alternatively, some duets of cantus and tenor secundus, but only a very few short and transitional trio passages. The tenor never takes part in a duet. The result is an alternation, over the whole cycle, between full sections *with* cantus firmus, and duets *without*. As the duets always interrupt the cantus firmus at analogous points and are of the same length or arithmetically proportioned to each other, they extend the repetition scheme of the cantus firmus itself. The whole cycle is built upon a proportioned alternation between tenor notes and tenor rests.

It is most probable that the 'Caput' Mass was really the first four-voice cycle written in this manner. Its technical solutions are interdependent with its peculiar cantus firmus – as if the symbolic 'Caput' melisma (referring to the head of St Peter, the head of Christendom) had required such a fundamental

---

[261] Generally on the phenomenon of more than one text being sung in Masses, see Planchart, 'Fifteenth-century Masses', 17–25; *idem*, 'Parts with words'.

effort. Once the technical ideas had been designed for this special purpose, they could be transferred to other works, and become part of the language. Of the several English and continental imitations of 'Caput' (see also p. 416), the English cycle 'Veterem hominem' exhibits not only the same texture (we might call it 'Caput texture') and arithmetic schemes, but also a cantus firmus in the seventh mode and in a high register. Was this composer influenced in his choice of cantus firmus by the technical procedures he had decided to adopt? Or was he *given* a similar cantus firmus for some extra-musical reason, and did he then feel impelled to imitate the successful solutions of the other Mass?

There is a chicken-and-egg question here, relating not only to individual works but to the origin of the genre as a whole. Bukofzer was convinced that composers chose their cantus firmi to suit their own musical ideas, in the manner of emancipated Renaissance artists.[262] By implication, the whole genre would have arisen in order to achieve purely compositional goals (such as 'unification'). This cannot, however, really explain the choice of a specific cantus firmus, because so many chants existed which were sufficiently similar to suit equally well.

On the other hand, the 'Caput' Mass triggered off a number of imitations that use cantus firmi with very different liturgical implications. It would have been an extraordinary coincidence if external forces (a commission, for example) had predetermined the choice of the antiphon 'Veterem hominem' for a composer who wished to follow the procedures of 'Caput' in any case. No: the composer did choose 'Veterem hominem' as his cantus firmus, because it accorded with his wish to imitate the music of the 'Caput' Mass. The commission, however, was to compose a Mass for the clerical feasts of the Christmas cycle: the antiphon belongs to the Octave of Epiphany, when these feasts came to a climax.[263]

Our conclusion must therefore be that liturgical and social considerations came first: the commission or endowment of festive polyphony for recurring or non-recurring functions such as annual clergy feasts, endowed Lady Masses, consecrations and courtly events, as well as their anniversaries. It was left to the composer and perhaps his liturgical advisers, however, to select a plainsong or make some other liturgical allusion that would suitably express the given function. Artistic freedom could be exercised *within* a framework of social reference. Enough choices were left open to the composer, including that of a compositional strategy: cantus firmus technique, isorhythm, and so on. The choice of the tenor Mass came to be considered, first in England and then also on the Continent, as a particularly stringent solution. But the problem which it solved was not so much an aesthetic one ('unification', for example)

---

[262] Bukofzer, *Studies*, 225 f. In a similar vein, Bowers, 'Obligation, agency and laissez-faire', maintains that aesthetic considerations had absolute priority in the emergence of the cantus firmus Mass.

[263] Later performances of either work need not have been limited to the original liturgical contexts, of course. Further on polyphonic Masses for clergy feasts, see Strohm, *Bruges*, 35, 46 and 127; Strohm, 'Music in recurrent feasts'.

as a functional and social one: the need for a single work which in all its parts spelled out the purpose for which it was composed and performed.

A sweep through Europe

It has often been considered an anomaly that so much English fifteenth-century music is known only through continental manuscript sources. Most of these were actually written within the relatively small geographical area approximately defined by the triangle Basle–Bologna–Vienna (see Map 2, p. 155). The conclusion that musicians in that area had particularly strong ties with England would be erroneous (although they did have some): not only does the situation arise from the fortuitous survival of sources, but it is also a fact that these sources contain even more music written elsewhere in Europe, above all in the Franco-Netherlands territories. It is to those territories – from which extremely few music manuscripts of this period survive – that we must look to discover earlier and stronger Anglo-continental interactions. English music first gained a foothold in Paris, northern France and the Low Countries: from there, it travelled further east and south, often in the luggage of chapel musicians and clerics, who disseminated it among their central European and Italian colleagues. As a result of this 'secondary' distribution of English music, it often exists only in second or more remote copies, obscuring its original form, genre, status or authorship.

Only three extant English music manuscripts of the fifteenth century reached the Continent in that period. One is a single leaf cut from a choirbook and containing a Kyrie in English discant. This was bound as a flyleaf into the personal Bible of St Vincent Ferrer, the Spanish Dominican preacher. He died in 1419 in Brittany (then under English control); his Bible ended up in the Dominican house in Pisa.[264] The second is a mid-fifteenth-century English 'Deo gratias' for two voices, possibly the contrafactum of a carol or secular song, added at the end of the Sarum gradual (*I-PAp MS 98*). The Sarum book seems to have reached Italy in the fifteenth century.[265] The third manuscript, found at Lausanne, comes from a mid-fifteenth-century English codex in black notation. It contains two fragmentary antiphon settings, at least one of which is in five parts.[266] Lausanne then belonged to the dukes of Savoy, who employed Dufay in the 1450s. They obtained a church benefice for him in Geneva, where

---

[264] Reinhard Strohm, 'Ein englischer Ordinariumssatz des 14. Jahrhunderts in Italien', *Mf* 18 (1965), 178–81. Günther, 'Unusual phenomena', 108 f, mentions the musical interests of St Vincent Ferrer.

[265] The piece is published in von Fischer–Gallo eds, *Italian Sacred and Ceremonial Music*, no. 34. The transfer of the Sarum gradual to Italy may have something to do with the English Carmelite John Hothby (see p. 588), who taught at Lucca from 1467: many codices of this part of the Biblioteca Palatina, Parma, were acquired from Lucchese private collections.

[266] Martin Staehelin, 'Neue Quellen zur mehrstimmigen Musik des 15. und 16. Jahrhunderts in der Schweiz', *Schweizer Beiträge zur Musikwissenschaft* 3 (1978), 57–83.

he actually spent some time.[267] Can the Lausanne MS have been known to him? It is just as likely that it reached the Lake of Geneva as binding material in a book, perhaps from Paris.

There are various clues to the presence of English musicians in *France*. As mentioned above (p. 205), the royal chapel was there several times from 1417 onwards, and in 1431 performed for the coronation of Henry VI in Paris. The regent in France, John of Bedford, had his own musicians, including John Dunstable and, in 1427, John Pyamour. The dean of Bedford's chapel, Alan Kirketon, attended the University of Paris in 1427; the French musicians serving Bedford included Thomas Hoppinel and Robert Pelé (Robinet de la Magdalaine), who later served the Duke of Burgundy.[268] Dunstable obtained church benefices in northern France.[269] It is likely that he spent some time in Paris and Rouen, Bedford's administrative centres, where much English music may have been performed. A continental composer who probably benefited from this experience was Binchois (see p. 246). Conversely, two French chansons by Dunstable may have originated in these circumstances: the rondeau 'Puisque m'amour' (copied in the Burgundian chansonnier *EscA*, possibly under Binchois' supervision) and the ballade 'Je languis en piteux martire'.

'Je languis' received an unlikely ascription to Dufay in the codex *Tr 92* (no. 1573) – over an earlier, erased one to Dunstable.[270] The English origins of sacred works, too, often got obscured in continental sources. A beautiful Kyrie setting in chanson style was attributed to Dufay in *Tr 92* (no. 1510) as the result of an apparent misunderstanding: the scribe thought it formed a pair with the following Dufay Gloria. It has now been claimed to be English;[271] its other copies are anonymous, including those in the Cambrai choirbooks *F-CA 6* and *11* which may well have been compiled under Dufay's supervision. The Kyrie seems to quote two rondeaux by Binchois: 'Se j'eusse un seul peu d'esperance' at the beginning and 'De plus en plus' at the beginning of the Christe. Since Lionel Power apparently based his 'Anima mea liquefacta est' on motives from 'De plus en plus' (see p. 190), he or Gilles may have composed the Kyrie. Dufay did use some English Mass music at Cambrai Cathedral in the 1440s: *F-CA 11* contains, for example, anonymously the Gloria from Benet's (?) 'Missa sine nomine'.

The Cambrai sources still eschew cantus firmus Masses, and when the first such works appear in continental sources in anything like a cyclic arrangement,

---

[267] His only extant autograph letter was written there: see Fallows, *Dufay*, 71. It remains puzzling in this very context that Martin le Franc, the Savoy court secretary and eulogist of the *contenance angloise*, was provost of Lausanne Cathedral from 1443.

[268] Pirro, *Histoire*, 95 f; André Pirro, 'Robinet de la Magdalaine', in *Mélanges de Musicologie offerts à M. Lionel de la Laurencie* (Paris, 1933), 15–18.

[269] Wathey, 'Dunstable in France', and *idem*, *Royal and Noble Households*, 184–247, with further information on the English chapel musicians in France.

[270] As reconstructed in Bent, 'Songs of Dufay', 458 f.

[271] Craig Monson, 'Stylistic inconsistencies in a Kyrie attributed to Dufay', *JAMS* 28 (1975), 245–67. The work is edited in *Opera omnia*, no. 19.

other deviations from the originals remain.[272] The English Kyrie settings underlaid with the long *prosulae* 'Deus creator omnium', 'Conditor Kyrie', 'Omnipotens pater' and 'Rex genitor' constituted a typical problem. As far as we know today, these four texts were not used in continental liturgies.[273] Often the scribes left them out or omitted the Kyrie settings altogether, even when copying other sections from the same cycle. Furthermore, some English Kyries may have never reached the Continent in the first place, having already been relegated to separate, indigenous manuscripts (see p. 200). For some such reason, the Kyries of the Masses 'Alma redemptoris' by Lionel and 'Salve sancta parens' have been lost, and those of 'Fuit homo', 'Caput' and 'Veterem hominem' arrived on the Continent separated from the other sections.

In the case of 'Caput', we have another misattribution to Dufay. It occurs in codex *Tr 88* (*c*.1460), above a copy of the Kyrie and Agnus only. The Kyrie is transformed from the English bipartite into a tripartite form, and only fragments of the prosula text 'Deus creator omnium' are left. An earlier copy of the cycle, in *Tr 93* (*c*.1452–3), lacks the attribution, but also the Kyrie – as do the other English works in this group of six Masses (see p. 242). Probably the Kyries were omitted when the cycles were first copied on the Continent. The attribution of the 'Caput' Kyrie to Dufay in *Tr 88* may indicate a Cambrai connection; in 1463 the 'Caput' Kyrie was copied there separately, perhaps in a similar tripartite arrangement.[274]

By the same token, the copying at Cambrai in 1463, which was surely necessary to complete an earlier incomplete copy, betrays an increased interest for complete English cycles in the area. This change of attitude followed in the wake of tenor Mass compositions also by continental composers (Dufay, Ockeghem, Domarto), and a general revaluation of the genre around 1450–55. The trend now carried more English Masses to the east and south, indeed as far as St Peter's, Rome. In Burgundian Flanders, under Charles the Bold, many English Masses were copied around 1470 in the Lucca choirbook (*I-Las 238*) and in *B-Br 5557* (see also pp. 405 f.).

By the fifteenth century the receptiveness of *Flanders* for English culture was something of an old tradition. English clerics, diplomats and particularly merchants, who had lived there for a long time, had acted as patrons of music and the fine arts.[275] Special significance must be accorded to the organization of the English Merchant Adventurers, who in 1344 founded their headquarters in Bruges, where they had their hôtel ('domus Anglorum') and a chapel dedicated to St Thomas Becket in the Carmelite friary. In this and other establish-

---

[272] Bent-Bent, 'Dufay, Dunstable, Plummer'; Strohm, 'Zur Rezeption'.

[273] Other Kyrie tropes, such as 'Fons bonitatis', 'Magne Deus' and 'Rex virginum', were frequently used on the Continent, however.

[274] Reinhard Strohm, 'Quellenkritische Untersuchungen an der Missa "Caput"', in Finscher ed., *Datierung und Filiation*, 153–76.

[275] Strohm, *Bruges*, particularly 63 ff; Malcolm Letts, *Bruges and its Past*, 2nd edn (London, 1926); Norman Francis Blake, *Caxton and his World* (London, 1969); Raymond A. de Roover, *Money, Banking and Credit in Medieval Bruges* (Cambridge, Mass., 1948).

ments of the city, English music and music theory were known in the fifteenth century. In the 1460s, two English singers taught *'contreyn und fauberdon'* in Bruges to the German musician (and later chapelmaster of the Count Palatinate at Heidelberg) Johann von Soest.[276] The English theorist John Hothby, a Carmelite, had contacts with Bruges, where the Lucca Choirbook was compiled around 1470 for his use at Lucca Cathedral.

The main musical establishment at Bruges, the collegiate Church of St Donatian, instituted a daily polyphonic Lady Mass ('Missa de Salve') in 1421; a cyclic work like the English Mass 'Salve sancta parens' may have been used. Documents suggest that the Mass was performed by the four specially trained choirboys and their master, who probably sang the tenor, plus one or two chaplains and a small organ. This practice was widespread in the Low Countries, and comparable to that of English cathedrals. St Donatian, the patron saint of Bruges, is the dedicatee of an English antiphon setting, 'O sanctissime presul Donatiane / O Christi pietas'. The work was written in the 1420s or early 1430s and closely resembles the style of Lionel or Forest.[277]

A certain 'Johannes Forster, Anglicus' held a canonry at St Donatian's from 1423 to *c.*1429; he had another benefice at Bordeaux (then in English hands). There is a possibility that he was the composer Forest, though it is not certain that this was also the John Forest, Dean of Wells, who was associated with Cardinal Henry Beaufort, a regular visitor of Bruges in those years.[278] 'O sanctissime presul' was copied in a group of English antiphons in *Tr 92* (no. 1506) around 1435–40; it may not have been the only English work to reach that manuscript from the Low Countries.

The paradigm of Bruges – characterized by the 'international' culture of trade organizations, merchant patrons, travelling clerics and musicians – may be reiterated within many other cities of the Low Countries. Extensive research has already been undertaken on musical life in Brussels, where the English element seems to play a lesser role.[279] A prominent confraternity of Lille, dedicated to 'Notre Dame de la Treille', was probably the original owner of the recently discovered fragment containing a Dunstable antiphon and other Marian compositions of Netherlands and possibly English origin (see p. 438). In Antwerp, the chaplains at the collegiate church of Our Lady sang polyphony from at least 1410. Several important lay fraternities were attached to this church.[280] The English merchants in Antwerp received trade privileges from the city in 1446 and founded a chapel in Our Lady's well before the Merchant

---

[276] Friedrich Stein, *Geschichte des Musikwesens in Heidelberg bis zum Ende des 18. Jahrhunderts* (Heidelberg, 1921), 14; Pietzsch, *Quellen und Forschungen*, 679; Heinrich Wiens, *Musik und Musikpflege am herzoglichen Hof zu Kleve* (Cologne: Volk, 1959), 54–8 (with further excerpts from the narrative).

[277] Strohm, *Bruges*, 118–20 and mus. ex. 6; *DTOe XL*, vol. 76, 82.

[278] Margaret Bent, 'Forest' in *The New Grove*; Strohm, *Bruges*, 79 and n. 12.

[279] Barbara H. Haggh, 'Itinerancy to residency: professional careers and performance practices in 15th-century sacred music', *Early Music* 17 (1989), 359–66; idem, *Music, Liturgy and Ceremony*.

[280] Forney, 'Music, ritual and patronage'.

Adventurers established themselves in the city in 1474.[281] It is possible that one or more 'Salve regina' settings in newly discovered fragments from Antwerp (see p. 438) are English. In the 1440s, the chaplains of the church included several prominent musicians.[282] Jean Ockeghem is documented there for the first time, in 1443–4; and so are the singer Jean Philibert, who afterwards served the Ferrara court of Leonello d'Este; the composer Jean Pullois, a papal chaplain from 1447; and in 1449 Pieter de Domar(t)o, another important composer. It so happens that all three composers – Ockeghem, Pullois and Domarto – based Mass settings on English models. As for Pullois, the similarities of his only surviving Mass ('sine nomine') with the 'Missa sine nomine' ascribed to Benet are so strong that it has been argued that the work is not by Pullois but in fact English.[283] It also has continental traits, however, such as a motto-like beginning in the tenor in long notes, very reminiscent of Loqueville's and Dufay's 'Vineux' settings (see p. 152). It is not much more than a formula of the first mode, but is used as a 'unifying device' in the absence of an actual cantus firmus. Pullois' work, furthermore, indulges in a particular stereotyped little motive also found in his French chansons, but rare in other composers:

Example 39 The 'Pullois fingerprint'

The Mass, and many secular compositions by Pullois, were copied at Trent Cathedral in the early 1450s – a remarkable coincidence of transmission which may be connected with the composer's journey to Italy in 1447. It is indeed possible that he was one of two 'Frenchmen' who sold six Masses to Jean Philibert (the former Antwerp colleague) in Ferrara shortly before June, 1447. A group of six Masses prefixed to *Tr 93* (copied *c*.1452–3) includes Pullois' 'Missa sine nomine' as well as an anonymous three-part cycle over 'O quam suavis' and the English cycles 'Caput', 'Fuit homo', 'Quem malignus spiritus' and 'Salve sancta parens': these may well be the very works sold at Ferrara in 1447, and brought there from Antwerp.[284] This seems corroborated by the fact that both Ockeghem and Domarto used the English 'Caput' Mass as a model for their own pioneering cantus firmus works of *c*.1450 (see p. 416). Even if the transmission to Italy remains a conjecture, the fact that English tenor Masses reached Antwerp in the 1440s is not in doubt.

Little is known about the musical repertory of Liège, although a stream of composers went from there to Italy before *c*.1430. A direct link with England

[281] O. De Smet, *De Engelse Natie te Antwerpen in de 16de eeuw (1496–1582)*, 2 vols. (Antwerp, 1950).
[282] Van den Nieuwenhuizen, 'Koralen'.
[283] Curtis, 'Jean Pullois'. The music is edited in Pullois, *Opera omnia*.
[284] Strohm, review of Lockwood, *Ferrara*, ML 67 (1986), 285.

may exist in the five-part motet 'Ave virgo lux / Sancta Maria' by Johannes Franchois. In its isorhythmic scheme and its use of upper-voice canon, the work resembles the five-part Gloria 'Johannes Jesu care' by Pycard in the Old Hall MS (no. 28).[285] Franchois, however, prefixes a 'trumpetta introitus' without text, consisting of two canonic upper parts and a lower voice with the range A-f'. This voice uses all the diatonic pitches of the scale, and produces many 'V-I' cadences, as in chansons by Fontaine and others of his generation. The parallels with works by Loqueville, Arnold and Hugo de Lantins and Dufay are as striking as those with Pycard's piece. Since it is now known that Jean Pycard was in fact a Frenchman from Picardy (see p. 205), this further exemplifies the difficulty in separating musical traditions on either side of the Channel in the early fifteenth century. It is still possible that Franchois got to know Pycard's work (or a similar one) through English contacts.

Franchois also wrote a Credo 'Alma redemptoris mater', whose antiphon tenor is rather songlike. This non-isorhythmic work does not necessarily point to English influence either; it would be interesting to compare it with a Gloria 'Ave regina celorum' by Bartholomeus Poignare of Douai, which can hardly predate 1425 (see p. 163). 'Ave virgo' by Franchois, on the other hand, could have been written when the composer was still in Liège, c.1418-20, as it is included in the earliest layer of the manuscript *Q 15*. Given the 'Liégeois bias' of this north Italian collection, – and the prominence of works by Ciconia and Arnold de Lantins – it is possible to infer that also its early copies of English works had something to do with Liégeois musicians.

The musical contacts between England and the Burgundian court are somewhat mysterious. The reign of Duke Philip the Good (1419-67) began in a pro-English vein, because of the conflict with royal France and the murder of Duke Jean sans Peur in 1419. Diplomatic and cultural links with England were forged in the 1420s. Duke John of Bedford married Philip's sister Anne; English and Burgundian administrators collaborated in the occupied French lands (at Rouen, for example); British prelates visited Flanders. Although Duke Philip personally disliked the English and had a private axe to grind with Duke Humphrey of Gloucester (whom he challenged to single combat), his court was open to Englishmen, whether diplomats, businessmen, musicians or spies.[286] His chaplain Guillaume Ruby could just possibly have been an Englishman by birth (see p. 425), and his chaplain Robert Pelé (Robinet de la Magdalaine), who entered in 1448, had been in the service of Bedford and then of Louis of Luxembourg, Archbishop of Rouen and Chancellor of France for the English.[287] After the Congress of Arras (1435), where English and Burgundian

---

[285] James T. Igoe, 'Johannes Franchois de Gembloux', *NRMI* 4 (1970), 3–50 (with edn of the pieces mentioned here), especially 13 f n. 31. On the Pycard Gloria, see also Bukofzer, *Studies*, 60–62.

[286] Vaughan, *Philip the Good*; Marie Rose Thielemans, *Bourgogne et Angleterre: Relations politiques et économiques entre les Pays-Bas Bourguignons et l'Angleterre 1435-1467* (Brussels, 1966).

[287] See n. 268 above, and Marix, *Histoire*, 202 f. Two manuscripts of apparently English polyphony were owned by the archbishop at the time of his death (1443): see Wathey, 'Lost books', nos. 160–61. Bedford, in turn, left one 'livre de motetz en la maniere de France' when he died in 1435; see *ibid*, no. 159.

musicians probably met, Philip's politics changed in favour of France. This may not have affected the music of his court, however, nor that of his cities. Philip's son Charles the Bold (r. 1467–77) could almost be called an Anglophile (see also p. 389).

The *sacred music of Binchois* might provide a test case for English influence on Franco-Burgundian composers.[288] There are about 60 extant sacred works by him. They may be a fair representation of his output, since they were being copied c.1435–50 in central Europe, an area where his reputation was so great that copyists would not intentionally have omitted a piece by him, and where his Latin-texted music could be even more easily absorbed than his famous songs. Among these works, there is a large proportion of simple, functional Mass and Vespers settings: music of this kind by other composers is rare today, because at that time it would only have been of local interest. There are Mass Ordinary settings (single and in pairs), some Mass Proper items, antiphons, processional and other hymns for the Office, five *Magnificat* settings, using the tones 1–4 and 8 (perhaps the remainder of a complete 'set': see p. 249), a *Te Deum* and a setting of the psalm 'In exitu Israel'. The last-named (no. 27) is significant for its austere, declamatory fauxbourdon style and close adherence to the plainsong (the *tonus peregrinus*), which is in the top voice.[289] In 1438 Binchois supplied the Burgundian court with a book of 'Passions en nouvelles manières' which he had 'composed';[290] the wording is strangely reminiscent of the 'novelties' and 'renewals' of his songs (see p. 193).

In most genres, Binchois uses fauxbourdon or fauxbourdon style. The plainsong is generally elaborated in the top voice, except in Glorias and Credos. Where syllabic chant occurs, or the text is lengthy (hymns, *Magnificat* and *Te Deum* settings), the plainsong tends to be less ornamented, whereas in melismatic items (Kyrie, Sanctus, Agnus) it is more richly paraphrased – although the details of Binchois' elaboration are quite unpredictable. Most of the works are for three voices, but two-voice subsections or passages are frequent. There are also whole pieces for two voices only. Soli–tutti alternation between two-part and three-part sections is found (*a versi* technique). There are some unusual pieces, including a chanson-style Sanctus (no. 52), the beginning of which resembles the Flemish song 'Al eerbarheit' in the Burgundian chansonnier *EscA*. Its ambitious series of mensurations (¢ – ○ – C – ¢) shows that it must be an early work. The single Gloria in *I-Bc Q 15* (no. 19) would appear to be early, but it is so Italianate that its authenticity must be doubted. It seems to form a pair, however, with a Credo that appears in *I-Bc Q 15*, *Ao* and *Tr 92*,

---

[288] Complete transcription and discussion: Parris, *Binchois*. (The works are numbered here according to this edition.) See also David Fallows, 'Binchois, Gilles de Bins dit' in *The New Grove*, 712 ('Binchois and England'), and the work-list and bibliography.

[289] The appended antiphon 'Nos qui vivimus' seems to point to the Sarum liturgy; but it was also well known on the Continent and is used for the music examples of the ninth-century Franco-Flemish treatise *Musica enchiriadis*.

[290] Marix, *Histoire*, 180.

labelled in the first two sources as 'Anglic(an)us', and ascribed in the last to 'J Bodoil'. This does not, however, prove the English provenance, or Binchois' authorship, of the Gloria.[291]

Except in the isorhythmic motet 'Nove cantum melodie' (and perhaps in 'Veneremur virginem'), there are no examples of borrowed tenors in Binchois' compositions. Arthur Parris attempted to assemble as many as three cyclic Masses[292] from extant individual sections or pairs, and made far too much of incidental melodic similarities. Some of the sections he assembled use their own chants, and their cyclic relationship depends largely on a supposed cyclic relationship between the plainsong melodies themselves. There are, however, many convincing Mass pairs, including the Gloria–Credo pairs nos. 18/43, 21/45, and 22/46, and the Sanctus–Agnus pairs nos. 53/2, 54/3 and 55/4.[293]

Several sacred works by Binchois only employ three low voices. They may have been written for the Burgundian chapel in the 1430s and later, when it used to perform without choirboys: this is virtually the only suggestion about chronology and destination which we can make for a substantial group of these works. The antiphon 'Dixit sanctus Philippus' would have been dedicated to the duke's patron saint; the motet 'Nove cantum melodie' dates from 1431, and 'Domitor Hectoris' probably from 1429, the approximate time the composer entered the Burgundian chapel (see p. 191).

It may be only a coincidence that no fewer than four works wrongly ascribed in the sources to Binchois are really by English composers – three antiphon settings by Lionel and Dunstable, and a motet by Standley. Whether compositions by Binchois were also wrongly attributed to these English composers is by no means established today. Some central European musicians seem to have been unable to distinguish the sound of English music from that of Binchois.

The vaguely 'English' flavour of his sacred works may result from specific textures (such as the frequent duets), melodic contours (triadic or 'pentatonic' outlines) or from Binchois' preference for 6–3 sonorities. There is no single work, however, that could confidently be called English in style, or that imitates a known English model.[294] Compositional technique or genre, and individual style, do not go hand in hand in this respect. Some Kyries or hymns have the regular phrase-shapes and gentle contours of the typical Binchois songs, whereas the ballade 'Dueil angoisseux' (see Ex. 30) has the triadic contours and expansive gestures characteristic of much Lionel or Dunstable. The motet 'Domitor

---

[291] Brian Trowell, 'Bodoil, Jo(hannes?)' in *The New Grove*; Bockholdt, *Messenkompositionen*, vol. 1, 188 f. I suspect that the 'English' labels in *I-Bc Q 15* and *Ao* are erroneous, and that the pair was written by a northerner in Italy.

[292] Parris, *Binchois*, 71–8.

[293] One Gloria (no. 23) is also ascribed to Jacobus de Clibano (in *Ao*), and furthermore paired with a Credo undoubtedly by him. Also an Agnus by Clibano and one by Binchois are related in the sources. Whether these are scribal errors or not – there are biographical links between Binchois and this Bruges composer who was, furthermore, acquainted with Dufay. Strohm, *Bruges*, 21 and 117 f and mus. ex. 5.

[294] The spurious 'Dufay' Kyrie no. 19, discussed above, would be Binchois' best English-sounding work if it were by him.

Hectoris', which has no cantus firmus, represents a genre rarely found in England, but recalls 'chanson-style' Glorias and Credos in the Old Hall MS (for example, by Cooke or Byttering):

Example 40 Binchois, 'Domitor Hectoris'

Binchois must have heard much English music in his early years, although in his secular status he cannot have been a member of an English chapel. After he became a Burgundian chaplain he had more opportunities to compose sacred music, though his English contacts petered out. This particular circumstance, and the likelihood that he was rather a gentleman–performer than a learned musician, combine to suggest that the English sounds Binchois re-created arose from a purely aural recollection.

If that is correct, it would be tempting to identify what kinds of English music he would have heard, and whether they included any unwritten English techniques such as faburden. First of all, most of the free, stylized fauxbourdon and the melodic stereotypes that sound English in Binchois show the influence of *written* Mass and antiphon settings by Dunstable and his generation. These models may be responsible for the predominance of fluent rhythms and O metre in Binchois' sacred works, whereas many of his songs are notated in ₵ .

(Alternatively, it is possible that most of the sacred works were composed later, and that here Binchois simply followed a trend of the 1430s.) Secondly, Binchois left more plainsong settings for the Office than any known English composer – although *anonymous* works of this kind in English sources such as the Egerton and Selden MSS are comparable in technique, genre, and sometimes style. It is likely that he knew such pieces: his frequent two-part writing suggests this, and his sacred works are, on the whole, close in style to the carol.[295] Thirdly, Binchois does not write faburden but *fauxbourdon*. His strict technique is identical to that of Dufay and other French composers; but deployed in pieces of such simplicity (the *Te Deum*, for example), that it resembles a continental variant of faburden practice (see p. 180).[296]

Binchois has the plainsong in the middle voice in the hymn 'A solis ortus cardine' (no. 1) and in the Kyrie no. 34. In both cases, it is not really a middle voice but a second cantus. Although fourths are admitted between the two cantus parts, this is hardly English discant technique, at least not more so than in two analogous pieces by Dufay (the Kyries nos. 12 and 17; see below). There is, however, Binchois' Agnus no. 6 (for four voices): it has a motet-like scaffolding of tenor and contratenor, with the tenor part predominantly in the higher register because of the high register of the plainsong it carries. This piece sounds very English; its attribution in the sole source (*Tr 92* no. 1548) is not necessarily reliable. The assertion that 'Gloria, laus, et honor' (no. 26) and the first setting of 'Inter natos mulierum' (no. 29) draw on Sarum plainsongs[297] must be treated with extreme caution – too many plainsong books from the Low Countries and northern France have as yet to be examined. Bukofzer noted that the Sanctus no. 53 is 'curiously similar' to a Sanctus in the Egerton MS, on the same chant.[298] In fact, the Sanctus no. 53 and Agnus no. 2 reappear as the respective movements in the Egerton Mass.[299] There is, finally, a very English-sounding Sanctus–Agnus pair (the same music serving both texts), though the attribution has been challenged.[300] In conclusion, tangible English connections in Binchois' liturgical works seem to suggest that either the piece in question is not by him anyway, or that, conversely, his music was used by English musicians. Binchois was, after all, too much of an individualist to be simply 'influenced' by others: he followed his own, aural version of the *contenance angloise*.

---

[295] Kenney, *Walter Frye*, correctly observes this, but then makes Frye the inventor of idioms which Binchois has in common with earlier English music: see p. 394 below.

[296] In the fauxbourdon hymn 'Ut queant laxis' (no. 59) in *I-Vnm it. IX 145*, the unwritten cantus has to be derived from the written contratenor, not vice versa. But the chant is in the top voice, not in the middle as in faburden. Reese, *Renaissance*, 90.

[297] Reese, *Renaissance*, 90.

[298] Bukofzer, 'English church music', 181. On the manuscript, see also p. 383.

[299] I am grateful to David Fallows for pointing this out to me.

[300] Not in Parris, but edited and discussed in Edward Kovarik, *Mid-Fifteenth-Century Polyphonic Elaborations of the Plainchant Ordinarium Missae*, Ph.D. Harvard U., 1973, 451–65. It is in *Tr 87* and in a concordant fragmentary source, *GB-Ob Mus. c. 60*, which is Austrian, too.

It is now easy to see why Binchois did not write a cantus firmus Mass or isorhythmic motets like Dunstable, and why he hardly ever employed borrowed tenors. This learned type of music did not interest him, and he may not even have had manuscript copies of such works on which he could have based his own imitations. This is in contrast to the approach of Dufay, and later composers (such as Ockeghem and Domarto), who studied English music in its written form, thereby assimilating procedures that could not be detected by ear. Binchois' aural approach to English music, on the other hand, must have been adopted by other continental musicians – Johannes Brassart, for example – who were attracted to the music before the manuscripts became widely available.

Dufay's response to English music is more complex, but this is because it was no mere 'reaction'. His attitude is most difficult to interpret in the genre of the isorhythmic motet. He must have known some Dunstable motets, which would have demonstrated to him, in the early 1430s, that the resources of the technique were by no means exhausted. I suggest that Dufay's transition from ambitious, multi-layered structures such as 'Ecclesie militantis' (1431) to simpler, but more developmental forms such as 'Supremum est' (1433) and 'Nuper rosarum' (1436) was partly due to this influence. Fauxbourdon is a different matter. When Dufay selected his version of the technique in *c.*1427 (see p. 180), he was probably familiar with both continental and English practices. His decision to make explicit and communicable what had previously been orally transmitted usages distinguishes him from Binchois as well as from the English themselves, and aligns him with the rational, Vitryan tradition. In Dufay's strict version involving a verbal 'canon' for the contratenor, fauxbourdon became an eligible technique for mensural composition, and was adopted by many composers from *c.*1430. Others restricted its use to liturgical plainsong settings; however, only Dufay extended its application to the motet ('Supremum est').

Fauxbourdon in plainsong settings implies the more general technique of cantus paraphrase. This was, in itself, rare on the Continent before the 1420s, but – possibly owing to Dufay's influence – enjoyed a great vogue around 1430. Dufay was probably the first composer to write whole groups of interconnected liturgical settings, which tended to use the device of a paraphrased plainsong in the top voice. These were not 'cycles' (Mass Ordinary, Mass Proper) but 'sets': groups of single Mass sections such as Kyries or Glorias; hymns; sequences; *Magnificat* settings.[301] The sets incorporated the various chants from the gradual or antiphonal over long stretches of the Church calendar. Chapel singers were provided with a different Kyrie or hymn setting from the same set on each Sunday or feast-day, to cover the needs of an established polyphonic practice. This usage differs from the functions of earlier individual, occasional pieces but also of votive antiphons or cyclic Masses, where the *same* setting was used weekly or daily. The individual items were often short and simple. In Kyries, hymns

---

[301] Dufay's works of this type are edited in *Opera omnia*, vol. 5.

and sequences, the performers alternated between plainsong and polyphony from verse to verse, making the liturgical melody prominent throughout.

The principle of this (the set formation as well as the cantus paraphrase) can already be seen in the hymns of the Apt MS, and in the Mass settings in the Old Hall MS, where even ferial (weekday) services are catered for by the use of their appropriate plainsongs. It is no coincidence that both codices served court chapels: actual sets of liturgical compositions tend to appear at first in connection with important establishments.[302] The practice not only reflects the fact that, in wealthy centres, written polyphony largely replaced plainsong or unwritten discanting; it also shows a new liturgical aesthetic. A systematic, uniform approach can be observed here. It is particularly striking in the case of the *Magnificat*, where the provision of one setting for each of the eight *Magnificat* tones became almost standard in the following generations.[303]

Early continental sets composed after the compilation of the Old Hall MS include the introits by Brassart, the sequences by Roullet, and the *Magnificat* settings by Binchois. Dufay's largest surviving set is of hymns, once believed to have been written for the papal chapel. They were certainly used there for decades, as documented by the late fifteenth-century papal choirbook *I-Rvat CS 15*, which contains many of them in revised versions, although the plainsongs used differ from the Roman melodies.[304] It is more likely that the set was composed as a result of a commission, either from the court of Savoy (in 1434–5) or of Ferrara, which Dufay visited in 1437.[305] The Ferrarese choirbook *ModB*, dating from the 1440s, contains the most complete surviving group of Dufay's hymns, although that does not rule out the possibility that they were taken over from another court.

Dufay's hymns are among his simplest settings of this kind. Their technique is intentionally varied, however: there are examples of chanson format with and without fauxbourdon, tenor cantus firmi, and two items resembling English discant. In the even-numbered verses of 'Christe redemptor omnium' (no. 24b) and in 'Audi benigne conditor' (no. 14), the chant is in the middle voice (or second cantus), and fourths are admitted between it and the top voice. The same happens in the sequence 'Veni sancte spiritus' (no. 6).[306] This work, with its predominantly syllabic declamation in full chords, comes closer to English discant than almost anything by Binchois or even Dunstable. The other seven sequences by Dufay lack this phenomenon, but vary between cantus paraphrase (with or without fauxbourdon sections) and cantus firmus use in the tenor or a high contratenor. Dufay's sequences were probably composed as a set, just like the hymns, and display varied plainsong treatments within the same

[302] Sources date from *c.*1435 onwards, but older manuscripts must be lost. See also pp. 436 f below.
[303] Edward Lerner, 'The polyphonic Magnificat in fifteenth-century Italy', *MQ* 50 (1964), 44–58; an exhaustive bibliography of settings is Kirsch, *Quellen*.
[304] Ward, 'Polyphonic Office hymn'; Fallows, *Dufay*, ch. 11.
[305] Lockwood, 'Dufay and Ferrara'.
[306] It also happens in two Kyries: *Opera omnia*, vol. 4, nos. 12 and 17.

genre. (This is an attribute not noticeable in Binchois.) Perhaps the hymns and sequences were intended for the same patron.

At least some of the isolated Kyries and Glorias by Dufay may have originated in circumstances similar to those described here.[307] Their plainsongs are less indicative of the individual feast to which they belong than of the rank or type of feast; in this way they reflect the procedure of the plainsong graduals.[308] The titles in the polyphonic sources are, for example, 'Kyrie paschale' (for Easter), 'de apostolis' (for Apostle feasts) or 'in dominicis diebus' (for Sundays). Some of the sources contradict each other in these labels, because different institutions sometimes assigned the same plainsongs to different feasts. Only a few melodies had an invariable application; for example, the Marian Gloria with the trope 'Spiritus et alme' (see Dufay's no. 24) or the 'Kyrie paschale' (no. 15). For the other settings, we would still have to find the gradual matching Dufay's plain-song – which might in turn lead us to the chapel for which he composed these graceful works. Apart from the liturgical use, the formal arrangement of the *alternatim* verses has been tampered with in many sources, with the result that there is still some controversy as to how the works were actually per-formed.[309] For some fauxbourdon Kyries there exist alternative settings with conventional contratenors: these must be authentic and show that from the very start Dufay offered more than one version.

Dufay travelled much in the 1430s, remaining in touch with several patrons. They may have requested sacred works from him: this was certainly true of motets. Only one of his late isorhythmic motets, 'Fulgens jubar / Puerpera, pura', seems to have been composed for Cambrai Cathedral, where he had taken residence in 1439. The work may be coeval with 'Moribus et genere', which was perhaps intended for the Burgundian court, as its text mentions the duchy's capital, Dijon.[310] 'Magnanimae gentis / Nexus amicitiae' was written in 1438 for a peace celebration between the Swiss cities of Berne and Fribourg. In the same year Dufay seems to have visited the Council of Basle with a Cambrai delegation. At that time he apparently wrote the satirical 'Juvenis qui puellam nondum septennem duxit' ('A youth who married a girl not yet seven years

---

[307] *Opera omnia*, vol. 4. A slightly different case seems to be that of the Sanctus–Agnus pairs nos. 6 and 8 (with plainsongs in the tenor). The Sanctus 'Papale' and the Agnus 'Custos et Pastor' (no. 7) are festive works; Fallows, *Dufay*, 46, relates them to the Florentine cathedral inauguration of 1436. Whether the anonymous Agnus (with retrograded and diminished tenor) is Dufay's, is hotly debated. Bockholdt, *Messenkompositionen*, vol. 1, 98 ff; Fallows, *Dufay*, 179–81.

[308] Not, however, of the *Liber Usualis*. The handful of melodies in this modern chant edition might be compared with the repertories catalogued in Landwehr-Melnicki, *Kyrie*, Bosse, *Gloria*, and Thannabaur, *Sanctus*. See also p. 324 below.

[309] See, respectively, Lia Laor, 'Concerning the liturgical use of Dufay's fragmentary Masses', *CMc* 37–8 (1984), 49–58; Edward Kovarik, 'The performance of Dufay's paraphrase Kyries', *JAMS* 28 (1975), 230–44.

[310] For the dating (c.1442 or 1448–9?), see Fallows, *Dufay*, 61 f, *Dufay*, rev. edn, 309. Duke Philip had actually reckoned the composer among his household servants (*familiares*) for the period June 1439 to February 1440: see Strohm, *Bruges*, 24; Planchart, 'Guillaume Du Fay's benefices', 135.

old').[311] The text is couched in the form of a legal dispute in court: the youth has abandoned the girl to marry her cousin instead, and the legitimacy of either bond is at stake. This must allude to the impossible relations between Pope Eugenius IV and the Council of Basle (opened in 1431) in the year 1438. Dufay's text concludes that the second marriage is illegitimate, and that the 'youth' must return to the first one. (Eugenius did not do that, although the Council of Ferrara – his 'second marriage' – was not a great success; in 1439 the Basle assembly deposed him and in 1440 elected Amadeus VIII of Savoy as Pope Felix V.) 'Juvenis qui puellam' is Dufay's last work using fauxbourdon: it depicts, in a comical fashion, the falsettos of three lawyers.

The *Council of Basle* was convened by Pope Eugenius IV, in observance of earlier agreements, immediately after his accession in 1431. The power struggle between the Basle assembly and the pope prolonged the sessions until 1449, after the antipope Felix V had abdicated and Eugenius had died (in 1447). European politics during these eighteen years progressed in such a way as to make many conciliar debates ultimately irrelevant. Eugenius's walk-out in 1438, his Council of Ferrara (where he reached an understanding with the Greek Church on matters of dogma), and his ability to sit out adverse circumstances, all contributed to a reaffirmation of the Roman papacy and to its consolidation as a European political power. Despite the intermittently huge attendance of the Basle sessions, and the massive interference of powers such as Savoy and Habsburg, this Council was more a protracted congress of theologians, unlike the Council of Constance. In the immense flood of writings that Basle generated – tracts, letters, edicts, commentaries, and indeed also music manuscripts – some resolutions concerning music are extant but little-studied. One of them requests the clear and complete singing of the Credo, without any textual omissions, in church services. This implies, of course, that such omissions, considered an abuse by the authorities, had been a widespread practice perhaps also in polyphony.[312] The English practice of 'telescoping' the text verses would fall under this verdict as well.

Although many composers were probably present at Basle at one time or another, only three names can be cited with confidence: Johannes Brassart from Liège served in the conciliar chapel in 1433, and in 1434 became a chaplain, in 1437 *rector capelle*, of King Sigismund, the secular overlord of the Council.[313] Nicholas Merques, a cleric from Arras, served in the conciliar chapel from November 1433 until at least 1436.[314] Dufay is believed to have visited Basle

---

[311] Ernest Trumble, 'Autobiographic implications in Dufay's song-motet "Juvenis qui puellam"', *RBM* 42 (1988), 31–82.

[312] The Basle resolutions have been printed (in the context of an excellent presentation of the writings of Jean le Munerat) in Don Harrán, *In Defense of Music: The Case for Music as Argued by a Singer and Scholar of the Late Fifteenth Century* (Lincoln, NE, and London: University of Nebraska Press, 1989), 107–13. On the Credo, see Ruth Hannas, 'Concerning deletions in the polyphonic Mass Credo', *JAMS* 5 (1952), 155–86.

[313] Mixter, 'Johannes Brassart' I, 47–50.

[314] Tom R. Ward, 'The structure of the manuscript Trent 92-I', *MD* 29 (1975), 127–47.

in 1438 (see above). The names of some minor musicians, singers in the conciliar chapel, are also known.[315] This chapel was in itself a novelty: whereas at Constance the musical part of the main services had been shared between the papal chapel and the local clergy, this time the Council employed its own chapel, because that of Pope Eugenius was absent. All the full sessions – which took place in the cathedral – were preceded by a solemn Mass service, and there were also Vespers services with processions and other ceremonies. The chapel must therefore have provided a great deal of functional polyphony, and probably Vespers motets as well.[316] Less is known about the presence in Basle of other chapels. The royal chapel attended with Sigismund himself, of course; but the long trips that he undertook elsewhere were not beneficial to it. In 1434 his choirboys were lured away in Basle by some 'great ones of the Council', who claimed that the boys did not want to go with him to Hungary![317] The Savoyard chapel may have been performing in Basle at least around the time when Amadeus VIII became antipope (1440). It is possible that some German princes deployed more musicians here than they would have sent to Constance, where a group of trumpeters or minstrels would have been considered sufficient. Some leading prelates may have employed musicians privately: Cardinal Louis Aleman, the former patron of Dufay; Alexander of Masovia, Patriarch of Aquileja and Bishop of Trent; Johannes de Segovia, Cardinal of Arles; Johannes Grünwalder, Bishop of Freising and representative of the Bavarian dukes. Chapels, or at least chaplains, of the Habsburg Dukes Albrecht V (elected King Albrecht after Sigismund's death in 1437; *d.*1439) and Frederick IV of Tyrol (*d.*1439) must have been there at least intermittently. There was a permanent to-ing and fro-ing between Basle and the princely residences at Prague, Vienna, Innsbruck, Graz, Chambéry; the imperial diets at Mainz (1443) and Nuremberg (1444); and the major commercial cities and episcopal Sees along the Rhine and in the general area. University theologians, clerics and humanists (including Enea Silvio Piccolomini, secretary to conciliar prelates and, later, to King Frederick III) visited Basle either as delegates or in the retinue of princes. That some of them exchanged not only theological arguments but also music can be taken for granted. Musical literacy, like the use of script in general, had rapidly progressed since Constance. Even the secular nobleman Oswald von Wolkenstein, who was in Basle with King Sigismund in 1432, now had his personal scribe.[318]

It is likely that the Tyrolean cleric Johannes Lupi (Volp) copied music

---

[315] Martin Tegen, 'Baselkonciliet och kyrkomusiken omkr.1440', *STMf* 39 (1957), 126–31.

[316] The ceremonial was largely the same as in Constance. Koep, 'Liturgie'; Schimmelpfennig, 'Zum Zeremoniell'. The standard history of the Council is Johannes Haller, *Concilium Basiliense* (Basle, 1896–1926).

[317] Pietzsch, *Fürsten*, 54.

[318] He mentions him in the song 'Wer die ougen wil verschüren' (*Lieder*, no. 103), which laments bad living conditions endured in Italy by Oswald and other members of King Sigismund's chancery, then at Piacenza (early in 1432). As established by Lorenz Welker, 'Wer die ougen' is an arrangement of Nicholas Grenon's 'La plus jolie et la plus belle'; on the implications, see p. 149 above.

manuscripts at Basle. He was from Bolzano, had studied at the University of Vienna, and from 1431 was chaplain to Duke Frederick IV (the Elder) of Austria, Count of Tyrol. Peter Wright has identified Lupi's hand in the manuscript units *Tr 87-I* and *Tr 92-II* as well as in the fragment *A-ZW*.[319] The last-named comes from a large choirbook of at least 200 folios, containing Mass Ordinary sections.[320] The extant pages show six Gloria settings by Loqueville, Grossin, Johannes Verben, Johannes Roullet and anonymous composers. All are notated in the old-fashioned ℭ metre; two works (by Loqueville and Grossin) use *a versi* technique and trompetta contratenors. Such music was around already at Constance (see p. 152). The manuscript *A-ZW*, however, is written on paper in 'white' notation and dates from the very early 1430s; it served a large, western-orientated chapel[321] with an extended Mass repertory. Nothing is known about contacts of Lupi with a French-speaking chapel; his employer, Duke Frederick, was not on good terms with the Emperor. Lupi probably compiled the codex for either Frederick himself or for the conciliar chapel at Basle.

Lupi also owned a manuscript unit not copied by him, *Tr 92-I*. This was an originally independent codex written about 1435–7; it features 15 of the 21 extant works by the Basle chaplain Nicholas Merques.[322] That some of his pieces in *Tr 92-I* are among the later additions, but others not, could mean that he himself used the manuscript. Its main contents are Mass Ordinary and Proper settings, arranged in 'plenary cycles'. There is the Marian cycle by Reginald Liebert (see p. 178); the other cycles are made up from individual sections and pairs by Dufay, Binchois, Lionel, Dunstable, Benet, Forest, Merques and Brassart.[323] Most of the Proper items are anonymous: it would seem that introits and offertories, at least, were newly composed at Basle to accompany the respective processions of the Council fathers in the cathedral. One introit is, in fact, attributed to Merques. Some added hymns make the codex a little more miscellaneous in character. Already its original plan, however, includes a group of English votive antiphons (by Dunstable, Lionel and anonymous composers) which were perhaps used for Vespers processions.

This remarkable reception of English music, and the presence of continental works that must date from the 1430s, can be explained as a reaction to the influx of Western delegates and musicians to Basle, whether or not the codex was used there.

Other manuscripts written in the *Austrian–Swiss area* can be linked, at least indirectly, to the Council and affiliated chapels. The Aosta Codex (*Ao*) is a com-

---

[319] Peter Wright, 'Compilation Tr 87-I and 92-II' (reporting the scribal concordance with *A-ZW*); *idem*, 'Origins Tr 87-I and 92-II' (Lupi's handwriting and biography). A thematic index of the Trent Codices *87, 88, 89, 90, 91* and *92* is in *DTOe VII*, vols. 14–15.

[320] Discovered by Kurt von Fischer; see Fischer, 'Neue Quellen', 94–7.

[321] The enormous staff height of the manuscript (*c*.26 mm) is exceptional at the time.

[322] Tom R. Ward, 'Merques, Nicolas' in *The New Grove*. Among his other works are four French songs, added about 1435–40 to the Strasbourg MS *F-Sm 222*, which they may have reached from Basle.

[323] The Credo and Sanctus from the 'Rex seculorum' Mass are used as well, copied on paper datable to 1435/7.

pound of four different units (I–IV) whose succession gives a clue to its history.[324] Common to all of them is the concentration on Mass music and motets, and the exclusion of vernacular texts and secular music (in contrast to *Tr 92-I*). There are some brief Latin tracts on notation. The codex must have belonged not to an individual but to successive institutions: the copying dates stretch from *c.*1434 to *c.*1442. Unit I begins with a series of ten polyphonic introits, followed by Kyries and Gloria–Credo pairs. The introits are by Brassart and de Sarto, composers in the royal/imperial chapels (see below). Units II and III, in which these composers are not represented, comprise a substantial Mass collection with an insertion (in unit III) of motets. Several works are by English composers chiefly or exclusively known from this source: Soursby, Neweland and Bloym (or Blome).[325] There is also a Gloria by Byttering (*OH* no. 17) and Lionel's 'Alma redemptoris mater' Mass *in cyclic order*, followed by two sections from Dunstable's 'Da gaudiorum premia'. After unit III was completed, its owners acquired unit I and prefixed it to the manuscript, appropriately for its contents. This was, in turn, preceded by a special fascicle with the index for all three units, which also contains music: Mass Proper items and Kyries – but the very first composition is the motet 'Argi vices Polyphemus' in honour of Pope John XXIII, deposed at Constance in 1415 by King Sigismund and the Council (see p. 111). The copying of such a piece at this time – the late 1430s! – makes political sense only if it was done for Frederick of Tyrol, King Sigismund's arch-enemy, who had supported John XXIII (almost forfeiting his lands for it), and was still unrepentant at the time of his death in 1439.

In the same fascicle of the codex, there is a contemporary note in German on organ-pipe measurements: the manuscript was obviously then used in a German-speaking chapel. This must surely have been Duke Frederick's chapel, then located either in Innsbruck or in the duke's territory along the Upper Rhine.[326] On the duke's death in 1439, the codex passed, with Lupi and other chaplains, and even his infant son Sigismund, into the hands of his cousin Frederick (the Younger), soon to be elected King Frederick III, who usually resided at Graz. At that time unit IV was added, which contains the funeral motet for King Albrecht II of Habsburg (*r.* 1437–9), 'Romanorum Rex inclite', most probably by Brassart. It also contains Brassart's motet 'O rex Fridrice / In tuo adventu' for the new king's accession (1440) or coronation (1442).[327]

Johannes Lupi is documented as having been in the royal service in 1440; around that time, he had just finished copying and assembling two large music

---

[324] See also Marian Cobin, 'The compilation of the Aosta Manuscript: a working hypothesis', in Atlas ed., *Dufay Quincentenary Conference*, 76–101; de Van, 'A recently discovered source'.

[325] On them, see Trowell, *Plantagenets*, and the respective articles in *The New Grove*.

[326] These territories were strategically important; they included Thann (Alsace), Freiburg i. Br., Stein a. Rh., and the fortress of Rheinfelden, just an hour's ride from Basle (see also Duke Albrecht's travel accounts of 1444, pp. 311 f).

[327] Both works are in Brassart, *Opera omnia*, vol. 2, and in Brassart, *Sechs Motetten*. See also Mixter, 'Johannes Brassart', I, 57 f. On the personnel and history of King Frederick's chapel, see p. 505 below.

collections for himself: the manuscript units *Tr 87-I* and *Tr 92-II*. This vast amount of somewhat miscellaneous material (totalling 240 pieces) was drawn, of course, from chapel manuscripts to which Lupi had access at court, including *Ao* itself.[328] In addition, he undoubtedly had access to secular sources and to miscellaneous collections like the one he was producing himself. The genesis of the manuscripts has been scrutinized on the basis of handwriting and repertorial types, as well as paper chronology; it is established that Lupi sometimes duplicated so-called 'fascicle manuscripts' – small independent units which passed from hand to hand.[329] Lupi's collecting zeal probably exceeded his repertorial needs. He may have left the court for a chaplaincy in Bolzano about 1443; in 1446/7, he obtained a rectorship in Caldaro and a chaplaincy at Trent Cathedral. But he was more a musician than a priest: in his will of *c*.1455, he bequeathed 'six books of *cantus figuratus*' to his church in Bolzano, and several instruments including two lutes and a *Schachtpret* (exchiquier) to colleagues. By that time he had become cathedral organist at Trent, where he died in 1467.[330]

Lupi's 'six books' of polyphony obviously included not only the units *Tr 87-I* and *92-II*, but also the matching ones with which he apparently bound them together, *Tr 92-I* (see above: he may have 'inherited' this manuscript from his time at Basle) and *Tr 87-II*. The latter, a small collection, was copied *c*.1435 in the area of Namur. Its only named composer (some pieces by Binchois and Dufay are anonymous here) is the otherwise unknown H. Battre. His motet 'Gaude exulta tu Ceunacum bona villa' praises the town of Ciney in the province of Namur, and its patron St Maternus; his strange canonic motet with the macaronic text in Latin and Greek(!), 'Chomos Chondrosi', alludes to the region around Ciney, the Condroz.[331] There is also some simple liturgical music, and two *lauda*-like cantiones that bring to mind the cultivation of such genres by Liégeois composers. In Battre's antiphon 'Gaude virgo', alternating sections are sung by '*mutate voces*' and '*pueri*', respectively – an *alternatim* performance between men and boys which may be behind many compositions in the *a versi* manner (see p. 152). Surprisingly, the motet contains the motet 'Inter amenitatis / O livor' from the *Roman de Fauvel*; this piece was by now 120 years old and may have been used by Battre himself for didactic purposes. If indeed he was a cantor or schoolmaster from the Condroz region, how did his manuscript reach Lupi? In the early 1440s King Frederick III replenished his chapel with Netherlands singers, and in 1443 he wrote to the Bishop of Liège to obtain benefices for several of them (including Brassart) who were from that diocese.[332] Battre may have come to Austria with this group, and Lupi could have acquired

328 Peter Wright, 'The Aosta–Trent relationship reconsidered', in Pirrotta–Curti eds, *Codici Musicali*, 138–57.

329 On these issues, see, respectively, Peter Wright, 'Compilation Tr 87–I and 92–II'; Saunders, *Dating of the Trent Codices*; Hamm, 'Manuscript structure'.

330 Further on Basle, Lupi, Bolzano and Trent, see p. 507 below; Peter Wright, 'Origins Tr 87–I and 92–II'; Strohm, 'Native and foreign polyphony', 219–23.

331 These and four other works are edited in *DTOe XL*, vol. 76.

332 Mixter, 'Johannes Brassart' I, 59; Pietzsch, *Fürsten*, 59 f.

the manuscript from him at the court in Graz. This opening-up to western influence went further than that: in 1442 the king even requested English singers for his chapel. Nicholas Sturgeon was asked to select six singers for Austria, but it is not known whether they ever set off.[333] However, English music did arrive, perhaps largely via Netherlands musicians.

Their own compositions were remarkable enough. Johannes de Sarto left three 'motets' in diverging styles: the canonic 'Verbum caro factum est', the cantio (or Latin *lauda*) 'Ave mater, o Maria'[334] and the very English-sounding antiphon 'O quam mirabilis'.[335] At some stage (possibly under Emperor Sigismund), he collaborated with Johannes Brassart on a set of polyphonic introits, a genre in which Brassart himself was highly accomplished.[336] Those were collected as part of *Ao-I*. Early introit compositions were essentially antiphons with tenor cantus firmus: the psalm verse and the Gloria Patri were left to plainsong.[337] With Brassart (and apparently with Binchois), the psalm (or at least its conclusion), and also often the Gloria Patri were assumed into the polyphony. Since the chant of these sections was declamatory, not melismatic like the antiphon, it was now placed in the cantus and accompanied in fauxbourdon or very simple, syllabic declamation by one or two lower voices. This resulted in little more than harmonized liturgical recitative, which foreshadowed later *falsobordoni*.[338]

In the output of known composers, such simple, functional styles appear with some frequency only in Binchois, whereas the central European sources have dozens of anonymous pieces of this type. This may be connected with the cultivation of primitive polyphony in the area (see p. 336): relative to *those* usages, Brassart's pieces were worthy of their demanding patron.

Brassart also left Mass Ordinary settings (including two Gloria–Credo pairs but no cycle), nine motets (four of them isorhythmic; all but one in four parts), three antiphon settings, the Christmas cantio 'Gratulemur Christicole' and a three-voice setting of the German *Leise* 'Christ ist erstanden'. Like the two ceremonial motets for Habsburg kings (see above), the *Leise* setting must have been written in Austria, where the tune was especially at home.[339] Brassart had also composed motets for the church of Saint-Jean l'Evangeliste, Liège, where

---

[333] Brian Trowell, 'Heinrich VI.' in *MGG* vol. 6, 67 f; Margaret Bent, 'Sturgeon, Nicholas' in *The New Grove*.

[334] A different setting of what is partly the same text was arranged by Oswald von Wolkenstein as 'Ave mueter, kuneginne': Pelnar, *Die mehrstimmigen Lieder Oswalds*, no. 35.109. See also Welker, 'New light on Oswald', 207–13.

[335] Edited in *DTOe VII*, vols. 14–15, 215.

[336] See his introits (plus the two by de Sarto) and other Mass music in Brassart, *Opera omnia*, vol. 1.

[337] Dangel-Hofmann, *Introitus*. This applies not only to the introits by Dufay, Arnold de Lantins and Johannes de Lymburgia in *I-Bc Q 15*, which she quotes, but also to the recently discovered 'Gaudeamus omnes' by Paolo da Firenze (ed. in PMFC, vol. 12, no. 30). The settings by Paolo, Arnold and Lymburgia all have *monorhythmic* cantus firmi.

[338] See Brassart, *Opera omnia*, vol. 1, and the first nine examples – by Brassart, Binchois (?), Lymburgia and anonymous composers – published in Dangel-Hofmann, *Introitus*.

[339] See p. 343 below.

he had been succentor between 1422 and 1431, and for the papal chapel in 1431 (see p. 164). The Corpus Christi hymn 'Sacris solemniis' could be connected with several major endowments for this feast made by King Frederick in churches in his realm in the early 1440s. By 1443 Brassart seems to have retired to his native Liège.

The biography of Johannes Roullet is unknown, but he must have been another Netherlander (perhaps from the Flemish town of Roulers) who found employment in the south Germanic area where all his fourteen extant works were copied (in *A-ZW*, *Tr 87* and *Em*). His most interesting pieces comprise four sequence settings that suggest Roullet was familiar with those by Dufay (which they follow in *Tr 87*), and a 'Benedicamus domino' reminiscent of Dufay's setting of the same chant. Some of the Dufay and Roullet sequences may even have been combined in a 'set' together. Their form consists of strict alternation between plainsong and polyphonic versicles, of which the latter use cantus paraphrase, fauxbourdon, and other techniques. In Roullet's setting of 'Laus tibi Christe', the sequence for St Mary Magdalene, the chant versicles are written in mensural rhythm in longs and breves (*modus perfectus*), suggesting a later-forgotten performance style for this liturgical genre. Also in Dufay's 'Letabundus', the sixth verse is notated with fixed rhythm (*tempus perfectum*).[340] Roullet's polyphonic versicles are not chordal and declamatory as were the psalm verse settings in Brassart's introits, but, like Dufay's, they form elegant, chanson-like phrases as befits their poetic texts. The plainsong is paraphrased freely, even in respect of its modal character (see Ex. 41).

We also have source evidence for the spread of English and French music further east. Thanks to the collecting zeal of Hermann Pötzlinger, a priest from Bayreuth who studied and taught at the University of Vienna in the later 1430s, there is a manuscript with 276 polyphonic pieces, compiled by Pötzlinger him-

Example 41 Johannes Roullet, Sequence 'Laus tibi, Christe'

---

[340] *Opera omnia*, vol. 4, no. 2.

Example 41 (*cont.*)

2a. Ce - li, ter - re, ma - ris,

Contratenor

Tenor

an - ge - lo - rum et ho - mi - num.

2b. Qui pec - ca - to - res ve - ni - sti ut sal - vos fa - ce - res.

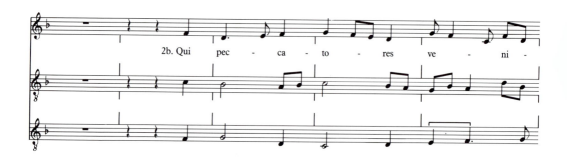

2b. Qui pec - ca - to - res ve - ni -

Example 41 (*cont.*)

self and some helpers between *c.*1435 and *c.*1443. He left the codex to the Regensburg abbey of St Emmeram, where he was schoolmaster in later life. The 'St Emmeram Codex' (*D-Mbs lat. 14274*; *Em*) is a private and informal collection like Lupi's Trent volumes. It must have been used mainly for teaching of (and performances with) boy choristers and students at the Vienna Bürger-schule – the collegiate school of St Stephen's (see p. 506) – and later, at St Emmeram.[341]

The sources from which the music was assembled must have come from many parts of Europe. The repertory available at the Council of Basle played an important role, since Vienna University had intense contact with the assembly; in the earliest fascicles of the codex, there is also a cluster of Bohemian pieces, some of them distinguished by notational symbols invented in Prague university circles.[342] During the Hussite wars, most Germans were forced to leave Prague University, and many ended up in Vienna: manuscripts with monophonic and polyphonic music reached Austria from Bohemia around this time (see p. 115). The codex *Em* has many items in common with the aforementioned collections *Ao*, *Tr 87* and *Tr 92* – confirming the expectation that the compositions were passed from the Habsburg chapels to cathedral musicians and schoolmasters. The collegiate school of St Stephen's and its *Kantorei* under Hermann Edlerawer (see p. 506), certainly performed much music copied in *Em*. Pötzlinger may have intended his music-book principally as a Mass collection, and even placed monophonic Mass Ordinary chants at the beginning (he later replaced the Kyrie plainsongs with polyphonic settings). But he went on to assemble Office music, antiphons, *cantiones*, motets and a good deal of secular music, most of which had Latin contrafactum texts or was without words.

---

[341] Thematic index: Karl Dèzes, 'Der Mensuralkodex des Benediktinerklosters Sancti Emmerami zu Regensburg', *ZMw* 10 (1927-8), 65-105; on its history, see Rumbold, 'Compilation of Munich Clm 14274'; Dagmar Braunschweig-Pauli, 'Studien zum sogenannten Codex St. Emmeram', *KJb* 66 (1982), 1-48; Reinhard Strohm, 'Zur Datierung des Codex St. Emmeram (Clm 14274): ein Zwischenbericht', in Finscher ed., *Datierung und Filiation*, 153-76; *idem*, 'Native and foreign polyphony', 217-19.

[342] Ward, 'A central European repertory', 326-30.

English compositions suddenly become prominent in fascicles copied *c.*1440; most of these are antiphons that may well have been imported from Basle. A number of works are local or regional products, of which some are attributed to Hermann Edlerawer and other German composers.

'International' polyphony of the kind known in Vienna is also found in the miscellany *A-Wn 5094* (*c.*1440) – a group of fragments bound into a codex that may have belonged to the Augustinian abbey of St Dorothy at Vienna.[343] Of the several discrete fragments, some contain Bohemian polyphony. Others contain keyboard arrangements, in Italian keyboard score as well as German letter notation, of pieces as old as the Ars nova motet 'Apollinis eclipsatur' and as recent as Dufay's ballade 'Ce jour le doibt'. We also find the exchiquier piece 'Qui contre fortune' (see p. 120) and 'Seigneur Leon', which may be by Dufay and was perhaps composed for the accession of Leonello d'Este of Ferrara in 1442.[344] The copyist's hand in 'Ce jour le doibt' is virtually identical with that of the last section of codex *Em*;[345] it may well have been the handwriting of a Viennese organist who – like Johannes Lupi – was interested in both vocal and keyboard polyphony.

The interaction between princely, academic, civic and monastic institutions that one finds in Vienna also characterizes other centres in *east central Europe* where foreign polyphony was cultivated.[346] (The indigenous music of these areas, and the later developments, will be discussed in Part IV, Chapter 3.) Especially Kraków, the seat of a famous university, the royal Polish chapel and perhaps an episcopal chapel, was a centre for musicians with international experience.

With one or more of these institutions, we may tentatively connect some composers whose names appear in the manuscripts. Magister Nicolaus de Radom (Mikołaj Radomski) seems to have worked at Kraków University for some time.[347] The music of his circle can be identified in the Polish sources *Kras* and *PL-Wn 378*, copied *c.*1440, where nine pieces are attributable to him. In the same context belongs a fragment now at Poznań University (*PL-Pu*; *Pu 2*), which is a little older and very probably of Italian origin.[348] The dominating style in these collections is that of the Ciconia generation in Italy. The fragmentary Gloria in *Pu 2* has an 'isorhythmic' tenor but only in the sense that the rhythms undergo mensural transformation (from C to Ɔ to C, actually meaning ₵ to C to ₡), whereas there is no exact melodic repetition. Technical analogies may be found in the works of Matteo da Perugia and others in codex

---

[343] Strohm, 'Native and foreign polyphony', 212 f and table I.

[344] Fallows, *Dufay*, 62 f.

[345] Ward, 'A central European repertory', 342 f.

[346] For the questions of repertoire and historiography in this area, see the contributions by Jaromír Čzerný and Mirosław Perz in Strohm (chairman), *Costituzione e conservazione*, 168–83. On the early sources, see also Brewer, *Ars nova*.

[347] Henri Musielak, 'W poszukiwaniu materiałow do biografii Mikołaja z Radomia' [In search of biographical material on Nicolaus de Radom], *Muzyka* 18 (1973), no. 1, 82–9.

[348] All these manuscripts are edited, in facs and transcription, in Perz ed., *Sources of Polyphony*.

ModA (see p. 205). In *Kras* and *PL-Wn 378*, we find fifteen pieces – mostly Mass settings – by Ciconia, Antonius Zacharias and Magister Egardus, plus anonymous works echoing their style. If Radomski is identifiable as Nicolaus Geraldi de Radom, documented at the Roman *curia* of Pope Boniface IX (*r.* 1389–1404), the connection with Zacharias and Egardus could be explained.[349] Alternatively, there may have been an influx of sacred music from the Council of Constance, or from St Stephen's, Vienna. Radomski comes close to Italianate idioms in a Gloria–Credo pair (*Kras* nos. 31–2), and a Credo in *a versi* technique with short duos for high voices (*PL-Wn 378* no. 8). Also a certain Nicolaus de Ostrorog (if that is the name of the composer) echoes the style of Egardus' Gloria (*Kras* no. 35) in *his* Gloria (*Kras* no. 36). A virelai or ballata with the contrafactum text 'Regina gloriosa' (in *Kras* no. 33) has tentatively been attributed to Ciconia: the echo imitations, repetitive rhythmic patterns and general motivic vocabulary are less reminiscent of Ciconia's Gloria–Credo pair nos. 3–4 (also in *Kras*) than of his virelai 'Aler m'en veus', which could be an early work.[350]

On the other hand, these Polish sources reflect influences and ideas which undoubtedly postdate 1420. There are three celebrative motets in chanson format with French-style contratenors: the anonymous 'Cracovia civitas' and Radomski's 'Hystoriographi aciem', both with texts by Stanisław Ciołek, Bishop of Poznań (the latter for the birth of Prince Kazimir Jagiełło, 1426)[351] and 'Pastor regis egregius' by Nicolaus de Ostrorog, a motet for St Stanisław but perhaps also a contrafactum of a virelai. These motets, or pseudo-motets, are more modern in style than the anonymous 'Nitor inclite claredinis', a Christmas cantio with alternative text (by Ciołek?) for the birth of another royal prince. It has the textual acrostic 'NICOLAUS' which may refer to an author, or to the saint and his feast (see p. 514 for similar pieces in the Strahov Codex). Musically, the work again resembles a reduction or recomposition of the Ars nova motet 'Apollinis eclipsatur'. Radomski's Gloria–Credo pair *Kras* nos. 22–3 is surely comparable to an Italian or Liégeois idiom after *c.*1420 with its combination of canon, free imitation and sequential patterning: Hugo de Lantins and Johannes Franchois come to mind.

The most modern stylistic layer in the *Kras* MS abandons the somewhat nervous rhythmic activity of previous pieces in ℂ mensuration in favour of songlike tenors and a broader rhythmic flow, often in ○. In this group of pieces, there are some *cantiones* (for example no. 21, 'Christicoli fecunditas', whose tenor repeats formulas of the first mode); and no. 19, the *lauda* 'Ave mater, o Maria', which appears in a version also transmitted in *BU*.[352] Three, possibly four, Mass settings in the *Kras* MS are by Etienne Grossin, one of which is his Kyrie in fauxbourdon (see p. 177). They are key compositions for this latest

---

[349] Perz, 'Carattere internazionale'.

[350] Ciconia, *Works*, nos. 3-4 (Gloria–Credo), 24 ('Regina gloriosa') and 44 ('Aler m'en veus'), respectively, with the editors' comments pp. 199 and 209.

[351] Perz, 'Carattere internazionale', 155 n. 6, maintains that the motet is a contrafactum of a ballata.

[352] This is the *lauda* also used by Oswald von Wolkenstein; see n. 334 above.

style in *Kras*. They can be grouped together with an anonymous Gloria in *PL-Wn* 378 (no. 11), which features a continuous canon for the upper voices and a repetitive tenor, and with the Sanctus 'Gustasti necis pocula' in *Kras*, composed by either Jacobus de Clibano (according to *Ao*) or Peter Sweikl (according to *Em*).[353] The inclusion of the last-named work suggests contacts with the Council of Basle and/or a Habsburg chapel. Radomski himself contributes to this stylistic group a *Magnificat* (*Kras* no. 13) in fauxbourdon, in which one can perhaps detect the influence of Grossin's Kyrie. The unwritten contratenor is prescribed in the Kyrie with the rubric '*a discantu contratenor*', but in the *Magnificat* '*per bardunum*'. The unorthodox as well as inconsistent nomenclature may suggest that the owner of the *Kras* MS did not yet have a standard term for the technique, and was not familiar with collections such as *Em* or *Tr 87*, where the term fauxbourdon is the norm. Radomski's technique in this work, however, is indistinguishable from that of Grossin or Dufay. He eschews the simplest, homorhythmic fauxbourdon style as found, for example, in the *Magnificat* settings of the Austrian sources. He sets the verses alternately in fauxbourdon and chanson format. In the latter sections, the plainsong (*Magnificat* tone I) is accompanied by relatively active lower voices:

Example 42 Nicolaus Radomski, *Magnificat*

---

[353] For Sweikl, see Dagmar Braunschweig-Pauli, 'Studien zum sogenannten Codex St. Emmeram', *KJb* 66 (1982), 38. For Clibano, see Strohm, *Bruges*, 117 f.

262

Example 42 (*cont.*)

A composer of the skill and experience of Radomski would perhaps also have absorbed English idioms, had they come his way, or emulated the sacred music of Binchois or Brassart. Apparently he did neither, but remained anchored in Italian styles. We may conclude that he was indeed connected with Italian music early in the century, and that his most recent contact with western music came about no later than *c.*1434 and by way of the Council of Basle.

One contemporary of Radomski who worked in Poland, but whose works are mostly known from Czech sources, was the mercurial Magister Petrus Wilhelmi of Grudencz, probably of German descent and a 'studiosus cracoviensis' from 1418 to 1430.[354] He is documented as a cleric of the diocese of Chełmno (Kulm) in 1442, when he was granted a royal safe-conduct to attend the imperial diet at Frankfurt – surely an indication of German courtly connections. Over twenty works have been attributed to him, several of which have topical or celebratory texts. His motet text 'Pontifices ecclesiarum' seems, in fact, to allude to King Frederick III and the Council of Basle, and his canonic motet for St Nicholas, 'Presulem euphebeatum', also occurs in the codex *Em*.[355] Wilhelmi cultivated the polytextual, non-isorhythmic 'Bohemian motet' which must be considered an outgrowth of fourteenth-century motet traditions in central Europe.[356] His declamatory, energetic style is indeed closer to that of Bohemian sacred music of his time – including its Ars nova precedents – than to the chanson idioms adopted by Radomski's circle. Wilhelmi signed his own name in the form of acrostics in at least a dozen works; no doubt the curiously-contrived Latin poems are by him as well. One of his several patrons was the Silesian Andreas Ritter (possibly the owner of the Glogauer Liederbuch of *c.*1480), for whom Petrus composed the satirical motet 'Probitate eminentem / Ploditando exarare' (see p. 502).

---

[354] Jaromir Černý, 'Petrus Wilhelmi de Grudencz: neznámý skladatel doby Dufayovy v českých pramenech' [An unknown composer of the age of Dufay in Czech sources], *Hudebni Veda* 12 (1975), 195–238; *idem, Petrus Wilhelmi*.

[355] Further on his life, see Rumbold, 'Compilation of Munich Clm 14274', 178 f.

[356] Černý, 'Mehrtextige Motette'. See also p. 337 below.

Italian reception of foreign music had always been a step ahead of that in central Europe. Apart from the papal chapel and its international connections, and the foreign dynasties established on Italian soil (the dukes of Savoy in Piedmont, and the Aragonese kings in Naples), several indigenous princes imported music and musicians from abroad. The Visconti of Lombardy had done so since the later fourteenth century, the branches of the Malatesta family of Rimini/Pesaro/Brescia since the time of the Council of Constance, and the Este family of Ferrara from about 1430, when Marquis Niccolò III was already in touch with the Burgundian court over the import of musical instruments, and possibly their players.[357] From Dufay he commissioned the celebratory ballade 'C'est bien raison', perhaps in 1433; Dufay visited his court in 1437. In the same context belongs the appointment of the German singer and instrumentalist Niccolò Tedesco (i.e. Nikolaus Krombsdorfer, see p. 519) in 1436. The famous virtuoso Pietrobono de Burcellis grew up in Ferrara as the son of northern immigrants. Marquis Leonello d'Este (*r.* 1441–50) founded an actual court chapel where his Italian and foreign chaplains celebrated daily Mass and Vespers, often with polyphony. His models may have been the chapels of Burgundy and Savoy; his patronage was imitated, in turn, by the Medici, Sforza and Gonzaga dynasties. The musical culture at the Este court itself was to develop into a major paradigm of a musical 'Renaissance'.[358]

The manuscript *ModB* (*I-MOe* α.X. *1. 11*), compiled towards 1448, is the only surviving music-book from Leonello's chapel, and demonstrates a systematic and comprehensive use of liturgical polyphony.[359] The 131 pieces include the largest set of Dufay's hymns found anywhere (23 settings), followed by other Vespers compositions mainly by Dufay and Binchois: psalms, 'Benedicamus domino' and *Magnificat* settings, and Vespers antiphons.

The last section comprises over 50 motets and votive antiphons, ascribed to Dunstable (30 works), Lionel (7), Forest (4), Benet (2), Polmier (i.e. Plummer: 4), Stone (2), Pyamour and Standley (1 each),[360] plus Dufay's isorhythmic motet 'Fulgens jubar'. This work, and those by Plummer, Stone and (probably) Standley, originated after *c.*1440. The whole section is headed by the rubric 'Hic incipiunt moteti' ('Here begin the motets'). This may betray a special pride in this motet collection; at least it indicated to the chaplains that the works did not belong to the regular Vespers liturgy to which the manuscript is dedicated up to that point. In fact, many of the pieces, such as the fifteen

[357] See, respectively, Strohm, 'Filipotto da Caserta', and pp. 58 f above; Allan W. Atlas, 'On the identity of some musicians at the Brescian court of Pandolfo III Malatesta', *CMc* 36 (1983), 11–20; Lockwood, *Ferrara*, 11–40.

[358] Lockwood, *Ferrara*.

[359] Charles Hamm and Ann Besser Scott, 'A study and inventory of the MS Modena, Biblioteca Estense, a.X.1.11', *MD* 26 (1972), 101–43; Ann Besser Scott, 'English music in Modena, Biblioteca Estense, a.X.1.11, and other Italian manuscripts', *MD* 26 (1972), 145–60. The date of 1448 has been proposed in Lockwood, *Ferrara*, 52.

[360] The number of works by little-known Englishmen would be even greater if the scribal attributions were not apparently slanted in favour of Dunstable.

isorhythmic motets by Dunstable, Benet and Forest, are not liturgical at all; others are Marian antiphons or similar pieces which could be sung in various circumstances.

In only one other extant source is there a similar cluster of English works: in part III of the Aosta Codex (see p. 254), which has many pieces in common with *ModB*. But the Ferrarese collection is more systematic and complete in all its aspects than any of the Germanic sources. It seems that an ambitious spirit was at work here similar to that at the unknown court which commissioned Dufay's hymns in the 1430s. In *ModB*, the *Magnificat* settings cover all but two of the *Magnificat* tones, and are thus an almost complete set. Two of the settings are Binchois *unica*, and so are his ceremonial motet for the Burgundian court, 'Nove cantum melodie', and his antiphons for St Philip, St Anthony Abbot, St John and All Saints. Further significant *unica* among the Vespers music include antiphons for saints venerated at Ferrara (St George, St Anthony of Padua, St Dominic) by Dufay and Johannes Fedé; these are slightly later additions to the codex. Fedé's pieces were surely written about 1445–6 when this composer from Douai was a member of Leonello's chapel.[361] Further additions were made much later, under Duke Ercole d'Este (*r.* 1471–1505), which suggest that at that time the codex was still used by court performers. The concentration on Vespers music and motets in this manuscript suggests that the chapel also owned a separate, large collection of Mass music. Perhaps it was not yet assembled in one volume by the time of Leonello's premature death in 1450.

In order to explain the surprising concentration of English works, Ann B. Scott has shed much light on contacts between England and Italy at the time,[362] especially through humanists and university students. None of these contacts, however, links the Este court with anyone who could have been in possession of such a large and up-to-date collection of English music. We cannot entirely separate the issue of the English material from that of the Dufay and Binchois groups. They all suggest that Marquis Leonello did not need to collect incidental pieces here and there, but had access (through his agents) to the richer-flowing sources of western European music. It is perfectly feasible that he wrote a letter to Duke Philip the Good asking for liturgical music by Binchois, or to Dufay requesting his hymn cycle and latest motets. As it is, Leonello rewarded Dufay for services unknown to us with a payment of twenty ducats in 1443, as his father had done in 1437.[363] The earlier payment could have been for the ballade 'C'est bien raison' in praise of Niccolò III, the later one for the ballade 'Seigneur Leon / Benedictus qui venit' for the enthronement of Leonello early in 1442 (see above). These would be extraordinary sums for single compositions; perhaps Dufay had also provided the court with sacred works on one of these occasions.

---

[361] Lockwood, *Ferrara*, 55.
[362] Ann B. Scott, 'English music' (n.359 above).
[363] Lockwood, 'Dufay and Ferrara', 1–3.

The English works were probably obtained in a similar way: by writing to a court or court chaplain who was in possession of such music. The court of Frederick III of Habsburg in Graz (then in possession of the Aosta Codex) is a possibility; but it is more likely that Leonello wrote to the court of Henry VI, to obtain the music at source and to outdo his continental competitors. An additional clue to a connection with Henry's chapel is that *ModB* is the earliest continental source to contain works by the younger Englishmen John Plummer, John Stone and Standley. Plummer is first heard of in 1440, when he joined the royal chapel; in 1442, he became Master of the Children.

The Este court occasionally bought music from visiting musicians, as in the case of six Masses acquired from two Frenchmen in 1447 (see p. 242). If these works are identical with the first six Mass cycles in the codex *Tr 93* (four of which are certainly English), then the Ferrara chapel must in turn have provided other courts with imported music. Its lost repertory of Mass music might well have to be sought in the Trent Codices of the 1450s (*93, 90* and *88*).

Among the foreign musicians whom Leonello employed for services outside the chapel, there was between 1448 and 1450 a certain 'Johannes de Anglia' or 'Johannes ab arpa de Anglia', and in 1448 a 'Johannes presbiter Londini' – perhaps the same man.[364] The English harper, and his possible identification with John Bedyngham, will occupy us in a later chapter (p. 546).

It seems that also the musicians of Ferrara Cathedral participated at this time in an international network of music distribution, perhaps encouraged by its archdeacon, the famous theorist and composer Ugolino da Orvieto.[365] Small fragments from a polyphonic choirbook of Ferrara Cathedral exist (*c.*1440). They contain the interesting four-voice motet 'Ibo michi ad montem mirre' which resembles English antiphon settings of this text, also in *ModB*.[366] The anonymous work survives complete in the Viennese codex *Em* (no. 94), where it was copied *c.*1440. This connection recalls the fact that 'Seigneur Leon' also exists in a contemporary Viennese source, *A-Wn 5094* (see above). If 'Ibo michi' is indeed English, it would reflect the style of the post-Dunstable generation, as represented by Plummer and Stone. The music also shares elements with Netherlands and even Italian settings, for example the two top voices singing in the same register. For the moment, it is one of the many beautiful works of uncertain authorship and origin, which demonstrate the stylistic fusion reached in European sacred polyphony by the 1430s and 40s.

---

[364] See the documents cited in Lockwood, *Ferrara*, 49 f and 60 f.
[365] Enrico Peverada, 'Vita musicale nella cattedrale di Ferrara nel Quattrocento', *RIM* 15 (1980), 3–30; Lockwood, *Ferrara*, 74–85.
[366] Lockwood, *Ferrara*, 74 ff (with facs).

PART III

THE COMMON TRADITIONS

I

MUSIC IN THE LIFE OF THE INSTITUTIONS

The Church and the world

Among the medieval institutions which cultivated music, the Church was unlike any other. It was not only the largest and most comprehensive of all the institutions, exercising a control that reached deep into the fabric of society, it also had a special musical mission. To sing God's praise was part of worship in the Jewish and Christian traditions, so that a religious incentive existed to expand and refine musical practice.[1] Furthermore, music had become a means for the other most important task of the Church, that of spreading the faith (*propagare fidem*), i.e. of propaganda. Church music addressed the world and this had enormous repercussions for its own development.

One could say that music 'entangled' the Church with the world: with the senses, in the first place. This was potentially dangerous. Theologians and Church administrators had the task of keeping this relationship in order – preserving a well-controlled hierarchy in which music, like all the other secular concerns, was kept in its proper place. The Church as a whole could neither reject music altogether as being 'too worldly' nor support it as an individual 'patron' could. Such choices had to be left to particular pressure-groups, organizations or individuals.[2]

Many of these were individual churchmen or other wealthy members of a parish or cathedral chapter. We have seen that the popes of Avignon and later of Rome employed composers in their chapels and drew on their abilities as composers and performers of secular music. Medieval bishops and abbots who held secular lordships often demonstrated this by maintaining trumpeters and other minstrels in their private households; song and dance were admitted to their palaces as to any other princely dwellings.[3] The earliest known name of a German composer of polyphony, 'Hermann the Monk of Salzburg' (see p. 345), may be nothing but a pseudonym for Archbishop Pilgrim II of Salzburg

---

[1] This is perhaps the main reason why the western musical tradition has become so different from those of other civilizations.

[2] For the controversy about the role of the Church, see the contributions by Bowers and Cattin in Fenlon ed., *MMEME*.

[3] The famous *Carmina burana*, a collection of goliardic songs of the thirteenth century, originated probably at the court of a Styrian bishop.

(*d*.1396). But the official reactions of the Church towards music could be quite different. At Notre Dame, Paris, polyphonic singing was outlawed in the fifteenth century.[4] A strange mixture of official and personal reactions to music is contained in Pope John XXII's Bull of 1324/5 (see p. 34); this condemnation of 'modern music' was to some extent at variance with tradition, but even in its very personalized form contributed to the huge task of defining the borderlines between ecclesiastical dignity and worldliness. The religious reformers and lay preachers of the late Middle Ages often condemned music far more harshly. The attitudes towards music within these partisan groups were often ambiguous, and depended on religious and church-political goals in each case.[5]

Locations for music in the church: choir, nave and chapel

Medieval thinkers took delight in classifying music (into *musica mundana*, *humana*, *instrumentalis* or *organica*, for example). In a more concrete sense, medieval church buildings are in themselves hierarchic structures where music and its subdivisions have well-defined places. The separation of the choir from the nave, for example, makes architecture serve a musical purpose; indeed it makes architecture define the order to which music is subjected. The choir serves for worship and the nave for propaganda, and the music made in either location corresponds to those functions. Of the other characteristic locations in a medieval church – among them the crypt, cloister and refectory – the *chapel* developed into the most important place for music-making.

'Choir' and 'chapel' are names given to architectural units as well as to musical ensembles. Obviously, the 'choir' comprises the clerics who sing and pray in the reserved space at the eastern end of a church building, the 'presbytery' or more generally the 'choir'. This they do in the Divine Office, i.e. the 'Hours' (Matins, Lauds, Prime, Terce, Sext, None, Vespers and Compline), or at Mass. The liturgical chant used there addresses God in the first place and the worshippers themselves (not an 'audience') in the second, as does the psalmist of the Old Testament. The psalms are the most typical example of the music performed in the choir, i.e. of 'choral' music. This can be seen in the 'antiphonal' mode of performing the psalms, because it is an alternation of two groups of singers, coinciding with the architectural layout of the choir itself.

Many other forms of music in the choir developed over the centuries, including 'responsorial' singing (solo–chorus response), as well as liturgical polyphony (*organum*) and organ music. Specialist members of the clerical community itself, such as 'vicars-choral' or choristers could be used to provide these genres, and even laymen could be hired to sing, conduct the specialist singers, or play the organ. Although they were largely soloist music, these more specialized

---

[4] See Wright, *Music and Ceremony*.
[5] See also pp. 298 f.

modern genres were performed in the choir. The designation 'choral', however, was retained for those items of the liturgy which represented the original type of singing in the choir (psalms, antiphons, hymns etc.), so that the term came to indicate rather a manner of singing, or a large ensemble. The split between the two meanings – location vs. performance type – did not happen all at once, and only from about the sixteenth century was the purely musical meaning of 'choir' and 'chorus' established. In German Protestant churches, 'chorale' (*Choral*) is actually the vernacular hymn tune sung by the congregation in the nave! This is understandable, because the parishioners in the nave had now become the main worshippers and had inherited the dignity of choral singing, formerly reserved for the clergy in the choirstalls.[6] Certain trends leading up to this great reversal of roles can be observed in the fifteenth century; the participation of unskilled or halfskilled lay singers in church music is an important development here (see p. 283). But on the whole, 'choral' music before the Reformation is to be understood as the plainchant sung in the choir by the full ecclesiastical chorus.

Before we look at the other main places for music-making in the church, the nave and chapels, it should perhaps be explained that all medieval churches were organized according to the same hierarchic principles, whether large or small. Only a difference of degree existed between a cathedral or collegiate church, where the members of the 'chapter' (the canons, *mansionarii* etc.) headed the sacred community, and a parish church, where that community consisted only of parish priests, chaplains and lower clergy. Collegiate churches were distinguished from cathedrals only by having no bishop or diocese; but in either type of church the canons and others had to sing the daily Office and High Mass under the guidance of the cantor and his assistant. (More often, the canons sent their vicars and left the music for the lower clergy to perform.) In many parish churches, especially in urban centres, the clergy were numerous enough to form a proper choir and the choirstalls were sometimes built in such a way as to resemble those of cathedrals. The choral singing of Mass and the Divine Office was, of course, most frequent in collegiate churches and cathedrals. Usually, the spoken Mass (*missa lecta*) was the staple fare for ordinary weekdays, and sung Masses occurred only on Sundays and higher feasts; the daily Office with all its 'seven Hours' (Matins and Lauds being counted as one) was sung in parish churches only where wealthy parishioners supported this costly exercise with endowments – as true 'patrons' of music and liturgy. Their support also went to genuine musical adornments such as polyphony. For that to happen, parish churches had to provide themselves with four things: 'a rood-loft, an organ, additional clerks or "conducts", and books of pricksong'.[7] In England, the Low Countries, probably in Paris, and in the central European

---

6 The Protestant churches demonstrated this musical continuity by converting many medieval hymns and antiphons into vernacular hymns.

7 Harrison, *Britain*, 197.

area between Basle and Kraków, parish churches introduced polyphonic music in the course of the fifteenth century.

In monasteries and friaries, the 'choir' was by definition that of the monks and friars. But the participation of lay clerks, and musical specialization, was widely admitted, enriching the music inside as well as outside the choir.

The nave is the place of assembly for the laity – princes and nobles were sometimes admitted to the choir for special ceremonies – and the services provided for the laity such as the 'parishioners' Mass' were also held in the nave. Here, music was not a high priority; in the fifteenth century, the Sunday sermon (preached increasingly in the vernacular) was more important. Also the music heard in the nave had the function of propaganda, and consisted mainly of organ music or processional music. Organs were variously positioned in medieval churches: the top of the choir-screen, or a rood-loft, were favoured locations, as may still be seen in many English churches. In this case, the organ could be heard, and often also seen, from inside the choir as well as from the nave, and could establish acoustic contact between the privileged and the common worshippers. Arnold Schlick (in 1511) recommended that the organ be placed next to the singers in the choir and also near the celebrant to ensure a good musical interaction during Mass; this implies that the organ still served the clergy in the choir and not the congregation. But Schlick also finds it laudable for the organ to be visible from the nave so that it can be an ornament of the church, its decoration and painting inspiring devotion.[8] The position of the organ on a side wall of the nave seems a very old custom, proving that the instrument was meant to 'address' the parishioners from early on. The main task of the organ in this position would have been to accompany processions through the nave. These were the rituals with a characteristic propaganda effect and sometimes full of music (the Palm Sunday procession, for example). Hymns, responds, antiphons, litanies and above all the *Te Deum* were liturgical genres often performed with the organ in processions (*alternatim* or simultaneously). Documents speak of the singing of the *Te Deum* in thanksgiving processions to the sound of the organ, and liturgical dramas and mystery plays usually ended with the *Te Deum* sung and played on the organ.[9] When events of great public importance were celebrated with a *Te Deum*, it is likely that the common people joined in the singing of this best-known hymn of the Catholic Church.

When instruments were allowed into church in such festive situations they were confined to the nave, even if the event they celebrated (a coronation, for example), was located in the presbytery. Trumpets, as the symbols of worldly

---

[8] Arnold Schlick, *Spiegel der Orgelmacher und Organisten* (1511), ed. E. Flade (Kassel etc.: Bärenreiter, 1951), 15.

[9] A description from Spain (1465) is in Lamaña, 'Instrumentos', 115: the *Te Deum* was performed *alternatim* during the procession; the participants walked when the organ played its verses, and stopped when singing theirs. For other uses, see Marix, *Histoire*, 82; Rokseth, 'Instrumental music', 424; Rokseth, *La musique d'orgue*, 50 ff; Strohm, *Bruges*, 87; Sabine Žak, 'Fürstliche und städtische Repräsentation in der Kirche (Zur Verwendung von Instrumenten im Gottesdienst)', *MD* 38 (1984), 243 ff, 249 f.

power, could be heard in the nave when the dignitaries to whom they belonged were present at a ceremony. The use of trumpets during the Gloria or in the offertory procession is documented.[10] Even more 'propagandistic', in a sense, were the liturgical dramas, the mystery plays and the forms of liturgical dancing which were excluded from the choir but admitted to the nave. Sahlin[11] reports an ancient ritual of the churches of Sainte-Marie-Madeleine and Saint-Etienne at Besançon, called *bergeretta*, which survived into the eighteenth century; on Easter Sunday, after lunch and after the sermon, the clergy performed round-dances (*choreae*) in the cloister or, 'in case of rain', in the middle of the nave, singing some chants as contained in the processional. In another source, the hymn 'Salve festa dies' is specifically indicated as being sung *alternatim* during this processional dance.

Similar uses of music can be observed in connection with the external part of the building. Processions go around the church (very often also around or across the cemetery); mystery plays or pageants are performed in front of the main portal – which is also the location where instrumentalists most often play, addressing large congregations at festivals.[12] When in Nuremberg in 1433 the city waits went 'on the choir' (*auf das kor*) of the main parish church to celebrate the emperor with fanfares, it was on the outer balcony around the building that they played. Many different forms of music – some of them secular – involved the portals and other external parts of the churches, because these were the locations where the Church and the world met. Last but not least, the church building and the outside world were acoustically linked by the sound of the church bells which were often used to underscore festive events. That they could be heard both inside and outside the building served to 'publicize' the ceremonies for which bells were rung, even if these were taking place in the seclusion of the choir.

Chapel music and its performance

The most important place for music-making in the late Middle Ages, however, was the chapel. It was only in the fifteenth century that this term assumed the meaning of a musical ensemble. Before, it was a sacred place, whether part of a church or an independent structure. The word '*capella*' allegedly originated as the name for the little building in which the cloak (*cappa*) of St Martin of Tours was kept. In any case, a chapel was not a meeting-place for worship but rather served to contain relics. In that connection it often had an altar at which private

---

[10] Examples in Žak, 'Repräsentation' (see n. 9). Despite assertions to the contrary, the question of instrumental playing in church (other than the organ) is far from settled. For some documents, see Moser, *Hofhaimer*, 16; Salmen, *Spielmann*, 77 f; Rastall, 'Minstrelsy', 87; Strohm, *Bruges*, 86.

[11] Sahlin, *Carole*, 147 ff. In Dubrovnik (Croatia), collective dancing in the church on the patronal feast-day was accompanied by pipers; the practice lasted until 1425: see Reese, *Renaissance*, 758.

[12] For pictures of processional music, see Bowles, *Musikleben*, plates 114–22.

Masses were read by a specially appointed chaplain. In the late Middle Ages, privately endowed Masses (very often Requiems) became the main purpose of the innumerable chapels built by individuals, families, fraternities and guilds. This expansion was due to the belief that the saying of Masses was a good work contributing to salvation, and that to pay for such services had the same effect; salvation was the nearer the greater the number of Masses said for somebody.[13] The effect which this belief had on the development of medieval churches defies description: they became sprinkled with 'chapels' and endowed altars, for most of which there was not actually any space. A chapel and chaplaincy was, in a sense, a legal concept only, meaning an identifiable income for the saying of certain Masses.

The richer benefactors, and indeed the princes, made sure that their chapels were well-defined structures, however: adorned with altars, liturgical vestments, works of art including statues and panel paintings, liturgical books, very often also a small organ (to be distinguished from the big 'choir organ') and sufficient personnel of officiating clergy. When services were held in guild chapels in Flemish churches, the space was cordoned off or closed with iron gates to keep non-members out. In princely chapels, the 'congregation' consisted of the prince, his friends and his household alone. This privatization of worship is understandable, because its main focus was usually the Masses for the soul(s) of one or more ancestors, or deceased members of the guild or confraternity, who were buried within the chapel. Many pictorial documents of the time show chapel services, suggesting that music-making was frequent in them.[14] It often involved specialized singers and a small organ; archival documents confirm that polyphonic music, mainly of the Mass Ordinary but also for Vespers, emerged in the context of private chapels in many fourteenth- and fifteenth-century churches.[15] The clergy who performed the music had often learned the necessary skills not for the sake of the official liturgy in the choir, but according to the wishes of well-paying confraternities and benefactors wanting the music for their chapels. As far as the famous Ghent altar panels by Hubert and Jan van Eyck reflect contemporary reality, the music panels show a typical chapel performance by specialized musicians. As is well known, the painting was made for a private chapel in a wealthy parish church.

Princely chapels served, in the first place, for the saying of Masses (and increasingly also the Divine Office) for the individual benefit of a ruler and his family. Many of them had a full complement of officiating clergy, chaplain-priests, servers, sacristan, sexton, organist and often also choirboys. As buildings, they could be splendid independent structures. They were not full churches, having neither cure of souls nor supervision of other churches. On

---

[13] Žak, *Musik als 'Ehr und Zier'*, 136.

[14] See Bowles, *Musikleben*, plates 100, 108 and 111.

[15] Representative examples are given in Strohm, *Bruges*, 15 (1417) and Forney, 'Music, ritual and patronage', 18–20 (1506). The practice was by no means confined to the Low Countries. For a case where not only the chapel and benefactor, but also the altar painting and the polyphonic Mass he endowed can be identified, see *New Obrecht Edition*, vol. 3 (1984), ed. B. Hudson, XI–XV.

the other hand, some of the largest institutions – such as the Sainte-Chapelle du Palais in Paris, the chapel of St George's, Windsor, that of St Stephen's, Westminster – were or became collegiate foundations with a full personnel of canons. To these 'permanently endowed Royal foundations'[16] correspond the various chapel buildings of the dukes of Burgundy. Plate 4 shows such a Burgundian chapel interior of *c*.1455, during a Mass service.[17] The prince is in attendance – in the curtained-off compartment to the right – and is engaged in prayer, while the priest and the ministers are officiating and other clergy in front are singing from a plainsong book, held by one of them. Four choirboys are visible. Many other people are in the chapel, some entering while the Mass is going on, or just looking in. These are household or family members; a door-keeper seems to prevent unauthorized people from entering. But the atmosphere is relaxed, almost as in a princely chamber when music was performed after dinner. It must be kept in mind that the miniature, if it refers to an actual Burgundian chapel, shows just one of the many buildings used for this purpose in the Burgundian territories (in Brussels, Ghent, Bruges, Courtrai, Hesdin, Lille, Dijon, Beaune etc.). Several of these were attached to the castles or city palaces which the dynasty owned. The chaplains shown in the picture, however, and also the choirboys, were one specific group that travelled with the duke, singing Mass for him wherever he went.[18] One could say, therefore, that the miniature shows 'the ducal chapel' (the musical ensemble) singing Mass in 'one of the duke's chapels' (the buildings).

Mass was sung daily in many royal and ducal chapels of the time. At the Burgundian court in the fifteenth century (but surely also in other places; see p. 178 for Bourges), there was a daily polyphonic Mass except on Mondays when there was a Requiem in plainsong. Also the Office was frequently provided, and princes liked to attend at least Vespers and Compline. Liturgical polyphony for these services (including hymns, antiphons, the *Magnificat* and the 'Salve regina') can have originated in the context of princely chapels as well as cathedrals. The richer establishments, however, were the earliest to provide themselves with large 'sets' of functional polyphony covering many days of the calendar. (See also pp. 248 f.)

In chapels of all kinds and sizes, the status of polyphony was not so restricted by liturgical considerations as it was in the choir, but there still had to be an orderly relationship. Ritual observances in private chapels could be partly

---

[16] Harrison, *Britain*, 21.

[17] See Bowles, *Pratique musicale*, pl. 133. To be compared with similar pictures in the same publication, especially with Bowles, *Musikleben*, pl. 102.

[18] Choirboys were apparently not part of the itinerant ducal household after *c*.1430; they used to go to school in Lille, Dijon and at The Hague where they also had endowed Masses to perform: see Marix, *Histoire*, 162 ff; Strohm, *Bruges*, 94; Higgins, *Busnois*, 81 f (with a document referring to the four choirboys at the 'domestic chapel' at The Hague, under Gauthier Vrankenzonne). The present miniature of *c*.1455, if intended to represent a Burgundian chapel, may show the building in Lille. The coat of arms in the circular window to the right is the lion of Flanders. The architectural style seems to belong to the fourteenth century; in the very similar miniature in Bowles, *Musikleben*, pl. 102, a romanesque building is shown.

4 The Burgundian chapel performing in a service. Jean Mansel, *La fleur des histoires*. (Bibliothèque Royale Albert Ièr MS 9232, fol. 269r.)

determined by the patrons; the French royal chapel was largely exempt from episcopal supervision but it did adhere to the liturgy of Paris which was recopied in the chapel books. The dukes of Burgundy followed this same liturgy, although none of their territories belonged to the diocese of Paris. The 'Mass of the Day' sung in those chapels would follow the missal and gradual of Paris. But in addition there would be a daily polyphonic Mass with 'votive' status, i.e. the Proper text of which was chosen from the formulas reserved for multiple use. It is most probable that the Burgundian chapel applied polyphony, in a weekly recurring pattern, to the following votive Mass texts (and the sets used in other western European chapels differed only slightly):

Tuesday:	Mass of the Holy Angels
Wednesday:	Mass of St Andrew (the patron saint of the House of Valois)
Thursday:	Mass of the Holy Ghost
Friday:	Mass of the Holy Cross
Saturday:	Mass of Our Lady
Sunday:	Mass of the Holy Trinity
(Monday:	Mass of the Dead – in plainsong)[19]

Returning once more to the miniature: we would, of course, like to know what music is being performed and whether the representation can be deemed 'realistic'. Unlike the illustrations of Richental's chronicle (see Plate 2), which aimed at recording extraordinary events, this picture represents daily practice. It shows a Mass service. The attitude of the celebrant and of his ministers is that of prayer, and the worshippers are mostly kneeling – so this might be the moment of the prayers of the 'canon of the Mass', before the Elevation of the Host. The chapel singers would thus be singing the Sanctus. The book in front of them, however, does not look like the Mass Ordinary section of a gradual (the 'Kyriale'), but rather like a hymnary with much text between the notes. It could be a Kyriale with trope texts, for example the Sanctus trope 'Ave verum corpus'; it certainly does not show polyphonic music. Of the nine individual musicians, two adults are not looking into the book and one boy cannot possibly see the music. In such miniatures it often seems that the singers are following the written plainsong only casually. They are either silent or singing by heart, probably because the melody is well known. Of the two raised hands of singers in front, one is clearly pointing to some notes near the end of the plainsong; the other hand is that of the leader of the group who is giving rhythmic signs. It is also of interest that the service takes place at night – as can be seen through the door to the left, where a man is entering with a burning torch. The service – if details can be understood literally – must therefore be a votive Mass, performed in the evening or early morning.

The polyphonic performance practice of chapel ensembles has been much investigated, but there was an enormous number of variations between the

---

[19] After Planchart, 'Guillaume Du Fay's benefices', 152.

institutions. The ordinances of the Burgundian chapel under Charles the Bold (of 1469) have been evaluated by David Fallows.[20] He concludes that only adult male voices were used, ideally fourteen of them, in uneven distribution over the voice-parts of a four-part setting:

(Cantus:)	six (*six haultes voix*)
(Contratenor altus:)	two (*deux moiens*)
(Tenor:)	three (*troys teneurs*)
(Contratenor bassus:)	three (*troys basses contres*).

This arrangement, Fallows argues, requires falsettists on the top line whose softer tone is balanced by their larger number. An alternative reading of the documentation, to the effect that only one singer per part was actually singing, would be possible but would open more serious questions about acoustic balance.

Other archival references tell us that tenors, and from 1450 at the latest also basses and trebles, were specialists in their respective ranges. A *tenoriste* was often the ensemble's leader. The range of the contratenor altus[21] was similar to that of the tenor – perhaps a little more extended above or (rarely) below. Contrapuntally this was the least important but melodically and rhythmically the least predictable line and therefore the most difficult to perform. It seems that few singers were usually assigned to that part, not because it was difficult but because it was deemed unimportant and even dispensable, whereas the high status of the tenor singers corresponded to the contrapuntal – and also symbolic – importance of their part.

Court chaplains were probably selected according to their ability to sing mensural music. Their salaries were handsome (particularly towards the end of the century in Italian chapels), and the quality of these princely chapels must have been well above that of most cathedral ensembles. Only the *petits-vicaires* of Cambrai Cathedral and of similarly important churches (for example St Donatian's, Bruges, Our Lady's, Antwerp; probably also the Lady Chapel singers of Canterbury Cathedral) formed highly self-confident 'professional' groups. The internal disruptions and the turnover of personnel were great, however: all these talented young men aspired to higher and thus 'non-musical' ranks in the church system.[22]

The chaplains and clerks, vicars-choral ('lay conducts'), *petits-vicaires*, or *socii de musica*, were the backbone of any chapel ensemble. Enlargements were made in many places, however, by the addition of a small organ, and/or choirboys with their master. Few establishments seem to have rejected organs and organists. This was the case at Cambrai Cathedral, which had no organ at all (not even for

---

[20] Fallows, 'Specific information', 110 ff.
[21] The designation *moien* in the ordinances is a little unusual; it certainly corresponds to the English mene and the Latin *medius*, the latter name being used also in central Europe.
[22] For a vivid sketch of the lifestyles of these singers, see Pirro, 'Cornuel'.

plainsong).[23] Since this institution was widely famous for its excellent singing, one must conclude that organ playing was considered by some not as an embellishment but as a crutch for weaker ensembles. On the other hand, there surely was a tradition in which the sound of the organ was positively sought after, in chant as well as in polyphonic music. As regards the precise modes of performance, each document has to be considered in its own right. Obrecht's 'Caput' Mass, for example, has been interpreted in such a way as to require the organ to play the cantus firmus throughout, but on changing pitch levels. The huge endowments made by Mary of Burgundy (*d*.1482), daughter of Charles the Bold, for the church of Our Lady in Bruges instituted three sets of Masses of different solemnity: the lowest-ranking Masses were sung in plainsong, the next higher with discant, and the highest-ranking with discant and organ. Since the exact terms of the endowment date from the time of Maximilian of Habsburg (1496), when it was first put in force, it is possible that the important role of the organ in connection with polyphony reflects Habsburg preferences.[24] But organ-playing was welcome in the Burgundian chapel, too. The *premier chapelain* of Charles the Bold, Philippe Syron, and several other chapel members were trained organists. It is likely that the ordinances of 1469 do not mention the organ because its role was fixed by traditional usage.

Boys' voices were, of course, traditional in church music throughout the Middle Ages. Schoolboys as well as choirboys (as far as there was a distinction between them) had specific musical tasks in the choir: the singing of lessons and responsory verses, for example. During the fourteenth century, some Franco-Netherlands institutions apparently began to train choirboys in polyphonic singing, especially in chapels. The polyphonic Lady Mass (*Missa de Salve*), performed in the Lady Chapel, became a characteristic task of the small ensemble consisting of the choirboys with their master and one or two assistants. By the 1420s, choirboys sang all kinds of sacred polyphony, whether in small chapels of collegiate churches, at secular courts (such as Burgundy) or the papal chapel. Roger Bowers traces their gradual admission to polyphonic singing in English 'choral' institutions from about the mid-fifteenth century, which is astonishingly late.[25] But already from about 1430, boy choristers had disap-

---

[23] See Wright, 'Performance practices'.

[24] See Planchart, 'Fifteenth-century Masses', 11–17 (on Ockeghem and Obrecht); Strohm, *Bruges*, 49 (on Maximilian). The central European traditions included by that time both the *alternatim* practice and organ accompaniment for polyphony, see p. 519. *Alternatim* practices are described in Leo Schrade, 'The organ in the Mass of the 15th century', *MQ* 28 (1942), 329–36 and 467–87; More, 'Organ-playing and polyphony'. Evidence for the organ accompanying polyphony in western Europe: Strohm, *Bruges*, 15 and *passim*; Forney, 'Music, ritual and patronage', 18 ff. Fallows, 'Specific information', appears unaware of the issue, but happens to quote (n. 40) a document in Marix, *Histoire*, 163, which I believe to refer to organ–discant collaboration (Mass endowment for the Sainte-Chapelle, Dijon, of 1425). For *solo polyphony* on the church organ, see pp. 373 f below.

[25] Bowers, *Choral Institutions*, *passim*; Bowers, 'Performing pitch', 22: 'Prior to *c*.1450/60, there is no evidence to suggest that the choristers were trained to participate in performances of composed polyphony'. But John Stele's contract at Durham, dated by Bowers himself *c*.1430, obliges him to teach 'pryksong' to the boys. See also Bowers, 'English church polyphony', 178 f, for the negative evidence concerning the fourteenth century.

peared from the papal chapel (see p. 163), whereas the Burgundian dukes sent their choristers to school in designated centres, where they also performed polyphony (see n. 18 above). The ordinances of 1469 do not mention them. Two years later, Duke Galeazzo Maria Sforza of Milan began to assemble a court chapel exclusively of adults. When requesting the chapel of his neighbour, the Duchess of Savoy, to sing for him (because he wanted to poach the best singers), he specified that he was not interested in the boys.[26] On the other hand, an institution such as Cambrai Cathedral relied on them for polyphonic music, certainly in chapels and perhaps in the choir. Dufay's will requested in 1474 that the choristers of the cathedral, with their master and two assistants, perform the four-part antiphon 'Ave regina celorum' at the composer's death-bed: this was the chapel ensemble.[27]

The main distinction between a princely chapel and one attached to a church is precisely that: the former is *not* attached to a church. In this case, the designation 'chapel' could become independent from the building and come to mean the musical ensemble itself.[28] A 'cathedral chapel', however, is properly the annex or little corner of the church where certain services are held by certain clerics. Even the relatively self-contained group of choirboys or vicars-choral who regularly perform a certain votive antiphon or Mass in a certain chapel are not therefore a 'chapel' themselves. They remain members of the choir, where they perform their main and – usually – their most onerous duties.

The obvious consequence is that the church musicians do their work in one or more chapels for extra remuneration. This they need, being among the lower-paid members of the cathedral choir; individual or collective patronage is the force behind chapel music. In that sense, the prince or prelate who maintains his own chapel is nothing but a more distinguished patron who has given his foundation a more permanent form. Unlike the citizens or guilds, a prince has to maintain all his chapel members throughout. He pays them a 'fixed salary' because he wants them to serve him exclusively and sing at least Mass and Vespers every day. Because of the many religious and ceremonial needs to be fulfilled in a princely chapel (one may think, for example, of all the Requiems for the ruler's ancestors), it is no surprise that many of them counted 10–20 men or more. These chaplains had to cater for everything, whereas the cathedral musicians were only a little group of specialists within a choir of canons and other priests, augmented by extra chaplains for extra Masses.[29] It is quite erroneous to claim that the number of three or four salaried singers of poly-

---

[26] Motta, *Musici*, 302 f (letters of 18 January and 30 October 1472).

[27] Houdoy, *Histoire artistique*, 410.

[28] Early unambiguous uses of the word with that meaning are contained in Duke Galeazzo Maria's 'recruiting letters' in Motta, *Musici*, 307 ff: for example, 'havere alcuni Cantarini per fare una Capella' (6 November 1472).

[29] Comparative figures for fifteenth-century Italian chapels are given in D'Accone, 'Performance'. They are very useful because the author does not, as others have done, jumble cathedral and courtly ensembles together. Under the conditions described here, the scale of Italian cathedral polyphony appears impressive.

phony in a cathedral account – as we have them for some Italian churches – reveals a low status for polyphonic music, in comparison with the two-figure personnel of princely chapels.[30] On the contrary: the four singers of Milan Cathedral about 1430, for example, were only the salaried specialists of polyphony (*biscantores*). To their voices, those of choirboys and other clerics could always be added as far as they were trained. (See also p. 587.) The system is not comparable to that of northern cathedrals either, where specialized singers may have been available, but besides the succentor nobody was engaged explicitly for polyphony.

Sometimes, one or two large confraternities dominated the life of a church so much with their spending power that they almost functioned as fixed employers of the musicians. This can be said, for example, of the *socii de musica* in some Flemish churches[31] and of the 'Singers of San Giovanni' at Florence.[32] The Florentine singers were named after their main (but not only) place of duty, the cathedral baptistry. This locale had the status of a chapel, or rather of an agglomeration of several chapels. The trade guilds of the *arte della lana* and the *arte di calimala*, i.e. of the wool and textile merchants, were responsible for the cathedral singers. The large parish church of St John at 'sHertogenbosch was culturally dominated by the *Illustre Lieve Vrouwe Broederschap*, a club of wealthy burghers who paid for the music. On account of this, mensural polyphony was performed here already in the 1330s.[33]

Choir music and chapel music compared

The distinction between the different localities within a medieval church, and its relevance for the respective music and its performance, may still have much to reveal.[34] 'Choir music' and 'chapel music' may one day become concepts as significant for fifteenth-century studies as *musica da chiesa* and *musica da camera* are for the study of Baroque music. Are we perhaps also dealing with different repertories?

There is, first, a strong likelihood that much of the provincial or primitive polyphony which will be described in the next chapter was performed in the choir. This repertory has older roots, was often cultivated in monasteries where musical specialization was not greatly encouraged, and also fits into the liturgical context of choir services. Significantly, no connections between this music and private patronage are known; the clergy or the monastic community introduced

---

[30] Pirrotta, 'Music and cultural tendencies', 129 and n. 7.
[31] See Forney, 'Music, ritual and patronage', 6 f.
[32] D'Accone, 'Singers'.
[33] Smijers, *Broederschap*, 5; see pp. 66 f above.
[34] The first suggestions in this direction have been made in Craig Wright, 'Voices and instruments in the art music of northern France during the fifteenth century: a conspectus', in Perkins, *Euphony*, 643–9.

this modest adornment on their own initiative, above all for the major feasts such as Christmas and Easter, and for liturgical genres which lacked a lay audience, such as lessons and responsory verses at Matins, or hymns. By contrast, privately endowed polyphony for a chapel (whether attached to a church or belonging to a prince) tends to be modern mensural music and to concentrate on Mass and Vespers as the two services which laymen will usually attend. Its liturgical application is either generic (votive Mass and votive antiphon) or it features specific patron saints, new feasts and devotions, secular allusions – such as lay patrons would be interested in. This is not only a contrast of styles. There are, for example, numerous cantus firmus Masses for Our Lady or for feasts of the Sanctorale, but (before the end of the fifteenth century) practically none for the highest feasts of the Temporale: the feasts of Our Lord and other seasonally fixed days, including Christmas and Easter. This must be due to practical conditions. Polyphonic Masses were endowed and caused additional duties for the clergy – and the clergy had more than enough to do on the highest feasts. Christmas, Easter etc. constituted an older layer of service music which had become statutory, whereas the younger layer was optional. These endowed ceremonies filled in the gaps in the calendar, encouraged new specializations among the clergy, created opportunities and answered personal wishes. I have argued above (p. 237) that the emergence of the polyphonic Mass cycle, and particularly of the cantus firmus cycle, is connected with this sphere of musical patronage. The motet and votive antiphon were even more characteristic 'chapel genres'. They were accretions to the liturgy and thus *a priori* not part of the choral duties, although they might sometimes have been inserted into Mass or Office services in the choir: in place of the sequence or offertory, or during the elevation or after the 'Deo gratias'. Much more often, motets were attached to votive services such as Marian Vespers or Compline in the Lady Chapel (especially settings of the 'Salve regina'), to suffrages and other brief endowed ceremonies in chapels, which comprised only a few prayers and chants, to *processions* when motets were sung at stations in front of special altars, and in more secular contexts in schools and refectories.

There must have been some overlap between these two types of music, of course. Endowments for services in the choir did happen, especially in smaller churches where there was still opportunity to expand and embellish. It is possible that Mass Ordinary settings of the fourteenth and early fifteenth centuries without cantus firmus were sometimes performed in the choir, and evidence for regular polyphonic singing in the choir on higher feasts is not lacking.[35]

In many areas, choral discanting must have been extemporized 'from the plainsong book' (*supra librum*), and this would be a reason why so little of this music has been preserved. The fauxbourdon and faburden repertories, as described above (p. 208), concentrated on Office and processional music as well as genres typically performed on or with the organ – hymns, *Magnificat* and

---

[35] Strohm, *Bruges*, 22.

Kyrie. Finally, in fifteenth-century England, central Europe and Italy, there is strong evidence for polyphonic singing of 'choral' items with at least the participation of unskilled clerics. Some of these items are late representatives of the more primitive practices of English discant; the continental pieces are analogously simple chant elaborations (*Choralbearbeitungen*). This type of music was performable with a virtually unlimited number of choir members who sang the plainsong from the book or by heart, whereas the musical specialists, and perhaps the organ, embellished and perhaps doubled the chant. This practice must be considered the beginning of 'choral' performance in the modern sense. It was used in the choir itself, or by the members of the choir in procession – in either case the great organ could be employed – and it could be heard and appreciated by congregation and bystanders. In this way, the collective music of the choir and the nave appealed to the community, whereas chapel polyphony was soloist music directed to *soloist listeners*.

Manfred Bukofzer tried to draw a distinction between soloist and choral polyphony in fifteenth-century sacred music.[36] Unfortunately, his criteria for 'choral polyphony' were weak: a homophonic–declamatory style can be observed in much fifteenth-century chapel music, but a large number of performers per part can rarely be shown to have been used. This problem arises, for example, with the English royal chapel, not a 'choir' but an ensemble of sixteen and more soloists, or with the ducal chapel of Ferrara, a particularly refined institution where specially composed double-chorus music for psalms and other Office chants inspired devotion in a tiny audience. (See also p. 604.) The label 'Chorus' in alternation with 'Unus' or an equivalent in works around the period of Ciconia and Dufay, and also in some carols, means something like 'ripienists' as opposed to 'soloists'. Cambrai Cathedral in the later fifteenth century had so many good singers of polyphony that the compositions were often copied in duplicate, so that everyone could see the music. Nevertheless, the performers were not a 'choir' but highly trained soloists. Finally, choral music does not simply arise where there is more than one singer per part, but rather where the music is of such a kind that potentially everyone, even the non-specialist, can join in.[37] This is at least how choral polyphony started in the fifteenth century, before it merged with chapel music (and *Kantorei* music, see below) in the Renaissance.

The functions of chapel music, and Dufay's last works

The cantus firmus Mass, the votive antiphon and the antiphon-motet of the later fifteenth century, as the main genres of chapel music, usually originated from endowments or other special commissions by individual or collective

---

[36] Bukofzer, *Studies*, ch. V ('The beginnings of choral polyphony').

[37] This latter definition is developed (although perhaps not consistently enough) in Hughes, 'Mensural polyphony for choir', and Hughes, 'Choir'.

patrons. It should therefore be possible to localize and date many more of these works than has hitherto been done, despite the usually very generic texts. Because there are technical features linking the isorhythmic motet to the tenor Mass, the latter genre has often been related to political events or other datable celebrations. The popular belief that a large number of Mass cycles were composed for dynastic weddings, coronations, peace treaties and so on is all the more convenient because any textbook of political history will tell us the exact date and place of the first performance. I suggest that such 'political' Masses do exist (see also p. 228) and may even constitute the origin of the genre, but that later on they are a minority. Contemporary chroniclers mention 'public' music of a very different spirit: trumpet fanfares, church bells, processional litanies, the *Te Deum*. What was performed in the chapel, we are not told.[38] Other types of documents, for example the contracts for endowments, must be consulted here. Inevitably, these lead us to ordinary and recurrent rather than extraordinary and unique events. It is unlikely indeed that the great Mass cycles and motets of the later fifteenth century were composed to be wasted on single performances.

This problem can now be illustrated by one particular case which may have extraordinary aspects but yet reflects general institutional customs: the case of Dufay's last works.

Alejandro Planchart's suggestion that Dufay composed his last Mass, 'Ave regina celorum', for the dedication of Cambrai Cathedral on 5 July 1472, has found wide acceptance, without there being any evidence.[39] Stylistically, the Mass seems to fit the date, and it was in fact copied into the Cambrai choirbooks in 1473–4. But the question is whether Dufay would actually have composed a Mass for this type of event – whether anyone would. The work is based on Dufay's motet of the same title with its very personal text insertion 'Miserere tui labentis Dufay' – musically, if not textually, recalled in the Agnus Dei[40] – and this motet was to be sung at Dufay's death-bed according to his will (see above). Since the motet, and therefore the Mass, are so obviously connected with a personal devotion, the possibility looms large that one or both of the works accompanied a personal endowment. We know of other such endowments by musicians.[41] It was simply a tradition in a medieval cathedral that each member of the choir left a bequest for at least a Requiem and if at all possible, donated more. Dufay made an endowment to Cambrai Cathedral well before making his will, and he stipulated, as other Cambrai canons had done before him, that music be sung annually for his personal patroness, the Virgin Mary. In the long lists of such memorial or 'obit' services, as exhibited by two contemporary obit

[38] The report about instrumental performances for the dedication of Florence Cathedral (1436) is scrutinized, with much additional material on such 'public' music, in Žak, 'Quellenwert'.
[39] Planchart, 'Fifteenth-century Masses', 20 ff; Fallows, *Dufay*, 78 and n. 20.
[40] Fallows, *Dufay*, 211.
[41] Strohm, *Bruges*, 40 f.

books from Cambrai,[42] known Cambrai canons occur in the role of benefactors: for example Symon le Breton, the Burgundian chaplain; Johannes Rodolphi alias Flamingi (he gave money for a motet); Egidius Flannel alias l'Enfant (a hymn and a motet); Michael de Beringhen (hymn and motet, 'Salve' and 'Inviolata' for the feast of the Visitation of Mary); the learned chapter dean and music theorist Gilles Carlier (a hymn 'Iste confessor', to be performed *alternatim*, and a motet for St Egidius's feast on 1 September; also a Mass 'de beata virgine'). Magister Gregorius Nicolai instituted a hymn and a motet for St Gregory; Magister Johannes Martini (not the composer) a Marian antiphon with *Magnificat* in plainsong, followed by a motet '*loco Benedicamus*', to be performed weekly by the six '*pueri altaris*' with their master and only one '*contratenens*'. Most of the endowments were for chapel performances. Dufay's is described thus in MS *B. 39*, fol. 56r:

> Die quinta Augusti in quaquidem solemnitas agitur sancte Marie ad Niues fiet de eadem beata maria missa celebris pro Magistro Guillermo du fay Canonico sacerdote quamdiu uiuet et post decessum eius obitus de xii lb. turon. distribuendis prout in missa domini decani continetur.

> [On the 5th of August, when the solemn feast of Saint Mary of the Snow is celebrated, will be sung a solemn Mass of the same Blessed Virgin Mary for Magister Guillermus Du Fay, canon and priest, throughout his lifetime, and after his death an obit, with 12 *livres* of Tours to be distributed in the manner as described in the Mass of the chapter dean.]

This is a very typical endowment for a polyphonic Mass cycle at the time. Comparison with other endowments recorded in this manuscript and in MS *B. 170* (including the one to which the entry explicitly refers: the Mass founded by the chapter dean, Gilles Carlier) suggests that: (a) Dufay's Mass 'de Beata Maria Virgine' was to be sung in polyphony by the *petits-vicaires* (*socii*) of the cathedral; (b) this was done annually on 5 August in the chapel of St Stephen where he had arranged for his burial; and (c) after his death (27 November 1474), the Marian Mass was replaced by an elaborate Office of the Dead, with vigil, and Requiem Mass in the morning, all celebrated in the chapel of St Stephen. This 'obit' is described in MS *B. 39*, fol. 31v, as including distribution of alms, candlelight, bellringing, the sequence 'Dies ire' sung by the choirboys, and other customary ceremonies. Apart from the *pueri altaris* with their master, the *petits-vicaires* also participated.

The total cost of the endowment would have been near 240 *livres* of Tours coinage, as the 12 pounds of distribution to the clergy corresponded to the

---

[42] Cambrai, Bibliothèque Municipale, MS *B.39* (fifteenth–sixteenth century) and MS *B.170* (fourteenth–fifteenth century). I examined both manuscripts in the autumn of 1982. Alejandro Planchart, whom I informed of these documents, discussed the endowment in his 'Guillaume Du Fay's benefices', 122 f, also reporting that Barbara Haggh concluded from later documentation that the endowment was in place in 1470.

annual interest only. For the obit, Dufay had to add another 97 *livres*. Dufay's will proves that he was a very wealthy man.[43]

From the handwriting and chronological order of the entries, it can be deduced that the endowment was made c.1470–72. It most probably preceded the dedication of Cambrai Cathedral on 5 July 1472. I suggest that Dufay composed his Mass 'Ave regina celorum' for his own endowment – which is also the reason why it is such a personal work – and in honour of Our Lady of the Snow, the same Madonna who had 'founded' Santa Maria Maggiore in Rome and had been invoked by 'Nuper rosarum flores' (see p. 169). The cult of *Notre-Dame aux Neiges* was widespread in the Low Countries at the time, and also in Germany and Bohemia, where many chapels and fraternities of *Maria Schnee* exist.[44] It had become popular during the Great Schism and afterwards, when northern churches and congregations demonstrated their attachment to Rome by celebrating the typically Roman feasts of the foundations of the city's basilicas. Probably, Dufay's choice of this particular devotion went back to his Roman years, or even to his youth.

An endowment for the dedication of Cambrai Cathedral, or rather for its anniversaries, exists as well (in MS *B. 39*). It was made by the canon Johannes du Rosut (*d.*1491), an executor of Dufay's will and thus closely acquainted with him. This elaborate endowment provides for a polyphonic motet and a hymn (a customary 'set', very probably performed in a procession) but *excludes* a polyphonic Mass Ordinary: du Rosut simply gave no money for it. Had the Mass 'Ave regina celorum' been composed for the dedication, then du Rosut, as an executor of the composer's will, would surely have seen to it that it was performed also on the anniversaries.[45]

If Dufay's work was used outside the terms of his own endowment, then it was most probably in chapel performances of other individual endowments – those of the canons Regnault de Lyons and Raoul Mortier, for example. Dufay had provided well enough for the posthumous fame of the Mass outside Cambrai by bequeathing a copy of it to Duke Charles the Bold. Certainly, with his own death and those of his colleagues, the work may have gradually disappeared from the cathedral repertory. Requiem Masses and Offices of the Dead inevitably replaced it.

The Requiem and the Office of the Dead complete this argument, because we know that Dufay composed polyphonic settings of both which are now lost.

---

[43] Fallows, *Dufay*, 216. See also Wright, 'Dufay at Cambrai', for the circumstances of his death. The will is published in Houdoy, *Histoire artistique*, 409–14. Dufay says in it that he has endowed seventeen annual Masses, of which he describes only sixteen: a fact that could have alerted scholars to the existence of a previous endowment. Of the sixteen Masses, that for St Anthony of Padua was also composed by Dufay himself, and was accompanied by ceremonies which included other performances of his works; see Fallows, 'Specific information', 117 f, and Houdoy, *Histoire artistique*, 412 f.

[44] For the musical activities of one such fraternity, see Strohm, *Bruges*, 47 f.

[45] The likelihood that the dedication on 5 July 1472 was celebrated with a ceremonial motet has increased, since Gerald Montagna connected Loyset Compère's motet 'Omnium bonorum plena' with that occasion: see Montagna, 'Caron, Hayne, Compère', 110–12.

The Requiem was copied at Cambrai in 1470–71, and Dufay states in his will that he left a manuscript containing it and his 'Missa Sancti Anthonii Viennensis' to the chapel of St Stephen – one would think that he wanted them to be performed in that chapel. Performances of the Requiem at Cambrai Cathedral itself are indeed documented between 1517 and 1521.[46] The Requiem also gained considerable external fame, as it was adopted by the courtly Order of the Golden Fleece and performed, together with Dufay's Office of the Dead, at its chapter meeting in Brussels in 1501. The chronicler reporting on the Brussels feast says of the composer (whom he does not actually name): 'having composed this Office of the Dead and a Mass for three voices, mournful, sad and very exquisite, he did not let them out during his lifetime, but left in his testament that they should be sung after his death for his soul'.[47] But the will, as we have it, does not actually say this. Dufay prescribes only one performance of the Requiem: on the day after his death (28 November). This is because the actual memorial service, the *anniversary* with Requiem Mass *and* Office of the Dead, was already stipulated in his endowment for 5 August and described in MS B. 39, fol. 31v, as the customary 'obit'. In the traditional terms of the endowment, the annual Mass for Our Lady of the Snow was to be replaced after Dufay's death with the annual Requiem and Office, 'sung for his soul'. Thus, the Mass 'Ave regina celorum' – Dufay's last surviving, splendid composition – yielded to the 'exquisite and mournful' three-part Office and Requiem for the first time on 5 August 1475. This is how Dufay had planned it, and we can be almost certain that the three works were composed by him together, some time about 1470–71.

Schools and the Kantorei

The many special duties performed by choirboys in chapels, in processions, in the choir – whether polyphonic singing or not – were possible only because these children were constantly being trained. Most of the larger medieval churches (including parish churches at least in cities) had a school. These parish, collegiate, cathedral and conventual schools offered virtually the only formalized education. The number of civic, non-clerical schools (teaching only in the vernacular) slowly increased in the fifteenth century.

The backbone of the medieval curriculum – with all its varieties – was music. The subject is too large for a full discussion here;[48] a few specific developments of the fifteenth century may be pinpointed. One of these is the remarkable growth of the musical curriculum and of its administration. The traditional system had been that one member of the choir (the *scholasticus*) was responsible

---

[46] Wright, 'Performance practices', 303.

[47] Prizer, 'Music and ceremonial', 133 ff.

[48] A useful survey is 'Education in music, §II and III' in *The New Grove*.

for all the educational needs; he may or may not have appointed deputies. By the fourteenth century, the involvement of the succentor (the assistant or deputy of the cantor) in the teaching of music had become regular in cathedral and collegiate churches, so that in many places he was henceforth referred to as the 'master of the children', although there was a separate teacher of grammar as well. The music lessons covered plainsong, extemporized discanting techniques, music theory (solmization, mensural notation, counterpoint) but also keyboard playing, for example.[49] It is no surprise, therefore, that even in a medium-size collegiate church such as St Gertrude, Bergen-op-Zoom, in addition to the grammar teacher two music teachers were needed by the 1460s: one responsible for plainsong and another for polyphony.[50]

The succentor, or master of the children, was often a 'professional', sometimes a layman. He was the reader, and occasionally the author, of manuscript and printed music theory (see also p. 595). Often he was a composer. His multiple tasks – to teach the children, to appear with them in services and 'public' performances, perhaps also to provide the music – is characteristic for the late medieval system. Whatever connection may now be discerned between music theory, education and practice in today's institutions, it is inherited from the medieval church schools.

In many churches, positions of succentors (or *magistri cantus* or whatever the term was) were created or consolidated in the early fifteenth century by special endowments. Correspondingly, the upbringing of the schoolboys themselves relied on generous donations and foundations, many of which established actual boarding schools. English colleges such as Winchester and Eton closely correspond to the many schools of the *bons enfants* in France and the Low Countries, or to establishments such as the famous *Mensa degli Accoliti* of Verona Cathedral, founded in 1440 with the consent of Pope Eugenius IV.[51] The latter was only one of a whole string of such foundations, commonly referred to as the *Scuole Eugeniane* (although the local bishops and citizens were usually the instigators and main benefactors), whose twofold purpose was that of providing charity to young people (in the form of free education) and better musical services to cathedrals. (See also p. 586.) The most important aspect is that the performance of music, often of up-to-date forms of polyphony, was requested from the boys and their teacher almost in return for the scholarships and housing received – whether they had to sing Masses and votive antiphons for the benefactor's soul, or be available for the more festive musical occasions the church had to observe. Since for many types of music adult voices besides that of the master were required, he often had to teach counterpoint to other

---

[49] Information about teaching duties is most readily available in Harrison, *Britain*, especially 177 ff and app. I and II; Bowers, *Choral Institutions*; Edwards, *English Secular Cathedrals*, 307–17; Becker, *Maîtrise*, ch. III; Wright, *Music and Ceremony*, ch. V.

[50] This is mentioned in the extremely interesting correspondence of the Flemish humanist Jan de Veere, *magister cantus* at Oudenburg; see Meersseman, 'L'Epistolaire', no. XXX.

[51] Paganuzzi *et al.*, *La musica a Verona*, 71 ff.

able clerics, particularly the younger ones. At the cathedral of León in 1467, the contract of the succentor (and composer) Alfonso de Belmonte obliged him to teach plainsong to practically the whole choir including the boys, but also 'Canto de órgano' (polyphony) and counterpoint to the gifted boys *and* canons and other beneficiaries of the choir.[52] This last stipulation is very significant, because it proves that clerics who were not statutorily responsible for the polyphony participated in it. The terms are very similar or even identical to those of the Italian cathedral foundations of the mid-fifteenth century.

But this was a truly European trend. The statutes of the *bonifanten* of St Pharahilde, Ghent (1423), are typical of many.[53] Here the schoolmaster was responsible to provide himself with a *cantere* who had to teach the boys 'discant, simple music' (i.e. plainsong) and 'good manners'. On the afternoons of Saturdays and of all days before feast-days, he and the schoolmaster together had to teach the schoolboys 'everything they have to sing in the choir' the following morning – which was essentially the plainsong repertory of the day. Those boys whose duty it was to sing daily in the choir – the actual choristers – were also taught daily, and their instruction included polyphony. The schoolmaster also had to appoint two *submonituers* (assistants) whose function in the school was a relatively humble one – only the teaching of 'good manners' is mentioned here – but who were musicians. They actually conducted the choirs (i.e. the general plainsong) in the dependent churches of St Michael's and St James's, and they appeared as musical specialists in endowed polyphonic Masses performed in the chapels of the main church itself.[54] No doubt they sang the contratenor parts there.

The *submonituers* of Ghent – young musicians who might have been choristers only a few years before, but who were already earning a living by conducting the music in peripheral churches – correspond to the assistants, 'helpers', vicars, *Astanten* in many other countries. They were the succentors and also the composers of the next generation. Many of them had received or were receiving a university education. Nicolaus Pfaldorff, one of the *Astanten* in the parish church of Bolzano, wrote, apparently for himself, an astronomical calendar (dated 1471) which is still preserved with his signature.[55] We know much about the music teaching in that particular parish school – for example, that the assistants did all the day-to-day work and that they used blackboards with music staves painted on them to teach counterpoint. The splendid polyphonic

---

[52] José M.a Álvarez Pérez, 'La Polifonia sagrada y sus maestros en la catedral de León (siglos XV y XVI)', *AnM* 14 (1959), 40. More specific even is the contract of the succentor of Ávila Cathedral of 1487: his duties included teaching 'canto llano e canto de órgano e contrapunto llano e dyminuydo' to four choirboys, but to other members of the choir only in so far as he could accommodate them. See Jaime Moll, 'El estatuto de maestro cantor de la Catedral de Ávila del año 1487', *AnM* 22 (1967), 89–95.

[53] Rijksarchief Gent, Sint-Veerle, S.228, fols. VIII ff.

[54] *Ibid* fol. XIX: 'and he also receives his share for the Masses sung with the choristers outside the high choir'.

[55] University College London, Ms. germ. I.

singing of choirboys in the area is documented, and the great mystery plays produced by the schoolmaster Benedikt Debs are another famous achievement of the Bolzano school. (See pp. 507 f.) In very similarly organized but bigger establishments such as the collegiate school of St Stephen's, Vienna, the parish school of St Jacob, Innsbruck, and the cathedral school of Trent, large and varied polyphonic repertories were collected (see pp. 506-11).

One could say that the schoolmasters, succentors and particularly their youngest assistants represented the cutting edge in musical progress of the day. The younger musicians had to be prepared to learn quickly and to take up jobs elsewhere at short notice like the travelling apprentices of other crafts and trades. Many manuscripts of polyphony and of theory originated in their hands: they compiled them in order to take advantage of the material in their next position. In this way, musical knowledge was disseminated to provincial areas as well. It is no surprise that the earliest documents of polyphonic music in Scandinavia are largely related to the business of schoolteachers.[56]

The little group of boys, adolescents and a singing-master who might be heard on Saturday evenings in a Lady Chapel or during processions in the streets, singing motets or carols, or performing mystery plays which their schoolmaster had written – it became a musical ensemble by itself: the *cantoria* or *Kantorei*. Whether or not a derivation of the term from the papal *schola cantorum* is accepted, the term 'Kantorey' appears in the fifteenth century as referring to the school building, often erected separately next to a church, where in some cases the choirboys lived. Just as with 'choir' and 'chapel', the term was then transferred to the musicians who performed and rehearsed there.[57] According to the circumstances, the group included not only the poor choristers who earned their bursary by singing, but also voluntary members, schoolboys as well as adults. In the urban environments of central and northern Europe, the *Kantorei* was soon so much a matter of public concern that the city magistrate took responsibility for it, sometimes engaging in long struggles for control with the Church authorities. The importance of the school and *Kantorei* for music history during the Reformation and Baroque periods may become immediately clear if we add to the examples of Bolzano, Trent, Innsbruck and Vienna that of St Thomas's of Leipzig.[58]

'Kantorei music' would have to be sought – if we can hope to isolate a repertory here – in the musical codices written by the schoolmasters and their assistants. The practice gets under way with the 'motet books' (*libri motetorum*) of

[56] See, for example, the large collection of the *Piae cantiones* (1582), which contain much medieval material; Norlind, 'Schwedische Schullieder'; generally on early Swedish polyphony: see Carl-Allan Moberg, 'On flerstæmmig musik i Sverige under medeltiden', *STMf* 10 (1928), 5-92.

[57] Pietzsch, *Fürsten*, anachronistically uses *Kantorei* to denote a princely chapel (ensemble), and *Kapelle* for princely instrumental bands. The identification of court singers as the *Kantorey* began in the sixteenth century.

[58] See Wustmann, *Musikgeschichte Leipzigs*; Knick-Mezger, *St Thomas*. For an important stretch of history between the fifteenth century and J. S. Bach, see Klaus W. Niemöller, *Untersuchungen zu Musikpflege und Musikunterricht an den deutschen Lateinschulen vom ausgehenden Mittelalter bis um 1600* (Regensburg: Bosse, 1969).

French and Netherlands churches in the fourteenth century. Although they contained not only motets (the term designated polyphonic art-music in general), it was especially the isorhythmic motet of Vitry and his followers which must have been handed down by schoolmasters in performance and instruction.[59] In the fifteenth century, the majority of the more extensive collections originating in central Europe seem to belong to this sphere. We may think of manuscripts such as the St Emmeram Codex (*Em*) of Magister Hermann Pötzlinger,[60] the Trent Codices 90, 88, 89 and 91 (the work of Magister Johannes Wiser), the large, miscellaneous Nicolaus Leopold Codex (*D-Mbs 3154*) which was probably compiled by a series of Innsbruck schoolmasters,[61] the Apel Codex (*D-LEu 1494*) of Leipzig University.[62] Equally interesting are smaller sources such as the tablature of the Stendal schoolmaster Adam Ileborgh of 1448,[63] the Kraków collection *PL-Kj 2464*, where the scribe Rambowski sarcastically annotates somebody else's compositions, and the collection of international favourites compiled by schoolmaster Johannes Greis of Benediktbeuern Abbey in 1495 (*D-Mbs lat. 5023*).[64] Common features are a rather miscellaneous nature and yet an unmistakable link with liturgical practice. The users had to perform in church every day, but many of the pieces served only for teaching purposes or for fun between school hours. Typically the manuscripts display many scribal hands, rounding out the work of one dominating scribe. This pattern of scribal collaboration is almost a portrait of the *Kantorei*. The assistants learned music and musical notation by filling the master's book.

The Benediktbeuern manuscript is one of the many which also evoke a monastic atmosphere (see below). As regards the musical education of women, the convent schools of nunneries were practically the only place where such an education could take place in a formalized manner.

Music books originating in schools must exist in other countries as well; they have only to be identified. Of the innumerable English fragments, some surely originated in colleges and for educational as well as performance purposes. The Pepys Manuscript (*GB-Cmc Pepys 1236*) comes close to what might be interpreted as an English schoolmaster's collection. In Italy and France, the situation seems different, or the manuscript losses in this particular sphere are greater.

The universities

The St Emmeram, Apel and Kraków codices are also linked to universities (Vienna, Leipzig and Kraków, respectively): institutions which were responsi-

---

[59] One of the latest Netherlands sources of this type seems to be the 'Battre section' of *Tr 87*, described above (p. 255).

[60] See p. 259; Rumbold, 'Compilation of Munich Clm 14274'.

[61] Noblitt ed., *Kodex Leopold* (edn in progress); see also p. 519 below.

[62] Gerber–Finscher–Dömling eds, *Mensuralkodex Apel* (complete edn).

[63] See C. Wolff, 'Ileborgh, Adam' in *The New Grove*; edn (unreliable) by W. Apel ed., CEKM 1.

[64] See, respectively, *CC*, vol. 2, 22 and 237.

ble for teaching music.[65] In the fifteenth century, their contribution to the development of music theory was strangely haphazard, as was that development itself. Whereas the works of Magister Prosdocimus de Beldemandis (*d.*1428) were a product of the Paduan university environment, the largest theoretical opus of the century, that of Johannes Tinctoris, originated at Naples under the influence of courtly and cathedral practice. While studying at the University of Orléans, Tinctoris had also been succentor at the local church of Sainte-Croix, where he may have developed his keen didactic sense.[66]

The fifteenth century was a period of great decentralization in the European university system, and this led to the transfer of music theory from one tradition into the other. It is most probable that Vienna, Kraków and Leipzig inherited a notational system developed at Prague University in the fourteenth century.[67] These universities formed a related group; musical learning was also exchanged with Bologna, Padua and Ferrara.[68] The encyclopedic *Liber viginti artium* by Paulus Paulirinus (Židek) is a typical product of these contacts. Paulus (1413– after 1471) was active at the universities of Vienna, Prague, Padua and Kraków. Music forms only a small section of his description of the liberal and other arts, although he is a sharp observer of contemporary practices.[69] In many university curricula containing music as one of the liberal arts, studies proceeded little beyond Boethius and Jehan des Murs' *Musica speculativa*. By a telling coincidence, the only written reflection of mensural theory as taught at Paris in Ockeghem's time are the lecture notes (?) taken down by the Austrian Georg Erber and preserved at Innsbruck (dated 1460).[70]

It seems that English, Italian and Spanish music theory were already in contact by the fourteenth century, and not only through Paris. A significant biography is that of the scholar John Hothby, who taught at Oxford in 1435, but then travelled widely before settling in Italy. His many treatises were disseminated in the university and monastic circles of Pavia, where he studied together with Johannes Legrense (Gallicus) from Namur, and of Florence and Lucca, where he later worked (see also p. 586). The University of Pavia seems to have had a significant tradition of music-making and music theory. Already in 1391 we find the name of an Englishman, Frater G. de Anglia, as a copyist of music theory at Pavia (see p. 58). In 1474 the humanist and musician Rudolf Agricola praised the new rector of the university, Johann von Dalberg, for his musical

[65] See the Round Table reports: Wright (chairman), 'La musica nella storia delle università'; and 'L'enseignement de la musique au Moyen Age et à la Renaissance' (Editions Royaumont, 1985). The most comprehensive survey is Carpenter, *Universities*. Archival data relating to central Europe are in Pietzsch, *Zur Pflege*; for France, see Pirro, 'Enseignement', for Salamanca, Gómez, 'Prehistoria'.

[66] Woodley, 'Tinctoris', 225–9.

[67] See Ward, 'A central European repertory'; Ward, 'Music and music theory'.

[68] F. Alberto Gallo, 'L'Europa Orientale e l'Italia tra il XIV e il XV secolo', in *Università di Bologna. Convegni sulla musica Italiana e Polacca* (Bologna, 1980), 29–44.

[69] See M. Velimirovic, 'Paulirinus, Paulus' in *The New Grove*; Rustena Mužiková, 'Pauli Paulirini de Praga Musica mensuralis', *Acta Universitatis Carolinae*, Philosophica et historica 2 (1965), 57–87.

[70] Federhofer-Königs, 'Proportionenlehre'; but see also Pirro, 'Enseignement'.

learning. This man was apparently known to Hothby's circle as the composer 'Johannes de Erfordia'.[71]

Music degrees were instituted at Cambridge and probably Oxford in the mid-fifteenth century; there is a claim that a 'chair of music' existed two centuries earlier at Salamanca.[72] A chair of music was endowed at Bologna in 1450, but the Spanish theorist Bartolomeo Ramos de Pareia failed to be appointed when living in Bologna between 1472 and 1482, and apparently nobody else was appointed either. From Ramos (and probably already from his teachers Juan de Monte and Pedro de Osma, the latter active at Salamanca) on the one hand, and Hothby on the other, two strongly opposed traditions of Italian theory descended, leading to the sixteenth-century discussions of the hexachordal and tonal systems (see also p. 596). A very influential figure in these debates was the composer and theorist Franchinus Gaffurius, who in the 1490s taught music in the Sforza *studio* of Parma / Milan. In other countries too, university teachers of this generation began creatively to engage in the development of the art.[73]

Little is known about extracurricular musical life in universities, grammar schools and colleges. Students sang and played many sorts of instruments in their dormitories; from time to time this had to be forbidden.[74] The humanist and scientist Hartmann Schedel of Nuremberg (1440–1514) collected the famous songbook carrying his name during his student years at Leipzig and Padua (1461–7); polyphonic love-songs, contrafacta and dance-tunes like these may have been circulating at almost any European university. Another story, which may sound more extraordinary to us than it really was, concerns the blind brothers Johannes and Karolus Fernandes, professors at Paris and widely reputed virtuosos on soft instruments. Tinctoris praised their playing, and the well-travelled motet 'Gaudent in celis' by Alexander Agricola was apparently part of their repertory.[75] Many university people had musical positions outside the university, or could enrich the institutional life with their musical expertise. At Kraków, for example, two members of the episcopal chapel, Blasius and Othmar Opilionis from Jawor, were registered students in 1441.[76] A textless

---

[71] Five pieces are ascribed to him in the Hothby-related appendix of the Faenza Codex (see p. 298). Dalberg had acquired his first degree in Erfurt, 1470; more on him in Pietzsch, *Zur Pflege*, 105 and 116.

[72] Stevenson, *Spanish Music*, 47 and n. 153. In 1254 not a professor of music but a *maestro en organo* is employed, comparable to a music master of a cathedral school. Music as a university discipline appears in 1313, and a *cátedra* in 1411. See Gómez, 'Prehistoria', 80 f.

[73] We might mention Johannes Cochlaeus of Cologne University, who from 1510 directed a humanist-inspired parish school at Nuremberg, and his student Heinrich Glareanus of Basle. For music at Basle University, see Nef, 'Basel'. The earliest of these south German musical humanists was Conrad of Zabern (*c.*1390–*c.* 1480), who taught at Heidelberg, Freiburg, Basle and Ingolstadt universities. His four treatises (see Gümpel, *Musiktraktate*) are practical manuals, but with wider educational goals.

[74] The manuscript statutes of a college of Freiburg University (1497) contain illustrations of the prohibited activities and thus become an iconographic source for the music: see Bowles, *Musikleben*, pl. 144.

[75] The piece is headed 'Cecorum' and 'Ferdinandus et frater ejus', respectively, in two sources, and also has the text incipit 'Cecus non judicat de coloribus' in one of them; see Strohm, *Bruges*, 143.

[76] Pietzsch, *Zur Pflege*, 44 and 55.

composition by the latter is in the codex *Tr 93*. At Vienna, Magister Thomas Oedenhofer of Munich taught music privately to students and citizens (including the burgomaster's daughter). One of his pupils, Andreas Kaufringer of Augsburg, was in contact with members of the imperial chapel as well as with Hartmann Schedel.[77] Princely chaplains very often attended the universities, and the master's degrees of Busnois, Obrecht and others remind us how much the universities were also potential meeting places for leading composers.

The regular duties of providing music for university feasts devolved, of course, mostly on a *Kantorei* attached to the university or college chapel. Its members must have included at least some of the poorer students. Annual feasts of the *nationes, bursen* (halls) or faculties often included polyphonic Masses. This may have been the case even in places such as Tübingen. In the year of this university's foundation (1477), two annual Lady Masses with organist, *rector scholarium* and indeed 'poor scholars' were instituted,[78] as well as a Mass for St Katherine, the patroness of scholars. As with the many English colleges, where a fine chapel ensemble performed regularly, educational institutions benefited from the greater influx of gifted students without there being any fundamental difference from cathedral or parish schools.

Singing in public

The poor students and schoolboys needed to earn a living beyond their small bursaries. Apart from catering for endowed Masses and other services in church, the *Kantorei* also developed a habit of singing for money to celebrate a visiting prince and in festal periods. This custom, called *Ansingen* in Germanic lands, was tolerated and even encouraged by the authorities; in some areas it expanded to many feasts of the calendar. Ecclesiastical and civic accounts document the sums which the students earned by this 'freelance' activity (and which they had to take back to their schoolmaster). The practice can be associated, of course, with the musical homages and pageants for festive royal visits, and for the nobility in general, which were provided throughout Europe by the younger members of the churches and schools in the hope of reward. The travel accounts of Duke Albrecht VI of Austria (see p. 309) record his many payments to local schoolboys and girls who 'sang before my Lord' (*die meins hern gnad angesungen habendt*). Between December 1467 and June 1470, the boy choristers of the following local churches sang Mass or secular music 'devant mondit seigneur', Charles the Bold:

> Louvain (City hall), Utrecht (dinner table), The Hague (ducal chapel), Louvain (St Peter's), Middelburg/Flanders (in the town of Aardenburg), Hal/Brabant (in church), Vere (Mass at the palace), Middelburg/Flanders (daily Masses), Nieuwpoort (Mass).[79]

[77] *Ibid.*, 30 f and 34 f.
[78] *Ibid.*, 139 f.
[79] Higgins, *Busnois*, 80 f n. 144. For further examples of *Ansingen*, see Moser, *Hofhaimer*, 73.

The repertories used by schoolboys and students when either honouring a prince in his lodgings or going from house to house and singing for money (a practice called the *Kurrende* in Germany), were surely quite varied. In central Europe, the Latin cantio (see p. 327) would probably constitute most of the material. Besides, there were of course vernacular carols or whatever corresponded to them in the various countries and on the various festive occasions: Czech and Polish *koledy*,[80] Spanish sacred villancicos, Italian *laude*, German *Weihnachts-lieder* and so on. A ceremony very probably instituted to benefit the youngsters was the carol singing (and often dancing) around a crib which was put up in the nave of parish churches, as documented in England, Flanders, Germany and Spain. This was usually referred to as *kindelwiegen* (child rocking).[81] A tradition common to several countries is that of macaronic texts – curious mixtures of Latin and vernacular, such as can have arisen in Latin schools every day.

Cantiones and carols – for various seasons and subjects – are increasingly found in artistic counterpoint (*cantus figuratus*); usually they are mixed together with figural music in the manuscripts, for example with hymn settings or Marian antiphons. The *Kantorei* used a good deal of music in its liturgical tasks and 'freelance' tours and any music could serve for its own entertainment and practice; as a result the stylistic division disappeared. A collection as comprehensive as the later Trent Codices includes pieces for the street concerts. The Swedish–Finnish *Piae cantiones* of 1582 (which contain much medieval material, monophonic and polyphonic) is probably a collection for singing in school and in the streets.[82]

It may be through lack of research that we know very little of these practices in France. In Italy, the type of music discussed here was cultivated not so much in the schools as in confraternities formed by adult citizens: the *laudesi*. The *lauda* repertory of this period is formally analogous to the other genres but has, on the whole, a less celebrative and more devotional, spiritual character (see also p. 593).

The most popular saints celebrated in carols, *koledy* etc. were St Martin, St Thomas Becket (in England) and especially St Nicholas. This reminds us that the whole tradition has its roots in the clerical feasts of the Middle Ages, mainly from the Christmas period. The 'Feast of Fools', or of the 'Boy Bishop', which focused on the days between Christmas and Epiphany (often with a climax on Holy Innocents' Day, 28 December) had the choirboys and young clerics as its main actors–performers. Their satirical impersonations of Church authorities ('Pope of Asses', 'Boy Bishop') and rituals (mock processions, mock

---

[80] See 'Koleda' in *The New Grove*; Kouba–Skalická, 'Koledy'; Anna Petneki, 'Die polnischen Kolenda-Lieder im Mittelalter', *SM* 15 (1973), 165–73.

[81] See Ameln, 'Resonet'; Greene, *Carols* ('The carol as dance song'); Walter Salmen, 'Weihnachtsgesänge des Mittelalters in westfälischer Aufzeichnung', *KJb* 36 (1952), 26–9. See also p. 329 below.

[82] Norlind, 'Schwedische Schullieder'. School songs and congregational songs are listed in the *Ord-nung* of a German school of 1480: see Johannes Janota, 'Schola cantorum und Gemeindelied im Spätmittelalter', *JbLH* 24 (1980), 37–52.

plainsongs), their Masses and banquets generated much special music including theatrical and convivial songs, of which little has been preserved or studied.[83]

By the fifteenth century, sacred pageants and theatre were no longer a unified tradition depending on the churches alone. Minstrels and ordinary citizens were actively involved; the divergent vernacular traditions transformed the common material. It should be remembered, however, that choirboys and schoolboys (and I believe, also schoolgirls), remained the foremost singers almost everywhere. In the play cycles of English guilds (such as the York cycle), the references to music regularly specify 'angels' or 'shepherd boys' as the singers. The surviving two-part pieces in the York Weavers' Play[84] are composed for two high voices alone. Where low voices were required, older students or 'assistants' who regularly sang with the choirboys can have provided them. In Flemish cities, the succentors of the churches were the authors of mystery plays, and the performers were their schoolboys. Rehearsals took place at school, performances in cathedral refectories and increasingly outdoors.[85] The large group of Tyrolean mystery plays from *c.*1500,[86] and the tradition of the humanist school drama,[87] are both products of this pedagogical sphere. In Florence under Lorenzo de' Medici, boy confraternities existed for the performance of *sacre rappresentazioni*.[88] An amazing variety of practices and repertory is found in the Iberian musical theatre.[89] These examples could be multiplied, but the subject of music in the theatre certainly goes beyond the realm of churches and schools, and diversifies into national, regional and stylistic threads that must be taken up one at a time.

Music in monastic life

The attitude of the 'regulars' towards music was more varied and more dynamic than some may assume. The different types of monastic orders held different opinions about the dignity or usefulness of music, and opinions also changed with time, in some cases radically.

The old monastic orders (Benedictines, Cistercians, Carthusians, Austin canons etc.) had outlived their great contributions to plainsong; the last of these had been the sequences of the Augustinian Abbey of St Victor, Paris, in

[83] Wulf Arlt, *Ein Festoffizium des Mittelalters aus Beauvais in seiner liturgischen und musikalischen Bedeutung* (Cologne, 1970); Heers, *Fêtes*.
[84] Wall-Steiner, 'York pageant'. See also Dutka, 'Mystery plays'; Carpenter, 'Mystery plays'.
[85] For examples, see Strohm, *Bruges*, 33-6, 44 ff.
[86] Partly edited, with music, in Walter Lipphardt and Hans-Gert Roloff eds, *Die geistlichen Spiele des Sterzinger Spielarchivs*, vol. 1 (Berne etc.: Lang, 1981).
[87] See, for example, Sternfeld, 'Schools'; Dent, 'Music and drama'; K. G. Hartmann and J. Bužga, 'Schuldrama' in *MGG*.
[88] Trexler, 'Ritual'.
[89] Fundamental: R. B. Donovan, *The Liturgical Drama in Medieval Spain* (Toronto, 1958). A detailed study of Catalan plays is Jésus-Francesc Massip, 'El repertorio musical en el teatro medieval Catalan', *Revista de musicologia* 10 (1987), 721-52.

the twelfth century. Nevertheless, there was a great deal of music-making in late medieval abbeys which was neither part of their chant traditions nor always compatible with their rule. In some areas (England, Austria) the Benedictines and Austin canons were often in charge of parishes and schools. Among their musical reactions to such tasks, the monks at least celebrated the clerical feasts (see above). Benedictine houses, in particular, also liaised with trade guilds, courts and the nobility, providing refined hospitality and, at times, a worldly musical environment.[90] The Trecento composer Vincenzo da Rimini was a Benedictine abbot and is depicted in his habit in the Squarcialupi Codex; another Benedictine was the composer Bartolomeo da Bologna, organist at Ferrara Cathedral *c.*1410. To higher-ranking members, these orders allowed the pursuit of music in all its aspects.

When a wave of monastic reforms reached the old orders in the early fifteenth century, it revealed, and unfortunately extinguished, much of the indulgence in contemporary musical trends. The Schottenkloster in Vienna probably ranked among the leading musical institutions of the city when changes began to be made in 1418. In the course of the Benedictine 'Reform of Melk'[91] in this region, visitation reports denounce secular or popular music in the abbeys, as well as liturgical dance. The guidelines imposed by the reforming superiors seem to have had two distinguishable effects: (a) vocal polyphony in general was banned, but not instrumental polyphony – this stimulated the polyphonic use of the organ, also in the liturgy; and (b) criticism of 'dance-like' triple metres in hymn singing resulted in a recognizably new style of hymn composition in duple metre ($\mathician{C}$) which suddenly appears about 1455–60 in Italy and Germany.

Giulio Cattin gives a vivid account of the changing attitudes at Santa Giustina, Padua, around 1410, when the reformers almost eradicated a flourishing musical life.[92] It had been supported by the local dynasty, the Carrara family, and by contacts with the cathedral and the university – institutions for which the monk Rolandus de Casale may have copied polyphonic music. After the reform, Italian Benedictines continued to cultivate only primitive polyphony and Latin *laude*. They eschewed vernacular texts, which were favoured by the mendicants.

The role of public preachers and missionaries, which the mendicant orders had assumed, directed them even more towards the cultural needs of the laity. But their more aggressive involvement in the world contrasts, elsewhere, with the most austere or anti-cultural attitudes. The typical strategy was that of the Franciscans who introduced vernacular sacred songs in order to make people abandon the secular texts. Whereas most of the radical Franciscans were anti-musical, the orders of the traditional observance greatly encouraged sacred song and simple polyphony in England, Ireland, the Netherlands, Germany

---

[90] For a few examples, see Strohm, *Bruges*, 61; Flotzinger–Gruber, *Musikgeschichte Österreichs I*, 105–16; Strohm, 'European politics', 313 f; Cattin, 'Ricerche S. Giustina'.
[91] See Angerer, *Melker Reform*.
[92] Cattin, 'Ricerche S. Giustina'.

and elsewhere. Many Italian manuscripts containing simple polyphony, or elements of music theory, are of Franciscan origin. The introduction of polyphonic music to Poland (in the thirteenth century) and to Hungary (in the fifteenth century) is apparently due to Franciscans. The leading medieval universities were largely dominated by mendicants, and musical friars are found in Oxford, Paris, Pavia, Salamanca, Vienna and Cologne. The Carmelites, inclined to scholarship in all the fields, were a particularly musical order.[93] One known Carmelite composer was Bartolino da Padova (perhaps also a university man). The reform of this order in the mid-fifteenth century resulted in an Italian 'Congregation of Mantua' which was musically productive, perhaps under the inspiration of the Mantuan court humanist Vittorino da Feltre. The Faenza Codex of early keyboard music (see pp. 90 f) was used and enlarged around 1470–74 in this circle. It contains several pieces by Hothby and Johannes de Erfordia, together with theoretical writings by Hothby and others, including the Flemish Carmelite Johannes Bonadies (Godendach), the teacher of Gaffurius, and Nicasius Weyts, a Carmelite schoolmaster from Bruges.[94] The related order of the Servites in Tuscany (*Servi di S Maria*) organized polyphonic performances in their Florentine house of SS Annunziata; they may even have had a scriptorium producing French chansonniers (see p. 560). The Carmelite church of SS Annunziata in Naples may have been a musical centre; Gaffurius was its choirmaster between 1478 and 1480. An important Carmelite centre of music around 1500 was St Anna in Augsburg. Its contacts with the Habsburg court and its chapel, its famous grammar school and its tradition of organ-playing, deserve further study.[95]

Surely the most creative activity of these orders with respect to music was the cultivation of lay confraternities. They were, in a sense, support groups, gathered around certain devotions promoted by the regulars, or seeking a spiritual home in the seclusion of the convents.[96] These mostly bourgeois, wealthy associations were receptive to artistic music. In England and the Low Countries, the earliest polyphonic Lady Masses were probably sung by lay clerks and friars together.

Reform movements within the mendicant orders grew strong in the fourteenth century. The *laudesi* associations in Italy (especially Florence), the central and south European flagellants and pilgrimage organizations were usually influenced by reformed friars. But even radical groups among the Italian flagellants (*disciplinati*) held elaborate ceremonies with the singing of Latin or Italian *laude* or such items as the 'Stabat mater' for Holy Week or the 'Tenebrae'

---

[93] Strohm, *Bruges*, 66.

[94] On him and his humanistic connections, see Strohm, *Bruges*, 43 f, 52 and 66; Meersseman, 'L'Epistolaire'.

[95] See Cuyler, *Emperor Maximilian*; Mahrt, *Missae ad organum*.

[96] See Strohm, *Bruges*, 60–73.

Offices.[97] Other Florentine *laudesi*, however, borrowed secular polyphonic songs for sacred contrafacta, thus initiating the polyphonic vernacular *lauda*. Some Trecento composers were in touch with these circles.[98]

One of the broadest movements which mixed monastic ideals and lay culture was the *devotio moderna* (new devotion). We really have two or three related groups, all arising in the late fourteenth century in the northern Netherlands. The 'Brothers of the Common Life', founded in 1391 by Geerd Groote in Deventer, were specifically a lay congregation, and were even initially in conflict with the official Church. Their devotion was to some extent detached from liturgical traditions, and their music developed in a spirit of great austerity and simplicity (see also p. 322). A model for Groote in spiritual and probably musical matters was the Carthusian monk and professor Heinrich Eger von Kalkar (1328–1408), whose *Cantuagium* (Cologne, 1380) teaches plainchant.[99]

The greatest wave of monastic reforms in this area took shape in the 'Windesheim Congregation' (and in a similar one with its centre in Bursfelde, northern Germany). This was a group of Augustinian priories, centred on the house of St Agnetenberg near Zwolle (founded in 1386). The Augustinian canons of the area (the diocese of Utrecht) had always been interested in music, and their chant books survive in hundreds. Although mensural polyphony was shunned by them, the whole range of semiliturgical tropes, *cantiones*, carols, and simple polyphony, was part of their tradition. The most famous later representative of the movement, Thomas a Kempis (1380–1471), the probable author of the *Imitatio Christi* (1441), was a keen musician. We have poems for music as well as probably the notated melodies from his own hand.[100]

Although the Czech religious reformers around Johannes Hus did not have monastic affiliations – Hus used to preach in parish churches – the strong congregational spirit in their movement was somehow analogous to that of the 'Brothers of the Common Life'. There is a number of musical links between the two movements, one being the pieces of Bohemian provenance collected in a manuscript from a Windesheim monastery near Treves.[101]

---

[97] Cyrilla Barr, 'Lauda singing and the tradition of the disciplinati. Mandato: a reconstruction of two texts of the Office Tenebrae', *L'Ars Nova* 4 (1978), 21–37.

[98] See von Fischer, 'Quelques remarques'; Kurt von Fischer, 'Stefani, Andrea' in *The New Grove*.

[99] Heinrich Hüschen ed., *Das Cantuagium des Heinrich Eger von Kalkar* (Cologne, 1952).

[100] *B-Br 3075–83*. A closely related manuscript from the Windesheim house of St Victor, Xanten, is *D-Mbs, Clm 28546* (with sacred songs by Thomas, and the two-part 'Ave pulcherrima regina': see p. 332). A central source for the customs of the Windesheim congregation is *B-Br 10876–83*, fols. 145–253: this contains the *ordinarius divini officii* of the congregation, and rules about music as observed in the Rooclooster nr. Brussels. 'Counterpoint' is forbidden (fol. 245v). Nevertheless, the manuscript was soon after bound together with some music treatises, including the famous chant manual *Flores musicae* by Hugo Spechtshart (printed edn, Strasbourg, 1487) as well as a little treatise on – counterpoint! On the *devotio* and music, see also Heinrich Husmann, 'Die mittelniederländischen Lieder der Berliner Handschrift 8°190', *IMSCR Utrecht 1952*, 241–51; Konrad Ameln, 'Geistliche Lieder der Devotio moderna', *JbLH* 2 (1956), 145–6.

[101] Ewerhart, *Handschrift 322/1994*. See also p. 337 below.

Music and the secular authorities

Medieval societies did not distinguish between the 'public' and 'private' spheres in the same way as we do. To have a sheltered sphere for oneself, filled with individually chosen pursuits such as music or literature, was a social privilege. The common people had no private sphere except, perhaps, the loneliness of the woods and plains where the shepherd boy would pipe his tune. The music of the common people was collective and 'public' in the sense that nobody was excluded from it. The Church did operate with exclusions, privileges and reserved spaces, but its activities were collective and not 'private'. Nobles and princes lived mostly in the same open world, surrounded by the official sounds of their trumpeters. They were able to carve out secluded spheres for themselves, however: chapel, hall and chamber within the palaces corresponded to increasing degrees of privacy (see below). The bourgeois and merchant classes – patrons of church music well before 1400 – gradually developed the individualist, home-orientated or humanist approaches which generated middle-class *Hausmusik* from the mid-fifteenth century onwards.

As long as these classes were struggling for political control, however, their use of music was mostly extrovert and assertive. Before music could embellish anyone's privacy, it had to help affirm his authority. The loud music (*alta musica, haute musique*) of trumpeters, pipers and drummers was used in the fifteenth century by civic authorities just as much as by princes, prelates and noblemen. This 'public' category of music also extended into church (into the nave only, to be sure) and into official buildings such as town halls and guild-halls, where more or less exclusive but collective banquets and balls were held. Soft music (*bassa musica, basse musique*) of stringed instruments, chamber organs, soft woodwinds and, of course, voices, could fill the chamber of a very rich man, but usually also served him in collective or 'public' activities such as a dinner with prominent guests. Whoever aspired to any kind of secular authority (and that certainly included city magistrates and craft guilds, English college provosts or Italian *condottieri*) needed the public honour and *decorum* provided by music in his service.[102]

Having said so much (or so little) about the patrons and organizers of 'public' music, who were the performers? The collective name of *minstrel* is appropriate to every type of professional musician serving secular patrons, whether he or she sings, dances to musical accompaniment, plays one or more instruments (alone or with others), and whether this music is sacred or secular. It is not the types of music that were divided, but rather the people who performed them. The city wait remained a minstrel when walking with the Corpus Christi procession and playing hymn-tunes as part of his official duties as a civic servant. On the other hand, a layman who sang in a princely chapel, who also played

---

[102] Thus, an important survey of music in the service of secular authorities, by Sabine Žak, is entitled *Musik als 'Ehr und Zier'* [honour and ornament].

instruments, and composed and performed chansons, was not a minstrel because of the sacred status of the chapel. The rift between minstrels and church musicians is very important for the fifteenth century, and can be followed through all the official documents such as payrolls. It was to some extent interdependent with social extraction and to a large extent with literacy. The ecclesiastical status was above the professional, whereas the minstrel's craft ranked at the lowest end of the professional scale, on the basis of a long discriminatory tradition.[103] The view that musical professionalism was a social disqualification lasted well beyond the Middle Ages. Bourgeois and noble musicians of the Renaissance were anxious to demonstrate their amateur status.[104]

Cross-overs surely did occur. A fourteenth-century friar is reported to have advised a boy *not* to learn instruments but rather to become a choirboy.[105] Such an option might have applied to a lowly born youngster who would normally have remained illiterate and learned a craft (such as the musical one), but had the gifts for a church career. The heir of a merchant family, on the other hand, would never consider a career in music. At the other end of the development, there were minstrels' families which, in the course of generations, levelled with the urban merchant class, for example the Nagel and Schubinger 'dynasties' in Augsburg and other trading centres.[106] They had started possibly as travelling minstrels and social outcasts, after which the most important step was the admission into service as official city waits and the acquisition of citizenship. From that point on, accumulating wealth was easy for good musicians in the prosperous cities. Their integration into the guild system is also shown, for example, by the existence of proper legal contracts between masters and prospective apprentices for instruction in one or several instruments.[107] More ambiguous are the courtly careers. Among the lay musicians at court, usually referred to as *valets de chambre*, there were composers such as Jacob

---

[103] For generalized approaches to the social history of minstrels, see Salmen, *Spielmann*; Werner Danckert, *Unehrliche Leute* (Berne, 1963); Rastall, 'Minstrelsy', 83–98; Heinrich W. Schwab, *Die Anfänge des weltlichen Berufsmusikertums in der mittelalterlichen Stadt* (Kassel etc.: Bärenreiter, 1982). A rich compendium is Whitwell, *Wind Band*. Most of the other literature is geographically focused. Significant contributions are Bridgman, *Vie musicale*; Zoltán Falvy, 'Spielleute im mittelalterlichen Ungarn', *SM* 1 (1961), 29–64; E. Faral, *Les jongleurs en France au moyen âge* (Paris, 1910/R 1964); Louis Gilliodts-van Severen, *Les ménestrels de Bruges* (Bruges, 1912); Marix, *Histoire*, 88–124; Pietzsch, *Fürsten*; Polk, 'Instrumental music'; Stevens, *Music and Poetry*, ch. 13 ('Professional musicians'); Edouard Van der Straeten, *Les ménestrels aux Pays-Bas* (Brussels, 1878); Wright, *Burgundy*, 23–53; Giuseppe Zippel, *I suonatori della Signoria di Firenze* (Trent, 1892). On the corporate life of professional musicians, see Hans Joachim Moser, *Die Musikergenossenschaften im deutschen Mittelalter*, Ph.D. Rostock, 1910; Baillie, 'London guild'. Lawrence Gushee, 'Minstrel' in *The New Grove*, understates the available information.

[104] See the testimonies, partly from Baldassare Castiglione's *Il Cortegiano* (1528), in Žak, *Musik als 'Ehr und Zier'*, 292 f.

[105] George Becker, *La musique en Suisse* (Geneva: Heron, 1923), 21.

[106] Polk, 'Instrumental music', 179–82.

[107] See Heartz, 'A 15th-century ballo', 372, and p. 348 below. Further on minstrels' biographies, families and social status, see Strohm, *Bruges*, 74 f and 88 ff, and Wilkins, *Chaucer*, ch. 5, which includes notices on women minstrels on p. 132 f.

de Senleches, Magister Baude Cordier, Jean de Noyers dit Tapissier, Gilles de Bins dit Binchois and Hayne van Ghizeghem; these were courtiers rather than minstrels. Their social distinction may often have been that of birth in any case, or it was supplied by a university degree or other intellectual distinction. In the Burgundian court accounts for 1467, Hayne van Ghizeghem is paid as a '*chantre et valet de chambre*' together with two other chanson composers, Antoine Busnois and Adrien Basin.[108] None of the three musicians was then a member of the chapel. Adrien Basin was a citizen of Bruges and in his later years a wealthy man; much of his later career was spent in high civic offices. His elder brother Jean was dean of the barbers' guild, and his other brother Pierre, also an accomplished musician, was a priest and 'sommelier' in the Burgundian chapel, later a court councillor and canon.[109] The barber–physicians were a highly respected if non-academic profession much inclined towards music. The famous virtuoso of the Ferrarese court, Pietrobono de Burcellis, was the son of a barber and still learned the craft himself.

Various public uses of music

The secular authorities, and also such semi-official groups as trade guilds, employed professional musicians to enhance the dignity, solemnity or festiveness of their public actions. These musicians usually wore liveries, and banners with the employer's coat of arms were attached to their trumpets. A public action in the widest sense of the word is – alas – warfare. Professional trumpeters and pipers took part in all the campaigns, battles, sieges, explorations, negotiations, victory and peace celebrations. The 'city waits' had a necessary function as watchmen on the walls or towers; unmusical though it may seem, the watchman's signal announcing an enemy's approach was one of the most vital military actions. The famous fifteenth-century song 'L'homme armé' (used in many polyphonic works) was derived from such a warning signal.[110]

The many types of public action for which music was appropriate can be gathered from contemporary pictures which show music and musicians. Edmund A. Bowles, in the collection *Musikleben*,[111] illustrates 'coronation', 'wedding', 'receptions and pageants', 'banquet', 'courtly dance', 'tournament', 'military

---

[108] Marix, *Histoire*, 260. Basin had already been in the service of Charles the Bold's former wife, Isabelle de Bourbon, in 1457 – probably as a musician: see David Fallows, 'Basin, Adrien' in *The New Grove*, where a connection with the minstrels' family Basin / Facien is also considered.

[109] Strohm, *Bruges*, *passim*.

[110] Strohm, *Bruges*, 130, and Ex. 73 below.

[111] Other significant iconographic publications are Bowles, *Pratique musicale*; Salmen, *Spielmann*; Isabelle Hottois, *L'iconographie musicale dans les manuscrits de la Bibliothèque Royale Albert Ier* (Brussels: Bibliothèque Royale Albert Ièr, 1982). See also Walter Salmen, 'Vom Musizieren in der spätmittelalterlichen Stadt', in *Das Leben in der Stadt des Spätmittelalters. Internationaler Kongress Krems a.D. 1976* (Vienna: Österreichische Akademie der Wissenschaften, Phil.-Hist. Klasse, Sitzungsberichte, vol. 325, 1977).

music', 'hunt', 'social music-making', 'church music', 'sacred music', 'theatre', 'town music', 'bourgeois dance', 'street buskers and beggars', 'peasant music'. The series of plates devoted to 'town music' alone (plates 131–51) exemplifies the variety of social applications of music. It begins with pictures of watchmen on the towers and of waits walking the streets with horns and other brass instruments, followed by trumpeters and nakerers playing for an Italian burgomaster's inauguration and a festal pageant of public notaries. A public proclamation is announced by city waits; heralds on horseback with a trumpet carrying royal arms make a public announcement. Public punishments and executions of criminals require trumpet fanfares, to signal the event, to display judicial authority, or perhaps even to entertain the watching crowd. Minstrels accompany religious processions; students make music in their college or in the streets; a lutenist enhances the sensual pleasures of a public bath-house. A young man, standing on a ladder under the window of his sweetheart, gives her a pot of flowers while three hired men in the street play flute and tabor, harp, and lute. It has been established that these serenades were an essential means whereby young burghers showed off and asserted their social success. The hired minstrels also demonstrated spending power; when a rival with his band appeared, street-fights were inevitable (and the musicians had to risk that).[112] Seasonal feasts such as May Day and carnival,[113] and of course the many guild festivals, generated performances that were the more elaborate because they were held recurrently in many cities; repetition and competition fuelled the quest for novelty. The testimony of pictorial sources is widely supported by archival evidence such as the account books of courts, city magistrates and guilds. The great annual feast of a wealthy trade guild, for example, would include, according to the combined evidence:

(1) a solemn Mass service in the guild chapel, possibly with polyphony and organ;
(2) a solemn procession through the town with the peal of the church bells, trumpets and shawms, guild banners in front, probably with singing of hymns etc., possibly with relics of the patron saint or disguisings;[114]
(3) a festal banquet (with loud as well as soft instruments);
(4) possibly a theatre performance afterwards, underscored by lutes, harps, organ, children singers, but also trumpet fanfares to silence the crowd;
(5) at night, a ball in the guildhall to the music of shawms or perhaps

---

[112] Robert Muchembled, 'Die Jugend und die Volkskultur im 15. Jahrhundert – Flandern und Artois', in Dinzelbacher-Mück eds, *Volkskultur*, 46 f.

[113] Heers, *Fêtes*, is partly explicit also about music on these occasions, which include elaborate Italian pageants, tournaments and horseraces carried out in competition by the urban youths.

[114] Various examples are found in Joseph Toulmin Smith, *English Guilds* (London, 1870), 148 ff and *passim*; for a detailed case see Wall-Steiner, 'York pageant'.

bagpipes and drums (round dances, and in the fifteenth-century increasingly the coupled *Hoftanz* or *basse danse*).[115]

In this feast, the music is provided by minstrels but also by churchmen, choristers, schoolboys and quite probably (in the procession and theatre) by 'amateurs', i.e. normal guild members.

Perhaps the most characteristic 'public' use of music in late medieval towns was that of the general processions, pageants, royal and ducal *entrées* and similar collective actions.[116] In those festive hours, everyone took to the streets: a ritual was being performed in which everyone believed (or had to believe). The action was embellished and integrated by music, whether played by the official band or particular groups, whether sung by the clergy or the schoolboys or vicars, or played and sung together by all the participants in the procession.[117] There was great variety in the choice of instruments and their combination. By no means were soft instruments (fiddles, psalteries, lutes, portable organs) excluded from processions outdoors. On the contrary, they were characteristic of Corpus Christi processions, for example.[118] The generalization can perhaps be made that the noise level of public and processional music increased with time. For analogous occasions, there would be string-players in the fourteenth century, trumpeters and shawmists in the fifteenth.

Among the most typical 'extensions' of the processional activity were (in order of importance): stops ('stations') in and before churches with prayers and other elements of worship; theatrical interludes which could be presented on a fixed stage along the way, or presented on a wagon while standing or moving;[119] singing from written music, including polyphony.

It can be argued that processional music – unless performed at stations – had to conform to a convenient walking rhythm. This is the obvious assumption already for *laude* and pilgrimage songs of earlier centuries. Syllabic hymns and sequences, the *Te Deum* and, above all, the litanies, could also be accommodated to a binary rhythm, and these tunes must have been played by the min-

---

[115] Heartz, 'Hoftanz', has interesting illustrations; see also pp. 355 f below.

[116] For an introduction to collective civic uses of music, see Strohm, *Bruges*, ch. 1 ('Townscape – soundscape').

[117] The last-named variety of 'choral singing' is rarely mentioned in the literature. The *Te Deum*, the litanies, and certain hymns, sequences and antiphons belonged to the common 'vocabulary' of European processions that was familiar to most members of society.

[118] Altenburg, 'Fronleichnamsprozession', especially 20 ff. Other studies of processional music include: Bowles, 'Civic processions'; *idem*, 'Musical instruments in the medieval Corpus Christi procession', *JAMS* 17 (1964), 251–60. The tendency to amass participants for Corpus Christi is shown in a city statute from Buda, 1421, which obliges all the minstrels in the town – fiddlers, lutenists, trombonists, pipers and kettledrummers – to appear before the main church on that feast-day; see Szabolcsi, 'Spielleute', 160.

[119] From the vast literature on sacred processional theatre, see in particular: Wolfgang F. Michael, *Die geistlichen Prozessionsspiele in Deutschland* (Baltimore and Göttingen, 1947); Hermenegildo Corbató ed., *Los Misterios del Corpus de Valencia* (University of California Press, 1932); A. M. Nagler, *The Medieval Religious Stage* (Yale University Press, 1976) (see especially ch. 4: 'Processional or stationary?').

strels while walking. An interesting item of processional music, which occurs many times in sacred as well as secular contexts, is the so-called *canticum trium-phale* 'Advenisti desiderabilis'. It has a trope (or 'verse') 'Triumphat Dei filius' with an obviously marching binary rhythm.[120] This plainsong belonged originally to Easter processions or rituals (the 'Harrowing of Hell' scene, when the forefathers in Hell greet the victorious Christ); but it was also used in receptions of secular rulers, for example of Emperor Sigismund at Heidelberg in 1414.[121] This was obviously a political use of music, and a very traditional one. In the fifteenth century, musicians increasingly came to serve political ends by composing specific works celebrating the authorities, for example the so-called 'Staatsmotetten'.[122] The majority of Ciconia's and Dufay's isorhythmic motets can be placed within this category.

Fixed theatrical presentations included the ubiquitous 'living pictures' (*tableaux vivants*), formed by still actors, which became extremely frequent in receptions (*entrées*) of secular rulers. They were usually accompanied by some music that was played next to the *tableau* by visible musicians, by musicians hidden behind it to make it appear as if the personages of the picture were themselves performing, or indeed by the actors. The last-named variety may apply to the elaborate living picture with Tubal (the mythical inventor of music) made for the wedding of Philip the Fair in 1496.[123] Splendid pageants, often linking displays of poetry to music, were created for royal entries in many cities of France.[124] Contemporary descriptions and illustrations sometimes exhibit a naive pictorialism or symbolism. Singing girls and boys appear as sirens or mermaids, shepherds or angels; allegorical figures represent the city welcoming the ruler, or the letters of his name, his virtues, coat of arms and more besides. The people used to shout 'Noël, noël!' in the streets, especially after coronations and the *Te Deum*. Children sang popular ditties as well as songs specially rehearsed at school. Among the former were probably the ones mentioned for Charles VI's entry into Lyon, 1389:

> Et en certains lieux en la ville avoit jusques a mil enffans, vestus de robbes royales, louans et chantans diverses chanssons de la venue du roy.[125]

[And in certain places of the city, there were up to 1000 children, clothed in royal robes, who said praises and sang various songs of the advent of the king.]

---

[120] See also p. 332.

[121] For the church ritual, see Chambers, *Mediaeval Stage*, vol. 2, 73 f; Schuler, *Osterfeiern*, 154 ff; for the secular use, Pietzsch, *Zur Pflege*, 97; Žak, *Musik als 'Ehr und Zier'*, 187–9; and Saunders, 'Liturgies', 182 f.

[122] A book on them is Dunning, *Staatsmotette*. It begins in 1480; as the author acknowledges, the practice was at least a century older.

[123] Bowles, *Pratique musicale*, pl. 128. Several more pictures are in Bowles, *Musikleben*, plates 123–30. See also Edmund A. Bowles, 'The role of musical instruments in medieval sacred drama', *MQ* 65 (1959), 67–84.

[124] The most comprehensive edition of texts and documents is Guenée–Lehoux, *Entrées royales*. For music, see particularly Stephen Bonime, 'Music for the royal entrée into Paris, 1483–1517', in Winn ed., *Musique naturelle*, 115–29. An analogous Burgundian *blijde inkomst* (happy entry) is described in Strohm, *Bruges*, 80–83.

[125] Guenée–Lehoux, *Entrées royales*, 144.

Among the latter, there were newly composed polyphonic chansons, as probably during the entry of Charles VIII into Paris, 1484. The verse chronicle of that event mentions: his *'garde riche et belle'* of *'trompettes et clairons'*; the general noise and the 'Noël' cries of the populace; the (very conventional) adornment of a fountain with the fleur-de-lys, and a statue of a naked girl squirting wine from her breasts. But around her,

> Y avoit bergieres bien chantans,
> Qui disoient chanson nouvelle
> De melodieux et doux chans.[126]

[There were Shepherdesses singing well, / who said new songs / with melodic and sweet tunes.]

The shepherdesses who sing 'novel chansons', probably in polyphony (and perhaps with a 'rustic' text), may seem a modern trait of the imagery. But there are many precedents for the pastoral taste in the poetic and musical tradition – from antiquity via the troubadour *pastorela* (and, at the same time, the shepherd plays of the Church) to the explicitly pastoral spirit of the famous Burgundian *banquet du voeu* (or 'banquet of the pheasant') held at Lille in February 1454, and the wedding festivities for Charles the Bold and Margaret of York at Bruges in 1468.[127] The imagery of these Burgundian feasts was borrowed from traditional book illumination, where plenty of singing or trumpet-blowing hares, donkeys or boars can be found. Pastoral, grotesque or exotic disguise was frequently worn by musicians in processions: it is not always 'unrealistic' when contemporary miniatures show such disguises.

Street pageants, living pictures and mystery plays were also the models for the most popular iconographic genre of the era: *angels' concerts*. Angels, acted by children, could perform almost any kind of music. Together with prophets, they could form complete ensembles for vocal polyphony. If the script of the pageant required them to play and display unusual instruments, these could be bought or made; if to form celestial choruses in symbolic numbers, the children would love to do so.[128]

It is difficult to imagine today how the 'hauts tons' of the trumpets and the cries of the people in a procession could coexist with the 'mélodieux et doux chans' of shepherdesses and angels. And yet, soloist singing and playing of soft instruments was heard in the thickest crowds, probably because people were able to fall silent at the right moments. Otherwise, neither the soloist performers of the three-part music in the Lichfield procession (see p. 386) nor the

---

[126] *Ibid.*, 112 f.

[127] See Marix, *Histoire*, 37 ff; Fallows, 'Specific information', 134 ff; Strohm, *Bruges*, 98 f.

[128] Many confident statements about the unreliability of iconographic evidence may need re-examination. The 'ancient Jewish musicians' in a miniature on King David in Bowles, *Musikleben*, pl. 143, may appear fantastic but are realistically possible in a pageant organized by *rhétoriqueurs* or Meistersinger, whose symbol King David was. On the grotesque and illusionistic aspects of civic festivals, see Heers, *Fêtes*.

polyphonic singers in the procession on St Mark's Square as painted by Gentile Bellini[129] would have been heard. In the latter, the three ensembles (soft ensemble of harp, lute and viol; vocal ensemble; wind band) are all shown playing – but in reality some kind of alternation must have been agreed.

On the whole, fifteenth-century public music was subordinate to other social activities – even if processions and theatre must have been enjoyed by many as mere entertainment. The transformation of music-making into an aesthetic activity respected in itself (and thus in a sense also the emancipation of the minstrel) was clearly foreshadowed in the urban sphere, however. The Netherlands *Lof* or 'Salve' performances – singing of the 'Salve regina' and other votive antiphons in the evening – were organized by fraternities but often displayed to the general public in the nave of the church. From one of these daily 'Salve' performances, the magistrate of Bruges developed the first *public concerts* involving the civic wind band in 1483. The trombonists and shawmists played every evening in the nave of the church (and thus for everyone), in praise of Our Lady but not as part of a service.[130] From this kind of practice descended the custom of the German *Turmmusiken* (wind band concerts from the church tower) as well as the famous *Abendmusiken* of Buxtehude's Lübeck.

The European scene

The lifestyle of the minstrel – if it can ever be defined – was originally that of a traveller, a *homo vagus* seeking employment or individual jobs wherever he could find them. The fourteenth century, which upset so many social patterns, could only intensify this one: long travels became part of the business of the successful musician. Many reports exist, for example, of the trips of musicians to and from the court of Aragon around 1400. German, Fleming and French instrumentalists were frequent there; the royal correspondence is full of the names of Everli, Ffrelich, Poncet, Colinet, Stroman and others, but also 'Galter el inglés' (Gauthier l'Anglois), employed in Burgundy, appears in Spain.[131] Another important exchange route of musicians connected Paris with the east.[132] The princes also sent their own minstrels away, either when requested by friendly powers or to make them learn new arts. The famous Flemish 'min-

[129] The picture has often been published and discussed. See Bowles, *Musikleben*, plates 120–21; Glixon, 'Scuole Grandi', 198 f. None of the commentators seems to note that the singers actually perform from mensural notation written on double sheets, one of which has the inscription 'CONTRA-TENOR' across the top of the pages.

[130] Strohm, *Bruges*, 85 f.

[131] Gómez, *La música, passim*; Salmen, *Spielmann*, 109 (and see this chapter in general for minstrels' travels); Wright, *Burgundy*, 123 f. A good survey is Higinio Anglés, 'Die Instrumentalmusik bis zum 16. Jahrhundert in Spanien', in B. Hjelmborg and S. Sorensen eds, *Natalicia Knud Jeppesen Septuagenario* (Copenhagen: Hansen, 1962), 143–64.

[132] André Pirro, 'Musiciens allemands et auditeurs français au temps des rois Charles V et Charles VI', in *Studien zur Musikgeschichte*, 71–7.

strels' schools' flourished in the late fourteenth century;[133] these were really congresses instituted by the musicians themselves, mainly during Lent,[134] when time could be set aside for training and for exchanges of ideas with colleagues from afar. The other times of the year were occupied with the many feasts, trade fairs, church councils, princely weddings and so on at home and abroad, where sometimes hundreds of musicians appeared seeking quick rewards. The assembly of a repertory was a serious task. Don Juan of Aragon lent his harper Johani to the Marquis of Villena, to serve at his son's wedding, and wrote: 'as he has come back from the school a short while ago, we want him to show your minstrels the new songs (*cançons novelles*) which he knows'.[135] The travels could be solitary ones, or in the company of wife and children (who had to take their share in the singing, playing and dancing, of course); they could be on horseback, on foot, in the wagon of the employer, or in the company of a merchant's *convoi*. Jacob de Senleches intended to travel with his harp alone to Aragon, France and Brittany (see pp. 55 f). This he says in a polyphonic chanson; firmer evidence is the contract made by the famous Anthoni Tallander alias Mossén Borra (1413) with a trumpeter Jacobus de Pina. Jacobus was to be his servant on the next trips 'to the kingdom of Aragon to the residence of the queen, and also to Portugal, and to other parts, for the way out and the return'.[136] Mossén Borra, famous as a jester, was an industry in his own right, and his trips were probably calculated investments. There is also much evidence of whole bands travelling together, particularly from town to town to appear at trade fairs and church festivals. In 1447, four trumpeters of the *signoria* of Florence appeared before Duke Philip the Good in Bruges. The Burgundian court was well known in all Europe for its hospitality to minstrels and was frequently visited by them.[137] International minstrelsy was, perhaps, the most common of all the musical traditions, and this music, of which little survives today, was probably the best known of all to fifteenth-century Europeans.

The employers of the minstrels travelled themselves, of course. Any trip which touched upon a ruler's authority needed to be underscored by at least a herald and some trumpeters: it was a matter of decorum.[138] Thus, the trips of the 'itinerant' households (England, France, Burgundy, Austria and others), plus the many military campaigns, diplomatic and pleasure trips, pilgrimages, and the missions of political and trade delegations all involved a movement of

---

[133] Greene, 'Schools of minstrelsy'; Salmen, *Spielmann*, 110–13.

[134] See also Smits van Waesberghe, 'Muziekboek'.

[135] Gómez, *La música*, doc. 31 (1377).

[136] Baldelló, 'La música', 42. This and other Iberian musicians who travelled abroad, are mentioned in Walter Salmen, 'Iberische Hofmusikanten des späten Mittelalters auf Auslandsreisen', *AnM* 11 (1956), 37–51.

[137] See Marix, *Histoire*, 54 ff.

[138] See on this point, in particular, Gerhard Pietzsch, *Archivalische Forschungen zur Geschichte der Musik an den Höfen der Grafen und Herzöge von Kleve-Jülich-Berg, Ravensberg* (Cologne: Volk, 1971), 118–22. The travels of the Ghent trumpeter Willem Obrecht in the 1450s (in this case to Mantua, 1459, with the Duke of Cleves) were, of course, significant for his son Jacob.

music. Trumpeters and pipers seem to have been essential personnel on ships –
perhaps less for practical purposes than as status symbols of the captain. Henry,
Earl of Derby (the future Henry IV), is often quoted for having taken six trumpeters with him to the Baltic and the Holy Land between 1390 and 1393. He
had little choice but to do so if he wanted to be a king; the case is by no means
exceptional. Wherever a travelling prince or delegate stopped over, he had to
reward the local musicians as well. The Earl of Derby's travel accounts regularly mention payments to minstrels; more unusual was a vocal New Year's
serenade given to him by clerics (probably students) in Gdańsk: a true case of
Ansingen. Conversely, the local city fathers had to reward *his* musicians.[139]

The account books of courts and cities are full of entries relating to minstrels;
this is surely the most abundant type of notice available relating to the music
of the age. To scrutinize and compare them is an immense task.[140] What shall
be given here as an example is a small, unpublished excerpt from an average
princely household account. It was made between 1443 and 1446 for Duke
Albrecht VI of Austria, and includes his expenses for music on travels from
Styria to his other residence at Freiburg im Breisgau (Upper Rhine) and
back.[141] (See also Map 2, p. 155.) Along the way, the duke visited territories
and cities with booming musical 'industries' – mainly of instrument-making
and performing – and he was met by minstrels from the most diverse and distant
courts. Albrecht VI was the younger brother of King Frederick III, with whom
he negotiated during this outward journey at the imperial diet of Nuremberg.

The accounts begin with Christmas 1443, which the duke spent in his residence of Judenburg (Styria); rewards were paid to:

> 'trumpeters and pipers of [the Archbishop of] Salzburg' (5 rg.);[142] a
> lutenist (32 d.); the local schoolboys (13 d.).
>
> New Year's day 1444, St Veit (Carinthia):
> the trumpeters of the king (8 rg.); the local schoolboys (14 d.); the
> trumpeters of Count Ulrich of Cili (Slovenia) (5 rg.).
>
> Lent (Tuesday after *Judica*), Wiener Neustadt:
> minstrels of Margrave Albrecht of Brandenburg (2 rg.).
>
> Easter week, Vienna:
> the singer *Nachtigal*[143] (1 rg.); the schoolboys for singing a Mass in
> Zemendorf (60 d.); the 'citizens' trumpeters' of Vienna (14 s.); one
> piper (3 s.).
>
> April, Vienna:

---

[139] See Lucy Toulmin Smith ed., *Expeditions to Prussia and the Holy Land made by Henry Earl of
Derby* (London: Camden Society, 1894), especially 111, no. 34.

[140] See Pietzsch, *Fürsten*, and Polk, 'Instrumental music'. Much primary material is offered and partly
discussed in Marix, *Histoire*, and Wright, *Burgundy*.

[141] Innsbruck, Tiroler Landesarchiv, Hs. 158 and Hs. 203.

[142] Currency: 1 *rheinisch gulden* (rg.) = 70 d. (pennies); 1 *thaler* (th.) = ?? d.; 1 shilling (s.) = 30 (!) d.

[143] Possibly the Nachtigall serving Duke Ludwig of Bavaria-Ingolstadt 1413–43 (Sterl, 'Regensburger
Stadtrechnungen', 298).

trumpeters of [the Bishop of] Trent (3 th.); trumpeters of [Count?] Georg Sisskra (3 th.); two boy trumpeters (28 d.).

May, Wiener Neustadt:

a minstrel of the Lord of Pappenheim (4 s.); a trumpeter (32 d.); 'little Martin', singer (14 s.).[144]

July, Vienna:

coats of arms to decorate the instruments of the duke's four trumpeters (16 rg.); annual salaries to them (28 th.). Departure for Germany.

July, Passau:

for a Mass, to organist and schoolboys (7 s.); the lutenist of the Count of Schaumburg (3 s.).

Straubing:

a minstrel of King Christoph of Denmark (7 s.); the town pipers of Straubing (2 th. 6 d.); the local schoolboys (28 d.).

Regensburg:

the city pipers (? rg.); the trumpeters of Duke Albrecht of Bavaria-Straubing (3 rg.).[145]

Neumarkt (Upper Palatinate):

schoolboys (21 d.).

August 2, Nuremberg (*imperial diet*):

the trumpeters of Margrave Frederick of Brandenburg (10 s. 24 d.); the city pipers and trumpeters of Nuremberg (10 s. 24 d.).

August 3:

a lutenist with a little boy (3 s.); the trumpeters of [the Archbishop of] Treves (2 rg.); the trumpeters and pipers of Duke Ludwig [IV, Count Palatinate] (6 rg.).

August 5:

three minstrels (42 d.); the singers of Duke Ludwig (1 rg.); the pipers of Margrave Johann of Brandenburg (2 rg.).

August 10:

the trumpeters and heralds of Margrave Albrecht of Brandenburg (6 rg.); pipers of [the Abbot of] Schwarzach (4 s.); a trumpeter of King Christoph of Denmark (1 rg.); a lutenist of Duke Johann of Neumarkt (42 d.); the singers of [the Archbishop of] Salzburg (79 d.).

August 25:

the trumpeters and pipers, the lutenist of Count Ulrich of Württemberg (7 people: 4 rg.); pipers of Georg of Schaumburg (1 rg.); the lutenist of the Bishop of Würzburg (79 d.); the eight trumpeters and pipers of the elector of Saxony (8 rg.); lutenist *Fuchs* and another with him (28 d.).

---

[144] On Martin, see also p. 505.

[145] The city of Regensburg, in turn, paid 4 rg. to Albrecht's own trumpeters (of whom there were four) on 25 July, and 5 rg. to those of the king the next month. (Sterl, 'Regensburger Stadtrechnungen', 274).

September 5:
> the trumpeters and pipers of Margrave Frederick of Brandenburg (see also August 2) (5 rg.); the 2 heralds of the Margraves Frederick and Johann (2 rg.).

September 6:
> the trumpeters of the king (7 gold ducats).

September 8:
> the trumpeters and pipers of [the Archbishop of] Mainz (5 rg.); two pipers of the king (2 ducats).[146]

September 13, Nördlingen (on the route to Freiburg):
> the city pipers (3 rg.).

September 15-18, Ulm:
> the city pipers (3 rg.); the lutenists of the Lord of Helfenstein and of the city of Ulm (1 rg.); a lady singer (1 rg.).

September 20, Reutlingen:
> the city pipers (11 s. 12 d.).

September 22, Rottenburg/Neckar:
> the city pipers (3 rg.).

Rottweil:
> the city pipers (2 rg.).

September 26, Villingen:
> the town pipers (1 rg.). (Arrival Freiburg October 1444.)

Remittals to Vienna, November 1444:
> to *Virgil*, singer of the Count of Cili (6 s.).

November 8:
> salaries to the servants in Vienna, among them 23 th. to the *cantores* [i.e. of the Vienna *Burgkapelle*]; 43 rg. to the trumpeters, for expenses (receipts submitted).

November 15, Strasbourg:
> the city pipers (1 rg.).

November-December:
> 24 rg. to the duke's trumpeters in Freiburg, for expenses; the city pipers of Winterthur (2 rg.); the pipers of the Bishop of Constance (2 rg.).

Christmas Eve, 1444, Stein a. Rh.:
> salary for the trumpeters (12 rg.).

Christmas, Constance:
> two lady singers (2 rg.).

New Year's day, 1445:
> three pipers (1 rg.).

---

[146] The city of Nuremberg, in turn, paid immense sums for gifts and gratifications to princely minstrels during the time of the imperial diet. They included 9 rg. to the royal trumpeters and pipers; 4 rg. to Duke Albrecht's 4 trumpeters; 6 rg. to those of the Saxon elector; 1 rg. (each) to the king's harper and Duke Albrecht's lutenist; 1 rg. to the poet and singer *Muskatplüt*, etc. See *Die Chroniken der deutschen Städte: Nürnberg*, vol. 3, 2nd edn (Göttingen 1864/R 1961), 398-401.

January, Stein a. Rh.:

> to the maidens of Stein, who sang before my lord [*die meins hern gnad angesungen habendt*] (10 s.); for four coats for the trumpeters (1 rg.).

Return travel, June 1445:

> the town pipers of Riedlingen (3 rg.); the city trumpeters and pipers of Villingen (10 rg.); the city pipers of Regensburg (24 d.). (Arrival by ship in Vienna, July 5.)

July, Graz:

> for Masses (?) paid through chaplain Hanns in Vienna (2 rg.); to a lutenist (3 rg.).

Christmas 1445, Salzburg:

> to *Poltzl*, harper (60 d.); schoolboys of Erding (6 d.).

Week after Christmas, Munich:

> lutenists (42 d.); the schoolmaster with the schoolboys (12 d.).

New Year's day, 1446, Landsberg:

> the schoolboys (6 d.).

January 5(?), Kempten:

> the town pipers (6 bohemian groats = 42 d.); the schoolboys 'who sat there singing for a long time' (2 bohemian gr. = 14 d.).

What emerges here, is in some sense a polarity between standard and casual ensembles or activities.[147] The princely wind band (trumpeters with or without additional pipers – that is to say shawmists), the town pipers (with or without additional trumpets),[148] the schoolboy singers, the individual lutenist – they are all combinations which the duke expected to meet everywhere. The tips paid to them were almost standardized: 1 rg. each for a princely trumpeter, for example; much less for schoolboys. More interesting are the casual, smaller groups of musicians (man and boy singer; a lutenist and his companion; three 'minstrels' etc.). The vocalists are least subject to standardization. There are individuals (Nachtigall, little Martin, a woman soloist, the Meistersinger Muskatplüt), a female duo,[149] and three 'court chapels': those of Salzburg, of Duke Albrecht himself, and of the Count Palatinate, Ludwig IV.[150] Duke Albrecht's accounts, and those of the cities he visited, also mention heralds and *persevanten* (mostly non-musical representatives but accompanied by trumpeters), as well as *sprecher* (poets who recite at court), fools, dancers, people showing bears or monkeys and so on. The duke spent much money on games, during which he

---

[147] For more extensive and systematic studies of ensembles, see Polk, 'Instrumental music'; Pietzsch, *Fürsten*.

[148] In all our documents, 'trumpeters' must be understood as using both natural trumpets and trombones. See also p. 359.

[149] Women appeared repeatedly as professional singers or players. For other examples, see Moser, *Hofhaimer*, 72 f; Salmen, *Spielmann*, 115; Polk, 'Instrumental music', 180, n. 37; Baldelló, 'La música', 8 f; and below.

[150] Each of these had about six singers. Duke Albrecht's *cantores* in Vienna, whose combined salary was 23 th., may have consisted of four men (paid 5 th. each) and three boys (1 th. each).

was probably entertained by minstrels. Presumably he often lost at cards, dice or chess. He left his *cantores* at home in Vienna, but often listened to local schoolboys and girls who sang for him. He must have been fond of secular song; in 1445, he acquired the manuscript 'A' of the collected songs of Oswald von Wolkenstein.

Various private uses of music

The problem surrounding the term 'private' has been mentioned above. The creation of a more intimate sphere for music was a cultural achievement, and a social privilege. Besides music, poetry and other intellectual pursuits filled the 'leisure' hours of nobles, prelates and rich citizens.

Music-making at court, when not 'public' and outdoors, could take place in one of three locations: the chapel, the hall and the chamber. The chapel has been discussed above: on Plate 4, the privacy of the prince in his worship seems by no means uncontested. A distinction between *hall* and *chamber*, as well as of the types of music appropriate to them, has been proposed by Christopher Page.[151] We shall adopt this distinction here, making some allowance for overlap, and add some remarks on outdoor 'scenes' of music-making (see below).

The hall of a palace is clearly a room where the prince receives guests for dinners, balls and other entertainments, but also for political receptions. In many contemporary miniatures, a throne is shown in the hall. Consequently, players of *haute musique* are regularly present at official dinners and festive balls.[152] For social dancing, the trio of shawms (or two shawms and one trombone) is standard in any case. In the modern, coupled dances, a soloist with one-hand flute and drum often directs the dancers. The traditional round dance (*carole, reigen*), accompanied by a stringed instrument or pipe and drum with or without singing, is a frequent iconographic type of the fourteenth century. It has a pastoral or popular connotation and becomes rarer in fifteenth-century pictures. Dances of burghers or peasants would often be accompanied by drum or bagpipe.[153] The wind band trio shown with the round dance in Plate 10

---

[151] See his commentary for his record *The Castle of Fair Welcome: Courtly Songs of the Later Fifteenth Century*. Gothic Voices; Hyperion Records Ltd. (London, 1986). (Unfortunately, the captions for the illustrations of 'hall' and 'chamber' are exchanged on the record sleeve.) Dr Page is expected to publish a monograph on the subject.

[152] See, for example, Bowles, *Musikleben*: jacket cover and pl. 36 (coupled dance in throne-room, with three shawmists on balcony), pl. 28 (banquet with shawmists and a herald on horseback), plates 33-5 (with mention of very loud music also in the commentary), plates 39 and 40 (dancing feasts; multiple scenes), plates 47-8 (the disguised dancing of 'wild men' with burning torches, which led to a fire in the hall of the *Hôtel de Saint-Pol*, Paris, in 1393). Bowles, *Pratique musicale*, p. 91 shows another torch dance, performed with accompaniment of flute and drum by trained dancers for a princely couple at the dinner table.

[153] See the open-air, bourgeois and peasant dances in Bowles, *Musikleben*, pl. 43, 154-7, 160; *idem, La pratique musicale*, pl. 88, shows informal round dances in an 'ancient Roman' countryhouse.

(p. 554) may indeed mark a transitional stage. There is much classical and medieval symbolism involved in such Italian miniatures.[154]

Softer music was more usual at dinners and is often mentioned in archival documents; in this context the court fiddler, a lutenist or harper, or a duo of string players appear, and quite often also vocalists, poets reciting their songs, children singing *chansonettes* and so on. Jean Molinet reports in 1486 of a young woman who appeared at supper before Maximilian of Habsburg:

> elle chanta seule chansons et motets, et jooit, en chantant, de luth, harpe, rebecque et clavechinbolon. . . .[155]

> [she sang alone chansons and motets, and played, while singing, the lute, harp, rebec and the harpsichord . . .]

When Leo of Rozmital visited the court of Edward IV in 1465, the practice seems to have been to let choristers of the king's chapel appear in the hall and sing before the guests after the dance (see p. 377 n.). The singing of 'caralls', and recitations and 'disguisings', took place in the banqueting hall at the early Tudor court. The great French–Burgundian festivities, such as the *banquet du voeu* (see p. 413), combined dinner, music and *entremets* (living pictures etc.). At the *Fête de paon* at Tours in 1457, in one *entremet* six boys sang polyphonic pieces, and in another four boys and a girl danced a morris dance with trumpets, flute and drum.[156] It is likely that some of the French polyphonic chansons with pictorial or symbolic texts accompanied *entremets*.[157] German courts seem to have been most eager to imitate the western celebratory fashions. At the ducal weddings of Amberg 1474, Urach 1474, and Landshut 1475, each time there was a pastry with singing musicians inside; in the first case, we are specifically told that in one half of the dish there was a boy who sang, in the other a boy who played the lute.[158] Although bourgeois feasts could not rival such ostentation, the civic weddings, in particular, were important musical feasts. Social distinctions in central European cities are reflected in the number of musicians which the magistrates allowed the various groups to employ at weddings for the procession to and from the church, for dinner and for the ball in the great hall of the guild house. Italian weddings are magnificently documented in painted *cassoni* (chests serving as wedding gifts) showing music and dance.

The most elusive type of music-making in the hall – iconographic evidence seems to be lacking – is the solo appearance of singer-poets.[159] The art of Alexander the Great's court singer Timotheus, of the Celtic bards, troubadours and

---

[154] See also pp. 549 f.

[155] Dupire, *Molinet*, 24 n. 1. This is just one of the more explicit testimonies for 'singing while playing'.

[156] Bowles, *Musikleben*, p. 48.

[157] See Gilbert Reaney, 'Music in the late medieval entremets', *AnnM* 7 (1964–77), 51–65.

[158] Gerhard Pietzsch, 'Die Beschreibungen deutscher Fürstenhochzeiten von der Mitte des 15. bis zum Beginn des 17. Jahrhunderts als musikgeschichtliche Quellen', *AnM* 15 (1960), 19–62.

[159] Possibly relevant are plates 83–5 in Bowles, *Pratique musicale*. The first two show duos of fiddle and harp, the last a soloist player of the *lira da braccio*. This *cassone* painting may be relevant for what is said below on Italy.

Minnesingers did not entirely die out in the fifteenth century. As far as epic song is concerned, there is evidence for the activity of bards, of Serbian, Hungarian, Italian, German, Lithuanian and Scandinavian singer-poets.[160] Another, more lyrical genre of solo song which just survived in the fifteenth century was the *lai* (previously cultivated by Machaut) and its German analogue, the *leich* (late examples are found in the works of the Monk of Salzburg and Heinrich Laufenberg, *c*.1400–20). The singer would usually appear during or after dinner in the hall and accompany himself on a harp or other plucked instrument (which could also be played by a companion). In the accounts of Duke Albrecht excerpted above, this was probably the function of the named individuals *Nachtigall*, *Virgil* and *Poltzl*. The assumption is not too far-fetched that *Virgil*, who served the Count of Cili (Celj, Slovenia), used native techniques of epic song. It is sometimes difficult to decide whether documents refer to lyric or epic poetry, to performances alone or with others, in the hall or in the chamber. The heroic and epic solo singer is often identified by terms such as 'sprecher', 'parleur', 'dichter' and 'faiseur'. A *sprecher* of Emperor Frederick III was Michel Beheim (1416–74), by whom an actual epic (*Das Buch von den Wienern*) survives with music.[161] But we have evidence of the terms 'dichter' and 'faiseur' referring to performers of lyrical poetry.[162] By the early fifteenth century, the epic–heroic genres must have widely yielded to ballads, *romances*, and love-songs in the fashionable sentimental mood. There is no evidence that Binchois performed any other genres than those in the *formes fixes*. Narrative singing, on the other hand, underwent a social decline which made it a genre heard in the streets and in bourgeois homes.

A 'renaissance' of the art may have taken place at Italian courts in the earlier fifteenth century, however. Poems in the only suitable form for such solos, the *sirventese*, are attributed to the famous singer–poet Leonardo Giustinian.[163] Italian humanist writers indicate that the *citharoedi* of their courts recounted the stories of famous lovers in their songs.[164] Singing to one's own accompaniment on the lute, viol or *lira da braccio* seems to have been frequent in the mid- to late fifteenth century; Pietrobono apparently excelled in this particular art. Precisely this kind of epic song is said to have flourished at the court of King Mathias Corvinus of Hungary (1469–90); the king was a friend of the Este family whom Pietrobono served, and Pietrobono actually visited Hungary in 1488. The Italian humanist Marzio Galeotto wrote about the Hungarian bards at Corvinus's court:[165]

---

[160] Salmen, *Spielmann*, 64 and 122 ff (with examples of musical patterns); Salmen, in *NOHM* 3, 357 f. For the Hungarian 'bards', see Szabolcsi, 'Spielleute', 162 f.

[161] See Christoph Petzsch, 'Beheim, Michel' in *The New Grove*.

[162] Strohm, *Bruges*, 84 (*dichtere*); Wright, *Burgundy*, 184 doc. 18 (*faiseur de rondeaux*).

[163] See Cattin, 'Quattrocento', 277 ff, and p. 543 below.

[164] This is explicitly claimed by Antonio Cornazano concerning Pietrobono and the year 1441: see Pirrotta, 'Music and cultural tendencies', 139 f, 144 f. Also Tinctoris's treatise *De inventione et usu musice* refers to the genre: see Weinmann, *Tinctoris*.

[165] Szabolcsi, 'Spielleute', 162; Fökövi, 'Musik', 2 f.

There are always disputations going on during his banquets, or speeches held about honourable or enjoyable subjects, or poems sung. There are in fact musicians and cythara-singers [*citharoedi*] who narrate in their native language the deeds of heroes, singing on the lyre at the dinner-table. This was the custom of the Romans, and from us has spread to the Hungarians. . . . Love-songs, however, are rarely performed there, and mostly the deeds against the Turks form the subject matter, not without fitting words.

We can only speculate which instrument was used by these bards as the chronicler uses apparently classical terms. By 'lyre', he may have meant something like the Italian *lira da braccio* – the equivalent of the Serbian *gusle* used in later centuries for epic singing. The whole practice was clearly an older tradition in Hungary[166] as well as in other countries, and Galeotto's claim that the Hungarians received it from Italy – because of the latter's descendance from the Romans – sounds unconvincing.

The royal chamber depicted in a miniature of Jean de Wavrin's *Chroniques d'Angleterre* (*c.* 1470)[167] does have a bed in it, but also a long table, at which the king is playing chess, and no fewer than fourteen other men are present. One of them is a Moorish ambassador or herald who is kneeling before the king. (The historical 'setting' is probably the twelfth or thirteenth century.) In this atmosphere, a royal harper or gitterner would be eminently fitting, or somebody who read or sang romances or *chansons de geste*. At fifteenth-century courts, the minstrels, chaplains, courtiers, or indeed the prince himself, might sing polyphonic chansons or perform them on soft instruments. In Charles the Bold's tent on the battlefield before Neuss, for example, the Milanese ambassador Pietro Panigarola could observe the duke's musical skill and his singing, 'though he does not have a good voice'.[168] More or less stereotyped 'disputations' on subjects such as famous lovers, or family trees and blazons, might be held in princely chambers, and rondeaux or ballades illustrating the arguments invented and performed on the spot. Also the Parisian/Burgundian *Cour d'amour* and other aristocratic or even high-bourgeois associations held such musical sessions in private rooms, where chansons for St Valentine's Day, the May festival or New Year (see also p. 64) were performed in the presence of ladies. This social music-making, and the participation of either sex in polyphonic singing and playing (of soft instruments only!) is abundantly documented. In private chambers of noble ladies, performing of chansons and especially poetry-writing must have been a widespread pastime.[169] Social games with

---

[166] Further evidence on the tradition in Hungary, including its inevitable popularization in the sixteenth century, is in Szabolcsi, 'Spielleute', 159–64.

[167] See Page, *The Castle of Fair Welcome* (n. 151), labelled 'Hall', a misprint.

[168] Vaughan, *Charles the Bold*, 162. The duke could not expose himself to public criticism, and the admission of the ambassador to his private quarters was a privilege. Molinet remembers the singing of the duke in similar terms: see Fallows, *Robert Morton's Songs*, 303 f. Also, more public music went on in the camp before Neuss, according to Molinet: see Pirro, *Histoire*, 117.

[169] Women of high social status are known as amateur performers and authors throughout this era – from the harp-playing princesses of the Valois-Visconti families to the Renaissance patroness of music, Isabella d'Este. See also Higgins, *Busnois*, ch. 4 ('The Hacqueville chansons') on Busnois' poetess Jacqueline d'Hacqueville, and generally on 'women's poems' in the known chanson literature.

music developed in such situations. Some surviving chansons of the period seem to form 'argument and response', as if they were results of amorous or witty debates.[170] Many others would fit the idea of a chanson contest at court, in which every participant tried to outdo the other with the same stereotyped motives, such as 'Serviteur' or 'Regrets' (see also p. 459).

The use of music manuscripts was common in such private pastimes. Pictures show music books, single sheets and scrolls, sometimes visible to only one performer,[171] sometimes shared by two or more.[172] During the performance of 'La harpe de melodie' by Jacob de Senleches, the patron will have had to see the harp-shaped music himself, otherwise the chanson would not have made sense to him or her (see p. 57). Many later chansonniers, and particularly the small, illuminated ones resembling Books of Hours in physical appearance, must have been read by the lady while the musician(s) performed the song. But well before 1500 we also encounter the polyphonic songbook serving for informal *Hausmusik* and as a poetry collection (or even 'poetry album'). It is characteristic that this type emerges first in German middle-class environments with the Nuremberg sources of the Lochamer and Schedel songbooks (see p. 495). Manuscripts of this type were used for singing and playing (particularly the lute), as suggested by the partbooks constituting the so-called Glogauer Liederbuch (see p. 362), with many instrumental as well as vocal pieces.

Pictures of social music-making often show outdoor scenes. The famous painting of the Burgundian court on a hunting picnic is one of them: it shows the professional wind band as well as the singing of noble amateurs. The various pastimes enumerated in this picture do not happen at the same time, of course. But some of them are just as 'private' as if they happened in a chamber.[173] It is no coincidence that many of the illustrations involving female musicians show garden or boating scenes. A lady could not be seen making music in public; the garden was sufficiently private for singing, dancing and other pleasures, and the only alternative to it was her chamber itself. One of the pictures of the type 'lady and knight in a chamber' shows an organetto player who accompanies himself while singing 'en lieu de messe chansonnectes' – probably to

---

[170] This is the case, for example, in a series of polyphonic 'rondels de refus' which form a dialogue between a proud lady and her unsuccessful suitor: see Strohm, 'Missa super "Nos amis"'. Other poetico-musical dialogues exist in the guise, for example, of letters between Busnois and his friend Jean Molinet: but although the chansons took the final form of letters, they can have originated – perhaps in extemporized form – during personal 'debates'. The 'Hacqueville chansons' set by Busnois (see previous note) have traits of just such a dialogue, including elements of the 'refus' group.

[171] Bowles, *Musikleben*, plates 75 and 81; *idem, Pratique musicale*, plates 107 and 110.

[172] Bowles, *Musikleben*, pl. 76, p. 100, plates 87–90 (singers sharing the music, instrumentalists playing without); 93 (the lady in front holds up a music sheet for the two players); Bowles, *Pratique musicale*, 112 (an ensemble of lady singers one of whom is conducting). In plates 75, 86 and 91 of the latter publication, the use of the manuscript is in doubt.

[173] Bowles, *Musikleben*, pl. 75. I believe that Duke Philip the Good himself is shown twice in two different pursuits: listening to music on the right and courting a lady on the left. Further suggestions on the picture are in Besseler, *Bourdon*, 50 and 165; David Fallows, 'Binchois, Gilles de Bins dit' in *The New Grove*, pl. 1.

steer his lady towards worldly thoughts.[174] 'Music in the home' (whether noble or bourgeois) was indeed an iconographic theme with erotic connotations, particularly when 'knight and lady' were shown making music together. The rather stereotyped boating scenes on city canals in Flemish miniatures of the Bening school (c. 1500–30) correspond to older traditions of courtship. The May festival was indeed celebrated in this way by wealthy youths, and a polyphonic chanson of c. 1400 explicitly mentions the ordering of a little ship for a pleasure trip.[175] Although the pastoral imagery cannot always be taken literally, the evidence linking music with gardens and Nature is credible. Eberhard von Cersne's work *Der Minne Regel* (1404) is for the most part a dialogue about love between the author and the 'Queen of Love', derived from an older Latin work. But Eberhard adds a new introduction where the author is in a secluded garden of love, listening to the music of the birds ('der fogel musica'), which he describes using a rich technical vocabulary.[176]

John Hothby tells us that Arnolfo Giliardi composed a piece (with symbolic implications) 'in insignibus tauxetis Cosmi', i.e. 'in the renowned taxus gardens of Cosimo (de' Medici)': from this we might conclude that the musical pastimes of this high-bourgeois family usually went on in their private gardens. In this, the Medici emulated the earlier practice of the Alberti, celebrated by Giovanni Gherardi's *Paradiso degli Alberti*, and of course the social pastimes narrated in Boccaccio's *Decamerone*.[177] In Mediterranean lands, the link between music and nature was an obvious idea and one which could be related to classical precedent.

There is another private use of music which we can distinguish from these collective pursuits. A solitary patron and his harper, or a musician alone in a chamber, are likely scenes of the late Middle Ages. In particular, a person confined to his or her room might have needed the consolation of soft music. King John of France, when a prisoner in England (1357–60), was perhaps given a chekker by Edward III because the instrument was reputed to relieve melancholy (see pp. 83 f). Later famous war prisoners include the song-writers Charles d'Orléans and William de la Pole. The last-named seems to have had his 'kithara-player' or 'Tymotheos' in Binchois.[178] Antoine Busnois is known to have performed for Duke Charles in his military camp, possibly in the privacy

---

[174] Bowles, *Pratique musicale*, pl. 104. Other examples of such 'chamber music' are *ibid.*, plates 94–7, and Bowles, *Musikleben*, plates 81–3. Compare the chivalric symbolism of the secluded garden (pl. 96) with the realistic living rooms of pl. 97, and the aristocratic-bourgeois contrast of plates 94 and 97. The miniatures showing clergymen playing soft instruments in their leisure hours (Bowles, *Pratique musicale*, pl. 78, for example), give a slightly humorous impression, although the intention may be serious and even realistic. According to Wright, *Music and Ceremony*, 34 f, Parisian canons owned instruments and secular music books for private purposes.

[175] 'Die mey so lieflic' by Thomas Fabri. See Strohm, *Bruges*, 109.

[176] The manuscript also contains four songs with melodies in letter notation. See Cersne, *Der Minne Regel*, and p. 350 below. Pirro, *Histoire*, 27 ff provides a context for the pastoral imagery in music.

[177] See p. 85. The performances of Solazzo and his aristocratic friends described by Prodenzani (see p. 90) take place indoors in the Christmas holidays.

[178] See p. 191 above, and Fallows, Review in *JRMA* 112, 132 f.

of his tent – another 'Timotheus and Alexander' image. Lorenzo de' Medici in his youth enjoyed singing to the *lira da braccio* in the evenings; his companion and model was the great Flemish *tenorista* Jean Cordier.[179] In some of his narrative or meditative songs, Oswald von Wolkenstein depicts himself in solitude, for example at a window of his mountain castle.[180] For Johannes Tinctoris, the preferred solitary instruments which chased melancholy were the viol and rebec.[181] The harp, and then keyboard instruments from the organetto to the harpsichord and virginal, were capable, as polyphonic instruments, of filling a solitary chamber. They were used for self-entertainment as well as for composition and theoretical meditations.[182] There is an iconographic tradition of showing famous musicians of antiquity and musical saints as solitary players: King David, the poetess Sappho,[183] St Cecilia and St Barbara. The last two, who suffered imprisonment, are usually shown with chamber organs. And finally, the tradition of blind organists and composers began with Landini and Paumann. Their blindness was a form of imprisonment, but they discovered in the polyphonic music of their age an open door to an inner world.

---

[179] Parigi, *Laurentiana*, 103 n. 6.

[180] According to Mayr, 'Liederhandschrift', the compilation of MS 'A' of his collected songs is directly connected with his time of imprisonment.

[181] Weinmann, *Tinctoris*, 45 f.

[182] Composition on the harp is mentioned in the prose romance *Cleriadus et Meliadice*: see Page, 'Performance'. The closest we get to 'composition sketches' in manuscripts of the period, are the fragments left by a Viennese keyboard player and arranger, *A-Wn 5094* (see p. 373).

[183] See Bowles, *Pratique musicale*, plates 73, 70 and 102. The Sappho miniature (pl. 70) shows her with books as well as with psaltery, organetto and harp.

2

MONOPHONIC SONG, SIMPLE POLYPHONY AND INSTRUMENTAL MUSIC

Developments of liturgical chant

It would not be fair to claim that the end of the Middle Ages was a brilliant period in the history of Western chant – but it is equally true that the achievements of this period have been considerably obscured. Most notably, the liturgical reform of the Council of Trent (1543–63) removed many feasts from the Roman calendar, and innumerable individual texts, melodies and melody versions from the Roman Mass and Office books.[184] This happened partly according to the principle 'last in, first out': the fourteenth- and fifteenth-century plainsongs were more systematically eliminated because a certain humanist tendency favoured the older Gregorian material over late medieval accretions. New, classicizing texts and melodies were also composed. At the same time, the centralizing trend of the Counter-Reformation eliminated many diocesan uses, or severely restricted them (to a few patronal plainsongs, for example).

The Reformation did away with much Latin sacred monody (Gregorian or not), although some ancient plainsongs have survived in the Lutheran liturgy until the present century, when the most radical liturgical iconoclasm affected Catholic and Protestant Churches alike.

Revivalist movements on both sides have not only restored parts of the ancient chant repertories, most impressively in the editorial work of the monks of Solesmes, they have also twisted the development further away from the late medieval plainsong heritage. Today the awareness of that heritage seems almost irrecoverable. For over a century, chant scholars and editors have taken Erasmus of Rotterdam's call '*Ad fontes!*' ('To the sources!') literally by studying *only* the wellsprings. Their concept of purifying or purging allegedly decadent traditions reflects the aesthetic of the same humanist chant reformers whose work they were undoing.

---

[184] The most conspicuous body of music to be abolished were the sequences, of which only four remained in the Roman books: 'Victime paschali laudes' for Easter, 'Veni Sancte Spiritus' for Pentecost, 'Lauda Sion Salvatorem' for Corpus Christi, and 'Dies ire' for the Requiem Mass. 'Stabat Mater dolorosa' for the Mass of the Seven Sorrows of Our Lady was reintroduced in the eighteenth century. The best access to the abolished texts is still provided by the series *AH*, which covers all rhymed and metrical poems.

The problem with fifteenth-century plainsong (apart from the fact that it is ignored) is that it inherited from earlier ages a dynamic of growth but no longer had the same space for expansion. Everyone serving in the ritual tended to be overworked in the fifteenth century. There were simply too many saints, chapels, altars and relics, too many commemorations, suffrages, processions, anniversary and Requiem Masses etc.: the negative side of the stimulating effect of private endowments. Although the calendars were full, new feasts were still being introduced. The older ones were continuously upgraded (for example, by giving them an octave, i.e. an additional service a week later) or otherwise embellished, most notably the Marian feasts and the ceremonies for the Holy Sacrament and for the veneration of relics.

The performances of music and text necessarily suffered in many churches. The best musical talents were now often absorbed by the task of singing and learning polyphony, or were lured away by chapels specializing in it. Complaints that the musicians neglected the regular liturgical services were frequent. Sessions devoted to liturgical reform at the Council of Basle were not the only occasions when stiff-worded admonitions against neglect of the sacred words had to be issued (see p. 251). This was taken very seriously in some circles, and movements such as the Bursfelde and Melk congregations simplified and 'purified' chant performances, anticipating the Tridentine reform in its care for text pronunciation.[185]

As regards new feasts, the most expansive area was still that of Marian devotion including the veneration of Mary's family – St Anne, St Joseph, the Holy Family, the Name of Jesus, the Three Maries (or Sisters of Mary). The more specifically Marian devotions widely introduced between 1380 and 1500 included the feasts of the Visitation (2 July), the Presentation (21 November) and – with less than unanimous support – the Immaculate Conception (8 December) and the subject of the Rosary.

The major steps in consolidating these feasts in the Roman calendar were taken (for clearly political reasons) during the Great Schism, at the Council of Basle, and particularly under the pontificate of Sixtus IV (1469–84) and later when the printing press (of L. A. Giunta in Venice, for example) began to disseminate the added liturgical material.

Many feasts received at least some new music. For a new Marian feast introduced at Cambrai in 1457, the 'Recollection of Feasts of Our Lady' (*recollectio festorum BMV*), none other than Dufay composed much of the necessary plainsong.[186] The Feast 'of the Seven Sorrows of Our Lady', promoted by a confraternity in the 1490s, was provided with a plainsong Mass and Office selected in a composing competition; the winner of the contest was Dufay's ex-secretary and provost of Condé, Pierre du Wez.[187] The idea of this feast was

[185] This is borne out, for example, by the Bursfelde Ceremonial (*c.*1500) D-As, *8ª Cod.62*. See also Angerer, *Melker Reform*.

[186] See Barbara Haggh, 'The celebration of the "Recollectio Festorum Beatae Maria Virginis", 1457–1987', *SM* 30 (1988), 361–73.

[187] See Robijns, 'Musikhandschrift'.

not new: many churches had celebrated it under the name of *Missa de compassione BMV* or similar ones. The 'Stabat mater' had served as its sequence for some decades. Similarly, the 'new' Feast of the Transfiguration (some chants of which were entered in the polyphonic codex *BU*), was promulgated by the pope in 1456, but had been celebrated long before, especially in the east.

As in earlier times, a new feast would usually require new texts for Mass and Office, often but not always containing borrowed elements, and the appropriate melodies, which were often but not always pastiche-work from older chants. The major task was the Office, of course, which could be about ten times as long as a set of Mass Proper texts. The metrical, *rhymed Office* (*historia*) of the late Middle Ages had become a special genre of sacred (mostly hagiographic) literature.[188] An English saint canonized as late as 1401, John of Bridlington, received a rhymed Office which has only recently been discovered;[189] it furnished the cantus firmus of the polyphonic Mass cycle 'Quem malignus spiritus'. Among the Mass Proper chants, the metrical, rhymed genre of the sequence was favoured for fresh creativity, which also focused on paraliturgical rhymed genres (see below). Large new sequentiaries, *cantoralia* and similar books to contain these genres were still being compiled in the early sixteenth century – many of them only to be thrown away a generation later.[190]

In many cases, it is impossible to say how or where music and text originated and whether they were original or borrowed. Even where authors can be named, their creations were quickly dismantled. To give one example: the Feast of the Visitation, promulgated by the Roman pope in 1389, received three different rhymed Offices almost immediately. For at least one of them, the music seems to have been newly written – by the papal cantor Henri Dézier de Latinnes (see p. 19). But the three sets of textual and musical material very soon became entangled in the various liturgies. Some churches, and particularly some monastic and mendicant houses, did not accept the flowery rhymed poetry of these Offices and partly replaced it by prose; this can be related to humanist or at least reformist attitudes. Others liked the new Offices so much that they arranged anthologies of them, mixing their contents together. Similar arrangements applied to the music. By the fifteenth century, there was no longer a consolidated tradition of the plainsong for this particular feast.[191]

---

[188] About 1000 individual poems are edited in volumes of *AH*. For brief introductions, see Andrew Hughes, 'Rhymed office' in *The New Grove*, and Karl-Heinz Schlager, 'Reimoffizien', in Karl Gustav Fellerer ed., *Geschichte der katholischen Kirchenmusik* (Kassel etc.: Bärenreiter, 1972), vol. 1, 293–7.

[189] By Andrew Hughes. See Bent ed., *Four Anonymous Masses*, xvi and 174 f, and p. 230 above.

[190] A model study of one such book and its contents is Labhardt, *Cantionale* (the manuscript in question is actually a gradual and antiphonal), with an edn of late or rare plainsong melodies, pp. 389–424. Other interesting graduals and sequentiaries – chosen at random – are the Cantorale of the Museo Diocesano of Palma de Mallorca, fifteenth–sixteenth century (*E-PAc*), and the MS *B-Br 9786–90* from Münsterbilsen, fifteenth century (see p. 333).

[191] An edn of text and music of a miscellaneous version prepared for the Carmelite order is given in James J. Boyce, *Cantica Carmelitana: The Chants of the Carmelite Office*, Ph.D. New York U., 1984 (UM 85-05471), vol. 2, 82–125. Further material on this Office is in Labhardt, *Cantionale*, 179 ff, and Strohm, 'Zur Rezeption', 29 f.

There were more important developments than the stitching together of new Masses and Offices. We may distinguish at least four:

(1) the expansion of the plainsong repertory for the Mass Ordinary;
(2) the infiltration of rhythmic and mensural performance practices into liturgical genres;
(3) a considerable surge of new creativity in certain areas of Europe; and
(4) a sweeping trend to paraliturgical and vernacular genres which appealed to wider audiences.

The creation of new melodies for the Mass Ordinary seems to have happened along a broad geographical band from the North Sea to Italy.[192] Particularly favoured were the Credo and Sanctus/Agnus melodies. By about 1400, central European and Italian sources register up to four Credo melodies (nos. 1–4 of the *Liber Usualis*), but fifteenth-century sources often contain far more, all of which disappeared in the following centuries.

A peculiar feature of the new Credos was that they were often rhythmicized in a simple manner known by the name of *cantus fractus*.[193] This syllabic, incisive text declamation and the regular metres must have sounded very powerful when performed by a monastic or cathedral choir.

Example 43 Credo in *cantus fractus*, D-Mbs *14274*, fol. 13v

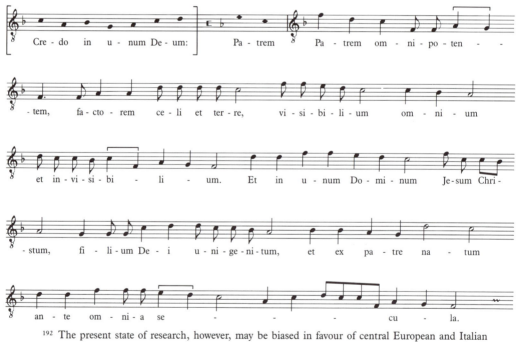

192 The present state of research, however, may be biased in favour of central European and Italian sources. The work of Bruno Stäblein and his students is reflected in the catalogues of Ordinary melodies: Landwehr-Melnicki, *Kyrie*; Bosse, *Gloria*; Thannabaur, *Sanctus* (the most elaborate and reliable volume); Schildbach, *Agnus*. An exhaustive study of the Credo is Miazga, *Credo*.
193 'Cantus fractis vocibus' is also a term referring to mensural music in general, and that is its meaning in some diatribes against polyphonic music.

Example 43 is taken from the codex *Em*, a polyphonic collection whose earliest gatherings (Vienna, *c*.1435) contain monophonic melodies of the Mass Ordinary of central European origin. The spread of such tunes, and the use of *cantus fractus*, was extremely wide. The phenomenon overlaps to some extent with that of simple polyphony (see below), and also with artistic Renaissance polyphony, because Heinrich Isaac and others used such melodies as cantus firmi for Mass settings.[194]

Monophonic chants found in English polyphonic sources such as the Pepys MS, often referred to as examples of *cantus fractus*, are usually melismatic and have flexible and sophisticated rhythms (see p. 385). Mensural Ordinary melodies also intruded into the Cambrai choirbooks written under Dufay, *F-CA 6* and *11*, and are found in other manuscripts of that area. In the context of Franco-Netherlands Mass polyphony, we encounter new Mass tropes such as Sanctus 'Qui januas mortis' or Kyrie 'Verbum incarnatum' – which have not yet been found in graduals of the traditional kind (see also p. 177). Mass Ordinary chants were also compiled or composed to form Mass cycles. Although this usage started with the Franciscans in the thirteenth century, it was widely adopted during the fourteenth and fifteenth particularly for Marian and votive Masses.[195]

Rhythmicized plainsong was also known for antiphons, sequences, the *Te Deum*, and especially hymns. These are choral genres, just like the Mass Ordinary. The often simple, alternating rhythmic patterns were a means of co-ordinating the singers, for example in a procession.

New plainsongs were created in the late Middle Ages, especially in the east and north.[196] On the basis of late medieval chant sources which seem to be lost today, Fritz Feldmann described many sequences, alleluia compositions, Mass Ordinary melodies and other items found in Silesia.[197] In Scandinavia, Poland, Bohemia and Hungary, the creation of new plainsongs was mainly a process of emancipation from western monastic models. For example, Cistercian and

---

[194] See Staehelin, *Messen*, vol. 3, 142 ff, Mother Thomas More, 'The performance of plainsong in the later Middle Ages and the sixteenth century', *PRMA* 92 (1965-6), 121-34; Frank Ll. Harrison, 'Two liturgical manuscripts of Dutch origin in the Bodleian Library', *TVNM* 32 (1982), 76-95; Bernhold Schmid, 'Chansonsatz und rhythmische Einstimmigkeit. Zu einer Gloria-Komposition aus dem St. Emmeram-Codex der Bayer. Staatsbibliothek', *Musik in Bayern* 30 (1985), 27-37. Many melodies are edited and discussed in Otto Marxer, *Zur spätmittelalterlichen Choralgeschichte St. Gallens. Der Codex 546 der St. Galler Stiftsbibliothek* (St Gallen, 1908).

[195] A fourteenth-century Swiss gradual cited in Jürg Stenzl, *Repertorium der liturgischen Musikhandschriften der Diözesen Sitten, Lausanne und Genf* (Fribourg (CH), 1972), no. 85, already contains six full Ordinary cycles (without Credos). See also Kurt von Fischer, 'Neue Quellen zum einstimmigen Ordinariumszyklus des 14. und 15. Jahrhunderts aus Italien', in *Liber Amicorum Charles van den Borren* (Antwerp, 1964), 60-68; Bruno Stäblein, 'Messe, A.' in *MGG*, vol. 9, col. 147-58; Martin J. Burne, *Mass Cycles in Early Graduals. A Study of the Ordinary of the Mass Cycles Found in Medieval and Renaissance Graduals in Libraries in the United States*, Ph.D., New York U., 1956; Hoppin ed., *Cypriot Plainchant*.

[196] See John A. Emerson, 'Plainchant', § II,7' in *The New Grove*, with bibliography p. 841 f. For various Eastern plainchant traditions, see Lissa ed., *Musica Antiqua Europae Orientalis*, vol. 1 (Warsaw, 1966); and especially *SM*, vol. 27 (1985).

[197] Feldmann, *Musik und Musikpflege*, 47-108.

Franciscan–Roman models had dominated Polish plainsong in the twelfth and thirteenth centuries; the Icelandic Mass and Office for St Thorlac (*d.*1193) was composed in the fourteenth century as a strict imitation of Dominican chants.[198] The influence of central European diocesan rites was also strong, for example in the southern Slavonic (Roman Catholic) area.[199] New plainsongs accumulated around the figures of local and national patrons such as Sts Stanislaw, Jadwiga (Hedwig), Jacek (Hyazinth) in Poland, Václav,[200] Adalbert and Ludmilla in Bohemia, Ladislas, King Stephan, Emeric and Elizabeth in Hungary,[201] Canute Lavard in Denmark,[202] Birgitta and Erik in Sweden, Henrik in Finland etc. Many patrons were 'shared' between several adjacent regions, for example Adalbert, Jadwiga and Elizabeth. An example is also the genesis of the oldest trope in the Polish language, the *Bogurodzica* ('Mother of God'), later a kind of national anthem (the first notated source dates from 1408). This was originally a Kyrie trope used for St Adalbert; a prototype of the melody is found in a Styrian source of the twelfth century.[203] A typical example of Czech plainsong with its strong triadic flavour in melodies on F (but also on E) is the *Magnificat* antiphon for St Ludmilla in the Hohenfurt (Vyšší Brod) Cantionale:[204]

Example 44 Antiphon 'O mater Bohemie', Hohenfurt Cantionale

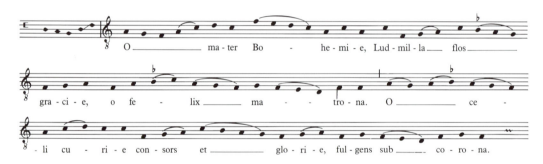

[198] Robert Abraham Ottósson, *Sancti Thorlaci episcopi officia rhythmica et proprium missae* (Copenhagen, 1959).

[199] See Janez Höfler, 'Rekonstrukcija Srednjeveškega sekvenciarija v osrednji sloveniji' [Reconstruction of the Medieval Sequencer in Central Slovenia], *Muzikološki Zbornik* 3 (Ljubljana, 1967), 5–15.

[200] See, for example, Jerzy Pikulik, 'Les offices polonais de Saint Adalbert', in *idem* ed., *Etat des recherches sur la musique religieuse dans la culture polonaise* (Warsaw, 1973), 306–72; Andrew Hughes, 'Chants in the Offices of Thomas of Canterbury and Stanislaus of Poland', in *Musica Antiqua Europae Orientalis* 6 (Bydgoszcz, 1982), 276–7.

[201] Dominique Patier, 'Un office rhythmique tchèque du XIVe siècle: Etude comparative avec quelques offices hongrois', *SM* 12 (1970), 41–131; a large collection of chants for St Václav (with facs and catalogue of sources) is Dobroslav Orel, *Hudební prvky Svatováclavské* (Prague, 1937).

[202] Zoltán Falvy, *Drei Reimoffizien aus Ungarn und ihre Musik* (Budapest, 1968); Kilián Szigeti, 'Denkmäler des gregorianischen Chorals aus dem ungarischen Mittelalter', *SM* 4 (1963), 129–72. On Denmark, see Angul Hammerich, *Mediaeval Musical Relics of Denmark* (Leipzig: Breitkopf & Härtel, 1912); Heinrich Husmann, 'Studien zur geschichtlichen Stellung der Liturgie Kopenhagens', *DAM* 2 (1962), 3–58; *idem*, 'Die Oster- und Pfingstalleluja der Kopenhagener Liturgie und ihre historischen Beziehungen', *DAM* 4 (1964–5), 3–62.

[203] Hieronim Feicht, *Bogurodzica* (Wrocław etc., 1957). For an example of Bohemian (Franciscan) influence in Denmark, see Bergsagel-Nielsen, 'Manuscript Copenhagen'.

The period around 1400, in particular, witnessed a rise in national self-consciousness in the field of liturgy and Latin chant. A gesture of the Roman Church towards Scandinavia was the canonization of St Birgitta of Sweden in 1414 – as the first major ceremony of the Council of Constance. St Birgitta herself had encouraged the creation of plainsong for her female order *Sanctissimi Salvatoris*. The sympathy of the Council fathers did not extend as far as the teaching of Johannes Hus, who in his own country recommended sacred song in Latin and Czech, congregationally and privately. The famous *cantio de corpore Christi* 'Jesus Christus, nostra salus', with acrostic 'JOHANNES', became in its Czech translation (see p. 340) an important congregational hymn of the Utraquist Church. On the other hand, its fifteenth-century melodic adaptations in diverse sources, and its transfer into the Lutheran *Gesangbuch* ('Jesus Christus, unser Heiland'),[205] also show that such music could not be contained within regional, national or confessional borders.

The late Middle Ages were also an important period of creation and transition in Jewish plainsong. While the hymns (*piyyutim*) of the Sephardic communities in Spain and other Mediterranean areas reflected mainly Arabic influences,[206] the Ashkenazic tradition in central and eastern Europe developed a peculiar blend of traditional and various local elements, in scriptural cantillation as well as other genres. According to Eric Werner, the *missinai* tunes – which were originally hymns and individualized laments but then became prayer melodies for high feasts – largely remind of models such as German *minnesang* and even of Burgundian polyphony. Many tunes are not so much imitations of specific non-Jewish models, but rather analogous expressions of the general spirit of late medieval monody.[207]

The Latin cantio and related forms

In the late Middle Ages, a tendency towards 'popular' forms of plainsong appeared in many European countries. The English cantilena and carol, the Italian *lauda*, and the central European cantio, *Leise* and *kolęda* are just the best-known results of what may have been a widespread tendency of creating religious lyrics which were less venerable, but more accessible to congregations, than liturgical chant. Sequences and tropes may have fulfilled such popularizing functions centuries before – for example by absorbing secular tunes. But these genres remained attached to the liturgy even in its more exceptional

---

[204] Rothe ed., *Hohenfurter Liederhandschrift*, 311 (fol. 117v).

[205] Ewerhart, *Handschrift 322/1994*, 61–6.

[206] See, for example, Higinio Anglès, 'La musique juive dans l'Espagne Médiévale', in *idem, Scripta Musicologica*, vol. 2, 735–51.

[207] Eric Werner, *A Voice Still Heard . . . The Sacred Songs of the Ashkenazic Jews* (Pennsylvania State University Press, 1976). The melody of 'Ma'oz Tzur', for example, analysed by Werner (p. 90 ff) for its links with sixteenth-century German hymns and folksongs, rather shares its main motives and general approach with a widely distributed fourteenth-century Credo in *cantus fractus*.

moments (the Feast of Fools, for example). They offered a means of identification with the ritual mostly to the performing clerics themselves, including the choirboys. By contrast, the late medieval genres mentioned here were all intended for, if not actually created by, the laity. They had no, or only ostensible, connections with the traditional liturgy.

This whole body of music was a 'common tradition' as far as its general types and functions were concerned; its specific branches were differentiated by region and, partly, by language. We shall discuss only a few examples and general procedures here, reserving further observations to the chapters on individual countries.

Not the only but perhaps the most important model genres for these sacred repertories were 'Benedicamus' and alleluia tropes, often called *versus* in the manuscripts. A frequent characteristic of the newer forms was in fact their strophic text. Several genres also had more direct secular roots, especially in dance-songs with refrain such as the ballata and *carole*.

Latin songs used in central European churches for paraliturgical ceremonies or in the Latin schools and for singing in the streets, were called *cantiones*, a noncommittal name mainly indicating that no liturgical identification was intended.[208] Many of these pieces occur again and again in their characteristic manuscripts (*cantionalia*) in German, Czech, Polish, Hungarian, Italian and Netherlands areas. The most exuberant production developed in Bohemia in the fourteenth century, and then, under the influence of the Hussite reforms, especially in the urban 'Rorate' fraternities of the fifteenth and sixteenth. Their plainsong codices were usually called *kancionály*, although they mostly contained liturgical items as well, such as Mass chants. Other regions strongly cultivating the cantio were Austria and southern Germany, and the Lower Rhenish and Dutch areas (where the convents of the *devotio moderna* contributed most). An old Christmas cantio of apparently French origin (i.e. a *noël*) which was used in several polyphonic settings, including one by Josquin, is 'Praeter rerum seriem'. In Italy the older vernacular genre of the *lauda spirituale* already fulfilled similar functions, so that no separate type of cantio developed – although the Latin *lauda* flourished in late medieval Italy under analogous circumstances to the central European cantio, and largely resembles it. In England it is the carol which catered for the respective needs, but the difference is that the cantio never reached the same artistic level of mensural three-part composition as the carol.

Latin *cantiones* were often translated into the respective vernacular languages (some travelled so widely that versions in several languages are found); quite frequently they also acquired a counterpoint to produce simple two-part polyphony. Most *cantionalia* contain at least a small number of such polyphonic pieces. Even if there was no polyphony, many melodies were composed – and

---

[208] See Ewald Jammers, 'Cantio' in *The New Grove*; Stäblein, *Schriftbild*, 74 ff. A representative if outdated edition of many pieces is *AH*, vols. 1 (with music), 20 (with a source catalogue), 21, 23 and 45.

this seems a distinctive feature – already with a specific rhythm matching the poetic metre of the text. The note-values were not always expressed precisely in the manuscripts, which show a bewildering number of notational systems from plainsong to mensural notation. (On all these characteristics of the cantio, which are shared with other forms, see also below.)

A relatively frequent source-type for *cantiones* is the plainsong gradual into which an enthusiastic cleric or schoolmaster had some of these pieces copied; these were intended to enrich the ceremonies and to distract the clerics and boys from secular song. A famous example of this is the Bavarian 'Moosburg gradual' of 1360 (*D-Mu 156*).[209] Its compiler explicitly states his aim of providing devotional substitutes for unwanted 'songs and debates' of his young clerics in church, especially during the clerical feasts of the Christmas period. Accordingly, many songs are intended as *Benedicamus* tropes for the Nativity, the Feast of the Holy Innocents and New Year. Concordances with much earlier repertories exist, for example with manuscripts of Aquitanian polyphony (twelfth century) and with thirteenth-century conductus settings. The forms are mostly strophic with three- or four-line stanzas, and a refrain. A Christmas song which was to have a celebrated later history (although its individual components were known earlier), is 'Resonet in laudibus'. This was not a song but a cluster of songs, often used in connection with the much older, rhymed antiphon 'Magnum nomen Domini' as 'tropes' for the *Nunc dimittis* on Christmas Day.[210] There are innumerable later sources, versions, translations and polyphonic settings of the song; together with 'In dulci jubilo',[211] it is perhaps the most popular and widespread Christmas carol that is still in use. One of the sources, shown in Plate 5 (*A-Wn 4494*, fols. 63v–4r), was the personal prayer-book of Emperor Frederick III (*c*.1460). This copy uses precise mensural rhythm; the breves preceding breves or longs are perfect. The song has the traditional single stanza:

	music	
Resonet in laudibus	A	4 bars
Cum jocundis plausibus	A	4
Sion cum fidelibus	B	4
Apparuit / Quem genuit / Maria.	C	6

and the triple refrain:

209 Franz A. Stein, *Das Moosburger Graduale* (Freiburg, 1956); see also *JbLH* 2 (1956), 93–7 (with facs); Walter Lipphardt, 'Das Moosburger Cantionale', *JbLH* 3 (1957), 113–17.

210 Wolfgang Irtenkauf, 'Die Weihnachtskomplet im Jahre 1345 in Seckau', *Mf* 9 (1956), 257–62. 'Magnum nomen domini' as antiphon for the *Nunc dimittis*, but in a two-part setting and with a Dutch translation, is also contained in the manuscript *B-Br II. 270*, fols. 138v–9r. Generally on 'Resonet', and on its connection with *kindelwiegen*: Konrad Ameln, '"Resonet in laudibus" – "Joseph, lieber Joseph mein"', *JbLH* 15 (1970), 52–112.

211 See Clytus Gottwald, '"In dulci jubilo": Morphogenese eines Weihnachtsliedes', *JbLH* 9 (1964), 133–43.

5 Christmas cantiones, Orationale of Frederick III. (Vienna, Österreichische Nationalbibliothek, Cod. 4494. fols. 63v–4r.)

I

Sunt impleta que predixit Gabriel.	D″	6
Eya, eya!	E	4
Virgo deum genuit,	D′	4
Quod divina voluit / clemencia.	D″	6

II

Hodie apparuit / apparuit / in Israel	F	8
Per Mariam virginem est magnus rex.	D″	6

III

Magnum nomen domini Emanuel	A′	6
Quod annunciatum est per Gabriel.	D″	6

Not only the lilting triple-rhythm and the triadic F major tune remind us of dance, but 'Eya, eya' is a specific 'call' which is also found as an insertion into dance-songs. The 'residual' text after the music adds the five stanzas – 'Cristus natus hodie', 'Pueri concurrite', 'Natus est Emanuel', 'Syon lauda Dominum' and 'Nunc voce prophetica' – after each of which the triple refrain is repeated in full, probably by a chorus. The multiple choral refrain or 'burden' is also a characteristic of English carols.

Although the manuscript was intended for private use, it seems that Frederick III had this and several other carols copied here to read them when attending Christmas performances by his chapel and, presumably, his choirboys.

With these German books we might compare two fourteenth- century graduals from the collegiate church of Aosta (*I-AO 9-E-17* and *9-E-19*). In his discussion of the latter codex, Harrison[212] emphasizes the European diffusion of the songs it contains. There are several Christmas tropes of the *Benedicamus domino* and the *Deo gratias* in liturgical order, plus four monophonic 'carols'. 'Verbum caro factum est / de virgine Maria' (no. 20) was known in Italy as a *lauda* and widely disseminated elsewhere. 'Fulget hodie / de l'espina la flour; / sol justicie / nos a donné s'amour' (no. 18) is a macaronic song in Latin and in the Franco-Italian dialect spoken in the Aosta region. For 'Noé, noé, iterumque noé', Harrison points to the French provenance of this acclamation.[213] Among the actual *Benedicamus* tropes, international favourites occur, such as the two-part 'Ad cantum leticie' (no. 1), the monophonic 'Verbum patris hodie' (no. 2), 'Johannes postquam senuit' and indeed our 'Resonet' – in the text version 'Resonemus laudibus / cum jocunditatibus...' but with almost the same melody.

At the beginning of the magnificent series of Bohemian cantio collections stands the Hohenfurt Cantionale of 1410 mentioned above. It was written for a Cistercian community – still uninfluenced by Hussitism – and contains many plainsongs for processions and similar ceremonies. Several *cantiones* are attached to a feast as if they were tropes. The wonderful melody of 'Ave yerarchia', for example, clearly an independent strophic composition, is here utilized as a

---

[212] Harrison, 'Benedicamus'. For further literature, see *RISM B IV/2*, 735–8.

[213] The piece appears again (without music) in the Liederbuch der Anna von Köln (c.1500). See Salmen–Koepp eds, *Liederbuch* (no. 7).

'Salve regina' trope. This was one of the fourteenth-century melodies carefully preserved by the reformed communities (as was 'Jesus Christus nostra salus'), and appearing in many Utraquist books. The melody also appears with a German text ('Ave Morgensterne') in our next source, the Neumarkt Cantionale, and it later entered the Lutheran hymn books with the text 'Gottes Sohn ist kommen'.[214]

The Neumarkt Cantionale (*PL-WRk 58*),[215] a Silesian source of 1474/84, and the codex *D-Z 119*, copied *c.*1520 by the Latin school rector Stephan Roth of Zwickau (Saxony), are typical collections of *cantiones* and other miscellaneous music made by local schoolmasters. Both also contain polyphony – the former an archaic gospel setting (*Liber generationis*), the latter settings of Mass Ordinary sections plus a fragment of Josquin's Mass 'L'ami Baudichon'. The repertory of the Neumarkt Cantionale spans the whole liturgical year, comprising mainly antiphons and songs for processions. A section for the Assumption of Our Lady (fols. 115v–18v) transfers well-known Easter chants to that feast (15 August). Thus the processional *canticum triumphale* 'Cum rex glorie Cristus infernum debellaturus intraret' appears as 'Cum regina glorie . . . ad celos migraret'. The original *canticum* is also known as part of a mystery play: the 'Harrowing of Hell' scene. In that context it was usually followed by the song of the forefathers in Hell, 'Advenisti desiderabilis', with or without the trope 'Triumphat dei filius'.[216]

Of the many other popular or widespread *cantiones* (or tropes or antiphons) in the Neumarkt MS, a good deal reappear in manuscripts from Bohemia, Germany (such as *D-Z 119*), and notably the Low Countries. It is often impossible to determine the origins of the songs, and it is in a sense immaterial. One of the most beautiful Marian *cantiones* of the fifteenth century often appears in manuscripts connected with the Netherlands *devotio moderna* and may well have originated in one of its houses: the *cantus ad Salve regina* 'Ave pulcherrima regina':[217]

Example 45*a* 'Ave pulcherrima regina'

A - ve pul - cher - ri - ma re - gi - na, gra - ci - a di - vi - na quam

tri - na be - a - vit, an - te nec post cre - a - vit ma - jo - rem te.

---

[214] Rothe ed., *Hohenfurter Liederhandschrift*, 366 (fol. 145r); Bäumker, *Kirchenlied*, vol. 1, 252.

[215] Description and inventory: Arnold Schmitz, 'Ein schlesisches Cantional aus dem 15. Jahrhundert', *AMw* 1 (1936), 385–423; *RISM B IV*.

[216] See Chambers, *Medieval Stage*, vol. 2, 74; Schuler, *Osterfeiern*, 154 f. For its adaptation for political use, see p. 305 above. Other sources are mentioned in Strohm, 'Native and foreign polyphony', 207 f.

[217] For a spurious attribution to Thomas a Kempis, see 'Thomas Hermerken a Kempis', *Opera omnia*, ed. H. J. Pohl (Freiburg i. Br., 1918), vol. 4, 324.

Example 45*b* B-Br 9786–90, fol. 26v

Om - nes   Mau - ri - ci - um pre - cen - tur,   cun - cti ve - ne - ren - tur ut

den - tur post mor - tem   re - gna no - bis in sor - tem ce - le - sti - a

Many copies of this song exist, mostly with some kind of simple counterpoint: in the Utrecht Songbook (*D-B 8° 190*), the Rostocker Liederbuch
(*D-Rou Mss. phil. 100/2*) the Cantionale of Thomas Kreß (*CH-Bu 46*), in the
manuscript *B-Br II. 270* and others. The two-part setting shown in Example
45*b*, with a contrafactum text for St Maurice, comes from a monastery in Münsterbilsen (*B-Br 9786–90*) (Limburg). A Dutch monophonic version is in the
Tongeren MS (*B-HAS*), a divergent Latin monophonic version in the Hussite
Cantionale of Jistebnice (*CS-Pn II c 7*).[218] The rhythmic stability of the main
melody in all these versions is remarkable. The rhythm is clearly invented to
suit the Latin words (note the lengthening of all the rhyme syllables), but
the melodic contour and motivic recurrences are also married to the poetry
('divina-trina' etc.). A distinctive first mode is used, with some uncertainty
about the flattening of the sixth. The form, in most of the copies, reminds one
of a sequence with its double-versicles 'aa bb', concluded by a single 'c'; the
repetition of the melody at 'c' is more genuine to refrain forms or *cantiones*.[219]

Simple polyphony

Some conceptual problems surround the phenomenon which we call 'simple'
here, and which has also been styled 'archaic', 'peripheral', 'primitive', 'organal',

---

[218] Two representative Netherlands sources (from Utrecht and Amsterdam) are ed. in Bruning-
Veldhuyzen-Wagenaar eds, *Het geestelijk lied*. See also Labhardt, *Cantionale*, 232. On *B-Br II.
270*, see *CC*, vol. 1, 96; on Münsterbilsen see Huglo, 'Séquences'; on other sources: Strohm,
'Polifonie', 91 f.

[219] See E. Bruning, 'De Middelnederlandse Liederen van het onlangs ontdekte Handschrift van Tongeren
(omstr. 1480)', *Koninklijke Vlaamse Academie voor Taal-en Letterkunde. Verslagen en mededelingen* 1
(1955), 95 (with facs of Tongeren); *AH*, vol. 1, 189 (from Jistebnice).

'usual', 'early' or simply 'liturgical' polyphony. A Latin designation derived (by F. Alberto Gallo) from a passage in Prosdocimus de Beldemandis is *Cantus planus binatim* ('plainchant twice').[220] This clever paradox expresses very well the intermediate position of the phenomenon.

All the cited terms have some bearing on the phenomenon itself: a survival, in the late Middle Ages, of composing and performing techniques which had been superseded by the Ars nova at the latest. In some areas the techniques survived into the Baroque period and even into the early twentieth century, as a recent research symposium has revealed.[221]

This already suggests that 'superseded' is not the best word for what happened to this type of music. It was not an object of artistic 'progress' in the same way as was other music – although it was not exempted from historical change either. It shared the delicate historicity of folklore.

The existence of simpler types of polyphonic music alongside the works of composers such as Machaut and Dufay would have to be postulated if it were not amply documented. Simple polyphony indeed represents, in later surroundings, primeval forms of Western liturgical polyphony, especially the organum of the ninth to eleventh centuries, and the earliest discant of the twelfth. The distribution of these practices over many parts of Europe was a slow process. The acceptance of organum and discant was not followed everywhere by further steps: in some places polyphonic singing remained simple for centuries. This was partly because these institutions were geographically peripheral (in eastern or northern Europe, for example), or provincial/rural (in central France, for example), or inclined to austerity (as in some monastic orders). The clerics in these places were less concerned with the advancement of the musical art than with the preservation of its ritual functions in the Mass and Office liturgy: to them, simple polyphony was a solemn manner of singing plainchant.

This function was equally welcome in some affluent, central and lively institutions. Abbeys and cathedrals such as Saint-Maur des Fossés, Le Mans or Padua used organum styles for certain ceremonies at Christmas and Easter, for *Benedicamus* tropes sung by young clerics, for the Mass Ordinary and especially the Kyrie, Sanctus and Agnus Dei.[222] Actually, these pieces became 'primitive' only by comparison when the same institutions accepted more modern polyphony in the fourteenth and fifteenth centuries.

---

[220] Gallo, 'Cantus planus binatim'. Other important literature: Geering, *Organa*; Göllner, *Formen früher Mehrstimmigkeit*; von Fischer–Gallo eds, *Italian Sacred Music*; F. Alberto Gallo and Giuseppe Vecchi eds, *I più antichi monumenti sacri Italiani* (Bologna: A.M.I.S., 1968) (facs edn of Italian sources); Benjamin Rajeczky, 'Spätmittelalterliche Organalkunst in Ungarn', *SM* 1 (1961), 15–28.

[221] Corsi-Petrobelli eds, *Polifonie primitive*. This conference report is of basic importance for the subject in general. See also Norman E. Smith, 'Organum and Discant: bibliography, § VII–XIV' in *The New Grove*.

[222] A primitive 'Benedicamus' trope was used even at Cambrai Cathedral (fifteenth century): Strohm, 'Polifonie', 90. For a large catalogue and bibliography of early 'Benedicamus' settings, see Huglo, 'Débuts'. The relationship to Notre Dame is discussed in Arlt, 'Symposium "Peripherie" und "Zentrum"'. For Mass repertories, see Max Lütolf, *Die mehrstimmigen Ordinarium missae-Sätze vom ausgehenden 11. bis zur Wende des 13. zum 14. Jahrhundert* (Berne, 1970).

Besides the basic note-against-note counterpoint to melismatic or troped plainsongs (discantus), a florid style over few held notes in the plainsong voice (*organum purum*) was also handed down, appearing as simple polyphony in later centuries (*Haltetonstil*, 'held-note-style'). This type may often have been improvised without being written down. It could serve as a kind of vocal prelude or interlude for discantus pieces. This mixture of techniques, typical for Notre Dame organa, is exhibited in a 'Benedicamus domino', written down in a south German fifteenth-century manuscript:[223]

Example 46 Benedicamus trope 'Benedicat, ympnum dicat' (two-voice section)
GB-Lbl add.27630, fol. 65r

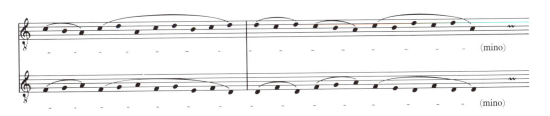

A third style, presumably the oldest, but which increasingly appears in manuscripts, is a strictly parallel chanting in two or three voices, mostly at the unison, fifth and octave. More elaborate introductory and cadential sections are often present. This is, of course, a manner of performing liturgical recitative, related to the more localized practices of faburden, fauxbourdon and *falsobordone*. The texts involved are most often the lessons, epistles and gospels of high feasts such as Christmas.[224]

[223] *GB-Lbl add.27630 (LoD)*, fol. 65. See Göllner, *Formen früher Mehrstimmigkeit*, 152. The manuscript has been edited in Dömling ed., *Handschrift London*.

[224] See Theodor Göllner, *Die mehrstimmigen liturgischen Lesungen*, 2 vols. (Tutzing: Schneider, 1969) (with an edn of all known pieces).

Simple polyphony can be interpreted as an orally transmitted practice which for some reason found its way into script.[225] Among the many innovations which it underwent (especially when cultivated in the larger centres), the first was the writing down of the pieces. In this process, the transmitted practice might be altered or incompletely reflected; pieces also 'developed' after they had acquired written status. Many of the early copies do not codify the rhythm which was known to the performers. Some pieces may have received mensural rhythms after they had already been sung for a while in equal values or simple alternations of long and short. In general, rhythm was inessential for the counterpoint of this music, and functioned as an external ornament only – one which did not need to be written.

Perhaps the greatest interest which all this music offers to the historian lies in its frontier position towards the unwritten and lost traditions of music. Extemporized performance practices existed in the great centres as well as in the provinces. The one most relevant in this context is *cantus supra librum*, the extemporizing of a counterpoint to a plainsong read from the liturgical book in performance.[226] Analogies between European simple polyphony and unwritten non-European polyphony have been noted. Within the Western hemisphere, this type of music-making was certainly 'supranational' even where it had a 'provincial' or socially modest outlook.

The distribution of the written sources in space and time shows that developments did take place in this practice – some of them drastic. There is still a great deal to be explained. After the early fourteenth century, the phenomenon virtually disappears from English sources, for example. The insular musicians used English discant and then faburden – extemporized practices mostly for two voices at a time – but they used the modern resources of mensural music when writing down plainsong settings in three parts.

Although many sources must have disappeared, it seems clear that in the fourteenth and fifteenth centuries this phenomenon was rarer in Spain, France and Flanders (i.e. the south-western Low Countries) than in Italy, the Empire and eastern Europe. This had to do with a degree of 'backwardness' in the sense that more institutions in western Europe had probably introduced mensural music by then and perhaps abolished earlier practices. The surviving medieval polyphony of Scandinavia is limited to the practices described here.[227]

Simple polyphony was sometimes related to written art-music, almost as a 'vulgarization' of it. German monks, for example, dismantled French three-part

---

[225] On relationships between unwritten and written practice, see Wulf Arlt, 'Repertoirefragen "peripherer" Mehrstimmigkeit: das Beispiel des Codex Engelberg 314', in Strohm (chairman), *Costituzione e conservazione*, 97–125; Theodor Göllner, 'Das Kyrie "Cunctipotens" zwischen Organum und Komposition', *Musik in Bayern* 22 (Tutzing, 1981), 37–57.

[226] It is discussed, for example, in Tinctoris's *Liber de arte contrapuncti*; see Bent, 'Res facta'; Sachs, 'Contrapunctus-Lehre', 210 and 248. The practice is mentioned at Cambrai Cathedral in 1485 (under Jacob Obrecht as succentor): see Pirro, 'Cornuel', 194.

[227] See Norman E. Smith, 'Organum and Discant: bibliography, § XII', in *The New Grove*; Bergsagel–Nielsen, 'Manuscript Copenhagen'.

motets into two-voice conductus or even monophonic lines. Italian manuscripts – for example those at Cividale (*I-CFm*) – contain reduced or simplified versions of Western art-music.

On the other hand, in some fourteenth-century centres, including the Swiss abbey of Engelberg,[228] a highly original motet style emerged, neither simple nor Ars nova in character, which was soon cultivated in various countries, above all in Bohemia.[229] Also due to further contacts with the French motet (for example at the Council of Constance), this central European motet style proved vigorous and developed a certain amount of sophistication. The repetitive schemes of these pieces are rarely so complex as to deserve the label 'isorhythmic'. Rather, the tenor is often sung with its own words in the same lively, declamatory style as the other voices. Any of the two to five voices (not all of which were necessarily sung at once) could be a pre-existing tune: for example, a Latin cantio or – in Bohemia – a Czech Utraquist song. This repertory is invariably sacred and was used for ceremonies and entertainment in schools, monasteries and civic fraternities. A particularly elaborate example is 'Crucifixum in carne / Also heylich', which is found in two German sources and in the Tyrnau MS (*H-Bn 243*) from Slovakia.[230]

Example 47 'Crucifixum / Cum rex glorie / Also heylich'

[228] Facs edn (with introduction) of the main source: Arlt, 'Engelberg 314'.

[229] An edn and study of a representative West German manuscript is Ewerhart, *Handschrift 322/1994*. An anthology of 41 pieces, mostly from Bohemia, is Jaromír Černý ed., *Vícetextová moteta 14. a 15. století (Moteti medii aevi)* (Prague: Editio Supraphon, 1989). See also *idem*, 'Mehrtextige Motette'.

[230] Edited in Ewerhart, *Handschrift 322/1994*, 21; Černý, *Vícetextová moteta* (see n. 229), no. 7; Mužik, 'Tyrnauer Handschrift' (facs).

'Cum rex glorie' (see Ex. 47) is the Easter chant for the 'Harrowing of Hell' scene (see p. 332). The text of the top voice is derived from the processional verse 'Crucifixum in carne laudate' – one of the most widely travelled pieces of this repertory. Settings appear in the Winchester Troper (eleventh century), in the Notre Dame MSS as well as in twelfth-century Sicily, in Germany in the fourteenth and fifteenth centuries,[231] in the English Pepys MS of *c*.1470–1520, and (in fauxbourdon technique) in the Genoese MS *I-Fn 112bis* of *c*.1460 (see p. 590). All these pieces serve the same ceremonial occasion of the Easter vigil. Our motet may refer to it as well, particularly since 'Also heylich' is nothing but the German translation of the processional hymn 'Salve festa dies'; another version of the same piece has a fourth voice declaiming the Latin hymn text itself. (A fifth voice also exists, with the cantio text 'Surgens mortis victor fortis'.)

Besides these motets, fourteenth-century developments also include the rise of two-part Credo settings – less often Gloria or sequence settings – in *cantus fractus* (for sources, see above). The voices are mostly equal in range and their vivid declamation of the long text is often in simple binary rhythms. Portions of the music are repeated within a piece in a rational pattern, just as in the Credo plainsongs, of which nos. 'I' and 'IV' of the modern books are regularly used. But there are also new Credo melodies, and freely composed settings. Partly or fully concordant versions of various Credos are strewn throughout Italian cathedral books; a network of such pieces connects Cividale, Rome, Pisa, Siena, Milan and Palma de Mallorca, and a few central European concordances are also known. One Gloria in this style in a Cividale MS (*I-CFm 79*) is attributed to Antonio da Cividale – presumably the papal chaplain who, for his own local cathedral, seems to have 'composed' simple polyphony.

Example 45 illustrates the convergence of simple polyphony with later monophonic genres such as *cantiones*. The earliest two-part setting of 'Ave pulcherrima' is probably the version of Münsterbilsen, despite its contrafactum text. Its contrapuntal features are typical for the majority of the sequences and Mass Ordinary sections in *cantus fractus*: parallel unisons, fifths and octaves in conspicuous positions ('cuncti', 'mortem', 'sortem'), and on the other hand, strict contrary motion in mirror-fashion with regular voice-crossings (the first phrase). The counterpoint really 'doubles' the original melody, and approximately shares its range. Other versions, not shown, add different counterpoints, mainly below the original voice and in mirror-fashion. This was a technique introduced already in eleventh-century plainsong settings. 'Ave pulcherrima', however, is a late cantio, composed with a fixed rhythm from the beginning. Thus, an older contrapuntal technique was applied here to a younger piece.

Not all the copies actually notate the rhythm, although it is clearly part of the piece.[232] The Cologne version (*D-KNa W 75*; *c*.1500), on the other hand,

---

[231] See Arlt, 'Symposium "Peripherie" und "Zentrum"'.

[232] In *D-Mbs 28546*, fols. 53v–4r, a two-part version comparable to that from Bilsen is notated in neumes without rhythmic values; the two voices are on two opposite pages of the manuscript, with different texts (alternate stanzas). It looks as if the piece had been disguised, to make it appear like plainsong for reasons of austerity. On the manuscript see Strohm, 'Polifonie'.

has rhythmic notation and a second voice in a very recent style. It regularly uses parallel thirds and sixths instead of fifths, but has little linear logic. It inappropriately assigns a perfect cadence to the unimportant resting point *c* ('beavit'); the cadence 'maiorem te' sounds like bad chanson-writing. Here simple polyphony is really on the decline.

European practices of vernacular song

The issue of vernacular song will also occupy us in the following chapters on national and regional developments of the later fifteenth century. What needs to be addressed here is the question of *shared traditions* and practices. Some of these were inherited from much earlier periods, some emerged only in the fifteenth century. Archaic or unwritten practices had an amazing potential to cross linguistic, ethnic and also social divisions. Art-music, especially written polyphony, was more deeply affected by these divisions, but it became more and more available for written transmission and conscious imitation.

It is the task of the ethnomusicologist rather than of the music historian to uncover the musical material that was common to various European song traditions, or that may have survived in the folksong of later centuries.[233] We may cast a glance, however, over the phenomenon itself. It is a fact that medieval European song exhibits widely known, shared melodic patterns or formulas. Some may have 'come naturally' with the mode, or with the textual form of songs, because vernacular poetic forms were also partly supranational. The wide distribution of song – of many kinds and in many languages – by travelling minstrels offers another, more concretely historical explanation. Through such common procedures and distribution channels, Eastern, Arab and Jewish influences also helped to shape Western vernacular song, just as they had contributed to Western liturgical chant. Salmen gives examples of melodic formulas known over wide distances, and makes the point that they also linked diverse social strata.[234] In any case, such 'shared substance' was transmitted orally, and among all kinds of people. Some of it may have had its origin in pre-historical or extra-historical (phenomenological) conditions of human life.

It is often difficult to draw a line between the more archaic types of 'substance sharing' (to be investigated by the ethnomusicologist) and more conscious 'borrowing' interventions by song composers (to be identified by the historian). As said above, conscious transfer procedures were more typical for art-song, whereas orally transmitted song adhered longer to its 'common roots'. Contrafacta, re-settings, borrowed material and so on are well represented, for example, in the courtly repertories of the troubadours, trouvères and Min-

---

[233] On this subject, see also Salmen, 'European song'; Salmen, *Spielmann*, 113–25. A statistical–analytical method for the comparison of melodies is developed in Meylan, *L'énigme*.

[234] Salmen, 'European song', 350 f, with music examples.

nesinger, but the less artful songs of minstrels and pilgrims were also carried far and wide and imitated consciously. Conversely, fifteenth-century art-song offers a good many 'glimpses of unwritten traditions'[235] – and with them, perhaps, of archaic material.

An example is the melodic identity of the first line of the 'L'homme armé' song (see p. 466) with the carol tune 'Princeps serenissime'.[236] We are dealing with a melodic cliché of the G mode. The rhythmic identity, however, speaks for musical contacts within a more definite geographical and chronological zone (perhaps Anglo-French minstrelsy and secular song of the early fifteenth century). The cliché could have been transported in some musician's conscious memory, although that was not a necessary condition for its appearance in different locations of the same zone.

More problematic is the case of another little phrase, shared between the Hussite hymn 'Jesus Christus nostra salus / Otče, bože všemohúci' (c.1400)[237] and the chanson 'J'ayme bien celui qui s'en va' by Pierre Fontaine of c.1420 (on which see also p. 148):

Example 48*a* Pierre Fontaine, 'J'ayme bien celui qui s'en va'

Example 48*b* 'Otče bože všemohúcı', Hohenfurt Cantionale

---

[235] Paraphrasing Nino Pirrotta, 'New glimpses of an unwritten tradition', *Words and Music: The Scholar's View, in Honor of A. T. Merritt*, ed. L. Berman (Harvard University Press, 1972), 271–91. For Pirrotta, unwritten traditions are nationally defined.

[236] Noted by Bukofzer, *Studies*, 160 f, and interpreted as a 'similarity of tone in the carol and certain Burgundian chansons'. The tenor of Grenon's ballade 'Je ne requier de ma dame' starts in the same way.

[237] See František Mužik, 'Systém rytmiky české pisně 14. století', *MMC* 20 (1967), 18, and p. 327 above.

This is presumably a case of 'shared substance': the D mode invites us to juxtapose the two triads $c'-a-f$ and $a-f-d$. Similar pentatonic structures are frequent and seem exactly the common, archaic type of material we are looking for. It is only worth mentioning that the hymn was probably heard at the Council of Constance, sung by Johannes Hus and his supporters. Apart from being a beautiful, elementary-sounding melody, the song gained European political significance. A sensitive musician who was then visiting Constance (and that may include Fontaine) would have been struck by it.

What makes these little questions arise is always the same big question: how much of the unwritten, archaic traditions was still alive in fifteenth-century art-music? In my view, this whole century is an enormous process of absorbing into art, or replacing by art, the shared archaic heritages. It is precisely the new, individualized art of this century – including the 'Burgundian' chanson – which shows the most distinctive signs of this ancestry.

We may now describe some of the common or analogous practices, i.e. uses and aspects of song that bridge national diversification including its actual languages.

Very characteristic for the period around 1400 is a sudden rise, in several countries, of *translations* from the Latin into vernacular languages. This supranational tendency was, at the same time, an important transmitter of shared musical material (liturgical plainsong) to the various nations and to the ordinary lay people. A main goal of the translators was to popularize the performance of plainsong, today a matter of course but in the high Middle Ages a precarious and exceptional idea.

Some such idea was in the minds of the first important translators into German: the Monk of Salzburg (*fl. c.*1390), Heinrich Laufenberg (*c.*1390-1460) and Oswald von Wolkenstein (1377-1445). All three also wrote original sacred lyrics inspired by liturgical models. The Monk of Salzburg worked at the court of Archbishop Pilgrim II of Salzburg, and his activities must have enjoyed the utmost support from this prelate.[238] The lay brothers of monastic houses, and probably also the population at large, were encouraged to sing these vernacular plainsongs, as is shown by the choice of items. They constitute 27 of the most popular sequences and hymns such as 'Mittit ad virginem', 'Mundi renovatio', 'Veni sancte spiritus', 'Ave preclara maris stella', 'Stabat mater', 'Christe qui lux es', 'O lux beata trinitas' as well as popular *cantiones* ('Uterus virgineus', 'Resonet in laudibus').[239] Laufenberg's oeuvre (eighteen translations) had fewer repercussions outside his local sphere of influence, the Upper Rhine

---

[238] Complete edn of his sacred songs: Spechtler, *Die geistlichen Lieder.* See also Burghart Wachinger, *Der Mönch von Salzburg. Zur Überlieferung geistlicher Lieder im späten Mittelalter* (Tübingen: Max Niemeyer, 1989); Mayer-Rietsch, *Mondsee-Wiener* (facs and transcriptions from the major manuscript source). A good commented edn of selected songs is Spechtler–Korth eds, *Der Mönch von Salzburg.* It is suggested there (p. 9 f) that the 'Monk' was really Pilgrim II himself.

[239] The latter with the German words 'Joseph lieber nefe mein' and with directions to perform it in a *kindelwiegen* scene (on which, see p. 295).

area. It includes famous songs as well, for example the 'Salve regina' ('Bis gruest, maget reine') and the cantio 'Puer natus in Bethlehem'. Oswald left only three texts, one of which is a version of the *lauda* 'Ave mater, o Maria' ('Ave muetter, kueniginne'). This polyphonic song is an excellent example of 'shared material': although it may well have originated, some time before 1430, as a Latin *lauda* in Italy, its motivic vocabulary reminds us strongly of such widely circulated Ars nova songs as 'En discort / Virginem mire' (see p. 122).[240] On the heels of these three poets there followed innumerable anonymous translators, largely working again with the same popular chants, up to the time of the Reformation.[241]

The analogy with England is striking. The monk and poet John Lydgate (*c.*1370–*c.*1450) wrote nearly as many translations, largely using the same type of models (hymns, sequences, Marian antiphons etc.), as the Monk of Salzburg, and also the number and character of his original sacred lyrics is comparable. In contrast to the German poets, Lydgate does not seem to have written his own melodies, however; the fact that few of his poems are transmitted with melodies indicates that he addressed them more to a reading public. Lydgate, too, is followed by many translators, for example the Franciscan James Ryman, and others who are anonymous today.[242]

In Bohemia before *c.*1410, a large number of sacred songs in the vernacular must have accumulated, partly – it seems – with original melodies not drawn from the Latin liturgy.[243] The reactionary Prague synod of 1408 rejected all but four of them, but with little effect. The Magisters Zavise of Zap and Johannes Hus wrote Czech translations, some apparently based on Latin originals by Johannes of Jenstein (who had resigned as Archbishop of Prague in 1398). The Hohenfurt Cantionale contains six Czech songs, including 'Jezu Kriste, štědrý kněže' which is probably an arrangement by Hus.[244] Also probably of Czech origin is the melody for the widely known rhymed prayer 'Patris sapientia, veritas divina'. The poem itself, attributed to Egidio Colonna (fourteenth century), was written for private recitation on the subject of the seven hours of the Passion; translations into several languages are documented. A vigorous

[240] See Kurt von Fischer, 'Die Lauda "Ave mater" und ihre verschiedenen Fassungen', *Colloquium amicorum: Joseph Schmidt-Görg zum 70. Geburtstag* (Bonn, 1967), 93–9; Welker, 'New light on Oswald', 207–13, where a northern origin (Limburg or Liège?) for the Latin version is proposed.

[241] No comprehensive survey is available. For the earlier translators, see Günther Bärnthaler, *Übersetzen im deutschen Spätmittelalter* (Göppingen: Kümmerle, 1983). For later songs, see Walter Lipphardt, 'Deutsche Antiphonenlieder des Spätmittelalters in einer Salzburger Handschrift (Michaelbeuren, MS cart. 1)', *JbLH* 27 (1983), 39–81.

[242] A good introduction to Lydgate is Walter F. Schirmer, *John Lydgate. A Study in the Culture of the 15th Century* (University of California Press, 1961). On Ryman, see Stevens, *Music and Poetry*, 48 ff.

[243] The most comprehensive (but outdated) study of Hussite and pre-Hussite song is Zdeněk Nejedlý, *Dějiny husitského zpěvu*, 2nd edn, 6 vols. (Prague, 1954–6). See also *idem*, 'Magister Zavise und seine Schule', *SIMG* 7 (1905–6), 41–69; Jan Kouba, 'Jan Hus und das geistliche Lied: Ein Literaturbericht', *JbLH* 15 (1969), 190–96.

[244] Rothe ed., *Hohenfurter Liederhandschrift*, 38–54. See also Ex. 48*b* for the Czech version of 'Jesus Christus, nostra salus'. Kouba, *Jan Hus* (see n. 243), suggests that in this case Hus only modified an original by Johannes of Jenstein.

melody in the E mode was composed for the Latin words, probably in the early fifteenth century. Translations into Czech and then German followed; the song entered the Lutheran hymn books and, from them, J. S. Bach's *St John Passion*.[245]

Translation was, of course, also a 'vehicle' for original vernacular songs; to the extent that a melody could be dissociated from the original verbal structure, it could travel almost anywhere. A famous example is the most ancient German *Leise*, 'Christ ist erstanden', first documented in Salzburg in the twelfth century. It shares melodic substance with – or quotes – the Easter sequence 'Victime paschali laudes'. From the fourteenth century onwards, it was disseminated to Bohemia ('Buoh vsemohúci'), then also to Hungary, Poland and many parts of Germany; a Latin re-translation 'Christus surrexit' was also known.[246]

Detaching a melody from its original words and providing it with new ones – the contrafactum procedure – was the simplest way to create a new song. It was often used by churchmen who exploited secular tunes for new devotional expression. In Italy from the fourteenth century onwards, vernacular *laude spirituali* were derived from secular ballatas or popular *strambotti*. Leonardo Giustinian is said to have written many *lauda* texts for his own secular songs. Later printed collections of *lauda* texts explicitly indicate these secular models with the rubric 'cantasi come' ('to be sung after the tune of').[247] It is interesting that the models are mainly polyphonic settings, including well-documented French chansons. Some models are popular songs, a few of which are otherwise lost. By comparison, the Dutch/Flemish cantio collections discussed above contain mostly original *cantiones* with a few interspersed folk-tunes such as 'T'Andernaken' (see also p. 361).

The identification of a melody with a tag like 'cantasi come' is, of course, a practice already known from liturgical books, where many melodies are used for more than one purpose. The same practice was observed in the sacred and secular theatre; instead of composing new tunes for their songs and interludes, playwrights gave the direction to sing, for example, a well-known antiphon – or a popular tune with adapted words. In French secular farces of the fifteenth and sixteenth centuries a whole world of native song was utilized: popular *chansons rustiques* and courtly *chansons musicales*.[248]

---

[245] See Strohm, 'Zur Rezeption', 30 ff.

[246] The *Leise* was an old strophic genre, sung in litanies and processions and ending with the invocation 'kyrieleis(on)'. The history of this particular song is studied in Walther Lipphardt, '"Christ ist erstanden". Zur Geschichte des Liedes', *JbLH* 5 (1960), 96–112; František Mužik, '"Christ ist erstanden – Buóh všemohúci"', *MMC* 21–3 (1970), 7–45. For an additional source, see Labhardt, *Cantionale*, 240 f. 'Christus surrexit' is not to be confused with the cantio 'Surrexit Christus hodie' (with German and Czech versions), which has a dance-like triple rhythm; it is found, for example, in *D-B 8º 190*.

[247] See William Prizer, 'Lauda spirituale' in *The New Grove*; Ghisi, 'Strambotti e laude'; Giulio Cattin, 'Contributi alla storia della lauda spirituale', *Quadrivium* 2 (1958), 45–75.

[248] See Brown ed., *Theatrical Chansons*; Brown, *French Secular Theater*. This book is the best introduction to the complex relationships between music and theatre in this period. See also the brief account in Reese, *Renaissance*, 150–52.

Very little original theatre music was needed for performances in this period. A type of piece with a specific theatrical function was the 'Pause', or 'Silete' ('be silent!') call, found in sacred and secular dramatic texts. This was either sung (in mystery plays by angels, for example) or played like a fanfare by instruments between scenes or at the beginning of a play. It became a stereotyped item; more or less elaborate polyphonic settings exist.[249]

The theatre was a place of encounter for many song traditions. Apart from Latin plainsong, however, we do not have much theatre music that transcended national borders. Certain types of sacred solos such as the planctus (lament) and its derivatives appear in most European countries; some melodies also seem to have travelled. The various *Marienklagen* (laments of the Virgin) of German-speaking areas have been said to descend from Italian *laude*; although this connection is no longer apparent in the transmitted fifteenth-century laments.[250]

Not surprisingly, the most 'supranational' elements of theatre music were apparently farcical and satirical texts, and musical caricatures of ethnic groups. There are instances of pseudo-oriental music which were widely popular in mysteries (mainly in saints' stories), and several German mystery plays have caricatures of synagogue chants. 'Cados, cados, adonay cherubim, cados sy singhen' is the beginning of a Franco-Netherlands three-part song – an elaborate anti-Semitic mock-song – which may reproduce some features of Hebrew music.[251] Two plays from the Bolzano group (*c.* 1500) also call for 'Cados' songs in stage directions.[252]

Monophonic art-song of the late Middle Ages has rarely been studied on a European scale. Is this actually possible, or did each language go entirely its own ways? Common traditions of poetic form and content did exist, for example the sequence/*lai*/*leich*/*estampie* or the virelai/ballata/lauda/villancico forms, or the *pastourelle* and *alba* types. But did singers of monophony still achieve any wider significance, such as the troubadours, trouvères and Minnesinger?

In the fifteenth century, the most durable and universal art-songs were polyphonic settings, appreciated as musical works. The polyphonic French chanson was the well from which the other nations drank. Monophonic art-song,

---

[249] Brown, *French Secular Theater*, discusses instrumental examples. For a vocal polyphonic 'Silete' in the 'Theophilus' mystery of the manuscript Trier (*D-TRs 1120/128*), see Peter Bohn, 'Theophilus', *MMg* 9 (1877), 3–4 and 24–9; Stevens, 'Medieval drama', ex. 21. Other pieces may be hidden in textless copies. Vander Straeten, *Musique*, vol. 3, 104 ff, gives stage directions from a Brussels mystery, 1444: 'Silete' and 'Pause' are either sung or played.

[250] Ancestors for both may be the Latin laments 'Planctus ante nescia' and 'Flete, fideles anime'. Whereas the Italian dramatic lament, 'Cum autem venissem ad locum', is a self-contained strophic *lauda*, the German *Marienklagen* are whole scenes incorporating chants, *Minnesang* melodies, recited texts, even dialogue. See Peter Bohn, 'Marienklage', *MMg* 9 (1877), 1–2 and 17–24; Stevens, 'Medieval drama', 40 f.

[251] See E. Werner, 'Jewish music, § I' in *The New Grove*, 625 f. This piece is found in the French Seville Chansonnier (*F-Pn n. a. f. 4379*) and therefore not of Spanish origin, as Werner seems to assume – with implications for the Jewish tradition it may reflect. It is surely a theatrical song. See Plamenac, 'A reconstruction', 523 f.

[252] See Lipphardt-Roloff eds, *Die geistlichen Spiele*, 338 and 408.

preserving the old unity of poet, composer and singer, somehow could no longer compete. There was also a social gravitation: the heritage of the trouvères had been carried into the fourteenth century partly by bourgeois societies of 'rhetoricians' attached to civic guilds; the courtly heritage of the Minnesinger in the fifteenth century became Meistergesang. The Meistersinger, organized as guilds in Nuremberg, Strasbourg, Augsburg and other cities, absorbed the individual songs of past masters such as Neidhart von Reuental, Heinrich Frauenlob, or Peter von Arburg (plus many songs only conventionally attributed to them) and collected and added others. Their outlook was that of a collective craft, not of poetic individuality. Many older melodies underwent a process of de-individualization, involving repeated changes of words: the courtly song became a collectively owned 'Ton'.[253] In other countries the role of the singer–poet also faded in comparison with that of the polyphonic song composer. Various stations along this road are occupied by four great collections of the decades 1390–1430: the songs of the Monk of Salzburg, of the 'Gruuthuse MS', of Leonardo Giustinian, and of Oswald von Wolkenstein.

The Monk of Salzburg was perhaps the last singer–poet whose creations were echoed down the century and achieved something like European significance. Oswald was much more of an aristocratic individualist whose strength was his independence from any school or social restraint. He did write great monophonic melodies which were tailored to his words, and to his own performances,[254] but unlike some of the simpler tunes of the Monk, these melodies remained a particular genre which others could hardly absorb; they did not become part of a tradition like the *Töne* of the masters mentioned above. The most significant pieces by either the Monk or Oswald seem to have been their pastoral and folkloristic songs, i.e. their more descriptive, detached statements. These pieces are often polyphonic: musical technique and subject matter disguise the poet's voice. Oswald's arrangements of foreign polyphonic chansons (see p. 120) are perhaps the most successful part of his output, because only western counterpoint could match the cleverness of his games with words and images, and because the arrangements reflected his wide horizon and intellectual enterprise.

Apart from these two masters, the scattered German and Dutch/Flemish lyrics from around 1400 amount to a substantial body of music.[255] Of even greater significance is the *Gruuthuse* MS *B-Bcaloen* of *c.*1390–1400, with 151 Flemish songs. These are the work of noble and bourgeois 'rhetoricians' of Bruges (*rederijkers*), organized in fraternities but also linked to Burgundian

---

[253] An example for this transformation is described in detail in Walter Röll, *Vom Hof zur Singschule: Überlieferung und Rezeption eines Tones im 14.–17. Jahrhundert* (Heidelberg: C. Winter, 1976). Generally on Meistergesang and its sources, see Horst Brunner, 'Meistergesang' in *The New Grove*; Christoph Petzsch, *Die Kolmarer Liederhandschrift* (Munich: Fink, 1978).

[254] See the fine analysis in Stäblein, *Schriftbild*, 178 ff.

[255] An introduction is Horst Brunner, 'Das deutsche Liebeslied um 1400', *Gesammelte Vorträge der 600-Jahrfeier Oswalds von Wolkenstein 1977* (Göppingen: Kümmerle, 1978), 105–46. See also Ewald Jammers, 'Deutsche Lieder um 1400', *AcM* 28 (1956), 28–59, and pp. 350 f below.

chivalric patronage. Apart from their interesting 'stroke notation' (see below), these poems and their monophonic melodies are significant because they share the aesthetic of both the Germanic and French traditions.[256]

Leonardo Giustinian cannot be compared with other authors well because we have no melodies by him. His authentic poetic voice, so clearly distinct from that of all his Italian predecessors, is not matched by any surviving music. When he performed his longer poems[257] for aristocratic Venetian listeners, he certainly used melodic patterns borrowed from unwritten epic songs. The so-called *giustiniane*, however, which Ciconia and others set so successfully, used succinct, lyrical forms of popularizing types: ballata, *strambotto, siciliana*. The texts, rarely by Leonardo himself but always overcrowded with his personal mannerisms such as emphatically repeated words, are only *poesia per musica*. (See also p. 103.) Monophonic art-song was no longer a tradition-building force in its own right, except in the limited environment of the Meistersinger schools.

Monophonic popular song, on the other hand, shaped much of the music of this era. It was a stock of poetic and musical ideas open to everyone; an object of reference in literature, theatre, and, of course, other music; building material for secular and sacred polyphony. Orally transmitted songs of this period typically surface in some form of adaptation within the written tradition, which does not mean that they have lost their identity. Nor should the problems of definition surrounding the romantic concept of 'folksong' cast doubt on the existence of musical entities which, with or without their 'own' words, were known to uneducated as well as educated people. Popular tunes were sometimes derived from artistic polyphony by simplification or extraction of individual lines – a phenomenon which could be called 'dismantled' polyphony. (A better but untranslatable term would be the German *zersingen*, literally 'sing to pieces'.) Most popular tunes were persistent travellers. That they were able to change genre, language, function and style, gave them a true European significance.

References to songs that are otherwise lost or rare can occur in literary sources (such as *Il Saporetto*, see p. 90), or in musical treatises.[258] More often they occur in polyphonic music. The tradition of quoting 'popular' cantus firmi in Masses, motets and, indeed, other chansons (the *chansons rustiques*; see p. 454), was old and persistent. Guillaume Dufay had a special flair for quoting or elaborating popular songs, some of which may have had an ancient history. He remodelled a polyphonic version of 'La belle se siet au pied de la tour', a song recalling a type of historical ballad known in thirteenth-century France as *chanson de toile* ('needlework-song'), analogies of which were known in many

---

[256] Karel Heeroma and Cornelis Lindenburg eds, *Liederen en Gedichten uit het Gruuthuse-Handschrift* (Leiden: Brill, 1966); Strohm, *Bruges*, 108.

[257] Collected in Bertold Wiese ed., *Poesie edite ed inedite di Lionardo Giustiniani* (Bologna, 1883). They are mostly passionate love-songs or dialogues in long *canzona* or *sirventese* forms.

[258] In a treatise attributed to Dufay which itself is known only through a citation, the composer quotes a lost Mass by Ycart over the Italian dance-tune 'Deh, vóltate in qua bella Rosina' (or 'Voltati in ça Rosina'): see F. Alberto Gallo, 'Citazioni da un trattato di Dufay', *CMH* 4 (1966), 149–52.

countries.[259] Dance-tunes – with and without words – also belong to this group. The most famous of them are found in various elaborations and can be considered part of a shared, supranational repertory, transmitted by the minstrels who used it in European ballrooms.[260] Many were derived from other genres, for example from artistic polyphony by way of *zersingen*.

There is the well-known case of the English square strongly resembling the *basse danse* tune 'La Portingaloise' and also found as the tenor of the ballade 'Or me veult Esperance mentir'. This song is attributed to Dufay in two sources and labelled 'Portugaler' in another.[261] Whereas this tune may not actually have come from Portugal, the ubiquitous 'La Spagna' (or 'Castille', or 'Re di Spagna') was probably a genuine Spanish melody which made an international career.[262] There is Binchois' use of the apparent dance-song 'Se tu t'en marias' as the tenor of his chanson 'Filles a marier' (the text of which was also applied to a *basse danse* tune); a Mass cycle over 'Se tu t'en marias' exists, and a theatrical use of this or a similar song is also likely.[263] More enigmatic is the possible link between the antiphon 'Te gloriosus' for All Saints, the apparent dance-tune 'Te gloriosus' or 'Te gratiorius' cited in two dance tutors, and an English Mass cycle over the antiphon tune.[264]

With the help of many secondary quotations, we can sometimes reconstruct the 'biography' of a famous tune. 'Rosty boully joyeulx' ('the merry boiled roast'), for example, was a *ballo* which may have originated as a kind of satirical song. It made its career as a dance-melody in France, Italy and then Germany, being used for both the stately *basse danse* and the lively or bawdy *pas de Brabant*. Many references in secular plays and other literature exploit its popularity and humorous name for comic effect.[265] A musician wishing to be hired for dancing festivities surely needed it in his repertory. We learn about the most requested tunes of this kind in a contract drawn up in 1449 between a student of the University of Avignon and a Jewish minstrel:

[259] See Michel Zink, *Les chansons de toile* (Paris, 1977) (Collection Essais sur le Moyen-Age, vol. 1); Samuel Baud-Bovy, 'Sur la ballade européenne', *SM* 19 (1977), 235–49. For the polyphonic version, see Fallows, *Dufay*, 130.

[260] Of the vast literature on late medieval dance, the best access to the music is given in Heartz, '*Basse Dance*'; Heartz, 'A 15th-century ballo'; Crane, *Materials*; Gallo, '"Ballare lombardo"'; to the choreographies in Brainard, *Art of Courtly Dancing*, and Heartz, '*Basse Dance*'; to the social aspects in Salmen, *Spielmann*, 113–20 and Lincoln Kirstein, *Dance. A Short History of Classic Theatrical Dancing* (New York, 1935 R Princeton, 1987).

[261] On this case and on the *names* for dance-tunes, see Strohm, *Bruges*, 115 f. I suggest now that the tenor was extracted from the chanson, whoever composed it, and *then* became an English square as well as a dance-tune (like 'Vostre tres doulx': see below). For the newly discovered second attribution to Dufay, see Helmut Hell, 'Zwei weitere Blätter zum Fragment Mus.ms.3224 in der Bayerischen Staatsbibliothek aus der Dufay-Zeit', *Musik in Bayern* 27 (1983), 43–9.

[262] See Bukofzer, *Studies*, ch. 6 ('A polyphonic basse dance of the Renaissance').

[263] Picker, 'The cantus firmus in Binchois' *Files a marier*', *JAMS* 18 (1965), 236 f; Strohm, *Bruges*, 115. Another good example of a popular dance-tune as tenor of a polyphonic chanson is 'La Triquotée': Brown ed., *Theatrical Chansons*, nos. 5 and 55.

[264] See Brown, *French Secular Theater*, 158 (for the plainsong and dance); Strohm, *Bruges*, 126 (for the Mass).

[265] See Heartz, 'A 15th-century ballo'; Brown, *French Secular Theater*, 157; Crane, *Materials*, 97–101.

Mosse of Lisbon . . ., Jew, promised and agreed to teach and instruct the aforesaid Anthonius in the playing, on the lute or harp [*cithara sive arpa*], of the following songs or tunes [*carmina sive cantinellas*]: First, *joyeux espoyr*; then, *sperance, rostit bollit, joyeux acontre, la bone volunté que j'ey*, in two metres [*a deux mesures*], including the *basse dance* [*l'aubedance*] and *le pas de breban*; two *bergeres*, i.e. *le joly vertboys* and *Jauffroit*, and the *entrée* that is accustomed in all dances.[266]

This probably means that the melodies from *joyeux espoyr* to *la bone volunté* were used in the 'two metres' of the *basse danse* and of the *pas de Brabant*, and it was necessary to specifically study their different rhythms in each version. The former requires, according to some scholars, all equal note-values for the tune (monorhythm), the latter probably a triple measure.[267] The two *bergères* may have been characterized dances for soloists, and the *entrée* a standard instrumental piece.

Aspects of transmission, performance and notation

The *basse danse* sources, for example the Franco-Burgundian court manuscript *B-Br 9085* from the end of the century,[268] contain many tunes which are either tenors extracted from polyphonic pieces or were used as tenors or cantus firmi. In fact, the *basse danse* was supposed to be based on tenor melodies, played in slow note-values (whereas the Italian *ballo* more often took its rhythm from a lively top line). The typical notation of the tunes uses equal black breves. Isolated tenors are also found outside the dance repertories, for example in the Venetian manuscript of *c.*1430, *PC III*. The tenors are good melodies, drawn from the best chansons of the day: by Dufay, Arnold de Lantins, Binchois. What happened to them may find its explanation in another Venetian manuscript, *GB-Lbl Cott. Tit. A. XXVI*. This was the pocket-book of a professional trumpeter, Zorzi Trombetta, who travelled on Venetian galleys all around the Mediterranean as well as to England and Flanders.[269] In his performances, for example for weddings along the Adriatic coast, he seems to have played chansons or only their tenors – which are notated in one part of his book. Several primitive two-part settings of the tenor of Dunstable's rondeau 'Puisque m'amour' fill another page of the manuscript.

To extract polyphonic tenors and re-use them in popular genres is the opposite of polyphonic composition over a popular tune in the tenor. The relationship of the two techniques must have been close. Composers (and poets, when they were not the same people) were mostly vocal performers, and they were mostly men, accustomed to singing a tenor part on its own. The cantus firmus

---

[266] Heartz, 'A 15th-century ballo', 372. The contract closely resembles the document on Cely's music and dance lessons from a minstrel in Calais (p. 393).

[267] Heartz, '*Basse Dance*'; Bukofzer, *Studies*, ch. 6.

[268] Facs edn: Closson ed., *Manuscrit dit des basses danses*. See also Heartz, '*Basse Dance*', 288 f and 327–30; Besseler–Gülke, *Schriftbild*, pl. 43.

[269] Leech-Wilkinson, 'Un libro'; Strohm, *Bruges*, 113 ff.

procedure, and the high social status of the tenor voice in sacred ensembles (see p. 278), are other aspects of the same phenomenon. Only England deviated somewhat: its detachable melodies were not always tenors but sometimes the counterpoints to them ('squares'). This was because in England, plainsongs were often performed by unskilled singers and it was the composer–specialist who provided the 'square'.

This hierarchy between the parts had an influence upon secular music. Secular monophony of the Middle Ages is usually notated in a tenor register – as is plainsong. Although the French chanson tradition gave priority – and words – to the cantus, which was sung at the top of the male register, that priority may have been rivalled by the tenor more often than we know. All-vocal performance of three-part chansons or, in fact, of two-part versions of chansons, is well documented. Although words are not necessary for a tenor singer to enjoy his line, texted tenors are frequent in Italian and German songs, and in certain French chanson types (two-part and double-texted pieces) as well. The German *Tenorlied*, where only the tenor needs words, seems to have originated with Oswald von Wolkenstein, but perhaps under the influence of Italian practice.[270] Later German songbooks, especially the Lochamer-Liederbuch (*D-B 40613*) (*c.*1452–60), transmit tenor parts which do not fit underneath 'their' cantus parts, and rather function as melismatic introductions for the song, or as some kind of related, independent melodies.[271] There was also a German–Italian tradition of playing a high part (on lute, harp or *chitarrino*, i.e. gittern) against a vocal tenor; performances of Pietrobono and uses of 'tenori todeschi' seem to belong to it (see p. 568). Iconographic and archival evidence is often ambiguous, but the least evidence supports the solution most favoured by traditional musicology: a vocal cantus over two instrumental parts. In reality the tenor was too important to be treated in the same way as the contratenor.[272]

Introductory melismas as in the Lochamer-Liederbuch occur regularly in monophonic and polyphonic song until the early fifteenth century. (See also Ex. 19.) Binchois used these apparently old-fashioned opening melismas only for a few very expressive songs. In monophonic song, they remained more standard. Scholars and performers have usually interpreted them as instrumental preludes. There is musical logic in this assumption: the instrument 'sets the tone'. By extension, intermediate textless passages would also have to be performed instrumentally, like ritornellos. Other arguments, however, speak for vocal performance: the scribal habit of placing the first syllable of the text, or only the first letter, at the beginning of the melismas; their presence in undoubtedly vocal compositions such as Italian madrigals and ballatas; the

---

[270] See Theodor Göllner, 'Landinis "Questa fanciulla" bei Oswald von Wolkenstein', *Mf* 17 (1964), 393–8; Pelnar, *Ars-nova-Sätze*.

[271] See Salmen–Petzsch eds, *Lochamer-Liederbuch*, nos. 2–5, 14a, 37 and 38. Of Oswald's arrangement 'Frolichen so wel', the tenor alone stands in MS '*B*', the cantus alone in MS '*A*' of Oswald's songs: the tenor of the original song 'N'ay je cause' (Ex. 8) was perhaps a detachable tune.

[272] Fallows, 'Specific information', 131 f, discusses several practices.

sometimes close motivic interplay with the texted lines. The Monk of Salzburg and Oswald von Wolkenstein favour *trompetta* contours for their melismatic introductions, which does not prove that they must be played on an instrument (certainly not a trumpet!). An average example is this little love-song by Eberhard von Cersne (*c.*1400):

Example 49 Eberhard von Cersne, 'Hilff, werde, suße, reyne frucht'

[Help, dear sweet pure fruit, well protected from any change, crowned with honourable modesty, illuminated by every virtue! I would have sworn that hardly a woman, when I was sitting alone and in sadness, could have stolen my heart out of my body in such a way, and placed it on the joyful road, making it overbearing with joy that was never imagined.][273]

Helmut Lomnitzer's transcription of this song had to solve some problems of the original notation. We may class it among the archaic or simplified notations which are typical for a vast amount of late medieval monophony or simple polyphony, and which inhabit the border areas of musical literacy. In this case

---

[273] Cersne, *Der Minne Regel*, 191 (with three other notated songs, from the manuscript *A-Wn 3013*).

the melody is written in letter notation only, separately from the words, and with 'orthochronic' indication of rhythm.

Letter notation is not a problem. As precise indicators of pitch, letters or numbers were used in medieval as well as later music theory, in practical sources of plainsong and, of course, in various types of tablatures. Two sources of German monophonic song also use letters: the Cersne MS (*A-Wn 3013*) with our song plus three others, and the Königsteiner Liederbuch (*c.*1470–76), where four songs have mixed letters and numbers as in a tablature for five-course lute.[274] In the Cersne songs, the letters resemble keyboard notation as they proceed through the octave from *c* to *b* (in the tenor register), and the upper octave is identified by a little stroke above the letters. It is a diatonic scale, as in staff notation. No distinction is made between 'b' (flat) and 'h' (natural): in lines 9 and 10, *b♭* should certainly be considered.

A much larger problem is the separation of the pitches from the words: the letters of the complete melody occupy their own line on the page, followed by the complete copy of the text. This format recurs elsewhere, for example in most melodies of the Gruuthuse MS. There is no 'text underlay' here: the singer has somehow to guess from the contours and phrase lengths of the tune where the words must go. The possibility of untexted melismas makes matters worse: in our case, the transcriber had to assume them simply because there were far too many notes for the syllables.[275] It is unlikely that this notation was useful to singers who were not already familiar with the tune or who could not at least predict the general phrase-patterns. The problem is not as rare as it may seem: we meet it in all those strophic songs where subsequent strophes differ in the number of syllables but are not underlaid to the music. Fifteenth-century scribes always leave this particular underlay problem to the performer – and this in addition to the general problem of rough or incomplete underlay.[276]

The letters in our song are used as 'orthochronic' symbols, i.e. each letter represents one unchangeable duration. For longer note-values, the scribe wrote the same letter twice. He could thus express the simplest ratio of note-values, 1 : 2, whereas he did not or could not express 2 : 3 or 3 : 4 etc. Also, his longer notes cannot easily be distinguished from repeated pitches because there are no underlaid syllables to mark the separation of the latter. Finally, the scribe took a liberty that was typical for Germanic verse: he did not notate the upbeats at all. The text lines 6, 7 and 9 of the example begin with upbeat syllables which

---

274 But they are not real lute music as has been claimed: see Fallows, 'Fifteenth-century tablatures'.

275 The question of untexted melismas is discussed in Biezen-Vellekoop, 'Aspects of stroke notation', 18 f, with the example of a similar German song.

276 The problem of text underlay in monophonic and polyphonic music of the time can only be signalled here. It is discussed in the writings of Don Harrán, especially his *Word-Tone Relations*, chaps. 3, 5 and 6. See also Leeman L. Perkins, 'Toward a rational approach to text placement in the secular music of Dufay's time', in Atlas ed., *Dufay Quincentenary Conference*, 102–14; Gilbert Reaney, 'Text underlay in early fifteenth-century musical manuscripts', in Snow ed., *Essays in Musicology*, 245–51.

are omitted in the music (the transcription adds them in pointed brackets). This is because upbeats are unaccented, 'supernumerary' syllables which can be omitted: when present, their note has to be 'subtracted' from the preceding longer note, repeating its pitch. The rhythmic grouping of the song falls easily in '4/4', suggesting the rhythm 'dotted minim–crotchet' across line-ends. The upbeat would then be subtracted from a quadruple, not duple, value. In the Gruuthuse songs, the suppression of unaccented syllables is almost the norm.

That this kind of notation was used far more often than its survival suggests is indicated by the variants found for the same tunes in different sources, where long notes are shortened and vice versa, and where repeated pitches are contracted to double note-values and vice versa. To some extent, these changes are caused by notational constraints, but sometimes it seems that a musical mind has intervened which worked on the same principles. This rhythmic flexibility was, indeed, part of musical practice: handing down melodies, 'dismantling' written music, or improvising over given tunes, involved precisely these stretching or contracting exercises. Even sources of mensural polyphony differ most often in the treatment of repeated pitches versus double note-values, and subsequent stanzas of strophic songs almost invariably do.

A comprehensive theory of the late medieval monophonic and primitive notations is a task for the future. Such a theory would have to elucidate the descendance of those late notations from earlier neumatic scripts, to explain how they were useful while looking 'deficient' to us, and to illustrate to what extent the 'deficiencies' were limitations of the music itself.[277]

The most interesting type was *stroke notation*, shown in Plate 6, and transcribed below (Ex. 50).

This notation is normally written on a five-line staff and instead of note-heads uses brief vertical strokes, similar to neumes. The external shape of these symbols varies in the sources; they can be dots, neumes or diamonds resembling semibreves. (The semibreve also had the status of a basic rhythmic unit in other monophonic notations, as for example in the Wolkenstein MSS.) Each symbol corresponds to an unchangeable note-value which has to be the smallest used in the piece (the 'pulse', as it were). The larger values are 'built up' by repeating the stroke in close succession. When these rules are observed, the stroke-unit is the only graphic symbol needed. The double (and sometimes triple) strokes resemble the *bistropha* and *tristropha* of neumatic notations, which had similar functions. The concepts of 'perfect' and 'imperfect' time do not exist, since everything is built up from one basic value. Dots of perfection, addition etc. are completely avoided. 'Strene notation' (found so far only in England) differs more in shape than in principle: the basic value is written as a square note-

---

[277] Wolff, 'Arten der Mensuralnotation', succinctly addresses the problem (and its link with keyboard tablatures). Of the various textbooks, only Rastall, *Notation*, 305 ff, and Wolf, *Handbuch*, vol. 1, 178 ff, pay attention to this subject. Very little is found in Ewald Jammers, *Aufzeichnungsweisen der einstimmigen außerliturgischen Musik des Mittelalters* (Cologne, 1975) (Paläographie der Musik, vol. I/4). See also the examples in Stäblein, *Schriftbild*, 208 ff and 218 f.

6 'VOTRE' and other music scribblings. (London, British Library, Harley 1512, fol. 2r.)

head, and double values are indicated by little strokes descending from both sides of it – so that there are two different symbols.

Plate 6 is a page from the private breviary *GB-Lbl Harley 1512*, once belonging to the Apsley Bee family. On fol. 2r–2v, somebody scribbled (*c.*1450) diverse melodies which he or she apparently liked. Of these, the melody labelled 'VOTRE' originated as the tenor of a Binchois rondeau, 'Vostre très doulx regart'. It is written at first in genuine stroke notation, but later on, mensural symbols are introduced. The transcription (see Ex. 50) compares the Binchois original with the version in Harley and with the tenor of a two-part setting in the English Ritson MS.[278]

Example 50 'Votre trey dowce regaunt': three tenors

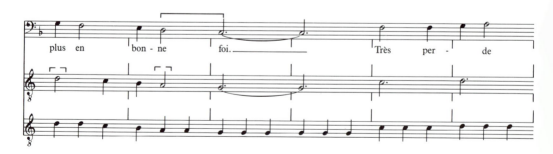

---

[278] The Ritson version, printed in Stevens ed., *Early Tudor*, no. 17, has been interpreted as polyphonic dance-music in Walter H. Kemp, '"Votre trey dowce": a duo for dancing', *ML* 60 (1979), 37–44.

Example 50 (*cont.*)

The idea that 'Votre' as notated in the Harley MS was played on an instrument, perhaps for dancing, seems reasonable. This would not be contradicted by the presence, on the same page, of the two-part hymn 'O lux beata trinitas', also in stroke notation. Hymn tunes were indeed used in England for instrumental exercises or entertainment. A similar page is found in the manuscript *GB-Ob Digby 167*, with three pieces: a plainsong hymn ('Eterne rex'), the *basse danse* 'Auxce bon youre de la bone estren', and a textless tenor apparently for the bagpipe ('Quene note'), with a florid upper voice.[279]

Stroke notation existed at least in England, the Low Countries, Germany, Austria and Italy – but something like it was probably known in yet other countries.[280] Significant sources of stroke notation are the large collection of the Gruuthuse MS and similar song sources from Germany, and the copies of nine songs, mostly French chanson tenors, on empty spaces of a county register

---

[279] See Crane, *Materials*, nos. 97 and 102. Facs in Stainer ed., *Early Bodleian Music*, pl. XCIII. Bagpipes are often shown in pictures of dancing.

[280] See Biezen–Vellekoop, 'Aspects of stroke notation', with excellent discussion and bibliography. To the eleven sources listed there, we can add: five other English sources, discussed in Bent, 'New and little-known fragments', and Hughes, 'Choir'; the Viennese collection *A-Wn 5094*; the Italian sources *GB-Lbl Cott. Tit. A. XXVI* (Zorzi Trombetta's book) and Bologna, S Petronio, fragment E (see Hamm, 'Musiche'); the appendix of the Lochamer-Liederbuch (fols. 44–5: see Ameln ed., *Locheimer Liederbuch*; Salmen–Petzsch eds, *Lochamer-Liederbuch*, 127–30).

of Namur.[281] Sacred polyphony is written in this manner in a four-part Mass cycle found in Saxilby (*GB-SA*) and Bologna (*I-Bsp* frg. E) (see p. 388), and in similar English sources. Zorzi Trombetta's book for instrumental performances, which uses single black semibreves, and the Viennese miscellany *A-Wn 5094* (which also uses letter notation) have partly simplified polyphonic pieces. The typical notation of the *basse danse* sources, in equal breves, is akin to stroke notation. The repertory appearing in this notation may be classified in three types:

> monophonic hymns, vernacular songs, and dance-tunes which may be 'adequately' expressed in a neumatic notation;
> 'dismantled' or simplified mensural music;
> polyphonic music composed *a priori* in simple rhythms that are suitable for this notation.

This is a very wide range of styles. If the different cases have anything in common at all, it is not a type of music, but a type of reader: the reader who was less informed (or was uninformed) about the rules of (French) mensural notation. This did not necessarily restrict the musical communication in genres which had no specific rhythm of their own (antiphons, for example), or whose rhythm was transmitted orally (metrical hymns, *cantiones*, monophonic art-song). Here the notation was not primitive, just as neumes are not primitive: the written symbols were intended to be complemented by a large supplement of unwritten information. We can speak of primitive notation, however, when pieces composed with the resources of mensural rhythm are transmitted without it, as in the case of dance tenors extracted from polyphonic chansons. An intermediate group are genuine dance-tunes, which lacked the rhythmic complexities of polyphonic voices. But their strict rhythmic continuity was also distinct from lyrical song with its freedom of phrasing, unmeasured rests between lines and so on. The last category comprises compositions such as the Saxilby Mass and the chanson arrangements in Zorzi Trombetta's manuscript, where the musical structure itself is kept simple for the benefit of halfskilled performers, as well as some sketches for settings of the hymn 'Ave maris stella' in *A-Wn 5094*.

The encounters between mensural and alternative notations were innumerable. The scribe of Plate 6, in copying a Binchois rondeau not composed with such restrictions in mind, unexpectedly found minims (quavers in modern transcription) and at that point switched to genuine mensural symbols. This kind of 'volatility' was typical. Many notational systems were created *ad hoc*, and a considerable input of oral information must have been necessary to understand some of them. Quite regularly, principles of orthochronic notation were mixed with symbols derived from neumes, or with square notations. This

[281] The chanson tenors of (Dufay) 'La belle se siet' and (Fontaine) 'Mon cuer pleure' are transcribed from this source in Biezen–Vellekoop, 'Aspects of stroke notation'. Another melody in Namur is the chanson tenor 'Je sui povere de liesse', of which polyphonic elaborations exist (see n. 293). On the manuscript, see Crane, *Materials*, 20.

happened often in simple polyphony when it was written in 'gothic' or 'German neumes' and 'Messine notation'.[282] The latter did not distinguish between *punctus* and *virga*, but had a normative unit which was often diamond-shaped. Some musicians looked upon this as equivalent to a mensural semibrevis unit. For smaller values (whether precisely half or not), they simply added an upward- or downward-stem. Ligatures were also used, and where an upward stem on a two-note ligature suggests to us specific mensural values (*cum opposita proprietate*), only an unmeasured melisma may be intended. In German and eastern sources, little dots or numbers above a square note are often used to indicate how many semibreves it lasts. This is also done with two-note ligatures in the ratios 2 : 1 or 1 : 2, as shown by the groupings of the dots. This device serves readers who do not know all the rules of mensuration. On the other hand, it is related to the orthochronic principle of tablatures, where dots or strokes above a note-head or letter indicate the durations. Most of these devices are also helpful for the keyboard player, and are therefore taken over in the developing keyboard tablature notation.[283]

Instrumental ensemble music

Instrumental performance and instrumental music were different issues in the Middle Ages: whereas the playing of vocal lines was ubiquitous, independent instrumental music seems to have been rare. We cannot be certain about this, since the professional players – the minstrels – who most probably developed genuine instrumental idioms were precisely those who were accustomed to perform without script. Where necessary, they could use vocal notation to learn the melodies. In contrast to keyboard music which developed its own notation, which was more often notated for its own sake and which is therefore more often preserved (see below), music for other instruments had no notation of its own and left few distinct traces. Conventional wisdom regards this music as an 'improvised' and therefore unwritten or even 'unwritable' art.

There is admittedly a scarcity of sources in the fifteenth century. The monophonic *estampies* of the Florentine Trecento manuscript *GB-Lbl add.29987* (see p. 90) are among the last notated specimens of independent instrumental music. In central Europe, the genres of *trumpetum* and *stampania* (*estampie*) are still mentioned in treatises and even found in music manuscripts – often with added texts, however.[284] Otherwise, we have only chanson tenors as in the

---

[282] For examples, see Stäblein, *Schriftbild*, 194 ff.

[283] See Wolff, 'Arten der Mensuralnotation'.

[284] On trumpet pieces, see below. Other witnesses are the Czech theorist Paulus Paulirinus (see p. 292) and the Bohemian (German?) fragment *D-WI* (*c.*1430): see Brunner-Ganser-Hartmann, 'Windsheimer Fragment', 194 ff with discussion of the three-part estampie 'Autentica hec regina'. For other sources, see Leo Schrade, *Die handschriftliche Überlieferung der ältesten Instrumentalmusik* (Lahr, 1931); Rokseth, 'Instrumental music', 414–19.

manuscript *PC III* (see above), or dance-tunes.[285] Generations of musicologists have combed the written sources for instrumental pieces. Criteria for their iden-tification (absence of words, 'unsingable lines' etc.) were proposed and duly rejected.[286] Most pernicious was the idea that contratenors of vocal pieces had to be instrumental in style. This research led – at best – to the recognition that practically every melody that was notated in the Middle Ages is singable, and that the instrumental drones, embellishments, 'improvised' tunes, the drumming, bellringing and other sundry noises as we know them from older recordings of early music can nowhere be found in the documents.

On the other hand, studies of the archival and iconographic sources[287] have not only demonstrated the importance and frequency of playing without writ-ten music, they have also suggested that pan-European traditions existed: prac-tices which everyone knew, tunes which everyone remembered. Are they all totally lost? Did illiterate minstrels conspire to deprive posterity of their art? Or have we simply been looking for the wrong thing?

There is evidence (provided by narrative sources, for example) that instru-mentalists did not always play typically instrumental idioms, but quite often vocal music – and this music we do have.[288] The most conventional public use of instruments took place in processions. We know what music was heard there, and we have it: sacred plainsongs. As regards the art of ensemble improvisa-tion, the improvisatory freedom of five wind players who perform while a hundred people sing the *Te Deum* is limited, to say the least. Embellishments did exist, of course, but could be premeditated. The tunes which the wind band played for dancing or dining were not always invented on the spot. The listeners must have wanted to recognize something.

We should abandon two misconceptions of our technological civilization. One of them is that music which has not come down to us was always 'unwritten' (as if all the written music of the time were preserved), and that 'unwritten music' was always 'improvised' (as if it were forbidden to carry a tune in your head). With our short memories, we tend to think that medieval musicians who performed without written music must have been improvising when they were just playing from memory. Leo Schrade recognized that if instrumental music was not written then this was not due to its style, form, technical aspects etc., but rather to the different status (the *ad hoc* character) of the performance

---

[285] Typical are the two 'carmina ytalica utilia pro coreis' ('Italian songs useful for round-dances') which Dr Schedel wrote into his songbook after returning from Italy in 1463: see Wackernagel ed., *Lieder-buch*, fol. 131. These textless tenors were well-known *basses danses*: see Heartz, 'Hoftanz', 19 f.

[286] See, for example, Arnold Schering, *Studien zur Musikgeschichte der Frührenaissance* (Leipzig, 1914). Despite a basically erroneous theory (Trecento madrigals with their melismatic lines are organ music), Schering's views on detail do not deserve the total neglect they are suffering today.

[287] See Bowles, *Musikleben*; Bowles, *Pratique musicale*; Salmen, *Spielmann*; Pietzsch, *Fürsten*; Polk, 'Instrumental music', as well as Brown, 'St Augustine'.

[288] A chronicler of Bruges recognized, without having any technical knowledge, that the city waits played 'Ave regina celorum, followed by several other musical songs': Strohm, *Bruges*, 87.

itself.[289] The instrumental piece could by all means be formally strict, premeditated and composed in the mind. It could sound like vocal polyphony.

The other misconception of our technological age is that instrumental or vocal character is an identifying, inalienable property of a piece, a substance as it were. But it is not the piece that was vocal or instrumental, but the activity. Just as the dividing line between the sacred and secular spheres was sometimes simply the threshold of the church door, so a chanson might be sung before dinner and played after. Narrative sources like *Il Saporetto* (see p. 90) document this pragmatic attitude towards media. The following is probable:

> instrumental music was largely borrowed vocal music;
> professional players were able to perform composed polyphony;
> instrumental idioms were often practised by singers.

Instrumental idioms are indeed found in the vocal 'trompetta' pieces of the early fifteenth century. The degree of their realism (fanfare style) seems irrelevant to the question of performance medium. Some pieces, and not the most realistic ones, might be genuine instrumental music, for example 'Tuba gallicalis' (see p. 108). Around 1415, polyphonic wind band performances imitated voices. The instruments themselves were well suited to the task; the trombone with some kind of slide mechanism had evolved in central Europe before *c.*1400.[290] Trumpet fanfares for war sounded different, of course. But vocalists of polyphonic chapels were able to sing like trumpets and thus we have written polyphony in this style, too.

The melodies played by minstrels in secular contexts (for dining, dancing, jousting etc.) were partly of vocal origin and partly 'genuine' instrumental tunes. The usual performance of these tunes in the early to mid-fifteenth century treated them as a kind of cantus firmus. The trombonist Zorzi Trombetta had in his book (see above) two types of music. The chansons or chanson tenors notated in black semibreves can have been played as written, or learned by heart and played with embellishments. The clumsy two-part versions of 'Puisque m'amour'[291] are Trombetta's attempts to write down a second voice against a given tenor as he would play it with a colleague.

'Votre trey dowce' in the Ritson MS is such a cantus firmus setting. To Binchois' tenor (see Ex. 50), an entirely new cantus has been added: a very florid line, which may have been played for dancing. Is it a frozen improvisation? It has been objected that Binchois' tenor is not dissolved into equal note-values as in *basses danses*, and that its rhythm was too irregular to allow for an improvised

---

[289] *Die handschriftliche Überlieferung* (n. 284 above), 14–20.

[290] See Polk, 'Instrumental music', especially 167–74, and *idem*, 'The trombone, the slide trumpet, and the ensemble tradition of the early Renaissance', *Early Music* 17 (1989), 389–97. The most authoritative earlier study (apart from the pioneering ones by Besseler, all quoted in it), is Janez Höfler, 'Der "Trompette de Menestrels" und sein Instrument', *TVNM* 29 (1979), 92–132. This view has partly been modified by Polk.

[291] Printed in Dunstable, *Collected Works*, n. 55.

counterpoint which itself is patterned.[292] The problem with this argument is, again, the concept of 'improvisation' as something totally unpremeditated. We can accept that the upper line of the Ritson piece is, or comes close to, a version which a good minstrel had worked out in his mind, and perhaps repeatedly tried out in performances. The version written down was the best or most difficult one. The same might be said of the several 'polyphonic *basses danses*' found in mid-fifteenth-century sources.[293] 'Auxce bon youre' and 'T'Andernaken al op ten Rijn' in *Tr 87* (*c.*1442) are cantus firmus settings in three parts, with florid top lines and intricate contratenors. 'T'Andernaken' is a complex piece of 37 bars length. Its chanson format and cadences resemble Binchois' style, although its motivic vocabulary is very different. A group of three shawms (one discant and two tenors), or two shawms and a trombone, would seem perfectly suited for its performance. This is not an improvised piece; it is even attributed to a composer: Tyling (a Netherlander?). In order to sing it one has to underlay the words to the folksong tenor itself. In the other voices words would sound futile:

Example 51 Tyling, 'T'Andernaken al op den Rijn'

[292] Litterick, 'Italian instrumental ensemble music', 125 n. 14.

[293] See Bukofzer, *Studies*, ch. 6; Southern, 'Foreign music', especially 268 ff; Crane, *Materials*, especially 62–7 (transcriptions of 'Quene note' and 'T'Andernaken'); Charles Hamm, 'A group of anonymous English pieces in Trent 87', *ML* 41 (1960), 211–15, with a reply by Brian Trowell and a counter-reply by Hamm in *ML* 42 (1961), 96 f; Meylan, *L'énigme*, plates V–VI; Biezen-Vellekoop, 'Aspects of stroke notation', 8 f (transcription of 'Quene note'); Fallows, *Dufay*, 130 ('Qui latuit / Je suis povere' perhaps by Dufay).

Example 51 (*cont.*)

All the ensemble music described so far seems connected with the tradition of wind bands.[294] This was partly a polyphonic tradition, for example in the major centres. Polyphonic elaborations of widely travelled tunes such as 'T'Andernaken' probably typify the repertories of sophisticated *musica alta* players around 1450. These musicians travelled widely themselves.

Some later documents can be interpreted retrospectively. One is the payment to Nicasius de Brauwere, a Bruges priest and succentor, for having 'notated and composed, at diverse times, certain motets for performance by the city minstrels' (1484–5).[295] Public concerts of the city waits of Bruges had been established in 1480, and the ability of these shawmists and trombonists to play 'motets' must have dated about a generation back. Another significant document from the Low Countries is the Maastricht fragment (*c.*1480) described by Smits van Waesberghe.[296] It contains a few plainsongs in neumatic notation, and – in mensural notation – the untexted cantus parts of ten polyphonic pieces including Dutch songs, French chansons and motets from Johannes Brassart to Josquin. Item no. VIII, the only tenor part, is the melody of 'T'Andernaken' in a mensurally rhythmicized version. Although the instrumental use of the manuscript cannot be proven, this isolated tenor suggests that the partbook served a discant shawmist who played the cantus parts as written, but played embellishments over 'T'Andernaken'.

By the end of the century, wind bands in many parts of Europe had polyphonic repertories, mainly consisting of chansons and motets. The best-known manuscript apparently containing such a repertory is the Casanatense Chansonnier (*I-Rc 2856; Cas*) of *c.*1480 (see p. 558). In Venetian processions of 1494 and later, a Mantuan wind band played mensural polyphony: 'motets' by Bus-

---

[294] See especially Polk, 'Instrumental music' (with further literature); Whitwell, *Wind Band* (compilation of documents).

[295] Bruges City Accounts, 1484–5: 'Betaelt heer Casin de Brauwer, priester ende cantor van den Kinderen van Sint-Salvators, . . . van ghestelt ende ghemaect te hebben, ten diverschen stonden, zekere motetten, omme die by den menestreulen van deser stede ghespeelt te werdene . . .' (after Vander Straeten, *Musique*, vol. 4, 99). For the context, see Strohm, *Bruges*, 86.

[296] Smits van Waesberghe, 'Muziekboek'.

nois and Obrecht.[297] The Bruges motets of 1484–5 were expressly composed for the civic wind band (the term 'motet' may have been applied loosely, meaning simply polyphonic pieces). They could have had a vocal 'basis' such as a folksong cantus firmus: many such pieces exist, for example by Obrecht and Agricola.[298]

In the mid- to late fifteenth century, a growing number of textless ensemble pieces appears in polyphonic sources. They are re-elaborations of voices from well-known chansons ('cantus firmus arrangements'), or imitative, freely composed pieces, sometimes referred to as 'fantasia', or – somewhat later – excerpts of sections from Masses or motets. One scholar, after having shown the origins of many pieces in chansons and Mass settings, dubbed them 'songs without words'.[299] This music could be vocal in origin, but was suitable for instrumental performance: the performance medium was here a question of choice or preference, not of intrinsic technical character. Voices and instruments shared contrapuntal and stylistic ideals.

It would appear that 'songs without words' were often played on soft instruments, and that the practice had an unbroken development in several countries from the 1460s until after 1500. An interesting early source is the Glogauer Liederbuch (*c.*1478–80) which also contains many polyphonic German songs and sacred works.[300] This is a set of three *partbooks*, which strongly suggests that the musicians played or sang directly from the written music – not the habit of professionals. The textless pieces, occurring in clusters, either have no titles but are identified by letters of the alphabet, or they have fanciful titles, the most striking one being 'schwanz' (tail). We find a *Pfauenschwanz* (peacock's tail), *Bauernschwanz* (peasant's tail), *Fuchsschwanz* (foxtail), but also further 'animal titles' such as *Katzenpfote* (cat's paw), *Eselskrone* (donkey's crown), *Krebsschere* (crab's scissors: a double canon) etc. In some slightly later Italian concordances, the titles are literally translated, for example *Fuchsschwanz* appears as *Coda di volpe*.

The name is thought to derive from the verb 'schwanzen' = 'tanzen', i.e. the pieces would be dances. In reality, however, many of them are literal transcriptions of French chansons and motets. *Bauernschwanz*, for example, is 'Entre Peronne et St Quentin', *Fuchsschwanz* is 'Ayme qui vouldra'. Another piece also called *Fuchsschwanz*, however, seems to be an instrumental elaboration of the same contrapuntal material, and there are other pieces which cannot easily be

---

[297] See Bowles, *Musikleben*, 128 f, with details from the Bellini painting (1496) discussed above (p. 307), and a letter (1494) by the Mantuan trombonist Giovanni Alvise, who says he has arranged two four-part motets, one by Obrecht and one by Busnois ('Gabrielem'), for six and five brass instruments, respectively, and has performed them with great success in the Christmas season in Venice. See Vander Straeten, *Musique*, vol. 8, 537; Higgins, *Busnois*, 9 f; Prizer, 'Bernardino Piffaro', 157 ff.

[298] See also Strohm, *Bruges*, 144.

[299] Edwards, 'Songs without words'. On this repertory, see also p. 568 below.

[300] Ringmann–Väterlein eds, *Glogauer Liederbuch*. Facs edn: *RMF* vol. 6. On its origin and other contents, see pp. 501 ff.

fitted to words in any of the *formes fixes*. It is even less easy to see how they could be used as dances. Some of them are long and intricately imitative. They are usually for three voices; there is a strong tendency towards strictly separate voice-ranges, i.e. with a bass instead of a conventional contratenor.

The oldest piece of the group (predating *c.*1465) seems to be the internationally famous *Pfauenschwanz* (*Coda de pavon*) by Barbingant, which is in four parts, and found in all its sources without words.[301] Its beginning suggests that it is neither a song nor a dance – but a genuine instrumental composition, not corresponding to a chanson form:

Example 52 Barbingant, 'Der Pfauenschwanz'

This piece apparently has a pre-existent tenor, perhaps a dance-tune, because another piece also entitled *Pfauenschwanz*, by Paulus de Broda (or Rhoda), is a similar elaboration of the same tenor.[302] Both pieces may reflect an earlier Franco-Netherlands style of wind band playing, documented by settings of popular tunes like 'T'Andernaken' (see Ex. 51). But the stylistic gap is large.

It may have been Barbingant's *Pfauenschwanz* that initiated a fashion for collecting such pieces for instrumental ensemble performances in Germany. By

---

[301] Barbireau (sic!), *Opera omnia*, vol. 2, 9. On the composer, see p. 444 below.

[302] On his probable identity with the Brabant composer Paulus de Rhoda, and his works, see Thomas Noblitt, 'Additional compositions by Paulus de Rhoda?', *TVNM* 37 (1987), 49–63. Both *Pfauenschwanz* pieces can be easily compared in Ringmann–Väterlein eds, *Glogauer Liederbuch*, vol. 4, 88 f.

implication, however, the works themselves may first have been composed in western Europe. A different textless piece by Paulus in the Glogau MS carries the generic name *carmen*. Although this really meant 'song' or 'poem', it became a frequent denomination for instrumental ensemble pieces in central European sources. This name is almost certainly linked to performances on soft instruments.

In Italian sources of *c.*1480–1500, the composers Martini, Agricola, Isaac and Josquin contribute most pieces. Some of these have titles such as 'La Martinella', referring to their respective composers or dedicatees.[303] 'La Martinella' is probably freely composed, and therefore needed a name like this. It initiates the development of the freely composed fantasia (see below).

Ensembles of *basse musique* were much less standardized than wind ensembles.[304] The soft instruments in processions, for example, could include portative organs, harps, lutes, flutes, gitterns, fiddles and psalteries. The iconographic and archival sources for private music-making in princely chambers, for example, reveal both 'whole' and 'broken consorts' – to borrow concepts from Elizabethan England. A slightly humorous depiction of instrumental music-making in a monastic or academic circle is shown in Plate 7. In the early and mid-fifteenth century, relatively standard combinations were:

> duets of two lutes, lute and harp, or lute and gittern;
> fiddle duets or trios;
> trios of two bowed or wind instruments with one lute, harp or organ.

Later developments led towards the 'whole consort' principle, although iconographic sources do not favour 'whole consorts' because they offer the artist's imagination too little scope. Complete sets of four recorders or crumhorns or viols are known to have existed from *c.*1500, perhaps reflecting the new style of four-part polyphony with pervasive imitation.

Lute, harp and gittern were often combined with voices. Lute and gittern were played – until the later fifteenth century – monophonically with a plectrum. Two performers, a combination frequently encountered in archival documents, could reproduce the usual chanson format with these instruments if one of them sang and played at the same time, or if the contratenor was left out (irrespective of the performance of any words). This seems to have been the practice of famous vocal and instrumental soloists such as Pietrobono, who performed either alone or with a *tenorista*, i.e. an assistant player.[305] This helper almost certainly played a lute or tenor fiddle. Against this, Pietrobono

---

[303] This type of nomenclature is apparently borrowed from *basses danses*: see Strohm, *Bruges*, 115 f. See also p. 570 below.

[304] See Polk, 'Instrumental music'; *idem*, 'Vedel and geige'. The most frequent soft instrument, the lute, has a vast literature. See the periodicals *LSJ* and *JALS*; 'Lute' in *The New Grove*; Christopher Page, 'The 15th-century lute: new and neglected sources', *Early Music* 9 (1981), 11–21. On some other instruments: Laurence Wright, 'The medieval gittern and citole: a case of mistaken identity', *GSJ* 30 (1977), 8–42; Rainer Weber, 'Recorder finds from the Middle Ages, and results of their reconstruction', *GSJ* 29 (1976), 35–41; on the harp, see p. 44 above.

[305] See Lockwood, 'Pietrobono'; Brown, 'St Augustine', 44 f, and p. 349 above.

7 Music-making clerics (Initial 'E'). Flemish, late fifteenth century. (London, British Library, add.15426, fol. 86.)

could sing the cantus line, or play it on another lute or gittern (*chitarrino*). However, if he did not perform the tenor, then he would have taken a place in the hierarchy of the music less important than that of his assistant. It is more likely, therefore, that Pietrobono sang the tenor line himself and also played an embellished cantus above it – just as if he were performing the Ritson version of 'Vostre très doulx regart'. (He may, on occasion, have done the reverse: sing the cantus and play the tenor.) The *tenorista*, dispensable as he was, must have played the contratenor, which was increasingly a bass part in three-part music, or the contratenor bassus of four-part music, while the contratenor altus was left out.[306] If there were no *tenorista*, then the contratenor was left out, and

---

[306] The word 'tenorista' may derive from two-part music of the Italian Trecento, and may generically refer to a low part. In a Frankfurt procession (1467), a lute and a muted trumpet were used 'zu discantieren', and three other lutes 'zu tenorieren': see Žak, *Musik als 'Ehr und Zier'*, 129.

Pietrobono performed only the cantus and tenor, or one of these voices alone.

The greatest organological problem is presented by ensembles of bowed instruments. The terms 'vielle', 'vedel', 'vivola cum arculo' (Tinctoris), 'vihuela de arco', 'viol' and 'geige' may all have referred to different, even incompatible, instruments according to the time and place of their use. A much-discussed monograph by Ian Woodfield concludes that the essential division is between the arm-supported (*da braccio*) types which included all the fiddles as well as the medieval *vielle*, and the leg-supported (*da gamba*) type which developed in Spain in the later fifteenth century. This became known as *viola da gamba* in Italy and did not begin 'its migration northwards across the Alps' before the early sixteenth century.[307] The problem is a historiographical one: given the many musical contacts 'across the Alps' and other surmountable barriers of the European landscape, can it be maintained that an instrument was known for a long time in one country and 'unknown' in the next? Woodfield seems unconvinced that the French and Germans had much need for viols before *c*.1510. Documents presented by Keith Polk stress the opposite; his most striking finds relate to the appearance of groups of three and more string players in many south German centres from the 1440s onwards, and the tendency of wind players to learn stringed instruments from the 1470s.[308]

It is possible to agree with Woodfield in his interpretation of a famous passage in Tinctoris's *De inventione et usu musicae* where the theorist praises the rebec and the 'vivola cum arculo' as his preferred instruments.[309] According to Woodfield, the latter is not the viol but the fiddle. Tinctoris specifically remembers performances on this instrument by the blind brothers Johannes and Karolus Fernandes. One of them played the cantus, the other the tenor of various chansons. This was in Bruges, probably in 1482. One piece from the repertory of the blind men can be identified as the widely known motet 'Gaudent in celis' by Alexander Agricola.[310]

Evidence not discussed by Woodfield involves an untitled three-part composition in *Tr 89* (fol. 402v, *c*.1466), all notated on eight-line staves because the parts have huge ranges: the top voice has c–g'', the middle voice F–b', and the bottom voice D–c'. As Disertori has shown, these ranges precisely fit a trio of viols according to the tunings listed by Silvestro Ganassi in his *Regola Rubertina* (1542).[311] This thesis would imply the existence of true viols, including a large bass viol, in the Tyrol about 1466. We probably have to agree with Woodfield, however, and think of such pieces as having been performed on fiddles and lutes.

The earliest attributable and datable fantasia, already mentioned, is Johannes

---

[307] Woodfield, *Viol*, 99.

[308] Polk, 'Vedel and geige'; see also *idem*, 'Instrumental music', 181.

[309] Woodfield, *Viol*, 96; Weinmann, *Tinctoris*, 45. Generally on Tinctoris's references to instruments, see Anthony Baines, 'Fifteenth-century instruments in Tinctoris' *De inventione et usu musicae*', *GSJ* 3 (1950), 19–26.

[310] See Strohm, *Bruges*, 88 and 143.

[311] Benevenuto Disertori, 'L'unica composizione sicuramente strumentale nei codici Trentini', *CHM* 2 (Florence, 1956), 135–45 (with edn and facs).

Martini's 'La Martinella', which was to become a source of inspiration for a whole series of similar freely composed pieces. Its earliest copy is, again in *Tr 89* (no. 752, *c*.1466), just a few pages away from the previously mentioned piece. Also adjacent to it are other pieces in similar styles, for example *Pfauenschwanz* and *Fuchsschwanz* with Latin texts for singing (nos. 604 and 675, respectively).[312] This little collection was copied for the cathedral school of Trent, but has affinities with the clusters of 'Spielstücke' in the Glogauer Liederbuch. It surely draws on instrumental ensemble repertories, most probably those that were growing up at the courts just north and south of the Alps – Munich, Innsbruck, Milan and Ferrara (see also pp. 533 ff).

Keyboard music

The earliest sources of polyphonic keyboard music already demonstrate the special status of both the instruments and their music. Organists were not minstrels, but clerics or monks and mostly learned people. Francesco Landini was famous for his playing and composing on the *organetto*, and Guillaume Dufay is portrayed with a portative organ in a well-known miniature (see p. 191). Keyboard instruments had always enjoyed social privileges; the church organs, in particular, were objects of pride upon which communities were prepared to spend almost as much as upon the churches themselves. The organ underwent dramatic changes in the fifteenth century, some of which concerned the introduction of reed pipes and of the pedal, the extension of the keyboard (by 1450 it had reached a fairly standard *B–f″*), and the creation of independent sets of stops. By about 1500 two main types of organ had emerged which remained distinct for centuries – the northern (Dutch–German) and the southern (Italian) types. Since the most important fifteenth-century treatise on organ-building, by Henri Arnaut de Zwolle,[313] precedes this division, it is customary to consider this text as a turning-point. The scattered information about organs from *c*.1350–*c*.1450 (some of which is provided by Henri himself), however, places him in the midstream of a longer development.[314] There is some agreement that the north-eastern Low Countries were a particularly significant 'organ landscape'.[315] Henri Arnaut's home, Zwolle, lies in that area, and so does Groningen, where a fragment with very early keyboard music was recently discovered (see p. 74). Organ-builders travelled far, however, and spread their

---

[312] See Fallows, 'Songs in the Trent Codices', 178.

[313] *F-Pn lat.7295*. The treatise, which also discusses the harpsichord and several other instruments, was written for the Duke of Burgundy, probably about 1440. See G. Lecerf and E.-R. Labande eds, *Les traités d'Henri-Arnaut de Zwolle et de divers anonymes* (Paris: Picard, 1932).

[314] See Peter Williams, 'Organ, § IV and V, 1–2' in *The New Grove* (with further literature); Karl Bormann, *Die gotische Orgel zu Halberstadt: Eine Studie über mittelalterlichen Orgelbau* (Berlin: Merseburger, 1966).

[315] See Cleveland T. Johnson, 'A modern approach to the historic organ', *Early Music* 8 (1980), 173–9.

expertise to different countries: the Flemish builders travelling to Spain, for example. Like printing from movable type a little later, organ-building was an internationally successful, dynamic business.

For use in private chambers and also together with other instruments, small organs such as portatives (Francesco Landini's *organetto*) and positives, sometimes even with parchment pipes, are amply documented in word and image. From before *c.*1400, we must reckon with at least two other main types of keyboard instrument, the clavichord (with its forerunner, the monochord, and possible relative, the chekker) and the harpsichord.[316]

All these instruments were used to support voices in one way or another. The daily life of a church organ was undoubtedly filled with plainsong performances; the smaller keyboard instruments counted with *basse musique* and could be used for secular music like strings or winds. Not surprisingly there are no written musical sources documenting these ancillary functions; the keyboard player either did not have written music or he played from the plainsong book. What distinguished the keyboard group, however, was the attraction of solo performance. Solo playing must have been an unwritten tradition for a long time. The earliest surviving sources of the period *c.*1360–*c.*1420 are found in England, the Netherlands and Italy, documenting the wide distribution of the practice; the extant manuscripts of the period *c.*1420–*c.*1460 are all from Germany, but many sources must be lost.[317]

These written sources are only the façade of the playing practices.[318] They were probably produced by keyboard players themselves and fulfilled their performance needs. The presence in them of didactic examples (*fundamenta*) ties the manuscripts to teaching and learning processes. In fact, what is written here represents a major alternative to conventions observed in vocal polyphony of the time.

Already the notation stands out:[319] it is always in score with two or three

---

[316] See Edwin M. Ripin, 'The early clavichord', *MQ* 53 (1967), 518–38; for the harpsichord and exchiquier, see also p. 92 above. Interesting testimonies on keyboard instruments are found in the *Liber viginti artium* of the Czech theorist Paulus Paulirinus: see Standley Howell, 'Paulus Paulirinus of Prague on musical instruments', *Journal of the American Musical Instrument Society* 5–6 (1979–80), 9–36; Wilson Barry, 'Henri Arnaut de Zwolle's clavichordium and the origins of the chekker', *Journal of the American Musical Instrument Society* 11 (1985), 5–13.

[317] Listed in John Caldwell, 'Sources of keyboard music to 1660' in *The New Grove*. For additions, see Apel ed., *Keyboard Music*, source B (*GB-Ob Douce 381*); Strohm, 'Native and foreign polyphony', 212; Klaus Hortschansky, 'Eine unbekannte Tabulaturaufzeichnung für Tasteninstrumente aus dem 15. Jahrhundert', in Finscher ed., *Renaissance-Studien*, 91–101; Hans Schmid, 'Ein unbekanntes Fragment eines "fundamentum organisandi"', *Musik in Bayern* 7 (1973), 135–43 (*D-Mbs Clm 14311*); Staehelin, 'Münchner Fragmente', 179–85. See also p. 260 above.

[318] Fundamental for the following paragraphs are Rokseth, 'Instrumental music', 419–32; Göllner, *Formen früher Mehrstimmigkeit*, 61–105; Kugler, *Tasteninstrumente*, 1–82; Zöbeley, *Buxheimer Orgelbuch*. A not very reliable edn of early sources is Apel ed., *Keyboard Music*.

[319] See Wolff, 'Arten der Mensuralnotation'. For facsimiles, see Rokseth, 'Instrumental music', 420; van Daalen-Harrison, 'Two keyboard intabulations'; Ziino ed., *L'Ars Nova*, vol. 5, jacket cover; Besseler-Gülke, *Schriftbild*, plates 28, 29 and 105; and the complete facs edns listed in Caldwell, *Sources of Keyboard Music*.

systems referring to the right and left hand, or hands and feet, of the player himself. Thus, the vertical axis of the score represents the simultaneity of the player's actions, and by implication, the horizontal axis becomes the symbol of the time lapse of the performance. The horizontal space is filled with the note symbols which 'take up time' as they take up space. This is not so in vocal polyphony, where notes of very long and very short duration can occupy about the same horizontal space. The actual shapes of the note symbols vary, and so do the means of indicating pitch. The Italian and Groningen sources have both systems in 'mensural' notation with diamond-shaped notes. The English and German/Austrian sources have letter notation for the lower system(s), often with additional durational symbols in the form of dots, note-heads or strokes. The most distinctive symbols in both types of notation are vertical 'barlines' which correspond to precise points in time, holding notes (which are usually of the same total duration) between them. These 'bars', or better 'time-boxes', are not germane to vocal music, even when it is notated in score. Their closest equivalent are the fourteenth-century Italian *divisiones* of the breve (by four, six, eight, nine or twelve minims): the dots of division have been replaced by 'barlines'. This is confirmed by the earliest source, the Robertsbridge MS (*GB-Lbl add.28550*), which has dots of division instead of 'barlines'. The most frequent numbers of minims between the lines are six, eight and twelve, corresponding to the Italian *senaria* (6/8 or 3/4), *octonaria* (4/4) or *duodenaria* (3/4, twelve semiquavers) divisions. Many manuscripts indicate the metre of a piece by the number of notes within a 'bar': there are pieces of 'three notes' ('trium notarum') as well as two, four, six and twelve. The durational unit which is counted in each case can differ, and so can the choice of note-value levels in any case. The Groningen scribe labels a piece as being 'de xii semiminimis' (*duodenaria*), although he actually writes twelve minims per bar. Others use the minim, not the semibreve, as the basic pulse of 'three-note' or 'four-note' pieces. The author of the Munich treatise calls the semibreve 'longa' (equivalent to two minims!), and the breve 'duplex longa'.[320] This confusion does not matter in a basically orthochronic system which does not depend on duple or triple subdivisions, but collects equal units in 'time-boxes'. It is more like the modern additive metres than the hierarchic subdivisions of the mensural system. Significantly, black notation is used in all these sources (white notation begins in the later parts of the Buxheim Organ Book, *D-Mbs 3725, olim Cim.352b*; *Bux*, *c.* 1460). There is no void coloration, but flags and double flags for the smaller values abound. 'Cut signatures' (¢, ⊘) are unknown; tempos are established as the case may be.

The letter notations, although slightly different in each case, all repeat at the octave (after *g*) and thus conform to the octave system of the keyboard rather than the vocal system of overlapping hexachords. These notations are not (as is

---

[320] This must be linked to the fact that he uses Messine neumes, which do not distinguish 'long' and 'breve'. See the edn in Göllner, *Formen früher Mehrstimmigkeit*, 155–94.

sometimes believed) secure guides to *musica ficta* usages: despite being applied
to a chromatic keyboard, they are essentially diatonic. Some sources distinguish
between 'b' = *b♭* and 'h' = *b♮*. Apart from this, all require special signs or 'accidentals' for the upper keys, but – just like vocal sources – often omit this
information.[321] It is true that we find, on the whole, more accidentals than in
vocal sources, mostly sharps. These are written as sharps or crossed stems
added to mensural notes, or as little hooks added to letters (*e♭* is written as '*d*'
with a little hook in the Robertsbridge MS, as remained customary for another
400 years). The abundance of sharps may relate to specifically 'organistic' practices or sound ideals, which deserve investigation; it cannot simply be used
as a guide for vocal *musica ficta*.[322]

Most keyboard notations transmit *ad hoc* transcriptions of actual playing,
not independent compositions. When they use existing vocal compositions
as the basis for 'arrangements', then the transcription is only one of several
ways of playing that piece. The largest fifteenth-century source of keyboard
arrangements (over 200) is the Buxheim Organ Book.[323] Here, many different
arrangements of the same vocal pieces can be found, demonstrating varied
solutions to the given contrapuntal or fingering problems. The book documents the work of a circle of organists – from Nuremberg and Munich,
*c.*1450–60 – whose master was the blind Conrad Paumann (see p. 489 and Plate
8). Teacher–student relationships can be detected in the way that the book often
has one arrangement immediately followed by another of the same model.
Above these further attempts, the main scribe usually writes in dog's Latin:
'adhuc semel, noch einmal', i.e. 'once more'! The linguistic joke apart, he
clearly thinks not of a second piece or second version of the piece, but of a
second 'try' at arranging it.

The repertory of all these sources can be classified in

(1) arrangements of polyphonic pieces (mostly songs);
(2) settings of vocal tenors or dance tunes;
(3) settings of liturgical chants;
(4) genuine instrumental genres such as *estampie* and *praeambulum*;
(5) *fundamenta* and *clausulae*.

The last-named category appears only in the German sources. A *fundamentum* is a written-out exercise, or set of exercises, in performing formulas, figura-

---

[321] The keyboard-player has in fact no greater need for this information than the singer. The argument
changes with later tablature systems (from *c.*1490), which are *essentially* chromatic notations: when
f is given as '3' and *f♯* as '4', there is little reason left *not* to specify the inflection.

[322] Mark Lindley, 'Pythagorean intonation and the rise of the triad', *RMARC* 16 (1980), 4–61, maintains that theorists and the early keyboard music itself favoured a tuning in which all the fifths are
pure except *B–F♯*, offering pure triads on *D*, *F♯*, *A* etc. This was gradually superseded by meantone
systems in the later fifteenth century.

[323] Wallner ed., *Buxheimer Orgelbuch*. Facs edn: Bertha Antonia Wallner ed., *Das Buxheimer Orgelbuch*
(Kassel etc.: Bärenreiter, 1955). Studies: Southern, *Buxheim Organ Book*; Zöbeley, *Buxheimer
Orgelbuch*.

tions, contrapuntal problems and the like, over a given tenor progression. A *clausula* is an example of a typical or recommended cadential approach. Both are 'raw material', as it were, to be memorized for extemporized playing. Some of these examples are extremely short; the largest *fundamentum* for organ, the *fundamentum organisandi* by Conrad Paumann, has 43 pages in the edition. One of the simpler *fundamenta* comes from a Silesian source of *c*.1440–50:[324]

Example 53 Fundamentum bonum p[edaliter] in C d e

[324] Feldmann, *Musik und Musikpflege*, app. II, 5 f; Apel ed., *Keyboard Music*, no. 11. The title 'in cda' as given by Feldmann and Apel must be an error for 'cde' (referring to the melodic pattern of the tenor?).

The purpose of the exercise is to find a connecting upper line for stepwise tenor ascents and descents, the staple fare of most *fundamenta*. While the left hand, apparently together with the pedal, moves forward step-by-step = bar-by-bar, the right hand ornaments this progress by a generally parallel motion. There are indeed many parallel fifths and octaves. Sometimes the upper part runs in contrary motion, or jumps. The striking energy of the fingerwork characterizes most organ pieces of this period. Dissonance is not avoided and is sometimes apparently sought after (see the appoggiaturas at the beginning of bars). Despite some recurring figurations, the upper line is by no means schematic. Not every tenor note receives equal attention; corresponding approaches connect the 'bars' 3–4 and 6–7 (*e–f* and *a–bb*), 8–10 and 11–13 (*a–g–f* and *e–d–c*), creating longer goal-directed stretches. The piece is not modal in a conventional sense, but rather 'in C'. The player freely indulges a little in the *bb* zone, and in the *f♯*s which are used as a pre-cadential flavour. Other *fundamenta*, especially those by Paumann, are often more consonant, and use even faster runs (semiquavers); the voice-leading tends to be more correct in the slightly later examples. Paumann and a certain 'Wolfgangus de Nova Domo'[325] also introduce more complex tenor patterns, for example ascending and descending thirds, fourths, fifths etc. Paumann has ornamented tenor lines as well.

Instead of Paumann's longest or most complex didactic *fundamenta*, we may consider one of his briefest, an exercise over 'repeated bass notes' (*redeuntes*) in 'six beats' (*voces*):[326]

Example 54 Conrad Paumann, Fundamentum

[325] In a lost source perhaps of the Paumann circle (Apel no. 28). Wolfgang's home, 'Neuhaus', could be the village of that name east of Nuremberg.

[326] From his 'Fundamentum organisandi Magistri Conradi Paumann Ceci de Nürenberga Anno 1452' in the Lochamer-Liederbuch. Apel ed., *Keyboard Music*, no. 41, p. 38. The manuscripts attribute to Paumann no fewer than four *fundamenta*, which constitute a chain of a developing practice rather than separate works. See Christoph Wolff, 'Conrad Paumanns Fundamentum Organisandi und seine verschiedenen Fassungen', *AMw* 25 (1968), 196–222.

This is no longer an exercise only, it is also a little composition, displaying something like a poetic mood. The technical task is, of course, the appropriate distribution of the middle voice among the hands (the pedal is not used), and perhaps the two ornaments.[327]

The *praeambula*, of which the tablature of Adam Ileborgh (dated 1448) has interesting examples, are comparable to the *fundamenta* in their primarily technical function, but have freely invented tenors without any particular pattern. The keyboard *estampie* is the only genre that uses the left hand largely in the same, repercussionist fashion as the right, often in alternation.[328] The genre occurs in the Robertsbridge MS and is mentioned in *Il Saporetto* (see p. 91). From that source, we also know that such pieces were performed for listening, and in secular environments. In all probability, the free *praeambulum* was also more or less a piece for listeners, but for performance in church, where its musical function was analogous to that of the later organ toccata.

Secular music 'for listeners' increasingly consisted of settings of well-known tenors and arrangements of vocal pieces. The tenors are sometimes called 'tenor bonus' (implying that other players had tried them out before) or are even attributed to composers: 'bonus tenor Leonhardi', 'tenor bonus Petri'.[329] Widely travelled melodies such as *basse danse* tunes also abound in the Buxheim Organ Book; its elaborations of 'La Spagna' or 'Votre très doulx' could be compared with the ensemble versions mentioned above (p. 356). The arrangements of chanson models in this manuscript favour international 'hits' by Binchois, Dufay etc.[330] The Viennese musician who collected parts of *A-Wn 5094* arranged vocal pieces in score, stroke notation or letter notation; they include Dufay's (?) 'Seigneur Leon' – but also the Ars nova motet 'Apollinis eclipsatur'.[331] The processual character of the organists' activity notwithstanding, their choices suggest that they did perform to audiences.

Plainsong settings are found in all the areas. They resemble the didactic examples, as well as each other. Already the Kyrie, Gloria and 'Benedicamus' settings in the Faenza Codex[332] establish the principles of this truly European genre. In the Gloria, only alternate verses are set; the plainsong in the left hand or pedal is untransposed and has simple rhythms or 'monorhythm'; the harmony is often unadventurous. These pieces were surely performed during the service, alternating with or accompanying the choir. By implication, most

---

[327] Trills? The symbol in this manuscript, as elsewhere, is a downward stem bent to the left. Its precise meaning is not known.

[328] Apel ed., *Keyboard Music*, nos. 1–3.

[329] Apel ed., *Keyboard Music*, nos. 19 and 20. The tenors in question could have originated in German polyphonic songs.

[330] See Southern, *Buxheim Organ Book*, 84 ff; Southern, 'Foreign music'; Fallows, 'English song repertories'; B. Thomas ed., *Music from the Buxheim Organ Book I. Chanson intabulations and basse danse settings* (London: Pro Musica Edition EK4, *c*.1983) (companion volume: *Ten French songs of the fifteenth century*, EK4a).

[331] Strohm, 'Native and foreign polyphony', 212 f and 227 f.

[332] See Kugler, *Codex Faenza*, 122 ff.

of the *fundamenta* with their monorhythmic, patterned tenors can be considered exercises in the performance of plainsong. In that case, the extant plainsong settings would only be 'worked-out' specimens of a much wider practice, and polyphonic organ playing in church would have been far more frequent than is conventionally assumed, at least in the areas from which we also have *fundamenta*. It would have been a formulaic, potentially unwritten type of polyphony, which required much practice but no composer.

PART IV

EUROPE AFTER 1450: DIVERSITY
AND PARTICIPATION

BRITAIN: HOMEGROWN GLORIES

Writers on English music history have noted – some with embarrassment – an apparent lapse into insularity after the age of Dunstable. Gustave Reese, for example, states that the English then lost prestige in Europe and retreated into 'insular conservatism'.[1] Contemporary support for such a global verdict seems to be forthcoming from none other than Johannes Tinctoris, in the same passage of his *Proportionale musices* which also yields the praise for Dunstable's 'new art' (see p. 127). Continuing from that praise, the theorist evaluates composers of his own generation.[2] Whereas Ockeghem, Busnois, Regis and Caron are 'the most outstanding of all composers I have heard', he says,

> the English cannot be compared with them, even if there is a popular saying that they jubilate, whereas the French sing. And yet, the French invent new songs in new manners every day, whereas the English go on using one and the same kind of composition, which is the sign of an impoverished mind.[3]

It has been observed that Tinctoris's statement about English singing reflected a widespread opinion, and that the term 'jubilate' referred to the 'florid' (or melismatic) style which English music had reached by the 1470s and which is impressively documented by the contents of the Eton Choirbook of *c*.1500 (*GB-WRec 178*).[4] 'Jubilare' means 'to vocalize' (as in the melisma of the alleluia, the *jubilus*). As far as English singing is concerned, its fame had obviously not diminished since the days of King Sigismund's visit in 1416.[5]

But Tinctoris goes on to criticize uniformity, and lack of invention, in English compositions. This judgement certainly demonstrates the 'loss of prestige' as diagnosed by Reese; but is it true that the English were so one-sided?

It seems that Tinctoris was, for once, incompletely informed. He could not have been familiar with the richness and diversity of English liturgical poly-

---

[1] Reese, *Renaissance*, 763.

[2] Tinctoris, *Opera theoretica*, vol. IIa, 10.

[3] For another translation, see Strunk, *Source Readings*, 5; Harrison, *Britain*, 257.

[4] Harrison, *Britain*, 258 and 171.

[5] See p. 197 above. In the travel diary of Leo of Rozmital and his companions, 1465–6, the diarist Gabriel Tetzel of Nuremberg describes the banquet and dance at the court of Edward IV. 'After the dance the King's choristers entered and were ordered to sing. We were present when the King heard Mass in his chapel. . . . I do not think that I have heard finer singing in this world.' Letts ed., *Travels*, 47 f.

phony of his own time, because so little of it reached the Continent. As far as it did, much of it circulated anonymously and its origin may not have been recognizable even to contemporaries. Secular songs by Bedyngham and Frye passed under Tinctoris's eyes when he compiled the Mellon Chansonnier (*US-NH 91*) *c*.1475 (see p. 461), but he may not have known that these pieces were about twenty years old. Judging them by contemporary standards, he may have concluded that English attitudes in composition had not changed much.

The problems have remained almost the same until the mid-twentieth century. Reese stated in 1954 that 'investigation has not yet revealed a missing link that will provide really great music between Dunstable and Fayrfax'.[6] Thanks to the work of Bukofzer and Harrison, and to further research on musical and archival sources, this verdict can now be challenged. Much more can now be said about the generation of composers immediately following Dunstable, and about the continuing English impact on European music at least in the mid-fifteenth century. Evidence grows thinner as the century progresses. It is still an arduous task to piece together a portrait of English music in the mid- to late fifteenth century from little more than snippets of evidence, distributed on both sides of the Channel.[7]

Musical institutions

The fifteenth century was a period of great expansion among English choral institutions, and polyphonic singing was introduced in many of them, from cathedrals to parish churches. The cultivation of artistic polyphony was most intense in princely and royal household chapels, and in the various collegiate foundations: grammar schools, university colleges and collegiate churches with schools attached to them.

Household chapels existed in the service of the king as well as of other royal and ducal magnates. In the early to mid-fifteenth century, some of these chapels must have helped to distribute English music abroad. Among the last English composers of the century whose names were known abroad, most had royal contacts. John Plummer served the household chapel from 1440 to 1460, for most of these years as Master of the Children; John Stone seems to have been a chapel member in the 1460s;[8] John Hothby was recalled from Lucca in 1486 to serve the court of Henry VII. Ordinances for the household musicians of Edward IV, for example in the *Liber niger*, partly reflect the Burgundian

---

[6] Reese, *Renaissance*, 764.

[7] See Harrison, *Britain*; Bukofzer, 'Popular and secular music'; Harrison, 'English polyphony'; Benham, *Latin Church Music*, chaps. 1–7; Ernest H. Sanders, 'England: from the beginnings to c.1540', in F. W. Sternfeld ed., *Music from the Middle Ages to the Renaissance* (London: Weidenfeld & Nicolson, 1973), 255–313. The best summary of secular music, especially at court, is Stevens, *Music and Poetry*. Studies of documents include Bowers, *Choral Institutions*; Trowell, *Plantagenets*; Wathey, 'Lost books'.

[8] See Brian Trowell, 'Stone' in *The New Grove*.

ordinances of 1469 (on them, see p. 278), although the chapel was larger with 24 chaplains and clerks.[9] The care for the eight choristers is characteristic: they were to continue their education at the royal colleges of Oxford and Cambridge if no household position could be found for them at the age of eighteen. The household chapel was flanked by the (Lancastrian) foundations of the chapels of St Stephen's, Westminster, and St George's, Windsor. Notable composers were employed there, too, again mainly as masters of the choristers (*informatores choristarum, succentores*). These chapels had collegiate status, but did not have their own teaching institutions. Education was most importantly represented by the famous 'twin foundations': New College, Oxford, and Winchester College, as founded by William of Wykeham (statute 1400), and Henry VI's foundation of King's College, Cambridge, and Eton College (1440–41). From archival sources we learn that all four institutions had an intense musical life. Music has survived only from Eton, in the Eton Choirbook. Like the Old Hall MS from the beginning of the century, this source contains English music on the highest artistic level of its time, although by the same token it represents only one segment of the musical production in the country as a whole.

The real breadth of the English musical scene can only be hinted at by naming a few more of the institutions cultivating polyphony which were newly founded in this century.[10] There were the university colleges such as Magdalen College, Oxford (1458), Lincoln College (1429), the independent colleges or grammar schools Higham Ferrers (1422), Jesus College Rotherham (1483) and New Romney; the collegiate churches attached to princely or baronial castles such as St Mary's, Warwick (Beauchamp), Arundel (1386), Fotheringhay (Henry IV), Ewelme (de la Pole, 1437) and Tattershall (Cromwell, 1439).

Among the cathedrals and abbeys, records of polyphonic practice in this period favour Lincoln, St Paul's, Wells, Lichfield, Exeter, Canterbury, Durham, Worcester, Westminster and Leicester. Perhaps more significant is the large number of parish churches known to have owned books of polyphony, especially in the London area. What happened here may well be compared with developments in the urban areas of Flanders and Italy. The middle classes, above all the merchant fraternities and the richer trade guilds, supported their parish churches and their private chapels to such an extent that musical practice was almost institutional. Also, individuals endowed churches, hospitals, colleges and almshouses with positions for musical clerks or choristers. The requested ceremonies often concentrated on the great outdoors processions,

---

[9] Edward IV was, of course, the brother-in-law of Charles the Bold and had visited Flanders in 1471–2. On the household musicians (minstrels and chapel singers), and the *Liber niger* ('Black Book'), see Wathey, *Royal and Noble Households*, and Stevens, *Music and Poetry*, ch. 13 ('Professional musicians').

[10] Much of the evidence for their music comes either from statutes and contracts or from inventories mentioning music books. See Harrison, *Britain, passim*; Wathey, 'Lost books'. The most thorough investigation of English musical establishments is Bowers, *Choral Institutions* (especially chaps. 4.2.1–3 and 5.2.1–4).

which displayed the wealth and the patronage of the guilds or benefactors.[11] 'Singing men' were often hired from cathedrals or even princely chapels to perform sophisticated musical works for parish feasts. There was also a concern to reach 'audiences' and to serve their needs. In Richard Whittington's college in London, the chaplains, clerks and choristers sang a Marian antiphon – not necessarily in polyphony – at nightfall for the benefit of the working population in the area.[12] Church musicians in London were organized in the St Nicholas Fraternity of parish clerks which dated back to 1240.[13] The fifteenth-century list of members reveals the names of many known musicians such as (in 1449) John Plummer, John Bedyngham, John Burell and John Benet. Elsewhere in Europe, church musicians were not organized on such a large scale, whereas minstrels' fraternities were frequent. The London minstrels were incorporated by royal privilege in 1469.

Musical institutions in Scotland can be traced only in the highest levels of society. The royal court must be reckoned as the most important centre for music-making. The institutionalization of a Chapel Royal in Stirling Castle is mainly due to James III (*r.*1460–88). Other collegiate foundations practising polyphony were Aberdeen, Dunkeld and St Andrews University.[14] The earliest surviving source of sacred polyphony, the Carver Choirbook or 'Scone Antiphonary' (*GB-En 5.1.15*), postdates 1500 but may reflect musical contacts with the Low Countries or France happening much earlier, as the presence of Dufay's Mass 'L'homme armé' suggests.[15] The foundation of Trinity College, Edinburgh, by James III (1462) was perhaps instigated by his queen, Mary of Guelders. The collegiate church and hospital had eight prebendaries who performed daily 'Matins, High Mass, Vespers and Compline, with notes'. None was appointed 'unless he shall be capable of reading and singing in plainchant and discant' ('legendo concinendo plano cantu et discantu').[16] The first College provost, Edward Bonkil, was portrayed, together with the magnificent organs he had ordered (with royal subsidies), by Hugo van der Goes *c.*1470.[17] At court, musicians came and went: James III hired the English musician William Rogeers (possibly a minstrel), and he sent his servant John Browne to Bruges for instruction on the lute in 1472.[18]

[11] See Harrison, *Britain*, especially 197 ff.

[12] Harrison, *Britain*, 86.

[13] Baillie, 'London guild'. See also Hugh Baillie, 'Some biographical notes on English church musicians chiefly working in London (1485-1569)', *RMARC* 2 (1962), 18-57.

[14] Harrison, 'English polyphony', 337. For a survey, see Kenneth Elliott and Frederick Rimmer, *A History of Scottish Music* (London: BBC, 1973), 12-15.

[15] See also Strohm, *Bruges*, 65 and 131.

[16] See J. D. Marwick ed., *Charters and Documents relating to The Collegiate Church and Hospital of the Holy Trinity, and the Trinity Hospital, Edinburgh. A.D.1460-1661* (Edinburgh, 1871), 23 ff.

[17] David McRoberts, 'Notes on Scoto-Flemish artistic contacts', *The Innes Review* 10 (1959), 93; Strohm, *Bruges*, 65 and n. 31.

[18] For further details, see Strohm, *Bruges*, 65. If John Browne was an Englishman too (or indeed if not), the supposition that he could be the composer of this name in the Eton Choirbook might not be totally unwarranted.

The primary layer of insular sacred polyphony comprised endowed Masses and votive antiphons, performed recurrently for benefactors and their patron saints or devotions. Some of this 'chapel music', whether composed at court or elsewhere, travelled to foreign countries. It also crossed social boundaries. An 'organbook' (1449) of the parish church of St James Garlickhithe, London, began with a 'Ridlington Kyrie'[19] which may well have been the Mass 'Quem malignus spiritus' for St John of Bridlington – probably a work from the royal chapel. Some compositions by Dunstable, Lionel, Bedyngham and Plummer were copied in apparently provincial sources, but at least one of them was considerably simplified for the lesser skill of the singers.[20]

Much of the polyphony sung in parish churches and in provincial institutions may have been performed in faburden or related discanting practices, also by using 'squares'. These techniques allowed for the participation of unskilled or halfskilled singers who would sing the plainsong by heart or double a given line in strict fashion. Many pieces were written in simplified notation, for example in chant notation, performed monorhythmically in all voices, or in 'stroke' or 'strene' notation. The collaboration between skilled and unskilled singers is indeed the common denominator of all the 'typically English' practices from squares and faburdens to simplified notations. The phenomenon bridges the realms of 'primitive' and 'artistic' music, which were distinguished more sharply on the Continent. The very diversity of terms used in England for notation ('pricked note, strene note, square note', for example) and for voice relationships (discant, counter, faburden) suggests the depth of these musical activities.

We are speaking here of a large 'secondary layer' of English music which served in the choir or in the nave on higher feasts or patronal feast-days, in pageants and processions, in schools, and for sacred drama. Almost nothing of this layer reached the Continent, in contrast to the 'chapel music' mentioned above. This is also the music which Andrew Hughes convincingly identified with the beginnings of 'choral polyphony'.[21] The development of vocal ensembles apparently moved in two opposite directions. Bowers maintains that ensembles increased their total range by the admission of boys' voices for the treble, and low basses.[22] The ranges observed in written compositions indeed grew from *c*.12–15 notes in the early fifteenth century to *c*.21–3 notes in the late fifteenth century. Five-part music was standard in the larger institutions by *c*.1470 and about that time the characteristic English tendency towards 'multi-part music' began (six and more voices – as opposed to the continental polychoral medium). But by the same token, this remained soloistic music, even if an establishment like the royal household chapel could muster as many

---

[19] Wathey, 'Lost books', no. 44.
[20] In the Ritson MS (*GB-Lbl add.5665*): see p. 387.
[21] See Hughes, 'Choir'; Hughes, 'Mensural polyphony for choir'; Bent, 'New and little-known fragments'.
[22] Bowers, *Choral Institutions*; *idem*, 'Performing pitch'.

as six performers for each of the five parts. The opposite tendency was to admit a potentially unlimited number of non-specialized singers, perhaps from among the schoolboys, the congregation, or the guild members, to the polyphonic performances. Thus, the true forerunners of modern choral music were created, but the compositions had to remain in few parts and relatively simple.[23]

The sacred repertory at home

It is almost no surprise that those music manuscripts which survive complete belong mostly to the 'secondary layer' of musical practice, containing liturgical music and carols. The chapel manuscripts of the larger institutions perished in the Reformation or later, whereas the more informal music books of local priests or schoolmasters survived. Of the numerous fragments, only a few can be mentioned here; their provenance and function are often unclear.[24]

The Selden MS (*GB-Ob Selden B. 26*)[25] was written perhaps about 1440 and is possibly linked with the Lancastrian foundation of St Mary in the Newarke, Leicester.[26] It contains votive antiphons and polyphonic carols – a significant combination. Most of the pieces are composed in chanson format but written in 'score'. Perhaps the notation was a concession to performers' reading habits. The fifteen antiphons, joined by a three-part drinking song 'Tappster, dryng-ker', could fit a collegiate or even monastic environment. The presence of one work each by Dunstable, Lionel and Plummer suggests metropolitan or courtly contacts. Most antiphons exhibit an old-fashioned chanson idiom in major pro-lation, with thick textures (except for duet passages) and florid melodic embel-lishments in semiminims. This style is akin to antiphon settings in the Old Hall MS, for example by Lionel. His own 'Ave regina' here, however, does not belong to that group, being in four voices with treble duets. Apparently, local composers trailed after Lionel's stylistic development. In some of their pieces, the floridity is so uninhibited that mensural units are disregarded – resulting, for example, in 7/8 units in no. 6. Dunstable's 'Beata mater' and an anonymous 'Speciosa facta es' appear more advanced; they make at least sectional use of perfect time and have an easier flow and a clearer phrase structure. The same could be said of the carol-like 'Gaude terra', on a strophic poem with verse and refrain, sung by one, two and three voices in succession. Almost incompatible with these idioms is John Plummer's 'Tota pulchra es', a long antiphon-motet

---

[23] See also p. 283 above for the objections to Bukofzer, *Studies*, ch. V, and partially to Hughes, 'Mensural polyphony for choir'.

[24] But see the excellent descriptions of many of them (with references to other descriptions) in *EMH* 3 and 4.

[25] Edited in facsimile and transcription in Stainer ed., *Early Bodleian Music*. A more modern edition of the antiphons is Hughes ed., *Fifteenth-Century Liturgical Music I*; of the carols: Stevens ed., *Medieval Carols*.

[26] Harrison, *Britain*, 300. This is a likelier provenance than Worcester.

in two sections but without mensural contrast. The form and growth of the piece relies entirely on the word-setting with its increasingly dramatic points of imitation. By contrast, 'Sancta Maria virgo' (no. 2) is an example of genuine English discant. The plainsong migrates between the lower voices but is most often in the mene in long note-values (see also p. 201). There are two more settings of this text in the Selden MS. The antiphon was used for memorial and votive purposes by a variety of institutions, as were 'Nesciens mater' and 'Mater ora filium', also represented in this manuscript. The use of all three texts together seems to concentrate in the diocese of Lincoln, which included Leicester and Oxford at the time.

The Egerton (*GB-Lbl Egerton 3307*)[27] and Pepys MSS (*GB-Cmc Pepys 1236*)[28] are different in so far as they contain strictly liturgical settings, mainly for Holy Week. Egerton also inserts carols as does Selden; Pepys lacks this ingredient. From the style of the new Egerton carols alone (i.e. those not shared with Selden), one can see that the manuscript is younger than Selden.[29] These carols are often in three parts and in perfect time; the lower voices are usually in the same range and cross frequently. A carol like 'Ave rex angelorum' (Stevens no. 52) could almost be regarded as an antiphon setting in the style of the Dunstable generation.

The liturgical settings in Egerton are mostly in chanson format, and less florid than the Selden antiphons. They comprise hymns ('En rex venit', 'Gloria, laus et honor', 'Salve, festa dies') and other liturgical settings for Vespers and processions, especially in Holy Week. They show signs of *alternatim* performance, partly with boy trebles. The plainsong is mostly in the top voice and never in the middle. As in the Selden MS, the notation in score is somewhat at odds with the chanson format of the settings. Also part of the liturgy of Holy Week are a ferial Mass (Kyrie, Sanctus and Agnus only; the Sanctus/Agnus pair is perhaps by Binchois, see p. 247) and two Passion settings according to Matthew and Luke. These are the earliest polyphonic Passion settings to survive in written form. The practice of singing Passions, like Holy Week lessons, in discant of some kind must be older.[30] The Egerton MS Passions are in a chordal, declamatory style suitable for liturgical recitative, but the plainsongs (Passion tones) are not used. It must be for this reason that there is neither English discant nor faburden. The polyphony covers only the opening words ('Passio domini'), the *turbae* (choruses of crowds) and the speeches of characters other than Christ and the Evangelist; the latter were performed by

---

27 The carols are in Stevens ed., *Medieval Carols*; the other contents are edited in McPeek ed., *Egerton*.

28 Complete edn: S. R. Charles ed., *The Music of the Pepys MS 1236*. See also Charles, 'Provenance'; Harrison, 'Sarum Rite'.

29 McPeek ed., *Egerton*, dates the manuscript 1430–44. 1430 is a very generous *terminus post quem*; the grounds for choosing 1444 as *terminus ante quem* are unconvincing.

30 The early history of the Passion, in plainsong and polyphony, is described in Kurt von Fischer, 'Die Passion von ihren Anfängen bis ins 16. Jahrhundert', in Wulf Arlt *et al.* eds, *Gattungen der Musik in Einzeldarstellungen: Gedenkschrift Leo Schrade* (Berne and Munich: Francke, 1973), 574–620; English translation in: von Fischer, *Essays*, 9–65 (on Egerton and Shrewsbury, see p. 27 f).

soloists in the appropriate Passion tone. This 'semidramatic' manner of performance would be very much in the spirit of the Egerton music in general, which appears to be linked to ceremonies and processions.

Two contrasting suggestions have been made about the origin of the manuscript. Neither Meaux Abbey in Yorkshire[31] nor St George's, Windsor,[32] seem to fit entirely. Three particular Latin texts towards the end of the manuscript have been used (among other arguments) to support the rival claims, but deserve further scrutiny. The carol-like 'Comedentes convenite' (no. 49) appears to be inviting women to a lavish dinner. The drinking song 'O potores exquisiti' (no. 51) is isorhythmic and makes use of an old goliardic poem. The two-section motet 'Cantemus domino, socie' (nos. 52–3) with tenor 'Gaudent in celis' is associated with a vision of St Dunstan: he is said to have watched Holy Virgins rejoicing in heaven and singing these texts.[33]

The explanations which have been given for these pieces all assume that the situations described by the respective texts were real. 'Comedentes convenite' is said to be a real invitation of women to dinner, 'O potores' a real drinking song composed for use in taverns, and 'Cantemus domino, socie' a motet to be sung by members of a Ladies' association. But music, and especially polyphonic art-music, is far more often figurative than real in its applications. It is hardly likely that drinkers in a tavern would stop to perform an isorhythmic motet describing their merriment! The source of the poem, the *Carmina burana* (thirteenth century), is a collection famous for its poetic–parodistic spirit. The vision of St Dunstan, which gave rise to the motet, is in turn related to the biblical story of the Wise and Foolish Virgins, who are remembered on the feasts of Virgins and All Saints: 'Gaudent in celis' is an antiphon for All Saints. According to the Sarum Breviary, on that feast a little performance was attached to the eighth lesson of Matins, which recited the story of the Wise and Foolish Virgins: five boys, all dressed in white tunics and holding burning candles, represented the Wise Virgins. They sang the solo sections of the eighth respond, 'Audivi vocem', including the verse 'Media nocte clamor factus est: Ecce sponsus venit'.[34] This liturgical moment had already been expanded into a play in eleventh-century France;[35] the dramatic subject was known in fifteenth-century England. The motet 'Cantemus domino' probably belonged to just such a dramatic context. It is in five parts, of which the upper two (a treble divided in two) can be sung by boys, the lower parts by other young clerics. It so happens that the Egerton MS itself contains two settings

[31] Manfred F. Bukofzer, 'Holy-Week music and carols at Meaux Abbey', in Bukofzer, *Studies*, 113–75 (= ch. IV); Richard L. Greene, 'Two medieval musical manuscripts: Egerton 3307 and some University of Chicago fragments', *JAMS* 7 (1954), 1–34.

[32] Bertram Schofield and Manfred F. Bukofzer, 'A newly discovered fifteenth-century manuscript of the English Chapel Royal', *MQ* 32 (1946), 509–36; 33 (1947), 38–51; McPeek ed., *Egerton*, introduction.

[33] Greene, 'Two medieval musical manuscripts'.

[34] See Young, *Drama*, vol. 2, 361 ff and 368 n. 6.

[35] The *Sponsus* Play: see Young, *Drama*, vol. 2, 361 ff.

of 'Audivi. Media nocte'. The strange text 'Comedentes convenite' may also belong here. In Greene's reconstruction, the poem actually mentions wax tapers. It is otherwise an invitation to spend a night at the dinner-table: very appropriate for the Foolish Virgins of the play. Furthermore, the textual metre of this song is modelled after that of 'O potores' – which, in turn, may have served the same dramatic context. The idea that the goliardic poem is put to a dramatic and moralizing purpose here is supported by the fact that the manuscript has two miniatures showing drinking scenes at this point. Also mystery plays tend to dwell on the details of sinful life. As a result of these suggestions, the provenance of the Egerton MS should again be considered an open question: religious drama and the Salisbury Rite coexisted in large parts of England.

The Pepys MS[36] was probably compiled between 1465 and 1475 in a school or college in Kent.[37] The contents of this small-size, personal volume show provincial as well as metropolitan connections.[38] The amateur composer of some pieces was Sir William Hawte, a cousin of Edward IV's Queen Elizabeth Woodville. Well-known composers represented here are Walter Frye (his St Nicholas sequence 'Sospitati dedit egros' is an unicum and his only work surviving complete in an English source), Gilbert Banaster (*d*.1487) of the Chapel Royal, and J. Nesbet (*d*.1488?) who was Master of the Lady Chapel singers at Canterbury, 1475–88. Works by Banaster and Nesbet appear also in the Eton Choirbook. On the other hand, many of the 121 pieces in Pepys fulfil only the minimum requirements of the craft. Sixteen are still written in 'score' notation; many are for two voices only or in *cantus fractus* (mensural monophony).[39] The pieces are all in Latin and are largely liturgical, following the Rite of Salisbury. There are no fewer than eighteen settings of the 'Benedicamus domino', possibly intended as short responds for the end of Vespers, and many alleluia settings. Harrison[40] uncovered a clue to parish church repertories: settings of the 'Propheta' trope of the hymn 'En rex venit'. This was sung in civic Palm Sunday processions by actors disguised as prophets – a typical lay entertainment also documented in the *rederijkers* organizations of the Low Countries (see p. 306). Other material can be related to semi-dramatic contexts as well. There are, for example, three settings of the respond 'Audivi. Media nocte' for the Wise Virgins' ceremony (see above), and four of the responsory verse 'Gloria in excelsis Deo'. The latter is sung by five boys, analogously to the

---

[36] Edition: Charles ed., *The Music of the Pepys MS 1236*.

[37] Charles, 'Provenance'. More recently, Roger Bowers suggested the Chapel of the Almonry, i.e. a foundation for boy choristers, of Canterbury Cathedral: see his contribution on the manuscript to Iain Fenlon ed., *Cambridge Music Manuscripts, 900–1700* (Cambridge University Press, 1982), 111–14.

[38] For more detailed descriptions, see Harrison, 'Sarum Rite'; Benham, *Latin Church Music*, 99–105.

[39] Doubts remain that these single voices may belong to polyphonic settings, and that the manuscript functions as a partbook in these cases. For the essentially different continental uses of *cantus fractus*, see p. 324.

[40] Harrison, 'Sarum Rite', 124 ff.

Wise Virgins' ceremony, with the first respond at Matins on Christmas Day, according to the Salisbury antiphonal:

> The foregoing verse is to be sung by five boys in choir frocks, with veiled faces, burning candles in their hands, from a high position behind the high altar but directed towards the choir.[41]

The boys represented the angels of Christmas night, of course.

The composer of the three 'Audivi. Media nocte' settings, as well as of some other pieces including the amazing Lamentations in *cantus fractus* was John Tuder, bailiff of New Romney, Kent, in 1466, and a member of Parliament for New Romney in 1472. Apparently an amateur like William Hawte, he might have composed for his local community only, and the grammar school (or college) of St Nicholas at New Romney would be an obvious destination. The manuscript contains several settings of the St Nicholas sequence 'Sospitati dedit egros', and other music for the schoolboys' feasts (the Blessing of the Boy Bishop, for example). New Romney – then a seaport for channel crossings – is not an unknown place in the history of the theatre. Together with the neighbouring town of Lydd, it had a tradition of performing plays or 'interludes'. A Passion play and one of the Resurrection are specifically documented; the town was a meeting-place for minstrels' bands at least in 1480.[42] *Pepys 1236* could have supplied many an insertion for the New Romney mysteries. They were probably performed by members of the Guild of St George's, but the singers might have been local schoolboys.

Another witness to the liturgical and ceremonial life in smaller centres is Shrewsbury School MS VI.[43] This is a partbook used for processions and mysteries by one of the singer–actors. It was probably copied for Lichfield Cathedral around the middle of the century. Together with fragments of two other processionals, this source (in Rankin's reconstruction) combines

(1) processional chants sung monophonically or in faburden;[44]
(2) *alternatim* three-part settings of processional hymns;
(3) three-part semi-dramatic Passions (as in Egerton);
(4) liturgical plays performed by three actors.

Correspondingly, the user of this partbook was

(1) a member of the procession participating in all the plainsong;
(2) the soloist of the treble part ('triplex') in the polyphonic hymn stanzas and similar settings;

---

[41] Frere ed., *Antiphonale Sarisburiense*, 47: 'Iste versus precedens cantetur a quinque pueris in suppellectis amictibus capita velatis cereos ascensos singulis deferentibus in loco eminentiori sed ultra magnum altare ad chorum conversis.'

[42] Chambers, *Mediaeval Stage*, vol. 2, 385 f; W. A. Scott Robertson, 'Passion play and interludes at New Romney', *Archaeologia Cantiana* 13 (1880), 217 ff; and Stevens, *Music and Poetry*, 299.

[43] See Rankin, 'Shrewsbury'.

[44] On this subject, see also Denis Stevens, 'Processional psalms in faburden', *MD* 9 (1955), 105-10.

(3) the performer of the treble part in the polyphonic *turbae* of the Passions (St Matthew and St John), and of some other speaking characters;

(4) the actor of the third shepherd, the third of the three Marys and the third disciple in the respective Christmas and Resurrection plays which had musical insertions for three voices also.

Unfortunately, the other two partbooks are lost;[45] but the isolated survival of this one emphasizes its status. The manuscript served not one particular performance or work, but one person who assumed specialized functions in various kinds of ceremonies. He was an adult singer with the approximate range of *f-a'*. Sixteenth-century partbooks, especially of processional music, are similarly tailored to the performer and named after him; the practical value of having one's own book in a procession should be obvious.

A much larger source with more varied contents than all the others is the Ritson MS (*GB-Lbl add.5665*),[46] which was compiled during the period *c.*1470–1520. It consists of five distinct sections and comprises liturgical settings, antiphons, Masses, carols and secular partsongs. The priests Richard Smert of Plymtree and John Trouluffe of Exeter, both connected with Exeter Cathedral before 1477, were involved in the collecting and partly in the composing of the earliest layers. This collection is probably typical of English provincial music towards 1480 for its deliberate simplicity but also its aural ingenuity. Many Latin-texted pieces are written in 'strene notation', and several votive antiphons have monorhythmic tenors. 'Nesciens mater' by Trouluffe (no. 51) is a late but genuine example of English discant over a monorhythmic plainsong. Similar pieces in somewhat freer techniques are other antiphons by Trouluffe, a 'Regina celi' by Richard Mower, and a 'Stella celi' by Sir W. Hawte which is also in the Pepys MS. Among the anonymous settings, the four-part 'Ave regina celorum, mater regis' (no. 56) comes closest to the sophisticated style of the Eton antiphons. On the other hand, the Dunstable/ Lionel 'Salve regina' occurs here but with simplified rhythms.[47]

The Mass 'Gaudete in Domino' by Thomas Packe observes a total range explicitly limited to twelve notes. Despite this concession to halfskilled singers, it is a beautiful work. This Mass and another labelled 'Rex summe', also by Packe, require some *alternatim* performance. Neither seems to be based on plainchant, but they frequently quote the same songlike motive (*d-f-e-d-a*) – known from French *chansons rustiques* of the time.[48]

Most unusual are Packe's five-voice 'Lumen ad revelationem' (for a Candlemas ceremony) and his carol with burden 'Te dominum confitemur', with

---

[45] The (fragmentary) text of the plays is edited, with an appendix on the music including transcriptions by Frank Ll. Harrison, in *Non-cycle Plays and Fragments* ed. N. Davis (Oxford University Press, 1970). Some of Harrison's conclusions have been revised by Rankin.

[46] Edition in Catharine Keyes Miller, *A Fifteenth-Century Record of English Choir Repertory: B.M.Add. Ms.5665; A Transcription and Commentary*, Ph.D., Yale U., 1948.

[47] Hugh Benham, 'Salve Regina (Power or Dunstable): a simplified version', *ML* 59 (1978), 28–32.

[48] For example, 'Adieu, mes amours' (a setting by Josquin and a Mass by Obrecht exist) and 'Une filleresse d'estouppes' (a chanson by Busnois).

the upper voices paraphrasing the *Te Deum* in Latin and English. In this piece, sections vary between one, two, three, four and five voices! Perhaps the best explanation for the extraordinary form would be a dramatic context: the *Te Deum* is a frequent conclusion to vernacular mystery plays.

'Strene notation' and 'stroke notation' have been explained above as concessions to halfskilled performers. Sometimes, only one voice (usually the one carrying the plainsong) was given to them, sometimes all the voices. In the Ritson MS, the 'Playn Song Mass' by Henry Petyr carries this title because all three voices are notated in 'stroke notation'. Only two different note-values are used (represented by single stroke and double stroke). A similar Mass in this respect, and also in modality and melodic style, is the 'stroke notation Mass' in the Saxilby fragment.[49] This work is somewhat older and might actually have been a model for Petyr (who graduated at Oxford in 1516 after 30 years of musical studies); it might have originated at Lincoln Cathedral. Amazingly, this Mass also survives in a manuscript found at the Basilica of San Petronio, Bologna, in a fascicle manuscript datable perhaps to *c*.1490.[50]

Practically all the Mass codices from the leading institutions between 1440 and 1500 are lost, including the Mass codex which Eton College must surely have owned. If we are to judge from the provincial sources, English Mass polyphony 'at home' followed varied customs. There are *alternatim* settings (we do not know whether plainsong or the organ took over the missing verses); there are cycles lacking the Kyrie (such as Petyr's; was this sung in plainsong or only notated elsewhere?); and there are 'short' or 'ferial' Masses comprising only two or three sections. The great 'festal' Mass (the nomenclature is Harrison's) might have a troped or untroped Kyrie, a plainsong cantus firmus or none. Almost all these varieties are included in the York MS, with fragments of Masses by John Cuk, William Horwood and anonymi.[51] Whereas Cuk may be identified with a York *succentor vicariorum* of 1452-5,[52] Horwood's career was spent in London (1459-74) and Lincoln (1476-84).[53]

The repertory of the royal chapels is totally unknown from direct sources. Some of it may have filtered down to other institutions and be preserved in

[49] Margaret Bent and Roger Bowers, 'The Saxilby fragment', *EMH* 1 (1981), 1-28.
[50] Hamm, 'Musiche' (Fragment E). It is most tempting to relate the Bologna concordance to the presence there of Robertus de Anglia (1467-74); see p. 591 below. D. Fallows, 'Robertus de Anglia' in *The New Grove*, connects the style of his 'O fallaze e ria fortuna' with the part-songs of the Ritson MS.
[51] Baillie-Oboussier, 'York Masses'.
[52] Harrison, *Britain*, 161 and 457. The melodic-rhythmic style and free cantus firmus technique of his Mass 'Venit dilectus meus' would be very advanced for that time. The anonymous pair 'Custodi nos domine' in York resembles the 'quotation' technique in Packe's Ritson Masses.
[53] Horwood was a member of the musicians' guild of St Nicholas in 1459 and, interestingly, its dean in 1474 (see Baillie, 'London guild'). This position he exchanged in 1476 for a simple vicarship at Lincoln Cathedral, where he became *informator choristarum* the following year. The contract obliged him to teach plainsong, pricksong, faburden, discant and counter as well as organ- and clavichord-playing to the choristers: see Harrison, *Britain*, 177.

their manuscripts – the fragments *GB-Lbl Add. 54324*[54] and *GB-Ob add. C. 87* are possible candidates here. There we find music of the highest rank by anonymi, Dunstable, Benet, Bedyngham and Plummer (the last-named, long associated with the royal household chapel, appears in both sources). A significant proportion of this music was also copied abroad: royal or baronial connections must have facilitated the 'export' of certain works. From about 1460, the wars affected the royal institutions; but it was precisely in those years that the Yorkist party forged new continental links, and musical influences must have travelled in both directions. Edward IV gave his sister Margaret in marriage to Charles the Bold (1468); when he had to flee England in 1471, he was well received in Flanders, and may have begun to import musicians, just as he imported Burgundian fashions, including illuminated books. During his reign, Eton Chapel was provided with magnificent grisaille frescoes by Flemish artists.

The introduction of continental music manuscripts to England is said to have begun under Henry VII (there is, for example, the so-called 'Prince Arthur Chansonnier', *GB-Cmc Pepys 1760*). In the following list of royal household expenses in 1493, there may be a reference to a Franco-Netherlands Mass. The list as a whole seems characteristic for the mixed tastes at the court of Henry VII:[55]

Jan.	1	To the choristers at St Paul's and St Stephen's, 13s. 4d.
	6	To Newark for making a song, £1.
March	25	To one that brought the King a Mass of the Passion of Our Lady, in reward, 13s. 4d.
May	13	To the waits of Northampton in reward, 13s. 4d.
	16	To Padesey piper on the bagpipe, 6s. 8d.
Aug.	5	To the young damsel that danceth, £30.
Sep.	24	To him that had his bull baited, in reward, 10s.
Nov.	12	To one Cornish for a prophecy, in reward, 13s. 4d.
	30	Delivered to a merchant for a pair of organs, £30.
Dec.	6	To the King of France's fool, in reward, £4.

The choristers were probably paid for performances on Holy Innocents' Day (28 December) or other festivities just before the New Year, and the Master of the Children of the chapel, William Newark, had probably composed a new song for such an occasion.[56] We know, in any case, that the custom of singing 'caralls' at dinner, and of watching 'disguisings' and 'interludes' performed by the choristers or court minstrels, began in this period.[57] It is also possible that one of the famous Twelfth Night revels had been performed (the

---

[54] See Bent-Bent, 'Dufay, Dunstable, Plummer'.

[55] After P. J. Helm, *England under the Yorkists and Tudors 1471–1603* (London: G. Bell & Son, 1968), 33.

[56] The composition of *nova carmina* for these feasts was at this time the regular duty of Bruges succentors; see Strohm, *Bruges*, 54.

[57] See Stevens, *Music and Poetry*, ch. 11 ('Music in ceremonies, entertainments and plays'). On interludes in general, see Chambers, *Mediaeval Stage*, vol. 2, 179 ff.

first unambiguous evidence for them appears in 1494) and that William Cornysh had written a new text for it. The 'prophecy' which he delivered before 12 November may have been part of the 'interlude' to be played in the banqueting hall. The Mass of the Passion can hardly have been anything other than a Mass of the Seven Sorrows of Our Lady. A confraternity of this new devotion had been founded just a year before in Flanders under the tutelage of Duke Philip the Fair. A magnificent choirbook produced somewhat later (*B-Br 215–16*) contains the new Mass and Office in plainsong, two motets and two Mass settings 'of the seven sorrows' by Pipelare, Josquin and La Rue.[58] Perhaps the Mass brought to Henry VII was one of these settings.

Secular polyphony

Not only Mass music, but also some of the most significant secular compositions by Englishmen have to be sought in continental sources, which may indicate that this kind of composition was mostly cultivated in court circles. English secular lyrics of the fifteenth century were closely attached to French precedent, and the dominating figure was Charles d'Orléans.[59] For the use of the largest part of society, the carol efficiently served its purpose of public and private entertainment. Secular partsongs that are no longer carols appear for the first time around 1500 in sources such as the Ritson MS, but the (earlier) carols of the same manuscript demonstrate how this genre had absorbed much of the French chanson idiom as well. A random example is the setting of the popular text 'Man assay', perhaps from the 1460s:[60]

Example 55 'Man assay', Ritson Manuscript

[58] Robijns, 'Musikhandschrift'; Strohm, *Bruges*, 149.
[59] See also p. 190. A study of the texts is Julia Boffey, *Manuscripts of English Courtly Love Lyrics* (Woodbridge: D. S. Brewer, 1985). See also the important review by D. Fallows in *JRMA* 112 (1987), 132–8, with additional attributions and reconstructions of songs.
[60] Stevens ed., *Mediaeval Carols*, no. 110. Earlier tunes and settings using this text exist; see no. 17 in the same edn.

Example 55 (*cont.*)

The opening may remind one of Dufay's late song 'Malheureux cuer',[61] but the simple continuation and the low level of floridity are more a reflection of Binchois' earlier songs; this style trails behind the Burgundian chanson by about a generation. On the other hand, the piece also demonstrates the distance the polyphonic carol itself had travelled from uniformity to individuality.[62]

The documentation of secular polyphony by English manuscripts is very scarce around the middle of the century. In an impressive study, David Fallows has combined the English and foreign source evidence to produce a picture of forms and styles.[63]

The main genre was that of an English *ballade*, continuing the life of this French Ars nova form which continental composers had all but abandoned by *c*.1430; the insular 'rhyme-royal stanza' (beginning with two alternating rhyme-pairs) was its poetic equivalent. We have three-voice ballade settings of

---

61 Dufay, *Opera omnia*, vol. 6, no. 24.
62 Some of Bukofzer's statements about the stylistic development are still valuable: see Bukofzer, *Studies*, 148–69; *idem*, 'Popular and secular music', 121–33.
63 Fallows, 'English song repertories'. This study also mentions the earlier song sources *GB-Cu 5943*, *Ob Douce 381* and *GB-Ob Ashmole 191*, for which see *CC*, vol. 1, 131 f, vol. 2, 381 and 271, respectively.

English words by John Bedyngham ('Fortune alas',[64] 'Myn hertis lust'[65]), Walter Frye ('Alas, alas', 'So ys emprentid'[66]) and anonymi. A remarkable piece is the anonymous 'Princesse of youthe', the words of which may be by John Lydgate.[67] For two other songs by Bedyngham, the original (perhaps English) words have not been found. A piece with the macaronic text 'Agwillare habeth standiff, in lanten this tale me told' is also probably an English ballade. The same is true of a textless two-part piece attributed to 'Watlin frew' (i.e. Walter Frye) in the Strahov Codex.[68] Typical for these songs is the identical melismatic extension of both the first and second part, a musical refrain or 'rhyming melisma'. The pieces are generally melismatic and have a peculiar way of eschewing strong metrical accents. There are many imperfect consonances between cantus and tenor in sometimes intricate rhythmic displacements. Also characteristic, especially of Frye, are crossings and pitch-exchanges between cantus and tenor.

Fallows also identifies English uses of the *rondeau* and *virelai* (*ballata*) forms, although not always orthodox ones. In these genres, Englishmen did set foreign texts. 'Anglo-Italian' songs exist, for example, by Robertus de Anglia who lived in Ferrara and Bologna in the 1450s and 60s, and by Galfridus de Anglia whose whereabouts are not documented, but who may have been in Ferrara before 1450.[69] There are, furthermore, Dunstable's rondeau 'Puisque m'amour' and Bedyngham's rondeau 'Mi verry ioy'. Frye's piece surviving only with the text 'Trinitatis dies' is most probably a rondeau, but we do not know in which original language. The rondeau 'Durer ne puis', perhaps the most French-sounding piece of all these, exists with attributions to both Dunstable and Bedyngham; the younger man is the more likely composer.

The ballata 'O rosa bella', whose attribution, whether to Dunstable or Bedyngham, has long been disputed, must be by Bedyngham. This piece, one of the most famous songs of the century, originated about 1450 in northern Italy as a new setting of the well-known *giustiniana* already set by Ciconia. This setting is connected with the Este court of Ferrara (see p. 545), from where the best manuscript copy of the song derives, attributing it to Bedyngham.[70] The

---

[64] Better known with the contrafactum text 'Gentil madonna'.

[65] Also known with the contrafactum text 'Mon seul plaisir'. This contrafactum has been attributed – unconvincingly – to Dufay. Fallows, 'Words and music', identifies Charles d'Orléans as the author of the text of 'Mon seul plaisir', but shows that the music fits the English translation of the poem better, i.e. it was composed for the English words. A study of this and related pieces by Bedyngham suggests that the composer tried to make the music suit *both* languages: see Leslie Kearney, *Emerging Humanism in Fifteenth-Century Chansons*, unpubl. seminar paper, Music Department, Yale University, 1985.

[66] Given to Bedyngham by David Fallows, 'Bedyngham, Johannes' in *The New Grove*, where the unusually complex transmission is discussed briefly. For editions, see Frye, *Collected Works*.

[67] Fallows, 'Words and music'.

[68] See Snow, *Manuscript Strahov*, no. 232; transcribed in Plamenac, 'Browsing', 109. The anonymous, textless three-part piece preceding it (ed. in Snow, no. 231) may be an English ballade as well.

[69] See Fallows, 'English song repertories'; *idem*, 'Robertus de Anglia'; Lockwood, *Ferrara*, 110–18.

[70] The Oporto MS (*P-Pm 714*), which also contains the songs by Robertus and Galfridus; see Fallows, 'Robertus de Anglia'. Editions of 'O rosa bella' are in Dunstable, *Works*, no. 54, and *DTOe VII*, vols. 14–15, 224–34 (including related settings and arrangements).

many repercussions of the setting (imitations, elaborations, added voices, three cantus firmus Masses based on it etc.) seem to have their origin in northern Italy, but soon appear in the north as well.[71] It is strange that the setting seems to ignore a well-known convention of the virelai–ballata form: the middle cadence, which is the last when all the stanzas are sung, does not have a full tonic close. This imperfect ('D major') chord is, in my opinion, due not to the composer's 'ignorance of the form', as has been claimed, but to a strong rhetorical intention – a characteristic of Bedyngham and his generation. When this chord is reached for the last time, the simple addition of a final chord $g-d'-g'$ will suffice – as indeed it does in the Mass–motet cycle over this tenor.[72]

Very little is known about the biographies of Frye (*d.*1475) and Bedyngham (1422–60), except that they were both active in London at some stage. They may have been attached to the court or another institution with foreign links, but the wide distribution of their music may be entirely due to the authors themselves. Their songs had an enormous impact on professionals and amateurs everywhere, rivalling the influence of Binchois' chansons whose procedures they inherit and develop. 'O rosa bella' is mentioned alongside Binchois' rondeau 'Votre tres douce' as one of many tunes which the merchant George Cely learned to sing, or play on harp and lute, from the harper Thomas Rede in Calais, 1474.[73] It is likely that the extant songs by Walter Frye were popular in the Franco-Netherlands area by *c.*1460. His rondeau 'Tout a par moy' is given to Binchois in the *Nivelle* Chansonnier (*F-Pn Rés. Vmc. ms. 57*);[74] it was sung one day outside Chartres Cathedral by a certain Gerardus de Brabant alone in two voices. Performances of this 'ventriloquist' are mentioned by Tinctoris and Jean Molinet.[75] The beginning of the second half, 'Faisant regretz de ma dolente vie', served Josquin as the cantus firmus for a Mass, and also seems to connect Frye with the fashion of 'chansons de regretz' of the 1470s and later. Like the songs of Binchois, those of Frye and Bedyngham were used in Masses and motets by two generations of Franco-Netherlands composers. The very

---

[71] Bukofzer's conclusion in 'Popular and secular music', 128 f, that the added voices in codex *Tr 89* were expressly attributed to Bedyngham, thus indirectly supporting Dunstable's authorship of the original setting, is in error. The caption for these voices 'Concordantie O rosa bella cum aliis tribus ut posuit Bedingham et sine hiis non concordant' must be interpreted thus: 'the concordances' (i.e. added voices) 'of O rosa bella for the other three voices *as Bedingham has set them* and without these they do not work'. It is a warning to use the three new 'concordances' only with the three voices of Bedyngham's setting and not any other of the various 'O rosa bella' settings. For editions of various arrangements, see *DTOe VII* (vols. 14–15), 224–34, and Trowell ed., *Invitation to Medieval Music 4*, no. 1.

[72] See p. 426.

[73] He also learned 'Go hert, hurt with adversite', 40 dance-tunes, and the essential dance-steps. See Alison Hanham, 'The musical studies of a fifteenth-century wool merchant', *The Review of English Studies*, new ser. 8 (1957), 270–74.

[74] David Fallows, 'Binchois, Gilles de Bins dit' in *The New Grove*, accepts this attribution. I believe that the song is by Frye (see also p. 442).

[75] Weinmann, *Tinctoris*, 34; Molinet, *Faictz et dictz*, vol. 1, 313 ('Recollection de merveilleuses advenues' LXXXVI: the implied date is *c.*1480–83). Molinet does not name the performer. The technique is also known in other cultural zones.

idea of composing Masses over chanson tunes may have originated with the English (see p. 413).

In her book on Walter Frye, Sylvia Kenney emphasizes what she calls a 'duet style' in his songs, and which she relates to the fact that two-part songs (with only cantus and tenor) are frequent not only in France but also in the few English song sources of the early fifteenth century.[76] She also compares this with the earlier polyphonic carols for two voices. Now, all the songs surviving with attributions to Frye have contratenors, but Kenney argues that their cantus and tenor framework is of a special, 'egalitarian' type, which she further identifies with English discant. This last identification is certainly erroneous, since the practice of English discant always presupposes the extemporizing against a given plainsong, which is the opposite of an 'egalitarian' relationship. In English and French song-writing in three parts at the time, the contratenor is always dispensable (if present at all), and Frye's use of the texture, which we call chanson format, is in no way special.[77] Just as Dunstable and Lionel forged their masterpieces in the continental chanson and motet idioms, so Walter Frye accepted the three-part chanson format of Binchois and Dufay. His songs are 'English' in other respects – form, melodic clichés, leisurely declamation – but not in harmonic technique.

Antiphon settings

It is ironic that Kenney overlooked the one work by Walter Frye where his technique does resemble English discant, the Mass 'Summe trinitati' (see below). Before turning to Mass compositions, however, we may cast a glance at the development of the genre in which Walter Frye and his English contemporaries created another aesthetic model of European significance. The point about Frye's most famous composition, 'Ave regina celorum, mater regis angelorum', is its rather anonymous beauty (see Ex. 56).

The work exists today in almost twenty manuscripts of Franco-Netherlands, German, Italian and Hungarian origin, and its notes are also depicted in two panel-paintings and a wall-painting.[78] An English source has not been found. The manuscripts are often chansonniers, not chapel choirbooks: the piece served for private devotions. The paintings show the Assumption of Our Lady (15 August) and seem to relate to Marian confraternities who performed the

---

[76] Kenney, *Walter Frye*, ch. 7 ('The chansons of Frye'). The English sources are *GB-Cu 5943*, *GB-Ob Ashmole 191* and *GB-Ob Douce 381* – see n. 63 above.

[77] Kenney, *Walter Frye*, 148, claims that about mid-century, the duet style superseded a different, older idiom, and that Frye was mainly responsible for this. Her interpretation of the earlier French chanson as 'accompanied solo song', derived from Besseler's concept of 'Balladenstil', is the root of all the other misunderstandings. Never had tenor and contratenor formed an accompanying 'duet' together. See also p. 44.

[78] See Kenney, *Walter Frye*, illustrations and ch. 4; Carapezza, 'Regina angelorum'.

Example 56 Walter Frye, 'Ave regina celorum'

Example 56 (*cont.*)

piece in their chapels as a votive antiphon. Its form, however, is not the free, prose-like structure of earlier English antiphon settings, but is identical to that of an English ballade with musical refrain (aBcB). Since the songs by Frye occur in continental manuscripts so regularly with substitute words (sometimes sacred), Sylvia Kenney plausibly suggests that 'Ave regina celorum' is a contrafactum of a ballade as well.[79] The problem is that in 'Ave regina celorum' the *text* is repeated within the stanza (aBcB), which contradicts the poetic form of the ballade. The repeat is not simply a final melisma, but is tailored to the words 'O Maria flos virginum, velut rosa velut lilium'. The brief, declamatory imitation at 'flos virginum' further emphasizes these words, as the tenor is texted as well. The form seems to be planned to enhance the devotional text. No hint of a vernacular text has been discovered in the sources, not even in fragmented or garbled form as is so often the case with other English songs.[80] The Latin words could thus be the original ones, after all, and the piece might have been written as a votive antiphon (in the form of a liturgical responsory) for a confraternity or similar group with contacts abroad.

In that case, Walter Frye would admittedly have conceived of the antiphon genre in a novel manner. His melodic–rhythmic vocabulary abounds with the courtly clichés of the late Binchois and early Ockeghem songs. The contour of the cantus, bar 2, is the most important cliché, and it generates others. The spare but incisive declamatory imitation recalls a few late Binchois songs. Frye's own songs, and those of Bedyngham, also belong in the stylistic context of this work. Its 'Englishness' lies rather in the generally melismatic style, the control of dissonance, and the shifting of cadential downbeats to other positions in the bar (see bars 11 and 13). A popular cadential motive in bars 6–7, 19–20, 24–5, 30 and 42–3 resolves the diminished fifth *e–b♭* inward to *f–a*. This had been much used by Lionel; it was well known also to Dufay and Baude Cordier (see p. 143). Similarly, the use of thirds and full triads for internal cadences, often with the third degree on top (bars 4, 10, 15 and 39) and the 'double-octave' cadence ('V–I') in the contratenor (bars 35–6) had become part of the international chanson language by *c.*1450.

The piece is much more than a collection of clichés, however. Whatever Frye's material, he has put it together with incredible skill to form a wonderful balance. Despite certain points of rhetorical emphasis, not a single element remains unconnected or unanswered. The fermata which concludes the opening phrase (in itself a well-known device in English antiphons and songs) isolates the word 'Ave' like a separate, emphatic gesture. But see how the contratenor in bar 8 echoes the first tenor entry, as if the first phrase were to be repeated. I believe that we may credit the composer after all with a creative role in the musical idiom found here. 'Ave regina celorum' could in fact be a

---

[79] See also Sylvia W. Kenney, 'Contrafacta in the works of Walter Frye', *JAMS* 8 (1955), 182–202. The 'rhyming melisma' for an antiphon setting is not unique: the widely known 'O gloriosa regina mundi' by Johannes Touront also has one, albeit with different proportions.

[80] Examples are collected in Fallows, 'English song repertories'.

work of the 1440s – although we have no biographical data for Frye before 1456/7 (when he entered the London St Nicholas Guild). He would then be an initiator of a European 'mixed style' between chanson, votive antiphon and motet. His modernity seems to have misled Tinctoris into believing that his pieces were composed in the 1460s.

A date of *c.*1440 or even earlier must be assigned to 'Tota pulchra es' (II) by John Plummer.[81] The clear distinction which this work maintains from all music by Dunstable and Power, lies not so much in the abundant use of imitation (in this way Hugo de Lantins differs from Dufay), as in the sharpening of rhetorical effects despite a simple motivic vocabulary. Both are features shared with Walter Frye. As Plummer was a member of the royal household by 1441, he may have been older than Frye, although he died later (*c.*1484). Three antiphon settings by Plummer occur in the codex *ModB* of *c.*1448 (see p. 266), where there are also two similar works by John Stone and one by a certain Standley which must predate 1443. Stone served the chapel of Edward IV in the 1460s. We have only these two pieces by him, which are of the same standard as the best of Frye and Plummer. Standley also left a canonic Mass cycle and other sacred pieces. They survive only in central European sources: this may have some significance for his biography. His extant works are – the canonic artifice apart – more routine than those of the others.

This whole group of composers and works is to be classed as 'post-Dunstable' in outlook: they developed an aesthetic of devotional word-setting which Dunstable only skirted with his famous 'Quam pulchra es'. Their music is essentially supranational in style and almost seems intended for continental distribution. Much of it found its way via Flanders to Italy, and Franco-Netherlands or Italian imitations may exist: for example, among the anonymous antiphons of the north Italian manuscript *I-Fn 112bis* (*c.*1460), which also contains Frye's 'Ave regina' and works by Dunstable and Power,[82] or in the Lucca Choirbook (*I-Las 238*; *c.*1470) with nine antiphon motets including one each by Stone and Plummer.[83]

We have only two more pieces by Frye with original Latin texts.[84] The sequence 'Sospitati dedit' in *Pepys 1236* uses many formulas from secular song: the beginning of the tenor, for example, is identical with that of 'So ys emprentid'. More independent in style is 'O florens rosa', which is surely a votive antiphon – although the beginning of the cantus, this time, echoes Dufay's 'Par le regart'. Perhaps the most elegant piece of this group is the anonymous 'O pulcherrima mulierum' which occurs in eight sources, including chansonniers.

---

[81] It is in the Selden MS (see p. 382), and edited in Hughes ed., *Fifteenth-Century Liturgical Music* I, 28. For other antiphons, see Plummer, *Four Motets*.

[82] See Kenney, 'In praise of the lauda', and p. 590 below.

[83] Inventory and description in Strohm, *Bruges*, 192–7 and 120–36.

[84] On 'Trinitatis dies', see p. 392 above; on 'Salve virgo' n. 106 below.

Because of the poignant imitations and the intense rhetoric of the setting, I attribute it to John Plummer whose 'Tota pulchra es' (I) it resembles most.[85]

Antiphons of this type have sometimes been called 'song-motets' or even '*lauda*-motets'. With the exception of the refrain repetitions of Frye's 'Ave regina', the English antiphon settings are formally free, and treat even metrical Latin poetry as free-flowing prose. This is the opposite procedure from that of all song genres before the modern era, which observe strict repetition patterns. Kenney's term '*lauda*-motet'[86] refers to certain affinities between the Latin *lauda* and other genres around the time of the young Dufay (see also p. 160). Latin *lauda* texts were still set as 'motets' by later generations, for example by Josquin des Prez. Such *rapprochements* between Latin-texted genres and also between antiphon and chanson were, in a sense, typical for the mid-century crisis of the motet genre.

Votive antiphons and *Magnificat* settings are so rare in English sources between the Selden and Eton MSS that a general picture of the stylistic development is not yet available. It is uncertain how far continental sources can help us here.[87] The transparent, often declamatory text setting of Plummer and Frye attracted more continental attention than other idioms which, from an insular point of view, were perhaps more advanced. The theorist John Hothby (*d.*1487) was insignificant as a composer; but the florid, intricate and rather shapeless appearance of his pieces (two *Magnificat* settings, one antiphon 'Que est ista', and some secular pieces) may reflect a real English trend of the 1450s and 60s. These pieces survived on the Continent only because the composer himself took them there. A development towards the 'Eton style' seems to be documented also by the Lausanne fragment[88] (with two antiphons, probably both for five voices), by the fragment *GB-Lbl add.54324* and by some of the anonymous antiphon fragments in the Lucca Choirbook. Furthermore, the type of the multisectional cantus firmus antiphon for five voices of fairly equal floridity does exist on the Continent: in the works of Ockeghem and Regis (see p. 481), in some works in codex *Tr 89* (*c.*1462–6) and in the second layer of the Nicolaus Leopold Codex (*c.*1476). A feature which some of these continental works have in common with the Eton antiphons is multiple cantus firmi. The matter is complicated by the fact that some anonymous works in the continental sources are actually English, for example a 'Gaude flore virginali' in *Tr 89*.[89] Certainly continental are, however, various 'Salve regina' settings with borrowed secular cantus firmi.[90]

---

[85] Strohm, *Bruges*, 133 and mus. ex. 12. I reject, on the other hand, an 'Ibo michi' in *Tr 88*, because it is far too clumsy for this composer. The attribution was suggested by Ann B. Scott, '*Ibo Michi ad Montem Mirre*: a new motet by Plummer?', *MQ* 58 (1972), 543–56.

[86] Kenney, 'In praise of the lauda'.

[87] But the problem is exactly analogous to that of secular music, which has been successfully treated by Fallows, 'English song repertories'.

[88] See Martin Staehelin, 'Neue Quellen zur mehrstimmigen Musik des 15. und 16. Jahrhunderts in der Schweiz', *Schweizer Beiträge zur Musikwissenschaft* 3 (1978), 57 ff, and pp. 238 f above.

[89] See Harrison, *Britain*, 307.

[90] See p. 438 below.

The Eton composers[91] can be grouped stylistically and chronologically in something like three overlapping generations. The oldest is represented by Richard Hygons, William Horwood, Gilbert Banaster, J. Nesbet and Baldwyn. Two four-voice *Magnificat* settings by Baldwyn are lost from the manuscript. He may have been John Baldwin, King's scholar between 1448 and 1452, and also the 'Baldwin' quoted by John Hothby in his *Dialogus* (*c*.1475).[92] Hothby mentions him as one of the (mainly English) composers who used the pitch *g''* in their 'cantilenae'. This statement recalls the practice of 'monitoring' the ranges of compositions, as does the index of the Eton Choirbook: for each work, the range is given in numbers of notes.[93] Baldwyn's *Magnificat* settings had 22 notes, i.e. conceivably a range of *G–g''*. A 'Bawldwyn' is documented at Tattershall College in 1498/9 as having composed a seven-part 'Gaude'.[94]

The increase in voice-numbers and total ranges for polyphony, which presupposed the addition of boy sopranos and low basses (see p. 381), was perhaps led by institutions such as Eton itself. The lost 'organ book' of the College's inventory of 1465[95] had a motet beginning on fol. 2 with the words 'laris qui'. The quotation seems to fit the contratenor altus of a motet fragment in the Lucca Choirbook: 'O rex gentium et desideratus earum, lapisque angularis, qui facis mirabilia'. This complex and florid four-voice setting of an 'O-antiphon' for Advent[96] seems to have had a range descending to *D* and ascending at least to *a'* (19 notes). A mysterious case is that of a lost 'Gaude flore', which the Eton index gives to Dunstable, describing it as a work for five voices with a total range of 21 notes. This texture would be drastically different from all of Dunstable's known works; a misattribution is likely.[97]

The earliest Eton composers are not a stylistically close group. As far as can be judged from biographical data on Hygons, Banaster and Horwood, their works were composed for various other institutions. Nevertheless, compositional traditions were rather coherent, particularly in *Magnificat* settings. Harrison quotes five motivically related *Magnificat* openings, in which settings by Horwood and Nesbet in the Eton Choirbook seem to have been imitated by younger colleagues elsewhere.[98] The first two works, however, are more closely related to each other than to the others. I believe it is Nesbet who quotes Hor-

---

[91] Edn: Frank Ll. Harrison ed., *The Eton Choirbook*, MB 10–12 (London: Stainer & Bell, 1973). A detailed investigation of the styles cannot be attempted here. See Harrison, *Britain*, 307–29; Benham, *Latin Church Music*, 58–97; Harrison, 'English polyphony', 308–27.

[92] Hothby, *Tres tractatuli*, 65.

[93] See also n. 119.

[94] Wathey, 'Lost books', no. 100.

[95] Harrison, *Eton Choirbook*, 161 f.

[96] See Strohm, *Bruges*, 134.

[97] An anonymous, fragmentary 'Gaude flore' using 21 notes in the MS *GB-Lbl add.54324* stands next to Dunstable's 'Descendi in ortum', one of his latest known works. Bent–Bent, 'Dufay, Dunstable, Plummer', transcribe the 'Gaude flore' and discuss its authorship (399 ff), inclining towards John Browne or Walter Lambe. In any case, the fragment has some connection with the Eton music.

[98] Harrison, 'English polyphony', 324 ff.

wood in his *Magnificat*, especially at the beginning and at the end, for example in the passage 'Sicut erat in principio'.

A more closely-knit group of composers comprises Walter Lambe, John Browne, Richard Davy and John Sutton. The last-named was at Eton in 1477–9, and his 'Salve regina' with the cantus firmus 'Libera nos' for seven voices (23 notes) seems to be written for the College itself. A certain John Browne was an Eton scholar, aged fourteen, in 1467. The Browne of the choir-book is with fifteen works the most prominent composer – followed by Lambe, also an Etonian and King's scholar, and later a member of St George's Chapel, Windsor, with twelve works. The slightly younger Richard Davy, by whom we have nine works (not all complete, but including a complete *St Matthew Passion*) is the last famous composer whose style still belongs in every respect to the fifteenth century. He worked at Magdalen College, Oxford, from about 1483 to at least 1492, and later at Exeter Cathedral; pieces by him were copied at Tattershall in 1498/9.[99] Little or nothing is known on Hugh Kellyk, Fawkyner, Edmund Turges and others, who also seem to belong to this chronological group.

With these composers, we reach the peak of a continuous stylistic development that had originated three generations earlier. Most striking – particularly in comparison with continental music – are the rich textures and the varied 'vocal orchestration',[100] an outgrowth of Lionel's, Cooke's and Byttering's 'reduced scoring' but now applied to four to seven voices of practically equal importance. In the prevailing traditional metres O and C, the semiminims (semiquavers in transcription with quartered values) are the main melismatic element, and the minim is largely treated as consonant. This high degree of 'euphony' may at times stand in the way of dramatic expression, particularly when combined with some form of imitation. But this is also a problem with some continental composers around 1500, Isaac and Mouton, for example. The melodic–rhythmic vocabulary of the Eton composers, however, seems richer, less regulated by constraints of metre and declamation, and more play-ful. Syncopations and proportions (triplets etc.) embroider the lines; the most forceful passages are often those of the greatest rhythmic excitement in all the voices, not – as more usual with Josquin – those in chordal declamation. The cantus firmi are usually 'borrowed' and combine with the main text to com-pound liturgical statements; more than one plainsong is sometimes used. The settings similarly conflate plainsong modes and melodies. 'Double cursus' (the cantus firmus being stated exactly twice) is usual, but the given melodic material can appear in any voice in various forms of paraphrase.

Apart from less important names, the latest Eton composers include Robert Fayrfax and William Cornysh (whose careers were linked to the royal house-hold), as well as William Brygeman and Robert Wylkynson, who were both connected with Eton. Wylkynson wrote what seems to be the latest work in

---

[99] Wathey, 'Lost books', no. 102.
[100] See the diagrams in Harrison, *Britain*, 316.

the manuscript, perhaps in his own hand: the thirteen-voice 'Jesus autem transiens / Credo in Deum' (Apostles' Creed). Also by him is a nine-part 'Salve regina', in which each voice symbolizes one of the nine choirs of angels (according to the pasted-down initials of the voices).[101] As Master of the Choristers at the College from 1500, he composed nine works for the choirbook (six of which are incomplete or lost) and was obviously responsible for this magnificent collection. One wonders whether it fell out of use when he left or died in 1515.

Mass settings

The richness and variety of English Mass music of this whole century is largely documented in continental manuscripts. But certain phenomena – such as *alternatim* performance, squares, stroke notation, and the form of the 'shorter' or 'ferial' Mass – are much more frequent in the few remaining insular sources. Perhaps these simpler or provincial types failed to reach the Continent because they failed to reach establishments in England that had any foreign connections. Alternatively, continental scribes may have rejected them because they were looking for more complex works.

In the 1440s, the English practised three types of cyclic Mass: one type for three or four voices with strict ('isorhythmic') cantus firmus treatment; another for three voices with free cantus firmus treatment, and the Mass without cantus firmus. From *c.*1450, the free type became increasingly popular; strict tenor Masses for three voices are no longer found. The model status of the 'Caput' Mass, a strict tenor Mass for four voices, probably contributed to the longer cultivation of this type in England ('Veterem hominem') and even more on the Continent (Domarto, Dufay, Ockeghem etc.). After *c.*1455, the leading English composers seem to have abandoned this type as well.

The music of Walter Frye (*d.*1475) is symptomatic of this development. The relatively strict tenor Mass 'Nobilis et pulchra', for three voices, is his most conventional cycle. As in 'Rex seculorum', the plainsong tenor is slightly varied in rhythm, but not in pitch, in the five sections. The chanson format, the short head-motive and the total range of sixteen notes could well fit a work written about 1450, although the rhythms of the outer voices are unusually lively in comparison with Dunstable's generation. The Kyrie has the prosula 'Deus creator omnium' for high feasts, whereas the cantus firmus is an antiphon for St Katherine of Alexandria. If this combination means anything, then it is perhaps that the Mass was written for a school or university college; St Katherine was the patroness of scholars, and her feast-day was often celebrated as the annual feast of arts' faculties.

---

[101] Harrison, *Eton Choirbook*, 147. These two 'symbolic' works may have served for semidramatic performances.

Together with a fragmentary 'Nesciens mater' Mass by Plummer,[102] Frye's 'Flos regalis' may be one of the earlier specimens of the free four-voice tenor Mass. Its cantus firmus (which has not yet been identified) is one of those plain-songs in mode seven that seem to emulate the 'Caput' tenor.[103] But Frye's step away from this model is considerable. Although his texture and layout appear similar, his tenor is differently varied in each section and in such a way that the lengths of passages in full and reduced scoring also vary. (The Kyrie is missing.) In the Gloria and Credo, there are duets between the tenor and lower contratenor where the former seems to carry the plainsong (not yet a usual technique). This four-part type of tenor Mass was to become the most frequent in Europe.

The adoption of secular cantus firmi for Mass cycles probably follows an English initiative. Frye's fragmentary Kyrie 'So ys emprentid' in the Lucca Choirbook (*I-Las 238*), which is surely part of a cycle, literally quotes the tenor of his ballade, preserving even its original rhythm. According to the reconstruction by Brian Trowell, the extant cantus also moves like a free paraphrase of the top voice of the ballade.[104] Dialectically related to the rhythmic freedom of Frye's Mass tenors cited above, this one might not have changed rhythm at all in the five sections. But the melody is not handled like an isorhythmic framework as in 'Caput': it moves at the same pace with the other voices and is simply 'followed through' during the whole section, without determining layout or mensurations.

'Literal quotation' is also the technique employed in Frye's three-part Mass 'Summe trinitati'.[105] Although it has an antiphon tenor (in the seventh mode and reminding one of 'Caput'), the specific rhythm given to it in the Kyrie is maintained throughout all five sections.[106] This pedantic repetition seems pointless as the lively rhythms in all the voices entirely disguise the shape of the tenor. Nor do the sectional divisions contribute to a recognizable structure. The whole cycle uses only one mensuration (C). The tenor carries the plainsong when participating in duets. The texture looks at first like chanson format but is not (see Ex. 57).

As can be seen from the first full cadence of the Sanctus in bar 10, the tenor moves to the fifth degree. This it does many other times in the work, always requiring the contratenor to support it with a third or fifth below. Contrapuntally speaking, this is the technique of English discant in three voices – or one could argue that it is derived from motet format for four voices, as in the 'Caput' Mass. But the many duets between any pair of voices, and their rhythmic

---

[102] See Brian Trowell, 'Plummer, John' in *The New Grove*.

[103] Others were 'Veterem hominem', 'Tu es Petrus', Frye's 'Summe trinitati' and the anonymous (English?) 'Thomas cesus' in *I-Rvat S Pietro B 80* (*SP*).

[104] Strohm, *Bruges*, 124 f.

[105] For continental uses of literal quotation, see p. 474.

[106] The Kyrie is preserved with the contrafactum text 'Salve virgo' (*Collected Works*, no. 9) – a recognition first published in Brian Trowell, 'Frye, Walter' in *The New Grove*. See also p. 429 below.

Example 57 Walter Frye, Mass 'Summe trinitati': Sanctus

equality, make it unlike either technique. Frye has probably developed his procedure from English discant and from more primitive types of Mass composition where the more complex perfect tempus was also avoided for the sake of halfskilled performers.[107]

John Bedyngham's two surviving cycles (both known at Trent Cathedral before 1455) represent two more types of Mass composition. One is without cantus firmus: a beautiful 'sine nomine' Mass in the first mode, with little structure or motivic recurrence to hold it together except for two different headmotives and generally tripartite layouts. The work has specific motives in common with the cycle by Jean Pullois (see p. 242) and a common precedent can be sought in the 'Missa sine nomine' by (Dunstable or Lionel or) Benet, but Bedyngham may have had direct access to Pullois' work, or vice versa.

Bedyngham's Mass 'Dueil angoisseux'[108] is the earliest complete 'parody Mass', i.e. a cycle over a secular chanson of which more than one voice is uti-

---

[107] It has been suggested that the Mass was intended for a royal occasion, as 'Summe trinitati' is sometimes sung at the reception of king and queen. But Trinity Sunday is also the conventional feast-day of civic guilds.

[108] Edited in *DTOe XXXI*, vol. 61. The Kyrie of this cycle is missing. The 'Benedicamus domino' mentioned by Fallows, 'Bedyngham, Johannes' in *The New Grove*, is a contrafactum of the 'Cum sancto spiritu'.

lized. Its technique is as different from Frye's 'So ys emprentid' fragment as can be. The chanson tenor is almost totally disguised by the varying ornamentations; some sections are omitted, others are repeated. The cantus line quotes from the model cantus – which is not an inevitable result of the tenor's presence because the respective appearances are so haphazard. The work is written in chanson format (the fourth voice added to the Credo is not authentic).

Bedyngham's variation technique is so bold and exuberant that a suspicion remains that his 'Missa sine nomine' has an extremely well disguised cantus firmus as well. It is more likely, however, that this work simply plays with modal clichés in the tenor, like the cycles by Benet and Pullois.[109]

Perhaps the most sophisticated work known today that belongs to this type is John Plummer's 'Missa sine nomine' in the Brussels Choirbook (*B-Br 5557*; *BR*).[110] It is in simple three-voice chanson format and has the conventional binary layout in 'O' and 'C' subsections. There are, however, an intriguing number of melodic and rhythmic recurrences and a beautifully shaped textural layout. Head-motives appear in several voices and at the beginnings of subsections. In the Gloria, for example, the initial motive of the second introductory duet ('Gratias agimus') appears later in inverted counterpoint to open the full section 'Domine fili'. There is much imitative and canonic play between the voices and the lines are often embroidered with ornaments in the smallest note-values. Interest is also provided by the fluctuating mode – or rather chromaticism – based on a combination of Mixolydian and Dorian on the finals *c*, *g* and *c'*: any of these finals can have the major or minor third and even sixth above it. The texts of Credo, Gloria and even Kyrie are considerably shortened.

BR is a precious document for the presence of English music at the court of Charles the Bold (*r.* 1467–77).[111] A self-contained group of five English Masses, perhaps collected for Charles's bride Margaret of York, was here combined with a Burgundian chapel repertory. The wedding of Charles and Margaret was celebrated in Damme and Bruges in July 1468, with the participation of many Flemish, French and English minstrels. It is quite probable that English chaplains also performed.[112] The five English Masses in *BR* comprise the three by Walter Frye that survive complete, and one each by Plummer and Riquardus Cockx – who may well be Richard Cokkes, an Eton scholar in 1440, and/or the Cokkes at King's College in 1457.[113] No English material contained in *BR* survives in earlier copies, but the contrafactum of the Kyrie 'Summe trinitati' was copied at Trent before 1460. It is unlikely that the five Masses were brought

---

[109] The attempts of Curtis, 'Jean Pullois', to reconstruct underlying plainsongs for the Benet and Pullois cycles seem unsuccessful to me.

[110] See Curtis ed., *Brussels Masses* (no. 5).

[111] On its origin, see Warmington, 'A very fine troop of bastards?'; Rob C. Wegman, 'New data concerning the origins and chronology of Brussels, Koninklijke Bibliotheek, Manuscript 5557', *TVNM* 36 (1986), 5–25.

[112] For some documents, see Strohm, *Bruges*, 98 f.

[113] Harrison, *Britain*, 456. The five Masses are edited in Curtis ed., *Brussels Masses*.

to the Continent with Margaret of York in 1468. Rather, they were already in use in Flanders, for example in the chapel of the English Merchant Adventurers in Bruges, an organization which could even have contributed the music as a wedding gift. Furthermore, other Netherlands institutions had cultivated English music for some time (see pp. 241 ff).

The English music of the Lucca Choirbook, already mentioned several times, belongs in a closely related context. These works were available to establishments in Flanders and were copied in Bruges about 1470.[114] Besides the works in these two major choirbooks, the codices *Tr 90* (copied *c*.1454-8), *Tr 88* (*c*.1458-62) and *Tr 89* (*c*.1462-6), as well as the choirbooks *I-Rvat SP B 80* and *I-VEcap 759*, also contain English Mass cycles, giving us a representative picture of developments in the 1450s and 60s.[115]

Very few works are attributed. Henry Thick (Henricus Tik) emerges as a particularly fine composer. His Marian Mass,[116] which opens the Lucca Choirbook and also appears in the Trent Codices (the Sanctus already by *c*.1458), seems at first glance to represent simpler or provincial idioms. But the three-voice chanson format, the modal unity (Dorian on *g*) and the frequent faburden-like progressions disguise artful text-setting, canon, declamatory imitation, and sometimes striking patterns of voice-exchange or melodic sequence:

Example 58 Henricus Tik, 'Missa de Beata Virgine': Gloria

---

[114] Strohm, *Bruges*, 120–36 and 192–200.

[115] Dates for *Tr* after Saunders, *Dating of the Trent Codices*; for *SP* after Reynolds, 'Origins'.

[116] There is no Marian cantus firmus, but allusions to the Kyrie de BMV (Vatican edition no. IX) in the head-motive as well as the tenor beginnings from the Gloria onwards. The head-motive is identical to the incipit of a Gloria by Johannes Franchois (Borren ed., *Polyphonia Sacra*, no. 13). Thick wrote another (lost) Marian Mass, mentioned in the Spanish treatise *E-E c.III. 23*.

Example 58 (*cont.*)

Triplet passages (in black notes in the manuscript) in canon recur in subsequent sections.[117] There can be little doubt that Thick was an Englishman. The telescoping of the Gloria text in the Flemish source would be exceptional for a continental work at this time, and the spelling of the composer's name as 'Fich' in Hothby's *Dialogus* (see also p. 596) can only have arisen from an Italian

---

[117] Tinctoris objected to blackened notation for triplets together with the reversed sign of *prolatio major* in a 'sine nomine' Mass by Barbingant: see Hamm, 'Another Barbingant Mass'. The passage in Barbingant's Mass is also in canon and generally very similar to that by Thick.

transliteration of 'Thick'. This master may have lived on the Continent for some time, perhaps in Flanders or Spain.

About 15–20 English Mass cycles have been identified in anonymous continental copies of the second half of the fifteenth century.[118] Quite regularly, they are not transmitted in their original forms. A cycle without cantus firmus appears in fragments in *Tr 90* (labelled 'Anglicum') and *Tr 88*, and complete in *SP* and *Verona 759*. There are three different versions of the Kyrie, because the scribes tried to 'complete' the English bipartite Kyrie in different ways (using the music of the Agnus Dei, for example). This modest three-voice cycle in the seventh mode, the motivic material of which may be compared with Frye's Mass 'Summe trinitati', was apparently popular in Italy.

We do not know whether more English Masses on secular models exist. Neither the anonymous 'O rosa bella' Masses nor 'Soyes aprantiz' ('So ys emprentid') by Guillaume Le Rouge are English as such, but their choice of models, and their style, point to English models. A remarkable four-voice cycle on Dunstable's rondeau 'Puisque m'amour' requires further scrutiny as to its origin.

An important work was the Mass 'Alma redemptoris', of which fragments exist in the Lucca Choirbook (no. 8) and in *GB-Lbl add.54324*. It represents a later stage than the other English 'Alma redemptoris' cycles or sections, but may yet predate 1455. The plainsong is very freely varied and takes part in duets. The great equality of the four voices, the snatches of imitation, repeated cadencing and the tonal sweep of the F mode remind one of Walter Frye.

The most recent English Masses preserved in any continental fifteenth-century copy are possibly the two fragmentary five-part cycles in the Lucca Choirbook (nos. 6 and 7). They existed by 1470 and are probably the earliest genuine five-voice cycles known. A gap of at least 30 years is left between them and the next comparable works that survive – the festal Masses by Davy and Fayrfax. In both cycles, the tenor (a freely varied plainsong) is much less florid than the other voices, and in no. 7 it is almost 'monorhythmic' in breves, which is an archaic trait. In all three lower voices of both works, few semiminims (semiquavers in transcription) occur. The layouts are bipartite, as convention dictated. No. 6 is a Mass 'Te gloriosus'[119] on an All Saints' antiphon, which is derived from the *Te Deum*; the Kyrie prosula is 'Conditor Kyrie'. The connection with the *Te Deum* may be important. A possibly English Mass on the *Te Deum* melody itself (strict four-part type with mensural and proportional transformations) is in *Tr 89*,[120] and a 'Missa de gratiarum actione' copied in Bruges in 1455 may also have been a 'Te Deum' Mass. Hugh Aston's work

---

[118] A study which accepts more Masses as English is Rob C. Wegman, 'Concerning tempo in the English polyphonic Mass, c.1420–70', *AcM* 61 (1989), 40–65.

[119] Hothby mentions the work, which uses the *g* clef and probably had a range of *c–g″* (nineteen notes), in his *Dialogus* (*Tres tractatuli*, 65); he probably knew it from the Lucca Choirbook itself.

[120] Nos. 546–50. See Gottlieb, *Masses*.

of this title may have been submitted to Oxford University in 1510 for the B.Mus. degree.[121]

The other five-part cycle is a Mass 'Sancta Maria virgo'. The cantus firmus begins with the first phrase usually set in polyphony, i.e. 'Maria virgo', the word 'Sancta' being intoned in plainsong. The Mass tenor is not identical with the antiphon, but is almost the same as the mene of an English discant setting in the Selden MS (no. 2), which is also given in Example 59.

Since the plainsong migrates in the Selden setting, the mene contains some plainsong pitches, but in other passages it is a counterpoint to the plainsong. A lost 'Sancta Maria' setting very similar to that in Selden must have furnished the Mass cantus firmus. This cantus firmus, then, is not precisely a 'square', but relates to the original plainsong in a similarly derivative manner. The style of the Mass is almost naive; typical are the pseudo-imitations within the triad and a rhythmic activity enlivening stable sonorities in fully scored passages. The lowest voice is more melodically than harmonically conceived ('V–I' cadences are surprisingly rare); the total range was probably $A–e''$ (nineteen notes). Nevertheless, the general floridity and freedom of phrasing seem to anticipate the Eton style. While that music can be regarded as the closest insular equivalent to the 'cosmopolitan' art of the Josquin era, it has significantly stronger roots in national and even provincial traditions not shared by other countries.

Example 59 Sancta Maria virgo: antiphon setting and Mass

Selden MS, no. 6

Lucca Choirbook, no. 7

[121] Harrison, *Britain*, 335.

Example 59 (*cont.*)

Example 59 (*cont.*)

2

FRANCE AND THE LOW COUNTRIES: THE INVENTION OF THE MASTERWORK

The enterprising 1450s

The beginning of the second half of the fifteenth century was as innovative a period for music as was the beginning of the first half. The political context mattered less this time, at least in western Europe. Of the three great rivals, England, France and Burgundy, surely the French benefited most from the return to an awkward balance of power. One of the last conquests of the strengthened Charles VII, the recovery of Bordeaux from the English in June 1451, was celebrated with the performance of the grand political motet 'Adoretur beata trinitas / Pacem Deus reddidit'. This anonymous five-part work is as significant for its ostensible link with the isorhythmic tradition – especially with Dufay's 'Ecclesie militantis' of 1431 – as for the fact that it is not itself isorhythmic. It is in two sections, as are many later motets; the cantus firmus is stated twice with variations ('double cursus'). By analogy with 'Ecclesie militantis', it has a second contratenor with an independent hexameter text referring to the French royal arms, 'Lilia nunc flores'.[122] But Dufay's last isorhythmic motets, 'Fulgens iubar' and 'Moribus et genere', had been composed several years earlier.[123] Now, the demise of the genre was only one factor in a large-scale reshuffle of genres, languages, regional styles, and of sacred and secular images.

Ironically, most of these changes had been prepared for by the losing partner in the international power game, England. English composers had been the first to transfer strict cantus firmus techniques from the isorhythmic motet to the Mass cycle (as in Lionel's 'Alma redemptoris' and the 'Caput' Mass); to use

---

[122] Printed in *DTOe XL*, vols. 76–7. See also Sparks, *Cantus firmus*, 191 f. Although Charles VII was not in Bordeaux, it is possible that the work was commissioned from a composer in the king's own service. See Perkins, 'Musical patronage', 522, concerning 'the appointment, perhaps already in the closing months of 1450, of Johannes Okeghem to a place among the singers in the king's employ. Okeghem was at that point the only member of the chapel now known to have been a composer of polyphony. . .'.

[123] Fallows, *Dufay*, 60 f gives 1442 for both works; but see his *Dufay* rev. edn, 309, for a new suggestion of 1447–8.

secular songs as Mass tenors (as in Bedyngham's 'Dueil angouisseux'); to merge the styles of antiphon settings, chansons and motets (as in the works of Frye and Plummer). They had employed non-isorhythmic cantus firmi in liturgical genres, as in Forest's 'Ascendit Christus' and the anonymous 'O sanctissime presul', or in non-liturgical works, such as 'Cantemus domino / Gaudent in celis' of the Egerton MS.

The 1450s were the years of the 'O rosa bella effect'. The fame of this single chanson, an 'English *giustiniana*', shot through Europe like lightning. Immediately, other composers began to reset or adapt it, and everyone else learnt to play and sing it on harp or lute. (See also p. 393.) The effect was soon to be repeated by other English as well as continental songs. On the 'O rosa bella' tune, and on Frye's ballade 'So ys emprentid', Franco-Burgundian composers constructed not simply Mass cycles but Mass–motet cycles – compounding genres at a time when the secular Mass tenor was itself an absolute novelty. This spirit of enterprise, and the international 'success stories', were most probably the artists' own doing, and not simply the outcome of inevitable cultural or political developments.

An occasion no less symbolic than the surrender of Bordeaux was the often-described Burgundian *banquet du voeu* held at Lille on 17 February 1454. (See also p. 306.) Its ostensible political aim – to rally support for a crusade against the Turks who had taken Constantinople in 1453 – was coated with sweet pastoral lyrics and lavish *entremets*. The more serious matter was addressed by the recitation of a lengthy lament on the fall of the eastern Empire. It was probably not identical with one of the four such laments composed by Dufay (on texts sent to him from Naples). Only one of these survives, the four-part *Lamentatio Sancte Matris ecclesie Constantinopolitane*; it has the texts 'O très piteulx de tout espoir fontaine / Omnes amici spreverunt eam'.[124] There is a new hybrid or mannerist attitude in this work and its text. The non-isorhythmic tenor is taken from the liturgical Lamentations of Jeremiah and is stated twice, first in perfect and then in imperfect time, as in the 'Caput' Mass. The melodic idiom resembles liturgical recitative and, at times, fauxbourdon, but is interwoven with chanson and motet styles.

We should investigate the purpose for which Bedyngham wrote his Mass cycle over Binchois' famous ballade 'Dueil angouisseux', the text and music of which had been written as laments (see p. 193). The lament on Binchois' own death (20 September 1460) was composed by Jean Ockeghem, certainly the new star of the 1450s. 'Mort, tu as navré' is a four-part ballade (as is 'Dueil angouisseux' in at least one version), with striking fauxbourdon sounds as in much of Binchois' sacred music.[125] The tenor 'Miserere' quotes the sequence 'Dies ire' of the Requiem. The piece connects the aesthetic of 'Dueil angoisseux' and of Dufay's 'O très piteulx' with the many later *tombeaux* for princes or artists in

---

124 Dufay, *Opera omnia*, vol. 6, no. 10; see also Fallows, *Dufay*, 71 and 130.
125 Marix ed., *Musiciens*, no. 54; Pope-Kanazawa eds, *Manuscript Montecassino*, no. 107.

Renaissance and Baroque culture; we may follow its traces to Josquin's lament on Ockeghem's death in 1497 ('Nymphes des bois'), to Isaac's for Lorenzo de' Medici in 1492 ('Quis dabit', p. 636) or to Obrecht's 'obituary motet' for his own father in 1488 ('Mille quingentis', p. 487). Thus, 'Mort, tu as navré' has two aspects. One is that it amalgamates the humanist and medieval tradition of praising a forerunner by imitating him, and the poetic-musical genre of the planctus or *complainte* for a deceased person. Landini's praise of Vitry comes to mind, or Andrieu's lament on the death of Machaut (see p. 53). The other aspect is new: it is the legend-building which inevitably takes place when the *premier chapelain* of the French king and new treasurer of St Martin of Tours – not just a student – places himself on the shoulders of Binchois and Dufay – not just his teachers. Also, Ockeghem takes into account their earlier laments, not just any of their music. In this way he consolidates a genre: later laments for composers have from now on to take into account earlier ones. Ockeghem 'tells music history', of which he himself is the subject. This new attitude could be compared with the surely impressive body of obit compositions which Dufay was to build around himself like a funeral monument (see p. 283). Dufay's works, for all their ambition, fulfilled liturgical traditions; Ockeghem's lament was the freely chosen, secular action of an artist.[126]

Mass and motet to c.1465

The winds of change had been blowing since about 1450, and Dufay and Binchois certainly felt them. Dufay's career took surprising (or indeed 'enterprising') turns. He was absent from Cambrai in 1450 and for most of the years 1452–8, mainly at the court of Savoy in Chambéry, with visits to Geneva and Turin. Probably in 1450, he composed the Mass for St Anthony of Padua ('Missa Sancti Anthonii'), which would have been intended for the inauguration of Donatello's altar for the saint in the basilica at Padua.[127] This is a three-part cycle in chanson format without cantus firmus; the Sanctus and Agnus Dei paraphrase plainsong in the top voice. It is a suave but intricate work, with many passages in proportion, and in some ways stands apart from the context of Franco-Netherlands Mass composition of its day.

It is difficult to reconstruct this context because many sources are lost. In the extant sources, the species without cantus firmus is well represented. The

---

[126] According to David Fallows, 'Two more Dufay songs reconstructed', *Early Music* 3 (1975), 358–60, and 4 (1976), 99, Dufay's rondeau 'En triumphant de cruel deul, *Deul angouisseux est mon acueil*' could also be a lament on the death of Binchois. There does not seem to be a musical allusion to Binchois, and the textual quotation is rather hidden, which would make this a very private statement.

[127] See Fallows, *Dufay*, 66 f and 182 ff; Fallows, 'Dufay's most important work: reflections on the career of his Mass for St Anthony of Padua', *MT* 123, no. 1673 (July 1982), 467–70. It was believed to be his 'Missa Sancti Anthonii Viennensis', until Fallows identified its true title. Apart from the *Opera omnia*, the work is also edited in Bockholdt, *Messenkompositionen*, vol. 2, 68.

'Missa sine nomine' by Jean Pullois of the mid-1440s, and its connection with the cycles by Benet (?) and Bedyngham have been mentioned (p. 242). Pullois, then a singer at Our Lady's, Antwerp, obviously had access to English music, and in his Mass cycle combined English with continental traits. Also Jean Ockeghem, who sang in the same church from June 1443 to June 1444, was probably familiar with both traditions. His earliest extant Mass setting (although contained only in later sources) may reflect experiences from that time: the 'Missa sine nomine' in G-Dorian.[128] This is largely an exercise in textural smoothness: despite the high tessitura of the cantus, which reaches *g″*, all three voices cross constantly. Ockeghem also cultivates declamatory imitation, especially in the Gloria and Credo. The initial motto of all the sections is the formula *g′–bb′–a′–d″* (see p. 444); it returns, in a very expressive manner, at the end of the Credo. A contemporary of this work is the 'Missa tube' by Jean Escatefer dit Cousin, a cycle without cantus firmus, which adheres to the outmoded trumpet-style tradition.[129] Cousin was a colleague of Ockeghem on two separate occasions: between 1446 and 1448 in the chapel of Duke Charles of Bourbon at Moulins, and between 1461 and 1475 in the French royal chapel.

Charles Hamm rightly stressed the continuous tradition of the cycles without cantus firmus when attributing an anonymous specimen to the little-known composer Barbingant, on evidence provided by a quotation in Tinctoris.[130] The striking similarities between this work and the 'sine nomine' Masses by Bedyngham and Ockeghem suggest that Barbingant knew them both; but his Mass must predate 1463. Its proportional passages (the notation of which was criticized by Tinctoris) and much of the modal style are also reminiscent of the Marian cycle by the Englishman Henricus Thick, known on the Continent before *c*.1458 (see p. 406). It is possible that all these works are votive compositions for saints or the Virgin, which were performed quite regularly in side chapels.

In the early 1450s, and in some connection with a Savoy wedding, Dufay composed his first cantus firmus Mass, 'Se la face ay pale'.[131] In this four-part cycle he uses the tenor of his own famous ballade setting which had perhaps itself been composed for a Savoy wedding in 1434. The cantus firmus, literally retaining the rhythm of the original song tenor, is strictly repeated in the five sections, although at times with twofold and threefold augmentation of its values. The Mass is thus one of the earliest non-English strict tenor cycles – perhaps the earliest. It clearly imitates the 'Caput' Mass in its contrapuntal technique, liberally allowing fourths between the tenor and the top voice. It

---

[128] Ockeghem, *Collected Works*, vol. 1, no. 2.

[129] Published in Flotzinger ed., *Trienter Codices. Siebente Auswahl.* Tinctoris cites, in his *Proportionale musices*, a Mass 'Nigra sum' by Cousin.

[130] Hamm, 'Another Barbingant Mass'.

[131] See Planchart, 'Guillaume Dufay's Masses', 38 ff; Fallows, *Dufay*, 68 ff. Planchart's original opinion was that the work celebrated the wedding of the Dauphin Louis of Savoy (1451). It may, however, have been composed within a year or so after the event.

almost equals the 'Caput texture' of two inner parts of the same range, flanked by a cantus which reaches a sixth higher and a contratenor bassus reaching a fifth (here a sixth) below. Also borrowed from 'Caput' is the contour of the opening motto.

On the other hand, 'Se la face' is also, with one exception, the earliest non-English cycle over a secular tenor.[132] Bedyngham's Mass 'Dueil angoisseux' may have preceded Dufay's, and Frye's fragment of a 'So ys emprentid' Mass could have been written around the same time (see p. 404). The combination of the two elements, however – a cantus firmus of secular origin but treated in a strictly motet-like, four-part format – is about the only solution which the English had not attempted by then. Augmentation or diminution of the tenor's values had also become rare in English Masses; we have to go back as far as Dunstable's 'Jesu Christe' pair for that technique. Dufay's first cantus firmus Mass is a bold departure as well as a synthesis.

Nevertheless, in the genre of the strict tenor Mass,[133] the 'Caput' Mass was still the most admired model in Europe. The work had reached Trent Cathedral by *c.* 1452, possibly via Antwerp and Ferrara (see p. 242). It was probably at Our Lady's, Antwerp, that Petrus de Domarto[134] and Jean Ockeghem became acquainted with the English 'Caput' Mass. Domarto's Mass 'Spiritus almus' and Ockeghem's 'Caput' are both closely modelled on the English work, albeit in different ways.

Domarto begins all five sections with duets and a common motto. The motto is the beginning of an ancient introit trope of the plainsong Mass of the Holy Ghost, 'Spiritus almus adest'. The cantus firmus 'Spiritus almus' is, like 'Caput', a concluding melisma from a highly symbolic chant. It comes from a respond for the Nativity of the Virgin:

> R. Stirps Jesse virgam produxit, virgaque florem;
> Et super hunc florem requiescit *spiritus almus*.
> V. Virgo Dei genitrix virga est, flos filius ejus.[135]

[The Tree of Jesse produced a branch, and the branch a flower / and above this flower reposes the Holy Ghost. / The Virgin, bearer of God, is the branch, the flower her Son.]

The Tree of Jesse was a well-known Marian symbol, often shown in mystery plays, street pageants and manuscript illuminations. The responsory (written

---

[132] The exception is the anonymous Mass of the Cyprus Codex (see p. 37), which may have been written for the Savoy wedding of 1434: a link with 'Se la face ay pale'?

[133] See especially Sparks, *Cantus firmus*, ch. 4 ('The structural cantus firmus').

[134] 'Pieter de Domaro' sang in the choir of Our Lady's in the second half of 1449; see Van den Nieuwenhuizen, *Koralen*, 38. I tentatively identified Domarto with the Burgundian chaplain Pierre Maillart, dict Petrus, in *Bruges*, 124.

[135] *Antiphonale Romanum*, 129*. R = responsory (choral), V = verse (soloistic). The second line of the responsory (*repetenda*) is repeated after the verse, followed by the Gloria Patri on the melody of the verse. The melodic version used in the Mass contains variants found in Netherlands and English service books. It is almost identical with the tenor of Busnois' motet 'Anima mea liquefacta est / Stirps Jesse': see Sparks, *Cantus firmus*, 227.

in hexameters) had a venerable reputation; its melismas on the words 'spiritus almus' and 'flos filius ejus' were known as melodies in their own right, the latter as the tenor of clausulae and motets of the Ars antiqua. Domarto transposes the second-mode melody (original range *A–a*) up a fifth; the lower contratenor (sometimes the upper) supports fourths between the tenor and the cantus. This technique is employed more cautiously than in 'Caput'. At the beginning of the Kyrie (where the 'Caput' tenor entered on the fifth degree), the *a* of the tenor is a fifth above the bottom voice, but the upper *d'* is avoided. The only fourth between tenor and cantus in this example occurs in the final chord:

Example 60 Petrus de Domarto, 'Missa Spiritus almus': Kyrie I

Example 60 (*cont.*)

Domarto's Mass faithfully observes the 'Caput texture': all four voices have almost precisely the same ranges as in the earlier work, except that they are written a minor third lower. The tenor, for example, has the range of *e–e'* instead of *g–g'*. By transposing the plainsong up a fifth, but by using it as the fifth degree at cadences, the composer maintains the overall Dorian character although the plainsong is now on *a*. This technique has itself an English tradition (see the fourteenth-century 'Paradisi porta', Ex. 9). Accidental sharps emphasize the 'major dominants' of both *d* and *a*. A surprising effect is the early turn to the 'major dominant' in bar 6. It does not lead to a 'tonic' but is abruptly followed by a cross-relation (*c♯–c*).[136]

The Mass 'Spiritus almus' is pathbreaking in a different respect. It varies the rhythm of its cantus firmus by *strict rhythmic transformation*. The cantus firmus is written identically for the five sections, but is performed under ever-changing mensural signs, some of which imply augmentation. The tenor line thus undergoes considerable changes, both in total length and in the rhythmic relationship between individual notes; these changes are not free variations but are precisely controlled by the time-signatures. (See Table 3.)

Table 3: *Petrus de Domarto, 'Missa Spiritus almus': Mensuration table*

Sections	Tenor signature	Equivalence tenor / outer voices	Outer voice signature
Kyrie I	O	□ = □	O
Christe	C	□ = □□	¢
Kyrie II	O	□ = □	O
Et in terra	⊙	□ = □·□·	O
Qui tollis	O	□ = □□□	O2
Cum sancto	C3	◇·◇· = □□	C2
Patrem	⊙	□· = □□□	O
Crucifixus	O	□ = □□□	O2
Et in spiritum	C3	◇·◇· = □□	C2
Sanctus	⊙	□ = □·□·	O
Pleni	tacet		O
Gloria tua–Osanna	⊙	□ = □·□·	O
Benedictus–Osanna	C	□ = □□	¢
Agnus I = III	O	□ = □	O
Agnus II	tacet		

---

[136] A very similar gesture opens all five sections of Johannes Regis's Mass 'Dum sacrum mysterium': see p. 469.

The technique had been a device of Ars nova motets (see 'Porcio nature / Ida capillorum', Ex. 3). As far as we know, it was never used in Masses before, and was, in this extreme fashion, not popular in England. There is an English precedent only for the implied augmentation under the sign ℂ: a minim under ℂ in the tenor equals a semibreve under ○ in the other voices, as shown here in the Gloria, for example.

Domarto's strict rhythmic transformation was adopted by other composers (see below). It implies not only the 'proportional transformation' of Dufay's 'Se la face', where all the cantus firmus notes are simply doubled or tripled in length, leaving their rhythmic relationships intact. In Domarto's work, the note-value relationships of the notes change under varying time-signatures, a technique which could be called 'mensural transformation'.

Domarto's influence was noted by Johannes Tinctoris who, in his *Proportionale musices*, criticizes 'Spiritus almus' several times for errors in the use of proportions and time-signatures. Tinctoris dislikes the use of the sign ℂ to signify augmentation – i.e. without an explicit verbal direction such as 'crescit in duplo' ('to be doubled in value'). This omission he criticizes in Domarto's Gloria, and adds:

> If de Domarto was imitated in this error by Regis, Caron, Boubert, Faugues, Courbet and many others, as I have seen in their works, I am not surprised because I have heard that they are poorly educated [*minime litteratos*]. And who, without a literary education, would be able to attain the true essence [*veritatem*] not only of this but of any liberal art? But that those composers have been equalled, in the Masses 'De plus en plus' and 'L'homme armé' [respectively], by Ockeghem and Busnois, whose Latin education is known to be quite competent, fills my breast with more than average astonishment.[137]

Much as Tinctoris may have complained about it, Domarto influenced Jean Ockeghem (*c*.1410–1497) and Antoine Busnois (*c*.1430–1492) with regard not only to proportional signs but also to rhythmic transformation. Busnois' Mass 'L'homme armé' uses it, and Ockeghem's 'Missa Prolationum' is altogether an exercise in strict rhythmic transformations. Each of its four voices is in a different metre, but only two are notated; the other two have to be derived from them by reading the notated lines under different time-signatures.[138] 'Mensural imitation' is hinted at in one of the earliest chansons by Ockeghem, 'Ma maistresse' (see p. 447). The strict form of a 'mensuration canon' occurs in Dufay's early motet 'Inclita stella maris', and in his late chanson 'Les douleurs'. The Mass 'Spiritus almus' belongs in the intellectual company of Dufay, Ockeghem and Busnois, and documents its composer's pioneering position in the 1450s.[139]

[137] Tinctoris, *Opera theoretica*, vol. IIa, 49. On Busnois, see below. In Ockeghem's Mass 'De plus en plus', ℂ with the meaning of augmentation occurs in the Sanctus (not in the Credo, as Seay erroneously comments). When writing his *Proportionale musices* (*c*.1473-4?), Tinctoris probably did not yet know Ockeghem's Mass 'L'homme armé', which uses this device in all sections.

[138] On this work, see Reese, *Renaissance*, 133 ff.

[139] Further on the Mass, see Strohm, *Bruges*, 123 f and 193. Domarto's other extant cycle is a 'Missa quinti toni irregularis' (i.e. in B♭), copied in *SP* from an exemplar of *c*.1458; see Reynolds, 'Origins', 298. The work seems to have an unidentified cantus firmus. The Kyrie, attributed to Egidius Cervelli, has been added by a later hand.

Ockeghem's 'Caput' Mass, to be sure, is a very different kind of work.[140] It exhibits neither formal nor rhythmic ambitions, but literally reproduces the cantus firmus of the English model: both its rhythms and its generally bipartite layout (double cursus). Apart from a short omission of cantus firmus material in the Agnus Dei, only the Kyrie stands apart by lacking an introductory duet and by having a tripartite layout of the cantus firmus.[141] These aspects of the work are rather conventional.

On the other hand, Ockeghem introduces dazzling harmonic artifice. He writes the cantus firmus precisely as it looks in the English 'Caput' Mass, but requires it to be transposed an octave down with the laconic words: 'Another Caput by lowering the tenor by an octave' (*Alterum Caput descendendo tenorem per dyapason*). This simple octave transposition generates drastic departures from the model. The other three voices are now all composed above the cantus firmus, not around it. Thus for a start, the composer has undone precisely what had been the innovative feature of the older work. Then, the unsuitability of the 'Caput' melody as a cantus firmus is dramatically increased: the near absence of stepwise descents, and the total absence of falling or rising fifths, makes this virtually the least suitable melody to serve as a bass voice. Finally, Ockeghem does not even compose the work in the Mixolydian mode of the plainsong but in the Dorian mode on *d*. This may partly be because he has so few stepwise descents, and no falling fifths towards the final *G*, but it is also a result of mere fancy. Cadences on *d* usually occur when the cantus firmus is silent; on the other hand, few downward steps in the cantus firmus are actually used for cadences! (This last tendency recurs in Ockeghem's later works.) Where the 'Caput' melody is present, the harmonization is awesome, even in the first bars:

Example 61 Jean Ockeghem, 'Missa Caput'

---

[140] Ockeghem, *Collected Works*, vol. 2 no. 11; Planchart ed., *Missae Caput*. Older discussions of the work are Borren, *Etudes*, 196–9, Bukofzer, *Studies*, 278–92.

[141] Perhaps Ockeghem rejected the English bipartite form for liturgical reasons (see also p. 240). It is possible, however, that he did not know the 'Caput' Kyrie, which may have been removed from the cycle (in Antwerp?) because of its form.

Example 61 (*cont.*)

In the English 'Caput' Mass (see Ex. 37), the tune had entered as the fifth of 'E minor' and after a longer introduction. Here, it enters in bar 2 as the root of a 'B minor' chord. This seems not only anomalous, but contrary to reason: the Dorian harmony of the upper voices is hardly established in bar 1, when in bar 2 the bass entrance on *B* shatters it. The tension between the implied 'D minor' of the first chord and the 'B minor' of the second, which remains throughout the work, exaggerates the modal tension found in the 'Caput' Mass. Instead of the Dorian fifth *d–a* and the Mixolydian fifth *g–d'*, the contestants are now the triads *d–f–a* and *B–d–f♯*. The contest *f/f♯* is not part of a great tonal symmetry as found, for example, in Dufay's 'Nuper rosarum flores' (see p. 169). Rather, the harmony is off balance, because the work is predominantly Dorian except for the recurring *B* in root position.

The Mass has other uncommon traits, such as the many inescapable tritones, or the English trait of 'telescoped texting' in the Credo (the verses 'Et resurrexit' and 'Et in spiritum' are performed simultaneously). The opening motto of the Gloria etc. resembles that of 'Caput' but is transposed down a third – the same interval by which Domarto transposed the whole texture.

These three cantus firmus Masses – by Dufay, Domarto and Ockeghem – form a context. All three are consciously indebted to English precedent, even to the same work. (Dufay quotes the motto of 'Caput'.) All three, however, are different and individual. Each of them adds something new: Dufay the secular tenor, Domarto the rhythmic transformations, Ockeghem the unprecedented harmonies. These new traits are, at the same time, the most important ones of each work, and in Ockeghem's case, they undo the very achievements of their model. This is a more explosive mixture of tradition and innovation than we know from earlier ages. It is like an attempt to defeat tradition, to demonstrate how it can be subverted. It is possible that the composers knew of each other and felt that they were competing with each other as well as with the past. Faced with masterworks, nothing less than a masterwork would do.

In Franco-Netherlands Mass compositions from the 1450s onwards, we witness the rediscovery of deliberate, 'artificial' manipulations of the cantus firmus material: an aspect of the so-called 'Art of the Netherlanders'. Similar procedures had already been typical for the isorhythmic motet, but this medieval tradition was now superseded. Cantus firmus technique from now on had to be learned from the Masses of Dufay and Ockeghem. Every new cantus firmus composition strove to be a masterwork and to outdo the others; the pace of innovation and individualization accelerated. From the astonishing inventions of Ockeghem and Busnois to the manipulations of Obrecht's tenors and the endless varieties of sound-play in Josquin's and Isaac's works with borrowed material – this type of composition reached its historical peak before the century was over. The idea which remains of it today is the association of musical artifice with cantus firmus composition – and more generally, the concept of composing musical masterworks as a problem-solving and intellectual as well as an aesthetic procedure.

Table 4 documents the early history of this kind of Mass, giving a chronological conspectus of cycles in which the cantus firmus is literally repeated or modified according to a strict rule. Although composers and places of origin are largely unknown to us, it is likely that some of the works are direct derivations or imitations of others.

Table 4: *Four-part Mass cycles with strict cantus firmus treatment*

Composer	Title	Origin	Earliest copy[142]
anon.	Caput	England, c.1440–45	*Tr 93* (c.1451–2)
	c. f. = final melisma; mode 7; double cursus		
anon.	Veterem hominem	England, c.1445–50	*Tr 88* (c.1458)
	mode 7; double cursus; 'Caput texture'		
Dufay	Se la face ay pale	Savoy, 1451–27	*Tr 88* (c.1458)
	Literal quote; proportional transformation; 'Caput texture'		
Domarto	Spiritus almus	Netherlands, c.1455?	*Tr 88* (c.1462)
	⊙ ; c. f. = final melisma; mensural transformation; 'Caput texture'		
anon.	Pax vobis ego sum ?		*Tr 88* (c.1458)[143]
	Gloria–Credo pair only; double cursus; strict c. f. canon		
Ockeghem	Caput	France, c.1455?	*Tr 88* (c.1462)
	Literal quote; transposition		
anon.	Meditatio cordis ?		*Tr 88* (c.1462)[144]
	Double cursus; 'Caput texture'		
anon.	Se tu t'en marias ?		*Tr 88* (c.1462)[145]
	c. f. varied, but also mensurally transformed; transposed		
anon.	Te Deum ?		*Tr 89* (c.1462)[146]
	⊙ ; proportional and mensural transformation		

[142] Copying dates from Saunders, *Dating of the Trent Codices*; Reynolds, 'Origins'.
[143] Published in Feininger ed., *MPLSER*, ser. I, tom. II, 2 (1952).
[144] Published in Snow, Manuscript Strahov.
[145] See Strohm, *Bruges*, 141 ('M. Filles a marier').
[146] On the works in *Tr 89*, see Gottlieb, *Masses*.

Table 4 (*cont.*)

anon.	Groß senen	Germany, *c*.1460	*Tr 89* (*c*.1462)[147]
	⊙ ; mensural transformation		
anon.	Christus surrexit	Austria, *c*.1460	*Tr 89* (*c*.1464)[147]
	Double cursus; 'Caput texture'		
Touront	Monyel	Bohemia?	*Tr 89* (*c*.1464)
	Mensural transformation		
anon.	Quand ce viendra	France, *c*.1462?	*Tr 89* (*c*.1464)[148]
	⊙ ; proportional transformation; parody of model		
anon.	Du cuer je souspier	France, *c*.1462?	*Tr 89* (*c*.1464)[149]
	Double cursus; mensural transformation; multiple transposition		
Ockeghem	L'homme armé	France, *c*.1460–65? (see p. 467)	*CS 35* (*c*.1490)
	⊙ ; proportional transformation; transposition		
Dufay	L'homme armé	Cambrai, 1460s? (see p. 467)	*Las 238* (*c*.1469–70)
	Proportional transformation; retrograde		
Busnois	L'homme armé	Burgundy, *c*.1468? (see p. 467)	*CS 14* (*c*.1475)
	⊙ ; proportional transformation; inversion		

Dufay's 'Se la face ay pale' cycle was soon followed by several other continental Masses based on secular songs. They exhibit a very different stylistic tendency, however: that of a cantus firmus freely varied from section to section. The earliest of them existed by *c*.1456 at the latest (copies in *Tr 90*). English precedent looms large in these works, too: Guillaume Le Rouge's Mass 'Soyez aprantiz' is composed over the tenor of Frye's ballade 'So ys emprentid',[149] and two anonymous Masses are based on Bedyngham's famous ballata 'O rosa bella'. None of these works, however, follows Bedyngham's method in the Mass 'Dueil angoisseux', that of richly elaborating and paraphrasing the borrowed tenor.

The work by Le Rouge has been described as a paradigm of the 'isomelic' technique (which we have encountered, for example, in Walter Frye's Mass 'Nobilis et pulchra'): the tenor cantus firmus is altered rhythmically but not melodically.[150] Besides the 'So ys emprentid' tenor, other elements of the song are also reflected in this Mass: the three-part chanson format is retained and the musical phrases and cadences often fall in analogous places to those of the chanson. The cantus line of the ballade is occasionally echoed in the Mass, foreshadowing parody technique, for example at the end of the Credo. The contratenor is different throughout. The tenor notes are at times considerably lengthened, for example in the Gloria and Credo where surplus text has to be accommodated. There are also duets without cantus firmus. The opening duets of the Gloria, Credo, and that of 'Et incarnatus est / Et in spiritum' quote the

---

[147] See Strohm, 'Meßzyklen'. 'Christus surrexit' is printed in Feininger ed., *MPLSER*, ser. I, tom. II, I; one flat at the clef should be added to all the voices.
[148] See also p. 471.
[149] Published in Flotzinger ed., *Trienter Codices. Siebente Auswahl.*
[150] Eduard Reeser, 'Een "iso-melische mis" uit den tijd van Dufay', *TVNM* 16 (1942), 151–76, 312 f.

tenor incipit in the upper voice like a motto; other sections start with a similar contour as well (scale degrees 1–3–2–5).

The work exists in two rather different manuscript versions. In *Tr 90*, the last section of the Credo begins with three different text incipits in the three voices, suggesting 'telescoped' texting. This is not enough evidence to make the Mass an English work, as has been claimed (see above on Ockeghem's 'Caput' Mass), although the nationality and even identity of its author are not absolutely certain. Documents mention him as 'Guillaume Ruby' or 'Guillaume Le Rouge'; he was apparently taught organ-playing at Rouen in 1399 and served the Burgundian court from 1415 to 1451, perhaps with interruptions. If our candidate was indeed the composer, he then worked at the court of Duke Charles of Orléans at Blois until the duke's death in 1465.[151] The idea that he was an Englishman (and therefore not identical with the Rouen musician?) cannot be entirely dismissed, but that would hardly matter for his style after 35 years of Burgundian service. Tinctoris in his *Proportionale musices* mentions a lost Mass by him over Pierre Fontaine's rondeau 'Mon cuer pleure', and sheds light on his position with regard to England. He gives two examples where major prolation signs are wrongly used to express *sesquialtera* and *sub-sesquitertia* proportions, respectively (i.e. 3/2 and 4/3), and adds:[152]

> Although Le Rouge and Puyllois do this in the Mass 'Mon cuer pleure' and in a Gloria of the transposed authentic Lydian mode,[153] [respectively], it is intolerable.

He then quotes from Dufay's 'Missa Sancti Anthonii' to show how a major prolation sign is properly employed against another mensuration in another voice, and concludes:

> As regards this [mensuration] sign, since these three famous composers disagree, you must believe Dufay more than the other two, of whom the first is the most arrogant of all those using proportions. He has been seduced by the error of the English [*Anglorum errore labefactus*] and has, ignorant of all proportions, anticipated all the other composers. The second [above-mentioned composer], however, is simple-minded [*simplicissimus*].[154]

The mistakes made by Le Rouge and Domarto (see p. 420 above) are not exactly the same, but they both concern the sign of major prolation and its erroneous use by the English. Tinctoris implies that Le Rouge was not himself an Englishman, but that he was misled by English precedent in a Mass cycle over a Burgundian chanson and that, like Domarto (see above), he was ahead of other continentals in this kind of work except for Dufay. It is legitimate

---

[151] See Higgins, *Busnois*, 251 n. 521. Le Rouge's only other extant work, the bergerette 'Se je fayz dueil', may have been written for that court.

[152] Tinctoris, *Opera theoretica*, vol. IIa, 47 f.

[153] *In quodam 'Et in terra' plagalis autenti triti irregularis*: i.e. a Gloria in B♭ extending down to *F* (the reading 'plagalis autenti' is suspect or at least pleonastic); an unknown work by Pullois. The words referring to Le Rouge's Mass should be 'in Missa Mon cuer pleure', not 'Missis' as in the edition.

[154] The passage has been garbled in the edition (and consequently misunderstood) by the placement of a comma before, instead of after, the word 'crede'. The famous *error Anglorum* is also discussed in Oliver Strunk, review of *MPLSER* in *JAMS* 2 (1949), 107–10.

to place his 'Soyez aprantiz' cycle closely to the Burgundian–Cambrai orbit around 1450.

Of the three Masses over 'O rosa bella' that are known today,[155] the first two (nos. I and II of the edition) are dialectically related. They form a 'pair of Mass cycles' – which is a novelty – and are probably by the same composer. Mass no. I uses the tenor of the chanson as its tenor with freely varied rhythms – the 'isomelic' procedure – and also retains its three-part chanson format and mode (G-Dorian). The cycle moves entirely in perfect time (O), reminding one a little of Frye's 'Summe trinitati' which is entirely in imperfect time. The Kyrie, Sanctus and Agnus state the ballata tenor once, but the Gloria and Credo state it one and a half times, repeating the first half (*ripresa*) just as a performer of the ballata would do.[156]

Stylistic details in Mass no. I, such as pitch-exchanges between outer voices, point to a chanson composer familiar with Frye and Le Rouge. The stylistic similarity with Le Rouge's Mass 'Soyez aprantiz' is particularly close. As for Bedyngham, it is not his Mass 'Dueil angoisseux' but his ballata 'O rosa bella' that is the contrapuntal prototype for this work. It is not actually a parody Mass, as only the chanson's tenor is consistently used. The opening of the cantus furnishes an opening motto only, which in the Kyrie anticipates the tenor entry by one bar:

Example 62 John Bedyngham, 'O rosa bella'

Mass 'O rosa bella', *Trent 88*

*) MS: cantus *c''*, contra *b flat'*.

[155] Printed in *DTOe XI/1*, vol. 22. For editions of the ballata, see n. 70 above.
[156] Since the first half does not end on a tonic chord, our composer simply adds a final G chord: this must have been what performers of the ballata did when having reached the end of all the stanzas (see p. 393).

The 'narrow miss' of the cantus and tenor openings resembles the first cantus firmus entry of Ockeghem's 'Caput' Mass.

'O rosa bella' no. II uses not the tenor but the cantus of the model, transposes it down a fourth and quotes it literally in rhythm and pitch. Despite the transposition, a three-part chanson format results, because the quoted voice is now in the tenor range: the source calls it 'contratenor'. A new cantus is added above it, with which it forms a structural duet. The voice labelled 'tenor' is really a contratenor bassus, grammatically inessential but often mimicking a cantus firmus voice with extended, plainsong-like melodies – for example at the beginning of the Kyrie, Credo and Sanctus. Duets occur between every pair of voices (this is a difference from no. I). The cycle is in imperfect time throughout (C) as is the ballata, notwithstanding a proportional passage at the end of sections. These contrasts to no. I suggest that the cycle originated not for its own sake but as a match to the other, more conventional cycle. Without its precedent, no. II would hardly have come into being. Nevertheless, no. II has independent links with Ockeghem's 'Caput' Mass (strict transposition; literal quotation) and Frye's 'Summe trinitati' (literal quotation; one mensuration only).

Walter Frye, however, cannot be the author of these Masses; nor can Le Rouge or Bedyngham. None of these composers cultivates canons, stretto imitations and other elements of strict patterning as do the 'O rosa bella' Masses. In that respect, they rather resemble the Marian Mass by Henricus Thick (see p. 406). Motives of the model are often imitated, and not only where the ballata setting itself does so. Compared with Ockeghem, however, his 'Missa sine nomine' no. 2 for example, the 'O rosa bella' cycles are contrapuntally simple. In conclusion, this 'pair of Mass cycles' was written by someone close to all these other composers, and perhaps to the circle in which the ballata itself originated.

An early elaboration of the famous song outside the Mass genre, a new set of two lower voices against Bedyngham's cantus, is found in *Tr 90* (c.1458) with the attribution 'Hert'. The name could be English, but there was also a chaplain of Bruges in 1453, Bartholomaeus Hert. One of his musician colleagues at the church of St Donatian's, the later 'Burgundian' composer Gilles Joye, strikingly fulfills some external conditions for being the composer of the 'O rosa bella' Masses. Documents describe him as an intelligent and loquacious dialectician – which seems borne out also by his amusing chanson 'Ce qu'on fait a quatimini' – and as a mind who would enjoy devising this kind of 'dialectic Mass pair'. Joye was perhaps in touch with the Anglo-Italian circles in which Bedyngham's setting originated, because he is the composer of another *giustiniana*, the ballata 'Poy che crudel fortuna', in the Porto Chansonnier. This piece, and a textless rondeau by him in *Tr 90* (fol. 295r),[157] are stylistically compatible with the Masses, whereas his three extant chansons with French texts, all in the Mellon Chansonnier, are later and different.[158] In Bruges,

---

[157] Printed in Marix, *Musiciens*, no. 57.
[158] See Perkins–Garey eds, *Mellon Chansonnier*, no. 9 ('Ce qu'on fait'), 13, 23.

Joye had access to works of Frye and Thick, and probably also Bedyngham, Le Rouge and Ockeghem. It adds spice to this theory that in 1454 he had a mistress with the nickname 'Rosabelle'.[159]

For both the Masses 'Soyez aprantiz' and 'O rosa bella' no. I a companion motet exists, forming a 'Mass–motet cycle'. Robert Snow identified a total of six cycles of this kind in central European sources.[160] The motets are built over the same tenors as the respective Masses and have other structural elements (for example a bipartite layout) in common with them, although according to their texts they are Marian antiphon settings without individual characteristics. The motet which belongs to the three-part Mass 'Soyez aprantiz' has the words 'Stella celi extirpavit', an antiphon often sung against the plague and especially popular in England. It is unmistakably composed over Frye's ballade tenor – unless for some reason the tenor itself was also used for the words 'Stella celi'[161] – but is in four parts, with introductory duets in the English manner, and on a grander scale than the individual Mass sections.

The same relationship obtains between the Mass 'Esclave puist-il devenir' (on Binchois' rondeau) and its antiphon-motet 'Gaude Maria virgo' in *Tr 88*, and between the Mass 'O rosa bella' no. I and its antiphon-motet 'O pater eterne' in the Moravian codex Strahov (*CS-Ppp D.G.IV.47*). 'O pater eterne'[162] is, in my opinion, by the same composer as the two 'O rosa bella' Masses. His busy but unadventurous counterpoint just about fills the large scale. He betrays his closeness to chanson style by avoiding fourths between cantus and tenor – despite the four-part texture. An English composer would hardly have done this, nor would Dufay, Domarto or Ockeghem.

Of Snow's six 'Mass–motet cycles', these three were surely composed as such, even if perhaps the antiphon texts found in the surviving sources are not the original ones. The three cycles seem Franco-Burgundian in origin and are among the very earliest Masses built on chansons. 'Esclave puist-il' is notable, in addition, for its elements of 'parody' (see below). A fourth cycle in the Trent Codices can perhaps be added to the group: the three-part Mass by Johannes Pullois (see p. 242) and his four-part motet 'Flos de spina'. Although the Mass is not built over a cantus firmus, recurrent modal gestures seem to connect it with the bipartite tenor of 'Flos de spina'.[163] In this case, too, the

---

[159] Further on him, see Strohm, *Bruges*, rev. edn, 27 ff, 126 and new note for p. 126.

[160] Snow, 'Mass–motet cycle'.

[161] On this problem and the many 'Stella celi' settings in England, see Bent, 'New and little-known fragments', 147 f n. 15. Bent identifies another setting of this 'Stella celi' tenor (or a similar one) in the manuscript Strahov, no. 217.

[162] Printed in Snow, 'Mass–motet cycle', 315–20. Also found, with the text 'O admirabile commercium', in the later manuscript *I-Md 1(2269)*. Snow assigned the four-part motet to the four-part Mass 'O rosa bella' no. III. But the opening motto and the cantus firmus layout prove its link with the Mass no. I: see Wegman, 'An anonymous twin', 36.

[163] The English composer Standley (see also p. 398) wrote a Mass cycle that is canonic throughout, and an antiphon 'Que est ista' in the same technique (Richard Loyan ed., *Canons in the Trent Codices*, CMM 38 (Rome: AIM, 1967) 40 ff). They may have been intended as a Mass–motet cycle, too.

Mass is in three parts, the motet in four, and the connection between them is structural.

Snow's other three cycles, all built on plainsongs, are 'made up', as it were. The 'motets' found for the Masses 'Summe trinitati' (Frye; see also p. 403), 'Meditatio cordis' and 'Hilf und gib rat' are more likely to be contrafacta of the otherwise missing Kyries. In these cases, the number of voices of the 'motet' equals that of the Mass. It is possible that the re-texting of Kyries which, for some reason, were not liturgically acceptable, was a widespread practice.

Whether re-texted Kyries or not, it is very probable that all these motets were sung during or after a Mass service. A motet composed by Charles the Bold himself was sung at Cambrai Cathedral after Mass on 23 October 1460.[164] In 1451, Philip the Good made an endowment at Our Lady's, Bruges, for a polyphonic Mass 'with a motet afterwards', to be sung annually on 16 August (i.e. it was a Lady Mass, following the day of the Assumption).[165] Of course these documents could conceivably refer to the old-fashioned genre of 'Deo gratias' motets (see p. 83), but it is more likely that this practice at Bruges, Cambrai and the Burgundian court was associated with cantus firmus works. A date close to 1451 for the three Mass–motet cycles over chanson tenors is likely in any case.

The impressive four-part motets of the genuine group have the textures of 'Caput' or 'Se la face' but also anticipate the formula for the late fifteenth-century motet: two sections, each introduced by a long duet and provided with its own climax, and a cantus firmus in double cursus or interrupted in the middle. Few other motets composed on this scale survive from the 1450s (some in *Tr 88* and *89*). Celebrative or political works (such as 'Adoretur / Pacem Deus', see above) must have largely disappeared with the royal and ducal manuscripts of western Europe. The surviving devotional and liturgical antiphon-motets, on the other hand, were still usually written in chanson format and in simpler styles (see also below). The practice of the Mass–motet cycle, however, initiated the resurrection of the great cantus firmus motet after the end of isorhythm.

The Mass with freely varied tenor cantus firmus became the standard form of Franco-Netherlands Mass composition throughout the 1450s and earlier 1460s. Chanson tenors outnumbered liturgical tenors by far. Four-part writing soon replaced three-part, and the English innovation of allowing fourths between tenor and cantus was accepted everywhere.[166] Table 5 lists significant tenor cycles written on the Continent until about 1465.

---

[164] Wright, 'Dufay at Cambrai', 209.

[165] Strohm, *Bruges*, 46. The archival source is the Planarius (obit-book) of Our Lady's, Archief O. C. M. W., Bruges, reg. 179, penultimate (unnum.) folio, verso: 'cantantibus Kyriel. Et in terra. Patrem. Scs. Agnus cum moteto post missam'. The performance may have conformed to established practice.

[166] The composer of the Mass 'Rosel im gortn' in *Tr 88* (c.1462; no. 423 ff) seems still unaware of this expedient. He was surely not English, but cannot otherwise be located. On the possible cantus firmus and origin, see Strohm, 'Meßzyklen'.

Table 5: *Mass cycles with free cantus firmus treatment*

Composer	Title	Origin	Voices	Earliest copy[167]
anon.	(Terribilis?)	?	4	*Tr 93* (c.1452)[168]
Le Rouge	Soyez aprantiz	France, c.1450–55	3	*Tr 90* (c.1456)
anon.	O rosa bella no. I	Bruges, c.1454?	3	*Tr 88* (c.1462)
anon.	O rosa bella no. II	Bruges, c.1454?	3	*Tr 90* (c. 1456)
anon.	La belle se siet	?	3	*Tr 90* (c.1456)
anon.	Puisque m'amour	?	4	*Tr 88* (c.1458)
Domarto	(Quinti toni irreg.)	Netherlands?	4	*SP* (c.1458)
anon.	Esclave puist-il	Burg. court?	3	*Tr 88* (c.1462)
anon.	(De S.Andrea?)	Burg. court? c.1460	4	*Las 238* (c.1470)[169]
Simon de Insula	O admirabile	Lille?	4	*Tr 88*(c.1462)
Faugues	Le serviteur	France, c.1460	4	*Tr 88* (c.1462)[170]
anon.	Le serviteur	?	3	*Tr 88* (c.1462)
anon.	Le serviteur	?	3	*Tr 89* (c.1464)
anon.	Grune linden	Germany	3	*Tr 88* (c.1462)
Ockeghem	Ecce ancilla	France, c.1460?	4	*Chigi* (c.1498)[171]
Ockeghem	Ma maistresse	France, 1460s?	4	*Chigi* (c.1498)
Ockeghem	De plus en plus	France, 1460s?	4	*CS 14* (c.1470s)
Ockeghem	Au travail suis	France, 1460s?	4	*CS 41* (c.1490s?)
Cornago	Ayo visto	Naples?	3	*Tr 88* (c.1462)[172]
Caron	L'homme armé	France?	4	*SP* (c.1463)
anon.	D'ung altre amer	France?	4	*SP* (c.1463)
anon.	Pour l'amour d'une	France?	3	*SP* (c.1463)
Barbingant	Terriblement	France?	3	*SP* (c.1463)
Dufay	Ecce ancilla	Cambrai, c.1463	4	*Br 5557* (c.1470)
anon.	Puisque je vis	France, 1460s?	4	*CS 14* (1470s)[173]
anon.	(Terribilis?)	?	3	*Tr 89* (c.1462)
Flemmik (?)	Veni creator	Netherlands?	4	*Tr 89* (c.1462)[174]
anon.	Hec dies	Bruges?	4	*Las 238* (c.1470)[175]
(Tinctoris?)	Nos amis	France?	4	*Tr 89* (c.1462)[176]

[167] Copying dates as before (n. 142), and from *CC*.

[168] C.f. perhaps 'Terribilis est locus iste', freely varied. Sections distributed over *Tr 93, 90* and *88*; no Kyrie. See Strohm, 'Zur Rezeption', 23 ('M. sine nomine II').

[169] See Strohm, *Bruges*, 126 f; the work could have served for a meeting of the Order of the Golden Fleece, as described in Prizer, 'Music and ceremonial'.

[170] Probably the anonymous work copied at Cambrai in 1462–3; see Houdoy, *Histoire artistique*, 192. See also p. 171.

[171] On the Ockeghem cycles, see p. 473.

[172] See p. 572.

[173] This work has been edited, and tentatively ascribed to Dufay, in Feininger ed., *MPLSER*, ser. I, tom. II, 4 (1952). See also Sparks, *Cantus firmus*, 136.

[174] Ed. in Snow, *Manuscript Strahov*, 385–405.

[175] See Strohm, *Bruges*, 127 f.

[176] See Strohm, 'Missa super "Nos amis"'.

Table 5 (*cont.*)

anon.	O rosa bella no. III	?	4	*Tr 89 (c.1464)*
Caron	Clemens et benigna	France?	4	*Tr 89 (c.1464)*
Philipus	Hilf und gib rat	?	4	*Tr 89 (c.1464)*
anon.	'Deutscher Lieder'	Austria?	3	*Tr 89 (c.1466)*[177]

This list includes the earliest continental specimens of what has come to be called the 'parody Mass'.[178] This is a type of Mass cycle based on a polyphonic model which incorporates more than one voice of the model simultaneously, at least for some passages of the work. It thus makes use of already composed counterpoint, not only pre-existent melody or rhythm. Individual Mass sections in this manner had been written already in the fourteenth century, and in Italy at the beginning of the fifteenth (see p. 100). The earliest extant cycle of this kind is Bedyngham's Mass 'Dueil angoisseux'; an apparently coeval work was Frye's 'So ys emprentid' (see p. 403). The idea was taken up at once on the Continent; the rather casual or tentative quotations of the cantus in the Mass 'Soyes aprantiz' are first signs of this. More obvious quotation occurs in the Mass 'Esclave puist-il devenir', written like Bedyngham's cycle on a Binchois chanson. In this Mass, copied *c.*1462 but surely older, the rondeau tenor is treated in the 'isomelic' manner. In the Osanna II, however, the tenor quotation is almost literal and complete – a few bars of the model are skipped – and the cantus line is simultaneously paraphrased in the top voice.

The next step is documented in the Mass 'Terriblement' by the enigmatic Barbingant.[179] This three-part work clearly reproduces the style, texture and even form of its secular model, and it uses more than one of its voices at a time, occasionally all three. The model is an anonymous setting of the *bergerette layée*, 'Terriblement suis fortunée' (a complaint of a betrayed woman).[180] At the time the song was composed (before *c.*1456), the bergerette form was a new fashion, apparently centred on French royal circles. Ockeghem might have been an early instigator of this fashion, for his two earliest datable chansons, 'Ma maistresse' and 'Ma bouche rit' (see p. 447), are both bergerettes. The genre was distinguished from the older virelai only by its pastoral name (which is actually misleading as the earlier virelais had often been pastorals, whereas the later bergerettes seldom were), and had the monostrophic form:

A b^{1}b^2 a A.

[177] See Schmalz, *Mass Ordinaries*; Strohm, 'Meßzyklen'.

[178] Objections to the term 'parody' with the meaning of 'imitation of a polyphonic model' appear in the literature with some periodicity. See Jack Allan Westrup, 'Parodies and parameters', *PRMA* 100 (1973-4), 19-31; Burkholder, 'Johannes Martini' (with ensuing discussion).

[179] Not identical with Jacob Barbireau, choirmaster at Antwerp 1484 (sic)-1491, whose works are edited in the same volume (Barbireau, *Opera omnia*): see Charles W. Fox, 'Barbireau and Barbingant: a review', *JAMS* 13 (1960), 79-101. As a result of the 'splitting' of the two masters, no information about Barbingant remains; but see p. 444.

[180] Text in Löpelmann, *Liederhandschrift*, no. 322. Music in *DTOe XI/1*, vol. 22, 112.

(The refrain, 'A', often had five lines, and each half-stanza, 'b', three.)

'Terriblement' is unusual in that its melody quotes the introit 'Terribilis est locus iste' (*d–d–c–A–c–d*) for apparently no other reason than the verbal similarity. But the low texture caused by this quotation serves for text-painting in this mournful song. The refrain and the stanza are in triple and duple metre, respectively, a contrast which was to characterize many later bergerettes. There may be a connection between the modernity of the chanson itself and the modern type of elaboration in the Mass. The chanson material is so comprehensively and consistently utilized that even the typical repetition patterns of the bergerette form can be recognized (see Ex. 63).

The stanza ('b¹b²') appears in the second Kyrie in its original doubled form. The second ending is a continuation, not a replacement, of the first. (The sources of the chanson do not tell us this.) The harmony of the parallel passages is strikingly contrasted: Barbingant forces the singers to solmize the same tenor figure in bar 3 as 'ut-re-mi' (*g–a–b*) and in bar 9 as 're-mi-fa': *b♮* the first time and *b♭* the second. Noteworthy also is the melodic design *d–f–e–a* (bars 1–2 and 5–6 in the cantus), which is not present in the chanson and was surely placed here intentionally.

I believe that there is a line from the Mass–motet cycles and the early parody Masses to Dufay's motet and Mass 'Ave regina celorum'.[181] The motet, copied in Cambrai in 1464–5, is a splendid example of the new four-part cantus firmus motet, in two sections of contrasting metre, with introductory duets and various formal breaks suggested by the text. But unlike motets on this scale by younger composers (Busnois, for example), it has no strict ground plan and makes no use of imitation to speak of. It rather belongs to the type of four-part antiphon-motets as found in the Mass–motet cycles. The text insertions, beginning with 'miserere tui labentis Dufay' ('Have mercy on thy dying Dufay'), and the sudden intrusions of *e♭'* and even *a♭* into the 'C major' context, which belong to the unforgettable moments of fifteenth-century music, resuscitate devotional antiphons of Dufay's early Italian years. This tone also resonates in some of his early and late chansons. In the Mass, which Dufay composed for a personal endowment about 1471 (see p. 286), each section reproduces the bipartite layout of the cantus firmus as in the motet, and the Agnus Dei quotes from the actual polyphonic fabric of the passage with Dufay's personal text insertion. The other allusions to the motet are insignificant by comparison.[182] This type of 'parody' relationship – block quotation in only one section – has just been seen in the Mass–motet cycle 'Esclave puist'. The Mass 'Ave regina celorum', however, has as its model not a chanson but a motet. A sixteenth-century tradition is first encountered here (see p. 486).

Dufay might have derived the idea from the 'made up' cycles with Kyries arranged as antiphons; he might have remembered the cycle 'O pulcherrima

---

[181] Printed in Dufay, *Opera omnia*, vol. 5 (motet), vol. 3 (Mass); Feininger ed., *MPLSER* ser. I, tom. II, 3 (Mass and motet).

[182] See Fallows, *Dufay*, 208 f.

Example 63 anon. / Barbingant, Bergerette 'Terriblement' (second section), and
Mass 'Terriblement': Kyrie

Example 63 (*cont.*)

Example 63 *(cont.)*

mulierum' by Arnold de Lantins. He did not intend the motet for performance immediately after Mass as with the Mass–motet cycles, nor did he use it only as a compositional model as did Arnold. Rather, he composed the Mass for annual performances on 5 August during his lifetime and stipulated in his will that the motet should be sung at his death-bed. However, both compositions have as their focus a personal devotion to the Virgin, and this unity of intent is as relevant to the composer as are the musical relationships.

Liturgical and devotional music; some sacred institutions

The growth of polyphonic practice in princely chapels and cathedrals during the earlier fifteenth century had already led to the production of large-scale 'sets and cycles' of liturgical compositions, often intended for the major feasts of the church year. This music was presumably sung in the high choir, replacing or enhancing the choral performance of the plainsong items. The pieces usually elaborated their appropriate liturgical plainsongs: a three-part setting of the introit 'Spiritus domini', for example, would normally incorporate the chant melody 'Spiritus domini' in the top voice or tenor. Dufay's hymn cycle (see p. 249) is one of the few bodies of this music that has survived with apparent completeness. Other repertories from that period – such as the daily poly-phonic Masses for the Sainte-Chapelle, Bourges (see p. 178) – have disappeared with their manuscripts, which were presumably kept in constant use at their home institution and later thrown away.

In sources of the 1450s and 60s, however, this kind of music appears with some regularity. There are groups of hymns, antiphons or *Magnificat* settings (i.e. music for Vespers), or introits, graduals, sequences etc. (i.e. music for the Mass).[183] Most of the pieces are anonymous, and it is never known for which institution they were originally intended. Since these genres had to fit local liturgies, however, and these liturgies were so different from each other – for example, in the precise allocation of texts and melodies to certain services – we can sometimes reconstruct a plausible provenance for them. If imported from outside, some liturgical adjustments could be made for their performance, or they could just be sung for enjoyment or instruction – at school, for example.

Of the polyphony for Vespers – hymns, *Magnificat* settings and antiphons – found in central European and Italian sources of the later fifteenth century, only a small proportion was composed in France or the Netherlands after 1450. Instead, the older Vespers compositions by Binchois, Dufay and Dunstable were copied many times over, and local anonymous works were added to them. This suggests that these particular genres were not intensely cultivated in western Europe at the time. The accounts of Cambrai Cathedral after 1450 repeatedly speak of the copying of new hymns, *Magnificat* settings and anti-phons (as well as Mass Proper items), but they tend to mention only one work at a time.[184] Some indication of the rate of production is provided by the Cam-brai hymnal *F-CA 29*, where a total of thirteen polyphonic hymns was entered, mostly on blank pages, during the whole course of the fifteenth century.[185] Accounts from St Donatian's, Bruges, mention the copying of *Magnificat* set-tings in large groups and of some *Te Deum* settings – otherwise a rarity in polyphonic sources.[186]

The largest, and perhaps the only surviving, Franco-Netherlands contribu-tion to be mentioned here is a series of Mass Proper settings (introits, graduals, alleluias, offertories and communions), which are grouped in Mass cycles and preserved anonymously in the Trent Codices, mainly *Tr 88* (*c.*1458–62).[187] They

[183] See Kanazawa, *Vespers*; Ward, *Office Hymn Catalogue*.

[184] Houdoy, *Histoire artistique*, 193 ff; Wright, 'Dufay at Cambrai', 198 f. The accounts mention lost works by Dufay (a *Magnificat*, an offertory, a tract, a sequence, a hymn) and the extant antiphon 'Ave regina celorum' (no. III). An attempt at identifying the hymn 'O quam glorifica' copied in 1463–4 with an anonymous work in the much earlier manuscript *F-CA 6* is the otherwise valua-ble study by Rudolf Bockholdt, 'Die Hymnen in der Handschrift Cambrai: zwei unbekannte Vertonungen von Dufay?', *TVNM* 29 (1979), 75–91; see also Fallows, *Dufay*, 288 n. 10.

[185] See *CC*, vol. I, 124 (with a wrong date), and p. 66 above.

[186] Strohm, *Bruges*, 30. A bibliography of *Magnificat* and *Te Deum* settings is Kirsch, *Quellen*. For a stylistic discussion, see Chris J. Maas, *Geschiedenis van het meerstemmig Magnificat tot omstreeks 1525* (Groningen: V.R.B., 1967).

[187] The cycles are described in detail in Gerken, *Polyphonic Cycles*, 36–102. Sequences – a genre of the Mass Proper – are lacking in these cycles; manuscripts of this period contain isolated sequence settings, however.

are mostly for three voices, not in fauxbourdon but in chanson format, with the plainsong paraphrased in the cantus. Psalmodic sections such as the verse and the 'Gloria patri' of the introit are often in declamatory block chords resembling later *falsobordoni*, although this convenient style has already been observed in Brassart's introits (p. 256). According to recent research, eleven or more of these cycles seem to have been composed in the 1440s by Guillaume Dufay.[188] Alejandro Planchart proposed that some of this music for the Proper of the Mass may have been copied in two lost Cambrai choirbooks of 1449–50 which contained music for the Ordinary and the Proper. He also showed that five cycles could have originated as a votive series for weekly Masses at the Sainte-Chapelle of Dijon – the seat of the Burgundian Order of the Golden Fleece.[189] Two of the cycles, for St Anthony of Padua and St Francis, are musically related and seem connected with the Mass Ordinary for St Anthony of Padua of apparently 1450 (see p. 414). Dufay's Proper sections and his Mass Ordinary for this saint could have been performed together as a so-called 'plenary cycle', perhaps in Padua.

'Plenary cycles' had existed earlier (see p. 253); one such cycle for St Anthony Abbot in *Tr 89* (c.1462–6) has tentatively been linked to Dufay because it is known that he composed a Mass for this saint.[190] The Gloria of this cycle is attributed to a certain 'Piret', however. Also, many individual sections and some Proper cycles in *Tr 88* have been judged on stylistic grounds not to be by Dufay.

Dufay's settings – whether for Cambrai Cathedral or for the Burgundian court – probably pioneered a wider interest in the polyphonic Mass Proper in western Europe and elsewhere. The works in the Trent Codices not composed by him were probably added to this collection at some intermediate institution which had adopted Dufay's settings, presumably in the 1450s. A court such as Savoy cannot be ruled out, but the best candidates seem to be the papal chapel and that of St Peter's, Rome: chapels employing northern singers and composers.[191]

In contrast to the strictly liturgical genres, devotional polyphony (such as votive antiphons performed in side chapels or in processions), was widely culti-vated, and we have mentioned it several times already (see especially p. 219). For France and the Low Countries, the performance practices are better known than the pieces themselves, because archival documents survive but most musi-

---

[188] See Feininger ed., *MPLSER*, ser. II, tom. I (1947), with the edition of sixteen cycles, 11 of which Feininger attributes to Dufay; Fallows, *Dufay*, rev. edn, 188–92 and 309 f; David Fallows, 'Dufay and the Mass Proper cycles in Trent 88', in Pirrotta-Curti eds, *Codici Musicali*, 46–59; the whole argument is developed in Planchart, 'Guillaume Du Fay's benefices', 142–62.

[189] Planchart, 'Guillaume Du Fay's benefices'; the document on the copying of the Cambrai volumes is in Wright, 'Dufay at Cambrai', 197 f. For the Golden Fleece, see Prizer, 'Music and ceremonial', 116–22.

[190] See Fallows, *Dufay*, rev. edn, 192 and (withdrawing the suggestion) 310.

[191] See Starr, *Papal Court*, and Reynolds, 'Origins', respectively; for the Italian contribution to the choirbook of St Peter's (*SP*), see p. 588.

cal sources are lost. The Columbia fragments (*US-NYcu 21*)[192] provide a good example of the devotional music of a typical institution: the fraternity of Notre Dame de la Treille at St Peter's, Lille. This wealthy association controlled in its chapel one of the most important burial places of the counts of Flanders. For its music, it was able to use the succentor and choirboys of the collegiate church. Also, by 1460–61 at the latest, a polyphonic Lady Mass was performed in the chapel every Monday by eight adult singers and the organist, Jacques Hourier.[193] Performances of Vespers polyphony and votive antiphons can be surmised. An endowment for the chapel, dated 8 May 1461, calls for the solemn performance of the prose 'Inviolata, integra et casta es' daily after Vespers between Christmas and Candlemas, with the stipulation that the congregation should kneel at the words 'O benigna'. It also instituted a solemn 'Regina celi' in Paschaltide, and the rank of a double feast for the day of St Bernard (20 August).[194] This links the fraternity to the Columbia fragments, because they contain, among *Magnificat* settings and other antiphons (three of which are of English origin), a setting of St Bernard's hymn 'Dulcis Jesu memoria', a 'Regina celi' and an 'Inviolata' with long-held chords on the words 'O benigna, o regina'.

Many similar examples could be mentioned of the spread of devotional polyphony through the Low Countries, usually encouraged by local patronage.[195] To give just one: another recently discovered set of fragments contains 'Salve regina' settings probably used in the fraternity of the Salve, later of Our Lady, at Our Lady's, Antwerp, in the 1460s to 80s.[196]

Two of these 'Salve regina' settings, which must date from the 1450s, were copied in *Tr 90* (by *c.*1456) in close vicinity to many works by Johannes Pullois, who had himself been at Antwerp until 1447. Also, other anonymous settings in the Trent sources must have arrived there – sometimes very quickly – from western Europe, including England.[197] A beautiful four-voice 'Salve regina' in *Tr 89* (no. 727) is attributed to Dufay in a later source, but Besseler tacitly excluded it from the *Opera omnia*.[198] If this work is not by Dufay, it is certainly a Franco-Netherlands composition of the 1450s. In a similar context, it would

---

[192] Discovered by Steven Bonime. See *CC*, vol. 2 , 259 f.

[193] Lille, Archives Départementales du Nord, 16 G 551, fol. 37r.

[194] Edmond Hautcoeur, *Cartulaire de l'Église collégiale de Lille*. 2 vols. (Lille, 1894), vol. 2, 1030 ff.

[195] The investigation has hardly begun, but see Bloxam, *Late Medieval Service Books*; Forney, 'Music, ritual and patronage'; Smijers, *Broederschap*; Strohm, *Bruges*; C. C. Vlam and M. A. Vente eds, *Bouwstenen voor een geschiedenis der toonkunst in de Nederlanden*, 1 ff (VNM, 1965–); Wegman, 'Bergen-op-Zoom'. See also p. 68 above.

[196] Discovered by Jaap van Benthem. See *CC*, vol. 4, 222.

[197] The Antwerp settings of *Tr 90* (nos. 1025 and 1038), are printed in *DTOe XXVII*, vol. 53, nos. 8 and 9. Other Franco-Netherlands works in this volume may be the 'Alma redemptoris mater' settings no. 2 (Phrygian; a contrafactum?), no. 3 and no. 4 (the plainsong combines with apparently a litany melody as cantus firmus); and the 'Salve regina' settings nos. 2–5 (no. 5 uses Dufay's tenor 'Le serviteur') and 7.

[198] Published as Dufay in *DTOe VII*, vols. 14–15, 178–83. Besseler's rejection of the work was based on Karl Dèzes, 'Das Dufay zugeschriebene "Salve regina" eine deutsche Komposition: stilkritische Studie', *ZMw* 10 (1927–8), 327–62 – an overambitious analytical effort not based on much knowledge of German polyphony of the time.

be interesting to know the place of origin of certain works by Johannes Touront, who seems to have been active in central Europe (see p. 511). His two Masses in *Tr 89* (*c*.1462-4), especially the three-part Mass 'Tertii toni', emulate or even antedate some of Ockeghem's modal procedures. His famous antiphons 'O gloriosa regina' and 'O florens rosa', in chanson format, are perfect examples of a contemplative but ornate idiom developed in western Europe from English models in the 1450s and 60s.[199] They exceed their models (except Plummer) in pervasive imitation and sequential patterning, quite comparable in this regard to the 'O rosa bella' Masses nos. I and II. Also Touront's large-scale motet 'Compangant omnes' (*Tr 89* no. 579) is comparable to works of the early Ockeghem circle.

Much liturgical and devotional music which is unknown or lost must have been composed for the princely chapels and sacred institutions of France which are so little investigated, with the exception of Notre Dame of Paris, as recently studied by Craig Wright.[200] The University of Paris must have sponsored significant festal and extracurricular musical activities, as attested, for example, by the presence of the musicians Johannes and Karolus Fernandes as professors in Paris from the 1470s.[201] It has been suggested that Antoine Busnois earned his master's degree at Paris; that he and Jean Ockeghem actually met there; or that Loyset Compère (*c*.1445-1518) befriended Jean Molinet (1435-1507) at the same university.[202]

The eventful career of Johannes Tinctoris (*c*.1435-1511) touched the University of Orléans, where he was a student and simultaneously succentor at the cathedral in the 1460s, and Chartres, where he seems to have occupied the same musical position later. At Orléans, he may well have met Eloy d'Amerval, and at Chartres, either Gilles Mureau in the 1460s, or Antoine Brumel in the 1480s.[203] Brumel was to become perhaps the most important composer of this group. His works are not easily datable; some at least must have been written between 1486 and 1492 when he was Master of the Children at the cathedral of Geneva. This ancient institution had a vigorous musical tradition of its own, supported by the dukes of Savoy with whom it shared some leading musicians in the 1450s, for example the tenor and composer Jacques Villette (son of Jean), the chapelmaster Barthélemy Chuet and, apparently in 1456, Guillaume Dufay.[204]

[199] Published in *DTOe VII*, vols. 14-15, 217-20. For the Masses, see Gottlieb, *Masses* (with edition). 'Tertii toni' has, in my opinion, a freely varied cantus firmus.

[200] Wright, *Music and Ceremony*. A brief survey of some other institutions is in Cazeaux, *French Music*, 40-52.

[201] Strohm, *Bruges*, 88.

[202] See Montagna, 'Caron, Hayne, Compère', 117. Jean Molinet (see p. 459 below) took a master's degree at Paris towards 1461; from *c*.1463, he served the Burgundian court.

[203] See Woodley, 'Tinctoris', 225 ff. On Eloy, see p. 472 below. On Mureau, see André Pirro, 'Gilles Mureau, chanoine de Chartres', in *Musikwissenschaftliche Beiträge: Festschrift für Johannes Wolf* (Berlin, 1929 R 1973), 163-7. On Brumel, see Barton Hudson, 'Brumel, Antoine' in *The New Grove*.

[204] See Marie-Thérèse Bouquet, 'La musique dans le culte catholique romain au temps des évêques, 1418-1535', in *Musique à Saint-Pierre*, préface de B. Martin (Geneva: Clefs de Saint-Pierre, 1984), 5-23; *idem*, 'Savoia'; Fallows, *Dufay*, 71.

The history and personnel of the royal chapel of France, which was based at the Sainte-Chapelle du Palais in Paris, has been reconstructed by Brenet and Perkins.[205] In the later reign of Charles VII (*r.* 1422–61) and under Louis XI (*r.* 1461–83), the importance of this performing body grew. There was, of course, Jean Ockeghem, *chapelain* in 1450–51 and *premier chapellain* from 1454 (modified to *premier chaplain de chant* in 1456, probably because Ockeghem did not become a priest and thus could not hold the highest liturgical rank). There were the composers Jean Cousin (from 1461; see above), Jean Fresneau (from 1469–70) and the well-travelled Jean Sohier dit Fedé (1473–4; see also p. 265). There were specialized singers of polyphony, such as Jean de Fontenay (1461–75), an ex-pupil of Dufay at Cambrai, and the *teneurs* Martin Courtois (from 1451) and David de Lannoy (from 1461).[206] Fedé also served in the separate chapel of Queen Mary d'Anjou (1462–3), and so did Pierre Basin, who joined the Burgundian court in 1460. The *teneur* Mathias Cocquiel (or Coyniel) was a king's chaplain from 1451, but in 1461 replaced Binchois in the Burgundian chapel, and was still active at court and in Bruges in 1480–81.[207]

The two most significant sacred institutions outside the court chapel itself, but patronized by the court, were the church of Saint-Martin at Tours, and the Sainte-Chapelle at the ducal palace of Bourges. The former abbey of Saint-Martin was, in the fifteenth century, the largest collegiate church of France. It was also a royal institution, the king himself being its titular abbot. Ockeghem was appointed treasurer shortly before July 1459.[208] It is likely that Ockeghem occasionally resided at Saint-Martin and that he composed for this church. He probably was a teacher or mentor of Antoine Busnois in Tours in the 1460s, since the latter is documented as a choir clerk at Saint-Martin in 1465.[209] This also means that the earlier compositions by Busnois are likely to have been written for Tours and for French courtly circles, before the composer joined the Burgundian court *c.* 1467 (see p. 450).

The Sainte-Chapelle of Bourges, too, was a sphere of activity for significant composers. In documents from this institution, Paula Higgins found the names of Jean Cousin (1458–9), Guillaume Faugues (1462–3), Jean Ockeghem (who visited in 1462), Charles de Launay (1472–87), and Philippe Basiron, whose career she traces there between the years 1458 and 1473.[210] The extant music by these composers can be assessed in new ways since their French courtly connections have become known.

---

[205] Brenet, *Musique et Musiciens*, 21–82; Michel Brenet, *Les musiciens de la Sainte Chapelle de Palais* (Paris: Picard, 1910/R1973); Perkins, 'Musical patronage'. See also the obit-book published in Auguste Molinier, *Obituaires de la province de Sens*, tom. 1, 2e partie (Paris, 1902), 814–24.

[206] Cambrai connections of Fresneau, Fedé, Fontenay, Courtois and indeed Ockeghem are demonstrated in Wright, 'Dufay at Cambrai', 204–8.

[207] On Basin, see Marix, *Histoire*, 260–62; Strohm, *Bruges*, *passim*. On Cocquiel, see Marix, *Histoire*, 211 f.

[208] Perkins, 'Musical patronage', 523–8; Higgins, *Busnois*, 125–34 and 143.

[209] Higgins, 'In hydraulis', 70 f. Further evidence that Busnois was there earlier has been discovered by Pamela Starr (personal communication).

[210] Higgins, 'Music and musicians'; Higgins, 'Tracing the careers'.

Secular song

In 1455, Dufay was apparently present at the conclusion of a treaty between France and Savoy at Saint-Pourçain, where he met Duke Charles d'Orléans as well as perhaps King Charles VII and his new *premier chapellain*, Jean Ockeghem. In this context, Dufay seems to have composed several chansons, partly on texts by poets of this circle. A distinctly different tone is heard in these and other 'late songs' by Dufay;[211] one might also call them 'new songs'. There is a suavity or mannered melancholy in their slightly over-ornamented melodies that emulates the refined taste of the poems themselves. They use much contrapuntal and imitative artifice. 'Les douleurs', for example, has a mensuration canon between the two top voices; they start in a stretto imitation which resembles the beginning of the 'St Anthony' Mass. In other late songs, clearly heard imitation also introduces internal or opening phrases. The tendency is shared with Frye and Binchois, but so is its unpredictability. The richest use of imitation, as in 'Adieu, m'amour', exceeds that of the other composers. Dufay takes great care at internal and final climaxes. These can be melodic (a series of upward leaps as in 'Par le regard', for example), rhythmic (increasing ornamentation) or contrapuntal (for example stretto imitation, as in 'Vostre bruit' and 'Belle, vueillés moy vangier'). But the composer's strategies are mostly unpredictable; obvious patterns are avoided. Textural experiments link several songs with Morton and Frye; in 'Du tout m'estoie abandonné' the voice-ranges are separated and the contratenor does not cross into the middle.

These songs are also highly individualized. In the most famous new song, 'Par le regard de vos beaux yeux', every single melodic and rhythmic effect in the cantus happens only once until bars 9–10, when suddenly the same falling gesture is reiterated (a'-g'-e'; d'-c'-a). Another extremely famous piece, 'Le serviteur hault guerdonné', shares with Ockeghem's early works the bold exploration of an irregular mode (C-Dorian, but with important Phrygian cadences on D).[212] The rotating imitations and bold crossings through intervals larger than the octave might resemble Frye and Ockeghem, but it is almost a harmless piece in comparison with the surely authentic 'Belle, vueillés moy vangier', which is not only in C-Dorian but also exploits false relations, various types of imitation and drastic changes of rhythmic and melodic language. I wonder if the surprising beginning of the second half (in *sesquialtera* proportion) is not an intentional reference to 'Faisant regretz' in Frye's 'Tout a par moy':

---

[211] Identified and described in Fallows, *Dufay*, ch. 12 ('The late songs').

[212] Besseler rejected the manuscript attribution, declaring that the song was too modern for Dufay(!). This was refuted in Fallows, *Dufay*, 159. Besseler also rejected an attribution to Dufay of 'Departez-vous, Malebouche' in one manuscript (Montecassino): another attribution, to Ockeghem, is probably wrong as the counterpoint is too conservative. Texture and metre are enterprising enough. Fallows, *Dufay*, rev. edn, 311, now prefers Dufay.

Example 64 Guillaume Dufay, 'Belle, vueillés moy vangier'

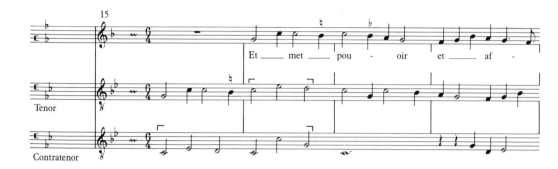

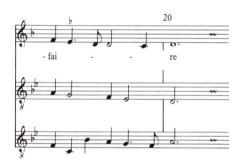

Binchois' career took no new turn, as far as we know, and this adds considerable interest to signs of a style-change in his works. According to manuscript evidence, seven songs attributed to him may have originated after *c*.1445, and stylistic peculiarities indeed separate five of these from the bulk of his output: the rondeaux 'Pour prison ne pour maladie', 'Seule esgarée' (his only song in duple metre), 'Comme femme desconfortée', 'Je ne vis onques la pareille' and 'Tout a par moy'.[213] 'Je ne vis onques' also exists with a less likely attribution to Dufay; it was performed (in two parts) at the *banquet du voeu* in 1454, and probably composed then. 'Tout a par moy' (see also p. 393) must be by Walter Frye: its imitative entries and quasi-sequential restatements of phrases are identical in character to those of Frye's English ballade 'Alas, alas is my chief song'. Even in the circumstances under scrutiny here, an imitation of someone else's style as close as this would be most improbable. These conflicts of attribution, and others mentioned above, are nevertheless symptomatic: some copyists of the 1450s seem to have lost sight of the differences between Dufay, Ockeghem, Frye and Binchois! Many of them refrained from naming any com-

---

[213] Binchois, *Chansons*, nos. 35, 42, 56, 57 and 58. The other two songs, 'En sera il mieulx' and 'Mon doulx espoir', survive only in the chansonnier *RU* (*c*.1455?) – in copies so full of errors that style judgements would be hazardous.

poser. For 'Pour prison' and 'Comme femme', Binchois' name appears in only one of respectively eight and nine sources.

Almost predictably, but unjustifiably, the authenticity of 'Comme femme' has come under suspicion among modern scholars.[214] This is an extremely important song – whose music is used about a dozen times in later Masses and motets. The words, put into the mouth of a mourning woman, could easily be referred to Mary. Binchois' setting features an imitative first entry, a strongly 'harmonic' contratenor, several cadences with the third on top, and excessive use of his favourite device, the *note échappée* (which is conspicuous also in 'Seule esgarée'). The small note-values and the nervously ornamented lines, which often curve back after only one bar and within limited intervals, suggest a slower performance tempo than in his older songs. (This characteristic also distinguishes some of Dufay's late songs.) Since 'Comme femme' is a lament, its preference for descending parallel sixth chords may be text-related. We somehow miss the sweep of Binchois' earlier tunes here – which in 'Pour prison' and 'Je ne vis onques' is still recognizable. 'Comme femme' offers, as compensation, an intricate web of 'pregnant' motives and pitch-exchanges among all the three voices, definitely resembling songs by Walter Frye. Also, 'Pour prison' recalls Frye – more than 'Tout a par moy' recalls Binchois. A similar relationship may have obtained between Dufay and Ockeghem: the more experienced men seem to have learned from their younger colleagues. We are witnessing a moment in history when Franco-Netherlands composers began to select their models or stylistic goals quite independently from their own respective backgrounds. English, French and Burgundian traditions suddenly crossed.

This is also borne out by some secondary composers, with whom eclecticism and unpredictability become, paradoxically, a fixed manner. The most prominent of them was Johannes Pullois (*d*.1478). He sang at Our Lady's, Antwerp, from 1442 to 1447, and afterwards became a member of the papal chapel and an incredibly busy careerist. The trail of his own prebends, as well as of those he helped to procure for his friends – who included Ockeghem and Busnois – was endless.[215] If it was important for a musician at this time to be 'well connected', Pullois overdid it. This is to some extent reflected in his music which often reminds us of other composers. Traces of Benet and Bedyngham in the Mass have been mentioned above (p. 242). A textless 'Le serviteur' (incompletely preserved) quotes the famous Dufay song, and Binchois is offered the homage of a 'Pour prison' which quotes him literally at 'ne vous peut mon cuer oublier'.

Pullois is an interesting composer in his own right. In 'Pour prison' he weaves together idioms of Binchois and Frye, but does not forget to add his own motivic 'fingerprint' (see Ex. 39). Ockeghem (and Regis?) seem anticipated rather than emulated in the florid and varied motet 'Flos de spina'. This is a four-voice com-

---

[214] Atlas ed., *Cappella Giulia Chansonnier*, 364 f; Binchois, *Chansons*, no. 56.

[215] See Starr, *Papal Court*, 167–75 (biography) and 287 f (a list of seventeen benefices). For his works, see Pullois, *Opera omnia*. An evaluation of the songs is Gerald Montagna, 'Johannes Pullois in the context of his era', *RBM* 42 (1988), 83–117.

position in two sections, in the grand manner as used in Mass–motet cycles, although without cantus firmus. (The tenor behaves sometimes as if it carried one.) The Dutch song 'So lanc so meer' seems at first to quote the beginning of Dufay's 'Par le regard', but then proceeds with a simple imitative text phrase. The most complex Pullois songs are 'De madame' and 'Je ne puis', which are anonymous in the sources but again contain his 'fingerprint'. Both occur in close connection with seven attributed works in the later fascicles of *Tr 90*, which were copied by *c.*1456. Only five other works (including the remarkably modern 'He, n'esse pas') can at all be later than this, appearing in Italian chansonniers of the 1460s.

Pullois must have known Ockeghem at Antwerp in the 1440s. Another man whose path Ockeghem seems to have crossed (perhaps at the court of Bourbon, where he stayed at least from 1446 to 1448) is Barbingant. His songs are surely as significant as his other works, described earlier, particularly if we can include among them the rondeau 'Au travail suis'. This excellent piece, composed in the 1450s, is attributed to Ockeghem in one source but is probably by Barbingant.[216] The bold contour of its first four notes ($a'-c''-b'-e'$) immediately captures the ear. It is the '1–3–2–5' contour, with the last note falling a fifth. In the form with the last note rising a fourth, it was an extremely popular cliché of the 1450s. It was known from the beginnings of Barbingant's Mass 'Terriblement', of Frye's 'So ys emprentid' tenor, and consequently as the beginning of the tenor and the head-motive in Le Rouge's Mass 'Soyez aprantiz'. It also is the head-motive of the 'sine nomine' Masses by Pullois (Kyrie, Agnus I and Agnus II), Bedyngham (Kyrie, Credo and Agnus I), Ockeghem (all sections) and Barbingant himself, as well as of 'Summe trinitati' by Frye. The motive with the last note falling is found only in 'Au travail suis' and in the most successful anonymous French song of this period: 'J'ay pris amours a ma devise':[217]

Example 65 'J'ay pris amours', Nivelle, fol. 70v

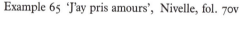

[216] Printed, for example, in Barbireau(!), *Opera omnia*. The attribution to Ockeghem must have arisen because he was much more famous, and because he wrote a Mass over Barbingant's rondeau. The case also involves Ockeghem's chanson and Mass 'Ma maistresse': see n.222 below.

[217] Printed in Droz–Thibault eds, *Trois Chansonniers*, no. 2. Montagna, 'Caron, Hayne, Compère', 125 f, makes a case for its attribution to Caron.

Example 65 *(cont.)*

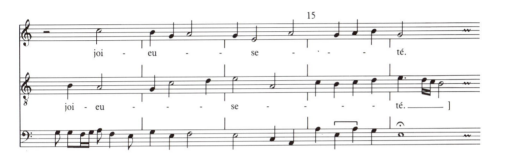

It is characteristic for this new kind of song that the opening motive is cut off from the continuation by a rest, where the words have completed a self-contained statement.[218] Both 'J'ay pris amours' and 'Au travail suis' lead on with imitation.

Tunes like these have a novel kind of vigour. Probably, contemporaries could hear in the '1-3-2-5' design something like a bolder, more explicit reference to a tonal structure than in the opening formulas of earlier songs – such as the more gently arched '1-2-4-3' so dear to Frye and Binchois. In the new design, the early appearances of the minor '3' and of the '5' immediately convey a characteristic flavour without taking recourse to a known modal formula. In 'Au travail suis' and 'J'ay pris amour' especially, the falling fifths combine the power of a Dorian 'dominant' with the expressivity of the minor third left by a semi-tone step. These pieces could be considered as being in the Dorian mode trans-posed to *a* – a transposition rarely found in chant – or they could indeed be considered modern minor mode pieces.

The search for such expressions was a conscious one. A similarly strong tonal feeling is conveyed by Ockeghem's bergerette 'Ma bouche rit et ma pensée pleure',

218 From such 'four-pitch-figures' based on the opening four syllables of the verse, there originated the four-note opening with the rhythm 'long-short-short-long' of countless sixteenth-century chansons and *canzoni*.

which opens with the imitative, rising fourths 'la-mi-la-sol-fa' ($a'\text{-}e'\text{-}a'\text{-}g'\text{-}c''$), but then nevertheless collapses into the falling fifth 'mi-mi' ($b'\text{-}e'$):[219]

Example 66 Jean Ockeghem, 'Ma bouche rit'

The main cadence of this song (the refrain ending) is Phrygian on E, and only the secondary cadence (the stanza ending) is on A. In the rondeaux 'Au travail suis' and 'J'ay pris amours', the relationship of the cadences is the reverse.[220] It is possible to look at 'Ma bouche rit' as a Phrygian song, but its similarities with the other two songs are so conspicuous (for example, the similar use of the falling fifth $b'\text{-}e'$), that all three might better be assigned to the same mode. The pieces balance two established modes, Phrygian and Dorian, to create a new one: the 'minor mode'.[221]

---

[219] The complete piece is printed in *HAM*, no. 75.

[220] An interesting derivative from 'Ma bouche rit', musically as well as textually, is the anonymous bergerette 'Mon corps gemist et mon coeur se lamente' (?; text garbled) in the manuscript *Pix* (no. 66): see Pease, *Pixérécourt Manuscript*, 223. Here, the cadences are on A and E as in 'Au travail suis'. For another derivative, 'Ma bouche plaint les pleurs de ma pensée', see Brown ed., *A Florentine Chansonnier*, no. 36.

[221] One wonders whether Glarean's 'Aeolian mode' on *a* (in his *Dodecachordon*, 1547) was really an expedient to accommodate in the traditional system a musical phenomenon which had existed since the mid-fifteenth century. Its existence is, however, not accepted in the expert study of 'Modal structures' in Perkins-Garey eds, *Mellon Chansonnier*, vol. 2, 24–52. Specially on the Phrygian, see William P. Mahrt, 'Guillaume Dufay's chansons in the Phrygian mode', *Studies in Music (Ontario)* 5 (1980), 81–98.

A feature not present in 'Au travail suis', hinted at by 'J'ay pris amours' and developed in 'Ma bouche rit', is the declamation in equal, repeated notes in duple metre. This somehow stubborn, 'parlando' style of word-setting was becoming a fashion towards 1460, affecting also Dufay ('Vostre bruit'), and surfacing in Ockeghem's early 'Missa sine nomine' (no. 2). It was perhaps derived from the declamatory style of *chansons rustiques* – genuine or imitated folk-tunes – which in themselves were now often used as chanson melodies (see also below). On the other hand, in 'Ma bouche rit' the simple openings of both the refrain and stanza sections are followed by some of the most complex part-writing in the repertory. The lower voices sneak in and out almost imperceptibly at times; it is as if Ockeghem had transferred to the chanson the textural unpredictability cultivated by Dunstable and Power.

'New contours, new harmonies, new textures' – this could be the motto of the French chanson around 1460, and this impetus was to last for about a generation. Apart from Barbingant, Ockeghem was very much at the head of the development. His bergerette 'Ma maistresse et ma plus grande amie', is not only a very early specimen of this chanson genre (see p. 431), but also shatters aesthetic expectations.[222] The rich, intricate part-writing (the many sequential and imitative patterns are started off with a brief 'mensuration canon'), the full, sweet harmonies (often with third degrees on top), the high register (f to f'') and the rapid melodic ascents and descents convey an almost feverish excitement despite the underlying serenity of the fifth (Lydian) mode.

There was a conscious exploitation of the Lydian mode at this time, and also a trend to transpose it flatwards to 'B flat'. In contrast to the conventional view of the fifth mode as 'joyful' or even 'voluptuous', Lydian chansons of this time often have melancholic or plaintive words.[223] Barbingant contributed the rondeau 'L'homme banny de sa plaisance, Vide de joie et de liesse', the words of which describe a sorrowful mood. The piece (ascribed in a later source to Jean Fedé) starts with sweet-sounding, pentatonic parallels of cantus and contratenor around a pedal point in the tenor. Barbingant repeats this idea in his 'Esperant que mon bien viendra'. 'L'homme banny' also introduces varied and skilful imitations. Jean Boubert, a minor composer active in Bruges between 1452 and 1461, wrote a Lydian rondeau which in the sweetest triadic style describes an adverse temperamental state: 'L'homme enragé, hors du sens forcené, Excervelé, impacient, frenaticque'. The anonymous rondeau 'L'homme qui vit en esperance' has a text opposing that of Barbingant, but almost literally

---

[222] Printed in *HAM*, no. 74. The song was copied in the manuscript *Tr 93* before *c.*1456. Its beginning quotes words and music from the last line of Barbingant's rondeau 'Au travail suis'. Ockeghem composed Mass settings on both 'Au travail suis' and 'Ma maistresse'; on the relationship of the four works, see Fallows, 'Johannes Ockeghem'.

[223] 'Modal ethos', i.e. expressive qualities attributed to the individual modes, was discussed at the time. See p. 596 below, on Ramos de Pareja and Italian theorists, and Harold S. Powers, 'Mode ♯III, 1' in *The New Grove*.

quotes his main musical ideas and even, at the end, his first line of text.[224] Some kind of poetic-musical game seems to be going on here, the nature of which eludes us. In a more general sense, these groups of related chansons belong to the category of 'chanson families' which accumulated quite naturally in poetic and musical circles (see also p. 459).

A major chanson composer of this period, who distinguished himself through his uses of contour, mode and texture, was the Englishman Robert Morton. He served at the Burgundian court from 1457 until at least 1476. In 1464–5 and 1466, he was in the household of the future duke, Charles of Charolais, as were the chamber valets and chanson specialists Hayne van Ghizeghem and Adrien Basin in 1467, and as was Antoine Busnois (see below). Of the songs attributed to Morton in the sources, David Fallows accepts eight as authentic, defining their context as that of the Burgundian court.[225] The two most famous pieces are the rondeaux 'N'aray je jamais mieulx que j'ay?' and 'Le souvenir de vous me tue', transmitted in sixteen and fourteen musical sources, respectively. 'Le souvenir' and the much less circulated 'Mon bien, m'amour, ma joye' are in a 'voluptuous' fifth mode with much play on the F major triad and its pentatonic satellites *g* and *d*.

'Mon bien, m'amour' shares with 'C'est temps perdu' a voice distribution that was characteristic of these years: cantus and tenor are almost precisely in the same range, and the contratenor remains always below. The 'trio sonata' idea of two high voices against a lower one had been familiar to the early fifteenth century; the difference here is that one of the high voices is the tenor. In these and other Morton songs, we also find canonic imitations between cantus and tenor. The contratenor sounds more like a bass:

Example 67 Robert Morton, 'N'aray-je jamais mieulx?'

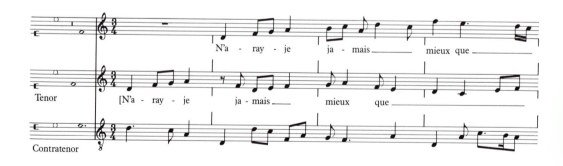

[224] Boubert's rondeau is in Droz-Thibault eds, *Trois Chansonniers*, no. 47, the anonymous one in Pease, *Pixérécourt Manuscript*, no. 156.
[225] Fallows, 'Morton, Robert' in *The New Grove*. See also Fallows, *Robert Morton's Songs*; and the edn: Morton, *Collected Works*.

Example 67 (*cont.*)

The example also shows Morton's concern for motivic economy and characteristic contours – in this case a line which quickly traverses the full range, actually accelerating the ascent by the double leap of a fourth. As often in Morton, the rhythm is simple, even conservative.

A contrapuntal side-effect of a voice distribution with low contratenor is that no structural fourths occur between any pair of voices: not between cantus and tenor anyway, and not with the contratenor because that voice is always at the bottom. The phenomenon of 'non-quartal harmony' has been singled out as a peculiar development of the later fifteenth century, although all that happened was the registral separation of the lowest voice.[226]

If unpredictability or elusiveness were characteristics of Dufay's late songs, the younger chanson composers of the 1460s and later perform precise and sometimes obvious strategies of surprise and drama. Jean Ockeghem (*c.*1410–1497), whose sacred music is breathtaking by design, left 22 songs with French texts, each of which is different from all the others.[227] He was a pioneer and a perfectionist at the same time: certainly an artist who hated routine. In the long years of his service in the French royal household – from 1450 to his death in 1497 – Ockeghem became the revered master for all those working after Dufay, as we may see from the several extant laments on his death.[228] He had a celebrated low contratenor voice, which must be related to the low range and melodic interest of his bass parts. Ockeghem was learned, although he did not have a

---

[226] Fox, 'Non-quartal harmony'. I think that the primary idea was not contrapuntal but textural. Fox mentions pieces without fourths where the lower voices do cross; these cases are coincidental, however. For the separation of the lowest voice, see also p. 533.

[227] Bibliographical guides to his life and works are Leeman L. Perkins, 'Ockeghem, Johannes' in *The New Grove*, and Picker, *Ockeghem and Obrecht*. Both can be used to find editions of the secular works and motets, still missing in the *Collected Works*.

[228] The best known are Guillaume Crétin's *Déploration*, a long poem which mentions many other composers as mourning their master (E. Thoinan ed., *Déploration sur le trépas de Jean Ockeghem* (Paris, 1864 / R London: Baron, 1965)); Jean Molinet's poem 'Nymphes des boys' which was set by Josquin, and a Latin poem 'Ergo ne conticuit' by Erasmus of Rotterdam, set by Johannes Lupi a generation later. Crétin's poem begins: 'Chargé de dueil par desmeseuré faix', which compounds Christine de Pisan's 'Dueil angoisseux, rage desmesurée' and an anonymous bergerette in Nivelle and later sources, 'Chargé de dueil plus que mon fais'.

449

master's degree as had Busnois.[229] Chroniclers, music theorists and early music historians see Ockeghem as a genius of counterpoint, and speak about him with the awe inspired by a great old master. But his early reputation was rather based on his bold, pioneering chansons which he wrote in the 1450s: 'Ma maistresse', 'Ma bouche rit', 'S'elle m'amera / Petite camusette' and 'Fors seulement'.

Antoine Busnois was presumably a student of Ockeghem at Tours in the early 1460s (see above), before he moved to the Burgundian court between 1465 and 1467. He stayed in that service as its most prominent composer and performer until the end of the dynasty in 1482 (the death of Duke Charles's daughter Mary of Burgundy). He was retained under the Habsburg regime, but died ten years later in the modest position of cantor at the parish church of Saint-Sauveur of Bruges – admittedly an institution patronized by Archduke Maximilian. With his Latin-texted works, Busnois is an important mediator between the Dufay era and Josquin des Prez. Even more significant are his French chansons, more than 60 in number. If Ockeghem's chansons are touching and individualistic, those of Busnois have, in addition, a brilliance and stylish beauty shared with the most memorable songs of any age. They are intellectually exciting, complex works, relying for their effect on the whole fabric of the three or four voices. Their invention is as rich as that of Dufay's isorhythmic motets or Ockeghem's Masses.

Around Ockeghem and Busnois, a wider circle of composers seems to have existed which was connected with the royal French court, with the sacred establishments at Tours and perhaps Bourges, and with ducal households centred in the Loire valley, such as Bourbon and Orléans. This circle included Jean Fresneau, Jean Fedé, Jean Delahaye (who set François Villon's 'Mort, j'appelle de ta rigueur'), and perhaps Barbingant, Jean Molinet, Gilles Mureau, Johannes Tinctoris, Convert (about whom nothing is known except that Tinctoris knew him) and the younger Philippe Basiron. Their secular music is concentrated in a number of chansonniers of the 1460s and 70s, which have traditionally been regarded as 'Burgundian'. In reality, they contain only some of the best-known pieces from that court (such as Morton's), whereas the core repertory is 'royal French'; the manuscripts themselves were compiled in the area along the Loire.[230] Most important for the development of the style are the chansonnier Nivelle de la Chaussée (*F-Pn Rés. Vmc ms. 57*; formerly *F-Pthibault*), which was probably copied at the ducal palace of Bourges in the early to mid-1460s, and the Dijon Chansonnier (*F-Dm 517*), which is about ten years younger but contains

---

[229] See also the passage from the *Proportionale musices* quoted above (p. 420). Tinctoris calls Busnois 'magister' in the dedication, to both Ockeghem and Busnois, of his *Liber de natura et proprietate tonorum*, in *Opera theoretica*, vol. I, 65–104.

[230] Jeppesen ed., *Kopenhagener Chansonnier*, is the major publication representing this older view. The revision was first proposed in Joshua Rifkin, 'Scribal concordances for some Renaissance manuscripts in Florentine libraries', *JAMS* 26 (1973), 305–26, and Louise Litterick, *The Manuscript Royal 20.A.XVI of the British Library*, Ph.D. diss., New York U., 1976; and developed in Higgins, *Busnois*, 269–308, and Gutiérrez-Denhoff, *Wolfenbütteler Chansonnier*.

the largest number of pieces, 160.[231] The related manuscripts Laborde (*US-Wc M 2.1.L 25 Case*), Copenhagen (*DK-Kk Thott 291⁸*) and Wolfenbüttel (*D-W 287*) stand between those two in size and probably in age.[232] Also important are some manuscripts containing only the poetic texts.[233]

Even before Busnois joined the Burgundian court, and surely after, the chanson production in that circle was interlocked with the music of Cambrai, Brussels, Bruges or Lille – just as the French court had its outposts at Tours, Orléans or Bourges. Burgundian song composers after Binchois, and besides Morton, were Magister Simon le Breton (a chapel member 1431-64), Constans Breuwe de Languebroek (1442-79), Gilles Joye (see p. 427), Adrien Basin (see p. 302), Duke Charles the Bold himself,[234] possibly Firminus(?) Caron and, notably, Hayne van Ghizeghem. Hayne was a young boy in 1457 when he lived, and probably studied, at the court with Constans Breuwe. He became a key figure of the 'Burgundian chanson' through the legendary success of just a few songs – 'Allez regretz', 'De tous biens pleine' and 'Amours, amours'.[235] It seems that only the first two of these were composed in his Burgundian service as a chamber valet, which he seems to have left sometime after 1476 for the French court. As far as is known, he never took sacred orders or became a chaplain. Like Binchois in his early years, Hayne seems to have accompanied the duke in a military capacity, probably as a squire, but also as a singer on the lute. Some of his compositions could be said to recall Binchois' music and his aural, spontaneous approach. Together with Morton, he sang and played to great applause at Cambrai; Crétin's *Déploration* for Ockeghem of 1497 makes him – as one of the deceased – play Ockeghem's 'Ut heremita solus' on the lute.[236]

The true identity and the correct Christian name of Caron are as yet unknown. For reasons of age, he was most probably not Philippe Caron, a Cambrai choirboy from *c*.1469, nor Jean (le) Caron, a Burgundian court *sommelier* 1436-74. The choice hinges between a Jean Caron, *petit vicaire* at Cambrai 1455-8, and a Firminus Caron, named by Tinctoris as the author of several distinguished works.[237] The five Masses and twenty chansons preserved under the name of

---

[231] See, respectively, Higgins ed., *Chansonnier Nivelle* (with important introduction); D. Plamenac ed., *The Chansonnier Dijon, Bibl. Mun. 517*, in Publications of Mediaeval Musical Manuscripts, vol. 12 (Brooklyn: Institute of Mediaeval Music, n. d.).

[232] Jeppesen ed., *Kopenhagener Chansonnier*; Gutiérrez-Denhoff, *Wolfenbütteler Chansonnier*.

[233] Available in modern editions are the Rohan Chansonnier (*c*.1463-75), with 663 poems, edited in Löpelmann, *Liederhandschrift*, and the print of 1501, *Le jardin de plaisance*. Poetry, language and text sources are discussed in Perkins-Garey eds, *Mellon Chansonnier*, 63-128 and 149-85.

[234] See Fallows, *Robert Morton's Songs*, 308-12.

[235] Hayne van Ghizeghem, *Opera omnia*, ed. B. Hudson, CMM 74 (Rome: AIM, 1977). A discussion of his style is Montagna, 'Caron, Hayne, Compère'.

[236] See Marix, *Histoire*, 207, and p. 480 below.

[237] See James Thomson, *An Introduction to Philippe(?) Caron*, MS 9 (Brooklyn, 1964); Geneviève Thibault, 'Caron, Philippe' in *The New Grove*. The Cambrai 'Jean Caron' has been proposed in Wright, 'Dufay at Cambrai', 205. 'Firminus' (a name typical for Amiens) has the advantage of an attribution 'F. Caron' for the Mass 'L'homme armé' in the manuscript *SP*: see Reynolds, 'Origins', 290. As this manuscript uses no Italian but only Latin, the reading 'F(ilippo)' is out of the question.

'Caron' are almost without exception safely attributable to the same man (for an evaluation, see below).

Secular music from the Burgundian court and its territories such as Flanders is widespread in European sources, especially in the many Italian chansonniers of the 1470s to 90s (see p. 558). The transmission to Italy, mainly through singers, was traditional and did not imply that the compilers of these sources had particular ties to the Burgundian court. They did of course not exclude music from royal France, such as Ockeghem's or Basiron's.

The strongest musical radiance in these repertories comes from Ockeghem's and Busnois' chansons. The glowing harmonic colours of Ockeghem's 'Ma maistresse' and 'Ma bouche rit' are also found in his Phrygian bergerette 'Presque transi', which derives incredible effects from the constant juxtaposition of C major and E minor sonorities. The tritones *f–b* or *b–f'* often act as pivots between them. The falling fifth in the bass at the beginning hardly establishes a feeling of 'V-I', also because of its inconclusive, dropping rhythm:

Example 68 Jean Ockeghem, 'Presque transi'

The gesture is repeated several times in the chanson, and at unexpected moments, also in transposition and in other voices. The (often dissonant) anticipation of the second pitch is a basic idea of the song. There are other motivic recurrences. The peaceful rhythms and expressive contours, especially the descents in bars 13–17 and 44–6, remind one very much of Binchois. (The refrain ends with the words 'De plus fort en plus fort'.)[238]

Ockeghem's externally most successful song was the rondeau cinquain 'Fors seulement l'attente que je meure'. It surfaces in several versions and in dozens of later adaptations.[239] It is the basis of his own five-part parody Mass and is quoted in his motet 'Intemerata' and in his late chanson 'Fors seulement contre

[238] Printed in Droz–Thibault eds, *Trois chansonniers*, no. 48 (with incorrect flats).
[239] See Helen Hewitt, '"Fors seulement" and the cantus firmus technique of the fifteenth century', in Snow ed., *Essays in Musicology*, 91–126. The original and 30 adaptations are in Picker ed., *Fors seulement*. The *eb* in bar 5 (contratenor) is incorrect: the scribe added the flat sign following the convention of notes *extra manum*, because it happened to be on a ledger line above the staff.

ce qu'ay promis'. 'Fors seulement l'attente' is in the 'Aeolian' mode and both its halves cadence on A, although there is a playful use of *bb*. The song is characterized by its parlando declamation; the opening rhythm became a stereotype in the song production of the age (see Ex. 69). Cantus and tenor, both texted, are

Example 69 Jean Ockeghem, 'Fors seulement'

in quasi-canon at varying distances, so that some text-lines are clearly heard twice over, whereas in other passages the canon obscures the words. The text is a 'woman's poem', i.e. the speaker is a lady, as in a great number of Ockeghem's chansons.

Other songs from the years around 1460 are 'D'ung aultre amer mon cuer s'abesseroit', often adapted and probably famous also for its clever text; 'La despourvue et la bannie' in B♭, which may belong to the Lydian group described above (p. 447); the canon 'Prenez sur moi' and the combinative chanson 'S'elle m'amera / Petite camusette'.

'Prenez sur moi vostre exemple, amoureux' is a musical brain-teaser whose words have to be understood both erotically and as a symbolic performance direction. The point of this three-voice canon is as follows. The second and third voices enter twice at the upper fourth, so that the piece would rapidly modulate flatwards and soon get 'out of hand', if literal (real) answers were employed. The singers must, therefore, find the right points at which to change the semitone structure of the subject (i.e. find tonal answers) to stay within the gamut. These points have to be determined by a proper use of vertical consonances, by avoiding tritones etc. In each phrase one of the two canonic voices has to change 'fa' into 'mi' at one appropriate point. The greatest fun probably lies in sorting out which of the two singers concerned has to carry out this task. The piece is not only a canon but, according to Glareanus, also a *catholicon* ('all-embracing work'), because no clefs are notated and it can be sung on any of the four modal finals. This it has in common with the Mass 'Cuiusvis toni' (see below).[240]

'S'elle m'amera / Petite camusette' combines a regular rondeau cinquain with the words and music of a popular tune. The tradition of building a polyphonic song around a monophonic tune was not special as such. In Ockeghem's generation, however, it developed into a major fashion among composers, singers and amateur musicians at large. In many of these pieces, a 'folksong' (*chanson*

[240] Joseph S. Levitan, 'Ockeghem's clefless compositions', *MQ* 23 (1937), 440–64; Reese, 'Musical compositions in Renaissance intarsia', 81–5.

rustique) and an art-song are performed simultaneously and 'at cross-purposes', as it were. If more than one type of song was involved, these settings are called 'combinative'. Most of the French specimens of this generation are in four parts, and in a marching duple rhythm, as in our case. The cantus sings a relatively conventional courtly rondeau text, while the tenor pronounces the borrowed tune:

'Petite camusette – a la mort m'avez mis.
Robin et Marion – s'en vont au bois jouer.
Ilz s'en vont bras a bras – ilz se sont endormis.
Petite camusette – a la mort m'avez mis.'

[Little snubnose, you've put me to death. / Robin and Marion are going to the wood to play. / They are going off, arm in arm; they've gone to sleep. / Little snubnose . . . .][241]

Ockeghem derives the music of the outer voices from the tenor by strict imitation. Cantus and contratenor 1 are a fifth above, contratenor 2 a fourth below the tenor. The tenor enters with the first syllable 'Pe-', followed by a rest, as if it had entered too early by mistake, and then begins properly in bar 2. Later on, the two incongruent text forms (five verses against four) are more and more in conflict, and the dance-tune sweeps past the mid-point of the rondeau. The phrases come together again at the end in the same imitative pattern. The music of bars 1–7 is thus repeated in bars 17–23, apart from the surprisingly added final chord. But in reality there are slight changes of counterpoint in the corresponding sections – almost voice-exchanges. Their effect is that in bar 21 the tenor finds itself in parallel fourths with the cantus, which violates the rules of chanson format (see p. 460). The piece marks the beginning of genuine four-part writing in secular song, although apart from Busnois, other composers were slow to take up the suggestion.

From the 1460s onwards, popular tunes (*chansons rustiques*) were increasingly cited in polyphonic settings, whether simple or 'combinative'. These settings are precious documents because the tunes they use are rarely found in written form on their own; only two manuscripts exist of an intermediate repertory of monophonic but mensural, courtly chansons.[242] The combinative songs, already practised by earlier generations (see Binchois' 'Filles a marier / Se tu t'en marias'), developed into true pot-pourris (*fricassées*), whose purpose was often the caricature of well-known chansons or indeed sacred music.[243] These

---

[241] Perkins-Garey, *Mellon Chansonnier*, no. 4.

[242] Gustave Reese and Theodore Karp, 'Monophony in a group of Renaissance chansonniers', *JAMS* 5 (1952), 4–15; Paris-Gevaert eds, *Chansons*; Théodore Gérold ed., *Le Manuscrit de Bayeux* (Strasbourg, 1921). Generally on the *chanson rustique*, see Howard M. Brown, 'The chanson rustique: popular elements in the 15th- and 16th-century chanson', *JAMS* 12 (1959), 16–26; Brown, *French Secular Theater*, 105–13; Brown ed., *Florentine Chansonnier*, vol. 1, ch. IX.

[243] Maria R. Maniates, 'Combinative chansons in the Dijon Chansonnier', *JAMS* 23 (1970), 228–81; idem, 'Combinative chansons in the Escorial Chansonnier', *JAMS* 29 (1975), 61–125. An early quodlibet quoting Dufay's 'Par le regard' is reconstructed in Jaap van Benthem, 'Ein verstecktes Quodlibet des 15. Jahrhunderts in Fragmenter 17/I der Kongelige Bibliothek zu Kopenhagen',

complex and witty pieces sometimes incorporated genuine folksongs (this is true also for their Italian and German counterparts, the *incatenature* and quod-libets), and they provided their authors and performers with outlets for irreverent or erotic feelings. One of the eight combinative chansons by Busnois, 'Vous marchez du bout du pied, Marionette', seems to string together two or three texts with the music of one tune, and has no overlying text in any of the *formes fixes*.[244] Like 'Petite camusette', it has the layout 'ABA', and it also starts with a 'wrong entry' in the tenor. Marching and riding, mentioned in the text and heard in the music, are perhaps to be taken as erotic symbols. A related piece is the anonymous 'Puisqu'aultrement / Marchons la dureau' in the Dijon Chansonnier (*F-Dm 517*), fol. 168v and later sources. It incorporates a real marching song, well known at the time and also used as a dance-tune.[245]

Not all combinative chansons are funny or obscene, nor are all popular chansons combinative. One of the two extant secular songs by Johannes Regis, 'Puisque ma damme / Je m'en voy' in the Mellon Chansonnier, combines two courtly themes. Comical contrasts, where intended (for example between lofty and lowly expressions), were achieved in many different ways, and some of the jokes are now lost on us. An anonymous piece in the Seville Chansonnier (*E-Sco 5-1-43*) fol. 15v has apparently a nonsense text: 'La parente Nostre Dame, la parente Dominus'. The simple tune, in largely syllabic declamation, wanders in repetitions through all the four voices. Of these repetitions, the opening and closing statements are in duple metre, the middle ones in a triple proportion.

That most of these pieces are in four parts seems to accord with the presence of two different texts. Three-part settings apparently arose a little later. An example is the anonymous 'Orsus, orsus' in the Pavia Chansonnier (after 1470), which has only one text given to the tenor, plus untexted outer voices above and below. Technically speaking, then, the chanson is a *Tenorlied*.[246] Example 70 gives the tenor.

Two famous and enigmatic pieces belong in the context of these popularizing traditions: 'Il sera pour vous / L'homme armé' which is probably by Robert Morton (see also p. 470), and Ockeghem's 'L'autre dantan'. 'Il sera pour vous' is a combinative chanson which exists in a three-part and a four-part version,

---

TVNM 24 (1984), 1–11. For a manuscript with combinative and popular songs in French, Flemish and Italian, see Nanie Bridgman, 'Paroles et musique dans le manuscrit latin 16664 de la Bibliothèque Nationale de Paris', in Günther–Finscher eds, *Musik und Text*, 383–409.

[244] Printed in *DTOe VII*, vols. 14–15, 236. A copy in a late Austrian source is erroneously attributed to Isaac.

[245] Albert Vander Linden, 'La musique dans le Chroniques de Jean Molinet', in *Mélanges Ernest Closson*, ed. C. van den Borren (Brussels, 1948), 176 f; Crane, *Materials*, 95 f and 112. The piece is printed in Maria R. Maniates, 'Mannerist composition in Franco-Flemish polyphony', *MQ* 52 (1966), 17–36.

[246] See *RMF* vol. 16, fol. 67r. The tenor appears in almost identical form in the monophonic chansonnier *F-Pn fr. 9346*. Johannes Martini wrote a parody Mass over the Pavia setting; see also Burkholder, 'Johannes Martini', 482–4.

Example 70 Tenor 'Orsus, orsus', *Pavia 362* fol. 66

Or - sus, or - sus, de per - sus tous les aul -
- tres be - noît soit le cou - cu, qua - ron - ques tiel oy - seau ne fut. Je -
- mi, je - not, e - stu point Ma - ri - e? Ou - y, beau si -
- re, que dieux en ait bon gré. A u - ne fil - le qui d'a - mours m'a
ple. Ja - ni, ja - not, e - stu point Ma - ri - e?

the latter of which is attributed to 'Borton'. The piece uses the traditional, monophonic 'L'homme armé' song (see p. 466) as tenor, against a newly written rondeau text in honour of 'Maistre Symon le Breton', a Burgundian chaplain, as a conqueror of the Turks. Various interpretations of this amusing text have been attempted. According to David Fallows, it was a farewell for le Breton's retirement from the court in 1464.[247] The musical idea of this combinative setting is the tension between the simple ABA form of the borrowed tune, and the rondeau. The borrowed tune imposes its quick triple metre and its old-fashioned rhythmic–melodic style on the newly composed voices.

Ockeghem's rondeau 'L'autre dantan' is related to this style, although it is not a combinative chanson.[248] The clever text about the failure of a love affair is couched in mostly military terms. It also mentions dance: the music is like an old-fashioned dance-song. In this sense, it is a 'mock *chanson rustique*'.

---

[247] Fallows, *Robert Morton's Songs*, 202–33; opposing views are expressed in Lockwood, 'Aspects'; Perkins–Garey eds, *Mellon Chansonnier*, no. 34; Taruskin, 'Antoine Busnoys'.

[248] See especially Perkins–Garey eds, *Mellon Chansonnier*, no. 20, with a discussion of Tinctoris's criticism of the proportion sign which implies a fast performance tempo. In one Italian manuscript, the song is labelled 'La trentana' – a distortion of the first text words – which in Renaissance Italy was the type of title given to instrumental pieces. This would seem to carry out some of its stylistic implications.

Even in 'folksong', rhythmic preferences can change with the generations. Marching duple metres came to dominate French popular tunes at this time, although they did not entirely oust the triple metre. Some tunes in this more old-fashioned metre still appear in the sources, whether as survivors from older repertories or because they were needed for round dances, or both. (Round dances were themselves an older fashion.) A lovely song in genuine triple metre, probably a dance-song, is 'Au chant de l'alouette', hitherto only known as the cantus firmus of an anonymous Mass in the codex *SP*.

A dance-song in triple (or 6/8) rhythm is 'Filles a marier', also known as a *basse danse*. (Binchois used only its text, not its melody, for his combinative chanson.) A four-part canonic setting of it, dating from the 1460s, is written in a fast triple proportion.[249]

Since we have no certain details relating to Caron's life, we might give his music the benefit of the doubt and assume that he did not have all the major Busnois songs before him when composing his. In this case, Caron would emerge as a major chanson composer.[250] Several of his songs had the usual 'successful career' with many copies and derivative settings, for example the rondeaux 'Accueilly m'a la belle', 'Cent mille escus', 'Helas, que pourra devenir' and 'Le despourveu infortuné'. Other significant pieces are the four-part combinative chanson 'Corps contre corps', where the two lowest voices have two different popular tunes, with many repeated staccato notes; the rondeau cinquain 'Pour regard doeul';[251] the tiny but expressive *rondeau layé* 'Morir me fault' which owes much to Binchois; and the flowing, widely arched 'Mort ou merchy'. Whether writing canonically or not, Caron often fragments his subjects into small splinters. Since he also likes stretto canons and small triadic motives, his imitative passages tend to become thickets of reverberating chords. This effect is often counteracted by very irregular phrase-lengths, and by vast divergences in average note-values from phrase to phrase. The excessive patterning of 'Helas que pourra' must have been famous – it is indeed a prototype for 'typically instrumental' sections of later Mass music – but it dominates only the middle phrases of the rondeau; see Example 71.

One of the earliest songs by Busnois is, according to the source transmission, the *rondeau layé* 'Quand ce viendra au droit destraindre'. (A competing attribution to Ockeghem can be read as a compliment to the younger master.[252]) This amazing composition borrows, as it were, the melodic–rhythmic vocabulary of late Binchois, Frye or Morton and organizes it twice as tightly. From line 3 onwards ('et mon cuer feindre'), there is a strict canon between cantus and tenor, five bars later to be superseded by free imitation between all three voices. In the

---

[249] See Plamenac, 'A reconstruction', mus. ex. no. 2. Also ex. no. 3 is a combinative song using fast triple metre (a proportion).

[250] This is approximately the opinion expressed in Montagna, 'Caron, Hayne, Compère', 117–29. The songs are edited in Caron, *Oeuvres complètes*, vol. 2.

[251] Incorrectly transcribed as a bergerette in Caron, *Oeuvres complètes*.

[252] Perkins–Garey eds, *Mellon Chansonnier*, no. 16.

Example 71 Firminus(?) Caron, 'Helas, que pourra devenir'

second half, free imitation comes first but then turns into a strict canon which works with almost the same motives as in the first half. Both canons are at the octave and at two semibreves' distance, conflicting with the perfect tempus.

The voice-ranges are radically separated; there are no structural fourths, although tenor and contratenor cross once. The latter voice often emphasizes just the first and fifth degrees of the mode (Dorian on G) in bass-like fashion. One manuscript source contains a second contratenor which was added to fill the space between cantus and tenor. It is so skilful and motivically so consistent with the other voices that Busnois himself might be its author.

Canonic or pervasive imitation seems to come naturally to Busnois; but he does not always use it in a declamatory fashion to pinpoint new text lines (as in 'et mon cueur feindre'). The bergerette 'A une damme j'ay fait veu' has declamatory imitations or canons between cantus and tenor, three in the first half and one in the second. Unlike 'Quand ce viendra', the piece is in imperfect tempus, and the distances of canonic entry (in semibreves) change in the following way: 4–2–3–2. The texture is very similar to that of 'Quand ce viendra' but is higher, beautifully balancing its sonorities in the second mode.

A paradigmatic problem is posed by a group of Busnois songs which are dedicated to, or have texts written by, a certain Jacqueline d'Hacqueville, whose name is present in acrostics, anagrams or cryptograms.[253] Jacqueline's identity is not established beyond all doubt, but she certainly was a member of high society in Paris. The texts of the songs do imply that she sent her own 'woman's poems' to Busnois who then set them, or that she received his songs like musical 'love letters'. The rondeau 'Ha que vile', with the most obvious allusion to her name, is an outburst of reproach, however. Critical or adverse sentiments are not necessarily concealed in poetic–musical exchanges at the time: a kind of social game developed around the so-called 'rondels de refus' which present imagined debates between lady and lover. A Burgundian group of such chansons (the 'Nos amis' family) involves Robert Morton, Adrien Basin and possibly Duke Charles the Bold himself.[254] During his Burgundian period, Busnois exchanged poems with Jean Molinet, the court poet and chronicler, who also set one of his poems himself ('Tart ara mon cuer').[255] I suggest that some of the numerous derivative songs – re-settings of the same text, but more often textually or musically related or opposed settings – originated in 'correspondences' or 'debates' between their authors. They may have to be distinguished from more openly satirical 'anti-chansons' such as 'Le serviteur infortuné' in the chansonnier *EscB* (no. 20) which quotes Dufay's 'Le serviteur hault guerdonné',

---

[253] They are 'A vous sans autre me viens rendre', 'Ha que vile et abominable', 'Ja que lui ne si attende', 'Je ne puis vivre ainsi toujours', and 'Pour les biens qu'en vous je parçoy'. Perhaps, her colours (blue and white) are those mentioned in 'A une damme'. See Leeman L. Perkins, 'Antoine Busnois and the d'Hacqueville connection', in Winn ed., *Musique naturelle*, 49–64; Higgins, *Busnois*, 161–212 (with much new material).

[254] See Strohm, 'Missa super "Nos amis"'.

[255] Molinet, *Faictz et Dictz*, vol. 2, 795 ff.

or indeed the rondeau 'O infame desloyauté' in Dijon (fol. 151v) which begins exactly like Bedyngham's 'O rosa bella'!

A *bergerette layée* which Busnois dedicated to Jacqueline, 'Je ne puis vivre ainsi toujours', has been singled out by Gustave Reese for its 'altogether extraordinary beauty'.[256] It must have sounded more strange to contemporary listeners than to us, because its harmony is very close to our C major – although flats dramatically intrude into the end of the second half. The piece is superbly constructed. Busnois derives canons, sequential patterns and almost invertible counterpoint from the harmonic concept of piled-up thirds and their octave displacements. One of the canonic voices (cantus and tenor) is almost invariably accompanied in parallel thirds, sixths or tenths by the contratenor; when and how, seems unpredictable. A rising sequential pattern in the first half leads to a climax when all three voices move rapidly in contrary motions through the C major octave, surprisingly ending on the tripled tonic degree, to the words: 'Amours jusqu'a la mort'.

The first phrase of 'Je ne puis vivre' is in strict imitation between cantus and contratenor, while the tenor is silent for the whole first line of text. This chanson could not therefore be well performed without the contratenor, although that would be grammatically possible. (There are no structural fourths between cantus and tenor requiring its presence.) The song has the tenor in cantus position – but whereas in the first half the two high voices are intertwined in a symbolic love duet, in the second the tenor remains in a slightly lower register, and almost consistently below the cantus. This is surely another symbol, because here the poet humbly addresses his plea to the 'Noble femme de nom et d'armes'.

The rondeau 'Pour entretenir mes amours' explicitly uses invertible counterpoint; it begins with a contratenor solo against a countersubject written into the same staff in two of the sources.[257] The countersubject is then passed to the contratenor while the tenor enters with the subject.

Imitative techniques occasionally led Busnois to abolish the hierarchy of the voices in the three-part chanson. In 'Bel acueil' and 'A vous sans aultre', all three imitative voices are in the same range and exchange their scale-degrees at cadences, so that the tenor repeatedly finishes a fourth below another voice. This had happened in Ockeghem's 'Petite camusette' (see above); other examples in this generation seem to be extremely rare.

A chronology of the chansons of Busnois is a task for the future. The pieces not present in the earliest sources (the Nivelle and perhaps Wolfenbüttel chansonniers, and *Tr 88* and *89*) could all have been written *c.*1470 and later, and would thus include the three last-mentioned, canonic pieces. 'Bel acueil le ser-

---

[256] Reese, *Renaissance*, 104. Printed in Perkins–Garey eds, *Mellon Chansonnier*, no. 12. See also the discussion in Higgins, *Busnois*, 42 ff.

[257] Perkins–Garey eds, *Mellon Chansonnier*, no. 15. On this and other Busnois songs, see also Catherine Brooks, 'Antoine Busnois, chanson composer', *JAMS* 6 (1953), 111–35.

gant d'amours' opens the Mellon Chansonnier, which was compiled *c*.1475 under the supervision of Tinctoris as a wedding gift for the Neapolitan princess Beatrice of Aragon.[258] About ten chansons appear only in sources which are even later than this, but the pieces themselves could all be earlier. They include the four-part 'Je ne demande autre degré', which for its rich harmony, racy passage-work and ever-changing textures could pass as a work of the next generation. But a relatively early source has recently been discovered,[259] and the restriction to cantus–tenor canons may point to an early stylistic phase. This song was often copied, arranged and cited at the time, and its popularity may have been connected with a feature pinpointed as a fault by our 'Beckmesser', Johannes Tinctoris: the liberal use of the tritone *e–bb*, even for the duration of a whole breve.[260] These tritone sonorities in the F mode give a persistent feeling of a harmonic dominant, and contemporaries were undoubtedly attracted to this sound. The ¢ metre requires a fast tempo here; declamatory phrase-openings in long notes contrast with running countersubjects. This combination points very much to Obrecht, who learned the technique from Busnois, and indeed composed a Mass over 'Je ne demande'.

In the four-part chansons, Busnois maintains the hierarchic order of the voices, despite his experiments in three-part writing mentioned above. The emergence in secular music of a genuine bass function, and of harmonic four-part writing, will occupy us later (p. 562). One particular tradition of the late fifteenth century, the reworking of three-part chansons into four-part pieces, was by definition not the direct way towards a bass-orientated four-part harmony: the predominance of the cantus–tenor duet was already part of the given structure. When Ockeghem arranged Johannes Cornago's 'Qu'es mi vida, preguntays' for four voices, he changed the existing contratenor and added another below, but did not touch the cantus–tenor duet.[261] Neither did he change the primary duet when rearranging the whole texture of his four-part chanson 'Je n'ay dueil'.[262] In the chansons of this generation we look more or less in vain for the contrapuntal revolution which, in the Mass, had already taken place with 'Caput'. Nevertheless, some interesting experiments were made, and the number of beautiful-sounding, harmonically conceived four-part pieces was steadily increasing. One of them, which seems to take the late work of Dufay as its point of departure, is the intensely poetic 'Ou lit des pleurs' in the Mellon Chansonnier. Anonymous, but surely written by a master, this melancholic *rondeau layé* indulges in all the full triads along the Dorian C minor scale, plus the tonic and dominant major triads. A 'tierce de picardie' briefly lightens the final chord.[263]

258 Perkins–Garey eds, *Mellon Chansonnier*, vol. 1, 17–26; Benthem, 'Concerning Johannes Tinctoris'; Higgins, *Busnois*, 199.
259 See Fallows, 'Johannes Ockeghem'.
260 Tinctoris, *Opera theoretica*, vol. II, 144.
261 See Pope–Kanazawa eds, *Manuscript Montecassino*, nos. 10 and 103.
262 An excellent analysis of this reworking is Litterick, 'Revision'.
263 Perkins–Garey eds, *Mellon Chansonnier*, no. 48.

Secular polyphonic song in western Europe was not confined to the French language. There are English-texted pieces which play an important role in the continental development (as, for example, Walter Frye's 'Alas, alas') – and there is, of course, the tradition of Dutch–Flemish song. Polyphonic settings began well before 1400 in Flanders and at the Netherlands courts (see pp. 69 f); they are rare in the early fifteenth century. The 1450s brought a revival of Dutch polyphonic song: we have two pieces by Pullois and several anonymous ones in a number of sources. The rondeau-refrain 'Ein vrouleen edel von natueren' survives with Germanized text in the Lochamer-Liederbuch of Nuremberg, *c*.1455 (see p. 493). It could pass for a piece in the later manner of Binchois or perhaps Gilles Joye.[264] Only the Josquin generation, however, witnessed a full-scale revival of song composing in this language. Jacob Obrecht alone left nineteen songs with Flemish texts, Johannes Ghiselin-Verbonnet and Matthaeus Pipelare four each, Alexander Agricola contributed 'Mijn alderliefste moesekin' and a particularly successful arrangement of 'In mynen sin' (another is by Busnois). From Japart (or Obrecht), we have 'Tmeiskin was jonck', by Barbireau 'Een vrolic wesen' – other contemporary 'hits' which were also used as Mass tenors.

Many of these pieces are either arrangements of folk-tunes (*chansons rustiques*) or they have newly written texts, but not in the usual *formes fixes*, so it is not always easy to know whether the words are supposed to be sung at all, or whether the piece is intended for instruments. The many settings of the folk-tune 'T'Andernaken op den Rijn', for example, are probably intended for instruments. In the case of Obrecht, it so happens that most of his Flemish songs are collected in the Spanish Segovia Choirbook (see p. 606), whose copyists were unable to transmit more than incipits. The pieces themselves, mostly for four voices, are rich in sound and invention, and often in two large sections of which the second can be in a contrasting metre.[265] Characteristic for them (although not present in all of them) is a homorhythmic, strongly 'harmonic' idiom, with 'V–I' cadences in the low contratenor. If pre-existing tunes can be identified, then they are in the tenor in augmented note-values. It is very likely that these songs were written for civic wind bands, and played for entertainment in public places.

Mass and motet from c.1465 to c.1480

There is reason to call these years the 'late Burgundian age'. The death of Duke Charles the Bold on the battlefield of Nancy in 1477, and his daughter Mary's premature death in 1482 after a riding accident, dealt final blows to a

---

[264] Salmen–Petzsch eds, *Lochamer-Liederbuch*, no. 18.
[265] Bibliography in Picker, *Ockeghem and Obrecht*, 81 ff. Ten songs are edited in Smijers ed., *Van Ockeghem tot Sweelinck*, fasc. 3, nos. 16–25. Generally on Dutch / Flemish songs, see the introduction of René Bernard Lenaerts, *Het Nederlands polifonies lied in de zestiende eeuw* (Amsterdam, 1933).

fascinating culture: an 'autumn of the Middle Ages' (Johan Huizinga). It seems, however, that drama and achievement did not entirely coincide. Burgundian culture was neither unified nor unique. In many respects, it was simply eclectic, derivative and hardly distinguishable from that of royal France. In other respects, it was not actually a product of the court but of the cities, churches and schools of the ducal territories, especially in the Low Countries. The splendidly illuminated manuscripts of the famous Bibliothèque de Bourgogne, which fortunately have survived to capture our imagination, are an example. The duke cherished his books, and hired his illuminators from many parts of France and the Low Countries; this was a Valois family tradition.[266] The contents of these codices are largely chivalric romances and French translations of standard medieval prose: they are hardly great literature. Major developments in the fine arts and architecture bypassed the court of Charles the Bold – sometimes by a near miss. It is mainly the enormous attention given to heraldry and etiquette at court which has impressed the image of the Burgundian world so firmly into the European memory. The Habsburg, Sforza, Aragon, Saxon dynasties, and even England under Edward IV, imitated Burgundian courtly manners – preserving what could be called a shadow of the medieval feudal tradition.

The Valois had a lucky hand with musicians, however. If the rest of Burgundian civilization was largely flamboyant decoration, its music belonged to a younger, much more vigorous current. For this current no name has yet been found. It was civic and courtly, intellectual and popular; it was French and Netherlandish in origin but European in effect.[267]

What was its most characteristic musical expression? If only a single work were admitted to represent it, my choice would be the 'L'homme armé' Mass by Antoine Busnois.[268] The rational irregularity of its melodic–rhythmic surface and the disguised constructivism of its cantus firmus scaffolding evoke comparison with Flemish painting and architecture of the time, but also represent the high level of an art which Tinctoris could compare with that of Homer or Vergil.[269]

At the beginning of the Agnus Dei (see Ex. 72), the two-voice motto (bars 1–3) is followed by increasingly intricate and imitative patterning, which reaches a stretto canon in bar 10. Here, the entry distance of one minim (crotchet

---

[266] Music manuscripts are cited in the interesting catalogues by Jean Barrois, *Protypographie, ou librairies des fils du Roi Jean* (Paris, 1830); Gabriel Peignot, *Catalogue d'une partie des livres composant la bibliothèque des ducs de Bourgogne au XVe siècle* (Dijon, 1841); Pierre Champion, *La Librairie de Charles d'Orléans* (Paris, 1910). See also Wright, *Burgundy*, 139–60.

[267] I accept the view of Henry Leland Clarke, 'Musicians of the northern Renaissance', in LaRue ed., *Aspects of Medieval and Renaissance Music*, 67–81 – but I object to the term 'Renaissance' in this context: see p. 542 below. An overview of Franco-Burgundian courtly music (excerpted from French historiographers) is Dahnk, 'Musikausübung'. Stylistic considerations are offered in Sparks, *Cantus firmus*, chaps. 6–8.

[268] Printed in Feininger ed., *MPLSER*, ser. I, tom. I, 2.

[269] Tinctoris, *Opera theoretica*, vol. II, 12 f.

Example 72 Antoine Busnois, 'Missa L'homme armé': Agnus Dei

Example 72 (*cont.*)

in transcription) and the length of the sequential motive of four minims are both in conflict with the underlying metre. Thus, tension is created and the cantus firmus entry is dramatized. When it appears in the tenor in bar 14, it proves to be the 'L'homme armé' tune in inversion: from its initial *g*, the tune falls rather than rises a fourth. In the previous Mass sections, the tune had retained its original contour, but had been augmented proportionally in the Gloria and Credo, and also transposed down a fourth in the Credo. Both transposition and strict proportional transformation had been techniques of Ockeghem's and Dufay's earlier Masses. Through the inversion in the Agnus Dei, the tenor becomes the lowest voice, stretching a major ninth downward from *g*, whereas the transposition to the lower fourth had only produced the range *d–e'*. Also, the cantus firmus is sounded in double augmentation in the first Agnus Dei, in quadruple augmentation in the third, where it becomes a mighty series of pedal points. The inversion prevents regular cadential approaches, because the melody now rises to its final. But it is exactly this that leads to grandiose effects, for example in the cantus firmus ascent to *g* in bars 16–17 and 21–2, where it is accompanied a tenth above by the cantus. At the end of the Mass, the harmonies are strongly on the flat side, and the tenor ascent *d–eb–f–g* turns the bright, trumpeting tune into a severe and gloomy *Memento*. Busnois, who liked Latin and Greek terms such as 'barycanor' for 'contratenor bassus', explains the inversion in a Latin 'canon': 'Where sceptres are next to a fall, there is a rise, and vice versa'. The notion of 'sceptres' (i.e. note symbols?) must have an extra-musical meaning, most probably that of the rise and fall of the mighty, and of the wheel of Fortune.

The 'L'homme armé' tune was a monophonic *chanson rustique*, or rather an artistic imitation of it, in the tradition of medieval narrative song genres:

465

Example 73 'L'homme armé' *I-Nn VI. E. 40*, fol. 58v

The motive of the falling fifth, which interrupts the song phrases, quotes an alarm signal sounded on a trumpet or horn. The connection between trumpet signalling and the sighting of 'men-at-arms' is documented: the 'L'homme armé' song is a realistic reference to warfare.[270] It originated in an urban, northern, French-speaking environment in the early fifteenth century: this is suggested by the notation in *prolatio major* in all the sources, and by the melodic-rhythmic similarity with some convivial songs from northern sources (see the combinative song 'Hu, hula hu! / Au debot de no rue', Ex. 7); even a *Maison de l'homme armé* at Cambrai can be quoted.[271] The song exists mostly in polyphonic adaptations; there are Masses and chansons, the latter including Morton's humorous version (see above) and a quodlibet cited and perhaps invented by Tinctoris (see p. 544).

The 'L'homme armé' Masses form what is perhaps the most famous musical tradition of this age and they have often been discussed.[272] The earliest datable specimens are: a 'messe sus l'ome arme' by Johannes Regis, copied into Cambrai choirbooks in 1462–3, and the Mass by 'F. Caron' in the codex *SP*, extant no later than 1463.[273] Interestingly, Tinctoris says that Busnois and Regis, in their

---

[270] See Strohm, *Bruges*, 129 f; Brenet, *Musique et Musiciens*, 6.

[271] Wright, 'Dufay at Cambrai', 210 f.

[272] See Lockwood, 'Aspects'; Planchart, 'Fifteenth-century Masses', 5–11; Leeman L. Perkins, 'The "L'homme armé" Masses of Busnois and Ockeghem: a comparison', *JM* 3 (1984), 363–96; Taruskin, 'Antoine Busnoys' (with ensuing discussion). A list of the chanson adaptations is in Fallows, *Robert Morton's Songs*, 238 f. On mode and motive in Dufay's 'L'homme armé' cycle, see Leo Treitler, 'Dufay the progressive', in Atlas ed., *Dufay Quincentenary Conference*, 115–27.

[273] See, respectively: Houdoy, *Histoire artistique*, 84 (Regis's Mass is probably lost: see p. 469 below); Caron, *Oeuvres complètes*, vol. 2, and Feininger ed., *MPLSER*, ser. I, tom. I, 3 (date established by Reynolds, 'Origins').

'L'homme armé' Masses, had followed Domarto in the inappropriate use of the sign O2 (perfect minor mode, '3/2').[274] As said above (p. 420), he also criticizes Busnois in his 'L'homme armé', with Ockeghem and many other musicians including Regis, for their incorrect use of ₵ to produce augmentation, after the model of Domarto's 'Spiritus almus'.

The 'L'homme armé' Masses tend to share strict transformation techniques. (Other famous cantus firmi, such as 'Le serviteur', had always been treated freely.) To some extent, this is a consequence of the quasi-crystalline structure of the tune. But strict transformation may also have become a habit in courtly Masses, inspired by cycles such as 'Spiritus almus' and 'Se la face'. Ockeghem's 'L'homme armé' was copied in Bruges in 1467–8, that of Dufay in the Lucca Choirbook (also in Bruges) c.1469–70. It is tempting to speculate that both works originated for the Burgundian court – where, as we remember, Morton's song setting was already known – and specifically for the Bruges festival of the Golden Fleece in May 1468. This was the first major meeting of the Order held under Charles the Bold as duke, and a prelude not so much to his wedding in July 1468 as to his reckless military campaigns of the following years. The knightly order could indeed see itself and its prince represented in the figure of the 'armed man'. It was no hindrance that the song had a more complex origin – civic rather than courtly – and that it may have had satirical or ironic connotations. The eclectic culture of this court was wont to appropriate but not quite integrate traditional ideas.

Antoine Busnois, the French-trained composer 'appropriated' by Charles the Bold, represents the combined Franco-Netherlands tradition. Whatever the destination of the 'L'homme armé' Masses by Regis, Caron, Dufay and Ockeghem, the work of Busnois very probably originated for a Burgundian ceremony. Dufay's and Ockeghem's are its obvious models. Ockeghem's 'L'homme armé' has the strictest type of cantus firmus treatment in all his works except 'Caput', but he uses only two types of transformation: augmentation by prescribing ₵ (in all the sections), and transposition. The cantus firmus is lowered by a fifth in the Credo and by an octave in the Agnus, where it reaches low *G*. This is the point of departure for Busnois, who with his inversion in the Agnus Dei reaches low *F*. Dufay has double and triple augmentations, but also other types of transformation such as the excision of all rests and the halving of all note-values. In Dufay's third Agnus, the tune is sung in retrograde and then once more 'forward' but in halved values (according to the witty canon: 'The crab goes forward whole but returns half'). Busnois answers Dufay's manipulations with fourfold (i.e. greater) augmentation in the last Agnus Dei, together with seemingly irrational variations not of the tune but of the rests between the phrases. As for augmentation, by prescribing ₵ he has that too, in addition to all the other techniques.

---

[274] *Opera theoretica*, vol. IIa, 55: 'non obstantibus Busnois et Regis in *Missis L'homme armé* et per omnia sequentibus illum excusari non poterit': '(Domarto) will not be able to be excused for this, notwithstanding Busnois and Regis, who in their Masses "L'homme armé" follow him in everything'.

467

It is more difficult to say how the 'L'homme armé' Masses of Dufay and Ockeghem relate to one another, but in an artistic constellation like this Ockeghem would hardly have written his relatively simple work if he had known Dufay's versatile showpiece. Whatever the date and destination of Ockeghem's cycle, the other two seem to me to have been composed after *c*.1465.

A Burgundian document of the 'L'homme armé' tradition is a splendid manuscript at Naples of six related Masses over the tune. The codex (*I-Nn VI. E. 40*) was presented, according to a dedicatory poem, to Beatrice of Aragon, the Neapolitan princess who in 1476 married King Mathias Corvinus of Hungary. Its previous user, and surely also its previous owner, is identified in the same poem as Charles the Bold.[275] The manuscript must have been compiled for him as a glorification of the courtly 'L'homme armé' cult. The song is written down monophonically at the beginning of the codex like a motto, and the six Masses then manipulate, segment and strictly transform it in all possible ways, which are explained by cryptic-symbolic instructions in Latin hexameters. This anonymous 'cycle of six Masses', a feudalistic and humanistic 'super-set', originated perhaps for the Order of the Golden Fleece: its statutory number of members, then 31, seems to be built into the numerical structure of at least one of the Masses (no. III). This might provide an argument to tie the works to Busnois, for we may look favourably on the suggestion that his 'L'homme armé' Mass alludes to the number 31.[276] On the basis of style, Caron has also been proposed as the author of the Neapolitan Masses.[277] Although his 'L'homme armé' Mass, with its free variations, is a far cry from the strict techniques of the Neapolitan set, his Mass 'Jesus autem transiens' does contain them. However we do not know the purpose for which these two works were written, nor whether that may have influenced the style. Caron's other three Masses ('Clemens et benigna', 'Sanguis sanctorum' and 'Accueilly m'a la belle') resemble his 'L'homme armé'; if they were composed for the same institution it may well have been a cathedral.

Even more of a riddle is the Mass 'Dum sacrum mysterium' by Johannes Regis. This important composer lived most of his life, from at least 1451-2, as a succentor and then as a canon/schoolmaster at Soignies (Hainaut); he apparently kept in touch with Dufay and is said to have been his secretary. Certainly in 1460 he was offered the post of *magister puerorum* at Cambrai Cathedral, but it seems clear that he ultimately refused it.[278] His Mass 'Dum sacrum mysterium' quotes the text of an antiphon for St Michael, but combines it repeat-

---

[275] Cohen, *L'homme armé Masses*; Judith Cohen, 'Munus ab ignoto', *SM* 22 (1980), 187-204. The Masses are printed in Feininger ed., *MPLSER*, ser. I, tom. III, 1-6. See also Woodley, 'Tinctoris' Italian translation', 178-86.

[276] See Taruskin, 'Antoine Busnoys'. The Mass is otherwise built on multiples of three, but the 'Et incarnatus est' section reaches 31 longs before the last ligature (which is in the bass). The evidence is inconclusive.

[277] Don Giller, 'The Naples L'Homme Armé Masses and Caron: a study in musical relationships', *CMc* 32 (1981), 7-28; *idem*, Communication, *JAMS* 40 (1987), 144 f.

[278] For much more detail of his newly reconstructed biography, see Fallows, 'Life of Johannes Regis'.

edly, and in several voices, with the melody of 'L'homme armé'. This unusual
approach is not unique in Regis's work (see p. 484 on his motets) and suggests
here a quasi-mysterious presence of the warrior angel. The cantus firmus treatment is not strict, but the Gloria and Credo incorporate an identical stretto
canon of the tune on *a* and *d*, which points to a late stage in the tradition. The
harmonic effects are surprisingly modern, including the opening three-voice
gesture of all sections, which moves immediately to a fermata on the major
dominant:[279]

Example 74 Johannes Regis, Mass 'Dum sacrum mysterium'

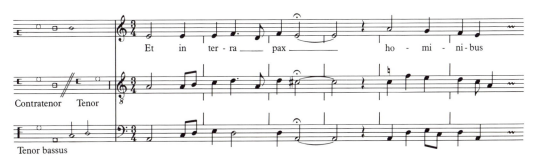

This work can hardly be the 'L'homme armé' Mass cited by Tinctoris, since
it contains neither the mensuration O2 as he says (see above), nor augmentation
of ₵ as he implies elsewhere. Regis must have composed a lost 'L'homme armé'
Mass with these features, and thus closer to the mainstream tradition. It was
probably the work copied in Cambrai in 1462–3.

The 'L'homme armé' Masses by Guillermus Faugues and Philippe Basiron
belong together, because the former was apparently the teacher of the latter at
the Sainte-Chapelle of Bourges.[280] Both works have strict canons of the tune as
has Regis. Faugues derives the contratenor altus by a stretto canon throughout
the work; Basiron's Mass (which was cited as new in Italy in 1484), adds a
number of transformations in the manner of Dufay.

An ambitious masterpiece is the 'L'homme armé' Mass (with trope 'Cuncto-
rum plasmator') by Johannes Tinctoris, in which all the artifices of the tradition
are put together: canons, transpositions, augmentations (correctly notated, of
course) and also the performance of extraneous plainsong texts as in Regis. In a
word, Tinctoris tries to carry out as a composer what he advocates as a theorist:
variety (see below). Tinctoris seems to have left France for the court of Naples
about 1472–3 and it is interesting that King Ferrante of Naples, having become

---

[279] See also p. 419 above. Printed in Regis, *Opera omnia*, vol. 1, and Feininger ed., *MPLSER*, ser. I,
tom. I, 5. All Mass sections must have a *c♯'* under the fermata.

[280] Higgins, 'Tracing the careers', 14. Printed in Feininger ed., *MPLSER*, ser. I, tom. I, 4 and 8.
See also Faugues, *Collected Works*.

a member of the Order of the Golden Fleece in 1473–5, commissioned from him an Italian translation of the statutes of the Order. The Mass may have originated in that context.[281]

An often-quoted contribution by Oliver Strunk of 1937 seemed to establish that the origin of the 'L'homme armé' settings was connected with Busnois' Mass. The 'Cum sancto spiritu' (or 'Tu solus dominus') section, Strunk argued, is so similar to Morton's combinative chanson 'Il sera pour vous' (see above) that they must have a common model or one must be derived from the other. This constellation seemed to justify the statement of the sixteenth-century theorist Pietro Aaron that Busnois was the 'inventor' of the tune. Here we are dealing with an error of translation, however. Aaron really says: 'it is believed that by Busnois was found that song called "the armed man", notated with the dotted sign [ⓒ] and that by him was taken the tenor', i.e. Busnois found the 'L'homme armé' song and took it as tenor.[282] David Fallows has shown that Aaron cannot have referred to 'Il sera pour vous' (i.e., there is no testimony for its being by Busnois rather than Morton). He argued that the similarities between 'Il sera pour vous' and the Mass section result from contrapuntal necessity rather than explicit borrowing, and that the earlier three-part version of the song is much less similar to the 'Cum sancto spiritu' than the later four-part version. According to this view, Morton reflected Busnois in the four-part reworking of his song only. In my opinion, there is not sufficient evidence that either Morton or Busnois was the original author of the 'L'homme armé' song, or that Busnois began the Mass tradition.[283]

The 'Cum sancto spiritu' of Busnois' Mass is remarkable, however, in that it quotes the old song literally, and performs its original note-values at something like their original, faster speed, prescribed by the proportional sign C3 (*sesquialtera*). It is the only such section in the Mass, distinguished by its literalness from the transformations like a theme from its variations. (The other sections use ₵ meaning augmentation.) Sections like this 'Cum sancto spiritu' are an interesting tradition in the history of the *parody Mass*. We have already encountered one of the earliest examples: the anonymous Mass 'Esclave puist' from before *c*.1462, where in the Osanna II with the most literal tenor quotation the cantus of the model is also quoted (see p. 431). The same thing happens in the three-part cycle 'Nos amis', probably an early work by Tinctoris, in the

---

[281] Atlas, *Aragonese Court*, 72 f; Woodley, 'Johannes Tinctoris'; *idem*, 'Tinctoris' Italian translation'. The Mass is in Tinctoris, *Opera omnia*.

[282] Oliver Strunk, 'Origins of the *L'homme armé* tradition', *Bulletin of the AMS* 2 (1937), 25–6; Lockwood, 'Aspects', 98 n. 6: 'Si esistima, che da Busnois fussi trovato quel canto chiamato lome armé, notato con il segno puntato, & che da lui fussi tolto il tenore . . .' 'Trovato' is 'found', not 'composed': the perfect participles 'chiamato' and 'notato' suggest that the song already had a name and a mensuration when Busnois found it. If they had been invented by Busnois, Aaron would probably have written 'che chiamò lome armé e notò . . .'.

[283] Fallows, *Robert Morton's Songs*, 221–33. Aaron may imply that Busnois was the first to have *used* the tune in another work. Taruskin, 'Antoine Busnoys', accepts this. Higgins, *Busnois*, 18–21, uses the late testimony of Cerone (1613) to maintain that Busnois 'wrote' the tune – and that Ockeghem composed the first Mass on it. But Busnois' primacy rests, in Aaron, only on a belief ('si esistima') reported from hearsay. This belief was mistaken, I think. See also Strohm, *Bruges*, 129 f.

Agnus Dei.[284] It also happens in three 'strict transformation' Masses with Flemish-Burgundian connections: 'Pour quelque paine' by the Bruges composer Cornelius Heyns, and the cycles 'Quand ce viendra' over Busnois' chanson and 'Nos amis' over the rondeau by Adrien Basin. The last two Masses may well be by the composers of their respective chanson models.[285] Each of these four-part works has only one section without augmentation of the tenor (labelled 'ut jacet'), which is a genuine parody with respect to the other voices.

Parody was by no means restricted to this particular tradition, of course. Three cycles over Dufay's 'Le serviteur' are known today which all make use of more than one voice of the model, although not consistently.[286] A four-part cycle in *Tr 88* significantly expands the imitations inherent in the model and thus involves all the voices in the derivative process. It is attributed to Ockeghem, but is most probably by Guillaume Faugues.[287] Because of its unusual length, it may have been the anonymous Mass 'Le serviteur' copied at Cambrai in 1462–3 on no fewer than sixteen folios. Faugues was then active at Bourges, but apparently known to Ockeghem (see p. 440), who visited Cambrai in 1462.[288] The other two 'Le serviteur' Masses are in *Tr 88* and *Tr 89*, respectively; the last-named has definite parody sections quoting all three voices of the model (Kyrie II and 'Cum sancto spiritu'). These works apparently originated in French royal circles – hence perhaps the erroneous attribution of the Faugues work to Ockeghem – and are survivors of what must have been a rich, diversified cultivation of the chanson Mass. Two other Masses by Faugues ('Je suis en la mer' and 'La basse danse') are significant for their ever-varied approach to the secular models.

For Tinctoris, variety was the highest ideal of counterpoint, according to the precepts of Horace and Cicero. Musical works fulfilling such precepts were for him, in this order:

Dufay, Mass 'L'homme armé';
Faugues, Mass 'Vinnus vinna';
Regis, motet 'Clangat plebs';
Busnois, motet 'Congaudebant' and other motets;
Ockeghem, chanson 'Ma maistresse';
Caron, chanson 'La Tridaine a deux'.[289]

---

[284] See Strohm, 'Missa super "Nos amis"'; and Strohm, 'Meßzyklen'. The model, not identical with the rondeau by Adrien Basin, is also known with the German words 'Wunschliche schone'.

[285] Strohm, *Bruges*, 128 and 131. In 'Nos amis', the literal quotation is so reliable that the 'Cum sancto spiritu' section can be reconstructed from only two voices (p. 248 f). On 'Quand ce viendra', see also Gottlieb, *Masses*, 83–90. Prof. Richard Taruskin kindly informs me that he accepts Busnois' authorship as likely and will publish the Mass in the appendix of his Busnois edition.

[286] The first two are printed in *DTOe XIX/I*, vol. 38. The third is in *Tr 89*, nos. 606–10.

[287] According to an attributed quote in Tinctoris, *Opera theoretica*, vol. II, 143. See also Faugues, *Collected Works*, and George C. Schuetze jr., *An Introduction to Faugues* (Brooklyn: Institute of Mediaeval Music, 1960).

[288] Wright, 'Dufay at Cambrai', 208.

[289] *Liber de arte contrapuncti* (1477): see *Opera theoretica*, vol. II, 155 f. 'Congaudebant' and 'La Tridaine' (a setting of a popular tune?) seem to be lost.

It is therefore possible to be reasonably confident that the resourceful, long and varied Mass 'Vinnus vinna', copied anonymously in *CS 51*, is indeed by Faugues, although doubts have been raised.[290] Like the Masses securely attributed to Faugues, 'La basse danse' and 'L'homme armé', it uses a monophonic tune as tenor, expanding its impact over several voices by canons and imitations. 'Cantus firmus in more than one voice' is characteristic of this composer.

Masses over plainsong tenors were apparently becoming rarer after *c.*1465, although many must have been lost. Almost in a reversal of the state of affairs compared with 1460, free variation was now more frequent in plainsong Masses than in chanson-based Masses. However, a strict, conservative approach governs the second Mass with a secure attribution to Busnois, 'O crux lignum triumphale'.[291] The cantus firmus, a stanza from the Holy Cross sequence 'Laudes crucis attollamus', is subjected to proportional and mensural transformation, although not segmented or further manipulated as in 'L'homme armé'. The mensural scheme of the Mass is close to that of 'Spiritus almus' (see Table 3). The contrapuntal surface, on the other hand, is as richly embroidered as in any of Busnois' more complex works.

The strict tradition is also represented by the Mass 'Dixerunt discipuli' by Eloy, copied in *CS 14* and lauded by Tinctoris; this work uses the first seven notes of a St Martin antiphon as an ostinato and in strict transformations. The composer must be the musician–poet Eloy d'Amerval, known to have worked at Savoy in 1455-7 (under Dufay), at the court of Charles d'Orléans between 1464 and 1471 and later at the cathedral of Orléans, where Tinctoris presumably came to admire his 'learnedness in the mensural modes'.[292]

Three Masses on antiphons connected with the theme of the Annunciation form an individual complex: Dufay's 'Ecce ancilla Domini / Beata es Maria' (copied 1463-4), Regis's 'Ecce ancilla Domini / Ne timeas Maria' and Ockeghem's 'Ecce ancilla Domini'. Dufay presents his two cantus firmi in the tenor in an almost symmetrical manner, reminiscent of the double cursus of 'Caput'. The two plainsongs are melodically related (untransposed Mixolydian; but the final chords are all 'C major'). The chants are as little paraphrased as they can be, which is probably necessary since they are sung with their original antiphon texts.[293] Regis evidently knew and emulated Dufay's work, using not only his two plainsongs but adding five others, some of which are again melodically similar, especially 'Ne timeas Maria'. He complicates the modal character by leaving some chants on *g* but transposing others down to *c*, and prescribing

[290] Printed in Feininger ed., *MPLSER*, ser. I, tom. IV, 1. On the title, see Strohm, *Bruges*, 176 f n. 150.

[291] Edited by D. W. Shipley in *Das Chorwerk* 123 (Wolfenbüttel, 1977).

[292] His epic *Livre de la deablerie* (printed 1508) is famous for mentioning the names of nineteen composers, many of whom were active in French royal circles. See Reese, *Renaissance*, 263, and especially Higgins, *Busnois*, 262-9.

[293] The same is true for Dufay's last Mass, 'Ave regina celorum' and a number of other works: see Gareth R. K. Curtis, 'Brussels, Bibliothèque Royale, MS 5557, and the texting of Dufay's "Ecce ancilla domini" and "Ave regina celorum" Masses', *AcM* 51 (1979), 73-86; Planchart, 'Parts with words', 246 f.

b♭ for all the voices: instead of a Mass 'in C' with tenors on *g*, we now have a Mass with seemingly Dorian tenors on *g* and Mixolydian basses on *c*. Also, the symmetrical form is gone, and the seven cantus firmi appear unpredictably, sometimes simultaneously. During long stretches of the cycle, the tenor or both lower voices can be sung with both the Mass and antiphon texts. Ockeghem has only one cantus firmus, the second half of the antiphon 'Missus est Gabriel angelus', also a Mixolydian chant. He leaves the chant untransposed except in the Credo, where he transposes it down a fifth, adds a general flat signature and produces a Mixolydian on *c*. This is probably an early work by Ockeghem, and it was known to both Dufay and Regis when they composed their related Masses.

The liturgical place of these works has to be sought in a specific ceremony: the 'Golden Mass' or 'Missus Mass', usually celebrated on Wednesday of the Ember days in Advent. It was not only a Mass, for it included solemn readings of the gospel 'Missus est Gabriel angelus', often with dramatic recitations of the Annunciation dialogue between Mary and the Angel, as shown in countless altar paintings. The 'Missus Mass' was increasingly popular and was often endowed by citizens; polyphony for the occasion is documented from about the 1460s.[294] The plainsongs used by the three composers all have their places in the Advent cycle according to various northern French and Netherlands liturgies. The destination of Dufay's and Regis's Masses can perhaps be circumscribed more closely on the basis of a melodic variant in their cantus firmus 'Ecce ancilla Domini'. Both composers begin the melody with *g–c'*, whereas the current version omits the initial *g*. Although it has been suggested that Dufay's and Regis's version is unique and a compositional alteration, precisely this variant for 'Ecce ancilla Domini' is found in the gradual–antiphonal (*incipitarium*) of St Peter's, Lille.[295]

The remaining Masses by Jean Ockeghem may conclude this chapter. They are his most significant works and perhaps the most important of his whole generation, although they seem to run counter to the general historical development. In some ways Ockeghem stands apart from the great historical line Dufay–Busnois–Josquin/Obrecht, particularly for his different attitude to large-scale construction. His deep concern with mode, tonality, range, register and harmonic progressions, on the other hand, added important elements to the European tradition which Dufay had not systematically cultivated. Ockeghem's approaches are extremely varied, however, and cannot be easily generalized. Stylistically some of the Masses stand quite on their own (for example 'Au travail suis'). The master sets himself the greatest canonic and mensural difficulties but then conceals his tracks; he evades cadences, smooths out contrasts, enjoys contradictions and surprises. His melodies are often of an astounding

---

[294] See Strohm, *Bruges*, 52 f and no. 40 (with correction in revised edn).
[295] Lille, Bibl. Municipale, MS 26, fol. 49v and 50v. The 'Missus' ceremony was regularly celebrated at St Peter's during this time.

beauty, even in his most 'artificial' creations such as the Mass 'Cuiusvis toni'. Ockeghem is surely not a northern, 'gothic' mystic, as earlier writers have made out, but a French royal composer of the highest refinement and individuality.[296]

The 'Caput' Mass contains the germs of several techniques which recur in later works. The most important of them is transposition; Ockeghem uses it to open up tonal space or to separate modal character from range. The second most important is literal quotation of a model. Both techniques are found in the short four-part Mass on his own bergerette 'Ma maistresse' (see also p. 447), consisting only of a Kyrie which has the tenor of the model as its bass, rhythmically varied, and a Gloria which has the cantus of the model as its contratenor. There are occasional references to the cantus of the model in other voices. This kind of borrowing corresponds exactly to what happens in the two 'O rosa bella' Masses nos. I and II, respectively. In both of Ockeghem's sections, the given material is transposed down an octave. Also 'O rosa bella' no. II involves a downward transposition (by a fourth). These striking analogies could mean that 'Ma maistresse' was composed as a 'Missa brevis' to match or contradict the pair of Masses over 'O rosa bella'. The quotations of the chanson tenor are 'summed up', as it were, at the end of the Gloria with a brief quotation repeating only the first phrase (bars 124-31).

Brief concluding statements are also found in the Mass 'De plus en plus', the only one which is otherwise a conventional tenor Mass over a chanson model. It has neither transpositions nor literal quotations. In the tenor, Ockeghem gives florid paraphrases of Binchois' tenor, but emphasizes its incipit $g-b-c'-e'$ always in longer notes, and seems to observe the rhythmic proportions of Binchois' first line (4 + 2 + 1 units). There are also occasional quotations of other voices and in other voices. The Sanctus begins with what sounds like the incipit of 'O rosa bella' – but then turns out to be the second cantus phrase of 'De plus en plus'. (A brief but unmistakable quotation of 'O rosa bella' opens the Benedictus of Ockeghem's Mass 'L'homme armé'.) The Agnus Dei has a 'first' and 'second' ending. The second is for the Agnus III performed 'ut supra', but adding eighteen additional bars of 'Dona nobis pacem', on a brief statement of the complete tenor in faster note-values. The resulting scheme of the Agnus Dei, 'AB A ab', is similar to rondeau form.

While 'De plus en plus' and 'Ma maistresse' may belong to the early 1460s, another reminiscence of old songs, the Mass 'Au travail suis', could well be a decade younger. It is not a parody Mass but simply quotes at the beginnings of sections the famous contour of Barbingant's rondeau incipit: '1-3-2-5' (or sometimes '2-3-2-5'), partly combined with a rising '1-3-2-1-5' motive, also

---

[296] The older view, concentrated in the writings of Besseler and continued in those of Bukofzer and Sparks, makes him a mystic or at least 'irrationalist'. A good matter-of-fact description of the Masses is in Reese, *Renaissance*, 124–36. The edition by Plamenac (Ockeghem, *Collected Works*, vols. 1 and 2) has an instructive commentary. An attempt at presenting the Masses as thoroughly rational, arithmetically planned structures is Marianne Henze, *Studien zu den Messenkompositionen Johannes Ockeghems* (Berlin: Merseburger, 1968).

known from the popular chanson 'Adieu mes amours'. The Kyrie goes a little
further in its borrowings from the rondeau. The transposition of the motto in
the tenor down a fifth to *d* produces a regular second-mode layout. Since no
flat is added at the clef, the Mass is more correctly Dorian than the 'Aeolian'
chanson. Most of the work is dedicated to harmonic and gestural effects, some
of which are breathtaking, especially in fermata-held passages. A mensural
peculiarity (also found in the later 'Missa Quinti toni') is the presence of only
the duple metres C and ₵ in each section. This implies a tempo increase in the
second halves of sections, offset at first by longer note-values, but not at the end
where the motion speeds up dramatically.

Ockeghem's later Masses are all dedicated to technical devices and problems,
even where they rely on some borrowed material. The 'Missa Cuiusvis toni' is a
catholicon which can be performed on any of the four modal finals. It sounds
best in the Phrygian mode (*Deuterus*), because in order to work in that mode at
all, it regularly avoids 'V–I' cadences. The plagal cadence and the Phrygian
mode, however, are Ockeghem's favourites also in other works, and the beautiful, melancholic gestures of this particular modal language are found in his
chansons as well. Even superior to 'Cuiusvis toni' in melodic and harmonic
beauty are the 'Missa Mi-mi' and the 'Missa Quinti toni' for three voices. 'Mi-
mi', which is in the fourth mode, has convincingly been shown to be based on
the bergerette 'Presque transi' (see p. 452), although Ockeghem's manner of
utilizing the voices of the model is predictably unpredictable.[297] Often, approximations, inversions or retrogrades of the chanson's melodies are used. The texture is thick and fairly imitative, with some strict canonic writing. The main
motto is the repeated pitch *e–e* (or *e'–e'*), solmized as 'mi – mi'; this motto is
underpinned in most places by a falling fifth in the bass, *e–A*. The latter is not
only a succession of two pitches, but also a rhythmic gesture, characterized by
the anticipated low *A* – which makes the motive unusable in a 'V–I' cadence.
The cantus and tenor lines are partly taken from the beginning of the bergerette, partly (Gloria, Credo, Agnus Dei) from the second half, whose incipit
e–a–g–a–b–c' is almost a competing Leitmotiv of the work. The characteristic
melos of this and other lines reminds one of the *Te Deum*: the song that could
be called the 'ideal type' of Ockeghem's Phrygian melodies.[298]

'Mi-mi' was copied (under this name) at St Donatian's, Bruges, in 1475–6,
together with Ockeghem's isolated 'Patrem de village'.[299] The latter received
its name from the use of the plainsong Credo no. I, called 'de village' perhaps
because it belongs to ferial Masses.

The canonic 'Missa Prolationum', in the fifth mode, is probably of the same

---

[297] Haruyo Miyazaki, 'New light on Ockeghem's Missa Mi-mi', *Early Music* 13 (1985), 367–75.

[298] A strikingly similar use of it occurs in Wreede's 'Nunca fué pena mayor': see p. 578.

[299] Strohm, *Bruges*, 30. The composer is not mentioned but there can be little doubt that he is Ockeghem; the Mass 'Mi-mi' ('Petite camusette') by Marbriano de Orto is a later work. An entry in
the same archival document, formerly read as referring to Ockeghem's 'Missa Cuiusvis toni', in
reality cites an unidentifiable 'Missa 3. toni' (communication from Dr R. Wegman).

period or a little later, especially as it employs the largest range of all four-part Masses by Ockeghem: 22 notes. The Credo 'de village' and 'Cuiusvis toni' have 21, 'Mi-mi' has 20 like all other four-part cycles except 'Caput' (19 notes). Other compositions apparently of the 1470s are the three-part 'Missa Quinti toni', and two five-part works consisting only of Kyrie, Gloria and Credo each: 'Fors seulement' and another 'sine nomine'. In 'Fors seulement', traditionally described as an 'early' parody Mass, the harmonic and partly declamatory interest is overwhelming.[300] The Kyrie and Gloria are notated a fifth lower (*C–bb'*) than the Credo (*G–e"*) – conceivably a case of transposed or *chiavette* notation, although it recalls the cantus firmus transpositions of the Credo in 'Ecce ancilla Domini' and 'L'homme armé'. The five-part 'sine nomine' is declamatory and compact; the Credo is here notated a third higher than the other two sections.

The 'Missa Quinti toni' experiments with the Lydian mode. The contratenor has two flats at the clef, against one flat in the other voices. The tenor overlaps with the contratenor at the critical point *e/eb*. Many unavoidable tritones and nearly missed cross-relations result. The three voices are spaced about a fifth apart from each other, so that the contratenor becomes a bass, and fourths occur only where the tenor crosses underneath. Characteristic for the divided ranges are the invariable cadences on a unison *f* in three octaves.[301] While each voice seems to perform its own variant of the Lydian mode, the harmonic effect is surprisingly close to 'Bb major' – because of the important role played by the subdominant region and by the tritones in cadential sonorities. The incredibly beautiful, placid flow of the voices can only be described as 'pastoral'; the Christe starts with a harmonic progression whose later history reaches Beethoven's 'Les adieux':

Example 75 Jean Ockeghem, 'Missa Quinti toni'

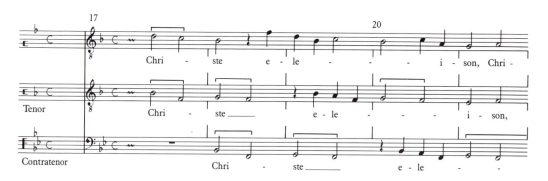

---

[300] See Sparks, *Cantus firmus*, 155–65. Interesting remarks about the work are found in Gottwald, 'Lasso-Josquin-Dufay', 55–61.

[301] The basic type of texture has been labelled 'reduced motet texture' in Wegman, 'An anonymous twin'. Although Wegman's term and description misrepresent the history of this device – it originated in the chanson of the 1450s – he is right in connecting the anonymous Mass in *SP* with 'Quinti toni' on the basis of this and other criteria.

Example 75 (*cont.*)

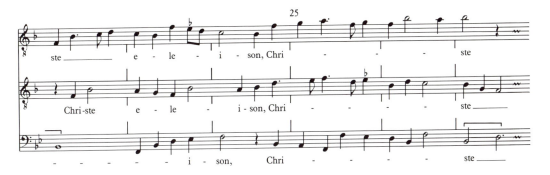

The development of the Franco-Netherlands motet from 1465 to 1480 could be characterized by the establishment of the large cantus firmus type, in two or more sections, and for four or more voices. It could also be characterized as the emergence of the fully imitative style, and as a further amalgamation of the motet and liturgical forms (hymn, antiphon etc.). All these are vague approximations; the problem is that tests against datable works are rarely possible.[302] Furthermore, only a fraction of the works that once existed is extant.

Busnois is much affected by this loss of sources. His motets 'Congaudebant' (praised by Tinctoris, see above), 'Animadvertere' (criticized by Tinctoris)[303] and 'Gabrielem' (cited in an Italian document, see p. 362), all apparently well known at the time, are lost. His extant eleven motets or similar works include three or four great cantus firmus motets as well as simple, declamatory and occasional pieces such as 'Noël, noël' (for the welcome of a visiting prince, or for Christmas). There are also two liturgical hymns, a respond for Christmas ('Alleluia Verbum caro factum est'), a sequence ('Victime paschali laudes'), a *Magnificat* and two antiphons ('Regina celi letare').[304] Busnois must have provided liturgical and devotional music for court and cathedral chapels; most of his surviving functional works are contained in the Burgundian chapel manuscript *Br 5557*, which apparently served for performance use. Busnois himself seems to have been responsible for the codex at some stage.

The compositional effort in each of these works seems almost unrelated to the genre at hand. The hymn 'Conditor alme', for example, is an exercise in varied mensurations (probably a brain-teaser for choirboys), although Vespers hymns are traditionally simple, functional settings. The Easter sequence 'Victime paschali laudes' is a large-scale four-part motet in two sections with in-

---

302 A flaw in the useful discussions in Stephan, *Motette*, and Sparks, *Cantus firmus* (chaps. 7 and 8) is their relative indifference to, or ignorance of, chronology.

303 *Opera theoretica*, vol. IIa, 52.

304 See the discussion of several works in Stephan, *Motette*, 17–23; Edward (*sic*) H. Sparks, 'The motets of Antoine Busnois', *JAMS* 6 (1953), 218–26; and Sparks, *Cantus firmus*, 212–29. A more recent contribution is Higgins, *Busnois*, 45–59.

troductory duets and statements of the cantus firmus in more than one voice. The 'anticipatory' statement in the opening duet of the second section ('Angelicos testes') is followed by another statement in the next duet, in literal quotation an octave higher. The tenor, which carries the cantus firmus for most of the time, is in the same high register as the cantus and contratenor, against one lower 'basistenor'. In this way, traditional voice-hierarchies are also obliterated in cantus firmus composition. A fifth voice joins the low register towards the end, participating in a passage of almost pervasive *Stimmtausch* imitation. This passage seems prefigured in some melismatic sections of the Mass 'O crux lignum'. Doubled quotation of the cantus firmus, as in the 'Angelicos testes' passage, is also found in Busnois' probably earlier motet 'Anima mea liquefacta es / Stirps Jesse', which is, however, in three-part chanson format.[305] The 'Regina celi' settings are both ambitious cantus firmus works, one with a continuous canon and the other with a migrant cantus firmus which is mostly in the bottom voice (labelled 'Thematenor').

'Anthoni usque limina' is a motet for St Anthony Abbot in which Busnois' own name is hidden at the beginning and end of the text ('Anthoni us / que . . . omni / bus noys').[306] It is likely that the composer himself wrote the text, which has the shape of an Ambrosian hymn and mixes many stereotyped formulas from the liturgies of St Anthony. The work has the curious feature of a fourth 'voice' for a bell – the attribute of the saint – which plays only one note (d') in alternate measures, according to a cryptically worded canon. Besides, there are two high voices and one low, but the openings of both sections are enriched by a third high voice. This is comparable to 'Victime paschali'. The absence of a genuine cantus firmus in this case allows for an even more pervasively canonic and imitative counterpoint, as well as for powerful harmonic gestures. The second section has particularly fine examples of pervasive imitation, generated by each new line of text.

The artistic purpose of the bell – as distinct from the symbolic one – may be to demonstrate how the harmonically limiting effect of the 'pedal point' can be overcome. This is also the musical point of some later works over artificial ostinati or *soggetti* (see p. 612), and indeed of Busnois' best-known motet, 'In hydraulis quondam Pithagora'.[307] This work stands in the tradition of the 'musicians' motets' and is in praise of music, of its 'inventor' Pythagoras, and generally of musicians. It is special, however, in that it pays homage to only one of

[305] Printed in Smijers ed., *Van Ockeghem tot Sweelinck*, vol. 1, which also offers the canonic 'Regina celi'.
[306] The work is unreliably edited and discussed in Walter Boer, *Het Anthonius-Motet van Anthonius Busnois* (Amsterdam, 1940). Boer's facsimiles show that the text underlay and other features of the only source, *Br 5557*, have been tampered with. The 'arranger' was Fétis, who in the same codex apparently changed existing composer attributions to read 'G. Binchois' and 'Okegan', respectively. See also Flynn Warmington, 'A Busnois-Fétis collaboration: the motet "Anthoni usque limina"', Paper Read at the 52nd Annual Meeting of the AMS, Cleveland, 1986. A theory on the destination of the work is advanced in Rob C. Wegman, 'Busnoys' "Anthoni usque limina" and the Order of Saint-Antoine-en Barbefosse in Hainaut', *Studi Musicali* 17 (1988), 15-31.
[307] Printed in *DTOe VII*, vols. 14-15, 105-11.

them – Jean Ockeghem, 'who sings before all others in the court of the King of France'. It is dedicated to him by 'his offspring' Busnois, who calls himself an 'unworthy musician of the count of Charolais'. The work thus antedates June 1467, when Busnois' employer ceased to be just 'Count of Charolais' and became Duke of Burgundy, and postdates April 1465, when the composer was last documented at Tours.[308] The two sections of the motet are built on the simple *soggetto* given in Example 76, which can be sung to solmization syllables.

Example 76 Antoine Busnois, 'In hydraulis': cantus firmus

This ostinato is performed twice in each section, undergoing strict proportional diminutions; it seems to me that the actual statements of the *soggetto* relate to each other in length like 6 : 4 : 3 : 2, although the mensuration signs read 'O C C2 O3'. The rests between the statements vary in length. The work is built on a large scale and has an exuberant contrapuntal surface with many patterned imitations and sequences. But the text–music relationship is less stringent than in 'Anthoni usque limina', and 'In hydraulis' sounds more monotonous despite the slightly more complex ostinato.

A descendant of 'In hydraulis' is evidently the musicians' motet 'Omnium bonorum plena' by Loyset Compère, which implores the Virgin for a whole series of composers.[309] Praising Dufay in the first place as 'the moon of all music and the light of singers', it is connected with Cambrai Cathedral, whose minor musical figures (Hemart, Dussart and George de Brelles) are also mentioned alongside Busnois, Caron, Tinctoris, Ockeghem and others. Compère perhaps regarded himself as the artistic 'offspring' of these 'magistri cantilenarum', just as Busnois was the 'propago' of Ockeghem. Compère ingeniously uses Hayne van Ghizeghem's chanson tenor 'De tous biens pleine est ma maistresse' as cantus firmus, which allows the *valet de chambre* an implicit place of honour among the named masters of sacred music. This original but unbalanced work was probably written for a celebration at Cambrai, perhaps the consecration of the cathedral in July 1472.[310] Compère left for Milan almost immediately after that time; the new task he was to face there (see p. 608) isolated 'Omnium bonorum plena' from his later oeuvre.

308 Higgins, *Busnois*, 137. On the music, see also van den Borren, *Etudes*, 255 ff, and Stephan, *Motette*, 22.

309 Printed in Compère, *Opera omnia*, vol. 4. On the work, see van den Borren, *Etudes*, 231 ff; Sparks, *Cantus firmus*, 208; Finscher, *Loyset Compère*, 131–40.

310 Montagna, 'Caron, Hayne, Compère', 110 ff.

A strange connection exists between 'In hydraulis' and Ockeghem's motet 'Ut heremita solus'. This astounding work, in the Aeolian mode and full of harmonic beauty, begins with the same two-bar motive as found at the beginning of Busnois' second section, on the words 'Haec Ockeghem'.[311] This must be an intentional quotation – but whose?

'Ut heremita solus' has a cantus firmus *soggetto* to be derived from a bewildering set of canonic instructions; it is monorhythmic (like the bell's notes in 'Anthoni') and stays within the hexachord *g-e'*.[312] The title 'Ut heremita solus' itself, read as 'ut re re mi la sol ut', serves as a solmization 'key' to decipher the tenor: this derivation of a tune from syllables was later called *soggetto cavato*. It is therefore unlikely that 'Ut heremita solus' was the beginning of a text, which is not supplied in the only source (Petrucci's *Motetti C* of 1504). Scholars seem to agree that the work had no text but was instrumental. The extremely rapid, syncopated ornamental passages (in *fusae* and *semifusae*) are unparalleled in vocal music of the period. Nevertheless, the four-part texture is fairly imitative; there are beautifully patterned passages and clear cadences. The layout is in the usual two sections with diminution of the *soggetto* to half its length in the second half; perfect time changes to imperfect and back in each section. This rich and complex piece was played, according to Guillaume Crétin's 'Déploration' on Ockeghem's death, by Hayne van Ghizeghem on the lute to greet the master in heaven. It is unlikely indeed that anyone on earth could play the piece on the lute!

The composer of 'Ut heremita solus' also wrote a canonic motet for 36 voices, which was mentioned by several contemporaries, including Crétin. A 36-part 'Deo gratia(s)' was printed in 1542 with an attribution to Ockeghem, and this may indeed be the genuine work, although the authenticity has been doubted;[313] it is in four nine-voice canons. This musical counterfeit of the heavenly hosts, far from being a product of Ockeghem's 'mysticism', was probably written for a performance in a *tableau vivant*. (See also p. 306.) The motets 'Caeleste beneficium', 'Gaude Maria' and 'Vivit Dominus', however, for which there are no good testimonies, may be spurious.[314]

Apart from the late four-part 'Ave Maria' (probably a liturgical work) and the splendid, complex 'Salve regina',[315] we have only two more motets by Ock-

[311] Higgins, 'In Hydraulis', 76 ff. The continuation of Busnois' phrase, interestingly, is the '1-3-2-5' motive, which may here refer to its use as a motto in Ockeghem's 'Missa sine nomine' no. 2. 'Ut heremita' is printed in Schering ed., *Geschichte*, 44–8. See also Stephan, *Motette*, 43 f.

[312] This description follows Andrea Lindmayr, 'Ein Rätseltenor Ockeghems: des Rätsels Lösung', *AcM* 60 (1988), 31–42, where earlier interpretations are also discussed.

[313] Picker, *Ockeghem and Obrecht*, 11 f; Edward E. Lowinsky, 'Ockeghem's canon for thirty-six voices: an essay in musical iconography', in Snow ed., *Essays in Musicology*, 155–80. Lowinsky also considers Josquin's 24-part 'Qui habitat'. Both works are edited by Edward Stam in *Exempla Musica Neerlandica* VI (Amsterdam: VNM, 1971). The authenticity and sources of all Ockeghem motets are discussed in Andrea Lindmayr, *Quellenstudien zu den Motetten von Johannes Ockeghem* (Laaber: Laaber-Verlag, 1990).

[314] Picker, *Ockeghem and Obrecht*, 28 f. A discussion is Stephan, *Motette*, 39–42.

[315] Ed. by John Milsom in *Mapa Mundi*, ser. B. 5 (London, 1978).

eghem which can stand beside his Masses. 'Alma redemptoris mater' is for four voices, the plainsong being carried in a lyrical paraphrase by the next-to-top voice.[316] (Josquin borrowed the beginning of the paraphrase for his 'Alma redemptoris / Ave regina celorum' setting.) This voice beautifully intertwines with the cantus and is largely, but not consistently, treated as the tenor; in bars 34 and 74, for example, it takes the fifth degree of the chord, supported by the bass. The low contratenor and the bass are eminently singable as well; the whole piece stands as a masterwork of pure vocal music, without any motivic, imitative or even modal artifice.

This style is also found in 'Intemerata Dei mater',[317] but here forms only one ingredient of a larger panorama. The motet is for five voices and in three sections. The first two sections begin with quotations – of the 'Mi-mi' motive and 'Fors seulement l'attente', respectively. In all the sections, there is a contrast between declamatory, chordal passages and melismatic mazes of all five, non-imitative lines. The work as a whole goes through various modes, but begins and ends in the Phrygian; the very low total range (C–a') could have to do with mourning.[318] The text, a desperate supplication to the Virgin, consists of Latin hexameters of a humanist brand, and the declamatory sections endeavour to pronounce the correct scansion over some stretches. They are also at times laid out as textural contrasts between groups of three voices. 'Intemerata' seems to sum up a life's endeavour; whereas some traits recall the early chansons, others are so modern that for this reason alone the motet might be considered a late work. Some surprising analogies with Poliziano's and Isaac's 'Quis dabit capiti meo aquam' (see p. 636) might be explained if Ockeghem's motet, too, were interpreted as a work in the shadow of death. It is perhaps no coincidence that the two quoted chansons are 'Presque transi ung peu mains qu'estre mort' ('Mi-mi') and 'Fors seulement l'attente que je meure'. While Ockeghem's polyphonic Requiem, the first work of its kind to survive, is said to have been composed on the death of King Charles VII (1461), 'Intemerata' may be a more personal work. If Ockeghem knew Dufay's four-voice 'Ave regina celorum' (and there can be little doubt that he did, since he visited Dufay in 1464 when the motet was being composed), he may well have thought of writing the same kind of motet for himself.

Regis and Obrecht

According to Wolfgang Stephan, Ockeghem's harmonic language is more varied than that of Busnois and Johannes Regis, although the latter's 'Clangat plebs'

---

[316] Heinrich Besseler ed., *Altniederländische Motetten* (Kassel etc., 1970).

[317] Smijers ed., *Van Ockeghem tot Sweelinck*, vol. 1, no. 2.

[318] See also Kenneth Kreitner, 'Very low ranges in the sacred music of Ockeghem and Tinctoris', *Early Music* 14 (1986), 467–79.

received the *varietas* prize from Tinctoris himself.[319] A difference with the younger composers is the adherence to a single mode – major or minor – in most chord formations, which from their perspective reflected perhaps a more modern attitude. Edward Lowinsky has given Regis enormous credit for his modern harmonic attitude, for example his 'splendour of full triadic harmony with the root in the bass', and he thought that these qualities made Regis an important link between Dufay and Josquin.[320] Stephan and Lindenburg had similar ideas about him, particularly in view of his great cantus firmus motets.[321]

'Modern' harmony is a difficult concept to substantiate. Full root-position triads, or the predominance of one particular sonority, seem insufficient criteria, since these features are quite widespread in late medieval polyphony. Certainly a criterion for tonal harmony would be the arrangement of the chordal sonorities in a goal-directed order – not just the predominance of one final, but its conclusiveness. There is, furthermore, the differentiation of the major and minor modes, and the use of certain conventions of cadential approach (subdominant preparation, dominant seventh, major dominant in the minor etc.). The opening gesture of the Mass 'Dum sacrum mysterium' (see Ex. 74) does seem to convey a 'tonal' harmonic feeling, and there are many other such gestures in Regis's work.

For all this, Johannes Regis as a motet composer seems at first glance much more concerned with cantus firmi, texts and textures. The five-part texture with one or two borrowed cantus firmi in the middle is the norm for him; of his nine extant motets, apparently six are composed in this manner. 'Apparently', because 'Salve sponsa' and 'Ave Maria . . . virgo serena' survive only in Petrucci's print *Motetti a 5* (1508), of which one partbook – for an inner voice – is missing. It may in this case have contained the borrowed cantus firmi of the two works. 'Ave Maria . . . virgo serena' is a lovely work, abounding in beautiful duet passages. Even the solo passages left over because of the missing voice are convincing melodies. The opening has been emulated (and surpassed) in Josquin's famous 'Ave Maria . . . virgo serena' (on which see p. 608). Josquin's predilection for paired imitation seems to owe something to Regis, although its use by the older master is more restrained and unpredictable, as shown in this work.

Another 'Ave Maria', on the biblical prose text and with some use of the plainsong melody, is in three parts only, two high and one low. The contrapuntal

---

[319] Stephan, *Motette*, 61 f and n. 10. The Tinctoris reference (of 1477) provides the earliest *terminus ad quem* for a motet by Regis. Several are preserved only in the Chigi Codex (c.1498) or even later sources. On the composer's biography, see Fallows, 'Life of Johannes Regis'.

[320] Edward E. Lowinsky, 'Canon technique and simultaneous conception in fifteenth-century music: a comparison between north and south', in *Essays on the Music of J. S. Bach and Other Divers Subjects: A Tribute to Gerhard Herz*, ed. Robert L. Weaver (Louisville, 1981), 181–222 (especially 194). An attempt to develop these ideas while revising their shortcomings is Blackburn, 'On compositional process'. See also pp. 584 f.

[321] Cornelis W. H. Lindenburg, *Het leven en de werken van Johannes Regis* (Amsterdam, 1939), 70 ff; Stephan, *Motette*, 26–35. Edited (unreliably) in Regis, *Opera omnia*, vol. 2. See also Sparks, *Cantus firmus*, 196–202.

ingenuity and disguised patterning of this piece remind one very much of Busnois' chansons.

The great five-part motets have borrowed cantus firmi and are usually in two sections. 'Celsitonantis', a Marian motet in humanistic hexameters, displays the hymn 'Abrahae fit promissio' in long notes in the tenor in the middle, often like an axis between an upper and a lower duetting pair. Towards the end of each section, the tenor becomes rhythmically more active, reaching the same level of floridity as the other voices. The tenor is notated identically for both sections, but the tempus changes from perfect to imperfect. This results at first in only proportional transformation, because no note-values shorter than breves appear (i.e. cases of alteration and imperfection do not arise), but towards the ends of the sections also in rhythmic transformation, because of the appearance of smaller note-values: a successful combination of symmetry and climax. 'Lauda Sion salvatorem' on the text of the Corpus Christi sequence, with plainsong tenor 'Ego sum panis vivus', has the same kind of texture, although the cantus firmus is not repeated. The same is true of 'Clangat plebs / Sicut lilium', where the main text is again a humanistic poem, the cantus firmus a Marian antiphon. In the second section, an ongoing duet of the top voices contrasts repeatedly with full chordal declamation; the cantus firmus appears only in the full passages and is, therefore, fragmented. Later, the cantus firmus begins to join in a varied succession of duets and, finally, a declamatory tutti. 'Lux solemnis adest / Repleti sunt omnes', for Pentecost, works in a similar way; it could be the latest of the extant five-part motets and is certainly the most developed. Here, the declamatory passages strongly support the impact of the humanistic hexameters, and the setting of individual words is also a major concern. This motet is modally very much like the Mass 'Dum sacrum mysterium', with its emphasis on the major dominant in the Dorian mode, and other 'tonal' uses of accidentals up to the 'tierce de picardie' at the end. Magnificent in this work (and prefigured in 'Lauda Sion' and 'Clangat plebs') is the use of the wide range of D-c''.

'O admirabile commercium' goes beyond the standard structure. It is in three sections. In the first two, the paired voices in the middle begin like a cantus firmus in canon at the upper fifth, but then develop into freer phrases. The text of these voices is, in both sections, a combination of the Christmas respond 'Verbum caro factum est et habitavit in nobis' with lines from the cantio 'Resonet in laudibus' (see p. 329). Also, the melody of the two voices is one of those current with this very popular cantio. The outer voices sing the antiphon text 'O admirabile' and paraphrase its melody. In the second and third sections, these voices have new text in elegiac couplets, interrupted at the beginning of the third section by the introit 'Puer natus est nobis' which also appears as a cantus firmus imitated in all the voices. This huge Christmas pie, reminding one of the multiple cantus firmi in the Masses, poses questions beyond those of technique. Did a certain environment prompt Regis to habitually combine and integrate texts as well as tunes?

The most striking work of this kind is the six-part sequence-motet 'Ave rosa speciosa', preserved anonymously but certainly by Regis.[322] Here the cantus firmus axis is a canon at the fifth of the antiphon 'Beata mater et innupta virgo'. The lowest voice, however, begins by singing the words 'Ave regina celorum, ave domina' on the 'L'homme armé' tune! Both the texts and the tunes are later varied, redistributed and interrupted. The third section ends with a massive climax where all the elements are present.

Regis was a canon at the collegiate church of St Vincent, Soignies, a post which he apparently did not want to exchange for Cambrai Cathedral (see p. 468). It seems that he composed for very sophisticated performers and audiences. The 'omnipresence', as it were, of liturgical and non-liturgical chant material, and on the other hand the humanistic texts, which Regis uses for church feasts as a matter of course, have as a common denominator the ceremonial practice of a *Kantorei* in a collegiate school. We do not know whether this place was Soignies only, or whether Regis also provided other centres of this kind with his demanding works. (Far too little music of the time can definitely be traced to specific places anyway.)

An anonymous five-part work, 'Ista est speciosa', seems remarkably close to the Regis group.[323] The only extant motet by the Antwerp succentor (1484–91) Jacob Barbireau, 'Osculetur me', does not really go beyond the scope of the older devotional motets. Gaspar van Weerbeke, however, who left for Italy as early as *c*.1470, composed some cantus firmus motets in this style; the well-known 'Stabat mater / Vidi speciosam' and 'Dulcis amica Dei / Da pacem Domine' may have originated in the papal chapel in the 1480s (see p. 640), but resemble pieces by Regis.[324] Josquin and Isaac certainly inherited elements of the style.

Most of these experiences flow together in the Masses and motets by Jacob Obrecht (*c*.1450–1505), to whom we will return in the last chapter. As a prolific composer, he seems to have acquired compositional routine rather early in his career, probably at Utrecht where he apparently taught the young Erasmus of Rotterdam (*c*.1476–80), and at Bergen-op-Zoom where he was succentor *c*.1481–4.[325] By this time, he was widely famous for his compositions (although he is never referred to as an outstanding performer, in contrast to Ockeghem and Dufay). Tinctoris cited him as a generally known master in the preface to his *Complexus effectuum musices* – probably not in its original version of *c*.1473–5, but about five to ten years later.[326] Obrecht then served for one year as succentor of Cambrai Cathedral, and from 1485 to 1491 held the same posi-

---

[322] Printed and reliably described in Edward F. Houghton, 'A "new" motet by Johannes Regis', *TVNM* 23 (1983), 49–74, where also a special affinity with Josquin's motet 'O virgo prudentissima' is noted.

[323] In the Leopold Codex, no. 48; see Stephan, *Motette*, 44 f.

[324] Stephan, *Motette*, 34 and 36.

[325] The present state of knowledge on Obrecht's life and works is succinctly reported in Picker, *Ockeghem and Obrecht*; see also Wegman, 'Bergen-op-Zoom'. The *NOE* has progressed to 9 volumes (all of Masses) in 1990.

[326] Tinctoris, *Opera theoretica*, vol. II, 176; Woodley, 'Tinctoris' Italian translation', 192–4.

tion at St Donatian's, Bruges. Duke Ercole I d'Este invited him to Ferrara in 1487–8 (see p. 604) and tried to keep him with the enticement of ecclesiastical benefices. Obrecht returned to the Netherlands, however, despite the political tensions there. After a difficult period of wars and famine, he was 'graciously dismissed' from his appointment at Bruges in January 1491, apparently for administrative faults.[327] About six months later, he became the successor of Jacob Barbireau (*d*.7 August 1491) at Our Lady's, Antwerp.[328] In 1499–1500, he returned to Bruges, then again to Antwerp. Obrecht started his last travel south in 1503, with an apparently significant pause at the Habsburg court of Innsbruck, and was the master of the Este chapel of Ferrara in 1504–5 until he died of the plague in July 1505.

Obrecht had a master's degree (it is not known from which university). In his Latin-texted works he displays a perfect mastery of musical techniques, mathematical insight and a tremendous depth of liturgical experience. He is the 'cantus firmus' composer *par excellence*, not only for the ingenious transformations he applies to his cantus firmi but also for the spiritual fervour with which he projects them and, often, their texts.

Obrecht composed more than 30 Mass cycles, but four have only recently been ascribed to him on mostly stylistic evidence; his cantus firmus techniques, in particular, are distinctive enough to encourage identification. One of them is the splintering of a melodic line into small fragments or even single notes, which are then laid out as a rigid scaffolding for the long Mass sections. Also characteristic of his approach is the literalness with which he cites borrowed musical material, for example – as in the 'Missa L'homme armé' – a cantus firmus throughout a whole Mass cycle. In this case, his cantus firmus is not the tune itself, but the tenor of Busnois' 'L'homme armé' Mass with all its rhythmic peculiarities. He also pays tribute to Busnois in the Mass 'Je ne demande', and to Ockeghem in the Mass 'Sicut spina rosam'. In this work, long stretches of voices are quoted from Ockeghem's 'Missa Mi-mi', and it has been suggested that it was composed in memory of Ockeghem (*d*.1497).[329] The cantus firmus, a phrase of the responsory 'Ad nutum Domini' for the Nativity of Mary, is also the motto of the Confraternity of Our Lady of 'sHertogenbosch. The work may have been commissioned by the brethren. Ockeghem is also behind Obrecht's 'Caput' Mass, of course: a composition that, with all its fidelity to the letter of the venerable cantus firmus, is unashamedly in C major.[330]

Obrecht reacted to the music of his own contemporaries as well, and took as models for his Masses not only Agricola's 'Si dedero' (which seems to have another offspring in Obrecht's motet 'Si sumpsero'), but also the four-part

---

[327] This period is described in more detail in Strohm, *Bruges*, 38–41 and 144–8.

[328] Important data for this period are in Forney, 'Music, ritual and patronage'.

[329] Barton Hudson, 'Obrecht's tribute to Ockeghem', *TVNM* 37 (1987), 3–13. Wegman, 'Another imitation', attributes to Obrecht an anonymous 'Missa de S Johanne Baptista' whose c.f. precisely reproduces the tenor rhythms of Busnois' 'L'homme armé' Mass.

[330] Planchart ed., *Missae Caput*. See p. 279 above on Planchart's theory that in Obrecht's work the cantus firmus must be performed on the organ throughout.

chanson setting 'Adieu mes amours' by Josquin. He must have admired Frye's 'Ave regina celorum', which he used not only as the basis of a tenor Mass (the tenor of the model permeates all the voices), but also reworked into a motet with the same text. In the latter case, however, he unaccountably transposed the borrowed material down a third converting its Lydian into a Dorian mode. This work, and the Mass 'Si dedero', belong to an as yet small group of cycles built over a pre-existing *motet* rather than a chanson or plainsong; others were Dufay's Mass 'Ave regina celorum' and Johannes Vincenet's 'O gloriosa regina mundi' (over Touront's famous song-motet). These cases may be significant in so far as the sixteenth-century parody Mass was to depend so much on the imitative motet as a model.[331]

At least twenty Masses by Obrecht are based on secular songs, of which he often uses more than one voice in the texture of his work. Nevertheless, his derivations concentrate more on individual voices, which are often quoted literally over long stretches. A significant example is Obrecht's derivation of his 'L'homme armé' Mass from that of Busnois; the quotation technique has been used to ascribe anonymous cycles to him.[332] Quotation involving more than one voice simultaneously (parody technique) is found, for example, in the Masses 'Rose playsante' and 'Fortuna desperata' (on which see pp. 620 ff).[333]

A general trait of Obrecht's sacred works is the tendency, appearing at first in the 1480s, to combine several cantus firmi, or at least to quote other melodies besides a liturgical tenor ('Missa de Sancto Martino', 'Missa de Sancto Donatiano' and 'Missa Sub tuum presidium'); this tendency is then taken over in the cycles based on secular material ('Missa Plurimorum carminum' I and II). Slightly younger composers such as Matthaeus Pipelare and Pierre de La Rue continued and expanded the 'multiple cantus firmus' technique.[334]

Several of Obrecht's 26 or more motets, antiphons and hymns have bearings on the composer himself. The combinations of seemingly heterogeneous cantus firmi, for example, may relate to events in his life or at least point to special liturgical circumstances. Apart from two undoubtedly political or personal works ('Quis numerare queat' and 'Inter praeclarissimas virtutes', see p. 633), seven motets use more than one liturgical or otherwise pre-existing melody and text. Some of these more or less 'enhance' the devotional intent, as in 'Beata es Maria / Ave Maria', in 'O beate Basili / O beate pater Basili', in 'Salve crux / O crux lignum', or in the huge pastiche of Advent plainsongs, 'Factor orbis'. Obrecht reminds us here not only of Regis, but beyond him of English motets

---

[331] See Lewis Lockwood, 'A view of the early sixteenth-century parody Mass', in A. Mell ed., *Twenty-Fifth-Anniversary Festschrift, Department of Music, Queen's College, CUNY* (New York: Queen's College Press, 1969), 53–77.

[332] See Tom R. Ward, 'Another Mass by Obrecht?', *TVNM* 27 (1977), 102–8, where the anonymous Mass 'Je ne seray plus vert vestus' is related to Obrecht's Mass 'Fors seulement' (with literal statement of the model's superius).

[333] Further on the music of the Masses and motets, see Sparks, *Cantus firmus*, ch. 9. See also *idem*, 'Obrecht, Jacob', in *The New Grove*, for an introduction to the music.

[334] On its musical, historical and liturgical aspects, see Bloxam, *Late Medieval Service Books*.

with multiple cantus firmi and, in a sense, even of Dunstable's isorhythmic motets. Other such combinations may have been brought about by special commissions, for example in the cases of 'O preciosissime sanguis / Guberna tuos famulos' (for the confraternity of the Holy Blood at Bruges?) and 'Salve sancta facies / Homo quidam' (for a 'table of the poor' endowed by a cloth merchant of Bruges?).[335]

A 'compound' motet in a more traditional sense is the work he wrote in 1488 on the death of his father, Willem Obrecht. This very beautiful work was long known without text, except for a tenor 'Requiem aeternam' – which is the introit of the Mass of the Dead but transposed down a semitone from F to E. Accordingly, the work is in the Phrygian mode, and Obrecht clearly exploits this for its sombre mood. Also, secular uses of the mode seem to be alluded to: for example, the bassus begins the first of the two sections of the work with the motive *e–f–e–A* in long-held notes, the second with *e–e–A*. This is as if both 'Au travail suis' and 'Presque transi (Mi–mi)' were called to mind and perhaps also 'Malheur me bat', another Phrygian song variously ascribed to Martini, Ockeghem and Malcort (and thus probably by Malcort).[336] The motet is imbued with gestures and motives from this stylistic sphere of the earlier chanson; the emphatic fall of a fifth ending a phrase as in Ockeghem's 'Ma bouche rit' (see Ex. 66) is everywhere.

Only the discovery of the Segovia MS in 1922 has unearthed the text of the upper voices in Obrecht's work, which reveals its destination:

> Mille quingentis verum bis sex minus annis
> Virgine progeniti lapsis ab origine Christi
> Sicilides flerunt Musae, dum fata tulerunt
> Hobrecht Guillermum, magna probitate decorum,
> Ceciliae ad festum, qui Siciliam peragravit.
> Os idem Orpheicum Musis Jacobum generavit.
> Ergo dulce melos succentorum chorus alme
> Concine, ut ad caelos sit vecta anima et data palme.
> Amen.[337]

This text has been discussed in various ways, always with the conviction that it reveals biographical detail relating to Jacob Obrecht. It is, however, an epitaph for his father, the well-travelled city wait of Ghent, Willem Obrecht. It was therefore unwise to expect it to reveal information on the place and date of birth of Willem's *son* – when does an epitaph give such information? Jacob is mentioned, after the *vita* of his father, to introduce the subject of music (both earthly, i.e. that of the Muses, and heavenly, i.e. that of the succentors), which indeed connected father and son. Here is a translation of these hexameters, which were probably written by Jacob himself:

---

[335] Bloxam, *Late Medieval Service Books*, ch. 16; Strohm, *Bruges*, 144–8.
[336] Printed and discussed in Brown ed., *A Florentine Chansonnier*, no. 11.
[337] Text as given in Picker, *Ockeghem and Obrecht*, 40, with slight emendations.

1500 minus twelve years after the birth of Christ from the Virgin, the Sicilian Muses wept, as Fate took away Willem Obrecht, a man of great righteousness, who travelled in Sicily, on the feast of St Cecilia. He begat with the Muses Jacob, the mouth of Orpheus.[338] Therefore, generous choir of succentors, sing sweet melody, so that his soul be carried to heaven and be assigned to triumph. Amen.

Earlier commentators were certainly right to maintain that this text alludes to a journey by Willem Obrecht to Sicily. It probably means that Willem died on the feast of St Cecilia (whose name is juxtaposed with that of Sicily for the sake of the pun), i.e. on 22 November 1488, while on a trip in Sicily; alternatively, the trip may only be mentioned as a memorable event of his life, and not in connection with the date. In any case, the date does not reveal anything about Jacob.[339] While it seems likely that the composer was born in Ghent, we continue to know nothing about the date of his birth or the circumstances of his youth and early career.

---

[338] The word 'os' as reconstructed here has been read as 'coram' or 'ceram', neither of which makes any sense.

[339] It could be that Josquin modelled on this work a *déploration* on the death of Jacob Obrecht himself: see Willem Elders, 'Josquin's *Absolve quesumus, Domine*: a tribute to Obrecht?', *TVNM* 37 (1987), 14–24.

3

CENTRAL EUROPE : MASTERS AND APPRENTICES

Organists and song collectors

An evocative portrait of Magister Conrad Paumann, carved into his tombstone (Plate 8), shows the blind artist and craftsman in his workshop: sitting on a low stool, surrounded by the instruments which he plays, concentrating on the performance on his portative organ. The inscription states:

> Anno 1473, on the eve of the Conversion of St Paul [24 January] died and was buried here the most artful master of all instruments and of *Musica*, Cunrad Pawman, knight, born blind in Nuremberg, whom God forgive.

The original location of the red marble slab was outside the south door of Our Lady's Church in Munich, the magnificent gothic brick building erected between 1468 and 1488 around an older structure by the master builder Jörg of Halspach. Paumann was buried at the doorstep of the church where he performed in his capacity as court organist, and not far away from the palace of his ducal employers – Albrecht III, Sigismund and Albrecht IV – where he exercised his art in secular instrumental and vocal music.[340]

Paumann and Jörg are typical representatives of central European culture at this time. They were craftsmen whose medium was eminently physical – wood, metal, stone and clay – and masters whose art was 'quadrivial', i.e. numerate, systematic and comprehensive. They served a prosperous and productive community, where instrument-makers and -players were numerous, poets rare. Paumann's 'masterworks' are not his various keyboard arrangements of songs, three of which are signed with his initials ('M. C. C.' = 'Magistri Conradi Ceci') in the Buxheim Organ Book, nor his skilful, courtly *Tenorlied* 'Wiplich figur' inscribed into the songbook of the Nuremberg physician Dr Hartmann Schedel (see p. 495). Paumann's most important contribution are his four interrelated *fundamenta*, technical and contrapuntal exercises for keyboard instruments, through which his whole art can be acquired and appreciated (see also p. 372). Paumann is a founder figure of German polyphonic keyboard music. It is no coincidence that 'fundamentum' is a term recalling architecture, and it is a fitting coincidence that 'Paumann' means 'builder'.

---

[340] See also Christoph Wolff, 'Paumann, Konrad' in *The New Grove*.

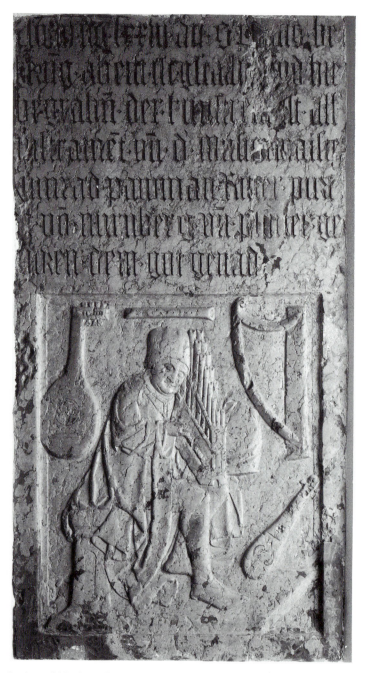

8 Tomb-plate of Magister Conrad Paumann, 1473; Frauenkirche, Munich.

Born *c*.1410, the master had joined the Munich court from his native Nuremberg in 1450, yielding to the entreaties of the wife of Duke Albrecht III of Bavaria–Munich, whose love of music (surely among other arguments) persuaded the reluctant city fathers of the free imperial town to part with their city organist. In that capacity, Paumann will have played for civic ceremonies such as Mass services and receptions of princely visitors. Since 1446 at the latest, he had also served on the newly built organ of the parish church of St Sebald's. The patrician families, Meistersinger and town officials of the wealthy merchant city were proud of him.[341] His departure from the bourgeois to the courtly sphere foreshadowed developments to come: princely patronage was beginning to replace civic control over the arts in the large urban centres of the Holy Roman Empire and beyond. Parish clerks became court chaplains, master craftsmen were knighted.

Not that the Nuremberg and the Munich of 1450 were drastically different communities. The Nurembergers were extremely proud of their imperial status and of their role as hosts of all the German princes during the frequent imperial diets and congresses (see also p. 311). They were not ordinary shopkeepers. Their *convois* travelled all over Europe; the silverware, jewellery, weapons, clocks and nautical instruments which they produced were seen at the courts of France and Italy, and sold at the fairs of Venice, Flanders and the Levant. These 'princes among burghers' competed with the other imperial towns in southern Germany of similar wealth and culture: Augsburg, Regensburg, Rothenburg, Nördlingen, Ulm, Ravensburg, Frankfurt and so on. (See Map 2, p. 155.) The citizens of ducal Munich were, on the whole, less sophisticated; their mercantile wealth and cultivation of the arts could not be compared with that of neighbouring Augsburg. But Munich did have bourgeois and intellectual families who were looking after their cultural interests independently from the court. We know, for example, of splendidly endowed musical services held at the church of Our Lady on behalf of the local physician Dr Sigmund Gotzkircher. In personal household accounts of *c*.1460, Gotzkircher documents his patronage for, or contribution to, almost twenty feast-days during the year, celebrated 'with trumpets and drums, organs, pipers and other instruments, with *cantores*, with clerics and laymen'.[342] Most of this music was probably heard in processions, but organ and singers may well have performed polyphonically in the church itself and they may have included the court organist Paumann and the court chaplains. We know of such courtly-civic interaction with regard to sacred vocal music from other places of the Empire, specifically the ducal residences of Innsbruck and Vienna (see p. 519). Other princely resi-

---

[341] The Meistersinger Hans Rosenplüt, in a poem on the city of Nuremberg (1447), praised his mastery of all the chant repertory, but also of motets, *rundellus*, counterpoint and *faberdon*: see Moser, *Geschichte*, vol. 1, 338 f.

[342] 'Cum tubis et timpanis et organis et fistulatoribus et aliis instrumentis musicalibus et cum cantoribus, cum clericis et laycis'. See Otto Ursprung, *Münchens musikalische Vergangenheit von der Frühzeit bis Richard Wagner* (Munich, 1927), 26.

dences such as Freiburg and Landshut, or episcopal cities such as Passau, Constance, Basle, Strasbourg, Augsburg and Trent still await investigation. As regards Paumann, his 'audiences' were not essentially different in Nuremberg and Munich: church congregations, wealthy patrons, guests of his workshop, colleagues at court, paying students and apprentices. Some of their names occur over pieces of the Buxheim Organ Book: Jo. Götz (no. 52), Boumgartner (no. 110), (Ulrich) Füterer (no. 107).

The last-named was a celebrated poet, Meistersinger and painter at the courts of Bavaria–Landshut and (from 1465) Bavaria–Munich. Since he is not credited with keyboard skills as well, the piece inscribed with his name ('Der füterer') may be a setting of a monophonic tune by him, or simply be dedicated to him. The year when Füterer moved to Munich, 1465, does not provide a *terminus post quem* for the dating of the codex,[343] since he might well have been in touch with Paumann's circle while still in Landshut. Paumann himself must have encountered the artists of this rival Bavarian court in 1454. On 9 May of this year, he played before Duke Philip of Burgundy at the imperial diet in Regensburg, as did several musicians and entertainers of Duke Ludwig of Landshut; Füterer could have been among them. The celebrated event, attended by minstrels from many territories and hosted by Duke Ludwig, has been recorded in the Burgundian travel accounts.[344] The city accounts of Regensburg, in turn, mention Paumann's appearance as a lutenist, together with two other lutenists of Duke Albrecht of Bavaria–Munich, in 1459.[345] Paumann's achievements on the lute – an instrument naturally represented on his tombstone – will occupy us further on.

The keyboard intabulation inscribed 'Boumgartner' – a common name in Nuremberg – is one of the signs that the Buxheim Organ Book draws on repertory first heard in circles of that town. Like several untitled pieces in the manuscript, it has a concordance in a Nuremberg source of *c.*1452–60: the Lochamer-Liederbuch (*D-B 40613*; *Loch*) so named after one of its later owners, the Nuremberg patrician Wolflein von Lochamer. In the second section of the manuscript, an organ tablature containing Paumann's *fundamentum organisandi* and dated 1452,[346] we find this 'Boumgartner' piece. It looks very much like an arrangement of a rondeau cinquain, with three of the five phrases entering in imitation as in the more modern French songs of the 1450s. On the other hand, as many as three of the phrases end on the final F, which would presumably not happen in a genuine French song. Perhaps the original three-

---

[343] As claimed in Wallner ed., *Buxheimer Orgelbuch*, IV. The date of the manuscript may be nearer 1460; see Zöbeley, *Buxheimer Orgelbuch*, 18 f.

[344] Marix, *Histoire*, 70 ff. Pietzsch, *Fürsten*, 159, and Wallner ed., *Buxheimer Orgelbuch*, 26 f, report that the relevant pages of Marix's document are missing (on the film only?).

[345] Pietzsch, *Fürsten*, 154; Sterl, *Musiker*, 27.

[346] The actual Liederbuch and the *fundamentum organisandi* are sometimes referred to as separate sources; but they served the same owner. See Ameln ed., *Locheimer Liederbuch* (facs); Salmen–Petzsch eds, *Lochamer-Liederbuch* (critical edn of vocal section only).

part song was indeed composed by Boumgartner and intabulated by one of his friends in the Paumann circle.

Jo(hannes) Götz is not otherwise known, but his arrangement 'Vil liber zit' follows the same vocal model as no fewer than eight other pieces in Buxheim and a ninth in Lochamer, some of which have the title 'Annavasanna' or some such. The model is the rondeau cinquain – and *basse danse* – 'Une fois avant que mourir', found in two older sources.[347] It was perhaps in Paumann's circle in Nuremberg that this particular tune led a prominent existence as a kind of test piece for organ students.

Much of the material in the Buxheim Organ Book, on the other hand, was probably collected by students or friends of Paumann in the 1450s in Munich. Any ambitious young organist of that town would have rushed to make the blind master's acquaintance or to study with him. We do not know whether among these apprentices there was 'Johannes organista de Monaco', who matriculated at Vienna University in 1454, or Johannes Wiser of Munich, from 1455 active at Trent Cathedral as succentor, schoolmaster and scribe of the later Trent Codices.[348]

In the sources mentioned so far in this paragraph – the Buxheim Organ Book, the Lochamer-Liederbuch and the Schedel Songbook – German organ playing meets European song. Between the *fundamenta, praeambula* and plainsong settings of the Buxheim Organ Book, and in the tablature section of the Lochamer-Liederbuch, there are arrangements of about a hundred German and several dozen foreign songs, polyphonic and monophonic. (Several of the latter are *basses danses*.) In the vocal section of the Lochamer-Liederbuch, there are 48 German songs, six of which seem to be derived from foreign models. The Schedel Songbook contains 127 musical pieces with German, Latin or French titles; at least 30 of them are French and English songs or 'song-motets'. Dufay and Binchois composed most of the polyphonic models used in all three sources; fifteen other composers from Ciconia to Robert Morton are represented.[349] Particularly striking is the presence of English pieces, some of which have not survived elsewhere, by Frye, Bedyngham, Dunstable and anonymi. There are apparently remote English pieces, such as the virelai 'Love will I without variaunce' which figures as 'Luffile' (Buxheim, no. 198), and a carol(?) which has been turned into a carnival song.[350] Since many pieces of these manuscripts

---

[347] See Fallows, 'Two equal voices', 234 f; Crane, *Materials*, no. 94. The copy in Zorzi Trombetta's book (*GB-Lbl Cott.Tit. A XXVI*) demonstrates that the piece was carried around by minstrels; see Leech-Wilkinson, 'Un Libro', and p. 348 above.

[348] See Pietzsch, *Zur Pflege*, 186, and p. 509 below. It is possible, indeed, that the two were the same man.

[349] Foreign pieces in the three manuscripts are listed in Eileen Southern, 'Foreign music in German manuscripts of the 15th century', *JAMS* 21 (1968), 258–85; for important additions, see n. 350.

[350] See Fallows, 'English song repertories'. This carnival song, 'Wann ich betracht die vasenacht' in Buxheim (no. 175) which also surfaces as 'In mentem veniunt cucumeres' (no. 4), could well have accompanied the traditional carnival pageants called *Schembartlaufen* (on which see Heers, *Fêtes*).

have contrafactum texts, not all the foreign models have been identified. The contrafactum practice demonstrates, on the other hand, that we are dealing with living, often-heard music.

The Schedel Songbook contains many songs without complete texts, plus 23 texts without music. Several times, otherwise known texts (German and Latin) are assigned to music which appears only here. These are signs that the match of music and poetry was partly *ad libitum* in this collection: some compositions were entered without text, in order to receive words recorded elsewhere in the book, and some new poems were probably written down to be sung with any suitable music that came to hand. The texts are virtually always strophic (type of *Kanzone*); the form of the individual stanza often recalls the so-called *Barform*, better *Gesätz*, which roughly corresponds to a French ballade form (AAB, with or without an extra refrain line C). The stanza forms are more varied than the French *formes fixes*.[351]

At least twelve items in the Lochamer-Liederbuch are monophonic tunes. The decision 'polyphonic or monophonic?' is difficult in about ten other cases, where an untexted line, usually labelled 'tenor', precedes the texted sections: it could be used as a prelude, interlude or even accompanying line. (On this problem, see p. 349.) Also, the notation of the tunes is often 'primitive', whether unmeasured or a-rhythmic. There are, however, only two or three tunes which might deserve the ambiguous name of 'folksongs': the dance-song 'Ich spring an diesem ringe' ('I dance in this round', no. 42), the farcical 'Es fur ein paur gen holz' ('A peasant drove to the woods', no. 45) and just possibly the satirical 'Mir ist mein pferd vernagelt gar' ('My horse has got wrong shoes', no. 28). The other items, overwhelmingly love-songs addressed to a woman, must be considered art-songs in the tradition of the *Hofweise* ('courting song'), which in German society held a status analogous to that of the French ballade or virelai.[352] (A monophonic example is the Cersne song, Ex. 49.)

The main scribe and owner of the Lochamer-Liederbuch identified himself, in his last dated entry of 1460, as 'frater Judocus de Windsheim'. The editors believe that he was an organ student of Paumann in Nuremberg, that he was a learned man and the author of several songs in his book, and that, after having become a friar in 1459, he ceased to devote himself to secular music.[353] The function and message of the Lochamer poems is non-individualistic but by no means 'popular'. In the cultivation and, admittedly, intensification of older stereotypes of love-song (the lament of the parting lover, for example), middle-class circles documented for themselves their ability to share aristocratic tradi-

---

[351] On text forms, see Salmen–Petzsch eds, *Lochamer-Liederbuch* (comments on individual items); Salmen, *Lochamer Liederbuch*; Rosenberg, *Untersuchungen*.

[352] See Christoph Petzsch, 'Hofweise' in *The New Grove*; *idem*, 'Weiteres zum Lochamer-Liederbuch und zu den Hofweisen: ein Beitrag zur Frage des Volksliedes im Mittelalter', *Jahrbuch für Volksliedforschung* 7 (1972), 9–34.

[353] Salmen–Petzsch eds, *Lochamer-Liederbuch*, LVI–LXI. Windsheim, a small town 30 miles west of Nuremberg, is also the home of an earlier polyphonic fragment (see p. 121 n.).

tions. It is unfortunate that, in the past, the Lochamer-Liederbuch has been exploited to exemplify the 'German people's soul' to nostalgic or chauvinist audiences.

The general musical type of the polyphonic pieces is surprisingly near to the chanson format as practised at the same time in the west. Socially, however, the circles cultivating this music differed somewhat from the French or Burgundian courtly environments.

The Schedel Songbook (*D-Mbs cgm 810*; *olim Mus. ms. 3232*; *Cim. 351a*) is the most comprehensive and sophisticated of all German sources of polyphonic song in this period.[354] It was owned by the most learned man: Dr Hartmann Schedel (1440-1514), a physician and humanist in Nuremberg, and author of the famous *Weltchronik* printed in 1493. Schedel's library – now in the Bavarian State Library – documents his comprehensive taste and erudition, and so on its small scale does the songbook itself. Although it may appear rather monotonous as a collection of German poetry, and although its Latin hexameters and meteorological annotation can be discarded as standard curiosities, its musical repertory is of European breadth and very much up to date for the 1460s. The manuscript was a private pocketbook (a 'vademecum'), written largely by Schedel himself. It accompanied him, *c.*1459-61, during his student years at Leipzig University; the dates of 1465 and 1467 later in the manuscript fall in and after the time he studied in Padua (1463-6). Clearly the musical repertory benefited from Schedel's travels, although it is not certain whether the book itself was with Schedel in Italy. He used it as a repository, from which he would extract pieces at will to prepare them more carefully for a performance. It can be presumed that he used to sing himself and had friends to accompany him. For many pieces, he wrote no words – either because he had no access to them, or because they were in a foreign language and he wanted to reserve the music for a German or Latin contrafactum text.[355] Schedel seems to differentiate between songs with text in the cantus and *Tenorlieder* by placing texts or incipits accordingly. These decisions are not always reliable. For example, 'Elend du hast umbfangen mich' (no. 11) has more text in the tenor than in the cantus; but the piece is also known with the rondeau text 'Vive ma dame par amours', and is attributed in a textless version to Robert Morton with whose style it is not incompatible. Can it be a German *Tenorlied*?[356] If so, its appear-

---

[354] See Wackernagel ed., *Liederbuch* (facs), introduction; Heinrich Besseler, 'Schedelsches Liederbuch' in *MGG*, vol. XI, col. 1609-12. A critical edn is announced in *EdM* (vols. 74 and 75).

[355] In many central European collections (for example Strahov and Trent), textless pieces are those designated to receive a contrafactum text, which has however not yet been chosen or underlaid. Further on contrafacta, see Friedrich Gennrich, *Die Kontrafaktur im Liedschaffen des Mittelalters* (Langen bei Frankfurt, 1965), 202-7; Christoph Petzsch, 'Geistliche Kontrafakta des späten Mittelalters', *AMw* 25 (1968), 19-29; Martin Staehelin, 'Zur Begründung der Kontrafakturpraxis in deutschen Musikhandschriften des 15. und frühen 16. Jahrhunderts', in *Florilegium Musicologicum. Festschrift H. Federhofer zum 75. Geburtstag* (Tutzing: Schneider, 1988), 389-96.

[356] The discussion of this case has involved Heinrich Besseler (Besseler-Gülke, *Schriftbild*, 101), Allan W. Atlas (Morton, *Collected Works*, 95-101) and David Fallows (*Robert Morton's Songs*, 383-420). The last-named offers the most convincing arguments for a misattribution (!) to Morton.

ance in foreign sources, once with the incipit 'Elend' (in *I-Fr 2356*), merits
further consideration (p. 568). The 'Elend' (i.e. 'misery', literally 'outland')
does not need to be taken too seriously. Other sources, including Buxheim and
Lochamer, have this or similar titles for different music: *Ellend* is the condition
of a lover who is far away from his beloved, possibly abroad: an idea that fits a
good many songs. Other standard incipits were 'Gross senen' ('High desire')
which in the Glogauer Liederbuch (see below) is given to several different
pieces, and 'Le serviteur' or something similar, which was occasionally given
to pieces quite unconnected with Dufay's rondeau.

The historically most significant aspect of Schedel – which was, after all, a
student's book – lies in the assumption that the repertory was circulating at the
universities visited by its owner. The first 103 items would have been available
to him at Leipzig before *c.*1463: they include works which he carefully attributes to 'Ockegheim' ('Ma bouche rit'), 'Tauront' or 'Thourot', 'Berbigant', 'Pil-
lays', 'Wal Frey', 'Jo Bodigham' and 'Binzois' (no. 62, a textless, unedited rondeau). Dufay's name is absent, but Schedel knows his late song 'Malheureux
cuer'. Le Rouge's bergerette 'Se je fays dueil' receives the full French text for
its second half (no. 21a), which curiously is copied far away from the first (no.
89). Schedel knew these pieces sometimes only a few years after the probable
dates of composition. The composers 'Walterus Seam', 'W. Ruslein' and 'Wenz
Nodler', who contributed German songs, could have been his college companions at Leipzig; Conrad Paumann's 'Wiplich figur' (no. 23) came probably
from Munich.

What is the relationship between the many German songs in Schedel's book,
and the foreign art, which he and his companions performed with the same
zeal? Paumann's 'Wiplich figur' may be exceptional.[357] This piece is like a first-
degree cousin of Robert Morton's songs, especially 'N'aray-je jamais mieux'
and 'Le souvenir' – the latter of which is twice intabulated in Buxheim (nos. 250
and 256). But the complex question of indigenous German trends[358] may gain
more profile when we consider the anonymous *Tenorlied* in Example 77, of
which a variant version exists in the slightly earlier codex *Tr 90*.

Example 77*a* 'Mein herz in steten trewen', *Tr 90*, fol. 294v

---

[357] Printed in Robert Eitner, *Das deutsche Lied des XV. und XVI. Jahrhunderts* (Berlin, 1880), 161 f.
[358] It has often been discussed, for example in Helmuth Osthoff, *Die Niederländer und das deutsche Lied
(1400–1600)* (Berlin, 1938), 1–48; Rosenberg, *Untersuchungen*; Salmen, 'European song', 371–7.

Example 77a (*cont.*)

Example 77*b* 'Mein herz in steten trewen', Schedel, no. 26

Example 77*b* (*cont.*)

gan - gen,   het   mich   die   zart   ge - wert.

There is obviously a pre-existing tune in the tenor, because this voice is almost identical in the two versions, whereas the other voices differ. The cantus of *Tr 90* is hardly a tune at all; its tritone leap in bar 2 results from contrapuntal necessity. The tenor's metrical irregularity, a somewhat free alternation between groups of three and four beats, seems to be original to this tune. In fact, German songs of the later fifteenth century often ignore the unit of tempus. Also typical is the relative freedom of the first and last note-values of each phrase; virtually every phrase could end with a fermata.[359] But the rhythm is strong and convincing, also because of its several repetitions. The rhythmic jolts are enhanced by the tendency of the cantus – in both versions – to accompany the repeated 'triple metre passage' (bar 3 etc.) in strict parallels above. It is as if the cantus did not dare contradict the tenor in this incisive passage. Elsewhere, its independence is much greater (in the *Tr 90* version in the lengthened bar 4 for example). At the beginning of phrases, the structural voices have identical rhythms, but are melodically more independent. In the second half of the Schedel version, the cantus goes its own ways; all the more striking is its faithful return to the established formulas in bar 21. The contratenor of *Tr 90* produces several dissonances, especially with the cantus. It seems to have been fitted only against the tenor – an old-fashioned and by now provincial approach (see also p. 110). The stanzaic form (AAB; 2 × 2 and 2 + 2 + 1 lines) is a conventional type of the fourteenth-century ballade. It is the same as in 'Medée fu' (Ex. 5), although here we find more melodic recurrences: ab ab; ab (transposed), a′ a″ b.

It is hard to prove how the difference between the two versions can have arisen. A written reworking in Schedel of the earlier version in *Tr 90* seems implausible at first. Some impact of aural memory must have played a role. The Schedel contratenor, however, is composed against the other two written voices, not by ear. The Schedel arranger might have decided to rewrite the contratenor because he saw the incorrect version of that voice as transmitted in *Tr 90*, or something like it.

---

359 See the remarks on the 'optional upbeat' in Cersne's song (p. 351).

There would be plenty of material for a history of German song in the late Middle Ages. The fifteenth-century sources are more numerous than appears from any published discussion of them; a few remarks must suffice here.[360]

From the era of the Minnesinger onwards, every generation of German art-song is represented by written sources.[361] From the early fifteenth century, polyphony is found in major collections, such as the manuscripts of Oswald von Wolkenstein and the 'Mondsee-Wiener Liederhandschrift' with many pieces by the Monk of Salzburg (see p. 345). Monophonic codices and smaller sources remain frequent, however, for both the *Hofweisen* (as represented by Schedel) and the *Töne* of the Meistersinger, which were sung monophonically. The largest source of *Hofweisen* is the Königsteiner Liederbuch with 169 songs, of which only four are notated. The largest source of late *Minnesang* is the Colmarer Liederhandschrift (*D-Mbs cgm 4997*). Both collections date from *c.*1470.[362] Typical of the many fifteenth-century sources of German sacred song are the codex *D-Mbs cgm 716* (from Tegernsee, *c.*1430; also containing primitive polyphony), the Wienhäuser Liederbuch (1460) and the songbook of Anna von Köln (*c.*1500).[363]

A source which is very different from the foregoing is the Rostocker Lieder-buch of *c.*1468–87 (*D-ROu Mss phil. 100/2*).[364] It is a miscellany of 60 popular, amorous, sacred, political and goliardic songs in German and Latin, which apparently served a member of Rostock University (founded in 1419). Among the popular and love-songs there are significant concordances with Lochamer, pointing to a similar social environment. Musically, the compiler was a true apprentice. His notation is very rough, and the last material he tried to notate is the two voices 'Dixit iracundus homo' and 'Quoniam secta latronum' – a variant version of the famous *Roman de Fauvel* motet 'Tribum quem / Quoniam' which is probably by Vitry (1315). The late occurrence is not entirely surprising for this genre, and this particular region.[365]

---

[360] Generally, see David Fallows, 'Sources, MS, #III, 5: Secular monophony, German' in *The New Grove*; Böker-Heil, *Tenorlied*.

[361] 21 sources up to *c.*1450 are listed in Salmen, *Lochamer Liederbuch*, 7 f. To this may be added the songs in the Cersne MS (see p. 351); the Windsheim fragment (see p. 121 n.); the source described in Staehelin, 'Münchner Fragmente', 177 ff; the Silesian source *D-LEu 1305*, with four songs including Conrad of Queinfurt's (*d.*1382) 'Du Lenze gut'. The manuscript is not dated 1382, as stated in *The New Grove*, but is of the early fifteenth century. See also Wolfgang Jungandreas, 'Das Ms.1305 der Universitätsbibliothek Leipzig eine Handschrift aus Schlesien', *JbLH* 17 (1972). New information on Salmen's no. 2, the 'Sterzing Miscellanies MS', is given in Welker, 'New light on Oswald', 210 f.

[362] Paul Sappler ed., *Das Königsteiner Liederbuch. Ms.germ.qu.719 Berlin* (Munich: Beck, 1970). For *Minnesang*, *Meistersang* and their sources, see p. 345.

[363] See, respectively: John Emerson, 'Über Entstehung und Inhalt von MüD', *KJb* 48 (1964), 33–60; Heinrich Sievers ed., *Das Wienhäuser Liederbuch*, 2 vols. (Wolfenbüttel, 1954) (facs and transcription of the fifteen melodies); Salmen–Koepp eds, *Liederbuch*.

[364] Friedrich Ranke and Joseph Müller-Blattau eds, *Das Rostocker Liederbuch* (Halle, 1927). Not listed in *CC*, but see *RISM B IV 3*, 383 f.

[365] A lost manuscript of Lübeck, City Library, 152, contained the same motet, along with other Ars nova pieces and a motet by Petrus Wilhelmi (on him, see also p. 263).

In polyphonic song, the balance and interaction between the native *Tenorlied* and the western chanson as displayed in Schedel remained characteristic for German-speaking areas for another three generations. The genre and function of polyphonic song seem to have been well established by mid-century: the *Hofweisen* are used as 'Gesellschaftslieder' ('social songs')[366] serving for collective entertainment, performed with or without audiences, in bourgeois, courtly and also monastic environments.

A large collection of songs which fit this definition is contained in the Glogauer Liederbuch of *c.*1478-80 from Silesia, a set of three partbooks (*D-B 40098*, long unavailable, now Biblioteka Jagiellónska, Kraków).[367] It is a very important source for German song despite the facts that it is not really a Liederbuch, and that it has few complete German texts. It is, in the first place, a sacred collection; 162 of a total of 292 items are Latin-texted. The German songs (about 70 in number) are recognizable only by their titles or text incipits, and the French chansons (about 30) are never identified as such: all these pieces usually have no words underlaid or have contrafactum texts in Latin. The textless pieces, including about 30 items without even a title, might have served for instrumental ensemble playing (as *carmina*: see p. 364). On the other hand, the texts may have been omitted – as in Schedel – in order to keep the music available for varying texts, according to demand.

The Glogau songs belong to an international repertory[368] which immediately precedes the development of the four-part chanson of the late fifteenth century. Less than ten secular pieces are for four voices (the fourth voice usually being added in the contratenor partbook), and the forms, textures and rhythmic conventions of the Busnois generation are observed throughout. Some of the songs with German titles or incipits can be identified as settings of popular tunes ('Es leyt eyn schlos yn österreich', no. 50; 'Es suld eyn man kein mole farn', no. 80; 'Elzeleyn, lipstis Elzeleyn', no. 250). Popular songs are also quoted in the four quodlibets (nos. 39/46, 117, 118 and 119), of which the last three have Bedyngham's 'O rosa bella' in the cantus and an amusing medley of song fragments in the lower voices. Most of the pieces, however, look like *Tenorlieder* on amorous subjects, save that no full text is recorded.

The main question is: were the German texts sung at all? I believe that most of them served only as 'tags', to identify the tune, perhaps only for the purpose of indexing (there are two indexes in each partbook). It is strange that of the many original French songs in the collection, only one piece has received a German 'tag' (Dufay's 'Dieu gard la bonne' appears here as 'Trag frischen

---

[366] A term created by Hoffmann von Fallersleben in the early nineteenth century, which has come under scrutiny since but seems hardly replaceable.

[367] Facs edn: Brown–D'Accone–Owens eds, *RMF*, vol. 6 (1986). Full transcriptions and commentary: Ringmann–Väterlein eds, *Glogauer Liederbuch*. My numbering follows Ringmann–Väterlein. A study of the German songs is Hans-Jürgen Feurich, *Die deutschen weltlichen Lieder der Glogauer Handschrift (c.1470)*, 2nd edn (Wiesbaden: Breitkopf & Härtel, 1973).

[368] In the manuscript as a whole, I count 66 musical concordances with manuscripts from Germany (mainly Schedel), Austria, Italy, Bohemia, Poland and other countries.

muth', no. 180) – whereas the others have Latin contrafactum texts or none at all. Many of the settings with German titles appear to be abstract arrangements of pre-existing tenors, not genuine songs. This suggests that the compiler, who did most of the copying and surely was the first owner, exploited a rich tradition of German song but did not intend his manuscript for actual song performances. He and his friends either sang the pieces in Latin or played them on instruments. Who was this compiler?

The manuscript itself suggests that he was a learned musician, who wrote impeccable Latin and had a secure musical hand. He was a systematic, skilful bibliophile, as evidenced by the calligraphy and the elaborate foliating and indexing system. He spent a lot of time on the compilation of the book and he had (or expected to have) friends or students with whom he could perform the pieces. His literary tastes might be illustrated by some non-liturgical items of which he did write out the full texts: the many stanzas of Conrad of Queinfurt's sacred spring song 'Du lenze gut', set as a three-part *Tenorlied* (no. 90);[369] the cantio 'Sempiterna ydeitas' (no. 138) which prays for the ducal couple of Silesia and their newly born son (*b.*1477); the four witty quodlibets; and two hexametric poems on the seasons, 'Viminibus cinge' for New Year (no. 142) and 'Alga jacet humilis' for Ascension Day ('cum scandit Christus Olympum'; no. 140). In the last-mentioned pieces, the syllables are written on the music staves of the tenor book without note-values, receiving a musical rhythm strictly from the long and short syllables of the Latin scansion. The pieces are thus the earliest specimens of the so-called 'humanist ode'.[370]

The composition which leads us closest to the owner's personality is also the most unusual and the most amusing: the satirical four-voice motet 'Probitate eminentem / Ploditando exarare' (no. 111). The tenor is 'isorhythmic' by virtue of consisting of four identical statements; the two texted upper lines keep alternating their texts in a *hoquetus*-like fashion. In this way, an ostensible praise of the blameless life of a certain Andreas Ritter unfortunately turns into the opposite, because the texts keep interfering with each other, as here at the beginning of the third section:

Et in templo	---------- est devotus	---------- pro veniaque supplicat.
------------	Raro manet -------------	in tabernis, pro se et suis cogitans.
[In church	------------ he is devout	------- and prays for forgiveness.
-----------	He is seldom -----------	in taverns, caring for his family.]

The author, who in the last section mentions his relationship to the dedicatee ('He generously treated the author of this work'), has hidden his name, 'Petrus', in an acrostic established by the first words. There is little doubt that he was Magister Petrus Wilhelmi de Grudencz, whom we have encountered before

---

[369] See Feldmann, *Musik und Musikpflege*, 150 f; Moser, *Geschichte*, vol. 1, 177.
[370] It is likely, however, that they did not originate in Silesia (see p. 538).

(p. 263). In a reconstruction of the life and works of this fascinating individual, Jaromir Černý proposes that he was not only the composer of this motet, which is in his style, but also the scribe and owner of the partbooks.[371] But Wilhelmi entered Kraków University in 1418, and his works are rooted in the style of the Ciconia period. The compiler of the Glogauer Liederbuch, on the other hand, appreciates composers like Busnois, Touront and Caron, and cannot have been working any earlier than 1477 (Wilhelmi would by then have been about 80 years old). I suggest he included the strange and old-fashioned motet because it was a personal souvenir. In other words, the owner of the partbooks was not the composer of the motet but its dedicatee: Andreas Ritter.

We know that Ritter was born c.1440 as the son of a schoolmaster of Grünberg (Zielona Góra), and that he was a scholar in nearby Glogau until c.1465, when he became a canon in the Augustinian abbey of Sagan (Zagań) under the music-loving abbot Martin Rinkenberg (1468–89 +). Rinkenberg, who had a master's degree (1441) from Leipzig University, is said to have introduced mensural music into the liturgy and the pastimes of the abbey. A chronicler reports, for example, musical endowments made by Rinkenberg. One of them stipulated that the students of the abbey school had to sing the antiphon 'Ave regina celorum, mater regis angelorum' on all feast-days before procession, 'with tenor, discant and contratenor'.[372] Walter Frye's setting, which of course answers this description, is in the Glogauer Liederbuch (no. 144). Polyphony was also practised in the Augustinian monastery of Grünberg, as well as in St Nicolaus of Glogau and other parishes of the area.

The musical and intellectual atmosphere of centres like Grünberg, Glogau or Sagan Abbey cannot easily be recalled to our imagination today.[373] A person like Ritter might have typified it; a highly educated musical amateur, a local man who must have been to a university – he was enough of an intellectual to have befriended Magister Wilhelmi. Like his contemporary Schedel (whom he could have met if he went to Leipzig University), he would have collected music throughout his student years. Later, he would have spent his empty days in the Augustinian abbey – a typical retirement place for wealthy burghers – on his manuscript, and performed the music together with other canons in this 'unreformed' community. Ritter died in 1480, committing suicide after a dispute with the abbot.

Chapels, schools and their music books

One aspect of central European sacred polyphony of the later fifteenth century, often overlooked, is its enormous quantity. We are dealing, in fact, with the

---

[371] Černý, 'Petrus Wilhelmi', 93. The attribution of 'Sempiterna ydeitas' to Wilhelmi is without stylistic foundation; the fact that 'Probitate' also stands in the Polish source *PL-Pu 7022* (see p. 515), hardly proves that Glogau had anything to do with him. See also Feldmann, *Musik und Musikpflege*, 139 n. 404.

[372] Pietzsch, *Zur Pflege*, 86 f.

[373] See Feldmann, *Musik und Musikpflege*, 128 f, 138–42, 205, and pp. 363 f above with pl. 7.

large geographical area between the Baltic Sea and the Alps, the Lower Rhine valley and the Hungarian plains: politically, the Holy Roman Empire (with Bohemia) plus the kingdoms of Poland and Hungary. Centres that were likely to cultivate art-music were the *c*.50 episcopal Sees, the big merchant cities (hanseatic and imperial free cities foremost), the residences not only of the emperor and the kings of Poland, Bohemia and Hungary, but of most of the greater and smaller territorial lords as well.[374] There were also the universities, and the cathedral and monastic schools, which alone seem to have generated more than half of the surviving manuscript sources.[375] Measured against the survival rate of the institutions and cities themselves, the transmission of their music is very good. We have literally thousands of compositions – native and foreign – in the codices of the area.[376]

In the earlier fifteenth century, however, organized polyphonic chapels were still rare. Outside the imperial court and some prominent ducal households (possibly the Tyrol, Bavaria and the Palatinate), the use of sacred polyphony was due to individual initiatives, for example the appointment of a succentor, in the bigger churches and monasteries. Great changes took place around mid-century, however, when western European models were adopted for the constitution of court chapels as well as for the repertory which they were expected to contribute. At the same time local musicians, who were or were not attached to these chapels, were busy copying the music for their own purposes as schoolmasters, cathedral succentors and university magisters. This is how foreign music spread to provincial *Kantoreien* in the mid-fifteenth century, and how it became mixed with modest and not-so-modest local imitations.

The development began – so it seems to me – in the *Habsburg* dominions, where the imperial court chapel and those of the dukes of Austria had imported western polyphony well before 1450. (See also pp. 253 f.) King Albrecht II (*r.* 1437–9) had Netherlands singers, among whom was Johannes Brassart of Liège, the *magister capelle* of his predecessor Sigismund. The funeral motet for King Albrecht, 'Romanorum Rex' (1439), mentions seven chapel members by name:

> Ergo Brassart cum Erasmo
> Adam serva, Io. de Sarto

---

[374] A documentary overview of courts cultivating music is Pietzsch, *Fürsten*.

[375] Pietzsch, *Zur Pflege*, is a guide to the music at 'German' universities. The author inappropriately (if usefully) includes Prague and Kraków. See also Ward, 'Music and music theory'.

[376] The following cities listed in the *Census Catalogue* still hold in their libraries significant fifteenth-century music manuscripts of local or regional origin: Augsburg, Basle, Berlin (supra-regional, but including central–north German sources), Dresden (1/D/504–6), Hradec Králové, Jena (Saxon court choirbooks), Klatovy, Kraków (2464), Leipzig (1236, 1494), Munich, Prague, Regensburg (C98, C120), Saint Gall, Trent, Vienna (international, Habsburg court repertoire, regional sources), Warsaw, Weimar (Saxon court choirbooks), Wrocław (U 428), Zwickau (Stephan Roth MSS). Supplement: Bratislava (33, 318), Leipzig (U 1084), Linz (529), Poznań. See also 'Sources, IX, 6' in *The New Grove*.

Iohannisque pariter
Tirion, Martin et Galer,
cantores celeriter
psallentes Cristo regi . . .[377]

[Therefore, serve, Brassart with Erasmus, Adam, Johannes de Sarto, and Tirion, Martin and Galer, all equally called Johannes, you *cantores* singing for Christ the King...]

The chapel, now under Frederick of Austria, most probably included choir-boys, as it had done under Sigismund (see p. 252). Their names, if present, would have to be sought at the end of the list. I suggest that they were Johannes Tirion, Johannes Martin and Johannes Galer. If not choirboys, these three will in any case have been the youngest chapel members.

It is not entirely speculative to identify 'Tirion' with Johannes Touront, the important composer whose extant works were all known in the Habsburg terri-tories and Bohemia (see p. 511). They must have been composed in the 1450s and 60s; thus he can well have been ten to fifteen years old in 1439.

Johannes Martin is probably the 'little Martinus, singer' to whom Duke Albrecht VI gave a reward in May 1444 in Wiener Neustadt (see p. 310). Just a month earlier, King Frederick III (Duke Albrecht's brother) had founded a col-legiate church in his castle-chapel of Wiener Neustadt, endowing among other services a daily Mass of the Trinity sung by four 'scolares'.[378] Time and place are compatible with the idea that this singer was born about 1430 and was the same person as Johannes Martini, who surfaces in 1471 at Constance Cathedral, already a known composer and heading for an appointment in Ferrara.[379] This musician from Brabant (or Armentières, Flanders), died in Ferrarese service in 1497. He would have come to Austria in his youth.

King Frederick's collegiate foundation in Wiener Neustadt was probably intended as a 'reservoir' for the training of his court chaplains. This resident foundation was, of course, not identical with his itinerant household chapel. There are analogies here with Burgundy and England; a specific model for the household chapel was probably that of Leonello d'Este in Ferrara. We have seen above (p. 254) that the royal chapel regularly sang sacred polyphony and pro-bably used the Aosta Codex; that the king sought to replenish it with Nether-lands and even English singers, and tried to obtain church benefices for them.[380]

---

[377] De Van, 'A recently discovered source', 57. The list is often quoted with the incorrect conflations 'Erasmus Adam' and 'Martingale'. On Brassart, de Sarto, Adam and the manuscript *Ao*, see p. 253.

[378] See Pietzsch, *Fürsten*, 60.

[379] See Manfred Schuler, 'Beziehungen zwischen der Konstanzer Domkantorei und der Hofkapelle des Herzogs Ercole I von Ferrara', *AnMc* 15 (1975), 15-20; Lockwood, *Ferrara*, 131 f. The identi-fication with the Habsburg singer was first suggested to me by Brian Trowell. Most documents spell Martini's surname as 'Martin' or 'Martinus'; no evidence supports the assumption that he was born *c*.1440. Further on him, see p. 613.

[380] Pietzsch, *Fürsten*, 59 f. The king's privileged requests for church benefices were called the 'preces primariae'. See Georg Reichert, 'Die preces-primariae-Register Maximilians I. und seine Hof-kapelle um 1508', *AMw* 11 (1954), 103-19.

The names of about fifteen chaplains, Netherlanders and Germans, are known between the years *c*.1440 and *c*.1470, plus that of an Italian organist, Anton Kcharfrey ('Carveri'? from 1465). On his journey to the coronation in Rome, in 1451-2, Frederick was accompanied by fifteen *cantores*.[381] It appears that from *c*.1466 the German and Netherlands singers were separate groups.

The king usually resided in Graz or Wiener Neustadt. *Vienna* was the residence of his brother Albrecht VI (d.1463) and, in 1455-7, of King Ladislas Postumus (1440-57), son of King Albrecht II and thus heir to the duchy of Lower Austria as well as the thrones of Hungary and Bohemia. In the Vienna *Burgkapelle*, about six or seven *cantores* sang under Duke Albrecht VI in 1444 (see p. 311). Frederick, on behalf of the young Ladislas, renovated the chapel building and in 1455 endowed it with benefices for the resident clergy, plus four (adult) *cantores*. The three further singers were apparently boys, just as in the motet of 1439. As with the collegiate foundation of Wiener Neustadt, these singers were not household chaplains.[382] Another important foundation was the 'citizens'' school and *Kantorei* of the collegiate church of St Stephen's. This was a civic institution and had its own building, erected in 1440 near the church; its earliest statute, of 1446, mentions the functions of cantor and subcantor. The regulations of 1460 explicitly prescribe the teaching of *cantus figurativus* as well as *conducten* to the boys according to ability.[383] Cantor from 1440 to 1449 was the composer Hermann Edlerawer.[384] Archival documents relating to him, to the school of St Stephen's, the university to which it was attached, the city and the ducal court, reveal an intricate network of administrative links. The cantor, as an official of the magistrate, appeared (and probably performed) in the city hall at receptions of noble guests, at annual feasts and dinners of the magistrate which were held, for example, on *Reminiscere* Sunday. He had to sing the respective Masses together with his assistants and choirboys. Later city cantors of St Stephen's were Conrad Lindenfels (first cited 13 November 1449; also in 1486), Thomas List (1464, 1467), Hans Payr (1476, 1477), Wolfgang Goppinger (1486, 1492) and Thomas Wiener (1509). Their assistants included Michael Wülfing (1457), Hans Richter (1465) and Sigmund Örtl (1473). The magistrate also had a foundation for four *scolares* in the chapel of the city hall, where they had to sing Mass regularly; the cantor and the boys

---

[381] See Pietzsch, *Fürsten*, 60-71; Helmut Federhofer, 'Die Niederländer an den Habsburgerhöfen in Österreich', *Anzeiger der Österreichischen Akademie der Wissenschaften, Phil.-Hist. Klasse*, vol. 93 (1956), 102-20. The accounts for *c*.1445-66 are missing. Hans Boubay, who joined *c*.1461, can have been Jean Boubert (see p. 447). Hans von Blidemberch also served in 1481 in Maximilian's 'Burgundian' chapel: see Higgins, *Busnois*, 111.

[382] Coelestin Wolfsgruber, *Die k. und k. Hofburgkapelle und die k. und k. geistliche Hofkapelle* (Vienna, 1905), 36-41.

[383] Josef Mantuani, *Die Musik in Wien. Von der Römerzeit bis zur Zeit des Kaisers Max I.* (Vienna, 1907, repr. Hildesheim: Olms, 1979), 285 f; Strohm, 'Native and foreign polyphony', 207 f.

[384] Rumbold, 'Compilation of Munich Clm *14274*', 169-76. I believe that Edlerawer still held the function of cantor in 1449, with a salary of 52fl. p.a. (Stadtarchiv Vienna, Oberkammeramtsrechnungen I, 10 (1449), fol. 32r). This and the following notices are drawn from the city accounts, and from Anton Mayer *et al.*, *Quellen zur Geschichte der Stadt Wien*, 10 vols. (Vienna, 1895-1937).

were further responsible for a major Corpus Christi procession with music, endowed by King Frederick *c.*1445. A university scholar, Thomas Oedenhofer, gave private lessons in *cantus figurativus*; among his students (*c.*1460) were the Augsburg patricians Andreas and Paul Kaufringer, and even burgomaster Gossembrot of Vienna and his daughter Sibilla.[385] Of other musical institutions in Vienna, the Benedictine 'Schottenkloster' with its school and *Kantorei*, and the Augustinian abbey of St Dorothy, are worth mentioning, especially since polyphonic fragments exist which seem to have belonged to these houses after *c.*1460.[386]

The enormous music collection of the seven *Trent Codices* (*c.*1700 pieces, if Mass sections are counted individually) has been studied for a century now, but its significance is still inadequately defined. The existence of so much European polyphony in a place as seemingly remote as Trent has been widely considered a mere accident of transmission or survival; few scholars have asked why so much music was copied there, and what it was needed for.[387]

The oldest two codices (*Tr 87* and *92*) were created around 1440 by the priest and organist from Bolzano, Johannes Lupi.[388] In his will of *c.*1455, he bequeathed his splendid collection of musical instruments to personal friends and colleagues, but his 'six books of *cantus figuratus*' to the parish church of Bolzano, where he held a chaplaincy. In doing so, he probably identified the place for which his music books had originally been compiled. The parish of Our Lady at Bolzano was then the cultural centre of a lively town with international trading connections, and its parish school was a centre of musical education, controlled and subsidized by the magistrate. In assembling his codices, Lupi probably hoped that his protector Duke Sigismund of Tyrol would make him parish rector or at least schoolmaster of Bolzano – positions for which the music collection would be useful indeed.

The wealth and ceremonial activity of this parish is documented by the inventories of its liturgical books,[389] by the fact that between 1484 and 1487 the famous Burkhart Distlinger of Bressanone could build two new organs (one small, one large), that around 1480–1500 its schoolmasters, especially Benedikt Debs, started to develop the most exuberant series of mystery plays ever seen in central Europe,[390] and indeed by civic records referring to continuous music-

---

[385] Pietzsch, *Zur Pflege*, 30 f and 33 f.

[386] Flotzinger-Gruber, *Musikgeschichte Österreichs*, 212–17; Strohm, 'Native and foreign polyphony', 212 f and 223 f.

[387] This is not to deny the importance of other studies. A blend of recent philological and stylistic enquiries is offered in Pirrotta-Curti eds, *Codici Musicali*. The best general description of the codices is still that by Adler and Koller in *DTOe VII*, vols. 14–15.

[388] See Wright, 'Origins Trent 87-I and 92-II', and p. 255 above.

[389] Hannes Obermair, 'Die liturgischen Bücher der Pfarrkirche Bozen aus dem letzten Viertel des 15. Jahrhunderts', *Der Schlern* 50 (1985), 516–36.

[390] Anton Dörrer, 'Tiroler Passionsspiele' in *VL* 3, 741–835, and 5, 870; Walter Lipphardt, 'Musik in den spätmittelalterlichen Passionsspielen und Osterspielen von Bozen, Sterzing und Brixen', in Egon Kühebacher ed., *Tiroler Volksschauspiel* (Bolzano: Athesia, 1976), 127–66.

making at the parish school itself.[391] They tell us how the magistrate employed the schoolmaster, succentors (*Junkmeister*), assistants (*Astanten*) and boys for ceremonial music, and quote countless 'sung anniversaries' endowed by citizens and guilds.[392] In a dispute between the city and the parish rector over the choice of schoolmaster (*Ratsprotokoll* of 1475), the magistrate told its candidate, Albrecht Weinreich, not to bother about singing in church if the priest did not want to give him his food; his cash salary would be paid to him as long as he fulfilled his civic singing duties.

One of them was the customary *Ansingen* with the boys on the higher feasts. The *Kantorei* went out in the streets, especially to the houses of nobles and wealthy burghers, but also to taverns and the hospital, and sang seasonal sacred hymns, motets and other compositions. The money received was delivered to the church wardens as representatives of the magistrate. For each festal period, the schoolmaster accounted for earnings six or seven times his own annual salary – after expenses paid for a good meal for the boys, assistants, organist and sexton. It is this custom which surfaces in an account of Venetian ambassadors travelling through the Tyrol in 1492:

> In Chiusa (Klausen), during dinner, there came two music masters with five boys, who sang various songs and one in particular, which sounded like a battle piece with trumpets . . . especially one boy, smaller than the others, distinguished himself by his voice. The listeners were excited to observe these boys sing together with their masters without seeing the music. The ambassadors gave each of them a sixpence, and much more to the masters, encouraging them to continue with their musical education . . . .
> In Vipiteno [Sterzing], the ambassadors again enjoyed the singing of five boys and three masters.[393]

The admiration expressed for singing by heart, and other clues, make it certain that the singing was polyphonic. *Ansingen* had to have an artistic appeal which distinguished it from plainchant and folksong. The practice relied on musical patronage; the princes or the wealthy merchants of a city showed their largesse by paying for skilled musical performances. As evinced by Duke Albrecht's travel accounts of 1444, such performances were regular occurrences in Austria and southern Germany. The schoolboys had sometimes to travel to sing before a prince in his lodgings: the Vienna *Kantorei* sang for Duke Albrecht in Zemendorf, the Erding *Kantorei* in Salzburg (see pp. 309, 312).

The courts were also keen to assemble their own groups of choristers – and that included older students, who could sing tenor and bass. Duke Sigismund sent his agents from Innsbruck to the schools of the area to fetch choirboys. In 1466, for example, he poached one boy from Merano and four from Trent.

---

[391] City Archives, Bolzano, no. 171 ff: Rats-, Burgermeister- und Amtsrechnungen (from 1465); no. 639 ff: Kirchprobstrechnungen (from 1470); no. 4 ff: Ratsprotokolle (from 1469); charters.

[392] Such as the guild whose chaplain Johannes Lupi was, the basket-makers ('cotzel pinters' as named in Lupi's will: I owe the explanation of the term to Dr Hannes Obermair, Bolzano), or the guild of Corpus Christi, founded in 1463.

[393] Moser, *Hofhaimer*, 12 f (with other important notices).

Once accepted, the choirboys were carefully educated, and travelled widely
with the duke or his chaplains.[394] In 1487, Margrave Johann Cicero of Brandenburg had three choirboys brought to him from as far as the Tyrol.[395] In 1472-3,
Ercole d'Este of Ferrara hired what would have been a whole *Kantorei* – nine
boys and their master – from Constance Cathedral and elsewhere: no doubt he
paid their churches well to let them go.[396]

Johannes Wiser joined this educational 'industry' at Trent Cathedral, an
ancient foundation within a busy Italian/German merchant city, ruled by a
German prince-bishop with Habsburg support. (See Plate 9.) Wiser is first
cited as succentor of the newly appointed schoolmaster, Johannes Prenner, on
30 July 1455.[397] By 1459, he had himself obtained the position of schoolmaster,

9 Trent Cathedral, view from the north

[394] Senn, *Musik und Theater*, 11 and 14.

[395] Pietzsch, *Fürsten*, 132.

[396] Lockwood, *Ferrara*, 318 f; see also p. 604 below.

[397] Wright, 'Origins Trent 87-I and 92-II', 261 n. 42. Wright reads an impossible 'suonatore' for 'suc-
centore'. Usually, the *Junkmeister* came with the schoolmaster. The document styles the schoolmaster as belonging to the city ('scholaris in dicta civitate'): like elsewhere, the citizens regarded
the school as theirs.

which he held until 1466. It is during these years (1455–66) that Wiser and a few assistants copied the codices *Tr 90, 88* and *89* (*Tr 91*, the latest of the series, was copied *c.*1468–80 incorporating only some of his work). The heaviest amount of copying was done in the early years. Wiser first copied the contents of a manuscript that was already there, the Mass collection *Tr 93*, into *Tr 90*. Then followed miscellaneous pieces, later bound at the end of both codices. By *c.*1459, over 400 pieces were assembled. Obviously Wiser tried to build a personal collection for his career as a cantor or schoolmaster. Had he not been appointed at Trent itself, he would have taken his copies with him – except for *Tr 93* which was not his. Instead, he remained and was able to enlarge the collection further over the years, as well as use much of the material in performances. These usually led to corrections in the often hastily written copies, whereas pieces that remained uncorrected were perhaps never performed under Wiser. The copies, whether bound or not, would serve the succentor and assistants in the rehearsals and perhaps performances of the works, but the boys would all sing by heart (as observed by the Venetian ambassadors).

Not only the physical status of the codices,[398] but also their musical contents match the needs of a *Kantorei*. The largest ingredient, Mass cycles and individual sections, would have been performed not so much at the daily services in the cathedral choir as for endowed Masses in guild chapels, of which Trent must have had even more than Bolzano. There must have been Masses for civic ceremonies – whether in the cathedral or the city hall – plus private services for visiting nobles. (Trent was a natural stopover between Venice and Innsbruck.) Masses were surely also requested by the bishop, who had his private chapel in the castle, or by other nobles such as the Tyrolean captain Balthasar von Liechtenstein who resided in Castel Beseno out of town. Endowed ceremonies in which the *Kantorei* participated must have included civic processions, Vespers and 'Salve' services, as in any urban centre of the time. For such purposes, Wiser collected innumerable Vespers hymns, *Magnificat* and 'Salve regina' settings, and other antiphons and responds. These pieces, furthermore, were suitable for *Ansingen* tours, as were the various *cantiones* and other popular festal songs, for example seven settings of the *Leise* 'Christ ist erstanden / Christus surrexit' for Easter, three 'Resonet in laudibus' and two 'Dies est letitie / Der Tag der ist so freudenreich' for Christmas. The over one hundred secular pieces may have been performed without words or with contrafactum texts; they remind us that at least the prince-bishop would have the right to hear the boys sing in his dining hall like any secular ruler. For certain political events, special performances were commissioned, an example being the five motets celebrating Bishops Georg Hack (1444–65) and Johann Hinderbach (1465–86).[399] Most (or all) of these occasional pieces are contrafacta, and the poem 'Clerus istius venerandus urbis' for Bishop Hinderbach is entered in *Tr 89*, fol. 199r,

---

[398] Some of this can even be seen from the facs edn: see *Trent Codices*.
[399] See *DTÖe VII*, vols. 14–15, plates II, III, V and VI, and pp. 81–8.

without music – a sign that local composers were rare. The local patron saint, St Vigilius, did not receive a single original composition. What Wiser's group could sing in his annual procession and services on 26 June, were two hymns 'Ut queant laxis' with a contrafactum text for St Vigilius, 'Gaudio summo celebrare festa' (nos. 594 and 1090).[400] The latter piece was composed by Christofferus Anthony, who was in all likelihood the nobleman and public notary Christophorus Anthonii de Molveno, a member of the Italian upper class in Trent and possibly a patron of music.[401] The codices also contain attributions to the possibly local composers Hainricus Collis (nos. 203 and 1073: fragments of a Mass cycle?) and Ludovicus Krafft (no. 1007). For the most part, however, the music of the codices was of external origin.

Where did it come from?[402] Above all, the Tyrolean-north Italian commercial centres saw so many long-distance travellers that they must have had access to music from virtually anywhere. In addition, a university-trained schoolmaster in Trent with Habsburg backing could deploy his own connections. The role of the provost – and then bishop – Johann Hinderbach has never been clarified. He was more interested in plainsong books, but it is likely that he helped his schoolmaster to find polyphonic music as well: for example in Vienna which was really Hinderbach's home (several of his cousins were connected with the university there), or in Rome, where he repeatedly stayed as a personal envoy of the emperor. It is likely that much liturgical music from France and the Low Countries reached Trent via Italian institutions, for example St Peter's, Rome, and Verona Cathedral. But these links account for only some of the foreign 'clusters' or individual works in the codices. A more important reason why so many European repertories – or fragments thereof – are merged here, is the existence or development of an *inner network* of court chapels and great cathedrals in south-east central Europe: from Trent to Kraków, from Esztergom and Buda to Leipzig and Torgau. We know little about these institutions, but repertorial research suggests that the Trent Codices, together with about a dozen similar sources from Austria, Moravia, Bohemia, Slovakia, Saxony, Silesia and Poland, indeed reflect the musical practices and repertories of these places.

An illustration of our insufficient knowledge of this 'inner network' is provided by the career of Johannes Touront. His works are found in virtually all of the central European choirbooks, with a concentration in two sources from Czechoslovakia: the codices Strahov and Speciálník (see below). Is it reasonable, then, to assume that he worked in Bohemia?[403] A piece by him which is found in both manuscripts, 'Chorus iste, pie Christe', contains the

---

[400] (Nos. refer to the thematic indexes in *DTOe VII*, vols. 14–15 and *XXXI*, vol. 61.) The divergence between a 'local liturgy' and the polyphonic collection has been demonstrated in Saunders, *Dating of the Trent Codices*, ch. III.

[401] Documents on him as well as issued by him are known from 1449 to 1468, for example Bayer. Haupt- und Staatsarchiv, Munich, HL Trient, vol. IV, fol. 100v.

[402] On the subject of this paragraph, see also Strohm, 'Native and foreign polyphony', 221–4.

[403] As suggested by Tom R. Ward, 'Touront, Johannes' in *The New Grove*.

words 'sit pax bone voluntatis nobis in Bohemia'. This text, however, is found only in the later codex Speciálník, whereas in Strahov, the piece is textless (no. 233). It is possible that Touront wrote it for a different text and that the words referring to Bohemia are a contrafactum. As said above (p. 505), there is a likelihood that the composer was a choirboy or younger chaplain under King Albrecht II in 1439. If he ever left the Habsburg sphere for Bohemia, he may have served under King Georg Podiebrad (r. 1458–71), who favoured music and supported the theorist Paulus Paulirinus. In October 1481, the 'singers of the King of Bohemia' received a gift of 84 pennies from the magistrate of Regensburg – as did the 'Burgundian singers'.[404] The sum paid to the two groups suggests that there were seven singers in each. Apart from speculating that Busnois may have visited Germany on this occasion, we must admit uncertainty as to the Bohemian chapel. The young Wladislaw Jagiełło, son of King Kasimir IV of Poland, had been elected king as successor to Podiebrad in 1471, but Mathias Corvinus, King of Hungary, had forced the Czechs to accept him as nominal King of Bohemia in treaties of 1469 and 1479. Both these magnates must have had chapels following western traditions. The latter, married to Beatrice of Aragon since 1476, idolized Italian Renaissance culture and accordingly employed Netherlands singers (see p. 605). The former was a grandson of Albrecht II of Habsburg, whose daughter Elisabeth had married King Kasimir IV of Poland. The political and cultural alliance of the Jagiellonian dynasty with Habsburg may imply, after all, that Touront worked in Kraków and Prague.

No music collection of the royal Bohemian chapel is known. On the other hand, an abundant – and essentially different – picture of Czech music results from the numerous choirbooks of the associations of *literati*.[405] These middle-class fraternities, who adhered to the various streams of Bohemian Protestantism, were somewhat analogous to Italian *laudesi* or Franco-Netherlands *rhétoriqueurs* in their spirit of collective devotion and cultivation of the arts. Socially, they were also comparable to the German Meistersinger and their schools. They sang themselves, but also employed civic schoolmasters and schoolboys. Active *literati* groups are documented in Prague, Hradec Králové, Klatovy, Rakovník, Kutná Hora, Sedlčany, Tábor, Chrudim and many smaller towns. Their splendidly illuminated manuscripts (the most famous is the 'Franus cantional' of Hradec Králové) are usually *cantionalia*, or graduals with Mass chants. Many of them contain simple liturgical polyphony – especially Credos, also in the vernacular, and other Mass Ordinary settings. In the *cantionalia*, one finds almost any kind of monophonic and polyphonic sacred songs in Latin and Czech; there are conductus-like *cantiones* (also called *cantilene*), antiphons,

---

[404] Sterl, 'Regensburger Stadtrechnungen', 288. This trip of the Burgundian singers (by command of Archduke Maximilian?) has not been noticed before.

[405] For an introduction, see: Černý, 'Zur Frage'; Černý-Mikan, *Pearls of Old Parchments*; Orel, 'Stilarten'; Jaromir Černý, 'Die mehrtextige Motette des 14. und 15. Jahrhunderts in Böhmen', in Rudolf Pecman ed., *Colloquium Musica Bohemica et Europea*, Brno, vol. 5 (1972), 71–88; (and a contribution by Kurt von Fischer in the same volume, 55–61). For the older styles, see pp. 328–33 above.

hymns, and the peculiar multi-textual 'Bohemian motets' derived from Ars nova idioms, for example by Petrus Wilhelmi (see p. 263). In this musical sphere, traditional and advanced polyphonic repertories co-existed in separate layers or sometimes in interaction. Most strikingly, this culture survived without any major changes until the early seventeenth century (when Bohemian Protestantism was broken by the Habsburgs).

The only two codices which contain substantial amounts of modern mensural music, Strahov and Speciálník, are in many ways typical for the diverging aspirations of Moravian and Bohemian circles at this time. They are also typical for the quantity of music which single institutions in central Europe used or needed.

The Strahov Codex (*CS-Ppp D.G. IV. 47*) is a collection of 328 mostly Latin-texted pieces including contrafacta of chansons (the only vernacular texts belong to three German songs).[406] The codex was compiled between *c.*1475 and 1480 for an important church or school, possibly Olomouc Cathedral (Moravia). It does not contain a single Czech word, and its sacred music is strictly Roman Catholic, i.e. it cannot have been used in Bohemia, except perhaps at the court of Wladislaw Jagiełło. The repertorial overlap with Austrian sources, especially *Tr 90, 88* and *89*, points to Habsburg influence. Connections with the court chapel of Mathias Corvinus are also probable, and would explain the presence of works composed in Naples. In this manuscript, Tourout (with fourteen pieces) almost appears as a 'local' composer. Nothing is known about 'Philippus Francis', by whom there is the Mass–motet cycle 'Hilf und gib rat' and two other pieces in the codex, nor about 'Flemmik', with three Mass sections.

The first half of the collection focuses on Mass music: introits, Mass Ordinary sections and cycles. Many pieces recur in other sources of the 'inner network', as well as abroad, but it is symptomatic that the Mass 'O rosa bella' (III) – unrelated to the Masses I and II on this tune (on which see p. 426) – coincides in its texture not with the copy in *Tr 89* of *c.*1466, but with another copy made at Ferrara *c.*1481 (*Mod D*).[407] The style resembles that of Johannes Martini, who reached Ferrara from Constance in 1473 (see p. 520). The Strahov–*Mod D* version has a much smaller total range than that of *Tr 89*, where the second contratenor is notated a fifth lower. As *Tr 89* is the oldest source, *Mod D* and Strahov may represent a revision for an ensemble lacking low-pitched voices, perhaps the Ferrara chapel.[408]

The second half of the codex concentrates on Office hymns, *Magnificat* settings, antiphons and *cantiones*. There is material for ceremonies, processions and *Ansingen* tours on high feasts. Many pieces are textless: the usual reservoir

---

[406] Full inventory and description, partial edition in Snow, *Manuscript Strahov*. See also Strohm, 'Missa super "Nos amis"', on date and provenance.

[407] See Lockwood, *Ferrara*, 217.

[408] Snow, *Manuscript Strahov*, 99–101, argues the opposite. But see Lockwood, *Ferrara*, 239: 'the versions of a number of Masses in *Mod D* by Martini, Faugues, and Caron differ substantially from the versions found in contemporary MSS, copied at Trent, Verona, and Rome . . .'.

for contrafactum texts fitting various occasions. Others have Latin texts mostly for Christmas, including a setting of the *lauda* 'In natali domini' (no. 183; the widely known tune is in the cantus). Six pieces are for St Nicholas whose name is hidden in acrostics – for example in no. 234:

[Nova instant cantica, omnes laudes attollite, vestris sonis . . . .[409]

Almost all these texts are newly made (by the schoolmaster?) and in some pre-humanist kind of Latin. They served for the schoolboy ceremonies around Christmas. 'Nova instant cantica' is attributed to Touront, and at closer inspection appears to be a French rondeau. A textless piece by Tourout (no. 236), which was probably intended for a similar contrafactum use, looks very much like a German *Tenorlied*. 'Nobis instat carminis' (no. 217) is based on the tenor 'Stella celi' also used by Walter Frye (see p. 428). This section of the codex, with several other English and French works (including two by Frye), is the simplest in function but 'international' in repertory. There is an interesting analogy here with the fragments of Košiče (*Kassa*), found in books of a monastery in Upper Hungary (now Slovakia). One of them contains a number of *cantiones* – including 'Christ ist erstanden' in four languages – which is characteristic of this Hungarian/German/Slovakian/Polish region. A younger fragment from the same place contains liturgical pieces (among which is a 'Kyrie paschale' with monorhythmic plainsong tenor) and *cantiones* such as 'Dies est letitie', 'Surrexit Christus hodie' etc., plus Frye's 'Ave regina celorum'.[410]

This work is also contained in the Speciálník Codex of Hradec Králové (*CS-HK II A 7*), left to us by *literati* from Prague as an impressive document of their widespread musical interests. The manuscript, with 201 pieces, was written between *c.*1480 and *c.*1540, and combines the types of gradual, *cantionale* and modern mensural codex.[411] The mensural repertory includes Tourout, Isaac, Josquin, Tinctoris, Weerbeke, Pullois, Philippon, Agricola, Frye ('Ave regina celorum' with an added fourth voice, p. 406) and even Plummer ('Tota pulchra es', p. 368). Busnois is not named, but a five-part Sanctus uses the tune 'Dieu quel mariage' from his chanson 'Corps digne / Dieu quel mariage' as double cantus firmus in simultaneous forward and retrograde motion.[412] It would be interesting to know in what relation this work stands to the Agnus Dei of Josquin's 'Missa L'homme armé sexti toni' (see p. 617). Many other pieces in Speciálník seem to be taken over from the Strahov Codex.

Bishop Zbigniew Olesnicki of Kraków may already have had a polyphonic

---

[409] Ed. in Snow, *Manuscript Strahov*. The other acrostics are in nos. 211, 216, 217, 218 and 235. Snow's description, pp. 146–54, overlooks this phenomenon.

[410] *CC*, vol. 5, 292 f ('BratisM 33' and 'BratisM 318'); Benjamin Rajeczky, 'Mittelalterliche Mehrstimmigkeit in Ungarn', in Lissa ed., *Musica Antiqua*, 223–36.

[411] For an interpretation of this multiplicity, see Černý, 'Zur Frage'. Inventory in Dobroslav Orel, *Der Mensuralkodex 'Speciálník': Ein Beitrag zur Geschichte der Mensuralmusik und Notenschrift in Böhmen bis 1540* (Vienna, 1914) (typescript). See also Orel, 'Stilarten'.

[412] Černý–Mikan, *Pearls*, after pl. 17. Busnois' chanson is also in *D-B 40021*, no. 24. David Fallows informs me that p. 255 contains Busnois' song 'Vous marchez du bout du pied'.

chapel in the 1440s. At any rate, he employed in 1441 the *cantores* Othmarus Opilionis and his brother Blasius, of Jawor, both students at Kraków University.[413] A three-part chanson attributed to Othmarus Opilionis survives without text in *Tr 93* (no. 1831), a good example of the cohesion of the 'inner network'. Some late fifteenth-century fragments of uncommon interest have recently been found in Poznań (*PL-Pu 7022*); they contain the remains of Masses by Dufay, Petrus de Domarto and Josquin des Prez, and Wilhelmi's 'Probitate eminentem' (see p. 502). The handwriting, and a concordance with *Linz 529* (see p. 523), suggest Austrian connections. The fragments were found in town registers of Lwów (Lemberg; now Ukraine), and perhaps belonged originally to a codex at the episcopal court of Lwów.[414]

The royal Polish chapel, where Touront could have spent some time, was the main sphere of activity of the German composer Heinrich Finck. Born in Bamberg *c.*1445, he was a choirboy at the Kraków court from 1454, matriculated at Leipzig University in 1482, and served various members of the Jagiellonian dynasty until at least 1505. Between 1510 and 1514 he was court Kapellmeister in Stuttgart, and later worked in Salzburg and Vienna, where he died in 1527. No fewer than 113 compositions by him can be documented. Only some of the extant works are of the fifteenth century: a three-part 'Missa sine nomine' and several motets and hymns.[415]

The appearance of Finck marks a major transformation in the central European sacred repertory. At the stage of the Trent Codices and Glogau, the artistic superiority of the western masters and the apprentice-status of local composers had been unquestionable. Not that all the production was provincial: some successful native pieces travelled widely within the 'inner network', appearing in places as far apart as Trent and Sagan. A few foreign composers worked in the area: Touront; perhaps Philippus Francis, Flemmik, Martini and Paulus de Rhoda (see p. 363). Sacred styles were derived largely from the idioms of the Dufay–Ockeghem orbit. Around 1480, this picture changes suddenly with the appearance of the sacred music of the Josquin generation and a striking number of Germans emulating it. This 'earliest generation of German composers'[416] must be measured with the same yardstick as their colleagues abroad. Direct interaction and, in some cases, a reversal of influences becomes possible.

This can be seen in four large codices from Saxony, Silesia and the Tyrol, which have often been compared with each other: *D-LEu 1494* (the codex of the Leipzig Magister Nikolaus Apel), with 163 pieces; *D-B 40021*, which combines repertory from Nuremberg and Saxony, altogether 151 works; *PL-Wu*

[413] Pietzsch, *Zur Pflege*, 44 and 55.

[414] See Perz, 'Lvov fragments'.

[415] See Lothar Hoffmann-Erbrecht, 'Finck, Heinrich' in *The New Grove*; idem, *Henricus Finck – musicus excellentissimus* (Cologne, 1982); see also the contributions by Eric F. Fiedler and Lothar Hoffmann-Erbrecht in Finscher ed., *Renaissance-Studien*.

[416] So named in the title of Ehmann, *Adam*. The label is not entirely fair to the Monk of Salzburg, Oswald von Wolkenstein, Wilhelmi, Edlerawer, Paumann, etc.

Mf. 2016 (*olim Rps. mus. 58*), from Wrocław, with 95 works; and *D-Mbs 3154* (the codex of the Innsbruck school rector Nicolaus Leopold), with 190 pieces.[417] These sources have in common with each other – and to some extent with Speciálník – that they are compiled over a longer time-span, largely from previously independent manuscript units, and that they reflect ongoing exchanges with other centres.[418]

We encounter here the music of the great Franco-Netherlanders of Josquin's generation. Although we shall discuss these composers in the last chapter, it is just as well to pay attention to them now from this angle. Apart from about ten (mostly minor) composers, by whom our sources contain only one or two works each, there is a remarkable concentration on the following masters:

	Apel	*40021*	*Mf. 2016*	*Leopold*	*total*
Isaac	9	10 (or 12)	6 (or 7)	6	31 (34)
Agricola	1	8 (or 11)	5 (or 7)	2	16 (21)
Obrecht	2	3	–	6	11
Josquin	1	4	2 (or 3)	2 (or 4)	9 (12)
Martini	–	1	(2?)	7 (or 9)	8 (12)
Weerbeke	2	1	3	(1?)	6 (7)
Compère	1	2	2	2	7
Ghiselin	1	2	1	–	4

Several compositions appear in more than one of the sources, which may be taken to mean that the work rather than the composer was widely appreciated. For example, Josquin's 'Ave Maria . . . virgo serena' and Agricola's 'Gaudent in celis' stand in all four sources, partly with contrafactum texts. In three sources are found Weerbeke's Mass 'O Venus bant' (or sections thereof), Compère's 'Magnificat sexti toni' and a 'Salve regina' by Isaac.

Whereas these works were equally popular in other countries, Isaac's 'Ecce sacerdos magnus' is a different case: it occurs in Leopold, Apel and *40021*, but in no other source. Some other works by him are also not distributed outside the area: were they composed there? The problem is that most of these copies predate Isaac's first employment in Germany (1496/7, see below): how is it that German musicians were aware of him so early? Three of his works in *40021* are headed '(H.Isaac) de manu sua', and two of these (nos. 144 and 150) seem to be autographs. The composer, when active in Saxony towards 1500, seems to have

---

[417] See, respectively, Gerber–Finscher–Dömling eds, *Mensuralkodex Apel* (complete edn); Just, *Mensuralkodex Mus. ms.40021* (discussion, inventory); Feldmann, *Codex Mf. 2016* (discussion, inventory, partial edn); Noblitt ed., *Kodex Leopold* (edn in progress). A discussion of all four is Martin Just, 'Bemerkungen zu den kleinen Folio-Handschriften deutscher Provenienz um 1500', in Finscher ed., *Formen und Probleme*, 25–45.

[418] Their dates are partly known: Noblitt, 'Datierung', establishes *c.*1466–*c.*1511 for Leopold; Just, *Mensuralkodex Mus. ms.40021*, arrives at *c.*1485–*c.*1501 for *40021* (both on the basis of watermarks). Apel was probably finished when bound at Leipzig in 1504; *Mf. 2016* was completed before the year 1517 recorded in the book.

sent all three pieces to the then owner of *40021* – by letter.[419] Agricola's and Obrecht's relationships with Germany are even more mysterious. What is striking this time is that so many different works by them were copied here: fifteen by Agricola, and eleven by Obrecht, of which nine are Mass cycles or parts thereof. Agricola seems more favoured by the Saxon codices, whereas the Leopold Codex stands apart in its preference for Martini. For some of these sources, the institutional backgrounds can be reconstructed.

Leipzig University, founded in 1409 in the refectory of the Augustinian monastery of St Thomas, was a considerable centre of music. With the manuscript named after him, Nikolaus Apel inherited the work of more than one generation of musicians – whether they were professors or students, members of the *Kantorei* of St Thomas which served the university, or clergy responsible for the university's church services.[420] By 1439, at the latest, the *rector scholarum* of St Thomas's, with succentor, assistants and choirboys, had to sing 'Salve' services, and, in Masses for the Dead, the offertory 'Recordare virgo mater'.[421] (Polyphonic settings of this offertory, with the trope 'Ab hac familia', exist in virtually all central European codices of the time.) The Apel Codex, and also *40021*, transmit music not only from Leipzig, but also from the cathedral of the diocese, Merseburg,[422] from the two ducal courts of Saxony which resided at Meißen and Torgau, respectively, and from places such as Rothenburg, Ulm and especially Nuremberg, whence had come scholars and students.[423] The Silesian codex *Mf. 2016* can be regarded as a cathedral book, perhaps from Wrocław where it was found.

Of the German composers named in these manuscripts, the best represented is Adam von Fulda (*c*.1445–1505), with a total of twelve works. They are a chanson Mass over the *Tenorlied* 'Seit ich dich herzlieb meiden muß', a *Magnificat* and (in the Apel Codex) ten smaller liturgical works. In his treatise *De musica*, which he wrote towards 1490 in a monastery near Passau, Adam demonstrates his knowledge of traditional theory and music by Dufay and Busnois. As a composer, he reveals himself to be up to date with the Netherlands idioms of Isaac, Obrecht and their contemporaries. This probably earned him the position of Kapellmeister of Duke Frederick the Wise of Saxony (1498); he also served the Torgau court as a singer (from 1489), historiographer and music professor at Wittenberg University.[424] Apart from Heinrich Finck, several other German masters surface in these sources but are little known:[425] Conrad

---

[419] Martin Just, 'Ysaac de manu sua', in *Congress Report Gesellschaft für Musikforschung, Kassel, 1962* (Kassel etc., 1963), 112–14 (with facs).

[420] Wustmann, *Musikgeschichte Leipzigs*, 12–30. For documents on music, see Knick–Mezger, *St Thomas*, 41–56, and Ward, 'Music and music theory'.

[421] Pietzsch, *Zur Pflege*, 70 f.

[422] Probably of local origin is the Merseburg fragment of the earlier fifteenth century (*CC*, vol. 2, 140 f.).

[423] See Just, *Mensuralkodex Mus. ms.40021*, 88–95 on the composers Volckmar, Nachtigall and Beham.

[424] Further on him, see Ehmann, *Adam*; Just, *Mensuralkodex Mus. ms.40021*, 73 ff.

[425] Information on most of them is in Just, *Mensuralkodex Mus. ms.40021*, 75–95.

Rupsch (a singer at the Torgau court from 1504), the older Magister Nicolaus Gerstman from Lemberg (Lwów), as well as the totally unidentified Aulen, J. Jacobit, 'B. H', 'E. O.', 'C. von P.', 'Rud. H.', 'M. S.' and Egidius Rossely. The last two, and Ulrich Flordigal from Stuttgart, are represented in *Mf. 2016* with works suitable for Czech liturgies; perhaps they worked in that area.

A curious musician was Bartholomäus Frank, cantor from Berne (Switzerland), who in the years 1479–88 travelled widely, offering princes and imperial cities his celebrative 'isorhythmic' motets, text and music of his own eccentric invention, like a latter-day Wilhelmi.[426]

The musical patronage of the Habsburgs

Cantor Frank also visited Innsbruck in 1479, together with five 'companions'. This makes him one of a long series of travelling singers, composers, chaplains, minstrels, schoolboys, organists, musical priests and women performers, who found employment or at least a gratification at the Tyrolean court of Duke Sigismund of Austria (*r.* 1446–90).[427] Music, literature, dancing, hunting and minor warfare, luxury goods bought in Venice, the building of palaces and churches were the pastimes of this extravagant ruler; his financial lifeblood was the silver coming from the recently developed mines in the north Tyrol. When he had spent his riches (in 1490), his nephew King Maximilian I sent him into retirement and relieved him of his land, including his court chapel and its famous organist, Paul Hofhaimer. Also Heinrich Isaac, whom Maximilian was to appoint court composer in 1496/7, had already attracted the curiosity of Duke Sigismund, who rewarded him in September 1484. The document – it is the earliest known for Isaac's biography – calls him 'componist'. The same designation is given in the account books, in 1483 and in 1484, to a 'composer Arnold', who may have been the imperial chaplain Arnold Fleron from Liège, or the blind organist of the Count Palatinate at Heidelberg, Arnold Schlick.[428]

---

[426] See Staehelin, 'Neues zu Bartholomäus Frank'. Frank's 'Venus stella splendens' in the manuscript *Mf. 2016* praises a Silesian duchess; a similar motet without text is in Speciálník; a motet in honour of the merchant city of Ravensburg (nr. Constance) is in an Augsburg manuscript of *c.*1490. See Martin Staehelin, 'Das Augsburger Fragment', *Augsburger Jahrbuch für Musikwissenschaft* 4 (1987), 7–63.

[427] Senn, *Musik und Theater*, 9 f. See also Manfred Schneider, 'Vom Musikleben am Hof Herzog Sigmunds des Münzreichen', in Gert Ammann ed., *Der Herzog und sein Taler* (exhibition catalogue) (Innsbruck: Ferdinandeum, 1986), 57–66.

[428] Schlick was a composer, and travelled and played before princes; he was later connected with Habsburg, the Tyrol and a bishop of Trent, Bernardo Cles: see Renato Lunelli, 'Contributi trentini alle relazioni musicali fra l'Italia e la Germania nel Rinascimento', *AcM* 21 (1949), 48 ff. The important musical tradition at the Heidelberg court, with its chapelmaster Johann von Soest, cannot be expanded here; but see 'Heidelberg' in *The New Grove*, and Gerhard Pietzsch, *Quellen und Forschungen zur Geschichte der Musik am kurpfälzischen Hof zu Heidelberg bis 1622* (Mainz and Wiesbaden, 1983).

The visit of both musicians in 1484 was probably connected with the sumptuous wedding of Duke Sigismund and Katharina of Saxony in the carnival of that year. This event alone may explain some circumstances of music history, such as the visits of Isaac to the Saxon court in c. 1497-1500, and the repertorial links of the Leopold Codex with the Saxon sources. More importantly, the origin of the codex itself remains to be explained.[429]

When the Innsbruck schoolmaster Nicolaus Leopold assembled about a dozen independent fascicles and larger units of mensural music in 1511, he simply inherited the work of his own predecessors. This codex is not a chapel manuscript, but due to the peculiar organization of the Innsbruck court it does contain music performed for the court by the *Kantorei* of the parish church of St Jacob. We can demonstrate this with the known history of this church, and the continuous flow of payments in the account books, which went to the schoolmaster and boys for the courtly services in St Jacob's.[430] There was no actual 'court chapel' to match the *Kantorei*, but rather many individual chaplains who were hired rather indiscriminately by the spendthrift prince against the protests of his financial advisers. They read and sang Masses for him, whether on his many travels or in his chapel of St Maurice in the Innsbruck palace (the *Mitterhof*), but the musical specialists among them presumably also supported the *Junkmeister* and choirboys in services at St Jacob's. So did, in any case, Paul Hofhaimer (1459-1537), court organist from 1478, who used to perform on the great organ in St Jacob's as well as privately in the palace. It may partly be due to Hofhaimer's activity in Innsbruck (although we should not forget Paumann's in Munich and Schlick's in Heidelberg) that German princes became so fond of combining the organ with polyphony. Maximilian's chapel made much use of the organ, and Isaac composed about twenty *alternatim* Masses or 'Missae ad organum' for the court.[431] We have already mentioned Duke Sigismund's care for singing boys, who were educated at court and joined the *Kantorei* of St Jacob's.

The most important figure in this system was Nicolaus Krombsdorfer. Possibly a native of Kronstorf in Upper Austria, he was organist and cantor of Duke Sigismund from 1463, took holy orders in 1470 and became court chaplain; from 1479 until his death in 1488 he was curate of St Jacob's. Many documents refer to his widespread activity as a musician and educator of the boys, whom he taught singing, organ- and lute-playing. He was undoubtedly the head of the church music, and, together with the schoolmasters, the organizer of endowed ceremonies, *Ansingen* performances, courtly Requiems and the like.[432] The most fascinating aspect of him is that he spent the years 1436-62 at the Este

---

[429] Noblitt ed., *Kodex Leopold*; Noblitt, 'Chorbuch' (inventory). Numbers here follow the inventory, not the edn.

[430] Senn, *Musik und Theater*, 15-18. I am preparing a more detailed study on the church and court.

[431] The fundamental study of Hofhaimer and organ music of his time is Moser, *Hofhaimer* (with edn of his works). On the Isaac Masses, see p. 532 below.

[432] Some references are quoted in Senn, *Musik und Theater*, 11 f and 15 f.

court of Ferrara under the name of 'Niccolò Tedesco, *cantor et pulsator*' (i.e. singer and player of organ and lute).[433] What it meant for the music at Innsbruck that its most important representative had served Leonello and Borso d'Este for 26 years can only be guessed. Krombsdorfer seems to have visited Ferrara again in 1466, perhaps in the company of a 'Giovanni d'Alemagna cantore', since both their names are listed in the court records for that year.[434] The latter could well have been Johannes Martini, who transferred from Constance Cathedral to Ferrara in 1472/3. This probably happened with the support of Krombsdorfer and Duke Sigismund, either of whom can have known Martini's music – an obvious assumption if Martini had been the 'little Martin' at Frederick's court – and recommended him to the Ferrara court. The connection with Krombsdorfer and Innsbruck explains, of course, why Johannes Martini knew Hofhaimer and was asked in September 1489 to bring him to the court of Beatrice of Aragon at Buda.[435]

In 1465, a servant of Duke Francesco Sforza of Milan visited Innsbruck with six singers.[436] The cantor and later chaplain Wilhelm Perger, who seems to have directed the Innsbruck court singers from 1464, disappears from the records in 1472, only to reappear the following year as 'Guglielmo Pergier' in the chapel of Galeazzo Maria Sforza in the company of Gaspar van Weerbeke and Josquin des Prez.[437] The Este and Sforza dynasties were the closest Habsburg allies in Italy; in 1482–4, Ercole d'Este and Sigismund together conducted an unsuccessful war against Venice. Occasional exchanges of court singers between Innsbruck, Ferrara and Milan, and more of instrumentalists (see p. 567), are no surprise.

In 1471, Sigismund appointed 'Herr Hanns Wiser von Triendt' as one of his many non-resident court chaplains;[438] an ecclesiastical career probably did not prevent the former schoolmaster from sharing his music with Innsbruck colleagues. A certain 'W. Raber', composer of a Corpus Christi communion in the Leopold Codex (no. 128), may well have been Vigil Raber, poet, painter and play director at Sterzing, who inherited the Bolzano play manuscripts of Benedikt Debs (see p. 507).

Schoolmasters of St Jacob's who must have collected music for the *Kantorei* include Augustin Bürckl (until 1465), Wolfgang Unterstetter from 1466 (who was replaced or assisted 1478–86 by Mathias Sekeresch, but pensioned as late as 1485)[439] and Valentin Unger (1486–9).

---

[433] See Lockwood, *Ferrara, passim*, and esp. 95–7; Strohm, review of Lockwood, *Ferrara* in *ML* 67 (1986), 285, with the identification Tedesco–Krombsdorfer; Strohm, 'Vierstimmige Bearbeitung', 170 f.

[434] Lockwood, *Ferrara*, 318.

[435] The request was unsuccessful, because by late 1489, Hofhaimer had already joined the service of King Maximilian. The documents are printed in Fökövi, 'Musik'; and Moser, *Hofhaimer*, 173 f. n. 40.

[436] Senn, *Musik und Theater*, 9.

[437] Motta, *Musici*, 334; Sartori, 'Josquin', 64–6.

[438] Tiroler Landesarchiv, Innsbruck, Cod.324, fol. 82v; he is thus distinguished from Hanns Wiser of Rheinfelden, a secretary of the duke from 1463 to c.1480.

[439] HHStA (State Archives) Vienna, Copialbuch H (1485) no. 7, fols. 170v–71r.

Unger (Honger) served from 1492 until 1505 as 'tenoriste' in the chapel of Archduke Philip the Handsome – Maximilian's son – in the Netherlands. This service led Unger back to Innsbruck, during Philip's visit there in 1503, when the singers of the archduke and the emperor – with Pierre de la Rue, Alexander Agricola and Heinrich Isaac among them – met and performed.[440]

The first 171 folios of the Leopold Codex were copied by a single scribe from *c*.1466 to 1482.[441] In this phase, the musical contents resemble those of the latest Trent Codices, especially *Tr 89*, and also Strahov. I suggest that Wiser in Trent and the Innsbruck scribe exchanged material in the 1460s. This may have happened in August 1466, when Krombsdorfer rode to Trent to fetch two choirboys. Rather precisely about this time, two unusual pieces were entered at the end of *Tr 89*: the song setting 'Heya, heya, nu wie si grollen' (no. 751), and Martini's instrumental fantasia 'La Martinella' (no. 752). Did Krombsdorfer take these pieces to Trent, and is he perhaps himself the composer of 'Heya, heya'?[442]

A large group of copies, made *c*.1476, includes three motets by Isaac, two hymns by Martini, Agricola's 'Gaudent in celis' and Josquin's 'Ave Maria'. These spectacularly early copying dates – the earliest for any work by Josquin, Isaac or Agricola, none of whom is represented at all in the Trent Codices – can partly be explained by the links to Milan and Ferrara; perhaps Martini and Krombsdorfer were the transmitters. How Isaac's music arrived at Innsbruck eight years before the composer himself is, as yet, unexplained. It is possible that he met with members of the imperial chapel in the Netherlands. As for Agricola, it is likely that he spent some time in Habsburg lands before *c*.1470–74, when he first appeared at Milan and Ferrara.[443] It has been argued that several works by Agricola are 'German' by destination (see p. 529). Obrecht's only documented contact with Habsburg happened in 1503; when stopping at Innsbruck *en route* to Ferrara, he received a reward for the Mass 'Regina celi' which he had composed for the court (it is now lost). The work had been commissioned previously in Namur. Four other Masses by Obrecht were copied in the Leopold Codex already in 1487–93, and two more in the Linz fragment which probably originated at Innsbruck *c*.1490–92 (see below). One wonders whether these were also commissioned from far away, or brought to Innsbruck by the composer himself on his trip to and from Ferrara in 1487–8. Obrecht's Mass 'Maria zart' uses as cantus firmus a German sacred song, apparently composed

---

[440] Pietzsch, *Fürsten*, 131; Doorslaer, 'Chapelle', 51 f and 147.

[441] Noblitt, 'Datierung'; see also his introduction to *Kodex Leopold*, vol. 1. Perhaps it will be possible some time to identify this scribe; both Wolfgang Unterstetter and Nikolaus Krombsdorfer would qualify very well.

[442] Strohm, 'Vierstimmige Bearbeitung'. Krombsdorfer's trip is documented in Tiroler Landesarchiv, Innsbruck, Raitbuch 4, fols. 114r and 116r.

[443] For his visit to Ferrara, 1474, see Lockwood, *Ferrara*, 156. He could also be identical with the 'Alessandro d'Alemagna, cantore e suonatore de viola', who was at the court in 1470 (pp. 97 and 318). For his Milanese service, see Motta, *Musici*, 532. Motta mentions a document of 1471 concerning a brother-in-law of Alexander, 'Pietro da Vienna'. This certainly speaks for Austrian connections.

in 1500 and soon known in more than one polyphonic setting.[444] The earliest of them, by a certain Pfabenschwanz of Augsburg, exists in three sources, including *B-Br II. 270* (fols. 123v–4r) where it has Dutch words.[445] An anonymous second Mass on the song, for three voices, is in the Leopold Codex (no. 129; copied *c.*1504–6). The absence of vocal works by Hofhaimer from Leopold (whereas *40021* has his 'Ave maris stella') may mean that he did not write vocal music before he left Innsbruck in 1489.

When the Czech nobleman Leo von Rozmital and his companions arrived at the court of Emperor Frederick III in 1467, concluding their two-year travel around Europe, they brought a gift for the Empress Eleanora: dance-songs from her native Portugal. After Rozmital's lutenist had played them to her, she ordered that her eight-year-old son Maximilian should learn the songs on the lute.[446] Despite later claims that he did not speak until he was nine years old, the young archduke may have received a musical education just like other young princes, for example Galeazzo Maria Sforza (see p. 544). His main governor and teacher was Jacobus de Fladnitz, rector of the 'Citizens' College' of St Stephan. Maximilian later recorded his musical education and musical inclinations in two propaganda publications. They were a fanciful autobiography written at his behest, the *Weißkunig*, and the famous series of woodcuts by Hans Burgkmair called the *Triumphzug Maximilians*, representing such an idealized pageant or 'joyous entry' into a town as had become the fashion in Burgundian and French territories (see also p. 305).[447] Maximilian's musical patronage was worthy of an emperor, going hand in hand with his support for humanists and care for his chapel.[448] He made his organist Hofhaimer a knight, and his first chaplain, Georg Slatkonia, Bishop of Vienna. The imperial chapel was a complex structure, of course, as it grew out of several elements:

> the household chapel of Frederick III which may not have been a functioning body at his death in 1493;
> the musicians of Sigismund of Tyrol, with very able individuals who included Hofhaimer;
> the 'Burgundian' chapel which Maximilian commanded as the widower of Mary of Burgundy (from 1482) and governor of the Netherlands, until his son Philip the Handsome took it over in 1494;
> an apparently intermediate, travelling body (perhaps the 'oberländische Kapelle' of Frederick III), situated at Augsburg in the early 1490s;
> resident foundations in Wiener Neustadt, Vienna etc. (see pp. 505 f).

---

[444] Burkhart Wachinger, 'Maria zart' in Kurt Ruh *et al.* eds, *Die deutsche Literatur des Mittelalters: Verfasserlexikon*, 2nd edn (1978), vol. 5, col. 1264–9.

[445] See Strohm, review of the edn by B. Hudson (*NOE* vol. 7). On the manuscript see *CC*, vol. 1, 96.

[446] Letts ed., *Travels*, 162.

[447] See Cuyler, *Emperor Maximilian*, *passim*. The *Weißkunig* picture (8 and pl. 2) shows him as a youth, but reflects instruments of the 1510s, of course (including a viol). On the instruments in both series, see Christine K. Mather, 'Maximilian I and his instruments', *Early Music* 3 (1975), 42–6.

[448] A brief introduction is Martin Picker, 'Habsburg, 2' in *The New Grove*.

There seems to be a musical document for Maximilian's inheritance of Sigismund's court music: the fragments *A-LIs 529*. They are not fully investigated yet; apparently they come from two major manuscripts, one of which consisted of partbooks. Two Obrecht Masses and a motet by Isaac ('Argentum et aurum', already found in a 1476 copy in Leopold) are associated here with anonymous Masses, hymns, *Magnificat* settings, *cantiones*, German songs and a good deal of French chansons or cantus firmus arrangements thereof.[449] Concordances reach from the Dijon Chansonnier to the Lwów fragments (*PL-Pu 7022*). The source reflects the last stage of Tyrolean court music at the moment when Maximilian took over (1490); the city of Linz, where the fragments were found, was his first residence of the 1490s. Many of the vocal pieces seem to have been copied here for the use of instrumentalists. This also seems the case with a small collection of mostly textless songs in Trent, *I-TRc 1947–4*, which corresponds in several aspects (including a very similar scribal hand) to the Linz fragments.

Maximilian and his councillors made efforts in the late 1490s to unify the administration, and to put music on a secure footing in various parts of the Habsburg territories. The appointment of Isaac in 1496/7 as court *componist* helped the provision with new sacred music; the first chaplain was not Isaac because he was a married layman, but Hans Kerner and then Georg Slatkonia. At the same point, the household chapel, then including '12 knabn unnd gesellen' (i.e. boys and assistants), was transferred from Augsburg to Vienna.[450] Probably under Isaac's direction, Adam Rener of Liège and Ludwig Senfl of Zurich sang as choirboys; all three composed sacred music for Maximilian. Senfl also produced countless *Tenorlieder*.

A great deal of money was spent on endowments for church rituals. At Our Lady of Bruges, the endowments in the testament of Mary of Burgundy were finalized by Maximilian in 1496 with daily polyphonic Masses, on Sundays and feast-days with organ.[451] In 1497, he endowed the parish church of Hall, near Innsbruck, with stipends for schoolmaster, organist, *Junkmeister*, assistants and schoolboys, who, in addition to a daily polyphonic 'Salve regina' instituted by the local patrician Waldauf, had to sing polyphonic Masses with organ every Sunday and feast-day.[452] The emperor was fond of the St Nicholas church of Hall and its famous relics; the town's salt mines paid many of his courtiers' salaries. In 1498, the constitution of the Vienna chapel followed. But Maximilian resided more often in the other musical centres of his orbit: Innsbruck, Hall, Augsburg and Constance. Paul Hofhaimer, resident in Augsburg from 1507 on the emperor's behalf, was surrounded by students, later called 'Paulomimes' ('imitators of Paul'). Many of them became well-known organists:

---

[449] A preliminary list of contents is in Strohm, 'Native and foreign polyphony', 229 f. Martin Staehelin is preparing a detailed study.

[450] The document is discussed in Staehelin, *Messen*, vol. 2, 43 ff.

[451] See Strohm, *Bruges*, 49.

[452] Walter Senn, *Aus dem Kulturleben einer süddeutschen Kleinstadt* (Innsbruck etc.: Tyrolia, 1938), 51.

for example Hans Buchner at Constance, Hans Kotter at Fribourg, Wolfgang Grefinger at St Stephan's, Vienna, and Dionisio Memmo at St Mark's, Venice.

Kotter had studied with Hofhaimer between 1498 and 1500 at the expense of the Elector of Saxony, Frederick the Wise. The friendly rivalry of Frederick and Maximilian in musical matters and other conspicuous ways of spending money is entirely comparable to the fancies of Italian Renaissance princes. It certainly extended to the collection and production of precious books: several of the famous 'Habsburg–Netherlands' court manuscripts produced by Petrus Alamire and his affiliates went into the chapels and libraries of Vienna and Torgau.[453] Further sacred works as well as *Tenorlieder* from Maximilian's household sphere were copied in Austria and southern Germany, many of them through the mediation of the chapel member Lucas Wagenrieder, who after the emperor's death went with Senfl to serve the Bavarian court at Munich.[454]

Some particular developments of central Europe

Certain 'native' traditions of sacred polyphony emerge for the first time with the original nucleus of *Tr 93*, a systematically ordered codex with music for the Mass. Its repertorial mix, with much English and Franco-Netherlands music, points to the use of the imperial chapel and its models: the Este chapel at Ferrara, and the chapel of the Council of Basle. *Tr 93* was copied about 1450–54 by a German scribe, conceivably a friend of Lupi or Wiser in the imperial household who made this chapel repertory available to the Trent musicians.

There must be some native compositions among the 61 polyphonic introits and 38 isolated Kyries of this source; they are mostly settings of the appropriate Mass plainsongs, and ordered according to the church year. This separates them from the other Mass sections which often use borrowed cantus firmi. The polyphonic introit, a genre introduced at the Habsburg court by Brassart and de Sarto (see p. 256), was perhaps not much cultivated in Italy or western Europe after *c.*1450. Here, the production increases. It remained characteristic of central Europe – as witnessed, for example, by the later Trent Codices and the Strahov MS.[455] Also the Kyrie plainsong setting had all but disappeared from the western tradition.

A number of plenary cycles and Proper cycles (i.e. the Mass Proper items with and without the Ordinary, respectively) were imported to Austria, apparently via Italian chapels, about 1460 (see p. 436). This was also to remain a musical fashion in central Europe. *Tr 91* and the Leopold Codex contain very many settings for the Mass Proper, suggesting that the genre was especially

---

[453] See Kellmann, 'Josquin and the courts', 210–16. A full inventory of the Saxon choirbooks is Karl Roediger, *Die geistlichen Musikhandschriften der Universitäts-Bibliothek Jena*, 2 vols. (Jena, 1935).

[454] Martin Bente, *Neue Wege der Quellenkritik und die Biographie Ludwig Senfls* (Wiesbaden: Breitkopf & Härtel, 1968).

[455] A comprehensive study is Dangel-Hofmann, *Introitus*.

welcome in the south of the Empire. This leads without complication to Heinrich Isaac's monumental collection of Mass Propers, the *Choralis Constantinus*. Printed in three books as late as 1550 and 1555 at Nuremberg, this is a composite of cycles written partly for the imperial chapel of Maximilian and partly commissioned by Constance Cathedral in 1508. The three books together cover all the major feasts and Sundays of the church year; introit, alleluia, sequence and communion are regularly provided.[456]

At about the same time, the Saxon court at Torgau provided itself with large sets of Proper cycles, some of them composed by Isaac's student Adam Rener.[457] There can be little doubt that the genre had never ceased to be cultivated in Austria since the days when it first entered *Tr 88* – and surely also the lost Habsburg choirbooks of that time.

Among the Mass Proper chants, the sequence has a special position, mainly because of its post-Gregorian musical and textual style. Polyphonic settings came to central Europe around 1440 with works by Dufay and Roullet (see p. 257), and fifteen settings surface in *Tr 93*.[458] One work, 'Lauda Sion' (no. 1761), is by Dufay. But the preceding 'Lauda Sion' (no. 1760) is by Hermann Edlerawer. Several others are in a primitive style with a 'monorhythmic' plainsong in the middle voice, written in chant notation:

Example 78 'Congaudent angelorum chori', *Tr 93*, fols. 205-6

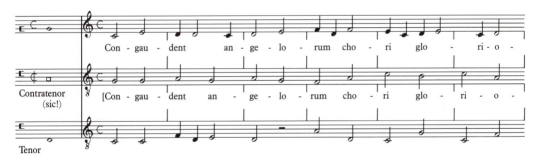

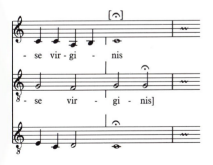

---

[456] Complete list in Martin Staehelin, 'Isaac, Heinrich' in *The New Grove*.
[457] See Gerken, *Polyphonic Cycles.*.
[458] There is no musical connection between them and the introits at the beginning of the same collection.

The fact that the plainsong is in the middle voice ('contratenor'), admitting fourths between it and the cantus, and the monorhythm itself, strongly suggest a link with English discant (see pp. 77 f). Or, is it 'European discant', a practice which was not extinguished but only buried by more refined Franco-Netherlands techniques? However that may be, the *monorhythmic cantus firmus style* remained a hallmark of German plainsong settings (*Choralbearbeitungen*) for generations.[459]

In the Trent series, it recurs in varied guises, soon being applied also to a cantus firmus in the top line (from *Tr 88* onwards). It is frequent in antiphon and especially hymn settings. The incidence of this technique even increases in *Tr 91*; typical of its further development here are the three-part 'Salve regina' settings nos. 1203, 1206 and 1317, and the 'Pange lingua' no. 1330.[460] The last-mentioned work is probably of Saxon or Silesian origin; Glogau and the Apel Codex offer more examples of this specific three-part style with a long drawn-out plainsong in the top voice and active, often florid and patterned lower voices. A particularly beautiful example is the *Leise* 'Nu bitten wir den heil'gen Geist' (Glogau no. 123), which in the last sections abandons monorhythm to form a long imitative pattern as a climax.[461]

Some settings around 1480–1500 seem to emulate each other also by their choice of similar plainsongs, preferably in the seventh mode. Two examples are the textless four-voice settings the Apel Codex nos. 104 and 106.[462] In both of these, the cantus firmus is first stated in the cantus, then in the bass, and last in the tenor. The motivic–harmonic fabric of the free voices is shot through with smaller and larger patterned imitations, whether of syncopated or straightforward scalic motives. Exactly the same 'migrant cantus firmus', distribution of voices, mode and general style characterizes Heinrich Isaac's motet 'Argentum et aurum' (Apel no. 145), a work not transmitted in sources outside central Europe. Who influenced whom? 'Argentum et aurum' appears first in the '1476 group' in the Leopold Codex and seems to have chronological priority over the similar settings, which also include at least one fragmentary piece in *A-LIs 529* (no. 7). But if Isaac was not yet present in the area how could he have invented such an ingenious, logical development of the German monorhythmic style?

The masterwork of this manner of chant-setting is the four-voice Trinity sequence 'Benedicta semper sancta sit Trinitas'.[463] The piece enjoyed spectacular success, being found in all the major collections of the area, including Leopold and Speciálník. The earliest sources are *A-LIs 529* and *40021* (both

[459] See Staehelin, *Messen*, vol. 3, 19 ff, 124 ff and 129 ff; Just, *Mensuralkodex Mus. ms.40021*, vol. 1, 137–96. Glarean (1547) called the technique *contrapunctus floridus seu fractus*.

[460] All printed in *DTOe XXVII/1*, vol. 53. The 'Salve regina' no. 11 has proportional transformation of the cantus firmus (in the top voice). See also the 'Christe redemptor' no. 3. More primitive are the hymns in *Tr 91*, nos. 1324–8, where already the thematic index shows the chant notation of their top voice.

[461] Ringmann-Väterlein eds, *Glogauer Liederbuch*, vol. 4; also in *NAWM 1*, no. 46.

[462] No. 104 is headed 'H.F(inck)' in the edn – erroneously? No. 106 is by Adam von Fulda; see Ehmann, *Adam*, ex. V (with the words 'Salve decus virginum').

[463] Printed in Gerber-Finscher-Dömling eds, *Mensuralkodex*, no. 85.

c.1490–95). This long work, consisting of ten versicles, abounds with ideas
how to embellish, interpret, emphasize or disguise the monorhythmic chant
which is mostly in the tenor, but also conducted in canon with the cantus,
or as the lowest of only three voices. The opening gambit is a skilful overlapping of syncopated repetition patterns around the tenor, inspired by its repeated
steps:

Example 79*a* 'Benedicta semper', Apel Codex, fols. 103v–8r

This seemingly abstract or constructivist approach, which repeats cadential formulas like building blocks, recalls instrumental techniques. In some later versicles, there are extended repercussive zones with all the voices oscillating back and forth between two harmonies (versicles V and VI). The beginning of VI is an inspired illustration of the joyful calls and 'musical chants' quoted in the text:

Example 79*b*

Martin Just, who discusses the work at length, believes that it may have been composed in Nuremberg.[464] But the setting relates to a particular liturgical usage more typical of the diocese of Merseburg and especially its musical centre, St Thomas's of Leipzig. In many regions, the individual versicle VII, 'O veneranda unitas, o adoranda trinitas' was sung as a specially solemn moment during the Elevation at Mass, when everybody had to kneel. But only in Leipzig did performances of the whole sequence also include a solemn and length-

464 Just, *Mensuralkodex Mus. ms.40021*, vol. I, 168–78.

ened performance of this versicle.[465] In our setting, versicle VII is nothing but a series of fermata-held chords: an awesome effect in this otherwise lively or even playful work. Despite its Leipzig origin, the sequence soon became known to Isaac, whose Mass 'Salva nos', composed *c.*1492 in Florence, contains many motives from 'Benedicta semper' in a slightly more elegant patterning.[466]

Office hymns are in a sense the most consistently 'native' ingredient in the central European sources, especially the later ones. The choice of hymn texts in this area contrasts with Italian or French liturgical uses; techniques such as fauxbourdon, formerly typical of the genre and developed further in Italy, were abandoned in central Europe after mid-century.[467] A development concerning all the minor liturgical genres is the ready acceptance of pervasive imitation (i.e. of all the voices). After the experiments of composers from Liège (Hugo de Lantins, Johannes Franchois), the technique may have been transferred to central Europe by Johannes Touront, whose four-voice 'Pange lingua', with two phrases entering in pervasive imitation, was copied in *Tr 88* (no. 463) by 1462.[468] The piece is remarkable not for the incidental similarity of its opening with Josquin's 'Pange lingua' Mass, but for its model status within the central European tradition. Pervasive imitation was tried but also simplified in various local compositions, for example a 'Kyrie Cunctipotens' in *Tr 93* (no. 1683), or in the exciting four-part cantio 'Resonet in laudibus' in *Tr 89* (no. 660). A more ambitious but related style is found in the 'Pange lingua' and other hymns by Adam von Fulda and Heinrich Finck, which are part of the large hymn collections in *40021* and the Apel Codex. Hymns and *Magnificat* settings were very important in German churches and were apparently among the first genres to be sung polyphonically in smaller centres.[469] Among the works by Alexander Agricola which Edward Lerner interprets as 'German', there are two hymns. 'A solis ortus cardine' has the peculiarity of using two different plainsongs – the hymn itself and an unrelated antiphon – a technique known only in works by Adam von Fulda and other Germans.[470] Nevertheless, Johannes Regis springs to

---

[465] The practice originated in 1464 at St Thomas as a votive usage against the plague, and was ordered for all churches of Leipzig in 1468. See Knick–Mezger, *St Thomas*, 52 f. The singing of 'O veneranda' at Mass is also mentioned in Wustmann, *Musikgeschichte Leipzigs*, 16.

[466] Heinrich Isaac, *Missa 'Salva nos'*, ed. Walter Pass (Vienna and Munich: Doblinger, 1971); see especially Kyrie I, bars 1–7 and Kyrie II, bars 62–6.

[467] Tom R. Ward, 'The Office hymns of the Trent manuscripts', in Pirrotta–Curti eds, *Codici Musicali*, 112–29. I believe that the Benedictine reform of Melk (see p. 297) is indirectly responsible for the disappearance of triple metre hymns from *c.*1460 (*Tr 88*), whereas Italian settings continue to use the metre.

[468] *DTOe XXVII/1*, vol. 53, no. 2. A rather weak imitation of his style is the 'Veni creator' no. 5 in the same volume (from *Tr 89*, no. 720).

[469] An interesting case is reported in Ehmann, *Adam*, 27–9: the parish priest of Görlitz, in 1489, failed to obtain the magistrate's permission to perform hymns and *Magnificat* 'in mensuris'.

[470] Lerner, '"German" works', 61 f. The author's point about 'Ave maris stella', however, is unconvincing: canonic duets between two tenors are part of the Franco-Netherlands tradition, for example in Regis, in settings of *chansons rustiques* ('Marchons la dureau') and the 'L'homme armé' complex. Also 'Ave pulcherrima regina' is probably not a German work, since this cantio was of Lower Rhenish or Dutch origin: see p. 332.

mind. A variant of the technique was known to Johannes Martini, whose 'Salve regina' in the Leopold Codex (no. 57), is set over multiple extraneous cantus firmi.[471] This codex also preserves antiphons and hymns incorporating secular tunes, a 'Salve regina' by 'Ar. Fer.' (see below) and two hymns: no. 79, a 'Veni creator' with the famous 'Tannhäuserlied' in the bass, and no. 84, 'Jesu corona virginum' where the altus sings – perhaps appropriately – the tune 'Einen frischen Buhlen muß ich haben' ('I must have a new lover').[472]

Two Gloria-Credo pairs and one Gloria over regional cantus firmi in *Tr 93* show that the western tenor Mass was being imitated in central Europe by 1450.[473] We do not know when the first complete cantus firmus cycle was composed in the area, but some specimens exist in Wiser's codices *Tr 88* and *89*. (See also tables 4 and 5.) The Masses 'Christus surrexit' in *Tr 89* (nos. 723–6) and 'Grune linden' in *Tr 88* (nos. 482–6) are composed over regional cantus firmi: the former over the traditional *Leise* 'Christ ist erstanden' and as a strict imitation of the 'Caput' Mass, the latter on a dance-song of apparently Silesian origin ('Nun laube, Lindlein, laube') and in the manner of the western chanson Masses of the early 1450s. There are four more cycles on German song tenors in the Trent codices and related sources antedating *c*.1470. Their techniques are surprisingly diverse, comparing, for example, the strict transformational 'Groß senen' (*c*.1462) with the fully fledged parody Mass 'Sig, säld und hail' (*c*.1470).[474] A less ambitious but efficient work is the four-part Mass 'Seit ich dich herzlieb meiden muß' by Adam von Fulda in *40021*.[475]

These cycles make no use of monorhythm at all. Rather, the borrowed song tenors or cantus parts often quote their original rhythms literally. Monorhythm applied to liturgical plainsong settings and was not suitable for works with borrowed tenors; it was a 'mensural interpretation' of non-rhythmic plainsongs in the first place.

By the same token, we find the technique in a few polyphonic arrangements of monophonic secular songs which lacked a mensural rhythm. The four-part 'Heya, heya, nu wie sie grollen' (see p. 521) is based on such a song by Oswald von Wolkenstein. The cantus firmus technique adopted here was to enjoy a great development: each line of the song is stated in the tenor monorhythmically, surrounded and 'pre-imitated' by the highly figurative counterpoints of the other voices. This was to be, of course, the technique of the German organ chorale in the period of Buxtehude and Bach. Several German song arrange-

---

[471] Printed, with a *Magnificat* and an 'Ave maris stella', in *Chorwerk*, vol. 46. A typical hymn with extraneous cantus firmus is Heinrich Finck's five-part 'Veni creator spiritus / Veni sancte spiritus' in *Chorwerk*, vol. 32, and *HAM*, no. 80.

[472] Printed in *Chorwerk*, vol. 32, nos. 9 and 8. The *Tannhäuserlied* is also set independently as no. 35.

[473] Nos. 1738/1784, 1739/1786 and 1716. See Strohm, 'Zur Rezeption'.

[474] See Gottlieb, *Masses*; Schmalz, *Mass Ordinaries*; Strohm, 'Meßzyklen'. The Mass 'Rosel im gorten' is a doubtful case (see p. 429). The German title (only in the Strahov MS) may be a translation of 'O florens rosa'.

[475] Kyrie printed in Ehmann, *Adam*, ex. I. The song is in Schedel, Buxheim, Glogau and Seville / Paris (no. 136).

ments in the Leopold Codex are of the same kind (nos. 32–7); especially similar to 'Heya, heya' is no. 32, 'So stee ich hie auff dieser erd'.

In the last decades of the century, central European Mass cycles were at the forefront of several developments. One was the use of *multiple secular cantus firmi*. The earliest-known 'Missa Carminum', an anonymous four-part cycle using at least two German songs as cantus firmi, survives in *Tr 89* (*c.*1466).[476] The next known examples are the two cycles by Obrecht, one of which ('Plurimorum carminum II') is also found in *A-LIs 529*, and the other ('Scoen lief') in the Leopold Codex. They are followed by the cycles of Isaac and his student Adam Rener.[477] This seems to provide a Germanic genealogy for the species: but we do not know its relationship to the use of multiple sacred cantus firmi as known in the Low Countries and England. Two remarkable works copied *c.*1476 seem, again, to focus this practice on the Tyrol. Leopold no. 57 is Martini's beautiful 'Salve regina' over five different, extraneous chants in the lower voices (see above); no. 60 is a 'Salve regina' whose top voice quotes six secular songs – two French and four German: 'Le serviteur', 'Zu jagen', 'Gene pris amor' (i.e. 'J'ay pris amours'), 'Glück walt der reyß', 'Wunschlich schon' and 'Weß ich mich leid'. A virtuoso feature is the almost monorhythmic quotation of the 'Salve regina' plainsong in the tenor against the almost literal quotations of the songs. The piece is headed 'Ar. Fer.', once erroneously interpreted as Isaac ('Arrigo Ferrarese').[478]

Further Masses on German song tenors in the Leopold Codex are 'O Österreich' (a rather gloomy piece), 'Ein maid zu dem brunnen' and Isaac's six-part 'Comment peut avoir joye / Wolauff gut gsell von hinen'. The last-named Mass was composed (*c.*1500–10?) over one of several 'bilingual songs' which served as Mass tenors. The French words were used in a famous setting by Josquin, but there is some agreement that the German words were original, too – whatever that may mean.[479] It seems that there were plenty of song translations or contrafacta in circulation *c.*1500, especially in Italy and in places with German influx such as Florence, Ferrara, Milan or the universities of Padua and Bologna. 'Bilingual songs' occur already in the collection of Hartmann Schedel, who studied in Padua. A book with 'tenori todeschi' was used at Ferrara in 1495, and well-known German songs were copied in Italian chansonniers. Foreign masters could use them as cantus firmi. This is perhaps the background for the Mass 'Wunschliche schone / Nos amis' by Tinctoris (?),[480] and for the recently identified Masses 'In feuers hitz' by Martini and 'Zersundert ist das junge herze mein' by Vincenet (see p. 601). A Mass on the popular song

---

[476] Entitled 'Missa Deutscher Lieder' in Schmalz, *Mass Ordinaries*, 120 ff.
[477] Edited, respectively, in *Chorwerk*, vol. 7 and 101.
[478] Refuted in Staehelin, *Messen*, vol. 2, 18 f. Allowing for a slip of the pen, the abbreviation could mean the imperial chaplain Arnold Fleron from Liège.
[479] See Osthoff, *Josquin*, vol. 2, 198.
[480] Strohm, 'Missa super "Nos amis"'; *idem*, 'Meßzyklen'.

'Rosina, wo war dein gestalt' has been cited in connection with Josquin and Isaac, but was composed by neither.[481]

Some other variants of cantus firmus composition may be mentioned briefly. A European trend towards 'plainsong Masses' (i.e. composed over plainsongs of the Ordinary itself, not borrowed tenors) seems to start earlier in the Austrian–German territories than elsewhere, although many specimens from the Ockeghem–Busnois generation may be lost. An early contributor to the most popular type, the 'Missa Paschalis' (based on Easter plainsongs), is Agricola, and Edward Lerner has identified his plainsongs with those used in the diocese of Passau, i.e. Vienna.[482] Related to this practice, and a specific development around 1500, were the *alternatim* Masses over plainsongs which Isaac and anonymi wrote for the Habsburg court ceremonial. In these works, polyphonic vocal sections alternated with polyphonic sections ('versets') played on the organ.[483] It is a major question whether this genre also had an unbroken (and unwritten?) tradition in central Europe since the Dufay period. Of course, alternation between polyphony and plainsong in the Mass and other liturgical items was well known in earlier times, for example around Dufay in the 1430s (see p. 250). The alternation between organ and plainsong was widespread but seems to have had special importance at Augsburg, where Hofhaimer may have extemporized in the Mass services. That Masses 'in discant and with organ' were of the highest solemnity in Maximilian's Bruges endowment of 1496 (see above), points in the same direction.

Busnois' motet 'In hydraulis' is found in both *Tr 91* and the Leopold Codex (no. 22).[484] The interest in this work may have to do with its didactic or scholastic flair, and its ostinato cantus firmus. 'Solmization' and ostinato tenors were adopted in the area in other guises as well.[485] Something about the idea of regulating the musical flow by 'mechanical means' appealed to the instrumental-inspired musicians of central Europe. But following 'In hydraulis' in the Leopold Codex (no. 23), and perhaps inspired by it, is the amazing achievement of the eight-voice motet 'Ave mundi spes Maria / Gottes namen fahren wir'.[486] The

[481] Tom R. Ward, 'A newly-discovered Josquin attribution', *TVNM* 33 (1983), 29–48. The idea of Moser, *Hofhaimer*, 170 n. 24, to refer the underlying song to Archduke Maximilian's first mistress Rosina (before his marriage in 1477), might be extended to the Mass.

[482] Lerner, '"German" works'. The argument that the Passau plainsongs, as printed in 1511 by Winterburger (see Väterlein ed., *Graduale Pataviense*), were also used at the Habsburg court, had already been adopted in the interpretation of the *Choralis Constantinus*. Some questions of detail remain unresolved.

[483] Mahrt, *Missae ad organum*, succinctly demonstrates this performance practice. See also Staehelin, *Messen*, vol. 3, 107–51. Also the simultaneous combination of organ and voices was frequent by 1500; see some references in Moser, *Hofhaimer*, 16 f.

[484] A facsimile of the copy in Leopold (where the words are not underlaid to the notes, but written at the end like a 'canon') is in *MGG*, vol. 9, pl. 116.

[485] Josquin's Mass 'L'ami Baudichon', for example, which has an ostinato tenor of the melodic type of 'Three blind mice', occurs in Speciálník and a Zwickau codex. It has been imitated in a Mass in *Mf. 2016* ('Missa anonyma II', no. 14): see Strohm, 'Missa super "Nos amis"', 50 f. The apparently unrelated Agnus Dei has an ostinato cantus firmus clearly inspired by that of 'In hydraulis'.

[486] Printed in *DTOe VII*, vols. 14–15, 266–8. The copy in *Tr 89* is earlier: *c.*1466!

opening three duets, repeating a well-rounded phrase of six bars, strikingly remind one of Josquin's 'Illibata Dei virgo nutrix' (see p. 640), although they are not imitative. Given the German tenor, a *Leise* which was very popular in Austria, the motet may have originated at the Tyrolean court. It is a beautiful work, and not monotonous harmonically, partly because the cantus firmus is presented on three different pitch-levels. It can hardly have originated without a western model, which would have to be sought in the Ockeghem–Busnois circle around 1460–65; perhaps in addition to 'In hydraulis' there existed such a multi-part motet which is lost today.

Central Europe also contributed to the old type of the three-voice Mass without cantus firmus as known from Benet, Pullois, Bedyngham, Ockeghem and Barbingant. There are interesting examples in the Apel Codex: no. 133 by 'M S', no. 154 by 'Rud. H.', and no. 158; in *Mf. 2016* (no. 55) and in the Leopold Codex (no. 74). In any of these cases there could be an underlying chanson which has not been recognized. This is unlikely, however, in the case of Apel no. 110: the cycle by (Johannes?) Aulen. Like 'Benedicta semper' and Josquin's 'Ave Maria', it is found in all the major central European sources, usually headed 'Officium Auleni' and never with any allusion to a cantus firmus. It also appears in the Spanish Segovia Choirbook, where it is attributed to Agricola.[487] The problem of authorship is intriguing, because it is suspected that Agricola worked in Germany (see above), and because the Mass is so excellent. A long and flowing three-voice motto, which opens all the sections, is continued in the Sanctus in a rather strict sequential pattern as might seem 'typically German' (see Ex. 80).

The counterpoint and melodic–rhythmic idiom, otherwise very flexible, are much more reminiscent of the Ockeghem–Busnois generation than of Agricola's. On the other hand, could this be the style with which Agricola began his career, perhaps in Germany?

The 'Aulen Mass' belongs to a specific group of three-part works with three distinct voice-ranges. The contratenor remains consistently under the tenor, providing many 'V–I' cadences. As a consequence, fourths are extremely rare (restricted to exceptional crossings of the contratenor into the middle) and parallel tenths between the outer voices abound. I believe I have shown above (p. 448) that this three-part texture – which is strongly represented in central European sources of *c.*1460–80 such as *Tr 89* and Glogau – goes back to the French chanson composers of the 1450s and early 1460s. The impact of these composers in central Europe (also testified by Adam von Fulda who praised Busnois) has been underestimated.

The history of *instrumental ensemble music* in the late fifteenth century is very complex. The subject has already been discussed and may be taken up briefly here with regard to central Europe. Around 1440, Johannes Lupi col-

---

[487] Printed also in *Chorwerk*, vol. 31. See Stanley Boorman, 'Aulen, J' in *The New Grove*; Just, *Mensuralkodex Mus. ms.40021*, vol. 1, 82 f.

Example 80 Aulenus, 'Missa sine nomine'

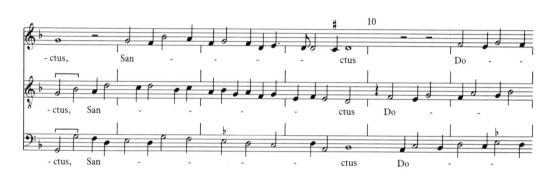

lected foreign instrumental compositions: the 'trebulus' pieces and Tyling's setting of 'T'Andernaken' in *Tr 87* (see p. 360). Perhaps he played the pieces with
friends at Trent Cathedral on some of his instruments: harpsichord, clavichord,
two lutes, 'schaffpret' (exchiquier) and portative organ.[488] Small keyboard
instruments were perfectly conducive to ensemble playing.[489] The conversion of

---

[488] He did, in fact, bequeath the instruments to his Trent colleagues in his will of *c.*1455: see Wright,
'Origins Trent 87-I and 92-II', 270.
[489] An amusing report on such playing, of 1492, is in Moser, *Hofhaimer*, 11.

organ pieces into ensemble pieces and vice versa was only a matter of transcription; most works by Hofhaimer are suitable for the procedure. Organ and lute were Krombsdorfer's instruments, and he also directed singers. Paumann was an important lutenist; an arrangement by him is intended alternatively for organ or 'cytharis', i.e. lutes (see also p. 492). We have seen that the Bavarian courts fostered such ensembles, and that Paumann performed together with two other players of stringed instruments. The instruments which they used may have varied. As Keith Polk has shown, 'geigen' and 'lauten' are not always clearly differentiated in the account books, and were certainly combinable; also, wind players increasingly doubled on soft instruments.[490]

It is in this context that we have tentatively placed Barbingant's 'Pfauenschwanz' and the ensemble pieces of the Glogau partbooks, passing on to Martini's 'La Martinella' and other pieces from *Tr 89*, one with enormous ranges for all three parts (see p. 366). Also in *Mf. 2016*, there is a two-part setting (no. 13) of Hayne van Ghizeghem's 'De tous biens pleine' with the lower part copied on a nine-line staff, and using the space in a 'typically instrumental' manner.[491]

Although traces of a rondeau form can be detected in Martini's piece[492] (and why should they not?), a suggestive factor is the 'instrumental' type of title which the piece received in *Tr 91* about ten years later. By that time, Martini had already shown his skills at such compositions in Ferrara. If any one man is to be mentioned as the initiator of the instrumental fantasia it is Johannes Martini, which makes it all the more interesting where he may have spent the years before 1471, when he surfaces at Constance Cathedral.

Instrumental ensemble pieces, as discussed by Warwick Edwards,[493] occur in three typical forms:

> the freely composed type as in the Glogau partbooks and *Tr 89*, mostly for three voices, which may or may not retain a likeness with the *formes fixes*;
> a type which consists of excerpts from motets and Masses, preferably melismatic sections such as the Christe or Benedictus;[494]
> the arrangement of, or addition of new voices to, one or more voices from a famous chanson, such as 'J'ay pris amours', 'Le serviteur', 'Comme femme', 'Fors seulement' and 'De tous biens pleine' ('cantus firmus arrangement').

The production of such pieces flourished when the Franco-Netherlanders adopted it: especially 'Isaac and Agricola, with Josquin, Ghiselin, Japart and

---

[490] Polk, 'Instrumental music', 174 and 180 ff; *idem*, 'Vedel and geige', 560 ff and 527 ff.

[491] See also Fritz Feldmann, 'Zwei weltliche Stücke des Breslauer Codex Mf.2016', *ZMw* 13 (1930–31), 252–66. The piece is, as David Fallows informs me, concordant with the manuscripts Segovia and *Perugia 1013*; in the former, it is ascribed to 'Roellrin' or 'Roelkin'.

[492] See David Fallows, review of Lockwood, *Ferrara* and Strohm, *Bruges* in *EMH* 6 (1986), 295 f.

[493] Edwards, 'Songs without words'.

[494] On this type, often found in connection with Masses by Isaac, for example 'Chargé de deuil' and 'Quant j'ay au coeur', see also Staehelin, *Messen*. Relevant in this context seems the discovery of two such excerpts from the Mass 'Coda di pavon' (!) by Martini in *Tr 91* (nos.1288 and 1289): see Fallows, 'Songs in the Trent Codices', 179.

Obrecht contributing smaller quantities'.[495] The central European sources need to be more thoroughly considered. There is, for example, the strictly imitative and patterned 'Sanctissima virginum' in *Mf. 2016* (no. 48); the Latin text is not original, but the piece cannot be a song.[496] There is the textless no. 117 in the Apel Codex, a lively piece with a loose texture and mostly only two-voice imitation in the early manner of Martini, ending after a big sequential climax around a stepwise ascending 'cantus firmus' in long equal notes. Both are 'German works', but perhaps 'German works' by somebody like Martini or Agricola? New source discoveries have added to this evidence. The fragment *A-Ws 355* has excerpts from two Masses, perhaps for instrumental use,[497] and *A-LIs 529* provides us with several new or little-known specimens of all three subgenres, including seven cantus firmus arrangements of famous chansons.[498]

Some of these are quite extreme pieces, for example a 'Le serviteur' which recurs in *Fn 229* (no. 258, following Isaac's 'Le serviteur' arrangement).[499] Very slow, augmented cantus firmi against ever more rapid and formulaic passage-work seem to denote an increasing virtuosic pride of the performers. Organists would have practised this as well, of course: the monorhythmic style of plainsong settings could have been used by instrumentalists as a training ground for improvisation. Paumann's *fundamenta*, and those of his apprentices, paved the way for codification and consolidation of improvisatory practices over cantus firmi with predictable rhythm – the easiest of which to handle is monorhythm.

Equally predictable, at least for a good German wind or string player who sought his fortune at Ferrara or Florence, were the cantus and tenor lines of the six or seven most famous chansons of his age. He knew all of them by heart, of course. The practice of literal quotation of the borrowed voice (even in augmented values) suits him perfectly: when performing with new colleagues, he might well ask them to be allowed to prove himself with new figurations against a universally known tune which they can play to him.[500]

Virtually all the 'particular developments' of central Europe, which we have described, were based on western precedent.[501] Another, discussed before, was the *Tenorlied* structure which can be traced beyond Oswald von Wolkenstein into fourteenth-century Italy. Nevertheless, the cultivation of these practices was such that it changed the course of music history. It affected, in particular, the instrumental genres of the Renaissance – and consequently European instrumental music in general.

[495] Edwards, 'Songs without words', 82 f. Martini's name is rather undeservedly omitted. See Martini, *Secular Pieces*. Otherwise, the list is of course correct.

[496] See Feldmann, *Codex Mf.2016*, vol. 1, 129 ff, and 2, no. 19, for discussion and edn.

[497] Martin Staehelin, 'Bemerkungen zu den Musikfragmenten im Wiener Schotten-Codex 355', *AcM* 58 (1986), 117–29.

[498] See Strohm, 'Native and foreign polyphony', 229 f.

[499] See Brown ed., *Florentine Chansonnier*.

[500] The idea of connecting cantus firmus arrangements and travelling instrumentalists is owed to Keith Polk, to whom I am most grateful. See also p. 568 below.

[501] All, in fact, if it is not assumed that monorhythmic cantus firmi emerged independently in England, Italy and Austria.

The developments described here had nothing whatsoever to do with national character. They did not depend on a specific language – whereas the rondeau, for example, could be said to depend on the French language. These practices are found in a coherent area where at least five different languages were spoken – German, Polish, Czech, Hungarian and Italian – but the techniques in question had nothing to do with linguistic structures.

By way of conclusion, we have to mention one practice which does seem 'typically German', although it is based on the least national language – Latin – and even depends on its linguistic structure. This is the so-called 'humanist ode', a song, mostly polyphonic but in simple chordal style, on metrical Latin verse. The scansion in long and short syllables as fixed by classical models is exactly transferred to the music, so that the asymmetrical succession of long and short syllables of the Latin metres leads to a strangely irregular rhythm.

Example 81 Paul Hofhaimer, 'Tu ne quaesieris' (Horace, Od. I, 11)

Systema
Asclepiadeum
quintum

[Do not enquire – it is forbidden to know – what end the Gods have chosen for me and you, Leuconoe; do not search the Babylonian ciphers . . .]

Example 81[502] is one of 35 'model settings' by Hofhaimer for the odes of Horace, published in 1539. Several well-known musicians 'composed' such pieces before and after him, including Ludwig Senfl. 'Musique mésurée à l'antique' became very important in the schools and churches of Germany and France in the age of the Reformation.[503] Hofhaimer's endeavour seems to be not only to

---

[502] After Moser, *Hofhaimer*, 119.

[503] See the comprehensive study of Edith Weber, *Musique et théâtre dans les pays Rhénans*, 3 vols. (Paris(?): Klincksieck, 1974). See also Sternfeld, 'Schools', 106–8.

express the rhythm but also the affect of the Latin words, and even an allusion to presumed ancient modes can be perceived if the whole collection is examined. It is usually said that the origin of this genre has to do with the humanist Conrad Celtis (1459–1508), a member of Maximilian's circle of advisers. Teaching at Ingolstadt University between 1491 and 1497, he encouraged or even 'commissioned' a student of his classes on Horace, Petrus Tritonius, to set the nineteen different metres of the Horatian canon in four-part music in this way. The settings were printed in 1507.[504]

They had an interesting prehistory, however.[505] Tritonius was a schoolmaster from Bolzano by the original name of Treibenreiff, who had studied at the University of Vienna from 1486. Besides him, the south-west German scholars Peter Schott and Jakob Locher also play a role in this story. The Paduan professor Franciscus Niger, in his *Grammatica* of 1480, had already printed musical note symbols exemplifying the long and short syllables of five Latin metres. Schott and Locher composed polyphonic odes in classical metres for school plays before 1490 and in 1495, respectively. The whole genre is a didactic one: Celtis's school play *Ludus Dianae* of 1501 ends each act with such a chorus.

Other evidence has been overlooked. The two hexametric poems 'Alga jacet humilis' and 'Viminibus cinge tristantem' in the Glogau partbooks, the second of which also appears in the Strahov Codex, have their tenors rhythmicized in precisely this way. These pieces antedate Niger's grammar of 1480. Where did they come from?

At least the later manifestations of this schoolmasterly fashion, as it can duly be called, have a common denominator: Habsburg patronage. This is obviously the case with Celtis and also with Locher, who worked at the Habsburg-founded (and -funded) University of Freiburg/Breisgau, and who wrote poems in neo-classical Latin for Maximilian, including in 1496 a *nenia* (lament) on the death of Duke Sigismund of Tyrol. This prince seems to have encouraged the trend. A precious and large collection of neo-Latin poems was put together in 1484 as a wedding gift for his bride, Katharina, by his chancellor Hans Fuchsmagen.[506] As if this were not enough, Franciscus Niger himself dedicated to the duke a collection of *Epithalamia* in this style for the wedding, didactically specifying the different metres as do the later musical settings.[507] It was the humanist Fuchsmagen who rewarded Isaac as a composer in September 1484, and Isaac's humanist compositions – the *nenia* for Lorenzo the Magnificent 'Quis dabit capiti meo aquam' and its twin 'Quis dabit pacem populo timenti' – seem to have been known in Habsburg circles (see p. 638). Moreover, the

---

[504] See James Haar, 'Ode, II' in *The New Grove*.

[505] Haar (see n. 504) mentions improvisations by Italian humanists; Moser, *Hofhaimer*, 162, points to similar attempts in the *Flores musicae*, a treatise by Hugo von Reutlingen of 1332. Most of the strings are pulled together in Karl-Günther Hartmann, *Die humanistische Odenkomposition in Deutschland. Vorgeschichte und Voraussetzungen* (Erlangen: Palm & Enke, 1976).

[506] The manuscript is in the Innsbruck University Library. See Gert Ammann ed., *Der Herzog und sein Taler* (n. 427 above), no. 1.24, p. 106.

[507] *GB-Lbl IA. 30050* (printed Padua, c.1484).

earliest polyphonic setting of a Horatian ode had already existed in the area since at least 1466: it is 'Tu ne quaesieris' in *Tr 89* (no. 616).[508] In four parts and in a rather stodgy, chordal style, the setting does manage to convey the Horatian verse audibly, although it does not yet have the strict scansion of the later pieces. A speculation that it has to do with Krombsdorfer and with the aforementioned Innsbruck–Trent–Ferrara traffic, would lead us back to Italy: not only to Ferrara with Pietrobono's improvised courtly recitations, but also to the University of Padua, where Hinderbach had earned his doctorate and where Niger taught.

We might say that, in this case, the Germans had turned an Italian humanistic idea into something rather too rigid and systematic. That was a manner which they applied to western European music as well. But by doing this, they have managed to push us all the way into our Renaissance chapter.

[508] Printed in *DTOe VII*, vols. 14-15, 89 ff. Martin Staehelin, 'Trienter Codices und Humanismus', in Pirotta–Curti eds, *Codici Musicali*, 158-68, mentions the piece in a similar context.

4

ITALY AND SPAIN: THE ENCOUNTER OF MUSIC AND RENAISSANCE

The Italian Quattrocento and the music historians

Italy was the cradle of the Renaissance, but she did not give birth to what is often called 'Renaissance music'. That happened in western Europe; Italy was just a wonderful foster-mother of that music. Embarrassment over the adopted (abducted?) child did not arise until Romantic historians had coined the term 'Renaissance' and had requested that age to conform, in all or most of its manifestations, to an ideal, homogeneous type of civilization – in other words to foster only its own children. For fifteenth- and sixteenth-century Italy they had reserved the imagery of a fertile, innovative, emancipated culture addicted to beauty, which had finally broken its medieval shackles of scholasticism and otherworldliness: all cultural activities had to answer to this description.

The *music* of the Italians did not seem to conform to this ideal organic unity, however. For one thing, it was slow to emerge at all: in Italy, the end of the Ars nova was followed by almost a century of foreign domination in music. When, as a new and splendid musical contribution to Renaissance culture, the Italian madrigal was created around 1520, the Renaissance in other arts was past its prime. What was to do with the fifteenth century when all the other arts flourished in Italy? To adopt the term 'Renaissance' for music[509] – as favoured by many music historians but with rather flimsy arguments – was to map out a chronologically separate development for music alone: Italian 'Renaissance music' began a century later than Italian 'Renaissance architecture', for example. The alternative was to integrate the music of the Franco-Netherlanders into the concept. This inevitably blurred the integrity of the Renaissance concept itself: Renaissance *music* – alone among the arts – would then have taken its origins from English cathedrals. Some scholars (especially non-Italians) began to feel that the meliorative term 'Renaissance' was not so useful for music after all; some adopted it in their titles but did nothing with

---

[509] For an introduction to the history of the term in music, see Lewis Lockwood, 'Renaissance' in *The New Grove*. A significant, controversial view is offered in Edward E. Lowinsky, 'Music in the culture of the Renaissance', *Journal of the History of Ideas* 15 (1954), 509–53.

it.[510] Other scholars (especially Italians) began to wonder whether northerners like Dufay and Josquin, let alone Dunstable, could actually represent Italy in the contest of nations for that beauty prize, the 'Renaissance' label. Should not Italian Renaissance music be something very different from an isorhythmic motet or tenor Mass: something simpler and more rounded, more relaxed and perhaps also more showy? Something with all its qualities on the surface? Something, in a word, more 'Italian'?

That Dufay's and Josquin's polyphony did not fulfil Romantic expectations about cultural homogeneity on a national basis would not have been so embarrassing had the Italians themselves produced music which, in some way at least, seemed to express their own Renaissance attitudes. But most researches into Italian fifteenth-century polyphony produced almost the opposite result: clumsy, rudimentary, clerical or otherworldly materials. Devotional *laude*, much primitive polyphony, little books with elementary music theory written by Franciscans and Benedictines, the occasional setting of French poems (particularly in the early part of the century), harmonizations of possibly popular tunes but in awkward emulation of foreign contrapuntal idioms. The fifteenth century in Italy – the Quattrocento – seemed a mysterious, dark age, if not a desert, from the musical point of view. What was clear as the sun, however, was the great appreciation the Italians had for the most complex and spiritual foreign music.

A major representative of Italian musicology, Fausto Torrefranca, decided in the 1920s that 'what is not allowed to be, cannot be' (C. Morgenstern). In his erudite and eloquent work, 'Il segreto del Quattrocento' ('The secret of the fifteenth century') of 1939, he re-dated the beginning of the four-voice villotta/nio, a very popular polyphonic genre of the sixteenth century, to the mid-fifteenth century. Thus, the four-voice villotta became the ancestor of the frottola, the madrigal and various other genres and musical devices (for example the quodlibet of folk-tunes): Italian musicians became leaders in the Renaissance movement.[511]

Other scholars, among them Knud Jeppesen, Alfred Einstein, Walter Rubsamen, Nanie Bridgman, Federico Ghisi and Nino Pirrotta, proceeded with more caution and a sounder methodology in their reconstructions of Italian secular music of the Renaissance.[512] They, and their students and collaborators, have largely filled the perceived void in Italian fifteenth-century music. Pirrotta still sees a need to explain 'why the age that saw an enormous display of native ingenuity in architecture, the fine arts, and all minor artistic crafts should have leaned so heavily on foreign talent only for music. The undisputed prestige of the French musical tradition cannot be made to account alone for the im-

---

[510] For example Besseler, *Musik des Mittelalters*; Bukofzer, *Studies*.

[511] Torrefranca's main piece of evidence was a north Italian villotta manuscript (*I-Vnm It. IV, 1795-8*), which has since been dated *c.*1520: see *CC*, vol. 4, 73 f.

[512] Their major publications are: Jeppesen–Brøndal eds, *Laude*; Jeppesen, *La Frottola*; Einstein, *Italian Madrigal*; Rubsamen, *Literary Sources*; Bridgman, *Vie musicale*; Ghisi, *Studi e Testi* (collection of essays); Pirrotta, *Music and Culture* (collection of essays); *idem, Music and Theatre*.

balance'.[513] Pirrotta, who also characterized the fate of Italian art-music in the Quattrocento as a 'sharp decline',[514] goes on to explain that the same forces which generated the Italian Renaissance in the arts and letters – by and large, the cultural trends spearheaded by the humanists – were averse to northern polyphony as it was cultivated in exclusive ecclesiastical circles. As a result, 'secular society simply reverted entirely to kinds of music which were mainly committed to oral tradition'.[515]

This solution to the perceived 'imbalance' between the Italian Renaissance and the fate of its music is brilliant in so far as it turns an alleged cultural weakness (rejection of written polyphony) into a strength (rise of unwritten practice). It is the more ingenious as it uses the men of letters, the humanists, as heralds of a potentially illiterate practice. Pirrotta maintains that, at least in the eyes of the humanists and their followers, the unwritten practice of music reflected Italian 'native ingenuity' just as did the novel works of architecture, painting or literature, whereas the rejected northern polyphony represented the scholasticism of the Middle Ages.

The concept of 'Renaissance' underlying this idea is the Romantic, organicist and national-orientated concept, of course. Italy's music has, after all, been integrated into this concept. There are minor questions remaining: for example whether it is actually true that the humanists despised written polyphony, or whether Italy's unwritten music-making was in itself so typically Italian. The major problem, however, is that the written polyphony of a Dufay or Josquin has been expelled from the Italian Renaissance. Whether or not we give the laudatory title of 'Renaissance' to Dufay and Josquin (their music can live without it), there is no doubt that northern polyphony was part of Italian culture; it belonged to it and grew with it. It was the adopted child whom the Italians loved and fostered.

This book is not a study of the Renaissance in music, but tries to do justice to European music over wider geographic and chronological stretches. Our final chapter will have to accommodate both the climax of a long artistic development *and* the particular conditions of a geographic area of Europe which is not limited to the Italian peninsula. This I see as a happy combination, although it is neither a logical nor a necessary one. The Renaissance concept is not needed to explain a development of the musical art; in fact it falls far short of explaining it. It can be used to describe, on the other hand, what happened to the musical art in places such as Italy and Spain in the later fifteenth century. The essence of the art itself, and what people do with it, are separate questions: but we shall attempt to understand them by holding them against each other.[516]

---

[513] 'Music and cultural tendencies', 128 f.

[514] *ibid*, 135.

[515] 'Italy, #I, 3' in *The New Grove*, 365.

[516] This path has already been pursued, with great success, in Bridgman, *Vie musicale*. See also the excellent survey of Cattin, 'Quattrocento'.

Courtly fashions: education and humanism

In some corners of Italy at least, secular society after the demise of the Ars nova did not 'simply revert entirely to kinds of music which were mainly committed to oral tradition'. What happened was more complex. The popularizing trends which had led to polyphonic settings of *siciliane* and *giustiniane* (or *viniziane*) in the age of Johannes Ciconia (see p. 103), remained strong, producing more popularizing songs in newer polyphonic idioms. The reference to unwritten practice, or at least to poetry and tunes also familiar to illiterate musicians, remained a frequent gesture in the *beau monde* of the Veneto and its neighbouring courts. Thus, it is possible to find pieces resembling *giustiniane* in the polyphonic codices of the Dufay era, some indeed by Hugo de Lantins and Dufay himself (see p. 157). Pirrotta has also found echoes of the *viniziane* in polyphonic songs by Bartolomeo da Bologna, Prepositus Brixiensis and Petrus Rubeus (*d*.1438), all transmitted in *GB-Ob 213*.[517] When needed, these songs could be turned into sacred *laude*: substitute texts were easy to find where the originals were in ballata form. This was the practice of Leonardo Giustinian at the end of his life. There is, furthermore, documentary evidence for the continued vogue of the *viniziane* beyond mid-century; occasionally it has been possible to connect this evidence with actually transmitted music. The ballata-*viniziana* 'Ayme sospiri', has been identified in an edition of 1505 (Petrucci's *Frottole libro 6*) in a more ornamented version.[518] Art-music also began to absorb other popular forms such as the *strambotto* (a monostrophic eight-line song usually with the rhyme-scheme of the *ottava rima*, ababahcc), whereas the traditional strophic–epic genre, the *sirventese*, which is never found in polyphonic settings of this time, was no longer mentioned in the metrical treatise by the Paduan professor Francesco Baratella of 1448.[519] Many other types of song, including French polyphonic chansons, were continuously performed for entertainment in the area. We are indeed told in a dialogue of 1448 by Giannozzo Manetti, the Florentine *orator* (ambassador) in Venice, how after a banquet some young aristocrats performed 'gallicas cantilenas et melodias', followed by 'venetis cantiunculis et symphoniis'; finally somebody sang Sicilian 'symphonias et cantilenas'.[520]

To broaden our picture somewhat geographically: the chansonnier *Escorial IV. a. 24 (EscB)* - a source which mixes French and Italian songs in just such a manner as might have suited the musical pastimes of a north Italian court –

---

[517] Nino Pirrotta, 'Echi di arie veneziane del primo quattrocento?' in *Interpretazioni Veneziane. Studi di storia dell'arte in onore di Michelangelo Muraro*, ed. David Rosand (Venice: Arsenale, 1984), 99–108.

[518] Rubsamen, 'Justiniane'.

[519] Cattin, 'Quattrocento', 282. This is in itself a sign that unwritten practice and the genres of art-music may sometimes develop analogously. A good introduction to the verse-forms used for music throughout the century is Prizer, *Courtly Pastimes*, 63–92.

[520] Rubsamen, 'Justiniane', 173. Rubsamen adds: 'The French songs were probably chansons by Dufay, Binchois, or their co-nationals, but the Venetian and Sicilian pieces are harder to identify'.

has been analysed by Nino Pirrotta for the role of native song genres.[521] Not by coincidence does the manuscript contain several *giustiniane*, among them 'Ayme sospiri'.

No fewer than three documents are known which prove that songs of this kind, mixed with French chansons, were in great demand at the Sforza court of Milan – probably because this family had to catch up with the culture of old-established houses such as the Este of Ferrara. In contrast to his father, the ex-condottiere Francesco Sforza, Galeazzo Maria Sforza (1444–76) was given a careful musical education. In March 1452, his singing studies with Guiniforte Barzizza are sufficiently advanced that 'he has already learned eight French songs, and is learning a new one every day'.[522] Better known is the memorandum by Cicco Simonetta, secretary of Galeazzo Maria, who in c.1471–5 recommends that the Milanese ambassador in Venice be asked to provide a manuscript with all the poems by Giustinian and all the other good Venetian songs, plus the music for two or three of them, so that the Venetian type of melody can be understood ('per intendere l'aere venetiano'). This is to be carried out by the specialist Filippo Macerata, a Venetian musician who had joined the Sforza court as early as 1454 (probably to sing just this type of music to the courtiers). What is more, Macerata is to send a boy of fourteen or fifteen years who can sing these pieces, has a good voice and some theoretical knowledge of music ('fondamenta et raxone del canto'), who can play the lute well, and sing with the lute as well as without.[523] Finally, on 16 November 1472 Galeazzo Maria orders his ambassador in Savoy to ask the Savoy chapelmaster for a song which he identifies as 'Robinetto notato su l'ayre de O rosa bella'; he is to send it quickly, with exactly the same words underlaid as the above-said chapelmaster says when singing 'Robineto'.[524] This song may well be extant: it is either the 'O rosa bella' quodlibet with the tenor 'He Robinet, tu m'as la mort donné' found on the first music page of the chansonnier *EscB*[525] – or the quodlibet mentioned in Tinctoris's *Proportionale musices*, which quotes underneath the 'O rosa bella' tune not only 'Robinet' but also 'L'homme armé'.[526] Whichever the source of the 'O rosa bella' quodlibet – Savoy or Naples – it was probably put to the same use as the *viniziane* and the singing boy: for the musical education of the younger members of the Sforza family, for example Ascanio Sforza, the later cardinal and probable patron of Josquin.[527]

Ippolita Maria Sforza (1445–88) was so well trained in singing and dancing that she made a great impression on her contemporaries at the time of her marriage to Alfonso, Duke of Calabria (1465). Galeazzo Maria's brother and factual

[521] Pirrotta, 'Su alcuni testi'.
[522] Barblan, 'Vita musicale', 818.
[523] Rubsamen, 'Justiniane', 173; the complete original is in Motta, *Musici*, 554 f.
[524] Motta, *Musici*, 303.
[525] See Pirrotta, 'Su alcuni testi', 133 f, edited 153 f; Hanen ed., *Chansonnier El Escorial*.
[526] *Opera theoretica*, vol. IIa, 51. See Lockwood, 'Aspects', 101.
[527] See Lowinsky, 'Ascanio Sforza's life', 45 f, for evidence on Ascanio's musical education.

successor in power, Ludovico Sforza, and his wife Beatrice d'Este, were also accomplished musicians. The Florentine noblewoman Clarice Tornabuoni, who married Lorenzo de' Medici in 1469, had several dancing masters, including the famous Giovanni Ambrosio from Pesaro (see below) and a certain Filippus.[528]

It is not known what kind of songs the Fleming Jean Cordier played and sang in 1467-8 to Lorenzo de' Medici on the *lira da braccio* (see p. 319). He obviously accompanied himself in a manner not recoverable from written documents, but frequently alluded to in literary sources. The musical education of Lorenzo de' Medici (1449-92) had begun much earlier, perhaps with Antonio Squarcialupi and John Hothby in the 1450s (see p. 318). There is a possibility that the manuscript *I-Rvat 1411* (*ROu*), a chansonnier with nineteen French- and Italian-texted songs, was used by the young Lorenzo: it belonged to his father Piero de' Medici who gave it to a relative before his death (1469) – perhaps when Lorenzo had learned all the songs in it.[529] They are largely by Binchois and Dufay, but two of them are settings of the *giustiniana* 'O rosa bella': the Ciconia setting and the one which is here attributed to Dunstable.

Although the Sforzas and the Medicis were catching up quickly, around 1460 some corners of Italy could still boast more competence in the *aere venetiano* than others. In that year, Marquis Lodovico Gonzaga of Mantua had to ask at the court of Borso d'Este for a good singer who could teach his own servants. The person he wrote to was Niccolò Tedesco (Nikolaus Krombsdorfer, see p. 519), and the person recommended was Giovanni Brith, whose nationality is unknown.[530] According to Niccolò, this Giovanni knew well the manner of 'modern singing, above all the Venetian type' (*cantare moderno et maxime de l'aëre venexiano*). In honour of two members of the Gonzaga family, two musicians in Verona performed for them 'many Venetian *canzoni* and *strambotti*' with a lute.[531] And, when it came to expertise in instrumental performance, an unwritten practice, the Sforzas knew whom to approach: a whole series of letters went back and forth in the 1450s between Milan and Ferrara concerning the instrumental training of Francesco Sforza's servant, the German Stefano da Monaco, with the great Pietrobono.[532]

Very little more needs to be said about 'O rosa bella' itself. The song, as set by Bedyngham, is an English tribute to the vogue of the *giustiniane* or *viniziane*, and as such it is a product of the Este court. Leonello d'Este (*r.* 1441-50) and his father, Niccolò III (*r.* 1393-1441), had not only fostered vocal music but also developed a specially Ferrarese tradition of instrumental ensemble music

---

[528] Timothy J. McGee, 'Dancing masters and the Medici court in the fifteenth century', *Studi Musicali* 17 (1988), 201-24. 'Medici court' is a misnomer, of course.

[529] On the manuscript, see *CC*, vol. 4, 68; Pirrotta, 'Ricercare', 64 f. Although written in black notation, the manuscript should not be dated *c.*1440 but in the mid-fifties.

[530] Prizer, *Courtly Pastimes*, 4. 'Brits' or 'Vrits' was the name of a Burgundian chaplain (Marix, *Histoire*, 211). It is just as possible that the name meant 'the Briton'. Brith also knew counterpoint and held cathedral positions before and after 1460.

[531] Prizer, *Courtly Pastimes*, 4 and n. 26.

[532] Lockwood, *Ferrara*, 100 f.

– loud as well as soft. Marquis Niccolò III also hired, probably in 1436, Niccolò Tedesco, and he must have discovered the talent of Pietrobono, who first appears at the court in 1441. Why would the marquis have employed precisely these two specialists of secular song and lute-playing? For the musical education of his son Leonello, of course, which was supervised, but not carried out in detail, by his teacher the humanist Guarino da Verona. The young man learned to play the lute and received songbooks plus a book of elementary music theory ('regole de canto').[533] During Leonello's enlightened reign, the chapel was formed and a sacred polyphonic repertory with a strong English ingredient was created (see p. 264). It was also during that reign that foreign minstrels and chaplains appeared at court to try their luck. Two Frenchmen who sold to the court a 'book of six new Masses' in 1447 may have come from Antwerp, carrying the 'Caput' Mass and other English works. It is hardly surprising to find at least one English musician directly serving Leonello's court: 'Johannes cantor quondam alterius Johannis presbiter Londini' (in 1448), and 'Johannes ab arpa de Anglia' (in 1448–50) – possibly the same man.[534]

I suggest that this musician was the composer John Bedyngham, and my reasons are as follows. How can Bedyngham have set 'O rosa bella' without personal contact with Italy? The *viniziana* was definitely not a fashion outside Italy. Whether he composed the piece during the stay at Ferrara itself or after having returned home, sending it by letter, we do not know. But he must have visited Ferrara also because the sources of his other works, sacred as well as secular, are so surprisingly concentrated on the area near Ferrara in the 1450s and early 1460s: the codices *Tr 93, 90* and *88*, the songbooks *EscB*, Schedel and Oporto.[535]

The Oporto Chansonnier is the best source of Bedyngham's setting of 'O rosa bella'; it also contains 'Anglo-Italian' songs by Robertus and Galfridus de Anglia, and another *viniziana* by a distant musician, Gilles Joye of Bruges ('Poy che crudel fortuna').[536] The date of this manuscript may be as late as the early to mid-sixties.[537] It seems to draw together the fashionable songs which

---

[533] Lewis Lockwood, 'Dufay and Ferrara', in Atlas ed., *Dufay Quincentenary Conference*, 24; Lockwood, *Ferrara*, 46.

[534] Lockwood, *Ferrara*, 49 ff, 60 f, 80, 115. The exact designations for the *presbiter* are slightly different in the various references. This priest had a benefice at the cathedral and taught the clerics, a frequent function of foreigners in Italian churches.

[535] Both Lockwood, *Ferrara*, and Fallows, 'Bedyngham, John' in *The New Grove*, consider but then reject the possibility that the London musician in Ferrara was John Bedyngham. It is unlikely that another English visitor to Ferrara had his luggage packed full with Bedyngham's works – unless he was perhaps a relative. According to Fallows, a certain John Bedyngham was a London parish clerk in 1449. This should not have prevented him from visiting Italy; but as the Ferrara records speak of a father and a son, both called Johannes and the son a priest, yet other solutions seem possible.

[536] For Galfridus, Robertus and the Oporto Manuscript, see Fallows, 'Robertus de Anglia'; Nino Pirrotta, 'Two Anglo-Italian pieces in the manuscript Porto 714', in *Speculum Musicae Artis. Festgabe für Heinrich Husmann zum 60. Geburtstag*, ed. H. Becker and R. Gerlach (Munich, 1970), 253–61. For Joye, see Strohm, *Bruges*, 126 (I am no longer sure that the original words could not be Italian after all: the song may have been written for an Italian in Bruges).

[537] See Fallows, 'Robertus de Anglia', and Lockwood, *Ferrara*, 109–18.

had accumulated over the years at the Ferrarese court of Borso d'Este (1450–71). It also reflects another young nobleman's musical education, in this case that of Rinaldo Maria d'Este (*c.*1430–1503), a younger bastard brother of Leonello and Borso. This education most probably took place at the hands of Robertus de Anglia, who had entered the service of the young man in 1454 and who is, if not the scribe, at least the later owner of the songbook. The necessary element of *ragione de canto* is present in the book in the form of theoretical tracts at the beginning (including two by Ugolino da Orvieto, formerly archpriest of Ferrara Cathedral).[538] The traditions sketched here extended, of course, into the era of Ercole I d'Este (*r.* 1471–1505). Very touching is the desire for musical education in his daughter Isabella (1474–1539), who immediately after her marriage to Francesco II Gonzaga of Mantua in 1490 still requested lessons from her former teacher at Ferrara, Johannes Martini: 'Io desidero imparare rasone de canto . . .'.[539]

It may seem a little monotonous if so much of courtly musical culture has been related here to education. But the Italians, and their aristocracy, are stubbornly conservative when it comes to family matters. The pattern of providing a son or daughter with the best possible musical training had been firmly established by the late Middle Ages. It also related, of course, to the ideas of the *humanists*.[540]

For them, music was an art which needed to be exercised for the perfection of the character and manners. Although time-honoured authorities of music theory (Boethius included) were accepted, for the young nobleman or noblewoman it was best to have as much theory as necessary and as much practice as possible. This kind of attitude seems to transpire from the writings of all the humanists who educated princes – Vittorino da Feltre at Mantua, Guarino da Verona at Ferrara and Giacomo Borbo at Naples in the earlier fifteenth century,[541] Marsilio Ficino at Florence under Piero and Lorenzo de' Medici. Ficino, in particular, is said to have performed songs on the lute in his Platonic academy at Florence.[542] Most humanists, whether they were princely educators, 'orators' or administrators, mentioned music in their speeches and writings with an invariably friendly tone, although they sound sometimes bland and sometimes uninformed.[543] Their overriding concern was not so much what

---

[538] See Lockwood, *Ferrara*, 112 f and 118 n. 31: another manuscript cited in 1453 seems to have contained 'razone de canto' (not 'drago de cento' which is nonsense). It was another educational book.

[539] Prizer, *Courtly Pastimes* 11 f and n. 32.

[540] On the subject of the following paragraph, see most generally Palisca, *Humanism*, ch. 1; Pirrotta, 'Music and cultural tendencies', 135 8; Cattin, 'Quattrocento', 273–7. As will be seen, my views differ in some respects, owing to a different evaluation of the facts. See also Bridgman, *Vie musicale*, chaps. 4 and 6.

[541] F. Alberto Gallo, 'Musica, poetica e retorica nel Quattrocento: l'*Illuminator* di Giacomo Borbo', *RIM* 10 (1975), 72–85.

[542] Paul O. Kristeller, 'Music and learning in the early Italian Renaissance', *JRBM* 1 (1947), 255–74, also in his *Renaissance Thought*, vol. 2 (New York, 1965), 142–62.

[543] See the statements in Karl Müllner, *Reden und Briefe italienischer Humanisten*, 2nd rev. edn (Munich, 1970) (index: 'musica'); and in Pirrotta, 'Music and cultural tendencies', 138.

constituted the musical art in itself but what it did to the human soul. This curiosity furthered, indeed, those theories of modal ethos – of the 'effects of music' – which utilized ancient precedent as well as initiated more modern theories of the affections.[544] Wherever classical opinions on music could be found, of course, the humanists adopted them. The most impressive work was perhaps done in the rediscovery of ancient music theory, especially of the Greeks. There is an undeniable connection between these efforts, represented, for example, by Giorgio Valla (1447–1500),[545] and a renewed practice and theory of the tone system as debated between Hothby, Ramos, Gaffurius and Spataro (see p. 596). The more elementary tutors ('ragione de canto' etc.) with their humanistic, educational or sometimes quadrivial orientation[546] could be a far cry from professional music theory. The latter became, in the hands of Tinctoris and Gaffurius, very much a theory of what constitutes the musical *art*. Humanists who looked at music more as a *practice* were predictably diffident about such theory.

On the other hand, while they may have sneered at scholastic authors such as Guido of Arezzo or Johannes de Muris for their non-classical Latin, there is no evidence that the Italian humanists of the fifteenth century despised the practice of written polyphonic music. As far as they were actually exposed to it – which would have happened to those humanists who worked at the courts of Ferrara, Naples, Milan, the papal court in Rome or under the Medici in Florence – we cannot find that they protested. If they did (as has been claimed), they had in any case not the slightest effect. On the contrary, these particular centres cultivated polyphonic music just as much as humanistic literature or philosophy.

The discussion of this issue has become confused through the mistaken assumption that Italians in general had little or no access to polyphony, that all polyphony was entrenched in monastic and cathedral circles, and that, consequently, there was *a priori* a gulf between 'Italian' and 'northern' types of music and attitudes to music.[547] This is not true. Nobody denies, of course, the social barriers which excluded large segments of the population from the fine arts in general. Apart from this qualification, however, written art-music, Italian and not, was a gladly accepted and enthusiastically studied subject in Quattrocento Italy.

We are indebted to the humanists not so much, perhaps, for their opinions about music-making as for their descriptions of it. Their freshness of observa-

---

[544] See pp. 596 f.

[545] Palisca, *Humanism*, ch. 4, and *passim*.

[546] A typical tutor for a prince – Ascanio Sforza, in fact – is described in Albert Seay, 'The "Liber musices" of Florentius de Faxolis', in *Musik und Geschichte. Leo Schrade zum 60. Geburtstag* (Cologne: Volk, 1963), 71–95. Medieval authorities and theories are by no means shunned in this tract. See also Lowinsky, 'Ascanio Sforza's life', 47 f.

[547] Palisca, *Humanism*, 10, rightly stresses that counterpoint was not a prerogative of the Netherlanders. It would be a misunderstanding to transfer the sixteenth-century 'campaign against abstract polyphony', as perceived by him (p. 16), into the fifteenth.

tion, journalistic eloquence and general curiosity have given us the first 'realistic' accounts of the performance and reception of music. Caution is in order, of course. While the fragment that survives of Johannes Tinctoris's most genuinely humanist work, *De inventione et usu musice*, abounds with pertinent and novel observations about his musical environment,[548] others who wrote in a similar vein lacked technical knowledge. Moreover, the desire to express everything in Ciceronian Latin curiously distorted terminology. Paolo Cortese's *De cardinalatu libri tres* of 1510 is a case in point. The author incorporates music in this encyclopedia of manners befitting a prelate in the section 'How passions should be avoided, and music used after meals'.[549] He takes his descriptive task seriously enough, however, to give us a survey of the effects and genres, the instruments, modes, major performers and composers, written and unwritten, monophonic and polyphonic music. His problem – the fundamental problem of 'Renaissance and music' – is that the object described is unknown to antiquity. Thus, in his determination to admit only classical vocabulary and concepts, he replaces established medieval musical terminology with neo-Latinisms, for example 'lembum' for 'lute' and 'canendi ratio' for 'mode'. Tinctoris had spoken of 'lyra populariter leutum' and of 'toni', respectively.

A related problem occurs with descriptions of performances. The humanist clothes as much as possible in a classical garb. Thus, every singer becomes automatically an Orpheus or, more fashionably, a Timotheus who rouses the passions of his Alexander. (The story was not very novel either – see also p. 191 – but was extremely popular through the account of Aulus Gellius's *Noctes Atticae*, a late classical chivalric epic often copied for Italian courts at the time.) It is little surprise to see who is most consistently likened to this prototype of musicians: Pietrobono 'del chitarrino' (1417–97).

Among the many eulogies which Pietrobono de Burcellis received from his literate contemporaries,[550] one of the most elaborate is an account by the humanist, secretary and dancing teacher of the Sforza court, Antonio Cornazano (*c.*1430–1484). He describes (under the fictitious date of 1441, probably to be read as 1456) an appearance of the famous lutenist–singer at the dinner-table of Francesco Sforza, performing improvised epics of heroes and lovers – modern rather than ancient.[551] The report can be read in two ways. One is to expect from the well-instructed musician Cornazano a matter-of-fact account. In that case, the author's spirited language, and his sheer enthusiasm for the effects of Pietrobono's singing and playing on the audience, strongly emphasizes the esteem in which such performances were held. The other way would be to expect from this servant of the Sforza dynasty, in his commissioned eulogy *La Sforziade*, a hyperbolic praise of the greatness of everything that went on

---

[548] See Weinmann, *Tinctoris*, and p. 595 below.

[549] Edited, translated and commented on in Pirrotta, 'Music and cultural tendencies', 146–61.

[550] A survey is in Lockwood, *Ferrara*, 98–102.

[551] Edited and discussed in Pirrotta, 'Music and cultural tendencies'.

at Francesco Sforza's court. One of these things was the traditional minstrels' performance at the dinner-table – a situation where splendour was the convention. We would then take the classical comparisons ('Apollo', 'Orpheo', 'Amphion') as literary niceties giving fresh colours to a convention shared with many other countries and centuries. Pietrobono, according to Cornazano, masters learned mensural music: he keeps 'syncopating', 'using proportions', 'imitating the tenor' on the lute. Thus, he outdoes many earlier colleagues, especially in Italy.[552]

The improvvisatori; dance music

Performers such as Pietrobono were usually called 'improvvisatori', a term which should not simply be translated as 'improvisers', because their art was largely premeditated and wholly mnemonic. They relied on textual as well as musical patterns which they knew by heart. The musical patterns, which in performance needed little adjustment or melodic elaboration to fit changing texts, were most probably not grounds nor bass lines as in the sixteenth century, but *tenori* – melodic lines in the range of the tenor voice which characterized all European secular and sacred monophony (see p. 349). These melodies were also sometimes called *aëre* ('modes or manners of singing').[553] Pieces printed by Petrucci (*Frottole libro 6*, 1505) were identified with these patterns by being headed 'the manner of singing (strambotti, sonnets, capitoli, odas etc.)'.[554] The musical *aëre* could be applied to any poem as long as it had the respective *forme fixe*. The principle as such was an old tradition, in Italy as well as in other countries, and had a sacred counterpart in the psalm-tones and related *differentiae* which could be adapted to many different words. Analogously, the secular *improvvisatori* sang by heart. The audience – patrons and humanists – were not interested in knowing whether the tune had been learned from a written copy or not, and to the musician this made no difference either. In rehearsal and for transmission, writing could always be useful.

Much of the music performed by these musicians must have been polyphonic. Petrucci's examples are polyphonic; we gather from Cornazano's and other descriptions that Pietrobono sang to his own accompaniment on the lute (or gittern, *chitarrino*), and that therefore two lines were sounded. Pietrobono probably sang a tenor line – his own register – while playing an ornamented

---

[552] Pirrotta, 'Music and cultural tendencies', 146, is unwilling to believe this: I concur. But it is one thing to doubt these statements, and another to notice *in what terms* Cornazano hopes to glorify the minstrel and his employer. A German lutenist and singer of Ferrara, Nicolaus Schefer (or Nicolaus Sch. Fer.?) was apostrophized as *alter Orpheus* on a medal struck in 1457 by Johannes Boldin: see Pirro, *Histoire*, 154.

[553] The *aëre veneziano* quoted above could be either a specific tune or a type of melody, which comes to the same if the tune is used to accommodate different 'songs' i.e. poems. On the term 'aëre' or 'ayre', see also p. 193.

[554] 'Modo de cantar strambotti (etc.)', in later sources often called 'aëre da cantar . . .'. See Prizer, *Courtly Pastimes*, 64 ff.

discant line on the instrument. This was also the practice of the singer on the *lira da braccio*, a characteristically Italian instrument, with the sole difference that the *lira* could be bowed, producing simple chords above and below the voice. Singers like Pietrobono were occasionally assisted by a *tenorista*, in this case the term for a second instrumentalist who could take an optional third line, i.e. a contratenor. (See also pp. 364 f.)

Not surprisingly, similar reports concerning bards and improvisers emanate from the self-consciously humanistic court of Matthias Corvinus of Hungary (see p. 315) and also from the Castilian and Aragonese courts, where Italian and French influences met.[555] Singer–poets were particularly active in a centre like Naples, where the Aragonese kings (Alfonso 'il Magnanimo', 1442–58 and Ferrante I, 1458–94) gathered humanists and musicians like no other dynasty on Italian soil. Several members of Italian aristocratic houses were given an education there that included music, the later Duke Ercole I d'Este among them. Under Ferrante, Catalan literature and song was gradually replaced by Neapolitan, typified in the example of the Catalan Benedetto Gareth ('il Charitheo'; *d.*1514) who was an 'improvvisatore' of his own poems on the lute. A *strambotto* by Chariteo, 'Amando e desïando io vivo e sento', was printed in Petrucci's *Frottole libro 9* (1509), the polyphonic setting being attributed to the poet as well. Ferrante also rewarded visiting humanists and poets, among them the great Serafino de' Ciminelli dall' Aquila (1466–1500).[556] His education in singing and lute-playing was predominantly received at Naples – from the Fleming Guillaume Guarnier – but he served many other courts as well, including the household of Cardinal Ascanio Sforza in company with Josquin (see p. 598). Serafino is said to have been induced to the recitation of *strambotti* by Chariteo in Milan, when he heard some of them performed by the Neapolitan singer Andrea Coscia.

The *improvvisatori* of *strambotti*, sonnets, epics (and in Spain, romances) dealing with love and heroic deeds were not too dissimilar from the saintly preachers of penitence who attracted enormous crowds to the piazzas, such as Vicente Ferrer of Valencia (*d.*1419) or Bernardino da Siena (*d.*1444). The preachers had, of course, audiences from all social classes, rather comparable to those of the popular masters of the same rhetorical art, the 'bench singers' – *saltimbanchi* or *cantinpanchi*. One of the most famous of these was the Florentine Antonio di Guido, who began his career in 1437 and was praised by the Medici poet Angelo Poliziano in a Latin sonnet.[557] It is so difficult to ascertain what some of these popular performers actually did, that the discoveries of the cultural historian Peter Burke are most welcome. He has found printed broadsheet collections of poetry, which Florentine performers, including the *cantampanco* Bernardino Ciurmadore, commissioned from the printing shops in large

---

[555] See Anglès, *La música*, 27–36.
[556] Atlas, *Aragonese Court*, 82 f and 102.
[557] B. Becherini, 'Un canta in panca Fiorentino: Antonio di Guido', *RMI* 50 (1948), 241–7.

numbers, for example 500 copies of a single item. No doubt, Burke argues, these sheets were sold at a low price to the listening audience, like libretti; the poems themselves sometimes disclose that they were addressed to listeners rather than mere readers. The poetic forms are the same as those of the courtly improvisers: *strambotti*, sonnets, *terze rime*, strophic forms, *canzoni* etc. The poems have mostly religious, legendary, chivalric or satirical topics, i.e. those suitable for audiences without a humanist education.[558]

A perfect example of the use of memorized patterns in performance is, of course, *dance*. The Italian courts – but also the non-Italian courts and the Italian and foreign urban middle class – were extremely fond of stylish dancing, which they did themselves or had performed for them by male and female minstrels. Dancing is performed without written aids and relies on rhythmic patterns to which the music (and, quite regularly, the words of the dance-song) has to conform. The teaching, rehearsal and transmission of dance-steps, tunes and more complex choreographies was best entrusted to writing, of course. This was first done in Italy by the dancing master Domenico da Piacenza (*d.* after 1472), in his treatise *De arte saltandi et choreas ducendi* (Of the art of dancing and leading collective dances).[559] He first describes four basic steps: *bassadanza, saltarello, quadernaria* (also called *saltarello todesco*) and *piva* – terms which have reminded scholars of the rhythmic classifications of Italian Trecento notation. The steps can be mixed within the same dance. Domenico then gives elaborate choreographies for twelve and more people, even creating two little ballets or 'dance-dramas'. The author worked for Francesco Sforza's court and from 1456 mostly for the Este family. He had a number of students, the most important of whom were Antonio Cornazano (see above) and the Jew Guglielmo Ebreo da Pesaro. Cornazano's treatise *Libro dell'arte del danzare* of 1465 (only the dedicatory sonnet survives of a first version of 1455, dedicated to his student at Milan, Ippolita Sforza) is in many ways indebted to Domenico's, but addresses his courtly audience rather than the professional colleague.[560] He uses mensural notation – monophonically – to convey the tunes and rhythms, which are of very varied complexity. He gives eight *balli* (relatively elaborate choreographies for more people), notating their tunes as 'Giove in canto', 'Bereguardo in canto' etc., and three *tenori da bassadançe et saltarelli*, notated in equal semibreves according to the principle of stroke notation: 'Tenore del re di spagna', 'Cançon de pifari detto el Ferrarese' and 'Tenore Collinetto'. He also mentions many other titles of dances of all genres, old and new, for which he gives no

---

[558] Peter Burke, 'Mündliche Kultur und "Druckkultur" im spätmittelalterlichen Italien', in Dinzelbacher-Mück eds, *Volkskultur*, 59–71.

[559] See Ingrid Brainard, 'Domenico da Piacenza' in *The New Grove* (with further literature). Other instructive articles by Brainard in *New Grove* are dedicated to Antonio Cornazano and Guglielmo Ebreo (see below). See W. Thomas Marrocco, 'Fifteenth-century ballo and bassadanza: a survey', *Studi Musicali* 10 (1981), 31–41. Brainard gives the date of Domenico's treatise as *c*.1420; but he was still alive in 1472: see David Fallows, Review, Lockwood–Strohm in *EMH*, vol. 6, 299.

[560] Printed in C. Mazzi, 'Il "libro dell'arte del danzare" di Antonio Cornazano', *La Bibliofilía* 17 (1915), 1–30 (with facs).

music. The distinction *ballo / bassadança* affects the musical performance practice: the stately, elaborate *balli* may have to be combined with dance-songs, whereas the tenors for *bassadanza* and *saltarello* are clearly instrumental – they are tunes on which minstrels improvised everywhere in Europe. The *balli* tunes are notated in the tenor register as well (*Bb–g″*). That the dancers sang some of the tunes is suggested by Plate 10, a miniature from Ferrara, where the dancing is accompanied by a wind ensemble. Lute and *lira da braccio* are actually more often seen in miniatures of Italian dancing; in the treatise *De pratica seu arte tripudii vulgare opusculum* (1463) by Guglielmo Ebreo, there is even a harp. Guglielmo (also called Giovanni Ambrosio) was perhaps the most famous of these intellectuals and artists of dance; he taught at Ferrara, Naples and Montefeltro, developing the choreographies of Domenico and adding to them.[561]

The dance melodies, their titles and rhythmic character, are a cross-section of European informal – but not necessarily 'unwritten' – music. Much work has been done on their ancestry and connection with other known music.[562] A number of titles – but not always the tunes – recur in the Burgundian *basse danse* repertory and other 'stroke notation sources' (see p. 347). Some tunes seem to be mentioned in Prodenzani's *Il Saporetto* (see p. 90). There is also the Ferrarese *Belfiore* dance of which a keyboard version is notated in the Faenza Codex of *c*.1410–15. One of the more frequently employed items is 'La figlia gullielmino' (*canto*), which comes from a French *chanson rustique*, 'Hélas la fille Guillemin'.[563] The *balli* 'Franco cuore gentile' (Dufay, 'Franc cuer gentil'), 'Lezadra' (Ciconia, 'Liçadra donna'), 'Rostiboli gioioso' and other items had descended from the international, often polyphonic, repertory.

The references to music in these treatises are the tip of an iceberg. Dancing was practised everywhere, and dance melodies often found their way, in elaborated form, into written sources. The two-part setting of the 'La Spagna' tune in the manuscripts *Per (I-PEco 431)* and *I-Bc Q 16*, entitled 'Falla con misuras' and 'La bassa Castiglya', respectively, may actually have been used for dance-music, as it is attributed to 'M(agister) Gulielmus'. A three-part arrangement of the same tune is the 'Alta' by the Aragonese chaplain and later succentor at Seville Cathedral, Francisco de la Torre (*fl.* 1483–1504).[564] (Probably not intended for dancing are the 'La Spagna' settings attributed to Josquin and

---

[561] On him, see especially Otto Kinkeldey, 'A Jewish dancing master of the Renaissance', in *Studies in Jewish Bibliography and Related Subjects in Memory of A. S. Freidus* (New York, 1929), 328–72; F. Alberto Gallo, 'L'Autobiografia artistica di Giovanni Ambrosio (Guglielmo Ebreo) da Pesaro', *SM* 12 (1953), 189–202.

[562] See, for example, Gallo, 'Ballare lombardo'; Barbara Sparti, 'The 15th-century *Balli* tunes: a new look', *Early Music* 14 (1986), 346–57.

[563] Printed, together with 'Collinetto', in Pope–Kanazawa eds, *Manuscript Montecassino*, app. I and II.

[564] For 'Falla con misuras' see Bukofzer, 'A polyphonic basse dance of the Renaissance', in *idem, Studies*, ch. 6, surveying almost the whole field and its literature. More recent data are in Atlas, *Aragonese Court*, 103, 153 and mus. ex. 18, and Stevenson, 'Spanish musical impact', 162 ff. De la Torre's piece is printed, for example, in *HAM*, no. 102a. His 'Dime triste coraçon' (Stevenson, *Spanish Music*, 244) quotes the 'Folia' tune in the top voice; Juan del Encina's villancico 'Señora de hermosura' quotes it in the bass.

10 Round dance with *musica alta* accompaniment. Bible of Borso d'Este. (Modena, Biblioteca Estense, V. G. 12, fol. 280v.)

Ghiselin, and of course the cantus firmus Masses on the tune by Weerbeke and Isaac.) Elements of dance rhythm are preserved, however, in two settings – by Johannes Martini and Johannes Japart – of the popular dance-song 'Nenciozza mia, Nenciozza ballarina' (see Ex. 82). A Tuscan girl of this name has been immortalized in Lorenzo de' Medici's poem 'La Nencia da Barberino'. It is possible that Martini's setting originated in Florence, where he apparently stayed in 1485 (see n. 741).[565]

Example 82 Johannes Martini, 'Nenciozza mia'

[565] After *Sev/Par*, fols. 130v-31r; another source is Petrucci's *Canti C*, fols. 101v-2; see Martini, *Secular Pieces*, 55-7.

Example 82 (*cont.*)

[My little Nencia, Nencia ballerina, who does a *passo e mezzo*, then makes a bow and arrives there.]

The 'correct' text, possibly a refrain of a strophic song, would be of two hendecasyllabic lines: 'Nenciozza mia, Nenciozza ballarina, / che balla un passo e mezzo e poi s'inchina'. The words 'e arriva là' must be an interpolation, shouted by the company, as they are frequently found in medieval dance-songs ('olà!', 'et puis holà!' 'Heya!' etc.). The melody is used by Martini as a cantus firmus in a strict sense: it is written out only once, but performed twice – first in duple, then in faster triple metre (*proportio sesquialtera*). This mensural transformation provides, nevertheless, the succession of the dance-steps *passamezzo-saltarello* which was now becoming more standard. This form can be found in several textless (instrumental?) pieces of the time, but also in texted songs, for example by Obrecht. If one imagines the tenor as performed very fast, one can hear the characteristic lilt of the tune, a 3/2 with hemiolas at the beginning of the phrases. Quite possibly the composition was played as fast as this – on lutes or fiddles – and the tenor was sung as in a *Tenorlied*. Whether people really danced to it, we cannot say. The other setting of the 'Nenciozza' tune, by Johannes Japart, is also interesting as it lets the tune migrate from the tenor to the cantus, and finally repeats its second half in the bassus.[566]

Foreign secular music

The culmination of Italian secular genres at the end of the fifteenth century was the polyphonic frottola with its subgenres and analogous types. In an attempt to trace the origins of this type of music, William Prizer has concluded that it was 'the direct outgrowth of what Nino Pirrotta has called "the unwritten tradition"', and he specifically related the peculiarities of this four-part genre to its ancestry in singing on the lute.[567]

We will discuss this technical aspect below, but we first have to ask what *written* genres circulated in late fifteenth-century Italy and could also have influenced the frottola. It would be a misunderstanding to assume that the frottola, unlike any other known Italian secular genre, was practised for a long time, without ever being written down, until it emerged about 1500, like Athena from the head of Zeus, fully equipped and developed in written four-part polyphony. Unwritten and written procedures were much more intertwined. The performance of secular music of all kinds usually happened without written aids, especially among professionals (*improvvisatori* or instrumentalists). That they did not perform from a book is no proof that what they played was never written down. Written-ness is not a quality of the music itself but a stage through which it passes: the good musician learned written music by heart and delivered it in a spontaneous and possibly ornamented fashion. This is

---

[566] See Brown ed., *A Florentine Chansonnier*, no. 103. Pirrotta, *Music and Theatre*, mus. ex. XII, gives the extracted melody (plus two similar songs).

[567] Prizer, *Courtly Pastimes*, 63; *idem*, 'Frottola'; Nino Pirrotta, 'The oral and written traditions of music', in *idem*, *Music and Culture*, 72–9.

what must have happened regularly, in fact, in courtly chambers as well as in the streets. The humanists in the audience may not always have got it right when they described the performance as 'improvised'. The question is rather this: if the 'unwritten tradition' was more a matter of performance than of musical style – if musicians transmitted, learned and rehearsed written music as well as unwritten – where is the written music they reproduced?

Much of it is lost today – the type of music manuscript serving a minstrel must usually be presumed lost – but by no means all. It is present, to a large extent, in the written sources of secular polyphony we have always known. It was not always performed precisely as written, of course, but then 'typically' written music such as French chansons and Latin motets was not always performed precisely as written; their individual voices could be extracted and re-elaborated, for example. Unwritten and written procedures were not strictly divided along genre lines.

The Italian musical *chansonniers* of the later fifteenth century provide an overwhelming testimony to the widespread and profound interest of Italians in complex written polyphony. These manuscripts are more numerous, individually larger, geographically and socially more varied than any group of secular music sources in any other country of Europe. It is impossible even to survey them here; the following table gives a selection of the most significant items only.[568]

Table 6 *Polyphonic song collections from fifteenth-century Italy*

Sigla	Provenance	Date	French songs	Italian	Other
EscB[569]	Naples or Lombardy	*c.*1455–1470	93	23	6
BerK[570]	Naples or Florence	*c.*1465	*c.*25	*c.*8	*c.*10
Pavia[571]	Piedmont	*c.*1470	36	7	1
Sev/Par[572]	Naples, Rome?	1470s	127	25	15
Mellon[573]	Naples	*c.*1475	47	3	5
Fn 176[574]	Florence	late 1470s	67	12	7
Cas[575]	Ferrara	*c.*1480	103	9	9

[568] Data after *Census Catalogue* (*CC*), simplified. Music with exclusively Latin words is excluded. Most sources are also described, especially for their Italian contents, in Jeppesen, *La Frottola*, vol. 2.

[569] *E-E IV. a. 24. CC*, vol. 1, 211 f and vol. 5, 368; Hanen ed., *Chansonnier El Escorial*.

[570] *D-Bk 78. C. 28. CC, vol.* 1, 59 f; Peter Reidemeister, *Die Chanson-Handschrift 78 C 28 des Berliner Kupferstichkabinetts* (Munich: Katzbichler, 1973) (with edition of the unidentified pieces).

[571] *I-PAVu Aldini 362. CC*, vol. 3, 42. Henrietta Schavran, *The Manuscript Pavia, Biblioteca Universitaria, Codice Aldini 362: a Study of Song Traditions in Italy Circa 1440–1480*, Ph.D., New York U., 1978.

[572] *E-Sco 5-I-43* and, part of the same manuscript, *F-Pn n. a. f. 4379 (Part I)*. The source contains at least two distinct layers, stemming from drastically different places and times. See *CC*, vol. 3, 29 f and 139 f; Plamenac, 'A reconstruction'; Dragan Plamenac ed., *Facsimile Reproduction of the MSS Sevilla 5-I-43 and Paris N.A.Fr.4379 (Pt.I)* (Brooklyn: Institute of Mediaeval Music, 1962).

[573] *US-NH 91. CC*, vol. 2, 248 f. Perkins–Garey eds, *Mellon Chansonnier* (with facs); Benthem, 'Concerning Johannes Tinctoris'.

[574] *I-Fn Magl. XIX, 176. CC*, vol. 1, 229 f.

[575] *I-Rc 2856. CC*, vol. 3, 112 ff. Edn and commentary in Arthur S. Wolff, *The Chansonnier Biblioteca Casanatense. Its History, Purpose, and Music*, Ph.D., North Texas State U., 1970. See also Lockwood, *Ferrara*, 225 f and 269–77.

Table 6 (*cont.*)

Ric 2[576]	Florence	early 1480s	55	4	6
Pix[577]	Florence	early 1480s	143	20	5
Per[578]	Naples or vicinity	*c.*1485	18	47	20
MC[579]	Naples or vicinity	1480s	35	29	11
Q 16[580]	Rome?	1487 ff	95	19	10
C.G.[581]	Florence	*c.*1492–4	85	10	11
BR 229[582]	Florence	1492–3	64	15	87
Fn 178[583]	Florence	1490s	62	5	4
Odh[584]	Venice (O.Petrucci)	1501	76	5	13
			1172	236	216

We may also mention the heart-shaped French chansonnier Cordiforme (*F-Pn Rothschild 2973*) of the 1470s, with 44 songs of which thirteen at the beginning have Italian texts.[585]

What do these figures tell us? In so far as the chansonniers can be assumed to reflect a living practice, they would suggest that polyphonic songs were performed regularly up and down the peninsula. This is essentially correct. It is also true that only a few of these – often richly illuminated – manuscripts were made for princely houses. Far more seem to have served the aristocracy and wealthy merchant bourgeoisie of the largest cities. None of the Florentine chansonniers in this list, for example, is known to have been owned by the Medici family; all belonged to aristocratic or bourgeois households that did not have professional musicians on the payroll. This is an important consideration for the state of music-making in Florence at the time. The sources *Per* and *I-MC 871* once belonged to Benedictine monasteries and may even have originated

---

[576] *I-Fr 2356*. Dragan Plamenac, 'The "second" chansonnier of the Biblioteca Riccardiana (Codex 2356)', *AnnM* 2 (1954), 105–87, and 4 (1956), 261–5.

[577] *F-Pn f. fr. 15123*. *CC*, vol. 3, 23 f. Edward J. Pease, *An Edition of the Pixérécourt Manuscript: Paris, Bibliothèque Nationale, Fonds Fr. 15123*, Ph.D., Indiana U., 1960.

[578] *I-PEco 431*. *CC*, vol. 3, 43 f; Atlas, 'Provenance MS Perugia'.

[579] *I-MC 871*. *CC*, vol. 2, 173 f. Pope-Kanazawa eds, *Manuscript Montecassino*.

[580] *I-Bc Q 16*. *CC*, vol. 1, 70 f and 4, 275 f. Edward Pease, 'A report on Codex Q 16 of the Civico Museo Bibliografico Musicale', *MD* 20 (1966), 57–94; Sarah Fuller, 'Additional notes on the 15th-century chansonnier Bologna Q 16', *MD* 23 (1969), 81–103.

[581] *I-Rvat Cappella Giulia XIII 27*. *CC*, vol. 4, 18 f. Atlas, *Cappella Giulia Chansonnier*.

[582] *I-Fn B.R.229* (*olim Magl. XIX, 59*) ('Braccesi Codex'). *CC*, vol. 1, 219 f and 4, 370. Brown ed., *Florentine Chansonnier*.

[583] *I-Fn Magl. XIX, 178*. *CC*, vol. 1, 230.

[584] Print: *Harmonice Musices Odhecaton A*. See *RISM B I*, vol. 1, 1501. Hewitt ed., *Odhecaton*. Stanley Boorman, 'The "first" edition of the *Odhecaton A*', *JAMS* 30 (1977), 183–207. Facs. edn: Milano, Bollettino Bibliografico Musicale, 1932.

[585] Edward L. Kottick, *The Music of the Chansonnier Cordiforme: Paris, Bibliothèque Nationale, Rothschild 2973*, Ph.D., U. of North Carolina, 1963; *idem* ed., *The Unica in the Chansonnier Cordiforme*, CMM 42 (Rome: AIM, 1967) (partial edn).

in monastic (or Franciscan) circles – although their links with the Aragonese court of Naples are also evident. *I-Fn Magl. XIX, 176* and *I-Fr 2356* share a scribal hand which seems connected to the Florentine Servite convent of SS Annunziata (see p. 298). An aristocratic and middle-class clientele was probably envisaged for the expensive printed edition of Petrucci; he was obviously successful with his choice of predominantly French chansons for his first publication, because he issued another two similar books, *Canti B* (1502) and *Canti C* (1504). After that, however, he ceased to publish French chansons. The many books of frottole issued by Petrucci and others responded to, and fuelled, a great fashion for the Italian genre – rather like the short blossoming, supported by printing privileges, of the English madrigal a century later.

The chanson repertory comprised fewer actual pieces than the above figures suggest because there are many concordances between the Italian sources (as well as with foreign manuscripts). In any case, the number of French chansons circulated in fifteenth-century Italy is astonishing. Was the genre really so much favoured at the expense of Italian and other song?

Let us begin with the third column: it comprises textless, untitled pieces, and songs provided with texts or incipits in the following languages (in order of frequency): Spanish, Dutch, English and German. 'Italian songs' are those found in the sources with only an Italian text, incipit or title. Some of them may be contrafacta, as yet unidentified, of French or, indeed, English, Dutch, Spanish or German songs. The whole group of sources abounds in contrafacta; many pieces are included in our statistics as French songs which are actually textless, or have an Italian incipit, but for which a French original has been traced. Textless items for which no original is known have been relegated to the third column, but they might just as well have been French (etc.) songs. Two entire manuscripts (*Cas, I-Rc 2856*, and *I-Bc Q 16*) have no complete texts underlaid at all, only incipits, and it has convincingly been argued that they were intended for instrumental use.[586] Also, most of the other manuscripts, and the Petrucci print, rarely offer more than an incipit. One source, *BerK* (*D-Bk 78. C. 28*), is without words altogether except for one song, 'Le serviteur'. The chansonnier has not been completed; except for some initials, the texts were never entered. Nevertheless, a substantial number of unidentified pieces in this source may have been intended for instruments, too. Textless items are also frequent in *I-Fn B.R. 229*. Some of them are true instrumental fantasias, others not.

Perhaps more importantly, the words underlaid to the French songs are predominantly ungrammatical and often incomprehensible. One and the same song may have several different titles or incipits in the various sources, of which only some bear some kind of resemblance to the original verse. Some individual incipits, for example 'Le serviteur', are given to several different pieces that have nothing to do with Dufay's chanson nor its various derivatives. We have encountered this 'indiscriminate titling' in Germany as well. It is unknown

---

[586] See especially the discussion in Lockwood, *Ferrara*, 269–72.

what text might effectively have been sung to these pieces. Some pieces exist in different musical versions (particularly with regard to the number of voices); the composer attributions – if there are any – also vary. Most importantly, words in a different language may be underlaid or suggested in the title. Here is an example chosen at random. The rondeau 'Mais que ce fust sécrètement' by the French composer Pietrequin Bonnel is found in several sources, of which three attribute it to him, and one (*Odh*) to Loyset Compère instead.[587] The piece exists in essentially three different musical versions, two of which (*Cas* and *C.G.*, *I-Rvat C.G. XIII 27*) are distinguished by the addition of several bars of music at the end. One of these (*C.G.*) furthermore incorporates an added fourth voice, a contratenor bassus.[588] As regards the text, three Italian sources have the correct French words or an acceptable approximation to them, one has no text (*Cas*), and one (*Fn 176*) has the 'reconstruction' in Italian 'Meschin che fuis secretament' ('Wretched man that I was, secretly'). The source with four voices, however (*C.G.*), has the incipit 'Donzella no men cul-peys' (correctly: 'non me culpeys'), which is a slightly Italianized version of a well-known villancico text. A completely different musical setting of this Spanish text is known from three sources, two of them Italian (*MC* and *Pix*).[589]

What happened here is obviously a multiple process of transformations, one of which was the addition of a pre-existent Spanish text. Note, however, that the Spanish words are not actually underlaid, just identified by an incipit. Similarly, of the Italianized version 'Meschin che fuis' there is only a first line – one wonders how this almost Beckmesserian reading of the elegant original might have continued. It is clear that the piece was sung in Italy in different versions, and only exceptionally with the correct words; it must have been performed more often without words (vocally or instrumentally or both) or with some known contrafactum text people could actually pronounce. We may go a little further and surmise that the addition or substitution of contratenors – as borne out by many written sources – was as much an everyday procedure as the tasteful ornamentation of the individual lines.[590] Three divergent copies of 'Mais que ce fust' were copied in Florence within a few years (*Fn 176*, *BR 229* and *C.G.*): it is possible that in one Florentine household the piece was known as an instrumental fantasia, in another as a rondeau and in the third as a villancico.

As regards stylistic development, the cultivation of French songs in Italy seems to follow a clearly delineated route. Until *c.*1475, the 'Burgundian' composers Binchois, Dufay, Morton but also Frye and Bedyngham are eagerly performed; their pieces circulate in many variant versions and contrafacta,

[587] Printed in Compère, *Opera omnia*, vol. 5, 67 f.

[588] Multiple attributions, versions and musical revisions are discussed in Atlas, 'Conflicting attributions'. (For Bonnel's piece, see ex. 11.)

[589] See the discussion in Atlas, *Cappella Giulia Chansonnier*, vol. 1, 113–20 (no. 41).

[590] See Howard M. Brown, 'Improvised ornamentation in the fifteenth-century chanson', *Quadrivium* 12 (1971), 235–58.

also as sacred *laude* (see p. 593). Only some of the most famous pieces of this group reappear in a second band of sources, of *c*.1475–85 (from *Fn 176* to *Cas*). In this group of sources, Busnois and Caron predominate so suddenly and drastically[591] that trips to Italy have been hypothesized for both composers. On the other hand, most of their works in Italian manuscripts also exist in earlier French sources and must have been composed well before 1475. The same is true for the secondary favourites, Robert Morton and Hayne van Ghizeghem. It was probably the greatly increased influx of French singers in the 1470s – see also p. 602 – which swept this music to centres such as Florence, Milan, Naples and Ferrara. Agricola, Martini and Isaac (in that order) are the most frequently represented composers in the sources from *c*.1485, but Agricola and Martini had entered the country in the early 1470s. Agricola's enormous secular output corresponds to his leading role in the later sources; he must have composed much of this music while in Italy. Of several younger musicians conforming to this particular pattern, for example Johannes Japart[592] and Johannes Ghiselin,[593] it can be suspected that they learned the art of chanson composition from colleagues in Italy, not in France. Admittedly, we know little about the biographies of Franco-Netherlands composers before they appear in some Italian chapel in the 1470s and 80s. Some of them may have been in the country already, singing in a cathedral choir as did Josquin at Milan (see p. 608). Although Josquin composed fewer chansons than his immigrant colleagues, some of his greatest achievements in the genre must have originated there. This is significant for an assessment of the 'transformation of the chanson'.[594]

The main trends in chanson composition can be described thus. A textural transformation, initiated by Ockeghem and Busnois, aligned the chanson with the four-voice, imitative and more or less widely spaced textures of motet and Mass. Whereas three-part chanson format (including its extension by adding a second contratenor, and its variety with 'disentangled' ranges) never permitted fourths between tenor and cantus, the 'motet texture' did so since the days of the 'Caput' Mass. For the chanson, the transformation process was a slow one, however. Most of the pieces copied in the above-mentioned sources are still either in chanson format or, increasingly, have an added fourth voice (usually a high contratenor), which does not alter the essential relationship between tenor and cantus. Long after the advances of Ockeghem and Busnois towards con-

---

[591] Although with surprising variations such as the absence of Busnois from *Ric 2*, whereas in *Pix*, copied a few years later also in Florence, he is the best-represented composer. On the two Italian songs ascribed to Busnois, see p. 620 below.

[592] Ralph W. Buxton, 'Johannes Japart: a fifteenth-century chanson composer', *CMc* 31 (1981), 7–38. His original Flemish name was Happaert.

[593] Gottwald, *Johannes Ghiselin*.

[594] On the subject of the following paragraph, see especially Hewitt ed., *Odhecaton*, introduction; Howard M. Brown, 'The transformation of the chanson at the end of the fifteenth century', in *IMS Report of the 10th Congress, Ljubljana 1967* (Kassel etc., 1968), 78–94; *idem*, 'Chanson, #2' in *The New Grove*.

trapuntal equality of the voices in four-part songs (see p. 454), the new texture was more widely adopted. In a representative source such as *BR 229* with 268 pieces (not all of them secular), I have found seventeen which permit fourths between cantus and tenor – mostly only incidentally. But it is noteworthy that the composers of these pieces are Busnois (three), Martini (two), Isaac (two), and Josquin, Obrecht, Stokem, Compère, Agricola and Japart (one each); thus, the development seems fairly widespread. The device concentrated at first (notably with Busnois) on settings of popular tunes and cantus firmus arrangements. It is also found, for example, in Josquin's cantus firmus chanson 'Fortune d'estrainge plummaige / Pauper sum ego' (extant only in sources after 1500), although this is a three-part song.

A related aspect of this development was, of course, pervasive imitation and the emancipation of the contratenors so that they became indispensable voices. This gave the performers of the contratenor parts something more important to do and undermined the hegemony of soloists. It also affected the musical form: whereas in older *forme fixe* compositions each text phrase more or less corresponds to one musical phrase, now the long distances between imitative entries can inflate each phrase into a complex unit, with changing textures and internal cadences: see, for example, no. 129 of *BR 229*, by Isaac.[595] When cantus firmi are used, possibly in augmentation or other strict transformation, the phrase structure can be distorted even more. Isaac's re-setting of the cantus part of 'J'ay pris amours' (no. 8) broadens the dimensions of the tune by accompanying it with much faster, lower voices, but Martini's setting (no. 179) uses the complete original cantus–tenor framework in augmentation, underpinned by a racing canonic duet of contratenors. Although the text could still be sung in the top voices, this is no longer really a song but an instrumentally conceived cantus firmus arrangement. In such a case, the social function of the piece has also apparently changed: it is to be performed by professional players, whose virtuosic show mocks the simplicity of the old tune.

Literally quoted song lines from the Busnois–Ockeghem–Hayne generation are now 'dressed up' in all kinds of manner. The amount of derivative and emulatory composition is stunning. Some pieces simply try to outdo another, as might be the case between Isaac's three-part 'Le serviteur' and the anonymous four-part piece which follows it (nos. 257–8). Many subtle allusions can also be detected, for example in Agricola's 'Je n'ay dueil que de vous viegne' (no. 174). This four-part bergerette (of gigantic dimensions) uses the opening motive of the bassus from Ockeghem's rondeau 'Je n'ay dueil que je ne suis morte', but in such a way that the exact quotation at the right pitch is the last of the four imitative entries.[596] The titles for these arrangements are often haphazard. Martini's textless piece no. 126 uses the same tenor as Isaac's no.

---

[595] This and the following examples are found in Brown ed., *A Florentine Chansonnier*. See also the stylistic comments, arranged by composer, in chaps. X and XI of the same work.

[596] The model is Ockeghem's own revision of the piece, analysed in Litterick, 'Revision'.

138, entitled 'Serviteur suis'. But neither Dufay's 'Le serviteur', nor the sacred words 'O intemerata' given to Martini's piece in another source, have anything to do with the underlying tenor; Martini's piece is called 'Der newe pawir schwancz' in Glogau (no. 257). There may be a dance-song involved here as well.

Dance-tunes, popular songs, *chansons rustiques* and, last but not least, tunes with texts in other languages, invade and transform the French chanson repertoire in Italy. Many of the poetic forms of these borrowed tunes were incompatible with the surviving *formes fixes* – rondeau and bergerette. Dutch and German songs, frequently copied in Florentine chansonniers, tend to be in ballade form or *Barform* approximately like AABC. Popular French tunes often involved final repeats ('ABA' and its variants). Such playing with formally incompatible material was traditional in French song, of course, but the tradition (as represented by Dufay, Morton, Ockeghem and especially Busnois) stipulated that the *forme fixe* be left intact. A famous *chanson rustique* setting by Josquin is his satirical 'Adieu mes amours, on m'attent / Adieu mes amours, adieu vous command' (no. 158). The borrowed tenor has three 'strains' of two decasyllables each, melodically ABA (plus more internal repetitions). The bass imitates it and sings its text; the cantus, supported by the textless contratenor altus, sings a rondeau cinquain, with midpoint in the middle of line four of the tenor. In two other *chanson rustique* settings, however, Josquin lets the original poem run its course. One of them is 'Bergerette savoyenne', a charming regional idyll;[597] the other is 'Une mousse de Bisquaye' (no. 145). This is a strophic song in ballade form with an eight-line stanza including a one-line refrain (in Basque). The piece, a *pastourelle* with exotic (Basque) appeal, is found in ten sources, all Italian, and must have impressed many musicians in the country. It has also been used as a dance-song.[598] The borrowed melody and text is sung in canon at the fourth (!) by the upper voices, supported by tenor and bass. Already bar 1 violates the cantus–tenor framework, requiring a true bass (see Ex. 83).

The stretto canon, symbolizing a 'chase' perhaps in the erotic sense, must be the greatest fun for the performers themselves. Its impact is enhanced by other stretto imitations involving also the lower voices (bars 2–3). This leads to repeated tonal surprises. Every single cadence is duplicated: depending on the choice of *musica ficta*, one can hear one or two authentic cadences, the second of which always turns flatwards (see the first cadence in bars 3–4). The individual phrases end, as established by the original tune, on the finals g-f-g-f-bb-g-f-bb. Thus, Josquin's double cadences carry out the same flatward turns as the given succession of finals f-bb. The concluding refrain line, with the girl's dismissing words 'Soaz, soaz, ordonarequin', is dramatically

---

[597] See Josquin, *Werken*, fasc. 53 (Wereldlijke Werken no. IV), no. 36.

[598] See Brown ed., *A Florentine Chansonnier*, commentary on no. 145, with further literature, including Beatrice Pescerelli, 'Una sconosciuta redazione del trattato di danza di Guglielmo Ebreo', *RIM* 9 (1974), 50–53.

Example 83 Josquin des Prez, 'Une mousse de Biscaye'

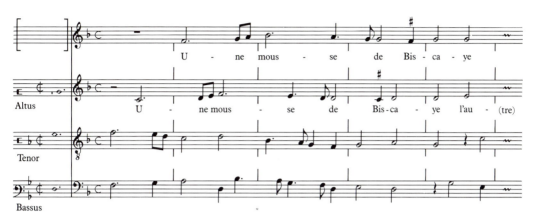

separated from the preceding line by a hiatus (bars 29–30), until the upper voices conclude in a higher register than before and end in B♭ despite the prevailing 'F major' of the piece. Josquin apparently wanted to suggest how the girl's words strike the narrator as strange.

Folklore in all degrees of stylization, foreign and strange tunes, Dutch and German dance-songs, derivative composition, cantus firmus arrangement and canonic artifice – these are some of the agents of change in the French chanson as it grew within the Italian climate. None of these agents was, precisely speaking, new, but their development was massive.

How were these repertories actually consumed? In two ways, essentially: by singing as much of the originals as was possible, and by playing them on instruments. Most often, voices and instruments will have collaborated. In aristocratic or bourgeois amateur circles, the sometimes precious manuscripts would have been used. The Italian sixteenth-century paintings of the iconographic type 'The concert' (usually showing men and women singing and playing from written music) surely reflect older customs. When professionals performed this repertory, however, they would not use written music. They would work out – possibly very precisely – their own versions, adapted to their skills and circumstances, and provided with their own texts. If we try to imagine the concrete situation, some conceptual difficulties disappear. A professional such as Pietrobono would not be caught mumbling a garbled or incomplete French bergerette or rondeau, as the Ferrarese manuscript *Cas* has it. Instead, he would work out a suitable Italian text – a barzelletta or other ballata species for the bergerette,[599] a *strambotto* or any other symmetrical pattern for the rondeau quatrain, treated as two strains. Any rondeau, provided it was not too long, could furthermore

---

[599] It is surprisingly seldom noted that barzelletta is actually derived from bergerette.

serve him *en bloc* for the strophic quatrain types called *oda*. Whether performed by professionals or not, the polyphonic song might lose dispensable contratenors, or only one structural voice (cantus or tenor) might be used, provided with a possibly improvised instrumental accompaniment. This could be chordal and simple – when played on the bowed *lira da braccio* – or melodic, such as a new, ornamental cantus line played on the lute against a given vocal tenor. This 'dismantling' of pre-existent polyphonic music had happened for at least a century by then; no doubt, it happened now. As the century progressed, the contratenor bassus gained in importance and was usually performed by a *tenorista*, for example on the lute. In this way, much of the written polyphonic repertory in the Italian chansonniers could enter the realm of 'unwritten' practice.

It may be asked why there are so few written specimens of 'dismantled', reduced or simplified polyphonic songs. The answer lies in the nature of the surviving manuscripts and in the nature of writing music in general. A chansonnier, a valuable object, was used only as a matrix for the versions made up in performance. These 'ephemeral' versions were not usually written down. There was no need to fix them; written monophonic versions were unnecessary in any case, because everyone could memorize them. As in other European musical traditions, only the 'artful' version, for example in four-part counterpoint, seemed worth writing down. From such an 'optimum version' (albeit without much ornamentation), performers would work out their personal versions. When the piece had to be transmitted – to somebody in a distant place, for example – it was not the personal but the written, official version that was copied, and with great accuracy.

This is not to deny the existence of striking variants within the written tradition which attest to the dismantling and rebuilding processes. Johannes Cornago's 'Morte merçe, gentile aquila altera', for example, exists in at least two versions with different lower voices and other modifications. As in our German song from Schedel and *Tr 90* (Ex. 77), one of the versions was perhaps 'recomposed' from memory.[600] 'Morte, merçe' is, notably, not a popular tune, where such modifications might happen as a matter of course, but a courtly *canzone* by a significant composer (see p. 574).

The input from memory was essential at least for the words. Garbled or incomplete texts in the chansonniers imply that the chosen texts were supplied from memory, as people usually do with subsequent stanzas of strophic songs, in any case. It was easier for the copyists not to bother about texts, or the niceties of a version as actually heard, but only to transcribe the written version note by note. (Literature, when recited, could similarly be modified in ways rarely committed to paper.) Thus, the notated polyphonic songs stand for many times their number of performance versions heard.

Another way of consuming this music was to entrust it to professionals who

---

[600] Both versions are printed in Cornago, *Complete Works*, 43 f and 63 f. In the Chansonnier Cordiforme, the first and second sections of the song are copied separately.

performed written polyphony but without written music in front of them: the courtly instrumentalists. We have discussed the wind bands before (p. 361); suffice it to say here that Italy's princes and city republics were extremely proud of their bands and fostered performances of high quality. This must have meant that polyphonic playing caught on as well. In many centres, trumpeters (*trombetti*) and shawmists (*piffari*) were maintained separately. Even a cursory glance through the documents demonstrates the financial importance of these bands, and the international character of their staff.[601] In Milan and Florence, German and Dutch players were already frequent in the earlier fifteenth century. In Florence, the Flemish and German musicians were prominent members of the fraternity *dei Fiamminghi*.[602] Also many Italians, and some French and Spanish players, served Italian cities. The evidence for these groups at the Iberian courts is less well researched but conclusive enough.[603]

The number of foreign players increased with the development of ensembles of soft music. It was also strengthened by continuous import of instruments from foreign makers.[604] German players such as Stefano da Monaco at Milan (who studied the lute with Pietrobono, see above) often mastered more than one instrument. The Schubinger dynasty of Augsburg sent players who doubled on stringed and wind instruments to Ferrara for generations, beginning with 'Michele Tedesco' (i.e. Schubinger) under Leonello d'Este.[605] The advance of soft music can be shown at Ferrara under Borso d'Este, who in the 1450s and 60s employed many lutenists or *suonatori de viola*. The 'della Viola clan' (a musical family which, in the sixteenth century, also produced composers) began its collective career at Ferrara in 1467, and the *viola* player 'Alessandro de Alemagna', with his companion Antonio, visited in 1470.[606] This Alessandro may have been Agricola who arrived then from Germany or Austria (see also p. 521).

The network of foreign players and composers in Italy, circulating between the major courts and cities, is in some sense mirrored in their musical repertory. Derivative works and compositions that emulate others, new arrangements of the same tunes, progressive and virtuosic trends – these are the kind of thing to be expected from groups and individuals who never work together

---

[601] Well-researched centres are Florence, Ferrara, Milan, Mantua. See Giuseppe Zippel, *I suonatori della Signoria di Firenze* (Trent, 1892); Luigia Cellesi, 'Documenti per la storia musicale di Firenze', *RMI* 34 (1927), 3–55 (also separate Torino: Bocca, 1927); Keith Polk, 'Civic patronage and instrumental ensembles in Renaissance Florence', *Augsburger Jahrbuch für Musikwissenschaft* 3 (1986), 51–68; idem, 'Instrumental music', 175 f and 182–5; Lockwood, *Ferrara*, 268–77; Motta, *Musici*, 35–56; Gaetano Cesari, 'Musica e musicisti alla corte sforzesca', *RMI* 29 (1922), 1–53; Prizer, 'Bernardino Piffaro'; Atlas, *Aragonese Court*, ch. 5. For a general study based on iconographic evidence, see Victor Ravizza, *Das instrumentale Ensemble von 1400 bis 1550 in Italien* (Berne: Haupt, 1970).

[602] See Strohm, *Bruges*, 139.

[603] The only detailed documentary study is Gómez, *La música*, vol. 1. The importance of stringed instruments, and the development of the viol in Aragon, is amply documented in Woodfield, *Viol*, chaps. 2–4.

[604] For the collection of mostly Flemish-made instruments owned by the Medicis, see Parigi, *Laurentiana*, 33. Generally on this issue, see Bridgman, *Vie musicale*, ch. 12.

[605] See Lockwood, *Ferrara*, 68 f; Polk, 'Instrumental music', 179 ff.

[606] Lockwood, *Ferrara*, 97.

for long in the same place but who regularly meet to perform 'against each other' in new combinations, as directed by their patrons' wishes. The cantus firmus arrangements typify the practice: even if a musician had not learned the 'latest' new contratenor yet, having just arrived in Florence from elsewhere, he could immediately join in by playing a cantus firmus which he already knew. Sometimes, cantus firmi were kept together in special manuscripts (comparable to the *basse danses* sources): a lost Ferrarese book of 'Tenori todeschi et altre cantiones' ('German tenors and other songs'), recorded in 1495, may have contained precisely those extracted tenors which the German players had imported and over which they used to improvise.[607]

In a remarkable study, Louise Litterick suggests that the instrumental fantasia (under which term she includes cantus firmus arrangements) arose in Italy at this time because the foreign composers had not enough other opportunities to show their contrapuntal skills.[608] I reject the argument that, because of a dearth of vocal polyphony, there was not much else for composers to do in Italy. Furthermore, instrumental ensemble music did not originate in Italy; it existed in central Europe before *c.*1470, probably based on western precedent (Barbingant: see p. 363). Nevertheless, there must be a reason why several foreign composers arriving in Ferrara, Milan and Florence in the 1470s and 80s (Martini, Agricola, Isaac) concentrated so much on writing 'songs without words'.[609] It seems that they composed for the instrumental groups, and particularly the foreigners in them, who were already acquainted with the practice. Martini's 'Martinella', composed before *c.*1466, probably in Austria (see p. 367), and other early pieces still lack 'typical instrumentalisms' such as rapid passage-work or repetitive patterns of small motives.[610] 'Martinella' is the title given to at least five different pieces, three of them by Martini himself; if they have anything in common stylistically then it is the ostensible adherence to the phrase structure of the *formes fixes*. Their instrumental destination, however, must be deduced from other clues. The original 'Martinella', for example, is a bipartite piece like a rondeau cinquain, but with an inserted *saltarello* section in the second half. In the imitative four-part piece 'Non seul uno', Martini observes the outline of a rondeau quatrain; but at the end states precisely the same four-bar motive four times, in double counterpoint and on different pitches. So much repetition, although disguised, would not be proper for a rondeau.

Isaac's famous 'La morra' (*BR 229*, no. 12) begins like some French or Italian three-part song with reasonably rounded phrases – but after the third or fourth phrase suddenly explodes in so many splinters of motivic patterning:

---

[607] *Ibid.*, 268.

[608] Litterick, 'Italian instrumental ensemble music', especially 125 f. See also Dietrich Kämper, *Studien zur instrumentalen Ensemblemusik des 16. Jahrhunderts in Italien* (Cologne: Böhlau, 1970) (*AnMc* 10).

[609] For editions, see Martini, *Secular Pieces*; Agricola, *Opera omnia*, vol. 5; Isaac, *Weltliche Werke*.

[610] For a comparison of 'La martinella' with Josquin's (?) 'Ile fantazies de Joskin', see Lockwood, *Ferrara*, 273–7, and the reviews by Fallows in *EMH* 6 (1986), 295 f and Strohm in *ML* 67 (1986), 286.

Example 84 Heinrich Isaac, 'La morra'

It is good to see some Italian use being made of a northern 'monorhythmic' style of cantus firmus elaboration. In fact, bars 36–43 are strikingly similar to a piece by Obrecht (*BR 229*, no. 210).[611] It is equally intriguing to consider the piece, as has been suggested, as a celebratory composition for the Spanish victory over the Moors at Granada in 1492.

Greater instrumental virtuosity, perhaps involving the use of bowed instruments, typifies many cantus firmus arrangements by Agricola and a group of interconnected pieces which might have been intended for north Italian courts: 'La Alfonsina' by Johannes Ghiselin,[612] 'La Bernardina' by Josquin[613] and 'La Stanghetta' by Gaspar van Weerbeke.[614] Josquin's work, which shares ideas with his 'Bergerette savoysienne', superbly demonstrates how rhythmic drive, sharp motivic contrasts and sequential patterning can be brought to a conclusion without any external formal signposts.

Among the various types of ensemble music, there are also extracted sections from Masses and motets. This variant of the contrafactum practice gave the professional players access to sacred music for outdoor performances.[615] It also provided the sacred work with new and larger audiences – the court chapels were private – and it is possible that the Mass and motet composers favoured this use of their music as a kind of advertisement. Although the practice apparently started with melismatic sections lacking cantus firmi, later 'excerpts' often involved cantus firmus sections. Many Masses by Agricola, Weerbeke, Martini and Isaac were written over the same well-known cantus firmi as the 'genuine' ensemble arrangements, and could have been planned for this multiple use.[616]

Native secular music in Italy and Spain

The practice of setting Italian texts polyphonically was never really interrupted since the time of the Ars nova. *GB-Ob 213*, completed in the 1430s, contains a considerable number of such settings – some by foreigners, others not.[617] If we gather the *giustiniane* composed by Bedyngham and Joye, the 'Anglo-Italian' songs by Robertus and Galfridus de Anglia, some pieces scattered in foreign sources and some anonymous pieces in *ROu*, Oporto and *EscB*, we can

---

[611] Both pieces are edited in Brown ed., *Florentine Chansonnier*.

[612] *Opera omnia*. vol. 4, no. 21; Gottwald, *Johannes Ghiselin*, 107 f; the piece might be for Alfonso d'Este, eldest son of Ercole I.

[613] Josquin, *Werken*, fasc. 53, no. 42; Osthoff, *Josquin*, vol. 2, 232. Could the piece have to do with the Mantuan player discussed in Prizer, 'Bernardino Piffaro'?

[614] Hewitt ed., *Odhecaton*, no. 49; probably for a member of the Stanga family of Milan.

[615] Documented, for example, in Prizer, 'Bernardino Piffaro'. See also p. 361 above.

[616] See also Edwards, 'Songs without words', 83–7. Multiple use could be the motivation for stylistic tendencies which have been dubbed 'instrumental', for example in Dietrich Kämper, 'Instrumentale Stilelemente bei Alexander Agricola', *TVNM* 28 (1978), 1–13.

[617] See Gilbert Reaney, 'The Italian contribution to the Manuscript Oxford, Bodleian Library, Canonici Misc. 213', *L'Ars Nova* 3 (1970), 443–64.

state that at least the ballata (which includes, formally speaking, the *giustiniana*) continued to be a polyphonic genre in mid-fifteenth-century Italy. From the 1460s, the dominance of this flexible lyrical genre is undermined by song-types of a more popular ancestry.

This development (*c.*1460–1500) may now be characterized briefly, using only a few examples of the repertory.[618] Italian song genres – especially of a popularizing kind – were much cultivated at Naples, the residence of the Aragonese kings and a thriving commercial metropolis.[619] A favourite of high society was 'Hora may che fora son', a long strophic song put into the mouth of a young nun who has escaped from the cloister. This song was also well known in other parts of Italy, as attested by many sources of the text, whereas the only copy with (polyphonic) music is the chansonnier *EscB*.[620] In 1465, it was danced for (and by?) the newly wed Ippolita Sforza in Siena, by twelve dancers in a choreographed *moresca*. (This event has no bearing on the date or provenance of *EscB*.) The song is, formally speaking, a barzelletta. It has two musical strains, A (bars 1–10) and B (bars 11–16). They are sung in the order ABBA for the first stanza, then BBA for all the subsequent ones (a restatement of the first 'A' is optional). Four text-lines are sung under the first 'A', the *ripresa*, two each under the 'Bs', the *piedi* or *mutazione*, and again four under the repeated 'A', the *volta*. The last three text-lines of the *volta* are identical or similar to the *ripresa* lines, 'leading back' to the refrain. In the barzelletta, there are always these identical lines which connect the *volta* and the *ripresa*; their number can vary, as can the total number of lines in each section.

What we have briefly described is also a basic form of the ballata and bergerette, of the Spanish canción and villancico, and – with possible modifications – of the frottola.[621] These forms differ from each other only with regard to the number of lines, their asymmetrical or symmetrical distribution among the sections, and by having more or less different music for the various textual sections. In Spanish terms, 'Hora may' would be a canción, because it has a four-line *ripresa* (*estribillo*), whereas that of the villancico has fewer lines. Significant also is the verse-type: the *ottonario* (eight-syllable line), which strongly resembles the trochaic tetrameter of the classical tradition and is also used for most Spanish musical poetry.

An interesting barzelletta which is not preserved in its original form has been

---

618 A still valuable introduction is in Pirro, *Histoire*, 155–67. The best Italian survey is Cattin, 'Quattrocento', 277–313; see also Francesco Luisi, *La musica vocale nel Rinascimento* (Turin: ERI, 1977), part II. For the period of *c.*1490–*c.*1520 in Italy, see Brown, *Renaissance*, ch. 4.

619 The general cultural background is well characterized in Atlas, *Aragonese Court*, ch. 1; see also pp. 140–54 and mus. exx. 9–17.

620 See the edition in Atlas, *Aragonese Court*, no. 12, and the description p. 144 f. I am quoting the words in the more widespread, north Italian spelling.

621 For Spanish genres, see Isabel Pope, 'Musical and metrical form of the villancico', *AnnM* 2 (1954), 189–214; for the frottola, William F. Prizer, 'Performance practices in the frottola', *Early Music* 3 (1975), 227–35; *idem*, *Courtly Pastimes*, ch. 3.

reconstructed by Rebecca L. Gerber.[622] Of this monophonic song, 'Ayo visto lo mapamundo', only the text of the *ripresa* survives in a poetry manuscript. There is a *lauda* contrafactum of the full text, and the melody has been used as cantus firmus in Johannes Cornago's three-part Mass 'Ayo visto'. This work, copied in *Tr 88*, antedates *c.*1462, which is remarkably early for a chanson Mass in Italy.

Atlas edited and described a typical *strambotto* from the Neapolitan repertory, 'Sufferir so disposto onne tormento' on a text by Serafino dall'Aquila.[623] It is a *strambotto siciliano* with the rhyme scheme ababababab, as distinguished from the *strambotto toscano* with abababcc. The music has two strains, repeated four times. It is characteristic of the *strambotto* that it uses only *endecasillabi* (eleven-syllable lines) which, despite their weightier character and descendance from the Latin hexameter, are typical for popular genres, particularly in southern Italy. The long lines, with flexible caesuras, can bear many improvisational variants; many different verse lines can be underlaid to the same music, which makes this an ideal metre for epic song. *Endecasillabi* are the only admissible verse-type in epics with *ottava rima* stanzas (as used by Ariosto and Tasso) and in *terza rima* or *capitoli* (as used in Dante's *Divina commedia*).

An important source for *strambotti* is the south Italian collection *MC*, with sixteen specimens among the 29 Italian-texted pieces.[624] Seven *strambotti* are written out for four voices. As elsewhere in this manuscript, the part-writing is not very interesting and is often clumsy. It is as if some musicians had been asked to provide the counterpoint because the pieces were to be codified in a written collection, not because the songs needed it. On the other hand, it is possible to hear in many four-part songs in *MC* a characteristic sound, which we are going to investigate.

Example 85 'Cor mio volonturiuso', *MC*, no. 129

[622] Cornago, *Complete Works*, ix. On the subject of the song, see Stevenson, 'Spanish musical impact', 141 f.
[623] *Aragonese Court*, no. 14 and p. 147 f.
[624] Described in Pope–Kanazawa eds, *Manuscript Montecassino*, 68–86.

Example 85 (*cont.*)

*) cancelled and replaced by ' ℂ '

[My wishful heart, hold firm, hold firm! My running blood, cool down, cool down!]

The music of the *strambotto* in Example 85[625] has some features that are typical for the Italian pieces in *MC* and other south Italian collections: the low, dense voice-registers; a certain metrical ambiguity around the cadence points; the active contratenor lines which have no melodic shape but often ornament a static pitch; the emphatic stops (fermatas), including the non-cadential 'half close' at midpoint. The third of the chord is regularly provided, also at the end. On the other hand, it is always the altus which provides that scale-degree,

[625] Full text and comments in Pope–Kanazawa eds, *Manuscript Montecassino*, no. 129. The original manuscript mensuration, *tempus perfectum*, is correct, although it was later replaced by *tempus imperfectum*. I have halved the rest in bar 4 (semibreve rest in manuscript) and the contratenor altus in bar 11 (manuscript rhythm corrupt).

and this voice is for all other purposes dispensable. Cantus and tenor form an ironclad framework, with many passages in parallel sixths. The bassus takes the 'root' of the chord from time to time, but also 'defects' from this role in the authentic cadences (with octave leaps). Often, the inner voices move back and forth in faster notes just to demonstrate rhythmic energy, with no harmonic consequences. There is a very consistent D minor modality, with only the fewest excursions into more remote harmonies such as E (bar 12).

The historical status of this compositional technique is identical to that of the western chanson of the 1450s and early 1460s. A fourth voice, as included here, was often added to these pieces also. In this and all the other Italian-texted songs in these manuscripts, the harmonic style and the part-writing are not distinguishable from a 'northern style' as has been claimed. The chordal declamation is a rhythmic and textural 'mode of presentation', not a harmonic idiom. It must not deceive us into thinking that the sonorities are brought about in a different way from, for example, those of an imitative piece.[626] We should also remember that (optional) full harmonies or chordal declamation are by no means confined to popular genres, especially not in the 1480s when this piece was copied.

Cornago's 'Morte merçe', mentioned above, is a *canzone* with a relatively long, irregular stanza lacking a refrain and involving *endecasillabi* as well as *settenari* (seven-syllable lines). The genre is that of Petrarch's *Canzoniere*, and single stanzas of the *canzone* were to become the usual poetic genre of the sixteenth-century madrigal. Cornago's piece is in two sections, with the rhyme scheme abc/cdef; the change of metre in the middle recalls the bergerette. The rather strict syllabic declamation of cantus and tenor, however (in both versions), is striking. This device seems to be of Spanish origin and can well be compared with Cornago's Spanish-texted songs, for example his beautiful-sounding canción '¿Donde estas que non te veo?'.[627]

Spanish music seems to have been a model for Italians, at least in Naples where the Aragonese rule had imported Spanish poets and musicians since the earlier part of the century. Secular compositions exist today by the Spanish court singers at Naples, Johannes Cornago, Pere Oriola and Bernardo Ycart.[628]

---

[626] The descriptions of this musical technique in Pope–Kanazawa eds, *Manuscript Montecassino*, 80, and Pirrotta, *Music and Theatre*, 26 f, are forced and anachronistic. Pirrotta construes a contrast between 'clear definition of vertical harmony' – as allegedly found here – and 'contrapuntal thinking' (p. 27 n. 63). The vertical harmony in a piece by, say, Busnois is as clearly defined as anywhere. Kanazawa claims that the *strambotto* harmony originated with two-part songs in the unwritten tradition, where an instrumental tenor supplied 'the notes essential to the harmony' (p. 80). This is not how *strambotto* harmony worked. Underneath *f'*, the notes *bb*, *a*, *f* and *d* were all equally 'essential'.

[627] See Cornago, *Complete Works*, 43 f, 63 f and 38 f; Pope–Kanazawa eds, *Manuscript Montecassino*, no. 16 ('¿Donde estas'); also the editions and commentary in Haberkamp, *Vokalmusik in Spanien*, no. 99, no. 10 and p. 37 ff. Isabel Pope, 'The secular compositions of Johannes Cornago', *Miscelánea en Homenaje a Monseñor Higinio Anglés* (Barcelona, 1958–61), 689–706.

[628] On them and their secular music, see Atlas, 'Provenance MS Perugia'; *idem, Aragonese Court*, 60–69 and 77–80; Stevenson, 'Spanish musical impact', 139–51. See also Isabel Pope, 'La musique espagnole à la cour de Naples dans la seconde moitié du XVe siècle', in *Musique et poésie au XVIe siècle* (Paris: C.N.R.S., 1954), 35–61.

A wealth of secular song is spread out before us in the great Castilian song collections, the Cancionero musical de la Colombina (*E-Sco 7-I-28; CMC*) with 95 pieces, the huge Cancionero musical de Palacio (*E-Mp 1335, olim 2-I-5; CMP*) with 458 pieces, and the secular part of the Segovia choirbook (*E-SE*, no shelf-mark), with 38 songs (plus 51 French, 33 Dutch, 3 Italian and 4 textless pieces). All three were compiled under the reign of the 'Catholic monarchs', Ferdinand V of Aragon and Isabella of Castile (1474–1516). *CMC* contains the oldest repertory, connected with Seville; *CMP* was produced for the royal court, reflecting its (truly catholic) tastes and favourite composers, above all Juan del Encina. (For Segovia, see p. 606.) The language in these Iberian sources is predominantly Castilian, whereas traces of Catalan occur in the Italian, Aragonese-influenced sources. Among them, the chansonniers *MC* and *Q 16* are the most important. Small groups of Spanish songs exist also in *Pix*, *Per*, Mellon, *Fn 176*, in several Petrucci editions of frottole and elsewhere.[629]

In Spain, the polyphonic song genre with the oldest roots was perhaps the *romance*, a strophic song of epic or proverbial character which was considered low class. For this reason, the courtly poets and musicians apparently rejected it in the early but adopted it in the later fifteenth century.[630] Only one specimen appears in *CMC*, but there are 44 in the somewhat later *CMP*. This is something of an analogy with Italian genres, especially the *strambotto*, which became a major fashion with professional composers only around 1500. An 'international folksong' (!) resembling a *romance* (or perhaps better: an *alba/romance* posing as a folksong) is 'Dindiridinridin rindayn. . . Me levay un domatin' in *MC* (no. 127) and *CMC* (no. 101). It was probably of Catalan or Provençal origin and was known in various linguistic and musical forms, and also as a monophonic song.

Monophonic *romances* were probably improvised according to musical patterns, but not much is known about the practice.[631] Their metres follow textual and musical stereotypes which would have been of assistance in extemporized performances, at least for the improvised addition of further text units, as is typical in popular epic forms. The rhyme scheme does not define a stanza but runs in the open progression abcbdbeb etc.; the musical setting usually provides four strains, each for one line of text. Several *romances* refer to historical

---

[629] The best complete edition is Anglès–Romeu eds, *Cancionero Musical de Palacio (CMP)*; for *CMC*, see Robert C. Lawes, *The Seville Cancionero: Transcription and Commentary*, Ph.D., North Texas State U., 1960; Miguel Querol Gavaldá ed., *Cancionero Musical de la Colombina* (Barcelona, 1971); Haberkamp, *Vokalmusik in Spanien* (edn of *CMC* and pieces in Italian sources; useful introduction). Inventories are in Anglès, *La música*, 95–112. For styles, genres and composers, see Stevenson, *Spanish Music*, 201–305; Pope-Kanazawa eds, *Manuscript Montecassino*, 86–99.

[630] Haberkamp, *Vokalmusik in Spanien*, 19–24.

[631] Walter Starkie, *Spain: A Musician's Journey through Time and Space* (Geneva: Kister, 1958), 52, says he heard the ancient monophonic ballad or *romance* 'Quien hubiese tal ventura' with its complete text from Sephardic Jews in Morocco. 'In this way, the Jewish exiles have in their exile preserved the ancient traditions which link them to the land they so enriched by their culture.'

events, especially in the war against the Moors – i.e. they have a function which elsewhere in Europe was left to courtly 'improvisers'. In this context, a piece datable to 1466 is often quoted: 'Lealtat ¡o lealtat!' was dedicated to the heroic deeds of the Condestable Don Miguel Lucas de Iranzo.[632] Its thick four-part harmony and chordal declamation lends weight to the emphatic words. There is a superficial similarity with 'Cor mio volonturioso' (see above). The cantus-tenor framework is made more flexible, however, for example by exchanging the cadential melodic progressions between these two voices. A musically more exciting *romance* is 'En memoria d'Alixandre', composed by Juan de Anchieta in 1489 in honour of the taking of Baza:[633]

Example 86 Juan de Anchieta, 'En memoria d'Alixandre'

---

[632] See Haberkamp, *Vokalmusik in Spanien*, no. 104; Stevenson, *Spanish Music*, 204 ff.
[633] Stevenson, *Spanish Music*, 246.

The initial repercussions – the only hint at 'imitation' – can be found also in the two Cornago songs mentioned above. The 'double upbeat' is produced by the trochaic metre, in which the third syllable carries the first strong word-accent. Correspondingly, the last trochee of each line (a feminine rhyme) is typically set on equal pitches, so that the cadential dissonance occurs before the penultimate chord. Both features became stereotyped musical formulas for the Italian *ottonario* too; the 'double upbeat' survived as a peculiarity of Italian music well into nineteenth-century opera. Its first full bloom occurred in the frottola repertory. As Haberkamp has shown, some other trochaic *romances* have a completely stereotyped line-rhythm, with the double upbeat and a characteristically hemiolic cadence (see Ex. 87).[634]

Example 87 Typical rhythm of the *romance*

If there is any musical genre which plays on this rhythmic scheme even more consistently than do the *romances*, it is the frottola.

The canción/villancico was the genre with which a large number of composers gained a high profile in the 1470s and 80s. This type of song provided much more scope for expression and rhythmic variation than the *romance*: variation through its contrast of refrain and stanza, expressivity through its subjective, amorous texts, many of which were provided by the noble amateurs in whose houses the pieces must have been sung. At first, the French chanson of the Ockeghem–Busnois generation was the constitutive influence for the villancico. It has been claimed that Ockeghem actually visited Spain in 1469 and that it was then that he arranged Cornago's canción '¿Qu'es mi vida preguntays?' for four voices.[635] Ockeghem's 'Petite camusette' is found in *CMC* (no. 87).

---

[634] *Vokalmusik in Spanien*, 22–4. Other *romances* are printed in Stevenson, *Spanish Music*, 247.

[635] The four-part version is in *CMC*, both versions in *MC*. See Pope–Kanazawa eds, *Manuscript Montecassino*, nos. 10 and 103; Stevenson, *Spanish Music*, 218–23.

Pieces by Juan de Triana (*fl.* 1478–83) occasionally recall French chansons, for example 'Ya de amor era partido' (*CMC* no. 35) or the wonderful four-part song 'Quién vos dio tal señorio' (*CMC* no. 34). Triana is the preferred composer of *CMC*, probably because the manuscript originated at Seville, where he was Master of the Children at the cathedral. Pieces in the same vein have been written by Alfonso de Belmonte, succentor of León Cathedral (see also p. 289), by Pedro de Lagarto, Master of the Children at Toledo Cathedral 1490–1507, by Francisco de la Torre and by the otherwise unknown Hurtado de Xeres.[636] As for Enrique – possibly a singer at the court of the Aragonese prince Charles of Viana – his villancico 'Pues serviçio vos desplase' has an attribution to Robert Morton in the Italian source *Per*. It is a very sensible attribution;[637] one of the problems is that the form of the poem in this case is identical to that of a bergerette. It would have been easy for the poet, Pero Toroella, to shape his contrafactum words on a French bergerette.

The most immediate model for these composers was, however, neither Ockeghem nor Morton, but a northerner living in Castile: Johannes Wreede (Urreda). He served the chapel of García Álvarez de Toledo, first Duke of Alva, in 1476, where he was specially rewarded for teaching three negro boys. From 1477 until at least 1481 he was Master of the Chapel of King Ferdinand V. Historians have for some time not quite believed that he was a foreigner, given the skill with which his works seem to blend into the Castilian environment, and given his leadership, which was acknowledged also by Spanish theorists such as Ramos de Pareja. In a copy of Wreede's Kyrie and Gloria 'de Beata Virgine' in the codex *CS 14*, his name is followed by the indication 'Brugen(sis)', i.e. from Bruges. It is now established that he was the son of Rolandus de Wreede, organist of St Donatian's, Bruges, and that he held clerical positions in Bruges churches from 1451 to 1460. Then he disappears – obviously because he has departed for Spain.[638] Wreede's three Spanish-texted works are all significant, but none can rival the almost mythical renown of his canción 'Nunca fué pena mayor' – perhaps the last of the great international success stories of the Ockeghem generation. It is found in *CMC* (no. 9), *CMP* (no. 1) and about twenty other sources. Masses were composed over it by Pierre de la Rue and Francisco Peñalosa, a motet by Matheus Pipelare. Alfonso de Belmonte quoted its cantus literally as the tenor of his 'Pues mi dicha non consiente', and Hurtado de Xeres seems to recall its melodic outline in 'No tenga nadie sperança' (*CMC* no. 40).[639] His textually related 'Con temor de la mudança' (*CMC* no. 42) is in the same 'mood'. The stark, melancholic tone of these pieces in the Phrygian or Aeolian mode has become what we may hear as a peculiarly Spanish idiom. Also, Wreede's three settings of 'Pange lingua', based

---

[636] On all of these and Enrique, see Stevenson, *Spanish Music*, 229–34.

[637] Accepted in Atlas's edition of Morton, *Collected Works*, no. 12, but rejected in Fallows, *Robert Morton's Songs*, 369. See also Stevenson, 'Spanish musical impact', 162.

[638] Strohm, *Bruges*, 43.

[639] See Stevenson, *Spanish Music*, 229–34.

on Spanish plainsongs, seem close relatives in mood and style. We have seen, however, that Ockeghem indulged in precisely this tone in the 1450s (p. 446).

The seemingly greater independence of Hurtado's 'Con temor' over 'No tenga' lies in the ¢ metre of the former against the French-style ○ of the latter. Instead of the potentially hemiolic cross-rhythms and small subdivisions of the more traditional metre, the duple division allows for simpler voice-leading and a somewhat thicker flow of consonances, because only about half of the beats are unaccented and can therefore carry passing dissonances. Another element which became typical for the villancico and canción, was a kind of precious asymmetry of phrases which never quite fall in 4 + 4 patterns despite the octosyllabic verse metre.[640] Triana, and several composers prominent in the *CMP*, demonstrate this. In this collection, the only significant composers (of 53), whose activity still focuses on the fifteenth century, are Juan de Anchieta (*c*.1462–1523), *maestro de capilla* of Prince Juan from 1489, and the poet–musician Juan del Encina (1468–*c*.1529). Only four songs by Anchieta are in *CMP*, but they include the influential 'En memoria d'Alixandre'. A report of 1490 tells us that Prince Juan sang tenor for two hours with his chapelmaster Anchieta and four or five choirboys, providing the tenor against their *tiple* (treble) and *corral* (contralto). The prince also owned many instruments.[641] Encina, an uncle of Ignatius de Loyola, served the Duke of Alva, then from 1498 the Spanish Pope Alexander VI (Borgia) and his successor Julius II (della Rovere), returning to Spain for ever higher ecclesiastical benefices as a reward for the mostly secular works he wrote for the Renaissance prelates. The other composers represented in the *CMP* were partly members of the splendid chapels of Ferdinand, Isabella and their relatives.[642] Most of their secular music should be compared with that of Josquin and his contemporaries, against whom the Spanish royal composers surprise by their relative uniformity and fear of dissonance.

This music, however, did not have to stand on its own; it largely served social purposes. It was performed by noble amateurs in courtly plays and 'revels' as well as by the chaplains. In few fifteenth-century repertories are there so many poets' names known as in this one: often the poets were the patrons themselves.[643] Encina, the son of a shoemaker from Salamanca, rivalled his masters by being a poet and dramatist himself. His *Cancionero*, printed in 1496, comprises lyrical and celebratory poems, mystery plays, 'Triumphs' (texts for pageants) and his famous treatise *Arte de poesía castellana*. He called his smaller, semidramatic plays 'eclogues', to honour the mythological poetry of his great model, Vergil, whose *Bucolics* he also arranged in Castilian. Pastoral or folkloristic tones are usual both in his sacred and secular plays. In his musi-

---

[640] Compare, for example, the Spanish pieces in *HAM*, nos. 97 and 98, with the immediately preceding Italian pieces.

[641] Lamaña, 'Instrumentos', 116 ff.

[642] See Stevenson, *Spanish Music*, 253–305, for a discussion of the composers in *CMP*.

[643] For them, see chapter XX in Anglés–Romeu eds, *Cancionero Musical de Palacio*.

cal works[644] Encina favoured the villancico as a standard genre, which he used for dramatic as well as for all other courtly occasions. Encina is a figure who would quite naturally be called a 'humanist composer' if he were Italian. (It is mainly his works that Petrucci selected from the Spanish repertory for his later frottola volumes.) To compare his music with that of the frottolists, and his poetry with that of a Poliziano or Sannazaro, seems an interesting task for the future.

Dramatic eclogues (mythological plays) with music, and other theatrical uses of vernacular song, were the great fashion at Italian courts around 1500 as well. If the musico–dramatic entertainments at the court of Henry VII (see p. 389) are rarely compared with those of the Italian Renaissance, those of the Mediterranean sister nations at least would seem to deserve the effort.

According to Wolfgang Osthoff, the aesthetic attitude of much Italian song around 1500 was 'dramatic', or in a wider sense, 'representational'. Such a quality would be independent from the actual use of this music, but many pieces were used in dramatic performances and combined with shows.[645] Concentrating more on the poetry and the genres of courtly theatre, Nino Pirrotta and Elena Povoledo have researched Italian theatre music from Angelo Poliziano's *Orfeo* (Mantua, probably 1480) to that of Striggio and Monteverdi.[646] Besides, there is all the music which accompanied street performances and pageants, as for example in the Florentine tradition of carnival and May songs (*canti carnascialeschi*).[647] The chansonniers and other musical sources are laced with individual pieces that can be linked to these various types of theatre. We may again give only some examples from this vast field.

A representational quality can be observed in some Italian celebrative songs for political events, functionally but not musically similar to *romances*. In *MC*, there is the celebratory four-part song 'Viva, viva rey Ferrando' which apparently originated at the Neapolitan court in the 1460s.[648] Although the text is a Spanish canción, the vivacious music was surely written in Italy. A more famous 'Viva' acclamation is the four-part barzelletta printed in 1492 at the end of a drama – the Latin *Historia Baetica* by the papal chamberlain Carlo Verardi – with the notes and the words 'Viva el gran Re Don Fernando'. (The woodblock print is one of the earliest printings of polyphonic music.) This time, the king

---

[644] Juan del Encina, *L'opera musicale*, ed. C. Terni (Florence, 1974). A critique of this and another edition is in Stevenson, 'Spanish musical impact', 160. See also Miguel Querol, 'La producción musical de Juan del Encina (1469-1529)', *AnM* 24 (1969), 121-31.

[645] Osthoff, *Theatergesang*.

[646] Nino Pirrotta and Elena Povoledo, *Li Due Orfei: da Poliziano a Monteverdi*, 2nd edn (Turin: Einaudi, 1975). Translated as Pirrotta, *Music and Theatre*.

[647] The fundamental study is Federico Ghisi, *I canti carnascialeschi nelle fonti musicali del XV e XVI secolo* (Florence, 1937); for editions, see *idem* ed., *Feste musicali della Firenze Medicea (1480-1589)* (Florence, 1939); Joseph J. Gallucci ed., *Florentine Festival Music 1480-1520* (Madison: A-R Editions, 1981). A good introduction is Frank D'Accone, 'Canti carnascialeschi' in *The New Grove*.

[648] See Pope-Kanazawa eds, *Manuscript Montecassino*, no. 111, with ample comment.

thus celebrated is Ferdinand V and his triumph is the fall of Granada: an event for which many other plays and performances were staged.[649]

Two of these, for example, were written by the Aragonese court poet Jacopo Sannazaro. The first, a *farsa* called *La presa di Granata*, concluded with a song by the allegorical character of Gaiety (*Letizia*), accompanied by three girls with cornamuse, viol and flute. A general dance of the *bassa* and *alta* followed. In the second play, Apollo appeared, singing 'certain verses in praise of the victory' to his own accompaniment on the viola (probably *vihuela de mano*).[650]

This gives us two contrasting types of representational music. The first is *collective*, performed by people who can appear as singing or shouting in a play or pageant, who address a patron or the audience in direct speech, and whose polyphonic singing can easily be made a symbol of their own multiplicity. If instruments are allowed to join in, they are most likely to be winds. The other type is *soloistic*, has a more distanced or epic quality, belongs to mythological or otherwise lofty figures, professional actor–singers or named characters in a play. If this type of song is polyphonic, then the cooperation between solo voice and soft instrument(s) is the ideal medium.[651]

Much of the Florentine carnival music was of the first kind. This sturdy polyphony, often in four parts, was usually addressed to a watching crowd by performers on carriages, disguised as representatives of crafts and professions. These songs were also called *carri* or *trionfi*: the circumstances of their performance (*trionfo* = pageant, procession) gave them their name. Other songs were part of staged *mascherate* in the street. These carnival processions and farces were, of course, another pan-European tradition, characteristic of the bigger commercial towns; Nuremberg and the Flemish cities come to mind. But only Florence developed this special musical repertory, surviving in a few large song collections (for example, *I-Fn B. R. 230*, *I-Fn Magl. XIX, 121*). Most of the pieces were composed after the fall of Savonarola (who had forbidden all secular feasts) in 1498 and under the restored Medici rule, but some go back to the earlier period under Lorenzo 'il Magnifico' (1469-92), when Isaac and Agricola also contributed pieces. Lorenzo himself took an active role in the development of the festivities and contributed poems. The names of native composers emerge in this genre at an early date, for example those of Alessandro Coppini (c.1465-1527) and Bartolomeo degli Organi (1474-1539), both active for a long time at the Servite convent of SS Annunziata.[652] Coppini is the composer, for example, of a *canto de' Giudei*, 'La città bella et conforme

---

[649] Einstein, *Italian Madrigal*, vol. 1, 35 ff. Osthoff, *Theatergesang*, 15-29, compares the various pieces, plus Josquin's 'Vive le roy'.

[650] Atlas, *Aragonese Court*, 104.

[651] Pirrotta, *Music and Theatre*, devotes his first chapter to the soloistic *strambotto* sung on stage, for example by *Orfeo*, and the second to the more varied field of *intermedi*. Additional interesting material is presented in Lockwood, *Ferrara*, 278-87 ('Music for court festivities and theatre').

[652] Frank D'Accone ed., *Music of the Florentine Renaissance*, CMM 32/2 (Rome: AIM, 1967): works by Coppini, Bartolomeo degli Organi and Serragli. See also Frank d'Accone, 'Alessandro Coppini and Bartolomeo degli Organi: two Florentine composers of the Renaissance', *AnMc* 4 (1967), 38-76.

natura', in which the Jews (impersonated by actors, of course) describe their legal and social situation in Florence with astonishing frankness. A good anonymous example for the fresh, declamatory style of the *canti* is 'Orsù, orsù, car' signori', the song of the chancery scribes.[653] Its harmonic style is remarkable, not because the voices are put together in some revolutionary way, but because tonic, dominant and subdominant functions are clearly distinguishable. The main cadences on C are all reached through the chord series 'I–IV–I–V–I'. As in much music of this kind, duple and triple metre are contrasted as in the *passamezzo–saltarello* combination already favoured by the dance tutors, and facilitated here by the barzelletta form.

Some pieces were intended for larger dramatic contexts. There is, for example, a whole group of collective songs or choruses of the type of 'A la battaglia' (sung by soldiers), 'Alla caccia' (hunters), 'Alla pesca' (fishermen) and so forth. Several of these were inserted as 'genre pieces' in dramatic representations of an established character, for example sacred plays. A piece used in this way was Isaac's famous 'Battaglia', the origins of which have recently come under scrutiny.[654]

It is also legitimate to draw the north Italian (?) 'Scaramella' song into this context. The name derives from an imaginary comical figure, the scarecrow-soldier Scaramella; the famous tune gave rise to imitations, so that it became synonymous with a whole group of mock-songs, often heard from schoolchildren in the streets. Professional musicians also cultivated the type, for example Pietrobono.[655] One of the most frequently performed secular pieces by Josquin today is his bristling 'Scaramella fa la guerra' (*BR 229*, no. 171); other settings of the same tune exist, one by Compère and one by Antonio Stringari; there are various other references to the tune and text.[656]

Like other nations, the Italians loved the fun inherent in pastiche and confusion. Quodlibets or, as they were called in Italy then, *incatenature* (chain-songs) or *insalate* are frequent in the song collections. Some are written, again, by famous immigrants; the best known is Isaac's 'Donna di dentro alla tua casa' (*BR 229* no. 150), where several songs circulate within the *al fresco* harmony like actors on a stage.

Many contrapuntal and improvisational experiences came together in the frottola, which might rather be called a fashion than a genre. It was also, with this label, a marketable product from the point of view of the publisher, whose business surely fuelled the activity of composers in the first two decades of the sixteenth century. The frottola was not only mass-distributed but also mass-produced. The most fertile frottola composers were Marchetto Cara (*c.*1470–*c.*1525) and Bartolomeo Tromboncino (*c.*1470–*c.*1535), both hailing

---

[653] Printed in *NAWM*, no. 47, and *HAM*, no. 96.
[654] Timothy J. McGee, '"Alla Battaglia": music and ceremony in fifteenth-century Florence', *JAMS* 36 (1983), 287–302. Osthoff, *Theatergesang*, 30–109, analyses the musical insertions in Florentine sacred dramas.
[655] Lockwood, *Ferrara*, 107 f.
[656] See Gallico, 'Josquin and the frottola', 446–50.

from Verona but active for many years at the Mantuan court of Isabella d'Este, the great patroness of 'frottolists'. Also worth mentioning among the older 'frottolists' are the Venetian organist Francesco d'Ana (*d.c.*1502/3), and the Veronese musicians Giovanni Brocco and Michele Pesenti (*c.*1470–*c.*1524).[657]

Since Petrucci and other printers gathered so many different musical and poetic genres under the title 'frottola', music historians have agreed to distinguish this wider use of the term from a narrower use, which defines only certain barzelletta forms. Besides these, possible genres or forms were *strambotto*, *oda*, *capitoli*, *sonnets*, *canzoni* and yet others. In his major contributions to the history of the frottola, William Prizer emphasizes the 'mnemonic' quality of the verse patterns, i.e. their dense repetition schemes which facilitated improvising texts on some given musical schemes.[658] It is as if the French *formes fixes*, now on the way out, had found an Italian heir. The rondeau and virelai patterns had been welcomed by the Franco-Burgundian singer–composers, or indeed 'improvisers', a century before.

The words were extremely important in the frottola, and were usually given to the cantus line in clear, declamatory rhythms with some melismatic extensions. Partly because of the regular use of the *ottonario* metre in the text, the musical phrases tend to be metrically even, and often have the rhythmic stereotype of double upbeats and hemiolic cadences (see p. 577). Not all the poems were significant; the rhythmic regularity gives many frottole an insistent or even dictational tone which does not always suit the amorous texts. But the frottolists and their patrons devoured poetry on all subjects; besides the angry complaint of the rejected lover, the debate with the unfaithful Lady Fortune was a typical frottola subject (albeit not limited to this genre). Classicizing poems and Petrarchan *canzoni*, or their imitations, were frequent in the frottola before they came to characterize the Renaissance madrigal.[659]

Prizer claims that the frottola descended from the practice of singing on the lute, played polyphonically. Given a particular affinity of the frottola to lute performance (which is, however, only a claim), this would explain why the genre was almost invariably written in four voices rather than three.

According to Prizer, Pietrobono and the lutenists of his generation played with a plectrum, producing only a single line. About the same time, however, polyphonic playing on the lute was being developed in the north. Tinctoris says that Conrad Paumann ('orbus ille Germanus') excelled in polyphonic playing on instruments, and the context implies that he meant plucked instruments, not the organ.[660] Paumann visited Italy, especially Mantua, in 1470, and his art

---

[657] A still valuable introduction to the frottola is Einstein, *Italian Madrigal*, vol. 1, 34–115, with emphasis on Tromboncino and Cara. Specifically for the latter, see Prizer, *Courtly Pastimes*. Brocco, Ana and Cara are represented in the most important early frottola manuscript, *I-MOe α.F. 9. 9*, copied in Padua in the 1490s. See *CC*, vol. 2, 164.

[658] Prizer, *Courtly Pastimes*; idem, 'Frottola'.

[659] On this subject, see Rubsamen, *Literary Sources*.

[660] Weinmann, *Tinctoris*, 45. In *Bruges*, 165 n. 38, I incorrectly related this passage to the organ.

– with which he may not have been alone among Germans – was admired all over Italy. His polyphonic arrangement of 'Je loe amours' in the Buxheim Organ Book (no. 17: 'In cytharis vel etiam in organis'), perhaps a polyphonic lute piece, has been connected with the claim that he invented German lute tablature.[661] Shortly afterwards, polyphonic playing of plucked instruments seems to have spread. The earliest Italian lute manuscript (in 'French lute tablature' notation), the Pesaro MS (*I-PESo 1144*), contains some early frottole in arranged form.[662]

What was the significance of the new style of lute-playing? It accompanied the development from predominantly three-part to predominantly four-part textures in such a way that no more performers were needed than before. The combined tenor and bass were now playable on a single instrument. Pietrobono, Niccolò Tedesco and other German–Italian professionals needed a *tenorista* for three-part music. In the chanson format cultivated by them, the contratenor (whether high or low) had to be dispensable. With the advent of the new style, the bassus could be advanced to an essential voice, and the basic framework became three part. The altus remained inessential. What this means, however, is that performance practices developed by analogy to composing styles. Paumann's playing developed simultaneously with the four-part settings of Busnois, whose music was appreciated in Germany. The bassus became an essential voice in four-part chansons of the Josquin generation (see p. 563), which circulated in Italy well before 1500. Thus, the frottola does not necessarily owe more to unwritten practice than to known compositional techniques of its time.

Pirrotta and Prizer seem undecided whether to make more of the idea, already considered by Lowinsky, that tonal harmonies emerge in the frottola, and that this is connected with the chordal style.[663] They do emerge, as they emerge in other genres and other countries. Tonal harmony, which is not so much a manner of putting voices above each other as a manner of connecting subsequent sonorities, developed in secular music of several countries simultaneously. Unwritten traditions neither furthered nor delayed it: the performers followed the same stylistic trends as the composers. Despite significant differences flowing

---

[661] See Fallows, 'Fifteenth-century tablatures'. Around 1470, two other blind musicians, 'Zohane Orbo' (apparently a German as well) and 'Francesco Cieco da Ferrara', fascinated Mantua and Ferrara with improvised playing on polyphonic instruments: see Lockwood, 'Pietrobono', 131 f; Atlas, *Aragonese Court*, 43 f n. 116. I cannot help suspecting that 'Johannes Orbus' may have been the blind Johannes Touront.

[662] See Walter H. Rubsamen, 'The earliest French lute tablature', *JAMS* 21 (1968), 286–99; Allan W. Atlas, 'The Foligno fragment: another source from fifteenth-century Naples', in Finscher ed., *Datierung und Filiation*, 181–98. Atlas maintains that the early part of *I-PESo 1144* originated at Naples, *c.*1480–1500.

[663] See Prizer, *Courtly Pastimes*, 155. In this chapter on 'harmony' and in 'Frottola', 18, Prizer makes contradictory comments on the role of the bassus. On the one hand, he states that the cantus-tenor framework is intact (no fourths), and on the other he claims that a 'cantus–bassus framework' has developed, or indeed a three-part framework. Even if the bassus 'consistently provides the harmonic underpinning' ('Frottola', 18), it is not an essential voice where no fourths need to be supported. Fourths *are* admitted in many frottole after 1500.

from the different languages, European polyphonic song around 1500 was developing along parallel lines.[664]

Music in the cathedrals and cities; music theory

It will probably take music historians a while to catch up with the recognition of other historians that Italian Renaissance culture was not exclusively courtly and aristocratic. A particular liking for feudal and other pre-democratic societies seems to prevail among lovers of early music in any case, and it sometimes seems as if 'Music fit for a prince' were all they wanted to hear. In reality, music for lesser patrons could be quite magnificent. The Medici family (of the ancient regime until 1494) were burghers, not princes; they had neither a 'court' nor a 'court chapel'.[665] Their family chapel was in the abbey of S Lorenzo, which was not a musical centre in the later fifteenth century. The Florentine 'chapel' that represented the highest artistic standards was the group referred to as 'the Singers of San Giovanni', supported by the city magistrate and the wool and cloth guilds. They also served the Servite friary of SS Annunziata, and at times the cathedral of S Maria del Fiore – an example of civic, ecclesiastical and monastic cooperation as it was bound to develop in a large commercial city.[666]

Another problem is the indifference with which the cathedral and monastic spheres have been regarded among students of Italian music. This attitude has been fuelled by the writings of Pirrotta, who spoke of a 'sharp decline' in Italian art-music in the mid-fifteenth century (see p. 542), in order to bounce off it his theory about the flourishing of unwritten practices in the secular field. In reality, both sides of music enhanced each other, and sacred polyphony was a frequent, welcome contribution to Italian civic, ecclesiastical and courtly life. Our knowledge of Italian cathedral music in the Quattrocento, and particularly in the problematic decades *c.*1440–*c.*1480, is scantier than it could be. At least the archival sources are quite rich, and have been made available by Italian historians.[667]

From the documents we learn that between 1440 and 1480 a striking number of Italian cathedrals had professional singers of polyphony on the payrolls, not only the succentor and organist, as was usual in the north. These *biscantori*, as they were often called, had to appear in the choir for the polyphonic singing of regular liturgical items such as Mass sections, Vespers hymns and *Magnificat*

---

[664] See also Herbert Rosenberg, 'Frottola und deutsches Lied um 1500. Ein Stilvergleich', *AcM* 18–19 (1946–7), 30–78.

[665] See J. R. Hale, *Florence and the Medici: The Pattern of Control* (London: Thames & Hudson, 1977). For some important aspects of musical patronage see Parigi, *Laurentiana*.

[666] See D'Accone, 'Music and musicians'; *idem*, 'Singers'; and p. 600 below.

[667] Surveys of this material are Cattin, 'Church patronage', esp. 30–33; S. Boorman and I. Fenlon, 'Italy, bibliography of Music to 1600 #B IV' in *The New Grove*. See also Bridgman, *Vie musicale*, 40–45.

settings. This was already the case at the duomo of Milan in 1402, when Matteo da Perugia was appointed *biscantor*.[668] One of the specialists, the *magister cantus* or succentor, usually had to teach plainsong and *cantus figuratus* to the boys of the *cantoria*, and to other clerics under certain circumstances. This was a regular condition, whether we look at the appointment of Nicolò Fragerio (recte: Frangens or Françeis) from Liège in 1419 at the cathedral of Chioggia – a small town near Venice – or the appointment of John Hothby in 1467 at Lucca Cathedral. In the former case, the Netherlands musician is required to:

> say Requiems every day in a special chapel;
> sing chant and polyphony (*cantar e biscantar*) in the service whenever necessary (i.e. probably on Sundays and feast-days);
> appear in all the services, day and night;
> teach chant and polyphony to all those clerics who wanted to learn it.

For these duties, he was promised a salary of 60 ducats p.a., provided by a chaplaincy of St Martin in the same town.[669] At Lucca in 1467, the noble family de Noceto endowed a chaplaincy of S Regolo in the cathedral with 36 ducats p.a., accorded to a chaplain called *magiscolo*, who was obliged to teach plainsong and *canto figurato* for free to the clerics.[670]

In many cathedrals, the vocal performances were supported or augmented by those of organists skilled in polyphony, for example Antonio Squarcialupi of Florence (1416–80), the long-time servant of the Medici and friend of Dufay, and his students Antonio Coppini and Bartolomeo degli Organi, or Jacopo Fogliani of Modena Cathedral (1468–1542) and his brother Lodovico, the music theorist (*d.*1539). Also Ferrara seems to have had a significant tradition of organists.[671]

A matrix for the provision of music and musical education were the papal Bulls of Eugenius IV, which resulted in musical appointments and subsidised instruction – the so-called *Scuole Eugeniane* – in the following cathedrals: Vicenza 1432; Turin 1435; Florence 1436; Bologna (Basilica di S Petronio) 1436; Treviso 1437; Padua 1439; Urbino 1439 and Verona 1440. Similar appointments were made at Brescia, Ferrara, Udine, Modena, Parma, Arezzo and Rieti. These were not endowments for plainchant only: the provision of a professional musician among the clergy enabled the cathedral chapters to introduce polyphony if they so wished. At S Petronio, it was confirmed in 1464 – not newly introduced – that the cantor had to teach up to 24 clerics daily, and to

---

[668] Cattin, 'Church patronage', 29.

[669] I. Tiozzo, 'Maestri e organisti della Cattedrale di Chioggia fino al XVII secolo', *NA* 12 (1935), 288. Nicolaus 'Frangens' was probably Nicolaus Simonis. See Petrobelli, 'Cattedrali e città', 467 f, and p. 117 above.

[670] Luigi Nerici, *Storia della musica in Lucca* (Lucca, 1870), 42 f.

[671] See, respectively, Gino Roncaglia, *La Cappella Musicale del Duomo di Modena* (Florence: Olschki, 1957), 14–20; Enrico Peverada, 'Vita musicale nella cattedrale di Ferrara nel quattrocento: note e documenti', *RIM*, 15 (1980), 3–30.

perform on all Sundays and double feasts including their vigils '*cantus figuratus* or *contrapunctus* with the boys and others'.[672]

This system, which also seems to have prevailed in Spanish cathedrals,[673] had a multiplying effect because it was so firmly tied to teaching. By no means all of the 'clerics' – the term included the schoolboys – remained in this state, and thus the musical education provided at the many small-town cathedrals filtered into civic and secular life. Similarly, the performances themselves could be executed by as many as 24 people, i.e. beyond the specialists by all those half-skilled clerics who were being taught music. And certainly, the performances were heard by audiences of hundreds. It is here that Italian polyphonic *choral* music originated, somehow analogous to the English development (see p. 381). In fact, a discernible departure from Franco-Netherlands usage is the frequent appearance of the *cantoria* in the choir for regular services. Endowed polyphonic Masses in side-chapels, a standard feature of Flemish churches, were not absent but were none the less rare in mid-fifteenth-century Italy. A little later, the custom of the private chapel Mass in polyphony reappeared; in 1484, the singers of S Giovanni in Florence obliged themselves to sing 'la messa di canto figurato' every Saturday morning at SS Annunziata, which corresponds to the tradition of the polyphonic Lady Mass.[674]

Even where the documents do not unambiguously refer to mensural polyphony, this was often the kind of music required from the succentors. Why, otherwise, would so many churches have hired Frenchmen and Englishmen to teach and perform music? At Vicenza, Bertrand Feragut and Johannes de Lymburgia (see p. 160) were followed, in the 1460s, by Johannes de Francia; at Treviso, Raynaldus *tenorista* and Nicolaus *de traconibus tenorista* (1438/9) were followed in 1441 by *cantores francigenae*, in 1448/9 by Giovanni Brith (who was at the Este court in 1460 and who became succentor of Udine Cathedral in 1474), in 1463 by Gerardus de Lisa from Ghent, who was joined in 1465 by Guilelmus *francese cantor*, etc.[675] Sometimes the archives tell us about lost manuscripts of polyphonic music, for example at Milan Cathedral, where an inventory of 1445 lists a book of *cantus figuratus* – in a period when little is known about the musical personnel.[676]

Proof of polyphonic practice in these cathedrals must, in fact, be sought in musical sources. Although the choirbooks of many big institutions – in Venice

[672] Osvaldo Gambassi, *La Cappella Musicale di S. Petronio* (Florence: Olschki, 1987), 10 f; *idem*, 'La scuola dei "Pueri cantores" in S. Petronio (1436–1880 ca.)', *NA* new ser. 3 (1985), 7–53.

[673] See p. 289 above. Documents from a major centre are published in Josep M. Gregori I Cifré, 'Mateu Ferrer, *tenorista*; mestre de cant de la seu de Barcelona (1477–1498)', *Recerca Musicológica* 3 (1983), 7–37.

[674] D'Accone, 'Singers', 334.

[675] Gallo-Mantese, *Ricerche*, 33; D'Alessi, *Treviso*, 44 ff.

[676] Marco Magistretti, 'Due inventari del Duomo di Milano del secolo XV', *Archivio Storico Lombardo* ser. 4, vol. XII, anno 36 (1909), 348 (no. 248). On this period at Milan, see Claudio Sartori, 'La cappella del Duomo dalle origini a Franchino Gaffurio', in *Storia di Milano*, vol. 9 (Milan: Fondazione Treccani, 1961), 723–86.

and Florence, for example – are lost, the situation is not as bad as has been claimed. There is, for example, the choirbook *SP* which belonged to the Basilica of St Peter's, Rome – written in the 1470s but incorporating discernible layers of the 1450s and early 1460s. In a conspicuous cathedral such as this, foreign singers were much appreciated; several of them were exchanged with the papal chapel.[677] Cathedrals further afield also provided singers as well as compositions. A certain 'Guglielmus de Francia' shuttled between St Peter's and Padua Cathedral between 1455 and 1461; he sang tenor and composed and copied music.[678]

SP contains a double-sided repertory: its seventeen Masses and few motets were probably used for specially endowed chapel services, but its dozens of hymns, *Magnificat* settings and antiphon settings must have been performed 'in the choir' and 'by the choir'. The Masses and motets may all be of western European origin; a certain Egidius Cervelli added a Kyrie of his own to Petrus de Domarto's 'sine nomine' Mass. Cervelli was surely an Italian, perhaps identical with Egidius Egidii who sang soprano ('qui cantat supra') at the Basilica between 1474 and 1481.[679] The Office compositions, the presence of which is typical for Italian cathedrals, include the admired models in these genres by Dufay and Binchois, but far more anonymous music. As suggested above (p. 437), some pieces may have been imported from France, but Italian musicians must have helped to complete the liturgical sets. The hymns, in particular, are most probably choral music, connecting traditional liturgical practice with the choral polyphony of the Renaissance as cultivated at Ferrara (see p. 604).[680]

Two Italian composers of the mid-fifteenth century have left enough attributed works to constitute 'Opera omnia': Johannes de Quadris and Antonius Janue. Johannes de Quadris[681] was a priest of the Veneto, surely active by the 1430s: his four-voice *Magnificat* is entered in *GB-Ob 213* with the (composition?) date 'May 1436 Venec(iis)'. It is the most complicated of his extant works, still indebted to the Ciconia tradition. Then, there is a three-voice hymn 'Iste confessor', extant by *c.*1450 but still copied in north Italian provincial sources *c.*1500. Most characteristic is a cycle of two-part pieces for Good Friday processions, including a setting of the extremely popular dramatic *lauda* 'Cum autem venissem ad locum' (the lament of the Madonna). Quadris also wrote a cycle of two-part *Lamentations* which existed already in the 1440s but were printed by Ottaviano Petrucci in his first book of Lamentations (1506) – together with

---

[677] Reynolds, 'Origins'. (See also p. 406 above.) For singers, see Haberl, *Bausteine* III, 48 ff n. 1. The total number of specially appointed discant singers rose from about three in 1450 to about five in 1460 to seven and more in 1475. At least twelve more resident clerics including boys would have performed with them, according to the practice described above.

[678] Reynolds, 'Origins', 283 f. He may be the Guilelmus later found at Treviso (see above).

[679] Haberl, *Bausteine* III, 49 f n. 1.

[680] Fifteenth-century Italian Vespers music has been studied in Masakata Kanazawa, *Polyphonic Music for Vespers in the Fifteenth Century*, Ph.D., Harvard U., 1966. See also Ward, *Office Hymn*; Edward R. Lerner, 'The polyphonic Magnificat in 15th-century Italy', *MQ* 50 (1964), 44–58.

[681] On his life and works, see Cattin, *Johannes de Quadris*. Cattin is also the editor of Quadris, *Opera*.

the Lamentations of Agricola! Petrucci must have known that there was a 'market' for this publication. The Lamentations and the processional set by Quadris are simple, but rhythmically varied and melodically graceful music; the plainsong is paraphrased in the upper voice as was usual in the Dufay era. The background for the processional set is the simple liturgical music in *cantus planus binatim* style, used in many Italian churches, which Quadris's mensural setting apparently superseded. If sung with the proper style and measure by a choir of men and boys, this music has beauty and force like other manifestations of Renaissance art. As an example, we may consider the little piece which concludes the procession cycle:

Example 88 Johannes de Quadris, Processional song

En brevissimo in tumulo te recondimus. Heu, heu, domine.

[Do not disdain, our saviour, the sighs of thy young children. See, in a narrow tomb we bury thee, oh Lord.]

The anonymous liturgical polyphony of mid-fifteenth-century Italy must generally be understood as a more artful replacement of more primitive styles. Much of it is found in the larger collections *Per* and *MC* – manuscripts with monastic or Franciscan backgrounds which we have encountered as song collections.[682] *MC* now contains 67 sacred pieces (there were originally more), *Per* contains 46. There are many hymns, *Magnificat* settings, verses from Lamentations, litanies, a few Mass items, and *laude*: just the music which smaller and larger cathedrals and monasteries 'consumed' in their ceremonial life in the

---

[682] On their connections with the Neapolitan sphere, see Atlas, 'Provenance MS Perugia', and most recently Giulio Cattin, 'Il repertorio polifonico sacro nelle fonti napoletane del Quattrocento', in Lorenzo Bianconi and Renato Bossa eds, *Musica e Cultura a Napoli dal XV al XIX secolo* (Florence: Olschki, 1983), 29–45.

choir and in processions. It would not be surprising if composers' names were entirely absent since this kind of music tends to be recorded anonymously everywhere in Europe at that time. Nevertheless, the two codices furnish the names of Aedwardus de Ortona, Serafinus (Baldessaris?) and Damianus, apart from those of the Spanish chaplains at Naples: Pere Oriola, Bernardo Ycart and Johannes Cornago.

Antonius Janue[683] was a more ambitious and perhaps better-trained composer. The only known fact of his life is that he was a 'cantor magiscolae' at the ducal palace of Genoa in 1456; this must mean that he helped the school rector in instructing the choirboys attached to the chapel of the doge. Possibly, Janue is to be identified with a certain 'Antonio da Genova' documented at Ferrara Cathedral in 1462.[684] Most of his thirteen attributed works, and several others which may also be by him, are three-part hymn settings in a style that takes its direction from Dufay but partly abandons fauxbourdon and homorhythmic declamation in favour of imitation. Occasionally, the contratenor behaves more like that of a chanson than like a texted voice. Janue's pieces are all found in *I-Fn 112bis*, a collection of 48 sacred pieces copied in the 1460s – by Antonius Janue himself, according to Kanazawa.[685] Significantly, other named authors of this manuscript include Dufay, Dunstable, Power and Quadris; there are also works by Frye and Binchois. That the compiler of the manuscript was well connected, especially with commercial centres of the Low Countries and England, is also suggested by his concentration on votive antiphons in the manner of Frye's 'Ave regina celorum'. No wonder, since Genoa, like Florence and Naples, was a trading partner of Bruges, Southampton and similar centres, where such antiphons were appreciated.[686] The document which cites Antonius Janue in 1456 also mentions, among the nine other musicians in the ducal service (probably trumpeters and singers), three Flemings ('Flamengus'). In a similar document of 1448, five Flemish musicians are mentioned.[687]

I-Fn 112bis is only one of the many private collections that must have served cathedral succentors and civic musicians in Italian towns. The kind of manuscript and repertory which we should expect to have existed in various Italian centres must have resembled the Trent Codices in character, if not in size. These codices, too, must contain some Italian music among the liturgical anonymi. Other material from cathedral uses has been preserved in later manuscripts, for example the newly discovered choirbook of Siena Cathedral, written largely in 1481, or the music fascicles of S Petronio, Bologna.[688] We have observed

---

[683] Masakata Kanazawa, 'Antonius Janue and revisions of his music', *Quadrivium* 12 (1971), 177–94; Kanazawa is also the editor of Janue, *Opera omnia*.

[684] Lockwood, *Ferrara*, 317.

[685] *I-Fn Magl. XIX, 112bis*. See *CC*, vol. 1, 225.

[686] See Sylvia W. Kenney, 'Four settings of "Ave regina Celorum"', in *Liber Amicorum Charles van den Borren* (Antwerp, 1964), 98–104; Strohm, *Bruges*, 140.

[687] Remo Giazotto, *La Musica a Genova* (Genoa, 1951), 103 f and 273 ff.

[688] See, for Siena: Brown-D'Accone-Owens eds, *RMF*, vol. 17 (1986); Frank D'Accone, 'A late 15th-century sacred repertory: MS K I.2 of the Biblioteca Comunale, Siena', *MD* 37 (1983), 121–70; *CC*, vol. 4, 475 f. For Bologna: Hamm, 'Musiche'.

that one of these fascicles contains an English Mass cycle in 'stroke notation', a fragment of which has also been found in Lincolnshire (see p. 388). From 1467, Robertus de Anglia served as *magister cantus* at S Petronio, followed in 1474 by Ogerio de Borgogna (Roger Saignand) from Dijon. Both these men may have collected music for the church. The fourth fascicle contains a Mass 'O gloriosa regina', built on the tenor of Johannes Touront's famous motet, but not identical with Johannes Vincenet's work of the same title (see p. 601). At about the same time, John Hothby in Lucca injected challenging western poly-phony into a traditional cathedral. The Lucca Choirbook, produced in Bruges *c*.1467-72 (perhaps with Hothby's advice), served his students and their per-formances for a number of years, as the many text revisions and other additions to the codex by Italian hands testify. In the cathedral inventory of 1492, the codex surfaces under the telling description: 'A book of *cantus figuratus* in modern style, called the book of the *cantori*'.[689] Of the composers whom Hothby mentions in his *Dialogus in arte musica* (before 1480), some were perhaps per-sonal acquaintances. 'Micheleth' may be the same person as the author of a piece in the Florentine chansonnier *I-Fn 176*, and 'Pelagulfus' is probably Antonio Peragulfo, succentor at Lucca Cathedral from 1507 and author of a piece in the manuscript *I-Fn Panc 27*.[690]

Similarly relevant is the manuscript collection in Verona, once belonging to the *Mensa degli Accoliti*, the cathedral school where Marchetto Cara, Michele Pesenti and perhaps Giovanni Brocco were trained.[691] Although copied in the 1480s and later, the codices contain much music composed and performed since the mid-century, when the personnel of Italian churches enthusiastically began to learn and perform mensural polyphony for the same ceremonies for which they had previously used *cantus planus binatim*. These were not 'dark years' of Italian polyphony, but years of enlightenment.

The four choirbooks (*I-Md librone 1–4*)[692] which Franchinus Gaffurius (1451-1522) compiled for the cathedral of Milan in the years after 1484, trans-mit much music by the northern composers employed at the Sforza court: Josquin, Compère, Weerbeke, Martini and Agricola. They also contain works by Tinctoris, Isaac, Brumel and notably by Gaffurius himself. More than 130 compositions, however, are anonymous, and many of them are not very compat-ible with courtly practices, the simple, homorhythmic settings of Latin *can-tiones* and *laude*, for example. Very little of this music has been studied as yet; some of it may go back to the time when Josquin himself was *biscantor* in the same cathedral (1459-72; see below).

[689] Strohm, *Bruges*, 120 ff. See also p. 406 above.
[690] On the treatise, see p. 596 below. On *Panc 27*, see *CC*, vol. 1, 232.
[691] The Verona choirbooks *755*, *758* and *759* are local compilations including some Franco-Netherlands music. For literature and inventories, see *CC*, vol. 4, 76-9 (note the predominance of anonymous, probably local works). Only MS *757* contains mainly foreign polyphony, and MS *756* is a Netherlands codex. See also Enrico Paganuzzi *et al.*, *La Musica a Verona* (Verona, 1976), 71-93.
[692] *CC*, vol. 2, 150-54. A facs edn of choirbooks 1-3 is Brown-D'Accone-Owens eds, *RMF*, vol. 12 (1987).

Music in the monasteries and cathedrals was particularly favoured by middle-class patronage. The burghers of the great cities paid for, and often participated in, performances of sacred music which met their developing tastes. The middle classes were more influenced than the aristocracy by religious radicalism, the calls for austerity and a return to Christian virtues which the mendicant preachers requested from them. This affected the music. Since the late thirteenth century, the *Laudesi* confraternities had been characteristic of this environment: groups which met in a chapel or oratory every night to sing devotional polyphonic songs, or have them performed by paid musicians.[693] The Florentine associations of S Maria Novella or Pietro Martire, of S Zanobi, of Orsanmichele, have been researched in great detail by D'Accone;[694] similar groups in Venice, called the *Scuole grandi*, have been identified as patrons of religious music of similar kinds.[695] A member of the Venetian congregation of the *Salvatoriani*, Innocentius Dammonis, is the sole author of the polyphonic *laude* published in the first of Petrucci's two books (1508). By this time, the genre had become very popular in northern Italy; the frottolists Marchetto Cara, Bartolomeo Tromboncino, Filippo da Lurano and Giovanni Brocco contributed to it, and Petrus Hedus (Capretto) provided his confraternity of S Maria dei Battuti at Pordenone with his own *lauda* compositions.[696] Naples was also a centre for polyphonic *laude*. In a number of monastic houses they became part of the ceremonies, for example during Holy Week; when they were sung in more voices, the polyphony could well be of a primitive type. This practice is also found in cathedrals, even in some major centres.[697] Among the various stylistic or institutional traditions, we can first identify a stricter, monastic approach as maintained by Benedictines adhering to the reform of S Giustina and Subiaco. These houses (for example in Venice and Pavia) tolerated, in practice as well as in theory, only Latin texts and the most austere types of counterpoint, i.e. *cantus planus binatim*. Controversies over the permitted limits in music-making were frequent. Two-voice ceremonial items, for example the Lamentations and processional songs of Holy Week, were their typical polyphonic repertory.[698] A different, more diffuse trend was led by the mendicants, especially the Carmelites (whose many contributions to music theory have already been alluded to), the Tuscan order of the Servites (*Servi di S Maria*) with its motherhouse of SS Annunziata at Florence, and, to some extent, the

---

[693] A good introduction is William F. Prizer, 'Lauda spirituale, 2.' in *The New Grove* (in the bibliography note contributions by Jeppesen, Ghisi, Cattin, Damilano, D'Accone). On the earlier history, see also p. 343 above (with further literature).

[694] Frank D'Accone, 'Alcune note sulle compagnie fiorentine dei laudesi durante il Quattrocento', *RIM* 10 (1975), 86–114.

[695] Glixon, 'Scuole Grandi'.

[696] Jeppesen-Brøndal eds, *Laude* (the sources are described on pp. LV–LXIV).

[697] See, for example, the processionals of Padua Cathedral (*I-Pc C 56*) and of Florence, S Maria del Fiore (*I-Fd 21*).

[698] Giulio Cattin, 'Tradizione e tendenze innovatrici nella normativa e nella pratica liturgico-musicale della Congregazione di S. Giustina', *Benedictina* 17 (1970), 254–99.

Franciscans of the less rigid branches. These orders encouraged the Italian polyphonic *lauda* and also mensural music of more modern kinds; contrafacta of chansons were heard on their premises all the time. Of the various manuscript collections of polyphonic *laude*, a significant example is the manuscript Grey (*SA-Cp*) of Cape Town, which contains at least eighteen sacred contrafacta of secular songs.[699] This source might be connected with Florentine mendicant houses. The writing of *laude* as contrafacta of secular polyphonic pieces was an almost universal practice. Even Girolamo Savonarola agreed to it, although he opposed all other polyphony. He wrote such texts himself; others were written by Lorenzo de' Medici, by his mother, Lucrezia Tornabuoni, and by members of their circle such as Angelo Poliziano and Feo Belcari. From *c*.1485, collections of *lauda* texts were printed, often with the indication 'to be sung like . . .' ('cantasi come . . .') identifying the secular melody.[700] The religious plays, *sacre rappresentazioni*, offered many opportunities to perform some well-known and possibly secular music under the guise of a sacred chorus; examples from mystery plays given in Florence and Urbino have been reconstructed and discussed.[701] Much original music was created for the *lauda* as well. There is in some of these short compositions a tone which, beyond the purely devotional, sets the words in an 'expressive' and almost theatrical pose. Their attitude is often indistinguishable from that of secular laments. Consider, for example, this sacred *strambotto* setting from a north Italian collection, *c*.1490:[702]

Example 89 'Alta regina', *I-MOe F. 9. 9*, fol. 61v

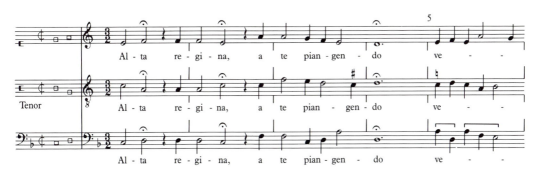

[699] See Cattin ed., *Italian Laude*.

[700] See Ghisi, 'Strambotti e laude'. Foreign songs, especially French chansons, were often used: see Giulio Cattin '"Contrafacta internazionali": Musiche europee per laude italiane', in Günther–Finscher eds, *Musik und Text*, 411–42.

[701] Bianca Becherini, 'La musica nelle sacre rappresentazioni Fiorentine', *RMI* 53 (1951), 193–241; Osthoff, *Theatergesang*, 30 ff.

[702] After Cattin, 'Contributi', no. 14. I have interpreted the mensuration as a large triple (*modus minor perfectus*), and adjusted the fermata length in bar 4. The resulting 'saraband' rhythm seems genuine to the piece.

Example 89 (*cont.*)

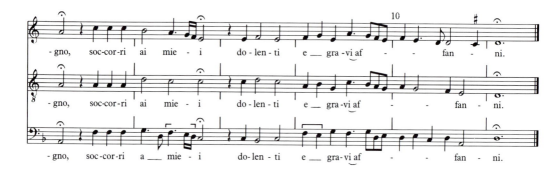

[High queen, to thee I come weeping; relieve me in my painful and grave complaints.]

The great flowering of *music theory*, indeed a 'music-theoretical madness' (Jeppesen), in fifteenth-century Italy – and Spain – can be described here only briefly.[703] Like music itself, music theory has its own traditions and developments beyond the conditioning by a certain time and place. An important stage, reached in Italy by the earlier fifteenth century, was the creation of a scientific language, nourished by the study of classical texts. If there was no ancient music to be studied, there certainly were ancient scientific writings about it which could be imitated. Another condition was, of course, princely patronage. We have already mentioned the connection between some theoretical writings and princely education (p. 547). It is strange that we do not know when and why the greatest theorist working in Italy in this century, Johannes Tinctoris (*c.*1435–1511), was called to the court of Naples.[704] Did King Ferrante actually want a theorist, rather than a purely practical musician? It seems so, because Tinctoris could be useful to a court with his knowledge of law and mathematics and he was an expert in the use of language.[705] But how did the king find him? Had Tinctoris already made himself known in France through his writings? I have suggested (p. 292) that a background for Tinctoris's theoretical interest was his pedagogical practice, and he was a teacher at Orléans Cathedral as well as, probably, at the Neapolitan court. Three of his treatises are dedicated to King Ferrante's daughter, Beatrice of Aragon, before her departure for Hungary in 1476. They could be called propaedeutical within a humanist education: the *Tractatus de regulari valore notarum* (one of five small tracts on mensural notation), the *Diffinitorium musices* (his most famous work, a dictionary of musical terms, printed in 1495 by the ex-cantor of Treviso Cathedral, Gherardus de Lisa) and his most classicizing work, the *Complexus effectuum musices*. A further

---

[703] See Palisca, *Humanism*, ch. 1, especially 7 ff.
[704] For the date of his arrival, see Atlas, *Aragonese Court*, 72. See also p. 605 below.
[705] See also Woodley, 'Tinctoris' Italian translation', 173 ff.

eight extant treatises combine with these to form a full course of instruction in the musical art, at its most critical and personal in the *Proportionale musices*, but culminating in the magisterial *Liber de arte contrapuncti*, dedicated to King Ferrante and dated 11 October 1477.[706] As far as we know, only *De inventione et usu musicae* followed this; the *Complexus* was incorporated into this *Hauptwerk*.[707] With these two major books, Tinctoris breaks the mould of medieval music theory. The 'Art of counterpoint' is the first book written to show how first-rank composers use – or should use – musical techniques, and *De inventione* (of which only a small part is extant) is essentially a history and criticism of music and musical performance. This work, at least, could not have been written without the experiences of Italian humanist writing about contemporary reality, pioneered by such men as Leon Battista Alberti.

A humble foundation for professional Italian theory was the craft of church-men and especially regulars (above all Benedictines, Franciscans and Carmelites), who left innumerable small tracts on plainsong, solmization, modes and psalm-tones, proportions and simple discant rules including extemporized discant 'from the plainsong book' (*supra librum*).[708]

Music theory was also traditionally an occupation in civic, cathedral and, of course, university circles. These qualifications are partly applicable to Ugolino da Orvieto (*c.* 1380–1457), a priest at the cathedrals of Forlì and Ferrara, whose five-volume *Declaratio musice discipline* (*c.*1430–35) is in its first books of particular interest for the discussions of the tone-system.[709] They are fully applicable to the Carthusian Johannes Gallicus (Legrense) from Namur (*c.*1415–73), and to John Hothby (*c.*1410–87), the English Carmelite who was Legrense's fellow-student at Pavia University before going to Florence and Lucca. Legrense stresses in his own writings that he had learned musical practice in France but music theory under Vittorino da Feltre, the humanist and educator of the Mantuan court. It is difficult to discover a 'humanist bent' (C. Adkins) in either Legrense's works or Vittorino's attitude to music, except that they esteemed Boethius above all later authors.[710] Legrense became the teacher of Burtius and Gaffurius (see below). Mantua, and the Carmelites in that town who in the 1470s collected some of the treatises in the Faenza Codex (see p. 298), are probably another link between Vittorino, Legrense and Hothby. A product of similar circles is perhaps the treatise *De preceptis artis musice* by a certain Guillelmus Monachus who discusses and contrasts English and Italian discant

---

[706] A description – not in chronological order – is in Reese, *Renaissance*, 140–48. The most recent edition (but not the last, it is hoped) is Tinctoris, *Opera theoretica*.

[707] Weinmann, *Tinctoris*; Ronald Woodley, 'The printing and scope of Tinctoris' fragmentary treatise *De inventione et usu musice*', *EMH* 5 (1985), 239–68.

[708] As an example of many, see the treatises discussed in Pier Paolo Scattolin, '"La regola del grado" nella teoria medievale del contrapunto', *RIM* 14 (1979), 52–74.

[709] See, for example, Andrew Hughes, 'Ugolino: the monochord and musica ficta', *MD* 23 (1969), 21–39; Berger, *Musica ficta*, 124 f.

[710] See Cecil Adkins, 'Legrense, Johannes' in *The New Grove*; Palisca, *Humanism*, 280–82; Gilbert Reaney, 'The musical theory of John Hothby', *RBM* 42 (1988), 119–33. The study at Pavia together with Hothby is mentioned in the latter's *Dialogus in arte musica* (Hothby, *Tres tractatuli*, 51 f).

practices, notably fauxbourdon and falsobordone.[711] This practical bent, and the fact that *falsobordoni* were then used for extemporized liturgical music in Italian cathedrals, makes it likely that Guillelmus was one of the many foreigners serving as *magistri cantus* in these institutions. That he describes the *falsobordoni* as being used 'among us' ('apud nos') does not prove that he was an Italian himself.

Hothby's treatises are known in partly overlapping manuscript versions, some of which are in Faenza; some may be revisions by his students or colleagues.[712] (He himself revised the first book of Ugolino's *Declaratio*.) The *Dialogus in arte musica* seems to have originated at the cathedral of Lucca in the form of orally delivered lectures which students wrote out. In this treatise, Hothby quotes compositions and authors he and his students knew, partly from the Lucca Choirbook which he was using in performance (see also p. 591). Hothby's major work is entitled *Calliopea legale*, an explanation of the tone-system which he wrote in, or had translated into, Italian. He allows hexachords to be transposed to several scale-degrees other than G, C and F, in order to legitimize accidentals. This approach was attacked by the Spanish theorist Bartolomeo Ramos de Pareja (*c.*1440–*c.*1491) in his important *Musica practica*. This book was printed in 1482 at Bologna, where Ramos had settled in 1472, hoping to obtain a university chair of music, and where he had apparently gathered a circle of students at the Spanish College. Ramos's main point was a vehement criticism of the (Pythagorean) interval system as established by Boethius, and of the solmization system as designed by Guido of Arezzo. In place of the former, he proposed the harmonic division of the fifth, resulting in just tuning for the major and minor thirds (5 : 4 and 6 : 5). In place of the latter, he suggested new solmization syllables (*Psal-li-tur per vo-ces is-tas*), covering a full octave and fully transposable.[713] Both innovations have, with some modification, been accepted by the musicians of later centuries, thanks not least to the defence of Ramos by his student Giovanni Spataro, choirmaster at S Petronio of Bologna between 1505 and 1541. Ramos's opponents were the circle of Hothby, with his followers Gaffurius and Nicolaus Burtius of Parma (*c.*1450–after 1518), as well as Hothby himself in two small treatises, the *Excitatio* and the *Epistola*. (Hothby's *Dialogus in arte musica* is not directed against Ramos as has been believed, but was written in the 1470s without any reference to Ramos.) Ramos owed his new ideas partly to his teacher at Salamanca University, Pedro de Osma (probably Pedro Martínez de Osma, *d.*1480). His practical training in music had begun under Juan de Monte, a papal chaplain 1447–57; he knew the composers Tristano de Silva and Johannes Wreede. Another significant aspect of Ramos's thinking was his identification of the eight modes not only with

---

[711] Andrew Hughes, 'Guillelmus Monachus' in *The New Grove*.

[712] See John Hothby, *De arte contrapuncti*, ed. Gilbert Reaney, CSM 26 (Rome: AIM, 1977), with an inventory of the theoretical contents of the Faenza Codex; Reaney, 'The musical theory' (see n. 710).

[713] Clemente Terni ed., *Música práctica de Bartolomé Ramos de Pareja*, 2 vols. (Madrid: Joyas Bibliográficas, 1983) (facs edn Spanish translation and commentary), vol. 1, 108–14 and 191–7.

ancient deities but also with human passions allegedly governed by these deities: a construction which was to influence later theories of affections.[714] Ramos's Spanish–Italian circle in Bologna was apparently the addressee also of a conservative tract, the *In enchiridion* by Guillermo Despuig (de Podio); the same author's larger work *Ars musicorum* was printed in Valencia in 1495.[715]

A similarly conservative but much more widely informed approach was that of Franchinus Gaffurius.[716] Although most famous as a music theorist, he had a cathedral career; in his youth he sang at the cathedral of his home town, Lodi, where he also studied music theory with Johannes Bonadies (Godendach), a Carmelite friar of the circle of John Hothby. From 1474 to 1476, he was at Mantua – conceivably to pursue his studies with the Carmelite theorists (see p. 298). This was followed by brief appointments at Verona and Genoa. From 1478 to 1480, Gaffurius lived in Naples, frequented the court, befriended Tinctoris, published his *Theoricum opus* and directed the music at SS Annunziata, the Carmelite church. Then he returned north to teach singing boys at the castle of the Bishop of Lodi, to direct the cathedral music at Bergamo, and finally (1484) to obtain the position of *magister cantus* at the duomo of Milan, where he also lectured on music in the *studio* founded in 1492 by Duke Lodovico Sforza.

Several of Gaffurius's important works were printed, for example the *Theoricum opus* of 1480, the *Theorica musicae* of 1492 and the *Practica musicae* of 1496. The theoretical books have a long ancestry in speculative thinking about music. More precisely, such an ancestry is being recovered here, as Gaffurius is one of the first writers to give a comprehensive survey of Greek thinking about music with respect to the aesthetics of music-making as well as the structure of the tonal system. He omits all reference to newer theories promoting, for example, non-Pythagorean divisions of the scale. The *Practica musicae* follows Tinctoris's pathbreaking approach in designing a course in composition from the rudiments to artistic counterpoint, save that Gaffurius is side-tracked in mathematical proportions – his favourite subject in the *Theorica musicae* – and does not explore new aspects of the musical art.

Sacred polyphony in the courtly sphere

For many observers today, the most characteristic manifestation of 'Renaissance in music' is the sacred music with which Franco-Netherlands composers

---

[714] See Palisca, *Humanism*, 12 f and 232 f, and Harrán, *Word-Tone Relations*, 92 ff, on Tinctoris, Gaffurius and Burtius.

[715] Reprint edn by Giuseppe Vecchi (Bologna: Forni, 1976); Terni ed., *Música práctica* (n. 713). On Ramos, Despuig and other Spanish theorists of the period, see Stevenson, *Spanish Music*, 50–101; *idem*, 'Spanish musical impact', 125–37. Tinctoris, in turn, influenced Spanish theory, as seen in the manuscript treatise *E-E c. III. 23*, dated Seville, 1480.

[716] For a worklist and evaluation, see Clement A. Miller, 'Gaffurius, Franchinus' in *The New Grove*; *idem*, 'Early Gaffuriana'. Essentially different aspects of Gaffurius's standing as a theorist have been stressed in Walter Kreyszig, *Franchino Gaffurio's Theorica Musicae (1492): Edition, Translation, and Study of Sources*, Ph.D., Yale U., 1989.

celebrated the patronage of Italian princes. What was there to be celebrated? Maecenatism celebrates itself; the prince pays the artist to create a work which celebrates the prince's paying of the artist.[717] This slightly paradoxical situation can also be viewed from a negative angle. When Josquin's patron, Cardinal Ascanio Sforza – so the story goes – failed to pay him in time, the composer set the frottola 'El grillo è buon cantore': a song about the never-tiring cricket who sings 'for love' even when he receives no food. According to others, Josquin then set the frottola 'In te, Domine, speravi' ('I have set my hope in thee, oh Lord').[718] In this way does he celebrate the fact that the prince was *not* paying him? This and similar anecdotes are as true or untrue as anecdotes usually are. Patronage could even have been involved if the story was fabricated, for posterity's sake: 'Please, Josquin, write me a piece that makes it look as if you needed more money – and you'll get it.' If Ascanio had really been mean, I wonder whether Josquin would have composed even 'El grillo' for him.

Although there was a Milanese singer Karlo Grillo,[719] the article 'el' in the song text conforms with Roman or southern dialect, and thus with a poet such as Serafino dall'Aquila. He was a 'compagno' of Josquin when the composer was in the service of Ascanio, perhaps *c.*1490.[720] The barzelletta with the refrain 'Lassa far a mi', often attributed to Serafino, is supposed to have given Josquin the idea of his Mass 'La sol fa re mi'. Another anecdote, reported by Glarean, turns this word-play once more into a charge of 'procrastination' of the cardinal in paying his musician.[721] It seems that it was not so much the patrons themselves who are relevant to art, but how people thought of them and how they have been received by posterity.

The humorous poem 'El grillo', set by Josquin in an onomatopoetic manner, says of the cricket that it does not behave like other 'birds' (!) who come and sing a little, but then move on. This recalls a letter by Duke Ercole d'Este of 1476, first published by David Fallows: 'My singers cannot pay their tithes just now because they are all people who live from day to day like the birds on the branches.'[722] Northern singers and instrumentalists frequently 'moved on' in Italy, sometimes of their own volition, sometimes being forced by their patron's sudden change of mind or by political circumstances. One such circumstance was the spectacular murder of Galeazzo Maria Sforza at Mass on St Stephen's Day, 1476. By manipulating the numbers which musical works inevitably comprise, it can be found that Josquin's Mass 'Ad fugam' encodes the date of

---

[717] See also Nanie Bridgman, 'Mécénat et Musique', in *IMS, Report on the Eighth Congress, New York, 1961* (Kassel etc., 1962), vol. 2, 19–30.

[718] This anecdote is accepted in Osthoff, *Josquin*, vol. 2, 204 f, mainly because copies of the two frottole are headed 'Josquin Dascanio'. Lowinsky, 'Ascanio Sforza's life', does not have it. See also Gallico, 'Josquin and the frottola', 450 ff.

[719] Barblan, 'Vita musicale', 826.

[720] Lowinsky, 'Ascanio Sforza's life', 51–60, covers every detail of that story.

[721] See Haar, '"Missa La sol fa re mi"', 564–6.

[722] Fallows, 'Contenance angloise', 189.

Galeazzo Maria's death as well as Josquin's own name. Similar methods reveal that his motet 'Illibata Dei virgo nutrix' which undoubtedly incorporates his name in an acrostic (see p. 640), refers, in *gematria* (number alphabet), to the Sforza patron as a male *nutrix* (feeder), and to his untimely end.[723] There is evidence, therefore, that artists and those who consume art – including modern scholars – are fascinated by the images of patrons and father-figures. If the fantastic wealth of the Italian Renaissance rulers, their lavish spending on art and fine understanding of it, had not existed, art enthusiasts might have invented them anyway. The possibility exists, of course, that some of these *are* actually fairy-tales not facts.

Lewis Lockwood has probably directed the sharpest focus on musical patronage of the Italian Renaissance in his comparative 'portraits' of Ercole d'Este and Galeazzo Maria Sforza.[724] Relevant here also are Galeazzo Maria's 'recruiting letters', in which the word 'cappella' is first used with the meaning of 'a team of singers in princely service' (see p. 280), and which reveal rather than disguise the intention of robbing the Savoy chapel of its best musicians. The chapels were the direct objects of rivalry between the courts, and rivalry was one half of a dynasty's *raison d'être*, the other being war. As has already been said, the Sforzas and the Medicis had to catch up with the genuinely aristocratic houses in Europe; Italian chapels in general had to catch up with those of France, England and the pope – for no better reason than that they were not yet their equals.

It does seem, therefore, as if the Renaissance in music had been invented and intentionally created simply because people wanted it to happen. It was an idea of harmony, an artificial environment like the cool and beautiful fantasy towns designed in Italian paintings and intarsias. This was a good environment for music, especially the music of foreigners. Italian patrons put up with their instability, let them shuttle between courts or leave altogether (unless their self-esteem was hurt by a poaching rival). They probably did not want their foreign musicians to feel too much at home, preferring the Church to pay for their retirement pensions. In fact, they tried quite hard to get church benefices for them.[725]

But whose 'home' was Italy anyway? The peninsula was not a nation yet; a Roman was a foreigner in Milan or Venice. Some patrons were foreigners themselves, of course. Three major chapels on Italian soil – and they happened to be the oldest, with the most 'organic' development – were attached to foreign rulers: Savoy, Aragon and the papacy. The Savoy chapel was essentially a French body, and orientated towards the west. It had seen better days under Dufay in the 1430s and 50s; around 1470, the music practised in Chambéry and Turin

---

[723] Gösta Neuwirth, 'Erzählung von Zahlen', in Heinz-Klaus Metzger and Rainer Riehn eds, *Josquin des Prés* (Munich: Edition Text & Kritik, 1982), 3–38.

[724] Lockwood, 'Strategies'.

[725] Lowinsky, 'Ascanio Sforza's life', 34–40; Lockwood, 'Strategies', 238–41.

could no longer compare with that of Burgundy.[726] In the *Regno di Sicilia*, as the Anjou/Aragonese kingdom in southern Italy was traditionally called, the royal chapel developed as a huge and complex agglomeration of ecclesiastical and musical personnel coming from Iberian and Italian towns.[727]

The papal *curia* was not an Italian institution. As shown in our first chapter, the idea of having northern singers was based on the Avignonese tradition, transferred to Rome. The history and structure of papal benefices was inter-related with the success of the Netherlanders at the *curia*: the pope's ability to reward his chaplains and other servants was greatest if they came from the north-western corner of the Holy Roman Empire.[728] These accidents of church history were principally responsible for the model status of the papal chapel in Italy, and for the Italian flowering of Franco-Netherlands music from *c.*1470 onwards. Just as they had grabbed the papacy itself – being entitled to it, of course – thus the Italians appropriated the northern music and musicians.

Looking at the Italian cultural landscape before *c.*1470, one would have expected the practice of sacred polyphony to grow naturally as it did elsewhere. What happened in fact was a total transformation of the role of music in Italian society. It was the result of a conscious, and partly long-planned, cultural campaign.

In the Aragonese chapel of *c.*1440–70, and in Florence, energetic leaders had looked after the wellbeing of their musical services. King Alfonso of Aragon, and his son Ferrante I (*r.* 1458–94), cultivated their private chapel in the fortress of Naples in the inherited royal forms. The Medici did not actually figure as the employers of church musicians: this task devolved upon the two civic guilds who were the overseers of the church, the *arte della lana* and the *arte di calimala* (the wool and cloth merchants). But the Medici, as the most powerful banking family in Florence, efficiently deployed their international connections to find the best chapel singers in the north. Angelo Tani and Tommaso Portinari in Bruges regularly helped to find singers; special agents such as Fruoxino and Simone Nori were sent to France and Flanders for the same purpose.[729] The Aragonese of Naples, in turn, drew on their Iberian hinterland as well as on trade connections in France and the Netherlands; their main agents were the ex-Florentine banking house of the Strozzi.

Almost casually, Dufay had become a correspondent of both cities; the laments he composed on the Fall of Constantinople in 1453 were sent to him from Naples (by a Strozzi agent?), and in 1456 he wrote to Piero and Giovanni de' Medici, almost as if seeking employment.[730] One of his patrons was the Floren-

---

[726] For a brief overview, see Marie-Thérèse Bouquet, 'La cappella musicale dei duchi di Savoia', *RIM* 3 (1968), 233–85.

[727] See the excellent discussion in Atlas, *Aragonese Court*, ch. 2.

[728] See Starr, *Papal Court*, ch. 1 ('Ars et praxis beneficiorum'). A detailed case study is Christopher Reynolds, 'Musical careers, ecclesiastical benefices, and the example of Johannes Brunet', *JAMS* 37 (1984), 49–97.

[729] See D'Accone, 'Singers', especially 310–24, about the vicissitudes of those decades.

[730] Fallows, *Dufay*, 71.

tine banker Francesco Sassetti, for some time a Medici agent in Flanders. In 1467, Dufay's friend the Florentine organist Antonio Squarcialupi asked him to set a poem by Lorenzo de' Medici. More officially, Dufay must then have assisted in sending singers from Cambrai and Douai. The Medici agent Simone Nori in Bruges, and the resident Medici banker Tommaso Portinari, were the main actors in this episode which brought one of the best Flemish singers, the *tenorista* Jean Cordier, to Italy.[731] This happened in the context of a 'reopening' of the chapel in 1467 after a short period of decline. Generally, the Florentine tradesmen imported people like other goods, such as works of art and musical instruments.[732]

Also characteristic of this period is the inner-Italian circulation of musicians, some of them assuming the role of agents or double-agents in the rival dealings of the princes. The French singers at the Neapolitan court, Filippo da Dortenche and Jachetto di Marvilla, fall in this category.[733] Whenever it seemed convenient, musicians were sent from one court to another as a diplomatic favour – for example the Neapolitan organist Joan Corbatò to Milan in 1463, or the famous organist and organ-builder Isaac Argyropoulos from Florence to Naples in 1472.[734]

This period is further characterized by the only occasional appearances of composers. Even they were appreciated, it seems, first and foremost as singers. From *c.*1450 to *c.*1470, the papal chapel had only one composer in its ranks (as far as we know today): Johannes Pullois. No sacred music by him is extant that can have been composed after 1455. The situation in Naples was a little different. The Spanish composers Johannes Cornago and Pere Oriola worked there in the 1450s.[735] Johannes Vincenet may have been in the chapel as early as 1458; he was dead by 1479.[736] His four cantus firmus Masses and four secular works can all have been written before *c.*1470. His excellent chanson 'Fortune, par ta cruauté' appears to echo 'Ma maistresse' (bars 18–22); in the Masses, there is much parody and paraphrase of the models as might be sought in Ockeghem and Faugues. Interestingly, three of his cantus firmi have central European connections: the 'Missa sine nomine' is based on a song in Glogau, 'Zersundert ist das junge herze mein';[737] the models 'Entrepris suis' (a rondeau by Bartolomeus Brolo of *c.*1430) and 'O gloriosa regina mundi' by Johannes Tour-

---

[731] D'Accone, 'Singers', 322 f; Strohm, *Bruges*, 37 f.

[732] Further details are in Armand Grunzweig, 'Notes sur la musique des Pays-Bas au XVe siècle', *Bulletin de l'Institut historique belge de Rome* 18 (1937), 73–88; Abi Warburg, *Flandrische Kunst und Florentinische Frührenaissance*, in A.W., *Gesammelte Schriften*, vol. 1 (Leipzig, 1932), 185–206 and 370–80.

[733] Atlas, *Aragonese Court*, 37–40; Lockwood, *Ferrara*, 166 f.

[734] Atlas, *Aragonese Court*, 42.

[735] For further details, see *ibid.*, 58–71.

[736] Vincenet, *Collected Works*, introduction. The editor, Bertran E. Davis, favours an identification with the papal chaplain of 1429, Johannes Vincinetti, who was a priest, whereas the Neapolitan singer was married.

[737] As identified by Adelyn Peck, *The Manuscript Trent 91: A New Assessment*, Unpublished paper, AMS, 53rd Annual Meeting, New Orleans, 1987.

ont (before 1460?) were well known in central Europe. Unless Vincenet was perhaps in Austria himself, he could have had contacts with centres like Ferrara and Modena Cathedral, where German musicians worked and where German tunes were heard.

Music for the chapels was still largely being imported. We do not know much on the circumstances, but singers travelling to Italy for employment probably carried many works with them. Four Masses by Dufay were carried southwards from Picardy by the singer Gile Crépin in 1468/9.[738] The Aragonese chapel had, among other music books, one 'Liber regius' which contained a Credo by Binchois, quoted in Tinctoris's *Proportionale musices*.[739]

This situation was now going to change radically. Around 1466–71, three young rulers came to power who must have planned long beforehand to establish themselves in the great series of musical patrons. Their polyphonic chapels were to outdo even England, royal France and Burgundy. We have already said something about the musical interests of Lorenzo de' Medici who came to power in 1469.[740] Under him, the number and quality of the singers of S Giovanni increased significantly. From 1478, the (mostly Italian) cathedral singers were separated from them; the more specialized group served S Giovanni and the SS Annunziata. In the 1480s and early 1490s, we find in the latter group foreign composers such as Arnolfo Giliardi, Giovanni Pintelli, Arrigo d'Ugo (= Isaac), 'Martino' (= Johannes Martini, 1485), Alexander Agricola (1491–2), Pietrequin Bonnel and Hermannus de Atrio.[741]

Galeazzo Maria Sforza became duke in 1466, Ercole I d'Este in 1471. The wealth and political power gathered by their predecessors, and the more refined education which they had been accorded themselves, combined to a form of patronage which was as informed as it was irresponsible. Already in 1469, Galeazzo Maria had two French singers sent to him from Naples, Antonio Pons and Raynero. By October 1471, the priest Raynero 'our musician' is sent to England to recruit 'musicos et cantores'. The letter of introduction to King Edward IV emphasizes Galeazzo's wish to 'adorn his chapel with perfect musicians and singers, who can satisfy Us in singing and music' (three times in

---

[738] Fallows, *Dufay*, 75–6 and 245. We do not know whether Crépin left the works in Savoy where he stayed, or took them as far as Rome where he was heading for.

[739] Tinctoris, *Opera theoretica*, vol. IIa, 45. It must be assumed that many works quoted by Tinctoris in his writings up to 1476 were extant in Aragonese chapel books. The claim that he quoted from the papal codices *CS 14* and *CS 51* (see n. 752) is the more unlikely as these manuscripts are probably a little younger.

[740] It should not be forgotten that Lorenzo himself travelled to France and Flanders in 1466. See A. Rochon, *La jeunesse de Laurent de Médicis (1449–1478)* (Paris, 1963) (with details on music).

[741] See D'Accone, 'Singers', 331 ff; *idem*, *A Documentary History of Music at the Florentine Cathedral and Baptistry during the 15th Century*, Ph.D., Harvard U., 1960; *idem*, 'Heinrich Isaac in Florence: new and unpublished documents', *MQ* 49 (1963), 464–83. 'Martino', who sang in 1485 at S Giovanni, is not Piero Martini; the reference to this man in *A Documentary History*, 203 and 212 n., has been overlooked as strong evidence that the composer Johannes Martini was also briefly employed in Florence, and did not only visit there in 1487 on his way to Rome.

this letter, 'singing' and 'music' are distinguished).[742] Galeazzo then makes various attempts, partly successful, to depopulate the chapel of Duchess Jolanda of Savoy, sends in 1472 the experienced singer Thomas Leporis to the court of France with a letter to Ockeghem ('Domino Johanni Oken') to help him 'conduct a few singers' into Galeazzo's service, and starts a particularly well-prepared campaign in the Netherlands, where he sends the musician Gaspar van Weerbeke on two trips in April 1472 and January 1473, equipped with letters of introduction to Duke Charles the Bold and to the Medici bank in Bruges, as well as with money to give to the recruitees for the travel. The success of these efforts is well known. The two groups of singers which Galeazzo Maria maintained under the names of 'chapel' and 'chamber' singers,[743] included by the end of 1474 a total of 40 outstanding singers, among them Loyset Compère, Josquin des Prez, Alexander Agricola, Johannes Martini, and the masters Antonio Guinati (*cappella*) and Gaspar van Weerbeke (*camera*), who were called 'abbate' and 'vice-abbate', respectively. The pay was high – an average of 10 ducats per month – but in addition, ecclesiastical benefices were provided for some singers, including one for Josquin in 1473.[744] Josquin was, unlike Weerbeke and others, almost a local man, having sung in the cathedral choir, under the chapelmaster Santino Taverna, from 1459 until December 1472 (with interruptions).[745] Galeazzo Maria's chapel foundation in the Castello Sforzesco was intended to give the duke private access to artistic service music; it is logical that in the years before, he took recourse to the cathedral services. He would not perhaps have considered hiring Josquin, and giving him a church benefice almost immediately, had he not known his abilities well before 1473. Despite the assassination of Galeazzo Maria in 1476, and a partial dissolution of the chapel, its development was not essentially harmed until the interruption of Sforza rule in 1499.

The building of the Ferrarese chapel, more or less from scratch, was the heartfelt wish and great achievement of Ercole d'Este (1431-1505), probably since his youthful years when he heard the chapel of Leonello.[746] Ercole I is a very interesting figure in this context because his patronage overlaps in a strange way with his religious fervour (see also p. 612). There is a touch of escapism to Ercole's cultural efforts; less powerful than his rival and ally Sforza, more threatened by national and international tensions (Venice, the Empire, the papacy, France), the Este family had to show splendour and strength without offending anyone.

Ercole's campaigns were not aggressive but very well prepared, it seems. Like Galeazzo Maria Sforza, he was from the start interested in good singing as well

---

[742] This and the following notices after Motta, *Musici*, 301 ff; Barblan, 'Vita musicale', 820 ff.

[743] This probably followed Burgundian precedent; at least in the 1490s, the Burgundian chapel was organized in this way. See Doorslaer, 'Chapelle'.

[744] Lowinsky, 'Ascanio Sforza's life', 33-40.

[745] Sartori, 'Josquin', especially 68 ff.

[746] On all these matters, see Lockwood, *Ferrara*, chaps. 12-16.

as composing skills. In 1471, he wrote to Constance for one particular singer and composer, Johannes Martini; he got him and also another, Johannes Bon, plus many choirboys (see p. 509), for whom Galeazzo notably did not compete (see p. 280). Ercole used the German boys as a chorus in alternation with the men; later, he had a double choir of adults at least for Vespers services, and an impressive repertory of double-choir music was assembled, composed largely by Martini (see p. 612). Already a recruitee of 1471, the Frenchman and first *maistro de cappella* Johannes Brebis, was a composer as well. Later came Alexander Agricola (1474 if not already 1470), Johannes Japart (1477–81), Jacob Obrecht (1487–8), Johannes Ghiselin-Verbonnet (*c.*1489–92), Josquin, who was chapelmaster in 1503–4, and finally again Obrecht, who succeeded Josquin but died in 1505 of the plague. An often-told story is that of the invitation of Obrecht from Bruges in 1487. In order to persuade the chapter of St Donatian's to give Obrecht a leave of absence, Duke Ercole sent Johannes Cordier, not only a highly respected singer but also a priest and canon of that same church, and a personal friend of Obrecht, plus Cornelius de Lilloo (Laurenti), one of the best-known singer–agents at Ferrara and Florence. What seems most telling is that Ercole told the Bruges canons that he already knew and loved Obrecht's music.[747] This evidence matches the famous correspondence of the duke with his agent Gian in 1502, in which the latter compares the respective merits of Josquin and Isaac, both of whom were considered as new chapelmasters. Everything the agent says about them favours Isaac, except that he has to admit that Josquin 'composes better'. As a result, Josquin was hired.[748] In these and other cases, it is the music to be newly composed which this patron was pursuing. Inducements and rewards to his composers included the promise of church benefices as well as pay; the duke's efforts were only partly successful.[749]

The fourth important centre of sacred music, the papal chapel, is not very well studied for this particular period. Recruitment campaigns in the north must have taken place; the popes also found many singers in Italian chapels, for example when they were being restructured or disbanded (such as the Sforza chapel in 1477).[750] Pope Sixtus IV (1471–84), the founder of the Sistine Chapel, and his successors Innocent VIII (1484–92) and Alexander VI (1492–1503), employed the composers Guillaume Garnier (*c.*1474–83), Gaspar van Weerbeke (1481–9), Marbriano de Orto (1483–*c.*1499), Bertrand Vaqueras (1483–1507), Josquin des Prez (1486, 1489–94), Johannes Stokem (1487–9), Crispin van Stappen (1493–1507) and Juan Escribano (1502).[751]

The Este court and the papal chapel are the only courts of this period in Italy for which we have a number of polyphonic choirbooks documenting their

---

[747] The circumstances of Obrecht's visit are all recapitulated in Picker, *Ockeghem and Obrecht*, 43–6.
[748] Lockwood, *Ferrara*, 203–5.
[749] See Lockwood, *Ferrara*, chaps. 17 and 18.
[750] See Lowinsky, 'Ascanio Sforza's life', 40 f. The pope had already in 1450 'inherited' singers from a disbanded chapel, that of Ferrara: see Starr, *Papal Court*, 96 ff.
[751] See Haberl, *Bausteine* III, 42–60. A comprehensive account of the later period is Richard J. Sherr, *The Papal Chapel ca. 1492–1513 and its Polyphonic Sources*, Ph.D., Princeton U., 1975.

repertories. The 'Cappella Sistina' choirbooks – so named because of their presumed use in Pope Sixtus IV's new private chapel which was later decorated by Michelangelo – are a long series of manuscripts beginning with chantbooks. The earliest codices with polyphony are the Mass codices *CS 14* and *51* (both *c*.1475–80, plus later additions), the motet and hymn collection *CS 15*, and the codices *35* and *26* (*c*.1485–1500). Music performed before 1500 is still contained in several later manuscripts.[752]

In June 1471, Our Lady's Church at Courtrai (Flanders) paid for the wine of some 'singers from out of town, who sang discant in the church on their way to the king of Naples' (*cantoribus extraneis discantantibus in hac ecclesia pergentibus penes Regem neopolitanum*).[753] The emigration of Franco-Netherlands musicians to the chapels of other countries was in full swing. We know some of the reasons: in 1482, the singer Johannes de Vos of Bruges threatened to leave for the chapel of King Matthias Corvinus of Hungary, having been promised much better pay there, whereas in Bruges he could 'hardly live on his salary'.[754] It is not known whether Matthias and his Queen Beatrice launched an aggressive recruitment campaign, but in the early 1480s they apparently reconstituted their chapel at Buda, previously resembling central European models, and now emulating the Italian manner. Its new master became Johannes (de) Stokem from Liège, a good composer and friend of Tinctoris; the theorist's influence on Queen Beatrice of Aragon has been made responsible for this appointment which seems to have lasted from *c*.1483 to *c*.1487. Pietrobono de Burcellis visited the court in 1488 (at Vienna and Buda), and Barbireau from Antwerp visited in 1490, apparently on a recommendation to Beatrice from Maximilian of Habsburg.[755]

What is known on the Spanish and Portuguese royal chapels of *c*.1450 to *c*.1500 suggests a greater independence from France and the Netherlands than in Italy. Whereas King Alfonso of Aragon, when residing in Barcelona (1416–42), had employed northern singers, organists and minstrels, in the list given for the chapel of the 'Catholic monarchs' in 1477 the *maestro* Urrede is the only foreigner among thirteen members; no foreigner at all seems to be present in 1498-9.[756] The chapel of Philip the Fair, who in 1496 had married Juana of Spain and was thus the heir apparent to the realm, visited the country

---

[752] See *CC*, vol. 4, 28–63; Adalbert Roth, *Studien zum frühen Repertoire der päpstlichen Kapelle unter dem Pontifikat Sixtus IV (1471-1484) Die Chorbücher 14 und 51 des Fondo Capella Sistina der Biblioteca Apostolica Vaticana*, Ph.D., Frankfurt/Main, 1982, who reconstructed some of the early history of these books, hypothesizes that *CS 14* and *51* were written in Naples and used by Tinctoris, *c*.1474. They must be younger, however, and Tinctoris used only some of their works in different copies, as I hope to show in a forthcoming study. On the choirbooks of the Este court, see Lockwood, *Ferrara*, 213–27, and below.

[753] Rijksarchief, Kortrijk, Onze-Lieve-Vrouw, Computus prebendarum 1471, p. 12.

[754] Bisschoppelijk Archief, Brugge, Acta Capitularia S.Donatiani, reeks A.2, vol. 55, 14 August 1482.

[755] See, respectively: José Quitin, 'Stokem, Johannes de' in *The New Grove*; Elly Kooiman, 'The biography of Jacob Barbireau (1455–1491) reviewed', *TVNM* 38 (1988), 36–42; Fökövi, 'Musik'.

[756] Anglés, *La música*, 49 (see also 50–61). Voice designations are 'triple', 'tenor', 'contra' and 'contrabaxus'.

in 1501 and 1505. Although these were pompous occasions, they cannot account for much Netherlands musical influence in Spain at that particular time. The many indigenous composers of sacred music, headed by Juan de Anchieta and Francisco de Peñalosa, were able to supply the liturgical repertory for the court, the emphasis of which resembles that of Naples: much music for Matins and Vespers, Holy Week services, hymns.[757]

The over 150 Netherlands works in the Segovia MS (c.1500) still demand a convincing explanation. There are 33 songs, mostly by Obrecht, with Dutch/Flemish incipits, and apart from these, the preferred authors are (in this order) Obrecht, Isaac, Agricola, Compère and Tinctoris. These masters had nothing to do with Spain except for Alexander Agricola, a member of the chapel of Philip the Fair, who died, like his suzerain, in Castile in 1506. The name of Pierre de la Rue, another prominent member of that chapel, is totally absent. Many of the secular pieces are florid arrangements of famous chanson tunes in an instrumental style. In the sections with sacred music, the only indigenous composer whose works are intermixed with the foreign ones, is Juan de Anchieta.[758] I suggest that the manuscript was compiled (perhaps by a person close to Anchieta) from a number of previous sources, which happened not to include the most recent sacred music sung at the Habsburg court.

Pierre de la Rue (c.1450–1518) and his early career are a mysterious subject in any case. He seems to have been in circulation as a *tenoriste* in Netherlands churches in the 1470s and early 1490s, but apparently was also at Siena Cathedral in the 1480s; he joined the Habsburg–Burgundian chapel about 1492. It is difficult if not impossible to prove that any extant work of this great master was written before c.1498, when two works by him were entered in the Chigi Codex.[759]

Whatever may be said about Italian influences on Franco-Netherlands composers after c.1470, the greater opportunities for the composition and performance of sacred music were an undeniable factor. The chapels at Milan, Ferrara, Florence and elsewhere needed *repertories*: new Mass and Office music, devotional and liturgical pieces. All this they got; only a small part of it was now brought from beyond the Alps. The repertorial requirements at Milan and Ferrara were special. Ferrara introduced the practice of double-choir singing, which does not seem to have played an important role in the north. At Milan, the court chapel used so-called *motetti missales*, substitute motets replacing Mass Ordinary items. In the sources (mainly the cathedral choirbooks assembled by Gaffurius), they are usually labelled 'in place of the Gloria, Credo' (*loco Gloria, loco Credo*) etc. and grouped in cycles, so that no doubt exists as

---

[757] A description, arranged by composer, is in Stevenson, *Spanish Music*, 127–200. Anglés, *La música*, contains six Mass cycles by Anchieta, Peñalosa, Pedro de Escobar and Alonso de Alba.

[758] See *CC*, vol. 3, 137; Anglés, *La música*, 106–12.

[759] See Jozef Robijns, *Pierre de la Rue (circa 1460–1518). Een bio–bibliographische studie* (Brussels, 1954); Martin Staehelin, 'Pierre de la Rue in Italien', *AMw* 27 (1970), 128–37. I am preparing a study on some documents likely to refer to his early career.

to when they were sung.[760] Six cycles are found in Gaffurius's books I–III: three by Loyset Compère, two by Weerbeke and one by Gaffurius. Two anonymous cycles have been found in the Leopold Codex of Innsbruck – that is to say in its layer datable *c.*1476.[761]

The usual make-up of these cycles is seven or eight motets, to replace the introit, Gloria, Credo, offertory, Sanctus, Agnus Dei and Deo gratias; there is normally also an extra motet for the Elevation of the Host. There is no Kyrie substitute: a precious clue that the performances took place in services following the Ambrosian rite (as established in Lombardy by St Ambrose in the fourth century), in which there is no independent Kyrie section. There are no other pointers to the Ambrosian ritual in the music; this 'problem' recurs with single motets and other Masses also written under the Sforza rule. It is not really a problem, however, because Ambrosian and Roman rites had coexisted in Lombardy for centuries, and the court chapel was not subject to the diocesan rite in any case.[762] Gaffurius himself, who collected these works for use at the cathedral, refers to them also as 'mottetti ducales', which seems to prove that they were not of cathedral but courtly origin.[763] The texts of the *motetti missales* and also of many single Milanese motets are peculiar: almost always they are pastiche-work, composed from sections of plainsong texts and prayers or *cantiones*, and they give the impression of having originated in a free, even whimsical selection. They were apparently the result of ducal wishes, not of a liturgically sanctioned practice. Gaffurius, who worked under Sforza rule, honoured the fashion by collecting the cycles; other editors such as Petrucci tore them apart and treated them as ordinary single motets.

Josquin des Prez, a chapel member like Weerbeke and Compère, apparently composed one such cycle, 'Vultum tuum deprecabuntur', which is nowhere preserved in its complete form of seven (or eight) sections. Besides, Josquin also included in his cantus firmus Mass 'D'ung aultre amer' a motet for the Elevation of the Host, 'Tu solus qui facis mirabilia'. This motet is typical of the Milanese style with its homorhythmic declamation, emphatic pauses, textural contrasts and short phrases.[764]

---

[760] See Thomas Noblitt, 'The Ambrosian Motetti Missales repertory', *MD* 22 (1968), 77–103; Ward, 'Motetti missales'.

[761] See the edition: Noblitt ed., *Kodex Leopold*. Some blatant scribal errors in the text of the first cycle have not been emended. This cycle is called 'Patris sapientia' and is a complete setting of the rhymed prayer on the seven Hours of the Passion by Egidio Colonna. See also Strohm, 'Zur Rezeption', 30–32. The existence of further possible cycles, all gathered in the half-destroyed fourth codex of Gaffurius, has been proposed in Ward, 'Motetti missales'; this would give us more cycles by Compère, Weerbeke and Gaffurius.

[762] Jacquelyn A. Mattfeld, 'An unsolved riddle – the apparent absence of Ambrosian melodies in the works of Josquin des Prez', in Lowinsky ed., *Josquin des Prez*, 360–67.

[763] Miller, 'Early Gaffuriana', 380–82.

[764] Josquin, *Werken*, fasc. 23, no. 11; also printed in *NAWM*, no. 29. The six-part 'Qui velatus facie fuisti' is probably not a *motetti missales* cycle. A convenient locator of Josquin's works, their sources and literature, is Charles, *Josquin des Prez*.

Music by Josquin and his competitors in Milan and Ferrara

The music written for Galeazzo Maria Sforza's chapel has often been discussed because such a strong 'team' of composers worked there together: with Josquin, Weerbeke, Compère, and the short-term visitors Agricola and Martini. Their music does seem to follow a common stylistic orientation.[765] Of these composers, only Josquin had been in Milan long before: he had been a singer of polyphony (*biscantor*) at the cathedral since 1459. He was an adult when reaching Milan from the north, perhaps from his presumed native area, Picardy. Thus, he may very well have composed for the cathedral, or even for the court, in the 1460s. There is no reason why some of his works which style criticism considers to be 'early' should not antedate 1472. His famous 'Ave Maria . . . virgo serena' was copied in the Leopold Codex *c.*1476 (see p. 521). It has traditionally been dated to the 1490s, by which time – so scholars thought – Josquin had reached the summit of his art. The text of 'Ave Maria . . . virgo serena' is exactly the kind of pastiche so often encountered in early Milanese motets.[766] The chronology of Josquin's works has to be remade from the beginning, and it will take a long time until some conflicting views can be reconciled and some old confusions cleared up.[767]

It is conceivable that Josquin alone had prepared some typical traits of the 'Milanese' style. This style can perhaps best be seen in the music of the younger and lesser composer, Loyset Compère. Not all of his works are in this style, of course; there is the earlier 'Omnium bonorum plena' (p. 479) and many pieces probably written for other French and Italian institutions. Compère must have been shuttling between Italy and the French court several times in the 1480s and 90s, before taking residence in northern cathedrals about 1500.

In Milan, he wrote much music on the pastiche texts just described. Of his three cycles of *motetti missales*, the earliest may be 'Ave Domine Jesu Christe' for four voices. There is also a four-voice Marian cycle for Christmas, 'Hodie nobis de Virgine', and a five-voice Marian cycle which is called 'Missa Galeazesca' in the source: perhaps a votive Mass commissioned by Duke Galeazzo Maria.

Little can be added to the style analyses of Finscher and Hudson.[768] Compère agrees with Weerbeke and Josquin in his declamatory, almost parlando word-setting, in small-motive imitations which are often pervasive and wander through the texture as in a *rondellus*; he has dramatic fermatas, simultaneous rests,

---

[765] An important contribution to this problem is Ludwig Finscher, 'Zum Verhältnis von Imitations-technik und Textbehandlung im Zeitalter Josquins', in Finscher ed., *Renaissance-Studien*, 57–72. The author speaks of a 'Milanese workshop'.

[766] Jacquelyn A. Mattfeld, 'Some relationships between texts and cantus firmi in the liturgical motets of Josquin des Pres', *JAMS* 14 (1961), 159–83, esp. 171–3.

[767] For the biographical basis, see Charles, *Josquin des Prez*; Jeremy Noble, 'Josquin Desprez' in *The New Grove*. Noble rejects the 1476 date for 'Ave Maria . . . virgo serena' without giving reasons. The composer's presence in Milan, 1459–72 (demonstrated in Sartori, 'Josquin', in 1956), has not sufficiently reoriented the traditional chronology which had placed the earliest works in the 1470s.

[768] Finscher, *Loyset Compère*; Joshua Rifkin and Barton Hudson, 'Compère, Loyset' in *The New Grove*.

changes of metre and sudden tutti entries, and also the constant variation of the texture pitching duets against duets, duets against trios, and so forth. Particularly in works for more than four voices, the complexity of events happening, for example, in a Regis motet, seems rationalized into a series of predictable, medium-sized phrases. Example 90 gives a series of 'chunks' from 'Ave Domine Jesu Christe':

Example 90 Loyset Compère, Mass 'Ave Domine Jesu Christe': Gloria

This type of music, particularly the pastoral dance-like section with its consonant sweetness and clear, word-dictated articulation, is not entirely unlike Josquin's 'Ave Maria...virgo serena'. Both are related to the musical type of the *lauda* given in Example 91:

Example 91 'Verbum caro factum est', MS Grey, no. 16

This Christmas carol is actually a cantus firmus setting of some merit. What Compère's piece derives from it, however, is the lilting, simplistic tone of the *lauda*. This tone pervades much Milanese music, and is a further clue that it was not liturgical tradition but individual taste that shaped the repertory here. Simplicity and humility was the aesthetic goal: but simplicity and humility displayed by masters of the art who had been fetched from across the Alps for high salaries.

Gaspar van Weerbeke (c.1445–after 1517) was at first the most successful of them. Unfortunately, he is one of those Netherlanders about whom we know nothing before they appear in Italy.[769] We do not know on what recommendation he made his rapid career at Milan in 1471–4 – being sent twice to Flanders to recruit singers, and appointed master of the *cappella da camera* in 1473. Glimpses of Gaspar's native environment are afforded by documents referring to a visit he paid to his home town, Oudenaarde. This was in 1489, and he was by then a seasoned member of the Sforza and papal chapels, having accumu-

---

[769] For his biography, see Gerhard Croll, 'Gaspar van Weerbeke: an outline of his life and works', *MD* 6 (1952), 67–81; *idem*, 'Weerbeke, Gaspar van' in *The New Grove*; Vander Straeten, *Musique*, vol. 6, 1–50. Pirro, *Histoire*, 210–14, discusses some of his music.

lated church benefices in Italy as well as in Flanders.[770] From 1495, he worked intermittently for the court of Philip the Fair, without severing his contacts with Milan, where he was enormously appreciated. After the fall of Ludovico il Moro in 1499, he returned to the papal chapel for the rest of his life. Weerbeke wrote several cantus firmus Masses and about twenty motets which were apparently appreciated, because Petrucci printed them; of his three cycles of *motetti missales*, the one for the Holy Ghost was printed in Petrucci's *Motetti libro quarto* (1505) alongside Josquin's cycle 'Vultum tuum deprecabuntur'.[771]

Weerbeke's independent motets are surely the most impressive part of his output, whereas the Masses show little beyond a somewhat bland and busy counterpoint. (His techniques there are closer to Ockeghem and Martini than to Dufay.) An excellent brief composition, which made an impression as early as Ambros, is the motet 'Virgo Maria, non est tibi similis', printed by Petrucci in 1502 but probably from Weerbeke's early period at Milan.[772]

After repeated hearing, it can be appreciated that the simplicity of form and declamation results from conscious compositional strategies. The first words 'Virgo Maria' are rhythmicized in all the four voices in such a way that the accented syllables 'Vir²' and '-ri²' receive the longest note-values. Even if the text underlay of the source were faulty, no different declamation could possibly be envisaged. Singers must have appreciated this – for example the bassus singer, whose first six bars are a crystal-clear motive. The tenor singer has the beautiful Phrygian ascent of the *Te Deum*, of Wreede's 'Nunca fué pena mayor' or Ockeghem's 'Missa Mi-mi' (see p. 475); surprisingly, the altus singer is given a well-rounded melody with the expressive conclusion of a falling fifth, and the cantus has an almost mystic tone, reiterating *e'* with only the slightest but an extremely expressive undulation a semitone above on the word 'Maria'. (This little undulation is echoed by the altus at the very end of the piece, on 'Christum'.) More dramatic events are reserved for the middle of the piece, for example the sudden opening into a B♭ sonority in bar 4, then the exciting climb of a tenth in the altus on 'similis' (bars 6–7), which is rhythmically patterned 3 + 2 + 2 + 2 + 3, or the florid lines of the same voice in bars 8–11. The imitation of cantus and tenor on the words 'inter omnes mulieres' involves two differentiated and somehow descriptive motives, leading to the midpoint cadence on the Phrygian tonic, E. The second half begins with paired imitation, a device which obviously reflects the word-pairs 'florens ut rosa', 'fragrans ut lilium'.

From bar 18, the full tutti takes over in mostly homorhythmic declamation – obviously, since the speakers identify themselves as 'we'. This piece, with its

---

[770] It seems that Gaspar is mentioned in other documents in Oudenaarde: in membership lists of the fraternity of Our Lady's (Kerkerchief Sint Walburga, Oudenaarde, Doos AA, no. 13, fol. 2v and 5v, and no. 14), 'her Jaspaert van den Kerchove, presbiter' is cited three times, once (no. 14) as 'for our Lady of Milan' ('voor onser vr(ouwen) van Milanen'). The lists are undated but may belong in the time when Bona Sforza was Duchess of Milan and officially Weerbeke's employer (1476–80).

[771] On Weerbeke's cycle, see Ward, 'Motetti missales', 503–8.

[772] Lenaerts ed., *Netherlanders*, no. 15.

simplicity of declamation and form, takes the attitude of a beautified but real prayer of real people, whether professional singers or the believers whom they represent. The devotional tone is also achieved by a certain modal sweetness – Phrygian mode interacting with 'C major' – which goes back to Ockeghem but now sounds forth with Italian clarity.

Ferrara had another challenge to offer to composers, and again one created by its duke. Ercole d'Este is described by contemporary chroniclers as a very devout man who liked nothing better than to be in church among his chapel singers and to pray – or in fact, to sing. On 7 December 1481, an agent of the duke of Mantua wrote home that he had found Ercole in the chapel 'in the midst of several singers, and after having sung a little at his leisure – not a song but *la sol fa* from Mass books – he drew me over to the window and listened to what your Excellence has written'.[773] It would not seem far-fetched to think that Ercole was actually trying out the *soggetto* of a newly composed Josquin Mass. There is a strong likelihood that Josquin des Prez was at Ferrara from early in 1480 to 30 September 1481 with his patron, Ascanio Sforza, and that he composed his celebrated Mass 'Hercules Dux Ferrarie' then.[774] The work is based on a little game with solmization syllables: the vowels of the formula 'Hercules Dux Ferrarie' are equated with the solmization syllables 're–ut–re–ut–re–fa–mi–re', which melody is used as cantus firmus. This technique of 'extracting' a melody from words (*soggetto cavato*) was probably widely known, since Ockeghem had contrived an enormous cryptic puzzle with it in his 'Ut heremita solus' (see p. 480). Duke Ercole might well be credited with having set the subject to Josquin, as Frederick the Great gave J. S. Bach his *thema regium*. In the Mass, Josquin repeats the theme as an ostinato, always in the tenor and in equal note-values (the monorhythm of central European chant settings?). He places it on the scale-degrees *d*, *a* and *d'*, recalling Busnois' ostinato tenor of 'In hydraulis'; he also retrogrades it. The contrapuntal web of the other voices successfully circumvents the limiting influence of the subject – a victory over severe limitations typical of Josquin.[775]

A striking contrast to this and other Ferrarese Masses is provided by the devotional, even austere, tone of most of the Office music which Ercole commissioned in large amounts and which he had ordered to be copied in special choirbooks. This music was performed by his chaplains *alternatim* – verse by verse – in a double-choir arrangement. A manuscript containing this music, *I-MOe α.M. I. 11–12 (olim lat.454 and 455)*, actually comprises two volumes, one for each choir. According to Lockwood, the set was completed in 1481.[776] The 65 anonymous psalm settings – about half of them for Holy Week – are

---

[773] Lockwood, *Ferrara*, 136. The translation given there is not entirely correct in so far as it implies that the singers only were singing.

[774] Lockwood, 'Josquin at Ferrara', in Lowinsky ed., *Josquin des Prez*, 108.

[775] A good discussion of the work is Lockwood, *Ferrara*, ch. 23.

[776] See *CC*, vol. 2, 166 f; Lockwood, *Ferrara*, 219 ff and ch. 24; Bukofzer, *Studies V*, 181–6.

mostly written in fauxbourdon in the manner of Dufay; besides, there are some Vespers hymns, *Magnificat* and two Passion settings. In the Passion of St Matthew, the choruses (*turbae*) are set for six voices in 'falsobordone style'.[777] As stated above (p. 283), this was not genuine choral music, because it was performed by a select chapel of specialists; but the roots of the style are certainly in Italian cathedral repertories, which were performed by the accomplished *biscantores* together with a choir of boys and clerics whom they taught. The Ferrarese psalms and Passion settings are all anonymous, but may well be the work of the chapelmasters Johannes Brebis (*d*.1479) and Johannes Martini, who is credited with about half of the other pieces.[778]

Of Martini's sacred works found in other sources, some must have been written for Ferrara. He worked there from 1473 to his death in 1497. His visits to Milan in 1474, to Florence in 1485, and to Rome in 1487 may have occasioned further sacred or secular compositions (see also below). It would be interesting to know when and where he wrote his splendid 'Salve regina' over 'Da pacem, Domine' and five other cantus firmi, which is not found in Ferrarese sources (presumably because the antiphon collection is simply lost).[779]

We have encountered the practice of setting the 'Salve regina' over extraneous cantus firmi in the Leopold Codex where Martini's setting was copied *c*.1476. I suggest that it belongs, together with the 'Salve regina' over secular songs by 'Ar. Fer.', to a repertory cultivated in the early 1470s among three related courts: Innsbruck, Ferrara and Milan. An exquisite specimen exists by the other composer besides Martini who also circulated in this area: Alexander Agricola. His 'Salve regina' (II)[780] – not found in the Leopold Codex but in other German sources – is built over the tenor of Jacob Obrecht's motet 'Ave regina celorum': a particularly complex derivation as Obrecht's work is in itself based on Walter Frye's antiphon setting of that name. Unlike Obrecht's Mass 'Ave regina celorum', which also uses Frye's setting, his motet transposes Frye's tenor down a third throughout, from the original Lydian to the Dorian mode. This, in turn, suited Agricola, who could now combine the (literally quoted) cantus firmus in the tenor with his paraphrases of the Dorian plainsong of the 'Salve regina' in the other voices (see Ex. 92).

It would be facile to interpret some of these lines as betraying 'Agricola the virtuoso of instrumental pieces' which he undoubtedly was. Rather, there is an effort here to combine irregularity with clarity. The extreme contrasts of contour and note-value in the various voices serve to articulate a large-scale work. Under the plainsong beginning of the cantus in long notes, the excited sequen-

---

[777] See Bukofzer, *Studies* V, mus. exx. 1 and 2.

[778] See also Masakata Kanazawa, 'Martini and Brebis at the Estense Chapel', in *Essays Presented to Myron Gilmore*, ed. S. Bertelli and G. Ramakus (Florence, 1978), 421–36.

[779] Lockwood, *Ferrara*, 258 f. The work is printed in *Chorwerk*, vol. 46. Further on the motets and *Magnificat* settings, see John G. Brawley, *The Magnificats, Hymns, Motets and Secular Compositions of Johannes Martini*, Ph.D., Yale U., 1968.

[780] Agricola, *Opera omnia*, vol. 4, no. 6. A useful *précis* of his life and music is Pirro, *Histoire*, 201–10.

Example 92 Alexander Agricola, 'Salve regina' II

Example 92 (*cont.*)

tial pattern of the altus leads surprisingly into another quote of the plainsong itself (at an eighth of its duration), but this gesture ties up the first phrase 'Salve' in a clear cadence. Imitation points follow, each sharply contrasted from the next: 'regina' for two voices, slow; 'misericordiae' nervous, for three. With the solemn tenor entry, rhythmic calm also returns to the other voices, which cease imitating in order not to obscure the cantus firmus. The work as a whole abounds with motivic ideas, all laid out in contrasts but in transparent textures which allow each voice to breathe. This flexible style is less rationalized or pervasively imitative, more flamboyant and surprising than the 'Milanese' idiom, but it holds its own significant position between Ockeghem, Regis and Josquin.

On the last few pages we may have given the impression that Ferrara and related centres had little use for cantus firmus Masses. This is by no means the case; but the repertory is strange. Of Martini's twelve cycles in this category that are known today (one, 'Nos amis', is attributable on stylistic grounds only), two are functional settings based on Mass plainsongs ('de feria', 'dominicalis'). All the others are written on secular subjects – and what subjects: 'Coda di Pavon', 'La Martinella', 'Or sus', 'Dio te salvi Gotterello', 'In feuers hitz', 'Cu cu' and so on. The first two models are not only secular, they are instrumental pieces. The 'Missa Cu cu'[781] is an ostinato cycle in which the one motive of the falling third is heard well over 200 times in the tenor: the hard-working bird is employed throughout the Mass service. It must have been fun for the singer because the call has dozens of different rhythmic shapes, is often transposed and is sometimes embedded in longer melodies. The Sanctus has a melodic cantus firmus apparently developed from the motive, and then strictly diminished a second time. The cuckoo is also mentioned in the *chanson rustique* 'Or sus, or

---

[781] Printed in Flotzinger ed., *Trienter Codices* (*DTOe*, vol. 120).

sus', which is the tenor of another Martini cycle (see Ex. 70).[782] The Mass 'Dio ti salvi' seems to be based on a popular song or *lauda* on S Gottardo, patron of Lombardy and much venerated at the Sforza court. Also the anonymous cycle 'La mort de Saint Gothard', which survives, like most of the other works, in a Ferrarese choirbook, might well be a work by Martini for Milan. On some of the other Masses, Burkholder based his claims that Martini was a major promoter of the 'Imitation Mass', which I prefer to call more simply 'parody Mass'.[783] Burkholder also reports Howard M. Brown's identification of the cantus firmus of a three-part Mass by Martini as the German song 'In feuers hitz, da brennet mein herz'. It remains to be determined whether this work originated in central Europe, or whether Martini found the tune in a Ferrarese copy of 'tenori todeschi' (see also p. 568).

The contrast between an austere, liturgically strict Vespers repertory and a secular-minded, playful Mass repertory is not characteristic of Ferrara alone at this time. The Milanese *motetti missales* and devotional motets were flanked by some of the most lighthearted cantus firmus cycles ever written. The Masses in the Gaffurius choirbooks are mostly in declamatory, chordal styles, shun word-painting or imitation, prefer the 'major modes' and rid themselves of the Gloria and Credo texts with parlando chatter at breakneck speed. Most of them have secular tenors, including dance-tunes as in Isaac's 'La Spagna'. Typical are tenors such as 'Cento mila scudi', 'Tant que nostre argent dura', 'Adieu mes amours', 'O Venus bant', 'Wolauff, gut gsell, von hinnen' – the convivial songs of clerics and travelling apprentices. The style was not confined to Milan, as the Isaac items show; probably the Florentine Mass repertory was similar. It is likely that daily Mass services, as celebrated in the court chapels, served for the musical delectation of the chaplains rather than for any particular religious message.

The Roman repertories of the *Cappella Sistina* choirbooks, by comparison, concentrate on sacred or at least serious chanson tenors. Much attention is paid to the words and their proper underlay in the manuscript; sections are added where the original composers had omitted text phrases.

The two greatest Mass composers of the period both visited Ferrara – not simultaneously, it seems – and the idea of making them compete by composing a Mass each over the same tenor might have occurred to many a colleague or courtier. It was an old idea. In a place very close by, somebody had encouraged Dufay and Hugo de Lantins to compose a Mass pair together (p. 157); Ockeghem and his circle had developed elaborate modes of imitating, emulating

---

[782] In the Lucca Choirbook, the same Italian hand added (*c.*1485–90) the 'Missa Or sus' and Isaac's Mass 'Chargé de deuil'. In a forthcoming edition of the manuscript (New York, Pendragon Press), I link the two works with the Florentine house of SS Annunziata.

[783] J. Peter Burkholder, 'Johannes Martini and the imitation Mass of the late fifteenth century', *JAMS* 38 (1985), 470–523. Burkholder says important things about Martini, but misconstrues the history of the 'Imitation Mass', which developed in the 1460s in France and Germany, not in the 1480s in Italy. See the replies to the article in *JAMS* 40 (1987), 130–39 and 576–79.

and outoing other composers' works, preferably over the same cantus firmi. Probably about a third of Josquin's and Obrecht's sacred works stand in some relationship of emulation to those of Busnois, Ockeghem and their colleagues – but also to each other.[784] Three Masses each by Josquin and Obrecht exist which are based on the same cantus firmus, and which have Ferrarese connections: the Masses 'Fortuna desperata', 'Malheur me bat' and 'L'homme armé'.[785]

Duke Ercole d'Este liked Obrecht's music, and this was one of the reasons why he invited him to Ferrara in 1487, as we have seen. The new works which the prolific composer may have produced during his stay there of somewhat less than eight months are nowhere documented. Lockwood has argued convincingly, however, that a Ferrarese choirbook with five (or seven) Obrecht Masses (*I-MOe α. M. 1. 2; olim lat.457*) was produced about 1504-5 mainly in his honour.[786] If this is the case, then the works he wrote for this court must surely be present in it. Interestingly, the only other composers represented in the source are Ockeghem (with the Mass 'Ecce ancilla Domini') and Josquin, whose Masses 'L'homme armé super voces musicales' and 'Fortuna desperata' are copied next to the homonymous cycles by Obrecht. Barton Hudson and others have claimed that not only 'Fortuna desperata' but also the Masses 'Malheur me bat', 'Schoen lief', 'Scaramella', 'Cela sans plus' and 'O quam suavis (O lumen ecclesie)' originated in Ferrara in 1487-8; the list of proposed works for this brief period has grown dangerously long.[787]

It is unlikely that a direct connection exists between the two 'L'homme armé' Masses in the Ferrarese choirbook or between the 'Malheur me bat' cycles of the two composers. The latter works do not share a common source; musically they seem quite unrelated. Obrecht's 'Malheur me bat' is a good example of his 'segmentation technique': each section of the cycle is based on a different phrase from the chanson tenor. In his 'L'homme armé' cycle, Obrecht is much indebted to that of Busnois, a major representative of the 'L'homme armé' tradition; he quotes the tenor of Busnois' work literally.

Of Josquin's two Mass cycles over the song, the 'Missa L'homme armé sexti toni' is a work defined by its modality and by the flexible variations of the cantus firmus melody, and thus opposed to Obrecht's procedures. It is also very much concerned with duets, canons and voice-pairs. The six-part Agnus Dei III pulls out all the stops of artifice, although it is at the same time a miracle

---

[784] Howard M. Brown, 'Emulation, competition, and homage: imitation and theories of imitation in the Renaissance', *JAMS* 35 (1982), 1-48, links similar observations to Renaissance ideals and rhetorical theory. I hesitate to accept *imitatio* as a key concept for specific Renaissance attitudes in music. See also Wegman, 'Another imitation', for thoughtful comments.

[785] Josquin, *Werken*, Missen I, no. 4; II, no. 8; I, no. 1 ('L.a. super voces musicales'); Obrecht, *New Obrecht Edition*, vols. 4, 7 and 6.

[786] Lockwood, *Ferrara*, 226 f.

[787] Barton Hudson, 'Two Ferrarese Masses by Jacob Obrecht', *JMus* 4 (1985-6), 276-302; for further suggestions, see Picker, *Ockeghem and Obrecht*, 74 no. 9, 76 no. 18, 83 no. 13; Brown, 'On Veronica'. On 'Malheur me bat', see Strohm, review of Obrecht, *New Obrecht Edition*, vol. 7, in *Notes* 46 (1990), 552-4.

of harmony: it compounds two canons in the two upper voice-pairs with two simultaneous forward and retrograde statements of cantus firmus sections in the low voices. In the 'Missa L'homme armé super voces musicales', Josquin uses the famous tenor only to exercise an entirely different principle: that of transposing ostinati. The famous tune is heard on all six steps of the hexachord: on Ut in the Kyrie, Re in the Gloria, Mi in the Credo, Fa in the Sanctus, Sol in the first Agnus Dei, and on La in the third. 'Ut' is always *c*, but the overall mode of the work is Dorian/Aeolian; the Kyrie, Credo and Sanctus conclude with cadences on *d* after the last cantus firmus note – very much like the Dorian conclusion of Ockeghem's 'Caput' Mass. The Credo 'in Mi' also alludes to the plainsong Credo 'de village' in the cantus. The rhythms of the cantus firmus are strictly organized; the Agnus Dei II (without tenor) is an intricate mensuration canon. In the Kyrie, the cantus firmus is strictly derived by way of mensural transformation first from the cantus (Kyrie I), then from the altus (Christe), and then from the bassus (Kyrie II). Gloria and Credo have sections with the cantus firmus in retrograde. The tune is always in the tenor, except in the third Agnus Dei when it suddenly appears in doubled values in the cantus. This and other happy surprises, as well as the ingenuity with which the wandering tune is contained within a single mode, earned the work an enormous reputation. In his first print of Josquin Masses in 1502, Ottaviano Petrucci placed this Mass at the beginning; the volume had to be reprinted four times.

Antecedents for this kind of transposing ostinato do exist; there is at least the anonymous Mass 'Du cuer je souspier' in *Tr 89* – almost certainly a French work – where the tune is heard on four ascending steps in each Mass section. We shall encounter further examples of transposing ostinati such as the famous 'Miserere' (see below). Almost more relevant, however, would be a comparison with the 'Missa de Beata Virgine', one of Josquin's most celebrated masterworks. It is built on Marian plainsongs in such a way that each section employs a different combination of final and mode.[788]

Obrecht's sacred works, particularly his Masses, are sometimes compared with those of Josquin and judged to retain a more conservative attitude. This is undoubtedly more a question of genres than of style, and might be applied, for example, to the contrast between the complex polytextual cantus firmus motet of the north (*à la* Regis) and the smoothly imitative or declamatory motet cultivated more in Italy. But even in this genre there are many overlapping elements, for example the predilection for declamatory tuttis found in Regis. Obrecht did cultivate constructivist, schematic or 'cryptic' procedures in his cantus firmus Masses which may occasionally have been over-interpreted.[789] Techniques such as strict mensural and proportional transformation, all sorts

---

[788] On these issues, see especially Leeman L. Perkins, 'Mode and structure in the Masses of Josquin', *JAMS* 26 (1973) 189–239.

[789] See the extreme theories of Marcus van Crevel concerning Obrecht's numerical constructions, expanded in his edition of the Masses 'Sub tuum presidium' and 'Maria zart': Obrecht, *Opera omnia*, vols. 3 and 4.

of canons, fragmentation of tenors, literal quotation, inversion and retrograde are typical of his Masses.[790] Some of these techniques – not all – were equally dear to Josquin's heart, whose canon techniques, in particular, surpass even the most complex inventions of his predecessors (see also below). Edgar Sparks has developed the most clear-cut view of Obrecht's and Josquin's cantus firmus technique in styling the first an 'uncompromising rationalist' and contrasting him sharply with Ockeghem, while considering it Josquin's achievement to have integrated and transcended both these orientations.[791] Few scholars have proposed interpretations, in terms of cultural history, of Obrecht's more obvious habits and surface procedures, such as his ubiquitous parallel tenths between outer voices, or the inclination towards strict sequential patterns. These devices contradict the ideal of *varietas* as pronounced by Tinctoris, and could best be accommodated within a 'poetics' of musical composition as *licences* for special expression. Repetitions occur regularly in Obrecht, however, and for no special purpose – i.e. the licence is taken too often. This is also the case in much anonymous music from central Europe. Josquin, on the other hand, repeats with enough deliberation to suggest that his overriding goal was *varietas*. Josquin's sequential patterns and ostinati almost always produce special effects, even when they characterize a complete work. The Mass 'Hercules Dux Ferrarie' is one of these works, with its particular starkness of construction and repetition.[792]

It is more difficult to compare masters like these when more abstract qualities are in question, for example 'tonal harmony', 'symmetry' or 'rhetoric'. I have commented on tonal harmony in connection with Regis and Obrecht. 'Symmetry', an architectonic metaphor, is easily over-used in describing music – music exists in time, and there can be no symmetry between sooner and later. But in connection with other interpretative strategies, thinking in terms of quantities and their relationships can reveal much of the music itself. Linguistic analogies, such as 'musical rhetoric' (the new-found land of Renaissance musicology in the 1970s), have always been held in high esteem for the interpretation of music of other ages, for example the Baroque period. The problem here is that rhetorical means and ends tend to be very predictable, and that composers from Gregorian chant to the present day have usually made some kind of premeditated 'rhetorical' effort in order to accomplish their ends.[793] It is probably no coincidence that a study which tries to identify Renaissance elements in Obrecht and Josquin ends up in tying the former more to architecture, the latter more to language and affect:[794] Josquin's greater flexibility is seen

---

[790] A good study of canon and other 'serial' techniques is Todd, 'Retrograde'.

[791] Sparks, *Cantus firmus*, 254 and 312 f.

[792] See some examples in Sparks, *Cantus firmus*, 332–4.

[793] Such predictability looms in the title of Christopher Reynolds's essay 'Musical evidence of compositional planning in the Renaissance: Josquin's *Plus nulz regretz*', *JAMS* 40 (1987), 53–81. The study has much to tell on rhetoric and symmetries.

[794] Myroslaw Antonowytsch, 'Renaissance-Tendenzen in den Fortuna-desperata-Messen von Josquin und Obrecht', *Mf* 9 (1956), 1–26.

as a more innovative, more human, and thus in our circumstances a more 'Renaissance-like' approach. It would be possible, however, to read in Obrecht's less balanced music elements of a nascent mannerism or even *seconda pratica* (mediated by Willaert and de Rore), while Josquin's 'classicism' may be said to have been ultimately exhausted in Palestrina.

The model for Obrecht's and Josquin's 'Fortuna desperata' Masses is a three-voice Italian song whose genre, meaning or origin have not been established.[795] Of the many versions of the song, most have an added fourth voice; the three-part version is attributed in the Segovia MS to Antoine Busnois, whereas three other sources are anonymous.[796] (The Segovia attributions have often been shown to be incorrect.) 'Fortuna desperata' is unlikely to be a contrafactum of a French song (which Busnois' only other Italian song, 'Con tutta gentilezza', almost certainly is). I suggest that it originated in Italy, perhaps in Naples, *c.*1480, and that its supposed connection with Busnois is an error; the style of the piece is a far cry from anything produced by that French master. The somewhat enigmatic frottola text is known from other sources.[797] The first two lines read: 'Fortuna desperata, iniqua e maledetta, che di tal donna eletta, la fama hai denigrata' – but might have to be emended to read 'la grazia hai dinegata' ('Desperate Fortune, unfair and cursed, who has denigrated the good name' – alternatively: 'denied me the mercy' – 'of that chosen woman').

The great popularity of the song may owe something to the general inclination of the time to curse Fortune, but it owes most to the music. A rhythmically simple, melodically naive F major tune in the tenor is accompanied, with some disguised artifice, by a similar melody in the cantus, even in imitation. The phrases of the various voices overlap in a curious way, and the cantus has no midpoint stop; the words fit really only the tenor. The F major harmony sounds very modern, and the subdominant preparations of several cadences are striking. The 'harmonic' contratenor also contributes to this effect. The leap of a tritone in the bass in the last phrase (bars 27–8), which cannot be removed by *musica ficta*, is unthinkable for Busnois. This last phrase was to become a stereotype of the frottola: the descent of the cantus is underpinned alternately by a fifth and third of the lower voices (see Ex. 93).

Obrecht approached his task in the strictest tradition of the tenor Mass. His whole cycle is based on the tenor of the song whose rhythms are quoted literally, but which are at times transformed. Literal quotation is facilitated by the fact that the basic mensuration of the Mass is that of the song, ₵. The first

---

[795] It is printed with the editions of the Masses themselves: Obrecht, *Opera omnia*, vol. 1, fasc. 3 and *New Obrecht Edition*, vol. 4; Josquin, *Werken*, Missen I, no. 4. For the sources and arrangements of the song, see Higgins, *Busnois*, 318–20, and Julie E. Cumming, 'The goddess Fortuna revisited', *CMc* 30 (1980), 7–23 (this study focuses on the later settings).

[796] Many settings (without the recently discovered ones) are compared in Otto Gombosi, *Jacob Obrecht: eine stilkritische Studie* (Leipzig, 1925), 99–116, who curiously concludes that Obrecht's Mass emulated Josquin's, not vice versa. This is accepted in Osthoff, *Josquin*, vol. 1, 144–8, whose only argument is the greater length of the Obrecht cycle!

[797] See Torrefranca, *Segreto*, 297.

Example 93 anon. (Busnois?), 'Fortuna desperata'

Example 93 (*cont.*)

Kyrie presents the cantus firmus in the tenor in the original shape and values from bar 7 – preceded by two pre-imitations in altus and cantus (see Ex. 94*a*).

Example 94*a* Jacob Obrecht, Mass 'Fortuna desperata'

(a) Kyrie I

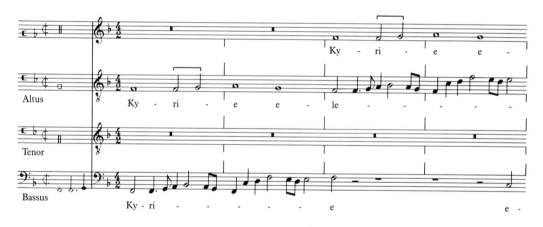

Example 94*a* (*cont.*)

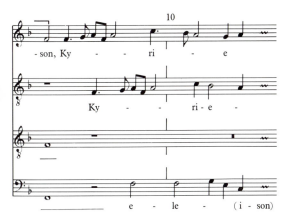

Pre-imitation was well known in cantus firmus settings, for example of popular songs; in this case it is striking that the two earlier statements are identical to that of the real cantus firmus: they are deceptively 'false' entries. The tenor then carries the melody to the end of its first phrase. There follows a postlude of the other voices (bars 31–48 of the edition), using invertible counterpoint with the following distribution of motivic material:

Cantus	A	C				A
Altus	B		A	D	F	H
Tenor				A	A	D
Bassus		A	C	E	G	I

Motive 'A' appears in all four voices, the fixed counterpoints 'C' and 'D' in two each. This whole conclusion of Kyrie I is a strong climax through the repetition and build-up of voices.

We have hardly heard anything of the tune yet, and already the Christe is without it, in three voices. It abounds with patterned repetitions, partly in cross-rhythms. Triple metre (*sesquialtera* proportion) is introduced at bar 66, and this proportion will be used throughout the Mass for intermediate or concluding passages.

In the second Kyrie, Obrecht suddenly makes an effort to pay tribute to his model. He quotes all its voices in compact 'parody' (see Ex. 94*b*).

Even the fourth added voice of some versions of the song is reflected in the altus here. In all voices but the tenor, however, the similarity with their respective model gradually dissolves. Already in bars 4–5, the harmonies of the song are altered. The altus in bars 8–9, over the organ point, is something like a paraphrase of the original contratenor.

Example 94*b*

(b) Kyrie II

The Gloria and Credo are very different. They both work through the literally quoted song tenor twice forward and in *retrograde*. The technique is old and may be expected from Obrecht, who uses it also in his Masses 'De tous biens pleine' (an early work),[798] 'L'homme armé', 'Petrus Apostolus' and 'Graecorum'.[799] Two things are peculiar, however. The first is extreme symmetry: under the canon instruction 'In medio consistit virtus' ('Virtue takes its stand in the middle'), the tenor begins first from the midpoint of the song line backwards, then from the midpoint forward (i.e. to the end); the whole is repeated. In the Credo, the tenor goes backwards from the end to the same midpoint, then forward from the beginning to midpoint; the whole is again repeated. The repeats are in the same note-values – not in diminution as happens so often elsewhere. Thus, the Gloria and Credo consist of four equal subsections each, and have the same total number of bars, 218.

The other peculiar thing is that the 'midpoint' is a specific long note, the high f', which is trumpeted out like a signal and set apart from the remainder of the tune by long rests. In the Gloria, of course, it opens all four subsections because they all begin at midpoint. In the Credo, it should conclude all four subsections, but Obrecht transfers the isolated note to the beginning of them, omitting it at the ends. Thus it stands even more isolated, like a pointing finger (the real tenor entry is at bar 8), see Example 94c:

Example 94c

(c) Credo

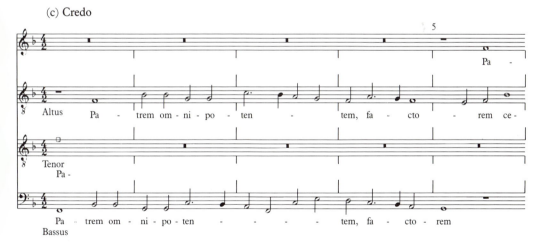

---

[798] Discussed in Sparks, *Cantus firmus*, 288–94.

[799] See Todd, 'Retrograde', 73 f. The most relevant models for the technique as used here were probably the Agnus Dei sections in the Masses 'L'homme armé' by Dufay and 'Pour quelque paine' by Cornelius Heyns.

Example 94c (*cont.*)

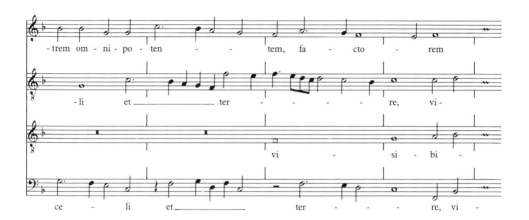

This 'Pa-' strikes us almost as a joke. Its model was the isolated 'Pe-' in the tenor of Ockeghem's 'Petite camusette' (see p. 454), which Obrecht had preserved in this form when using Ockeghem's chanson at the beginning of the Credo of his Mass 'Plurimorum carminum I'.[800]

The Sanctus and Agnus expand the range of cantus firmus techniques. In the Sanctus, the song tenor is heard a fifth higher in the cantus, but from bar 59 (edition) the first phrase of the original cantus concludes the section: a remarkable breakthrough, it seems. The Osanna has the tenor tune an octave lower in the bassus, complete. The first Agnus presents the tenor tune complete in the tenor, followed by a statement in halved values. The Pleni, Benedictus and second Agnus are three-voice sections, full of games with invertible counterpoint and sequential patterns. The third Agnus is a full-voiced 'parody' like the second Kyrie. This time, however – and this seems very important – the tenor is freely invented (the song tenor is sung by the altus), and after the similarities with the model in the other voices have gradually disappeared, it is the cantus that remains identical to its model voice. Thus, in the Mass as a whole, the cantus of the song has ousted the tenor as cantus firmus. This process (into which the Gloria and Credo were interposed like erratic blocks) may express the elusiveness of Fortune, and is certainly concerned with the question which voice of the song is actually the main tune. By making the ear accustomed to steady, literal quotations, Obrecht makes the process transparent. To distinguish allusions from 'true entries' is the main listening task which Obrecht has set us in this Mass.

When looking at Josquin's 'Fortuna desperata' Mass with these conclusions

---

[800] See Thomas Noblitt, 'Filiation vis-à-vis its alternatives: approaches to textual criticism', in Finscher ed., *Datierung und Filiation*, 114.

in mind, no doubt will remain that Josquin knew Obrecht's work and commented on it. This also implies that its date is not *c*.1480–82 as suggested by Lowinsky, who was keen to tie Josquin's works alluding to misfortune to a period when Ascanio Sforza was exiled.[801]

The mensurations are elusive: in the Kyrie and Gloria, the simple duple-metre song is adjusted to perfect time in the opening sections; but from the Credo onwards, the composition is always in imperfect time, with only one sub-section in triple rhythm for 'Cum sancto spiritu'. This inconsistency irritates: did the composer simply give up on a mensuration scheme?

The character of Josquin's work is apparent from the very beginning (see Ex. 95*a*):

Example 95*a* Josquin des Prez, Mass 'Fortuna desperata'

(a) Kyrie I

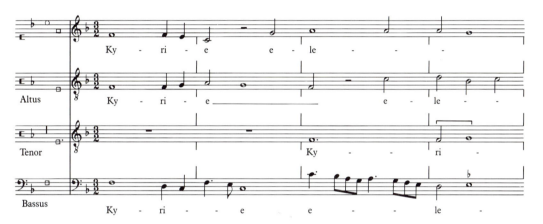

---

[801] Lowinsky, 'Ascanio Sforza's life', 65–7, grouping 'Fortuna desperata' with the cycles 'Malheur me bat' and 'Faysant regretz'. The 'Fortuna' Mass was printed by Petrucci in 1502 and thus composed before Josquin was appointed at Ferrara.

The first two bars seem to initiate a parody Mass, where each voice retains the material of its model voice – until the true tenor entry shatters these conclusions: this is a tenor Mass! Clearly, the model is provided by the 'false entries' of Obrecht's individual voices, here compounded to the false entry of a whole Mass. Since the distance of cantus and tenor entry is only two breves, the idea has also a forerunner in the 'near miss' entries of Ockeghem's 'Caput' and of 'O rosa bella I' (see pp. 426 f).

In the following bars, the outer voices 'forget' to echo their respective models, indulging instead in beautiful non-imitative filigree. The Christe is largely chordal and explores harmonic ideas which come perhaps from the song – for example the E♭ harmony. The tune in the tenor now appears in something like literal quotation, albeit in doubled values. In the second Kyrie, some melodic allusions to the tune can be spotted in the outer voices, but not to that part of the tune which is just sounding in the tenor. The Gloria advances a step further in this processual art:

Example 95*b*

(b) Gloria

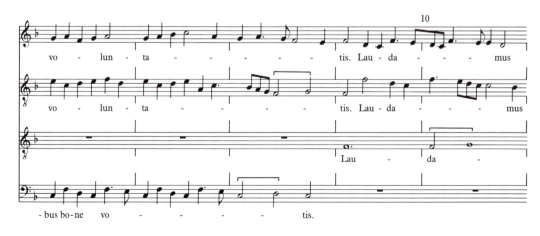

Example 95*b* (*cont.*)

Again, we have the 'false entries', this time of two voices only. The altus has the false entry of the tenor line, as before; the cantus motive is a contraction of the openings of both cantus and bassus (see the previous example). The peculiar thing this time is that the bassus is heard as late as bar 3 with its proper bassus material, as if faking a true (i.e. delayed) entry. This material differs, of course, only rhythmically from the 'contracted' motive in the cantus. Another rhythmic variant of the same motive is being proposed simultaneously (in bar 3) by the altus, who has thus abandoned the task of announcing the cantus firmus. Even the bassus catches on to this motive, repeating it four times with increasing speed as a kind of ostinato. This utter failure to produce a cantus firmus is made good when, in bar 9, the true tenor appears, greeted by the cantus in bars 9–10 and by the bassus in bars 11–12 with the ostinato motive ('Laudamus te').

At 'Gratias agimus tibi', there appears in all three outer voices a pre-imitation of the second tenor phrase, in a simplified but livelier form ($c'-c'-c'-d'-c'-a$) which cannot be confused with a true entry. It corresponds to the moment in the song when the contratenor and then the cantus pre-imitate the second tenor phrase (bars 8–11). Another, more elaborate version of the same motive pre-imitates the next section, 'Qui tollis', save that in the 'Qui tollis' the cantus firmus actually begins from the top again, as a second statement (in duple metre); the pre-imitation is curiously misplaced this time. Yet another misplaced pre-imitation of the same motive opens the 'Cum sancto spiritu' before the last statement of the tenor, which is in halved values.

The beginning of the Credo echoes that of the Kyrie, reversing roles. The three lower voices together parody the full three-part song for two bars. After this 'false entry', the cantus appears with its cantus line, literal and in augmented values:

Example 95c

(c) Credo

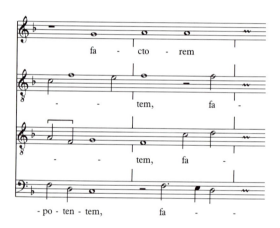

After the initial false entry, the other voices have little more to do with this melodic material.

The Gloria and the Credo are matched in this way: in the Gloria, the tenor carries the song tenor, presenting it three times in accelerating speeds; in the Credo, the cantus carries *its* respective tune, the cantus of the song, presenting it four times and in four different speeds. In the Sanctus, the choice of borrowed voice and 'host voice' is more surprising: the bass line of the song is now heard a fifth higher in the altus – not without the usual misleading pre-imitation. In this section, the cantus suddenly catches on to an ostinato motive, an insignificant formula of five notes which is repeated (on two different pitch levels) 23 times, and gradually a little expanded. Since it cadences on *f'* and *c'*, the section gains a particular tonal consistency, but many motives of 'Fortuna desperata' tend to reinforce an F major sonority in any case. Obrecht's Mass, too, can be regarded for the most part as a string of F major cadences; ostinato and repetition techniques are important to both cycles, and most of the motives have some cadential implication.[802]

The hunt for 'Fortune' goes on, however. The Pleni is in three parts, and accordingly lacks a cantus firmus. The Osanna denies us the tune as well, although it is in four voices. This is highly unconventional: usually only three-voice sections are allowed to go without the cantus firmus. Ostinato motives play a role in the Osanna, particularly a version of the 'contracted' motive from the Gloria with which it starts. The Benedictus, for three voices, is freely imitative again.

There are only two Agnus Dei sections. In the first, three voices take off with the 'contracted' ostinato motive a fifth higher, as if it had become the 'theme' of the Mass. (The upper voices seem to sing in C major, however.) The bass has a pedal point *c*. Uncannily, this is very slowly being revealed to be 'Fortuna', turned upside down and in *fourfold* augmentation:

Example 95d

(d) Agnus Dei

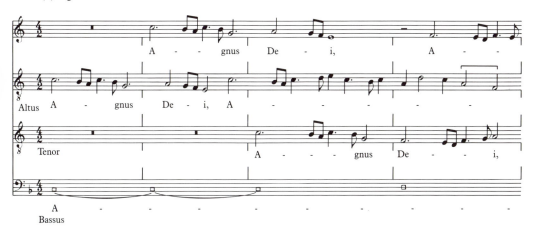

[802] It is no coincidence that Obrecht's work has been used to demonstrate his advances towards tonal harmony. See Arnold Salop, 'Jacob Obrecht and the early development of harmonic polyphony', *JAMS* 17 (1964), 288–309, esp. 303–8. A critique is in Dahlhaus, *Untersuchungen*, 75 f. I believe that the Lydian mode was already used in ways practically indistinguishable from tonal harmony by this time; distinctive signs are the subdominantic cadential preparations in Obrecht's work. Josquin's Mass 'Fortuna desperata' has furnished examples to Saul Novack, 'Tonal tendencies in Josquin's use of harmony', in Lowinsky ed., *Josquin des Prez*, 317–33, esp. 328 ff.

Example 95*d* (*cont.*)

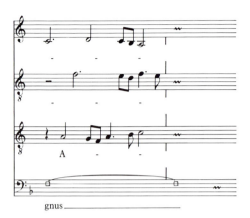

gnus

The cantus firmus had been lying in ambush for the first eight bars or so. Who would have thought Fortune would be *there*? The inversion is, of course, a symbol of the position of the hapless on the mythical wheel. It is perhaps not worth speculating whether Josquin had by this time already written his intriguing 'Fortuna d'un gran tempo', which, with its dangerous modulatory drive (inspired by Ockeghem's 'Prenez sur moi', no doubt), has been interpreted as a harmonic simile of the wheel.[803] In the Mass, the symbol for the downturn of the wheel is textural rather than harmonic; it seems cruder and more conventional. But the musical effect is awesome. The excited, lamenting ostinati of the upper voices seem to react to it.

The upper voices behave similarly in the second Agnus Dei, when the tenor melody is now heard in the correct speed and version, but an octave lower, in the bassus. This arrangement, which is borrowed from Obrecht's Osanna, including the initial point of imitation, leads now to a convenient ending as the bassus descends to low *F* at the end of the section for the final cadence. However, the upper voices continue for four more bars, forming a new cadence by themselves, into which the bassus drops an isolated, last and lowest *F*. In no other section before has Josquin split a single note away from the cantus firmus. He obviously does it here with reference to Obrecht's Mass: the isolated signal *f'* in his Gloria and Credo, treated with a somewhat pedantic constructivism, and its downturn with the single lowest note in the Osanna, have provoked Josquin's totally unwarranted, haphazard last gesture – really only a glorified exclamation mark.

[803] See Edward E. Lowinsky, 'The goddess Fortuna in music', *MQ* 29 (1943), 45–77; and, contradicting, Jaap van Benthem, 'Fortuna in focus: concerning "conflicting" progressions in Josquin's "Fortuna d'un gran tempo"', *TVNM* 30 (1980), 1–50.

I suggest that both Masses are somehow seeking a compromise between the systematic structure of a tenor Mass – a 'masterwork' – and a more humanistic idea: the depiction of something living and developing. Obrecht still treats his ideas, including his 'false entries', systematically. Josquin goes beyond that: he not only portrays the elusive Fortune but also makes his voices represent real people with their inconsistencies and addictions (ostinati). He hands over the structure to process, mixing it with surprise, fun and a little terror.

Faces of musical humanism

Two genres which have been scrutinized for Italian Renaissance elements are the political motet or *Staatsmotette* (for obvious reasons: more humanist poets served the State than the Church), and the motet setting of classical poems. Examples for the first category are settings, by Compère and Obrecht respectively, of the text 'Quis numerare queat / Audivit ipse tamen / Fundent preces Itali', which celebrates the peace of Bagnolo between Ferrara (plus its allies) and Venice on 7 August 1484.[804] In the second category, we have the exquisite settings of verses from the *Aeneid*, by Josquin ('Dulces exuviae', 'Fama malum'), Ghiselin ('Dulces exuviae') and younger composers. The cultivation of 'Vergil motets' might have been connected with the Mantuan court of Isabella d'Este, although the papal chapel, the French royal court and even northern cathedral schools also possibly cultivated the type.[805] We also have Horatian poems with music, mostly but not exclusively in the strict metrical style of the 'humanist odes' (see p. 537): there is, among other examples, Michele Pesenti's graceful frottola-style setting of 'Integer vitae scelerisque purus'.[806]

A more complex problem is posed by sacred works with humanistic texts or mixtures of classical and Christian imagery. Obrecht's Mass cantus firmus 'Salve diva parens' belongs in this category, and Josquin's six-voice motet 'Huc me sydereo descendere jussit Olympo', on an extraordinary, classicizing speech of Christ written by Mapheus Vegius. The manneristic imagery of the poem elicited a particular effort of word-painting from Josquin, who did not give up a complex cantus firmus construction, however.[807] Effortless and pleasing,

---

[804] Obrecht's work may have originated in 1487–8, when he was in Ferrara. Also probably of that period is his address to the pope, 'Inter praeclarissimas virtutes'. On both works, see Dunning, *Staatsmotette*, 9–20. For Compère's setting, see also Finscher, *Loyset Compère*, 121–4; and 118–21 on his political motet 'Sola caret monstris / Fera pessima'.

[805] See Helmuth Osthoff, 'Vergils Aeneis in der Musik von Josquin des Prez bis Orlando di Lasso', *AMw* 11 (1954), 85–102; Gottwald, *Johannes Ghiselin*, 108–11; Strohm, *Bruges*, 155 n. 85. A manuscript which focuses on such texts is *GB-Lbl Royal 8. G. VII*, a Netherlands ('Alamire') codex originally compiled for Louis XII of France and Anne of Brittany. Three works are also in *B-Br 228*, copied for Margaret of Austria: see Picker, *Chanson Albums*, 95 f.

[806] See Reese, *Renaissance*, 161.

[807] A melodically identical cantus firmus is used in 'Ave nobilissima creatura', a companion piece. See Osthoff, *Josquin*, vol. 2, 90 ff, and Elders, 'Plainchant', 526 f.

by comparison, is Compère's four-part work 'Sile fragor ac rerum tumultus', despite the particularly involved and (for us) tasteless combination of the Virgin Mary and Bacchus in the text.[808]

Musical constructivism and word-setting were the two (potentially opposed) ideals of this period. There was a different tension now between these principles than there had been, for example, in Dufay's 'Nuper rosarum flores'. The word-setting there had been complementary or even subordinate to the isorhythmic construction; within a constructive framework, Dufay had caught the opportunities to bring words into focus. Some of these opportunities were of a rhetorical kind (contrast, repetition, climax and so on), others were simply created with the part-writing.

In the non-isorhythmic motet – with or without cantus firmus – of the Josquin period, there is always the possibility that large-scale contrast or climax are entirely the poet's doing (or, the composer's reaction to the poet). The text of a motet can dictate the growth of the music. Furthermore, modes and poetic 'moods' – the connection between which had been a discovery of the 1450s – are available to music on a plane that is entirely independent of words. This can create miracles of word–tone interaction.

It would be possible to demonstrate this with some of Josquin's most famous motets, such as the 'Miserere' which was requested from him by Duke Ercole d'Este, not in order to fulfil a certain liturgical observance, but to express a certain religious attitude.[809] As Macey has shown, Josquin's huge three-section motet is less a setting of Psalm 50 than a musical reflection of Savonarola's meditation on that text: 'Infelix ego omnium auxilio destitutus, qui coelum terramque offendi. Quo ibo? Quo me vertam? ad quem confugiam?. . .' ('Wretched I am, deprived of all men's help, as I have offended Heaven and Earth. Where shall I go? Where turn? To whom may I flee?').[810] The rhetorical repetitions of this text, which also uses the psalm quote 'Miserere mei deus' like a refrain at the ends of paragraphs, are mirrored in the musical structure of the motet. The 'Miserere' refrain becomes a musical ostinato, repeated 21 times:

Example 96 Josquin des Prez, 'Miserere mei, Deus'

808 Compère, *Opera omnia*, vol. 4, 49–51. Finscher, *Loyset Compère*, 191–3, dates the work together with 'Propter gravamen' just before 1500.
809 See Lockwood, *Ferrara*, 261 ff.
810 Patrick Macey, *Josquin's Miserere mei Deus: Context, Structure, and Influence*, Ph.D., U. of California, Berkeley, 1985, ch. 1 and pp. 42–8; *idem*, 'Savonarola'.

In the first section of the motet, this ostinato descends by step through the octave *e′-e*; in the second, it ascends in halved note-values through the whole octave again, and in the third, it descends a fifth from *e′* to *a*. The resulting tonal asymmetry should be kept in mind: two longer sections beginning and ending in E (i.e. Phrygian), a third, shorter section ending in A (Aeolian). It is notable, furthermore, how the stark, almost monotonous sound of the refrain – materially only a murmured liturgical recitative – becomes musical and expressive first of all through the hidden potential of the upper semitone (aided by rhythmic emphasis) on the strongest and most meaningful syllable, and secondly through its contrapuntal decoration by the other four voices, lamenting, praying, exclaiming and mourning.[811]

It is strange that, in music of this period, there is so often an ostinato when serious matters such as life and death are addressed. There is also a worldly or frivolous side to the phenomenon, of course. Dufay used ostinati in his dance-song 'Resvelons nous, resvelons amoureux' and in his hilarious and pictorial song 'Je ne puis plus / Unde veniet auxilium mihi' (see p. 133). With the latter piece, he may have founded the tradition of the so-called motet-chanson, in which Ockeghem's lament for Binchois 'Mort, tu as navré / Miserere' could be placed (see p. 413).[812] In Josquin's time, the motet-chanson was a strangely ambiguous genre which combined a French secular text with a Latin cantus firmus, and according to the interplay of meaning of both texts, could be interpreted in a worldly or a spiritual fashion. Compère, Josquin and Agricola, among others, contributed to the genre. Least complicated are pieces such as 'O devotz coeurs / O vos omnes' by Compère, a song on the Passion of Our Lady which continues the Marian interpretations of 'Comme femme desconforté' and 'De tous biens pleine'. No fewer than nine motet-chansons occur in the chanson albums of Margaret of Austria, *B-Br 228* and *B-Br 11293*. In that context, they must be interpreted as spiritual transformations of chansons, and some of them are actual laments; although Finscher goes perhaps too far when interpreting the whole genre as a motet in both form and spirit.[813] The main compositional game of this genre is the interplay of two different formal structures – just as in the chanson with a secular cantus firmus (for example, a *chanson rustique*) or other forms. Clearly, such games could result in a play with religious concepts or religious emblems. In Josquin's Mass 'Di dadi', a game becomes itself the frivolous symbol of sacred–secular ambiguity. This cycle, with Morton's melody 'N'aray-je jamais mieux que j'ay' ('Will I never have any-

---

[811] The 'humanization' of music through imitation of human speech – or rather the musicalization of speech? – has often been observed in music of Josquin's time. For a summary of the issues, see Harrán, *Word-Tone Relations*, ch. 4.

[812] Picker, *Chanson Albums*, 83–8; two anonymous works of that kind have sometimes been ascribed to Ockeghem as well: see Picker, *Ockeghem and Obrecht*, 38. David Fallows, 'Motet-chanson' in *The New Grove*, does not describe this established meaning of the term, but the so-called 'song-motet'.

[813] Finscher, *Loyset Compère*, 205–30.

thing better than I have?') as cantus firmus, develops as a symbolic dice-game between the Holy Sacrament and the devil.[814] In a not altogether different manner, Josquin makes fun of ambiguity in his chanson-motet 'Ce povre mendiant / Pauper sum ego'. Here, he draws together the ambiguity of the ostinato principle and the ambiguity of the two-language text, to demonstrate that he is penniless (as he did elsewhere, for example in the double-texted chanson 'Adieu mes amours'). The money problem is so serious for him that he expresses it in Latin, with a melodic formula taken from the psalm tones, and repeated as a transposing ostinato in the contratenor.[815]

The connection with the stepwise descending ostinato 'Miserere mei Deus' is clear, and also corroborated by the meaning of the texts; both are spoken by a beggar.

This may set the scene for another ostinato composition, often discussed and surely representative of the age: Heinrich Isaac's lament on the death of Lorenzo de' Medici, 'Quis dabit capiti meo aquam'. The text was written by Angelo Poliziano (1454–94), Lorenzo's household poet, and obviously set to music very quickly after the death, which occurred in Florence on 8 April, 1492.[816] The demise of 'Il Magnifico' was an extremely important and serious event (even if it could not be foreseen that the years 1494–5 would bring the banishment of the Medici, the French invasion and Savonarola's ascent to power). An ostinato composition to commemorate the Medici patron must have seemed an obvious choice. This is what Isaac did: from his Mass 'Salva nos' (see p. 529), he took the last phrase of the cantus firmus, which is an antiphon for the *Nunc dimittis*. The last phrase, with the words 'et requiescamus in pace' ('and let us rest in peace'), becomes the ostinato subject of his motet, appearing on successive steps of the scale (see Ex. 97). A very similar transposing ostinato is found in the chanson-motet 'Que vous madame / In pace in idipsum' by Josquin, where the cantus firmus phrase 'et requiescam' appears successively on four different scale-degrees. The work is related by its cantus firmus to Agricola's famous three-voice motet 'Si dedero sompnum oculis meis'.[817]

---

[814] See the striking and convincing interpretation of Michael Long, 'Symbol and ritual in Josquin's Missa Di Dadi', *JAMS* 42 (1989), 1–22.

[815] Picker, *Chanson Albums*, no. 51; Josquin, *Werken*, fasc. 53, no. 46.

[816] For the historical circumstances and an edn of the poem, see Staehelin, *Messen*, vol. 2, 36 f. The music (Isaac, *Weltliche Werke*, vol. 28, 45–8) is discussed in Osthoff, *Theatergesang*, vol. 1, 177–9; Dunning, *Staatsmotette*, 20–22; Allan W. Atlas, 'A note on Isaac's "Quis dabit capiti meo aquam"', *JAMS* 27 (1974), 103–10; Martin Staehelin, Communication, *JAMS* 28 (1975), 160; Allan W. Atlas, Communication, *JAMS* 28 (1975), 565–6; Richard Taruskin, 'Settling an old score: a note on contrafactum in Isaac's Lorenzo lament', *CMc* 21 (1976), 83–92. Atlas claimed that the motet was originally composed on the text 'Cantantibus organis' given in the earliest source (*C.G.*), and its material transferred to the Mass. Staehelin and Taruskin, however, showed that the priority of the Mass is far more likely. Osthoff points out a constructive link with Josquin's 'Miserere' and 'Ce pauvre mendiant'.

[817] See Picker, *Chanson Albums*, MS 11239, nos. 22 and 23.

Example 97 Heinrich Isaac, 'Quis dabit capiti meo aquam?'

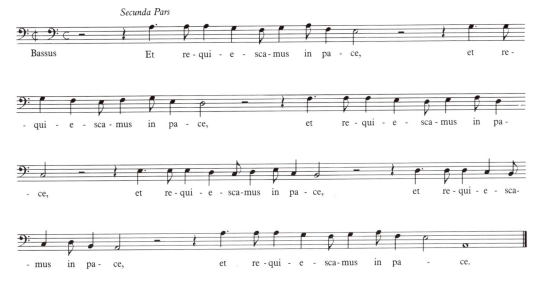

The rather beautiful if not novel idea of likening death to peaceful sleep in God was only the beginning of Isaac's task. Because of the pressure of time and perhaps influenced by his convenient habit of self-borrowing, the composer re-utilized three polyphonic sections of the Mass (contained in the Kyrie II, 'Cum sancto spiritu' and Osanna II) in the first, second and fourth sections of the motet. These contrafacta do not detract from the amazing new unity into which the composer has welded them. 'Quis dabit' is, at the same time, a large-scale 'political' motet and a *complainte* on a humanist text with its own formal ambition and peculiar imagery; an ostinato motet, a work in the Phrygian / Aeolian mode and expressing a 'sad' poetic mood. It is also an early example (with Ockeghem's 'Mort, tu as navré' as a possible precedent) of the use of descending chains of 6–3 chords (fauxbourdon style) with an obviously affective meaning.

There exists a related Latin lament by Isaac which is without ostinato: the motet 'Quis dabit pacem populo timenti'. This important work is based on verses (Sapphic hendecasyllables) from a funeral chorus in Seneca's tragedy *Hercules Oetaeus*. An anonymous poet has added more lines and arranged them in such a way that they seem to refer to Lorenzo de' Medici once more. The text of the second half, where the distinguishing names are mentioned ('dive pax orbis medice'; 'redde Laurenti'), could be a contrafactum, however. Wolfgang Osthoff thinks it is possible that the piece was composed as a chorus for a spoken tragedy.[818] Given the frequency, however, with which German musi-

---

818 *Theatergesang*, vol. I, 170–79. The work is printed in Isaac, *Weltliche Werke*, vol. 28, 49–52.

cians – for example Jakob Locher and Ludwig Senfl – adopted textual elements from 'Quis dabit pacem' etc. for laments on their princes, it is possible that Isaac's work had already been composed for one of them, perhaps Duke Sigismund of Tyrol (*d.*1496). The 'Medici arrangement' would then have been made, for pious reasons, by the compilers of the Florentine source; it may be significant that the only German source of the motet has a sacred contrafactum text only.[819]

The subject of ostinati leads us to some more compositions of great artistic profile and historical significance. Isaac wrote another such piece of this kind for the Medicis: the textless motet 'Palle, palle'.[820] This composition of *c.*1484–92, whose title refers to a famous battlecry of Medici supporters, *pictorially* represents the dynasty's coat of arms.[821] The emblem consists of six *palle* (balls or roundels) on a shield, arranged in an approximately elliptic contour. The lower five balls are red; the uppermost is blue and is decorated with three French fleur-de-lys – the permission to use them having been given to Piero de' Medici by Louis XI of France in 1465. This picture is musically represented by an ostinato tenor consisting of the pitches 'ut-re-mi-re-ut', symbolizing the five lower balls on the shield, plus three higher notes, 'sol-fa-sol', for the three fleur-de-lys. The ostinato sounds three times, with the lower five notes ascending by step. The interpretation of Allan Atlas goes so far as to suggest that the total number of symbols in the tenor, 18 (breve) rests plus 24 notes = 42, is the number expressing the name MEDICI in *gematria* (the method of substituting numbers for the letters of the alphabet), and that Isaac chose as his mensuration for the piece the by then relatively unusual perfect time, ○, because of its external shape. It might further be asked whether the length of the piece, 66 breves before the final, has anything to do with the six symbols in the coat of arms.

Many associations would be possible here – from number symbolism to *soggetti cavati*, and from Busnois' 'In hydraulis' as an obvious compositional model to the genre of 'motto' compositions and others that represent heraldic devices.[822] This piece does not exercise 'word-painting' but actual 'picture-painting'; it is not word-bound but an instrumental composition presenting a visual shape. Its outer voices play around the tenor in more or less patterned diminutions, articulated by many cadences. Also, despite the partial transpositions of the ostinato tenor, the piece remains in C-Ionian, with only occasional excursions into adjacent harmonies. The theatrical task of this music is fulfilled by the premeditated construction, not by the motivic surface of the added voices.

---

[819] For Isaac's motets and their sources, see Martin Just, 'Heinrich Isaacs Motetten in italienischen Quellen', *AnMc* 1 (1963), 1–19.

[820] Isaac, *Weltliche Werke*, vol. 28, 98–9.

[821] A full description is Allan Atlas, 'Heinrich Isaac's Palle, Palle: a new interpretation', *AnMc* 14 (1974), 17–25.

[822] Examples for the latter are discussed in Klaus Hortschansky, 'Eine Devisenkomposition für Karl den Kühnen', in *Festschrift Martin Ruhnke zum 65. Geburtstag* (Neuhausen and Stuttgart: Hänssler, 1986), 144–57; Staehelin, 'Neues zu Bartholomäus Frank'.

Isaac is a composer who somehow connects with everything around him. One further ostinato composition happened to bolster his reputation in direct comparison with Josquin. In the letter already quoted above which the Ferrarese agent Gian sent to Duke Ercole on 2 September 1502, he mentioned that Isaac, when staying in Ferrara shortly before, had composed a motet over the 'fantasia La mi la sol la sol la mi' in only two days.[823] The 'fantasia', in the terms of the writer, was the *soggetto* indicated by these solmization syllables. Isaac's work exists, both in textless form and with a perhaps inauthentic text 'Rogamus te, piissima virgo'.[824] Its ostinato tenor is $e'-b-e'-d'-e'-d'-e'-b$. This clever theme begins like Ockeghem's 'Ma bouche rit', and then retrogrades itself. It is carried through Isaac's four-part piece in strict proportional and mensural transformations; the main effect is a speeding up of the ostinato and a great climax over the two sections of the work. Moreover, the other voices also imitate or paraphrase the ostinato motive. Monotony is successfully avoided but a pentatonic sound like the ringing of many bells results, not entirely incomparable to the music for the walk to the Holy Grail in Wagner's *Parsifal*.

Busnois' 'In hydraulis' forms the backdrop for this ostinato technique, but the free variations of the simple motive in the outer voices also resemble the varied calls of the cuckoo in Martini's 'Cu cu' Mass. The piece further belongs in the Italian context of playing with solmization syllables and stitching poems together from them, and in the tradition of abstract ostinati as represented by Josquin's Mass 'La sol fa re mi'. This work and – as usual – the uncertainty of its date have often been discussed.[825] It is a glorification of the ostinato principle and a demonstration of Josquin's mastery over his material: although the five-note ostinato is sounded incessantly in the tenor and often in other voices, the four-part counterpoint flourishes uninhibited. Josquin does seem to follow Martini's 'Cu cu' Mass in his striving for ever new and free rhythmic variations. Thus, the connection between the Mass and Isaac's 'La mi la sol' (composed, as we have seen, 1502 in Ferrara) may be more than coincidental. When Isaac expanded his motet into a Mass cycle later, he surely thought of Josquin's cycle as a point of departure.

Josquin's two most famous *soggetto* or ostinato compositions, both biographically significant, are 'Ut Phebi radiis' and 'Illibata Dei virgo nutrix'.[826] It seems that the many riddles of 'Ut Phebi radiis' are now more or less solved, although weighty theories have been heaped on to this slender work.[827] The first part of

---

[823] Staehelin, *Messen*, vol. 2, 56 f: '. . . ha facto uno moteto sopra una fantasia nomata La mi la so la so lami, lo qualle e molto bono, et hallo facto in dui jorni'.

[824] Printed without text in Isaac, *Weltliche Werke*, vol. 28, 87–9. For the history and later uses of the motet – in a Mass cycle, for example – see Staehelin, *Messen*, vol. 3, 63–7.

[825] A thorough evaluation of the Mass and its repercussions is Haar, 'Missa "La sol fa re mi"'. I wonder whether Ercole d'Este was singing the tenor of *this* Mass when approached by the Mantuan agent on 7 December 1481 (see p. 612).

[826] Josquin, *Werken*, fasc. 7, no. 22, and 14, no. 27, respectively.

[827] Most convincing is the theory of a link with a projected meeting (1479/80) of the Order of the Golden Fleece, reflecting its symbols: see Prizer, 'Music and ceremonial', 129 ff; Jaap van Benthem, 'A waif, a wedding and a worshipped child: Josquin's *Ut Phebi radiis* and the Order of the Golden Fleece', *TVNM* 37 (1987), 64–81.

the text of 'Illibata Dei virgo nutrix' contains Josquin's own 'signature' as an acrostic: IOSQVIN DES PREZ.

It has also been claimed that there is an acrostic in the second part of the text referring to 'Aqua Escauga', the river Escaut, implying Josquin's birthplace in one of the towns along this river, such as Condé (where he died as provost of the collegiate church).[828]

'Illibata Dei virgo nutrix' is a large work in two sections and for five voices. Its cantus firmus is one of the simplest of ostinati: 'La mi la' – sounded alternately on the pitches $d'-a-d'$ and $g-d-g$. The choice of the theme, and its strict treatment in four different speeds (one in the first section, three in the second), are particularly reminiscent of 'In hydraulis'. As there, the mode (G-Dorian) is so clearly outlined by the ostinato that the harmonic monotony is considerable. The younger master acts very much in the spirit of Busnois and Regis by insisting on this modal austerity and by decorating the sound with the contrapuntal motion of the voices rather than seeking variety through extraneous sonorities. Much of the effect of the piece lies in the melodic lines. Within this orientation, the stylistic display is incredibly rich and varied. Antonowycz and Sherr[829] are probably correct in detaching the work from the early Milanese years where most other scholars had placed it: its 'archaisms' are intentional, its innovations disguised. As regards the latter, there is, for example, a genuine dominant-seventh chord in bar 112 for the words 'tota pulchra'.

Richard Sherr is also right in stressing the close contact of the papal chapel with Netherlands sacred genres – a contact continuously renewed by northern singers who joined the chapel and surely supplied more music from the north. In this case, we are dealing with the genre of the great five-voice cantus firmus motet in the manner of Regis and Obrecht. I believe that a singer such as Jean Cordier from Bruges, who entered the chapel in 1469, must have brought with him an anthology of tenor motets. New motets were still being written at Rome in the 1480s and 90s, for example by Weerbeke. Josquin's work might well have been composed at the time of his entry in 1486. Josquin is humbler than the other masters, as it were, in that he chooses as his cantus firmus one of the simplest possible subjects: 'la mi la'. But this *soggetto cavato* really means: Maria. Josquin's motet is a personal prayer signed with his name, and a singers' prayer.

The many duets have been said to be close to Dufay and the 'Burgundian' school, supporting the early dating that is conventionally assumed. Apart from the fallacy of placing a Josquin work early because it contains reminiscences of older music (what would have to be said, in that case, of the Mass 'Pange lingua'?), the opening duet of the motet already shows that here there is a different aesthetic:

[828] See Herbert Kellman, 'Josquin and the courts of Netherlands and France', in Lowinsky ed., *Josquin des Prez*, 181–216, esp. 206 ff.

[829] Myroslaw Antonowycz, '"Illibata Dei Virgo": a melodic self-portrait of Josquin des Prez', in Lowinsky ed., *Josquin des Prez*, 545–59; Richard Sherr, 'Illibata Dei Virgo Nutrix and Josquin's Roman Style', *JAMS* 41 (1988), 434–64.

Example 98*a* Josquin des Prez, 'Illibata Dei virgo nutrix'

[Unblemished virgin, mother of God]

The canonic duet is both too lively and too insistent for Dufay. It circles in itself, a hidden ostinato. Dufay and his contemporaries would not have repeated the rhythms almost identically from bar to bar – the 'almost' is important – and they would not have accepted such angular gestures as the transition from bars 3 to 4. In many works, Josquin cultivates leaps of a fifth and larger intervals in one voice around a held note in the other – with or without octave displacement. Characteristic, however, and aurally obvious is the balanced total shape of the phrase. It is a line of poetry: a beautifully articulated line in three phrases, which concludes as safely on to itself as if it were rhymed. One could call these six bars of music 'superbly timed'; they are exactly as long as they should be. This last quality is only hinted at by the similar phrase in 'Ave mundi spes Maria' (see pp. 532 f).

This opening duet, which is immediately repeated an octave lower by the altus and bassus, takes a carefree attitude to the words. Not so the long duet in the middle of the first section:

Example 98*b*

Example 98*b* (*cont.*)

[Safe intercessor for man's crime]

Here there are two very different duetting sections, although they are both canonic. The first plays with the syllables 'vi-ri ne-fas' etc. in such a transparent way that each syllable is actually *heard twice*. This is not what usually happens in older duets! The technique was also known to Obrecht, who uses it to great effect in his large cantus firmus motets (for example in the unforgettable canonic duets of 'Salve crux arbor / O crux lignum'). The second section is a sequential pattern of two motives, not one: the dotted figure descending straight, three minims long (bars 32–4), and then a four-minim motive which is different in the two voices. In the remainder of the first section, imitations like these – more of the declamatory type – are sown through the structure, seemingly regardless of the 'la mi la' in the tenor.

The meaning of 'la mi la' emerges more and more forcefully in the second part of the work. In this part, Josquin starts with paired imitation and, for the first time, homorhythmic declamation. Here – not before – he reveals his Milanese background.

From bar 100 onwards, more and more individual words, brief and pregnant, receive their own imitative entries and thus expressive attention. Even without giving the music it can be demonstrated what happens: the verbal units are 'flos humilium' (5 syllables), 'virgo decora' (5), 'Vale ergo' (4), 'tota pulchra' (4), 'ut luna' (3), 'electa' (3), 'ut sol' (2, or 1 + 1), and 'clarissima gaude' (6). Thus, the units – corresponding to points of imitation – become shorter in pairs, until the section is rounded off by a large gesture. Furthermore, during this climax, the speed and frequency of 'la mi la' has increased. After bar 125, there follows a '*lauda*-like' section in declamatory style and triple metre, which, however, soon thickens into a canonic maze. 'La mi la' is now sung by all the voices except the cantus, according to the words 'Console the *singers* of la mi la'.[830] The notes have become real people. Here is this genuine 'singers' prayer':

Example 98c

[Hail thee, only friend, console those singing 'la mi la' in thy praise.]

---

[830] In bars 126-7, the 'cum sola' of the sources (which seem to read 'Salve tu sola *cum sola* amica') must be omitted. It does not make sense textually and distorts the metrical regularity, which in this passage is of four hendecasyllables.

The company arrives on the D major chord like prisoners stepping out into the sunlight, overwhelmed by Her presence. In this moment, they can only utter 'la mi la'. The continuing repercussions on *A* and *a* sound like self-forgotten prayers. There is a precedent in Dufay for this D major chord: the overwhelming appearance of the D major sonority at 'grandis templum machine' in 'Nuper rosarum flores'. But unlike here, Dufay at that point wants to draw our attention away from human beings and to greater things.

For the singers of 'la mi la', the excitement recedes with the broad melody of 'in tua laude'. Taken together, the whole double phrase 'consola la mi la canentes in tua laude' again is wonderfully timed and lands safely on its rhyme and cadence. The circling quasi-ostinatos in all the voices have prepared this.

The following and last section, again in duple metre, is a series of four grand, almost identical invocations whose words paraphrase the 'Ave Maria'. The repetitions are so beautiful that they could go on eternally. They are *also* a convincing structure. A harmony is somehow found between architectonic or rhetorical means (balance, repetition, climax) and expressive ends. It is as if 'ostinato' had become 'the pulse of the praying soul'.

MUSIC MANUSCRIPTS

1. By countries

A: Austria

A-HEI: Heiligenkreuz, Archiv des Zisterzienserstifts, MS without shelf-mark 122 n., 145

A-Iu n.s.: (*Wolkenstein* MS *B*; *WolkB*). Innsbruck, Universitätsbibliothek, MS without shelf-mark 119, 352

A-LIs 529: (*Linz* fragments). Linz, Bundesstaatliche Studienbibliothek, MS 529 (frg) 521, 523, 526, 531, 536

A-M 749: Melk, Stiftsbibliothek, MS 749 (frg. from the same MS as *D-Nst 9 and 9a*) 115

A-Wn 2777: (*Wolkenstein* MS *A*; *WolkA*). Vienna, Österreichische National-bibliothek, Handschriftensammlung, Cod. 2777 119, 313, 319 n., 352

A-Wn 2856: (*Mondsee-Wiener Liederhandschrift*). Vienna, Österreichische National-bibliothek, Handschriftensammlung, Cod. 2856 341 n., 500

A-Wn 3013: (*Eberhard von Cersne* MS). Vienna, Österreichische National-bibliothek, Handschriftensammlung, Cod. 3013 350–51, 500 n.

A-Wn 4494: (*Orationale of Frederick III*). Vienna, Österreichische National-bibliothek, Handschriftensammlung, Cod. 4494 329–30 (Plate 5)

A-Wn 5094: Vienna, Österreichische Nationalbibliothek, Handschriftensamm-lung, Cod. 5094 116, 120–21, 260, 266, 319 n., 355 n., 356, 373

A-Ws 355: Vienna, Schottenstift, MS 355 (frg.) 536

A-ZW: Zwettl, Bibliothek des Zisterzienserstifts, MS without shelf-mark 152, 253, 257

B: Belgium

B-Amp M6: Antwerp, Museum Plantin-Moretus, MS M6 (frg.) 242

B-Bcaloen: (*Gruuthuse* MS). Private collection Baron Ernest van Caloen, Casteel Ten Berghe, Koolkerke (Bruges), MS without shelf-mark 345–6, 351, 355

B-Br 215–216: Brussels, Bibliothèque Royale Albert Ièr, MS 215–216 390

B-Br 228 and *B-Br 11293*: (*Chanson albums of Margaret of Austria*). Brussels, Bibliothèque Royale Albert Ièr, MSS 228 and 11293 633 n., 635

B-Br 5557: (*BR*; *Br 5557*). Brussels, Bibliothèque Royale Albert Ièr, MS 5557 240, 405, 430

F-CA 1328: (*CaB*). Cambrai, Bibliothèque Municipale, MS 1328   65–6

F-CH 564: (*Chantilly* MS; *Ch*). Chantilly, Musée Condé, MS 564 (*olim* 1047)   25, 37, 40, 46–7, 58–60, 67, 82 n., 132 n., 140, 141

F-Dm 517: (*Dijon* Chansonnier). Dijon, Bibliothèque Municipale, MS 517   450–51, 455, 460, 523

F-Dm 2837: Dijon, Bibliothèque Municipale, MS 2837   137

F-Lm: (gradual-antiphonal). Lille, Bibliothèque Municipale, MS 26   473 n.

F-Pn fr.146: (*Roman de Fauvel*; *Fauv*). Paris, Bibliothèque nationale, fonds français, MS 146   19 n.

F-Pn fr.1584: (*Machaut* MS *A*; *MachA*). Paris, Bibliothèque nationale, fonds français, MS 1584   67 n.

F-Pn fr.9221: (*Machaut* MS *E*; *MachE*). Paris, Bibliothèque nationale, fonds français, MS 9221   67 n.

F-Pn fr.9346: (*Bayeux* MS; monophonic chansonnier). Paris, Bibliothèque nationale, fonds français, MS 9346   455 n.

F-Pn fr.12744: (monophonic chansonnier). Paris, Bibliothèque nationale, fonds français, MS 12744   455 n.

F-Pn fr.15123: (*Pixérécourt* MS; *Pix*). Paris, Bibliothèque nationale, fonds français, MS 15123   446 n., 559, 561, 562 n., 575

F-Pn 568: (*Pit*). Paris, Bibliothèque nationale, fonds italien, MS 568   75, 89

F-Pn n. a. f. 4379 (part I): (= *Seville* Chansonnier; see *E-Sco 5-1-43*). Paris, Bibliothèque nationale, nouv. acq. fr., MS 4379, part I   344 n., 558 n.

F-Pn n. a. f. 4379 (part II): (*PC II*). Paris, Bibliothèque nationale, nouv. acq. fr., MS 4379, part II   137

F-Pn n. a. f. 4379 (part III): (*PC III*). Paris, Bibliothèque nationale, nouv. acq. fr., MS 4379, part III   137, 348, 358

F-Pn n. a. f. 4379 (part IV): (chansonnier). Paris, Bibliothèque nationale, nouv. acq. fr., MS 4379, part IV   137

F-Pn n. a. f. 4917: (*Pz*). Paris, Bibliothèque nationale, nouv. acq. fr., MS 4917   137

F-Pn n. a. f. 6771: (*Reina* Codex; *PR*; *Rei*). Paris, Bibliothèque nationale, nouv. acq. fr., MS 6771   75, 90–91, 103, 137

F-Pn n. a. f. 10660: Paris, Bibliothèque nationale, nouv. acq. fr., MS 10660   137

F-Pn n. a. f. 23190: (*F-SERRANT*; *Trémoïlle* MS). Paris, Bibliothèque nationale, nouv. acq. fr., MS 23190

F-Pn Rés. Vmc. ms. 57: (*Nivelle de la Chaussée* Chansonnier; *Niv*; formerly *F-Pthibault*). Paris, Bibliothèque nationale, Département de la Musique, MS Rés. Vmc. 57   393, 449 n., 450, 460

F-Pn Rothschild 2973: (*Cordiforme* Chansonnier; *Cord*). Paris, Bibliothèque Nationale, Collection Rothschild, MS 2973   559, 566 n.

F-Sm 222: (*Str*). Strasbourg, Bibliothèque municipale, MS M 222 C 22 (burnt in 1870)   108, 111, 112 n., 115–16, 118, 120–21, 137, 140, 243 n.

GB: Great Britain

GB-SHRs: Shrewsbury, Shrewsbury School, Ms. VI (*olim* Mus. III. 43) 386–7

GB-WRec 178: (*Eton* Choirbook). Windsor, Eton College, MS 178   377, 379, 380 n., 385, 387, 399

GB-Yi: (*York* Masses). York University, Borthwick Institute of Historical Research, MS Music 1   388

H: Hungary

H-Bn 243: (*Tyrnau* MS). Budapest, Országos Széchenyi Könyvtár, MS lat. 243   337

I: Italy

I-Ac 187: Assisi, Biblioteca comunale, MS 187   91

I-AO: (*Ao*). Aosta, Biblioteca del Seminario Maggiore, Cod.15 (*olim* A^I D 19)   117, 137, 244, 245 n., 253–6, 259, 262, 265–6, 505

I-AO 9-E-17 and 9-E-19: (graduals). Aosta, Biblioteca del Seminario Maggiore, MSS 9-E-17 (= C 3) and 9-E-19 (= D 16)   331

I-Bc Q 15: (*BL*; *Q 15*). Bologna, Civico Museo Bibliografico Musicale (*olim* Liceo Musicale), MS Q 15 (*olim* 37)   118, 136, 140, 141, 145, 160, 161, 171, 173–4, 176, 212, 243, 244, 245 n.

I-Bc Q 16: (*Q 16*). Bologna, Civico Museo Bibliografico Musicale (*olim* Liceo Musicale), MS Q 16 (*olim* 109)   553, 559–60, 575

I-Bsp frg. A-E: Bologna, Archivio Musicale della Fabbriceria di San Petronio, MS without shelf-mark, frg. A-E   355 n., 356, 388, 590–91

I-Bu 2216: (*BU*). Bologna, Biblioteca Universitaria, MS 2216   137, 181, 261, 323

I-CFm 57, 63, 79, 98, 101, 102: Cividale del Friuli, Museo Archeologico Nazionale, MSS LVII, LXIII, LXXIX, XCVIII, CI, CII   93–4, 337–8

I-Fd 21: Florence, Archivio Musicale dell'Opera di S. M. del Fiore, MS 21   592 n.

I-Fl 87: (*Squarcialupi* Codex; *Fl*; *Sq*). Florence, Biblioteca Medicea-Laurenziana, MS Med. Pal. 87   90, 297

I-Fl 2211: Florence, Biblioteca Medicea-Laurenziana, Archivio Capitolare di San Lorenzo, MS 2211   61 n., 90

I-Fl plut. 29.1: (*F*). Florence, Biblioteca Medicea-Laurenziana, MS plut.29. 1   19 n., 100 n.

I-Fn B. R. 229: (*Braccesi* Codex; *BR 229*; *Fn 229*). Florence, Biblioteca Nazionale Centrale, MS Banco Rari 229 (*olim* Magl. XIX, 59)   536, 559–61, 563, 570, 582

I-Fn B. R. 230: Florence, Biblioteca Nazionale Centrale, MS Banco Rari 230 (*olim* Magl. XIX, 141)   581

I-Fn Magl. XIX, 112bis: (*Fn 112bis*). Florence, Biblioteca Nazionale Centrale, MS Magl. XIX, 112bis   338, 398, 590

I-Fn Magl. XIX, 121: Florence, Biblioteca Nazionale Centrale, MS Magl. XIX, 121   581

I-PAVu 362: (*Pavia* Chansonnier). Pavia, Biblioteca Universitaria, MS Aldini 362   455, 558

I-Pc C 55 and 56: (processionals). Padua, Biblioteca capitolare, MSS C 55 and C 56   592 n.

I-PEco 431: (*Per*). Perugia, Biblioteca Comunale Augusta, MS 431 (*olim G. 20*)   553, 559, 575, 578, 589–90

I-PEco 1013: Perugia, Biblioteca Comunale Augusta, MS 1013   535 n.

I-PESo 1144: (lute book). Pesaro, Biblioteca Oliveriana, MS 1144   584

I-PIca s.n.: Pisa, Biblioteca Cateriniana del Seminario, gradual without shelf-mark   30

I-PIca 176: Pisa, Biblioteca Cateriniana del Seminario, MS 176   238

I-Pu 1475: (*PadA*). Padua, Biblioteca Universitaria, MS 1475   94

I-Rc 2856: (*Casanatense* Chansonnier; *Cas*). Rome, Biblioteca Casanatense, MS 2856   361, 558, 560, 562, 565

I-Rvat C. G. XIII 27: (*Cappella Giulia* Chansonnier; *C.G.*). Rome, Biblioteca Apostolica Vaticana, MS Cappella Giulia XIII 27   559, 561, 636 n.

I-Rvat CS 14, 15, 26, 35, 41, 51: (*CS 14, 15, 26, 35, 41, 51*). Rome, Biblioteca Apostolica Vaticana, MSS Cappella Sistina 14, etc.   *14*, 424, 430, 472, 578, 602 n., 605, 616;   *15*, 249, 605;   *26*, 605, 616;   *35*, 424, 605, 616;   *41*, 430;   *51*, 602 n., 605, 616

I-Rvat Chigi C. VIII 234: (*Chigi* Codex). Rome, Biblioteca Apostolica Vaticana, MS Chigi C. VIII 234   430, 606

I-Rvat SP B 80: (*San Pietro* MS; *SP*). Rome, Biblioteca Apostolica Vaticana, MS San Pietro B 80   406, 408, 430, 437 n., 457, 466, 476 n., 588

I-Rvat 1411: (*ROu*; *RU²*). Rome, Biblioteca Vaticana, MS Urb. lat. 1411   545, 570

I-Rvat 1419: (*RU¹*). Rome, Biblioteca Vaticana, MS Urb. lat. 1419   93

I-Tn J. II. 9: (*Cyprus* MS; *TuB*). Turin, Biblioteca nazionale, MS J. II. 9   37, 416 n.

I-TRc 1947-4: Trent, Biblioteca Comunale, MS 1947-4   523

I-TRmd: (*Trent* Codex 93). Trento, Museo Diocesano, MS B. L., now *I-TRmn 93*

I-TRmn 87 (*I and II*), *88, 89, 90, 91, 92* (*I and II*), *93*: (*Trent* Codices; *Tr 87* etc.). Trento, Museo Provinciale d'Arte, Castello del Buonconsiglio, MSS 87, etc. (MS 93 formerly *I-TRmd*)   *87*, 92, 137, 178, 239, 241, 244, 247, 253–5, 257, 259, 262, 291 n., 360, 507;   *88*, 240, 253, n., 266, 291, 399 n., 406, 408, 423, 428–30, 436–7, 460, 510–11, 513, 525–6, 529–30, 546, 572;   *89*, 253 n., 291, 366–7, 393 n., 399, 406, 423–4, 429–31, 437, 438, 460, 510–11, 513, 521, 529–30, 533, 535, 618;   *90*, 253 n., 266, 291, 406, 424–5, 427, 430, 438, 444, 496–7, 499, 510–11, 513, 546, 566;   *91*, 253 n., 291, 510, 526, 532, 535;   *92 see 87*;   *93*, 240, 242, 253 n., 266, 294, 423, 430, 447 n., 510, 524–5, 529–30, 546

I-VEcap 755, 756, 757, 758 and 759: (*Verona* choirbooks). Verona, Biblioteca Capitolare, MSS DCCLV, DCCLVI, DCCLVII, DCCLVIII, DCCLIX   406, 408, 591

I-Vnm It. IV, 1795-8: Venice, Biblioteca Nazionale Marciana, MS It. IV, 1795-8 (10653-10656) 541 n.

I-Vnm It. IX, 145: Venice, Biblioteca Nazionale Marciana, MS It. IX, 145 (7554) 156

NL: *Netherlands*

NL-Lu 2720: Leiden, Universiteitsbibliotheek, MS B. P. L. 2720 69, 73-4, 151, 190, 195

NL-Mr: (*Maastricht* fragments). Maastricht, Rijksarchief van Limburg, MS without shelf-mark 361

NL-Uu 37 I, II: Utrecht, Bibliotheek der Rijksuniversiteit, MS 6 E 37/I, II (*olim* 1846) 68, 69, 95, 99, 100, 122

P: *Portugal*

P-Pm 714: (*Oporto/Porto* Chansonnier). Oporto, Biblioteca Pública Municipal, MS 714 392 n., 427, 546-7, 570

PL: *Poland*

PL-Kj 2464: Kraków, Biblioteka Jagiellońska, MS 2464 (*olim* DD X 12) 291

PL-Kj 40098: (*Glogauer Liederbuch*; *Glog*). Kraków, Biblioteka Jagiellońska. Formerly Berlin, Deutsche Staatsbibliothek, Mus. ms. 40098 263, 317, 362, 367, 496, 501-3, 515, 526, 530 n., 533, 535, 538, 601

PL-Pu 7022: (*Lwów* fragments). Poznań, Biblioteka Uniwersytecka, MS 7022 503 n., 515, 523

PL-Pu: (*Pu 2*). Poznań, Biblioteka Uniwersytecka, Music Division, frg. without shelf-mark 260

PL-Wn 8054: (*Kras*). Warsaw, Biblioteka Narodowa, MS III. 8054 (*olim* Krasiński MS 52) 115, 122, 138, 177, 260-62

PL-Wn 378: (*StP*). Warsaw, Biblioteka Narodowa, MS Lat. F. I. 378 (lost, but microfilm held at *PL-Pu*, MS 695) 115, 260-62

PL-WRk 58: (*Neumarkt* Cantionale). Wrocław, Biblioteka Kapitulna, MS 58 332

PL-Wu Mf. 2016: Warsaw, Biblioteka Uniwersytecka, Oddział Zbiorów Muzychnych, MS Mf. 2016 (*olim* Rps. mus. 58), from Wrocław University 515-18, 532 n., 533, 535-6

SA: *South Africa*

SA-Cp: (*Grey* MS). Cape Town, South African Public Library, MS Grey 3. b. 12 593, 610

US: *United States of America*

US-Cn 54: (*Pavia* MS of 1391). Chicago, Newberry Library, MS 54 57-9

US-NH 91: (*Mellon* Chansonnier; *Mel*). New Haven, Yale University, Beinecke Library, MS 91 378, 427, 455, 461, 558, 575

US-NYcu 21: (*Columbia* fragments). New York, Columbia University, Smith Western MSS, MS Add. 21   241, 438

US-NYpm 978: New York, Pierpont Morgan Library, MS M 978   84 n.

US-PHci: (*Ileborgh* tablature). Philadelphia, Curtis Institute of Music, MS without shelf-mark   291, 373

US-Wc 14: Washington (D. C.), Library of Congress, MS M 2.1. C 6a. 14   81

US-Wc M 2. 1. L 25 Case: (*Laborde* Chansonnier; *Lab*). Washington (D. C.), Library of Congress, MS M 2. 1. L 25 (Case)   451

2. Informal titles and abbreviations

Anna von Köln Songbook: *D-Bds 8° 280*

Ao: *I-AO*

Apel Codex: *D-LEu 1494*

BarcB: *E-Bc 971*

Bayeux MS: *F-Pn fr.9346*

BerK: *D-Bk 78. C. 28*

BL; *Q 15*: *I-Bc Q 15*

BR; *Br 5557*: *B-Br 5557*

Braccesi Codex; *BR 229*: *I-Fn B. R. 229*

BU: *I-Bu 2216*

Bursfelde Ceremonial: *D-As 8ᵃ Cod. 62*

Buxheim Organ Book; *Bux*: *D-Mbs 3725*

CaB: *F-CA 1328*

Cancionero musical de la Colombina; *CMC*: *E-Sco 7-I-28*

Cancionero musical de Palacio; *CMP*: *E-Mp 1335*

Cappella Giulia Chansonnier; *C. G.*: *I–Rvat C. G. XIII 27*

Cappella Sistina Codices; *CS 14 etc.*: *I-Rvat CS 14 etc.*

Casanatense Chansonnier; *Cas*: *I-Rc 2856*

Cersne MS: *A-Wn 3013*

C.G.: *Cappella Giulia* Chansonnier: *I-Rvat C. G. XIII 27*

Ch; *Chantilly MS*: *F-CH 564*

Chigi Codex: *I-Rvat Chigi C. VIII 234*

CMC; *Cancionero musical de la Colombina*: *E-Sco 7-I-28*

CMP; *Cancionero musical de Palacio*: *E-Mp 1335*

Colmarer Liederhandschrift: *D-Mbs cgm 4997*

Columbia fragments: *US-NYcu 21*

Copenhagen Chansonnier; *Cop* : *DK-Kk Thott 291*[8]

Cordiforme Chansonnier; *Cord*: *F-Pn Rothschild 2973*

CS 14, 15, 26, 35, 41, 51: *I-Rvat CS 14 etc.*

Egerton MS: *GB-Lbl Egerton 3307*

Em: *D-Mbs lat.14274*

Eng: CH-EN 314

Escorial V. III. 24; *EscA: E-E V. III. 24*

Escorial IV. a. 24; *EscB: E-E IV. a. 24*

Eton Choirbook: *GB-WRec 178*

F: I-Fl plut. 29.1

Faenza MS; *FA: I-FZc 117*

Fauv; *Roman de Fauvel: F-Pn fr. 146*

Fl; *Squarcialupi* Codex; *Sq: I-Fl 87*

Fn 112bis, 176, 178: I-Fn Magl. XIX, 112bis etc.

Fn 229; *Braccesi* Codex; *BR 229: I-Fn B. R. 229*

Fountains fragments; *LoF: GB-Lbl add.40011 B*

FP; *Panciatichi* Codex: *I-Fn 26*

Fr 2356; *Ric 2: I-Fr 2356*

FZ: I-FZc 117

Gaffurius Codices: *I-Md librone 1–4*

Glogauer Liederbuch; *Glog: PL-Kj 40098*

Grey MS: *SA-Cp*

Gruuthuse MS: *B-Bcaloen*

Hohenfurt Cantionale: *CS-VB 42*

Ileborgh Tablature: *US-PHci*

Ivrea MS; *Iv: I-IV 115*

Jistebnický Cantionale: *CS-Pn II C 7*

Königsteiner Liederbuch: D-Bds 4° 719

Košice/Kassa fragments: *CS-BRmn 33, CS-BRu 318*

Kras: PL-Wn 8054

Kress Cantionale: *CH-Bu 46*

Laborde Chansonnier; *Lab: US-Wc M 2. 1. L 25*

Leopold Codex: *D-Mbs 3154*

Llibre Vermell: E-MO 1

Lo; *LoC: GB-Lbl add.29987*

Lochamer-Liederbuch; *Loch: D-Bds 40613*

LoD: GB-Lbl add.27630

LoF; *Fountains* fragments: *GB-Lbl add.40011 B*

Lucca Choirbook; *Lu: I-Las 238*

Lucca MS; *Mancini* Codex; *Man: I-Las 184*

Lwów fragments: *PL-Pu 7022*

Machaut MS A; *MachA: F-Pn fr.1584*

Machaut MS E; *MachE: F-Pn fr.9221*

Mancini Codex; *Man*; *Lucca* MS: *I-Las 184*

MC; *Montecassino* MS; *I-MC 871*

Mellon Chansonnier; *Mel: US-NH 91*

ModA, B, C, D, E: I-MOe

Mondsee-Wiener Liederhandschrift: A-Wn 2856

Montecassino MS; *MC: I-MC 871*

Moosburg Gradual: *D-Mu 156*
MüD: D-Mbs cgm 716
Münsterbilsen MS: *B-Br 9786-90*
Neumarkt Cantionale: *PL-WRk 58*
Nivelle de la Chaussée Chansonnier; *Niv: F-Pn Rés. Vmc. ms. 57*
O; Ox: GB-Ob 213
Old Hall MS; *OH: GB-Lbl add. 57950*
Oporto/Porto Chansonnier: *P-Pm 714*
Orationale of Frederick III: A-Wn 4494
Ox; O: GB-Ob 213
PadA: I-Pu 1475
Panciatichi Codex; *FP: I-Fn 26*
Pavia Chansonnier: *I-PAVu 362*
Pavia MS of 1391: *US-Cn 54*
PC II, PC III: F-Pn n. a. f. 4379 (part II, III)
Pepys MS: *GB-Cmc Pepys 1236*
Per: I-PEco 431
Pit: F-Pn 568
Pixérécourt MS; *Pix: F-Pn fr. 15123*
Porto/Oporto Chansonnier: *P-Pm 714*
PR; Reina Codex; *Rei: F-Pn n. a. f. 6771*
Pr : CS-Pu
Prince Arthur Chansonnier: *GB-Cmc Pepys 1760*
F-Pthibault: F-Pn Rés. Vmc. ms. 57
Pu 2: PL-Pu
Pz: F-Pn n. a. f. 4917
Q 15, Q 16: I-Bc Q 15, Q 16
Reina Codex; *PR; Rei: F-Pn n. a. f. 6771*
Ric 2; Fr 2356: I-Fr 2356
Ritson MS: *GB-Lbl add. 5665*
Robertsbridge fragment: *GB-Lbl add. 28850*
Roman de Fauvel; Fauv: F-Pn fr. 146
ROu; RU ² : I-Rvat 1411
RU ¹: I-Rvat 1419
San Pietro MS; *SP: I-Rvat SP B 80*
Schedel Songbook; *Sche: D-Mbs cgm 810*
Segovia MS; *Seg: E-SE*
Selden MS: *GB-Ob Selden B 26*
F-SERRANT; Trémoille MS: *F-Pn n. a. f. 23190*
Seville Chansonnier; *Sev/Par: E-Sco 5-1-43*
SP; San Pietro MS: *I-Rvat SP B 80*
Speciálník Codex: *CS-HK II A 7*
Squarcialupi Codex; *Sq: I-Fl 87*
St Emmeram Codex; *Em: D-Mbs lat. 14274*

StP: *PL-Wn 378*
Str: *F-Sm 222*
Strahov MS; *Strah*: *CS-Ppp D.G. IV.47*
Theophilus mystery: *D-TRs 1120/128*
Tongeren MS: *B-HAS*
Tournai Mass: *B-Tc 476*
Trémoille MS; *F-SERRANT*: *F-Pn n. a. f. 23190*
Trent Codex '93': *I-TRmd*, now *I-TRmn 93*
Trent Codices; *Tr 87, 88, 89, 90, 91, 92, 93*: *I-TRmn 87* etc.
Trinity roll: *GB-Ctc 0.3.58*
Tyrnau MS: *H-Bn 243*
Utrecht Songbook: *D-Bds 8° 190*
Vatican MSS: *I-Rvat*
Verona choirbooks *755, 756, 757, 758, 759*: *I-VEcap*
W; *Wolfenbüttel* Chansonnier: *D-W 287*
Wolfenbüttel Chansonnier; *W*: *D-W 287*
Wolkenstein MS *A*; *WolkA*: *A-Wn 2777*
Wolkenstein MS *B*; *WolkB*: *A-Iu*

BIBLIOGRAPHY

All bibliographical abbreviations follow the usage of *The New Grove*. Others are listed here in the alphabetical sequence.

Abraham, Gerald, ed.: *The Age of Humanism (1540-1630)* (NOHM IV) (Oxford and New York: Oxford University Press, 1968)

Adler, Guido, *et al.* eds: *Sechs Trienter Codices: Geistliche und weltliche Kompositionen des XV. Jahrhunderts* (DTOe VII, etc.) (Vienna, 1900-24 R Graz: Akademische Druck- und Verlagsanstalt, 1959) (Denkmäler der Tonkunst in Österreich, Jahrgang VII = vols. 14-15; XI/1 = vol. 22; XIX/1 = vol. 38; XXVII/1 = vol. 53; XXXI = vol. 61)

Agricola, Alexander: *Opera omnia*, ed. Edward R. Lerner, 5 vols. (Rome: American Institute of Musicology, 1961-70) (CMM, 22)

AH see Dreves-Blume eds

Altenburg, Detlev: 'Die Musik in der Fronleichnamsprozession des 14. und 15. Jahrhunderts', *MD* 38 (1984), 5-24

Ameln, Konrad: '"Resonet in laudibus" – "Joseph, lieber Joseph mein"', *Jahrbuch für Liturgik und Hymnologie* 15 (1970), 52-112

Ameln, Konrad, ed.: *Locheimer Liederbuch und das Fundamentum Organisandi von Conrad Paumann* (facs edn) (Kassel etc.: Bärenreiter, 1972) (Documenta Musicologica, 2nd ser., vol. 3)

Angerer, Joachim F.: *Die liturgisch-musikalische Erneuerung der Melker Reform. Studien zur Erforschung der Musikpraxis in den Benediktinerklöstern des 15. Jahrhunderts* (Vienna: Verlag der Österreichischen Akademie der Wissenschaften, 1974)

Anglès, Higinio: *La música en la Corte de los Reyes Católicos*, vol. 1: Polifonia Religiosa, 2nd edn (Barcelona, 1960) (Monumentos de la Música Española, I)
Scripta Musicologica, ed. José López-Calo, 3 vols. (Rome, 1975-6)

Anglès, Higinio, and Romeu Figueras, José, eds: *La música en la Corte de los Reyes Católicos, Cancionero Musical de Palacio (Siglos XV-XVI)*, 3 vols. (Barcelona, 1947-) (Monumentos de la Música Española, V, X and XIV)

Antiphonale Sacrosanctae Romanae Ecclesiae pro diurnis horis (Paris etc.: Desclée, 1924)

Antiquitates Musicae in Polonia see Perz ed., *Sources*

Apel, Willi: *The Notation of Polyphonic Music 900-1600*, 2nd edn (Cambridge, Mass.: The Mediaeval Academy of America, 1944)

Apel, Willi, ed.: *French Secular Compositions of the Fourteenth Century* (FSC), 3 vols. (Stuttgart: American Institute of Musicology, 1970-2) (CMM, 53)
French Secular Music of the Late Fourteenth Century (FSM) (Cambridge, Mass.: The Mediaeval Academy of America, 1950)

Keyboard Music of the Fourteenth and Fifteenth Centuries (Rome: American Institute of Musicology, 1963) (CEKM, 1)

Apfel, Ernst: *Studien zur Satztechnik der mittelalterlichen englischen Musik*, 2 vols. (Heidelberg: Winter, 1959)

Archivum Musices Metropolitanum Mediolanense, 13 vols. (Milan: Veneranda Fabbrica del Duomo, 1958-)

Arlt, Wulf: 'Repertoirefragen peripherer Mehrstimmigkeit: das Beispiel des Codex Engelberg 314', in A. Pompilio *et al.* eds, *Trasmissione . . .*, vol. 1 (Round Tables), 97-123

Arlt, Wulf (chairman): 'Symposium "Peripherie" und "Zentrum" in der Geschichte der ein- und mehrstimmigen Musik des 12. bis 14. Jahrhunderts' (with F. Reckow, M. Huglo, D. G. Hughes, J. Stenzl, M. Haas, L. Gushee), in H. Kühn and P. Nitsche eds, *Bericht über den internationalen musikwissenschaftlichen Kongress Berlin 1974* (Kassel etc.: Bärenreiter, 1980), 13-170

L'Ars Nova Italiana del Trecento (Certaldo: Comune di Certaldo, 1959-)

Atlas, Allan W.: *Music at the Aragonese Court of Naples* (Cambridge: Cambridge University Press, 1985)

The Cappella Giulia Chansonnier (Rome, Biblioteca Apostolica Vaticana, C.G.XIII.27) (Brooklyn etc.: Institute of Mediaeval Music, 1975) (Musicological Studies and Documents, 27)

'Conflicting attributions in Italian sources of the Franco-Netherlandish chanson, c.1465-c.1505. A progress report on a new hypothesis', in Fenlon ed., *MMEME*, 249-93

'Pandolfo III Malatesta mecenate musicale: musica e musicisti presso una signoria del primo quattrocento', *RIM* 23 (1989), 38-92

'On the Neapolitan provenance of the MS Perugia, Biblioteca Comunale Augusta, 431 (G 20)', *MD* 31 (1977), 45-105

Atlas, Allan W., ed.: *Dufay Quincentenary Conference. Brooklyn College 1974* (New York: Brooklyn College, 1976)

Bäumker, Wilhelm: *Das katholische deutsche Kirchenlied in seinen Singweisen von den frühesten Zeiten bis gegen Ende des 17. Jahrhunderts*, 4 vols. (Freiburg i.B., 1893)

Baillie, Hugh: 'A London guild of musicians, 1460-1530', *PRMA* 83 (1956-7), 15-28

'Squares', *AcM* 32 (1960), 178-93

Baillie, Hugh, and Oboussier, Philippe: 'The York Masses', *ML* 35 (1954), 19-30

Baldelló, Francisco de P.: 'La música en la casa de los Reyes de Aragón', *AnM* 11 (1956), 37-49

Barbireau, Johannes: *Opera omnia*, ed. Bernhard Meier, 2 vols. (Rome: American Institute of Musicology, 1954-7) (CMM, 7)

Barblan, Guglielmo: 'Vita musicale alla corte sforzesca', in *Storia di Milano*, vol. IX (Milan: Fondazione Treccani, 1961), 787-852

Becker, Otto Frederick: *The Maîtrise in Northern France and Burgundy in the Fifteenth Century*, Ph.D., George Peabody College for Teachers, Nashville, Tenn., 1967

Benham, Hugh: *Latin Church Music in England, c.1460-1575* (London: Barrie & Jenkins Ltd, 1977)

Bent, Margaret: 'A contemporary perception of early fifteenth-century, style: Bologna Q 15 as a document of scribal editorial initiative', in Günther ed., *1380-1430: An International Style?*, 183-201

Dunstaple (London: Oxford University Press, 1981)

'New and little-known fragments of English medieval polyphony', *JAMS* 21 (1968), 137-56

'The progeny of Old Hall: more leaves from a Royal English choirbook', in *Gordon Athol Anderson (1929-1981) in Memoriam* (Henryville etc.: Institute of Mediaeval Music, 1984) (Musicological Studies, 39), 1-54

'"Res facta" and *cantare super librum*', *JAMS* 36 (1983), 371-91

'The songs of Dufay: some questions of form and authenticity', *Early Music* 8 (1980), 454-9

'The transmission of English music 1300-1500: some aspects of repertory and presentation', in Lütolf ed., *Studien . . . Fischer*, 65-83

Bent, Margaret, ed.: *Fifteenth-Century Liturgical Music II: Four Anonymous Masses* (London: Stainer & Bell, 1979) (EECM, 22)

Bent, Margaret, and Bent, Ian: 'Dufay, Dunstable, Plummer - a new source', *JAMS* 22 (1969), 394-424

van Benthem, Jaap: 'Concerning Johannes Tinctoris and the preparation of the Princess's chansonnier', *TVNM* 32 (1982), 24-9

Berger, Karol: *Musica ficta. Theories of Accidental Inflections in Vocal Polyphony from Marchetto da Padova to Gioseffo Zarlino* (Cambridge: Cambridge University Press, 1987)

Bergsagel, John, and Nielsen, Niels Martin: 'A reconsideration of the Manuscript Copenhagen A.M.76, 8º. Its significance for Danish cultural history in the 15th century', in *Festskrift Henrik Glahn 1919-1979* (Copenhagen, 1979), 19-33

Besseler, Heinrich: *Bourdon und Fauxbourdon: Studien zum Ursprung der niederländischen Musik*, 2nd rev. edn (Leipzig, 1974)

Die Musik des Mittelalters und der Renaissance (Wildpark-Potsdam: Athenaion, 1931) (Handbuch der Musikwissenschaft, 2)

Besseler, Heinrich, and Gülke, Peter: *Schriftbild der mehrstimmigen Musik* (Leipzig: VEB Deutscher Verlag für Musik, 1973) (Musikgeschichte in Bildern, III, 5)

van Biezen, Jan, and Gumbert, J. P., eds: *Two Chansonniers from the Low Countries: French and Dutch Polyphonic Songs from the Leiden and Utrecht Fragments (Early 15th Century)* (Amsterdam: VNM, 1985) (Monumenta Musica Neerlandica, 15)

van Biezen, Jan, and Vellekoop, Kees: 'Aspects of stroke notation: the Gruuthuse Manuscript and other sources', *TVNM* 34 (1984), 3-25

Binchois, Gilles: *Die Chansons*, ed. Wolfgang Rehm (Mainz: Schott, 1957) (Musikalische Denkmäler, 2)

Blackburn, Bonnie J.: 'On compositional process in the fifteenth century', *JAMS* 40 (1987), 210-84

Bloxam, Mary Jennifer: *A Survey of Late Medieval Service Books from the Low Countries: Implications for Sacred Polyphony, 1460-1520*, Ph.D., Yale University, 1987

Bockholdt, Rudolf: *Die frühen Messenkompositionen von Guillaume Dufay*, 2 vols. (Tutzing: Schneider, 1960) (Münchner Veröffentlichungen zur Musikgeschichte, 5)

Böker-Heil, Norbert, *et al.* eds: *Das Tenorlied. Mehrstimmige Lieder in deutschen Quellen 1450-1580*, 3 vols. (Kassel etc.: Bärenreiter, 1981-7) (Catalogus Musicus, 9)

Boorman, Stanley, ed.: *Studies in the Performance of Late Mediaeval Music* (Cambridge: Cambridge University Press, 1983)

van den Borren, Charles: *Etudes sur le quinzième siècle musical* (Antwerp, 1941)

van den Borren, Charles, ed.: *Pièces polyphoniques de provenance liégeoise (XVe siècle)* (Brussels, 1950) (Flores musicales belgicae, 1)

Polyphonia Sacra: a Continental Miscellany of the Fifteenth Century (London: The Plainsong and Mediaeval Music Society, R 1962)

Bosse, Detlef: *Untersuchung einstimmiger mittelalterlicher Melodien zum 'Gloria in excelsis Deo'* (Regensburg, 1955) (Forschungsbeiträge zur Musikwissenschaft, 2)

Bouquet, Marie-Therèse: 'La cappella musicale dei duchi di Savoia dal 1450 al 1500', *RIM* 3 (1968), 233–85

Boutet, Dominique, and Strubel, Armand: *Littérature, politique et société dans la France du Moyen Age* (Paris, 1979)

Bowers, Roger: *Choral Institutions within the English Church: their Constitution and Development, 1340–1500*, Ph.D., University of East Anglia, 1975

'The performing ensemble for English church polyphony, c.1320–c.1390', in Boorman ed., *Studies*, 161–92

'Obligation, agency and laissez-faire: the promotion of polyphonic composition for the Church in fifteenth-century England', in Fenlon ed., *MMEME*, 1–19

'The performing pitch of English fifteenth-century church polyphony', *Early Music*, 8 (1980), 21–8; see also correspondence in *Early Music* 9 (1981), 71–5

'Some observations on the life and career of Lionel Power', *PRMA* 102 (1975–6), 103–27

Bowles, Edmund A.: 'Musical instruments in civic processions during the Middle Ages', *AcM* 33 (1961) 147–61

Musikleben im 15. Jahrhundert (Leipzig: VEB Deutscher Verlag für Musik, 1977) (Musikgeschichte in Bildern, III, 8)

La pratique musicale au Moyen Age (Geneva: Minkoff, 1983)

Brainard, Ingrid: *The Art of Courtly Dancing in the Early Renaissance* (West Newton, Mass.: Author, 1981)

Brassart, Johannes: *Opera omnia*, ed. Keith E. Mixter, 2 vols. (Rome: American Institute of Musicology, 1965–71) (CMM, 35)

Sechs Motetten, ed. Keith E. Mixter (Graz: Akademische Druck- und Verlagsanstalt, 1960)

Brenet, Michel (i.e. Marie Bobillier): *Musique et Musiciens de la vieille France* (Paris, 1911 R Paris: Presses Universitaires de France, 1977)

Brewer, Charles E.: *The Introduction of the Ars nova into East Central Europe: a Study of Late Mediaeval Polish Sources*, Ph.D., City University of New York, 1983

Bridgman, Nanie: *La vie musicale au Quattrocento et jusqu'à la naissance du madrigal (1400–1530)* (Paris: Gallimard, 1964)

Brown, Howard M.: *Music in the French Secular Theater 1400–1550* (Cambridge, Mass: Harvard University Press, 1963)

'On Veronica and Josquin', in J. Wright ed., *New Perspectives on Music. Essays in Honor of Eileen Southern* (Michigan: Harmonie Park Press, 1992), 49–61

Music in the Renaissance (Englewood Cliffs: Prentice-Hall, Inc., 1976)

'St Augustine, Lady Music and the gittern', *MD* 38 (1984), 25–65

'On the performance of fifteenth-century chansons', *Early Music* 1 (1973), 3–10

Brown, Howard M., ed.: *A Florentine Chansonnier from the Time of Lorenzo the Magnificent: Florence, Biblioteca Nazionale Centrale, MS Banco Rari 229*, 2 vols. (Chicago and London: University of Chicago Press, 1983)

Theatrical Chansons of the Fifteenth and Early Sixteenth Centuries (Cambridge, Mass.: Harvard University Press, 1963)

Brown, Howard M., D'Accone, Frank, and Owens, Jessie Ann, eds: *Renaissance Music in Facsimile (RMF)*, vols. 6, 12 and 17 (New York: Garland Publishing, Inc., 1986–7)

Bruning, E., OFM, Marie Veldhuyzen and Helene Wagenaar-Nolthenius eds, *Het geestelijk lied van Noord-Nederland in de vijftiende eeuw* (Amsterdam: VNM, 1963) (Monumenta Musica Neerlandica, 7)

Brunner, Horst, Ganser, Hans, and Hartmann, Karl Günther: 'Das Windsheimer Fragment einer Musikhandschrift des 15. Jahrhunderts', *Jahrbuch der Oswald von Wolkenstein Gesellschaft* 1 (1980/81), 185–222

Bukofzer, Manfred F.: 'English church music of the fifteenth century', in *NOHM III*, 165-213

'Popular and secular music in England (to c.1470)', in *NOHM III*, 107-33

Studies in Medieval and Renaissance Music (New York: Norton, 1950)

Burkholder, J. Peter: 'Johannes Martini and the imitation Mass of the fifteenth century', *JAMS* 38 (1985), 470-523; see also correspondence in *JAMS* 40 (1987), 130-9 and 576-9

Burstyn, Shai: 'Power's *Anima mea* and Binchois' *De plus en plus*: a study in musical relationships', *MD* 30 (1976), 55-72

Caldwell, John: *Editing Early Music* (Oxford: Clarendon Press, 1985)

Carapezza, Paolo Emilio: 'Regina angelorum in musica picta: Walter Frye e il "Maître au feuillage brodé"', *RIM* 10 (1975), 134-54

Caron, Philippe (?): *Oeuvres complètes*, ed. James Thomson (Brooklyn etc.: Institute of Mediaeval Music, 1976)

Carpenter, Nan Cooke: 'Music in the English mystery plays', in John H. Long ed., *Music in English Renaissance Drama* (Lexington: University of Kentucky Press, 1968), 1-31

Music in the Medieval and Renaissance Universities (Norman: University of Oklahoma Press, 1958)

Cattin, Giulio: 'Church patronage of music in fifteenth-century Italy', in Fenlon ed., *MMEME*, 21-36

'Contributi alla storia della lauda spirituale', *Quadrivium* 2 (1958), 45-75

Johannes de Quadris, musico del secolo XV (Bologna: Forni, 1971) (Biblioteca di Quadrivium, serie musicologica, 12)

'Il Quattrocento', in *Letteratura italiana, vol. VI: Teatro musica, tradizione dei classici* (Turin: Einaudi, 1986), 265-318

'Ricerche sulla musica a S. Giustina di Padova all'inizio del Quattrocento I: Il copista Rolando da Casale. Nuovi frammenti musicali nell'Archivio di Stato', *AnnM* 7 (1964-77), 17-41

Cattin, Giulio, ed.: *Italian Laude and Latin Unica in the MS Capetown, Grey 3.b.12* (Stuttgart: American Institute of Musicology, 1977) (CMM, 76)

Cazeaux, Isabelle: *French Music in the Fifteenth and Sixteenth Centuries* (New York: Praeger, 1975)

CC see *Census Catalogue*

Census Catalogue of Manuscript Sources of Polyphonic Music, 1400-1550 (CC), ed. by the Illinois University Archives for Renaissance Manuscript Studies, 5 vols. (Stuttgart: American Institute of Musicology, 1979-88) (Renaissance Manuscript Studies, I)

Černý, Jaromír: 'Die mehrtextige Motette des 14. und 15. Jahrhunderts in Böhmen', in Rudolf Pečman ed., *Colloquium Musica Bohemica et Europea*, vol. 5 (Brno, 1972), 71-88

'Petrus Wilhelmi de Grudziadz – an unknown composer of the "Age of Dufay"', in *Musica Antiqua Europae Orientalis. Acta Scientifica*, vol. 4 (Bydgoszcz, 1975), 91-103

'Zur Frage der Entstehungs- und Verwandlungsprozesse der mehrstimmigen Repertoires in Böhmen', in A. Pompilio *et al.* eds, *Trasmissione . . .* , vol. 1 (Round Tables), 168-84

Černý, Jaromír, and Mikan, Jaroslav: *Pearls of Old Parchments: Musical Manuscripts of East Bohemia* (Hradec Králové, 1967)

Cersne, Eberhard von: *Der Minne Regel. Lieder*, ed. D. Buschinger and H. Lomnitzer (Göppingen: Kümmerle, 1981) (Göppinger Arbeiten zur Germanistik, 216)

Chambers, Edmund K.: *The Mediaeval Stage*, 2 vols. (Oxford: Oxford University Press, 1903)

Charles, Sydney R.: *Josquin des Prez: A Guide to Research* (New York: Garland Publishing, Inc., 1983)

'The provenance and date of the Pepys MS 1236', *MD* 16 (1962), 57–71

Charles, Sydney R., ed.: *The Music of the Pepys MS 1236* (Rome: American Institute of Musicology, 1967) (CMM, 40)

Das Chorwerk, ed. F. Blume *et al.* (Wolfenbüttel: Möseler, 1929–)

Ciconia, Johannes: *Works*, ed. M. Bent and A. Hallmark (Monaco: L'Oiseau-Lyre, 1985) (PMFC, 24)

CMM (Corpus Mensurabilis Musicae) see individual authors and eds

Cohen, Judith: *The Six Anonymous L'homme armé Masses in Naples, Biblioteca Nazionale, MS VI E 40* (Rome: American Institute of Musicology, 1968) (MSD, 21)

Cohen, Judith, ed.: *The Six Anonymous L'homme armé Masses in Naples, Biblioteca Nazionale, MS VI E 40* (Stuttgart: American Institute of Musicology, 1981) (CMM, 85)

Compère, Loyset: *Opera omnia*, ed. L. Finscher, 5 vols. (Rome: American Institute of Musicology, 1958–72) (CMM, 15)

Cornago, Johannes: *Complete Works*, ed. R. L. Gerber (Madison: A-R Editions, 1984) (Recent Researches in the Music of the Middle Ages and Early Renaissance, 15)

Corsi, Cesare, and Petrobelli, Pierluigi, eds: *Le polifonie primitive in Friuli e in Europa* (Congress Report, Cividale del Friuli, 1980) (Rome: Torre d'Orfeo, 1989)

Coussemaker, Edmond de, ed.: *Scriptorum de musica medii aevi nova series* (*CS*), 4 vols. (Paris, 1864–76 *R* Hildesheim: Olms, 1963)

Crane, Frederick: *Materials for the Study of the Fifteenth-Century Basse Danse* (Brooklyn etc.: Institute of Mediaeval Music, 1968) (Musicological Studies, 16)

Curtis, Gareth R. K.: 'Jean Pullois and the cyclic Mass – or a case of mistaken identity?', *ML* 62 (1981), 41–59

'Stylistic layers in the English Mass repertory, c.1400–1450', *PRMA* 109 (1982–3), 23–38

Curtis, Gareth R. K., ed.: *Fifteenth-Century Liturgical Music III: The Brussels Masses* (London: Stainer & Bell, 1989) (EECM, 34)

Cuyler, Louise: *The Emperor Maximilian I and Music* (London: Oxford University Press, 1973)

van Daalen, Maria, and Harrison, Frank Ll.: 'Two keyboard intabulations of the late fourteenth century on a manuscript leaf now in the Netherlands', *TVNM* 34 (1984), 97–108 (with facs. and transcriptions)

D'Accone, Frank A.: 'Music and musicians at Santa Maria del Fiore in the early Quattrocento', in *Scritti in onore di Luigi Ronga* (Milan and Naples: Ricciardi, 1973), 99–126

'The performance of sacred music in Italy during Josquin's time, c.1475–1525', in Lowinsky ed., *Josquin des Prez*, 601–18

'The singers of San Giovanni in Florence during the 15th century', *JAMS* 14 (1961), 307–58

Dahlhaus, Carl: *Untersuchungen über die Entstehung der harmonischen Tonalität* (Kassel etc.: Bärenreiter, 1968)

Dahnk, Emilie: 'Musikausübung an den Höfen von Burgund und Orléans während des 15. Jahrhunderts', *Archiv für Kulturgeschichte* 25 (1934), 184–215

D'Alessi, Giovanni: *La cappella musicale del Duomo di Treviso (1300–1633)* (Vedelago, 1954)

Dangel-Hofmann, Frohmut: *Der mehrstimmige Introitus in Quellen des 15. Jahrhunderts* (Tutzing: Schneider, 1975) (Würzburger musikhistorische Beiträge, 3)

Dannemann, Erna: *Die spätgotische Musiktradition in Frankreich und Burgund vor dem Auftreten Guillaume Dufays* (Strasbourg: Heitz, 1936 *R* Baden-Baden: Koerner, 1973)

Davison, Archibald T., and Apel, Willi, eds: *Historical Anthology of Music*, vol. 1 (Cambridge, Mass., 1950)

Dent, Edward J.: 'Music and drama' (rev. F. W. Sternfeld), in *NOHM IV*, 784-820

Després (Desprez), see Josquin

Diederichs, Elisabeth: *Die Anfänge der mehrstimmigen Lauda vom Ende des 14. bis zur Mitte des 15. Jahrhunderts* (Tutzing: Schneider, 1986) (Münchner Veröffentlichungen zur Musikgeschichte, 41)

Dinzelbacher, Peter, and Mück, Hans-Dieter, eds: *Volkskultur des europäischen Spätmittelalters* (Stuttgart: Alfred Kröner, 1987)

Dömling, Wolfgang, ed.: *Die Handschrift London, British Museum, Add. 27630 (LoD)*, 2 vols (Kassel etc.: Bärenreiter, 1972) (EDM vols. 52-3)

van Doorslaer, Georges: 'La chapelle musicale de Philippe le Beau', *Revue Belge d'Archéologie et d'Histoire d'Art* 4 (1934), 21-57 and 139-61

Dreves, Guido Maria, and Blume, Clemens, eds: *Analecta Hymnica Medii Aevi (AH)*, 52 vols. (Leipzig, 1886-1909) (Register ed. Max Lütolf, 2 vols. (Berne and Munich: Francke, 1978))

Droz, Eugénie *et al.* eds: *Trois chansonniers français du XVe siècle* (Paris: Droz, 1927)

DTOe (Denkmäler der Tonkunst in Österreich) VII, XI/1, XIX/1, XXVII/1, XXXI: see Guido Adler *et al.* eds

DTOe (Denkmäler der Tonkunst in Österreich) XL: see von Ficker ed.

DTOe (Denkmäler der Tonkunst in Österreich) vol. 120: see Flotzinger ed.

Dufay, Guillaume: *Opera omnia*, ed. H. Besseler, 6 vols. (Rome: American Institute of Musicology, 1951-66 R 1978) (CMM, 1)

Dunning, Albert: *Die Staatsmotette, 1480-1555* (Utrecht: Osthoek, 1970)

Dunstable, John: *Complete Works*, ed. M. F. Bukofzer (London: Stainer & Bell, 1953; rev. edn M. Bent, I. Bent and B. Trowell, 1970) (Musica Britannica, 8)

Dupire, Joël: *Jean Molinet: La vie – les oeuvres* (Paris: Droz, 1932)

Dutka, Jo Anna: 'Music and the English mystery plays', *Comparative Drama* 7 (1973-4), 135-49

EDM (Das Erbe deutscher Musik) see individual authors and eds

Edwards, Kathleen: *The English Secular Cathedrals in the Middle Ages* (Manchester: Manchester University Press, 1967)

Edwards, Warwick: 'Songs without words by Josquin and his contemporaries', in Fenlon ed., *MMEME*, 79-92

EECM (Early English Church Music) see Bent, Curtis, Hughes eds

EFM (Early Fifteenth-Century Music) see Reaney ed.

Ehmann, Wilhelm: *Adam von Fulda als Vertreter der ersten deutschen Komponistengeneration* (Berlin, 1936)

Einstein, Alfred: *The Italian Madrigal*, 3 vols. (Princeton, N.J.: Princeton University Press, 1949)

Elders, Willem: 'Plainchant in the motets, hymns and Magnificat of Josquin des Prez', in Lowinsky ed., *Josquin des Prez*, 522-42

EMH (Early Music History) see individual authors

Ewerhart, Rudolf: *Die Handschrift 322/1994 der Stadtbibliothek Trier als musikalische Quelle* (Regensburg: Bosse, 1955) (Kölner Beiträge zur Musikforschung, 7)

Fallows, David: 'The contenance angloise: English influence on continental composers of the fifteenth century', *Renaissance Studies* 1 (Oxford, 1987), 189-208

Dufay (London: Dent, 1982)

Dufay, rev. edn (London: Dent, 1987)

'English song repertories of the mid-fifteenth century', *PRMA* 103 (1976-7), 61-79

'Fifteenth-century tablatures for plucked instruments: a summary, a revision and a suggestion', *LSJ* 19 (1977), 7-33

'French as a courtly language in fifteenth-century Italy: the musical evidence', *Renaissance Studies* 3 (Oxford, 1989), 429-41

'Johannes Ockeghem: the changing image, the songs, and a new source', *Early Music* 12 (1984), 218-30

'The life of Johannes Regis, ca. 1425 to 1496', *RBM* 43 (1989), 143-72

Review of Lockwood, *Music in Renaissance Ferrara*, and Strohm, *Music in Late Medieval Bruges*, *EMH* 6 (1986), 279-303

Robert Morton's Songs: A Study of Styles in the Mid-Fifteenth Century, Ph.D., University of California, Berkeley, 1978

'Robertus de Anglia and the Oporto Song Collection', in *Source Materials and the Interpretation of Music. A Memorial Volume to Thurston Dart* (London: Stainer & Bell, 1981), 99-128

'Songs in the Trent Codices: an optimistic handlist', in Pirrotta-Curti eds, *Codici Musicali*, 170-79

'Specific information on the ensembles for composed polyphony, 1400-1474', in Boorman ed., *Studies*, 109-59

'Two equal voices: a French song repertory with music for two more works of Oswald von Wolkenstein', *EMH* 7 (1987), 227-41

'Words and music in two English songs of the mid-fifteenth century: Charles d'Orléans and John Lydgate', *Early Music* 5 (1977), 38-43

Faugues, Guillaume: *Collected Works*, ed. G. C. Schuetze (Brooklyn etc.: Institute of Mediaeval Music, 1959)

Federhofer-Königs, Renate: 'Ein Beitrag zur Proportionenlehre in der zweiten Hälfte des 15. Jahrhunderts', *SM* 11 (1969), 145-57

Feininger, Laurence, ed.: *Documenta Polyphoniae Liturgicae Sanctae Ecclesiae Romanae* (Rome: Societas Universalis Sanctae Ceciliae, 1947-)

Monumenta Polyphoniae Liturgicae Sanctae Ecclesiae Romanae (MPLSER), series I, tom. 1-4, series II (Rome: Societas Universalis Sanctae Ceciliae, 1947-)

Feldmann, Fritz: *Der Codex Mf. 2016 des Musikalischen Instituts bei der Universität Breslau*, 2 vols. (Breslau, 1932)

Musik und Musikpflege im mittelalterlichen Schlesien (Breslau: 1938 *R* Hildesheim and New York: Olms, 1973)

Fenlon, Iain, ed.: *Music in Medieval and Early Modern Europe* (MMEME) (Cambridge: Cambridge University Press, 1981)

Ficker, Rudolf von, ed.: *Sieben Trienter Codices. Geistliche und weltliche Kompositionen des XIV. und XV. Jahrhunderts, Sechste Auswahl*, in *Denkmäler der Tonkunst in Österreich* (DTOe), Jahrgang XL = vol. 76 (Vienna: Universal-Edition, 1933)

Finscher, Ludwig: *Loyset Compère (c.1450-1518). Life and Works* (Rome: American Institute of Musicology, 1964) (MSD, 12)

Finscher, Ludwig, ed.: *Datierung und Filiation von Musikhandschriften der Josquin-Zeit* (Wiesbaden: Otto Harrassowitz, 1983) (Wolfenbütteler Forschungen, 26)

Formen und Probleme der Überlieferung mehrstimmiger Musik im Zeitalter Josquins Desprez (Munich: Kraus International Publications, 1981) (Wolfenbütteler Forschungen, 6)

Renaissance-Studien. Helmuth Osthoff zum 80. Geburtstag (Tutzing: Schneider, 1979) (Frankfurter Beiträge zur Musikwissenschaft, 11)

Fischer, Kurt von: 'Bemerkungen zur Überlieferung und zum Stil der geistlichen Werke des Antonius dictus Zacharias de Teramo', in Günther ed., *1380–1430: An International Style?*, 161–82

 Essays in Musicology (New York: The Graduate School and University Center, CUNY, 1989)

 'Neue Quellen zur Musik des 13., 14. und 15. Jahrhunderts', *AcM* 36 (1964), 79–97

 'Quelques remarques sur les relations entre les Laudesi et les compositeurs florentins du Trecento', *L'Ars Nova Italiana del Trecento* 3 (1970), 247–52

 Studien zur italienischen Musik des Trecento und frühen Quattrocento (Berne: Haupt, 1956)

 Handschriften mit mehrstimmiger Musik des 14., 15. und 16. Jahrhunderts (RISM B IV), 2 vols. (Munich: Henle, 1972) (Répertoire International des Sources Musicales, Ser. B/IV, 3–4)

Fischer, Kurt von, and Gallo, F. Alberto, eds: *Italian Sacred and Ceremonial Music* (Monaco: L'Oiseau-Lyre, 1987) (PMFC, 13)

 Italian Sacred Music (Monaco: L'Oiseau-Lyre, 1975) (PMFC, 12)

Flotzinger, Rudolf, ed.: *Trienter Codices. Siebente Auswahl* (Graz and Vienna: Akademische Druck- und Verlagsanstalt, 1970) (DTOe, vol. 120)

Flotzinger, Rudolf, and Gruber, Gernot: *Musikgeschichte Österreichs, vol. I (Von den Anfängen bis zum Barock)* (Graz etc.: Styria, 1977)

Fökövi, Ludwig: 'Musik und musikalische Verhältnisse in Ungarn am Hofe von Mathias Corvinus', *KmJb* 15 (1900), 1–16

Forney, Kristine: 'Music, ritual and patronage at the Church of Our Lady, Antwerp', *EMH* 7 (1987), 1–57

Fox, Charles W.: 'Non-quartal harmony in the Renaissance', *MQ* 31 (1945), 33–53

Franzen, August, and Müller, Wolfgang, eds: *Das Konzil von Konstanz. Beiträge zu seiner Geschichte und Theologie* (Freiburg i. Br.: Herder, 1964)

Frere, Walter H., ed.: *Antiphonale Sarisburiense*, 4 vols. (London: The Plainsong and Mediaeval Society, 1901–25 R 1966)

 Graduale Sarisburiense, 2 vols. (London: The Plainsong and Mediaeval Society, 1894 R 1966)

Frye, Walter: *Collected Works*, ed. Sylvia W. Kenney (Rome: American Institute of Musicology, 1960) (CMM, 19)

Gallico, Claudio: 'Josquin's compositions on Italian texts and the frottola', in Lowinsky ed., *Josquin des Prez*, 446–54

Gallo, F. Alberto: 'Il "Ballare lombardo" (circa 1435–1475)', *Studi Musicali* 8 (1979), 61–84

 'Cantus planus binatim'. Polifonia primitiva in fonti tardive (Bologna, 1966) (Biblioteca di 'Quadrivium', Serie Paleografica, 12)

 Music of the Middle Ages II (Cambridge: Cambridge University Press, 1985)

Gallo, F. Alberto, ed.: *Il codice musicale Panciatichi 26 della Biblioteca nazionale di Firenze: riproduzione in facsimile* (Florence: Olschki, 1981)

Gallo, F. Alberto, and Mantese, Giovanni: *Ricerche sulle origini della cappella musicale del Duomo di Vicenza* (Venice and Rome: Istituto per la collaborazione culturale, 1964)

Geering, Arnold: *Die Organa und mehrstimmigen Conductus in Handschriften des deutschen Sprachgebietes vom 13. bis 16. Jahrhundert* (Berne, 1952)

Gerber, Rudolf, *et al.* eds: *Der Mensuralkodex des Nikolaus Apel (Ms. 1494 der Universitätsbibliothek Leipzig)*, 3 vols. (Kassel, etc.: Bärenreiter, 1956–75) (EDM, 32, 33 and 34)

Gerken, Robert E.: *The Polyphonic Cycles of the Proper of the Mass in the Trent Codex 88 and Jena Choirbooks 30 and 35*, Ph.D., Indiana University, 1969 (UMI 70-7447)

Ghisi, Federico: 'Strambotti e laude nel travestimento spirituale della poesia musicale del quattrocento', in *idem, Studi e Testi*, 109-42

    Studi e Testi di Musica Italiana dall'Ars nova a Carissimi (Bologna: A.M.I.S., 1971)

Glixon, Jonathan: 'Music at the Venetian Scuole Grandi, 1440-1450', in Fenlon ed., *MMEME*, 193-208

Göllner, Theodor: *Formen früher Mehrstimmigkeit in deutschen Handschriften des späten Mittelalters* (Tutzing: Schneider, 1961) (Münchner Veröffentlichungen zur Musikgeschichte, 6)

Gómez Muntané, Maria Carmen: 'El manuscrito M 971 de la Biblioteca de Catalunya (Misa de Barcelona)', *Butlletí de la Biblioteca de Catalunya* 10 (1982-4), 159-317; also separately (Barcelona, 1969)

    La música en la Casa Real Catalano-Aragonesa durante los años 1336-1437, 2 vols. (Barcelona: Bosch, 1979)

    'Musique et musiciens dans les chapelles de la maison royale d'Aragon (1336-1413)', *MD* 38 (1984), 67-86

    'Prehistoria de la enseñanza musical en las universidades españolas', in *De musica hispana et aliis. Miscelánea en honor al Prof. Dr. José López-Calo, S.J.* (Universidade de Santiago de Compostela, 1990), 77-89

Gossett, Philip: 'Techniques of unification in early cyclic Masses and Mass Pairs', *JAMS* 19 (1966), 205-31

Gottlieb, Louis E.: *The Cyclic Masses of Trent Codex 89*, Ph.D., University of California at Los Angeles, 1958 (CU 3237)

Gottwald, Clytus: *Johannes Ghiselin – Johannes Verbonnet: Stilkritische Untersuchung zum Problem ihrer Identität* (Wiesbaden: Breitkopf & Härtel, 1962)

    'Lasso-Josquin-Dufay. Zur Ästhetik des heroischen Zeitalters', in H.-K. Metzger and R. Riehn eds, *Musik-Konzepte 26/27: Josquin des Près* (Munich: edition text + kritik, 1982), 39-69

Greene, Gordon: 'The schools of minstrelsy and the choir-school tradition', *Studies in Music (University of Western Ontario)* 2 (1977), 31-40

Greene, Gordon, ed.: *French Secular Music*, 2 vols. (Monaco: L'Oiseau-Lyre, 1982 and 1987) (PMFC, 20 and 21)

    The Manuscript Chantilly, Musée Condé 564, 2 vols. (Monaco: L'Oiseau-Lyre, 1981-82) (PMFC, 18 and 19)

Greene, Richard L.: *The Early English Carols*, 2nd edn (Oxford, 1977)

    'Two medieval musical manuscripts: Egerton 3307 and some University of Chicago fragments', *JAMS* 7 (1954), 1-34

Guenée, Bernard and Lehoux, Françoise: *Les entrées royales françaises de 1328 à 1515* (Paris: C.N.R.S., 1968)

Gümpel, Karl Werner: *Die Musiktraktate Conrads von Zabern* (Wiesbaden: Steiner, 1956)

Günther, Ursula: 'Datierbare Balladen des späten 14. Jahrhunderts', *MD* 15 (1961), 39-61; 16 (1962), 151-74

    'Problems of dating in Ars nova and Ars subtilior', in *L'Ars Nova Italiana del Trecento* 4 (1975), 289-301

    'Unusual phenomena in the transmission of late 14th-century polyphonic music', *MD* 38 (1984), 87-118

'Zur Biographie einiger Komponisten der Ars subtilior', *AMw* 21 (1964), 172–99

Günther, Ursula, ed.: *The Motets of the Manuscripts Chantilly, Musée Condé 564 (olim 1047) and Modena, Biblioteca Estense, α. M. 5, 24 (olim lat. 568)* (Rome: American Institute of Musicology, 1965) (CMM, 39)

1380–1430: An International Style? (Stuttgart: American Institute of Musicology, 1987) (MD 41)

Günther, Ursula and Finscher, Ludwig, eds: *Musik und Text in der Mehrstimmigkeit des 14. und 15. Jahrhunderts. Vorträge des Gastsymposions in der Herzog-August-Bibliothek Wolfenbüttel, 1980* (Kassel etc.: Bärenreiter, 1984)

Gutiérrez-Denhoff, Martella: *Der Wolfenbütteler Chansonnier. Untersuchungen zu Repertoire und Überlieferung einer Musikhandschrift des 15. Jahrhunderts und ihres Umkreises* (Wiesbaden: Harrassowitz, 1985)

Haar, James: 'Some remarks on the "Missa La sol fa re mi"', in Lowinsky ed., *Josquin des Prez*, 564–88

Haberkamp, Gertraut: *Die weltliche Vokalmusik in Spanien um 1500. Der 'Cancionero Musical de la Colombina' von Sevilla und außerspanische Handschriften* (Tutzing: Schneider, 1968) (Münchner Veröffentlichungen zur Musikgeschichte, 12)

Haberl, Franz Xaver: *Bausteine für Musikgeschichte, I. Wilhelm Du Fay, III. Die römische 'Schola Cantorum' und die päpstlichen Kapellsänger bis zur Mitte des 16. Jahrhunderts* (Leipzig, 1885/88 R Hildesheim: Olms, 1971)

Haggh, Barbara H.: *Music, Liturgy and Ceremony in Brussels, 1350–1500*, Ph.D., University of Illinois, Urbana, 1988

HAM (Historical Anthology of Music), see Davison-Apel eds

Hamm, Charles: 'Another Barbingant Mass', in Snow ed., *Essays in Musicology*, 83–90

'Manuscript structure in the Dufay era', *AcM* 34 (1962), 166–84

'Musiche del Quattrocento in S. Petronio', *RIM* 3 (1968), 215–32

Hanen, Martha K., ed.: *The Chansonnier El Escorial, IV. a. 24*, 3 vols. (Henryville etc.: Institute of Mediaeval Music, 1983) (Musicological Studies, 36)

Harrán, Don: *Word-Tone Relations in Musical Thought. From Antiquity to the Seventeenth Century* (Stuttgart: American Institute of Musicology, 1986) (MSD, 40)

Harrison, Frank Ll.: 'Benedicamus, conductus, carol: a newly-discovered source', *AcM* 37 (1965), 35–48

Music in Medieval Britain, 2nd edn (London: Routledge, 1963)

'English church music in the fourteenth century', in *NOHM III*, 82–106

'English polyphony (c. 1470–1540)', in *NOHM III*, 303–48

'Music for the Sarum Rite: MS 1236 in the Pepys Library, Magdalene College, Cambridge', *AnnM* 6 (1963), 99–144

Harrison, Frank Ll., ed.: *Motets of English Provenance* (Monaco: L'Oiseau-Lyre, 1980) (PMFC, 15)

Motets of French Provenance (Monaco: L'Oiseau-Lyre, 1968) (PMFC, 5)

Heartz, Daniel: 'A 15th-century ballo: Rôti Bouilli Joyeux', in Jan LaRue ed., *Aspects of Medieval and Renaissance Music. A Birthday Offering for Gustave Reese* (New York: Norton, 1966), 355–75

'The *Basse Dance*, its evolution circa 1450 to 1550', *AnnM* 6 (1958–63), 287–340

'Hoftanz and Basse Danse', *JAMS* 19 (1966), 13–36

Heers, Jacques: *Fêtes des fous et carnavals* (Paris: Fayard, 1983)

Hewitt, Helen, ed.: *Harmonice Musices Odhecaton A* (Cambridge, Mass., 1942)

Higgins, Paula: *Antoine Busnois and Musical Culture in Late Fifteenth-Century France and Burgundy*, Ph.D., Princeton University, 1987

'In Hydraulis revisited: new light on the career of Antoine Busnois', *JAMS* 39 (1986), 36-86

'Music and musicians at the Sainte-Chapelle of the Bourges Palace, 1405-1515', in A. Pompilio *et al.* eds: *Trasmissione . . .* , vol. 3 (Free Papers), 689-701

'Tracing the careers of late medieval composers. The case of Philippe Basiron of Bourges', *AcM* 62 (1990), 1-28

Higgins, Paula, ed.: *Chansonnier Nivelle de la Chaussée (Bibliothèque Nationale, Paris, Rés. Vmc.ms.57, ca. 1460)*, facs. edn (Geneva: Minkoff, 1984)

Honegger, Marc, and Meyer, Christian, eds: *La musique et le rite - sacré et profane (Actes du XIIIe congrès de la SIM, 1982)*, 2 vols. (Strasbourg: Université, 1986)

Hoppin, Richard H.: *Medieval Music* (New York: Norton, 1978)

Hoppin, Richard H., ed.: *An Anthology of Medieval Music* (New York: Norton, 1978)

Cypriot Plainchant of the Manuscript Torino, Biblioteca Nazionale J. II. 9: A Facsimile edition with Commentary (Rome: American Institute of Musicology, 1968) (MSD, 19)

Hothby, John: *The Musical Works*, ed. A. Seay (Rome: American Institute of Musicology, 1964) (CMM, 3)

Tres tractatuli contra Bartholomeum Ramum, ed. A. Seay (Rome: American Institute of Musicology, 1965) (CSM, 10)

Houdoy, Jules: *Histoire artistique de la cathédrale de Cambrai, ancienne église métropolitaine Notre-Dame* (Lille, 1880 R Geneva: Minkoff, 1972)

Hughes, Andrew: 'The choir in fifteenth-century English music: non-mensural polyphony', in Snow ed., *Essays in Musicology*, 127-45

Manuscript Accidentals: Ficta in Focus 1350-1450 (Rome: American Institute of Musicology, 1972) (MSD, 27)

'Mensural polyphony for choir in fifteenth-century England', *JAMS* 19 (1966), 352-69

Hughes, Andrew, ed.: *Fifteenth-Century Liturgical Music I: Antiphons and Music for Holy Week and Easter* (London: Stainer & Bell, 1964) (EECM, 8)

Hughes, Andrew, and Bent, Margaret: 'The Old Hall MS', *MD* 21 (1967), 97-147

Hughes, Andrew, and Bent, Margaret, eds: *The Old Hall Manuscript* (OH), 3 vols. (Rome: American Institute of Musicology, 1969-73) (CMM, 46)

Hughes, Dom Anselm, and Abraham, Gerald, eds: *Ars Nova and the Renaissance (1300-1540)* (NOHM III) (Oxford: Oxford University Press, 1960)

Huglo, Michel: 'Les débuts de la polyphonie à Paris: Les premières organa Parisiens', *Forum Musicologicum* 3 (Winterthur, 1982), 93-163

'Les séquences de Münsterbilsen (Bruxelles/Brussel, Bibliothèque Royale 9786-9790)', in *Gordon Athol Anderson (1929-1981) in Memoriam* (Henryville etc.: Institute of Mediaeval Music, 1984) (Musicological Studies, 39), 392-402

Isaac, Heinrich: *Opera omnia*, ed. E. R. Lerner, 7 vols. (Rome and Stuttgart: American Institute of Musicology, 1974-) (CMM, 25)

Weltliche Werke, ed. J. Wolf, 2 vols. (Vienna, 1907-9) (DTOe, XIV/1 = vol. 28 and XVI/1 = vol. 32)

Janse, Anthuenis: 'Het Muziekleven aan het Hof van Albrecht van Beieren (1358-1404) in Den Haag', *TVNM* 36 (1986), 136-57

Janue, Antonius: *Opera omnia*, ed. M. Kanazawa (Stuttgart: American Institute of Musicology, 1974) (CMM, 70)

Jeppesen, Knud: *La Frottola*, 3 vols. (Copenhagen, 1968–70) (Acta Jutlandica, XL/2, XLI/1 and XLII/1)

Jeppesen, Knud, ed.: *Der Kopenhagener Chansonnier: Das Manuskript Thott 291ᵉ der Königlichen Bibliothek Kopenhagen* (Copenhagen and Leipzig, 1927 R New York, 1965)

Jeppesen, Knud, and Brøndal, V., eds: *Die mehrstimmige italienische Laude um 1500* (Leipzig and Copenhagen: Breitkopf & Härtel, 1935)

Josquin Des Prés (des Prez): *Werken*, ed. A. Smijers *et al.* (Amsterdam, 1921–)

Just, Martin: *Der Mensuralkodex Mus. ms. 40021 der Staatsbibliothek Preußischer Kulturbesitz Berlin: Untersuchungen zum Repertoire einer deutschen Quelle des 15. Jahrhunderts* (Tutzing: Schneider, 1975) (Würzburger musikhistorische Beiträge, 1)

Kanazawa, Masakata: *Polyphonic Music for Vespers in the Fifteenth Century*, Ph.D., Harvard University, 1966

Kellmann, Herbert: 'Josquin and the courts of the Netherlands and France', in Lowinsky ed., *Josquin des Prez*, 181–216

Kenney, Sylvia: 'In praise of the Lauda', in LaRue ed., *Aspects . . .* , 489–99

    Walter Frye and the Contenance Angloise (New Haven and London: Yale University Press, 1964)

Kirsch, Winfried: *Die Quellen der mehrstimmigen Magnificat- und Te Deum-Vertonungen bis zur Mitte des 16. Jahrhunderts* (Tutzing: Schneider, 1966)

Knick, Bernhard, and Mezger, Manfred: *St. Thomas zu Leipzig: Schule und Chor* (Wiesbaden: Breitkopf & Härtel, 1963)

Koep, Leo: 'Die Liturgie der Sessiones Generales auf dem Konstanzer Konzil', in Franzen-Müller eds, *Konzil von Konstanz*, 241–51

Korth, Hans-Otto: *Studien zum Kantilenensatz im frühen 15. Jahrhundert* (Munich and Salzburg: Katzbichler, 1986) (Berliner musikwissenschaftliche Arbeiten, 29)

Kouba, Jan, and Skalická, Maria: 'Koledy v předbelohorských písňových pramenech' [Koledy in Bohemian Song Sources], *Miscellanea Musicologica Universitatis Carolinae Pragensis* 30 (1983), 9–37

Kugler, Michael: *Die Tastenmusik im Codex Faenza* (Tutzing: Schneider, 1972) (Münchner Veröffentlichungen zur Musikgeschichte, 21)

    Die Musik für Tasteninstrumente im 15. und 16. Jahrhundert (Wilhelmshaven: Heinrichshofen, 1975) (Taschenbücher zur Musikwissenschaft, 41)

Labhardt, Frank: *Das Cantionale des Kartäusers Thomas Kreß: Ein Denkmal der spätmittelalterlichen Musikgeschichte Basels* (Berne and Stuttgart: Haupt, 1978) (Publikationen der Schweizerischen Musikforschenden Gesellschaft, Ser. II, vol. 20)

Lamaña, José M.ª: 'Los instrumentos musicales en los últimos tiempos de la dinastía de la casa de Barcelona', *AnM* 24 (1969), 9–119

Landwehr-Melnicki, Margarethe: *Das einstimmige Kyrie des lateinischen Mittelalters* (Regensburg: Bosse, 1955)

LaRue, Jan, ed.: *Aspects of Medieval and Renaissance Music: A Birthday Offering to Gustave Reese* (New York: Norton, 1966)

Leech-Wilkinson, Daniel: 'Un libro di appunti di un suonatore di tromba del quindicesimo secolo', *RIM* 16 (1981), 16–39

Lefferts, Peter M.: *The Motet in England in the Fourteenth Century* (Ann Arbor: UMI Research Press, 1986) (Studies in Musicology, 94)

Lenaerts, René Bernard, ed.: *The Art of the Netherlanders* (Cologne: Volk, 1964) (Anthology of Music, 22)

Lerner, Edward R.: 'The "German" works of Alexander Agricola', *MQ* 46 (1960), 56–66

Letts, Malcolm, ed.: *The Travels of Leo of Rozmital* (Cambridge, 1957) (The Hakluyt Society, 2nd series, CVIII)

Liber Usualis pro diurnis horis, ed. by the Monks of Solesmes (Tournai: Desclée, 1934)

Lipphardt, Walter, and Roloff, Hans-Gert, eds: *Die geistlichen Spiele des Sterzinger Spielarchivs*, vol. I (Berne etc.: Lang, 1981)

Lissa, Zofia, ed.: *Musica Antiqua Europae Orientalis. Acta Scientifica I (Bydgoszcz 1966)* (Warsaw, 1966)

Litterick, Louise: 'On Italian instrumental ensemble music in the late fifteenth century', in Fenlon ed., *MMEME*, 117–30

'The revision of Ockeghem's "Je n'ay dueil"', in Winn ed., *Musique naturelle*, 29–48

Lockwood, Lewis: 'Aspects of the L'homme armé tradition', *PRMA* 100 (1973–4), 97–122

'Dufay and Ferrara', in Atlas ed., *Dufay Quincentenary Conference*, 1–25

Music in Renaissance Ferrara 1400–1505 (Oxford: Clarendon Press, 1984)

'Pietrobono and the instrumental tradition at Ferrara', *RIM* 10 (1975), 115–33

'Strategies of musical patronage in the fifteenth century: the Cappella of Ercole I d'Este', in Fenlon ed., *MMEME*, 227–48

Löpelmann, Martin: *Die Liederhandschrift des Cardinals de Rohan (XV. Jahrhundert)* (Göttingen, 1923)

Lowinsky, Edward E.: 'Ascanio Sforza's life: a key to Josquin's biography and an aid to the chronology of his works', in Lowinsky ed., *Josquin des Prez*, 31–75

'Jan van Eyck's *TYMOTHEOS:* sculptor or musician? with an investigation of the autobiographic strain in French poetry from Ruteboeuf to Villon', *Studi Musicali* 13 (1984), 33–105

Lowinsky, Edward E., ed.: *Josquin des Prez. Proceedings of the International Josquin Festival-Conference New York, 1971* (London etc.: Oxford University Press, 1976)

Lütolf, Max, ed.: *Studien zur Tradition in der Musik: Kurt von Fischer zum 60. Geburtstag* (Munich: Katzbichler, 1973)

Macey, Patrick: 'Savonarola and the sixteenth-century motet', *JAMS* 36 (1983), 422–52

Mahrt, William P.: *The Missae ad organum of Heinrich Isaac*, Ph.D., Stanford University, 1969

Marix, Jeanne: *Histoire de la musique et des musiciens de la cour de Bourgogne sous le règne de Philippe le Bon (1419–1467)* (Strasbourg: Heitz, 1939) (Collection d'études musicologiques, 28)

Marix, Jeanne, ed.: *Les musiciens de la cour de Bourgogne au XVe siècle* (Paris: Droz, 1937)

Marrocco, W. Thomas, ed.: *Italian Secular Music*, 2 vols. (Monaco: L'Oiseau-Lyre, 1975–7) (PMFC, 9 and 10)

Marrocco, W. Thomas, and Sandon, Nicholas, eds: *Medieval Music* (London: Oxford University Press, 1977)

Martini, Johannes: *Secular Pieces*, ed. Edward G. Evans, Jr. (Madison: A-R Editions, 1975) (Recent Researches in the Music of the Middle Ages and Early Renaissance, 1)

Mayer, F. Arnold, and Rietsch, Heinrich: *Die Mondsee-Wiener Liederhandschrift und der Mönch von Salzburg* (Berlin, 1896)

Mayr, Norbert: 'Oswald von Wolkensteins Liederhandschrift A in neuer Sicht', in H.-D. Mück and U. Müller eds, *Gesammelte Vorträge der 600-Jahrfeier Oswalds von Wolkenstein, Seis am Schlern 1977* (Göppingen: Kümmerle, 1978), 351–71

McPeek, Gwynn S., ed.: *The British Museum Manuscript Egerton 3307* (London: Oxford University Press, 1963)

Meersseman, G. G. OP: 'L'Epistolaire de Jean van den Veren et le début de l'humanisme en Flandre', *Humanistica Lovanensia* 19 (Louvain, 1970), 119–200

Meylan, Raymond: *L'énigme des basses danses du quinzième siècle* (Berne and Stuttgart: Haupt, 1968) (Publikationen der Schweizerischen Musikforschenden Gesellschaft, Ser. II, vol. 17)

Miazga, Tadeusz: *Die Melodien des einstimmigen Credo der römisch-katholischen Kirche* (Graz: Akademische Druck- und Verlagsanstalt, 1976)

Miller, Clement A.: 'Early Gaffuriana: new answers to old questions', *MQ* 56 (1970), 367–88

Mixter, Keith E.: 'Johannes Brassart: a biographical and bibliographical study', *MD* 18 (1964), 37–62; 19 (1965), 99–108

Molinet, Jean: *Les Faictz et Dictz*, ed. N. Dupire, 3 vols. (Paris: Droz, 1937)

Montagna, Gerald: 'Caron, Hayne, Compère', *EMH* 7 (1987), 107–57

More, Mother Thomas: 'Organ-playing and polyphony in the fifteenth and sixteenth centuries, with special reference to the choir of Notre-Dame of Paris', *Journal of Ecclesiastical History* 18 (1967), 15–32

Morton, Robert: *The Collected Works*, ed. Allan W. Atlas (New York: Broude Bros. Ltd., 1981)

Moser, Hans Joachim: *Geschichte der deutschen Musik*, vol. 1, 4th edn (Stuttgart and Berlin: Cotta, 1926)

  Paul Hofhaimer: ein Lied- und Orgelmeister des deutschen Humanismus (Stuttgart and Berlin: Cotta, 1929)

Motta, Emilio: *Musici alla Corte degli Sforza. Ricerche e documenti milanesi* (Milan, 1887 *R* Geneva: Minkoff, 1977)

MSD (Musicological Studies and Documents) see individual authors

Mužik, František: 'Die Tyrnauer Handschrift (Országos Széchenyi Könyvtár c. l. m. 243)', *Acta Universitatis Carolinae, Philosophica et Historica* 2 (1965), 5–44

Nádas, John: 'Further notes on Magister Antonius dictus Zacharias de Teramo', *Studi Musicali* 15 (1986), 167–82

NAWM (The Norton Anthology of Western Music) see Palisca ed.

Nef, Karl: 'Die Musik in Basel von den Anfängen im 9. Jahrhundert bis zur Mitte des 19. Jahrhunderts', *SIMG* 10 (1908/09), 395–432

The New Grove Dictionary of Music and Musicians, ed. Stanley Sadie, 20 vols. (London: Macmillan, 1980)

New Obrecht Edition (*NOE*) see Obrecht, ed. C. Maas *et al.*

Newes, Virginia: 'Imitation in the Ars nova and Ars subtilior', *RBM* 31 (1977), 38–59

Noblitt, Thomas: 'Das Chorbuch des Nikolaus Leopold (München, Staatsbibliothek, Mus. Ms. 3154): Repertorium', *AMw* 26 (1969), 169–208

  'Die Datierung der Handschrift Mus. ms. 3154 der Staatsbibliothek München', *Mf* 27 (1974), 36–56

Noblitt, Thomas, ed.: *Der Kodex des Magister Nicolaus Leopold: Staatsbibliothek München, Mus. ms. 3154*, vol. 1 (Kassel etc.: Bärenreiter, 1987) (EDM, 80)

NOHM III (The New Oxford History of Music, III): see Hughes, Dom Anselm, and Abraham eds

NOHM IV (The New Oxford History of Music, IV): see Abraham ed.

Norlind, Tobias: 'Schwedische Schullieder im Mittelalter und in der Reformationszeit', *SIMG* 2 (1900/01), 552–607

Obrecht, Jacob: *New Obrecht Edition*, ed. C. Maas, B. Hudson and T. Noblitt (Utrecht: VNM, 1983–)

Opera omnia, editio altera, ed. A. Smijers *et al.*, 4 vols. (Amsterdam: VNM, 1953-64)

Werken, ed. J. Wolf, 8 vols. (Amsterdam and Leipzig, 1908-21)

Ockeghem, Johannes: *Collected Works*, ed. Dragan Plamenac, 2 vols., 2nd corr. edn (American Musicological Society, 1959) (Studies and Documents, 3)

OH (The Old Hall Manuscript) see Hughes, Andrew, and Bent eds

Orel, Dobroslav: 'Stilarten der Mehrstimmigkeit des 15. und 16. Jahrhunderts in Böhmen', in *Studien zur Musikgeschichte*, 87-91

Osthoff, Helmuth: *Josquin Desprez*, 2 vols. (Tutzing: Schneider, 1962-5)

Osthoff, Wolfgang: *Theatergesang und darstellende Musik in der italienischen Renaissance (15. und 16. Jahrhundert)* (Tutzing: Schneider, 1969) (Münchner Veröffentlichungen zur Musikgeschichte, 14)

Paganuzzi, Enrico, *et al.*: *La musica a Verona* (Verona: Banca Mutua Popolare, 1976)

Page, Christopher: 'The performance of songs in late medieval France: a new source', *Early Music* 10 (1982), 441-50

Palisca, Claude V.: *Humanism in Italian Renaissance Musical Thought* (New Haven and London: Yale University Press, 1985)

Palisca, Claude V., ed.: *The Norton Anthology of Western Music*, vol. 1: *Medieval-Renaissance-Baroque* (New York and London: Norton, 1980)

Parigi, Luigi: *Laurentiana. Lorenzo de' Medici cultore della musica* (Florence: Olschki, 1954) (Historiae Musicae Cultores Biblioteca, 3)

Paris, Gaston, and Gevaert, Auguste, eds: *Chansons du XVe siècle* (Paris: Firmin Didot, 1875)

Parris, Arthur: *The Sacred Works of Gilles Binchois*, 2 vols. Ph.D., Bryn Mawr College, 1965

Pease, Edward J.: *An Edition of the Pixérécourt Manuscript: Paris, Bibliothèque Nationale, fonds fr. 15123*, Ph.D., Indiana University, 1959

Pelnar, Ivana: *Die mehrstimmigen Lieder Oswalds von Wolkenstein*, 2 vols. (Schneider: Tutzing, 1981) (Münchner Veröffentlichungen zur Musikgeschichte, 32)

'Neuentdeckte Ars-nova-Sätze bei Oswald von Wolkenstein', *Mf* 32 (1979), 26-33

Perkins, Leeman L.: 'Musical patronage at the royal court of France under Charles VII and Louis XI (1422-83)', *JAMS* 37 (1984), 507-66

Perkins, Leeman L. (chairman): 'Euphony in the fifteenth century' (Round Table), in *IMS Report of the 12th Congress, Berkeley 1977* (Kassel etc.: Bärenreiter, 1981), 620-58

Perkins, Leeman L., and Garey, Howard, eds: *The Mellon Chansonnier*, 2 vols. (New Haven and London: Yale University Press, 1979)

Perz, Mirosław: 'Il carattere internazionale delle opere di Mikołaj Radomski', in Günther ed., *1380-1430: An International Style?*, 153-9

'The Lvov fragments: a source for works by Dufay, Josquin, Petrus de Domarto, and Petrus de Grudencz in 15th-century Poland', *TVNM* 36 (1986), 26-51

Perz, Mirosław, ed.: *Sources of Polyphony up to c. 1500*, 2 vols. (Warsaw: Warsaw University Press, 1973-6) (Antiquitates Musicae in Polonia, 13 and 14)

Petrobelli, Pierluigi: 'La musica nelle cattedrali e nelle città', in *Storia della cultura veneta. Il Trecento* (Venice: Neri Pozza, 1977), 440-68

Picker, Martin: *Johannes Ockeghem and Jacob Obrecht: A Guide to Research* (New York: Garland Publishing, Inc., 1988)

Picker, Martin, ed.: *The Chanson Albums of Marguerite of Austria* (Berkeley and Los Angeles: University of California Press, 1965)

Fors seulement: Thirty Compositions for Three to Five Voices or Instruments from the Fifteenth and Sixteenth Centuries (Madison: A-R Editions, 1981) (Recent Researches in the Music of the Middle Ages and Early Renaissance, 14)

Pietzsch, Gerhard: *Fürsten und fürstliche Musiker im mittelalterlichen Köln* (Cologne: Volk, 1966) (Beiträge zur rheinischen Musikgeschichte, 66)

Quellen und Forschungen zur Geschichte der Musik am kurpfälzischen Hof zu Heidelberg bis 1622 (Mainz and Wiesbaden, 1963)

Zur Pflege der Musik an den deutschen Universitäten bis zur Mitte des 16. Jahrhunderts (R Hildesheim and New York: Olms, 1971)

Pirro, André: 'Jean Cornuel, vicaire de Cambrai', *RdM* 7 (1926), 190-203

'L'enseignement de la musique aux universités françaises', *Mitteilungen der Internationalen Gesellschaft für Musikwissenschaft* 2 (1930), 26-32

Histoire de la musique de la fin du XIVe siècle à la fin du XVIe (Paris: Librairie Renouard, 1940)

La musique à Paris sous le règne de Charles VI (1380-1422) (Strasbourg: Heitz, 1930) (Collection d'études musicologiques, 1)

Pirrotta, Nino: 'Music and cultural tendencies in 15th-century Italy', *JAMS* 19 (1966), 127-61

Music and Culture in Italy from the Middle Ages to the Baroque (Cambridge, Mass.: Harvard University Press, 1984)

Music and Theatre from Poliziano to Monteverdi (Cambridge: Cambridge University Press, 1982)

'Ricercare e variazioni su "O rosa bella"', *Studi Musicali* 1 (1972), 59-77

'Su alcuni testi italiani di composizioni polifoniche quattrocentesche', *Quadrivium* 14 (1973), 133-57

'"Zacharus Musicus"', *Quadrivium* 12 (1971), 153-74; also in *idem, Music and Culture*, 126-44

Pirrotta, Nino, and Curti, Danilo, eds: *I Codici Musicali Trentini. Atti del Convegno 'Laurence Feininger: la musicologia come missione'* (Trent: Museo Provinciale d'Arte, 1986)

Plamenac, Dragan: 'A reconstruction of the French Chansonnier in the Biblioteca Colombina, Seville', *MQ* 37 (1951), 501-42; 38 (1952), 87-117 and 245-77

'Browsing through a little-known manuscript (Prague, Strahov Monastery, D. G. IV. 47)', *JAMS* 13 (1960), 102-11

Planchart, Alejandro E.: 'Fifteenth-Century Masses: notes on performance and chronology', *Studi Musicali* 10 (1981), 3-29

'Guillaume Du Fay's benefices and his relationship to the court of Burgundy', *EMH* 8 (1988), 117-71

'Guillaume Dufay's Masses: a view of the manuscript traditions', in Atlas ed., *Dufay Quincentenary Conference*, 26-60

'Parts with words and without words: the evidence for multiple texts in fifteenth-century Masses', in Boorman ed., *Studies*, 227-51

'The relative speed of tempora in the period of Dufay', *RMA Research Chronicle* 17 (1981), 33-51

Planchart, Alejandro E., ed.: *Missae Caput* (New Haven and London: Yale University Press, 1964) (Collegium Musicum, 5)

Plummer, John: *Four Motets*, ed. Brian Trowell (Banbury, 1968)

PMFC (Polyphonic Music of the Fourteenth Century) see individual authors and eds

Polk, Keith: 'Instrumental music in the urban centres of Renaissance Germany', *EMH* 7 (1987), 159-86

'Vedel and geige - fiddle and viol. German string traditions in the fifteenth century', *JAMS* 42 (1989), 504-46

Pompilio, Angelo, *et al.* eds: *Trasmissione e recezione delle forme di cultura musicale. Atti del XIV Congresso della Società Internazionale di Musicologia*, 3 vols. (Turin: Edt, 1990)

Pope, Isabel, and Kanazawa, Masakata, eds: *The Musical Manuscript Montecassino 871. A Neapolitan Repertory of Sacred and Secular Music of the Late Fifteenth Century* (Oxford: Clarendon Press, 1978)

Power, Leonel: *Complete Works*, ed. Charles Hamm, vol. 1: *The Motets* (Rome: American Institute of Musicology, 1969) (CMM, 50)

Powers, Harold, ed.: *Studies in Music History: Essays for Oliver Strunk* (Princeton: Princeton University Press, 1968)

Prez, Josquin des, see Josquin

Prizer, William F.: 'Bernardino Piffaro e i pifferi e tromboni di Mantova: strumenti a fiato in una corte italiana', *RIM* 16 (1981), 151–84

    Courtly Pastimes: The Frottole of Marchetto Cara (Ann Arbor: UMI Research Press, 1980) (Studies in Musicology, 33)

    'The *Frottola* and the unwritten tradition', *Studi Musicali* 15 (1986), 3–37

    'Music and ceremonial in the Low Countries: Philip the Fair and the Order of the Golden Fleece', *EMH* 5 (1985), 113–53

Pullois, Johannes: *Opera omnia*, ed. Peter Gülke (Rome: American Institute of Musicology, 1967) (CMM, 41)

Quadris, Johannes de: *Opera*, ed. Giulio Cattin (Bologna: A.M.I.S., 1972) (Antiquae Musicae Italicae Monumenta Veneta)

Ramalingam, Vivian S.: 'The *trumpetum* in Strasbourg M 222 C 22', in Honegger–Meyer eds, *La Musique et le rite*, vol. 2, 143–60

Rankin, Susan: 'Shrewsbury School, Manuscript VI: a medieval part book?', *PRMA* 102 (1975–76), 129–44

Rastall, Richard: 'Minstrelsy, church and clergy in medieval England', *PRMA* 97 (1970–71), 83–98

    The Notation of Western Music (London: Dent, 1983)

Reaney, Gilbert, ed.: *Early Fifteenth-Century Music* (EFM), 7 vols. (Rome and Stuttgart: American Institute of Musicology, 1955–83) (CMM, 11)

Reese, Gustave: 'Musical compositions in Renaissance intarsia', in John L. Lievsay ed., *Medieval and Renaissance Studies* (Durham, N.C.: Duke University Press, 1968), 74–97

    Music in the Renaissance, rev. edn (New York: Norton, 1959)

Regis, Johannes: *Opera omnia*, ed. C. W. H. Lindenburg, 2 vols. (Rome: American Institute of Musicology, 1956) (CMM, 9)

Rehm, Wolfgang, ed.: *Codex Escorial Chansonnier (Manuscript EscA)*, facs. edn (Kassel etc.: Bärenreiter, 1958) (Documenta Musicologica, II, 2)

Reynolds, Christopher: 'The origins of San Pietro B 80 and the development of a Roman sacred repertory', *EMH* 1 (1981), 257–304

Richental, Ulrich: *Chronik des Konstanzer Konzils, 1414–1418*, ed. O. Feger, 2 vols. (Constance: Bahn, 1964)

Ringmann, Heribert, and Väterlein, Christian, eds: *Das Glogauer Liederbuch*, 4 vols. (Kassel etc.: Bärenreiter, 1936–81) (EDM, 4, 8, 85 and 86)

RISM B IV (Répertoire International des Sources Musicales, B IV, 3–4) see Kurt von Fischer ed.

RMF (Renaissance Music in Facsimile) see Brown *et al.* eds

Robijns, Jozef: 'Eine Musikhandschrift des frühen 16. Jahrhunderts im Zeichen der Verehrung unserer lieben Frau der Sieben Schmerzen', *KJb* 44 (1960), 28–43

Robijns, Jozef, ed.: *Renaissance-Muziek 1400–1600. Donum Natalicium René Bernard Lenaerts* (Louvain, 1969)

Rokseth, Yvonne: 'The instrumental music of the Middle Ages and the early sixteenth century', in *NOHM III*, 406–65

La musique d'orgue au XVe siècle et au début de XVIe (Paris: Droz, 1930)

Rosenberg, Herbert: *Untersuchungen über die deutsche Liedweise im 15. Jahrhundert* (Wolfenbüttel and Berlin: Kallmeyer, 1931)

Rothe, Hans, ed.: *Die Hohenfurter Liederhandschrift (H 42) von 1410*, facs. edn (Cologne and Vienna: Böhlau, 1984)

Rubsamen, Walter H.: 'The Justiniane or Viniziane of the fifteenth century', *AcM* 29 (1957), 172–83

Literary Sources of Secular Music in Italy (c. 1500) (Berkeley and Los Angeles: University of California Press, 1943)

Rumbold, Ian: 'The compilation and ownership of Munich, Clm 14274', *EMH* 2 (1982), 161–235

Sachs, Klaus-Jürgen: 'Die Contrapunctus-Lehre im 14. und 15. Jahrhundert', in F. Zaminer ed., *Geschichte der Musiktheorie*, vol. 5 (Darmstadt: Wissenschaftliche Buchgesellschaft, 1984), 161–256

Sahlin, Margit: *Etudes sur la carole médiévale* (Uppsala, 1940)

Salmen, Walter: 'European song', in *NOHM III*, 349–80

Das Lochamer Liederbuch. Eine musikgeschichtliche Studie (Leipzig: Breitkopf & Härtel, 1951)

Der Spielmann im Mittelalter (Innsbruck: Helbling, 1983)

Salmen, Walter, and Koepp, Johannes, eds: *Liederbuch der Anna von Köln (um 1500)* (Düsseldorf: Schwann, 1954)

Salmen, Walter, and Petzsch, Christoph, eds: *Das Lochamer-Liederbuch* (Wiesbaden: Breitkopf & Härtel, 1972)

Sanders, Ernest: 'Cantilena and discant in 14th-century England', *MD* 19 (1965), 7–52

'England. From the beginnings to c. 1540', in F. W. Sternfeld ed., *Music from the Middle Ages to the Renaissance* (London: Weidenfeld & Nicolson, 1973), 255–313

Medieval English Polyphony and its Significance for the Continent, Ph.D., Columbia University, 1963 (UM 65-7472)

Sanders, Ernest, Harrison, Frank Ll. and Lefferts, Peter, eds: *English Music for Mass and Offices II* (Monaco: L'Oiseau-Lyre, 1985) (PMFC, vol. 17)

Sartori, Claudio: 'Josquin des Prés, cantore del Duomo di Milano (1459–1472)', *AnnM* 4 (1956), 55–81

Saunders, Elizabeth S.: *The Dating of the Trent Codices from their Watermarks, with a Study of the Local Liturgy of Trent in the Fifteenth Century* (New York and London: Garland, Inc., 1989)

'The liturgies of Trent and Brixen in the fifteenth century', *MD* 38 (1984), 173–93

Schering, Arnold, ed.: *Geschichte der Musik in Beispielen* (Leipzig: Breitkopf & Härtel, 1931)

Schimmelpfennig, Bernhard: 'Zum Zeremoniell auf den Konzilien von Konstanz und Basel', *Quellen und Forschungen aus italienischen Archiven und Bibliotheken* 49 (Tübingen, 1969), 273–92

Schmalz, Robert F.: *Selected Fifteenth-Century Polyphonic Mass Ordinaries Based upon Pre-existent German Material*, Ph.D., University of Pittsburgh, 1971 (UM 72-16, 134)

Schoop, Hans: *Entstehung und Verwendung der Handschrift Oxford, Bodleian Library, Can.*

misc. 213 (Berne and Stuttgart: Haupt, 1971) (Publikationen der Schweizerischen Musikforschenden Gesellschaft, Ser. II, vol. 24)

Schuler, Ernst August: *Die Musik der Osterfeiern, Osterspiele und Passionen des Mittelalters* (Kassel etc.: Bärenreiter, 1951)

Schuler, Manfred: 'Zur Geschichte der Kapelle Papst Martins V', *AMw* 25 (1968), 30–45
'Die Musik in Konstanz während des Konzils 1414–1418', *AcM* 38 (1966), 150–68

Senn, Walter: *Musik und Theater am Hof zu Innsbruck* (Innsbruck: Österreichische Verlagsanstalt, 1954)

Slavin, Dennis: *Binchois' Songs, the Binchois Fragment, and the Two Layers of Escorial A*, Ph.D., Princeton University, 1988

Smijers, Albertus A.: *De Illustre Lieve Vrouwe Broederschap te s'Hertogenbosch* (Amsterdam, 1932) (also in *TVNM* 11–14)

Smijers, Albertus A., ed.: *Van Ockeghem tot Sweelinck* (Amsterdam, 1939; 2nd edn, 1951)

Smits van Waesberghe, Joseph: 'Een 15de eeuws muziekboek van de stadsministrelen van Maastricht?', in Robijns ed., *Renaissance-Muziek*, 247–73

Snow, Robert J.: *The Manuscript Strahov D. G. 47*, Ph.D., University of Illinois, 1968 (UM 69-1456)
'The mass-motet cycle: a mid-fifteenth century experiment', in Snow ed., *Essays in Musicology*, 301–20

Snow, Robert J., ed.: *Essays in Musicology in Honor of Dragan Plamenac on His 70th Birthday* (Pittsburgh: Pittsburgh University Press, 1969)

Southern, Eileen: *The Buxheim Organ Book* (Brooklyn: Institute of Mediaeval Music, 1963)
'Foreign music in German manuscripts of the 15th century', *JAMS* 21 (1968), 258–85

Sparks, Edgar H.: *Cantus firmus in Mass and Motet: 1420–1520* (Berkeley and Los Angeles: University of California Press, 1963)

Spechtler, Franz Viktor, and Korth, Michael, eds: *Der Mönch von Salzburg. Ich bin du und du bist ich. Lieder des Mittelalters* (Munich: Heimeran, 1980)

Stäblein, Bruno: *Schriftbild der einstimmigen Musik* (Leipzig: VEB Deutscher Verlag für Musik, 1975) (Musikgeschichte in Bildern, III, 4)

Stäblein-Harder, Hanna, ed.: *Fourteenth-Century Mass Music in France*, Edition (CMM, 29) and Critical Text (MSD, 7) (Rome: American Institute of Musicology, 1962)

Staehelin, Martin: *Die Messen Heinrich Isaacs*, 3 vols. (Berne and Stuttgart: Haupt, 1977) (Publikationen der Schweizerischen Musikforschenden Gesellschaft, Ser. II, vol. 28)
'Münchner Fragmente mit mehrstimmiger Musik des späten Mittelalters', in *Nachrichten der Akademie der Wissenschaften in Göttingen* I, Phil.-hist. Klasse, Jg. 1988 no. 6 (Göttingen, 1988), 167–90
'Neues zu Bartholomäus Frank', in V. Ravizza ed., *Festschrift Arnold Geering zum 70. Geburtstag* (Berne and Stuttgart: Haupt, 1972)

Stainer, J. F. R., and Stainer, C., eds: *Dufay and His Contemporaries* (London, 1898 *R* Amsterdam: Knuf, 1966)
Early Bodleian Music, 2 vols. (London, 1901 *R* Farnborough, 1967)

Starr, Pamela: *Music and Musical Patronage at the Papal Court, 1447–1464*, Ph.D., Yale University, 1987

Stephan, Wolfgang: *Die burgundisch-niederländische Motette zur Zeit Ockeghems* (Kassel etc.: Bärenreiter, 1937 *R* 1973)

Sterl, Raimund W.: *Musiker und Musikpflege in Regensburg bis um 1600* (Regensburg: Author, 1971)

'Die Regensburger Stadtrechnungen des 15. Jahrhunderts als Quelle für fahrende und höfische Spielleute', in *Studien zur Musikgeschichte der Stadt Regensburg I* (Regensburg: Bosse, 1979)

Sternfeld, Frederick W.: 'Music in the schools of the Reformation', *MD* 2 (1948), 99-122

Stevens, Denis, ed.: *Venetian Ceremonial Motets* (Sevenoaks: Novello, *c.*1978)

Stevens, John E.: 'Medieval Drama, # I–V', in *The New Grove*, vol. 12, 21-58

Music and Poetry in the Early Tudor Court (London: Methuen, 1961; rev. edn, 1979)

Stevens, John E., ed.: *Early Tudor Songs and Carols* (London: Stainer & Bell, 1975) (Musica Britannica, 36)

Mediaeval Carols (London: Stainer & Bell, 1952; rev. edn, 1958) (Musica Britannica, 4)

Stevenson, Robert: *Spanish Music in the Age of Columbus* (The Hague: Nijhoff, 1960)

'Spanish musical impact beyond the Pyrenees (1250-1500)', in *Actas del Congreso Internacional 'España en la Música de Occidente'*, 2 vols. (Madrid: Ministerio de Cultura, 1987), vol. I, 115-65

Strohm, Reinhard: 'The Ars nova fragments of Gent', *TVNM* 34 (1984), 109-31

Music in Late Medieval Bruges (Oxford: Clarendon Press, 1985)

Music in Late Medieval Bruges, rev. edn (Oxford: Clarendon Press, 1990)

'Einheit und Funktion früher Meßzyklen', in N. Dubowy and S. Meyer-Eller eds., *Festschrift Rudolf Bockholdt zum 60. Geburtstag* (Pfaffenhofen: Ludwig, 1990), 141-160

'European politics, and the distribution of music in the early fifteenth century', *EMH* 1 (1981), 305-23

'Filipotto da Caserta, ovvero i Francesi in Lombardia', in F. Della Seta and F. Piperno eds, *In cantu et in sermone. For Nino Pirrotta on his 80th Birthday* (Florence: Olschki, 1989), 65-74

'Magister Egardus and other Italo-Flemish contacts', *L'Ars Nova Italiana del Trecento* 6 (1992), 41-68

'Meßzyklen über deutsche Lieder in den Trienter Codices', in *Liedstudien. Festschrift für Wolfgang Osthoff zum 60. Geburtstag* (Tutzing: Schneider, 1989), 77-106

'Die Missa super "Nos amis" von Johannes Tinctoris', *Mf* 32 (1979), 34-51

'Music in recurrent feasts of Bruges', in Honegger-Meyer eds, *La Musique et le rite*, 424-32

'Native and foreign polyphony in late medieval Austria', *MD* 38 (1984), 205-30

'Le polifonie più o meno primitive', in Corsi-Petrobelli eds, *Polifonie primitive*, 83-98

'Die vierstimmige Bearbeitung (um 1465) eines unbekannten Liedes von Oswald von Wolkenstein', *Jahrbuch der Oswald von Wolkenstein Gesellschaft* 4 (1986-7), 163-74

'Zur Rezeption der frühen Cantus-firmus-Messe im deutschsprachigen Bereich', in W. Konold ed., *Deutsch-englische Musikbeziehungen. Referate des wissenschaftlichen Symposions ... 1980 'Musica Britannica'* (Munich and Salzburg: Katzbichler, 1985), 9-38

Strohm, Reinhard (chairman): 'Costituzione e conservazione dei repertorii polifonici nei secoli XIV e XV' (Round Table II), in Angelo Pompilio *et al.* eds, *Trasmissione ...* , vol. I, 93-184

Strunk, Oliver: *Source Readings in Music History: The Renaissance*, paperback edn (New York: Norton, 1965)

Studien zur Musikgeschichte. Festschrift für Guido Adler zum 75. Geburtstag (Vienna and Leipzig: Universal Edition, 1930; 2nd edn, 1971)

Szabolcsi, Benedikt: 'Die ungarischen Spielleute des Mittelalters', in F. Blume ed., *Gedenkschrift für Hermann Abert* (Halle: Niemeyer, 1928), 154-64

Taruskin, Richard: 'Antoine Busnoys and the L'Homme Armé tradition', *JAMS* 39 (1986), 255-93

Thannabaur, Peter Josef: *Das einstimmige Sanctus der römischen Messe in der handschriftlichen Überlieferung des 11. bis 16. Jahrhunderts* (Munich: Ricke, 1962)

Tinctoris, Johannes: *De inventione et usu musicae* see Weinmann
  Opera omnia, ed. W. Melin (Rome: American Institute of Musicology, 1976) (CMM, 18)
  Opera theoretica, ed. Albert Seay, 3 vols. (Rome: American Institute of Musicology, 1975) (CSM, 22)

Todd, R. Larry: 'Retrograde, inversion, retrograde-inversion, and related techniques in the Masses of Jacobus Obrecht', *MQ* 64 (1978), 50–78

Tomasello, Andrew: *Music and Ritual at Papal Avignon 1309-1403* (Ann Arbor: UMI Research Press, 1983) (Studies in Musicology, 75)

Torrefranca, Fausto: *Il Segreto del Quattrocento* (Milan: Hoepli, 1939)

Toulmin Smith, Lucy, ed.: *Expeditions to Prussia and the Holy Land Made by Henry, Earl of Derby (afterwards King Henry IV) in the Years 1390-1 and 1392-3 being the Accounts Kept by his Treasurer (Richard Kyngeston) during Two Years* (London: The Camden Society, 1894)

Trent Codices (facs. edn), 7 vols. (Rome: Vivarelli & Gullà, n. d.)

Trexler, Richard C.: 'Ritual in Florence: adolescence and salvation in the Renaissance', in Charles Trinkaus and Heiko A. Oberman eds, *The Pursuit of Holiness in Late Medieval and Renaissance Religion. Papers from the University of Michigan Conference* (Leiden: Brill, 1974), 200–70

Trowell, Brian: 'Faburden – new sources, new evidence: a preliminary survey', in E. Olleson ed., *Modern Musical Scholarship* (Stocksfield etc.: Oriel Press, 1978), 28–78
  Music under the Later Plantagenets, unpubl. Ph.D., Cambridge University, 1960

Trowell, Brian, ed.: *Invitation to Medieval Music 4* (London: Stainer & Bell, 1979)

Väterlein, Christian, ed.: *Graduale Pataviense (Wien 1511)*, facs. edn (Kassel etc.: Bärenreiter, 1982) (EDM, 87)

Van, Guillaume de: 'A recently discovered source of early fifteenth-century polyphonic music', *MD* 2 (1948), 5–74

Van den Nieuwenhuizen, J.: 'De koralen, de zangers en de zangmeesters van de Antwerpse O.-L.-Vrouwekerk tijdens de 15de eeuw', in *Antwerps Katedraalkoor: Gouden Jubileum Gedenkboek* (Antwerp: Choraelhuys, 1978), 29–72

Vander Straeten, Edmond: *La musique aux pays-bas avant le XIXe siècle*, 8 vols. (Brussels, 1867-88 R, with introduction by E. Lowinsky, 4 vols, New York: Dover, 1969)

Vaughan, Richard: *Charles the Bold* (London: Longman, 1973)
  Philip the Good: The Apogee of Burgundy (Harlow: Longman, 1970)

Vincenet, Johannes: *Collected Works*, ed. B. E. Davis (Madison: A-R Editions, 1978) (Recent Researches in the Music of the Middle Ages and Early Renaissance, 9–10)

Vitry, Philippe de: *Works*, ed. Leo Schrade (Monaco: L'Oiseau-Lyre, 1956) (PMFC, 1)

Vogeleis, Martin: *Quellen und Bausteine zu einer Geschichte der Musik und des Theaters im Elsaß 500-1800* (Strasbourg, 1911 R 1979)

Wackernagel, Bettina, ed.: *Das Liederbuch des Dr. Hartmann Schedel*, facs. edn (Kassel etc.: Bärenreiter, 1978) (EDM, 84)

Wall, Carolyn, and Steiner, Ruth: 'York pageant XLVI and its music', *Speculum* 46 (1971), 689–712

Wallner, Bertha Antonia, ed.: *Das Buxheimer Orgelbuch*, 3 vols. (Kassel etc.: Bärenreiter, 1959) (EDM, 37-9)

Ward, Lynn H.: 'The motetti missales repertory reconsidered', *JAMS* 39 (1986), 491–523

Ward, Tom R.: 'A central European repertory in Munich, Bayerische Staatsbibliothek, Clm 14274', *EMH* 1 (1981), 325-43

'Music and music theory in the universities of central Europe during the fifteenth century', in Wright (chairman), 'La musica nella storia delle universita', 49-57

The Polyphonic Office Hymn 1400-1520. A Descriptive Catalogue (Stuttgart: American Institute of Musciology, 1980)

'The polyphonic office hymn and the liturgy of fifteenth-century Italy', *MD* 26 (1972), 161-88

Warmington, Flynn: 'A very fine troop of bastards? Provenance, date, and Busnois' role in Brussels 5557', *Abstracts of Papers, AMS 50th Annual Meeting* (Philadelphia, 1984)

Wathey, Andrew: 'Dunstable in France', *ML* 67 (1986), 1-36

'Lost books of polyphony in England: a list to 1500', *RMA Research Chronicle* 21 (1988), 1-19

Music in the Royal and Noble Households in Late Medieval England. Studies of Sources and Patronage (New York and London: Garland Publishing, Inc., 1989)

Wegman, Rob C.: 'An anonymous twin of Johannes Ockeghem's Missa Quinti Toni in San Pietro B 80', *TVNM* 37 (1987), 25-48

'Another "Imitation" of Busnoys's *Missa L'Homme armé* and some observations on *Imitatio* in Renaissance music', *JRMA* 114 (1989), 189-202

'Concerning tempo in the English polyphonic Mass, c. 1420-70', *AcM* 61 (1989), 40-65

'Music and musicians at the guild of Our Lady in Bergen op Zoom, 1470-1510', *EMH* 9 (1989), 175-249

Weinmann, Karl: *Johannes Tinctoris, 1445-1511, und sein unbekannter Traktat 'De inventione et usu musicae'*, ed. W. Fischer (Tutzing: Schneider, 1961)

Welker, Lorenz: 'New light on Oswald von Wolkenstein: central European traditions and Burgundian polyphony', *EMH* 7 (1987), 187-226

Whitwell, David: *The Wind Band and Wind Ensemble before 1500* (Northridge, CA, 1982)

Wilkins, Nigel: *Music in the Age of Chaucer* (Cambridge: Brewer, 1979)

Winn, Mary Beth, ed.: *Musique naturelle et musique artificielle. In memoriam Gustave Reese* (Montreal: Gros, 1980) (Le Moyen français, 5)

Wolf, Johannes: *Handbuch der Notationskunde*, 3 vols. (Leipzig, 1913)

Wolff, Christoph: 'Arten der Mensuralnotation im 15. Jahrhundert und die Anfänge der Orgeltabulatur', in *Kongreßbericht Gesellschaft für Musikforschung, Bonn 1970* (Kassel etc.: Bärenreiter, 1971), 609-13

Wolkenstein, Oswald von: *Die Lieder*, ed. Karl Kurt Klein *et al.*, 2nd edn (Tübingen, 1975) (Altdeutsche Textbibliothek, 55)

Woodfield, Ian: *The Early History of the Viol* (Cambridge: Cambridge University Press, 1984)

Woodley, Ronald: 'Johannes Tinctoris: a review of the documentary biographical evidence', *JAMS* 34 (1981), 217-48

'Tinctoris' Italian translation of the Golden Fleece statutes: a text and a (possible) context', *EMH* 8 (1988), 173-244

Wright, Craig: 'Dufay at Cambrai: discoveries and revisions', *JAMS* 28 (1975), 175-229

Music at the Court of Burgundy 1364-1419: A Documentary History (Brooklyn etc.: Institute of Mediaeval Music, 1979)

Music and Ceremony at Notre Dame of Paris, 500-1500 (Cambridge: Cambridge University Press, 1989)

'Performance practices at the cathedral of Cambrai, 1475-1550', *MQ* 64 (1978), 295-328

Wright, Craig (chairman): 'La musica nella storia delle università' (Round Table I), in Pompilio *et al.* eds, *Trasmissione . . .* vol. 1, 27–89

Wright, Peter: 'The compilation of Trent 87–I and 92–II', *EMH* 2 (1982), 237–71

'On the origins of Trent 87–I and 92–II', *EMH* 6 (1986), 245–70

Wustmann, Rudolf: *Musikgeschichte Leipzigs*, vol. 1 (until 1650) (Leipzig and Berlin, 1909)

Young, Karl: *The Drama of the Medieval Church*, 2 vols. (Oxford: Clarendon Press, 1933)

Žak, Sabine: *Musik als 'Ehr' und Zier' im mittelalterlichen Reich* (Neuss: Päffgen, 1979)

'Der Quellenwert von Giannozzo Manetti's Oratio über die Domweihe von Florenz 1436 für die Musikgeschichte', *Mf* 40 (1987), 2–32

Ziino, Agostino: '"Magister Antonius dictus Zacharias de Teramo": Alcune date e molte ipotesi', *RIM* 14 (1979), 311–48

Zöbeley, Hans Rudolf: *Die Musik des Buxheimer Orgelbuchs. Spielvorgang, Niederschrift, Herkunft, Faktur* (Tutzing: Schneider, 1964) (Münchner Veröffentlichungen zur Musikgeschichte, 10)

INDEX